Africa Since Independence

Also by Paul Nugent

Big Men, Small Boys and Politics in Ghana: Power, Ideology and the Burden of History, 1982–1994

Smugglers, Secessionists and Loyal Citizens on the Ghana–Togo Frontier: The Lie of the Borderlands Since 1914

African Boundaries: Barriers, Conduits and Opportunities (co-edited, with A. I. Asiwaju)

Ethnicity In Ghana: The Limits of Invention (co-edited, with Carola Lentz)

Africa Since Independence

A Comparative History

PAUL NUGENT

First published 2004 by
PALGRAVE MACMILLAN
Houndmills, Basingstoke, Hampshire RG21 6XS and
175 Fifth Avenue, New York, N. Y. 10010
Companies and representatives throughout the world

PALGRAVE MACMILLAN is the global academic imprint of the Palgrave
Macmillan division of St. Martin's Press, LLC and of Palgrave Macmillan Ltd.
Macmillan® is a registered trademark in the United States, United Kingdom
and other countries. Palgrave is a registered trademark in the European
Union and other countries.

ISBN 0–333–68272–6 hardback
ISBN 0–333–68273–4 paperback

This book is printed on paper suitable for recycling and made from fully
managed and sustained forest sources.

A catalogue record for this book is available from the British Library.

Library of Congress Cataloging-in-Publication Data
Nugent, Paul, 1962–
　　Africa since independence : a comparative history / Paul Nugent.
　　　　p. cm.
　　Includes bibliographical references and index.
　　ISBN 0–333–68272–6 (cloth) – ISBN 0–333–68273–4 (paper)
　　1. Africa – History – 1960– I. Title.

DT30.5.N84 2004
960.3′2—dc22   2004044503

10　9　8　7　6　5　4　3　2　1
13　12　11　10　09　08　07　06　05　04

Printed by Creative Print & Design (Wales), Ebbw Vale

Transferred to digital printing 2005

Contents

List of Maps and Tables

Maps

Tables

Acknowledgements

This book has taken rather longer to complete than I had expected. I am most grateful to Terka Acton and her colleagues at Palgrave Macmillan for applying just the right amount of pressure to see that it was delivered and for being flexible over word limits. In the course of carrying out the underlying research, I was able to visit Ethiopia and Senegal with the generous support of the Hayter Travel Fund, and South Africa with the assistance of the then Faculty Group Research Fund, both of the University of Edinburgh.

As a West Africanist, I have found myself leaning heavily on the expertise and insights of others with different regional specialisms. I would like to thank Steve Kerr for various discussions about Tanzania while stoking up the braai, and I only regret that I have not been able to incorporate his imaginative suggestions about unlikely Scottish-Congolese comparisons with Rémy Bazenguissa–Ganga. I have also tapped into Tom Salter's enthusiasm for the intricacies of the Congolese musical diaspora. The Centre of African Studies has had a good crop of research students and staff over recent years, and I have also drawn a lot from the annual cycle of seminars and conferences. Special thanks go to Ken and Pravina King, Alan Barnard, Sara Rich Dorman, Sarah Vaughan, Lawrence Dritsas, Jude Murison, Rachel Hayman and John Lwanda. In History, I am indebted to past and present colleagues, namely Paul Bailey, Crispin Bates, Markus Daechsel and Ian Duffield. Luke Staniland kindly helped with the production of many of the statistical tables.

Not surprisingly, Ghana features very prominently in the pages of this book and as usual my thanks go to Pip and Gareth Austin, Tom McCaskie, Lynne Brydon, Emily Asiedu, Carola Lentz, Alhaji Mohammed Abukari, Harry Asimah, Moses Agbovi, Nana Soglo Allo IV, and the whole of the Department of Political Science at the University of Ghana. In the Gambia, special thanks are due to Ernest Aubee for assistance in facilitating the correction of the final manuscript from Banjul.

Finally, I would like to thank all the members of the Nugent and Ngoué diasporas for their interest: especially Tony, Colleen, Gabriel and Phoebe in Oranjezicht; San, Fergus and Alec in Fish Hoek; Peter, Hilde, Fionuala, Medhbh and Aoife in Ballajura; Diddy, Marc, Jordan and Audrey-Rose Skinner in Houghton; Marie Ngoué in Lolodorf; Annie Ngoué, Dénis Ngoué and Carole Bureau in Paris; Rosine Soguia in St-Louis (Senegal), and, of course, Eliane and Kwally in Edinburgh itself.

Edinburgh
October 2003

Abbreviations

AAC	All Anglophone Conference
ABAKO	Alliance des Bakongo [Congo-Kinshasa]
ABN	Association for a Better Nigeria
AD	Alliance for Democracy [Nigeria]
ADB	African Development Bank
ADF	Allied Democratic Forces [Uganda]
AFDL	Alliance of Democratic Forces for the Liberation of Congo/Zaire
AFL	Armed Forces of Liberia
AFORD	Alliance for Democracy [Malawi]
AFPRC	Armed Forces Provisional Ruling Council [Gambia]
AFRC	Armed Forces Revolutionary Council [Ghana, Sierra Leone]
AFRC	Armed Forces Ruling Council [Nigeria]
AG	Action Group [Nigeria]
AIDS	Acquired Immune Deficiency Syndrome
ANC	African National Congress [South Africa]
ANC	African National Council [Rhodesia/Zimbabwe]
APC	All People's Congress [Sierra Leone]
APL	Armée Populaire de Libération [Congo-Kinshasa]
APO	African People's Organisation [South Africa]
APP	All People's Party [Nigeria]
APRC	Alliance for Patriotic Reorganisation and Construction [Gambia]
ARPB	Association of Recognized Professional Bodies [Ghana]
AZACTU	Azanian Congress of Trade Unions [South Africa]
AZAPO	Azanian People's Organisation
BAC	Basutoland African Congress [Lesotho]
BAD	Bantu Affairs Department [South Africa]
BBC	British Broadcasting Corporation
BCP	Basutoland/Basotho Congress Party [Lesotho]
BDP	Botswana Democratic Party
BNF	Botswana National Front
BNP	Basutoland/Basotho National Party [Lesotho]
BPC	Black People's Convention [South Africa]
CAFM	Christian Action Faith Ministries [Ghana]
CAMPFIRE	Communal Areas Management Programme for Indigenous Resources [Zimbabwe]
CANU	Caprivi African National Union [South West Africa/Namibia]
CAR	Central African Republic

CCCCN	Comité Coordonnateur Pour la Convocation d'une Conférence Nationale [CAR]
CCM	Chama Cha Mapinduzi [Tanzania]
CCN	Council of Churches of Namibia
CCZ	Christian Council of Zambia
CDR	Coalition for the Defence of the Republic [Rwanda]
CDR	Committees for the Defence of the Revolution [Benin, Ghana, Burkina Faso]
CDR	Revolutionary Democratic Council [Chad]
CELU	Confederation of Labour Unions [Ethiopia]
CFA	Communauté Financière Africaine
CGCE	Comptoir Guinéen du Commerce Extérieur [Guinea]
CGCI	Comptoir Guinéen du Commerce Intérieur [Guinea]
CGT	Confédération Générale du Travail
CIA	Central Intelligence Agency [United States of America]
CIDA	Canadian International Development Agency
CIO	Central Intelligence Organisation [Rhodesia]
CCJP	Catholic Commission on Justice and Peace [Zambia]
CMB	Cocoa Marketing Board [Ghana]
CNDD	Conseil National Pour la Defense de la Démocratie [Burundi]
CNGT	Confédération Nationale des Travailleurs Guineéns [Guinea]
CNL	Conseil Nationale de Libération [Congo-Kinshasa]
CNN	Cable News Network
CNR	Conseil National de la Révolution [Congo-Brazzaville]
CNTS	Confédération Nationale des Travailleurs Sénégalais
CODESA	Convention for a Democratic South Africa
CONAKAT	Confédération des Associations Tribales du Katanga [Congo-Kinshasa]
CONCP	Conference of Nationalist Organisations of the Portuguese Colonies
COPWE	Commission for the Organisation of the Ethiopian People's Workers Party
COSAS	Congress of South African Students
COSATU	Confederation of South African Trade Unions
CP	Conservative Party [South Africa]
CPDM	Cameroun People's Democratic Movement
CPLF	Community of Portuguese-Speaking Countries
CPP	Convention People's Party [Gold Coast/Ghana]
CPSA	Communist Party of South Africa
CUF	Civic United Front [Tanzania]
CUT	Comité de l'Unité Togolaise [Togo]
DA	District Assembly
DP	Democratic Party [Uganda, South Africa, Kenya]
DRC	Democratic Republic of Congo
DTA	Democratic Turnhalle Alliance [South West Africa]
DUP	Democratic Unionist Party [Sudan]
DWM	December 31st Women's Movement [Ghana]

EC	European Community
ECOMOG	ECOWAS Monitoring Group
ECOWAS	Economic Community of West African States
EDU	Ethiopian Democratic Union
ELF	Eritrean Liberation Front
ELM	Eritrean Liberation Movement
EPDM	Ethiopian People's Democratic Movement
EPLF	Eritrean People's Liberation Front
EPRDF	Ethiopian People's Revolutionary Democratic Front
EPRP	Ethiopian People's Revolutionary Party
ERA	Eritrean Relief Association
ERP	Economic Recovery Programme
ESAF	Enhanced Structural Adjustment Facility
ESAP	Enhanced Structural Adjustment Programme
EU	European Union
FAN	Armed Forces of the North [Chad]
FAO	Food and Agriculture Organisation
FDD	Forum for Democracy and Development [Zambia]
FDD	Forces de la Défense de la Démocratie [Burundi]
FEA	French Equatorial Africa
FEDECO	Federal Electoral Commission [Nigeria]
FESTAC	Black and African Festival of Arts and Culture [Nigeria]
FGCEI	Fonds de Garantie des Crédits Accordés aux Enterprises Ivoriennes [Côte d'Ivoire]
FGOR	Former Government of Rwanda
FIDES	Fonds d'Investissement pour le Développement Economique et Social
FLEC	Front for the Liberation of the Cabinda Enclave [Angola]
FLING	Front for the National Independence of Guinea
FLN	National Liberation Front [Algeria]
FLNC	Front Pour la Liberation Nationale du Congo[Zaire/Congo-Kinshasa]
FNLA	National Front for the Liberation of Angola
FORD	Forum for the Restoration of Democracy/Kenya & Asili
FOSATU	Federation of South African Trade Unions
FPI	Front Patriotique Ivoirien
FPC	Forces Politiques du Conclave [Zaire]
FRELIMO	Front for the Liberation of Mozambique
FRODEBU	Front Pour la Démocratie au Burundi
FROLINAT	Front for the National Liberation of Chad
FROLIZI	Front for the Liberation of Zimbabwe
FWA	French West Africa
GBA	Ghana Bar Association
GBM	Green Belt Movement [Kenya]
GDP	Gross Domestic Product
GEAR	Growth, Redeployment and Redistribution[South Africa]
GECAMINES	Générale des Carrières et des Mines [Zaire/Congo-Kinshasa]

GEMA	Gikuyu, Embu and Meru Association [Kenya]
GNP	Gross National Product
GNPP	Great Nigeria People's Party
GNTC	Ghana National Trading Corporation
GRO	grassroots organisation
GRVC	Groupements Révolutionnaires à Vocation Coopérative
GSU	General Service(s) Unit [Kenya, Uganda]
GUNT	Transitional Government of National Unity [Chad]
HIV	Human Immunodeficiency Virus
ICDC	Industrial and Commercial Development Corporation [Kenya]
ICGC	International Central Gospel Church [Ghana]
ICJ	International Court of Justice
IFI	International Financial Institution
IGNU	Interim Government of National Unity [Liberia]
IMF	International Monetary Fund
INPFL	Independent National Patritotic Front of Liberia
ING	Interim National Government
INM	Imbokodvo National Movement [Swaziland]
IOM	Indépendants d'Outre-Mer
JFM	June 4 Movement [Ghana]
JMNR	Jeunesse de la MNR [Congo-Brazzaville]
JMPR	Jeunesse de la MPR [Zaire/Congo-Kinshasa]
JNS	Junta of National Salvation [Portugal]
JRDA	Jeunesse de la Révolution Démocratique Africaine [Guinea]
JRDACI	Jeunesse du Rassemblement Démocratique Africain de Côte d'Ivoire
KAU	Kenya African Union
KADU	Kenya African Democratic Union
KANU	Kenya African National Union
KNDP	Kamerun National Democratic Party [British Cameroon]
KPU	Kenyan People's Union
KNTC	Kenya National Trading Corporation
KY	Kabaka Yekka [Uganda]
LCD	Lesotho Congress for Democracy
LD-MPT	Ligue Démocratique-Mouvement Pour le Parti du Travail [Senegal]
LLA	Lesotho Liberation Army
LPC	Liberian Peace Council
LPP	Liberal Progressive Party [Eritrea]
LURD	Liberians United for Reconciliation and Democracy
MANU	Mozambican-Makonde Union [Mozambique]
MCDDI	Mouvement Congolais Pour le Développement et la Démocratie Intégrale [Congo-Brazzaville]
MCP	Malawi Congress Party
MDC	Movement for Democratic Change [Zimbabwe]
MDJT	Movement for Democracy and Justice in Chad
MDR	Rwandan Democratic Movement
Meison	All-Ethiopian Socialist Movement
MFA	Armed Forces Movement [Portugal]

MFDC	Mouvement des Forces Démocratiques de Casamance [Senegal]
MFJ	Movement for Freedom and Justice [Ghana]
MFP	Marematlou Freedom Party [Lesotho]
ML	Muslim League [Eritrea]
MLC	Mouvement de Libération du Congo [Democratic Republic of Congo]
MLSTP	Movimento de Libertação de São Tomé e Príncipe
MMD	Movement for Multiparty Democracy [Zambia]
MNC	Mbandzeni National Convention [Swaziland]
MNC	Mouvement National Congolais [Congo-Kinshasa]
MNR	Mouvement National de la Révolution [Congo-Brazzaville]
MNSD	Mouvement National Pour une Société de Développement [Niger]
MOJA	Movement for Justice in Africa [Liberia]
MORENA	Mouvement de Redressement Nationale [Gabon]
MP	Marematlou Party [Lesotho]
MP	Member of Parliament
MPCI	Mouvement Patriotique de Côte d'Ivoire
MPD	Movimento para a Democracia [Cape Verde]
MPLA	Popular Movement for the Liberation of Angola
MPLC	Mouvement Pour la Libération Centrafricain [CAR]
MPR	Mouvement Populaire de la Révolution [Zaire/Congo-Kinshasa]
MRS	Mouvement Républicain Sénégalais
MRND(D)	National Revolutionary Movement for Development (and Democracy) [Rwanda]
MRP	Mouvement Républicain Populaire [France]
MYP	Malawi Young Pioneers
NA	Native Authority
NABSO	Namibian Black Students' Organisation
NACP	National AIDS Control Programme [Uganda]
NAD	Native Affairs Department [South Africa]
NADECO	National Democratic Coalition [Nigeria]
NAL	National Alliance of Liberals [Ghana]
NARC	National Rainbow Coalition [Kenya]
NATO	North Atlantic Treaty Organisation
NAYO	National Youth Organisation [South Africa]
NCD	National Commission on Democracy [Ghana]
NCCK	National Council of Churches of Kenya
NCCR	National Convention for Construction and Reform [Tanzania]
NCNC	National Council of Nigeria and the Cameroons/National Council of Nigerian Citizens
NCO	Non-Commissioned Officer
NCWK	National Council of Women of Kenya
NDA	National Democratic Alliance [Sudan]
NDC	National Democratic Congress [Ghana]
NDM	New Democratic Movement [Ghana]
NDP	National Democratic Party [Rhodesia]
NDP	National Development Party [Kenya]

NEC	National Electoral Commission
NEC	National Executive Committee
NEPAD	New Partnership for Africa's Development
NEPU	Northern Elements People's Union [Nigeria]
NERP	New Economic Recovery Programme [Zambia]
NFD	Northern Frontier District [Kenya]
NGO	Non-Governmental Organisation
NIC	Natal Indian Congress [South Africa]
NIF	National Islamic Front [Sudan]
NIP	National Independence Party [Ghana]
NLC	National Liberation Council [Ghana]
NLM	National Liberation Movement [Gold Coast/Ghana]
NNA	Nigerian National Alliance
NNGO	Northern Non-Governmental Organisation
NNLC	Ngwane National Liberatory Congress [Swaziland]
NNOC	Nigerian National Oil Corporation
NNP	New National Party [South Africa]
NORAD	Royal Norwegian Embassy Development Corporation
NOVIB	Netherlands Organisation for International Development Co-operation
NP	National Party [South Africa]
NPC	Northern People's Congress [Nigeria]
NPFL	National Patriotic Front of Liberia
NPN	National Party of Nigeria
NPP	New Patriotic Party (NPP)
NPP	Nigerian People's Party
NPRC	National Provisional Ruling Council [Sierra Leone]
NRC	National Redemption Council [Ghana]
NRC	National Republican Convention [Nigeria]
NRC	National Resistance Council [Uganda]
NRM/A	National Resistance Movement/Army [Uganda]
NRP	National Reform Party [Ghana]
NUGS	National Union of Ghanaian Students
NUKEM	National Union of Kenyan Muslims
NUM	National Union of Mineworkers [South Africa]
NUP	National Unionist Party [Sudan]
NUPENG	National Union of Petroleum and Natural Gas Workers [Nigeria]
NUSAS	National Union of South African Students
NUTA	National Union of Tanganyika Workers
OAU	Organisation of African Unity
OCA	Office de Commercialisation Agricole [Senegal]
ODP/MT	Organisation pour la Démocratie Populaire/Mouvement du Travail [Burkina Faso]
OECD	Organisation for Economic Co-operation and Development
OFY	Operation Feed Yourself Programme [Ghana]
OFN	Operation Feed the Nation [Nigeria]

OLF	Oromo Liberation Front [Ethiopia]
ONCAD	Office National de Coopération et d'Assistance au Développement [Senegal]
ONUMOZI	United Nations Organisation for Mozambique
OPEC	Organisation of Petroleum Exporting Countries
OPC	Ovambo People's Congress [South West Africa/Namibia]
OPDO	Oromo People's Democratic Organisation [Ethiopia]
OPO	Ovambo People's Organisation [South West Africa/Namibia]
PAC	Pan-Africanist Congress [South Africa]
PAI	Parti Africain de l'Indépendance [Senegal]
PAICV	Party for the Independence of Cape Verde
PAIGC	African Party for the Independence of Guinea and Cape Verde
PALIPEHUTU	Party for the Liberation of the Hutu People [Burundi]
PAMSCAD	Programme of Action to Mitigate the Social Costs of Adjustment
PARMEHUTU	Parti du Mouvement de l'Emancipation Hutu [Rwanda]
PCD-GR	(Partido da Convergência Democrática - Grup de Reflexão) [São Tomé and Príncipe]
PCP	People's Convention Party [Ghana]
PCT	Parti Congolais du Travail [Congo-Brazzaville]
PDC	Parti Démocratique Chrétien [Burundi]
PDCI	Parti Démocratique de Côte d'Ivoire
PDG	Parti Démocratique de Guinée [Guinea]
PDG	Parti Démocratique Gabonais
PDP	People's Democratic Party
PDS	Social Democratic Party [Rwanda]
PDS	Parti Démocratique Sénégalais
PF	Patriotic Front [Zimbabwe]
PFP	Popular Front Party [Ghana]
PHP	People's Heritage Party [Ghana]
PLAN	People's Liberation Army of Namibia
PMAC	Provisional Military Administrative Council [Ethiopia]
PNC	People's National Convention [Ghana]
PNDC	Provisional National Defence Council [Ghana]
PNP	People's National Party [Ghana]
POGR	Presidential Own Guards Regiment [Ghana]
POMOA	Provisional Office for Mass Organisational Affairs [Ethiopia]
PP	Progress Party [Ghana]
PP	Progressive Party [South Africa]
PPP	Progressive People's Party [Liberia]
PPP	People's Progressive Party [Gambia]
PPT	Parti Progressiste Tchadien [Chad]
PRA	Parti du Regroupement Africain [Senegal]
PRC	People's Redemption Council [Liberia]
PRE	Programme of Economic Rehabilitation [Mozambique]
PRL	Pouvoir Révolutionnaire Locale [Guinea]
PRP	People's Redemption Party [Nigeria]

PRPB	Parti Révolutionnaire du Benin
PRS	Social Renovation Party [Guinea-Bissau]
PRSP	Poverty Reduction Strategy Paper
PS	Parti Socialiste [Senegal]
PSA	Parti Solidaire Africain [Congo-Kinshasa]
PSD	Partido Social Democrata [São Tomé and Príncipe]
PUDEMO	People's United Democratic Movement [Swaziland]
PUP	Parti de l'Unité et du Progrès [Guinea]
P/WDCs	People's and Worker's Defence Committees [Ghana]
RCC-NS	Revolutionary Council of National Salvation [Sudan]
RCD	Rassemblement Congolais Pour la Démocratie [DRC}
RCD-ML	RCD-Mouvement de Libération [DRC]
RDA	Rassemblement Démocratique Africain
RDA	Ruvuma Development Association [Tanzania]
RDC	Rural District Council
RDP	Reconstruction and Development Programme [South Africa]
RDR	Rassemblement des Républicains [Côte d'Ivoire]
RENAMO	National Resistance of Mozambique
RF	Rhodesian Front
RFI	Radio France Internationale
RPF	Rwandan Patriotic Front
RPT	Rassemblement du Peuple Togolais [Togo]
RTLMC	Radio Télévision Libre des Milles Collines [Rwanda]
RUF	Revolutionary United Front [Sierra Leone]
SAAWU	South African Allied Workers Union
SACP	South African Communist Party
SADC	Southern African Development Community
SADF	South African Defence Force
SAL	Structural Adjustment Loan
SAL	Sectoral Adjustment Loan
SANU	Sudan African National Union
SAF	Structural Adjustment Facility
SAP	Structural Adjustment Programme
SASM	South African Students Movement
SASO	South African Students Organzation
SCNC	Southern Cameroons National Council
SDF	Social Democratic Front [Cameroun]
SDP	Social Democratic Party [Nigeria]
SDP	Swaziland Democratic Party
SDSF	Somali Democratic Salvation Front
SFC	State Farms Corporation [Ghana]
SFIO	French Socialist Party
SIDA	Swedish International Development Authority
SLPP	Sierra Leone People's Party
SMC	Supreme Military Council [Ghana and Nigeria]
SNACS	Swaziland National Association of Civil Servants
SNAS	Swaziland Association of Students

SNAT	Swaziland National Association of Teachers
SNM	Somaliland National Movement
SONAFI	Société Nationale de Financement [Côte d'Ivoire]
SPLA/M	Sudan People's Liberation Army/Movement
SPM	Somali Patriotic Movement
SSLM	Southern Sudanese Liberation Movement
SSRC	Soweto Students Representative Council [South Africa]
STD	Sexually Transmitted Disease
SWA	South West Africa
SWANLA	South West African Native Labour Association
SWANU	South West African National Union
SWAPO	South West African People's Organisation
SYL	Somali Youth League
SYL	SWAPO Youth League
TANU	Tanganyika African National Union
TPLF	Tigrayan People's Liberation Front [Ethiopia]
TRC	Truth and Reconciliation Commission [South Africa]
TUC	Trade Union Congress
UANC	United African National Council [Zimbabwe]
UBC	Urban Bantu Council [South Africa]
UCZ	United Church of Zambia
UDENAMO	National Democratic Union of Mozambique
UDF	United Democratic Front [South Africa, Namibia, Malawi]
UDI	Unilateral Declaration of Independence [Rhodesia]
UDP	United Democratic Party [Tanzania]
UDPS	Union Pour la Démocratie et le Progrès Sociale [Zaire]
UDSR	Union Démocratique et Sociale de la Résistance
UEMOA	West African Economic and Monetary Union
UGCC	United Gold Coast Convention
UGFCC	United Ghana Farmers' Co-operative Council
ULIMO	United Liberation Movement for Democracy in Liberia
UMBC	United Middle Belt Congress [Nigeria]
UMHK	Union Minière du Haut-Katanga
UN	United Nations
UNACOIS	Union Nationales des Commerçants et Industriels du Sénégal
UNAMI	National Union of Independent Mozambique
UNAMIR	United Nations Assistance Mission to Rwanda
UNAMSIL	United Nations Mission in Sierra Leone
UNAR	Union Nationale Rwandaise
UNC	United National Convention [Ghana]
UNC	United National Congress [Uganda]
UNDP	Union Nationale Pour la Démocratie et la Progrès [Cameroun]
UNECA	United Nations Economic Commission for Africa
UNESCO	United Nations Economic, Social and Cultural Organisation
UNHCR	United Nations High Commission for Refugees
UNICEF	United Nations International Children's Emergency Fund
Unigov	Union Government [Ghana]

UNITA	National Union for the Total Independence of Angola
UNLF	United National Liberation Front [Uganda]
UNIP	United National Independence Party [Zambia]
UNOSOM	United Nations Operations for Somalia
UNTS	Union Nationale des Travailleurs Sénégalais
UP	Unionist Party [Eritrea]
UP	United Party [Ghana, South Africa]
UPA	Union of the Peoples of Angola
UPADS	Union Panafricaine Pour la Démocratie Sociale [Congo-Brazzaville]
UPC	Uganda People's Congress
UPC	Union des Populations de Cameroun
UPGA	United Progressive Grand Alliance [Nigeria]
UPN	Unity Party of Nigeria
UPNA	Union of the Peoples of Northern Angola
UPND	United Party for National Development [Zambia]
UPRONA	Parti de l'Union et le Progrès National [Burundi]
UPS	Union Progressiste Sénégalaise
UPU	Uganda People's Union
USA	United Swaziland Association
USAID	United States Agency for International Development
USC	United Somali Congress
USOR	Sacred Union of the Radical Opposition [Zaire]
USTN	Union des Syndicats des Travailleurs du Niger
UTP	United Tanganyika Party
VAT	Value-Added Tax
VOA	Voice of America
WSLF	Western Somali Liberation Front
WWF	World Wildlife Fund
ZANC	Zambia African National Congress
ZAOGA	Zimbabwe Assemblies of God Africa
ZANLA	Zimbabwe African National Liberation Army
ZANU-(PF)	Zimbabwe African National Union (Patriotic Front)
ZAPU (PF)	Zimbabwe African Patriotic Union
ZCTU	Zambian Congress of Trade Unions
ZCTU	Zimbabwe Congress of Trade Unions
ZIPA	Zimbabwean People's Army
ZIPRA	Zimbabwe People's Revolutionary Army
ZLC	Zimbabwe Liberation Council
ZNP	Zanzibar Nationalist Party
ZUM	Zimbabwe Unity Movement

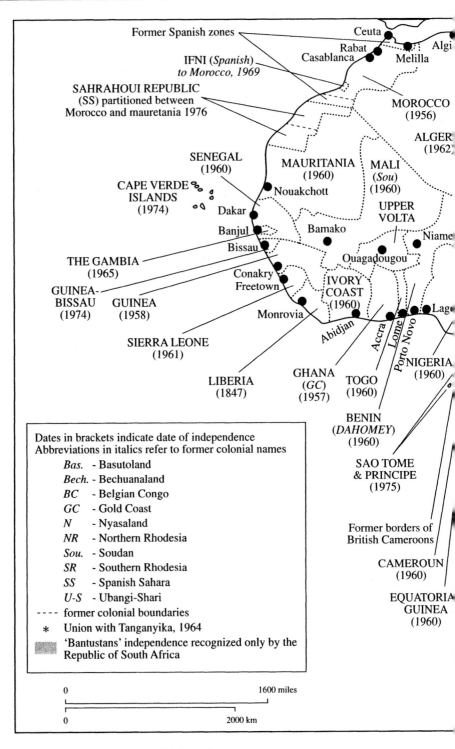

Former Spanish zones

Ceuta

Rabat · Algi

Casablanca · Melilla

IFNI (*Spanish*) to Morocco, 1969

MOROCCO (1956)

SAHRAHOUI REPUBLIC (SS) partitioned between Morocco and mauretania 1976

ALGER (1962)

SENEGAL (1960)

MAURITANIA (1960)

MALI (*Sou*) (1960)

CAPE VERDE ISLANDS (1974)

Nouakchott

UPPER VOLTA

Dakar

Niame

Banjul

Bamako

Bissau

THE GAMBIA (1965)

Ouagadougou

Conakry Freetown

IVORY COAST (1960)

GUINEA-BISSAU (1974)

GUINEA (1958)

Lag

Monrovia

SIERRA LEONE (1961)

Abidjan

Accra

Lome

Porto Novo

NIGERIA (1960)

LIBERIA (1847)

GHANA (*GC*) (1957)

TOGO (1960)

BENIN (*DAHOMEY*) (1960)

SAO TOME & PRINCIPE (1975)

Former borders of British Cameroons

CAMEROUN (1960)

EQUATORIA GUINEA (1960)

Dates in brackets indicate date of independence
Abbreviations in italics refer to former colonial names

Bas.	- Basutoland
Bech.	- Bechuanaland
BC	- Belgian Congo
GC	- Gold Coast
N	- Nyasaland
NR	- Northern Rhodesia
Sou.	- Soudan
SR	- Southern Rhodesia
SS	- Spanish Sahara
U-S	- Ubangi-Shari

- - - - former colonial boundaries

* Union with Tanganyika, 1964

'Bantustans' independence recognized only by the Republic of South Africa

0   1600 miles

0   2000 km

Map 1   Africa showing dates of independence

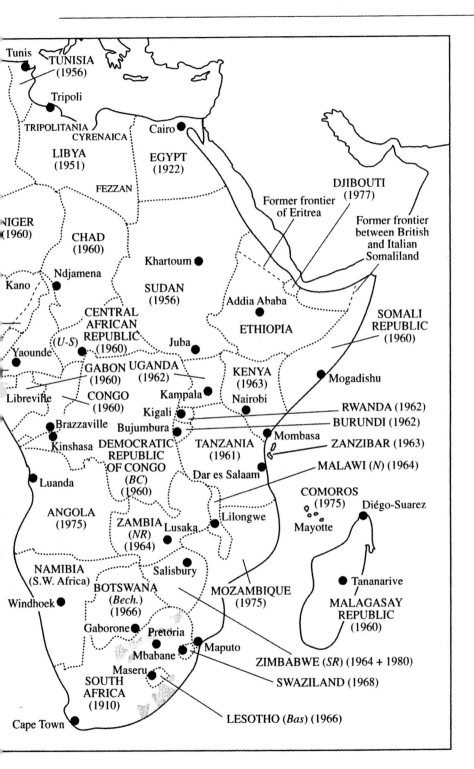

Tunis

TUNISIA
(1956)

Tripoli

TRIPOLITANIA
CYRENAICA

Cairo

LIBYA
(1951)

EGYPT
(1922)

FEZZAN

NIGER
(1960)

CHAD
(1960)

Ndjamena

Kano

Khartoum

DJIBOUTI
(1977)

Former frontier
of Eritrea

Former frontier
between British
and Italian
Somaliland

SUDAN
(1956)

CENTRAL
AFRICAN
REPUBLIC
(U-S)   (1960)

Addia Ababa

ETHIOPIA

SOMALI
REPUBLIC
(1960)

Yaounde

Juba

GABON UGANDA
(1960)   (1962)

KENYA
(1963)

Mogadishu

CONGO
(1960)

Kampala

Nairobi

Kigali

RWANDA (1962)

Libreville

BURUNDI (1962)

Brazzaville   Bujumbura

Mombasa

ZANZIBAR (1963)

Kinshasa

DEMOCRATIC
REPUBLIC
OF CONGO
(BC)
(1960)

TANZANIA
(1961)

Dar es Salaam

MALAWI (N) (1964)

Luanda

COMOROS
(1975)

Diégo-Suarez

ANGOLA
(1975)

ZAMBIA Lusaka
(NR)
(1964)

Lilongwe

Mayotte

NAMIBIA
(S.W. Africa)

Salisbury

Tananarive

BOTSWANA
(Bech.)
(1966)

MOZAMBIQUE
(1975)

MALAGASAY
REPUBLIC
(1960)

Windhoek

Gaborone

Pretoria

Maputo

Mbabane

ZIMBABWE (SR) (1964 + 1980)

Maseru

SWAZILAND (1968)

SOUTH
AFRICA
(1910)

Cape Town

LESOTHO (Bas) (1966)

Introduction: The Basis of Comparison

To embark on writing the history of an entire continent is inevitably a highly ambitious enterprise. Indeed, given the number of abandoned wrecks littering the historiographical roadsides, one might even conclude that it is foolhardy. To write a history of Africa is yet more ambitious, given the sheer size and complexity of the subject-matter. This remains the case even if one excludes North Africa and some of the islands, as I do here.[1] Despite a persistent belief that Africa is vast but pretty much the same – how else can people talk of travelling 'to Africa'? – it is far more diverse than Europe, whether measured in terms of language, social organisation, religion, environment or cultural expression. It has also undergone even more dramatic upheavals over the past half-century, which is saying something. Finally, Africa is the continent which has been subjected to the greatest distortions and wilful misunderstandings with respect to its past, and this still impedes our progress today. Before saying anything substantive, the historian has to spend much of his/her time simply trying to set the record straight. If North Americans find Europe bewildering, with all its historic enmities and obsessions, then they should be prepared for something even more taxing when it comes to Africa.

I have rendered the exercise more manageable by making certain calculated decisions. When I first embarked on the project, I was hoping to compose a history which would give adequate coverage to political, economic, social and cultural themes. This quickly became unworkable, and I have ended up producing an account which is dominated by politics – and hence, I am afraid, by conflict which tends to be its stock-in-trade. Nevertheless, I have sought to weave a consideration of popular culture (music, film, theatre and literature) into the fabric of the text. I have also examined the various development models which African states experimented with after independence, as well as those which have been externally imposed in more recent times. Unfortunately, I have not managed to incorporate much of what could properly be called social history, for which there is arguably a need, and many readers may feel that an explicit gender dimension is lacking. In mitigation, however, I do highlight the role of rapid urbanisation in fostering a highly assertive youth culture.

There is also a second set of problems which goes to the heart of debates about the practice of history. Although it is possible to reconstruct the first two decades of independence with a certain amount of confidence – decolonisation and the Cold War are in a sense completed history – it is far more difficult to assess the recent past. There is an enormous outpouring of writing about contemporary Africa, but a lot of it is unreflective and does not seek to place the

1

material in any kind of historical context. To choose an example which is salient at the time of writing, it is possible to accumulate innumerable facts about the crisis in Côte d'Ivoire, but what they add up to is not very clear. Journalists seek to make sense out of the jumble of information, which they gather at some speed, but it is by no means sure that they make the best sense of it. Often, their noses are pressed up too close to the events for them to be able to properly explain them. In the heat of the moment, certain ways of seeing an issue tend to hold sway, and it is only rather later that a greater sense of perspective becomes possible. The reportage of the Rwandan genocide in 1994 is a case in point. If one reads the accounts written closest to the events, they seem to privilege certain storylines to the exclusion of others which were arguably as important. After some time has passed, the full range of possibilities tends to become apparent and one starts to hear voices which were drowned out at the moment in question. As one stands back from the historical portrait, it becomes easier to appreciate how the intricate details contribute to the making of the larger picture.

This might sound teleological, in the sense of asserting that one has to know the end of the story before it can properly be told. It is precisely this kind of meta-narrative that postmodernists have attacked on the basis that the historian is imposing an order which simply does not exist. Far better, it is said, to take pleasure in the jumble, picking out a few pieces here and there without trying to fit them together in any systematic way. My problem is that while postmodernist historians might not seek to impose order, the historical subjects themselves do. Indeed, so too does the historical profession across Africa, which has shown little interest in such ideas, except in South Africa. Postmodernist writing cleverly exposed the historical boundedness of Enlightenment thought, but clearly its own insights have emerged under their own conditions of knowledge production. Postmodernism grew out of the professionalisation of the academic institution in North America and Europe, enabling academics to establish a measure of distance from the wider society, both in terms of what they produced and the conditions under which they did so. However, this is not the experience of those working within African institutions of higher learning. When historians are not struggling to make ends meet, they are writing texts which speak to the concerns of their constituency which demands usable history. It therefore makes little sense for the rest of us to shy away from attempting to interpret the historical experience of the past half-century. What one comes up with is likely to be contested, not least within Africa itself, but this is the point of the exercise. Historical consensus tends to emerge slowly as assertion and counter-assertion find their own fit, following which a new terrain of contestation emerges.

As Stephen Ellis points out, there is abundant commentary about Africa, but relatively little in terms of contemporary history writing.[2] This book is one attempt at a synthesis. In writing this text, I have found myself grappling with different kinds of subject-matter: some is safely 'historical', like the advent of Ghanaian independence; some is on the way to becoming so, including the Rwandan genocide and the ending of apartheid in South Africa; and finally, there is the live history which one approaches with some trepidation. The material which is available for the reconstruction of each is somewhat different, as I will explain below. None of it can simply be taken at face-value. It has to be critically evaluated, but crucially one is only able to make sense of it at all by passing it through some kind of interpretative filter. What one chooses to look at is itself conditioned by the kinds of questions one is seeking to answer, and this depends on one's sense of historical progression. One danger of 'presentism', of the type practised by aid agencies and many journalists (with honourable exceptions), is that it disconnects the present from its antecedents in a way that the actors themselves do not do. But if one wishes to reconnect the immediate present with the past, how far back should one go? One imagines that few readers would quibble with the proposition that independent Africa carried with it much of the baggage of colonialism. However, there are many who would argue that European rule was relatively shortlived and did not enjoy the luxury of starting with a blank slate. Hence, in order to make sense of the present, one has to have some conception of the *longue durée*. The reparations movement, which insists that Africa still bears the scars of the slave trade and colonialism, is clearly comfortable with adopting the long view. But Africanist scholars working in a variety of fields are increasingly doing so as well.

Hence, Jean-François Bayart maintains that the behaviour of someone like Mobutu in the Congo/Zaire – who cleverly exploited his favoured relationship with the West in the context of the Cold War – needs to be viewed in terms of a much longer history of 'extraversion' dating back some hundreds of years.[3] If Africa became economically dependent during the era of the slave trade, the relationship was also advantageous for those who managed to monopolise the position of gatekeepers to the external world. The contention is that this pattern continues to replicate itself down to the present. One might add that there is also a close similarity in the manner in which the holders of power have legitimated themselves by setting themselves up as the sole distributor of patronage. Mobutu, for example, promised to construct schools in particular communities not on the principle that it was the duty of the state to do so, but as if the resources were coming from his own pocket. Needless to say, there is a world of difference between Africa in the eighteenth and twenty-first centuries, but Bayart's reminder of the continuities is an instructive one.

A cognate point might be made with respect to the playing out of identity politics, which is such a feature of much of contemporary Africa. The colonial presumption that all Africans belonged to discrete 'tribes' seemed all too simple to historians looking at the record in the 1980s. Terence Ranger provoked a revisionist reappraisal which emphasised the agency of the colonial authorities and African cultural entrepreneurs in 'inventing tribes'.[4] Whereas Ranger's work was suitably nuanced, the 'invention' insight was sometimes pursued in a manner which suggested a rupture between pre-colonial and subsequent identities. It is difficult to dispute the extent to which identities have mutated over the course of the twentieth century – with dazzling speed in countries like Congo-Brazzaville – but the idea that colonial administrators, employers, missionaries and labour recruiters manufactured 'tribes' is problematic. Many colonial and post-colonial identities clearly do have pre-colonial roots – for example, that of the Ashanti in Ghana or the Baganda of Uganda – and what is becoming clear is the way in which disorientated Europeans often borrowed from African ways of seeing the world.[5] The role of interpreters, in both a literal and a figurative sense, was clearly important. Although this might have been a distorting lens, the likelihood is that pre-existing stereotypes and self-images were carried forward in a modified format. The colonial period may consequently be viewed as a bridge from the pre-colonial to the post-colonial periods rather than an abrupt break. Finally, scholars working on the African environment have disputed a presentist interpretation which saw the continent as heading for catastrophe at the end of the twentieth century – in the shape of desertification and land degradation – as a consequence of unprecedented population pressures.[6] Environmental historians are inclined to take the long-term view when it comes to matters of climate change, and to emphasise deep knowledge about maintaining sustainable livelihoods when it comes to resource use.[7] Consequently, many dispute whether there is, or necessarily needs to be, an ecological crisis at all.

If one accepts the logic of the *longue durée*, this is likely to inform the way one approaches the recent past. It does not, however, mean that one has to write one's history *as* the *longue durée*.[8] One might think of history as a complex machine in which a series of wheels propel progressively larger ones. The historian of the *longue durée* may be interested in the entire machine, but is ultimately concerned with the turning of the largest wheels which produce the final product. The contemporary historian is transfixed by the rapid revolutions of the very small wheels, without knowing whether they will be able to turn the next set of wheels, far less the really big ones at the other end. The two sets of historians are inclined to consult each other because history, like our imaginary machine, operates through the very interconnectedness of the process. This analogy does of course break down rather quickly. Evidently, the historical wheels turn larger ones *ad infinitum*. Moreover, when it comes to human history, there is likely to be a feedback effect. The actors respond to their own reading of past outcomes by seeking to mould future arrangements, but also by rewriting history to suit themselves – as has happened on a grand scale in the Great Lakes region. Although they cannot change what happened, they can try to dismantle parts of the machine and to substitute different components. Inevitably, therefore, the production process is characterised by much sputtering and discontinuity.

In this book, I am writing very close to many of the events, but in doing so I am informed by an understanding of the longer trajectory. As mentioned above, the sources for this study differ depending on the period concerned. There is a large corpus of documentary material covering the period before and immediately after independence. In the 1980s, however, the official record becomes far more patchy, while a veritable mountain of journalistic commentary, donor assessments and various shades of grey literature come into their own. The advent of the internet means that there is now more material 'out there' than ever before. Even groups which might seem marginalised and even technophobic are careful to construct their websites, in order that we can all see things from their own point of view.[9] I have made cautious use of much of this material, being aware of the problems associated with it.

Because this is primarily a work of synthesis, I have also relied on a large body of secondary literature, published in English and French, most of it derived from the Social Science disciplines. Engaging with this corpus entails problems of its own. The literature covering the first decade after independence is suffused with the assumptions and models associated with the modernisation paradigm, which posited that economies and social structures were caught up in the transition from tradition to modernity and that this was likely to impose certain strains on fledgling political institutions. Much of it does not make for pretty reading. During the 1970s and early 1980s, revisionists associated with the dependency/ underdevelopment school turned modernisation theory on its head and gave it a good shake. This was the tradition in which I myself was reared as a student at the University of Cape Town, and it has been quite an experience transporting myself back to the intellectual excitement of those bygone days. As with the paradigm which it replaced, however, one often has a feeling that the authors concerned were determined to make the empirical material fit the preferred model at all costs. The fit was often imperfect and it is possible to tear off the outer casing to get at the data which, to a much greater extent than now, was often gathered after lengthy periods in the field. Once fed through a different filter, the material remains very useful to the historian.

In writing this text for the student and general reader, I have found it useful to proceed by recalling what I dislike most about this genre and to practise the opposite. Hence I have tended to engage in 'thick description', based on specific case-studies, rather than serial comparisons which can too easily become superficial. The detail may often be overwhelming, but by way of compensation I trust that the book will serve as a resource which may be dipped into rather than necessarily being read from cover to cover. I have also cited my sources in detail rather than tacking a literature guide onto the end of the text. The latter may reduce publishing costs, but it tends to be of very limited utility to the reader. Moreover, if students of history are to be encouraged to interrogate their sources, it seems only right that they should be given the chance to dissect what I myself have done – to see what I have consulted and what I have ignored, and to assess the plausibility of my conclusions on the basis of the evidence provided. I assume that reading a history book is intended to be an intellectual exercise rather than a simple rendition of some objective 'truth'. I have therefore made a conscious effort to draw the reader's attention to areas of contention. By addressing specific debates, I highlight the manner in which the mode of gathering and processing evidence can lead to researchers coming to very different conclusions. I have often taken up a position of my own, and while I obviously hope the reader will be persuaded by the force of my argument, I accept that other readings are possible and trust that the reader will examine what I say with a critical eye.

Finally, it may assist the reader to know that the chapters are arranged broadly chronologically and according to theme. I begin by revisiting the end of British, French, Belgian, Italian and Spanish rule in the 1950/60s and the historical debates which have surrounded these events. In Chapter 2, I provide a brief overview of the colonial inheritance, before proceeding in Chapter 3 to a closer examination of irredentism, secessionism and Pan-Africanism in the aftermath of independence. The next chapter considers the fate of 'traditional rulers' over roughly the first two decades. Chapter 5 offers the reader a sustained comparison of the records of the socialist and capitalist-roaders through to the mid-1980s. Chapter 6 compares the record of military regimes, in various ideological guises, over the same time-period. In Chapter 7, I consider the consequences of the adoption of armed struggle in the Portuguese colonies and Zimbabwe, and the different path to liberation which was followed in South Africa. In Chapter 8, I address the unfolding of a new African (dis)order from the mid-1980s as structural adjustment, the AIDS pandemic and NGOs became the dominant features of a new continental landscape. In Chapter 9, I assess the impact of new forces favouring political liberalisation in the 1980s and 1990s. In the final chapter, I present a more mixed picture in which the demise of entrenched leaderships was often followed by a complete political breakdown. I finish with a brief discussion of efforts to reconcile truth and justice, whilst embracing the reality of Africa as a continent of marked diversity.

1

African Independence: Poisoned Chalice or Cup of Plenty?

We have done with the battle and we again rededicate ourselves in the struggle to emancipate other countries in Africa, for our independence is meaningless unless it is linked up with the total liberation of the African continent.

Independence speech of Kwame Nkrumah,
first Prime Minister of Ghana, 1957

In Africa, when children have grown up they leave their parents' hut, and build a hut of their own by its side. Believe me, we don't want to leave the French compound. We have grown up in it and it is good to be alive in it. We simply want to build our own huts.

Léopold Senghor, future President of Senegal, 1957

1.1   Interpreting African independence: the social sciences and the writing of history

Although this book is concerned with Africa since independence, there is a compelling case for adopting a somewhat longer-range perspective. Few historians would dispute that colonialism left a legacy which endured beyond independence day, and many would contend that its echoes still resonate at the start of the twenty-first century. Hence the clock cannot realistically be started in 1960 – the so-called 'year of African independence' – or, for that matter, in 1956 when an independent Sudan came into being. At the very least, one needs to take account of the protracted processes of decolonisation which unfolded in the aftermath of the Second World War, because the permutations prepared the ground for much which was to follow. The aim in this chapter is not to provide an exhaustive account of colonialism or of decolonisation, both of which have been the subject of substantial monographs in their own right.[1] It has a more limited remit, namely to convey some sense of what the rulers of newly independent states were actually inheriting and to examine how new languages were coined – of participation, development and a common humanity – which helped to shape the post-colonial world.

The inheritance consisted both of what was left behind when the tides of empire receded and the configurations which emerged in the course of achieving liberation. For that reason, decolonisation could never have simply been the negation of colonisation – a return to what had existed before. Although nationalists understood the point very well at one level, being committed modernists for the most part, it has taken time for the implications of the original sin of colonialism to fully register. The first generation of African rulers were typically sanguine about what independence would bring, even if they disagreed as to how far the break with the former colonial power ought to go. When Kwame Nkrumah uttered the immortal words, 'Seek ye first the political kingdom and all else will added unto you,' he was articulating a widely held belief that self-rule would make a profound difference. For Nkrumah and like-minded nationalists, the colonial state had functioned in the service of narrow coteries of European interests. Once commandeered by Africans, however, the state would deliver collective benefits and greater material prosperity for all. A general sense of optimism was also reflected in the writings of an emergent community of Africanist scholars. However, this optimism had mostly evaporated by the 1970s, at a time when the dependency paradigm captured the academic imagination, and was transformed into a pervasive sense of pessimism during the 1980s and 1990s. No-one better exemplifies the ground covered than Basil Davidson, who began as an enthusiastic follower of the independence movement in Ghana, then shifted his loyalties to successive guerrilla causes in the 1970s and early 1980s, and finally authored a book which argued that the entire independence project had been fatally misconceived because it was premised on an alien model of the nation-state.[2] Even Davidson, the eternal optimist in relation to things African, had begun to sound distinctly pessimistic by the 1990s.

The widespread feeling that flag independence had failed to deliver genuine liberation for the mass of the African population has led a variety of academic practitioners to take fresh stock of the twentieth-century record. While it would be misleading to suggest that anything like a consensus has emerged, diagnoses of the 'African condition' have tended to gravitate towards two poles. On the one side, there are those who point out that the colonial state was always an alien imposition, resting upon authoritarian modes of operation, which meant that it could not simply be appropriated as it stood. This is the substance of the most recent position of Davidson and is also the principal contention of a recent monograph by Mahmood Mamdani.[3] The latter insists that while the state was deracialised at independence, it was never effectively detribalised. The result was that a culture of authoritarianism, which alienated the mass of the population from the structures of power, was perpetuated. This kind of analysis does, of course, beg the question of why African political leaders should have colluded in the reproduction of these structures. One answer lies in the contention that external dependency and domestic authoritarianism have been mutually reinforcing, and have together served the interests of elites whose organic links to the mass of the population were always somewhat tenuous. This, in a nutshell, is what the dependency writers of the 1970s and early 1980s were arguing. In more recent times, it has resurfaced in the claim that 'extraverted' elites depend upon their ability to massage their links to the outside world, to the extent that they have positively benefited from conditions of endemic crisis.[4] On the other side, there are scholars who insist that the colonial state, and hence its post-colonial successor, was actually rather weak in relation to society. An early marker was laid down by Goran Hyden who insisted that African peasants had never effectively been 'captured' and – even more controversially – that genuine development might be impossible unless this historic task was completed.[5] More recently, Patrick Chabal and Jean-Pascal Daloz have contended that the colonial state itself failed to free itself from society, with the result that its post-colonial offspring was unable to function according to anything approximating the Weberian ideal.[6] There is also a suggestion in some recent writing that indigenous cultural forms, which had hitherto been suppressed, have begun to reassert themselves as state structures have become increasingly enfeebled.

For different kinds of reasons, the two broad approaches tend to downplay the significance of flag independence. For the first group, decolonisation provided a façade of change, behind which a continuity in unequal power relations was effected. For the second group, the record of independent regimes highlights the failure of colonial structures to make much of a dent on the African social landscape. Whether the state is seen as overbearing or weak in relation to social forces, the preferred model tends to draw upon a particular stock of examples which provide a neat fit and to bend the edges of others that do not. It is perhaps unavoidable that, in seeking to elaborate a model for an entire continent, the rich complexities are flattened out. Nevertheless, some attempts at presenting the big picture are more subtle than others. The problem with cruder versions of neo-colonialist interpretations is that they fail to take cognisance of the very difference courses charted by, say, a Côte d'Ivoire and a Tanzania. On the other hand, those interpretations which underline the weakness of the state sometimes fail to distinguish between countries where the state has ceased to function (like Somalia) and others where its operation has never really been in doubt (Senegal or Ghana).[7] The real challenge, which is taken up in this book, is to find some compromise between the urge to generalise and the desire to faithfully reflect the variety of historical experiences – or, to put it another way, to mesh the traditional craft of the historian with the concerns of the social scientist.

On the assumption that both the colonial inheritance and the particular route to independence did make a difference, the rest of this chapter is concerned with mapping out some of the variations. I will make quite detailed reference to specific territories because these threads will be taken up in subsequent chapters. In the first part, I will chart the differential experiences of decolonisation between, as well as within, the British, French, Belgian and Portuguese empires in tropical Africa. In the second part, I will examine the contents of the inheritance package in closer detail, drawing on a number of basic social, economic and political indicators.

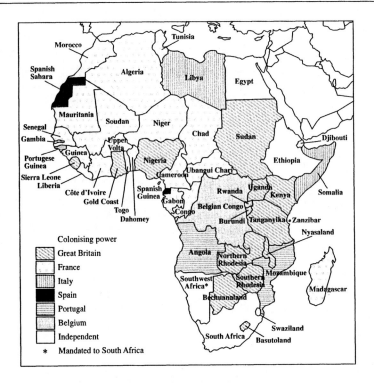

Map 2 Colonial Africa

1.2   Long walks and short cuts to freedom

1.2.1   The colonial contradiction

Was decolonisation in any sense inevitable? The answer is almost certainly yes, but it is highly unlikely that it would have taken place at the time and in the manner in which it did, had it not been for the outbreak of the Second World War. Whereas the colonial powers had ridden the storms of the Great Depression and appeared more firmly ensconced than ever at the end of the 1930s, they re-emerged in 1945 with their economies in tatters and their confidence severely dented. The country which profited most from this passage of events, the United States, was not a colonial power in Africa and had limited sympathy for European ambitions to resurrect imperial patrimonies – at least along pre-war lines.[8] Had it not been for the outbreak of war, it is conceivable that the African empires would have endured for some decades more, although one suspects that much would still have hinged on parallel developments in Asia. Nevertheless, it is unlikely that the empires would have made it as far as the new millennium, because of the deep-seated contradictions which lay at the heart of the colonial project. The significance of the war lay in exposing these to public view. Furthermore, the unsuccessful efforts of each of the colonial powers to carry out a repair job after 1945 demonstrated not just the depth of the contradictions but also the dangers associated with reform.

In referring to contradictions, I am using the term in broadly the same sense as Marxists refer to contradictions lying at the heart of capitalism: that is, as seeds which silently germinate within a given system of power relations and which eventually blow it open. As Homi Bhabha and others have contended, European imperialism embodied a fundamental tension between the desire to represent the colonised as innately different – which provided the rationale for conquest in the first place – and the need to consider them sufficiently alike as to make the effort worthwhile.[9] If the colonised acculturated too fully, this paradoxically posed a threat to the coloniser because it removed the justification for the exercise of power. The coloniser could either seek to apply the brakes, thereby appearing thoroughly hypocritical, or embrace a dynamic whereby colonialism eventually rendered itself superfluous. Bhabha goes on to suggest that the colonised were often mindful of this tension and could resort to mimicry as a means of destabilising the coloniser. This analysis is taken a step further in a reappraisal of colonial nationalism by Partha Chatterjee.[10] The latter argues that nationalist elites in Africa and Asia responded to the tension in two ways simultaneously. On the one hand, they insisted that they were indeed the same as Europeans, and ought therefore to be accorded the same political liberties. On the other hand, they had recourse to a rich field of cultural symbolism which underlined their essential difference from the Europeans and which could be used as a rallying point. In this way, the discourse of colonialism was turned back on the colonial power and placed in the service of a liberation which was as much cultural as political in character.

Can such insights be applied to colonial Africa? In the light of the peculiar trajectory of racial thought in relation to the continent, some might feel inclined to question whether Africans were ever regarded by Europeans as anything other than completely and utterly 'Other'. If that were the case, then the African model might be one in which Europeans phrased their right to rule purely in terms of their own needs and interests – whether in the form of minerals, land, or raw materials – and with little reference to the peoples of the continent. Africans, then, might be considered at worst as a nuisance and at best as beasts of burden. There are certainly periods and places where Africans were spoken of in these terms. At the time of the Scramble, when King Leopold enthused about acquiring large slices of 'this magnificent African cake', he exhibited no particular interest in the peoples living there: he was thinking of himself, in a quite literal sense. Again, the cavalier manner in which Africans were cleared off the land to make way for white settlers in Kenya and Rhodesia also highlights the self-referential aspect of British colonialism. Furthermore, when the Portuguese *Estado Novo* after 1926 depicted its African populations as beasts of burden, to be yoked to metropolitan progress, it came close to denying the common humanity of Africans. Finally, one should not forget that Germany's first genocide was conducted not at home, but in South West Africa where three-quarters of the Herero and half of the Nama people were killed between 1904 and 1908, in a systematic human cull.

Nevertheless, it would be an error to suppose that there was a fundamental difference between colonial discourse in relation to the African and Asian colonies. In Africa too, the innermost tension was apparent from an early stage. In the aftermath of the Scramble, a well-organised humanitarian lobby – consisting of a mixture of intellectuals, trading interests and mission organisations – argued for the primacy of African interests. Although they subscribed to the popular image of a benighted continent, the members of this lobby also believed that Africans could be bettered through the spread of education, commerce and the word of the Christian God. They also applied pressure upon each of the emergent colonial powers to justify their presence. This forced each of them to articulate a vision, which took the form of some variant or other on the conceit of 'the white man's burden'. Whether it was the Luso-tropicalism of Portugal or the *mission civilisatrice* of France, the claim was that Africans would derive some betterment from their engagement with Europeans. The adoption of a series of international conventions covering slavery, imported liquor and the arms trade put additional pressure on each of the colonial powers to demonstrate that they were genuinely concerned with the welfare of Africans. And after the terrible abuses of Leopold's Congo were brought to light, international surveillance became far more rigorous. Even if many practices such as forced labour and enforced cultivation continued, it became increasingly difficult to argue that these practices were actually perpetuated for the good of Africans. Moreover, the founding of the League of Nations in 1919, and the subjection of the former German colonies to the Mandates system, was a further watershed. Britain, France, Belgium and South Africa all assumed responsibility for African mandates, which required them to submit regular reports on their management of these territories. As Michael Callahan has persuasively argued, the mandates system gave birth to a new international discourse of trusteeship, which further circumscribed what could be done – not just in the mandated territories, but also in the colonies which formally lay outside the purview of the League.[11]

None of this is intended to demonstrate that colonial rule was benign. In the light of all the evidence to the contrary, the purpose is not even to highlight the hypocrisy of the grand programmatic statements. It is simply to point to the fact that by adopting the ideological pairing of guardian and ward, the colonial powers left open the possibility that Africans would one day 'grow up' and seek to go their own way. The question of what would happen then was potentially a very worrying one for committed imperialists who secretly hoped that their wards would never reach maturity. Indeed, by the inter-war period, one can identify a concerted effort to make sure that Africans remained under perpetual tutelage – creating what Christopher Fyfe has aptly described as 'Peter Pan children who can never grow up, a child race'.[12] As each of the colonial powers became more conscious of the colonial contradiction, therefore, they fell back upon what purported to be a gradualist approach – backed up by repeated warnings about the perils of too rapid change – but which really amounted to a desire to retard social transformation. There were many justifications advanced, but politically the hope was that the terminal point could be pushed back to such a remote future that any talk about an end to empire would amount to meaningless speculation. The underlying conservatism, which Anne Phillips describes as a 'colonial enigma', flatly contradicted the grand claims associated with the civilising mission.[13] This point was not missed by liberal critics of colonialism such as Joyce Cary, who insisted that if colonial regimes could not answer the question of what material benefit they were bringing to Africans, then they should not be on the continent in the first place.[14] The policy of stasis was also questioned by many Africans who had become the most closely implicated in the colonial project. Their mounting frustration arose from the fact that they had played by European rules, only to be penalised for their effort. Across Africa, the elites began to question whether there was not a cynical plot afoot to hold Africans back.

However, there were also significant differences in the way the contradiction was juggled with, which helps to explain varying African counter-responses. British involvement in Africa had initially revolved around trade, and had shifted towards direct control of small colonial enclaves in first half of the nineteenth century. The territory which was added during the Scramble was vast and required a more elaborate framework of governance. The British approach to the colonial question was distinctive in that it eschewed any desire to assimilate Africans, a path which – it was constantly reiterated – would merely lead to cultural alienation. The British posed as responsible guardians who were simply guiding Africans in their efforts to perfect their own institutions. A debate about the relative merits of direct and indirect rule was carried out within and between the various African colonies, and this was often extremely animated. However, the disagreement effectively boiled down to the issue of the amount of steerage that British officials ought to exercise in their dealings with chiefly authority. Whereas the followers of Frederick Lugard advocated a policy of minimal interference, on the grounds that this was the only way in which Africans would grow to have confidence in their own institutions, the supporters of direct rule generally argued that traditional rulers were in need of close instruction. Both sides shared an assumption that the majority of Africans were rural dwellers who would be forever locked into structures of chiefly rule.

The insistence that 'traditional rule' provided the most appropriate vehicle for Africans' political expression did, however, run up against certain practical realities. One was that the larger towns began attracting Africans from across a wide area. Whereas a system of 'tribal headmen' could be grafted onto the mining compounds, in most urban settings it was difficult to slot the new arrivals into existing chiefly hierarchies. Another difficulty was that several of the older towns, especially on the coast of West Africa, had spawned a cadre of merchants, doctors and lawyers who increasingly insisted that they ought to be accorded the same civic rights as British people – more or less along the lines identified by Chatterjee. Educated Africans rejected the leadership pretensions of the chiefs and demanded a direct say in their own governance and that of their countrymen. Paradoxically, however, those who had bought most completely into the civilising mission ended up being castigated by European officialdom as the very worst kind of Africans. They were derided as self-serving minorities who were out of touch with their own cultures and detached from the mass of the population. Indeed they came to stand as the living embodiment of what was to be avoided in areas where it was not already too late to chart a different course.[15]

The British understood only too well that increasing urbanisation and the uncontrolled expansion of education had the potential to undermine the foundations of their rule. In the 1930s, their response was to insist more stridently than ever that their goal was to assist in the organic evolution of indigenous structures, and that their job would not be considered complete until this was effected. This was expected to take a good many generations, and quite possibly centuries, to complete. Thus, whereas the ideology of British rule accepted a terminal point in principle, it was pushed far beyond the immediate horizon. The British did make some concessions to unpalatable realities, by granting elective municipal institutions and some elite representation on the Legislative Councils in West Africa. However, there was a determination, both in the Colonial Office and in the colonies themselves, to scotch any expectation that the future lay in the further elaboration of those institutions. At the same time, the British had recourse to more coercive instruments in order to keep 'bolshie' Africans in their place, especially during the 1930s when worries about the infiltration of Communist ideas reached levels bordering on paranoia. However, the failure of elite nationalism to fully connect with peasant movements meant that the challenges were contained with relative ease. Going into the war, the British genuinely believed that they would be able to regulate the pace of change in the African colonies once peace returned: there was to be no precipitous end of empire.

Although the French style of colonial governance always exuded a rather different air, and has frequently been contrasted with that of the British, it followed a comparable trajectory. Like the British, the French had longstanding commercial interests along the coast of West Africa. Their trading posts provided the nucleus for the first colonial possessions, notably along the coast of Senegal, where the towns of St Louis and Gorée were founded in the second half of the seventeenth century. These centres quickly became sites of creolisation in which Frenchmen and Africans conducted business and forged marital bonds. In French eyes these black-and-blue spots came to be regarded as an integral part of the metropole, under the ideology of *assimilation*. The theory was that France would bestow all the benefits of her civilisation upon blacks and *métis*, who would then become to all intents and purposes French. On this view, the historic rôle of France was that of an adoptive parent rather than a mere guardian. The promise of assimilation bore important practical implications. Africans who were born in what eventually became the four communes (St Louis, Dakar, Gorée and Rufisque) came to enjoy rights of citizenship. After 1791, they were granted the right to elect their own municipal councils and mayors, and in 1872 the communes were permitted to send a deputy to the French National Assembly. However, once France acquired vast swathes of Africa in the course of the Scramble, the terms of engagement were called into question.[16] To have conferred full citizenship rights upon all colonised peoples would have entailed the distasteful prospect of metropolitan Frenchmen being outnumbered – and, who knows, maybe even acculturated. Moreover, the practicalities of disseminating French culture across such an expansive and variegated empire were simply too complex to contemplate. It also has to be said that the intellectual climate within France had shifted away from the universalist ideas associated with the French Revolution towards a form of cultural relativism. In a manner which paralleled developments in Britain, contributors to imperial discourse began to stress that culture was something which was organic and could not therefore be transplanted willy-nilly from one context to another.[17] In the twentieth century, therefore, the ideology of *assimilation* formally gave way to a policy of *association*. Henceforth the expressed intention was that of taking what was best about African culture and improving upon it – which was precisely what the British themselves purported to be doing. In practical terms, a two-tiered system came into being. Those people born in the four communes continued to enjoy their citizenship, and were joined by the few Africans elsewhere who fulfilled the strict criteria for elevation. The rest of the Africans were classified as *sujets*, which meant subjection to chiefly rule, abridged legal rights and responsibility for a series of tax and labour obligations.

The change of direction inevitably raised the question of where the empire was now supposed to be headed. It would be reasonable to conclude that nobody was entirely sure any more, either in Paris or in the colonies themselves. Although the French had apparently jettisoned the idea of turning all Africans into Frenchmen, they had not abandoned the principle that the colonies constituted an integral part of France. What this added up to was the prospect of perpetual colonisation, in which the majority of Africans would be closely administered by colonial officials through chiefly intermediaries for time out of mind. In order to carry this off, it was necessary for the French to police the boundaries between citizen and subject, lest the demand for inclusion become more widespread. One means of so doing was to place controls upon African access to education: hence there was a conscious effort to impart a more practical dimension to primary education and to restrict access to secondary education. Like the British, therefore, the French drew back from the high-sounding mission of social transformation into a deeply conservative policy which was geared towards retarding change. The irony was not lost on those most assimilated of Africans who sincerely wished to see an extension of French institutions and practices – and especially high quality education – to the population at large. To them, cultural relativism sounded like a poorly concealed excuse to hold Africans back. Indeed Senegalese intellectuals like Blaise Diagne even began to suspect an intention to turn back the clock within the four communes. Janet Vaillant's biography of Léopold Senghor – a rare case of a *sujet* who managed to secure access to higher education and eventually citizenship – reveals how disillusionment and Francophilia could coexist within the same individual.[18] In the final analysis, the willingness of the elite to tackle the presumptions of imperialism was limited. Moreover, the bifurcation between elite and popular politics was, if anything, even more pronounced in the French colonies. As war loomed in 1939, therefore, the French had reason to believe that the security of their African empire was amongst the least of their worries.

The Portuguese, Spanish, Belgians and Italians brought their own obsessions to the colonial equation. In the case of the Portuguese, the ideology of Luso-tropicalism was one which purported to offer an alternative to the limitations of both the British and French models. The Portuguese liked to think of themselves as the most experienced of the colonial powers, and in the course of their longstanding colonial engagements in Brazil and in parts of Africa – namely in Luanda and along the Zambezi river – they claimed to have found the right balance. The ideologues of empire asserted that whereas the British and French imperial visions were underpinned by racism, they alone were genuinely interested in a creative fusion of peoples and cultures. The theory was that Portugal and its colonies would blend together to the mutual benefit of both sides. As was so often the case, Portuguese colonial theorists were rather more adept at exposing the cant of their rivals than in acknowledging their own shortcomings. Gerald Bender has identified a fundamental difference between the Brazilian version of Luso-tropicalism, which lauded the cultural give-and-take between Portuguese and African populations, and the Portuguese variant in Africa which envisaged a one-way process in which the colonised would eventually become acculturated.[19] The Portuguese model, which was deeply imbued with the kind of social Darwinism which had lost ground elsewhere in Europe, explicitly denied that Africans had anything meaningful to contribute. Consider, for example, the following categoric statement by Marcello Caetano, the future Prime Minister, at a time in the mid-1940s when he was Colonial Minister:

> The blacks in Africa must be directed and moulded by Europeans but they are indispensable as assistants to the latter. I do not affirm this out of prejudice – I merely formulate an observation ... The Africans by themselves did not know how to develop the territories they have inhabited for millennia, they did not account for a single technical discovery, no conquest that counts in the evolution of Humanity, nothing that can compare to the accomplishments in the areas of culture and technology by Europeans or even by Asians.[20]

In the words of Bender, the Portuguese envisaged a three-stage assimilation process: 'the destruction of traditional societies, followed by the inculcation of Portuguese culture and finally the integration of "detribalised" and "Portuguesised" Africans into Portuguese society'.[21] The Colonial Minister in 1933 intimated that this was a process which might take centuries to complete.

Like the French, the Portuguese set up a distinction between those Africans who could be considered as properly assimilated (the *assimilados*) and the rest of the population who were beyond the cultural pale (the *indígenas*). In order to be accepted as an *assimilado*, it was necessary to demonstrate fluency and literacy in the Portuguese language and to practise what was judged to be a civilised lifestyle. In other words, Africans were required to renounce their own cultures in order to avoid the many disabilities that went with being classified as an *indígena*. By its very nature, this requirement ruled out any possibility of cultural give-and-take. Furthermore, assimilation was a practical impossibility for the mass of the population in the colonies of Mozambique, Angola, Guinea-Bissau, Cape Verde, São Tomé and Príncipe because there was little access to education beyond the most basic level.[22] Not surprisingly, therefore, the ranks of *assimilados* remained pitifully thin during the inter-war period, being confined for the most part to individuals of mixed parentage.[23] To be African in the Portuguese colonies, as in the case of the French, was to be condemned to a perpetual minority. The reality of non-assimilation bore important implications in Portuguese Africa by virtue of the mercantilist policies pursued by the Salazar dictatorship. The African peasantry was obliged to cultivate cotton, to sell it at below the world market price and then to purchase

Portuguese cloth at inflated rates. In crude economic terms, these policies were extremely successful. Under conditions of rigid protectionism, the Portuguese textile industry underwent steady expansion.[24] The flip side was, however, the progressive impoverishment of the peasantry in Mozambique and Angola, whose ability to grow sufficient food was threatened by the labour requirements of cotton cultivation.[25] In spite of the ruthless exploitation, the Portuguese did not face a significant challenge to their position in the 1930s, whereas in Guinea-Bissau (which was less systematically exploited) there was a succession of rebellions. Peasants opted to escape across state boundaries, or to quietly subvert the regime of forced cultivation, rather than resorting to more overt forms of resistance. For their part, the *assimilados* were preoccupied with ameliorating the terms of their own incorporation into the colonial system.

Spanish involvement in sub-Saharan Africa was limited to a number of plantation islands, the largest of which was Fernando Po, and the tiny mainland enclave of Rio Muni. Like the Portuguese, the Spanish were primarily concerned with the economic exploitation of their colonial possessions. Insofar as they articulated an ideological position, it was one which dwelt on the 'childlike' nature of Africans who would be in need of perpetual guidance from their Spanish overlords.[26] The Belgians were more unusual in the extent to which they conspicuously failed to articulate a vision of where their colonial enterprise was heading. Part of the reason was that metropolitan opinion exhibited little real interest in matters of colonial policy. But as importantly, the Belgians felt disinclined to articulate a grand philosophy, on the grounds that incremental changes would generate their own dynamic. After the public relations disaster of Leopold's Congo, when large numbers of Africans had been killed or maimed in the pursuit of rubber quotas, the Belgian state assumed direct control and introduced what purported to be a less self-interested form of rule. The Belgian mission was cast primarily in terms of the material improvements it would bring to the lives or ordinary Congolese. The same applied perforce to Ruanda-Urundi, where the Belgians were answerable at the bar of the Permanent Mandates Commission. The concern with intervening purposefully lent a double edge to Belgian rule. On the one hand, they channelled considerable human and financial resources into health care – with a view to the eradication of sleeping sickness and other endemic diseases – and into primary education. The result was that many more Congolese had access to schooling than their counterparts in the other African colonies. On the other hand, Africans were subjected to intrusive interference in almost every aspect of their lives, through the joint operations of three sides of the colonial triad: that is, officialdom, mission organisations and the plantation and mining companies. In the assessment of Crawford Young:

> Through the combined efforts of bureaucracy, capital and Church, each of which fashioned a formidable organisational structure in its own sector of activity, a remarkable colonial system was constructed, unparalleled in the depth of its penetration into the African societies upon which it was superimposed and in the breadth of its control of nearly the whole spectrum of human activity.[27]

As in the Portuguese colonies, the package included compulsory cultivation of crops, especially cotton, and strenuous labour obligations.

To the question of what the ultimate destination might be, the Belgians did not offer a consistent answer. At particular moments, they embraced the ideology of indirect rule, which seemed to imply a desire to build upon indigenous institutions. But at the same time, they appeared to contemplate a permanent bond between Belgium and the Congo (if not the mandated territory). Hence in 1937, Pierre Ryckmans, the Governor-General, felt able to describe the Congo as the 'tenth province' of Belgium.[28] Nowhere was the confusion more apparent than in relation to the emergent *évolué* population. By effectively capping education at the primary level, the Belgians calculated that they would not have to accommodate the aspirations of highly educated Africans. However, post-primary education was available through the seminaries, of which there were quite a number in the Congo. By the 1930s, a cadre of educated seminarians had emerged and was starting to pose a dilemma for the authorities. Many administrators agreed that these individuals ought not to be treated on all-fours with the mass of the population. However, efforts to introduce an *immatriculation* decree, which would confer a distinct status on 'civilised' Africans, foundered due to a lack of consensus as to how widely the net should be cast. The result was that the issue remained in abeyance when war broke out. The assumption was that there was no great rush, and that it would be possible to revisit the issue at a more convenient moment. As for the rest of the population, colonial discourse was inclined to present a reassuring picture of infantile Africans who were growing up happily, but ever so slowly, under the benevolent gaze of Belgium.

Like the Belgians, the Italians were comparative late-comers to the imperial game. They established their first formal possession at Assab, on the Red Sea coast, in 1882. Over the course of the following decades, two colonies were carved out in the Horn, namely Eritrea and Somalia. From the start, the Italians struggled to define the place of the colonies in the greater scheme of things. The colonisation of Eritrea had originally been advocated as a means of relieving land hunger in southern Italy. However, the proposed settlement schemes produced derisory results, and Eritrea quickly fell into other kinds of support roles – as a transit point in the Ethiopian trade and as a supplier of troops for the military conquest of Libya and Somalia.[29] The settlement schemes had even less relevance for Somalia, with its shortage of arable land, and so here the Italians leaned heavily upon concessionary companies – again much like the Belgians and the Portuguese.[30] In both Eritrea and Somalia, the Italians implemented something approximating to French direct rule, in which chiefs were accorded recognition in return for carrying out the everyday tasks of administration. However, comparatively little thought was devoted to larger questions of colonial policy. Italian imperialism was premised on the notion that the colonies were potentially useful assets to the metropole, but there was little clarity beyond that point. As Tekeste Negash has demonstrated with respect to Eritrea, little effort went into trying to imbue the indigenous population with the 'civilising mission'.[31] School textbooks extolled the longevity of Italian civilisation, dating back to Roman times, but few Eritreans ever entered a classroom – and even fewer Somalis did so. In fact, there was a conscious policy of restricting access to education, and limiting it to the primary level, on the grounds that schooling had the potential to destabilise the colonial relationship. The explicit intention was to avoid the creation of educated elites along the lines of British West Africa.

In the first two decades of the twentieth century, Italian policymakers were happy to repeat a familiar paternalist mantra, according to which Africans would need to be ruled by Europeans in their own best interests and for the indefinite future. The rise to power of the Fascists during the 1930s did, however, lead to more overtly racist and self-centered justifications for the colonial project. Africans were now presented as members of a benighted race which needed to be physically segregated from Europeans and dominated by them in perpetuity. The Fascist period also witnessed the resurrection of grandiose plans for European settlement which had serious implications for the indigenous population. Whereas there were only 4188 Italians in Eritrea in 1931, that figure had jumped to 75,000 in 1939 – or 15 per cent of the total population.[32] Moreover, planned settlement of the highlands lay behind the invasion of Ethiopia in 1935, probably even more than Mussolini's desire to avenge the defeat at Adowa.[33] Once in control of Ethiopia, the Italians sought to govern with minimal reference to the indigenous aristocracy, many of whose members turned to guerrilla war. More tellingly, the Italians physically liquidated educated sections of the Ethiopian population who were held to pose a threat to Italian rule.[34] The massacres of 1937, which followed the cold logic of perpetual colonialism to its ultimate conclusion, revealed the colonial contradiction in its starkest form.

1.2.2 Traces in the dissolution of empire: nationalism, colonial planning and neo-colonialism

The Second World War has conventionally been seen as the turning point in the trajectory of colonial rule, and for some very obvious reasons. The fighting culminated in the defeat of one colonial power, namely Italy, and the loss of its empire. In the French and Belgian cases, the impact of the war could hardly have been more climactic, with the humiliating occupation of the metropole by the Nazis. Ironically, it was the African colonies which subsequently provided a secure base for the resistance. From Chad, the Guyanese governor, Félix Eboué, engineered a series of coups d'état which led to all of French Equatorial Africa as well as Cameroun being detached from the Vichyite fold in 1940. Two years later, French West Africa was won over to the resistance side. Similarly the exiled Belgian government relocated itself to the Congo. Although the British did not succumb, there is no question that the frailty of the largest empire was put on public display – most obviously in Asian theatres such as Singapore. Throughout the continent, Africans contributed to the war effort, either in a military capacity or through the contributions they made to wartime production. These were years of intense hardship, and there was widespread recognition that Africans would have to be offered some reward when the fighting eventually came to an end. Promises made, or even expectations raised, in the heat of the conflict could not so easily be withdrawn once the dust had settled. To a greater or lesser extent, therefore, each of the powers – with the exception of neutral Portugal – found themselves having to address the question of post-war reform. As I shall now demonstrate with reference to each of the empires, this brought the colonial contradiction into the open.

1.2.2.1   War as a solvent of empire

To make sense of the dismantling of the European empires, it would be wise to start with the weakest links – that is the territories which had ceased to be, or had never been, colonies in the conventional sense. On the one hand, the League of Nations mandates were transferred to the United Nations after the Second World War, which – in the spirit of the Atlantic Charter – vested the various trustees with preparing the territories for eventual independence. The one exception was South West Africa which South Africa refused to relinquish, preferring to install its own quasi-colonial system. As much as the European powers insisted on the distinct status of the colonies, the language of trusteeship was bound to resonate within these other domains as well. On the other hand, the post-1919 settlement also provided a model for dealing with the Italian colonies. In fact, the outcomes were not quite those which might have been predicted. Following victory over the Italians in 1941, in which Ethiopian combatants played their part, Haile Selassie returned from exile and made it clear that he would accept nothing less than a reversion to full independence. Largely because of American backing, this was achieved the following year. In fact, the emperor also hoped to claim slices of the Italian colonial cake if – as seemed likely – there was to be a fresh carve-up in the Horn. Although he was not entirely successful in his endeavours, Haile Selassie was able to stake a lasting claim to the whole of Eritrea on the basis of ancient historical and cultural affinities. In 1946, Britain had advocated the partition of Eritrea between Ethiopia and Sudan, which fell short of what the Emperor would ideally have wanted. Nevertheless he was prepared to accept such an eventuality given the lack of enthusiasm for his own claims on the part of the United States, the Soviet Union and France.[35] The Four Power Commission which visited Eritrea over 1947/48 found a very slim majority of local opinion in favour of independence or temporary international trusteeship, but estimated that as many as 48 per cent favoured union with Ethiopia. The Muslim League (ML) championed independence largely because of apprehension about domination at the hands of Christian Ethiopia. The Liberal Progressive Party (LPP), on the other hand, proposed unification of Tigrayans on either side of the Ethiopia–Eritrea border, in which independence would follow a ten-year period of British trusteeship.[36] The largest single party was the Unionist Party (UP), drawing most of its support from the Christian highlands, which advocated outright union with Ethiopia. Nobody supported partition at the time, although in 1949 Muslim Leaguers from the Western province realigned themselves with the UP after the latter endorsed the Bevin-Sforza proposal to unite that region with Sudan.[37] In subsequent years, the unionist position gained in strength, in large part because of internal divisions within the pro-independence camp. In 1949, the ML, the LPP and four smaller parties had joined hands in an Independence Bloc.

However, the breakaway of the ML of the Western province was followed by a rapid unravelling of the Bloc. Many historians have also attributed the advance of the UP to the willingness of the Ethiopian government to bankroll its activities, although Tekeste Negash denies that there is very much evidence for this.[38] Be that as it may, a further United Nations Commission in 1950 now found that 'a majority of Eritreans favour political association with Ethiopia', although it accepted that there was a large body of dissenting opinion. Quite what 'political association' meant in practice was open to interpretation.[39] Nevertheless, on 2 December 1950 the United Nations sanctioned a federal union between Eritrea and Ethiopia, which came into existence two years later after further consultations between the appointed Commissioner and the Ethiopian government.

An equally unexpected scenario unfolded in Somaliland. Having established their de facto control over most of the Somali peoples, with the exception of those in Djibouti, the British initially sought to perpetuate these arrangements under a trusteeship agreement.[40] When this bid was frustrated, in part through Ethiopian opposition, there was effectively a return to the *status quo ante*. The Western Somalis of the Ogaden and the Haud were handed over to Ethiopia in 1948, while the United Nations vested the Italians with trusteeship over their own former colony the following year.[41] In each case, however, riders were attached. The British were to retain a presence in the Haud, where British Somalis enjoyed grazing rights. In the Italian Trust Territory, crucial stipulations were written into the trusteeship agreement: namely that the Italian administration would endure only for a ten-year period, during which time it was 'to promote the development of the inhabitants of the territory towards independence'. The terminal point was precisely stated, and the Italians dutifully set about training a cadre of administrators and politicians who would take over the reins when the trusteeship was terminated. As that date approached, the parties which had emerged to contest elections agreed on one thing, which was that the Somali people who had been divided by colonial borders ought to be reunited in independence. The formation of the National Pan-Somali Movement in 1959 added greater momentum to the unification cause. In the British Protectorate of Somaliland, there was initially a lack of a sense of urgency. However, the final withdrawal of British officials from the Haud at the end of 1954, accompanied by an obvious Ethiopian determination to establish effective control, led to political restiveness within the Protectorate. Although the British could do nothing to reverse the Haud decision, they did decide to accelerate the pace of political change in their own territory.[42] They did not limit themselves to creating representative institutions, but also intimated that they would not stand in the way of a future union with the Italian territory. As independence for Somalia loomed, the administration hastily brokered a deal which provided for the independence of British Somaliland five days before. On 1 July 1960, an independent Republic of Somalia was forged out of the neighbouring territories. The euphoria was palpable, but there remained the issue of other Somalis in neighbouring states. As we shall see in the next chapter, the leadership of Somalia embarked on a collision course with the latter soon after independence.

The tractability of the British in relation to Somali affairs can partially be explained by their response to other kinds of events unfolding in the Sudan. The Sudan had always enjoyed a unique status, and it is this which helps to account for its early evolution in the direction of independence.[43] Although the Sudan was formally an Egyptian possession, the British claimed rights of administration after helping to defeat the Mahdist forces – an arrangement which was formalised under the 1899 Agreement. When Britain formally acknowledged Egyptian independence in 1922, the question of the status of the Sudan was posed once again. After the British insisted on the withdrawal of Egyptian troops in 1924, the co-domini found themselves at persistent loggerheads. The Egyptians sought recognition of their sovereignty over the Sudan, whereas British administrators made it clear that they would have preferred to abrogate the condominium altogether. The fact that the Sudan was a Foreign Office rather than a Colonial Office responsibility, and that the former was guided by wider strategic considerations, merely complicated matters further. In their efforts to offset Egyptian claims, the British desperately needed Sudanese voices to lend support to their own position, which explains why official policy diverged from that in the colonies proper. On the one hand, significant numbers of educated Sudanese were brought into administrative structures much earlier than in most of colonial Africa. On the other hand, the British encouraged different fractions of the Sudanese elite – traditional, religious and modern – to embrace the vision of a future apart from Egypt. In April 1942 when Stafford Cripps stopped off en route to make his famous offer to Indian nationalists, he was presented with a Graduates' Congress memorandum which, amongst other things, asserted the right of the Sudanese to self-determination.[44] Although this demand was regarded as premature, it did hasten the process of internal reform.

As part of their unfolding strategy, the British administration buried a very rusty hatchet by establishing a working alliance with the son of the Mahdi and head of the Ansar sect, Sayyid Abd al-Rahman al-Mahdi, whose anti-Egyptian sentiments could always be counted upon. Nevertheless, there were other sections of the population who saw things differently. Within the Graduates' Congress, the Ashiqqa faction espoused a vaguely unionist position, and was supported by the leader of the other influential Muslim brotherhood, Sayyid Ali al-Mirghani of the Khatmiyya. By 1945, Sudanese politicians (who were all from the North) were divided over the future of their country. The Umma Party, which was sponsored by Sayyid Abd al-Rahman, participated in the Advisory Council for Northern Sudan, and later the Legislative Assembly, with a view to hastening independence. By contrast, the unionists boycotted these institutions and continued to look to Egypt.[45] A major turning point followed in 1946 when the Foreign Secretary declared that the British goal was self-government leading to independence, and that the final dispensation had to be the choice of the Sudanese themselves.[46] This way of phrasing the question was an anathema to the Egyptians who continued to seek recognition of the sovereignty of King Farouk, and even went as far as unilaterally abrogating the 1899 Agreement in October 1951. The second turning point came with the military coup which overthrew Farouk in July 1952, marking the return of a more militant form of Egyptian nationalism. The primary objective of the Nasser regime was to secure the removal of foreign troops from the Suez Canal zone. The assertion of claims over the Sudan were consistent with the nationalist posture of the regime, but were of secondary importance. The new Egyptian government acknowledged that some form of self-determination for the Sudan was inevitable, but calculated that enduring links might still be retained if only the meddling British were removed from the equation. It therefore set about wooing Sudanese politicians of all persuasions and did so with such success that the British were forced to make concessions, which involved reduced powers for the Governor-General and the acceptance of a role for outside powers. There remained one fundamental sticking point, namely the future of southern Sudan which had been insulated from the North. The British administration initially sought to retain oversight over the South, but a series of mutinies there in 1955 seemed to demonstrate the folly of hanging on. As relations between Britain and Egypt deteriorated in the run-up to the Suez crisis, the former let it be known that it would be receptive to a Sudanese request for outright independence. When the request came in January 1956, it emanated from the National Unionist Party (NUP) which had finally come to recognise the advantages of going it alone. In that momentous year, Britain was forced to forfeit its pre-eminent position in Egypt, while Sudan was forever lost to the Egyptians.

The cases which I have considered so far were those where the fewest barriers to independence existed. In the colonies proper, things were not as straightforward, and it is these to which I now turn.

1.2.2.2   The setting of the sun on the British empire

Despite British assumptions that the colonial project had almost infinite amounts of time in which to play itself out, it was wound up in a historical flash. Because of the singularity of the Sudan, the independence of Ghana the following year was a more symbolic moment. Nigeria was to follow suit in 1960, followed by Sierra Leone and Tanzania in 1961. By 1968, the year of Swaziland independence, the remaining colonies had gone their separate ways. That left only Southern Rhodesia, but even here there was an independence of a sort, in that white settlers proclaimed their own Unilateral Declaration of Independence (UDI) in 1965. The rapidity with which the British empire in Africa imploded has frequently been commented upon. In their efforts to account for this unanticipated outcome, historians have invoked different kinds of causalities. There are broadly speaking three competing positions, each of which has enjoyed the ascendancy at a particular moment in recent history: for convenience these may be labelled as the nationalist, the neo-colonialist and the planned decolonisation theses.

The historical writing which followed hard on the heels of independence itself accorded considerable weight to the wartime experience in shaping nationalist responses. These early accounts told of how the scales fell from the eyes of Africans, and how the latter set about organising themselves into more purposeful nationalist organisations once peacetime conditions returned. The textbook case was the rise of nationalism in the Gold Coast – or what C. L. R. James dubbed more grandiosely 'the Ghana revolution'.[47] Standard nationalist histories typically posited a linear sequence of events: in the case of the Gold Coast, it was the grievances of ex-servicemen which led to the Accra riots of 1948, colonial repression and the emergence of a radicalised movement in the guise of the Convention People's Party (CPP). At the centre of this particular story – as told by C. L. R. James, Basil Davidson and others – stood the commanding presence of Kwame Nkrumah, who had learned the tactics of modern party organisation during his travels abroad.[48] It was conceded that while the British were reluctant to pack their bags, they had the good grace to recognise when the game was up. Nkrumah's victory in the elections of 1951, from behind the prison bars, clearly demonstrated where the loyalties of the mass of the population lay. A similar story has been told, often to the accompaniment of the jailer's keys, in respect of Tanganyika (Tanzania), Nyasaland (Malawi), Northern Rhodesia (Zambia) and Kenya.

Nationalist historiography was, however, the epic as political elites wanted it told. Indeed some leaders like Kwame Nkrumah contributed consciously to the telling in their own memoirs.[49] In the light of subsequent experience, when the same leaders often took on a less benign aspect, the liberational tone of this early writing began to seem more suspect. In the 1970s, the rise of the dependency paradigm brought a reappraisal of the entire decolonisation episode. Some commentators now questioned whether the high drama of the nationalist struggle was not more of a smokescreen, concealing a cosy compact between the departing colonial power and the African elites whom they had groomed for the succession. From the standpoint of *dependendistas*, flag independence amounted to the perpetuation of a dependent relationship in a slightly different guise – in other words, neo-colonialism.[50] In the 1980s, as the explanatory power of the dependency paradigm waned in its turn, historians with a decidedly empiricist bent claimed that the real answers to why decolonisation occurred were to be found in the Public Record Office in London as the 30-year rule expired.[51] The revisionists effectively reversed the order of causality, asserting that it was the British who had decided to embark upon the path of reform which led inexorably towards decolonisation, breathing life into the dormant forces of nationalism in the process.

The imputation that African nationalism was the by-product of British initiatives of course veered dangerously close to the neo-colonialist thesis. However, both John Flint and Robert Pearce set out to distance themselves from the latter on the grounds it was driven by theory rather than the hard evidence; that it wrongly assumed the prescience of the colonial power; and that the British actually eschewed the temptation to cultivate a tame *comprador* class, preferring instead to transfer power to nationalists who could demonstrate mass support.[52] Ironically, this desire to put clear blue water between themselves and the dependency school sometimes led the revisionists back into the terrain of nationalist history which they purported to have transcended. Hence, Flint finally concluded that colonial planning failed because of the exigencies of the war which 'proved fertile soil for the transformation of elite reformism into mass nationalism on challenging and not the cooperative lines envisaged by the plan. In the end this forced a policy of political decolonisation to replace that of colonial reform.'[53] By highlighting the catalytic effect of the war in stimulating mass nationalism, and by crediting the latter with shaping the final contours of decolonisation, Flint brings his readers full circle.

Where then does this leave the quest for an overarching explanation? This is not the place to construct a detailed answer. However, it would be remiss not to offer some guidance as to how the various interpretations might be reconciled. The first point to make is that a whiff of reform was indeed in the air towards the end of the 1930s. As Flint indicates, this involved a significant departure from two of the most deeply ingrained colonial orthodoxies. On the one hand, the strict insistence that budgets should balance and that the colonies should pay for themselves was replaced by a willingness to countenance investment in economic development and social improvement. The Colonial Development and Welfare Act of 1940 might reasonably be taken as the point at which the modern discourse of developmentalism – which has continued, through various mutations, down to the present day – was born.[54] On the other hand, Indirect Rule dogmas began to be jettisoned as second thoughts were expressed about the viability of chieftaincy as the building blocks for a future political dispensation. Although Colonial Office thinking remained sceptical about the leadership claims of the educated elites, there was at least a willingness to think again. As Flint has indicated, the job of mapping out an alternative course was handed over to Lord Hailey. The latter was not intellectually inclined to serve up cut-and-dried solutions, and firmly insisted that the course of economic and social change should be left to shape the contours of a future political dispensation.[55] In that sense, the empiricist tradition lived on. At the end of the day, the undoubted historical significance of these policy shifts lay in the abandonment of the presumption that Africans belonged to a separate political species. If Africans were not so different after all, that did raise fundamental questions about the basis on which they could be prevented from exercising full political rights. In that sense, reform brought the colonial contradiction to the fore.

Nevertheless, it would be fallacious to presume that reform pointed unambiguously in the direction of decolonisation. Indeed, it arguably had the opposite intention, namely to reconstitute empire on a more viable footing. If Africans belonged to *homo politicus*, it was still possible for the likes of Hailey to insist on the requirement of a lengthy period of induction. Flint claims that Malcolm Macdonald was the first to have made 'self-government for British African colonies...a central purpose of colonial policy' in a speech in 1938.[56] However, Pearce points out that this amounted to mere speculation on the part of the Colonial Secretary. He also disputes that Oliver Stanley's 1943 statement that the intention was 'to guide colonial peoples along the road to self-government within the framework of the British Empire' amounted to very much, both because of hidden ambiguities and because the Colonial Secretary expressed doubts that it could be applied to the majority of the colonies. Pearce concludes, convincingly enough, that 'there can be little real doubt that by 1943 "colonial reform" from the CO [Colonial Office] was in essence designed to conserve Britain's imperial control'.[57] This assessment is borne out in the internal debate surrounding Governor Alan Burns' proposal to include Africans on the Executive Council of the Gold Coast in 1942. The then Colonial

Secretary, Lord Cranborne declared himself in favour of this apparently radical step, not because he wanted to hasten independence, but for precisely the opposite reason:

> If we want the British Empire to endure, is it not essential that we should assume that it is to be a permanency, and that so far from teaching Colonial people to govern themselves, we should do the contrary, and welcome their participation in our administration?[58]

Pearce nevertheless concurs with Flint that the initiative ultimately rested with the metropole. For him, the turning point came not in 1938 or 1943, but in 1947. In that year, two memoranda were hatched within the Colonial Office.[59] The first was the Cohen-Caine report which explicitly envisaged constitutional development for the African colonies, according to which the Legislative and Executive Councils would be adapted to conform to the Westminster model. The report also spoke explicitly of a four-stage transition to self-government. The second document was the Local Government Despatch which clarified the relationship between central government and the structures of 'native administration'. The despatch envisaged replacing the old Native Authorities by elected local government bodies – thereby finally driving a stake through the heart of the Indirect Rule beast – and utilising these councils as electoral colleges for legislative assemblies at the centre. According to Pearce, '[T]he 1947 plans were a mature and systematic exposition of CO [Colonial Office] thinking, a consistent and conscious strategy of decolonisation.'[60] This is a significant claim because, if it were true, it would demonstrate that nationalist agitation post-dated British planning. However, it would seem that the very objection raised by Pearce against Flint's reading of history could be levelled at his own conclusions: namely that reform, however far-reaching, did not of itself point to a firm intention to pull out. If we take note of what Sydney Caine – one of the key architects of the plan – was saying in 1947, it is striking how limited the ambitions were. He stated that Britain 'must assume that perhaps within a generation many of the principal territories of the Colonial Empire will have attained or be in sight of the goal of full responsibility for local affairs'.[61] Almost every word is laden with hefty qualifications to the main proposition. Turned inside out, the statement could be taken as meaning that even after a generation many – even most – territories would remain firmly within the colonial orbit, and that the select few that were judged fit for internal self-government would still be constrained. In effect, policy-makers at the centre were still intent on consigning the terminal point to some conveniently distant spot on the political horizon.

Nor is it in any way surprising that Britain should have wanted to reinvigorate the empire. During the war, and in the years immediately following, the African colonies made an invaluable economic contribution by virtue of the dollars they earned through primary exports to the United States, which were then surrendered to the metropole. These enabled Britain to secure vital American imports, a consideration which gained added salience with the termination of Lend-Lease arrangements in 1945. The sterling crisis of 1947, which resulted from a premature effort to restore convertibility, underlined just how serious the foreign exchange constraints were – and thus how crucial the contribution of the colonies was.[62] Before the war, the African colonies had been considered as somewhat marginal to Britain's economic prosperity. However towards the end of the 1940s, the Gold Coast stood second only to Malaya in its dollar-earning performance.[63] And around 1952, it has been estimated that the African colonies as a whole provided over 20 per cent of the sterling area's reserves.[64] Although the colonies earned dollars, restrictions were placed on imports from outside the sterling area. Moreover, the sterling equivalents were not returned to the African colonies, but were banked in London and used to finance post-war reconstruction in the metropole. In the estimation of David Fieldhouse, colonial sterling balances rose from £760 to £920 million between 1946 and 1951, in addition to which the West African marketing boards accounted for a further £93 million.[65] If there was ever a time when the African empire was a paying proposition, this was surely it. Indeed, the point was not lost on the post-war Labour government. The Chancellor of the Exchequer, Stafford Cripps, hoped for a resolution to the structural weakness of the British economy by developing the colonial estates with greater vigour.[66] The expectation was that more substantial investment in the colonies would yield greater rewards both for Britain and her colonies. In an effort to avoid making concessions to the dependency school, Pearce makes two observations: that Cripps' vision of an African Eldorado proved to be utopian, and that political reforms evolved separately from the economic agenda.[67] On the first point, it is surely as questionable to extrapolate intentions from consequences as it is to deduce consequences from intentions (the essence of his critique of the dependency position). The second qualification may well be valid, but it nevertheless remains to be proven that there was a coherent plan for African independence in 1947.[68] If one were to meet the revisionists half way, one might accept that 'intimations of imperial mortality' had begun to register during the war years.[69] But if the thinking of 1947 was an advance on the perpetual colonialism of the inter-war years, it was surely a limited one. The telling words 'perhaps within a generation' do not suggest that very much thought had been given to a terminal point.

If the planned decolonisation thesis has its limitations, one is inevitably led to reconsider the impact of events within the African colonies themselves. It is all too easy to downplay the significance of the Gold Coast riots of 28 February 1948, which have stood as the centrepiece of standard nationalist histories: they were relatively shortlived in duration, geographically isolated and entailed fairly minimal loss of life and property.[70] Be that as it may, the riots did shake the local administration to its core and sent alarm bells ringing back in London. Fearing a Communist-inspired conspiracy, the authorities quickly rounded up the leadership of the United Gold Coast Convention (UGCC), including their young general secretary, Kwame Nkrumah. Because the Gold Coast had hitherto been regarded as something of a model colony, a good deal of soul-searching ensued. The Watson Commission, which was set up to look into the causes of the outbreak, identified insufficient scope for political participation as a root cause.[71] The Burns Constitution of 1946, which had conceded an African majority in the Legislative Council, was now adjudged to be 'outmoded at birth'. The authors made recommendations for constitutional reform which, as John Hargreaves observes, were still premised on the maintenance of the colonial nexus for the foreseeable future.[72] The Colonial Office did not accept the specific recommendations, but did take the general point that educated Africans needed to be given a more demanding role. The bold official response was therefore to create an all-African commission to draft fresh constitutional proposals. The Coussey Commission included the released UGCC leaders with the pointed exception of Nkrumah who defected to form the CPP in June 1949. As has been extensively documented, the CPP then proceeded to outbid the UGCC, which was prepared to endorse a steady progression towards greater autonomy under British tutelage.

Although it is difficult to put a precise date on it, it is at about this point that colonial certainties began to dissolve. This was not because the British actually lost control over the Gold Coast. On the contrary, the Positive Action campaign of the CPP was quashed with comparative ease. It was rather because issues of timing had begun to be phrased in a manner which undercut the British position. Prior to 1949/50, the Colonial Office had managed to discuss the principles of self-government in abstract terms, whilst studiously avoiding the question of timetables. The CPP leadership was astute enough to put the question of timing at the forefront of its campaign. The only possible response to 'Self-Government NOW' was 'as soon as practicable', which merely invited the subsidiary question of 'So when?'. The inevitable consequence of being placed on the spot was that the British entered into a kind of off-stage debate, which had the net effect of foreshortening expectations of the durability of British rule. When Nkrumah won the 1951 election in handsome fashion, Governor Charles Arden-Clarke bit the bullet and invited him to form a government. From this point onwards, the CPP cooperated closely with the British authorities, in the belief that power would thereby be transferred to African hands with greater despatch. By 1954, the British appear to have accepted that there was nothing that could justify resisting the demand for independence for very much longer. Although the regionalist backlash in Ashanti, the Northern Territories and Trans-Volta Togoland threatened to derail the smooth transition, the clear victory of the CPP in the 1956 elections prepared the way for the final handover on 6 March 1957.[73]

Standing back from all this detail, it evidently makes little sense to write Gold Coast nationalists out of the script, or to cast them merely as a by-product of Colonial Office initiatives. The reason is that the networks of collaboration, which had held the fabric of colonial rule together, were already tearing in the 1930s. Although the cocoa holdups were directed against the European buying firms rather than the state *per se*, they did point to a pervasive malaise surrounding the colonial system as a whole.[74] The acute hardships of the 1940s had an even more profound impact on the urban areas, where a culture of popular resistance was manifesting itself in consumer boycotts and labour unrest. Hence the 1948 riots did not come out of the blue, but were the culmination of a process of steady attrition in the relationship between ruler and ruled. Although the intelligence arm of the colonial state was aware of this trend, it took the riots to serve the administration with a wake-up call. The CPP played a double game, which involved tapping into popular discontent at the same time as it sought to persuade the British that it was led by reasonable men. The balancing act worked in part because there were no rivals to outflank the CPP on the left, and in part also because the British did not have the stomach for a fight. Once it had gained access to the corridors of power, the CPP was able to unravel what remained of the colonial project by tugging at the weakest threads. One does not have to accept the whole package of nationalist history – with its portrayal of the relationship between leaders and followers – to recognise that without the nationalists there would have been no Ghanaian independence in 1957.

Together, the unfolding of events in the Sudan and the Gold Coast created precedents for, as well as heightening expectations in, other parts of British Africa. In a nutshell, they made it difficult to justify withholding political entitlements from other Africans. The authorities in the other colonies were only too well-aware of the fact that their own room for manoeuvre was being circumscribed by developments in these two territories. Hence Governor Macpherson of Nigeria expressed dismay at the pace of change in the Gold Coast, and in 1953 went as far as soliciting a guarantee from Arden-Clarke that full self-government would not come to the Gold Coast before a period of four to five years was up.[75] Equally, the Governors in East and Central Africa repeatedly expressed their concern that reforms in the Gold Coast were creating 'unrealistic' pressures for political change in their own domains. As it happened, the Gold Coast precedent proved rather stronger in the context of West Africa than in East or Central Africa.

There had always been an underlying assumption that the fates of the Gold Coast and Nigeria were somehow intertwined. Nevertheless, the Nigerian authorities were generally more inclined to err on the side of caution when it came to political reform. The reason was partly that the Indirect Rule canon was more deeply entrenched in Nigeria than anywhere else, with the possible exception of Uganda. The situation was further complicated by the substantial variations in practice between different parts of the colony, which made for some passing similarities with the Sudan. Whereas the preservation of the emirate system in Northern Nigeria had sealed off the North from outside political influences and restricted access to education, the South-West had enjoyed a long acquaintance with mission education and was fast being caught by the South-East. The intrusion of a fresh wave of pan-Africanist ideas in the 1930s had also underlined the extent to which southern intellectuals still looked beyond the borders of Nigeria towards a wider Atlantic world.[76] The elites of the South had long been agitating for greater access to decision-making at the centre. In 1947, the Richards Constitution offered modest concessions, whilst bringing northerners onto the Legislative Council for the first time.[77] The disappointment registered in nationalist circles led the newly formed National Council of Nigeria and the Cameroons (NCNC) to embark on a political tour of the entire country for the first time. This period also witnessed a brief efflorescence of militant nationalism in the form of the Zikist movement, which was prepared to resort to violent methods in pursuit of independence and 'socialism'. However, after a bloody strike at the Enugu colliery, widespread rioting and an attempted assassination of the Chief Secretary, the Zikists were proscribed in April 1950.[78] As the initiative returned to more orthodox nationalists, bitter rifts within Nigerian politics (which were both ethnic and intensely personal) became increasingly apparent. In the mid-1940s, there had already been a Yoruba backlash against the leadership pretensions of Nnamdi Azikiwe, who was an Igbo and distinctly proud of it. In 1950, Obafemi Awolowo formally inaugurated the Action Group (AG) as a political party with the explicit aim of driving the NCNC out of the West and mobilising a Yoruba ethnic constituency. The emergence of the Northern People's Congress (NPC) in time for the 1951 elections set the seal on a tripartite division of the country. Whereas the NPC sought to delay independence in order to enable the more backward North to catch up, the NCNC and the AG competed in making demands for rapid independence.

The fracture within Nigerian politics was probably as decisive in guaranteeing a British retreat as if there *had* been a more cohesive nationalist movement. The spectre which hung over the British was that of a re-run of the partition of India. The administration found itself caught on the horns of a dilemma: to fail to keep pace with concessions in the Gold Coast risked antagonising southern nationalists, whereas seeking to keep ahead of the political game risked provoking the northern aristocracy. The scale of the problem was underlined in March 1953, when the AG proposed a legislative motion for self-government in 1956. The NPC representatives refused to back it and when they were subsequently heckled in Lagos, they returned to the North with threats of secession on their lips. Widespread rioting in Kano followed in May, after Awolowo had indicated his intention to embark on a tour of the North. At this point, the Northern House of Chiefs and the Northern House of Assembly demanded outright dissolution of the Nigerian federation. Faced with a serious crisis which might require the deployment of imperial troops, the British sought to create a breathing space. They brokered a new constitution in 1954, which devolved substantial decision-making powers onto Nigerians, but shifted the centre of gravity towards the three Regions within the federation. In the short term, this defused some of the tension, but in the longer run it merely created fresh sites of contestation. While the NCNC and the AG renewed their struggle for control of the Western Region, the AG lent its support to emergent minority movements demanding separation from the Northern and Eastern regions. The British response to the minorities question was to have fatal consequences for Nigeria after independence. Rather than endorse a federation of multiple units, the British insisted on the perpetuation of an arrangement in which minority voices were sidelined and the Northern Region was larger than the East and the West combined. This meant that if the NPC could establish a stranglehold over the North, it was well-placed to dominate the federation in perpetuity. Following an ill-tempered national election in 1959, the British choreographed their formal exit in 1960, transferring power to a highly unstable coalition between the NPC and the NCNC.

Once the Gold Coast was independent and Nigeria was heading in the same direction, the British embarked on what might fairly be described as a policy of scuttle in relation to the two remaining West African colonies. In Sierra Leone and the Gambia, where the forces of nationalism were distinctly weak, it was the British who forced the pace. The Gambia was a tiny sliver of territory, consisting of roughly ten kilometres on either side of the river by that name, and was poorly endowed. Whereas the best interests of Gambians lay in trying to wring as many resources as possible out of the metropole, the latter was reluctant to prolong the relationship for this very reason. The British recognised that the viability of the Gambia was doubtful, but placed their hope in some form of association with neighbouring Senegal.[79] The mineral wealth of Sierra Leone gave this territory more of a fighting chance. Here it was the division between Colony and Protectorate which was the dominant theme.[80] Whereas the Creoles of the Colony, with their tradition of educational achievement and enterprise, might have been expected to emulate their Gold Coast and Nigerian cousins, their posture was actually closer to that of the conservative Northern Nigerian establishment. They were generally opposed to the wholesale extension of the franchise for the reason that they would be outnumbered by up-country voters. They therefore sought to hold out for equal representation with the Protectorate, a demand which was not acceptable to the emergent up-country leadership or to the British. Sierra Leone was ultimately placed on the same constitutional track as the larger colonies, but with the one significant difference that chiefs were accorded separate representation in the legislature. The independence of Sierra Leone, under the leadership of Dr Milton Margai, followed in April 1961. The Gambia brought up the rear four years later.

When it comes to East and Central Africa, the planned decolonisation thesis carries even less explanatory weight because settler communities were able to dictate the pace and trajectory of change for much of the time. The Colonial Office consequently found itself responding to local pressures rather than shaping events according to some plan of its own. In Southern Rhodesia, the settlers had been granted a substantial measure of internal self-government as early as 1923 and were in no mood to accept renewed metropolitan interference at the end of the 1940s. Although the smaller settler community of Kenya (numbering around 130,000 in 1950) had tried and failed to wrest the same concessions from the British state, they had nevertheless managed to increase their representation within the Legislative Council and had gained entry to the Executive Council during the war.[81] From these strongholds, they were able to mount effective resistance against a replication of the processes they saw unfolding elsewhere. Across East and Southern Africa, settlers flatly contradicted the notion that the principle of universal adult suffrage might be applicable to Africans. Instead, they insisted that *their* Africans were incapable of appreciating, and thus sharing in, such entitlements – at least for the foreseeable future. In that sense, settler communities remained fixated on the discourse of perpetual colonialism. To a substantial degree, they enjoyed the sympathetic backing of local administrations. For example, Sir Philip Mitchell had been appointed Governor of Kenya because it was felt that he would stand up to the settlers, but he became pretty much captive to their viewpoint.[82] Like them, Mitchell was overtly critical of the Cohen-Caine proposals which he regarded as misguided and out of kilter with Kenyan realities.[83]

The election of the National Party government in South Africa in 1948, and the flirtation of settlers with influences from south of the Limpopo, persuaded the Colonial Office that it was essential to work with the grain of settler opinion, lest it lose their support altogether. Whereas the principles of majoritarianism won out in West Africa, the profoundly ambiguous concept of a 'multiracial partnership' was concocted to serve a number of ends. The name of the game was to keep the settlers on-side, whilst providing greater scope for African participation. Alongside partnership went an interest in federating neighbouring territories in East and Central Africa. At one level, federation was touted as a means of combining the complementary strengths of the different territories and rationalising the costs of their administration. Closer union for the three East African territories of Kenya, Uganda and Tanganyika – one with a dominant settler sector, the second with vibrant peasant economy and the third with a mixture of the two – had been mooted as early as the 1920s. After 1945, there was renewed interest in developing mechanisms to administer their common services. A similar rationale was put forward in respect of Central Africa, where there was talk of combining the mineral resources of Northern Rhodesia, the labour of Nyasaland and settler enterprise from Southern Rhodesia. At another level, the federation packages were also designed to recapture some of the political initiative for the metropole. Settlers in Kenya well understood the dangers of demographic dilution and opposed federation proposals for that reason, despite Mitchell's efforts to persuade them of the countervailing advantages.[84] In a nutshell, multiracialism and federalism were designed to win over incompatible constituencies amongst the settlers, the Asian community and the African population.

In East Africa, it took vigorous African opposition from within Uganda and Tanganyika to scupper the federation proposals. In both cases, the underlying fear was that land might be alienated to white settlers and that the racial hierarchy of Kenya might be imported from across the border. Tanganyikans had good reasons to be apprehensive, because the administration had set about soliciting European immigration after the war. In the decade after 1948 the number of whites virtually doubled from 10,648 to 20,598, although many of these were associated with the ill-fated groundnut scheme rather than being settler farmers in the conventional sense.[85] Given that there were plans afoot to quadruple the number of settlers entering Kenya as well, there was every possibility that federation would open the door to European encroachment.[86] In Tanganyika, the initial debate over Closer Union had led to the formation, as early as 1929, of the African Association, which was the first political organisation to aspire towards national coverage.[87] The post-war proposals similarly played their part in the transformation of the African Association into the Tanganyika African National Union (TANU) in 1954. In Uganda, the European and Asian business community had themselves opposed pre-war federation proposals on the grounds that they were subsidising the Kenyan settlers enough as it was through preferential freight rates and the unequal distribution of customs revenue.[88] However, opposition to federation was mobilised most resolutely from within Buganda, which had enjoyed a special status since 1900. When the British sought a land grant to build Makerere College and an agricultural station, the proposals were interpreted by a rising neo-traditionalist movement as the first step towards the expropriation of Baganda land.[89]

In 1953, when the Secretary of State, Oliver Lyttleton, raised the question of federation in general terms, this was interpreted in the most sinister way. In order to regain some of his waning authority, Kabaka Mutesa II did not simply insist that Uganda remain outside any projected federation, but seemed to lend his voice to calls for the separate independence of Buganda. His refusal to back down over this issue led to his deportation at the hands of none other than Governor Andrew Cohen, the supposed liberal of revisionist historiography. The first Buganda crisis was instrumental in putting the final nail in the coffin of federation. From this point onwards, attention focused on the question of balance of power within each of the East African territories.

In Tanganyika, Governor Twining was an enthusiastic advocate of partnership, and sought a means of reconciling the conflicting aspirations of Europeans, Asians and Africans. Like Mitchell in Kenya, he regarded the West African model as singularly inappropriate. Twining brokered a formula in 1949 which established parity of representation between the three populations, both at the centre and at lower levels of the administration. Given the demographic imbalance, this was regarded by Africans as a cynical attempt to cement minority dominance. In the late 1940s and early 1950s, there was much rural resistance to the heavy-handed interventionism associated with the agricultural 'improvement', to the attempted reorganisation of local government and to land seizures in Meru.[90] These various strands were drawn together by the new generation of activists who founded TANU. The latter insisted that Tanganyika was as much an African territory as the Gold Coast was and set about emulating the strategies of the CPP. Within the space of a few years, TANU had proved highly successful in establishing new branches, with separate youth and women's sections, across the length and breadth of the country.[91] By 1960, TANU may have recruited as many as a million members, which meant that a remarkable one in five adults belonged to the party.[92]

Although TANU set its face against Twining's vision, its leadership was also pragmatic. Nyerere and his colleagues spent much of their time seeking to cool down the militants in the provinces, lest an outbreak of violence lead to a repetition of the crisis which was unfolding in Kenya.[93] In 1954, Nyerere had spoken of independence in 25 years, and although he had foreshortened this prediction to ten years by the end of 1956, he was not seeking a precipitous termination of British rule.[94] Iliffe observes that his immediate priority was to undo the official attachment to multiracialism.[95] TANU did enjoy one advantage, which was that Tanganyika was a United Nations Trust Territory. This set limits on what the British could foist on Tanganyikans, whilst providing a platform for Nyerere, which he exploited to good effect. In 1956, Twining sponsored a multiracial party, the United Tanganyika Party (UTP), in an effort to undercut TANU. However, when elections were held in 1958/59 – under a bizarre formula which created separate seats for the three racial groups but a common electorate – the UTP scarcely put up a fight, and thereafter collapsed. A new Governor, Sir Richard Turnbull, was better placed to appreciate the risks of seeking to frustrate TANU at all costs, and to recognise the advantages of striking a deal. A conference of East African governors in 1959 still proposed an elongated timetable which would only have reached its climax in 1970. This was unacceptable to TANU, and with the unfolding crisis in Central Africa to contend with, the British government was forced to consider whether it was worth insisting on such a prolonged transition. After TANU won all but one of the seats in fresh elections in 1960 (which were held for the first time according to a non-racial formula) the game was up. The Colonial Secretary, Iain Macleod, consented to full independence in December 1961.

In Tanganyika, the forces of African nationalism had taken on the settler minority and won, and had achieved a remarkable measure of territorial unity in the process. In Uganda, once federalism was laid to rest, the dynamic could not have been more different. Here Africans were unrepresented in central institutions before the war, because the Buganda court – satisfied with its own measure of internal autonomy – pointedly refused to take part, while the rest of the population was adjudged to be too backward. Opposition to participation in nationwide institutions was to be restated by the Lukiiko (the Buganda parliament) as late as 1953.[96] Governor Cohen was, however, intent on bringing Uganda into line with the other non-settler colonies, to that extent remaining loyal to his reformist credentials. In 1955, the Legislative Council was restructured to comprise 30 government members and 30 representatives, of whom only five were from Buganda.[97] And on the eve of his departure in 1956, Cohen also unveiled plans for direct elections on a common voters' roll, which was duly implemented two years later. As in Nigeria and the Sudan, the sudden demarcation of a single political arena, after decades of partitioning colonial peoples from one another, created anxieties on all sides. The emerging spokesmen for the more deprived parts of the country were worried that the headstart enjoyed by Buganda would secure its permanent domination. At the same time, the traditional establishment within Buganda was concerned that the kingdom would forfeit its special privileges within a greater Uganda.

As the first coherent political parties crystallised, an extremely complicated patchwork of alliances was forged. The Democratic Party (DP) appealed to Catholics in Buganda, who had been marginalised within the heavily Protestant environment of the court, and across the country at large. The United National Congress (UNC) had been formed by mostly Protestant Baganda in 1952, but broke apart in 1958. One non-Baganda faction then joined with the Uganda People's Union (UPU) to form the Uganda People's Congress (UPC), under the leadership of Milton Obote (a Northerner). Meanwhile, the Buganda court desperately fought to insulate itself from the winds of change. In 1960, the Lukiiko made an ill-fated declaration of independence and then sought to enforce a total boycott of the 1961 elections, which merely helped to hand victory to the DP. The gamble for secession having failed, the court had to be content with extracting constitutional concessions on the eve of independence. The final dispensation granted a special federal status to Buganda, which included the selection of parliamentarians from an electoral college of the Lukiiko, whereas the neighbouring southern kingdoms were accorded a semi-federal status and the rest of Uganda was placed under a unitary form of government. The Buganda court then established its own political party, the Kabaka Yekka (meaning 'the King Alone'), which went on to win the majority of the seats in the Lukiiko elections of 1962. In a purely tactical alliance which was reminiscent of that between the NPC and the NCNC in Nigeria, the KY and the UPC joined forces to oust the DP from government in April 1962. Formal independence followed in October of that year, enabling the British to avoid the many banana skins which were strewn across their path. However, as we shall see, it did not take long for the underlying fissures to reveal themselves with the most tragic consequences.

In Kenya itself, it took the violent eruption of the Mau Mau revolt to break the settler stranglehold. It would be difficult to maintain that African opposition was anything other than the crucial factor here, even if nationalism assumed an ethnic form and if the metropolitan government was instrumental in the eventual handover of power. In the last decade and a half, there has been a veritable avalanche of publications reappraising the origins and course of the revolt.[98] This is not the place to embark on a detailed analysis of the current state of knowledge, but it is worth noting the consensus that Mau Mau was a movement of the predominantly Kikuyu dispossessed who broke free of the moorings of the elite nationalist leadership. The movement was composed of three strands which intersected by virtue of the movement of population, oathing ceremonies and the circulation of news and rumour. These were the squatters in the White Highlands who were being turned into rural wage-labourers; peasants in the land-hungry Reserves who were subjected to increasing levels of interference in their daily lives under the so-called 'second colonial occupation'; and the urban poor of Nairobi, whose ranks were constantly augmented by fresh recruits from the countryside. The elite nationalists of the Kenya African Union (KAU) purported to represent the aspirations of the African majority, but found it increasingly difficult to control their mass following. Meanwhile, trade union radicals managed to capture the Kikuyu Central Association and later the KAU, and set about coordinating the oathing ceremonies which obligated the recipients to violence. In response to a series of murders of perceived collaborators, the British declared a state of emergency in October 1952. They proceeded to round up the entire nationalist leadership, including both moderates as well as radicals. This was a crucial intervention because it broke the organic link between leaders and their mass base, whilst leading many poor Kikuyu to take to the forests to fight for 'land and freedom'.

The Mau Mau revolt, which was always destined to be something of a rear-guard action, was put down in part by Kikuyu loyalists, thereby lending a dimension of civil war to the proceedings. More crucially, the Kenyan government was forced to call on the services of the British army. This was crucial because it demonstrated that white Kenyans were not capable of running their own affairs. Although an official report highlighted the supposed inability of the Kikuyu people to cope with the pressures of modernisation, many were inclined to blame the intransigence of the white community for the outbreak.[99] By 1955, when the insurgency was effectively broken, the British government was reconsidering its options in Kenya. The search was now on for moderate African nationalists who might be persuaded to embrace a partnership with equally moderate white settlers. However, those who commanded the greatest African support were reluctant to accept any deal which might merely reinforce settler power. In the Lancaster House conference of January 1960, African delegates demanded the release of Jomo Kenyatta from jail and independence under conditions of majority rule. Following a familiar pattern, British concessions gave vent to internal schisms within nationalist ranks.[100] The Kenya African Democratic Union (KADU) was more inclined to play the 'partnership' game, and formed a government with white and Asian collaborators in 1961. However, the Kenya African National Union (KANU), which built a strong base in the Kikuyu and Luo areas, remained committed to the original position. Eventually, the authorities accepted the inevitable and released Kenyatta from jail. After a successful trip to the polls in 1963, it was KANU which formed the next government. To the delight of the British government, and the audible relief of the settler community, Kenyatta – who had once been described by Governor Renison as 'the leader to darkness and death' – made it clear that there would be a place for whites in an independent Kenya. At the end of that same year, Kenya became the latest member of an expanding club of independent states. The Kikuyu subalterns who had made independence possible by taking up arms were marginalised, while power was assumed by members of the elite who had played no part in the revolt. The prime beneficiary was Kenyatta himself whose popularity soared after having been confined by the British.

By comparison with their counterparts in East Africa, white settlers in Central Africa were in a relatively strong bargaining position. The greater proximity of South Africa enabled whites to exploit perceived threats to British hegemony, although sections of the European community in Southern Rhodesia were genuinely worried about Afrikaner imperialism. In return for their loyalty, settlers in Southern Rhodesia and their less numerous counterparts in Northern Rhodesia advocated some form of closer union, which later came to encompass the adjoining colony of Nyasaland as well.[101] The newly elected Conservative government consented to a federation at the end of 1951, and the Central African Federation duly came into effect in August 1953, despite misgivings in many quarters. Because of strict franchise qualifications and separate voters' rolls, whites were destined to hold the whip hand for the immediate future.[102] This analogy is especially apposite in the light of the infamous description by the Southern Rhodesian Prime Minister, Dr Godfrey Huggins, of a partnership akin to that between a rider and a horse. Critics of federation were concerned that there were few safeguards for African interests, not least in respect of the franchise. Pearce has suggested that the founding of the federation is compatible with the planned decolonisation thesis, in that 'a federation of Central Africa could preserve the possibility of future black self-government' – that is once Africans had caught up in terms of education and political awareness.[103] However, this is surely stretching a point: if the pace was being dictated from within Central Africa, this certainly demonstrates the limits of a metropolitan impulse to decolonise. Faint hopes and long-range planning are evidently not the same thing.

In the first few years of the federation's existence, African opposition in Northern Rhodesia and Nyasaland seemed to recede somewhat. There was also some evidence of the kind of economic growth which had been predicted by the enthusiasts for federation. However, it was Southern Rhodesia which benefited most from a stimulus to its manufacturing industry and the allocation of federal revenues. Nyasaland was relatively better off than it would have been without federation, but the transfer of resources was too limited to significantly redress the poverty of its population. Northern Rhodesia, with its strong mining sector, was the greatest loser from federation.[104] At the end of the 1950s, there was a perceptible shift in African attitudes in both Northern Rhodesia and Nyasaland. The reason was that a review of the federation provisions was supposed to follow within a period of between seven and nine years. In 1957, the British government announced that it would take place sooner rather than later – that is, in 1960. At the same time, it promised that consideration would be given to dominion status for the Central African Federation. Africans worried that this would mean the withdrawal of British oversight and the entrenchment of white power in perpetuity. An indication of where power really lay came with a proposed constitutional amendment in 1957, which sought to enlarge the membership of the Federal Assembly, but in such a way as to preserve separate categories of voters and in effect to preserve white dominance. When the African Affairs Board, which was supposed to protect African interests, objected to the amendment on the grounds of its being discriminatory, it was over-ruled by the British government.[105] This episode heightened anxieties about what lay in store after 1960. Furthermore, because of the restrictive franchises in each of the individual territories, it was whites who were likely to predominate at the review conference itself.[106] The aim of the nationalists in these two territories was therefore to secure an African majority within their own legislatures which could be used to state the majority case at the review conference – and hopefully secure termination of the federation itself.

Much like in Tanganyika, there was now a rapid acceleration of nationalist activity, both in town and countryside. In Northern Rhodesia, there was evidence of a cross-fertilisation of trade union militancy on the Copperbelt with the nationalist agenda of the African National Congress from as early as 1956. Two years later, the Zambia African National Congress (ZANC) was formed, under the leadership of Kenneth Kaunda. In that same year, Hastings Banda returned to Nyasaland, after an absence of over 40 years, to lead the Congress Party in its opposition to the existing constitution. In December 1958, both Kaunda and Banda attended the All-African People's Conference in Accra where they were heartened by the expressions of solidarity they received from Nkrumah and the other delegates. In 1959, there was evidence everywhere of mounting popular resistance – as manifested in strikes, a refusal on the part of peasants to obey agricultural officers, and the outbreak of rioting. In March 1959, parallel states of emergency were declared and substantial numbers of nationalists in Nyasaland and Northern Rhodesia were placed under arrest. The was followed by considerable disruption, loss of life and injury.[107] Although this was not another Mau Mau, it had a similar effect in impelling the metropolitan authorities to reconsider the wisdom of their earlier position. With Kenyan memories still fresh, and against the backdrop of events in the Congo, the British government doubted whether the federation was sustainable without resorting to increasing levels of repression. Its response was therefore to chart a pragmatic course in the face of settler intransigence. The review conference was postponed indefinitely, while new constitutions for Northern Rhodesia and

Nyasaland pointed in the direction of African self-government. After fresh elections were won by the same nationalists who had been incarcerated in 1959, the British government agreed to the principle of secession for Nyasaland and subsequently Northern Rhodesia over 1962/63. On 1 January 1964, therefore, the Central African Federation ceased to exist. Nyasaland became independent as Malawi and under the leadership of Banda's Congress Party, while Kaunda's United National Independence Party (UNIP) took power in Zambia.

The future of Southern Rhodesia still remained to be settled. Here, events took a radically different turn with the electoral defeat of the United Federal Party, which had hitherto dominated white politics, by the hardline Rhodesia Front (RF) in 1962. The latter had made a campaign issue of the willingness of the incumbent government to bring some African faces into the power structure. Feeling cheated by the collapse of federation, Winston Field now raised the question of outright independence, which the British government was not prepared to assent to unless it was preceded by black majority rule. When the more militant Ian Smith replaced Field as Prime Minister, the Rhodesians decided to force the pace. Having won a referendum on the question of independence and followed up with a thorough election victory in May 1965, Smith opted for an announcement of UDI in November of that year. Smith had calculated that the Labour government would be unwilling to commit itself to a costly war at this late stage in the imperial endgame. As it happened, this assessment proved well-founded. In accepting UDI as a fait accompli, the British government ceased to enjoy any real capacity to influence events within that country. Although international sanctions were imposed, the Smith regime was able to blunt their effect by establishing close ties with the National Party regime in South Africa – thereby realising the earlier fears of the British. The South Africans backed the Smith regime in the belief that the preservation of white rule in Rhodesia offered the prospect of a friendly buffer state to the north, whilst stemming the tides of African nationalism which threatened to spill over their borders. This outcome was a severe blow to African nationalists in Rhodesia who had believed that their chances of securing majority rule still lay in the application of British pressure. This was a glaring miscalculation on their part. Even before UDI was declared, the Zimbabwe African National Union (ZANU) had been banned. The lack of progress had led to mounting dissatisfaction with the leadership of Joshua Nkomo, and in August 1963 the ZANU had broken away to pursue a more militant agenda. At the end of the year, the leaders of both organisations were detained or restricted to remote rural areas. With the advent of UDI, therefore, it became clear that there was simply no mileage in pursuing a peaceful strategy in pursuit of liberation. As we will see in Chapter 7, it took a sustained guerrilla war before the nationalists finally had their way.

So far, I hope to have established three main points: that British planning for decolonisation has been exaggerated; that the forces of nationalism had an instrumental role to play in the attainment of independence in a number of crucial theatres; and that even where nationalism was inchoate, precedents elsewhere drove the process inexorably onward. It remains to consider whether a neo-colonialist deal was struck at the moment of independence, as some writers have averred.

In the light of what has already been said, it should be evident that the British did not succeed in handing power to mere stooges. Time and again, the very nationalists whom the authorities had tried to frustrate – from the CPP in the Gold Coast, through TANU in Tanganyika to the Congress Party in Malawi – were those who eventually moved into Government House. However, this does not of itself invalidate the neo-colonialist hypothesis, since it was credible leaders who were likely to be able to preserve British interests in the long run. It is also striking how the British repeatedly switched from dismissing figures like Nkrumah and Kenyatta as dangerous demagogues only to embrace them later on as popular leaders with whom they could do business. Whereas some like Milton Margai and Abubakar Tafawa Balewa were natural conservatives, Nkrumah was not – and yet he was apparently transformed in the course of working alongside the British. However, whilst wishing to take the neo-colonialist thesis seriously, one needs to insist on a modicum of specificity. At the very least, the thesis should be able to identify specific areas in which old power relations were perpetuated, as well as the mechanisms through which neo-colonial relationships were reproduced.

In West Africa, there was no pressing strategic or military interest which the British government felt the need to guarantee. This both smoothed the path to independence and ensured that the rupture would be more visible. The West African states retained links of affinity through the Commonwealth, but the latter did not offer an instrument for the preservation of British control. Apart from anything else, the more substantial member states of the Commonwealth, such as Canada and India, would not have been particularly well-disposed towards such a scenario. Although the African states became independent with the Queen as their head of state, they did not wait long before opting for the robes of republicanism (this was no less true for the East and Central African states). In the initial stages of decolonisation, Britain still retained some influence through the maintenance of the sterling area. In the 1950s, the British continued to expect the colonies to surrender their dollar earnings to a common pool, to limit their imports from beyond the sterling area and to uphold the practice whereby currency control boards would fully back local currencies with sterling reserves. However, these restrictions rankled with nationalist leaders, many of whom regarded them as tantamount to imperialist exploitation. In Nigeria and Gold Coast, nationalist pressures led to a grudging accession to demands for the creation of central banks.[108] This was initially a limited advance because the respective currencies continued to be pegged to the pound and still had to backed by sterling.[109] After independence, however, the Ghanaian and Nigerian governments wasted little time in running down their sterling balances in London and then disengaging from the sterling area altogether. In Nigeria, a good deal of effort went into nurturing a financial market, while the Nkrumah regime introduced foreign exchange controls in 1961. The devaluation of the pound in 1967 was not mirrored in Accra or Lagos, and from this point onwards Britain ceased to exercise much practical leverage.

When it came to private capital, the departing colonial power was not able to strike a lasting bargain. It is true that a capitalist framework was still in place, with all the openings for private investors which this implied, but there was no guarantee that the beneficiaries would be British. In the case of Nigeria, Robert

Tignor has revealed how the British tried, and ultimately failed, to underwrite the long-term dominance of metropolitan capital.[110] One reason was that there was considerable suspicion about British motives, dating back to the economic struggles of the inter-war period. Another was that the Nigerian political elite in each of the regions was intent on harnessing marketing board reserves to finance business ventures in competition with foreign capital. In the Gold Coast, it was equally clear that Nkrumah was intent on enlarging the scope of state enterprise, which was bound to have important implications for British business. For the most part, British capital struck its own deals rather than clinging onto frayed imperial coat-tails. Mining companies in Sierra Leone, the Gold Coast and Nigeria were in a relatively secure position because they held a monopoly on the relevant expertise and enjoyed access to global financial markets. However, the great trading firms occupied a niche which West Africans themselves were eyeing up. Firms like the United Africa Company were astute enough to vacate the field of produce-buying, and to place greater emphasis on manufacturing activity, sometimes in association with local capitalist interests.[111] This opened up a lucrative space for local capital or the state, or some combination of the two. If the expatriate firms prospered after independence, therefore, it was chiefly because of their ability to blend into the local surroundings.

In the eastern half of the continent, there were greater strategic interests at stake. However, these receded with time and ultimately, independence heralded much the same kind of political rupture as in West Africa. Currency controls remained in place for somewhat longer. In the case of Zambia and Malawi, one of the by-products of the Central African Federation was a federal reserve bank which tied these territories into the sterling area. This setup survived until 1965, when separate central banks were established.[112] Further to the north, the East African Currency Board continued to operate according to conventional principles until it was wound up in 1966 and replaced by separate central banks in Kenya, Tanzania and Uganda. Although the territories continued to hold sterling reserves, they increasingly charted a separate financial course from Britain. When it came to the interests of British capital, there were some significant differences with West Africa. Mining capital in the two Rhodesias enjoyed the same structural advantages as in the Western half of the continent. But much of the commercial sector lay in the hands of Asian rather than British entrepreneurs, and it was the former which was required to make adjustments to independence. The greatest difference, however, lay with the existence of settler communities whose long-term security needed to be secured. In the terminal phase, the greatest worry was that, against a backdrop of land hunger, settlers might become the target of land seizures. In Kenya, which was home to the greatest number of settlers outside of Rhodesia, the administration finally grasped the nettle of land redistribution. The exercise began in 1960, with the intention of carrying out resettlement in such a manner that economic stability would not be jeopardised.[113] However, it soon became obvious that this initiative had failed to take the heat out of the land issue, and that something much bolder was required. As a result, the ambitious 'million-acre scheme' was launched in 1962, under which the British government provided the Kenya government with a grant of £7.5 million and a loan of a further £9 million in order to finance the purchase of white farms and the resettlement of some 70,000 African families.[114] In essence, this exercise amounted to a very delicate balancing act. Those white farmers who wanted to leave were bought out rather than being expropriated or being forced to sell at bargain-basement prices. Many peasant families gained access to land, but so too did the emergent Kenyan elite. There was to be no flight of capital, and Kenya was made safe for commercial agriculture. The departure of the smaller mixed farmers was accompanied by the consolidation of the position of large multinational companies such as Brooke Bond which had established large estates of their own.[115] Many writers on Kenya have seen the independence settlement as a classic instance of neo-colonialism, in which foreign capitalist interests were shielded by the opening up subsidiary veins of accumulation for indigenous elites.[116] But given the multinational character of foreign capital in Kenya, it is questionable whether 'neo-colonialism' is the most appropriate term.

In general, therefore, it would be difficult to argue that Britain implemented a neo-colonial programme with very much success. The collapse of the sterling area, and the introduction of autonomous African currencies, signalled the final defeat of imperial ambitions. The Commonwealth remained, but here Britain increasingly found itself in a minority and embarrassingly so in respect of some of the unresolved issues of decolonisation. Following the Rhodesian declaration of UDI, African member states demanded that Britain act decisively against the 'rebel' regime. When Britain dithered, Ghana and Tanzania severed diplomatic relations in protest. The crisis could hardly have come at a worse time, because sterling was once again revealing its shakiness as an international currency. This frailty was exploited by the Zambian government, which was by now the greatest holder of sterling reserves. In a neat reversal of the logic of neo-colonialism, the Kaunda government threatened to pull the plug on sterling and to withhold copper supplies from Britain if the latter did not modify its position on UDI. Prime Minister Harold Wilson worried that if the latter threat was fulfilled, 'we would have two million unemployed within a matter of months'.[117] As it happened, Zambia was kept on-side with the promise of greater aid, but this episode clearly demonstrates that the tail was in danger of wagging the dog. The subsequent turbulent history of Britain's relations with its former African colonies further demonstrates that the former colonial power was rather inept at converting formal empire into informal influence – certainly by comparison with the French, to whom we now turn.

1.2.2.3 An ambiguous adventure: the end of the French empire in Africa

By comparison with its British sibling, there has been comparatively little controversy surrounding the termination of the French empire in Africa. No historian has been as bold as to postulate a conscious metropolitan plan to wrap things up until the very last moment. Instead, it seems pretty evident that the reforms which were advanced after the war were intended to provide moral rearmament for a revitalised empire. Equally, it is difficult to point to cohesive nationalist movements in French West Africa (FWA) or French Equatorial Africa

(FEA), which subverted the agenda of the colonial power. It is striking that as late as 1957, the year of Ghanaian independence, Léopold Senghor was still invoking the imagery of basically contented Africans who merely wanted to 'build their own huts' within the French compound. Only Ahmed Sékou Touré of Guinea and the militants of the Union des Populations de Cameroun (UPC) followed Nkrumah's lead in seeking to take outright ownership of the compound. In the light of the colonial consensus, the question which has most exercised historians is why the French empire was dissolved at all. For some, the answer lies in the playing out of inter-African rivalries, while others are inclined to argue that the empire was actually repackaged rather than dissolved. There is an element of truth to each of the propositions, as I shall seek to demonstrate. However, before doing so it is necessary to substantiate the earlier propositions in a little more detail.

The objective of rejuvenating the African empire was manifested even before the war came to an end. Over January and February 1944, General de Gaulle took time out to preside over a conference in Brazzaville, the capital of FEA, which was convened 'to determine on what practical bases it would be possible to found, stage by stage, a French community that included the territories of black Africa'.[118] The choice of participants spoke volumes about the perceived provenance of future change. The 50 or so contributors consisted principally of senior colonial officials. The only black face present was that of Félix Eboué – and he was Guyanese rather than African. The presumption was that the participants were not in Brazzaville to discuss plans for African autonomy, for as René Pleven, the Minister of the Colonies, put it 'the African peoples want no other liberty than that of France'.[119] Rather, the aim was to put the relationship between France and the colonies on a new, and firmer, footing. As with Colonial Office revisionism, this did entail a shift of ideological gears. There was the same realisation that greater attention needed to be paid to the advancement of economic and social development which had hitherto taken second place to day-to-day administration in the African colonies. Moreover, this was advocated on the same principle that closer economic integration would redound to the mutual benefit of both parties. Hence the pronouncement that:

> On the one hand, the quantity of raw materials produced by the colonies will make a possible contribution to the satisfaction of needs that will appear after the war. On the other, increasing the natives' purchasing power will result in new markets that will enable the merchandise of the industrialised countries to find new outlets.[120]

It is true that similar ideas had been floated in the inter-war period, most notably by Albert Sarraut, at one time Minister for the Colonies, in *La Mise en Valeur des Colonies Françaises* which was published in 1923.[121] But whereas such earlier musings had failed to engender concrete results, the creation of the Fonds d'Investissement pour le Développement Economique et Social (FIDES) in 1946 created a mechanism for purposeful intervention. The consensus amongst historians is that FIDES amounted to much more than an ideological figleaf. It did channel substantial resources into the African colonies – initially (as in the British case) into infrastructural development, but later also into industrial

enterprises and agricultural projects.[122] In the same vein, the Brazzaville conference also expressed a commitment to the expansion of access to education and
medical care. As part of the moral rearmament, the French also recognised the
need to redress some of the most unpopular aspects of French rule. The conference committed the French to phasing out the hated *indigénat* (the system of
arbitrary justice which applied only to *sujets*) as well as forced labour.

The trickiest aspect of reform was always going to be the issue of political
representation. The conference did recommend a greater voice for Africans, and
hinted at an expansion of representative institutions within the colonies.
However, de Gaulle and the other participants were distinctly vague about what
African participation in a French community would mean in practical terms –
simply put, did it imply the continuation of colonial domination in a more
benign guise or the reworking of the assimilationist project in such a way that
Frenchmen and Africans would meet as political equals? The issue was posed in
very practical terms once the war came to a close. The provisional government
needed to design a new constitution for France, and the question immediately
arose as to where the colonies would fit into the process. In the event, the government adopted a middle course, associating colonial peoples with the business
of constitution-making, but restricting their level of representation. The
colonies as a whole were granted only 64 out of a total of 586 deputies within
the Constituent Assembly, with ten going to West Africa and six to Equatorial
Africa and Cameroun. In Africa the seats were divided equally between citizens
and subjects.[123] Only those subjects who had achieved a certain level of education or held a position of responsibility could vote, which disenfranchised the
vast majority of the population. Of course, anyone born in the four communes
of Senegal counted as a citizen, but across the rest of French Africa very few
escaped the category of subject. In 1938, the number of African citizens
amounted to around 5000 in all of FEA as against 90,000 in FWA (the higher
figure here reflecting the importance of the communes).[124] The result was that
Frenchmen ended up being massively over-represented within the electorate.
When the delegates turned up for the start of the Constituent Assembly, there
were as few as nine African faces amongst the assembled ranks.[125] The proceedings of the Constituent Assembly also led to ambiguous results for the
African colonies. On the one hand, the legislative powers vested in the Assembly
enabled African deputies to break down important dimensions of the colonial
relationship. Félix Houphouët-Boigny from Côte d'Ivoire sponsored a law
which ended the regime of forced labour. Even more importantly, Lamine
Guèye (representing the citizens of Senegal) managed to secure passage of a law
which ended the status of *sujet* and made all of the inhabitants of the 'overseas
territories' citizens of the French Union. This one piece of legislation, passed
just before the adjournment, brought the colonial contradiction to the fore: if
all Africans were to be treated as citizens, that raised the question of the basis
on which people with white skins could claim to exercise authority over those
with darker skins. If pursued to its logical conclusion, common citizenship
in the French Union ought to have meant parity of representation in its
institutions. In reality, few French politicians had probably thought through the
implications, being much more preoccupied with metropolitan concerns.

Indeed, the very meaning attached to the French Union was left decidedly vague, and it would probably be fair to say that the majority of delegates did not expect anything other than an unequal relationship to continue for the foreseeable future. This was reflected in the final decisions about levels of representation within the French National Assembly. The first draft of the constitution was rejected by the electorate, and when the Assembly was reconvened to produce a second draft, the results could scarcely be considered generous towards the colonies. The number of African deputies to the National Assembly was reduced – in the case of FWA from 21 to 13 (later raised to 16). Moreover, the perpetuation of a separate voters' roll for Frenchmen in FEA, Madagascar and Cameroun called into question the principle of a common citizenship. Representation in the Assembly of the French Union, which was now to be a purely consultative body, was similarly skewed. Furthermore, the elected assemblies within each of the colonies were accorded strictly limited powers. To all intents and purposes, it was the French Governors and their civil servants who would continue to make the decisions affecting the lives of ordinary Africans. The Constitution of the Fourth Republic therefore tackled the colonial contradiction by asserting a common citizenship in principle, whilst maintaining virtually the opposite in practice. This should be seen not so much as a resolution as a postponement of the fundamental problem surrounding the relationship between France and its African colonies.

This brings us to the virtual absence of cohesive nationalist movements in the mould of the CPP in the Gold Coast or TANU in Tanganyika. This is not to suggest that the French colonies were entirely quiescent after the war. Indeed, there were unmistakable signs of popular discontent, most notably in FWA, which was fuelled in part by the exigencies of the war years and in part by the impression that the French were seeking a return to business as usual. In December 1944, there was a serious incident at a military camp in Thiaroye, on the outskirts of Dakar, when African ex-servicemen engaged in a stand-off over the payment of wartime benefits. The affair, which is the subject of a polemical film by Sembène Ousmane, led to the deaths of 24 ex-servicemen and numerous injuries. Within FWA, the plight of the 'mutineers' who were put on trial became a genuine *cause célebre*, to the extent that Lamine Guèye defended them in court, while Léopold Senghor was moved to poetry. There were also signs of unrest within the ranks of organised labour, where real incomes had declined substantially during the war years.[126] In late 1945 and early 1946, there was a general strike in Dakar and St Louis, straddling the traditional divide between manual and clerical grades. Significantly, the dispute turned not just on wages, but also on the principle of parity of employment terms with French workers. The same basic issues recurred in the West African railway workers' strike of 1947, which has been immortalised in Sembène's novel *God's Bits of Wood*.[127]

For all that, these various expressions of malaise failed to build into a movement aimed at the withdrawal of the colonial power. Organised labour did throw up one committed nationalist, in the shape of Sékou Touré who launched his political career as a trade unionist in Guinea. Labour activists were equally critical in the formation of the UPC which, under the leadership of Reuben Um Nyobe, insisted on the unique status of Cameroun, demanded outright independence and overtly sympathised with the liberation movements in Indochina and Algeria. After the UPC was officially proscribed, its leaders embarked on the path of guerrilla war in 1956.[128] However, for the most part the politics of each of the colonies was dominated by those individuals who were elected to the French National Assembly. They were almost all *évolués* who were prepared to play by French rules, even if they were critical of many of the decisions which were made in Paris. The machinations surrounding the Fourth Republican Constitution left many African politicians with a nasty taste in their mouths. However, their response was not to seek outright independence, but rather to put pressure on the French to honour the vision of a Union founded on the principles of equality and mutual respect. Hence the paradox of Senghor himself, who could express his suspicion of French intentions, but in virtually the same breath extol the virtues of French civilisation and defend the merits of an enduring Franco-African relationship.[129] In a manner which echoed assimilationist ideology of an earlier era, Senghor repeatedly advocated a *France-Afrique* – and beyond that a *Eurafrique* – in which the working out of mutual complementarities would enrich all sides.[130] It scarcely needs to be stated that any such suggestion would have been complete anathema to a Nkrumah or an Azikiwe.

The desire to advance the cause of a more symmetrical French Union helps to explain the behaviour of African politicians in Paris. From the time of the Constituent Assembly, African deputies chose not to go it alone, but instead to associate themselves with mainstream French political parties in a conscious effort to win influence at the centre. Lamine Guèye had been a member of the French Socialist Party (SFIO) as early as 1936, and was now joined there by his Senegalese colleague, Senghor, as well as by Fily-Dabo Sissoko from Mali, Yaçine Diallo from Guinea and S. M. Apithy from Dahomey. As the SFIO became increasingly unpopular, many deputies (including Senghor) switched to the Indépendants d'Outre-Mer (IOM) which was sponsored by the metropolitan Mouvement Républicain Populaire (MRP). Thirdly, Houphouët-Boigny opted to affiliate with the French Communist Party, which participated in a three-way coalition government until May 1947. These tactical alliances did, however, constrain as much as empower the African deputies in their efforts to renegotiate the colonial relationship. Hence, at the time of the 1947 rail strike Guèye did lasting damage to his reputation by succumbing to SFIO pressure to demand a return to work.[131] The SFIO also frustrated the one serious attempt at combining the strength of the emergent political organisations within Africa. In the wake of the disappointments surrounding the new constitution, a conference was scheduled for Bamako in October 1946 to discuss the formation of a pan-territorial political organisation. This initiative was driven by the realisation that only better coordination amongst African leaders would force the French to listen seriously to their demands. However, the SFIO enjoined its African members not to attend, fearing the possible extension of Communist Party influence. The result was that Guèye, Senghor and Diallo stayed away, although Apithy was present and Sissoko chaired the proceedings (with some reluctance). The absence of the Senegalese deputies was to herald the start of a longstanding rift with the Ivoirien leadership. The Rassemblement

Démocratique Africain (RDA), which was born out of this meeting, was severely weakened by the inclination of around half of the African deputies to put metropolitan political affiliations ahead of African solidarity. Under the leadership of Houphouët-Boigny, the RDA did manage to establish affiliates across West Africa. Hence it enjoyed some success in Upper Volta, Mali and, Guinea and patchy support in Niger, Togo and Dahomey. It also had a more limited presence in parts of FEA.

Once the Communists had been forced out of the governing coalition, the Socialists embarked on an undeclared war against its RDA fellow-travellers in West Africa. In Côte d'Ivoire, in particular, the Communist affiliation cost the Parti Démocratique de Côte d'Ivoire (PDCI) dearly. In 1948, Laurent Péchoux was despatched to the colony with the explicit mandate of breaking the PDCI. He duly embarked on an unrelenting campaign of repression, which included detentions and the systematic rigging of elections. As Hargreaves has indicated, the scale of the unrest which ensued dwarfed the 1948 riots in the neighbouring Gold Coast.[132] Nevertheless, it is difficult to construe these events in terms of the playing-out of nationalism. The PDCI was targeted not because it was nationalist, but because it was allied to the Communist Party. The latter was in no sense an advocate of African independence, and indeed was openly hostile to any suggestion that the link with France should be severed. Nor, it has to be said, was Houphouët interested in securing outright independence. Both believed in a greater French Union which would serve the interests of black and white, which was one reason why the UPC was expelled from the RDA in 1955. Houphouët, as both a chief and a substantial cocoa farmer, was also a rather unlikely Communist. Having entered into the alliance for tactical reasons, at a time when the Communists were partners in government, he now found it expedient to sever the link in 1950. He was persuaded by François Mitterrand to affiliate instead with his smaller socialist party, the UDSR (Union Démocratique et Sociale de la Résistance), thereby initiating an intimate relationship which was to endure for some four decades. Although this realignment was not to the liking of all parties (notably the UPC), most of the RDA affiliates, which had tasted official repression on a lesser scale, fell into line. Significantly, this was followed by a more conciliatory response by the local authorities, which enabled the PDCI to triumph in the 1956 elections.

At the start of the 1950s, the empire seemed able to limp along without any final resolution of the substantive unresolved questions. However, by the middle of the decade, pressures upon the French government had begun to accumulate, thereby forcing the issue. The most dramatic development was the commencement of the Algerian War in 1954, which increasingly came to underline the need for a more creative response to African aspirations south of the Sahara. The second source of pressure came from an apparently unlikely quarter, namely the tiny Trust Territory of French Togoland. Here, the Comité de l'Unité Togolaise (CUT), led by Sylvanus Olympio, was able to use the fora of the Trusteeship Council to argue both for the reunification of the Ewe people– divided by the border with British Togoland and the Gold Coast – and for separation from the French Union. The French had good cause to worry that the independence of Togoland would create a precedent for the colonies proper. For that reason, the local administration – significantly headed once more by Péchoux – set out to disarm the CUT by sponsoring pro-French parties, harassing CUT supporters and rigging elections.[133] These tactics were reasonably successful in themselves, but the problem was that as British Togolanders began to share in the political rights of Gold Coasters, so the French felt obliged to demonstrate that they too were advancing the scope for African participation in government. In 1955, the powers of the locally elected government was expanded, and the following year the territory became an 'autonomous republic' within the French Union. Now that French Togoland was effectively internally self-governing, a major psychological barrier had been breached. The movement towards Ghanaian independence also impacted upon the French empire in more direct ways. Some politicians from French Africa, most notably Sékou Touré, began to look with envy upon what was on offer in Ghana and to question the need to remain tied to the colonial power at all. In this, they were spurred on by Nkrumah who made every effort to persuade his Francophone colleagues of the need to cut the umbilical chord if Africa was ever to be truly free. The French found Nkrumah's pan-Africanist overtures deeply threatening, and hastened the process of remoulding the Franco-African relationship in a manner which would insulate the colonies from the sirens of the Anglophone countries. In the process of so doing, they unleashed rivalries between different sets of African interests, which contributed greatly to the final dissolution of empire.

The first significant watershed came with the passage of the Loi-Cadre in June 1956. This was partly an attempt to forestall a repeat performance of the Algerian debacle and partly an exercise in broadening the scope of the Togoland reforms.[134] The legislation, which was intended to be compatible with the 1946 Constitution, granted universal suffrage and, for the first time, a broad measure of autonomy to governing councils chosen by elected assemblies. Some of the most strategic areas of policy-making were, however, reserved to the centre: notably matters of defence, foreign policy, currency, tariff policy and higher education. Following elections in the colonies, the new governing councils became operational in 1957. This was France's measured response to the independence of Ghana that same year. Although the Loi-Cadre was in many senses an important break with the past, in other respects it simply added to the underlying malaise. By granting greater powers to the individual colonies, whilst failing to create a role for institutions at the level of FWA and FEA, the reforms shifted the balance of power within Africa. Committed federalists in West Africa, notably Senghor and Sékou Touré (from outside and from within the RDA respectively) concluded that the net effect would be the balkanisation of Africa. This had serious implications for the evolution of a future relationship with France, because in the absence of substantial African entities France was bound to dominate. Houphouët was as keen as anyone that the Franco-African nexus be preserved, but he preferred the African territories to federate individually with France. There was a very simple reason why he was happy to dissolve FWA: like Gabon in FEA, Côte d'Ivoire was the richest component unit and thus subsidised the rest of the federation. Houphouët was by now a member of the French government and was presumably banking on his ability to exert influence through alternative mechanisms.

The larger questions of empire came to a head in 1958, when the Algerian crisis brought de Gaulle back to power. The latter had been fiercely critical of the Fourth Republican Constitution from the start, and indeed had withdrawn from politics over its contents. Now he wasted no time in initiating plans for the drafting of a new constitution for France, which necessarily had implications for Africa. In July 1958 a Consultative Constitutional Committee was established which included Senghor, Guèye and Philibert Tsiranana who was from Madagascar and a trusted associate of Houphouët. Within this forum, Senghor argued the case for large African federations joined in a confederation with France. However, the final outcome was much closer to what Houphouët was advocating. The draft provided for a Community, in which France and the individual territories would supposedly come together as equal partners. As before, territorial governments would exercise control over most internal affairs, but a list of other policy areas were to be reserved to the Community as a whole. This included the reserved items from the Loi-Cadre era, but also added in finance, raw materials policy, justice, transport and telecommunications.[135] As Chipman observes, because the institutions of the Community were inextricably linked to those of the Fifth Republic, there was a sense in which French dominance was guaranteed.[136] Prior to the referendum on the draft Constitution, de Gaulle embarked on a tour of the major African capitals to drum up support for a 'Yes' vote. In Dakar and Conakry, where he met a hostile response, he hinted that a 'No' majority in any individual territory would confer independence, but at the cost of an absolute rupture of the connection with France. In the event, only Sékou Touré in Guinea and Djibo Bakary in Niger urged their voters to reject the Constitution, and it was only the former who was successful in swinging the result.[137] The French responded by pulling out of Guinea, removing everything from administrative files to the light-bulbs. Although Nkrumah stepped in with an offer of financial assistance, the petulant manner of the French withdrawal left Guinea in a severely crippled state. It reinforced the stern message that if Africans wanted their independence, it would come at material considerable cost to themselves.

Although the rest of French Africa had voted in favour of the Constitution, that did not mean any greater consensus as to what the precise relationship with France ought to be. In particular, the federalists had not given up on their dream of reconstituting the FWA in some form or other, and they took succour from the fact that the Constitution permitted the regrouping of member states. Towards the end of 1958, there were moves to establish a Mali Federation which would embrace Senegal, Mali, Upper Volta and Dahomey. After some backroom interference from Houphouët, the latter two decided to pull out. The following year, however, the leadership of the truncated Federation took the step of seeking full independence, whilst remaining within the French Community. Remarkably, in the light of the Guinean experience, de Gaulle consented and Mali formally became independent on 24 June 1960. From this point, the empire unravelled very quickly. Houphouët felt betrayed by this turn of events, complaining that de Gaulle had gone back on all previous understandings to the effect that independence and membership of the Community were incompatible. In a fit of pique, the Ivoirien leader announced his own independence on 7 August 1960, without even waiting to sign cooperation agreements with France.[138] By December, 14 African colonies had opted for independence as well – with the exception of Djibouti, the Comoros and Réunion – although Gabon virtually had to be pushed to accept it.[139] On the face of it, that was the end of the French imperial affair in Africa.

The final outcome was a curious one. The empire had dissolved despite repeated insistence that the destinies of France and Africa were inextricably linked, and in spite of the fact that it was de Gaulle – always a passionate defender of the imperial vision – who was at the helm. Even more strangely, independence arrived despite the fact that almost every African leader had professed not to want it. The fundamental reason is that there was no satisfactory halfway house between old-style colonialism with its culture of command and compliance – which was unacceptable to Africans – and the fusion of France and Africa, which was equally unacceptable to Frenchmen. In the final event, therefore, the colonial contradiction turned out to be insoluble. The wrangling between African politicians certainly hastened the process of dissolution, but was itself a reflection of the fact that the various halfway houses which had been constructed after 1946 were never considered satisfactory as home. There is also a further reason why the seemingly impossible transpired, and that has to do with the manner in which the French adapted to the realities of the situation. The Algerian disaster provided a salutary lesson as to the dangers of clinging on, which was only reinforced by the outbreak of armed insurgency in Cameroun and the playing out of increasingly bloody power struggles in Congo-Brazzaville.[140] In the final event, the sub-Saharan experience demonstrated the advantages of trading in formal rule for enduring influence. France signed detailed cooperation agreements with all of the newly independent African states (except Guinea), covering much of the same ground that had constituted reserved affairs under the 1958 Constitution. These agreements covered foreign affairs, enabling France to count on the support of its African allies in international fora, as well as defence, thus permitting France to retain military bases on African soil. The latter agreements provided the excuse for a string of interventions in the politics of post-colonial states.

On the economic front, the African states signed up to membership of either the West or Equatorial African currency zone, which ensured convertibility on the African side and leverage on the French side. The French also entered into technical agreements, which committed African states to the buying-in of their expertise across a broad front. African states were required to give preferential treatment to French business, at the same time as France sought to broker more favourable African access to the European market. This post-colonial dispensation provided such a satisfying resolution to the colonial contradiction precisely because the it could be presented as a partnership in which both sides gained. While France was able to maintain vestiges of its position as a global power, African leaders secured a measure of influence over French policy as well as the resources needed to cement their own power bases. In the eyes of many Francophone African intellectuals, such an arrangement amounted to neo-colonialism pure and simple. This is a question which we will have cause to return to in subsequent chapters. Suffice it to note here that the neo-colonialist cap fits the former French colonies more comfortably than the former British colonies.

1.2.2.4 A botched job: decolonisation Belgian-style

The final instance to be considered here is the winding up of the Belgian empire, covering the vast expanse of the Congo and the Ruanda-Urundi Trust Territory. In some respects, the Belgian model of decolonisation could be seen as a hybrid of the British and French prototypes. Like the French, the Belgians were determined to find a way of re-entrenching the colonial relationship after the war, but like the British they eventually fell back upon a policy of scuttle. In the process, the Belgians managed to accomplish the worst of both worlds. Their response to events was ostrich-like throughout the first half of the 1950s, but once cold reality dawned they panicked and then withdrew in a precipitous fashion. The eve of the Belgian retreat was characterised in each instance by conditions of political uncertainty, administrative confusion, and a good deal of violence and loss of life.

Such a scenario would scarcely have seemed conceivable to the Belgian authorities at the end of the war. As in Paris, the governing elite was not oblivious to the fact that the international climate had altered. But its response was to restate the colonial mission in a manner which ploughed most of the same furrows from the interwar years – if sometimes a little deeper. The underlying strategy was what Crawford Young has called 'controlled gradualism', which can be broken down into a number of core components.[141] First of all, the Belgians expressed a renewed commitment to assimilationist principles, but also continued to underline the importance of maintaining a measured progression. As has already been noted, they had come to recognise the need to offer some reward to the small number of Congolese who had embraced the values of the coloniser. After the war, many of the promises were carried through, but in a manner which specifically avoided making a radical break. The introduction of the *carte du mérite civil* and the *immatriculation* in the Congo were supposed to accord *évolués* the same rights as Belgians. However, the certificates were granted sparingly, and seemed to make little practical difference to the presumed second-class status of their recipients.[142] As in Cameroun, the racist overtones within European discourse were scarcely disguised. There was also a limited attempt at bringing the *évolués* into the structures of government. The Conseil du Gouvernement was expanded in 1947 to bring about an unofficial majority, but this included only two Congolese – although the figure was raised to eight in 1951.[143] A handful of Africans was also included in the provincial councils, where tuition in the arts of government was supposed to begin. However, most of the African representatives at these different levels were actually chiefs, besides which the councils merely performed an advisory function. To all intents and purposes, it was the Governor-General and his civil servants who continued to make the important decisions. As for the mass of the Congolese, they continued to be subjected to chiefly rule and the daily interference of Belgian officials. As for the rapidly expanding urban centres, municipal elections were finally held in seven of these over 1957/58, but by then it was far too late.[144]

In Ruanda-Urundi, the Trusteeship agreement was predicated on the eventual achievement of self-government, but this did not render the Belgians any more inclined to modify their overall vision. They remained wedded to a system of indirect rule in which they watched over a hierarchy of chiefs which stretched from the king (or *mwami*) down to the hill-chiefs in each of the twin-kingdoms. Educational access and chiefly positions were for the most part restricted to the Tutsi section of the population, which contributed in no small measure to a sense of exclusion on the part of the Hutu majorities. The Belgians had long operated on the premise of the so-called 'Hamitic hypothesis' which posited that the Hutus were racially distinct Bantu agriculturalists who had been conquered by cattle-keeping Tutsi Hamites. There is some disagreement as to whether proto-ethnic divisions existed in pre-colonial times, or whether they were purely a Belgian construct.[145] Be that as it may, the Belgians sought to freeze these categories and to govern through their Tutsi overlords. After the UN Visiting Mission of 1951 criticised the lack of political advancement, a hierarchy of councils was introduced in order to create the outward appearance of popular participation. However, it was not until 1956 that universal male suffrage was introduced at the sub-chiefdom level, and even then the *ex officio* representation of chiefs ensured that the established hierarchy remained in place. This was reflected in the fact that the highest council in Rwanda contained no Hutus, while in Burundi the latter comprised three out of a total of 31 members – despite the fact that the Hutus constituted an overwhelming numerical majority.[146] The Belgians hoped as far as possible to blunt the impact of new-fangled notions of democracy in these controlled monarchies.

The second dimension of Belgian policy was equally familiar from the pre-war period. It underscored the importance of conferring material improvements upon the African populations which would underline the advantages of European rule. The first ten years after the war were marked by rapid economic expansion in the Congo, based chiefly on the increased production of minerals – principally copper, cobalt, diamonds, tin, gold and manganese – but also on commercial farming, and to some extent, peasant agriculture. The commodities boom was associated with increased wage employment and some material improvement for much of the population.[147] The period of growth also enabled the Belgians to channel greater resources into social welfare. Expenditure on health care was quite considerable, yielding what was reputed to be the best medical infrastructure in tropical Africa by 1958.[148] Moreover, as the pressure for living space grew within the urban areas, the Belgians channelled significant resources into housing programmes. This contrasted with the niggardly British policy in Eastern and Southern Africa, where there was a reluctance either to accept the realities of urbanisation or to foot the bill for African housing. The educational system continued to be bottom-heavy, but it was at least broad-based. In 1959, 70 per cent of children between the ages of 6 and 11 were enrolled in Congolese primary schools, and the overall rate of attendance was reputed to be higher than in the Gold Coast, India or FEA.[149] Although mission schools still dominated, the first steps were taken to provide state education with effect from 1954. At the same time, the Belgians finally broached the sensitive issue of secondary and higher education which had previously been curbed on the basis that it was prudent to educate Africans only as far as was commensurate with the labour demands of the colony. As late as 1959, only 29,000 pupils were in secondary schools, but with the founding of the University of Louvanium in 1954 and the University of

Elizabethville in 1956 – the one Catholic, the other lay – the Belgians claimed to have made a start. Although many administrators had their doubts as to whether this was the wisest course of action – such was the presumed power of ideas – it was ultimately considered preferable to letting Congolese attend universities abroad.[150] In Ruanda-Urundi, by contrast, the pace of educational advance was slower. The first secondary schools opened in the 1950s and there were no universities at all prior to independence.

At an ideological level, controlled gradualism continued to presume that while Africans might eventually grow up, this was a process which was likely to take an extremely long time. In the mid-1950s, as Ghana was moving steadily towards independence and French Togoland was starting to acquire a measure of internal autonomy, the Belgians continued to behave as if they had all the time in the world. Their latitude was somewhat restricted in Ruanda-Urundi, and there was always the danger that developments there would complicate the situation in the Congo. Nevertheless, when it came to their one colony, the Belgians apparently believed that they had found a means of exempting themselves from the general trend towards decolonisation. As Stengers puts it:

> They were convinced, as they themselves often said, that they had 'found the right formula' – that is, a formula that guaranteed them against the miscalculations other colonising countries had made. It consisted in improving the native's material condition to the point where he would not dream of the right to vote. That was the 'formula': Keep the natives happy by looking after their welfare, their housing and their health.[151]

The extent to which the Belgians believed in their colonial immortality is revealed in reactions to a book published by a Belgian professor, A. Van Bilsen, in early 1956. In this treatise, the author contradicted official presumptions by predicting that the forces of nationalism which were on the move elsewhere would begin to manifest themselves in the Congo. He then proceeded to advocate a 30-year programme to prepare the way for a federal union between Belgium and the Congo – presumably somewhat along the lines of the French Union. This analysis could scarcely be considered radical – either in its prognosis or in its diagnosis of the situation – but in Belgium it produced a stunned reaction. By putting a date on the fulfilment of the Belgian mission, Van Bilsen had exposed the colonial contradiction to public view.

This belief in the efficacy of the magic formula was for some time fortified by the absence of any overt challenges to Belgian position. The Congolese *évolués*, seeking to elevate themselves above the rest of the population, wholeheartedly embraced the civilising mission, even as they smarted at the rebuffs they were subjected to on a daily basis. Stengers quotes the following arresting passage from a book by Patrice Lumumba in 1956:

> The day when the Congo has its own technicians in all fields, its doctors, agronomists, engineers, entrepreneurs, geologists, administrators, foremen, skilled workers… social workers, nurses, midwives: only then must we speak of independence and self-government, for then we shall be intellectually, technically, and materially strong enough to rule ourselves, should this be necessary.[152]

Whereas the bulk of this quotation suggests that independence might become an eventuality after a long haul, even that message is dramatically undercut by the final words. Of course, the apparent willingness of the *évolués* to wait their turn was not necessarily shared by the rest of their countrymen. However, it has to be said that there was no immediate sign of the activism that the Congolese people would later exhibit. In the mid-1950s, therefore, the colonial system still seemed to Belgian eyes pretty much impregnable. In June 1960, however, the Belgians made a precipitous exit from the Congo, preceding even the fulfilment of their trusteeship obligations in Ruanda-Urundi.

Stengers suggests that the key to understanding the unravelling of Belgian rule lies in the interplay between an upsurge in Congolese nationalism and metropolitan reactions which sought to head off an Algerian scenario at all costs.[153] As far as the former is concerned, the first steps were extremely hesitant. In 1956, a group of upriver (or Bangala) *évolués* reacted positively to Van Bilsen's intervention in a manifesto contained within the Catholic journal, *Conscience Africaine*. The tone of the manifesto attempted to mollify Belgian opinion, but at the same time it insisted that there ought to be plan for 'complete political emancipation within a period of thirty years'.[154] This precipitated a counter-demand by Bakongo intellectuals for 'immediate independence', and from this point onwards the tone of nationalist expression became more strident. The transformation was perfectly encapsulated in the person of Lumumba, whose earlier pro-Belgian sentiments gave way to a fierce critique of colonialism in the Congo and an insistence on total liberation. The wider African context had everything to do with this change of heart. In December 1958, Nkrumah convened the All-African People's Conference in Accra to spread the message of independence and continental unity. Lumumba was amongst the participants, and on his return his rhetoric increasingly echoed that of his Ghanaian mentor. On the Belgian side, there was at last an effort to respond creatively to the developments. The metropolitan government convened a 'working group' whose report proposed the creation of democratic institutions which would, at some unspecified time in the future, permit the Congolese to be given the choice between independence or a continued association with Belgium. But by the time the report emerged in January 1959, it had been overtaken by events. That month, an attempt to ban a political rally by the Alliance des Bakongo (ABAKO) in the capital, Leopoldville, led to rioting and considerable loss of life. This unexpected turn of events, in a colony whose tranquillity had been the proud boast of the Belgians, immediately brought worrying international parallels to mind. The Minister for the Congo responded with the promise of independence, which was reinforced by a speech from the king to the same effect. Although a specific timetable had not been mentioned – and Stengers suggests that the assumption was that it might take as long as 15 years – the offer of independence had been put on the table.[155] From this point onwards, it became a question of 'when' rather than 'if'.

The situation in the Congo in 1959 bore some similarities to India in the aftermath of the war. In each case, the offer of independence – made in the heat of the moment – circumscribed the colonial power's subsequent room for manoeuvre, not least because indigenous elites were thenceforth unwilling to collaborate on the same basis as before. At the same time, areas of each colony began to slip out of the effective grip of the colonial power. In the Lower Congo, the Belgian authorities encountered a novel situation in which the local population refused to accept the European writ, and professed to recognise only to the authority of ABAKO and its leader, Joseph Kasavubu. Moreover, the malaise began to manifest itself in other parts of the colony as well. With Algerian precedents uppermost in their minds, the Belgian public lacked the stomach for a fight to cling on to the Congo. That left only one option, namely to withdraw with as much goodwill as they could still muster. Hence, in December 1959 the Belgian government formally offered independence the following year. The Indian parallel is also apparent in the upsurge of sectarianism as nationalists turned to consider the balance of power in the state (or states) that someone was about to inherit. As in Nigeria, the ruptures occurred along ethno-regional lines.

The fractured political landscape is clearly reflected in the outcome of the first national elections held in May 1960, when 137 seats were contested in the central legislature. No political party managed to win votes across the country, although Lumumba's Mouvement National Congolais (MNC) came closest.[156] The MNC won the greatest overall number of seats (41 including those of its close allies), and had at least one seat in each of the provincial assemblies. But it was still a party whose support was concentrated in Orientale and neighbouring parts of Kasai province. The Alliance des Bakongo (ABAKO) adopted an overtly ethnic designation, which ensured that it was confined to winning 12 seats in its heartlands. Elsewhere in the province of Leopoldville, the Parti Solidaire Africain (PSA) won 13 seats on the strength of the support of smaller groups. Again, the Confédération des Associations Tribales du Katanga (CONAKAT) won a total of eight seats entirely on the basis of its strongholds in the south, whereas BALUBAKAT and its associates pulled in the Baluba vote in the north of Katanga. Hence, Crawford Young observes that Congolese parties were unique in Africa in their open use of ethnic nomenclature.[157]

Although Kasavubu and Lumumba put together a governing coalition, it was wrapped around the flimsiest of accords. Formal independence followed on 30 June, in an atmosphere of resentment towards the departing colonial power and mutual suspicions, bordering on paranoia, between the Congolese parties. Five days later, the army mutinied and within two weeks, Moïse Tshombe had declared the secession of Katanga. By leisurely traversing the stretches of open road and then suddenly accelerating when they reached the political corner, the Belgians caused the Congo to career off the road altogether. This could not be construed as planned decolonisation in any meaningful sense. As for Congolese nationalism, anti-colonial sentiments were profound enough to panic the Belgians into withdrawing, but there was insufficient commonality of experience to render nationhood much more than an abstraction. Moreover, as was often the case in late-colonial Africa, where peoples of different origins did rub shoulders in the rapidly expanding urban centres it tended to be as day-to-day competitors for customers, work and living space. Ethnic mobilisation consequently proceeded on the basis of lived experience, in a way that nationalism could not. Moreover, it tended to feed off violence and insecurity, whereas the dream of a liberated Congo evaporated in the melée.

In Ruanda-Urundi, Belgian strategy had equally disastrous consequences, although the road travelled was very different. In 1959, the Belgians finally recognised that it was untenable to stick to a policy of minimal change. Here too a 'working group' was convened and in November it advanced far-reaching reforms: it proposed the replacement of appointed chiefs by elected burgomasters at the local level and the transformation of the kings into something approximating constitutional monarchs appointable by elected kingmakers. Furthermore, the two kingdoms were to be separated from one another.[158] In Rwanda, the sudden opening up of the political arena led to the politicisation of ethnicity. The death of the *mwami* in July 1959 and the appointment of a successor by the Tutsi court clique was followed by an outbreak of ethnic violence, the overthrow of the existing chiefly hierarchy and the imposition of Hutu chiefs in their place. What began as opposition to the monarchy, crossing ethnic boundaries, quickly assumed an ethnic hue. In the electoral field, the Parti du Mouvement de l'Emancipation Hutu (PARMEHUTU) presented itself as the guarantor of the interests of the Hutu autochthons who had supposedly been enslaved to Hamitic Tutsi invaders and systematically discriminated against under Belgian rule. These appeals resonated so strongly because as subjective readings of history they were rooted in the objective reality of colonial policy which froze Hutu and Tutsi social categories and turned them into criteria for deciding on political and social advancement. To be a Hutu was to be a second-class citizen, which the mandatory identities cards (introduced in the 1930s) had made a fact of daily life. PARMEHUTU was aware of the demographic realities which would guarantee electoral victory provided no other party competed for Hutu votes. The party which represented Tutsi interests, l'Union Nationale Rwandaise (UNAR), struck an anti-Belgian posture and sought to enlist international sympathy for its cause.

When the date of a national election became the bone of international contention in January 1961, PARMEHUTU convened a mass meeting of local councillors and burgomasters and pronounced the birth of a 'democratic and sovereign Republic of Rwanda'. Significantly, the declaration of the abolition of the monarchy was not challenged by the Belgians, who had by this time come to embrace the inevitable. In September 1961, a national election was held alongside a referendum on the ending of the monarchy, both of which were easily won by PARMEHUTU. Although two ministerial positions were allocated to UNAR by way of a compromise, it was apparent that the country would remain in the hands of an explicitly ethnically based party. In the wake of the initial violence, some 22,000 Tutsi fled into neighbouring states and by 1963 the number of refugees had swollen to 130,000. The excision of nearly one-third of the Tutsi population may have seemed the perfect solution to PARMEHUTU ideologues, but it was hardly a guarantee of stability when those refugees continued to regard Rwanda as home.

In Burundi, the omens for a peaceful termination of Belgian trusteeship initially seemed somewhat better. Here, it was not ethnicity, but clan rivalries at court, linked to differences over relations with the Belgian administration, which drew the most attention. When the first political parties were formed, the more nationalistic Parti de l'Union et le Progrès National (UPRONA) identified itself with the Bezi chiefly faction, whereas the more accommodationist Parti Démocratique Chrétien (PDC) associated with the Batare faction. Both of these parties appealed to Hutus as well as Tutsis, and the figure who came to improve the fortunes of UPRONA, Prince Louis Rwagasore, was himself married to a Hutu.[159] Although they had the United Nations to contend with, the Belgians unsurprisingly sought to tilt the balance in favour of the PDC as the electoral principle was extended upwards. Nevertheless, UPRONA succeeded in sweeping the board when national elections were finally held in September 1961. The installation of Rwagasore should have set Burundi on a relatively smooth transition to independence, but the balance was upset when he was assassinated only a month later by members of the PDC/Batare faction. Although independence arrived without a full-scale conflagration, a process of selective assassination had begun which was a harbinger of worse to come.

By this point, it should scarcely need underlining that the Belgian imperial legacy was an extremely unfortunate one. Whereas the Belgians could run for cover, the people who were left to shoulder the consequences were ordinary people in the successor states of Congo, Rwanda and Burundi who had hardly been involved in the struggle over inheritance of the political kingdom. Many thousands of these people were to lose their lives over the next few years. However, it also needs to be said that the outcome hardly served the interests of the Belgians very well either. The shambolic manner in which they departed won them few friends in the sub-region, while their subsequent intervention in the Congo crisis may be considered an abortive attempt to recover some of the lost ground. Insofar as Belgian business interests were preserved, this had less to do with governmental support than with a strong sense of self-preservation within the ranks of big business. The largest mining company, the Union Minière du Haut Katanga, offered money to all sides, before finally deciding to plump for Katangan secession. Such was the might of the mining companies, that they were able to buy a measure of long-term security once the civil war came to close. If there was a Belgian neo-colonial strategy afoot, therefore, it can hardly be considered a very great triumph.

1.3 Conclusion

To the reader, it might appear anachronistic to devote so much of a book about independent Africa to the colonial period. After all, was a new chapter not begun as soon as the colonial powers packed their bags and headed for home, and moreover is it not pushing it to ascribe everything to the legacy of European rule? These are serious questions, but there are good reasons for tackling the subject in this fashion. To start with, decolonisation did not always represent a sharp rupture. In the French case, except in Guinea, the colonial relationship was exchanged for something which carried forward many of the same characteristics. In the British and Belgian cases, independence represented more of a clean break, but the colonial legacy remained in evidence for a long time afterwards. In Kenya, for example, many of the Europeans did not pack their bags at all, but remained and continued to enjoy possession of much of the best land. Again, many of the largest mining and trading companies continued as before. Some commentators would also contend that there are continuities in respect of the relationship between rulers and ruled. The culture of command was one which was often perpetuated within the organs of the post-colonial state, whereas the governed themselves resorted to many of the tried-and-tested repertoires of compliance, evasion and resistance. Finally, I wish to develop a larger argument as this book progresses: namely that the exposure of the colonial contradiction, which was premised on innate difference between Europeans and Africans, gave way to an international discourse of human rights and development after 1960 which was predicated on supposedly universal values. Ironically, however, the 'white man's burden' ended up being reinscribed.

2

A Profile of Africa at Independence

> In Africa, natural conditions, though clearly more difficult than in Europe and America, can certainly be conquered, particularly in view of the enormous reserves of energy and minerals, and the advances possible with modern agricultural techniques. Men alone are responsible for the economic backwardness of Africa.
>
> René Dumont, *False Start in Africa*, 1962

In the chapters which follow, we will consider how Africans made the best of the difficult legacy which had been bequeathed by the departing colonial powers. Whereas the rest of the text follows a broadly linear historical sequence, albeit within a thematic structure, this chapter provides a simple cross-section of post-colonial states as an aid to the discussion which follows.

2.1 A demographic profile of African states

In the aftermath of independence, the first wave of Africanist scholarship concerned itself with a continent supposedly 'in transition' from tradition to modernity. Although this literature now reads as faintly peculiar, stuck as it is in late-colonial ways of seeing Africa, the transition motif does have some relevance for a period when rapid social change was evident at many levels. One respect in which this was true was in the changing demographic profile of the continent. Although there were urban settlements of some antiquity in West Africa (such as Kano) and along the Swahili coast, the level of urbanisation in pre-colonial Africa was limited.[1] During the colonial period, many new urban centres came into existence. Some of these emerged from colonial design, as the respective powers founded centres of administration, often selected for their geographical convenience rather than their prior significance – the construction of Kaduna as the administrative capital in Northern Nigeria would be an example. Others blossomed because of their location at strategic points along the expanding road and rail networks and/or because of their attributes as coastal ports, as was the case with Mombasa in Kenya. Finally, other urban centres sprung up around the mining camps, notably on the Zambian and Congolese Copperbelts and on the South African Rand. Needless to say, some colonial cities performed more than one such function and when this happened it merely served to underline the dominance of the capital city over its nearest rivals. Hence Lomé and Lagos served as administrative capitals for their respective territories as well as the termini of the rail networks into the interior. In fact, as many as 23 of the 37 newly independent states which had a coastline also had a port city as their capital.[2]

During the first half of the century, urban growth proceeded at a relatively sluggish pace, in part because European rulers sought to set limits on permanent African settlement in the cities. In the settler colonies of Eastern and Southern Africa, there was a particular concern to preserve the city as an exclusive European domain, with whatever African presence there was being considered as essentially transient. However, after the war, an extraordinary acceleration of urbanisation ensued, reaching a peak in the decade leading up to independence. Hence, the population of Nairobi stood at 119,000 in 1950, but had swelled to 344,000 by 1960. Over the same period, Leopoldville (Kinshasa) mushroomed from 199,000 to 510,000, and Lagos from 250,000 to 600,000 inhabitants.[3] *Bidonvilles* and shanty towns sprang up in an uncontrolled fashion due to the inability (or unwillingness) of the authorities to keep pace with the demand for housing, and even in the approved townships overcrowding became endemic. The enforced intimacy of the city often spawned a vibrant popular culture, in which the influences were drawn from the widest possible orbit: migrants brought elements of their own cultures from the outlying regions, where they intermingled and were transformed in the process, whereas other influences were drawn from North America and Europe. This cultural cocktail brought forth some remarkable innovations in music, theatre and dress which European observers often found baffling. Moreover, the process of mutation was boundless as successive external influences were indigenised. The emergence of highlife music in Accra and its dissemination across urban West Africa, and the parallel efflorescence of Congolese music in Central and East Africa, are cases in point.[4] Cuban music became all the rage in the 1940s as records were made for the African market and then entrepreneurs on the continent began recording local artists. Gradually, Spanish lyrics gave way to African ones and local rhythms and were laid across the borrowed Cuban forms. The result was an exciting cultural hybrid. Again, when urban gang members dressed in cowboy attire, they were expressing themselves in a cultural idiom that combined global and local meanings. Finally, the proliferation of football and boxing clubs is a further illustration of the manner in which urban dwellers began to live their lives in a manner which differed from that of their country-cousins. To live in the city was to be quintessentially modern, which meant dressing, speaking and acting differently from villagers who had no reason to conceive of leisure time as something to be filled in a refracted image of work-time. Many a fresh arrival in the city had to endure the embarrassment of being regarded as a *villageois* before learning the rules of the aesthetic game. Those who returned to their rural homes typically went out of their way to demonstrate the extent to which they had transcended the rural milieu, thereby feeding the ambitions of the next cohort. If the villager was perceived to lie at one end of the spectrum of modernity, the 'been-to' – that is someone who had travelled abroad – lay at the other extreme. During the interwar period, the minority of Africans who had received the chance to experience the world outside gained enormous social respect. Although the number of beneficiaries expanded in the post-independence era, the cachet that came with being worldly-wise never evaporated. In the Zaire (Congo) of the 1970s and 1980s, young men did everything in their power to visit Europe with a view to purchasing flashy items of clothing for sartorial display when they returned home.

The underside to urbanisation was, however, the addition of a certain volatility to urban politics, as incomers jostled for living space and employment with each other and with the supposed indigenes. In a number of cities, competition assumed an overtly ethnic or nativistic flavour – for example in Ibadan where the NCNC enjoyed considerable success in tapping into local Yoruba antipathy towards Ijebu-Yoruba immigrants, despite the fact that it was normally identified as an Igbo party.[5] The same logic was also apparent in the spatial politics of Kinshasa and Brazzaville which faced each other across the Congo river. To sympathetic external observers at the time of independence, 'tribalism' represented an immediate problem, but many also considered it to be a passing phase which would subside as alternative solidarities took hold in the urban setting, notably class. In the post-war period, as we have seen, there were manifestations of worker consciousness, as exemplified by the strikes of French West African railway workers and East African dockworkers. The threat of crippling strikes in the public utilities, linked to perceived Communist plots, had led the British and the French to belatedly encourage 'responsible' trade unionism.[6] At independence, most African countries manifested some level of formal union organisation, although this was still largely confined to the mines, railways and ports. Although the number of urban employees was rising on the eve of decolonisation, as money from the colonial development funds fed through, formal employment could not absorb the annual influx to the cities. For most of the urban population, therefore, the only realistic prospects lay in trading, transport, artisanship or by activity bordering on the criminal: in short, getting by in any way possible.

Although the acceleration of urban growth was undoubtedly impressive, it still needs to be remembered that in absolute terms the cities were still relatively small (see Table 2.1). At the time of independence, the vast majority of Africans lived in settlements of fewer than 20,000 inhabitants: in South Africa, the figure for those who did not was relatively high at 30.7 per cent, but in Nigeria it was only 11.4 per cent and this fell to as low as 1.8 per cent in the case of Mali.[7] In some countries, there really were no cities to speak of. Because Mauritania had been governed from Saint-Louis in Senegal, the capital of Nouakchott had to be built virtually from scratch after independence. Botswana had similarly been governed from Mafeking in South Africa, and Rwanda from Bujumbura, with the result that Gaborone and Kigali respectively were tiny.[8] Malabo in Equatorial Guinea and Mbabane in Swaziland were equally minuscule capitals within micro-states. In Upper Volta (now Burkina Faso), Ouagadougou, with 70,000 inhabitants, had a reasonably close rival in Bobo-Dioulasso (numbering 55,000), but their combined total was still very small in a country where 96 per cent of the population remained rural. The everyday experience of the majority

Table 2.1   Growth of population of selected cities, 1931–60

City	1931		1950	1960
Accra	61,000		160,000	390,000
Addis Ababa	300,000	(1938)	350,000	500,000
Dakar	92,000	(1936)	180,000	380,000
Dar es Salaam	23,000		80,000	164,000
Douala	28,000		137,000	173,000
Ibadan	387,000		430,000	550,000
Khartoum	176,000	(1938)	210,000	380,000
Leopoldville/Kinshasa	27,000		199,000	510,000
Lagos	127,000		250,000	600,000
Nairobi	30,000	(1928)	119,000	344,000
Salisbury/Harare	26,000		140,00	176,000

Sources: Column 1 from William Hance, *The Geography of Modern Africa* (New York and London: Columbia University Press, 1964, p. 54); columns 2 and 3 distilled from Charles M. Becker and Andrew R. Morrison, 'The growth of African cities: theory and estimates', in Archie Mafeje and Samir Radwan (eds) *Economic and Demographic Change in Africa*, pp. 112–15, and Anthony O'Connor, *The African City* (London: Hutchinson, 1983), p. 48.

of Africans was therefore located far from direct access to the sights, sounds and (often hypothetical) amenities of the big city. The next best thing was typically the market town where a wide range of consumer goods could be purchased and where at least some of the attractions of urban life could be replicated.

Whereas there are common attributes of cities which make it possible to make blanket generalisations about the experience of living in one, the same cannot be said of the rural areas. All that these really had in common was that they were not part of the urban complex, but even this needs to be qualified in the light of the importance of the migrant labour system in parts of the continent. Large parts of rural Mozambique and Lesotho, for example, served as vast labour reserves for the South African mines, rendering the urban–rural distinction somewhat problematic. The marked differences in environmental resources across the continent had a profound importance for the manner in which Africans have made their livelihoods, constructed their living spaces and construed their social relations. Moreover, the opportunities for engaging profitably with the external world were unevenly distributed across the continent. With the exception of Kenya, Rhodesia, South Africa and Ethiopia, there was no great social inequality which hinged on access to land. And with the exception of Rwanda, Burundi, Zanzibar and parts of Ethiopia and Nigeria, Africa was characterised by a relatively low people-to-land ratio until the end of the twentieth century when pressures had become apparent in a number of countries. The real inequalities lay in the differential access to the most fertile and well-watered land and to basic infrastructure. These tended to be mutually reinforcing in that colonial road networks tended to be at their most dense in the areas with the greatest perceived agricultural potential. In regions with dependable and abundant rainfall, and where the infrastructure was in place, peasant households could hope to combine the cultivation of food crops, like yams, cassava, plantain and maize, with cash crops such as cocoa, coffee, palm-oil and groundnuts. By the close of the colonial period, some communities had proved themselves extremely adept at exploiting the advantages of their particular environmental niches. In Ghana, for example, cocoa provided the money which southern farmers used to sponsor their children's education, to purchase fine cloth and other items of personal consumption, as well as to invest in further income-generating activity, including yet more cocoa and transport. Coffee fulfilled a similar function for peasant households in Buganda and for the Meru of northern Tanzania. The years leading up to independence were generally characterised by high prices for cash crops, with the result that these farmers had considerable income at their disposal – although the share that went to the state also tended to increase at the same time.

In the savanna regions, there was generally less opportunity to engage in cash crop agriculture. The labour requirements of cotton competed with those of food crops (whereas in the case of cocoa they were complementary), which reduced the popular appeal of this particular crop. Groundnuts provided a valued source of income for farmers in Senegal, the Gambia and Northern Nigeria. In the case of the first two, the production zone was relatively close to the coastal ports, while in the third the railway provided the essential outlet. But in other parts of the Sahel there was neither the level of rainfall nor the infrastructure to support a similar expansion of cash crop cultivation. In the vast drylands of West Africa, the Horn, East and Southern Africa, agriculture was itself not an option except in close proximity to the rivers. As has already been noted, the population densities for Africa at the time of independence were generally low: whereas Rwanda and Burundi counted 88 per square kilometre, Mauritania, Botswana and South-West Africa (Namibia) counted one person each; Chad, the Central African Republic, Congo-Brazzaville and Gabon 2 each; and Djibouti and Somalia 3 each. In the first three cases, and the last two, these very low population densities reflected the extreme harshness of the environment. Even in Kenya, a country which is often pictured as a land of fertile highland valleys, the dominant reality is one of acute aridity. These environmental constraints help to explain why Africa is the continent characterised by the greatest attachment to pastoralism and hunter-gathering. Across Africa – from the West African Sahel, though the Horn East Africa and down to Southern Africa, settled agriculture either co-exists alongside pastoralism or gives way to it entirely. Hunter-gathering also continues to reproduce itself in parts of Southern Africa, especially Namibia and Botswana.

The populations of many African countries were spread extremely thinly across the landscape while pastoralists were frequently on the move, albeit along reasonably predictable paths of migration. The Fulani (or Fulbe) of West Africa, the Somali of the Horn and the Maasai of East Africa are perhaps the best known examples of peoples who have continued to herd their cattle across great distances in search of pasturage and water, without much regard to the positioning of international borders. Newly independent governments based in the capital cities aspired to reach all their newly acquired citizens, including the pastoralists. Some hoped to persuade the latter to adopt a sedentary lifestyle, in order that they might be provided with the benefits of schooling and medical facilities. However, the ostensibly benevolent promises of government assistance were often spurned. Hence the relationship with central authority was destined to be almost as fraught as it had been in colonial times. Even in countries, like Somalia, where pastoralism was the norm, political elites viewed this way of life as a barrier to 'development', a self-evident good. In countries, where the elites were drawn from agrarian backgrounds, pastoralism – and even more so hunter-gathering – was construed as tantamount to wallowing in backwardness. This brings us to the elites themselves.

2.2 The compression of elites

The imperative of 'nation-building' was on everyone's lips in the immediate aftermath of independence. It was generally understood that the colonial powers had done little to nurture a sense of emotional attachment to the administrative units they had created – in some cases, like Nigeria and Sudan, they had actually placed many practical barriers in the way of this occurring naturally. Hence, the African politicians who took over the reins of power based much of their own legitimacy on their claim to be actively forging a sense of nationhood where it existed only in outline. The outward manifestation of this drive included the fabrication of national symbols in the form of flags, anthems and so on, but it was also embodied in their claims to being inclusive of all the components of the nation-in-the making. Ironically, however, it was the elite itself which provided a highly unstable platform for the completion of the nation-building project.

The problem was partly one of the size of the elite and partly one of its regional distribution. During the colonial era, the pre-colonial ruling classes had been harnessed to the imperial state. At the same time, indigenous merchants had been squeezed out by the large European firms which were better capitalised and enjoyed direct access to the corridors of power. At independence, the traditional elites remained a visible presence, except in Rwanda and Guinea. However, their claim to legitimacy had been undermined by the belated introduction of the electoral principle. Most elected politicians were clear in their own minds that it was they and not the chiefs who were entitled to call the shots and they set about clipping the wings of 'traditional rulers' (see Chapter 3). During decolonisation, some African businessmen did move into the niches vacated by the European firms, but the greater beneficiaries were the Lebanese in West Africa and the Asians in East Africa who were better placed to take advantage. By their nature, these middleman minorities were on the fringes of the political system. An African business class consequently remained very small and prospered largely on the basis of access to political patronage from the centre. As we shall see, this fundamental weakness tended to turn business competition into a by-product of the struggle for state power. The elite which inherited power was not born out of economic strength, but out of access to the educational system. This had been rudimentary in most of Africa and remained so until the post-war promises of social improvement began to bear fruit. Secondary education tended to be very limited, and higher education even more so. Countries like Ghana and Nigeria could point to a solid core of

University graduates, but there was nothing comparable in most of Africa where the colonial authorities had been suspicious of 'overly educated' Africans. Many newly independent countries could only boast of one or two of people with any kind of higher education. Graduates were placed in an ideal position to translate educational attainment into political power. However, this further reduced the pool of skilled personnel available to service the administration. The French promised help to get around this little problem by means of technical co-operation agreements which left French personnel in charge of much everyday decision-making. Meanwhile, many more young people were sent overseas to complete their education, while governments busied themselves with building their own Universities to nurture home-grown graduates. But there was no disguising two facts: firstly, that, for the first decade or so, there was an absolute shortage of skilled manpower; and secondly, that education provided a gateway to power and prestige, so that a collective good also traded as a private perk.

There was a further problematic legacy of the colonial system, which is that whatever education had been provided tended to be unevenly distributed. The spread of primary education normally reflected the pattern of missionary penetration, which could vary greatly within the boundaries of a colony. In areas which had limited basic education, few students fed through to secondary and tertiary education. Hence in Uganda, the number of northern graduates from Makerere College was minute by comparison with the wealthier south, a pattern which was replicated at the University of Ghana despite Nkrumah's efforts to encourage northerners. Since education conferred such advantages on the recipient, whole regions were effectively disadvantaged from birth. The political ramifications were bound to be especially acute when the disadvantaged groups happened to be in a numerical majority. In Sierra Leone, the Creoles of the Colony initially fought hard to maintain their privileges, but were ultimately forced to concede political precedence to the emergent elite of the larger Protectorate. But things did not always proceed so smoothly.

In Nigeria, Catholic and Protestant missionary organisations had been given a relatively free hand in the South from the nineteenth century, but they had been kept out of the Muslim north. The result was northerners lagged far behind in terms of educational attainment. Oxford had graduated its first Yoruba woman in 1935, amidst a steady trickle of educational migration in the interwar years. In 1950, there were 938 Nigerian students in British Universities, and another 300 in American institutions, but these were overwhelmingly from the South. The first Northerners graduated as late as 1951.[9] This was one very good reason why the Northern People's Congress (NPC) sought to retard the pace of decolonisation in the 1950s. Once in power at the centre, the NPC set out to redress the balance through greater educational expenditure in the North and selective recruitment policies, which southerners regarded as discrimination. In the Nigerian case, the British intention had been to avoid antagonising the Muslim establishment, but in Rwanda and Burundi it was a conscious policy on the part of the Belgians to favour Tutsis over Hutus. As Mahmood Mamdani observes, their policy effectively created a two-tier system, in which Tutsi were 'introduced into a "civilised" French-medium education', while their Hutu counterparts 'were confined to a "nativised" second-rate Kiswahili-medium education'.[10] The inevitable result was that better-educated members of the Tutsi elite emerged with a reinforced sense of their own superiority, while the Hutus who did manage to advance through the Catholic seminaries had a highly developed sense of grievance against a system which was stacked against them. Unable to obtain jobs elsewhere, this Hutu 'counter-elite' found a home in the Catholic church, whose publications provided a forum for the first expressions of Hutu nativism. As in Nigeria, therefore, a fault line emerged which became imprinted on the psyche of the political elite, and which was to colour the subsequent history of that country. Whereas a large, wealthy and relatively cohesive elite in other parts of the developing world – for example India – has been conducive to stability, the elite in Africa was very small, insecure and prone to factionalism. South Africa was the only country which could really boast of an indigenous bourgeoisie, but here too the overlap between ethnicity and class created a dynamic which was hardly conducive to nation-building.

2.3 Variations in political geography

In this final section, it remains to consider the viability of the states which took the stage at independence. In the view of some commentators, as well as nationalist leaders like Nkrumah, African states were simply not workable in their existing form. For the realists, on the other hand, it was a question of playing the hand which was dealt with intelligence and pragmatism. In 1960, there was a case for arguing that the continent of Africa had sufficient mineral riches, and an abundance of land, to make rapid economic development a possibility. This is reflected in the initial assessment of René Dumont which introduces this chapter.[11]

In seriously addressing the colonial legacy, it has to be remembered that there was not a uniform inheritance. The new map of contained no fewer than 34 independent states in sub-Saharan Africa and the Horn, excluding those still under Portuguese (five) and white settler rule (three). Some of these countries were dealt an appalling hand, whereas others seemed to be reasonably well-placed to consolidate their independence. Needless to say, lurking behind any assessment of the prospects at independence is usually some assumption about what the optimal arrangement might have been. What is striking is the extent to which the assumptions differ. This is reflected in arguments about the importance of sheer size, both spatially and in terms of population. The variation in the dimensions of the newly independent states could scarcely have been greater. Including North Africa (which brings the total to 47 countries), Ieuan Griffiths estimates that fifteen states made up only one per cent of the continental surface area, whereas 81.7 per cent was accounted for by 22 of the states.[12] Hence, the Gambia was a tiny slither of territory located 10 km on either side of the river of that name, whereas the Sudan (like the Congo) was bigger than the combined size of what became the twelve member states of the European Union and was 238 times larger than the Gambia itself.[13] It should also be noted that geographical and population size was not always that closely correlated. In the case of the micro-states – the Gambia, Equatorial Guinea, Lesotho and Swaziland – the correlation was very close, as it was at the other end of the scale with Nigeria, the Congo, Sudan and Ethiopia. But some states were physically very large, but contained very small populations: such as Botswana, Mauritania, Mali and Chad. However, most of the continent was made up of medium-sized states with relatively small populations numbering less than ten million at independence.

This solid wedge of states is precisely what many have regarded as symptomatic of the balkanisation of Africa. Ieuan Griffiths makes a case for the importance of size and sees much of Africa as ill-served by its inheritance:

> The prospects for independent economic development are extremely poor for the very small economies encountered in Africa. Actual smallness is compounded by the fact that the economies comprise large rural sectors. Many African economies are smaller than the minimum threshold size for the establishment of any manufacturing industry other than small craft or repair and service industries, so a whole avenue of potential development is closed off. Such economies are too small to support even basic services.[14]

By contrast, coming from the standpoint of a political scientist, Jeffrey Herbst is sceptical of the claims that are advanced in favour of size, regarding this as an yet another European import with doubtful application to Africa. The performance of some the largest countries in Africa after independence – notably Sudan, the Congo and Nigeria – would in Herbst's views cast doubt on the assumption that big is best.[15]

There is a similar difference of opinion when it comes to shape. Scrutiny of the map of Africa reveals a number of countries which are very elongated. The historical roots of this legacy lie mostly in the fact that the European powers expanded inland from coastal trading ports, which sometimes created a ribbon effect. The singular case of the Gambia had already been referred to. The elongated shapes of Togo and Benin similarly resulted from competitive European imperialism. In south-eastern Africa, Mozambique emerged from the partition as a colony with a very long coastline, but not much of an interior. This occurred precisely because Portugal had been unable to translate its longstanding coastal claims into control of the interior where Cecil Rhodes was engaged in his own land-grab. Griffiths, who has gone to the effort of producing a shape index for each country, explains the importance of this factor in deriving the maximum advantage from infrastructural investments:

> Short feeders of unmade roads quickly and cheaply extend the hinterland, and it is generally reckoned that a major transport artery can positively affect development for at least 50 miles (80 km) on either side, plus a radius of 50 miles around the rail/tarred road. Thus a railway or tarred road 250 miles (400 km) long can open up as much as 29,000 square miles (74,000 square kilometres) of territory by accelerating economic development, giving access to markets and facilitating the diffusion of modern farming methods, the use of better seed, fertilizer and so on.[16]

The implication is that a ribbon-shaped country will not derive the optimal benefits from its infrastructural investments, and indeed feasibility considerations may tend to militate against such investments being made. Griffiths also notes that the extremities of such countries are likely to be feel especially remote from their capital cities.

Herbst, on the other hand, is no more impressed by this factor, contending that 'Shapes and sizes are not important in and of themselves; rather what is critical is the particular population distribution that they represent to national leaders.'[17] In other words, where the populations of a given country are divided into discrete pockets, this makes it difficult for states to 'broadcast' their power. The best-case scenario is where 'the highest concentration of power is found in one area, usually around the capital, and then the population densities become lower as distance from the capital increases'.[18] The substance of the difference between these authors is that whereas Griffiths appears to believe that the countries which were dealt the best hand were those which were as near to round in shape as possible, with a sufficient surface area and population to match, Herbst gives precedence to those states which were small and which had a relatively concentrated distribution of population. Herbst even produces a grid of countries according to how favourable or unfavourable their political geographies are. He lists no fewer than nineteen countries as fitting the favourable category, a list which includes Benin, Burundi, Congo-Brazzaville, Equatorial Guinea, Gabon, the Gambia, Guinea-Bissau, Lesotho, Rwanda, Sierra Leone, Swaziland and Togo. These are all small states which fall foul of the Griffiths criteria, although the latter does not produce a comparable league-table. Herbst's list of countries with difficult political geographies, on the other hand, includes those with the largest populations and/or land area, including Congo, Ethiopia, Sudan, Tanzania and Nigeria. There seems to be agreement between the authors that Mozambique, Chad, Mali, Mauritania and Niger had it tough, but otherwise Griffiths and Herbst seem to be at clear odds with one another.

Part of the reason for coming to different conclusions is that while Herbst accords primacy to political efficacy, Griffiths is concerned with the developmental implications of the territorial division of Africa. Nevertheless, it would be surprising if these two sets of criteria did not coincide to some extent. On the whole, the Griffiths model seems to have the greatest heuristic value because it builds more factors into the overall equation. The problem with the Herbst model is partly that it simply ignores many of the issues raised by Griffiths and others. The claim that small states have denser road networks, for example, glosses over the Griffith's point that the beneficial effects to the states in question will be greatly attenuated by the proximity of the borders. There is a certain circularity attached to privileging the proximity of the population to the centre of decision-making and then finding that small states are more viable. This methodology also leads to some peculiar conclusions, most notably that the Gambia enjoys a favourable political geography, whereas most people would probably agree that the size and shape of this country have created profound difficulties.

The oddities of size and shape do not tell the full story. In many cases, additional handicaps were heaped on already fragile states. The most important of these was perhaps the curse of being landlocked, which potentially reduced the benefits of external trade. A number of states in former French West Africa, and in Central Africa, had to contend with this particular legacy of decolonisation (see Table 2.2). In West Africa, Mali and Burkina Faso were connected to the sea by the railway network of the defunct federation, but Niger was not. In West-Central Africa, Chad had access to the sea through a very indirect route, while the Central African Republic was only connected to its neighbours by dirt road and river.[19] Burundi was equally cut off, whereas Rwanda had better road links. Uganda, on the other hand, was connected to the Kenyan seaboard by the former colonial railway. In Southern Africa, the dominance of the mining industry ensured that most of the landlocked states had rail access to the sea, although the fact that many the links passed through white-ruled Rhodesia, Mozambique and South Africa presented moral dilemmas for the governments of the newly liberated states.

In some cases, the various disadvantages were offset by the discovery of other valuable resources. These were not always immediately apparent at the time of independence – nobody, for example, could have predicted the future importance of oil reserves – with the result that some states actually ended up being better off than seemed likely in 1960. Gabon and Botswana, for example, were fortunate in ultimately being able to distribute some of the benefits of oil and diamond production across small populations. The second column in Table 2.2 lists the states which have significant mineral deposits and which were actually exploited

Table 2.2 The resource endowments of African states

Country (and other names)	Geographical anomalies	Mineral resources	Other main exports
Angola	No	Oil, diamonds	
Benin (Dahomey)	Shape	Some oil	Cotton, cocoa, palm products
Botswana	Landlocked	Diamonds	Cattle
Burkina Faso (Upper Volta)	Landlocked	Some gold, some diamonds	Cotton
Burundi	Landlocked	Unexploited deposits of nickel, vanadium and phosphates	Coffee
Cameroun	No	Oil	Timber
Cape Verde	Micro-state, islands	No	
Central African Republic	Landlocked	Uranium, some diamonds	Coffee, cotton, timber
Chad	Landlocked	Oil	Cotton, livestock
Congo-Brazzaville	No	Oil	
Congo (Zaire, Democratic Republic of Congo)	No	Diamonds, zinc, cobalt, copper, coltan	
Côte d'Ivoire	No	Some oil, and untapped iron ore, bauxite, diamonds, gold, nickel	Cocoa, coffee, pineapples, cotton, palm-oil, timber

Table 2.2 Continued

Country (and other names)	Geographical anomalies	Mineral resources	Other main exports
Djibouti	Micro-state	No	Livestock
Eritrea (from 1993)	No	No	Livestock
Ethiopia (formerly including Eritrea)	Part desert	No	Coffee
Equatorial Guinea	Micro-state, part islands	Oil (1990s)	Cocoa, timber
Gabon	Micro-state	Oil, manganese, iron ore, uranium	Timber
Gambia	Micro-state	No	Groundnuts
Ghana	No	Gold, diamonds	Cocoa
Guinea	No	Bauxite, gold, diamonds	Coffee
Guinea Bissau	Micro-state	No	Cashew
Kenya	No	No	Coffee, tea, sisal
Lesotho	Micro-state	No	
Liberia	No	Iron ore	Rubber, timber
Malawi	Shape	No	Tobacco, tea, sugar
Mali	Landlocked, part desert	Gold (1990s)	Cotton, livestock
Mauritania	Desert	Iron ore	Fisheries
Mozambique	Shape	No	Cotton, cashew, fisheries
Namibia (South West Africa)	Part desert	Diamonds, uranium	Fisheries
Niger	Landlocked, part desert	Uranium	
Nigeria	No	Oil	Cocoa, palm-oil groundnuts
Rwanda	Landlocked	No	Coffee
São Tomé and Príncipe	Micro-state, islands	No	Cocoa
Senegal	No	Little gold	Groundnuts, fisheries
Sierra Leone	No	Diamonds, gold	
Somalia	No	No	Livestock, fisheries
South Africa	No	Gold, diamonds	Various, plus manufacturing
Sudan	No	Oil	Cotton
Swaziland	Micro-state	No	
Tanzania (Tanganyika and Zanzibar)	No	Gold (1990s)	Cotton, tea, sisal, cashew
Togo	Shape	Phosphates	Cocoa, coffee
Uganda	Landlocked	No	Coffee, cotton
Zambia	Landlocked	Copper, cobalt	
Zimbabwe (Rhodesia)	Landlocked	Gold	Tobacco

within the first forty years of independence. The third column also lists other resources which made a significant contribution to the national economy. Reading the table as whole, it can be seen that a large number of states had disadvantages which were not compensated for: these include Benin, Burkina Faso, Cape Verde, Burundi, the Gambia, Guinea Bissau, Lesotho, Mozambique, Rwanda, Somalia and Swaziland. It is worth underlining that this list includes both the smallest states as well as some which were extremely large. Many of the other states had difficulties unique to themselves, but also enjoyed some of the means to redress them after independence. As we will see in subsequent chapters, mineral resources could be a curse as well as a boon. Alluvial diamonds became bound up with warlordism in Sierra Leone and Angola, while petroleum intensified political cleavages and social divisions in Nigeria and Angola.

With the exception of South Africa, most states had a negligible manufacturing base. This meant that even the most prosperous countries were dependent upon the export of primary commodities, both for government revenues and for foreign exchange earnings. The problem was that the range of commodities which most countries could export was limited, while international markets were highly vulnerable to price fluctuations. For example, the comparative prosperity of Ghana and Côte d'Ivoire was heavily dependent upon one commodity, cocoa, the world price for which was notoriously unstable. Whereas the world price reached a peak of £460 per ton in 1954, it had fallen to £222 by 1960 and then plummeted to a low of £138 in 1965. It was no accident that Ghanaian production peaked at the same time, because as the world's largest producer Ghana contributed directly to the glut on the world market. It was a similar story with copper, which provided 71 per cent of Zambian government revenues in 1965.[20] In this case, the world price remained buoyant until 1974 when there was a sudden collapse. Although a resource-starved country like Somalia might have envied these kinds of problems, the reality was that the economies of the wealthier states were built on fragile foundations. The possible solutions to monocrop dependency included the promotion of indigenous manufacturing (including domestic processing of primary products), export diversification and a concentration on maximisation of agricultural output. As we shall see in Chapter 5, African opinion divided at an early point between the advocates of gradualism and of a radical break with the colonial inheritance.

René Dumont was perhaps the most uncompromising of the early critics of the choices made by African governments in the immediate aftermath of independence. But Dumont himself acknowledged that it was simply not the case that newly independent regimes inherited full coffers and the kind of functioning institutions with which to remake their destinies as they saw fit. The altogether harsher reality was that the post-war period had thrown up a whole series of very complex problems which the departing European powers deftly avoided having to deal with. This was briefly obscured by the euphoria of the independence celebrations, but it did not take long for the truth to emerge. In the chapter which follows, I will consider the fate of successive efforts to return to the drawing board.

The Shape of Things to Come: Irredentism, Secessionism and the Pan-African Ideal

> To us, Africa with its islands is just one Africa. We reject the idea of any kind of partition. From Tangier or Cairo in the North to Capetown in the South, from Cape Guardafui in the East to Cape Verde islands in the West, Africa is one and indivisible.
>
> Kwame Nkrumah, *Africa Must Unite*

> Wherever the camel roams, that is Somalia.
>
> Somali proverb

> To Keep Nigeria One is a Task That Must be Done
>
> Nigerian government poster during civil war of 1967–70[1]

As we have seen in Chapters 1 and 2, the playing out of the colonial endgame gave rise to a territorially fragmented continent where the sheer viability of many of the constituent states was open to question. Although independence was seized with alacrity in most cases, there was a lack of consensus about whether the new map of Africa ought merely to be taken as a starting point or its contours should be considered immutable. In many cases, leaders clung on jealously to what was theirs, whilst others pursued irredentist claims against their neighbours. Some, like Kwame Nkrumah, expressed a keen interest in territorial mergers with a view to avoiding the perils of continental balkanisation, while demands for secession elsewhere threatened to break the continent into yet smaller pieces. Of all the weighty questions facing the first generation of post-colonial leaders, perhaps none was of greater moment than the configuration of the political map. With the benefit of hindsight, some have bemoaned their over-eagerness to perpetuate the terms of the European partition. But it would be a mistake to forget that over the first decade or so there were many efforts to chart a different course. In order to understand what eventually transpired,

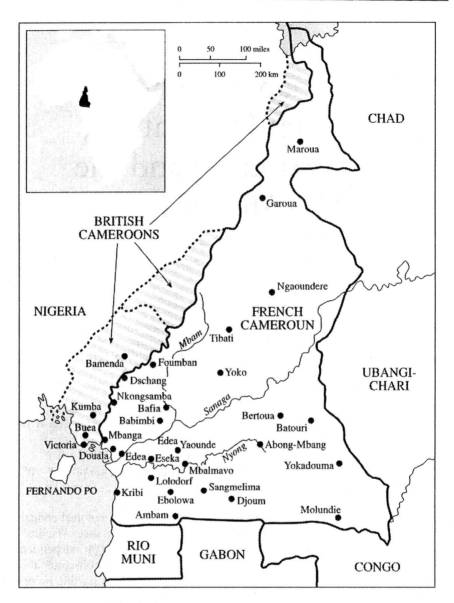

Map 3 French Cameroun and British Cameroons

Adapted from Richard Joseph, *Radical Nationalism in Cameroun: Social Origins of the UPC Rebellion* (Oxford: Clarendon Press, 1977), p. 6.

we need to take account of a combination of factors which tilted the balance in favour of one outcome rather than another: including the ambitions and resources of the leaders concerned, their levels of grassroots support, and the international environment in which they were forced to operate. There is an important story to be told here – a story of lost chances and partial successes. In this chapter, we start with the formation of political unions, then turn to consider the fate of various irredentist, secessionist and rebel movements, before finishing up with the formation of the Organisation of African Unity (OAU).

3.1 Africa Unbound: regrouping territories and states

For Pan-Africanists, it was an indictment of decolonisation that it had bequeathed a continent that was even more balkanised than colonial Africa itself. Of course, the Central African Federation continued to exist until the end of 1963, but this was hardly a model to emulate. There had also been functioning federations in French West and Equatorial Africa before they were broken up in the 1950s. And in British East Africa the idea of federation remained potent enough for Julius Nyerere to offer a postponement of Tanganyikan independence in order to make the dream of unity on equal terms a reality.[2] Although there remained some emotional attachment to these older projects in the 1960s, however, the most successful efforts at political union were those which came more out of the comparative blue. This was doubly counter-intuitive in the sense that one might have expected success to have hinged on a coming together of roughly equal partners, whereas the opposite was the case. What seems to have mattered more was that these steps towards union were simultaneous with the coming of independence, when there was still some flexibility, and that they bore the imprimatur of the international community.

Both conditions were operative in the fusion of former Italian Somaliland and British Somaliland to create the Republic of Somalia in July 1960. Here the territorial units were roughly symmetrical, but they lacked a common tradition of colonial governance. Still, there was no doubting the enthusiasm for union within the two territories, which meant that the British, the Italians and the UN could claim that they had honourably discharged their responsibilities. Elsewhere in the Horn, reconfiguration of the colonial map was destined to be a more fraught affair. As we have already seen, the UN struggled to find a satisfactory solution to the Eritrean puzzle for the reason that there was a lack of consensus between Muslim and Christians in the former Italian colony. After a series of Visiting Missions and debates, the UN finally came down in favour of a union with Ethiopia, which took practical effect in 1952. Eritrea was to constitute 'an autonomous unit federated with Ethiopia under the sovereignty of the Ethiopian Crown'. For sympathisers with the later Eritrean liberation movement, this was not a union which was freely entered into by both parties. On this reading, it was Ethiopia's requirement of access to sea which led it to pursue its claim to Eritrea in the first place, despite the references to close affinities between the peoples concerned. Furthermore, since Ethiopia was ruled by an Emperor, the democratic provisions written into the Eritrean constitution were bound to conflict with Ethiopian ways of doing things. Indeed the constitutional arrangements are often seen as a pragmatic compromise which Haile Selassie never intended to honour.

The Eritrean Constitution conferred responsibility for defence, foreign affairs, currency, finance, external and internal commerce and communications upon the Ethiopian government. The Eritrean executive was left with those areas of decision-making which were not reserved. The language of federation was misleading to the extent that there was no federal government as distinct from the government of Ethiopia. Moreover, the latter was the creature of the Emperor whose 'sovereignty' over Eritrea was also clearly stipulated in UN resolution 39(V)A of 1950. Equally, it is true that the United States wanted the best deal for Haile Selassie with a view to extracting the concession of the highly valued Kagnew military base in Asmara. It is also difficult to deny that the Ethiopian government displayed little interest in respecting the internal autonomy of Eritrea. Indeed its interpretation of the constitution was one which – with some reason – denied that there was a clearcut division between the two constituent parts. Nevertheless, Tekeste Negash has made a reasonable case for regarding members of the Christian political elite as the architects of their own fate.[3] They did not share the religious fears of their Muslim counterparts and many of them appeared to accept the potential advantages which would come with closer association with Ethiopia. If they had consistently supported the demand for Eritrean independence, it is unlikely that the territory would have been joined to its larger neighbour. To that extent, they walked knowingly into the federalist trap.

Ruth Iyob observes that the first three years of the federation were characterised by the maintenance of the appearance of democracy, whereas the reality was that real powers were progressively transferred to Addis Ababa. After 1955, she writes, the federation was effectively abrogated with 'the change of the name of the Eritrean government to that of Eritrean "administration", the adoption of the Ethiopian flag, and the introduction of a large number of Ethiopian administrators and teachers into Eritrea'.[4] In her view, these various acts effectively extinguished the separate identity of Eritrea and signalled that it was to be treated as just another region of Ethiopia. Tekeste does not differ greatly on this point, concluding that '[s]ince the last weeks of 1958 the constitution had definitively ceased to exist. Only its shadow remained; and it was to remain as long as it pleased the Eritrean head of state and the Ethiopian authorities.'[5] He credits the efforts of the Muslim League (ML) to defend the federation, by petitioning the Emperor and the UN itself, and gives due weight to the repressive response by the authorities. Where he parts company is in underlining the crucial part played by the UP (Unionist Party), which dominated the Eritrean assembly, and successive Chief Executives who were intent on terminating the separate status of the territory.[6] The implication is that if the UP had stood up for the separate status of Eritrea, the federation might well have found its feet – a point which Eritrean nationalist historiography conveniently ignores.

Wherever the blame is placed, there is a broad consensus that the weakness of the Eritrean administration and the inclinations of the Ethiopian government led to the demise of unionism in the long run. A policy of Amharisation had long been pursued across the empire, entailing the imposition of the Amharic language and the Orthodox Church upon subject peoples. The religious issue did not pose a problem for Eritrean Christians in the way that it did for Muslims, but the downgrading of Tigrinya did threaten to put them at a serious disadvantage. Moreover, government repression of peaceful protest tended to strip the political institutions of whatever legitimacy they enjoyed and led to an increased preparedness to resort to arms.[7] The resulting cycle of violence in turn led Haile Selassie to look to direct control as the means of ensuring order in an 'unruly province'.[8] On 14 November 1962, the Eritrean Assembly finally voted, in the menacing presence of imperial troops, for integration into the Ethiopian empire, thereby terminating the short-lived federal experiment.

Taking up Tekeste Negash's point, it is conceivable that if the Ethiopian government had been more accommodating it might have consolidated support amongst a solid wedge of Christian highlanders. However, its heavy-handedness alienated many of those who had hitherto been loyal allies. Prominent leaders of the ML like Ibrahim Sultan were the first to opt for exile, but they were soon to be joined by their Christian counterparts. At first, resistance was poorly co-ordinated, in part because of the religious divide. The Eritrean Liberation Movement (ELM) had been founded in 1958 by young Muslims living in the Sudan, who looked to an independent Eritrea in which Christians and Muslims could both feel at home. The ELM modelled itself on the cellular organisation of the Sudanese Communist Party, and according to Iyob it successfully tapped into elements of popular culture.[9] One of its shortcomings was the misguided (and costly) faith it placed in a military coup as a short-cut to liberation.[10] A further problem was the hostile reception extended by an older generation of Muslim activists who disliked the leftist rhetoric of the ELM and its explicit appeal to a Christian constituency. These came together to form the Eritrean Liberation Front (ELF) in 1960, which maintained that 'The Eritrean Revolution is, and must be, a Muslim Revolution, or a Revolution of the Muslims and for Muslims alone.'[11] The infighting between the ELM and the ELF eliminated any possibility of a co-ordinated challenge to Ethiopian rule, and greatly assisted the authorities in rounding up dissident elements.[12] In 1965, the war of words between the organisations escalated into a violent confrontation which virtually crippled the ELM and momentarily put paid to the vision of a Muslim–Christian alliance. Although the first shots in the war of liberation were fired as early as 1961, it took some years before the Ethiopian position was seriously challenged.

Another union of unequal partners, which was facilitated both by propitious timing and by a favourable international environment, was the federation of British Southern Cameroon with French Cameroun. Like the two Togolands, these had formed a single unit under German rule, been partitioned after the First World War and placed under League of Nations Mandates, before finally becoming UN Trust Territories. In the case of the Togolands, reunification was dealt a blow by the 1956 plebiscite in which the majority of voters in British Togoland voted for union with an independent Ghana. The Nkrumah regime expressed the hope that French Togoland would join later on, and in the 1958 elections it even provided moral and logistical support to Sylvanus Olympio against those parties which were both pro-French and hostile to reunification. Although Olympio won these crucial elections and took French Togoland towards full independence, it became apparent that he had no intention of merging with Ghana. And the more Nkrumah sought to force his hand, by for example sealing the border between the two countries, the more intransigent Olympio became. By 1961, nobody seriously believed that a union of Ghana and Togo was a possibility except by force of arms – and this was ruled out by the alliances which Olympio managed to reach with France and Nigeria.

In the case of the Cameroons, the dynamic was different. As in British Togoland, there was an administrative and cultural separation between the North and South of the British Trust Territory. But because the votes were counted together in the British Togoland plebiscite, the pro-union vote of the North outweighed the unificationist vote in the South.[13] Furthermore, the plebiscite took place before the grant of Ghanaian independence, whereas British Cameroon was separated from Nigeria when it became independent in October 1960. When the Cameroons plebiscite was finally held in February of the following year – with a choice between joining an independent Nigeria or an independent Cameroun – the votes of the northern and southern halves were counted separately. Whereas the peoples of Northern British Cameroon had much in common with those of Northern Nigeria, with whom they had been jointly administered, those of the South felt isolated from Southern Nigeria. Moreover, an influx of Igbo traders and civil servants did little to endear them to southern Cameroonians. In the event, the majority of the latter voted to join Cameroun, which had become independent in 1960, whereas their northern counterparts plumped for Nigeria.

In the former French territory, the new province was an unknown quantity in part because no large ethnic groups had been partitioned by the border. Nevertheless, the Union des Populations du Cameroun (UPC) had placed unification on the agenda in the 1950s, and although it was later banned, this particular plank was appropriated by the ruling party at independence. President Ahmadou Ahidjo was a convert to the unification idea, but was less than enthusiastic about federalism. The deal which Ahidjo struck with J. N. Foncha, leader of the majority KNDP (Kamerun National Democratic Party) in 1959, and subsequently confirmed in October 1960, was one which left him with the freedom to construe the relationship as he saw fit.[14] The federation of what became known as West and East Cameroun was almost as asymmetrical as that between Ethiopia and Eritrea. The Anglophone West was only one tenth the geographical size of the East, and contained about a quarter of its population. Moreover, it was attaching itself to an independent country which had all of its institutions already in place; which upheld quite different legal, administrative and educational traditions; and used a different official language. Moreover, whereas the plantation economy of the West depended heavily on preferential access to British markets, this was destined to end once it was integrated into the franc zone.

There were many problems of adjustment, most notably declining revenues and falling agricultural exports, but a commitment to gradualism reduced some of the teething troubles. Writing in 1967, Edwin Ardener commented favourably on the substantial infrastructural investments which ended the geographical isolation of the West, and an official commitment to bilingualism which helped to assuage the fears of the Anglophone minority.[15] Moreover, whereas the East was characterised by an increasingly authoritarian style of rule, there remained a greater measure of political pluralism in the West. This was reduced by the merger of the Anglophone parties with the ruling party in 1966, but for some years the separate identity of the West continued to be respected. In the rhetoric of the Ahidjo regime, the coming together of an Anglophone and a Francophone territory offered a model of Pan-Africanism at work which the rest of the continent could learn from. This was over-stating the achievement, but the Camerounian federation was more than a fiction until it was abruptly terminated by Ahidjo in 1972.

Our final case is the federation of the island state of Zanzibar with mainland Tanganyika. Here, there were historic and cultural ties which could be invoked, in that the Sultan of Zanzibar had once governed over the coastal strip and the Swahili language was spoken throughout. However, the Omani Arabs who ruled Zanzibar had constructed a rigid social hierarchy which survived the ending of slavery and which was further entrenched under the British Protectorate. In the 1950s, the Omani aristocracy continued to dominate politically, while an Asian minority controlled much of the business and the African majority made up the plantation and urban labour force. As Zanzibar approached independence in December 1963, politics polarised along ethnic lines.[16] Although Africans made up some three-quarters of the population, there was a division between the indigenous population of the islands, who defined themselves as Shirazis, and the descendants of slaves and more recent labour migrants who originated from the mainland. It was this fault-line which enabled astute Arab politicians to retain their grip on power. In the last elections before independence, the mainly Arab Zanzibar Nationalist Party (ZNP) allied itself to the Shirazi-based People's Party. Together they captured more seats than the Afro-Shirazi Party, even though the latter actually won more votes overall. Immediately before the election, however, a radical faction had broken from the ZNP to form the Umma Party, which immediately joined with the Afro-Shirazi party in attacking the regime as a cover for Arab oligarchy.

Within a month of independence, a full-blown crisis erupted on the islands. Africans who were broadly sympathetic to the opposition mounted a successful coup under the leadership of John Okello. Many of the protagonists were policemen of mainland origin who had been purged by the government or feared they were about to be. The principal intention of the coup-makers was to effect a transfer of political power from Arab to African hands, but in the aftermath of the coup many plantations were destroyed, some 5000 Arabs were killed and perhaps as many again were expelled or fled.[17] The revolution was not universally popular, especially amongst the Shirazis of Pemba, and the regime therefore needed to cement its legitimacy. For this reason, members of the Afro-Shirazi party and the Umma Party were invited to join the Revolutionary Council, which was headed by Abeid Karume of the former party. It was possibly for reasons of insecurity that the regime approached Tanganyika about forging a possible union. This was unexpected, but it was perfectly understandable since the regime saw itself as definitively non-Arab and was predisposed to identify with the peoples of the mainland who had previously manifested sympathy for the plight of the African majority. The TANU leadership responded positively to the overture, possibly hoping to contain the aftershocks of the revolution, as the Revolutionary Council turned to the Eastern Bloc. In April 1964 the union came into effect, bearing the name of the United Republic of Tanzania.

The arrangement was one which left Zanzibar with a remarkable level of internal autonomy. The Zanzibar authorities retained control over their own army, immigration policy on the islands, agriculture, health, education and trade.[18] The Revolutionary Council, which had a mind of its own, even drew up its independent Five Year Plan, with the assistance of East German economic advisors, without any reference to the National Assembly.[19] Moreover, although the population of Zanzibar constituted a mere three per cent of that of the mainland, the constitution provided for a Presidency which would rotate between the two halves of the federation. While Nyerere became the new President, Karume was installed as the First Vice-President. At the same time, the Zanzibaris received five Ministerial positions and as many as 52 seats in the National Assembly. These were generous terms indeed, and although there was periodic friction in the relationship, this explains why the United Republic endured without very much dissent until the 1990s.

The coming to fruition of the Camerounian and Tanzanian federations, contrasts with the failed efforts at reunification in former French West Africa. After the withdrawal of Upper Volta and Dahomey from the proposed Mali Federation, the latter had been reduced to Mali and Senegal. Although this was a disappointment for committed federalists, the rump stood a good chance of surviving: after all, Mali and Senegal shared an administrative and linguistic legacy, a common cultural inheritance and close economic linkages arising from labour migration and the Bamako-Dakar railway. Furthermore, when de Gaulle agreed that the Mali Federation was not incompatible with a continuing relationship with France, this ensured that external aid would be forthcoming. It was on these terms that independence was conferred on a single territorial entity in June 1960. Modibo Keita was installed as President, while Léopold Senghor became President of the National Assembly and Mamadou Dia was appointed Prime Minister and Minister of Defence. However, it did not take very long for the federation to come unstuck. The reasons lie precisely in the close affinity between the partners which made it all too easy for each to step on the other's toes. Keita offended his Senegalese partners by criticising Senghor and Dia on their home patch, and by making direct overtures to the Muslim brotherhoods on which their power base depended.[20] As rumours of plots abounded, Keita sought to replace Dia as Minister of Defence and then to march on Dakar. When Senegalese troops failed to comply, a stalemate ensued which ended with the declaration of a separate Senegalese independence in January 1961. Senghor now became President and Mamadou Dia headed the government of the successor state.

The collapse of the Mali Federation was not quite the end of the story. After the abrupt termination of French relations with Guinea, Nkrumah's generosity towards the stricken regime led to the proposal for a Ghana–Guinea union. This was nothing if not ambitious, given that the two countries had different colonial inheritances and were not even geographically contiguous. Yet in some respects this grand gesture of the pan-Africanist will made the union all the more attractive. The collapse of the Mali Federation provided the perfect opportunity for Nkrumah and Sekou Touré to make their paper union appear more credible (Mali at least shared borders with Guinea). On the other hand, it provided the Malian leadership with a alternative set of friends. After the acrimonious split with Senegal, part of the railway line to Dakar had been ripped up and Mali faced the prospect of being turned into a landlocked state. Part of what Mali hoped to gain from the new arrangement was an alternative rail link to the coast through Guinea.[21] Thus was born the idea of a Ghana–Guinea–Mali union – extolled in one of the more memorable highlife tunes of E. T. Mensah.[22] To have turned this paper union into a reality would have required a formidable amount of patience and political will. Sekou Touré, Keita and Nkrumah were ideological soulmates, but different official languages, currencies, administrative traditions and sheer physical distance created practical impediments which would have taken decades to overcome. Unfortunately the rhetoric outstripped the commitment, while the egos of the respective leaders inevitably led to a clash of heads. The result was that the union had withered on the vine by 1963, and the focus of pan-Africanist idealism shifted to other fora.[23] Over subsequent years, each of these states became ever more preoccupied with its own internal affairs, ironically bearing out Nkrumah's own prediction that unless political unions were effected during the molten phase of independence, vested interests and bureaucratic inertia would take hold.

3.2 What's yours is mine: irredentist Somalia

In *Partitioned Africans*, A. I. Asiwaju provides a checklist of 'partitioned culture-areas': that is, broad cultural groupings which were bisected by the boundaries of independent Africa.[24] Judging from the length of the list, one might have expected demands for the reunification of divided peoples to have proliferated after 1960. However, it has to be recalled that most African states enclosed a number of different peoples, with the result that the plight of particular groups was unlikely to command great attention unless they exercised leverage over the politics of the country concerned. In many cases, irredentism was unattractive to those in power because it threatened to disrupt the delicate ethnic arithmetic. Only four states came remotely close to being ethnically homogeneous at independence: namely Somalia, Botswana, Lesotho and Swaziland, although the first two did in fact include significant minorities. The leaders of the last three were well-aware of the existence of kinsmen across the border, but the neighbour in question was South Africa on which they were economically dependent and which would not look kindly on irredentist claims.[25] In the case of Somalia, however, the success of uniting the former Italian and British colonies nourished an appetite for the unification of all the Somalis under a single flag. Indeed the flag which was designed for an independent Somalia said it all: it consisted of a five-pointed star, the first two representing the British and Italian colonies which had already been unified and the other three symbolising Somalis still under 'foreign' rule in Ethiopia, Kenya and Djibouti.

In common with many such movements, Somali nationalism posited a timeless unity in the face of deep-seated divisions along clan lines.[26] As was graphically confirmed towards the end of the twentieth century, these clan distinctions could be every bit as divisive as ethnicity in other African countries. However, for the moment anyway, the myths surrounding Somali nationalism remained unchallenged by academics and political actors alike. The claim over Somalis in Djibouti was the most difficult to advance given the determination of France to protect its own perceived strategic interests in the Red Sea. However, the government of Somalia believed that it had greater bargaining power in relation to its other neighbours. Some 275,000 Somalis were to be found in the vast Northern Frontier District (NFD) of Kenya which had been cordoned off from the rest of the colony by closed-district provisions. This meant that right up until the final moments of British rule, the Somali population had been left out of the political equation. As negotiations over the shape of independence began in earnest, the British recognised the need for a Somali voice. Kenyan nationalists themselves regarded the Somali issue as little more than a side-show and made no effort to garner political support in the NFD. The small parties which sprang up in the NFD were divided along clan and ethnic lines, but shared a common opposition to incorporation within Kenya. At the 1962 Lancaster Conference, the Somali representatives asserted their right to join Somalia and managed to extract a British agreement to conduct an enquiry into opinion in the NFD. Although the report found majority support for joining Somalia, John Markakis observes that the British government was unwilling to stand up to Kenyan nationalists when they insisted on the indivisibility of their country. The upshot was that the NFD became a region of independent Kenya despite vociferous protests by the Somali government.[27] Somali nationalists in the NFD responded by boycotting the administration and soliciting Somali government support for an armed insurrection. Although Somalia had limited military means, it despatched some old rifles which were used to launch operations across the border. However, with the British military helping the Kenyans to conduct a ruthless campaign of reprisals against pastoralists who were suspected of backing the rebels, the crisis was brought under control. In August 1967, a more conciliatory Somali government signed an agreement with Kenya which effectively ended its irredentist claim upon its kinsmen across the border.

In the case of the Ethiopian Somalis, the early stages of the struggle for unification were much the same, but the subsequent trajectory diverged significantly. After the war, it appeared as if Haile Selassie might be forced to relinquish his claims to the Ogaden, but American support was crucial to reconstitution of the empire in 1948. The returning Ethiopian administration discovered, however, that the Somali Youth League (SYL) had begun to operate in the territory during the British occupation and was peddling the cause of a united Somali nation. Haile Selassie endeavoured to buy off local support by incorporating some Somali chiefs into his administration, but this did not stem the rising tide of nationalism in the Ogaden.[28] In 1963, an attempt to tax Somali pastoralists precipitated outright rebellion. Once again, the rebel forces fought with limited weapons acquired from Somalia, which they supplemented with rifles supplied by Egypt. The Ethiopian government rightly perceived that the chances of putting down the rebellion, which was spreading rapidly and which was compounded by a separate outbreak in Bale and Sidamo, depended on cutting off Somali government support. At the start of 1964, the first full-scale war broke out along the border between the two states. At this juncture, the Somalis lacked the military equipment to fight a sustained campaign, and in March 1964 they were forced to sign a peace treaty. A new government calculated that while a greater Somalia was a desirable goal, the rebels were threatening its own internal stability. It therefore sought to discourage further rebel activity to the disgust of the substantial refugee population which had gathered within Somalia. In July 1967, the election of Ibrahim Egal as the second Prime Minister marked a further distancing from the pan-Somali cause as the regime endeavoured to normalise relations with its neighbours.

In October 1969, the pendulum swung back again following a military coup which was to alter the course of Somalia's history in ways as yet unimagined. The head of the junta, General Siyad Barre, had been involved in efforts to aid Somali rebels in Kenya and had taken a leading part in the Ethiopian campaign.[29] For this reason, he might have been expected to adopt a resolute pan-Somali stance. However, the regime was initially preoccupied with its own internal problems and with its fleshing out of its programme for 'scientific socialism'. Moreover, it needed time to reinvigorate the armed forces with the Soviet aid which was flowing in. When Somali nationalism reared its head once more, it was in relation to Djibouti where the French had finally begun to time their exit. There was a problem, though, in that the Afar population were more concerned with the plight of their own kinsmen in Ethiopia than they were with Somali grievances. When independence came in June 1977, the main Somali party was a partner in government. However, its Afar coalition partner could hardly be expected to support a union with Somalia. The result was that the government distanced itself from the Pan-Somali cause and articulated an inclusive Djibouti nationalism instead. This put paid to the prospect of redrawing the borders in this part of the Horn.

The focus of Somali irredentism subsequently shifted back to the Ogaden. In the early 1970s, the Ethiopians were confronted by a series of guerrilla insurgencies which fed off each other: the normal pattern was that the opening up of a new rebel front required the withdrawal of government troops from other zones and so invited different sets of dissidents to take up arms themselves. In the Ogaden, the Western Somali Liberation Front (WSLF) began a fresh phase of the struggle against Ethiopian rule. The Barre regime initially kept its distance, but this changed as the WSLF demonstrated its capacity to make significant inroads. In 1977, the Ethiopian forces were in retreat across the Ogaden, as the WSLF first cut off and then occupied the main towns. However, the Ethiopian revolution of 1974 led to a radical turnaround. The new military regime was committed to defending the territorial integrity of Ethiopia, and in 1977 the Soviet Union agreed to supply it with arms. This led Somalia to sever its own links with the Soviet Union. The perception that the military balance was about to shift led to an intensification of the fighting, and in February 1978 Somalia threw its own forces directly into the war. By this point, it was too late, and direct Cuban and Soviet assistance in the form of tanks and MIG aircraft, tilted the advantage against the Somalis.

In March, Somalia was forced to withdraw its forces from the Ogaden. This defeat dealt a death blow to the ideal of a united Somali nation. It had demonstrated that, as a very poor state, Somalia lacked the wherewithal to tip the balance in favour of rebel movements in Ethiopia. Moreover, the chances of gathering in the Kenyan and Djibouti Somalis had faded even further from view by the end of the 1970s. On a diplomatic level, things had turned out equally badly. The United States, which was smarting from its expulsion from Ethiopia, happily stepped into the vacuum which was created by the rupture with the Soviet Union. But while the Americans were prepared to provide aid to their latest client, they insisted that Somalia should renounce its irredentist claims in the Horn. This stance was understandable given that the Americans had nothing to gain by antagonising Djibouti and Kenya. What was more demoralising was the lack of solidarity demonstrated by other Muslim countries. Hence while Iran and Saudi Arabia were sympathetic to the Somali cause, they were not in favour of reopening the vexed question of colonially derived borders.[30] This echoed the position of the OAU (see below). In subsequent years, Somalia itself fell apart as we will see in Chapter 10, underlining the fallacy that there was something uniquely cohesive about the Somali nation.

3.3   The limited allure of secessionism: Sudan, Congo, Nigeria and Chad

Although militant Somali nationalism posed a threat to the stability of the entire Horn, elsewhere it was secessionism which always seemed most likely to disrupt the post-colonial *pax*. No sooner had the national flags been run up the respective poles than rebel movements made their dash for 'freedom'. In the four most important cases which we will consider here – the Sudan, the Congo, Nigeria and Chad – the collapse of the independence consensus was hardly surprising in the light of the difficult colonial inheritance. All were geographically vast, culturally and religiously diverse and – most importantly of all – had never been effectively welded together by the colonial power. In the Congo and Nigeria, secessionist leaders were also emboldened by the shrewd reckoning that their proposed states would be resource-rich. Here, a sense of alienation from the political centre was reinforced by a belief that it would pay to go it alone. In Southern Sudan and northern Chad, by contrast, the absence of consistent plans for independence reflected the comparative poverty of these regions. In each case, the rulers of the states concerned were hardly likely to consent to the excision of large chunks of their national territory. Hence, the secessionist leadership needed to persuade its people both that victory was attainable and that the loss of life and other privations were worth the effort.

In the Sudan, as we have already seen, it had been British policy to isolate the South until as late as the 1940s. One consequence was that it lagged far behind in terms of every index of development. This was starkly apparent when it came to educational provision. Whereas male literacy stood at between 2 and 4 per cent in two of the three southern provinces, it reached 22 per cent in Sudan as a whole and hit 50 per cent in Khartoum province.[31] At independence in 1956, the constitutional future of the Sudan still needed to be fleshed out. Although southern politicians were led to expect that a federal solution would be found, their northern counterparts opposed such a concession on the basis that it might merely encourage separatism.[32] The integration of the Sudan along unitary lines therefore led to a heavy predominance of northerners within the administration, not just in the country as a whole (where southerners constituted a tiny minority of officials) but also in the South. The sensitivity about northern domination was heightened by virtue of the fact that northerners were predominantly Muslim, whereas some leeway had been given to Christian missionaries in the South. Many southerners worried that an independent government would seek to impose the Arabic language and Islam upon them. A portent of the crises yet to come was a mutiny by southern troops in Equatoria Province in August 1955 which was accompanied by attacks on northerners. The Sudanese government responded with heavy reprisals against perceived sympathisers. The worst fears of southerners were further confirmed when the first military regime of General Abboud in 1958 adopted an explicit policy of Islamicisation and Arabisation in the South, culminating in the expulsion of the Christian missions in 1964. The imposition of Arabic as the medium of instruction in schools was regarded with dismay by southern intellectuals, not least because it was a further step towards their marginalisation within the administration.

The alienation of a southern sub-elite was fundamental to the launching of guerrilla war and the tortuous trajectory which it eventually took. During the first civilian regime (1956–58), southern parties enjoyed some influence by virtue of the jockeying for power at the centre. After the 1958 elections, southern parliamentarians grouped themselves into the Federal Bloc which campaigned for the adoption of a federal constitution and equal status for Christianity. The Bloc allied itself with non-Arab groups from the North as well as with the Sudanese Communist Party. However, the coup of 1958 was followed by closure of the political system, which led many southern intellectuals and politicians to go into exile. In 1962, the newly formed Sudan African National Union (SANU) set up its secretariat in Kampala, where there was much sympathy for the plight of fellow 'Africans'. The following year, a guerrilla insurgency was launched by an organisation calling itself the Anyanya, which was loosely connected to the political wing of SANU. The attacks inside Southern Sudan provoked a predictable government backlash, leading to the flight of tens of thousands of refugees into neighbouring states. In 1964, the military regime was toppled, in large part because of its mishandling of the southern crisis. This ushered in a renewed bout of civilian rule between 1965 and 1969. Whereas some SANU leaders decided to enter into the political process, where they could bargain for concessions, others resolved to continue the armed struggle. At the crucial conference in Khartoum in March 1965, southern politics revealed itself in all its bewildering complexity as its spokesmen tabled demands ranging from regional autonomy to full independence. The conference broke up without finding a formula which was acceptable to all sides. Thereafter, various fractions of the rebel movement stepped up the insurgency from bases inside the Congo and Uganda. As Markakis observes, the retaliation of the civilian regime was more brutal than anything the junta might have unleashed.[33]

In May 1969, the Sudan experienced its second coup, ushering in a lengthy period of military rule under Colonel (later General) Nimeiri. One of the latter's key indictments of the previous civilian regime was that it had failed to find a solution to the southern problem. Nimeiri committed his regime to national reconciliation, and introduced a southern policy. Markakis writes that:

> It recognised the objective reality of historical and cultural differences between North and South, acknowledged the right of the people in the South to regional autonomy, established a Ministry of Southern Affairs, and pledged to promote economic and social development in that region within the framework of a socialist society.[34]

Members of the Communist Party were included in the government, and the first Minister of Southern Affairs was Joseph Garang, himself a southerner. The latter maintained that southern concerns could be satisfied by squarely address-ing the historic neglect of this part of the country. However, the rebels were reluctant to call off their insurgency at a time when they were making some headway. In the midst of the Middle East crisis, Israel was looking for ways to weaken its international enemies and to cultivate client states of its own. Because the Sudanese government identified with Egypt, Israel retaliated by training and directing an impressive arsenal of weapons to the soldiers of the Southern Sudanese Liberation Movement (SSLM) which had emerged out of one wing of the Anyanya. In the early 1970s, the SSLM was a reasonably well-drilled fight-ing force capable of causing considerable disruption at a time when Khartoum lacked access to external military aid. The reality remained, however, that the SSLM never possessed the might to seize control of the South. This meant that some kind of a negotiated settlement was always potentially on the cards.

In 1971, Nimeiri collided with the Communist Party and when the latter attempted to stage a putsch, a number of its leaders were executed – including Joseph Garang. A new Minister for Southern Affairs sought permission to enter into fresh negotiations with the rebels, and in February 1972, the two sides met in Addis Ababa. They ended by signing an agreement which granted a measure of autonomy to the South. The three southern provinces were consolidated into one region with an elected Assembly, which possessed responsibility for local affairs, and an executive which was partially responsible to it. At the same time, the Nimeiri regime incorporated 6000 Anyanya fighters into the Sudanese armed forces, extended a share of civil service posts in the central government to southerners and gave the southern administration control over its own recruitment. At the same time, the South was given assurances of protection for Christianity and the English language. The negotiated end to the rebellion was a considerable achievement. However, southern spokesmen had never been inflexible on the question of relations with the North. Because the South was both poor and ethnically divided, the preference of many southerners had always been for a formula which merely granted them a measure of autonomy. The Addis Ababa agreement was seductive because it gave southern intellectuals a stake in the idea of one Sudan. In Chapter 10, we will consider the subsequent fate of this negotiated settlement.

Turning now to the Congo, we have already seen that the Belgians had made no preparations for independence. Moreover, the vast expanse of the Congo had only been loosely integrated under their rule. The Western Congo faced towards the coastal port of Matadi and Leopoldville, on the lower reaches of the Congo River. The minerally rich regions of Kasai and Katanga were linked by rail to Zambia and South Africa, and in many ways revolved in their economic orbit.[35] Moreover, whereas Leopoldville attracted migrants from further upstream as well as from the coastal belt, the railways ferried a different set of migrants towards Elizabethville (Lubumbashi). As for the other major cities, Crawford Young observes that Matadi, Stanleyville (Kisangani), Coquilhatville, Bukavu and Luluaborg attracted most of their migrants from the surrounding area.[36] The net result was the makeup of these cities was significantly different. The prolific post-war expansion of the cities led to an increasing obsession with ethnic origin, as 'indigenes' jostled for jobs and living space with putative strangers. Hence in Leopoldville, the Bakongo identified themselves in opposition to the Bangala, a term which originally embraced migrants from upriver but eventually came to be used for anyone who was not Bakongo.[37] Similarly, in Elizabethville the Baluba, Lulua and other peoples from Kasai were lumped together as strangers by southern Katangans who construed themselves as the true indigenes. The contextual and highly fluid nature of Congolese identities illustrates the folly of regarding 'tribe' in essentialist terms.[38]

The implosion of Belgian rule resulted in the 'hothousing' of Congolese politics as the electoral principle was rapidly extended to urban councils, provincial and national assemblies. The political associations which sprang up to wage local struggles expanded their remit without seeking to significantly widen their support-base. As we have seen in Chapter 1, there was no political party which could claim national coverage. When independence arrived on 30 June, it was in a climate of mutual mistrust.[39] A coalition government had been stitched together, in which the Presidency was conferred on Joseph Kasavubu (the head of ABAKO) while Lumumba assumed the post of Prime Minister. However, this was a marriage of convenience rather than a genuine meeting of minds. Kasavubu had initially been the political frontrunner, but had been eclipsed by the charismatic Lumumba who enjoyed the favour of Nkrumah. There was even talk of the Congo joining the Ghana–Guinea union when the time was right. As against the Pan-Africanist message of the MNC, Kasavubu had flirted with the idea of breaking away to forge a greater Kongo with his ethnic kinsmen in Congo-Brazzaville.[40]

What brought matters to a head was a mutiny within the Force Publique on 5 July. General Janssens, who had held out against demands for Africanisation of the military, scribbled the following equation on a blackboard before an audience of non-commissioned officers: 'After Independence – Before Independence'. The effect was incendiary, and over the next few days mutiny spread across the Congo, accompanied by violence directed against Belgian nationals. The response of the Belgian government was to send in troops to protect its citizens, which the Congolese authorities grudgingly accepted as a short-term expedient to restore order. However, the Belgian presence quickly assumed a more ominous complexion. Having flirted with secessionism in the recent past, CONAKAT suddenly declared the breakaway of Katanga, calling on the practical assistance of Belgian troops. The complementary of their interests was not difficult to discern. On the one hand, the CONAKAT leadership wanted to secure the enormous mineral wealth of Katanga for the exclusive enjoyment of its constituency. On the other hand, Belgium possessed substantial economic interests in the copper mines of southern Katanga. The controlling stake in the largest company, Union Minière du Haut-Katanga (UMHK) was owned by Société Générale de Belgique.[41] The UMHK was worried about the radical rhetoric of the MNC and struck up a close relationship with CONAKAT as the best guarantor of its investments. For its part, the Belgian government did the bidding of UMHK not just by lending troops to Katanga, but also ordering its civil servants to remain at their posts. From the perspective of Leopoldville, Belgian intervention smacked of nothing less than an attempt to carve a neo-colony out of the ruins of empire.

The Katangan secession underlined the fundamental weakness of the Leopoldville government, which was forced to request United Nations intervention. The first contingent of Ghanaian and Tunisian troops arrived in mid-July and from this point onwards the UN became a leading actor in the unfolding drama. The crisis took a further turn for the worse on 8 August, when Albert Kalonji declared the secession of South Kasai. His justification was that the Baluba had been the targets of ethnic violence, especially on the Copperbelt, which justified going it alone. However, Kalonji was also acting on the belief that the diamond wealth of this area made independence a viable option – the choice of name of the 'Mining State' said it all.[42] In the same way that CONAKAT came to a sweetheart arrangement with UMHK, the South Kasai regime got into bed with Forminière, which helped to pay for the resettlement of its large refugee population and the fledgling secessionist administration.[43]

The breakaway of two regions placed severe strains on the unstable coalition in Leopoldville. Lumumba expressed understandable frustration at the decision of the UN to stop short of the restoration of the central authority. His decision to solicit Soviet backing and his sending of troops into South Kasai, who were accused of indiscriminate killings, further alienated Kasavubu. In September, the latter announced the removal of Lumumba and the appointment of a new Prime Minister in his place. By this point, Cold War rivalries had begun to play themselves out, with the Americans urging Kasavubu to break with Lumumba who they believed to be firmly in the Soviet camp.[44] When Lumumba reciprocated by dismissing Kasavubu, the Congo was thrown into a constitutional crisis. This had tragic consequences for the Congo, by creating a window of opportunity for one Colonel Joseph-Desiré Mobutu. The latter had been a close associate of Lumumba and had even served briefly in the government, before joining the armed forces. In the midst of the constitutional impasse, Mobutu announced that the army was imposing a 'truce' on the warring factions. This was presented as a holding operation, in which the powers of the administration would be vested in a College of Commissioners, made up of graduates and University students.

Lumumba continued to insist that he was the rightful leader, but found himself in a very weak bargaining position. He lacked the support of the military, he had no political constituency in Leopoldville itself and, to compound the insult, the UN recognised the legality of the Kasavubu putsch. Lumumba was reduced to the indignity of becoming a prisoner in his official residence, surrounded by a protective ring of Ghanaian soldiers (under UN command) and an outer ring of Congolese soldiers waiting to arrest him. He eventually decided to make a break for Stanleyville, where his supporters had formed a government-in-exile. However, he was captured en route, handed over to the Katangans and executed. The evidence clearly suggests that the CIA and the Belgians had a direct hand in the liquidation of someone who they regarded as a threat to their geo-political interests.[45] To this day, nobody has been placed on trial for this most calculated and cynical assassination.

The elimination of Lumumba signalled the splitting of the Congo into four different administrations: namely Leopoldville, where the College of Commissioners governed in the name of the Congo; Stanleyville, where the provincial government provided a home for the government-in-exile of Antoine Gisenga; Elizabethville, where Moïse Tshombe claimed to be the leader of an independent Katanga; and Bakwanga where Kalonji went on to declare himself king. The first two regimes remained attached to the idea of the Congo, whereas the second two insisted that it was consigned to history. The reconstitution of the Congo, in relatively short order, has everything to do with the same external forces which had eliminated Lumumba. The regime in South Kasai began to splinter when Kalonji made his bid for enthronement, after which some politicians restored their links with Leopoldville. However, Katanga was a harder nut to crack. The Belgian military was persuaded to withdraw, but Tshombe recruited innumerable mercenaries, whilst looking to his powerful allies to guard his back diplomatically. His problem was that the Americans really favoured the reintegration of the Congo under a friendly regime and were prepared to apply pressure. When a change of regime took place in Belgium in 1961, the incoming administration also began to withdraw its support.[46]

Crucially, the UN modified its own position. From attempting to keep the peace, it shifted towards a policy of bringing the Congo back under one administration. In February 1961, the College of Commissioners wound itself up and Kasavubu returned to centre-stage in Leopoldville. The following month, he chaired a conference at which Tshombe tabled proposals for a confederal Congo, in which substantial powers would have been vested in the provinces. Although this was actually accepted, Tshombe was reluctant to call off his secession and relations with Kasavubu thereafter deteriorated.[47] By contrast, there was a surprising rapprochement between Kasavubu and the Lumumbists who at least shared the ideal of a reunified Congo. In July, Parliament was reconvened with both the Lumumbists and the South Kasaians in attendance. This led to the installation of a new government headed by Cyrille Adoula, who was acceptable to most of the major protagonists.[48] That only left the Katangans on the outside. The UN finally lost patience with Kasavubu and decided that it was time to use military force to end the secession, which was precisely what it had failed to do for Lumumba. After the UMHK jumped ship and UN troops captured Elizabethville, Tshombe was forced to declare an end to the breakaway state in January 1963. While he went into retirement with a large stash of Belgian francs, the focus returned to the reconstruction of the Congolese state.[49]

After much wrangling, a constitution was produced and fresh elections were planned. But, not for the first time, Congolese politics took an unexpected turn.

President Kasavubu brought Tshombe out of retirement in July 1964 and asked him to head a provisional government. In short order, the administration was over-run with Katangans who had only recently been trying to secede. Not surprisingly, this was a source of some irritation in Leopoldville. Meanwhile, a fresh wave of rebellions was breaking out across the country. In the Kwilu district, Pierre Mulele, a Lumumba supporter who had spent some time in China, began mobilising a guerrilla army amongst the Mbundu and Pende populations in August 1963. The Mulelist insurrection marked a fresh addition to the Congolese political imagination. The Mulelists prefigured subsequent guerrilla movements in their blending of traditional and modernist themes. On the one hand, the leaders talked of social liberation using a vaguely Maoist vocabulary.[50] Their immediate aim was to create liberated zones in which an egalitarian society would be constructed from the bottom up, but the ultimate objective was to capture power at the centre and to disseminate this model more widely. On the other hand, the peasant fighters were encouraged by the belief that the observance of certain ritual practices and prohibitions would render them impervious to bullets – a theme which recurs across East and Central Africa, going back to colonial times.[51] With relatively few weapons at their disposal, the guerrillas scored a number of successes. Although the Mulelists occupied a relatively small area, and soon became internally fragmented, powerful myths grew up around the movement and Mulele himself.[52]

The Mulelist rising inspired other aspirant revolutionaries to take up arms in what became known as the 'second liberation'.[53] It is important to underline that the objective here was not to secede from the Congo, but to capture of power at the centre. A change of government in Congo-Brazzaville presented those Lumumbists who were dissatisfied with the Adoula regime with friends willing to back an insurrection. In October 1963, a Conseil Nationale de Libération (CNL) was formed in Brazzaville, and in April 1964 insurgents crossed the border from Burundi into the Uvira-Fizi area. They proceeded to seize Albertville, the capital of North Katanga, and Kindu, the capital of Maniema.[54] The youth of Maniema were then organised into the Armée Populaire de Libération (APL) which recaptured the former stomping grounds of the MNC with comparative ease. In September 1964, the APL felt confident enough to proclaim a People's Republic centered on the old MNC capital of Stanleyville.[55] With remarkable speed, the eastern half of the Congo had slipped from government control.

Once again, it was external intervention which was crucial to the outcome. The Americans were determined to prop up the Leopoldville government, and together with the Belgians, provided logistical support for the government forces, consisting of an eclectic mixture of Katangan gendarmes, European mercenaries and the rag-tag national army. The Belgians furnished paratroopers (flown in on American planes) who helped retake Kisangani, with considerable loss of life, at the end of November. By the end of 1964, most of the territorial gains had been reversed and the eastern rebellion dissolved into smaller pockets of resistance. Some of these became a more or less permanent fixture. The most famous was located around Fizi, where a rebel band – which was briefly visited by the Bolivian revolutionary, Che Guevara – held out for decades in difficult frontier terrain.[56] However, there was no doubting that the central authority had finally prevailed in the struggle against dissidents in the provinces. This could not be attributed to the legitimacy of the Leopoldville authorities, but rather to the willingness of foreign powers to prop up the regime in spite of its manifest unpopularity.

What was deeply ironic was that the victor appeared to be none other than the ex-secessionist, Tshombe, whose grip was further consolidated by the results of the March 1965 elections. However, the Congolese saga had one further twist in the tail. When Tshombe decided to seek the position of President for himself, this brought him into direct confrontation with Kasavubu. When the latter dismissed him as Prime Minister in October 1965, there was a re-run of the constitutional crisis which had brought about the downfall of Lumumba. The script, of course, had already been written. On 25 November 1965, the armed forces stepped in for the second time, on this occasion announcing that Mobutu himself would take over as President. There was to be no question of sharing power with the politicians, who were roundly castigated for their interminable bickering. Mobutu staked his legitimacy on the formal assent of Parliament, and on a promise to bring peace to a war-ravaged country. The first was a legal technicality, but the second had some mileage in it. It has been estimated that something in the region of one million people died as a result of the second round of rebellions alone.[57] As Crawford Young observes:

> Most Zaireans experienced in their personal lives some of its repercussions; the loss of a friend or relative; a brutal encounter with an ill-disciplined army patrol or rampaging gangs of youth; the depressing awareness that one's ethnicity defined the quarters of town it was safe to enter...[58]

After the turmoil of the first five years of independence, many Congolese were prepared to tolerate any government that could deliver a basic level of security. What the Congolese had not banked on was the darker side of the Leviathan they had invested with absolute power – but this is a story to be told in a later chapter.

The third country where secessionism became a live issue was Nigeria. The sheer size and cultural diversity of the country had always generated a certain scepticism about its viability. In 1947, Obafemi Awolowo famously wrote that 'Nigeria is not a nation. It is a mere geographical expression. There are no "Nigerians" in the same sense as there are "English", "Welsh" or "French"'.[59] British rule had not helped manufacture Nigerians, given that north and south had been effectively compartmentalised prior to the 1950s. Decolonisation was an ill-tempered affair in Nigeria, as a result of bitter rivalries between each of the three main political groupings.[60] These sought to monopolise power at the Regional level whilst angling for a constitutional dispensation which would be most favourable to themselves. As in the case of Sudan and the Congo, secessionist rumblings were already audible in the period leading up to independence. When Northern members of the House of Representatives drew the ire of the Lagos crowds in 1953, for having opposed a motion calling for self-government in 1956, rioting broke out in Kano which left some 36 people dead and many more injured (mostly Igbos). On this occasion, it was the Northern People's Congress (NPC) which asserted the right to secede from the rest of Nigeria.

The introduction of a federal constitution in 1954 conferred substantive powers upon the three Regional governments. In each case, the dominant party deployed resources derived from the Marketing Boards to build its patronage networks, whilst harassing the competition. The NPC, which was widely regarded as the vehicle of the Hausa-Fulani traditional elite, endeavoured to mobilise on a region-wide basis. The Action Group (AG) appealed to Yoruba voters in the Western Region, where it gradually succeeded in rolling back the National Council of Nigeria and the Cameroons (NCNC). In the Eastern Region, the NCNC held sway over its Igbo heartlands. In each of these Regions, smaller parties appealed to minorities on the basis of their demand for separate regions: these included the United Middle Belt Congress (UMBC) in the non-Muslim North; the Calabar, Ogoja and Rivers State Movement and the Niger Delta State Movement in the East; and the Mid-West State Movement in the non-Yoruba West. These demands for state-creation were, however, rejected by the Minorities Commission in 1958, thereby entrenching a lopsided federation in which the Northern Region was larger than the other two together.[61] Despite this setback, the NCNC and the AG continued to lend their support to smaller parties in the North in a bid to undercut the NPC.[62] As fierce rivals, they also sought to stir things up each other's minority problems. By contrast, the NPC displayed little interest in southern minority movements, which reflected its disdain for the South more generally. The NPC could afford to do so because it was assured of a governing majority if it managed to monopolise the northern vote. Alongside the rallying cry of 'One North, One People, One Destiny' the NPC resorted to naked coercion to cripple the Northern Elements People's Union (NEPU) and the minority parties.

This pattern of frantic ethnic politicking set the tone for the 1959 Federal election, the last before independence. The NCNC and AG aimed to chip enough support away from the NPC in the North to make victory possible, but failed miserably. The NPC fell short of achieving an overall majority, which presented a window of opportunity for a southern coalition to take power. However, the mutual antipathy between the NCNC and the AG and their respective leaders, Nnamdi Azikiwe and Obafemi Awolowo, was simply too great. When the NPC extended an offer to the NCNC, it was accepted and Nigeria became independent under an unlikely coalition between these parties. Significantly, though, the NPC leader, Ahmadu Bello, did not deign to involve himself with the federal government, preferring to remain Premier of the Northern Region. This spoke volumes about how the Northern establishment regarded their relationship with the rest of Nigeria. The position of Prime Minister was instead conferred on Abubakar Tafawa Balewa, while Azikiwe became the President.

Unlike in Sudan and the Congo, there was no immediate bid for secession after independence. Indeed, it took a full seven years for the political contradictions to play themselves out. Moreover, when the breakaway occurred it was not in the North (as had been widely anticipated), but in the South-east. In order to understand why, it is necessary to get to grips with the rancorous politics of the First Republic. As Larry Diamond has cogently argued, the politics of this era was characterised by a refusal to accept limits to contestation.[63] Any advantage was pressed home with a view to completely eliminating rivals from the political equation. This tended to make all sides feel extremely insecure and to imagine conspiracies where they did not exist. The NPC was prepared to use all the instruments at its disposal – some constitutional, others doubtful and still others thoroughly illegal – to disable its rivals. Given the determination of the AG to stir up the Northern minorities, it was perceived as the immediate threat. While the NPC plotted its downfall, the NCNC was only too happy to play along because it had its own scores to settle in the Western Region. The opportunity to strike presented itself not long after independence. Following the electoral disaster of 1959, a heated debate broke out within the ranks of AG about how the party should respond. Some argued that it would be suicidal to engage in a fight to the death with the NPC, and favoured reaching some kind of accommodation. This position came to be associated with S. L. Akintola, the Premier of the Western Region. On the other hand, others wanted to raise the stakes. Awolowo argued in favour of adopting a socialist platform which would appeal to the *talakawa* (the Hausa commoners) of the North as well as to the minorities. However, this had the effect of driving the more conservative elements in the party into the Akintola camp.

Because the Premier controlled the resources at the Regional level, he presented a serious challenge to Awolowo who was leader of the opposition in Lagos. Matters came to a head early in 1962, when the Awolowo faction attempted to replace Akintola with someone from their own side. Their opponents engineered a disturbance within the Regional Assembly, which provided the federal government with a pretext for declaring a state of emergency in the West. The Regional executive was dissolved and many members of the Awolowo faction were detained by the caretaker administration. In January 1963, Akintola was reinstated as Premier in return for agreeing to the creation of a separate Mid-West Region.[64] From this point onwards, the NPC could rely on a Western administration which was prepared to play ball. After the release of the Coker report on corruption in the Western Region, Akintola had a legitimate excuse to nail the Awolowo loyalists. Victory was complete when Awolowo himself was convicted of plotting a coup and incarcerated in June 1963.

Once the AG had been broken, the latent divisions between the coalition partners at the centre began to open up. All eyes were focused on the 1962 census, because this would determine the composition of the next federal legislature. The NCNC believed that the count would reveal that the population of the North was much smaller than had previously been supposed. If Northern representation declined significantly, the balance between the political parties could be expected to shift as well. For good reasons, therefore, the census became a highly politicised affair. Because each Regional government had a direct hand in the enumeration, there was a standing invitation to inflate the numbers. The NCNC administration in the East was evidently the most skilled because the provisional returns revealed that the population had jumped by 70 per cent in just ten years. The North woke up to the implications and quickly found another 8.5 million 'lost' citizens. Nobody believed any of these figures, and so it was decided to hold a fresh census in 1963. On the re-run, the Northern and Western governments made sure that their numbers were properly inflated, which guaranteed that the results were not acceptable to the NCNC.

The recriminations over the census ensured the collapse of the federal coalition. With a fresh set of national elections scheduled for 1964, there was a wholesale reconfiguration of alliances. The NCNC, the remains of the AG and their northern partners came together to form a new political umbrella, the United Progressive Grand Alliance (UPGA). On the other side, the NPC entered into a formal alliance with Akintola's party under the banner of the Nigerian National Alliance (NNA). The Federal election was a psychological watershed in that it signalled the complete abandonment of the rules of the game. The NPC made sure that candidates could not be put up in the Northern seats which UPGA planned to target. Since UPGA could not win without making substantial inroads into the North, it had effectively lost before a single vote was cast. It therefore resorted to the high-risk option of boycotting the polls. Unfortunately, the boycott was not very effective, which created the worst of all possible worlds. The NNA won many seats it might otherwise have lost and what is more it could claim to be the legitimate winner, having taken 198 of the 253 seats declared. This provoked a constitutional crisis in that President Azikiwe was required to ask someone to form the next government. His own party claimed that the whole exercise had been vitiated by fraud and intimidation, and expected him to stand by them. After a good deal of wrangling and political brinkmanship, a compromise was found. A government of national unity was established, and fresh polls were planned for areas where the boycott had been effective.[65] But it was only a matter of time before the struggle recommenced. The predictable battleground was the Western Region where the Akintola and Awolowo forces, who had yet to engage in a proper trial of strength, lined up against each other in the 1965 Regional election. When Akintola engaged in wholesale fraud and claimed to be the victor, UPGA supporters took the law into their own hands.

By the start of 1966, the First Republic had reached the crossroads. Each crisis seemed to render the underlying political problems more intractable, and on all sides there was a willingness to contemplate more unorthodox methods. The Police and Armed Forces found themselves being drawn into the fray. In 1964, the Army had been sent in to restore control in Tiv, a UMBC stronghold, and when the Western Region crisis broke it came as no great surprise when the soldiers were once again called upon. Rumours also abounded to the effect that the NPC was preparing a definitive strike against its opponents. On 14 January 1966, when Ahmadu Bello returned from Mecca he met with Akintola to discuss the matter more fully.[66] The following day, the first military coup – which may have been a pre-emptive strike – was unleashed in which Akintola, Ahmadu Bello and Balewa (amongst many others) were all murdered.

An extensive literature has grown up around the January 1966 coup, consisting initially of academic analysis and more recently of reminiscences by some of the key protagonists. One of the most revealing accounts is the sympathetic biography of Major Chukwuma Nzeogwu, the central figure in the plot, by Olusegun Obasanjo.[67] Whereas the coup was interpreted as an Igbo conspiracy carried out by a cabal of Majors seeking to accomplish by the gun what the NCNC had singularly failed to achieve through the ballot box, Obasanjo presents an altogether more nuanced picture. Although Nzeogwu was an Igbo, he had been brought up in the North and spoke Hausa fluently. Far from adopting a simple ethnic interpretation of the crisis, his diagnosis was that politicians of all parties were engaged in a destructive drive for wealth and power. What was worse was that they were drawing the Armed Forces into their fratricidal struggles. Nzeogwu apparently favoured a clean sweep in which all of the leading politicians would be liquidated, along with senior military officers who were held to be in collusion with them.[68] Not all the plotters agreed, and after some debate it was eventually decided 'to let every officer exercise his discretion in handling the matter'.[69] The net result was that while Nzeogwu ensured that Bello and other Northern politicians were killed, and Akintola was similarly eliminated in the West, the Premier of the Mid-West (Chief Dennis Osadebay) and the East (Dr Michael Okpara) were spared. Only one Igbo officer was killed, and he was the one guarding the keys to the armoury.[70] The Igbo head of the Army, General Aguiyi Ironsi, was one of those who was supposed to have been killed, but he survived when the Lagos takeover broke down.[71] However, the arithmetic of death was such that the Igbo conspiracy thesis took hold in the North.

The coup went according to plan in Kaduna, where Nzeogwu took charge of operations, but it misfired elsewhere. In Lagos, Ironsi was able to rally loyal troops and to take control of the capital. Realising the untenable nature of his position, Nzeogwu surrendered. The power vacuum at the centre was filled by Ironsi who persuaded the politicians to hand over to him. In the North, the perception was that this had been planned from the start. The fact that Nzeogwu was never put on trial seemed merely to confirm the suspicion of an elaborate conspiracy.[72] Once in control of the government, Ironsi took it upon himself to prepare the way for a thorough reform of the constitution. His reading of the recent past was that federalism had merely exacerbated divisions within the body politic. His solution was therefore to move Nigeria back in the direction of being a unitary state. Hence the Nwokedi Commission was appointed in February to formulate proposals for the integration of the civil service. Then in May, Ironsi announced Decree No. 34 which abolished the Regions at one fell swoop. In some respects, Ironsi and his advisors were justified in pointing to the unworkability of the independence constitution, but arguably the root problem lay in the peculiar federal structures which Nigeria had inherited. By pushing for a unitary state, at such a sensitive time, Ironsi appeared to be favouring an arrangement in which more educated Igbos would be the primary beneficiaries. The accelerated promotion of Igbos within the Army, where a quota system had protected less well-educated Northerners, merely added weight to the conspiracy theses.[73]

Three days after Decree No. 34 was announced, serious rioting broke out across the North. As had been the case in the 1953 Kano riots, Igbo migrants were targeted by urban mobs who knew exactly where to find them because of their residential segregation in the *sabon garis*. The situation was eventually brought under control, but only after many thousands were killed. Then, on

28 July a mutiny broke out in Abeokuta in which Northern troops turned on their Igbo officers and shot them. Before long, the mutiny had spread to Kaduna and Kano. Amongst the casualties of the mutiny was Ironsi himself who was arrested and secretly killed. The stage was now set for the final descent into civil war. The mutineers, who were loosely organised, demanded either the secession of the North or, at least the repeal of Decree No. 34.[74] After an interval during which the ship of state was entirely rudderless, Lt.-Colonel Yakubu Gowon, who had himself been arrested, was released and asked to become the interlocutor of the Northern troops. Brigadier Ogundipe, the senior officer who had been negotiating for the government, agreed to step aside and Gowon became the de facto head of the government in Lagos.[75]

However, it very quickly became apparent that Gowon did not command universal support. In the Eastern Region, the military Governor, Lt.-Colonel Odumegwu Ojukwu refused to accept the authority of someone he regarded as both a military and an intellectual inferior. The efforts of the Gowon regime to revisit the constitutional issue were bound to be controversial, especially as drawing in the 'leaders of opinion' meant consorting with the same vested interests who had wrecked the First Republic. When an ad hoc Constitutional Conference was convened in mid-September, there was broad agreement on the need for a looser union, but there was a lack of consensus over how many states the country ought to be broken into. When the Conference adjourned, everything was thrown into turmoil with the outbreak of fresh paroxysms of violence in the North. Once again, Igbos were targeted by urban mobs and killed with the utmost brutality. The precise number of casualties is unknown, but it must have run into tens of thousands.[76] Why did violence erupt with such ferocity twice over the course of 1966? There is some evidence of incitement by the very interests which felt most threatened by the Igbo presence – Northern civil servants and students – but the mass killings were not co-ordinated. The Igbos were clearly resented in the North for their visibility in formal employment and their competition in the market-place.[77] Hence they became convenient scapegoats for the everyday hardships experienced by northerners. Once the rioting began, it spiralled out of control, fuelled in part by rumours of killings of Northerners in the East.

The second wave of rioting was decisive in preparing the way for secession. For the leadership in the East it demonstrated that there was no mileage in a united Nigeria. Ojukwu ordered all strangers out of the East and urged all Easterners to make their way home by any means possible. The last chance of finding a solution was a meeting between Ojukwu and Gowon held in Aburi, Ghana, in January 1967. At this meeting, the two sides appeared to have reached some kind of an accord, in which Nigeria would become something much closer to a confederation. But when they returned home, the leaders recounted differing versions of what had transpired. Ojukwu was at least able to release a recording which appeared to support his interpretation of what had transpired. It seems likely that Gowon had conceded more than his own civil servants thought justified. When they sought to backtrack, Ojukwu insisted that there could be no going back on the Aburi accords. The impasse was therefore complete. On 31 March, Ojukwu declared that all revenues which had previously gone to the Federal government would be paid into the Eastern Regional treasury, to which Gowon responded with an economic blockade. At the end of May, the secession of the East finally became official with the announcement of a 'Republic of Biafra', timed to coincide with the outbreak of the first wave of rioting the previous year.

Various explanations have been given for the declaration of Biafran secession – by the protagonists, their partisans and by academic observers. The government in Lagos preferred to portray it as the outlet of the unbridled ambition of one man, Ojukwu, who wanted his own state to rule over. Although the ego of Ojukwu was legendary, this was hardly a satisfactory explanation. For its part, the Biafran government claimed that the conduct of a systematic pogrom against the Igbos, which the Gowon administration had failed to prevent, made continued membership of the Nigerian federation untenable. There can be no doubting the profound shock occasioned by the killings, but there was nothing inevitable about the breakaway. On the contrary, the government in the East made a calculated bid for secession on the basis of an assessment about the likelihood of success and the advantages which would follow. There are three factors which help to explain why the Ojukwu regime finally took the plunge. The first is the influence of the many Igbo refugees who made it back to the East. They had lost everything in the North, and were therefore inclined to argue that the East should cut its losses. Igbo military officers who escaped the killings were amongst the most insistent on this point. Secondly, there were rumblings of secessionism emanating from elsewhere within the troubled federation, which diminished the likelihood of a co-ordinated federal response. For example, Awolowo went on record to state in no uncertain terms that if the East seceded, the West and Lagos should follow.[78] And in the Mid-West, the Governor, Lt.-Colonel David Ejoor, pointedly distanced himself from both sides, stating that the Region did not intend to become a battleground between them. From a Biafran perspective, therefore, there was every chance that secession would provoke a *de facto* dissolution of the federation.

However, the most important factor in the equation was oil. Whereas the colonial economy of the East had once revolved around oil-palm exports, this paled into insignificance alongside the importance of petroleum. Between 1958 and 1968, the production of crude oil had jumped from 5000 to 415,000 barrels a day, and by the time of the Nzeogwu coup it accounted for about a third of total Nigerian export earnings.[79] This was as nothing compared to what was to follow in the 1970s, but it was already clear that the oil economy would soon dwarf agricultural exports. Crucially, this oil was all located in the South-east of the country. Northern separatism was tempered by the reality that the poorest Region of the federation was dependent upon the oil revenues which flowed into the federal coffers. By the same token, there was acute dissatisfaction in the East that the revenue-allocation formula denied the producing Region the bulk of the returns.[80] The Ojukwu regime believed that Biafra would be much better off going it alone, thereby following in the footsteps of Tshombe. Provided Biafra could persuade the oil companies to pay their revenues to Enugu, it would also have the money to sustain the war effort if that should prove necessary.[81] What Ojukwu conveniently forgot was that most of the oil was located in the Niger Delta, where the minorities had long been clamouring for separation from the East. Whereas the discourse of the Eastern government had focused on the Hausa-Fulani threat, that of the minorities had long pointed to Igbo domination. Because of petroleum, the federal government could not permit the East to go its own way. In order to drive a wedge between the Igbo and the minorities, Gowon announced the breaking up of the federation into 12 states on the eve of the declaration of secession. The Igbos were to have their East-Central State, but the minorities were awarded a Rivers State and a Southeastern State. The ploy appears to have worked. Ken Saro-Wiwa has revealed that the reception towards Biafran secession was decidedly lukewarm in the Delta, and this is confirmed by other sources.[82]

The Gowon regime apparently believed that the Biafrans could be brought to their knees within a matter of weeks. In reality, the fighting was drawn out from July 1967 to January 1970 and when victory came it was at enormous financial and human cost.[83] The campaign was conducted on two fronts simultaneously. First of all, there was the purely military dimension, in which the federal forces endeavoured to strike an early and decisive blow in the North; the Biafrans responded with a successful invasion of the Mid-West; and finally the Biafrans were driven back into a steadily shrinking enclave as the superior weight of federal numbers and military equipment took their toll.[84] Between July and October 1967, the federal troops chalked up decisive victories when they succeeded in capturing Bonny, which housed the export terminal, and Port Harcourt, which was the site of the only oil refinery.[85] Whereas mining companies in Katanga and South Kasai had backed secession from the start, the petroleum corporations in Nigeria had always been more equivocal. On the one hand, they were concerned about the threat of higher federal taxation; but on the other, they were wary of falling foul of the Lagos government. In June 1967, Shell-BP offered a token payment to the Biafrans, but this was later revoked after the intervention of the British government, which was a major shareholder.[86] The loss of the Delta oilfields ensured that the corporations would simply back the side that was evidently winning. From courting the companies, the Biafrans resorted to attacking the oilfields which was hardly likely to win them over. Deprived of access to the oil revenues, Biafra lacked the money to import the arms and munitions to maintain anything like parity. The seizure of Enugu in October 1967 also dealt a cruel psychological blow in that the Biafrans had lost their capital. In the later stages of the war, increasingly demoralised and undernourished Biafran soldiers went into battle with very few guns and with only a couple of rounds of ammunition between them. The Nigerian army, by contrast, continued to trundle forward, relying on weaponry supplied by friendly countries, notably Britain.

As the tide turned against the Biafrans, a second dimension assumed added importance: namely the propaganda war. The Biafrans perceived that their chances of success lay in winning international opinion to their side. A Geneva-based public relations company, Markpress, was recruited and performed sterling work on behalf of the Ojukwu regime. Indeed it is generally agreed that the Biafrans beat the Nigerians hands-down on this front at least. One early theme which was percolated through the Western media was that of a Christian minority being persecuted at the hands of a fanatical Muslim majority. When this failed to provoke the desired response, the focus shifted to images of mass suffering. As thousands of Igbos retreated into an ever-shrinking space, famine inevitably ensued. Markpress managed a media campaign which ensured that the image of starving children appeared on television screens and newspaper front-pages on an almost daily basis. The none-too-subtle message was that the Nigerian government, and by implication its Western backers, was murdering innocent children by the thousand. Sympathetic observers, most notably Frederick Forsyth, also offered highly articulate advocacy of the Biafran cause.[87] Much of their propaganda emphasised the pluck of the Biafran soldiers and the sheer ingenuity of ordinary people in the face of impossible odds.[88] The Nigerian government was much less skilful at presenting its own case, and foreign journalists did not enjoy the same ease of access to the frontline as in Biafra. The most lurid stories emanating from the enemy lines therefore remained largely uncontested. Greater energy went into persuading Nigerians that the war was worth fighting, and to a large extent the domestic propaganda hit the target. Not all Nigerian intellectuals were convinced that the Gowon regime was best placed to make the case for a united Nigeria, but at the same time there was limited sympathy for Ojukwu. The differential reactions of two Yoruba cultural icons is worth noting here. Whereas Wole Soyinka was imprisoned for his pro-Biafran stance, the musician Fela Kuti – who became the bane of all subsequent military governments – recorded 'Viva Nigeria' which argued strongly that Nigerians had to learn to live together.[89]

While some Western governments, notably Britain, continued to back the federal cause, there was definite slippage towards the Biafrans. Whereas the Katangans failed to secure any external recognition (not even that of Belgium), France and four African countries did recognise Biafra.[90] It was evident that France could only benefit from a weakening of her principal regional competitor, and it was widely suspected that French oil companies were angling for a cut of the action. However, the willingness of a reputable African government like that of Tanzania to take such a bold step was proof that the public relations effort was paying off. As a television documentary has since established, the relief effort which carried out by well-meaning foreigners provided the Ojukwu regime with some of the means to prolong the war – and hence the suffering of the Biafran people.[91] However, none of this was ultimately sufficient to stave off defeat. As the latter seemed inevitable, latent divisions within the Biafran leadership became more obvious.[92] Finally, as the federal forces moved in for the kill, Ojukwu fled the country, leaving Lt.-Colonel Philip Effiong and his fellow officers to conclude the peace agreement which finally brought Biafran adventure to an end.

After the peace, the Igbos re-entered Nigeria as a defeated people and there were wild predictions about the retribution which would follow. However, the Gowon regime won much credit by eschewing any temptation to exact revenge.[93] Easterners were slowly reintegrated into the civil service and the Armed Forces, although they never entirely regained their exalted positions, and many Igbos made their way back to the North. But if national reconciliation was actively pursued by Gowon, there can be no doubting the long-term effects of the defeat on the Igbo political psyche. In future years, Igbo leaders adopted a rather detached attitude towards the hurly-burly of Nigerian politics. During the 1970s, the war became virtually a taboo subject, especially within the official media. However, with the passage of time, the wounds healed somewhat and it became possible to discuss what the country had been through. It was mostly the Igbo and southern minority writers who felt moved to publish their personal and often highly poignant accounts. The historical profession has been rather slower to address this tragic episode, although the first tentative steps towards reconstructing the social history of the war have begun to be made.[94]

One important difference between Nigeria and the Congo was that state structures was much more effective in the former case. Hence the Nigerian crisis pitted two halves of an army against each other, whereas in the Congo it was relatively easy for guerrilla armies to claim territory in the absence of an integral state. The fighting in Chad, to which we now turn, bears greater similarities to the Congo and Sudan. But while there was a *de facto* collapse of central power for extended periods of time, none of the principal combatants was attracted to secession. On the other hand, the regional tensions in Chad were more like those in Nigeria, in the sense that the South had been exposed to colonial *mise en valeur*, Christianity and a modicum of education, whereas the arid north, where Islam predominated, had been largely left to its own devices. The civil servants, who represented a privileged elite, were overwhelmingly drawn from the South, whereas the few northerners who acquired a foreign education in the Arab world felt themselves to be marginalised. A special factor was the enclave status of the capital, Fort-Lamy (later renamed N'Djamena), in relation to the rest of the country.

In the prelude to independence in 1960, no political party had emerged which was capable of mobilising support across the vast expanse of Chad. The dominant party, the Parti Progressiste Tchadien (PPT), which was an affiliate of the Rassemblement Démocratique Africain (RDA), was elected on the southern vote and did nothing to dispel impressions that it was catering to its regional and ethnic (Sara) constituency. On the eve of independence, François Tombalbaye ousted Gabriel Lisette as Prime Minister and, playing a card which was later to be used in countries like Côte d'Ivoire and Zambia, stripped him of his citizenship.[95] Tombalbaye subsequently turned to the ruthless elimination of opponents within the PPT and the formalisation of a one-party state in which the party itself counted for little next to the cult of the leader.

In 1965, the first rebellion began in the Centre-East and spread to the North which had only just been removed from beneath a French military administration. The following year, the Front for the National Liberation of Chad (FROLINAT) was formed. It drew its principal support from the North and East, but eschewed a Muslim identity in favour of a vague socialist platform. Crucially, it indicated that it was fighting for control of the state rather than secession. In 1971, it clearly stated that: 'There will be no Katanga, no Biafra, in Chad. We will mercilessly eliminate any tendencies towards secessionism.'[96] Given the poverty of the North, perhaps it could not have chosen otherwise. As FROLINAT made substantial inroads against the Chadian army, Tombalbaye was forced to call on French military assistance in 1968. Within three years, the

French army had defeated the forces of a rebel movement which had received moral support from Sudan and Libya, but little in the way of proper training. However, Tombalbaye proved incapable of winning over northern support, despite investing in the legitimacy of the chiefs, and indeed he progressively alienated many in the South. As a result of successive purges, the circle of trusted confidantes narrowed, while the northern insurgency began to gather momentum once again. Tombalbaye made one crucial mistake which was to raise French suspicions about his loyalty to the country which was still (in effect) paying his civil servants and training his soldiers.[97]

After FROLINAT took a number of French nationals hostage, and executed the officer who had been sent to negotiate their release, the French government felt impelled to intervene directly in Chadian affairs once more. Tombalbaye had become a liability and, with the complicity of the French secret service, the regime was overthrown in a coup in April 1975 in which the President himself was killed.[98] The incoming military regime of General Félix Malloum (who had been released from prison), proved incapable of either conciliating northern dissidents or delivering the killer punch. To complicate matters, FROLINAT itself split as the Libyans attempted to impose their own leadership on the front. When Goukouni Weddeye was substituted for Hissein Habré, the latter broke away to form a separate movement, the Armed Forces of the North (FAN). This prepared the way for a pragmatic agreement between the Malloum regime and FAN in 1978 which brought Habré into government as Prime Minister. The new regime very quickly proved to be a pantomime horse with Habré posing as the champion of northern and Muslim interests against the presumed southern bias of Malloum. Before long the partners were fighting for control of the capital, with the French leaning towards FAN. Southerners emptied from the capital, many fleeing towards Cameroun, as Goukouni's own forces moved towards N'Djamena. By this point, Goukouni had clashed with the Libyans over ownership of FROLINAT, provoking yet another split in which the Qaddafi advanced the ambitions of Achmat Acyl.

Having just emerged from its own civil war, the Nigerian government was keen on promoting African solutions to Africa problems. Hence Goukouni, Habré, elements of the former military regime and other factions were prevailed upon to constitute a government of national unity. Goukouni and Habré quickly decided that they did not need the other partners who almost immediately resumed the fighting. The former military administration relocated southwards and created a separate administration – to all intents and purposes a state within a state, but not explicitly secessionist.[99] There was one final attempt at forming a Transitional Government of National Unity (GUNT) under the chairmanship of Goukouni, following the signing of an agreement in Lagos in August 1979. However, the commitment of the various factions was as weak as ever and it collapsed very quickly. By March 1980, the capital was once again the site of a vicious power struggle, as the forces of Goukouni and Habré turned on each other. While the Revolutionary Democratic Council (CDR) of Acyl and the southern leadership of General Kamougoué nominally remained members of GUNT, Habré's FAN was chased out of the capital with the help of Libyan troops.

Following the defeat of Habré, Goukouni signed an agreement with Qaddafi which anticipated movement towards a union between Chad and Libya. Qaddafi had spoken lovingly of creating a Great Islamic State of the Sahel, but he also had a more mundane interest in a thousand square kilometres of northern Chad known as the Aozou strip where uranium deposits were located. Qaddafi claimed the strip under a Franco-Italian treaty dating back to the 1930s. The irredentist claims of the Libyans provoked a furore amongst many other African leaders who began to take a more active interest in the internal affairs of Chad. As the French indicated their determination to thwart Libyan ambitions, Qaddafi withdrew his troops from the greater part of Chad in 1981. Without the support of his patron, Goukouni fell victim to a renewed FAN insurgency. Although the OAU endeavoured to bring the combatants to the negotiating table, and despatched peacekeepers to the country, their mandate was unclear. At the crucial moment in 1982, the peacekeepers stepped aside and permitted FAN to capture the capital. In a game of Chadian musical chairs, Goukouni regrouped in exile and began his own armed insurgency in 1983, while Habré captured control of the South and most of the North, except the Tibesti region in the far North. As GUNT made inroads with Libyan support, the Americans and the Mitterrand administration weighed in on the side of Habré in 1983. The French were reluctant to enter directly into fighting over of the Aozou strip, and eventually they reached an agreement for a scaling down of the conflict in 1984.[100] With the backing of the Western allies, Habré was able to establish a measure of control over most of the country once more. In reality, though, meaningful administration still tended to be confined to the capital and provincial towns. Unlike Nigeria, Chad still remained an aspiration rather than a functioning state.

3.4   A qualified success: the formation of the Organisation of African Unity

As we have seen, the achievement of flag independence was less about closure and more about the papering over of deep-seated problems which the European powers knew they had no real answer to. The first of the newly independent leaders, Nkrumah and Sekou Touré, regarded it as their mission to advance the liberation of the rest of the continent from European rule and to speak for Africa in international fora. In their assertion of a distinctively African perspective, in which imperialism was identified as the principal enemy, they found ready allies in Nasser's Egypt and in Morocco. However, when a large cohort of French territories joined the club of independent African states in 1960, unity became an altogether trickier proposition. Whereas the first Conference of Independent African States, held in Accra in April 1958, was largely dominated by Nkrumah, the second conference in Addis Ababa in June 1960 was noteworthy for expressions of dissent.[101] The leadership pretensions of Nkrumah were openly repudiated by the Nigerians, who were mindful of the leadership which their own size ought to confer, while the Francophone states hesitated to associate themselves with an anti-French posture over Algeria.[102] From this point onwards the club dissolved into three more or less fixed groupings, which have been described (somewhat vaguely) as the 'conservatives', the 'moderates' and the 'radicals'.[103]

The conservatives were made up of the former French territories in sub-Saharan Africa, minus Guinea, Mali and Togo. The leaders of these states had reconciled themselves to independence on the condition that their relationship with France would remain intimate. The recognition that they shared a common official language and the French colonial inheritance led them to group themselves together in a series of organisations geared to fostering co-operation in matters of defence, economic development and cultural exchange.[104] In December 1960, the leaders of twelve Francophone states met in Brazzaville with a view to harmonising their foreign policies as well. From this point onwards, the Brazzaville bloc became the embodiment of a particular tradition which eschewed confrontation with Europe and the United States and kept a safe distance from the Communist world. The so-called 'moderates', composed of Ethiopia, Liberia, Libya, Nigeria, Togo, Somalia, Sudan and Tunisia were more of a mixed bag. The group was composed of fairly conservative regimes which stood apart from the Brazzaville bloc by virtue of the fact that they were either Anglophone or, as in the case of Togo, ambivalent about the French connection. Four of them had an Italian link, but this failed to bind them together in a coherent fashion. Finally, there were the more 'radical' states of Ghana, Guinea, Mali, Algeria, Egypt and Morocco which remained as committed as ever to the struggle against imperialism. To them, the Brazzaville bloc was guilty of complicity with French neo-colonialism. The French decision to persist with nuclear testing in the Sahara in the face of African objections gave this critique added potency. In January 1961, the leaders of these countries, together with Libya and the provisional government of the FLN (National Liberation Front), gathered in Casablanca to launch a counter-blast to the Brazzaville group. Although they had made the early running, the Casablanca countries soon found that the initiative lay elsewhere. In May, the countries of the Brazzaville bloc participated in yet another conference in Monrovia which brought them into alliance with the 'moderates'. The Brazzaville grouping retained its own identity, but now became a sub-set of the Monrovia bloc. The Casablanca countries stayed away from Monrovia and henceforth found themselves in a clear minority.

During the early 1960s, the divisions between African states widened over two substantive issues. The first was the ongoing quest for the total liberation of the African continent from European rule. Whereas white minority rule in Southern Africa provided a common focus of opposition, the Algerian war divided the Brazzaville countries from their North African and Anglophone counterparts. The Casablanca states regarded the FLN campaign as both just and deserving of African support. However, the states which were hoping to benefit from French economic assistance could hardly afford to annoy their powerful patron. At the same time, Nkrumah alienated many of his Francophone colleagues by continuing to lend succour to left-leaning liberation movements which had lost out in the struggle for power. This included the UPC which claimed to be the only party struggling for the genuine liberation of Cameroun from the clutches of French neo-colonialism. There was also evidence to suggest that Nkrumah was backing internal opposition to Sylvanus Olympio in Togo. When the latter was assassinated by mutinous soldiers in January 1963, the Nigerians believed that the Ghanaian government was directly implicated and even threatened to send in troops to head off an anticipated invasion.

The second issue was the territorial partition of the continent which we have dealt with in this chapter. As we have already seen, the Somalis wasted little time in making the case for an adjustment which would bring international boundaries into alignment with ethnic realities in the Horn. The Moroccans staked their own claim to Mauritania which, they argued, had been granted a hollow independence for Machiavellian reasons, most notably the desire of the French to secure military bases and preferential access to the mineral resources.[105] From a quite different angle, Nkrumah maintained that it would be sheer folly to allow colonial boundaries to settle, because a balkanised continent would remain perpetually at the mercy of outsiders. The Ghanaian leader consistently argued for practical steps which would lead towards the ultimate creation of a United States of Africa.[106] These advocates of radical restructuring set alarm bells ringing in countries which felt they had something to lose. However, it was the unfolding Congo crisis which really divided African leaders on matters of principle. Nkrumah was a staunch supporter of Lumumba, who he regarded as the legitimate authority after the breach with Kasavubu. When Katanga seceded, Nkrumah agreed to send in Ghanaian troops under UN auspices in the hope that the Belgian meddling would be rebuffed and a splintering of the country avoided. The Casablanca bloc as a whole demanded that the UN recognise Lumumba, and when it declined to modify its stance the member countries withdrew their peacekeeping troops. On the other hand, the Brazzaville countries backed Kasavubu against Lumumba and failed to take a principled stand against Katangan secession.

On the face of things, the prospects for a continental consensus looked very bleak at the end of 1961. However, with surprising speed renewed efforts to bridge the ideological divide bore fruit, leading finally to the foundation of the Organisation of African Unity (OAU) in May 1963. The reason for this turnaround lies partly in the disappearance of the main bones of contention between radicals and conservatives. In 1962, France and the FLN came to an agreement on Algerian independence. At the same time, the formation of a Congolese government of national unity under Adoula enabled backers of the Leopoldville and Stanleyville regimes to put aside their differences. As Western governments themselves went cold on Katangan secession, a consensus began to emerge about the need to bring all parts of the Congo back into the fold. As Klaas van Walraven has also observed, both the Casablanca and the Monrovia blocs began to lose their internal coherence at about the same time. The rift between Mali and Senegal led Modibo Keita to look to Côte d'Ivoire – led by an arch-conservative – for possible routes to the coast. Moreover, as relations between Ghana and Guinea turned sour, Sekou Touré jettisoned the Soviet alliance and embarked on an unlikely rapprochement with France.[107] Within the Monrovia group, relations between Senegal and Côte d'Ivoire were as tempestuous as ever, while in Equatorial Africa Gabon and Congo-Brazzaville were at daggers drawn. As a Francophone country, Guinea was ideally suited to bridging the gap between the Brazzaville group and the Casablanca countries. The Guineans found a close partner in Haile Selassie who was a natural conservative, but was also able to trade on the symbolic capital of Ethiopia as a country which had repeatedly and successfully resisted European imperialism. Together the leaders of Guinea and Ethiopia coaxed members of the Casablanca and Monrovia blocs back into a dialogue. The fruits of their labour were finally realised when delegations from 32 African countries – excluding the Grunitzky regime in Togo which was debarred – converged on Addis Ababa in May 1963.

After a great deal of horse-trading which need not detain us here, the heads of African governments finally put their signatures to an agreement which brought the Organisation of African Unity (OAU) into existence. Given the earlier mistrust, this was something of an achievement in itself. However, the OAU fell far short of the expectations of many people – both at the time and since. On the one hand, committed pan-Africanists were disappointed that the OAU was not conceived of as a stepping-stone on the road to continental union, but rather the final resting point. Indeed, the Charter did not commit the member states to anything other than voluntary co-operation on the basis of 'the sovereign equality of all Member States'. Because it seemed to foreclose options, Nkrumah was very reluctant to sign the final document, although he finally relented. On the other hand, the OAU held out little encouragement to states and political movements which were hoping for a wholesale revision of the map of Africa. Article 3 of the Charter demanded adherence to the following principles:

1. the sovereign equality of all Member States;
2. non-interference in the internal affairs of States;
3. respect for the sovereignty and territorial integrity of each State and for its inalienable right to independent existence;
4. peaceful settlement of disputes by negotiation, mediation, conciliation or arbitration;
5. unreserved condemnation, in all its forms, of political assassination as well as of subversive activities on the part of neighbouring States or any States;
6. absolute dedication to the total emancipation of the African countries which are still dependent;
7. affirmation of a policy of non-alignment with regard to all blocs.[108]

Crucially, therefore, the OAU was constructed around the concept of state rights as opposed to group rights.[109] The second, third and fifth principles made it exceedingly difficult for secessionist and irredentist movements to stake a claim to political legitimacy. The OAU tied its hands in respect of the former, while it could little more than offer mediation when irredentist claims threatened to result in conflict.

The OAU Charter was a particular affront to the aspirations of Somali nationalists. The Somali government delegation had argued for boundary rectification to be included within the remit of the OAU, but failed to carry other states along with it. Having lost that battle, it shifted its campaign to the fora of the UN, but the latter merely referred the Somali case back to the OAU for consideration. After hearing evidence from all sides, the Council of Ministers fell back upon the principle of respect for the territorial integrity of member states. A further blow followed at the second OAU summit in Cairo in July 1964, when the Somalis failed to prevent passage of the Resolution on the Intangibility of Frontiers which stated that 'all Member States pledge themselves to respect the borders existing on the achievement of national independence'.[110] The Somali President was not present at the crucial meeting, and this enabled the Somalis to claim that they were not bound by its terms. However, from this point onwards the Somali unification campaign was regarded by most member states as in breach of OAU resolutions. At the Kinshasa summit in 1967, the Somalis accepted mediation and reached an agreement with Kenya, and this was followed by an accord with Ethiopia. When Siyad Barre became OAU Chairman in 1969, the Somali government even appeared to have accepted its defeat with relatively good grace. However, as we have seen above, the dispute was merely in abeyance and there was renewed recourse to arms over 1977/78 which the OAU was powerless to prevent.

The OAU was founded at the moment when the Congo crisis was temporarily in remission. However, the outbreak of the 'second independence' rebellions presented the OAU with a fresh dilemma. When Tshombe was installed as Prime Minister, certain states which recalled his earlier record preferred to accept the legitimacy of the shortlived Stanleyville regime. However, the reconquest of the liberated areas resolved this particular matter. When Mobutu staged his second coup in 1965 the principle of respect for national sovereignty resulted in the General becoming one of the central players within the OAU. In 1967, Kinshasa hosted a key summit where both the Somali and Biafran issues came up for discussion. Eritrean nationalists appealed to the sixth principle on the grounds that Ethiopia was a colonial power from which they wanted to be liberated. However, as Iyob has observed, the Ethiopians were able to counter that this was merely another instance of secessionism which could not be entertained under OAU rules.[111] The Ethiopians also won sympathy by pointing to their support for 'genuine' liberation movements and claiming that the states which were partial to the Eritrean cause, some of whom were not OAU members, were guilty of interference in Ethiopian domestic affairs. The southern Sudanese rebels were far less adept at raising awareness of their cause which meant that the Sudanese government was hardly forced to even defend its position.[112]

By contrast, Biafran secession set up a crucial test-case for the willingness of the OAU to abide by its own rules. While the Nigerian government repeated the Tshombe line that the crisis was purely an internal affair, the Ojukwu regime appealed directly to the OAU for intervention. When the matter was discussed at the Kinshasa summit, the language of secession served to discredit the Biafran cause.[113] However, Haile Selassie headed successive efforts at mediation, all of which came to grief over the issue of whether a ceasefire should precede negotiations. As the war ground on, the Biafrans won some influential friends. Nyerere, in particular, bearded the Nigerian government by arguing the case for Biafran secession at every opportunity. However, most of the OAU member countries remained wedded to the earlier assessment and the 1969 summit ended by reiterating the importance of keeping Nigeria as one country. When the Nigerian forces went in for the kill, OAU mediation was rendered entirely superfluous and the outcome was settled by force alone. If the Biafrans had won the war, the OAU might have been forced to reconsider the groundrules. However, the result tended to further reinforce adherence to Article 3 of the Charter.

The commitment to peaceful mediation was even evident with respect to the last bastions of white rule in southern Africa. The OAU had failed to head off UDI in Rhodesia by applying diplomatic pressure to Britain, and had made little headway in persuading the Portuguese of the need to reconcile themselves to decolonisation. Nevertheless, the Lusaka Manifesto of April 1969 expressed a preference for negotiated settlements and demonstrated flexibility over possible timetables towards black rule.[114] It was only when the various initiatives failed to make significant headway that the OAU openly endorsed the armed struggle. Even then, some conservative regimes such as those of Malawi and Côte d'Ivoire persisted with negotiations in the face of fierce criticism from their colleagues. Once again, it was force of arms which brought about the termination of Portuguese colonial rule and the implosion of white rule in Rhodesia. Here, the support of the OAU Liberation Committee was far less important than the willingness of countries like Zambia and Tanzania to provide bases for the conduct of guerrilla operations and to bear the brunt of the reprisals.

Assessments of the performance of the OAU have typically been unkind. At worst the organisation has been depicted as a trade union for African dictators, and at best it stands accused of failing to address the most serious problems afflicting the continent since independence. The failure of its attempted mediation in the Chad civil war in 1981 demonstrated that the hopes for a concerted continental approach were matched by neither the political will nor the logistical wherewithal to make its resolutions stick. Most of the weaknesses stem directly from the fact that the OAU was born of a difficult compromise between different ideological tendencies. A relatively loose alliance, held together by a weak bureaucratic structure, was all that could realistically have been expected in 1963. Although Eritrean secessionists and Somali irredentists bemoaned the unwillingness of the OAU to square up to the legacy of the partition of Africa, it is by no means clear that the continent would have been better served if it had charted a different course. The reality is that it would have been virtually impossible to come up with new boundary lines which would have been generally acceptable. The founders of the OAU prioritised harmony between states over everything else, and by enshrining the principle of *uti possidetis* it almost certainly spared the continent a rash of border wars after independence. In 2002, the African Union which replaced the OAU was founded on the promotion of closer integration between existing African states. The Constitutive Act spoke in the language of democracy and respect for cultural rights, and placed particular emphasis on conflict resolution, but it left little space for an acceptance of the right to secession. Whether the African Union will prove more imaginative than the OAU remains to be seen.

4

Modernity and Tradition, Power and Prestige: Monarchs, Chiefs and Politicians, 1956–74

A chief is a chief by the people.

Pedi proverb

If Africans have had chiefs, it was because all human societies have had them at one stage or another. But when people have developed to a stage which discards chieftainship, when their social development contradicts the need for such an institution, then to force it on them is not liberation but enslavement.

Govan Mbeki

In 1970, Pierre Alexandre, who had served a lengthy stint in the French colonial service, observed that:

The problem of chieftaincy in Africa would seem today, according to certain points of view, to be outmoded, a thing of the past relegated to the background by the more pressing questions of political, social and economic development which are more in tune with the modern world. Chiefs now appear to interest only the ethnologist, if not the archaeologist or even the paleontologist.[1]

More than three decades later, the suggestion that chieftaincy is destined for extinction seems decidedly misplaced. Although post-colonial chiefs have lost most of their formal powers, they have often carved out other niches for themselves. Towards the end of the twentieth century, the chiefs were also able to turn the clock back in many countries, by demonstrating the role they could play in conflict mediation and reconciliation. With the time-lag that is inevitable in academic writing, historians, political scientists and anthropologists have all begun to reappraise chieftaincy as post-colonial phenomenon.[2] As things stand, there is nothing which really serves as an adequate synthesis. This chapter therefore attempts to bring together some of the most recent research as well as drawing on an older literature, with a view to making some broad conclusions about the saliency of 'traditional' institutions in the first decade-and-a-half of independence.

4.1 The conceptual framework

Decolonisation was such a fraught affair because it involved a transfer of power at two levels simultaneously: that is, from European officials to African politicians and from chiefs to locally elected leaders. The electoral principle, which had never found favour amongst the colonial authorities, was now formally enshrined as the basis on which the right to command rested. In the last days of colonialism, there was almost constant electioneering as a myriad of decision-making bodies – local and urban councils, regional and national governments – were voted into office on the basis of universal adult suffrage. Office-holders now claimed legitimacy on the basis of their popular mandate. National governments were often reluctant to accept that locally elected leaders enjoyed legitimacy in their own right. A common pattern therefore was for the elective component of local councils to be watered down, as central governments installed their own nominees – normally comprising those who were loyal party members. However, it was not all one-way traffic. Elected politicians at the centre also faced challenges to their authority from different quarters. One was the newly indigenised Armed Forces, as we will see in greater detail in Chapter 6. The second challenge tended to be less dramatic and therefore attracted less attention and that emanated from the chiefs.

Throughout the first half of the twentieth century, chiefs had been the most trusted intermediaries of the colonial regimes, only to find themselves jilted at the altar of independence. Traditional rulers did not take rejection lightly and during the run-up to independence they often fought a rearguard action to recapture a political voice. They argued that, as the custodians of hallowed tradition, they embodied a deeper legitimacy than politicians who came and went like the changing of the seasons. Amongst other things, this meant that they were duty-bound to speak out on behalf of their people when the politicians got it wrong. In some countries, like Rwanda, the tussle between the chiefs and the politicians assumed an explicitly ethnic dimension, which was resolved through resort to force. In many others, however, chiefs continued to matter because aspiring politicians needed their backing at the polls. When soldiers seized power, they were even more desperate to find political allies and the chiefs were amongst the first groups they turned to for endorsement. The salience of chieftaincy therefore varied, depending on the skill with which the chiefs played their card as intermediaries between national leaders and their local constituents.

Mahmood Mamdani contends that colonial rule in the countryside was characterised by a 'decentralised despotism' exercised by chiefs who owed their authority to their European masters, and that this setup was never effectively dismantled.[3] Now, there is abundant evidence to suggest that colonial chiefs were never 'traditional' in any straightforward sense. Even where the incumbents (almost always male) could trace their claims to pre-colonial ruling lines, they were less dependent upon their councillors and survived on the basis of keeping their European superiors happy. Mamdani's distinction between urban and rural power structures is equally instructive. Nevertheless, his formulation is a curious one because it implies that the chiefs were scarcely affected by decolonisation, whereas the overwhelming weight of evidence would suggest that they were amongst the principal casualties of the independence settlement. The 'decentralised despots' of post-colonial Africa were not the chiefs, but rather the *préfets* and District Commissioners who administered rural peoples through local bureaucracies and appointed local councils. At best, the chiefs found themselves at one remove from the structures of decision-making.

Nevertheless, across the greater part of the continent the institution of chieftaincy did not enter a terminal decline. Indeed in the later twentieth century it even experienced something of a revival. This apparent paradox can be resolved by making some fundamental distinctions: namely between formal power, influence and prestige. By formal power we mean the inherent right to exercise and execute decisions. Whereas the latter is normally laid down in writing, often in the form of a constitutional provision, influence is altogether more elusive. Formal power almost always confers influence as well, but the latter may also derive from social networks which lie outside the formal structures altogether. Hence when a chief is courted at election time, it is not because he has the right to instruct voters, but because he is likely to know what themes will play well with the local electorate. Prestige is something different again. It arises in part from the conscious display much loved by traditional office-holders – such as the dazzling exhibition of gold and other artifacts surrounding the Asantehene in Ghana during traditional festivals – but it is also manufactured by the daily expressions of respect on the part of state officials and/or deference on the part of ordinary people. Where there is formal power, prestige is sometimes part of the package, although governments have often been inclined to treat chiefs as mere functionaries. But it is important to recognise that the prestige of chiefs in post-colonial Africa has often had very little to do with the possession of formal power. Indeed, some distancing from the power structure has helped chiefs to present themselves as the custodian of a quite separate sphere, bounded by 'tradition' which lies beyond the ken of the politicians. The latter have courted the chiefs precisely because they preside over a cultural commodity which they do not possess. Because certain governments played on a modern-traditional dualism after independence – revealing different faces to different audiences – this helped the chiefs to preserve their own role.

The relationship between formal power, influence and prestige is therefore a complex one, and the permutations vary from one country to the next. In this chapter, I aim to give some sense of the combinations which worked themselves out in the early years of independence. I have used the colonial legacy as an organising principle because this set the broad contours of what was to follow. I will begin with a discussion of those countries where a single monarchy, with substantive power, was in place during the terminal phase of colonial rule. I will then consider the fate of traditional rulers in the former British colonies where the Indirect Rule legacy was profound. I then turn to the former French colonies where there was a long tradition of regarding chiefs as mere instruments of administrative rule. Finally, I will consider the special case of South Africa, where Bantu Administration policies attempted to breathe life back into an Indirect Rule canon which had only just been abandoned elsewhere.

4.1.1 We four kings: Ethiopia, Burundi, Swaziland and Lesotho

In colonial Africa, European officials tended to think in terms of an ensemble of chiefdoms, which were more or less uniform in appearance and more or less hierarchical depending on the predilections and phobias of the powers concerned. However, there was a handful of territories in which a single monarchy held sway – namely Ethiopia, Burundi, Lesotho, Swaziland and Rwanda – and it is with these somewhat exceptional cases with which we begin.

Ethiopia falls into a category all of its own by virtue of the fact that its modern imperial system was the creation of the Emperors Menelik and Haile Selassie rather than the Europeans. The Italian occupation, which lasted from 1935 to 1941, brought the suspension of the monarchy and enabled some of the regional nobility to pursue their own ambitions in collaboration with the invaders. On the back of the Italian defeat, Haile Selassie picked up more or less where he had left off. Since becoming the substantive Emperor in 1930, Haile Selassie had embraced a modernising agenda, which included road-building, the creation of a professional standing army, the establishment of the Bank of Ethiopia, the founding of modern schools and administrative reforms. He even introduced Ethiopia's first written constitution in 1931, borrowing freely from the Japanese constitution of 1889.[4] This provided for a Parliament, comprising a Chamber of Deputies elected by members of the nobility and a Senate directly appointed by the Emperor. After 1941, the modernisation project was resumed with greater urgency across the board, with financial backing from the United States.[5] This entailed further improvements to communications and, although the expansion of educational was slow at the base (with only 52,965 school-goers in 1950), the opening of the University of Addis Ababa reflected a determination to nurture a cadre of skilled Ethiopians. This bore directly on the issue of administrative reform. Whereas the empire had previously been ruled through devolution of power to the nobility, Haile Selassie sought to nurture a new class of officials who would be loyal to their creator. These were individuals whose position rested less on high birth than on educational attainment. In the provinces, the Emperor was sometimes forced to make compromises with powerful families – including those that had collaborated with the Italians – but his ultimate objective was to break the hold of entrenched provincial interests and to concentrate decision-making on Addis Ababa. The conception of Haile Selassie as an arch-conservative, which was one of the many by-products of the Ethiopian revolution, is in many ways wide of the mark. The Emperor actively embraced reform on the understanding that the survival of Ethiopia, and hence his own patrimony, depended on it.

All the same, it would also be mistaken to think of the Emperor as committed to bureaucratic efficiency. As John Markakis has eloquently demonstrated, the reforms were intended to strengthen the hand of a resolutely absolutist monarch.[6] All decisions supposedly emanated from the will of the Emperor, as befitted the notional descendant of King Solomon and the Queen of Sheba. This was in spite of the fact that the Revised Constitution of 1955 introduced universal adult suffrage for elections to the Chamber of Deputies (if not the Senate) for the first time.[7] The Constitution vested full executive power in the Emperor and stipulated the responsibilities of Ministers towards himself.[8] Those who were supposed to implement the decisions had to interpret the wishes of the Emperor, even when these were not clearly stated. Ministers, who were given overlapping responsibilities, were appointed and demoted by Haile Selassie in a manner which was designed to keep them on their toes and to foster a culture of intense competition.[9] Reputations were typically made and unmade on the basis of rumour and intrigue carried out within the palace walls, where senior officials spent much of their working week.[10] All of this made for effective political control, but also for a less than efficient administration. The Cabinet almost never met because collective responsibility was not a presumption. The elaboration of the Ministry of the Pen was supposed to impart greater bureaucratic cohesion, but this was subject to the same vagaries as the rest of the structure. The Minister of Finance had a particularly thankless task because the Emperor invented new spending commitments as the whim seized him.[11]

Haile Selassie had, however, embarked on an enormous political gamble. By weakening the nobility, he neutralised a perennial threat to his position. But the nurturing of educated commoners as a counter-elite raised the possibility that the latter would acquire their own political ambitions. The Emperor's strategy of encouraging direct dependence on his person worked for as long as the modern elite was compact. But as the latter's numbers steadily expanded, the Emperor became dangerously detached from sections of society which were increasingly conscious of the gulf between global trends – not least African decolonisation – and what they experienced at home. The contradiction was an obvious one: how could men who had drunk at the well of modernity reconcile themselves with the divine right of kings? The Emperor's first rude awakening came in December 1960, when the head of the Imperial Bodyguard, Mengistu Newaye, and his brother Girmame, attempted to stage a coup while the Emperor was abroad. The Newaye brothers were both highly educated and close to the structures of power, and in that sense belonged to the very constituency which Haile Selassie had been so carefully cultivating. Girmame's experiences as a sub-provincial governor had, however, convinced him that 'feudalism' was to blame for the economic backwardness of Ethiopia and for institutionalised mismanagement in the provinces. The Emperor was not directly attacked and the plotters apparently envisaged the movement towards some form of constitutional monarchy.[12] But this would have amounted to a revolutionary transformation in itself.

On this occasion, the monarchy was saved by the failure of the Newaye brothers to win over the Armed Forces, although it is highly significant that University students took to the streets in their support. The coup attempt was crushed and Haile Selassie then set about restructuring his security apparatus to prevent a repeat occurrence. However, the habits and assumptions of imperial governance remained pretty much unchanged. The simple fact of the matter is that while the Emperor could be magnanimous, he could not share power without ceasing to be the King of Kings. Although the 1960 putsch was abortive, it represented a historic turning point because it was revealed that the Emperor was not in fact all-knowing and all-seeing. In subsequent years, students and urban workers became increasingly assertive, thereby preparing the ground for the cataclysm of 1974. In some respects, the 1960 coup was to the Ethiopian revolution what 1905 were to the Russian Revolution. In each case, a systemic crisis was laid bare in most of its essentials, but the right mix of conjunctural ingredients was absent.

In 1974, students, civil servants and workers were even more deeply alienated from the regime, but on this occasion what was crucial was that disillusionment was rife within the Armed Forces as well. The malaise was brought to a head by the convergence of three crises which the imperial regime singularly failed to deal with. The first was the outbreak of famine across northern Ethiopia over 1972/73. Although the failure of the rains was the underlying cause of mass starvation, as it was in West Africa at the same time, what turned it into a political issue was the failure of the Emperor to take the matter seriously. Despite the fact that up to 200,000 peasants had died by 1973, the attitude was that famine conditions constituted an embarrassment which was best swept under the imperial carpet.[13] Not only was the government painfully slow to mobilise internal resources and external assistance, but Ethiopia actually continued to export significant quantities of agricultural produce. However, after news of the scale of the human tragedy reached the outside world and was widely publicised, staff and students at Addis Ababa University were galvanised into action. Student demonstrations in sympathy with the peasantry led to clashes with the police, which further compounded the sense of outrage.

The second conjuncture was the steep rise in oil prices following the OPEC embargo of 1973, which hit the Ethiopian economy hard. The inevitable result was galloping inflation which left a large hole in the pockets of urban wage-earners. Taxi drivers came out on strike over pump prices in February 1974 and teachers followed suit.[14] This provided the cue for a medley of strikes and demonstrations within the capital, which brought public services and communications to a grinding halt. Even priests of the Orthodox Church took to the streets, demanding better remuneration.[15] Finally, there was the escalating war against Eritrean secession which was at least partly of the Emperor's own making. The hardships experienced by Ethiopian non-commissioned officers (NCOs) and the ranks contrasted with the comfortable lifestyles of senior officers who also tended to be Amharas. It was mutiny within the 24th Brigade at Neghele (in Sidamo) in January 1974 which actually ignited the revolution. The failure of the government to swiftly resolve this particular incident, after privates and NCOs had arrested their officers, led to a rash of mutinies across the country – first at Dolo on the Kenyan border and then at the Debre-Zeit Airforce base, some 50 kilometres from Addis Ababa.[16] Crucially, the mutineers remained in close contact with one other, thereby spreading the contagion from one unit to the next.

What brought about the downfall of the Emperor was the steady haemorrhaging of his moral authority over the course of 1974. A pattern was established whereby Haile Selassie, or his representatives, caved in to particular demands which merely galvanised other interest groups to table their own. With each fresh concession, the mystique surrounding the Emperor evaporated into thin air. Responding to ongoing restiveness within the Armed Forces, the government of Aklilu Habte Wolde offered substantial pay increases, but this was followed almost immediately by fresh acts of mutiny in Asmara and elsewhere. In April, the Emperor accepted Aklilu's resignation and installed Endelkatchew Makonnen as Prime Minister. Crucially, he also promised a new constitutional framework which would have made the Prime Minister account-able to Parliament rather than to himself. The Confederation of Labour Unions (CELU) wasted no time in presenting Endelkatchew with a list of demands which turned partly on wages and conditions, but also explicitly backed those of the student movement. When a General Strike was launched in March, followed by wildcat strikes, the new government was forced to concede sub-stantial wage and salary increases to workers.

The control of the new administration was, however, slipping as Armed Forces co-ordinating committees began to take a more active part in the political process. In June, militants formed a Military-Police Co-ordinating Committee which invited provincial police and military units to send represen-tatives to a meeting on the 28 June. The 106 delegates who attended consti-tuted the Co-ordinating Committee of the Armed Forces, the Police and the Territorial Army – the Derg ('Committee') for short. This committee began arresting members of the former Aklilu administration and then went a step further by rounding up Ministers, elements of the nobility and even members of the royal family.[17] This contributed to the power vacuum at the centre which the Derg itself proceeded to fill. In the last week of July, the Derg deposed Endelkatchew and installed Mikael Imru in his place. While work proceeded on the drafting of a new constitution, the Derg set about dismantling key institu-tions of Haile Selassie's government. The Emperor himself posed something of a dilemma, and he was placed under effective house arrest as the Derg consid-ered its options. In a fascinating reconstruction of the last days of Haile Selassie, Ryszard Kapuscinski paints a picture of an Emperor whose power evaporated daily as his officials melted away.[18] Having initially contemplated the retention of Haile Selassie in the role of a constitutional monarch, the Derg eventually decided that the octogenarian Emperor had to be got rid of. The anti-climax came on 12 September when Haile Selassie was removed from the palace and asked to join a waiting Volkswagen. After a brief protest at the indignity of it all, Haile Selassie was driven away, never to be seen again. He was murdered the following year and his body secretly buried. The Derg duly transformed itself into the Provisional Military Administrative Council (PMAC) under the formal chairmanship of Lt.-General Aman Andom. However, real power lay within the Derg itself, none of whose members ranked above Major. The extinction of the monarchy was now complete.

Haile Selassie's hopes of combining modernisation with absolutism proved an impossible trick in the latter half of the twentieth century when the basis of the Emperor's claims had come to be regarded as anachronistic. The cruel irony was that he was deposed by precisely the constituencies which he had so assiduously built up – namely, students, civil servants and soldiers. As Donald Donham suggests, the latter turned their back on the monarchy, which they associated with backwardness, and embraced what they construed as modernity.[19] A number of commentators have remarked on the narrow social base of the revolution. Apart from the mutinies, the high drama was confined to Addis Ababa. Andargachew estimates that the urban population comprised 3 million out of nearly 32 million people, of whom the civil servants, workers, students and soldiers made up a mere 300,000.[20] But while it is true that peasants did not topple the Emperor, Donham maintains that the language of modernity was no less seductive in remote rural locations.[21] To that extent, the demise of Haile Selassie was rooted in a tectonic shift within greater Ethiopia.

The monarchies of Rwanda and Burundi differed in that while they emerged out of pre-colonial kingdoms, they were remodelled in profound ways by the Germans and later the Belgians. As we have seen in Chapter 1, the 'Hutu revolution' culminated in the abolition of the Rwandan monarchy on the eve of independence. In Burundi, by contrast, it appeared as if the *mwami* might turn back the tides of republicanism. A crucial difference was that Hutus had been incorporated into the chieftaincy hierarchy to a greater extent than in Rwanda, despite Belgian reforms.[22] Hence the monarchy was never regarded as a purely Tutsi affair. Another related difference was that there were two fiercely competing ruling lineages in Burundi, the Bezi and Batare, creating a fault line which cut across the 'tribal' divide. In the 1950s, *Mwami* Mwambutsa IV from the Bezi line was under attack from Belgian administrators who toyed with the idea of installing a more pliable Batare candidate in his place. It was this, rather than ethnicity, which animated Burundian politics.

When political parties were formed in 1959 these replicated the divisions. After failing at the polls in the communal elections of 1960, the Bezi-oriented UPRONA was triumphant in the legislative elections of the following year, winning no fewer than 58 out of a total of 64 seats. The incoming Prime Minister, Louis Rwagasore, happened to be the eldest son of the *Mwami*, and so could be expected to accord due respect to the king. But at the same time, Rwagasore belonged to a younger, educated elite which was explicitly modern and nationalist in outlook. Lemarchand observes that Rwagasore also had an avid following amongst the 'Hutu masses'.[23] The political alignments which were taking shape were, however, shattered by the assassination of Rwagasore (with possible Belgian complicity) a month after the elections. The struggle over the succession took on an ethnic dimension, influenced in part by events across the border in Rwanda. Rival Tutsi and Hutu candidates emerged, splitting the ruling party into so-called Monrovia (Hutu) and Casablanca (Tutsi) factions. The impasse enabled *Mwami* Mwambutsa to step in, initially as an arbiter but increasingly as a player in his own right. In May 1965, following two years in which domestic political rivalries became intertwined with the fighting in the eastern Congo (see Chapter 3), the king agreed to arrange elections. Because Hutus were in a numerical majority, Hutu politicians had everything to gain by playing the ethnic card. However, the refusal of the king to appoint a Hutu Prime Minister after the polls fuelled the perception that he had become a captive of Tutsi interests.

A crucial turning point came in October 1965 when Hutu elements within the security forces killed the Prime Minister and attacked the palace. *Mwami* Mwambutsa fled across the border to the Congo, and it was left to Captain Michel Micombero to quash the rebellion. The reprisals taken against 'Hutus' as a category led to thousands of deaths, thereby adding a dose of objective reality to the perceived primacy of ethnicity. *Mwami* Mwambutsa never returned to the country, but appointed his son to act in his place, who formally assumed the throne as *Mwami* Ntare III in July 1966. The monarchy had been severely shaken, but it stood every chance of bouncing back because of its possible role in bridging the ethnic divide. Unfortunately for *Mwami* Ntare, his attempt to take an active part in proceedings was not to the liking of Tutsi militants, and the king soon found himself at odds with the military junta. The king waited for an official delegation to leave for an OAU summit and then, on 7 November, endeavoured to make a radio broadcast suspending the government by royal decree. This royal putsch misfired and on the 28th the Micombero regime declared the abolition of the monarchy.

This was not quite the end of the story. In the years that followed, the conflict became increasingly ugly as Hutu insurgents and their Congolese allies raided across the border and the military took reprisals against Hutu civilians. This culminated in the pogroms of 1972 when perhaps as many as 200,000 people were slaughtered and some 150,000 fled to neighbouring states. The deposed *Mwami* might have still have provided a focus for those Burundians who wished to see the conflict brought to an end. Possibly for that reason, Ntare was abducted from Uganda on 30 March, flown back to Bujumbura and secretly murdered by agents of the military regime.[24] Micombero later claimed that the former king had been conspiring with Hutu plotters whose attempted rebellion at the end of April provided an excuse for the killing. Although this is highly doubtful, it does support the contention that the monarchy was not regarded as the property of the Tutsis alone. Unlike in Rwanda, the Burundian monarchy was extinguished precisely because it had the capacity to straddle the ethnic divide.

In Southern Africa, the kingdoms of Basutoland (Lesotho) and Swaziland had been forged during the turbulent years of the nineteenth century. Swaziland was later reduced to a protectorate of the South African Republic and lost most of its land to white settlers. After the South African War (1899–1902), Britain converted Basutoland, Swaziland and Bechualand (Botswana) into High Commission territories under the joint administration of a Commissioner who was physically located in South Africa. All three territories remained closely tied to South Africa through the export of migrant labour to the gold mines, and there was a British expectation that they would ultimately be absorbed by their more powerful neighbour. The election of the National Party regime in 1948, however, put paid to that prospect in the short term. Nevertheless, deep-seated fears about annexation continued to animate the internal politics of these territories during the 1950s. Another feature which all three territories shared was a British attachment to Indirect Rule. Whereas eight Tswana paramount-cies were recognised in Bechuanaland, Basutoland and Swaziland were administered through a single monarchy. The British initially left considerable powers over the allocation of land, the dispensation of justice and the appointment of lesser chiefs to the respective kings. In the mid-1940s, these territories experienced their own version of the 'second colonial occupation' which was manifested in a greater European willingness to interfere in the daily lives of rural populations. However in Swaziland, a series of Proclamations in 1950 enabled the king to claw back many of his prerogatives. He was given powers to regulate many areas of Swazi life, to issue rules which did not conflict with British laws and to oversee the native courts.[25] Furthermore, the king held in trust the land which was formally allocated to Swazis as well as that which was later bought back from the white settlers. Because half of the total territory continued to lie in non-Swazi hands, there was considerable land hunger which placed the chiefly hierarchy in a powerful position vis-à-vis the peasantry.[26] In Basutoland, by contrast, the king was left in a rather weaker position. He lost the power to appoint and dismiss chiefs in 1946. The chiefs themselves lost their courts and the right to collect fines, which were taken over by government bureaucrats.[27] Crucially, however, the monarchy retained control over the system whereby chiefs allocated land.

When the winds of political change finally swept into this corner of southern Africa, the effect was as profound as elsewhere. The end result was, however, strikingly different in Lesotho and Swaziland. In Basutoland, the very large numbers of migrant workers who shuttled backwards and forwards from South Africa (around 200,000 per year by independence) had an important influence on local politics. Many of the founders of the first truly political organisation – the Basutoland African Congress (BAC), which was launched in 1952 – had been involved in the African National Congress (ANC) in South Africa, including its leader Ntsu Mokhehle. The BAC campaigned for substantial progress towards self-government lest Basutoland fall prey to South African imperialism. The BAC, which was largely composed of teachers and migrant labourers, also demanded a legislature in which the seats would be held by elected representatives rather than chiefs. At this time, the monarchy was in a transitional state because the heir to the throne, Bereng Seeiso, was pursuing his academic studies in Oxford, leaving the kingdom in the hands of an unpopular female Regent, Mantsebo.

After some resistance, the British agreed in 1958 to establish a legislature in which indirectly elected representatives would enjoy parity with nominated chiefs. Although this was a limited concession, it did confirm that Basutoland was not to be treated as an exception to the African rule. With an eye on the 1960 elections, the BAC reconstituted itself as the Basutoland Congress Party (BCP). Modelling itself on Nkrumah's Convention People's Party (CPP), the BCP consolidated its hold on the teachers union, and infiltrated a range of voluntary associations, including football clubs, youth and women's associations.[28] The image of the BCP as a radical nationalist party provoked consternation within the British administration, the upper echelons of the chiefly hierarchy and the Catholic Church, all of whom began looking for more palatable alternatives. One was the Basutoland National Party (BNP) which was formed in 1958 by Chief Leabua Jonathan (a minor chief), who enjoyed very close links to the Regent. The BNP advocated some modernisation of chieftaincy, but promised to do so in collaboration with the chiefs. Another was the pro-royalist

Marematlou Party (MP) which was formed in 1957 around the single issue of the enthronement of Bereng Seeiso. When this was achieved in 1960, the MP did not dissolve but continued to pose as the defender of royal interests.

On the basis of a very limited turnout, the BCP emerged with 32 of the 40 indirectly elected seats in the 1960 elections.[29] However, because half of the seats in the National Council were filled by chiefly appointees, it was possible to restrict it to a single representative on the executive. Mokhehle himself was pointedly frozen out. The BNP won a single seat, but Jonathan who had failed in his own electoral bid, was later appointed by Mosheshoe II as a chiefly representative.[30] The MP fared rather better, winning 5 seats on the National Council and taking one place on the executive. The BCP, which had been cut out of power at the centre, nevertheless enjoyed majority control of many District Councils where it endeavoured to take control at the expense of the chiefs. In the years that followed these first elections, the balance of forces tilted against the party which appeared to pose the greatest threat to royal interests. As happened in many other African countries, however, the politicians who appeared most supportive of the traditional power structure often turned out to be its nemesis. In the wake of the 1960 elections, the BNP continued to enjoy the patronage of the chiefly hierarchy, the Catholic Church and (covertly) the South African government. By contrast, the BCP experienced a damaging split which mirrored the breakaway of the Pan-Africanist Congress (PAC) from the ANC in South Africa.[31]

The formal powers of the monarchy had already been pared back, but Mosheshoe enjoyed some leverage by virtue of his prerogative of appointment. In 1963, however, representatives of the main parties sat on a Constitutional Commission which recommended the confinement of royal discretion to matters of land tenure and chiefly discipline.[32] Chiefly representatives in the legislature steered through amendments which were designed to swing the balance the other way, but the main party leaders were determined to stick by their republican guns. In 1964, Moshoeshoe was eventually forced to sign up to a constitution in which his powers were to be strictly nominal. Real power would henceforth be vested in a Prime Minister, who was accountable to a parliament elected under conditions of universal adult suffrage for the first time.[33] The lower house was comprised entirely of directly elected representatives, although chiefs were still nominated to the Senate. In the 1965 elections, the BNP won 31 seats in the National Assembly to 25 by the BCP and four by the Marematlou Freedom Party (MFP).[34]

When Chief Jonathan made a formal request for independence, the British Government convened a conference in London in June 1966 which was a bruising encounter. Jonathan insisted that the king should enjoy the status of a constitutional monarch, but without substantive powers. In particular, he maintained that the position of head of the Armed Forces should reside with the Prime Minister, rather than the king in his capacity as Head of State. The BCP which had consistently argued for strict limits to royal power now joined the MFP in arguing for a wider constitutional role for the king. Unfortunately for them, the British decided to back Jonathan.[35] Independence came in October 1966 and was followed by measures which were calculated to further weaken the monarchy. All tax-gathering responsibilities were transferred to the capital, and under the Chieftaincy Act the king lost his powers of discipline over lesser chiefs, who were henceforth accountable only to the Minister of Chieftainship Affairs.[36] But at the same time, the BNP regime also took the radical step in 1968 of dismantling the local government system, which had allowed people to elected their own village committees and District Councils. These reforms, which were intended to weaken the opposition parties as well as the monarchy, faced a crucial test in the upcoming elections in 1970.

When the BNP appeared destined to lose, Chief Jonathan simply suspended the constitution and declared a state of emergency. He arrested many opposition leaders, but significantly he also detained Mosheshoe himself, who stood accused of plotting a coup. The regime proceeded to dismiss swathes of officials at every level of the administration.[37] In place of local democracy, the BNP government substituted development committees and land development committees, both of which were made up of chiefly appointees. Although an electoral element was later reintroduced, chiefs and government nominees retained much of their dominance.[38] At the national level, Jonathan convened an interim parliament in 1973, in which all the main parties were supposed to be represented. However, the corporatist formula scarcely concealed Jonathan's intention to run the country single-handedly. The regime never went as far as abolition of the monarchy – although it toyed with forcing an abdication – primarily because it had no need to resort to extreme measures. Mosheshoe returned from eight months of enforced exile suitably chastened, and reconciled himself to his purely symbolic role – at least, for the time being.

On the surface, the BNP appeared to have undercut the powers of the king and the principal chiefs, whilst according greater prerogatives to village chiefs – thereby exploiting one of the fault lines within Basotho chieftaincy. However, this was an optical illusion. In 1975, Jonathan made it clear that chieftaincy at all levels was henceforth to be in the gift of the government:

> I would say that the chiefs are not as important any more ... But the institution of chieftaincy is an important arm of government. It is responsible for peace in the rural areas. We have a very small police force and it cannot cope with law and order. The chiefs work on behalf of government. To keep order is a function for which the chiefs are paid. If a chief does not fulfil this function he is dismissed.[39]

In this, the Jonathan regime conformed to a fairly typical pattern. Where Lesotho is perhaps unusual is in the extent to which local powers were usurped by development agencies and state bureaucrats especially with respect to land.[40] As James Ferguson has persuasively argued, development projects which were often a failure in purely economic terms nevertheless performed a critical function in enabling central government to strengthen its administrative grip over the rural areas.[41]

The outcome could hardly have been more different in Swaziland which diverged in two respects. On the one hand, white settlers were an important factor in the political equation. On the other, Sobhuza II (who came to the throne in 1921) was a shrewd operator with considerable experience in dealing with officials and settlers alike. As in Lesotho, the greatest threat emanated from the educated sections of society and workers who felt excluded from the structures of power.[42] In 1960, the Swaziland Progressive Party (SPP) was deliberately sidelined in the deliberations of a constitutional committee which was dominated by settlers and chiefs. After a series of schisms and realignments, the SPP transformed itself into the Ngwane National Liberatory Congress (NNLC). Like the BPC, the NNLC leadership was closely associated with the ANC in South Africa and drew inspiration from Nkrumah's brand of Pan-Africanism. Unsurprisingly, therefore, it was not to the liking of the settlers or Sobhuza, who perceived it as anti-white and anti-royalist respectively. Two other parties, the Swaziland Democratic Party (SDP) and the Mbandzeni National Convention (MNC) were regarded as more accommodating.

A turning point came in 1963 when the NNLC backed a general strike, which had begun on the railways and spread to the mines.[43] The strike, which was construed as a challenge to the moral authority of Sobhuza himself, was crushed with the assistance of British troops, following which NNLC leaders were put on trial. This weakened the principal challenger to the traditional power structure, just as the latter was beginning to regroup. The first constitutional committee had recommended vesting substantial powers in the king, such as control over mineral rights, which the British were reluctant to agree to. When the latter sought to water down these proposals, the monarchy mobilised to defend its interests. This culminated in the formation of the Imbokodvo National Movement (INM) which was to all intents and purposes the party of Sobhuza. To the alarm of the three existing parties, the INM contested the 1964 elections with the backing of the settler United Swaziland Association (USA). The INM made optimal use of the chiefs to get ordinary Swazis to rally behind the monarchy. The result was the INM won the elections comfortably, leading to the political capitulation of the SDP and the MNC.

The constitution under which Swaziland became independent was highly favourable to the monarchy. Control over mineral rights were indeed vested in the king who was also empowered to nominate one-fifth of the members of the House of Assembly and half of the Senate. Given the coercive resources underpinning the INC, it could also expect to win a majority of the elected seats. It made a clean sweep in the 1967 elections because of the peculiarities of the voting system.[44] Five years later, the NNLC won a single constituency which entitled it to three seats. Even this was unacceptable to the INM which did everything in its power to have one of the prospective MPs disqualified on the grounds of being an alien. When the Appeal Court failed to fall into line, a constitutional crisis resulted. This was resolved on 12 April 1973 when the king announced the suspension of the constitution and his assumption of all legislative, executive and judicial powers. Following a predictable script, the leadership of the NNLC was detained and opposition was effectively proscribed. King Sobhuza remained the absolute ruler of Swaziland until 1978 when a new constitution was introduced to give the stamp of legitimacy to what was in effect a royal coup. As before, Parliament was divided into a House of Assembly and a Senate. Forty members of the House were to be elected indirectly from local assemblies (or *tinkundhla*) which could be tightly controlled by royal officials, while the king was empowered to nominate ten others.[45] The House of Assembly in turn elected ten members to the Senate, while the king appointed an equal number. In practice, though, Sobhuza ruled by Orders in Council until his death in 1982.

The contrast between the destinies of the Basotho and Swazi monarchs could hardly have been starker. The one had been constitutionally emasculated and then publicly humiliated in the wake of a coup launched by the politicians; the other had extracted a constitution which was favourable to himself before launching his own coup against refractory politicians. However the king of Lesotho had fared comparatively well by comparison with his counterparts in Ethiopia and Burundi. Here, the monarchies were abolished outright and the last incumbents were murdered, providing spectacular illustrations of how the balance of power in post-colonial Africa had shifted.

4.1.2   *Breaking the indirect rules: Nigeria, Ghana, Uganda, Tanzania and Botswana*

The next set of countries are those where British Indirect Rule policies had conferred substantial powers upon chiefs prior to decolonisation. An obvious starting point is Nigeria because it was here that Indirect Rule provided the closest approximation to a British philosophy of governance. Although the British were eventually forced to concede that it could not be applied willy-nilly to the decentralised societies of the South-east, they did take the policy as far as they could in the North and West of the country. In the North, British Residents saw it as their duty to oversee the Native Authority (NA) system so as to ensure 'sound administration', and intervened in matters of succession, but to a large extent the Emirate structures were self-regulating.[46] Most northerners would therefore have encountered colonial justice in the form of Native Courts, presided over by Alkalis applying principles of Islamic law. As late as 1958, Sklar observes, there were only three Magistrates Courts for the whole of the Northern Region, with the result that 80 per cent of all criminal and 85 per cent of civil cases were transacted through the Native Courts.[47] At the same time, northerners paid their taxes – which were initially a continuation of earlier taxes, but were eventually consolidated into a flat-rate assessment – into the Native Treasuries through collectors appointed by the relevant NA. The erstwhile Sokoto Caliphate continued to be bound together by an elaborate administrative hierarchy of district and village heads and titled officials which stretched down to the smallest village. At the summit sat the Emirs, who claimed descent and thus legitimacy from the leaders of the jihads. In Yorubaland, which had been characterised by a distinct lack of unity in the nineteenth century, the British endeavoured to import the same setup. Obas with some claim to historical precedence – notably the Ooni of Ife and the Alafin of Oyo – were elevated over their neighbours and were invested with the status of Sole NA, with responsibility for the Native Courts and Treasuries.

There was some reform of the southern NAs during the 1950s, but for the most part the northern Emirs remained as firmly entrenched as ever. Hence, writing shortly after independence, Sklar could state that 'Within his jurisdiction, the emir possesses supreme executive and judicial power in addition to shared legislative powers.'[48] The introduction of representative institutions did, however, present a direct threat to the northern chiefly establishment which could not simply be ignored. An alarming prospect was that nationalist politicians would muscle in and lay claim to the powers which were had hitherto been the preserve of the Emirs. This challenge was met by stepping directly into the political arena in a bid to pre-empt unwanted change.

The Northern People's Congress (NPC) was founded independently of the Emirs, but it soon became the party of the Fulani aristocracy – or *Masu Sarauta*. Its initial advocacy of NA reform was quietly forgotten as the party campaigned for the preservation of traditional structures. Its principal rival was the Northern Elements Progressive Union (NEPU) which campaigned for a fundamental overhaul of the corrupt and authoritarian NAs. In an instructive analysis of the social composition of these two parties, Sklar observes that the NPC received the bulk of its active support from people tied in to the NAs, whereas NEPU was mostly supported by Hausa commoners (*talakawa*) – and in particular by petty traders and artisans in the cities – while many of its prominent leaders were Muslim scholars.[49] Whereas the NPC posed as the defender of the Islamic institutions upon which the Sokoto Caliphate had been founded, NEPU attacked the Emirates as a corruption of Islam.[50] Unfortunately for NEPU, the Emirs still controlled the Native Courts and were therefore in a position to systematically harass NEPU supporters with the connivance of the British authorities.[51] In this way, the NPC applied a stranglehold over the Northern Region and ultimately the entire Nigerian federation. The NPC made no secret of the close collaboration between politicians and Emirs. The most important of them, namely the Emirs of Kano and Katsina and the Sultan of Sokoto, even served in the Northern government which was headed by the Sardauna of Sokoto, Sir Ahmadu Bello – himself a direct descendant of Usman dan Fodio (the founder of the Caliphate) and a possible future claimant to the Sultanate.[52] Moreover, whereas the Lyttleton Constitution of 1954 provided for relatively weak upper chambers in the Eastern and Western Regions, the Northern House of Chiefs enjoyed legislative powers of its own.[53]

Significantly, however, tensions did develop between the Northern Regional government, which emphasised its electoral mandate, and the Emirs who regarded themselves as the sole repositories of customary legitimacy. Although their formal powers were not tampered with, Emirs detected an attack on their status. After the recognition of Provincial Commissioners in 1962, these political appointees were accorded formal precedence over the Emirs, and three years later the latter were required to seek permission if they wished to travel outside their provinces.[54] Furthermore, the Northern government conducted probes into a number of NAs which were accused of inefficiency and financial mismanagement. The definitive proof that the power balance was shifting came when the Emir of Kano, Sir Muhammadu Sanusi, was forced to abdicate in 1963 after an investigation into the affairs of the Kano NA. Although he had served in the Regional executive and was connected to Ahmadu Bello by marriage, this did not save his skin.[55]

In other parts of Nigeria, traditional rulers had never enjoyed the same measure of protection. In the Western Region, where a fierce struggle for power was played out between the Action Group (AG) and the National Council of Nigeria and the Cameroons (NCNC), the chiefs became directly embroiled. Obafemi Awolowo had played the Yoruba ethnic card against the NCNC. This resonated with senior Yoruba chiefs who saw themselves as the bearers of a great tradition. However, the AG was led by a confident modern elite which was less inclined to defer to traditional authority than in the North. When the Awolowo administration sought to advance local government reforms in 1952, which were designed to reduce chiefly representation in local councils, some of the leading Obas shifted their allegiance to the NCNC. This brought them into direct conflict with the Regional government which proceeded to use every means at its disposal to bring them into line. In 1956, the Alafin of Oyo was removed from office, and the following year the regional government passed a law which gave it to the formal right to appoint and dismiss chiefs. At the same time, customary courts in the Region were brought under the supervision of the Attorney-General, while greater controls were placed on chiefly management of communal lands.[56] The result was that chiefs became dependent on the goodwill of their political masters. When the Western Regional crisis broke in 1962, chieftaincy predictably became a key battleground. Akintola sought to cement his tenuous grip on Regional power by dissolving elected local councils and replacing them with appointed management committees to which loyal supporters could be assigned. He also rewarded chiefs who supported him and punished those who continued to side with Awolowo.[57] The Ooni of Ife was amongst those threatened with removal unless he modified his stance. Although the crises in the West also gave particular chiefs a measure of influence, this should not be exaggerated: a chief who found himself on the wrong side of the political fence could all too easily find himself deposed.

The abortive coup of January 1966 did not greatly disturb the pattern which had been established during the First Republic. Major Nzeogwu and his co-plotters had intended to strike a decisive blow against everything they regarded as 'feudal' and reactionary – but crucially they failed. Of course, they did bring about the collapse of the NPC regime, but the incoming Ironsi administration was forced to placate injured northern pride. In Northern palaces, there was particular resentment at the murder of NPC politicians, including Ahmadu Bello. The Regional Governor, Major Hassan Katsina, who also happened to be a son of the Emir of Katsina, spearheaded a campaign to win the Emirs to the side of the government by means of a series of consultations.[58] Having been openly courted in this fashion, the Emirs seized the opportunity to make some forthright demands of their own. Although the charm offensive was reasonably successful, Olufemi Vaughan adjudges that the Ironsi regime miscalculated by relying so heavily on the support of traditional rulers.[59] The latter failed to head off the mounting crisis which began with the May riots and culminated in the bloody overthrow of Ironsi in July. The Gowon regime, which stepped into the breach, did not repeat the experiment. Although it made a show of consulting important chiefs, this was a junta which was inclined to rely much more on professional civil servants.

The successor regime of Generals Murtala Mohammed and Olusegun Obasanjo exhibited reforming zeal on a number of fronts (see Chapter 6). Amongst other things, they decided that it was time to bring the different systems of administration into conformity with one another. In effect, this meant that many of the sacred cows of the North would have to be sacrificed in the interests of 'national unity'. In 1976 there remained basic differences in the systems of local administration, resulting both from the messy compromises surrounding decolonisation and the quality of the relationship between political parties and traditional rulers during the First Republic. The Mohammed/ Obasanjo regime introduced a three-tier system of government which would at last be uniform across the country. Below the Federal and state governments a tier of local government was created with its own sources of funding and responsibilities. In 1977, the federation was further broken down from 12 to 19 states, and these were subdivided into local council areas covering populations ranging between 150,000 and 800,000.[60] Crucially, chiefs and Emirs were excluded from the local councils, although purely advisory traditional councils were created as a sop. This radical reform was justified on the basis that chiefs ought to be above partisan politics.[61]

Although Nigerian chiefs had been stripped of their formal power, the greatest amongst them retained a measure of political influence because politicians and soldiers alike still needed to bask in their reflected glory. However, there was no disguising the fact that a veritable revolution had been carried out, especially in the North. The extent to which the chiefs had been tamed became fully apparent some years later, in 1984, when the Buhari regime confined the Emir of Kano and the Ooni of Ife to their home areas for having dared to make an unauthorised mission to Jerusalem in defiance of government policy.[62] As we have seen, the Bello administration had not hesitated to put an earlier Emir of Kano in his place, but the public manner in which the chastisement was carried out reverberated through Nigeria. The fact that the Buhari himself was a northerner underlined just how much the balance of power had shifted away from the palace and towards the barracks.

The same result was accomplished much earlier in Ghana because the dominant party was always much less beholden to the chiefs.[63] The CPP had been founded as a party of commoners who regarded the NA system, with some reason, as oppressive and corrupt. No sooner had the CPP taken office in 1951 than the first reforms of local government were introduced. In August, the Legislative Assembly passed a Local Government Ordinance which permanently altered the landscape of power. The NAs were replaced by elected local and urban councils, in which chiefs (or other appointees from the traditional councils) constituted only one-third of the membership. Moreover, the chiefs in Ashanti and the Colony were forced to cede the management of stool lands to these councils which collected the revenues. The perception that the chiefs were under attack helps to account for the emergence of overt opposition to the CPP from 1954. The National Liberation Movement (NLM) enjoyed the unconditional backing of the Ashanti chiefly hierarchy and cloaked much of its appeal in neo-traditional language. Not surprisingly, the CPP administration did everything it could to weaken the power-base of opposition chiefs. Although it was unable to push through reforms to the Native Court system until *1958, it was empowered to change the membership of the panels and did so in a manner which tended to replace chiefs with loyal commoners.[64]

By the time of independence, traditional rulers had already been forced to disgorge most of their formal powers, and their autonomy was further eroded in subsequent years. The CPP was able to justify its assault on the grounds that it was promoting sound administration, advancing democracy and even acting in the best interests of the chiefs themselves. The immediate concern was to dispense with chiefs whose loyalty was suspect. By withdrawing de facto recognition from the incumbents, the government invited communities to depose their chiefs. This stratagem was successful in Akyem Abuakwa, long considered a place where chieftaincy was impregnable, when Okyenhene Ofori Atta II was removed from office in May 1958.[65] These interventions were eventually given statutory force in 1959 when the Chiefs (Recognition) Act made government recognition the essential criterion for holding chiefly office as well as defining the hierarchy of offices in any given traditional area. In the same year, the chiefs were removed from local government bodies altogether. The CPP never went down the route of seeking to dismantle chieftaincy because it was able to secure compliance through other means. Indeed compliant chiefs might even help to cement party control at the local level. Across the country, though, opposition chiefs were replaced by more acceptable candidates. The government refrained from deposing the Asantehene, but it did whittle away his remaining powers and force him into a humiliating submission.[66] Within a few years of independence, therefore, the Nkrumah regime had brought even the most powerful traditional rulers to heel.

As in Western Nigeria, the next turn of the wheel of fortune created a dramatic break, but one which concealed a strong element of continuity. After the military coup of February 1966, the National Liberation Council (NLC) went out of its way to curry favour with groups which had been fallen foul of Nkrumah, including the chiefs. The NLC passed Decree 112 which was intended to restore traditional rulers who had been wrongfully deposed and to restore chiefly hierarchies which had been altered by the CPP regime. As a consequence, some prominent individuals regained their stools – notably in Akyem Abuakwa where Nana Ofori Atta II was returned to office. In all, Rathbone estimates that 'well over 100' chiefs who had been destooled were resurrected. However, this game of musical chairs merely underlined the fact that it was central government which was the arbiter of who was a chief and who was not. Many observers have commented on the continuing vitality surrounding chieftaincy in Ghana. This might seem surprising, given that the chiefs had forfeited most of their formal powers in the 1950s. However, much of their legitimacy stemmed precisely from the fact that they were not formally incorporated into decision-making structures. They continued to carry out certain duties in an informal manner – for example arbitration of local disputes.[67] Again, Akan chiefs remained the effective custodians of stool lands attached to their stools, despite efforts by the state to control the revenues.[68] But their performance was closely monitored by their communities who were all too aware of past abuses. Most importantly, the chiefs had to earn their respect, and it is this (together with the threat of destoolment) which tended to make them good listeners. Apart from local mediation, their most valued contribution was as interlocutors between rural communities and the government. It was well-understood that an effective chief could win official backing for local development projects such as a health clinic or a secondary school. This is an important reason why there was increasingly a preference for chiefs who were well-educated and/or well-heeled. The fact that Ghanaians deferred to their chiefs meant that state officials also had to treat them with a certain respect, as they do to this day.

The third instance which warrants closer attention is that of Uganda, which has some resonances with both the Nigerian and Ghanaian experiences. As in Ghana, a well-organised monarchy and a dominant political party locked horns. The Buganda kingdom was to Uganda what Ashanti was to Ghana – only more so. However, the CPP was far more cohesive than the Uganda People's Congress (UPC) ever was. Whereas the British had sought to disable Asante institutions after the 1900 revolt, before going into reverse gear in the mid-1930s, they had carefully nurtured the Buganda monarchy after the signing of the Buganda Agreement of that same year. Baganda chiefs had even been sent to administer other parts of the Uganda Protectorate, establishing a special relationship which persisted down to the 1950s. One result of the 1900 Agreement was that Baganda chiefs were granted private ownership over vast tracts of the kingdom, amounting to about one half of the total surface area, thereby turning peasants into tenants.[69] Although the exactions levied upon peasants were mitigated under the Busulu and Envujo Law of 1927, the landlord-tenant relationship itself remained in place. This model of land tenure was considered far too radical in the Gold Coast, where the principle of communal land tenure was upheld. A crucial difference, therefore, was that Buganda chieftaincy had a much stronger economic underpinning than in Ashanti. In line with the prescriptions of Indirect Rule, an elaborate hierarchy of chiefly offices linked the smallest village to the Kabaka's court in Mengo. The monarchy ran itself for most of the period until the 1950s, when the special status of Buganda became problematic in the context of decolonisation.

The introduction of elections posed a double threat to the monarchy: it created a competing basis for legitimacy in Buganda, and at the same time it forced the kingdom to engage on equal terms with the rest of Uganda. A refusal to accept the modified rules led to the enforced exile of the Kabaka in 1953, but thereafter the British lost the will to impose a solution. The independence constitution of 1962 represented a classic imperial compromise in which the Baganda monarchy won acceptance of most of its demands. Whereas Buganda was granted full federal status, the other kingdoms of Ankole, Bunyoro and Toro had to settle for a semi-federal arrangement, while the rest of the country (which mostly lacked a tradition of kingship) was divided into districts which were incorporated into Uganda on a unitary basis. To an even greater extent than in Nigeria, therefore, a plurality of systems of administration was carried over into independence. The Emirs of Northern Nigeria would have envied the Kabaka for a constitution which not only ceded extensive powers to the parliament of Buganda (the Lukiiko), including exclusive control over matters relating to land tenure, but also gave it the right to select the Baganda members of the National Assembly. It is true that the Lukiiko was mostly elected (68 seats in all), but 18 seats were reserved for the county chiefs.[70] Moreover, the political party which was founded to represent court interests, the Kabaka Yekka (KY), was virtually assured of winning the majority of the contested seats. In 1962, it actually took all 21 of the Buganda seats within the National Assembly.[71] Finally, much like in Northern Nigeria, the monarchy retained local power because it continued to appoint chiefs at the county and sub-county level, and retained its own parallel court system dispensing customary law.

A crucial difference is that whereas the NPC was assured of dominating the Nigerian federation for as long as it could monopolise the Northern vote, the Baganda were in an overall minority. The security of the monarchy therefore depended on active participation in a governing coalition at the centre, backed up by constitutional guarantees. The fact that the UPC was unable to command a legislative majority at independence initially worked to the benefit of the monarchy. By entering into a coalition with the UPC, the KY secured five out of 15 Cabinet positions. Prime Minister Milton Obote even installed the Kabaka as the President of Uganda, with the Paramount Chief of Busoga as his Vice-President. On the face of things, therefore, the Baganda monarchy seemed as comfortably placed as it could have ever have hoped to be. However, within five years disaster had struck: the monarchy was abolished and the Kabaka, along with much of his court, was forced to head into exile for a second time.

What went so terribly wrong? Part of the problem was that political allegiances in Uganda were based on relations of clientage which were inherently unstable. To be excluded from power at the centre was in effect to be cut off from material resources, which in turn risked a draining away of support at the constituency level. Soon after independence, opposition members of parliament began crossing the floor, enabling the UPC to establish an overall majority by August 1964.[72] This meant that Obote no longer needed the KY and in that year the coalition was finally abrogated. This had immediate consequences because the government set about holding a referendum in the so-called 'lost counties' which Bunyoro claimed as its own. Despite attempts to settle Baganda in the disputed area, the vote was lost and the counties were excised from the kingdom. The Kabaka appears to have realised that the tide was turning and decided to embrace entryism as a means of garnering influence in the UPC.[73] Hence many KY parliamentarians crossed the carpet in 1965 and pitched into a power struggle within the UPC.

Ironically, the UPC, which had been a loose alliance from the start, became increasingly fractured as its overall parliamentary representation increased. The KY defectors joined a conservative faction within the party and sought to protect Buganda's special interests. The 'radical' faction, which had a solid base in the trade union movement, argued for the adoption of 'scientific socialism' at home and a more militant foreign policy abroad. The 'moderate' faction was headed by Obote himself and espoused a version of 'African socialism' in which control of the commanding heights of the economy was presented as the immediate priority.[74] In the trial of strength which ensued, the radicals were the first casualties. The conservatives then directed their fire against Obote and his associates. A golden opportunity was presented by revelations that rebels in the

Congo, who enjoyed the patronage of Obote, had entrusted a large sum of money, ivory and gold to the safe-keeping of Colonel Idi Amin. The conservatives in the National Assembly waited until Obote was away and then levelled charges of corruption against Amin and a number of Ministers. The effect was devastating and for a number of days it appeared that Obote might be toppled. However, the failure of the conservatives to strike decisively presented Obote with the opportunity to regroup. At a Cabinet meeting convened to resolve the crisis in February 1966, Obote had the 'rebels' arrested by loyal troops. He also pronounced the suspension of the 1962 constitution and declared that he was assuming supreme power. In April, Obote tabled a new constitution which struck a lethal blow against the Buganda monarchy. The most crucial provisions were the exclusion of chiefs from sitting in district councils and kingdom legislatures; the abolition of the separate Buganda Civil Service Commission; the elimination of *mailo* estates tied to traditional offices; the ending of the rights of the Lukiiko to sit as an electoral college; the termination of the parallel judicial system; and more rigorous central control of finances of the former federal and semi-federal units.[75] The response of the Lukiiko was to instruct the central government to remove itself from Bagandan soil, while the Kabaka appealed for United Nations intervention.

The final showdown occurred on 23 May 1966. When rebels blocked the roads leading into Kampala and over-ran police posts, the Army responded by attacking the Kabaka's palace. Fighting continued for some days, claiming many hundreds of lives.[76] However, resistance collapsed when it became clear that the Kabaka and his Katikiro had escaped across the border into Burundi, from where they made it to Britain. The last act of the unfolding drama ensued a year later when the Obote regime finally pronounced the abolition of all the kingdoms and local legislatures. Whereas the Asante monarchy survived by making a humiliating peace with the Nkrumah regime, its Buganda counterpart was completely dismantled because it posed a greater threat to a weak leader. Of course, there remained a need for some authority at the village level to serve as an instrument of the government in power, but in 1970 Obote announced that the chiefs would henceforth be elected. It fell to Idi Amin to implement this policy three years later. This meant the ending of the ancien regime across southern Uganda, but most noticeably in Buganda where kingship had meant so much. When Amin began appointing soldiers as chiefs, the full scale of the revolution finally became apparent. It reduced chiefs in Uganda to something far more ephemeral than in either Nigeria or Ghana.

Whereas it was the political insecurity of Milton Obote which motivated the assault on chieftaincy in Uganda, much the same result was accomplished in Tanzania for the opposite reason. Here it was the emergence of the Tanganyika African National Union (TANU) as the party enjoying overwhelming African support which made it possible to envisage a world without chiefs. As in the rest of the British colonies, decolonisation was accompanied by the creation of elected local councils. When these reforms were initiated, it was intended that the chiefs would retain some representation at the local government level. However, this was unacceptable to TANU, in large part because the chiefs were believed to have been in league with the British in their efforts to weaken the party. Local TANU activists therefore took on the chiefs across Tanganyika in the years leading up to independence. In the Kilimanjaro region, Chagga modernisers had initially advocated the recognition of a single paramountcy in the early 1950s as a way of undercutting the divisional chiefs who had been the principal beneficiaries of British reforms. Chief Marealle was duly elected to the paramountcy. As an educated civil servant, he seemed to provide a perfect vehicle for the Chagga movement which also adopted a flag, an anthem and a national holiday.[77] The assertion of an intense local nationalism in Chaggaland posed a challenge to TANU which was seeking to create a Tanganyika-wide movement. Fortunately for TANU, many of the modernisers quickly became disillusioned with Marealle and began campaigning for the abolition of the paramountcy. This gave TANU a shoe-in to Chagga politics, and after the removal of Marealle there ceased to be much support for the notion of a paramount chieftaincy. This pattern was replicated across Tanzania over 1960–61, when local TANU activists succeeded in removing their chiefs.[78]

TANU equated chieftaincy with 'tribalism' and was determined to replace it with a structure which would put the party in direct contact with its rural constituency. In 1962, the chiefs lost their residual powers over law and order and in 1963 District Councils assumed all powers at the local government level. From that year onwards, chieftaincy in Tanzania ceased to exist, being replaced by elected local councils.[79] The manner in which Tanzanian socialism was played out at the local level will be addressed at greater length in the next chapter. Here it is merely worth underlining that Tanzania was unique amongst the former British territories for the lengths to which the government was prepared to go in neutralising competing sources of loyalty. As it was, TANU knew it could take on the chiefs and win.

In most former British colonies the chiefs lost almost all of the powers which they had exercised before the Second World War. They did not normally collect taxes; they were not empowered to extract forced labour, whether for local development or for their own fields; and they had no power to regulate markets. In a number of countries, the chiefs did retain some say over the allocation of land, although they were normally expected to share this responsibility with bureaucrats and local councils. Policing and adjudication had been amongst the most important functions associated with Indirect Rule, and they were amongst the first to be stripped away during decolonisation. In most countries, the chiefs had no powers of arrest and they were expected to leave criminal matters to the police. The formal court system, presided over by judges and magistrates, was vested with absolute jurisdiction in respect of crimes against the person and against property. In civil cases, the chiefs were sometimes allowed to carry out informal arbitration, but their rulings were not always considered binding by the courts. In concluding this section, it is important to take note of a partial exception to the rule, namely Botswana.

In 1964, the earlier system of 'native administration' was replaced by District Councils which were elected under conditions of universal adult suffrage. Ten years later, Anthony Sillery, a former Resident Commissioner, was struck by the dilution of chiefly prerogatives across the board.[80] However, the retention of certain judicial functions by the Botswana chiefs represented an important exception to the African rule. The chiefs' court, or *kgotla*, was formally incorporated into a national legal system which ran through the magistrate's court to the High Court at the apex. The state courts enjoyed primacy in the sense that they were also courts of first instance, while appeals from the *kgotla* were also heard at the magistrates' court and finally at the Customary Court of Appeal.[81] The jurisdiction of the *kgotla* was limited to relatively minor civil and criminal cases. Nevertheless, Anne Griffiths argues for not being taken in by formal appearances and for taking seriously the 'social contexts in which law is embedded'.[82] In a nutshell, litigants often preferred to turn to the chiefs' court rather than the magistrates' court, especially in divorce settlements. Although Griffiths is at pains to point out that women did not necessarily get a better deal from the *kgotla*, they were nevertheless able to choose the forum where they were most likely to receive a sympathetic hearing. Because the chief's court provided a setting where Tswana custom was constantly debated, contested and indeed reformulated, an astute litigant could effectively exploit his/her own local knowledge and social networks. On their side, the chiefs retained the respect of their people, but also a measure of national importance because ordinary Tswana actively chose the *kgotla* over the formal courts. In most African countries, this measure of chiefly autonomy would have been deemed threatening to state authorities. The reason why it worked in independent Botswana comes down perhaps to the relatively high level of social and political consensus in that country.

4.1.3   *Chieftaincy in Francophone Africa: Guinea, Senegal and Niger*

Having dealt with the former British colonies, I turn now to consider the fate of chieftaincy in the former French colonies. I do not wish to dwell unduly on an older debate as to whether or not British and French policies were really so different in practice. Suffice it to note that in the early days of colonial rule, all the European powers tended to act pragmatically, preserving political structures where they did not pose a threat and breaking them down where they did. But once the colonial regimes fell into their stride, there was greater scope for imperial preferences to intrude. Hence the British restored the Asante monarchy in 1935, whereas the Dahomean kings recaptured little of their power or status – a difference which is starkly apparent to this day. Again, comparative studies of partitioned Yorubaland and Hausaland have concluded that the chiefs were ultimately accorded much greater power and autonomy in British Nigeria than on the French side of the borders concerned.[83] On the whole, the French were inclined to treat their chiefs in a utilitarian fashion as instruments of European administration, whereas Indirect Rule was predicated upon a relatively autonomous sphere of chiefly decision-making. The French approach was famously stated by the Governor-General of French West Africa, Joost Von Vollenhoven, in 1917:

> The commandant de cercle alone is in command. He alone is responsible. The native chief is only an instrument, an auxiliary … The native chief never speaks or acts in his own name but always in the name of the commandant and when delegated formally or tacitly by him.[84]

The French system hinged upon a hierarchy of chiefs working beneath a European official: the village chief, the canton chief and (sometimes) the provincial chief. The French often appointed chiefs where they had never existed before and installed chiefs who were often not even from the same area as their subjects. At the same time, they frequently broke up established polities into smaller units. The chiefs were expected to carry out a range of administrative functions: including tax collection; monitoring population movements and land use; checking the spread of human and animal diseases; extracting forced labour and exercising judicial functions. If they failed to come up to scratch, they could be fined, suspended or removed from office. The measures which the chiefs were expected to enforce were often highly unpopular and because chiefs were not well-remunerated, they tended to live by exacting informal tribute and labour from their subjects.

As in the rest of Africa, decolonisation had lasting consequences for chieftaincy in the French territories. The role of the chiefs changed as the distinction between citizen and subject was abolished, along with forced labour. The French also embraced – albeit in a somewhat fitful manner – the principle of election to traditional office. In 1947, the French launched a fairly radical reform in Senegal by introducing elections for chiefs. The electors were to consist of men and women at the village level and a more select group of men at the canton level.[85] In 1957, the system actually became less democratic because the electorate was narrowed to male notables at the village level, while the candidates for election now had to come from recognised chiefly families. But it was in Guinea that the most far-reaching reforms were carried through. Here the chiefs continued to be imposed from above until 1957, which goes some way towards accounting for their singular unpopularity. When the Parti Démocratique de Guinée (PDG) gained control over the local legislature in the 1956 elections, it did so on the basis of a popular wave of anti-chiefly sentiment. In December of the following year, the PDG was able to pass a law which abolished the position of canton chief altogether. The village chief remained in place, but was henceforth to be an elected figure who carried out his duties alongside a village council.[86]

After independence, the Sekou Touré regime finally dispensed with chiefs altogether by introducing a hierarchy of elected committees. A number of villages were grouped together to form a single administrative unit, without any consideration being given to the character of earlier relationships. The elders of a given community elected a *comité de base* (base committee) while the young men and women elected a *comité de jeune* (youth committee). In an illuminating account of the operation of these parallel committees, William Derman notes that they carried out 'the organisation of co-operative work projects, collection of taxes, distribution of goods from the state, organisation of receptions for visiting dignitaries, and dispensing justice in inter- and intra-village disputes, divorce and theft'.[87] In other words, they performed most of the same functions which had previously been devolved upon the chiefs. In the highly dirigiste system which prevailed after independence (see Chapter 5), the committees were also intended to act as conduits for the flow of information and instructions from above. The area committees were grouped into sectional committees which were also elected by them. Here they came up against the *commandants d'arrondissement* who were appointed officials vested with responsibility for executing government policies as they were fed down from the provincial governors. The Guinean system was one which was tightly controlled at the top, but seems to have left some scope for local autonomy at the lower reaches. The institutionalisation of the distinction between youth and elders also built upon cultural norms at the village level. However, as Derman demonstrates, the social distinction between the old ruling elites and their former slaves was effectively eradicated as the latter came to fill most of the elected positions at the local level.

Much as Tanzania stood out from the rest of the Anglophone states, so Guinea was singular amongst the former French colonies. The country which bore some resemblance was Senegal. Here, the chiefs suffered from some of the same unpopularity as their counterparts in Guinea. In the early 1950s, Léopold Senghor skilfully presented himself as the defender of the poor peasants against the oppressive canton chiefs. Whereas the latter tended to favour the cause of Lamine Guèye, Senghor cultivated the leadership of the three Muslim brotherhoods: that is the Qadiriyya, the Tijaniyya and the Mourides.[88] Whereas chiefs had relatively little purchase over villagers, the same could hardly be said of the *marabouts* (or 'saints'). The greater societal leverage of the *marabouts* helped the Socialist Party to come out on top in the political contest. The Mourides became a particularly valuable ally as Senghor (a Catholic himself) attempted to consolidate his grip on power after independence – initially against his Malian rivals and subsequently against Mamadou Dia in 1962 (see Chapter 5). Having steered his way through successive crises, Senghor struck up a good rapport with the *marabouts*: the latter lobbied for rural amenities and in return they delivered rural votes to the ruling party. In 1960, a fundamental reform of the administration was embarked upon, which had a lasting impact on chieftaincy in Senegal. The country was divided into seven regions, headed by a governor, and these were broken down into *cercles* which more or less conformed to the earlier *subdivisions*. The real innovation lay in the creation of a third tier, the *arrondissement*, which was made up of two or three of the old cantons.[89] The canton chiefs were abolished and replaced by *arrondissement* heads. Some of the appointees had previously been canton chiefs, but this continuity was a transitory phenomenon. That left only the village chiefs, as the lowliest functionaries in the bureaucratic hierarchy. These chiefs commanded little influence or prestige, and were regarded by everyone concerned as secondary in importance to the *marabouts*, especially in the large number of villages which owed their origins to a founding religious leader.

The Malian experience ran parallel to that of Senegal, given that they did not go their separate ways until 1961. But elsewhere in Francophone Africa, the years immediately after independence were characterised by a broad measure of continuity. That is, chiefs continued to be regarded as auxiliaries of the governmental apparatus: they were merely serving a different set of political masters. They were expected to carry out official orders, and they could be sanctioned if they failed to comply.

4.1.4 Apartheid as decentralised despotism

There remains one final case which is worthy of examination in greater detail, and that is South Africa. Although the latter tends to be treated as exceptional, Mahmood Mamdani has made a convincing case for viewing apartheid as the lineal descendant of Indirect Rule.[90] Any anachronism lies merely in the fact that the NP was seeking to resurrect a formula which was in the process of being jettisoned in the British colonies. Apartheid did not come out of the blue, but amounted to a reworking of the main themes of segregationist discourse which took a tenacious grip in the 1920s, but whose origins can be traced back to the nineteenth century.[91] The central axiom was that Africans were to be treated as subjects, whereas whites were citizens bearing rights. This was why the qualified African franchise in the Cape could not be extended, and why it was ultimately extinguished in 1936. Perhaps the most crucial tenet of segregationism, which was carried over into the apartheid era, was that the cities were the exclusive preserve of whites and that Africans would only be tolerated as 'temporary sojourners' selling their labour.[92] At the end of their labour contracts, Africans were expected to return to their rural homes. Every effort was made to regulate the flow of migrant labour to the cities and to determine the conditions under which Africans lived and worked. Although *indunas* (or 'headmen') were recognised on the mines, urban Africans were without structures of representation because the authorities preferred the fiction that they really did not exist. In the rural reserves, which were construed as the true home of the African, the 'native' was to live under the authority of a chief who was, in turn, closely supervised by a Native Commissioner appointed by the Native Affairs Department (NAD).

The NP was elected in 1948 because the United Party government had failed to resolve problems with implementing segregationism. Growing impoverishment in the reserves was creating a situation in which Africans were in danger of being pushed off the land and drawn towards the cities. This threatened the foundations of cheap labour, which had always depended on the rural areas bearing part of the costs of reproduction of the labour force.[93] However, it was also threatening to ordinary whites who feared 'swamping' by a black majority in the urban areas. The Malan regime was therefore mandated to take decisive steps to restore the equilibrium. The 1913 Native Land Act had set aside a mere 7 per cent of the land for the reserves. This was raised to 14 per cent under the 1936 Native Trust and Land Act, which provided for the purchase of white farms and Crown lands by the South African Native Trust, but acute land hunger remained a face of life. Although the Native Economic Commission of 1930–32 recognised this fact, it chose to place greater emphasis on the supposedly wasteful manner in which Africans utilised the land. It therefore advocated a 'comprehensive reorganisation of rural society which would include significant reductions of stock, the fencing of lands, concentrated settlements, improved seed and the expansion of agricultural education'.[94]

In short, Africans were to be cajoled and coerced in an effort to head off the impending collapse of the reserve economy. This new technocratic mentality echoes the 'second colonial occupation' in post-war Kenya (and also in

Basutoland), and it was similarly resisted on the Trust lands and in the reserves proper.[95] One indictment of the Smuts government was that it had backed off in the face of resistance in places like the Zoutpansberg and Sekhukhuneland. The NP was also sensitive to complaints from white commercial farmers that they could not secure sufficient labour because poorer white farmers were encouraging Africans to squat.[96] The NP promised to beef up the operations of the NAD and to remove African families from white land who had not signed recognised labour contracts. The NP regime later dedicated itself to eradicating so-called 'black spots', that is areas outside of the reserves which had historically been farmed by Africans – whether on mission stations or on lands which had been purchased by them. The net effect was to push many African families into already overcrowded reserves.

Whereas the NP was initially rather pragmatic in its approach, apartheid became more ideologically driven in the later 1950s, and this had an important bearing on chieftaincy. The key figure in this transformation was H. F. Verwoerd, first in his capacity as Minister of Native Affairs and later as Prime Minister. Whereas the crude interventionism of the 1930s had tended to undermine the authority of the chiefs, Verwoerd understood that the latter were crucial to his strategy of 'retribalising' Africans – or, as he would have preferred it, of helping Africans to develop 'along their own lines'. Verwoerd regarded the partially elected district councils of the Eastern Cape and the purely advisory Native Representative Council as an anathema because they were not based on 'traditional' political forms. In their place, he advocated a return to a 'natural Native democracy'.[97] The Bantu Authorities Act of 1952 enshrined the chief-in-council as the basis on which rural Africans would henceforth be governed.[98] A three-tier system stretched from the 'tribal' authority at the bottom through the regional authority to a territorial authority for each ethnic group at the summit. These various Bantu authorities were expected to exercise a wide range of administrative, executive and judicial functions. Although this was trumpeted as promoting 'the supremacy of the Bantu in his own sphere', Native Commissioners were nevertheless expected to extend a guiding hand for the foreseeable future.[99] Moreover, once the Native Representative Council had been wound up, there was no voice for Africans at higher levels. In its commitment to an exaggerated form of cultural relativism, which conveniently precluded demands for electoral representation, Bantu Administration echoed British policies of the pre-war era.

Within the reserves, a struggle ensued over the entire raft of apartheid innovations, including conservation, Bantu Education, the extension of pass laws to women and an increase in rural taxation. The chiefs were caught between the (renamed) Bantu Affairs Department (BAD) who demanded their co-operation in New Bantu Authorities, and their people who regarded the latter as the thin end of the wedge. Alongside a physical battle for control of the countryside, in which violence was resorted to on both sides, a debate unfolded about what constituted tradition. Critics of the BAD programme pointed out that chiefs would be required to enforce unpalatable regulations and would become less accountable to their people. Such has been the fascination with urban politics that the struggles which were played out across rural South Africa have only recently begun to be properly documented. It is worth summarising some of the main findings here. In the case of Sekhukhuneland (northern Transvaal), Peter Delius has demonstrated how Pedi migrant workers were in the vanguard of opposition to the BAD. In 1955, they founded Sebatakgomo, an association whose aim was to persuade the paramount chief to stand against the creation of a Bantu Authority. The campaign in Sekhukhuneland, which enjoyed some support from the South African Communist Party (SACP) and the ANC, escalated into a attack on perceived collaborators, a number of whom were killed. The response of the state was to deport the paramount from Sekhukhuneland, while the full force of the state was used to intimidate the rebels. Once the government had re-established control, the BAD demonstrated its sound appreciation of the tactics of divide-and-rule by recognising 26 'independent' chiefs, thereby effectively downgrading the paramountcy.[100]

Another important site of struggle was in the Bafarutshe reserve on the Botswana border, where opposition to Bantu Authorities became intricately bound up with resistance to the pass laws in 1957.[101] Once again, the chief was won over to the opposition cause, which was co-ordinated by another association of migrant workers. The difference was that women played a more active part, by refusing to accept the new pass books or burning them in public. The authorities responded by deposing the chief and, in the face of physical attacks on perceived collaborators, resorting to brute force. The state had re-established effective control by 1958. A Bantu Authority was duly established and was headed by one of the loyalist chiefs, Chief Lucas Mangope. No sooner had the flames subsided than a further outbreak occurred amongst the Mpondo of the Transkei in 1960. Here a secret organisation called Intaba was formed with the aim of using violent action to forestall the creation of a Bantu Authority and the implementation of destocking, resettlement and other conservation measures.[102] The difference was that the Mpondo paramount chief – whose powers already greatly exceeded that of most of his peers – had already consented to the establishment of a Bantu Authority in 1958. The Intaba campaign was initially successful in bringing about the collapse of the local administration, but by January 1961 a police and army crackdown had reasserted the authority of the paramount chief.[103] Finally, there remains the instance of Tembuland in the Transkei/Ciskei. Here the creation of Bantu Authorities entailed the abolition of the partially elected General Council or Bunga.[104] In 1961, the paramount chief and most of the chiefs in Tembuland proper opposed this reform, but in Emigrant Tembuland (in the Ciskei) Chief Kaiser Matanzima agreed to co-operate.[105] The upshot was a very bitter struggle within Emigrant Tembuland, in which Chief Matanzima used intimidation to ensure compliance, whilst local dissidents and Poqo (the armed wing of the PAC) attempted to assassinate the chief and his allies. Whereas the ANC, the SACP and the PAC drifted in and out of the other struggles, the Tembuland case is singular because of its centrality in the PAC's plans for a general uprising. In crushing this revolt, the state put paid for all time to the thesis that South Africa was a country ripe for guerrilla warfare. The liberation movements thereafter concentrated more of their energy on mobilising an urban constituency.

After the efflorescence of rural resistance in the 1950s, the following decade ushered in a period of relative acquiescence, born of a combination of exhaustion and fear. With the banning of the ANC, the PAC and the SACP in 1960, and the issuing of detention orders against anyone construed as obstructing Bantu administration, many of the old forms of organisation (often established by migrant workers) became untenable. The strangulation of rural protest was accompanied by a further elaboration of apartheid ideology which went a step beyond the Indirect Rule canon. In 1959, the government passed the Bantu Self-Government Act which created eight (later ten) Bantustans out of the existing reserves, constituted on the principle that all Africans belonged to discrete 'tribes'. In view of the push towards decolonisation elsewhere, the Verwoerd regime felt the need to offer some kind of riposte. Given the hegemonic status of a new international discourse of equality, it was difficult for the government to simply deny its relevance for South Africa. What it did instead was to fall back upon an earlier line of colonial defence which contended that political institutions were organic and could not therefore be adopted and discarded like so many changes of clothing. The problem in South Africa, it was argued, was that white and black simply did not share a common political culture. Instead of trying to co-opt Africans into a parliamentary system which was thoroughly alien to them, would it not be better to help them to evolve their own institutions? Hence the NP's counterblast to European decolonisation was to insist that blacks would enjoy full rights within their own 'Bantu states' – dubbed Bantustans and later homelands. That this was in large part a response to external events was made clear by Verwoerd himself:

> The Bantu will be able to develop into separate states. That is not what we would have liked to see. It is a form of fragmentation that we would not have liked if we were able to avoid it. In the light of the pressure being exerted on South Africa, there is however no doubt that eventually this will have to be done, thereby buying for the White Man his freedom and the right to retain his domination in what is his country.[106]

Following suppression of the revolt in the Eastern Cape, Verwoerd pushed ahead with the grant of internal self-government to the Transkei, where he promised that chieftaincy would be safeguarded. The Transkei Constitution of 1963 provided for a Legislative Assembly in which 64 chiefly appointees outnumbered the 45 members who were popularly elected.[107] Chief Matanzima was elected Prime Minister on the strength of the chiefly vote and in the expectation that he would know how to make the most out of his client status with the South African government. Matanzima ensured that his grip on power never slipped in subsequent years. The Transkei government accepted 'full independence' from South Africa in 1976, followed by Bophutatswana in 1977, Venda in 1979 and Ciskei in 1981. In the case of Bophutatswana, the principal beneficiary was Chief Mangope, who clung to power with the same tenacity as Matanzima did. Some homeland governments stopped short of independence, most notably that of Kwazulu where Chief Gatsha Buthelezi realised that there were limited advantages to becoming 'independent' in name only. But in these homelands, the pattern of politics was much the same as in the notionally independent states. In Kwazulu itself, Buthelezi had beaten his brother to the chieftaincy because the BAD reckoned that he was more likely to support the formation of Bantu authorities. Like Matanzima and Mangope, Buthelezi became Chief Executive Officer in 1970 with support from the chiefly majority in the legislature. Where Buthelezi was singular was in the skill with which he set about turning Inkatha into a formidable political machine, reaching all the way down to the smallest settlement. Access to land, education and employment all became contingent on membership of Inkatha, which simultaneously functioned as the personal vehicle of Chief Buthelezi.[108] By refusing the offer of independence, Buthelezi signalled that he intended to act as a key player in the wider political game within South Africa.

The homelands policy suited the South African government and its homeland clients equally well. The latter were given a free hand to establish a system based on patronage, in which they could materially reward their supporters and bludgeon their opponents. The perks of office, which were underwritten by Pretoria, were also very considerable. Newell Stultz has estimated that by the time of Transkeian independence, chiefly members of the legislature were earning no less than 60 times the minimum stipend for a chief in 1963.[109] At the same time, Matanzima became the most highly paid political figure in all of South Africa.[110] On the other hand, the South African government could claim that it was within its rights to withhold citizenship rights from Africans who had other political homes to go to. In 1970, all Africans were assigned to a homeland on the basis of their presumed ethnicity, regardless of whether they even had any rural ties. The ultimate objective was to dispense of that category of Africans who had acquired urban residence rights by virtue of their birth or length of stay.[111] In their greatest flights of fancy, apartheid ideologues imagined they could whiten the cities, by forcing Africans to commute from their assigned homelands towards industrial zones created just within the boundaries of white South Africa. Any Africans who remained within the cities would be there on temporary labour contracts, having been directed there by a labour bureau. Other Africans would be channelled towards white farms by means of the same bureaucratic process. As we shall see in a later chapter, the gap between theory and reality became increasingly obvious towards the end of the 1970s, forcing significant modifications to the apartheid system.

At this juncture, it remains to consider precisely how much power the chiefs could really exercise within the homelands setup. Elsewhere in Africa, political leaders who aligned themselves with traditional rulers could not always be counted upon to respect their status once they were safely installed in office. In the homelands, this pattern was repeated. At the local level, chiefs were often able to wield considerable power over the people placed beneath them. In the case of Sekhukhuneland, which was absorbed into the homeland of Lebowa, Pedi chiefs regulated people's access to land, trading licenses, labour bureaux, and even the payment of pensions.[112] The same story was repeated in Kwazulu.[113] But while the chiefs gained leverage over their people, and ruthlessly extracted money from them through the exercise of these gatekeeping functions, it is a moot point whether the chiefs were powerful in their own right. In each of the homelands, the governing party jealously guarded its monopoly on the right to command. Chiefs were expected to toe the party line, failing which they could have their salaries suspended or be removed from office. The position of the Zulu monarchy is perhaps the crucial test-case.

King Goodwill Zwelithini came to the Zulu throne in 1971 at the very moment when deliberations over a constitution for Kwazulu were reaching a watershed. Whereas the draft constitution had made the king a member of the Assembly, an amendment was eventually adopted which reduced the king to the position of a constitutional monarch. The Chief Executive Officer was given the right to choose his cabinet unhindered, while the king was reduced to a largely ceremonial role.[114] This evidently rankled within the court, where hostility to Buthelezi ran surprisingly deep. Shortly after his coronation, Zwelithini despatched a delegation to Swaziland to study the constitutional position of Sobhuza. This was regarded as an affront to Buthelezi who set out to clip his wings. In 1975, the government insisted that all invitations to the king be sent through the cabinet who also needed to approve his travel plans. In 1979, Buthelezi even went as far as accusing Zwelithini of dabbling in party politics, and imposed strict reporting restrictions on him.[115] Unlike in Buganda, however, Buthelezi could not afford an all-out confrontation with the monarchy. After all, Inkatha positioned itself as the very embodiment of Zulu tradition in which the king was the focus of identification. In the event of a take-on, it was by no means certain that most Zulus would side with the Chief Executive rather than their king. The net outcome was similar to that in Lesotho, where the king was used as a nationalist symbol, but kept on a tight leash. As far as the chieftaincy as a whole is concerned, Buthelezi consistently stressed the importance of building upon Zulu culture, but as Maré and Hamilton suggest this vote of confidence in the chiefs was contingent on the latter's acknowledgement of his own pre-eminence.[116]

4.2 Conclusion

In this chapter, I have sought to give some sense of the different trajectories along which African chieftaincies were propelled from the 1950s. I have sought to draw an analytical distinction between formal power, influence and prestige. In Swaziland, Sobhuza II possessed all three in spades. But he was unique in the success with which he reinvented monarchy for the post-colonial age. Haile Selassie of Ethiopia ultimately failed in his attempt to marry tradition with modernisation, and paid with his life. In most African countries, the formal powers of traditional rulers were significantly reduced during decolonisation and after independence. Even regimes which were ostensibly pro-chief, such as the NPC in Northern Nigeria, found it difficult to tolerate a potential rival. Although their formal powers were reduced, chiefs nevertheless retained a measure of influence and prestige in the former British colonies. The exception was Tanzania where the Nyerere government abolished the institution outright.

In the Francophone states, the chiefs seemed to command more power, but this was not inherent in the institution but was, in a sense, borrowed from the central authority. In most Francophone states, the chiefs functioned as pliable instruments of higher authorities, pretty much as in colonial times. The exception was Guinea, where the Sekou Touré regime decided to dispense with their services altogether. Finally, I have sought to demonstrate that the NP regime sought to reinvent the notion that Africans were happiest when governed through their 'traditional' institutions. The duties which the South African chiefs were expected to perform were not unlike the unpleasant tasks devolved downwards by the French colonial authorities. According to the local defenders of chieftaincy, to comply with Bantu Administration would mean sowing the seeds of destruction of an institution rooted in consent. The defeat of these rural rebels paved the way for the further elaboration of the homelands policy, in which chiefs became the junior partners of regimes which were only loosely accountable.

5

'Ism Schisms': African Socialism and Home-Grown Capitalism, 1960–85

We are not socialists, in that we do not believe in giving priority to the distribution of wealth but wish to encourage the creation and multiplication of wealth first of all. Our major concern is with the human aspect of growth. Our system cannot be described as liberalism either, but it can be linked to a planned economy. We are following a policy of State capitalism.

President Houphouët-Boigny of Côte d'Ivoire

'Ujamaa', then, or 'Familyhood', describes our socialism. It is opposed to capitalism, which seeks to build a happy society on the basis of the exploitation of man by man; and it is equally opposed to doctrinaire socialism which seeks to build its happy society on a philosophy of inevitable conflict between man and man. We, in Africa, have no more need of being 'converted' to socialism than we have of being 'taught' democracy. Both are rooted in our past – in the traditional society which produced us.

President Julius Nyerere, 'Ujamaa – the Basis of African Socialism', April 1962

In the last chapter, we dealt with the rearguard action by 'traditional leaders' to cling to their once-exalted position in the face of the determination of politicians to concentrate and monopolise political power in the name of modernity. In this chapter, we will compare two versions of that modernist vision: namely 'African socialism' and 'African capitalism'. The African descriptor is not redundant here. As the above quotes demonstrate, the champions of each of these tendencies saw themselves as departing in significant ways from Western models – from pure economic liberalism in the one case and from classical Marxism in the second. With the benefit of hindsight, it is tempting to argue that these paths were not really so different after all, given the centrality of the one-party state in each case and the frequent use of public resources for private gain. However, this would be an overly reductionist reading, glossing over substantive differences. The fact of the matter is that Kenya and Tanzania did make very different choices after independence and these had real consequences for the citizens of both countries. Their freedom of choice ultimately proved to be much more limited than nationalist politicians imagined in the early 1960s, but it was also greater than at any other point thereafter.

There remains the problem of deciding on what basis to distinguish countries, given that many regimes spoke the language of African socialism whilst scarcely changing step after independence. In the words of Crawford Young: 'The capitalist pathway in Africa has numerous followers but few partisans.'[1] Such dissimulation is intriguing and demands an explanation. At independence, capitalism was deeply tainted by its associations with colonialism which perhaps explains a tendency to shy away from trumpeting its virtues. The capitalist-roaders preferred on the whole to present themselves as pragmatists who eschewed any ideological position – which was of course an ideological statement – but in countries like Kenya and Senegal the rhetoric of socialism was sometimes deployed by the leadership. The deeper reason appears to be that the leaderships were engaged in a dialogue at two levels simultaneously. On the one hand, they wished to convince their supporters that they were seeking to promote the welfare of the masses. On the other hand, they wished to blunt the impact of a new international discourse of human rights and democracy which could easily lend itself to interference in their internal affairs. Having just emerged from the darkness of colonialism, African leaders were reluctant to submit themselves to a new form of Western paternalism. Hence even those countries which retained close links with Europe and the United States were at pains to point out that African societies were modelled differently to Western ones, which implied that supposed universals like democracy were actually culturally relative. The countries which were closest to the West were often the most anxious to make these distinctions, because of the greater need to draw a line. This was true, for example, of Malawi where Hastings (later Kamuzu) Banda managed to manifest pro-Western sympathies at the same time as dressing in the garb of indigenous 'tradition' when it suited him. One might conclude, therefore, that the dualism identified by Partha Chatterjee did not cease to operate when independence was won: it merely mutated to fit the altered circumstances of living within the international system.[2] The socialist countries were also keen to assert their uniqueness, but for different reasons. They insisted that Western prescriptions amounted to imperialism in another guise – 'neo-colonialism' – and that Africans should have the courage to formulate their own solutions to their own special problems.

The rhetoric of capitalist and socialist regimes had a certain amount in common for the simple reason that they were dealing with a shared colonial legacy. But this is not a good reason for supposing that they boiled down to essentially the same thing. Although official statements should be taken seriously, it is far more fruitful to look at what governments actually did. Given that there were no socialist states which preached capitalism and practised the opposite, the problematic cases are the conservative regimes which spoke in the seductive language of African socialism. For the purposes of this analysis, four criteria are deployed to distinguish between regimes. The first is the perceived importance of national self-reliance. On the one hand, the socialist countries placed great weight upon breaking their ties of dependence on the former colonial power, and tended to favour non-alignment in Cold War politics. On the other, the capitalist-roaders were more prepared to co-operate with the former imperial power whilst sometimes balancing the ticket by seeking closer ties with the United States. The latter was simpler for the Anglophone than for the Francophone states because the French were extremely jealous about encroachment on what they still considered their patch. The second criterion is the extent to which the state was perceived as the leading engine of economic growth and social development. The lines are somewhat blurred by virtue of the fact that the capitalist states also envisaged a prominent role for the public sector – as evinced by Houphouët-Boigny's statement above. But an essential differences lie in the attitude towards the dominance of private (mostly foreign) capital and the willingness to promote the state and co-operative sectors at the former's expense.

The third criterion is the level of commitment to the furtherance of social equality. Although both kinds of state invested heavily in health and education, the socialist states generally sought to change the nature of the service provided and to link it to more egalitarian end-goals. The capitalist states, on the other hand, were aiming to provide more of the same, and were at best committed to achieving greater equality of opportunity (as opposed to establishing equal outcomes). Finally, the socialist regimes placed greater verbal store by the participation of the 'masses' in the political process. This is perhaps the most slippery criterion of all given that both types of state went down the route of one-partyism and tended to concentrate power at the centre. Nevertheless, there remained some differences when it came to moulding the political arena. Whereas the capitalist states tended to build their politics around patron-client relations, the socialist states sometimes endeavoured to build functioning party structures at the local level. Taken together, therefore, the application of these four criteria would place both Kenya under Kenyatta and Senegal under Senghor squarely in the capitalist corner, alongside countries like Malawi, Côte d'Ivoire, Cameroun and Gabon. Equally, they would place Nkrumah's Ghana and Nyerere's Tanzania in the African socialist corner, alongside countries like Guinea, Mali under Modibo Keita, Zambia under Kenneth Kaunda and Uganda (after Obote's move to the left).

In the next chapter, we will consider Afro-Marxist military regimes which exhibited significant differences from each of these models. Here we will examine what the socialists and the capitalist-roaders regimes sought to achieve, and evaluate their success in terms of economic performance, social development, political cohesion and cultural assertion. As an index of performance, some attention will focus on popular responses to state initiatives. Finally, rather than considering the two different types of states separately, the chapter is structured around a series of comparisons, in order to bring out the contrasts more effectively. Although the fit is never likely to be perfect, the pairings have been chosen because the countries concerned either shared a common colonial legacy (Senegal and Guinea; Tanzania and Kenya) or similar resources and potentialities (Ghana and Côte d'Ivoire). We have chosen not to consider those countries which enjoyed particularly favourable resource endowments – such as Botswana and Gabon – on the basis that this would skew the analysis.

5.1   The parable of the two brothers: Tanzania and Kenya

Our first comparison, which has become something of a standard in Africanist literature, is between the neighbouring states of Kenya and Tanzania.[3] Although they shared a common legacy of British rule, their regimes embarked upon significantly different trajectories after independence. Tanzania came to attract a great deal of international attention – often bordering on adulation – arising from Julius Nyerere's vision of an indigenous and non-doctrinaire form of socialism. By contrast, Kenya under Jomo Kenyatta came to stand for a relatively successful appropriation of capitalism.

As we will see, there is some basis to this contrast. However, none of this could have been foreseen at the time of independence. In the case of Tanzania (or Tanganyika as it was still called until 1964), the instincts of Nyerere were distinctly cautious at independence in December 1961. Nyerere, who was perhaps Africa's closest approximation to Plato's 'philosopher-king', was already thinking creatively about what kind of country he wanted to nurture. He was overtly critical of the assumption that Western models were necessarily applicable to Tanganyikan conditions. In particular, he disputed whether multi-partyism was the only meaningful index of democracy, maintaining that the African way was grounded much more in the search for consensus. In his 1962 pamphlet, 'Ujamaa – The Basis of African Socialism', Nyerere expressed his aversion to the untrammelled individualism of Western capitalist society, and argued for the extension of a communitarian ethic, which he believed still existed in rural society, to the nation as a whole.[4] The challenge was to encourage individuals to perceive their interests as lying within the pursuit of the collective good rather than in opposition to the rest of society.[5] Although Nyerere was working through his ideas at an intellectual level, TANU (the Tanganyika African National Union) was scarcely influenced by them at this early stage, although it signed up formally to the principles of socialism in 1962.

Furthermore, Nyerere was inclined to pragmatism in order to avoid a damaging rupture at independence. He imagined that the relationship with Britain would remain an intimate one, and he committed his government to the continuing employment of British civil servants for as long as it took to train up African replacements. As late as 1966, there remained as many as 400 British officers at post, almost all of whom were former colonial administrators who could look forward to pensions paid for by the Tanzanians.[6] The government also continued to recruit skilled personnel from abroad, with a heavy preponderance coming from Britain. Again, the economic orientation of the first government was striking only for its lack of ideological scruples. The Five Year Development Plan of 1964–69 continued in the same vein as the previous Three Year Plan which had aimed to promote indigenous entrepreneurship.[7] Most of the emphasis was placed upon social expenditure, especially an expansion of education which had been woefully neglected by the British.[8] Significantly, the regime expected that fully £33 million out of an anticipated £40 million designated under the new Plan would come from external sources.[9]

As Cranford Pratt has demonstrated, the switch of direction in 1967 arose from a combination of internal and external factors.[10] On the one hand, Nyerere became acutely disillusioned with the behaviour of his Western partners. In 1965, the government severed diplomatic relations with Britain over its failure to take decisive measures to head off Rhodesian UDI. This meant that Tanganyika had to go forego access to the development assistance (in the form of a £7.5 million loan) which had already been pledged. The West Germans similarly pulled the plug after the government agreed to the creation of a quasi-diplomatic mission for the East Germans on Zanzibar, while relations with the United States became strained over the latest chapter in the ongoing saga of the Congo. These various spats led the TANU regime to embrace a more independent and non-aligned position, in which the Chinese became important allies alongside middle-ranking Western countries like Sweden and Canada.[11] The initial motivations here were arguably much more nationalistic than socialist. Nyerere repeatedly insisted that if Western economic assistance had to come at the price of national sovereignty, then it was much better that the country soldier on with its own limited resources. The second reason Pratt offers for the reorientation of Tanzanian policy is Nyerere's own mounting concern about the direction which the country was heading in. Although the Five Year Development Plan chalked up some modest achievements, for example with respect of industry and cash crop production, a per capita increase in GDP of just 1.5 per cent was not likely to enable TANU to deliver on its promises of improved living standards for all.[12] Indeed, while civil servant salaries had risen substantially as Africanisation policies fed through, the living standards of the rural majority, which Nyerere consistently championed, were static at best. Nyerere regarded these signs of creeping stratification as incompatible with the furtherance of social equality, and warned that unless they were nipped in the bud the communitarian values of Tanzanian society would be eroded to the point where they would be lost forever. Moreover, Nyerere expressed increasing alarm at the manifestations of acquisitiveness and authoritarianism within TANU and the government bureaucracy.

It was, therefore, for a combination of reasons – some nationalist, others egalitarian in conception – that Nyerere tabled the Arusha Declaration of February 1967. His problem was to convince TANU that it needed to change tack. Although he enjoyed enormous respect by virtue of his combination of intellectual worldliness and practical simplicity – as reflected in his title of Mwalimu or 'teacher' – not all members of TANU were so enthusiastic about signing up to a programme which would clip their wings. As Pratt points out, however, Nyerere was extremely astute in playing the nationalist card in order to secure acceptance of socialist goals. After Nyerere first introduced the Arusha Declaration for discussion within the National Executive Committee (NEC) of TANU and received a mixed response, he announced a series of nationalisations which were guaranteed to garner public sympathy. This affected all the private banks, the leading food processing companies, the National Insurance Corporation and a number of manufacturing enterprises (where majority control was assumed).[13] There had long been an anti-foreign undercurrent within TANU, and it certainly helped that the net losers were Asian and European businessmen. Riding the wave of enthusiasm, Nyerere was able to insert other measures into the Arusha package which were less in harmony with the instincts of the party.

The Arusha Declaration, and the subsequent policy documents which fleshed out Tanzanian socialism or *Ujamaa*, consisted of five main components. The first was the principle of self-reliance which was born out of Nyerere's disillusionment with the experience of the first few years of independence. In the Declaration, Nyerere attacked the obsession with attracting external aid, which bred a dependency mentality and detracted from what Tanzanians could do for themselves by better harnessing their resources. Money, he claimed, was not the solution to Tanzania's problems:

> We are making a mistake to think that we shall get money from other countries; first, because in fact we shall not be able to get sufficient money for our economic development; and secondly, because even if we could get all that we need, such dependence upon others would endanger our independence and our ability to choose our own political policies.[14]

In a later speech, Nyerere clarified his stance when he declared that the intention was not to pursue a thoroughly autarchic path, cut off from the world economy. On the contrary, Tanzania would continue to accept foreign aid, but it had to be without political strings and in consonance with the country's priorities.[15] And these would have to be very different from those which had been taken for granted up until 1967. Whereas some variants of African socialism favoured rapid industrialisation, the Arusha Declaration proclaimed openly that 'We have put too much emphasis upon industries.' Nyerere argued that these required large-scale investments which Tanzania could not afford and which would have to be paid for by squeezing the peasantry. Long before it became fashionable to lament urban bias, Nyerere was warning about the danger of reaching 'a position where the real exploitation in Tanzania is that of the town dwellers exploiting the peasants'.[16] The Tanzanian path to development therefore, rested on keeping faith with the peasant majority.

Again, a commitment to self-reliance did not mean that there was any intention to withdraw from the production of cash crops for the global market. On the contrary, foreign exchange earnings from cash crops would remain essential to the promotion of appropriate industries. Hence the Declaration referred to the increased production of cash crops like sisal, cotton and pyrethrum, alongside food crops like maize, wheat, groundnuts as well as animal husbandry.[17] However, the task was to establish the right balance between different sectors of the agricultural economy (taking account of local conditions), as well as between agriculture and industry. Although self-reliance referred mostly to Tanzania's relations with the external environment, the Arusha Declaration also linked it to local initiative: if every tier from the ten-house cell up to the Regions became self-reliant, then the nation would itself become more so.[18] A new Tanzania was therefore to be built upon the foundations of tightly knit village communities working in close harmony to produce their wants and only calling on state resources when they really needed to.[19] By reducing their own dependency on the state, they would in turn reduce the latter's dependency on external donors, thereby creating a virtuous circle.

This brings us to the second strand within Tanzanian socialism which was the reactivation of supposedly latent socialist values. As has already been indicated, Nyerere proposed that rural society remained essentially communal in nature, although rural wage employment was on the increase in some regions. He differed from Marxist scholars at the newly opened University of Dar es Salaam because he did not believe that true class differentiation had emerged, although he accepted that the Five Year Plan had been a step in the wrong direction. The objective was therefore to bring to the fore those rural values which were in consonance with a socialist vision of modernity. His advocacy of the peasant way of life, which often bordered on romanticism, was not to be taken to mean that rural societies should remain untouched. Nyerere was too much a captive of his Western intellectual roots for that to sound like an attractive option. Like most African leaders, he was deeply steeped in a discourse of modernity which bought into the notion of progress – hence his much-quoted pronouncement that 'we must run while others walk' which assumed a clear historical destination – and indeed a manifest destiny. In practical terms, it sounded as if peasants needed to be given a nudge in the right direction. But in crucial respects, Nyerere was actually arguing for a fundamental reorganisation of rural society. Whereas peasants preferred to farm in individual family units, Nyerere contended that this was incompatible with socialism in which wealth ought to be collectively created and communally shared. He was adamant, therefore, that peasants should live together in villages rather than in a dispersed fashion as was the norm in Tanzania. They should farm collectively and assume joint responsibility for the management of social services – thereby becoming true *ujamaa* villages. The Arusha Declaration underlined the importance of 'hard work', but it was also unambiguous about what Nyerere saw as the limitations of hoe agriculture. He argued against quick-fix technical solutions in the form of expensive machinery, but he did advocate the judicious use of fertilisers and ox-ploughs and other 'modern' methods. In that sense, he remained susceptible to the sirens of modern science.

Thirdly, Nyerere placed overwhelming emphasis upon checking the emergence of acquisitive tendencies within TANU and the bureaucracy. The Leadership Code was written into the Arusha Declaration and came to be seen by many observers as a sign that the government was serious about socialism. The Code stated that no TANU or government leader – defined so as to include senior party officials, Members of Parliament, senior managers of parastatal organisations and middle and higher-ranking civil servants – could hold shares or directorships in a company, receive more than one salary or own rentable property. Although leaders were later allowed to transfer property into trust funds for their children, the Leadership Code was not watered down in any significant way. It was inscribed in the constitution of the CCM (which formally replaced TANU in 1977), and was only somewhat diluted as late as 1991. Although it may fairly be seen as 'a statement of minimum conditions of "right conduct" for leaders engaged in building socialism',[20] it altered the rules of the game in important ways. The contrast with the unfettered acquisition of wealth by the holders of power in Kenya is one that needs to be borne in mind (see below).

A fourth and related point is that the Arusha Declaration committed the government to the furtherance of social equality. Insofar as there was a tradeoff between growth and equity, Nyerere came down firmly on the side of the latter. This meant redressing the tendency for the incomes of government employees to grow faster than those of the peasant majority and beyond what the country could realistically afford. In a pamphlet entitled 'Education For Self-Reliance', which was part of the Arusha package, Nyerere developed his thesis that the inherited educational system fostered intellectual elitism and urban-centrism.[21] A radical reform of educational provision was therefore proposed which would reinforce collective values and a respect for manual labour. The post-Arusha policy framework also placed considerable emphasis upon widening access to basic education and correcting the historic disadvantages suffered by less advantaged communities. The small minority who entered University were seen as a vital national resource, but Nyerere also maintained that they represented a privileged group who owed a debt to their country cousins. The document therefore proposed that students should spend part of their time in the countryside, contributing to the national development effort. Again, the government proposed to redress the urban bias inherent in medical provision by widening access to primary health care in the villages, which would be preventative rather than purely curative in orientation. This chimed in with the mantra that it was the welfare of rural communities which would set the tone for the progress of the nation as a whole.

Finally, Nyerere maintained throughout that socialism was inseparable from the larger question of democracy which he took to be deeply ingrained in traditional society. Many Marxists argued that TANU, and later the CCM, ought to turn itself into a true vanguard party which would be better placed to foster ideological clarity and commitment. Nyerere demurred on the grounds that the party could not be democratic if it was not open to all Tanzanians. He even seemed to deny that there was a higher truth of which leaders could claim a superior knowledge. Hence while he forcefully articulated the case for the creation of *ujamaa* villages, he denied that there was any point in trying to force peasants to comply for the simple reason that 'socialist communities cannot be established by compulsion'.[22] The confidence of a community to chart its own destiny could only emerge from its own initiatives, and even when these faltered valuable lessons were learned. The first step was therefore to encourage the peasants to coalesce in village communities. There, they could be encouraged to adopt some collective practices as the first step along the road to the creation of communal farms which would be jointly owned, cultivated and managed.

However, Nyerere still did not accept that there needed to be a multiplicity of political parties. He contended that genuine democracy could thrive within a single party provided that it was solidly rooted within the primary communities; there was open debate within the party; and that the electoral principle was respected. In fact, the adoption of one-partyism predated the Arusha Declaration, reflecting Nyerere's earlier thinking on the subject. Moreover, as Pratt has suggested, Nyerere's conception of democracy was not very sympathetic to the representation of special interests.[23] The need to accommodate the Zanzibaris was a necessary compromise. But otherwise, all special pleading for ethnic and religious communities was regarded as taboo (unlike in Kenya). Nyerere argued that legitimate interest groups ought to be incorporated within the party and to strive along with everyone else for the pursuit of the common good. This legitimated the co-optation of the National Union of Tanganyika Workers (NUTA) and the co-operative movement which were turned into integral wings of TANU and the CCM. Many critics saw these measures as an attempt to muzzle potential sources of opposition, but Nyerere continued to deny that workers, for example, had an interest which could be separated from the common good. In his elaboration on the Arusha Declaration, he pointed out that wages had risen faster than was desirable, that this had contributed to falling employment levels, but most importantly that higher wages merely increased the burden on peasants.[24] Hence, the traditional trade union mentality was inappropriate when the leading employer was the public sector. Tanzanian workers forfeited their right to strike, but at the same time workers' councils were created to promote participation at the workplace. The TANU Guidelines of 1971 even invited workers to assume a more vigilant role in exposing management abuses within the public sector.

During the 1970s, when Tanzanian socialism was in its youth, there was considerable disagreement as to whether it amounted to a genuine attempt at a radical social transformation. Many commentators gave Nyerere the benefit of the doubt, in part because his case was put with such conviction and intelligence, and went on to debate the implementation. But some critics from the left, such as Issa Shivji, asserted that the Arusha Declaration was essentially a ruse which weakened the (Asian) commercial bourgeoisie to the benefit of the bureaucratic bourgeoisie.[25] Some three decades later, the heat has gone out of these debates and the import of the Tanzanian experiment is somewhat easier to gauge. It does not seem particularly illuminating – or for that matter necessary – to posit a class-based conspiracy for what transpired after 1967. Although many government directives were honoured in the breach, it is difficult to see how the Leadership Code could be construed as an optimal policy for a would-be 'bureaucratic bourgeoisie'. Equally, to blame everything on poor implementation rather downplays the agency of ordinary Tanzanians. At the heart of the tale of Tanzanian socialism lies the response of the peasants, in particular, who were supposed to be the primary beneficiaries, but who found themselves holding the short straw.

To what extent, then, did the regime succeed in fulfilling its stated objectives? Perhaps the most telling indication that all had not gone according to plan was Nyerere's tenth-anniversary speech commemorating the Arusha Declaration. On this occasion, Mwalimu – ever the teacher – issued a report card which read 'could do better'. He pointed to some notable successes, but in typically forthright fashion he pronounced that Tanzania had failed to achieve either socialism or self-reliance.[26] The mixed picture is worth examining in a little more detail. Arguably, the government went some way towards meeting two of the four core objectives identified above. First of all, it advanced some considerable way towards levelling out the social inequalities which had so perturbed Nyerere in 1967. After Arusha, the salaries of senior state officials were effectively capped, while the Leadership Code (backed up by an Enforcement Commission) narrowed the scope for moonlighting. According to Nyerere, the ratio between the highest salaries and the minimum wage fell from 50:1 in 1961 (after tax) to around 9 : 1 in 1976, which was in itself quite a feat.[27] In the countryside, the government undermined the basis for social differentiation. In some regions, party bosses interpreted *ujamaa* to mean a frontal assault on capitalist farmers whose roots lay in British rule. Goran Hyden goes so far as to conclude that over 1971/72:

> ... most of Tanzania's capitalist farming came to an end. More than half of the country's sisal plantations were nationalised. Many of the large-scale grain farms were turned into state farms or given to ujamaa villagers to farm. The last capitalist enterprise to go were the coffee estates in Kilimanjaro which were handed over to local co-operative societies in 1974.[28]

But TANU did not merely target the wealthiest enclaves of the rural economy. It also sought to reverse the policy of backing 'progressive farmers' which had been such a feature of the first two economic plans. Over 1975/76, the government finally closed down the co-operatives because they were regarded (correctly) as inefficient, but also because they were seen as the pre-serve of rural elites. In their place, the government substituted village structures which were expected to liaise with the parastatals responsible for purchasing at government-controlled prices. The government also rather rashly announced Operation Maduka which brought the sudden closure of private retail outlets in order to make way for village shops.[29] One indicator of rural equality which Nyerere repeatedly returned to was whether peasants controlled their own labour. If the ideal was for peasants to work together on communal farms, then the worst case scenario was one where poorer peasants sold their labour to richer ones. In registered *ujamaa* villages, wage employment was strictly prohibited. However, there was also a more general sense in which villagisation policies disrupted the accumulation strategies of richer peasants. Finally, there also seems also to have been some narrowing of the gap between urban and rural incomes. In 1977, Nyerere was able to report that the earnings of cash crop farmers, in particular, had risen relative to urban wages.[30]

However, while Tanzania was becoming a more equal society, the levelling tended to be downwards after 1974. In real terms, the minimum wage peaked in 1974 and then it fell precipitously, so that by 1980 the lowest wage-earner was receiving 21 per cent less than in 1970 while a middling civil servant earned 54 per cent less.[31] This trend continued during the 1980s, by the end of which the real minimum wage was about a quarter of what it had been at the time of the Arusha Declaration. Even if one takes a Byzantine array of allowances into account, the standard of living of urban workers had declined substantially. Amongst other things, this was bound to take its toll on morale and to breed illicit activity. Moreover, even if rural incomes improved somewhat relative to urban ones, the terms of trade were still running against the peasantry. McHenry suggests that the index of real producer prices for agricultural com-modities fell from 160 in 1971/72 to 108 by 1985/86.[32] At the time Nyerere tabled his report in 1977, prices had just been adjusted upwards. But in real terms, the cotton producer price still stood at 14.2 Tanzanian shillings per kilo-gram as against 17.7 cents in 1967, while the maize price remained at about the same level of 5.2 cents per kilogram. A further ten years down the road and the real cotton price had slumped to 11.3 cents while the maize price stood at 4.8 cents per kilogram.[33] Nyerere had repeatedly pronounced that Tanzanians were poor and that the most disadvantaged of all were the peasants. However, socialism was threatening to make the majority of the population even worse off in absolute terms.

A greater achievement lay in delivering basic education and health services to the hitherto neglected rural majority. The government remained true to its promise of counteracting the trend towards urban bias by building very few new hospitals, on the principle that they were expensive and served the urban minority, whilst expanding primary health care at the village level. In 1977, Nyerere could report that whereas there had only been 42 rural health centres in 1967, there were 152 of these in 1976 and still more were on the way. The number of rural medical workers had also more than doubled, and by 1978 some 8000 villages had been provided with their own dispensaries.[34] An important contribution towards checking water-borne disease lay in furnishing potable water. By 1978, some 7.7 million rural dwellers were the beneficiaries of piped water supplies.[35] Partly as a result of these various interventions, average life expectancy is estimated to have risen from 40 years in 1967 to 52 years in 1979.[36]

As a teacher, Nyerere was most heartened by the impressive strides which were taken in the educational field. Between 1966 and 1976 primary school enrolments tripled and they had tripled again by 1981. Primary education was made free in 1973 and the following year TANU committed itself to providing universal primary education by 1977. Although the target was not quite achieved, some 97 per cent of children were supposedly attending primary school by 1981. The results were the most impressive in those parts of the country which had historically received minimal access to education. Furthermore, the adult education programme succeeded in reducing illiteracy from 90 per cent at independence to 20 per cent by 1981.[37] However, the flip-side of the primary school expansion was the capping of secondary education. By 1980 Tanzania had one of the lowest secondary school attendance rates in the world.[38] This was defended on the questionable basis that very few Tanzanians would be able to acquire employment which required a secondary education. As impressive as the achievements in improving mass access to education and health facilities undoubtedly were, the capacity to sustain them depended crucially on the generation of sufficient resources to pay for them. Whereas Nyerere imagined that villagers would ultimately take responsibility for their own schools, the rural population typically saw them as the baby of government. With teachers caught in the salary squeeze, the country began to experience an endemic shortage of teachers while those who were employed inevitably spent much of their energy inventing new ways to make money.[39]

Although Nyerere spoke most passionately about equity, he did not neglect the underlying issue of economic growth. In fact, his constant reiteration of the point that Tanzania was a poor country underlined the priority of making rapid strides. This brings us to perhaps the crucial failing of the Tanzanian experiment, namely its inability to deliver the economic takeoff upon which everything else hinged. The 'modernisation' of agriculture within *ujamaa* villages was presented as the way forward. But the peasantry displayed little interest in a grand vision which required them to change their way of life in significant ways. In the wake of the Arusha Declaration, the concept of the *ujamaa* village was willingly embraced by some TANU Youth Leaguers – most notably in the Ruvuma Development Association (RDA) which had been formed as early as 1961 – and it was foisted upon peasants living in proximity to the unstable Mozambican border.[40] But across Tanzania, the idealised model of *ujamaa* villages was not taken up with any great enthusiasm. By 1969, only 400 had been recognised (alongside the 400 border villages), and most of these displayed a very token commitment to communal farming.[41] The feeling that greater urgency was required led to the launching of Operation Dodoma in 1970/71, which led to much of the population of that region being corralled into villages. By 1973, over two million Tanzanians were reported to be living in villages, but Nyerere was still unhappy and announced that all Tanzanians would be required to live in villages by 1976. This was the signal for a big push which led to more than 13 million people, representing 85 per cent of the rural population, living in villages by the conclusion of the exercise.[42]

This was undoubtedly a bureaucratic achievement of sorts, but it rested on the abandonment of the cardinal principle of consent – a point we will return to shortly. What transpires from the substantial literature on villagisation is that peasants were often simply rounded up and deposited in newly designated villages whose location was often less than optimal.[43] One gendered consequence was that women were often forced to walk further than before to find water and firewood. Peasants generally complied without overt resistance, but this did not mean that they were any more enamoured of *ujamaa* than before. Where the party or government officials applied sustained pressure, the peasants would grudgingly carry out the minimum work possible on communal fields whilst reserving their energies for their family farms. Because regional administrators were often under some pressure to show results, the very tractors which Nyerere depicted as an inappropriate technology were often thrown at the problem. However, peasants merely saw mechanised services as a chance to reduce the amount of labour-time they needed to devote to the communal farm. The evidence which exists on the relative productivity of the two types of farms is startling. Even when fertilisers were used on the communal plots, the average yields tended to be lower than on the family farms. At worst, therefore, the communal farms became a drain on resources, and at best they were a sideshow.

Quite why the government failed to transform agriculture is a matter of some debate. In a stimulating interpretation of these events, Goran Hyden argues that peasants were not particularly concerned with contributing to the national development effort. They were embedded in an 'economy of affection' which was itself rooted in the reproduction of social relations rather than a logic of economic maximisation. Hyden argues that because peasants retained control over their own land (even after villagisation) they remained 'uncaptured' and therefore impervious to government pressure.[44] The suggestion that they effectively subverted government policy by exercising their 'exit option' is broadly convincing. However, it would seem rather misplaced to argue that peasants were uninterested in growing a marketable surplus. There is no reason why

Tanzanian peasants should have been any more reticent than other African peasants in this respect. Indeed, in areas where positive support was given to peasant producers, in the form of better infrastructure and access to fertilisers, the results were often quite striking. In the southern highlands, where the World Bank participated in a programme to distribute free (later subsidised) hybrid maize seeds and fertiliser to peasant farmers, there was a marked increase in output and farm yields.[45] But in most of Tanzania, the inefficiencies of the marketing system meant delays in payment and difficulties with acquiring inputs. Hence peasants did not see any particular advantage in producing more under the conditions that pertained. If they had received attractive producer prices, been paid promptly, been provided with appropriate support services and been able to purchase a greater array of consumer goods, the story might well have been very different. However, giving the peasants the run of the market was an anathema to Nyerere who saw it as tantamount to sponsoring the twin evils of capitalism and individualism. Instead what happened was that most peasants experienced a reduction in incomes and restricted access to consumer items.

The government could fairly claim that many of its plans were blown off course by two external factors which could neither have been foreseen nor avoided. The first was the severe drought which hit Tanzania over 1973/74, which meant that from being a net exporter of maize in 1970 Tanzania became dependent upon food imports in 1974. But arguably this was less of a disaster than it seemed at the time. It may actually have helped to persuade peasants to reconcile themselves to villagisation. Moreover, food production increased markedly when better rains returned, probably because peasants were determined not to be caught short a second time. In fact by 1978 Tanzania was even exporting some foodstuffs to neighbouring countries. Because maize and cassava could be consumed within the household and easily traded on the black market, there was some incentive for farmers to switch their energies into these crops. By contrast, the production of other crops like wheat and rice remained more or less static despite a rate of population growth of around 3 per cent per annum.[46]

The second external factor was the oil price hike which struck first in 1974 and once more in 1979. The increase in the fuel import bill translated into a substantial deterioration in the terms of trade for Tanzania. This was, however, greatly compounded by the poor performance of cash crop production. This was partly a consequence of renewed peasant concern with food security, but it is also attributable to the unattractive prices which were offered to producers. In Tanzania, the real producer price for coffee was higher in 1977 than in 1967, but after 1979 it gave way. This was due to a conscious policy of taxing the crop very heavily to finance development, but it was also an indirect consequence of maintaining a vastly overvalued exchange rate.[47] The production of tea increased somewhat, while that of coffee stagnated. Cotton production declined from the early 1970s while cashew production imploded after villagisation. The official statistics are, however, inherently problematic because of the quantity of cash crops which were smuggled across national borders. The resulting squeeze on foreign exchange earnings posed additional difficulties for the struggling industrial sector. Because Tanzanian industries were engaged in import substitution, they were reliant upon imported equipment and raw materials which had to be paid for with cash crop earnings. The shortages were compounded by regular power cuts which often paralysed the industrial sector. With parastatals running at well below capacity, they became a further drain on an increasingly empty public purse. Between 1978 and 1985, the contribution of manufacturing to GDP slumped from 13.5 per cent to 6.9 per cent. The vicious circle was complete when peasants who could not acquire these goods through official channels traded their goods in neighbouring states or withdrew further from the market. Far from a vibrant rural economy stimulating the industrial sector, therefore, Tanzania found itself trapped in a cycle of negative entropy in which state industries failed to deliver the goods and peasant agriculture stagnated because it was effectively been taxed to make good the revenue shortfall. Nyerere had warned repeatedly about the iniquity of squeezing the peasants to support expensive industries, but this is precisely what transpired. Table 5.1 tells the story of economic failure in a stark and unambiguous fashion.

The implications for living standards have also been alluded to. But it is also important to observe that the downward spiral undermined one of the central pillars of Tanzanian socialism, namely self-reliance. In 1967, Tanzanian exports were sufficient to cover the import bill, but by 1976 they met only 62.6 per cent of the total and by 1985 this had fallen to 28.6 per cent.[48] The result was that Tanzania began to accumulate a substantial international debt from the end of the 1970s. Moreover, the government was unable to cover more than a small proportion of its total expenditure without recourse to foreign assistance. As Nyerere himself had predicted, dependency on donors exposed the country to

Table 5.1 Selected economic indicators for Tanzania, 1967–84 (per cent)

Indicator	1967–73	1974–78	1979–81	1982–84
Real GDP growth rate	5.2	2.5	2.1	0.6
GDP growth rate per capita	2.5	−0.9	−1.1	−2.9
Ratio of current account deficit to GDP	−2.9	−9.7	−11.7	−7.4
Ratio of debt to exports	120.6	187.1	261.1	513.1
Growth rate of real output in agriculture	2.3	4.7	−1.0	1.8
Growth rate of real output in industry	7.8	4.7	−10.2	−9.9
Growth rate of exports	3.6	−6.8	7.1	−16.7
Growth rate of imports	3.6	2.8	14.3	−8.4

Source: From the World Bank. Every effort has been made to trace the copyright holder and the publisher will be pleased to make the necessary arrangement at the first opportunity.

external pressures which might lead the country away from its chosen priorities. During the early 1980s, Nyerere resisted the aid conditionalities which the International Monetary Fund (IMF) insisted upon, on the grounds that these were incompatible with socialism. However, a country which was unable to service its debt was hardly in a commanding bargaining position. When Nyerere voluntarily retired from the Presidency in 1985, Ali Hassan Mwinyi (his successor) reopened negotiations which led to Tanzania signing up to a Structural Adjustment Programme the following year. As we will see in Chapter Eight, this committed the Mwinyi government to the abandonment of most of the policies which it had hitherto defined as integral to socialism.

Finally, it remains to consider the implications for the promise of mass democratic participation which Nyerere had always argued was vital to socialism. Nyerere had imagined that prospering village democracies would provide the stable foundations upon which institutions could be erected at the national level. But when he lost patience with the slow pace of villagisation, and accepted the need for greater coercion, this voluntarist vision was effectively abandoned. The decision to enforce socialism from above placed greater power in the hands of party officials whose popular mandate was questionable. An early warning sign came with the winding up of the RDA in 1969 because it was seen as a threat to party supremacy.[49] Although Nyerere bemoaned the authoritarianism and arrogance of party and state officials in his 1977 report, the fact of the matter is that he had helped to tilt the balance of power in their direction. From the mid-1970s, the regime seemed to be more interested in imposing its will on the rural population rather than allowing the latter to come to its own decisions. For example, when the government introduced a decentralisation policy in 1972, the goal seems to have been less about maximising participation and rather more about penetrating rural communities. Local residents were reduced to an advisory role in relation to Regional and area commissioners and development directors who decided on community priorities.[50] It was not only in the countryside where the ruling party deviated from its stated objectives. When workers responded to the revised TANU Guidelines with strikes and lockouts directed against corrupt management, the government was initially encouraging, but clamped down hard in 1973 when it seemed that the national economy might suffer. Nyerere thereafter exhorted NUTA members to concentrate on raising productivity rather than engaging in actions which the country could ill afford.[51] Partly for this reason, party structures atrophied amongst workers as much as amongst peasants.

In one residual respect, the government remained faithful to its populist roots. Although mainland Tanzania was a one-party state, legislative elections continued to be held every five years on the basis of a choice between candidates. The proportion of Members of Parliament (MPs) who failed to secure re-election was remarkably high: that is, 58 per cent in 1965, 61 per cent in 1970 and 48 per cent in 1975.[52] On each occasion, Ministers were amongst the casualties. In 1980, when economic conditions reached a nadir, voters once more rejected more than half of the sitting MPs whom they appeared to blame for their plight. These results demonstrate that voters did have some say in the choice of their leaders. Nevertheless, the problem was that Parliament itself became a relatively toothless body. Real power lay in the bureaucracy and in the higher echelons of the party. And although party officials were themselves subjected to the electoral test, when active party membership declined in the 1970s officials became less accountable in practice. We can conclude, therefore, that while democracy was sacrificed in the interests of a developmental agenda, the latter failed to produce the promised benefits. Even the improvements in health and educational provision began to recede as state coffers ran dry. If Nyerere's tone was suitably sombre in 1977, there was no disguising the pervasive sense of disillusionment by the time of his retirement eight years later.

The path which Kenya pursued after independence could not have looked more different. Here, the question of equity came to be subordinated to the quest for economic growth along overtly capitalist lines. This was no more pre-ordained than was the adoption of socialism in Tanzania. The grassroots radicalism which manifested itself during Mau Mau suggests that the country might have gone down a different path. The fact that it did not has everything to do with the comprehensive manner in which the rebels were defeated, the class character of the independence settlement and the strategies adopted by Kenyatta. Tanzanian socialism amounted to something because Nyerere was able to impose his will on a party which had, in turn, placed its stamp on the country at large. In Kenya, things panned out very differently for two related reasons. First of all, the transfer of power was linked to the equally delicate issue of land reform. The manner in which this was effected was crucial because it led to the deepening of capitalism in Kenya. And secondly, land reform unleashed fierce competition between rival parties and factional interests which rendered any concept of 'general will' highly implausible. These two distinctive features of the Kenyan experience are worth examining in a little more detail.

As has already been seen in Chapter One, the Million-Acre scheme was a cornerstone of the decolonisation package in Kenya. The objective was to allow those white settlers who wished to leave Kenya to dispose of their farms at favourable prices (taking 1959 as the base year), whilst redistributing enough land to take the sting out of the issue. The first was facilitated by external loans derived from the World Bank, Britain and West Germany. The second hinged on a closely managed pattern of resettlement based on individual title rather than communal tenure (as distinct also from state control which was asserted in Tanzania). In the process, two crucial distinctions were made. On the one hand, the so-called White Highlands were divided into areas which were suitable for large-scale plantation agriculture and ranching – which were expected to continue as before – and the mixed farming areas which were considered suitable for resettlement. Within the resettlement zones, a further distinction was made between 'high density' and 'low density' schemes. Under the first, which had the financial backing of the World Bank, white land was made available to African 'yeoman' farmers who had hitherto been prevented from owning land in the Highlands. 'High density' resettlement involved the allocation of smaller parcels of land to ordinary peasant families, many of whom had previously been squatters. The latter were subjected to conditions which included farm plans and a package of credit and services to meet the targets which was supervised by government officials.[53] The land resettlement programme was a delicate balancing act: although the intention was to assuage land hunger, this was not to come at the expense of production for the market. To all intents and purposes, then, land resettlement was about the spread of rural capitalist relations to include Africans who had previously been seen as merely fit for labouring jobs.

Who, then, were the beneficiaries and who were the casualties of land reform? Ordinary white farmers must be counted amongst the winners because they were given a choice between selling up at attractive prices or remaining on the land. Christopher Leo demonstrates that much of the land which ended up being classified as 'high density' was of such poor quality that it would otherwise have been unmarketable.[54] Equally, the future of the large plantations and ranches was guaranteed under this arrangement, and after independence substantial investments in tea, coffee and sisal were made by multinational companies such as Brooke Bond and Lonrho.[55] It was also the case that certain Kenyans (mostly those with good political connections) were able to raise loans to purchase the 'large farms' which had been excluded from the resettlement schemes – a practice which Ngugi wa Thiong'o drew attention to in his novel, *A Grain of Wheat*.[56] Indeed by 1977, 57.5 per cent of the large farms had changed hands.[57] Another important set of winners were the African farmers who received bank credit and better land in the 'low density' schemes. As a result, many were well-placed to take full advantage of the export market for commodities like coffee, tea and pyrethrum as well as the internal market for dairy produce and maize. But there were also many ordinary peasant families who benefited from land reform as well. By 1970, more than two-thirds of the European mixed farms had been turned over to Africans and seven years later only some 5 per cent of this land still remained in white hands.[58] This did not, however, resolve the phenomenon of landlessness. The real losers were the landless peasants who had lost access in the former reserves and who were not included in the resettlement programme. One might also mention many of the settlers who were forced to pay for sub-standard land. The poorest sections of Kenyan society were largely excluded from the fruits of the capitalist development path which was pursued with gusto by the Kenya African National Union (KANU). Although Nyerere believed that Tanzania had gone too far down this same path in the early 1960s, this was as nothing compared to the head of steam which was built up in Kenya in the early 1960s.

The lack of a political consensus in Kenya was closely related to the working through of land reform. An underlying factor is the very different quality of land in Kenya. Much of the country is either too arid for arable farming (89 per cent is unsuitable) and/or prone to tsetse fly, whereas the White Highlands, the Rift Valley and parts of the adjoining reserves were ideally suited for the production of a range of food and cash crops and livestock rearing. As the Highlands ceased to be 'white', it was perhaps inevitable that they would become the prize around which competition would centre. The Kikuyu had experienced the most acute land hunger and had moved into the Highlands as squatters during the inter-war period. Although they had failed to secure title to land, this looked set to change once land reform was squarely on the agenda. Because it was landless Kikuyu who had fought during Mau Mau, they were always the most likely to be targeted for resettlement. Hence the Department of Lands and Settlement, earmarked some 40 per cent of the resettlement land for the Kikuyu, although they made up only 20 per cent of the total population.[59] This was deeply resented by other peoples, especially in the Rift where the Kalenjin perceived the Kikuyu as interlopers. As Robert Bates has demonstrated, the fact that elected regional governments were given some control over implementation of land reform enabled Kalenjin politicians to frustrate plans for the settlement of Kikuyu.[60] The latter responded angrily with the resumption of the oathing which had preceded the Mau Mau outbreak.

The peoples who competed with the Kikuyu in the Rift Valley, namely the Kalenjin and the Abaluhya, mostly lined up behind the Kenya African Democratic Union (KADU). On the other hand, the Kikuyu and the Luo, who were not directly affected by the land issue in the Highlands, tended to support KANU. Ever the wily politician, Kenyatta was able to detach Abaluhya supporters from KADU by exploiting their own land rivalries with the Kalenjin in the Western Rift, and then to offer sweeteners to the remaining KADU politicians if they agreed to merge with KANU, which they did in November 1964.[61] As a result, much of the land designated for resettlement in the Rift Valley was designated as land suitable for large-scale farming, which enabled the Kalenjin elite to acquire their own substantial farms with bank loans.[62] This compact between ethnically based elites prevented the struggle over land from escalating into local warfare. But crucially for our purposes, it was contingent upon the advancement of rural capitalism. Whereas Tanzanian socialism was supposed to solidify attachment to the nation, it was the opportunity to pursue material gain which was counted on to smooth ruffled feathers in Kenya.

This is not to deny that there was also an undercurrent of ideological contestation. Within KANU, there was a solid core of MPs who argued that the party owed a responsibility to the rural poor. Amongst these was Bildad Kaggia who was one of the militants who had covertly organised oathing in the early 1950s. In June 1964, Kenyatta pressured Kaggia into resigning from the government after his repeated criticism of the implementation of land resettlement. Another was Oginga Odinga who was engaged in a tussle for influence within KANU with Tom Mboya, a fellow Luo and the most articulate spokesmen for a policy of continuity. Within Parliament, the leftwingers established a powerful backbench lobby which threatened to defect to KADU unless the government modified its stance and signed up to a socialist programme. Although the leftwingers were outmanoeuvred when the KADU leadership agreed to join KANU, the government was evidently rattled by the criticism and sought to repackage its policies. In 1965, the government published its master document entitled *African Socialism and Its Application to Planning in Kenya*. In the introduction, Kenyatta described government policy as a form of 'Democratic African Socialism', explaining that '[W]e rejected both Western Capitalism and Eastern Communism and chose for ourselves a policy of positive non-alignment.' However, it was clear from the small print that this was a conception of socialism which placed economic growth first and expected societal benefits to result from the trickle-down effect. Hence it was baldly stated that:

> Other immediate problems such as Africanisation of the economy, education, unemployment, welfare services, and provincial policies must be handled in ways that will not jeopardise growth.[63]

The critics within KANU were not satisfied with rhetorical commitments to socialism and in March 1966 they seceded to form the Kenyan People's Union (KPU). The KPU adopted an avowedly socialist platform, whilst attacking KANU for its cynical use of socialist language at the same time as its members were pursuing capitalism and amassing personal wealth. In the words of Odinga:

> These politicians want to build a capitalist system in the image of Western capital-ism, but are too embarrassed or dishonest to call it that. Their interpretation of independence and African Socialism is that they should move into jobs and privileges held by the settlers.[64]

The latter was actually a pretty accurate depiction of what KANU was seeking to achieve: that is, the aim was to dismantle the special advantages which had accrued to the Asian and European minorities and to open the doors of accu-mulation to Africans. This was apparent with respect to land, of course, but it was also true of commerce which had traditionally been dominated by Asians. Under the rubric of Africanisation, trading licenses were confined to citizens, which in practice meant Africans. The Kenya National Trading Corporation (KNTC), which assumed a commanding position in the import-export trade, channelled much if its transactions through approved African agents. This meant that a minority of Africans were able to break into the preserves of the Asian petite bourgeoisie and to prosper accordingly.[65] The KPU differed from KANU in advocating a greater measure of state control over the economy and a more equitable distribution of resources, in the direction both of the landless poor and the less endowed parts of the country (including the Luo areas). This was not exactly revolutionary stuff, but it was enough to present KANU with a problem. In 1969, this was resolved when the KPU was banned and its leaders detained. From this point onwards, Kenya became a *de facto* one-party state.[66]

Strikingly, though, the monopolisation of power by KANU did not mean the ending of political contestation. On the contrary, it simply led to the formalisa-tion of factions within KANU. Kenyatta swiftly centralised governing powers within the Office of the President, but unlike Nyerere he was not particularly averse to the existence of factions within the party. In fact, he rather enjoyed playing them off against each other in such a manner as to enhance his own dominance within the political arena. Politicians who were promoted today were likely to be cut down tomorrow if they over-reached themselves. Something of this nature may have happened to the hapless Mboya. The latter had assumed a leading role in defending government policies in the early years of independ-ence. With Odinga out of the way, his position was stronger than ever, which led to whispering within KANU about his leadership ambitions. Even Kenyatta was reputedly worried. In July 1969, Mboya was shot dead in the streets of Nairobi in one of the most notorious of a string of high-profile assassinations after independence.[67] As Kenyatta visibly ailed in the mid-1970s, the question of the succession set in motion a furious bout of internal jockeying for position which we will consider in greater detail below. Under the constitution, Vice-President Daniel Arap Moi (one of the KADU converts) would step in as acting President in the event that Kenyatta died in office. In 1976, a group of prominent Kikuyu MPs launched a campaign to amend the constitution in an attempt to forestall such an eventuality. The stakes were high because the losing side in the race for the succession might well find itself cut out of governmental office and therefore the patronage that came along with it. Business and politics were thoroughly intertwined by this point. Many of the members of the campaign to block Moi were also members of the Gikuyu, Embu and Meru Association (GEMA) which had been founded in 1971 as the business arm of powerful Kikuyu interests within KANU. For these politicians, the future of GEMA hinged upon having access to bank credit and other preferential treatment. They feared that Moi would shift patronage to his own supporters if he should succeed to the Presidency.

These intrigues did not take place only in smoke-filled rooms. Like Tanzania, Kenya retained a system of competitive elections under the regime of the one-party state. It was clearly in the interest of faction leaders to have as many MPs on their side as possible. However, parliamentary nominations came from the local party committee, which required prospective candidates to curry favour. With some surprising echoes of Nyerere's self-reliance, Kenyatta repeatedly insisted that government could not provide all the amenities which the population expected. Much would have to come through local self-help or *harambee*. Hence *harambee* rallies (or *barazas*) became an important political forum at which would-be candidates were expected to demonstrate their largesse. Those who did not have the material means to dig deep depended upon the help of others who did, and this is where the support of faction leaders came in. In fact, politicians spent much of their time attending and contributing to each other's *harambee* events, thereby establishing ties of political affinity and personal dependency. This system generated extended chains of clientage, leading from the remotest rural localities to the epicentres of power. To some extent, it forced 'big men' to justify themselves to the ordinary people, although the latter often had to struggle to make their voices heard – literally as well as figuratively.[68] This setup naturally reinforced the tendency towards private accumulation, by fair means or foul, because every MP had to continue giving generously lest he/she be jettisoned by the local party. Hence the kind of Leadership Code which Nyerere imposed upon Tanzania was simply unimaginable in Kenya where the entire political system was lubricated by money.

Above, we evaluated the success of Tanzanian socialism in terms of the criteria laid down by TANU/CCM itself. It would be clearly be pointless to judge KANU by the same criteria because it was attempting to do something very different. We need therefore to consider the success of KANU in terms of three criteria which were stipulated by the government itself: (1) to what extent did the government succeed in its quest for rapid economic growth? (2) to what extent did any of the benefits of that growth trickle down? (3) did the one-party system contribute to a sense of national identity whilst taking the edge off ethnic rivalries? To begin with the question of economic growth, the data is unambiguous. In the first decade after independence, GDP grew very rapidly at around 6.8 per annum. However, growth began to slow in 1973, falling back to 2.4 per cent in 1976. The economy bounced back during the next two years when tea and coffee prices were extremely buoyant, but when commodity prices dropped more sluggish growth rates returned, averaging around 3.2 per cent for the period 1981–85. If one takes the years of abnormally high commodity prices out of the equation, then the economy was actually growing slower than the rate of population increase from about 1974 onwards. This casts some doubt on Crawford Young's estimation that the growth rate was 'impressive'.[69] But if one compares Kenyan growth rates not just with those of Tanzania (which were appreciably lower), but with the rest of Africa its performance is placed into some kind of perspective. Between 1960 and 1970 Kenya recorded an average growth rate of some 6.0 per cent, compared to an average of 4.5 per cent for low-income countries and 5.9 per cent for oil-importing middle-income countries. Between 1970 and 1979, it actually averaged 6.5 per cent, as opposed to 5.5 per cent for its competitors amongst middle-income countries. This is significant because Kenya was struck by a number of adverse factors beyond its control. In 1973 and again in 1979, Kenya was hit by steep oil price rises. In 1977, the collapse of the East African Community and the closure of the Tanzanian border damaged much of its inter-regional trade. In 1984, the country also experienced a devastating drought.[70] Of course, many of the same factors impinged on other African economies as well. The point is, however, that Kenya withstood the external shocks with greater success than most (see Appendix 5.1).

The other point which needs to be made is that the growth was evident both in agriculture and in industry. Between 1965 and 1980, the agricultural sector grew at an average of 5 per cent per annum as against a mere 1.6 per cent in Tanzania.[71] There was a steady growth in output of cash crops like coffee and tea, and a more jagged upwards movement in the production of foodstuffs like maize. At the same time, the industrial sector underwent periods of very rapid expansion. Between 1968 and 1974, manufacturing was growing at about 9.3 per cent per annum, before slowing to almost nothing in 1975. The commodity boom years witnessed a renewed expansion in double-figures before falling back to an average of 4.1 per cent between 1981 and 1985.[72] These swings reflected many of the external factors already alluded to. On the whole, one can conclude that Kenyan economic performance was above-average in relation to the rest of Africa and well ahead of Tanzania.

However, an obsession with growth statistics can all too easily detract from the basic question of what development really means. Not everyone was so impressed by the Kenyan achievements, even at their apogee. There were many who wondered whether Kenya was not a classic instance of a country experiencing growth without development. Indeed, this lay at the centre of the so-called 'Kenya debate' which almost matched the debate about Tanzanian socialism for its intellectual intensity. In the 1970s, underdevelopment theorists like Samir Amin and André Gunder Frank were advancing reasons why capitalism could not be indigenised in the Third World. Many of those who studied Kenya were struck by the dominance still exercised by foreign capital. Kenya seemed to represent a classic instance of neo-colonial dependency in which the governing classes simply lived off the scraps that fell from the table of foreign capital rather than constituting a genuine bourgeoisie.[73] A second argument, which was often raised alongside the first, was that while limited growth had undoubtedly made some compradors rich, it had not benefited the majority of the workers and peasants. This point will be considered in greater detail when we come to evaluating government success in fulfilling the second criterion. But lets us first consider the first indictment of the Kenyan model.

It would be hard to deny that much of the wealth of the Kenyan elite was derived from unproductive activity such as speculation and the accumulation of nominal directorships on the boards of foreign companies. But Nicola Swainson has observed that while the initial African advances were made in farming and the retail trade, by the mid-1970s there was a shift into manufacturing activity where the rates of return were thought to be higher.[74] Most of the investment lay in what 'could best be described as "light industry": iron and steel products, pharmaceuticals, oil filters, leather, shoes, soap, radios, food and beverages'.[75] The Industrial and Commercial Development Corporation (ICDC), which had previously assisted African traders in displacing their Asian competitors, facilitated the transition with access to relatively soft loans. It has been estimated that by 1977 some 60 per cent of the equity in manufacturing actually came from Kenyans, although this included quite substantial state investments.[76] Interestingly, Swainson suggest that the GEMA Holdings Corporation, which began as an instrument of Kikuyu political interests, began to look like more of a business concern over time. It was managed by professional businessmen and maintained an increasingly diversified portfolio of investments in property, agriculture and manufacturing. She points out that while GEMA engaged in joint ventures with foreign capital, it also set up industries in direct competition with foreign firms. While foreign capital was always well-placed in Kenya, Swainson and others have argued that it would be a mistake to imagine that the state simply did its bidding. In reality, the Kenyan government was subjected to considerable pressure from indigenous entrepreneurs to rein in foreign capital. Hence multinationals were forced to sell a substantial proportion of their shares to Kenyans, while pleas for the protection of 'local' industries were sometimes entertained. Like Swainson, Colin Leys also argued that the Kenyan bourgeoisie showed definite signs of establishing itself as an autonomous force capable of performing the progressive role of national bourgeoisies elsewhere.[77]

Although much of the evidence is compelling, Steven Langdon argued very persuasively that none of this added up to the likelihood of sustained capitalist development in Kenya.[78] On the one hand, he revealed that a good deal of manufacturing activity continued to reside in the hands of the subsidiaries of multinational companies. These tended to be very capital-intensive and to rely on materials imported from their parent companies rather than delivered by local suppliers. On the other hand, he demonstrated that the Kenyan capitalists identified by Swainson were those who tended to mimic the strategies of the multinational firms, with whom they were often directly involved. The net result was that new industrial enterprises provided little employment, fostered few linkages with the internal economy and contributed to the pressure on foreign exchange. Although Langdon accepted that external factors sometimes impinged on the situation, his assessment pointed to deep-seated structural weaknesses in the Kenyan economy. When commodity prices were high, these were momentarily concealed, but the inevitable consequence of economic expansion was that imports flooded in and generated trade imbalances. The Kenyan authorities could only square the circle by increasing the export of man-ufactured goods. With the collapse of the East African Community, the regional market was effectively closed. Moreover, while there was some scope for penetrating the European market after the Lomé Convention, foreign capital displayed little interest in setting up export-oriented factories in Kenya.

By the early 1980s, the Kenyan government was evidently losing the economic battle as trade imbalances became endemic and as the debt burden accumulated at an alarming rate.[79] The point when the Kenyan miracle was definitely finished was when the Moi government was forced to embark on its own Structural Adjustment Programme in 1983. Although market reforms were in some respects less difficult to swallow than for the Tanzanians, the cap-italist fabric of Kenya was honeycombed with government controls of one kind or another. To give in to IMF conditionalities therefore amounted to an admis-sion that Kenya had got it (or parts of 'it') wrong. Hence Kenya and Tanzania ended up in more or less the same position in the 1980s, despite seeming to set out on very different routes.[80] In a sombre reassessment of the Kenyan experi-ence, Colin Leys concedes that the indigenous bourgeoisie had failed its historic mission of generating sustainable capitalist development:

> On the contrary, it remained deeply permeated and divided by ethnic conscious-ness, still strongly reliant on political influence (rather than market competitiveness) for its profits and security, and still rather ignorant of and unsympathetic to the needs of modern industry, hardly any of which it owned.[81]

But if Kenya never broke out of its import dependency, it was still in a far stronger bargaining position than Tanzania.[82]

At this point, we turn to consider whether there was any discernable trickle-down, as had been posited by the Kenyatta regime in 1965. One conclusion which is fairly uncontroversial is that Kenya became a much more unequal coun-try after independence. While the racial barriers were removed with little delay, nobody has seriously denied that the gap between the haves and the have-nots widened markedly – only attenuated by the somewhat notional responsibility of the haves to help their poorer kinsmen and 'tribesmen'. The wealthiest section of the Kenyan population, who tended to be politically well-connected as well, consisted of those who were able to acquire the best land for commercial farm-ing in the early 1960s and then diversified into other business activities. The poorest sections of society were the landless peasants, estimated at 17 per cent of all households in 1972, who were forced to work for others and whose num-bers were constantly augmented because of Kenya's rapidly expanding popula-tion. To them one needs to add the growing mass of urban dwellers who struggled to scrape a living as best they could within the informal sector, hav-ing fled the rural areas. By the 1980s, Nairobi was growing at 11 per cent per annum, but many other urban centres were swelling at an even faster rate.[83] In Kenya, as in many African countries, women tended to make up a small fraction of those in formal wage-employment and to be heavily concentrated in farming and the urban informal economy. Sharon Stichter concludes that '[T]hey are part of the underside of capitalism in Kenya, and are among those who lose out in the game of uneven development'.[84] In the middle of Kenya's class hierarchy was a solid wedge of peasant farmers, producing for the market as best they could, as well as petty traders and urban workers.

There has been some debate as to whether the Kenyan path to development tended to lead to absolute impoverishment. On the positive side, there is broad agreement that land resettlement was followed by a rapid expansion of peasant production for both the domestic and export markets. Indeed, the success story of Kenyan agriculture derived very largely from the ability of smallholders to take advantage of price incentives. Whereas the Tanzanian state squeezed rural producers, the Kenyan state maintained attractive producer prices and reaped the reward. Moreover, the key to the success was the middling sort of peasant family. Leo, for example, found that whereas the 'high density' farmers received some of the most marginal land, they were often far more productive than their 'low density' counterparts, many of whom became absentee farmers.[85] In a study of the Central Province (Kikuyuland), Michael Cowen has actually made a good case for regarding market-oriented production as a leveller in terms of the incomes of middle peasants.[86] But then middle peasants were only one section of the rural population. Leaving aside pastoralists, who tended to be left out of the reckoning, the path of rampant capitalism produced its casualties. Rising land prices precluded poorer peasants from ever being likely to buy land. Moreover, some of the least successful beneficiaries of land resettlement were forced to sell off part of their landholdings.[87] Within the peasantry, therefore, government policies led to a widening of income differentials which left the poorest sections of society on the very margins. When environmental vagaries suddenly threw an additional spanner into the works, as in 1984/85, the hardship was acute, even if famine was avoided. On balance, however, the majority of peasants probably found themselves somewhat better off by the end of the 1970s by comparison with the early 1960s.

The matter of equity cannot, of course, be reduced to income levels alone. It is also worth considering how well the Kenyan model served the needs of its population. The policy document of 1965 made no bones about the limited ability of the state to provide all of the social services which Kenyans expected of it. Its proposed solution was partly to expand the size of the economic cake, foregoing expenditure today in order to fund better services tomorrow. Its second solution lay in encouraging communities to fund as many of their own services as they could through self-help. Education was one service on which Kenyans placed particular importance, and it not too surprising that it came to consume anywhere between 11 and 20 per cent of the government budget. The Kenyan approach to educational provision inverted the priorities which were laid down by the Tanzanian government. Whereas the latter favoured expanding primary education, an official Commission in 1965 argued that the expansion of secondary education should come first. In fact, this pattern was already on the way to being established. Hence primary school enrolment only increased by 3 per cent between 1964 and 1966, whereas secondary school enrolments increased by 76 per cent. And in the period up to 1979, the number of secondary schools increased eightfold while primary schools less than doubled. Although primary education was not the stated priority, there was nevertheless a steady increase in enrolments, so that by 1978 over 85 per cent of children of primary school age were in schools where they no longer had to pay fees. The Kenyan government also made a conscious effort to expand University education. Two new Universities were created, and the Kenyan student body swelled from 536 in 1963/64 to 7000 by 1978/79.[88] Whereas the Tanzanians were keen to lower popular expectations of urban employment, the Kenyan Holy Grail of economic growth was itself contingent upon having a much more skilled workforce.

The considerable achievements on the educational front were slightly diminished by three considerations. One was that much of the educational expansion was in the form of *harambee* schools which entered the formal statistics, but which were poorly resourced. However, it is a moot point whether these were any worse than the crisis-ridden Tanzanian state schools by the early 1980s. The second is that the expansion tended to favour the wealthier parts of the country, notably the Central Province, whereas those regions which had historically been disadvantaged (such as the Coast and North-eastern Provinces) remained so. By contrast, the Tanzanian government embarked on a conscious policy of levelling out historic inequalities by means of quotas. Finally, whereas girls' education caught up substantially, boys still made up 53 per cent and 60 per cent of primary and secondary school enrolments respectively in 1978 (see Table 5.2).[89]

Next to education, health was the most important social service provided by the Kenyan state, consuming anywhere between 4 and 7 per cent of the annual budget. Here, all the indicators pointed towards significant improvements. Between independence and 1978, the number of doctors in the country increased from 948 to 1596 and the number of nurses rose from 2308 to 6388. Although there was an increase in the number of hospital beds, the government

Table 5.2 Comparative school enrolments in Kenya and Tanzania, 1962–91

Year	Kenyan	Tanzanian	Kenyan	Tanzanian
	Primary	*Primary*	*Secondary*	*Secondary*
1962	n/a	518,663	n/a	14,175
1963	892,000	n/a	31,000	n/a
1966	n/a	740,991	n/a	23,836
1968	1,210,000	n/a	101,000	n/a
1973	1,816,000	n/a	175,000	n/a
1976	n/a	1,954,442	n/a	39,947
1978	2,995,000	n/a	362,000	n/a
1981	n/a	3,538,183	n/a	38,524
1983	4,324,000	n/a	494,000	n/a
1988	5,124,000	n/a	540,000	n/a
1989	5,389,000	n/a	641,000	n/a
1991	5,456,000	3,507,3884	614,161	166,812

Sources: Adapted from Brian Cooksey, David Court and Ben Makau, 'Education for self-reliance and harambee', in Joel D. Barkan (ed.), *Beyond Capitalism and Socialism* (Boulder and London: Lynne Rienner, 1994), pp. 204, 209; Lene Buchert, *Education in the Development of Tanzania, 1919–1990* (Oxford: James Currey, 1994), pp. 110–11.

also went some way towards improving primary health care. Together with rising incomes for the majority, improved access to health care contributed to rising life expectancy. Whereas at the time of independence it stood at only 44 years, it had risen to 55 years in the 1970s. However, there were once again marked regional disparities. In the Central Province, the female life expectancy rose to as high as 63.6 years, whereas men ranked substantially below that figure in the poorer regions.[90] Some of these achievements displaced the problems elsewhere. For example, a declining infant mortality rate contributed to a galloping rate of population growth which was close on 4 per cent by the 1970s – reputedly the highest in the world. Inevitably, this created the need for a further expansion of schools and health facilities, as well as increasing land pressures.[91] By the mid-1980s, the Kenyan government was finding it difficult to manage its internal finances while growing food imports added to the accumulating trade imbalance. Although Kenya was not as stricken as Tanzania, it was nevertheless evident that a growth-led strategy had failed to generate the means to pay for expanding social services. When the IMF finally stepped in, its conditionalities required the paring back of government expenditure at the expense of much which had been achieved. On balance, therefore, one can conclude that there was a measure of trickle-down in Kenya. The living standards of most Kenyans improved appreciably in the two decades after independence: incomes were higher, social services were more in evidence and Kenyans were living longer. On the other hand, Kenya was a more unequal place than it had been in 1963, and for a sizeable minority conditions actually got worse.

Finally, the Kenyan model needs to be assessed in terms of its political dividends. Although Kenyatta presided over the creation of a one-party state, he gave it only a cursory ideological gloss. The principal defence of the one-party state was that it was more conducive to national unity, whereas multipartyism tended to breed 'tribalism'. But whereas allusions to ethnicity, region and religious difference were frowned on within TANU/CCM, these were the very stuff of internal politicking within KANU. After the winding up of KADU and the banning of the KPU, the struggle over resources was taken into the heart of the party and was played out there in part through the language of alterity. As David Throup and Jennifer Widner have both pointed out, Kenyatta succeeded in maintaining a delicate balancing act in the early years of independence.[92] He rewarded Kikuyu loyalists with land and business opportunities, but at the same time he endeavoured to buy off former Mau Mau sympathisers with the promise of land. Under Kenyatta, government spending tended to be disproportionately concentrated on the Central Province, while land reform in the Rift Valley equally benefited Kikuyus more than other groups. At the same time, Kenyatta constructed a network of support which rested heavily upon his Kiambu home-base. After his release from jail, he had married into two prominent Kiambu families, those of Koinange and Muhoho. He had also solidified his position by means of tactical alliances with Charles Njonjo, Arthur Magugu and Munyua Wanyaki, who were powerful local leaders whose forebears had profited from collaboration with the British. Finally, he drew in some prominent leaders from more marginal parts of Kikuyuland, notably Mwai Kibaki from Nyeri and Julius Kiano from Murang'a.[93]

The Kenyatta regime was heavily Kikuyu in complexion. According to Throup, around 30 per cent of Cabinet positions were held by Kikuyus, while the inner circle, known as the 'the Family', consisted of Mbiyu Koinange (his brother-in-law), Njonjo, Kiano, Kibaki, Njeroge Mungai and James Gichuru – all of whom were Kikuyus.[94] The danger was that non-Kikuyus would feel left out, but Kenyatta was adept at buying off those leaders who posed the greatest potential threat. Daniel Arap Moi was rewarded for his loyalty by being given the Vice-Presidency and Home Affairs, although he always remained outside the inner circle. At the same time, the continuation of land settlement in the Rift Valley and the rapid economic expansion in the decade after independence meant that the national cake grew sufficiently for non-Kikuyus to have something to gain by accepting the rules of the game. Although the Central Province received the lion's share of state expenditure, Kenyatta used the *harambee* system to ensure that some resources reached the non-Kikuyu areas.[95]

Although this setup functioned relatively well for some years, it began to break down when land available for redistribution began to dry up, the economy began to falter and Kenyatta became too enfeebled to rule the roost effectively. This led to the emergence of more entrenched divisions within KANU as outsiders took on the Family. This politicking did not assume a purely ethnic form because many of the more marginal parts of Kikuyuland equally felt that they were excluded by the Family. The fiercest criticism was actually launched by J. M. Kariuki, himself a former Mau Mau detainee and a junior minister. Although he was a millionaire with a dubious business record, Kariuki launched a sustained attack on government policy which he argued was rigged in favour of the rich and well-connected and discriminated against the poorer parts of the country. Although Kariuki was a Kikuyu, he was supported by other politicians from the Rift Valley, such as J. M. Seroney, who resented the neglect of their areas. Although Moi had done his best for his Tugen followers, other Kalenjin sub-groups felt left out in the division of the spoils. Kariuki was able to extend his influence into these non-Kikuyu areas through participating in *harambee* activities.

Some powerful ammunition fell into the laps of the dissidents when the International Labour Organisation (ILO), on the invitation of the government, published a report in 1972 entitled *Employment, Incomes and Inequality*. This report confirmed that Kenya had become a highly unequal country in terms of income distribution and the regional allocation of state resources. Amongst other things, the report recommended government intervention to assist the deprived regions and regional quotas in education and employment. This was music to the ears of non-Kikuyu politicians and an anathema to the Family. Whilst mobilising support within the Rift Valley, Kariuki appealed to landless peasants and former Mau Mau sympathisers within the Central Province. The advocacy of a fresh division of the national cake threatened the Kiambu heartlands and to reopen old wounds within the Kikuyu community. At first, GEMA responded by funding its own *harambee* activities in order to weaken its critics but thereafter more direct means were employed. Although Kariuki and Seroney were re-elected to Parliament in 1974, Kariuki was murdered in March of the following year, probably by the Police acting on behalf of the Family.[96]

Seroney was detained and other MPs were successfully ousted from their seats and expelled from the party. By the end of the Kenyatta era, therefore, the scope for political dissent had been substantially narrowed, while ethno-regional divisions had been pushed to the fore.

During the Kariuki affair, Moi had remained loyal. As Kenyatta weakened, the issue of the succession brought him into open conflict with the Family. The 'Change the Constitution' lobby was fronted by GEMA which bankrolled *harambee* activities across the country (especially in Luo country) in order to forge a broader coalition. On the other side, Njonjo (the Attorney-General), Kibaki and important non-Kikuyu politicians rallied to Moi's cause. The war of words was brought to a premature end when Njonjo announced that it was unlawful to speculate on the death of the President and received the backing of Kenyatta himself in October 1976. The period that ensued was nevertheless characterised by further jockeying for position which assumed an overtly ethnic character when non-Kikuyus formed their own ethnic unions in order to compete with GEMA on equal terms. This represented a significant departure from the earlier pattern of cross-ethnic alliances. When Kenyatta finally died in August 1978, there was nothing that the Family could do to prevent Moi from engineering the succession for himself.

At the start of his term of office, Moi was in a relatively weak political position and, because the Kalenjin were a small minority, he needed to work hard at constructing a coalition. The government won some favourable comment by releasing political prisoners, including Ngugi wa Thiong'o. Moi also embarked upon a conscious balancing act in which different interests would feel represented. Some Family members were given Ministerial positions, although it was only a matter of time before they were dispensed with. A number lost their seats at the 1979 elections when they were forced to campaign without access to official patronage. In July 1980, Moi intervened to ban ethnic associations, a move that was clearly intended to destroy GEMA as a political force. Although the latter transferred its assets into another holding company, it became much more difficult for the Family to use money to buy support. Moi had come to power with the support of two Kikuyu politicians, Kibaki and Njonjo, who had parted company with the Kiambu clique. Although Moi owed them a personal debt, he was also wary of allowing them to accumulate too much influence. In July 1983, Njonjo was forced out of office, and Kibaki was greatly weakened when two former Mau Mau organisers, Kariuki Chotara and Fred Kubai, were allowed to challenge him in his home area of Nyeri.[97]

By 1985, Widner suggests, Moi had created a new system in which MPs had lost much of their room for independent action. Politicians required permission before they could hold *harambee* rallies, while State House sought to closely regulate political activity at every level. The Kikuyu elite who had grown up around Kenyatta woke up to discover that they had been consigned to the margins by someone they had always been regarded as something of a nonentity. And it hurt, not least when plum postings and contracts started to pass the way of Kalenjin parvenus whilst they themselves found the avenues blocked. In August 1982, shortly after the declaration of a *de jure* one-party state, the Airforce attempted to stage a military coup with the backing of University students and sections of the Luo community. This was a coup which would almost certainly enjoy the sympathy of much of the Kikuyu political establishment. After the attempt was quashed, the Moi regime had an excuse to purge the senior ranks of the Armed Forces, the paramilitary General Services Unit (GSU) and the Police. Not surprisingly, this entailed the further weeding out of Kikuyu personnel.

The Moi regime was increasingly intolerant of dissent in the 1980s, but it displayed a particular aversion to criticism which emanated from within the Universities. The government was proud of its record in expanding higher education and expected gratitude, not carping, from its principal beneficiaries. But as Haile Selassie discovered to his cost, Universities represented the local assembly plants of global intellectual output and could not be so easily regulated. Although the Moi regime expressed a commitment to a cultural policy, in which indigenous languages and cultures would be given pride of place, it was unable to find common ground with its leading intellectuals lights, like Ngugi, who were actually saying many of the same things.[98] The problem was that when Ngugi talked of spreading his message to ordinary peasants through the Gikuyu language, the exercise was likely to smack of subversion. What the government wanted was cultural works which would 'unite the nation' in as blandly apolitical manner as possible. Any reference to the betrayals of Mau Mau, a favourite theme of Ngugi, or the growing gulf between rich and poor, was considered taboo. Intellectuals were considered as an especially dangerous species because they typically refused to play by the ground-rules of clientage and deference to authority which was the hallmark of the Kenyan political system. Thus whereas Tanzania actively promoted a cultural policy, based on the dissemination of Swahili as the national language and approved musical forms from coast and interior, a Kenyan equivalent was conspicuous by its absence.[99]

In conclusion, therefore, the relatively open political system which prevailed under Kenyatta became more overtly authoritarian under Moi. This may have reflected differences of temperament – the conciliator as opposed to the instinctive autocrat – but it also reflected the shrinkage of material resources from the mid-1970s. The capitalist path to development which had worked so well during the first decade was producing a much less bountiful harvest. Whereas Kenyatta could get away with distributing unequal slices of an expanding cake, Moi was placed in the more delicate position of managing scarcity when there were bound to be transparent losers. The fact that the losers had previously been the winners made the disjuncture particularly obvious. The fact that the intelligentsia was drawn disproportionately from Kikuyu ranks tended to make the Moi regime especially sensitive to criticism from this quarter.

5.2 The West African wager: Ghana and Côte d'Ivoire

The comparison between Ghana under Nkrumah and Côte d'Ivoire under Félix Houphouët-Boigny is almost as well-trodden as that of Tanzania and Kenya. In some respects, it was invited by the protagonists themselves who embarked upon a very public wager in April 1957 while Nkrumah was paying an official visit to Côte d'Ivoire. Nkrumah was strongly of the opinion that the French colonies needed to cut themselves free from the imperial apron-strings if they were ever to advance. The Ivoirien leader, on the other hand, continued to extol the virtues of 'a great Franco-African Community based on equality and fraternity'. During a speech in Nkrumah's honour, Houphouët acknowledged their difference of opinion and laid down a challenge:

> A wager has been made between two territories, one having chosen independence, the other preferring the difficult road to the construction, with the metropole, of a community of men in equal rights and duties. Let us each undertake his experiment, in absolute respect of the experiment of his neighbour, and in ten years we shall compare the results.[100]

Neither leader could have foreseen what was subsequently to transpire. Within a few years, Houphouët had decided to accept formal independence, albeit premised on the maintenance of an enduring relationship with France. And before the ten-year period was up, Nkrumah had been overthrown in a military coup and was languishing in exile in Conakry. Although the wager did not go quite as planned, this has not stopped the relative merits of the Ghanaian and Ivoirien paths to development from being hotly debated ever since.[101]

The comparison has also seemed attractive because these neighbouring countries shared comparable resource-endowments. Ghana was fortunate in having minerals (especially gold, diamonds, manganese and bauxite), while Côte d'Ivoire had a greater land mass. Their similarity lay in the considerable potential for cash crops, especially cocoa and coffee, which could be grown on peasant farms as well as on plantations in the southern forest belt. In the case of Ghana, European plantations had never been permitted a foothold. In Côte d'Ivoire the favouritism displayed to a small group of French planters was what had led to Houphouët taking the political stage. The end result was pretty much the same, namely the predominance of African smallholders. For anyone seeking to understand what practical difference it might make for the regime of a relatively prosperous African country to adopt one set of policies rather than another, the Ghana-Côte d'Ivoire comparison is instructive. Whereas the first represented a bold socialist experiment for some commentators – sheer folly for others – the second stood for a realist appropriation of capitalism – or alternatively, pure neo-colonialism. As in the last section, I will begin with this comparison with a discussion of the Ghanaian socialism, before turning to compare it with the case of Côte d'Ivoire.

Although Nkrumah's Ghana is often considered as a textbook example of African socialism, there were certain differences with, say, *ujamaa* in Tanzania. If Nyerere's vision was humanistic and egalitarian, Nkrumah's could be described as economistic and utilitarian. Unlike Nyerere, Nkrumah never talked about 'traditional' society in particularly positive terms, and certainly never considered it as socialist. His suspicion of 'tradition' was reinforced by the Ashanti backlash in the mid-1950s which appealed to this stock of ideas. In dealing with the National Liberation Movement (NLM) and its acolytes, the Convention People's Party (CPP) liked to imagine that it was uprooting a backward-looking tribalism. But more fundamentally, Nkrumah equated socialism squarely with modernity – to an even greater extent than Nyerere did. There was an interesting similarity in their use of metaphors, but whereas Nyerere spoke of running while others chose to walk, Nkrumah used far more technologically driven imagery:

> All dependent territories are backward in education, in science, in agriculture, and in industry. The economic independence that should follow and maintain political independence demands every effort from the people, a total mobilisation of brain and manpower resources. What other countries have taken three hundred years or more to achieve a more dependant territory must try to accomplish in a generation if it is to survive. Unless it is, as it were, jet-propelled, it will lag behind and thus risk everything for which it has fought. Capitalism is too complicated a system for a newly independent state. Hence the need for a socialist society.[102]

The last two sentences pretty much give the game away. The emphasis does not lie on universalist aspirations towards human equality, but on the fastest means of catching up with the developed world. Hence my advised use of the term 'utilitarian'. Again, Nkrumah's complaint about the Ghanaian bourgeoisie was not that its members were becoming unacceptably richer than everyone else. It was partly that they tended to side with the 'reactionaries' and partly that they lacked the requisite capital and entrepreneurial skills to propel the country forward. A version of self-reliance was articulated by both the leaders, but again its philosophical underpinnings were very different. Whereas Nyerere assumed that self-reliance was a desirable end in its own right, Nkrumah tended to see it as the inverse of (neo-)colonial exploitation in which Western capitalists fed off the wealth created by Africans. Roger Genoud has suggested that the instincts of the Nkrumah regime were actually much more nationalist than they were socialist.[103] But as Tony Killick has convincingly argued, nationalism, socialism and modernisation formed a single integrated package for Nkrumah.[104]

Although it is perhaps misleading to describe Nkrumah as a Marxist, there is no doubt that his early thinking was heavily influenced by his engagement with a pre-war discourse of anti-imperialism which originated with the European left. This was married to a discourse of racial self-assertion which he imbibed while studying in the United States. Although Thomas Hodgkin once described Nkrumah as someone who collected bits of theories like a squirrel gathers nuts, there was a certain consistency in his attachment to the twin themes of anti-imperialism and African unity, which for him were intimately linked.[105] In Nkrumah's view, only an independent and unified African continent stood a chance of keeping the forces of imperialism at bay. He remained firmly locked into a Marxist problematic in the sense that the imperialists were always assumed to be of the capitalist variety. During the last phase of his rule, that is from around 1961, he began to exhibit a more active interest in the Soviet model because it seemed to point to ways in which a backward country could make rapid economic strides.[106] By contrast, Nyerere instinctively rejected it for its gargantuan pretensions and its lack of attention to democratic principles. He was more attracted to the Chinese alternative because it seemed to eschew an urban industrial pattern in favour of a peasant agrarian one. But even then he had no particular wish to be seen as a Maoist. His real desire was to come up with a third way which was uniquely Tanzanian – and beyond that African. This was why *Mwalimu* spent much of his time committing his thoughts to paper. A lot of writings were attributed to Nkrumah as well – not all of which were actually penned by him – but these tended to consist of diatribes about imperialism, pitched in vaguely Leninist language.[107] Although Nkrumah sometimes referred to the 'African personality', in terms redolent of much of African socialist discourse, most of his writing was couched in the language of the international left rather than anything which was specifically African.

Although Nkrumah and Nyerere differed in interesting ways – and had their public spats as well – there was one respect in which their politics developed in parallel. Nyerere, as we have seen, was led to the Arusha Declaration out of a sense of disillusionment with the development path that had been followed immediately after independence, and as a consequence of his falling out with his former patrons. Nkrumah underwent a broadly similar set of formative experiences. For all his anti-imperialism, Nkrumah manifested a surprisingly pragmatic streak. He was willing to cohabit with the British between 1951 and independence in 1957 and was prepared to go along with much of the development agenda which the British were wedded to. The First Development Plan (1951–56) was drawn up by British officials, but taken over by the CPP, the only real modification being that it was telescoped into five rather than ten years.[108] Under this plan, most of the eventual spending was allocated to infrastructural development (36 per cent) and to social services (36 per cent), followed by administration (19 per cent) and productive activity (a mere 9 per cent).[109] The Plan was enthusiastically embraced by Nkrumah who insisted on chairing the committee which was responsible for implementation. This was compatible with his pursuit of the trappings of modernity. Moreover, the bias towards infrastructural improvement could be seen as laying the foundations for subsequent substantive development. The proposal to construct a dam on the Volta River was especially close to Nkrumah's heart because electrification held out the promise of developing home-grown industries. It so happened that many of the projects played well with an electorate which desperately wanted more roads, schools and hospitals. However, as critics of the Plan have frequently noted, it amounted to a 'shopping list' of projects without much sense of what was needed to generate sustained development.

Although the Plan had been completed by the time of independence in 1957, a consolidation period of two years followed in order for unfinished projects to be brought to fruition. By 1959, Nkrumah might have been expected to try his hand at something a bit more adventurous. However, when the Second Five Year Plan (1959–64) was launched, it reproduced the 'shopping-list' approach and once again allocated 80 per cent of expenditure to infrastructure and social services.[110] On this occasion, a distinction was made between projects which would be implemented at all costs (the 'inner plan') and others whose future depended on the required funds becoming available (the 'outer plan'). The Volta Project was placed in a separate category, signalling that for Nkrumah it was an unconditional priority. The peculiar configuration of the plan arose from the growing realisation that the ability to meet substantial levels of development expenditure was no longer assured. From 1955, the government began to run up substantial budgetary deficits which necessitated raiding the country's overseas reserves.[111] In 1961, the Nkrumah regime abruptly terminated the Second Plan and vested a new Planning Commission with responsibility for drawing up more ambitious Seven Year Plan.

Why had the government gone cold on the existing plan? As in the case of Tanzania, there was some dissatisfaction with the pace of economic growth in the 1950s. A growth rate of roughly 5 per cent per year between 1955 and 1960 was respectable, but less spectacular than the government had promised.[112] More crucially, the impact of unstable world cocoa prices upon government planning seemed to underline the structural weakness of the Ghanaian economy. When cocoa prices began to stall in the second half of the 1950s, this had an immediate knock-on effect given that the cocoa export duty contributed around 42 per cent of total revenues at the time of independence. Whereas falling prices might have been expected to instil a greater sense of caution, it actually had the opposite effect on Nkrumah. The latter came to the conclusion that only a 'big push' would free the country from a crippling reliance upon this one commodity and upon imported manufactured goods. Although the timing was less than ideal, Nkrumah was not necessarily going out on a limb. Tony Killick has argued that much of Nkrumah's thinking was actually shared by mainstream development economists of the period who asserted the need for Third World economies to overcome structural disequilibria through precisely such a 'big push'.[113] Indeed some very eminent economists of their period made their own input into the Seven Year Plan.

A second reason why Nkrumah drifted leftwards was that (like Nyerere) he had become mistrustful of the West. When the crisis in the Congo first erupted, Nkrumah stood by Lumumba and despatched 1000 troops under United Nations auspices, believing that their mandate would be to support the central government. When the UN appeared to connive with the Katangan rebels and then Kasavubu, Nkrumah became sharply critical of Western machinations. And after the assassination of Lumumba, Nkrumah openly attacked what he regarded as a Western plot to exchange formal colonial rule for neo-colonialism. Although he insisted that Ghana was wedded to a policy of non-alignment, most of his animus was thereafter directed at the Western powers, especially the United States.[114] At the same time, relations with the Soviet Union began distinctly warmer, as reflected by his decision to pay an official visit to Moscow in July 1961 and subsequent efforts to foster closer trade relations. Although foreign policy represented a specialist arena, the ratcheting up of anti-imperialist rhetoric was bound to have an impact at home. In particular, it strengthened the hand of leftwingers in the CPP and in the party press who were arguing for the adoption of a more overtly socialist position at home and abroad.

The socialist embrace was signalled in a number of actions taken by the regime over 1961 and 1962. In April 1961, Nkrumah delivered a Dawn Broadcast which signalled a break with the entrenched habits of the ruling party. He voiced his concern about the lack of discipline within the CPP and, in particular, the self-enrichment of government and party officials alike. Although he did not announce a formal Leadership Code, Nkrumah signalled that there were to be stricter limits placed on accumulation by officials in future.

By the end of the year, a number of the CPP old-guard had been dismissed because they were seen as being excessively pro-Western, corrupt or both. The casualties included Komla Gbedemah, the very able Minister of Finance who went into exile in 1961, Kojo Botsio, and Krobo Edusei whose conspicuous consumption was legendary. Into the breach stepped a group of younger men espousing a more radical position, like Tawia Adamafio. Although a commitment to socialism had been included in the 1951 party manifesto, the 'Programme for Work and Happiness' (1962) attempted to define the socialist orientation of the regime more explicitly. Freedom was defined so as to include freedom from material want, but more than that: 'Our Party is determined that the people of Ghana shall look forward to ever-increasing social benefits and ever-widening opportunities for the enjoyment of leisure and culture.'[115] However, what is really noteworthy about the document was the overwhelming emphasis placed upon economics:

> There is no half way to socialism. The total industrialisation of the country, the complete diversification and mechanisation of agriculture, and a national economic planning based on the public ownership of the means of production and distribution must be the order of the day.[116]

By contrast, the document said remarkably little about the participation of Ghanaians in the building of a socialist society. A section on labour relations urged trade unions to 'spearhead their efforts to raise production and productivity' and to shed their 'colonial mentality' now that they were no longer living in a capitalist society. Other than that, there was reference merely to the need for a 'strong, stable, firm and highly centralised government' to achieve socialism.[117]

This highly economistic conception of socialism meant that overwhelming importance was attached to the Seven Year Plan. In his launch speech of March 1964, Nkrumah repeated the observation that earlier plans had merely comprised 'a collection of various individual petty projects' and proudly proclaimed that the new document heralded the birth of 'the first integrated and comprehensive economic plan for Ghana's development'.[118] The Plan was presented as a radical leap beyond what had hitherto been attempted. On the one hand, the Plan was even more ambitious in its spending objectives, with an anticipated outlay of £G476 million as against a total of £G350 million under its predecessor (a sum which included the Volta Project). On the other hand, the Plan was supposed to direct a greater share of total investment into directly productive activity – that is, industry and agriculture. Although infrastructure and social services were destined to remain an important call on government expenditure, their share was scaled downwards.[119] Nkrumah had always been mesmerised by the vision of rapid industrialisation powered by the electricity produced by the Volta Dam. However, he had hitherto deferred to economic advisors like W. A. Arthur Lewis who had argued against premature industrialisation and in favour of encouraging improvements in agriculture. Under the Seven Year Plan, Ghana was to abandon this advice and to go for broke. The aim was to set up state manufacturing enterprises which would produce many of the goods which Ghana imported. In the longer run, the Plan also anticipated the promotion of heavy industries, beginning with metals, chemicals and synthetics and culminating in the production of capital goods (like machinery) and electronics.[120]

Although the avowed aim was to bring the means of production under public ownership – which made it formally socialist – the government did not push for nationalisation of foreign enterprises, unlike in Tanzania. Instead it envisaged that new state enterprises would be established and would eventually displace foreign ones through competition. In the short term, though, Ghana was to retain a mixed economy in which there would be a place for private capital. Indeed, the government actually expected half of the anticipated investment under the Plan to come from external sources. This acceptance of foreign capital was most obvious in the case of the Volta Project, which was half-financed by the government and half by loans from the World Bank, the United States and Britain. As originally conceived, the project was supposed to enable Ghana to turn its own bauxite into aluminium using the electricity generated by the dam. However, the government was eventually forced to sign an agreement with the Volta Aluminium Corporation (owned by the Kaiser and Reynolds Corporations) in which the latter built a smelter, but was permitted to import its alumina from outside and to purchase electricity at very cheap rates. This capitulation to the demands of these large multinational corporations was a bitter pill for Nkrumah to swallow, but he considered it necessary for the project to go ahead since the Soviet Union was unable to offer an equivalent package. Finally, insofar as agriculture was considered as important, the government proposed to pursue mechanisation upon specially created state farms. Although Nkrumah expressed his hope that the peasants would continue to enlarge their own output, he maintained a rather pessimistic opinion of their capabilities. It was anticipated that state farms would receive the lion's share of resources, which would be justified by their superior performance as well as their demonstration effect upon the peasantry. Whereas Nyerere attempted to harness his peasants, therefore, the Seven Year Plan aimed to bypass the Ghanaian peasants almost completely.

The pursuit of 'development' at all costs had implications for the political complexion of the Nkrumah regime as well. In the 1960s, when socialism was the official watchword, there was much talk of turning the CPP into an appropriate vehicle for mass mobilisation in association with the integral wings. In 1961, the Kwame Nkrumah Ideological Institute was founded at Winneba to instruct party cadres in the central tenets of Nkrumahism, while *The Spark* received official sanction to pursue a more Marxist line. In 1964, the country was formally proclaimed a one-party state. However, the presumed centrality of the CPP had a much longer history than the adherence to socialism. Nkrumah and other CPP bosses regarded the opposition as inherently illegitimate because their appeal was supposedly based on sectionalism rather nationalism. In 1958, the government introduced legislation which outlawed the formation of political parties on ethnic, regional or religious lines. This forced the existing opposition parties to merge as the United Party (UP). Although the UP was legal, the Nkrumah government did everything in its power to disable it at every level of the political system. At the local level, the CPP engineered the destoolment of anti-CPP chiefs (as we have seen) and established an iron grip over local government and the patronage which went with it. Its ability to choke off the opposition at this level was facilitated by the replacement of the old Regional and District Commissioners (who had been civil servants) with CPP politicians in 1958/59.

In 1958 the government passed the Preventive Detention Act and proceeded to use it against opposition politicians who were accused of plotting against the government or (as in 1961) with fomenting disorder.[121] Perhaps the most ignoble act of the Nkrumah regime was to preside over the death in detention of the veteran nationalist, Dr J. B. Danquah. Many opposition politicians fled into exile, while others did the smart thing and crossed the carpet to join the CPP. By 1961, Ghana had become a de facto one-party state. The adoption of a socialist platform the following year merely added ideological icing to the cake. Whereas Nyerere wrestled with what democracy might mean in the context of a single-party state, comparatively little thought was given to the issue in Ghana. A simple axiom stated that 'the CPP is Ghana and Ghana is the CPP'. There were no internal party elections and no competitive Parliamentary elections after 1956, which gave the rank-and-file limited opportunities to influence their leaders or to get rid of them. In theory party branches could pass their demands upwards, while the integral wings provided alternative avenues through which Ghanaians could influence decision-making. For those who were serious about socialism – and there were some – the CPP was actually a rather weak instrument for effecting social change. Once the opposition had been routed, the structures atrophied because there was not much left for them to do. Indeed Ghana looked like a classic no-party state, in which the bureaucracy, and increasingly the President's Office in Flagstaff House, assumed a far more important role than the party did.

There was, however, a need to win at least the compliance of the Ghanaian population because structural transformation promised a belt-tightening which was not likely to be warmly received. Although workers and peasants were supposed to be the beneficiaries of socialism, the 'big push' actually depended on squeezing their incomes. In some respects, Ghanaian socialism looked rather like Kenyan capitalism in the sense that they both placed economic growth first and expected the social benefits to follow further down the line.[122] The difference was that the public sector assumed a much higher profile in Ghana. During the 1950s, the cocoa farmers were chained up as the milch-cows of the state in the drive to mobilise resources for development. Because the Cocoa Marketing Board (CMB) fixed the price which was paid to the farmer, it was relatively easy for government to cream off the difference with the world market price. The proportion which was paid to the producer dropped from 94 per cent in 1949 to 33 per cent in 1954, before rising briefly to 70 per cent in 1957 and then falling back to 56 per cent in 1964. The years where the farmers received a higher proportion tended to be those when world prices were low, because there was a bottom limit, whereas in years of buoyancy the state appropriated much more. The government wanted to continue extracting resources from the cocoa farmers whilst keeping the farmers more or less agreeable. Its chosen instrument was the United Ghana Farmers' Co-operative Council (UGFCC) which squeezed out foreign buying farms and as well as the co-operative movement. The UGFCC was recognised as the sole representative of the farmers, and became one of the integral wings of the CPP. In theory, the UGFCC leaders were mandated to negotiate the producer price on behalf of the farmers. But the reality was that the UGFCC was batting for the CPP. When the government introduced a compulsory savings scheme in 1961, the UGFCC stage-managed rallies in which farmers supposedly donated the funds to government. And two years later, the UGFCC volunteered a special 'income tax' on cocoa farmers.[123] As Björn Beckman has demonstrated, the UGFCC was not led by farmers, but by officials whose interests actually lay in milking the producers. In consequence, it was highly unpopular with the farmers.

As far as urban workers are concerned, the relationship between the CPP and the trade union movement was fixed at an early stage. Over 1954/55, the government brokered the formation of a single Trade Union Congress (TUC) to be led not by the militants who had often challenged the CPP, but by party loyalists. The government ensured that John Tettegah became head of the TUC and survived repeated attempts to oust him. Tettegah was an enthusiastic advocate of a hierarchical union structure which would be tied to the CPP. In 1958, the government passed the Industrial Relations Act which made the TUC (rather than its constituent unions) the supreme arbiter of labour affairs. This restructuring was a double-edged sword for organised labour. On the one hand, all waged workers were required to become union members, and their dues were deducted at source. Minimum wages were standardised, and raised by 5 per cent in 1960, which benefited private sector workers who had often been prevented from forming unions.[124] On the other hand, the right to strike was withdrawn on the basis that the country needed labour stability in order to meet its development objectives. When socialism was enshrined as the formal doctrine of the CPP, workers were informed that they should contribute to debate within the party where they were fully represented: Tettegah was, after all, a Cabinet Minister. Workers were also admonished to concentrate on raising productivity rather than making unrealistic wage demands, given that any increases would have to come from the public purse unless supported by higher productivity. Whereas cocoa farmers had born the brunt of taxation in the 1950s, the collapse of the world market price after 1960 slashed this source of revenue. While the government resorted to bank lending and external loans to finance its 'big push', it also needed to apply downward pressure upon wages and salaries. The 1961 budget introduced a compulsory saving scheme for wage earners, the proceeds of which were to be invested by government. The Nkrumah regime hoped to sell austerity to workers on the principle that when the investment effort yielded its benefits there would be greater material prosperity for all. However, its ability to persuade workers was always likely to depend on the credibility of TUC leadership, a point we will come to shortly.

It should be evident by now that the Nkrumah regime wished its performance to be measured in terms of its acceleration of economic change. But there is a consensus amongst those who have looked closely at the record that the economic performance was very poor indeed. The judgements have typically been harsh: 'little short of catastrophic', 'ludicrously amateurish' and 'appalling' to mention only three damning assessments.[125] Even those who have seen merit in the Seven Year Plan, have bemoaned the poor implementation.[126] The problem was not that the Nkrumah regime failed to mobilise the resources it needed for the massive investment target. On the contrary, there is a consensus that through its mobilisation of domestic savings (in other words, squeezing Ghanaians) and external loans, it was able to achieve a level of investment which was very high by the standards of developing countries (22 per cent of GNP in 1965). The problem was that there was very little to show for the big push.

According to Killick, per capita GNP grew at only 0.2 per cent between 1958/59 and 1964/65, but from then until 1968/69 – when some of the returns from the big push might have been expected to feed through – it actually fell by 2.3 per cent.[127] The record of state industries was very poor for a variety of reasons: some were not really viable to start with; others laboured under weak management; and, as shortages of foreign exchange became a recurrent problem, many factories suffered from endemic shortages of raw materials and spare parts. The result was that most of the state industries operated at well below their notional capacity (around one-fifth on average) and at a financial cost to the state.[128] Other parastatals, such as the State Fishing Corporation and the State Gold Mining Corporation, constituted a further drain on the exchequer. Only the Ghana National Trading Corporation (GNTC) and the State Construction Corporation actually operated at a profit. In agriculture, the results were, if anything, even less impressive. The State Farms Corporation (SFC), which invested heavily in tractors and expensive inputs, consumed vast public resources, but its 105 farms contributed very little to national output. As in Tanzania, the peasant sector, which received minimal support, produced far more, but also managed a substantially higher yield per acre in the case of every crop.[129] The Workers' Brigade, which operated 10 mechanised farms of its own, provided employment for CPP loyalists at considerable cost, but contributed even less than the SFC did.

Having exhausted its external reserves, the government began to accumulate a substantial external debt arising mostly from suppliers' credits which bore higher rates of interest.[130] The problem here was that despite the existence of a State Planning Committee, which was supposed to monitor spending under the Plan, in reality, Ministries and parastatals spent at will. At the same time, the rapid expansion of import-substituting industries intensified the pressure on foreign exchange because of the requirement for imported machinery, spare parts and raw materials. Clearly, it did not help that this was precisely the moment when the world cocoa price was tumbling.

Beneath the grim economic statistics lurks the reality of declining living standards for most Ghanaians during the first part of the 1960s. On the plus side, there were some real improvements in the provision of public services. Between 1958 and 1965, primary school enrolments jumped from 471,000 to 1,145,000; middle school enrolments from 140,000 to 268,000; and secondary school enrolments from 13,200 to 46,800. The number of hospitals also doubled and this was exceeded by the expansion in the number of health workers.[131] On the other side, the incomes of most Ghanaians took a definitive turn for the worse as consumer prices doubled between 1960 and 1965.

Between these years of rapid inflation, the real minimum wage fell by 41 per cent, while the average income of the cocoa farmers is also estimated to have fallen by over 60 per cent.[132] Considering the steep increase in food prices, some other farmers may have benefited, but much of the increase would have reflected rising transport costs. It is also worth noting that, in the opinion of a number of observers, there was (unlike in Tanzania) an increase in social stratification. The wages of unskilled workers fell disproportionately by comparison with the top 20 per cent, who received as estimated 37 per cent of total income in 1956 and as much as 50 per cent in 1968.[133] What even these figures conceal is the extent to which the real opportunities for the accumulation of wealth lay in the manipulation of scarcity by those who had access to positions of authority. Those who gained access to import licences and scarce consumer goods were able to reap substantial rewards by selling them on. Senior government officials themselves amassed wealth through bribes and kickbacks. It is for this reason that some commentators have regarded Ghanaian socialism as a convenient cover for a petite bourgeoisie which was not entrepreneurial in any sense, and could only accumulate through state intervention.[134] This interpretation, which echoes that of Shivji, arguably rings truer for Ghana than for Tanzania.

This tale of mounting hardship for the many, set against increasing wealth for the well-connected few, is graphically illustrated in many of the cultural works from the period. Ayi Kwei Armah's classic novel, *The Beautyful Ones are Not Yet Born* (1968) tells the sordid story of a man struggling to maintain his personal integrity, against the demands of his wife and her brother (a CPP politician) that he partake in the corruption. Whereas this was a book with an explicitly political message, it was written a few years after the fall of Nkrumah and was geared to a relatively small audience. More telling perhaps are the themes which emerge within popular forms of entertainment, notably highlife music and concert party theatre, which became partially fused as art forms in the 1950s. During the heyday of nationalism, the CPP received a great deal of support from highlife musicians like E. K. Nyame, whose 'Honourable Man and Hero, Kwame Nkrumah' (in celebration of his release from prison) was an early hit. Another stalwart was E. T. Mensah who produced a number of popular praise songs to Nkrumah and the nationalist movement. Nyame went on to form a concert party troupe, the Akan Trio, which pioneered the use of Ghanaian languages and remained pretty committed to the CPP throughout.[135] The Nkrumah regime recognised the importance of remaining in touch with popular culture. It patronised concert party troupes and bands and founded others such as the Workers' Brigade Concert Party which were intended to pedal a more political message.[136] Although the plots dealt mostly with the relationship between lovers, families and tricksters, there is a sense in which many of the plays worked at more than one level. Catherine Cole gives the example of a production by the Ahanta Trio, entitled 'The Family Honours the Dead' (1961) which deals with a selfish lineage head who fails to carry out his duties. Cole concludes that 'the narrative is not only about individualistic greed in the extended family system but is also a parable about corruption in the larger arena of national politics'.[137] Ghanaian audiences would have been only too

well-aware of the coded references to the CPP, and part of the fun lay in exposing the hidden meanings. The tales of everyday hardship, which highlife songs
dwelt upon, were equally a powerful indictment of the regime.

As the problems multiplied, the CPP regime struggled to convince the
populace that the sacrifices were necessary in the interests of socialist development. In September 1961, the railway workers defied the TUC leadership and
the government and went on strike. Significantly, they were supported by the
wider community of Sekondi-Takoradi, including the unemployed and market
women who felt excluded from the charmed circle who enjoyed access to the
GNTC.[138] The grievances of strikers and their sympathisers were rooted not just
in the compulsory savings scheme, but also in a distaste for the selfish behaviour of the ruling elite. It was largely as a result of this strike that a number of
the old guard were briefly purged from the government and forced to disgorge
their ill-gotten gains. Although the government was able to reassert its authority through recourse to preventive detention and by banning public meetings,
Jeffries suggests that there was a deepening sense of malaise within the labour
movement in the years that followed.[139] In the countryside, there was little sign
of overt opposition, but there is plenty of evidence of a resort to tried-and-
tested strategies of evasion. Cocoa farmers who had seen their incomes shrink
over the past decade ceased to plant new trees or smuggled their loads into
neighbouring countries where the prices were substantially higher.[140]

Many Ghanaians learned that if one made the right ideological noises, it was
possible to do as one pleased. Hence cynicism abounded at all levels of the party.
The brief rise of the radicals was cut short after a bomb was thrown at Nkrumah
during a visit to Kulungugu. Adamafio was implicated (probably falsely), while
Botsio and Edusei were rehabilitated.[141] Thereafter Nkrumah did not feel he
could trust anyone outside a very small circle of confidantes, and he increasingly
confined himself to the safety of Flagstaff House. The promotion of the cult of
the leader, which was taken to extremes in the period after 1960, had helped to
breed a culture of sycophancy and dissimulation which meant that nobody, and
least of all Nkrumah, was sure of what party leaders really thought. When the
military struck on 24 February 1966, the CPP dissolved into thin air as the
urban and rural population alike (including many party members) came out to
cheer. For those who had watched the rot, this reaction did not come as a total
surprise, although many external observers had been taken in by the apparent
solidity of the ruling party.

Arguably, Ghanaian socialism was all back-to-front. On the one hand, the
country embarked on an ambitious structural economic transformation at the
very moment when the pool of available resources was running dry.[142] This
necessitated inflicting acute hardship on the people and accumulating an unsustainable debt. On the other hand, the commitment to socialism came at the
point when the regime had severely alienated the labouring classes, namely
urban workers (as shown by the 1961 strike) and peasants. 'Investment without development' and 'socialism by proclamation' were two criticisms of the
Ghanaian experiment which remain convincing to this day. The military coup
brought the socialist experiment to an abrupt end and it was not for close on
two decades before leftwingers tasted power once again.

News of the putsch was received with some satisfaction in Abidjan where the government suspected Nkrumah of sponsoring subversion. No doubt Houphouët-Boigny felt that the rejection of Nkrumah by his own people meant that he had won the bet (see Appendix 5.1). However, the adoption of a capitalist path to development in Côte d'Ivoire was not without its own little difficulties. After he severed his alliance the French Communist Party in 1951, Houphouët was pretty consistent in his assertion that the best hope for the country lay in a collaborative relationship with French capital and the French state. The Parti Démocratique de Côte d'Ivoire (PDCI) was, however, a loose coalition of occupational and ethnic interest groups which had been constructed from the top downwards. What this meant is that while Houphouët himself was clear about which direction the country should be heading in, this was not necessarily shared in all corners of the party. The first signs of internal discord became apparent in March 1959 when the secretary-general of the party, J.-B. Mockey was forced out of office and there was a crackdown on the youth wing of the party, the JRDACI (Jeunesse du Rassemblement Démocratique Africain de Côte d'Ivoire).[143] In 1963, there was an even more serious crisis when as many as 200 people were arrested – Cabinet Ministers included – of whom 64 were later found guilty of a conspiracy to seize power. This was closely followed by the revelation of yet another conspiracy in August, implicating no fewer than six Ministers.

It is somewhat difficult to get to the bottom of these events because of the element of blatant stage-management. Many still believe that the plots were entirely fictitious and that they provided a convenient ruse for Houphouët to reconfigure the regime as he saw fit. But if one reads between the lines in official statements, it appears that there may also have been genuine tensions which were ethnic, generational and ideological – all rolled into one. The first was rooted in northern resentment towards the prominent position occupied by Baoulés, the origin of Houphouët himself, within the PDCI. The second arose out of the frustration of younger members who were anxious to have a greater say and regarded the founding fathers as a conservative dead-weight. And finally, it was claimed that some of the plotters had retained close links with French Communists and wanted to adopt a more radical programme. The winning side also hinted that the plotters had enjoyed the support of the Nkrumah regime over the border. If any of this is true, it would suggest that there was support at the very heart of the PDCI for a programme which diverged from that which Houphouët was wedded to. The dissident elements were rooted out and the government proceeded to impose tighter regulation on those groups which posed the greatest threat, notably students and trade unions. There was one further alleged plot in 1964, executed by a former Communist who had studied in France, who had supposedly tried to harm the President through witchcraft. But thereafter, the leadership question was definitively over and Houphouët settled into the seat of power as the supreme overlord. Over subsequent decades, he came to be regarded with a mixture of reverence and fear. He was commonly referred to as *Le Vieux* (or Old Man), and the political style which he cultivated was that of the benevolent patriarch. But as Ivoiriens were well-aware, he also had his fingers on the pulse. Houphouët once famously invoked a different metaphor when he commented that he was like a crocodile: he always slept with one eye open.

What then was distinctive about the Ivoirien way? First of all, the Ivoiriens, like the Kenyans, accorded primacy to the achievement of rapid growth rather than immediate redistribution. Like virtually everyone else at the time, they accepted the need for economic planning, and within the plans there was an attempt to keep expenditure on social services and administration under tight control, thereby freeing up money for other things. The document which mapped out government objectives for the ten-year period, 1960–69, allocated 20.1 per cent of spending to social, educational and administrative infrastructure and another 30.4 per cent to economic infrastructure. This left 49.5 per cent for the directly productive sectors of the economy.[144] Despite the rhetoric surrounding the Ghanaian Seven Year Plan (where the equivalent allocation was only 37 per cent), the Ivoiriens were actually devoting a greater share of state resources to productive investment. The difference was that the Ivoiriens were much more cautious in the manner in which they went about spending. Planned investment was maintained well within what the country could afford. By contrast, Ghana planned for three times more investment than Côte d'Ivoire in the first decade.[145] As we have seen, actual spending in Ghana tended to outstrip the Plan, whereas in Côte d'Ivoire greater attention was paid to feasibility studies and the monitoring of expenditure. The result was that Côte d'Ivoire managed to have its plan and still maintain a budgetary surplus during the 1960s, whereas Ghana was unable to balance the books.

The second distinctive feature of the Ivoirien model was that the country became even more tied to the former metropole than in colonial times. Most obviously, the country chose to remain within the French economic orbit, adopting the CFA Franc which was pegged to the French Franc. This meant surrendering monetary policy to Paris in return for ensuring convertibility, whereas Ghana chose to launch its own currency, the cedi, which was de-linked from sterling. In 1961, France and Côte d'Ivoire signed a protocol under which France granted preferential tariffs to Ivoirien coffee, cocoa, bananas, pineapples and wood, in return for the protection of French imports.[146] This amounted to a substantial French subsidy, which was largely passed on to the producers. The Ivoiriens also permitted the French to retain troops on their soil for rapid deployment across Africa. And by the early 1980s, there were no fewer 50,000 French people living and working in Côte d'Ivoire, which was five times the number in colonial times, placing the country on par with Morocco and Algeria.[147] This substantial expatriate community was employed at the highest levels of administration and right across the private sector. At independence, Houphouët resisted pressure to rapidly Africanise the civil service, stating categorically that 'we refuse, as it were, to let our administration sink into mediocrity'.[148]

The first Minister of Finance, Raphael Saller, was from the Antilles, while the first real plan was largely devised by French experts. Even when top posts were handed over to Ivoiriens, French officials tended to be kept on as advisors (or *eminences grises*) and continued to play an active role in decision-making. Lower down the chain, some 20,000 French citizens were also deployed as school teachers and technicians, to compensate for the shortage of skilled Ivoirien personnel.[149] It was not only in the public sector that the French were a commanding presence. The regime gambled on attracting large amounts of foreign investment, and the investment code of 1959 offered very attractive concessions such as easy repatriation of profits and low corporate taxation. French companies became heavily involved in plantation production and in manufacturing, as well as in the established spheres of banking and the import–export trade. The inevitable result was that most management and technical positions tended to be occupied by Frenchmen rather than Ivoiriens, who accounted for a mere 10 per cent in industry by 1971. In 1965, non-Africans represented as much as 7 per cent of the total salaried workforce and most of these would have been French nationals, although some had become naturalised Ivoiriens.[150] It was not just a matter of employment and investment. The French constituted a very visible presence in Abidjan, and in an effort to maintain their lifestyles they carved out a privileged space for their own language, cuisine and cultural *mores*. The Gallicisation of the ultra-modern Ivoirien capital contrasted starkly with Accra or Lagos, where British culture was never more than a thin veneer.

Thirdly, the Ivoiriens (like the Kenyans) did not plump for rapid industrialisation, but placed greater emphasis upon increasing agricultural commodities for export – a policy which Nkrumah regarded as a fatal trap. At independence, Côte d'Ivoire was well-placed to expand the production of its traditional exports, cocoa and coffee, and it did so with considerable energy. The forest zone, which was ideally suited to the production of these crops, had a relatively small population. In 1963, the government passed a code which stipulated that land which was unused would revert to the state. This made it possible for aspiring farmers to move into the forests and to acquire land for cash cropping. After independence, there was a massive relocation of population towards the forest frontier – from other parts of the South, but also from the North and especially from neighbouring countries. Whereas Ghanaian cocoa farms had once been a Mecca for labour migrants from the Sahel, the increasingly unattractive conditions led many to relocate to Côte d'Ivoire where they were positively welcomed. The result was that no fewer than one-quarter of the population of the country were immigrants by the 1970s. The availability of a large and relatively cheap labour force was crucial to the expansion of output during the 1960s. Moreover, many of those who arrived as labourers were later able to acquire their own farms, thereby contributing to the process of peasantisation. The government did its bit by sponsoring research into improved crop varieties and by providing farmers with effective extension services. Although cocoa and coffee remained the key to success, the Ivoirien regime successfully diversified its exports. Smallholders were encouraged by the state and French support to turn to bananas and cotton production. Nevertheless, private companies were also encouraged to set up plantations specialising in export commodities like pineapples. Furthermore, the government created state agencies to produce palm-oil, sugar and rubber on plantations alongside the peasant sector.

Although the Ivoirien government placed the accent on agriculture, it nevertheless accepted the desirability of expanding manufacturing output. Whereas Nkrumah's attitude towards foreign capital was grudging, the Ivoiriens expected foreign companies to play a catalytic role in developing industries. The government initially shied away from establishing state-owned industries on any scale.[151] During the first decade after independence, the emphasis lay on the creation of private industries of the import-substitution variety. In the 1970s, there was a switch towards industries which could be expected to find an export market. To some extent, these gains were expected to come at Senegal's expense.[152] As far as the non-African market is concerned, a great deal of investment went into agro-processing – the production of tinned pineapples, soluble coffee, sawmilling and the like – which complemented the growth strategy based on smallholder agriculture.

To start with, foreign capital was very much in the vanguard. This is reflected in the fact that by 1971 an estimated 71 per cent of capital invested in the food industry and 92 per cent in textiles, shoes and clothing came from outside.[153] But as the decade progressed, Ivoirien capital became more directly involved with the state playing a nurturing role. Shortly after independence, Houphouët made statist noises, but in subsequent years this was presented as a temporary expedient until such a time as Ivoirien capitalists were ready to shoulder the responsibility.[154] But whereas the Ghanaian state was seen as filling a void, the Ivoirien vision was one in which the state was supposed to muscle in and create a space in which indigenous capitalism could develop. In 1963, the government established the Société Nationale de Financement (SONAFI) which was mandated to purchase shares in foreign companies with a view to eventually selling them on to Ivoiriens. And in 1968, the Fonds de Garantie des Crédits Accordés aux Enterprises Ivoiriennes (FGCEI) was set up to provide credit guarantees for majority-owned industrial enterprises which wished to take out bank loans. Other state agencies provided subsidies and direct grants to small and medium-sized Ivoirien enterprises.[155]

Finally, this particular developmental model had implications for the pursuit of politics. Côte d'Ivoire was already a one-party state on the eve of independence. But unlike in Tanzania, very little attention was paid to the question of how the PDCI might contribute towards the fulfilment of the goals which had been laid down. The most that was said to justify one-partyism was that it prevented Ivoirien politics from dividing along ethnic and religious lines. Because the PDCI was genuinely a vehicle for elites drawn from across the country, it could plausibly be presented as a unifying force. However, at the local level the party was actually organised along ethnic lines until 1970 and therefore tended to enshrine ethnicity as an organising principle. Moreover, it was not entirely clear what practical function the PDCI was expected to perform. Even more than in Kenya, the regime assumed a highly technocratic complexion. Experts formulated policy in Abidjan and administrators then went about implementing it in the country at large. This did not leave very much scope for the input of ordinary Ivoiriens who were expected to leave decisions to those who knew better, and to be grateful for whatever came their way. Philippe Yacé, the PDCI Secretary-General, summed this attitude up when he remarked that the participatory role of the citizen consisted of 'active acquiescence in the policies of government'.[156] However, *Le Vieux* was astute enough to recognise when the government was seriously out of step with the population. In 1969/70, for example, Houphouët convened a series of public 'dialogues' with powerful interest groups like teachers, unions and parents which signalled a willingness to listen, at the same time as underscoring his own supremacy.

By 1965, the country had been repartitioned into six *départements*, each headed by a *préfet*, and around one hundred *sous préfetures* headed by *sous préfets*. These administrative appointments were made by the President himself. The PDCI created its own structures in parallel with the administration: there were *sous-sections* which corresponded to the *sous-préfetures*, which were headed by secretary-generals, and below that there were village and ward committees. The secretary-generals were not elected, but chosen by the President's men, and were scarcely accountable to the committees below them. Their role was actually a rather circumscribed one, in that real decision-making powers lay with the administrative officers. Hence, writing in 1971, Stryker observed that:

> While the party is proclaimed to have an 'explanatory and persuasive role' in promoting local development, this is irregular at best, and the regime has placed little reliance on the PDCI for either educational or organisational tasks.[157]

There was nevertheless a structural tension between the secretary-generals and the *sous-préfets* in that they represented competing sources of local influence. Moreover, the former were indigenous to the area in question whereas the *sous-préfets* were almost always outsiders. Hence if the former had good political connections in Abidjan, they might come prevail in a local struggle for power. But then the *sous-préfets* had the *préfets* above them to back their cause, whereas there were no party offices at the *département* level. This missing link may have been a deliberate strategy to prevent the party from dividing along regional and ethnic lines. But what it meant was that there was a yawning gap between the local party and the PDCI at the national level.[158] In general, then, the PDCI had a marginal role in advancing the development goals of the government.

The overall intention was to make administrators and local party officials dependent upon the centre – and ultimately upon the President himself. In fact, Houphouët largely dispensed with formal structures altogether, choosing instead to convene an ad hoc national council – consisting of hundreds of party and government officials – when the occasion demanded it.[159] The dominance of the centre was also reflected in the fact that it effectively chose the candidates for the National Assembly. Although primaries were nominally held, the results were often not adhered to. The hand-picked favourites represented a narrow sub-stratum, of society, namely Ivoiriens who had acquired a University education (around half of the legislators) or at least a secondary education. The deputies were almost all male, as were the Ministers and the top PDCI officials. In fact, it was not until 1976 that the first woman Minister was appointed.[160] In general, the political elite constituted a small clique who played pass-the-parcel with governmental and party positions, subject to whim of Houphouët. According to Tessilimi Bakary, the sum total of all decision-making positions were shared out amongst 320 individuals between 1957 and the mid-1980s. Of that number, a mere 19 were women.[161] Within the inner circle, political and business relations overlapped and were cemented by ties of marriage. Houphouët was particularly careful to marry off his daughters to political and business associates.[162] In this respect, he behaved much like Kenyatta. However, Kenyatta saw some value in allowing political rivals to compete before the eyes of the nation. In Côte d'Ivoire, the deals tended to be done behind closed doors as Houphouët carefully balanced out competing sets of interests.

Let us now turn to consider whether the Ivoirien model lived up to the claims of its architects. In terms of the relentless pursuit of economic growth, there was a time when the words 'Côte d'Ivoire' and 'economic miracle' were seldom found far apart. Writing in 1971, Elliot Berg contrasted the weakness of Ghana's performance with the 'dazzling' record of its neighbour.[163] A decade later, Crawford Young commented that 'Ivory Coast is by some distance the most influential exemplary state on the African capitalist pathway', before going on to confirm that Nkrumah had been well-and-truly trounced.[164] But there have always been the gainsayers who, whilst admitting that there were years of rapid growth, pointed out to the structural weaknesses of the Ivoirien economy. One reason for being sceptical was that Côte d'Ivoire had vast reserves of forest land which made it possible to continue expanding peasant production until the land frontier closed. Ghana had started the process and had hit the buffers first, and some believed that it was only a matter of time before its neighbour followed suit. Hence, writing in the same volume as Berg, Reginald Green observed that 'the Ivory Coast in 1957 was rather more analogous to the Gold Coast of 1900 than to Ghana of 1957'.[165] Another consideration was that there was a finite market for most primary exports like cocoa and coffee, which meant that expanding production was likely to be counter-productive in the long run because it would merely undermine world prices. Finally, some pointed out that the domination of the industrial sector by foreign capital was merely likely to lead to the promotion of capital-intensive enterprises which fostered minimal linkages with the rest of the Ivoirien economy.

Miracle or mirage? In trying to disentangle the evidence, it is appropriate to begin with what is agreed upon: namely two decades of very rapid economic growth (at 8.1 per cent in the first decade and 6.7 in the second), followed by a marked slowdown in the 1980s. This is clearly reflected in Appendix 5.1. In the first period, there was a pretty spectacular increase in the production of export crops which lay behind the wider success. To quote John Rapley:

> Crop production expanded at sometimes massive rates: in the first decade and a half of independence, the volume of production of coffee and bananas almost doubled, that of cocoa increased sixfold, while pineapple production increased by over 4600 per cent. Even pineapple production, however, could not compare to the increases in palm oil production. Processing of these crops – representing secondary development – expanded even more quickly. By the early 1980s Côte d'Ivoire had become the world's largest producer of coconuts, its largest exporter of tinned pineapple, its third largest producer of palm oil, and Africa's second largest producer of cotton. No other West African country came close to duplicating this record.[166]

Hence Côte d'Ivoire managed to overtake Ghana in the production of its traditional export crops, but also to diversify very successfully. Ironically, it was

Ghana more than Côte d'Ivoire which continued to be dependent upon the vagaries of world cocoa prices.

Moreover, whereas the Nkrumah regime chose industrialisation over agricultural expansion, Côte d'Ivoire was able to have its cake and eat it. Hence, the industrial sector expanded fastest of all, and the country came to boast the highest value of manufactured export in sub-Saharan Africa (see Appendix 5.3). But perhaps the most remarkable part of the story, which is recounted in Rapley's book, is that Ivoirien capitalists became serious players in the game. The founders of the PDCI were large commercial farmers like Houphouët himself, but this agrarian capitalist class later moved into trade and urban real estate. With the support of the Ivoirien state, some began to buy shares in private companies during the 1960s. By 1971, Ivoiriens held minority shares in a number of large concerns, although foreign capital was still dominant. Rapley goes on to chart the irresistible rise of Ivoirien capitalists who acquired majority shareholdings in a large number of companies and moved into the manufacturing sector in a big way. Indeed by 1980, some two-thirds of their capital was invested in manufacturing: especially agro-industry, but also textiles, printing and the metal, mechanical and electrical industries.[167] Moreover, Rapley demonstrates that Ivoirien companies, or those with majority Ivoirien ownership, were far more likely than foreign ones to recruit Ivoiriens and rely upon local inputs rather than imported ones.[168] He also argues that the onset of more difficult economic conditions at the end of the 1970s and early 1980s tended merely to increase the attractiveness of a business career, leading to the emergence of a new cohort of young, graduate entrepreneurs. As against those who maintained that the African bourgeoisie was merely of the comprador variety – contributing nothing to real development – Rapley concludes that 'capitalism in Côte d'Ivoire is clearly Ivoirien and not merely a foreign branch of European capitalism'.[169] His figures, which use different base years to those of the Appendix, are reproduced in Table 5.3.

However, there were downsides to the Ivoirien 'miracle', even at its most miraculous. First of all, while rural Ivoiriens came to enjoy the benefits of an excellent road network – at the same time as that of Ghana was fast deteriorating – social services lagged behind. In particular, the expansion of access to schooling

Table 5.3 Average annual Ivoirien growth rates (per cent)

Sector	1965–80	1980–89
GDP	6.8	1.2
Agriculture	3.3	2.3
Industry	10.4	−1.7
Manufacturing	9.1	8.2
Exports	5.5	3.1
Imports	7.6	−1.1

Source: From the World Bank. Every effort has been made to trace the copyright holder and the publisher will be pleased to make the necessary arrangement at the first opportunity.

was considerably slower than in other countries. In 1965/66, some 56 per cent of primary age children in Ghana were in school, but only 35 per cent were in Côte d'Ivoire. Although the latter were conscious of the skills shortage, secondary school enrolments were also remarkably small: that, 28,100 as against 312,700 for Ghana.[170] The Ghanaians also had a much better record of promoting the education of girls, especially at the secondary school level. In Ivoirien schools, boys outnumbered girls by a ratio of four to one. Moreover, there was a much greater regional disparity in access to schooling, so that people living near Abidjan were eight times as likely to receive an education as residents of the North were. The Ivoiriens expected to buy in foreign skilled manpower, but the educational policy was publicly justified on the basis that the country did not want to provide a 'cut-rate education'. As René Dumont acidly remarked: 'so as not to be given a cut-rate education to the African peasants, they are given none'.[171] The one bright spot lay in the innovative provision of educational broadcasts through the medium of television, with support from UNESCO and the World Bank, with some positive consequences for reading and writing skills.[172]

The issue of income inequality is also worth considering in closer detail. The remarkable openness of the Ivoirien job market meant that those at the top and the bottom of the income scale – French managers at one end and Burkinabé (or Upper Voltans) at the other end – were typically foreigners, although many of these 'foreigners' sank permanent roots in Côte d'Ivoire. Those who have addressed themselves to issues of equality have tended to come to rather different conclusions. Whereas at least one analyst ranked Côte d'Ivoire as amongst the 'high inequality' countries Bastiaan Den Tuinder (writing in 1978) placed it amongst the 'low inequality' countries. He concluded that the lowest 40 per cent of the population received 10 per cent of the income in 1970 while the top 20 per cent received 67.1 per cent, but that the former had improved their share to 19.7 per cent by 1973/74 while the latter had dropped to 51.6 per cent.[173] On these figures, Côte d'Ivoire was a more unequal country than Ghana was, but by a lesser margin than might have been expected. However, it has to be recognised that these figures conceal marked regional inequalities. The gap between the earnings of most northern peasants and Abidjan wage-earners was very substantial indeed. Within the cocoa farming communities itself, it has often been assumed that income inequalities amongst the farmers were very great. But it has been demonstrated that farm size does not necessarily correlate with output because many of the smaller farms were worked more intensively.[174] The income disparities amongst the cocoa farmers were therefore less profound than those between cocoa farming and grain producing communities in the North, despite some channelling of resources from one to another. On balance, it would be fair to conclude that the Ivoirien path to development generated extremes of wealth and poverty, but not always in the places analysts have expected to find them.

Finally, if there was a 'miracle', the doubters were correct to predict that it would not last. Towards the end of the 1970s, the economy began to falter for a combination of reasons. The most obvious was the collapse of commodity prices. Côte d'Ivoire toughed out the oil price hikes of the early 1970s, and after the discovery of its own reserves it seemed that it might even become a modest exporter in its own right. Moreover, between 1975 and 1977 there was more than a doubling of the world cocoa price and more than a tripling of the coffee price. However, global overproduction thereafter helped to precipitate a price slide to the detriment of export earnings and government revenues alike. As Nkrumah himself might have predicted, the relentless expansion of cocoa production would ultimately prove self-defeating because there was a limit to how much the market could absorb. By 1980, Côte d'Ivoire had become the world's largest cocoa producer, but there had been a similar push in Brazil and Malaysia. The decline of Ghanaian production was something of a Godsend for everyone, but it could do no more than postpone the day of reckoning. The Ivoirien government had refused to sign the International Cocoa Agreement, which sought to reconcile the demands of producing and consuming countries, and hoped to be able to influence prices by playing the world market. During the 1979/80 seasons, the government withheld 150,000 tonnes from the market in an effort to push up the world price. The gamble failed when the world price continued to fall. Côte d'Ivoire was eventually forced to sell the cocoa at lower prices than she would originally have earned. In the wake of this financial disaster, Houphouët, who had always championed the virtues of capitalism, started to sound more like Nkrumah with his bitter denunciations of the iniquities of the global marketplace. The harsh reality was that the country's terms of trade had declined by 32 per cent between 1977 and 1980.[175]

The second overall problem was that there had been a rapid expansion of state expenditure during the 1970s, which yielded disappointing returns and put further pressure on strained public finances. Ironically, the Ivoirien regime was lured into a false sense of security by the short-lived cocoa and coffee booms, and began to borrow heavily from Western banks when credit was easy to come by. An example of ill-advised expenditure was the construction of six large sugar complexes whose routine operating costs amounted to between two and three times the world market price.[176] In the absence of a commensurate increase in foreign investment, Côte d'Ivoire began to run up a substantial foreign debt. By 1980, debt servicing amounted to as much as 26 per cent of exports and in 1984 if there had not been a rescheduling it would have reached more than 60 per cent.[177] Such high levels of debt repayment were clearly unsustainable and, having come to terms with the IMF, the government was able to reschedule its repayments. The resulting stabilisation programme aimed at making substantial cuts in government spending, especially amongst the under-performing parastatals. However, the leadership had not yet fully grasped the depth of the crisis. After an improvement in commodity prices in 1985, the regime appeared to believe that it was back to business as usual. However, this was followed by a renewed downturn which subjected Côte d'Ivoire to the ultimate humiliation of declaring its insolvency in May 1987. Ultimately, therefore, there was some convergence between the Ghanaian and Ivoirien experiences by the early 1980s.

Finally, it remains to consider the extent to which the Ivoirien political system contributed to the 'miracle'. The political system which Young describes as 'mildly authoritarian' was tolerated by Ivoiriens for as long as it delivered material benefits. For example, while trade union activities were quite narrowly circumscribed, the wages of Ivoirien workers were relatively high. Young cites an average monthly wage in 1974 of 20,700 CFA francs as compared to 10,000 in Singapore and half that in Taiwan.[178] However, as crisis conditions emerged, the lines of fracture became more obvious. In the urban areas, the lack of functioning local government structures contributed to housing shortages and the decline of public services as the central government budget came under strain. This was especially the case in Abidjan, which served as the primary urban magnet for rural migrants and foreign immigrants alike. Indeed Abidjan was the fast growing city in the world in the second half of the twentieth century. It did not help matters that the government pumped as much as one-third of urban investment into Houphouët's home-town, Yamoussoukro, which was proclaimed as the new capital in 1983.[179] The President's construction of a vast basilica, designed to rival St Peter's in Rome, was the most visible sign of misplaced priorities. During the early 1980s, the implementation of an austerity programme led to rising rents and to increased levels of urban unemployment. While certain anti-foreign sentiments had always lurked beneath the surface, they became more obvious as many ordinary Ivoiriens looked for scapegoats.

Houphouët was aware that the popularity of the government was shrinking, and it was in an attempt to renew the social contract with the Ivoirien people that he announced the first competitive elections in 1980. Although Côte d'Ivoire remained a one-party state, there was henceforth to be a choice of candidates for new local government bodies and the National Assembly. This culminated in a significant turnover of personnel: in the national elections of 1980, no fewer than 120 of 147 the winners were newcomers.[180] These elections did not, however, lead to the creation of a better gender balance: only eight women were elected, and only one was rewarded with a government post.[181] Moreover, the new politicians were drawn from much the same stratum of Ivoirien society. Yves Fauré suggests that an additional reason for implementing these political reforms was that Houphouët needed to bring the lines of patronage back under his control after some years in which members of the elite had been able to build their own patrimonial networks. On this view, the flushing out of the political stables, under the guise of eradicating corruption, was really about restoring an older system of Presidential patronage.[182]

Some intellectuals began to voice the unthinkable, namely that Côte d'Ivoire should abandon the one-party state. In 1982, Laurent Gbagbo, then a University lecturer, had been prevented from delivering a speech in favour of multipartyism and was forced to go into exile. However, a greater threat emanated from within the PDCI. In 1980, Houphouët turned 75 years old and it became increasingly apparent that he would not be around for ever. Yacé had seemed to be anointed heir, but he was unceremoniously dropped by his mentor. An amendment to the constitution was introduced which provided that the Vice-President would succeed if the President died in office. However, in vintage crocodilian fashion, Houphouët made sure that no-one filled that position. Nevertheless, prospective successors began to jockey for position, much like in Kenya. The language of ethnicity now became more audible as northerners sought to disqualify potential Baoulé candidates from assuming the mantle.

The institutional weakness of the PDCI was such that it did not provide a coherent mechanism for resolving the issue amicably. By the close of the decade, an escalating political crisis was added to the manifestations of economic distress, leading to some serious questions as to whether the Houphouët legacy was so benign after all.

5.3 A clash of styles: Senegal and Guinea

Our final comparison is between two other neighbouring states in West Africa – namely Guinea under Ahmed Sekou Touré and Senegal under Léopold Senghor. This is the trickiest comparison of them all because of the imbalance in the literature about these countries. After independence, the Sekou Touré regime closed the country off for long periods of time, making it difficult for researchers to go into the field. Both the quantity and the quality of what has been written about Guinea is consequently disappointing. By contrast, Senegal was welcoming towards the academic community, and this has helped to spawn a rich body of published research on that country. Ironically, this relates to the very ideological differences which form part of our concerns here.

Guinea was one of the better-endowed colonies in French West Africa. In addition to possessing considerable potential for agriculture and pastoralism across diverse ecological zones, the fact that the major rivers of West Africa have their source in the Fouta Djalon highlands meant that there were excellent prospects for the generation of hydro-electric power. Guinea was also particularly well-endowed with mineral resources: it contained two-thirds of the world's bauxite reserves, plus substantial quantities of iron ore and smaller reserves of diamonds and gold. During colonial times, French capital had invested in plantation agriculture and in the mining sector. Although Guinea could well have gone down the Ivoirien route, Sekou Touré came to disagree strenuously with Houphouët (a former colleague in the RDA) over relations with France. When the Guinean people followed their leader and voted against the constitutional proposals in 1958, de Gaulle acted on his veiled threats, despite Sekou Touré's attempts to mend fences.[183] The French swiftly dismantled their administrative machinery and pulled out as many of their nationals as they could persuade to leave in order to wreak the maximum havoc. Even then, Sekou Touré held out hope that a rapprochement might still be possible. Guinea remained within the franc zone and Sekou Touré hoped to sign bi-lateral agreements with France, as all the other African states were eventually to do. However, de Gaulle resolved that there would be no forgiveness and sought to precipitate an economic crisis in the belief that this would create a backlash against the leadership.[184] Guinea was cut off from further access to FIDES funding and the only French aid which remained on offer was targeted at the enormous aluminium complex at Fria which commenced operations in 1960. Having been cast out of the French compound – to recall Senghor's metaphor – the Touré regime set about seeking to manage the crisis. The government now adopted a defiant posture, accusing the French of wanting to perpetuate colonial exploitation and castigating those African leaders who had gone along with de Gaulle. Predictably perhaps, the Guinean leader became soul-mates with

Nkrumah who made a loan of £10 million at a critical juncture. Although the two leaders certainly had their disagreements, they always regarded each other as sharing a common agenda: that is, completing the independence of the African continent (Guinea made real sacrifices on behalf of Guinea-Bissau) and fighting neo-colonialism in all its disguises. Their collaboration was one of the few examples of African leaders who managed to bridge the Francophone/Anglophone divide.

If Nkrumah was a cherished ally, Houphouët and Senghor were vilified as the lackeys of Western imperialism. Sekou Touré was especially scornful of the Senegalese leader's speeches and writings on the subject of African socialism which he depicted as a convenient cover for policies which were neither truly African nor socialist. Sekou Touré was at pains to assert that Guinea was committed to 'scientific socialism', and to an even greater extent than Nkrumah he appropriated the language of Marxism. In fact, he modelled himself on the other great leaders of the Communist world: he published the mandatory volumes of his thinking on various subjects and revelled in lengthy speeches exhorting the masses to greater feats of endeavour. Guinea even embarked on its own version of China's Cultural Revolution, dubbed the 'Socialist Cultural Revolution', in 1967.[185] But for all the insistence on socialist purity, the reality was that the Guinean revolution was rooted in a gut nationalist impulse. Unlike Nkrumah, Sekou Touré had only finished primary school before going to work in the postal service, from where he rose to become the head of the Guinean chapter of the radical CGT union (Confédération Générale du Travail). To all intents and purposes he was a self-educated man, and even more than Nkrumah he accumulated a colourful array of intellectual baggage. In the later years of his rule, Sekou Touré was finally drawn back to his Muslim roots. Although the official tone of government rhetoric was decidedly Marxist, the underlying agenda was not that different to African socialist regimes elsewhere. Little attention was paid to questions of class or to the operations of capitalism on a global scale. Moreover, while Sekou Touré cosied up to the Eastern Bloc after his falling out with France, he nevertheless insisted on the maintenance of a non-aligned position. On more than one occasion, he crossed swords with the Soviet Union and China over what he regarded as attempts to disseminate their propaganda. At the same time, he was able to maintain surprisingly friendly relations with the United States.

The adoption of socialism had important consequences for the framing of economic policy after independence. The withdrawal of French planters and the perceived disloyalty of the French business community not surprisingly led Sekou Touré to look elsewhere for a developmental motor. As in the case of Ghana, it was argued that there was no indigenous capitalists who could perform the job, and those that there were could not be trusted. This meant that the state would have to assume the commanding role. In seeking to formulate an economic strategy, the regime turned to a French Marxist economist, Charles Bettelheim (known for his writings on Russia) for advice in 1959. The latter advocated the extension of state controls to cover trade, currency and credit; the nationalisation of certain utilities and the promotion of agricultural co-operatives.[186] The government took much of this advice on board, whereas

René Dumont received short shrift after an ill-fated attempt to proffer advice of his own. The first act of the regime was to assert control over the commercial sector which had hitherto been under the control of French business. The Comptoir Guinéen du Commerce Extérieur (CGCE) was given a monopoly on trade with the socialist world, over the importation of key consumer goods as well a guaranteed share of the export market for crops like groundnuts, palm-kernels, bananas and coffee.[187] In May 1960, the Comptoir Guinéen du Commerce Intérieur (CGCI) was established to take over many of the internal commercial operations of the CGCE. The attempt to centralise control over the import-export and wholesale trade led to economic chaos and hastened the withdrawal of French capital. As part of an attempt to refine statism, a series of separate parastatals were created in 1961 to take over the buying, selling and pricing of different types of commodities.[188] In November 1964, all foreign and wholesale commerce was finally nationalised. Another turning point came in February 1960 when the regime suddenly announced its breakaway from the franc zone and the creation of a new national currency, the Guinean franc, which was notionally pegged to the CFA franc. In 1972, the Guinean franc was in turn replaced by the *syli*, which was not a convertible currency. Finally, the government nationalised the national utilities, the gold, diamond and some of the bauxite mines, as well as shipping.

Although these policies seemed to confirm that the regime was hostile to foreign capital, it manifested a surprising willingness to solicit aid from the West. The country's first Three Year Plan (1960–63) aimed at increasing Guinean control over the national economy, raising living standards and modernising the social and economic infrastructure of the country. However, the plan assumed the injection of substantial quantities of foreign aid into the economy. Whereas the regime expected to find 6 billion Guinean francs from the profits of the CGCE, it expected another 23 billion to come from external sources.[189] The Seven-Year Plan (1964–71) and the next Five Year Plan (1973–78) did not significantly alter this dependency upon external sources of funding. Whereas Nyerere preached self-reliance while Tanzania became increasingly dependent in practice, Sekou Touré seems to have been entirely unconcerned about the implications of aid dependency. He calculated that Guinea needed external aid and it did not matter greatly whether this came from the East or the West.

The result was that the structure of the Guinean economy was highly segmented. Foreign capital invested heavily in the mining sector, often in partnership with the state. A good example is the Boké bauxite complex where two multinational corporations, the Harvey Aluminium Company and ALCAN, embarked on a joint venture with the state which owned 49 per cent of the shares. Similarly, at the Fria alumina complex the state assumed 49 per cent of the shares in partnership with a consortium of multinationals.[190] The close relationship with these companies was never regarded as problematic because they contributed so much to exports and the public coffer. Between 1948 and 1972, the share of exports accounted for by alumina (processed bauxite) rose from 46.8 per cent to 70.8 per cent of the total.[191] If bauxite is added in, their joint contribution comprised no less than 95 per cent of total exports in 1975.[192] However, foreign capital was squeezed out of the non-mining sectors.

The one exception was in agriculture where plantations producing pineapples provided Guinea with its second largest export commodity. But elsewhere, the state assumed the commanding role, with foreign aid often being used to establish state enterprises. Britain, Italy, the Soviet Union and China were all involved in the construction of industrial enterprises which were turned over to the state on completion. In agriculture, the regime followed a familiar obsession with modernisation, which was to be achieved through a combination of state and co-operative farms as a first step towards collectivisation. As in Ghana, 'socialist agriculture' was expected to achieve superior results through the application of 'modern' methods. Within the Guinean conception of socialism, there was little place for indigenous capitalists. The rough treatment meted out to them stands in stark contrast to the willingness to cut deals with multinational corporations. There was only one private Guinean firm listed as employing more than ten persons in 1971 and this closed down when the director was imprisoned by the regime.[193] The assault on the business community was taken to unprecedented levels in 1975 when the government declared the ending of all private trade and the closure of markets, with a view to strengthening the co-operatives.[194] Given the historic strength of the *dioula* (*dyula*) traders, this was a very bold and a very unwise move indeed.

There is little disagreement about the results which ensued, despite the almost total absence of reliable statistics. State intervention was often little short of disastrous, a reality which was somewhat concealed by the rapid expansion of production in the mining enclaves. Despite the existence of a formal planning machinery, state agencies spent at will. Recurrent expenditure accelerated so rapidly that there was often little left over to finance genuine development projects, with the exception of those which were directly funded from external sources. The investments which were made were often poorly conceived and state enterprises were poorly managed. The factories ran at a fraction of capacity and at a substantial loss. The scarcity of consumer goods, which was compounded by the inefficiencies of the state distribution system, discouraged peasants from selling their goods through official channels. Peasants were also resistant towards attempts to push them into collective production, while pastoralists were even more reluctant to embrace collective ownership of cattle. The smuggling of crops into neighbouring states – where consumer goods could be purchased and where the CFA franc was worth something – became endemic. Moreover, around a fifth of the population (mostly peasants) voted with their feet and settled in Senegal and Côte d'Ivoire.

The result of ill-chosen agrarian policies was that the production of rice, the staple of most Guineans, declined to a point where the country became dependent upon American food aid under the PL480 programme. The decline of cash crops production was even more dramatic: whereas bananas and coffee made up 60 per cent of exports by value at independence, their joint contribution, together with pineapples, only accounted for 27 per cent of the total by 1966.[195] To top it all, Guinea sank heavily into debt during the first decade. By 1967, the national debt was four times larger than the annual revenues of the state.[196] Without external assistance, including aid from the capitalist countries, Guinea could not have continued to import essentials like petroleum or maintain its spending commitments. Equally, it is only the mineral exports which made the economic figures look vaguely respectable (see Appendix 5.1).

In the case of Tanzania, the government could at least point towards real improvements in certain social indices, but in Guinea there was nothing positive to weigh in the scales. The government allocated relatively little of its expenditure to services like health and education. In 1964/65, it dedicated FG 2590 million of its recurrent budget (totalling FG 12,530 million) to defence as against FG 3280 million to education and FG 1420 million to public health. But by 1972/73, the share allocated to defence (FG 7470 million of a total of FG 18,200 million) was significantly greater than the totals for education (FG 2300 million), health (FG 1820 million) and agriculture (a pitiful FG 130 million) put together.[197] In the development budget, tiny sums of money were allocated to education and health, whereas communications and industry consumed almost everything. The proportion of children attending school appears to have increased somewhat. The percentage of children between the ages of seven and thirteen attending school rose from a mere 9 per cent in 1958 to 33 per cent in 1964 and 36 per cent in 1973, but this was still a minority.[198] Moreover, the schools were plagued by a shortage of teachers, books and buildings. Although the Guinean government prided itself on liberating the curriculum from French influences, the quality of education was poor. In the immediate aftermath of independence, voluntarism was enshrined as state policy under the so-called 'human investment' programmes. Communities were encouraged to engage in their own voluntary labour to construct schools and health centres. However, the enthusiasm for voluntary labour steadily declined and relatively little was achieved thereafter.

One reason why Guinean socialism delivered so little was that the regime was concerned above all with ensuring its political survival. In 1958, the French were seeking to destabilise the regime, and in 1970 the Portuguese sponsored an invasion force which came close to toppling it. The regime was also conscious of an undercurrent of hostility emanating from the Foulah of the North who had been amongst the last to join the PDG (Parti Démocratique du Guinée).[199] The siege mentality partly accounts for the substantial resources which were diverted into defence and national security. However, as most authors on Guinea have observed, the 'perpetual plot' also became a very convenient political device for Sekou Touré. By keeping the country on an almost constant state of alert, he could justify the arbitrariness of his rule – for this was a President who was determined to exercise the full range of his powers. Sekou Touré was also able to use a steady succession of supposed crises to intimidate potential opponents and to clear out the political stables from time to time. Even his closest allies lived in almost perpetual fear of the next purge.[200] The United States was always one of the most important purveyors of aid, and Sekou Touré aspired towards a rapprochement with France. Although relations with Senegal and Côte d'Ivoire were normally frosty, and the latter were blamed for number of plots, Sekou Touré could turn up the heat or turn on the charm as the mood caught him. In other words, this was a highly astute politician with a keen sense of political survival.

The internal organisation of the regime followed from the same logic. For Sekou Touré, it was essential that all potential sources of opposition be snuffed out. It has been suggested that the Guinea was the only real police state which emerged in sub-Saharan Africa.[201] After 1958, when the opposition parties merged with the PDG, Guinea became a de facto one-party state. The theory was that all Guineans would be members of the party and therefore have an input into decision-making. Writing in 1978, R. W. Johnson commented that 'its claim to be a true mass party has to be treated with some respect. Virtually every Guinean town-dweller is a member and attends party meetings or gatherings at least occasionally.'[202] He conceded, however, that party structures were more ephemeral at the village level. Although the party committees had replaced the chiefs (as we saw in the last chapter), the level of active participation was probably lower. In the first decade of independence, regional party bosses wielded a considerable amount of power, albeit in competition with the regional governors who belonged to the administrative branch. However, when the regime launched the 'Socialist Cultural Revolution' in 1967, it promised to restore power to the grassroots. The basic unit of the party was henceforth to be the Pouvoir Révolutionnaire Locale (PRL) of which there were some 8000.[203] The PRLs were often directed against the state and party bureaucracies, but they were also a handy instrument of central control. Similarly, in empowering the youth through the JRDA (Jeunesse de la Révolution Démocratique Africaine) and the Militia, the government was able to kill two birds with one stone: it diverted the energies of the youth into safe channels, whilst enabling the government to intimidate potential dissidents.

The government was especially suspicious of religious bodies. Although it attacked 'indigenous religion' as mere superstition, it had no more time for the Catholic Church or Muslim clerics. The French Archbishop of Conakry was expelled in 1961, and his Guinean successor was later sentenced to forced labour for life for his alleged role in a subsequent plot.[204] At the same time, the government attacked many prominent marabouts as being errant Muslims. The regime tried to force the Imams to preach on its own chosen themes, to reduce the number of daily prayers to two and to restrict pilgrims wanting to go to Mecca. Given that this was a predominantly Muslim country (about 75 per cent of the total), these were bold measures.[205] In fact, there was scarcely an area of Guinean life which was untouched by the centralising hand of the PDG. For a regime in search of modernity, culture had to be taken in hand and liberated from its dangerous traditional moorings. A pride in indigenous culture and history tended therefore to be expressed in a baroque fusion of socialism and traditionalism.

The main associational bodies were required to come under the wing of the single-party on the grounds that the PDG embodied the general will. Sekou Touré might have been expected to look kindly on the labour movement, given that this was where he started from. He was evidently proud of his background, but he was also aware of the potential threat which organised labour posed. Sekou Touré remained the nominal head of the Confédération Nationale des Travailleurs Guineéns (CNGT) for some years after independence, and when he finally relinquished the position he ensured that he was succeeded by political loyalists.[206] The CNGT was converted into an integral wing of the party and did little to back workers on the few occasions when they dared to challenge the government – such as in 1961 when the leaders of the teachers' union circulated a memorandum calling for higher pay and were put on trial for subversion.[207] The women's movement, which had been a powerful force within the PDG in the 1950s, was similarly subordinated. The government laid considerable emphasis upon the furtherance of women's liberation, and there was some basis to its gender claims. In 1962, it introduced a new law which made seventeen the minimum age of marriage and required the consent of the woman. It also ensured that the wife had rights of inheritance and provided for equality of access to divorce. More remarkably, the government outlawed polygamy except in special circumstances.[208] But while women were reasonably well-represented in the National Assembly (certainly as compared with Côte d'Ivoire), the regime provided little real space for women to organise themselves as women.

Nevertheless, it was women who eventually stood up to the President. In August 1977, market women in the provinces demonstrated against the decision to close village markets and abuses of power by the Militia. Their protests spread to Conakry, where the market women's grievances fed into a more general sense of malaise. On 27–28 August, thousands of women marched on the Presidential palace and many were killed in the standoff which ensued. Although control was restored with the aid of Cuban troops, the President was clearly shaken by the manner in which the women had 'spoken truth to power'.[209] The offending decree was quickly withdrawn, and thereafter the government seemed to recognise that it could not resolve the underlying economic crisis without shifting its ground somewhat. The retreat from doctrinaire socialism was signalled by subsequent efforts to mend fences with Guinea's sworn enemies. In December 1978, Giscard d'Estaing became the first French president to visit Conakry since de Gaulle, and there was a public reconciliation with Senghor and Houphouët.[210] However, while there was an opening up on the international stage, Sekou Touré could not relinquish his tight grip on power at home. When he died in March 1984 a power vacuum was inevitably created. The following month, before the PDG could meet to choose a successor, the army stepped in. A new military junta was formed under the leadership of Colonel Lansana Conté and the PDG was dissolved. Guinean socialism, which had failed to produce either greater material prosperity or freedom, was abruptly terminated – although the ghost of Sekou Touré lived on.

The trajectory which was followed by Senegal diverged in fundamental respects from that of Guinea. Whereas Sekou Touré (somewhat reluctantly) severed the link with France in 1958, Senghor regarded it as in the best interests of Senegal to retain the closest ties possible. Both in his intellectual pursuits, as one of the leading lights in the *négritude* movement, and as a nationalist politician Senghor was perpetually in search of the golden mean. *Négritude* amounted to an intellectual rejection of the supposed superiority of European culture, but as an affirmation of African values it often merely inverted the signs and ascribed positive values to Western stereotypes.[211] Senghor was not aiming to subvert Western hegemony, but to find an equal place for Africa at the table of world civilisation. Equally, as a politician Senghor sought to steer a middle course between militant nationalists who advocated a total break with France, and others such as Lamine Guèye who believed that the existing relationship could continue pretty much as before. In the 1950s, Senghor was an advocate of greater powers being devolved to the colonies, but without detriment to the maintenance of a harmonious Franco-African relationship. When the schism with Mali occurred, Senghor signed a series of accords which were designed to put the relationship on a new footing. These ensured that France would remain the main dispenser of aid and a guarantor of preferential trading arrangements. Senegal retained a large body of French technical advisors within key Ministries, and these numbered several hundred in the mid-1960s. Indeed, Jean Collin served as the Minster of Finance until 1970. The Senegalese also consented to the presence of some 7000 French troops. And finally, Senegal joined the CFA franc zone. In all of these respects, the Senegalese path closely mirrored the Ivoirien one whilst diverging from that of Guinea. Confusingly, though, Senghor spoke publicly in the language of African socialism, and even went as far as to convene a conference on the subject in 1962.[212] However, Senghor's approach corresponded more closely to that of Côte d'Ivoire and Kenya than Ghana or Tanzania.

The key to understanding the Senghorian method lies in appreciating the critical importance of alliances forged between the ruling party, the UPS (Union Progressiste Sénégalaise), and two sets of vested interests. The first of these was the French business community which had traditionally dominated the import-export trade and had begun to move into light industry in the 1950s. After independence, French firms were eased out of the groundnut trade, which was taken over by the state, but they retained highly favoured positions within the tightly regulated import-export sector. Moreover, they came to be regarded as the primary instrument of an industrial strategy which rested on import substitution. The concessions which were granted to French firms were extremely generous by any yardstick. The Investment Code of 1962 provided guarantees against nationalisation and assured the unfettered repatriation of capital and profits. Moreover, French firms were assured easy access to credit from within Senegal.[213] The largest firms were also granted a special status which protected them from changes in their tax and customs status for a 20-year period. Finally, the government introduced measures to protect industries which were set up on Senegalese soil. Customs duties were set at a level which discriminated against imports (especially Asian ones) which might compete with the locally produced product. Because of the heavy subsidies and low rates of corporate taxation, Catherine Boone observes that these French-owned enterprises contributed very little to government coffers, while there was actually a net outflow of capital and profits from the country.[214] This was a price the Senegalese regime was prepared to pay for the development path it had chosen.

The second alliance was with the marabouts (or Muslim clerics) whose societal influence cannot be over-emphasised. In his struggle with Lamine Guèye in the 1950s, Senghor astutely brought the religious authorities of the interior onto his side, whereas his rival relied on a narrower support-base in the four communes. The marabouts subsequently stood out against any leftward drift within the UPS and ensured that the latter remained committed to a policy of continuity. Soon after independence, they also inflicted a crucial defeat on the would-be technocrats when the latter threatened to meddle in their relationship with the peasantry. In the early 1950s, experts were already warning that wasteful methods of cultivation threatened to turn the groundnut basin into a dustbowl. Prime Minister Mamadou Dia proposed dealing with the problem by bringing the administration and the peasantry into closer proximity through decentralisation and the promotion of co-operatives which would improve production techniques. The government even toyed with the idea of promoting land reforms. These interventions threatened to weaken the position of the marabouts who responded by calling for the removal of Dia at the end of 1962. This precipitated a schism between the Prime Minister and his technocratic supporters, on the one side, and President Senghor, who sided with the marabouts, on the other.[215] The deadlock was resolved when Senghor deployed paratroopers and proceeded to arrest Dia and four of his Ministers, alleging their involvement in a coup plot.[216] This crisis underlined that nothing was more important to Senghor than the preservation of the strategic alliance with the marabouts, particularly those of the Mouride brotherhood which was dominant in the groundnut basin.

In subsequent years, the regime pursued a policy of maximising groundnut production despite the adverse environmental consequences which were predicted. The marabouts were crucial to this strategy because they tended to own the groundnut fields on which their disciples (or *talibés*) worked. But their compliance was also crucial because the creation of a statutory marketing organisation, the Office de Commercialisation Agricole (OCA), provided a mechanism by which resources could be extracted from the countryside and diverted to other purposes. This included the payment of bureaucratic salaries, which consumed as much as half of the recurrent budget by the mid-1960s, as well as infrastructure and social services.[217] If the marabouts had resisted the terms of the pricing policy, the government would have found itself in a very awkward position. Senghor went out of his way to court the *grand marabouts*, and ensured the continuing support of the head of the Mourides, Falilou M'Backé. The marabouts also received material inducements to play the game. The government created some 1500 producer co-operatives which were dominated by the marabouts, who received the lion's share of the credit, inputs and access to public lands.[218] The net result was many of the marabouts became extremely wealthy in their own right. In 1967, 27 of the 29 largest landholders were marabouts, and of these no fewer than 20 belonged to the Mourides.[219]

These two primary alliances were underpinned by a strategy of keeping other potential sources of opposition under wraps. After the 1963 elections, Senegal became a de facto one-party state, and political opponents were either co-opted into the ruling party, as was the Parti du Regroupement Africain (PRA), or repressed. The government was also conscious of the potential threat posed by students and intellectuals who were the least enamoured of the slavishly pro-French orientation of the regime. Here the UPS endeavoured to buy compliance through the expansion of state employment. Then there were urban workers and the residents of Dakar more generally. The regime favoured the maintenance of a low-wage economy in order to attract investment. It therefore dealt firmly with labour militants, while using some of the resources sucked out of the countryside to upgrade urban amenities. Finally, there was the Senegalese business community to reckon with. Because the regime was reluctant to go down the path of indigenisation, it was difficult for Senegalese to muscle in on the juiciest pickings which had been cornered by the French and the Lebanese. However, precisely because the gateway to accumulation was a narrow one, the UPS was able to trade political support for preferential access to resources. Traders required licenses and these were distributed on the basis of political allegiance. The government also brokered relationships between favoured Senegalese traders and the French commercial houses which ensured good business opportunities for the lucky few. Again, imported rice (the staple food) was channelled through selected Senegalese agents.[220] In his stinging attack on neo-colonialism in Senegal, *Xala*, Sembène Ousmane confronted the manner in which economic rents were made by the selling on of these allocations at handy markups.[221] In a country where patron-client relations were a crucial determinant of success, business and politics were inevitably closely intertwined.

When measured against the economic dislocation in Guinea, the Senegalese record might seem rather successful. However, when set against the record of Côte d'Ivoire the results seem much less impressive. Between 1960 and 1970, the economy grew at an unspectacular 2.5 per cent, which was probably at about the rate of population increase (see Appendix 5.1). Industry grew somewhat faster (at 4.4 per cent), but these results were not comparable to those of the Ivoiriens. Moreover, the rural economy remained heavily dependent upon groundnut exports, in a sector where yields were falling. Moreover, rice continued to be imported in large quantities, despite the untapped potential of the southern Casamance region. Moreover, there had been no deepening of Senegalese capitalism in the sense of the emergence of an indigenous entrepreneurial class. The favouritism shown to French business had stifled Senegalese business far more than in Côte d'Ivoire. Finally, the country had become a more unequal place. Government bureaucrats, numbering about 3 per cent of the population earned 7 times more than the average peasant and twice that of a skilled worker.[222] At the top of the social hierarchy sat the French and Lebanese business community and a small number of prosperous Senegalese merchants. In the villages and in the streets of Dakar, real poverty was there to be seen.

The growing sense that the Senghor government had got things badly wrong led to an eruption of popular resistance at the end of the 1960s which caught the regime by surprise. In the vanguard were the students who, in the spring of 1968, matched their Parisian counterparts by taking to the streets to protest against French domination of the economy and the educational policies of the government. The students were joined by trade unionists who went out on strike and demonstrated alongside many other citizens in the streets of Dakar. To top it all, Senegalese businessmen launched a damaging indictment of policies which had favoured French business interests to the exclusion of indigenous entrepreneurs. Meanwhile, in the countryside peasants were sullenly refusing to repay their loans or to market their crops through official channels – a phenomenon which came to be known as the 'peasant malaise'.[223] Part of the problem was that producer prices had fallen by 15 per cent when French groundnut subsidies were removed in 1967, but this was compounded by the fact that the state was pocketing the lion's share of the proceeds and was not prepared to cushion the fall. Furthermore, the yields on peasant plots declined as fragile soils showed definite signs of exhaustion.[224] The yields plummeted further as a result of the droughts which struck between 1966 and 1969 and again over 1972/73. Even the marabouts began to adopt a somewhat sulky position in relation to the regime. After the death of Falilou M'Backé in 1968, his younger brother, Abdou Lahatte M'Backé, succeeded to the head of the Mourides and pointedly distanced himself from the UPS.[225] He even went so far as to advise peasants to concentrate on subsistence crops in the place of groundnuts.[226]

The Senghor regime responded to the crisis with a familiar mixture of carrots and sticks. At the height of the protests in Dakar, a state of emergency was declared and the army was sent onto the campus. Many students and workers incurred injuries, around a thousand people were arrested and many were imprisoned. The government then set about seeking to dismantle the Union Nationale des Travailleurs Sénégalais (UNTS) whilst sponsoring a new Confédération Nationale des Travailleurs Sénégalais (CNTS) which was tied to the ruling party. At the same time, the regime modified its co-option strategy to bring new constituencies into its embrace. This necessitated a reworking of its entire policy framework in such a manner as to maximise the generation of spoils. In the process, the government took to heart some of the criticisms which had been levelled against it. After 1970, the French administrative presence was scaled down and greater numbers of educated Senegalese were employed in senior positions. This went together with the creation of seventy new parastatals with responsibility for managing a large portfolio of state investments in mining, fishing and tourism. The money increasingly came from the World Bank and private banking institutions in the Arab world. Aside from the economic spinoffs which were expected to ensue, the enlargement of the public sector provided employment for the large numbers of students graduating each year.[227] Furthermore, a number of other honeypots were created which tended to intensify the clientelist dimension in Senegalese life.

In this connection, the regime attempted to provide more of a leg-up to Senegalese businessmen. New financial institutions were created which provided preferential terms of credit for Senegalese entrepreneurs. Despite a new technocratic language of administration, these loans tended to gravitate towards those who were politically well-connected – in a manner which is strikingly reminiscent of the Kenyan experience. Moreover, whereas French companies had previously been permitted to monopolise the import–export trade, a select group of 100 Senegalese businessmen was henceforth to be allowed a cut of the action. Equally, Senegalese traders were given better access to the goods which were produced by local factories. More symbolically, the Dakar Chamber of Commerce, which exercised some control over import licence and quotas, was indigenised.[228] It was this episode which is mercilessly parodied by Sembène Ousmane in the opening sequence of his film, *Xala*, in which the French are turned out of the Chamber buildings only to return with suitcases full of money which secure their continued control behind the scenes.

Finally, the Senghor regime set out to rekindle its political links with the countryside, which was hit hard by successive droughts. When the marabouts proceeded to negotiate on behalf of groundnut producers, the government wanted to be seen to listen. In 1971 and again in 1973, when peasants complained of financial distress, the government wrote off their debts to the co-operatives. The President took personal responsibility for setting the producer price for groundnuts and raised it on a series of occasions. However, there was a limit to the generosity of the regime because groundnuts provided one of the few sources of government revenue. In 1972/73 the peasants were still receiving only 43 of the world price.[229] Moreover, by 1980–81, the producer price was 30 per cent lower than at the time of independence.[230] Interestingly, the government also turned something of a blind eye to the rampant smuggling of groundnuts into the Gambia (estimated at no less than 40,000–50,000 tons around 1970) which the Mouride marabouts were deeply implicated in. Their capital, Touba, became a state-within-a-state where the writ of the central administration did not run. It was from Touba that much of the contraband trade was organised. Although this was considered as a threat to the national interest, the regime did not feel it could clamp down too heavily for fear of alienating its principal allies.

The political calculations which underlay the second phase go some way towards explaining the disappointing results which ensued from the restructuring. Whereas Senegal desperately needed to find a way out of its monocrop dependency, there was little in the development plans which pointed to a meaningful strategy of diversification – other than the promotion of tourism. The pursuit of industrial development yielded some results, but only because of heavy levels of subsidy, which put additional strains on state finances, and protectionism which raised the cost to consumers.[231] Moreover, French companies continued to repatriate a large proportion of their profits, which meant that Senegal remained a net exporter of capital. As for the parastatals and the state financial institutions, these accumulated substantial losses, which is not altogether surprising because they made so many of their decisions on political grounds. During the 1970s, financial scandals within the public sector mounted, culminating in the spectacular financial collapse of ONCAD (Office National de Coopération et d'Assistance au Développement) in 1980, leaving a total debt of CFA 94 billion or a whopping 15 per cent of gross national product.[232] Meanwhile, the global economic downturn which followed the OPEC oil price rises hit Senegal as hard as anywhere. Over the course of the decade, the national debt rose to critical levels, so that in 1980 servicing accounted for 25 per cent of export earnings.[233] This meant that Senegal, like almost every other country was forced to come to terms with the World Bank and the IMF. Whereas the star of Côte d'Ivoire fizzled brightly and died, the Senegalese experiment with capitalism scarcely even fizzled.

Although the Senghor regime could not point to much success in economic terms, it was at pains to contrast its political stability with the predicament of other African states. Barring the jitters of the late 1960s, the UPS did manage to govern in a manner which did not require resort to heavy-handed methods. A case in point is the latitude which was extended to intellectual critics of the regime. Sembène Ousmane, Cheick Anta Diop (a historian) and Senghor himself could fairly be considered the intellectual giants of Senegal. The first two were relentless critics of what they regarded as an emasculating neo-colonialism, the physical impotence of the protagonist in *Xala* standing for the condition of the Senegalese ruling elite. Through his novels, and increasingly through his films, Sembène tackled what he regarded as the dishonesty of the Senghorian rhetoric of African socialism.[234] Although Sembène had his public disagreements with the President, and some of his work was banned, he was never actually victimised. It has to be remembered that no writer would have dared to mount the same critique in Guinea. And although Senegal became a one-party state in the early 1960s, it was also ahead of its time in permitting the formation of opposition parties. In 1974, the Parti Démocratique Sénégalais (PDS) was legalised and two years later the constitution was revised to allow for three (later four) parties, occupying specified points on the ideological spectrum. The UPS now became the Parti Socialiste (PS) and was supposed to stand for democratic socialism; the PDS became the party of liberalism; and the Marxist tendency was represented by the Parti Africain de l'Indépendance (PAI). In 1979, the conservative brief was extended to the Mouvement Républicain Sénégalais (MRS). This was democracy of a controlled kind, but it was accompanied by greater political freedoms.

Finally, Senghor did something which neither Houphouët nor Sekou Touré could bring themselves to do, and that was to voluntarily relinquish power. After the crisis of the late 1960s, Senghor recreated the position of Prime Minister, which had been abolished when Dia was removed. Instead of elevating one of the godfathers of the party, he appointed Abdou Diouf to fill the slot. Diouf was a young technocrat rather than a conventional UPS politician, and it was to him that Senghor handed the Presidential baton when he demitted office in 1980. But even this transition was laced with the Francophilia. Whereas other former heads of state in Africa made their successors nervous because they were always lurking in the background, Senghor retired to France with his French wife and left Diouf to get on with the job of governing. Hence it was Diouf who was left with the difficult task of selling Structural Adjustment policies to a reluctant population. Diouf was, however, able to capitalise on the euphoria which followed the transition. The new President legalised all opposition parties and won the 1983 elections on a landslide.

5.4   Conclusion

In this chapter, we have addressed the question of what practical difference it made when regimes opted for African socialism or attempted to indigenise capitalism. We have selected six countries for the comparison, but could quite easily have chosen others. Malawi and Cameroun might have stood equally well for the capitalist path, while Kaunda's 'Humanism' in Zambia could have furnished another example of African socialism at work.

What, then, are the broad lessons which emerge from this series of comparisons? The first is that the African socialist regimes chalked up less impressive rates of economic growth in the first decade-and-a-half of independence, but they tended to score more highly in the provision of health, education and other social services. The problem was that these investments could not be sustained in the face of rapid increases in population and sluggish economic growth. When the oil crisis struck in the 1970s, compounded by a decade of terrible drought, the socialist countries ran up substantial debts, while the amenities themselves fell into disrepair. The timing of the crisis differed from country to country, but it afflicted each in turn. Guinea scarcely had a bright patch whereas the problems of Tanzania became evident some time later. African socialism had always been closely associated with the quest for economic liberation, but each country ended up being less self-reliant in the long run.

The capitalist-roaders fared much better in crude economic terms over the first decade. In Kenya and Côte d'Ivoire it was even possible to point to the emergence of an indigenous capitalist class. Admittedly, the latter leaned heavily on its political crutches, but it began to compete with foreign capital. However, the emphasis on growth first predictably meant that social services expanded in a more haphazard manner, which tended to reinforce regional disparities. Moreover, the income gap between the richest and the poorest widened markedly. If we had chosen to consider the oil-rich states, this point would have emerged even more clearly. Although many observers believed that Kenya and Côte d'Ivoire had got it about right, they also began to struggle during the 1970s. The oil-price hike and unstable commodity prices threw government finances and the foreign trade balance out of kilter. Moreover, these regimes had also made substantial state investments which turned sour. Senegal, which was never quite the model state, exhibited the same fundamental problems, but at an even more profound level.

The second feature which is worth underlining is the close link between the development path that was chosen and the conduct of politics. The African socialist regimes tended to lay emphasis upon the primacy of the one-party state, to which trade unions, women's organisations and student associations were subordinated. This was typically justified on the principle that sectional interests ought not to be allowed to over-ride the collective good. In Tanzania, competitive elections were nevertheless retained and furnished a means of maintaining a modicum of public accountability. But in most cases the party ceased to depend on the active support of its citizens. Although these regimes preached participation, in practice they were more concerned with exacting compliance. The emphasis which was placed on the national interest also narrowed the scope for ethnically based competition, most notably in Tanzania. The African capitalist regimes also tended to favour the one-party model, and for broadly similar reasons, but within these structures there was often intense competition revolving around ties of clientage. Ethnicity was often an integral dimension thereof, but in the Kenyan, Ivoirien and Senegalese cases patron–client ties also cut across ethnicity. The capitalist states tended to nurture a culture of political competition which was frowned on in the socialist states.

Appendices

Appendix 5.1 Average GDP growth rates in selected African countries, 1960–87

Country	1960–70	1970–79	1980–87
Tanzania	6.0	4.9	1.7
Kenya	6.0	6.5	3.8
Ghana	2.1	−0.1	1.4
Côte d'Ivoire	8.0	6.7	2.2
Senegal	2.5	2.5	3.3
Guinea	3.2	3.6	2.1
Cameroun	3.7	5.4	7.0
Zambia	5.0	1.5	−0.1
Botswana	n/a	10.5*	13.0
Nigeria	3.1	7.5	−1.7

* 1973–80.

Appendix 5.2 Growth in agricultural production in selected African countries, 1960–87

Country	1960–70	1970–79	1980–87
Tanzania	n/a	4.9	3.8
Kenya	n/a	5.4	3.4
Ghana	n/a	−0.2	0.0
Côte d'Ivoire	4.2	3.4	1.6
Senegal	2.9	3.6	4.2
Guinea	n/a	n/a	n/a
Cameroun	n/a	3.5	2.4
Zambia	n/a	2.3	3.2
Botswana	n/a	0.6*	−7.8
Nigeria	−0.4	−0.3	0.6

* 1973–80.

Appendix 5.3 Growth in industrial production in selected African countries, 1960–87

Country	1960–70	1970–79	1980–87 (Industry and manufacturing separately)
Tanzania	n/a	1.9	−2.4
			−3.5
Kenya	n/a	10.2	3.0
			4.3
Ghana	n/a	−1.5	0.1
			−2.1
Côte d'Ivoire	11.5	10.5	−2.4
			8.2
Senegal	4.4	3.5	4.3
			4.3
Guinea	n/a	n/a	n/a
			n/a
Cameroun	n/a	6.5	11.0
			8.5
Zambia	n/a	1.5	−0.7
			0.8
Botswana	n/a	10.5*	19.2
			8.5
Nigeria	12.0	11.2	−4.4
			12.9

* 1973–80.

Source: Tables from World Bank, *World Development Report, 1981* (Washington: World Bank, 1981), pp. 136–7; World Bank, *Sub-Saharan Africa: From Crisis to Sustainable Growth* (Washington: World Bank, 1989), pp. 222–3.

6

Khaki Fatigue: Military Rule in Africa, 1960–85

When a chief takes a decision he decides – period. I have decided, in the name of the high command, that we will be in power for five years – full stop. A group of politicians therefore has no business playing the game of the financiers to provoke further disorders and troubles in the country.

General Mobutu, Congo, May 1966

We have dutifully intervened to save the nation from imminent collapse.

Major-General Buhari, Nigeria, January 1984

At independence, it was widely assumed that the Armed Forces would accept their support role in relation to the duly constituted civilian authority. However, it did not take very long before this assumption was called into question. The Congo crisis, which propelled Mobutu to the fore, provided an early indication that the men in khaki had the capacity to set themselves up as the arbiters of the fate of squabbling politicians. From here, it was but a short step to dispensing with the politicians altogether, as Mobutu and his Beninois counterparts were to do in 1965. The first substantive coup d'état took place in Togo in 1963, during which Sylvanus Olympio was assassinated as he attempted to escape into the American Embassy compound. This was followed by a rash of military takeovers across the continent, which consumed both the more fragile states like Benin, the Central African Republic (CAR) and Upper Volta, as well as those which seemed more viable like Ghana, Uganda and Nigeria. By 1984, there were only sixteen countries left which had not experienced a successful coup, whilst takeovers averaged three per year since 1963.[1]

As military rule ceased to be an aberration, political sociologists set about seeking to account for this transformation of the political landscape. The result is a large literature on coups and military rule, of somewhat variable quality. In this chapter, I will seek to distil some of the main patterns. As before, I will concentrate on a number of cases which best exemplify the underlying trends. We begin by considering the reasons for military intervention, before turning to consider four types of military regime: caretakers, reformers, radicals and usurpers.

6.1 The causation of coups

One of the questions which exercised political scientists in the 1960s and 1970s was why military intervention occurred with such regularity in both the Francophone and the Anglophone states. Some sought the answer in societal tensions which, it was argued, more or less sucked the military into the political vortex. Those who worked within a modernisation paradigm saw the problem as one of nascent political institutions which were unable to contain the effects of mass political mobilisation.[2] One intended consequence of the coup was therefore to narrow the political arena, thereby reducing the points of social friction. Some even regarded the military as the ideal instrument of post-colonial governance in the sense that it was supposedly a 'modern' institution which transcended ethnicity and which possessed skills which might assist the task of economic modernisation. The poverty of the modernisation paradigm emerged with particular clarity in relation to the military which proved no more efficient, 'modern' or development-oriented than the politicians it displaced. In the light of the evidence, other analysts such as Samuel Decalo asserted that the coup syndrome was rooted less in societal causes, and rather more in the military itself.[3] Corporate pride, ethnic jealousies and personal aggrandisement were seen as some of the factors which came into play. To this may be added the demonstration effect, because after the first takeovers it became apparent that mounting a coup was actually not that difficult. It merely required a tight-knit group of conspirators who could deploy enough soldiers to arrest key figures, and to take over strategic installations – notably the radio-station and the airports. If presented with a fait accompli and a plausible justification for acting, the rest of the Armed Forces would probably fall into line.

After four decades of military coups, each bearing its own unique attributes, one can conclude that the typical pattern was one in which the unpopularity of the incumbent regime provided the backdrop against which the soldiers felt empowered to act. Although military conspirators could technically overthrow a legitimate regime, they were much less likely to do so because they could not be assured of a measure of popular support and the compliance of other sections of the Army and Police.[4] But official justifications for a coup always need to be distinguished from the underlying reasons. Coup leaders almost invariably produced a list of justifications, centring on the corruption and incompetence of the incumbent regime, as well as the fact that a change of regime was impossible under the one-party state. But underlying the protestations of patriotic responsibility lurked other considerations of a more banal nature: these were sometimes corporate, sometimes ethnic and sometimes intensely personal.

At independence, most African countries inherited relatively small armies (alongside gendarmeries in the case of the Francophone states) and almost nothing in the way of an airforce and a navy. Up until the final stages of decolonisation, the officers had invariably been white whereas Africans could not rise above the rank of Non-Commissioned Officer (NCO). Once independence was won, there was intense pressure both to enlarge the Armed Forces and to Africanise the officer corps. In many instances, experienced NCOs were rapidly promoted to fill the positions vacated by European officers, but at

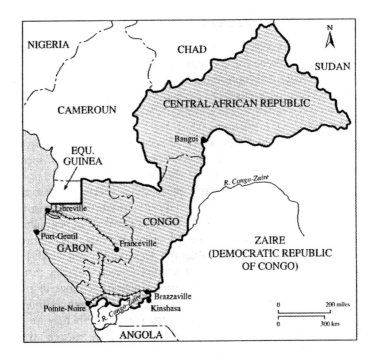

Map 4 Congo-Brazzaville, Gabon and the Central African Republic

the same time relatively new recruits were hastily despatched to overseas training academies like Sandhurst, Mons and St. Cyr. Here, they were encouraged to take a pride in their status as professionals. The memoirs of those who graduated from these academies suggests that they internalised much of the accompanying ideology: in the case of the former British colonies, newly minted officers learned to brandish their swagger-sticks with panache, took pleasure in drinking whisky and called each other 'chap'. They also forged friendships which cut across ethnicity and, for that matter, national boundaries. When they returned to their countries of origin, they expected to be well-remunerated and to be treated with respect. They also expected to be left to carry out their allotted functions, as defenders of the nation, without undue interference from the politicians. However, they also depended upon the latter for their salaries and for the purchase of the latest military equipment.

Not surprisingly, the politicians had their own preoccupations which did not necessarily coincide with those of the men in uniform. The friction which surfaced in many countries was related both to the struggle for material resources and for mastery over the military apparatus. The first came to the fore in a series of dramatic incidents over 1963/64. In the case of Togo, the army numbered no more than 250 men at independence and, as far as Olympio was concerned, that was as much as his tiny country could afford. His principal worry was that Nkrumah might seek to annex Togo, having failed to achieve unification by persuasion, but he was well-aware that the country would never possess the means to repel a Ghanaian invasion. He therefore signed agreements with the French and the Nigerians who would serve as the guarantors of Togolese sovereignty. But while Olympio was happy to make do with a token army, there were some 300 demobilised Togolese soldiers from the French army who demanded to be absorbed, including one Sergeant Etienne Eyadéma. When Olympio refused to give in, the ex-servicemen conspired with some of the serving soldiers and seized power. The inevitable consequence was that the army was expanded to 1200 which was far more than the number Olympio had been asked to take in the first place.[5]

The following year, the former British colonies in East Africa received a shock of their own when all three armies mutinied. Their demand was for improved rates of pay for privates and NCOs and for accelerated Africanisation of the officer corps. This episode was acutely embarrassing for the leaders of Kenya, Tanganyika and Uganda who had to request British troops to quell the mutinies.[6] Having restored control, the respective governments endeavoured to buy future compliance with increased levels of military expenditure. The capitulation was abject in the case of Uganda where hefty pay increases meant that even the lowliest private received an income fifteen times higher than the national average and twice that of his counterpart in Kenya.[7] Meanwhile, there was accelerated Africanisation of the officer corps, while recruitment to the Ugandan army was increased from around a thousand to close on 6000 in 1967. Each of the East African regimes was conscious of the need to avoid a repeat of the 1964 episode and was generous in its budgetary allocations. The problem was that these concessions risked wetting the appetite of the military for an even greater share of the resources. Whereas the Kenyan and Tanzanian governments found the right formula, the Obote regime in Uganda failed in spectacular fashion. Within a few years of independence, it was apparent that many African rulers had created a monster which they could not adequately feed or control.

However, civilian–military relations were not merely coloured by crude matters of funding. There was also the delicate issue of the relationship between the soldiers and their supposed civilian masters. One consequence of rapid Africanisation and expansion of the army was that politicians intervened directly in the military arena. When politicians made decisions about promotions or recruitment, they encroached on terrain which the soldiers regarded as their own. Moreover, when the politicians resorted to force to settle scores, this threatened to drag the military into sectional squabbles. The deployment of the Nigerian military in the Western Region crisis was a contributing factor to the January 1966 coup because the Majors concerned believed that the army was being asked to carry out the dirty work of the Northern People's Congress (NPC). The use of troops to settle the Buganda crisis in 1966 did not have the same direct consequences, but it did drag the army into partisan politics. For their part, African socialist regimes were held to have breached a mutual under-standing when they toyed with the introduction of political education into the barracks and when they created civilian militias. For those who had graduated from military academies, this compromised the primacy of the professional army. When governments subsequently decided to send some of their cadets to Communist countries, this was deeply resented by members of the earlier cohorts. Finally, as the first military takeovers occurred, the politicians often sought an insurance policy in the guise of special units and elite bodyguards who were entrusted with defence of the President. In Ghana, the creation of a better-equipped Presidential Own Guards Regiment (POGR) by Nkrumah was deeply resented. Similarly, Obote raised military hackles by creating a Special Force and a 1000-man General Service Unit (GSU) which was expected to shield him and to spy on the regular army. Ironically, by creating these parallel agencies, Nkrumah and Obote precipitated the very intervention which they had been seeking to avoid. Some of the Francophone states enjoyed greater success by billeting French troops who could be expected to back the incumbent regime in the event of an attempted putsch Hence, both the Senegalese and Ivoirien regimes were greatly reassured by the French military presence which kept their own armies in check.

However, as Decalo suggests, it is a mistake to place undue emphasis on the corporate identity of the military. The formal ideology of the institution was one thing, but reality was quite another. The rapid changes which have already been referred to generally had the effect of sowing the seeds of internal dissension. The result was that coups broke out precisely because of an absence of institutional coherence. Ethnic divisions were amongst the most pronounced and represent yet another of the pernicious legacies of colonialism. In very many countries, the rank-and-file of the army was recruited from particular ethnic groups and regions. These tended to be the most poverty-stricken because a military career was otherwise none too enticing. During decolonisation, the recruitment of African officers tended to favour groups who had greater access to colonial education. In the case of the Gold Coast/Ghana, this was the Ewe, Ga and various Akan sub-groups, and in Dahomey/Benin it was the Fon and the Yoruba, with northerners in each case making up the majority of the rank-and-file. In fact, one comparative study found that only a third of African armies were ethnically balanced in the late 1960s.[8]

There again, the efforts to establish greater equilibrium did not always help matters because it was all to easy to interpret intervention as ethnic favouritism or discrimination. In Nigeria, for example, the officer corps came mostly from the South, while the rank-and-file came primarily from the North and the Middle-Belt. When the NPC introduced regional quotas for the officer corps, Igbo candidates resented being passed over in favour of less qualified Hausas. In the case of Uganda, Obote was fortunate that there were relatively few Baganda in the army. They allegedly tended to fall foul of the height requirement, a British invention which favoured the Nilotic peoples of the North, but cash crop farming also happened to be far more attractive. Those Baganda officers who existed were swiftly marginalised, as were their perceived sympathisers like Brigadier Opolot (a Teso) who was removed from his position at the head of the army. At the same time, Obote sought to pack the army with peoples of his own ethnic origin, the Langi, who might be more loyal to him. This set him on a collision course with Idi Amin, Opolot's successor, who secretly recruited people from his own minority group (the Kakwa) and region (West Nile). By 1971, the Ugandan armed forces had become a seething cauldron of ethnic tensions. Whereas in Ghana and Nigeria, the officers who trained at Sandhurst built up some sense of camaraderie which cut across ethnicity, this did not occur in Uganda because few officers received any overseas training.

The ethnic factor was further complicated by the jealousies which surrounded promotions. The colonial NCOs who had finally achieved officer status typically resented the accelerated promotion of young officer recruits who were sent on crash-courses abroad. Equally, the latter were condescending towards those they regarded as ill-educated dinosaurs: General Ironsi in Nigeria and General Ankrah in Ghana were two cases in point, although each found themselves propelled to the fore of their respective post-coup juntas. The fast-track officers, in their turn, came to be resented by the cohort that followed in their slipstream. The latter found that their own prospects for rapid promotion were blocked by those who had got to the senior positions first. A familiar pattern was therefore one whereby the second cohort staged (or used) a coup as an opportunity to remove the blockages and promote themselves into the top slots. This set up the next stage of the cycle of competition because the junior officers who were pulled behind them similarly had their expectations of rapid career advancement raised. The grubby struggle over promotions frequently lay behind the exalted claims of many putschists – as the memoirs of the Ghanaian and Nigerian coupmakers of 1966 makes all to clear.

It stands to reason that in any particular instance, there was a particular political context in which the plot was launched and a complex mixture of motivations behind the seizure of power. To take one example, the Amin coup which toppled the Obote regime on 25 January 1971 arose out of the interplay between a number of factors. At one level, it arose from the knowledge that Obote was probably going to remove Amin when he returned from his trip to the Commonwealth Conference in Singapore, and possibly bring him to trial on charges of corruption and murder.[9] Amin felt impelled to strike first because he was confident of his standing amongst the rank-and-file. But there was also an ethnic dimension, in that rumours were circulating of a military purge which would benefit the Langi and Acholi at the expense of the West Nilers. However, these personal and ethnic motivations also need to be put in a context in which Obote had alienated large sections of Ugandan society. The Baganda harboured a particular grudge and many welcomed the coup as poetic justice. Moreover, wage earners were struggling with falling real incomes. In 1970, Obote had sought to rejuvenate a flagging economy and a fragile party by announcing his 'Move to the Left'. This appropriation of African Socialism was wrapped up in the 'Common Man's Charter' which promised Ugandans greater control over their economy, social equality and material upliftment. But the nationalisation of foreign enterprises merely had the effect of scaring the Indian community into withdrawing its capital. This merely exacerbated the crisis and made wage-earners appreciably worse off. The fact that some of the 'socialists' were doing rather well for themselves merely added insult to injury. When Amin struck, therefore, he could be reasonably assured of support from the wider society.

6.2   The performance of military regimes

In the same way that politicians have come in different ideological guises and disguises, so too have military regimes differed in their stated goals and political practices. For heuristic value, I have divided military regimes into certain broad types. Needless to say, particular regimes often bore the imprint of more than one of these. Here, we are merely seeking to convey some sense of the variation of military regimes which emerged after independence.

6.2.1   Caretakers

The first category is perhaps the simplest to grasp, representing as it does a temporary holding action on the part of the military. Caretaker regimes were those which continued to accept the premise that the military did not really belong in politics. But as part of their obligation to defend the interests of the nation, they claimed an obligation to remove civilian politicians who were driving the country to rack and ruin. The first coup in Togo was of the caretaker variety. The coup-makers had acted for self-serving reasons, but they were quick to justify the coup on the basis that the Olympio regime had become authoritarian. Eyadéma and his colleagues professed to have no interest in ruling and so turned to an alternative set of politicians waiting in the wings. Nicolas Grunitzky (the brother-in-law of Olympio) was installed by the Military Insurrection Committee as the provisional president, at the head of a broad-based coalition government. This arrangement was given the seal of popular approval at an election held in May. However, Grunitzky's tenure was a singularly unhappy one, being punctuated by internal wrangling along ethnic lines and a renewed challenge from Olympio's party. The paralysis of the regime provided both the context and the excuse for the second intervention which followed exactly four years later on 13 January 1967. Although there was initially talk of holding fresh elections, Eyadéma cleared up the confusion in April by declaring himself president. The new regime made it abundantly clear that it had no intention of handing power back to the civilians, arguing that the latter had proved themselves incapable of governing in an unselfish manner. This former Sergeant in the French army (and veteran of the Indochinese and Algerian colonial wars) promoted himself to General and promised to take the country in hand. At the time of writing (in 2003), Eyadéma is still there and still passing himself off as the indispensable helmsman of the Togolese nation.

In Benin also, it took some time before soldiers felt comfortable about claiming power. Even more than in neighbouring Togo, the post-colonial order was one which was highly fractured along ethno-regional lines. Because this was replicated in the military, it was very difficult for the armed forces to achieve any consensus about what regime the soldiers might want to create. The civilian arena was itself characterised by a split between the Fon of the South-west, the Yoruba of the South-east and the North, each of which produced its own political heavyweight: namely Justin Ahomadégbé, Sourou-Migan Apithy and Hubert Maga respectively. It was the inability of the 'big three' to work together which first drew the military into the political arena in October 1963. On this occasion, the logjam was broken when a wave of strikes and demonstrations led to President Maga being ousted and an Ahomadégbé-Apithy coalition being installed by the army. The same pattern was repeated in November 1965, when General Soglo clashed with President Ahomadégbé over how to deal with street protests in Porto Novo, and ended up dissolving the government and inviting the speaker of the assembly to form a government. When this failed, Soglo assumed power in his own right the following month. As in Togo, this was justified on the basis that the politicians had shown themselves incapable of rising above their petty jealousies. However, the Soglo intervention did not settle the matter and two years later he was deposed in a junior officer's coup, which followed a further round of strikes to protest against austerity measures. One consequence of this coup was that the ranks of Fon officers were thinned out, while the position of northerners improved appreciably.

The incoming junta decided to revert to a caretaker role and proposed holding fresh elections in which the old guard would be debarred from standing. The elections went ahead, but after Maga and Apithy (from exile) called for a boycott, a mere 17 per cent turned out to cast their votes. The legitimacy of any winner was clearly questionable and after toying with a resumption of military rule, it was decided to invite Emile Zinsou to form a new civilian administration for a period of five years. Zinsou, who lacked a solid ethnic constituency of his own (being of Afro-Brazilian extraction) lasted all of seventeen months before he was deposed by the person who had handed him the presidency, namely Major Maurice Kouandété. However, the latter failed to carry his colleagues along with him and he was forced to accept a diminished position in a junta which, after debating its options, finally decided to invite the 'big three' back again. The armed forces evidently realised that the bitter divisions in its own ranks made a resumption of military rule untenable. The outcome of the election was a victory for Ahomadégbé under highly controversial circumstances. The subsequent threat of northern secession was only staved off with a compromise formula according to which the 'big three' would rotate the presidency between them. Maga took the first turn and in May 1972, he was followed by Ahomadégbé. This experiment was, however, punctuated by attempted coups and assassinations and was finally terminated on 26 October 1972, when Major Mathieu Kérékou seized power. Kérékou had first come to prominence under the Soglo regime and he was one of the northerners who profited from the clearing out of the military stables. His accession finally established the claim of the armed forces (by now heavily northernised) to rule in its own right in the supposed absence of an alternative.

The textbook case of a caretaker military regime was the one which was established on Togo's other border on 24 February 1966. We have already examined the manner in which Nkrumah's attempt at a 'socialist' structural transformation had culminated in declining living standards for most Ghanaians (see Chapter 5). When a successful plot was finally hatched, it was (highly unusually) a joint operation between the police and the army, with the former rounding up the CPP politicians and the latter taking on the POGR. The reasons for the coup lay in a familiar combination of personal, corporate and (to some extent) ethnic grievances on the part of members of both institutions.[10]

The initial group of conspirators was composed of southern Ewes, that is John Harlley and A. K. Deku of the police and Lt-Col. E. K. Kotoka of the army, but the final circle was much more inclusive. Indeed, Simon Baynham has demonstrated the active or passive involvement of a greater part of the officer corps.[11] There remains a persistent belief that the CIA was intimately involved, although it is doubtful whether this was a necessary requirement.[12] However, the exaggerated pro-Western posturing of the National Liberation Council (NLC) did nothing to dampen suspicions.

In his first radio speech on the morning of the coup, Kotoka itemised the misdemeanours of the CPP regime which justified the coup. The spontaneous rejoicing of Ghanaians who revelled in the dizzy fall of CPP 'big men' imparted some legitimacy to the takeover. The junta promised that it would not seek to usurp power, but would secure the conditions for an orderly transfer of power back to a civilian government.[13] The NLC was composed exclusively of army and police officers, and headed by General Ankrah who had been sent into retirement by Nkrumah. Military officers were also sent to administer the Regions. However, it was senior civil servants who largely ran the show. Moreover, when the NLC established a series of committees to advise it, politicians of the former opposition were brought in, alongside academics and civil servants. The Political Committee was made up very largely of politicians of the former United Party (UP).[14] The NLC set itself a relatively modest agenda of reform which legitimised its decision not to hand power back prematurely. It promised to restore economic equilibrium which included striking a deal with the International Monetary Fund (IMF), privatising loss-making state enterprises and liberalising foreign trade. At the same time, it launched a series of commissions of enquiry to investigate the financial affairs of CPP politicians and the operations of a number of state enterprises. These predictably led to revelations of corruption and mismanagement at the highest levels. Finally, given that Ghana had been a one-party state before the coup, there was a need to frame a replacement constitution. The politicians of the former opposition were brought onto the Constitutional Commission, where they played a leading role in shaping the contours of the Second Republic.[15]

Although the NLC was not in a great rush to withdraw, there were early indications that it would be unwise to prolong its stay. The first warning came in 1967 with an attempted coup led by an ultra-ambitious Lieutenant Arthur, which brought about the premature death of Kotoka. Moreover, as the country began to move in the direction of civilian rule, individual members of the NLC began to strike up personal alliances with aspirant politicians. Ankrah was an early casualty of the political in-fighting, and it was increasingly apparent that the Ewe members of the NLC (Harlley and Deku) were not of the same mind as Akwasi Afrifa. Although the return of Komla Gbedemah was brokered by Harlley, a fellow Ewe, the real shoe-in was given to Professor Kofi Busia, the former leader of the UP. As head of the Commission on Civic Education, Busia could project himself to the country at a time when political parties were still proscribed. When elections were finally held in 1969, Busia's Progress Party (PP) won comfortably against Gbedemah's National Alliance of Liberals (NAL). The PP performed particularly well in the Akan areas, whereas NAL successes were mostly confined to the Volta Region.[16] The orderly conduct of the polls prepared the way for a return to the barracks, the historic task of the military apparently completed. Unlike in Benin, there was a reasonably good chance that the elite consensus which had been forged during the drafting of the constitution would hold, leaving the soldiers to return to their allotted tasks. However, it was doubtful whether it was really possible to write the CPP out of the script. The party was debarred from standing in 1969, but many of its sympathisers had not ceased to believe that theirs was still the party of preference for the majority of Ghanaians.

6.2.2 Reformers and redeemers: corrective regimes

The second category of military regimes differed in that they were explicit about their intention to govern for as long as they deemed necessary. The typical rationale was that national unity could not otherwise be maintained and/or that the military alone possessed the managerial competence to put the country back on track. The corrective regimes tended to rely heavily on civil servants, and sometimes drew on the moral support of traditional rulers, whereas the politicians were relegated to the background. Moreover, soldiers tended to insist not merely on heading the various Ministries, but also sitting at the head of public corporations.

Ghana provides a classic case of the switch from a caretaker to a reformist agenda within the armed forces. After the return to civilian rule in 1969, the officers who had headed the NLC went into early retirement. Their places were filled by promotions which seemed to represent political interference in the affairs of the military. Moreover, the Busia regime swiftly expended the political capital with which it entered office. On the one hand, its economic management was called into question when trade liberalisation led to a flood of imports and a foreign exchange squeeze. The attempt to impose austerity measures did not go down well with urban workers and, following a head-on confrontation, the government dissolved both the Trade Union Congress (TUC) and the National Union of Ghanaian Students (NUGS). Busia, who had always presented himself as a committed democrat, revealed an unexpected willingness to transgress the rules of the game. Following a decision to dismiss over 550 civil servants in 1970 (a disproportionate number of whom were allegedly Ewes), Busia launched an ill-considered attack on the judiciary when it ruled against him. When the regime tried to impose austerity on the Armed Forces, it went a step too far. On 13 January 1972, the military intervened for the second time – on this occasion without the assistance of the police.

Colonel I. K. Acheampong, who headed the National Redemption Council (NRC) justified the coup on various grounds: the authoritarianism of the PP government, its mismanagement of the economy, blatant tribalism and, most disarmingly of all, the complaint that Busia was removing the 'few small amenities' which the officer corps had enjoyed. Acheampong pointed to a national malaise which only the military had the capacity to resolve. This time, the NRC indicated that it would remain in office until such time as it had put the country back on an even keel. Acheampong declared 'war on the economy' and placed the pursuit of national self-reliance at the centre of its platform. The junta reversed the devaluation of the cedi which Busia had recently agreed to, declared that it would not pay any foreign debts which were vitiated by fraud and sought to reactivate many of the state enterprises which the NLC and the Busia regime had allowed to wither. The centrepiece of its economic strategy was the Operation Feed Yourself Programme (OFY), in which Ghanaians were enjoined to return to the land to free the country from its dependency on imported food. Colonel Frank Bernasko, who served as the Commissioner for Agriculture, established a reputation as a dynamic figure who exemplified the practical virtues of the men in uniform. There was much in the economic nationalism of the NRC which was redolent of Nkrumahism. Indeed, the NRC rehabilitated several CPP politicians and brought them into advisory roles. Moreover, when Nkrumah died in Romania, the Acheampong government won many plaudits when it ensured that his body was returned to Ghana and given a fitting mausoleum at his birthplace of Nkroful. But, despite the echoes with Nkrumahism, the NRC remained a military regime from tip to toe.

For the first few years, the NRC was remarkably successful at selling itself to the Ghanaian public. The nationalist pose which it struck rekindled memories of a time when Ghana was at the centre of international affairs. Moreover, there were some signs of economic recovery. The OFY programme, which students supported by going to the countryside to harvest and transport crops, registered significant increases in output. However, it did not take too long before cracks began to appear. The first plots against the regime could be explained away as efforts on the part of disgruntled politicians – of both the UP and the CPP variety – to resume their misrule.[17] However, by 1975 it became clear that rifts were emerging between Acheampong and some of the Ewe Colonels who had planned the coup.[18] In October, Acheampong announced that the NRC would be subordinated to a Supreme Military Council (SMC) which would compromise himself, the head of the Army, Navy, Airforce and the Border Guards. The Ewe members of the NRC resigned and were forcibly retired. In December, there followed an alleged Ewe plot in which both civilians like Kofi Awoonor and soldiers like Captain Kojo Tsikata were implicated.[19]

The creation of the SMC coincided with the evaporation of the early economic gains. The country was dealt a body-blow by the sudden hike in the oil-price in 1973. Furthermore, OFY ran into trouble when the rains failed in 1975, which led to the country reverting to the importation of food on a large scale. As conditions deteriorated, the soldiers were revealed to have feet of clay. For example, Acheampong's answer to fiscal stringency was simply to print more money, which had the predictable effect of driving inflation upwards. The price controls which were supposed to protect consumers were thoroughly unrealistic and mostly unobserved, with the result that urban workers saw a marked decline in their real incomes after 1975. The government also calculated the price paid to cocoa farmers at official rates of exchange, which meant that they received much less in real terms. The Cocoa Marketing Board (CMB) consumed the lion's share, mostly in the form of waste. Many farmers neglected their cocoa farms, while those in the Brong-Ahafo and Volta Regions smuggled their crops into Côte d'Ivoire and Togo respectively.[20] As foreign exchange became increasingly scarce and state industries struggled to sustain production in the face of a dearth of raw materials, consumer shortages became a fact of daily life. This was ideal for a proliferation of rent-seeking activities, which came to be known as *kalabule*. The recipients of import licences were able to make instant fortunes by selling the goods, or the licences themselves, at a substantial markup. To compound matters, it became common knowledge that senior members of the SMC were themselves profiting from such activity and/or were favouring relatives, wives and especially girlfriends.[21] The term 'bottom power' was coined at this time, alluding to the influence of young women with their bodily assets in one place and their financial assets in another.

It became abundantly obvious that the SMC was, if anything, less competent and even more venal than the civilian regimes which preceded it. The students were the first to call Acheampong's bluff and the campuses were variously raided, attacked and closed over 1975–76. In September 1976, the Ghana Bar Association demanded a rapid return to civilian rule. In June of the following year, the Association of Recognised Professional Bodies (ARPB) went a step further by openly criticising the corruption and mismanagement of the SMC and giving it until 1 July to resign. This ultimatum was followed up by a strike, which received some support from particular trade unions.[22] As the pressure mounted, Acheampong responded with his infamous Union Government (Unigov) proposal, under which the military would become permanent partners in a no-party system. It was argued that this was in accordance with indigenous cultural traditions and that it gave due recognition to the important contribution the military had to make. To put flesh on the bones, an Ad Hoc Committee on Union Government was set up to gather opinions from the populace and to hammer out concrete constitutional proposals. The report equivocated on many of the delicate issues, but the impression was left that it had endorsed the proposal for a permanent military stake in government.[23]

The civilian opposition was not slow in realising that Unigov amounted to a thinly veiled attempt at entrenching military rule. The battle lines were clearly drawn, therefore, when the proposals were put to a referendum in March 1978. Civilian opposition was co-ordinated by the People's Movement for Freedom and Justice, the Front for the Prevention of Dictatorship and the Third Force. For its part, the SMC bankrolled its own support groups. The referendum itself underlined the cardinal principle that if one is going to rig a poll then one has to do it properly. The SMC bungled the attempt, with the result that conflicting sets of results were released. Even if one were to accept the figures most favourable to the SMC, these revealed that the Ashanti, Eastern and Brong-Ahafo Regions had voted against the proposals, while less than one in four of the eligible voters had turned out to vote 'yes'.[24]

The SMC had been given a bloody nose, and it came as no great surprise when there was a palace coup on 5 July 1978. General Akuffo assumed the chairmanship of the SMC, while Acheampong and Major-General E. K. Utuka (the head of the Border Guards) were forced to step down. Akuffo attempted to manage a dignified retreat to the barracks, promising that national elections would be held prior to a full return to civilian rule in September 1979. The observation that nothing is more corrosive of military unity than military rule, was borne out in graphic detail at this point.[25] Junior officers and the rank-and-file, who had suffered from plummeting living standards along with everyone else, chafed at the gratuitous self-enrichment of the top brass. When Akuffo failed to punish Acheampong, it seemed that the worst perpetrators would escape with impunity. On 15 May 1979, therefore, a young airforce officer by the name of Flt.-Lt. Jerry Rawlings attempted to stage a coup in order to bring the wrongdoers to book. When placed on public trial, he defended his actions in a manner which won instant sympathy on the campuses and in the barracks. On 4 June 1979, radicalised junior officers and lower ranks decided to make their move. Following a mutiny, Rawlings was sprung from prison and brought in to head an Armed Forces Revolutionary Council (AFRC), made up of soldiers from different units. The SMC members were arrested and senior officers were publicly humiliated by the ranks.

The AFRC fell into the caretaker category, albeit of a very particular kind. Rawlings proclaimed that the AFRC had no intention of altering the date which had been set for a return to civilian rule, and the elections went ahead as scheduled. However, the AFRC proposed to carry out a 'housecleaning' exercise directed against all those who had been involved in *kalabule*. Unless a new moral standard was established, it was asserted, the Third Republic would be tainted from its inception.[26] No fewer than eight senior officers, including three former heads of state – Acheampong, Akuffo and Afrifa – were executed by firing squad in a country which had been largely free of political violence. Rawlings later claimed that if he had not allowed some blood to be spilled, the list of casualties would have been very much longer. Businessmen and market women accused of hoarding and selling above control prices were harshly punished, and a number of Lebanese businessmen were deported.

The elections themselves took the form of a three-cornered contest. The People's National Party (PNP) was formed by old Nkrumahists who put forward the unknown Dr Hilla Limann as their Presidential candidate. The Busia/Danquah camp split into two, with the majority entering the Popular Front Party (PFP), led by Victor Owusu, and the rest opting to follow Dr William Ofori-Atta into the United National Convention (UNC). In the Parliamentary polls, the PNP won reasonably comfortably, while Limann defeated Owusu in the second round of the Presidential election, becoming the first head of state to hail from the North of the country.[27] On 24 September, Rawlings formally handed over power to Limann and returned to the airforce with the same rank as before. There ended the first unhappy experiment with corrective government in Ghana. Military rule had evidently failed to deliver any of the goods and had led to the unravelling of the army itself. Although the return to civilian rule was welcomed, Limann was left with an unenviable legacy.

At this point, we turn to the Nigerian experience, which parallels that of Ghana, but with two significant differences. One is the fact that the Nigerian military had been thrown into active combat during the Civil War, creating a certain *esprit de corps* amongst the federal field commanders which never existed in Ghana (see Chapter 3).[28] Another, which was of even greater significance, is that whereas the Ghanaian junta was damaged by the OPEC price rises, the Nigerian military – or rather successive factions thereof – entrenched itself as a consequence of the oil boom. It is difficult to over-emphasise the impact of oil on Nigeria. Whereas petroleum provided half of government revenues in 1971/72, this had risen to 87 per cent by 1975/76. At this point, oil also accounted for 93 per cent of export earnings, with traditional exports like groundnuts, cocoa and palm-oil waning into insignificance (see Appendix 5.2).[29] However, these bald figures do not convey an adequate sense of the transformation of virtually every aspect of state and society.

While the Civil War was being fought, there was little realistic possibility that the armed forces would hand power back to the civilians. But there was a general expectation that when peace was restored, the military would do the right thing. Gowon initially flirted with something sounding very similar to Unigov, but later conceded that there ought to be a return to unadulterated civilian rule.[30] However, he also laid out a nine-point programme, which amounted to a lengthy list of tasks to be completed before a transfer of power could be completed. It would be fair to say that these eventually engulfed a regime which proved reluctant to take on entrenched interests. First of all there was the imperative of post-war reconstruction, which the military assumed was best carried out by itself. Then there was the question of the reconstitution of the Nigerian federation along more viable lines, given the unseemly collapse of the First Republic. Ironsi's movement in the direction of a unitary state was considered unacceptable, but the contours of a federal alternative was by no means a straightforward matter either. Following the creation of twelve states in 1967, which finally assuaged minority demands, there were requests for the creation of yet more states. This, in turn, was bound up with the question of how the oil revenues ought to be divided. Whereas the oil-producing states wanted most of the money to be allocated according to the principle of derivation, the rest of the federation wanted the money to be divvyed up in ways which assured them of a greater overall share. In 1975, the Gowon regime decided on a formula according to which 20 per cent of on-shore royalties and rents (but none of the off-shore revenues) were allocated to the states where the oil was located. This left as much as 80 per cent to be paid into a 'distributable pool', from which the subsequent allocation to the states was divided in two – half according to population and half to each of the states equally.[31] The demand for the creation of new states was therefore based on the rational expectation that these would be the recipient of a greater share of the oil bonanza. Because population comprised the second criterion, official statistics remained as sensitive an issue as during the First Republic. The Gowon regime promised that the military would preside over a properly conducted census which a civilian regime might find beyond its capacity. However, the 1973 census proved as controversial as that of 1962/63. Whereas the Northern states returned vastly increased population levels, and raised their overall share from 53 to 64 per cent of the national total, those of the Yoruba states supposedly declined. Westerners smelt a Northern rat and, such was the level of disputation, that Gowon was unable to ratify the figures – meaning that nobody was any the wiser as to what the population of Nigeria really was.

The final task which the Gowon regime set itself was the promotion of development. The flood of oil revenues meant that there was no shortage of money: the problem, according to Gowon, was how to spend it. Nigeria even began furnishing aid to other more benighted African countries, in an attempt to convert petro-naira into continental influence.[32] Under Gowon, senior civil servants (so-called 'super permanent secretaries') became the shapers of national development priorities, imparting a certain technocratic arrogance to the regime which irritated other sections of the elite. A four-year National Development Plan was launched in 1970, which was later extended until 1976. During this period, government expenditure increased nearly tenfold, as money was pumped into infrastructural development (especially roads and motorways) and countless prestige projects, while a programme for universal primary education was added to the list. The Nigerian state was also accorded a more dynamic role within the economy. Under the 1972 Indigenisation Decree, the state assumed a 40 per cent share in commercial banks, and reserved to itself the production of iron and steel. Moreover, the state took a majority of shares in a number of large oil companies, while a Nigerian National Oil Corporation (NNOC) was formed to engage in all aspects of the production and marketing of petroleum.[33] At the same time, the regime also claimed to be doing its bit to nurture Nigerian capitalists as in Côte d'Ivoire. The marginal sectors of the Nigerian economy were reserved for nationals only, while elsewhere foreign investors were expected to divest 40 per cent of their shares to Nigerians. Finally, the boom enabled the government to offer rewards to important urban constituencies. Hence the Udoji Commission which was set up to look into the salaries recommended 'stupendous increases'.[34] When workers in the private sector demanded equal treatment, the government went ahead and increased the minimum wage by much as 30 per cent.

The Gowon regime initially promised that its restructuring would be complete by October 1976. However, in a manner which was to become all-too-familiar, Gowon announced the postponement of the terminal point in October 1974. Although the transition was supposed to begin in earnest, Gowon argued that neither the political nor the economic climate were yet ripe for a handover of power. In July 1975, Gowon was overthrown in another military coup which led to the installation of Brigadier Murtala Mohammed, a longstanding critic of Gowon who had felt jilted by him after having gifted him the top slot.[35] It has also been suggested that the so-called 'Kaduna Mafia'– made up of a clique northern intellectuals, businessmen, soldiers and bureaucrats – resented the manner in which their own influence had been usurped by the 'super permsecs' who surrounded Gowon.[36]

The Mohammed regime functioned as a triumvirate, consisting of three Generals: Mohammed, Olusegun Obasanjo and T. Y. Danjuma. When Mohammed was killed in an abortive coup in February 1976, Obasanjo moved into the top slot without significantly altering the direction of what was a classic corrective regime. The junta prided itself on its no-nonsense style and military professionalism. Mohammed decided that the 'super permsecs' had been allowed to get above themselves, and they were henceforth subordinated to Commissioners appointed by the Supreme Military Council (SMC). Borrowing from an Acheampong script, the authorities launched Operation Feed the Nation (OFN) in 1976 which was an attempt to address the devastating impact of the oil boom on Nigerian agriculture. Two years later, the military introduced the controversial Land Use Decree which vested lands in the state, in order that these could be acquired for large-scale agricultural projects. In the industrial sector, the construction of the giant Ajaokuta steel complex went ahead, and a third oil refinery was constructed.[37] Then there was the commitment to ending the veritable explosion of corruption which had accompanied Gowon's spending spree. Panels were set up to investigate the financial affairs of top officials, and of twelve former state governors no fewer than ten were found guilty of corruption.[38] In the same vein, there was a wholesale purge of the public service. As many as 10,000 employees were compulsorily retired across the whole range of state institutions – from the civil service to the military and from the parastatals to the Universities – under 'Operation Deadwoods'. These purges made Busia's actions in Ghana look positively timid. Finally, the regime proposed to tackle the most controversial issues which Gowon had fudged. The 1973 census was formally scrapped and the country was divided into 19 states.[39] In October 1975, Mohammed announced a four-year transition programme, which would lead to the reorganisation of local government and the holding of elections at the state and federal levels, culminating in the withdrawal of the military on 1 October 1979.

Although this programme did not mean that the process would be completed any faster, the sense of a mission enabled the regime to retain a broad measure of popular acceptance. Indeed, there remains a popular myth that if Mohammed had not been so cruelly cut down, great things would have followed. This takes no cognisance of the fact that Mohammed had a background of ethnic particularism, having spearheaded the revenge killings in the military in 1966. Nor did he have a particularly firm grasp of economic complexities. Under the SMC, agricultural output continued to decline. As Gunilla Andrae and Bjorn Beckman have demonstrated, Nigeria became thoroughly dependent upon imported foodstuffs, notably wheat which she did not grow.[40] Moreover, the manufacturing sector did not receive much of a fillip because of the import mentality which prevailed. When the tides of the oil boom receded in 1978, therefore, the country was left high and dry. Most Nigerians experienced no noticeable improvement in terms of reliable access to water, electricity and other basic amenities. While rampant inflation made the lot of many Nigerians appreciably worse off, a small minority lived in a level of opulence which was unrivalled in Africa. The regular shortages of petroleum within Nigeria provided the clearest indictment of a system which was not working. It was also the soldiers who presided over the institutionalisation of a culture of waste and corruption in Nigeria. As the popular 'Afro-beat' musician, Fela Kuti, pointed out the Second World Black and African Festival of Arts and Culture (FESTAC) and OFN provided a cover under which large sums of money were spirited into private pockets.[41] It cannot even be said that the military healed its internal wounds, for as we have already pointed out military rule tended to spawn divisions. The Nigerian armed forces avoided the complete institutional meltdown which occurred in Ghana, but there was nevertheless a succession of plots, including the Dimka coup attempt which killed Mohammed and led to the execution of the Commissioner for Defence, General I. D. Bissalla.[42]

For the politicians, though, it was sufficient that the government kept to its timetable for the transfer of power. A Constitution Drafting Committee reported in 1976 and its report was then considered in detail by a Constituent Assembly, made up of a mixture of elected representatives, government appointees and delegates derived from special interest groups. The Assembly came up with a new document in record time, one which was full of the most elaborate checks and balances. The most significant innovation was the provision for a directly elected President and State Governors. There was also to be a two-tier Federal legislature, as well as state assemblies elected on the basis of single-member constituencies. Although there was a particularly fierce debate over the issue of whether there should be a Sharia court of appeal, the constitutional deliberations passed off remarkably smoothly. A Federal Electoral Commission (FEDECO) was entrusted with arranging an enormously complex series of elections. On 21 September 1978, the ban on party politics was finally lifted and within a week a number of parties had sprung into life. In reality, many of the politicians had been in their starter's blocks for some time. Whereas the military had talked about the emergence of a new breed of politician, the transition phase demonstrated how shallow the achievements of corrective government really were. The lines of party division tended to replicate those of the First Republic, while the leaders who came to fore were mostly familiar faces.

Obafemi Awolowo, who had been released from prison by Gowon to serve as a Federal Commissioner, had been awaiting this moment for years. He quickly established the Unity Party of Nigeria (UPN), which appealed directly to the Yoruba and the minorities. In the South-east, Nnamdi Azikiwe similarly came out of hibernation and established the Nigerian People's Party (NPP). This was a party of the Igbo as well as the Yoruba areas which had voted for him in the past. The re-entry of Azikiwe led to the breakaway of the Great Nigeria People's Party (GNPP) which was a party of other minorities in the North (Borno) and the South-east. The National Party of Nigeria (NPN) was a lineal descendant of the old Northern People's Party (NPP), and was led by Shehu Shagari who was one of its veterans. Finally, the People's Redemption Party (PRP), which was a leftwing breakaway from the NPN, was led by Aminu Kano and maintained some continuity with the populist roots of the Northern Elements Progressive Union (NEPU). Although there was formally an ideological difference between the parties – with the PRP and the UPN standing for socialism and the NPN remaining true to Northern conservatism – the parties were in reality Byzantine agglomerations of patronage networks.

In the Presidential polls, Shagari emerged triumphant, despite a wrangle over the stipulation that the winner should poll a majority in two-thirds of the states (the constitutional drafters having neglected to clarify what two-thirds of nineteen came to). The NPN also won a plurality of seats in the Senate and the House of Assembly, but not an absolute majority. Finally, the NPN won in only seven of the states, which ensured that the opposition parties were left with substantial power-bases of their own. The NPN ultimately triumphed because it was the party which managed to capture minority votes outside of its Hausa-Fulani heartlands.[43] Awolowo failed to even find a northern running-mate, with the result that the UPN was seen as a Yoruba party. The NPP was similarly stuck with the Igbo tag, and was also somewhat undercut by Shagari's choice of Alex Akueme as his running-mate. There was also an uncanny re-run of the First Republic when the NPP decided to enter into a Federal alliance with the NPN in return for certain Ministerial positions, and when Yoruba politicians fell out over the issue of whether it was better to strike a deal with the Northern elite or to fight them to the death. True to form, Awolowo resolved to go it alone, and having failed to overturn the results of the Presidential polls, the UPN state governments refused to acknowledge Shagari as President, to the extent of refusing to exhibit his photograph in public buildings.[44] But these were troubles yet to come. On 1 October 1979, Nigeria was returned to civilian rule – a little more than a week after Ghana. At the time, many believed that Africa's most populous country would be able to make a better go of civilian rule the second time around. How wrong they were.

One might have expected the politicians to have learned the lessons of the First Republic: that is, while the perks of office were always going to render political competition pretty unforgiving, creating an excuse for a subsequent coup would redound to the detriment of all concerned. The fact that the politicians failed to learn the lessons reflects a get-rich-quick mentality on all sides probably more than any naive belief that the soldiers would confine themselves to barracks. After all, the military had excised a clause which aimed to render military coups unconstitutional. Shagari himself once boasted that Nigeria only had two parties: the NPN and the military. When the next coup came on 31st December 1983, it was not unexpected, and indeed it was even welcomed by the opposition. In that sense, the national calamity which best Nigeria over the next two decades can be squarely laid at the doorsteps of the politicians as much as the military.

The Shagari administration contributed to its own demise by the thoroughly profligate manner in which it dissipated state resources. The temporary recovery of global oil prices in 1981, for example, led to a renewed spending spree, despite the fact that it was generally understood that the Eldorado years were over. The result was that Nigeria sank deeper into international debt. In 1980, the country was already indebted to the tune of $9 billion, but in 1983 this had climbed to a staggering $18 billion. Meanwhile, GDP shrank by 8.5 per cent in real terms between 1981 and 1983.[45] Alongside, the wasteful management of national resources, the Shagari administration exhibited a rapacious venality of its own, which emerged in all its ugliness in the show-trials which followed the coup.[46] The construction of a new Federal capital at Abuja, at the geographical centre of the country, was defensible in view of the notorious congestion of Lagos and its distance from much of the country. However, vast sums of money were paid out to contractors who paid off officials for a cut of the action and failed to execute the work. The opposition politicians in the states made their own contribution to the demise of the Second Republic, being no less corrupt or dissolute in their use of public resources. Moreover, they were often determined to pursue the politics of confrontation to the point that no give-and-take with the NPN was possible.

While the well-connected became fabulously rich – the private jet became a status symbol in Nigeria whereas most African elites had to make do with the

Mercedes Benz – the mass of the population was being urged to tighten its belts. When the government introduced austerity measures in 1982, the cutbacks hit the pockets of ordinary Nigerians, while the import, exchange and price controls merely provided fresh avenues for rent-seeking by the favoured few. During the Shagari years and afterwards, the glaring inequalities of wealth and power led to outbursts of popular discontent. In 1980, a millenarian Islamic movement (not the first) emerged under the leadership of Muhammadu Marwa, otherwise known as Maitatsine, and fought the security forces in pitched battles in Kano.[47] Although the leader died in this insurrection, the movement spread to other northern cities through to 1985. In successive clashes with the army and police, anything from 3000 to 10,000 people may have lost their lives.[48] The Maitatsine movement was undoubtedly unorthodox, given that the founder apparently disputed that Mohammed had been the prophet. However, its social roots lay amongst alienated Muslim youth in the cities.[49] Marwa championed the lot of the have-nots and preached against conspicuous consumption which the Northern Muslim elite had taken to with gusto. He even banned symbols of modernity like wristwatches, radios and money (or more than was absolutely necessary).[50] This movement demonstrated the fallacy that Muslims necessarily shared a sense of belonging to a common moral community, as well as the depth of class antagonisms in the North. An equally fascinating social phenomenon emerged in the South, in Benin City, where a gangster by the name of Anini was catapulted to the status of a folk hero when he declared war on the police.[51] Shagari had greatly increased police powers and the latter were regarded as highly corrupt. In the classic style of social bandits, Anini played to his mass audience, announcing the time when he was going to raid a bank and then throwing money to the crowds when he made his getaway. The Anini phenomenon was only terminated when he was finally caught and killed by the police. Clearly, neither of these movements was political in the conventional sense, but in each of them one can identify an acute sense of alienation from the system.

As in the case of the First Republic, it was electoral contestation which brought the military back again. The NPN had achieved some high-profile defections, including the former Biafran leader, Emeka Ojukwu. After the NPP broke off its alliance with the NPN in 1981, there was a prospect that it would join with the UPN in an opposition front. But not for the first time, the rivalries between Awolowo and Azikiwe took precedence, and the parties opted to contest the polls of August/September 1983 as separate entities. The elections descended into farce when the governments in opposition states began declaring their own results which conflicted with those announced by FEDECO. There is no reason to believe that either was particularly accurate given that all sides were determined to win at all costs.[52] As in 1964/65, it was in Yorubaland where the most heat was generated, given supposed 'gains' by the NPN. With the outbreak of rioting, the end of the Shagari regime was not long in coming. On 31 December 1983, Brigadier Sanni Abacha announced that the armed forces had intervened to pull the country back from the brink of collapse. The broadcast recited a familiar litany of charges, including 'squandermania, corruption and indiscipline'.[53]

A new SMC, headed by Major-General Muhammadu Buhari, pronounced that since the politicians had proven themselves incapable of addressing the problems of Nigeria, the armed forces would be forced to take the nation in hand. Buhari insisted that the scale of the crisis was such that the military would need to govern for some time before there could be any talk of a transition back to civilian rule. The first priority was to address the economic problems of the country. Although it continued with the austerity measures first introduced by Shagari, it displayed a greater willingness to implement unpopular measures. As part of an effort to curb public expenditure, for example, the regime trimmed Ministerial budgets, made substantial reductions in the state payroll and froze salaries. It also tightened up controls on the import-export trade in an effort to redress the adverse balance of trade. In the past, rampant smuggling had rendered these controls ineffective, so the government began by closing the borders and later introduced the death sentence for trafficking in specified items such as petroleum.[54] In order to squeeze a few more golden eggs out of the goose, the government subverted the OPEC production quota, by trading oil on barter terms, without formally leaving the cartel. Finally, the regime entered into negotiations with the IMF in an effort to secure fresh loans. However, these talks broke down over liberalisation conditionalities which the government was unwilling to concede. That left the regime with very little room for manoeuvre. At best, it could manage scarce resources more efficiently, but the structural weakness of the Nigerian economy ran too deep for tinkering to make very much difference.

The second plank of the regime was its attack on the spectacular corruption of the Second Republic. The regime embarked on the prosecution of politicians at the Federal and state levels, many of whom were forced to pay back millions of Naira and were given lengthy prison terms in special military tribunals. At one point, the regime famously attempted to abduct Umaru Dikko (a Shagari sidekick) from Britain in a crate. Apart from bringing some money into government coffers, the show-trials were intended to cement the legitimacy of the regime. Finally, with a naivety common to professional soldiers, Buhari and Brigadier Idiagbon concluded that the Nigerian condition was rooted in a lack of social discipline. The government therefore launched a War Against Indiscipline in which Nigerians were 'taught' to queue, turn up for work on time and clean up their communities. All of this was carried out in a hectoring tone and with a considerable amount of unnecessary violence.

The difficulty for any corrective regime is that Nigeria has spawned a sophisticated civilian elite which is prepared to embrace military rule as a temporary expedient, but quickly becomes impatient for a reversion to competitive politics. The Buhari regime attempted to secure its political base by striking up a working alliance with the traditional authorities.[55] The regime also attempted to establish its legitimacy by claiming to be a descendant of the corrective regime of Mohammed/Obasanjo. After a honeymoon period, criticisms began to be expressed about the heavy-handedness of the regime. Some observers also noticed the more lenient treatment meted out to NPN politicians. In the South, this seemed to confirm the northern complexion of the SMC. The Buhari government did not take kindly to these criticisms. A military decree was promulgated which authorised the detention of journalists who published any rumour which brought government officials into disrepute.[56] This further antagonised the journalists in a country which prided itself on having the freest press in Africa. The Nigerian Bar Association had its own run-in with Buhari over the powers of the military tribunals, while the National Association on Nigerian Students (NANS) was banned after leading student protests against the withdrawal of subsidies.

By 1985, popular support for Buhari had evaporated. On 27 August, there was yet another palace coup as Major-General Ibrahim Babangida, an important member of the SMC, seized the reins of power. Babangida cited the lack of collective decision-making under Buhari.[57] The two had apparently fallen out over Babangida's advocacy of greater defence allocations and over the direction of economic policy. Although the coup seemed to herald the advent of another corrective regime which hardly differed from the old one, the reality was that Nigeria was about to experience the third variant of military rule – that is outright usurpation by the Generals. By the mid-1980s, the Nigerian polity had reached something of an impasse. While elected politicians were widely mistrusted, the military had proven its lack of superior credentials. The armed forces could topple a civilian regime with comparative ease, but military regimes struggled to sustain consent in this most politicised of countries. It was left to Babangida to attempt something altogether more daring.

6.2.3 Usurpers in uniform

Our third category of is that of the usurpers. Whereas caretaker regimes generally promised a speedy, and corrective regimes a more prolonged, withdrawal there were a number of countries where soldiers had the temerity to declare themselves President – and, in one case, Emperor. In most cases, military usurpers cloaked themselves in civilian garb and founded political parties which enjoyed monopoly privileges, but their real power lay within the instruments of violence. The act of outright usurpation was a bold step which, once taken, could lead down many unexpected pathways. Indeed, usurper regimes have provided some of the most extreme examples of personal rule. This is exemplified by the two cases with which we will begin, namely the CAR under Jean-Bedel Bokassa and Uganda under Idi Amin. The personal excesses and sheer buffoonery of these two figures mesmerised Western journalists during the 1970s, for whom they served as symbols of a continent which appeared to be regressing to a pre-modern past.[58] By focussing on the bizarre and the grotesque, these contemporary accounts misread the evidence and failed to appreciate the method in the apparent madness. Fortunately, a deeper analysis has since emerged which enables one to penetrate beneath the surface.

Let us therefore begin with the CAR which was saddled with a legacy of French colonialism at its most rapacious. This landlocked country inherited little in the way of an infrastructure and had only a tiny number of skilled personnel (perhaps a hundred or so) at independence. Such business as there existed was owned by the French and consisted of plantations and mining companies. The colonial experience had also done to little to forge a sense of common identity. Barthélémy Boganda was the first (and only) leader to achieve a national following, but his premature death in 1959 created a vacuum. In the struggle for the succession, French interests backed David Dacko (a relative of Boganda) against the more nationalistic Abel Goumba despite the fact that the latter actually commanded greater support.[59] Dacko became the President of an independent CAR in September 1960, while Goumba and his allies hived off to form an opposition party of their own. Sensing his vulnerability at the polls, Dacko swiftly moved to outlaw the opposition in December, thereby producing an almost seamless transition from colonialism to the one-party state.

At independence, Dacko signed the standard list of bilateral agreements with France, which ensured technical co-operation, in the form of skilled manpower, and economic aid. Most state contracts went to French companies, while imports were derived overwhelmingly from the same source. Dacko leaned heavily on his French patrons, but when he became increasingly unpopular at home he became expendable. The regime was forced to double or treble taxes to pay for the ambitious spending plans of the administration which was largely manned by Frenchmen. In December 1965, it was evident even to Dacko that he would have to go, and the way was secretly prepared (with prior French knowledge) for the head of the gendarmerie, Jean Azamo, to take over the reins. However, the chief of staff in the Ministry of Defence, Colonel Bokassa, got wind of the plot. Fearing for his own life, Bokassa mobilised the army and seized power in his own name. Although this had not been in the original script, the French grudgingly accepted the *fait accompli* in July 1966. Bokassa had served in the French army from 1939 until 1960, leaving as lieutenant, and had been decorated for bravery in Indochina. He also happened to be a French citizen. For these reasons, he was unlikely to steer the CAR out of the French orbit. Nevertheless, Bokassa was kept waiting until September 1967 before he could take up a formal invitation by General de Gaulle to visit Paris. There, Bokassa proclaimed his enduring devotion to France and to de Gaulle, who he referred to as his former commanding officer and adoptive father.[60] The pact between the countries was sealed with a French agreement to locate paratroopers within the CAR.

Like many military despots, Bokassa started out with a measure of popularity which he added to by displaying a sensitivity to popular concerns. Thomas O'Toole writes that:

> He started construction of a large concrete central market in Bangui, to establish a public transport system, ordered buses from France, donated his first month's salary as president to the main hospital in Bangui, subsidised two national dance orchestras, and paid in cash the debts that Central African butchers owed Chadian cattle-breeders so that meat would be available once more in the markets. Such acts, though seemingly unimportant to outsiders, did create for the first time the sense for most Central Africans that the government could actually act in their interests.[61]

The team which he assembled contained some competent individuals, most notably Captain Alexandre Banza, who became the Minister of Finance, and

Ange Patassé, a young civil servant who was elevated to Minister of Development. However, a sign of things to come was the decision by Bokassa to assume both the position of President and three Ministerial portfolios, to which he had added two more in 1970.[62] Although the first three years were broadly successful, the rot quickly set in thereafter.

In 1969, Banza was removed from office, tortured and executed for allegedly plotting a coup. From this point, O'Toole observes, 'the distinction between Bokassa's personal accounts and those of the state ceased to exist'.[63] Bokassa set about creating a new system which orbited around his person. On the business side, he raided the Treasury at will and used its reserves to finance his own companies, which were given a virtual monopoly (for example in cement) and were not required to pay any taxes. He forced the managers of foreign companies to come up with the money to pay government employees and on a number of occasions he caused an uproar when he simply confiscated the assets of French enterprises. After he launched a new agrarian policy in 1970, Bokassa also set about expropriating all the farm machinery he could lay his hands on and sent it to his private plantations at his home town of Berengo.[64] It was literally the case that Bokassa drew no distinction between his property and that of the state. The clinching moment came when Bokassa had himself crowned Emperor in 1977, at a cost of $30 million, in a conscious attempt to emulate Napoleon I. Under the new monarchical constitution, it was formally stated that the Emperor (and those who would succeed to the throne) was the nation incarnate.[65]

Bokassa also took a weak state and, according to Didier Bigo, effectively dismantled it. In the place of functioning institutions, he created highly personalised relations of dependency on himself. Although Bokassa had come to power through the army, he wreaked havoc with its internal organisation by assuming the right to promote and demote officers on a whim.[66] With little regard for the consequences, he promoted soldiers of his own Mbaka ethnic group into top positions. However, the army and the gendarmerie were themselves superseded by a praetorian guard, which functioned more like a private militia owing absolute loyalty to Bokassa. A succession of attempted military coups between 1974 and 1976 seemed to underline the unreliability of the army and the gendarmerie. The bureaucracy equally ground to a halt because Bokassa insisted on taking almost every decision himself. Government officials were scared to act on their own, lest they displease the President. Hence, while Bokassa became bogged down in the minutiae of decisions which would normally be left to state officials, many items of government business simply fell off the agenda altogether. Indeed, Bigo suggests that out of sight was literally out of mind because Bokassa tended to concentrate on matters which came to his attention at Berengo. Much of the country was left to its own devices because it never crossed his field of vision. Moreover, Bokassa created a parallel structure within his court which shadowed the state administration. In reality, the courtiers wielded far more influence than the nominal Ministers, while the latter bore the consequences if things went awry.[67]

Bokassa was able to stay on top of things using a variety of stratagems. He elevated close members of his family to important positions, although he kept a close watch on their ambitions. He also neutralised potential threats by keeping his officials in a state of perpetual insecurity. Although the coronation was farcical, the parallel with imperial Ethiopia is actually rather apposite because, as in Haile Selassie's court, there was little scope for collective solidarity amongst officials. A climate of mutual mistrust was created by means of a dense network of informers who reported directly to Bokassa. This was underpinned by a fertile rumour mill which could see over-mighty courtiers cut down to size at a stroke. Thirdly, Bokassa was also astute at tapping into indigenous constructions of power. Revealing his benign side, he posed as the father of the nation – 'Papa' – who would listen patiently to the supplications of his subjects. But he also let it be known that he was well-versed in the occult, which incidentally provided a point of personal contact with Amin. After his overthrow, bodies parties were discovered in his fridge, allegedly for his consumption.[68] In all likelihood, Bokassa was fortifying himself spiritually, rather than engaging in acts of 'cannibalism'. According to Bigo, Bokassa also tapped into the supernatural powers which were thought to reside with women. He was astute enough to listen to the Bangui market women, who were powerful both as women and as the regulators of consumption. Bokassa's closest confidante was one of their number, Madame Domitien, who was greatly feared in the country.

Bokassa was highly effective in negotiating his relationship with France, with which he had a love-hate relationship. Whereas some have seen Bokassa as little more than a puppet of the French, Bigo argues convincingly that he was a good deal smarter than this would give him credit for. The manner in which he oscillated between expressions of friendship and denunciations of French imperialism might suggest outright irrationality. However, his principal campaigns against French business interests, in 1968 and 1971, were carefully timed to coincide with his efforts to squeeze greater economic aid out of the French.[69] Bokassa struck up a particularly close relationship with President Giscard d'Estaing, who came to the CAR to hunt and who (it was later revealed) was the recipient of diamonds from Bokassa.[70] His flirtation with the Eastern Bloc was motivated by a similar calculus, as was his shortlived adoption of Islam in the hope of unlocking Libyan largesse. At one point he frankly pronounced that he would adopt the ideology of whichever country would build him his beloved railroad.[71]

Although Bokassa's policies were disastrous, economic growth or sustainable development were not his concerns. In reality, he was merely interested in his personal aggrandisement which he could measure on a daily basis by the amount of genuflection to his greatness – especially by foreigners – and the size of his hoard (allegedly some $125 million), which he preferred to keep in the form of diamonds. What happened outside of Berengo and Bangui was of relatively little interest to him. The so-called agrarian reform was highly destructive and led to a reversion of much of the countryside to subsistence production, in the absence of motorable roads, inputs or attractive terms of trade. Not surprisingly, there was a flight of foreign capital although some carpetbaggers also entered the country in the hope of making a quick buck. Moreover, state finances were in a state of perpetual crisis. After the coronation, which consumed a third of the annual budget, there was nothing left to pay public servants with until he managed to extract a further tranche of aid from the French.[72]

Such systems of personal rule, which are arbitrary and brutal in the extreme, are also intrinsically fragile. The despot rules through (often rehearsed) displays of overt deference, and although he may be aware of the existence of sullen compliance at the margins, as long as the outward form is obeyed that is the important thing. However, as soon as dissent is openly articulated it has to be eradicated at once, lest it appear that the all-powerful ruler is after all human. Bokassa remained in power for no fewer than fourteen years, which is an indication that he understood the rules of the game very well. However, as the lot of the urban population progressively deteriorated, expressions of dissent slowly came to the surface and then multiplied at frightening speed. The catalyst for the final downfall came with a pronouncement that all school pupils should purchase a new uniform bearing his effigy and which happened to be manufactured one of his wives. In January 1979, pupils began demonstrating and what started as a specific grievance escalated into calls for the removal of Bokassa. In an attempt to quell the mounting challenge, Bokassa sent in the army and killed up to 200 people, most of them school pupils. When he withdrew the offending pronouncement, however, his position was weakened in the eyes of the population of Bangui. A wave of strikes followed against the backdrop of a proliferation of subversive tracts in Bangui. Over three days in April, there was a swoop on the youth of the affected areas. Around one hundred detainees were beaten to death 'in the presence of, and probably with the participation of, Bokassa himself'.[73]

This was the Emperor seeking to reassert his absolute authority. Unfortunately for him, the killings and secret burials soon became common knowledge and not only in Bangui. When the CAR Ambassador to Paris himself resigned over the issue, the French government was placed in a very awkward position. Giscard D'Estaing suspended military aid and supported the formation of an African Mission of Inquiry, made of representatives from mostly Francophone states. When the Mission confirmed that the alleged murders had indeed taken place, President Omar Bongo of Gabon was asked to broker the resignation of Bokassa. It was only when the latter refused to go quietly that the French military launched Operation Barracuda in September 1979 to physically depose the Emperor. The latter was refused a comfortable retirement in one of his many *chateaux* in France, and had to settle for Côte d'Ivoire, which resolved an embarrassment for Paris – until Houphouët eventually tired of his guest and he was resettled at Château Hardricourt near Paris. However, the French intervention scarcely resolved any of the deep-seated problems of the country because they merely brought Dacko back from exile. Dacko enjoyed some temporary legitimacy when he put Bokassa collaborators on public trial, but before long this began to wear thin. When Dacko reverted to type and attempted to crush political opposition, the new French government of François Mitterrand, in an effort to distance itself from the Giscard years, gave its tacit consent to another coup, which was led by General André Kolingba on 1 September 1981.[74] The new regime set itself up as a corrective government, but perhaps predictably found reasons for remaining in office. As for Bokassa, he surprisingly returned to the country to face trial and the inevitable death sentence in 1986. Defiant to the end, he blamed everything on the French.

Uganda differed insofar as it was comparatively well-endowed at independence, with a substantial educational and administrative infrastructure to boast of. However, as we have already noted, wealth and education were concentrated in the South, whereas political power gravitated towards the impoverished north. The inability of the main political players to resolve this contradiction created an opening for Idi Amin who, as we have seen, had his own personal reasons for seizing power. Like Bokassa, Amin had a limited education (to primary level) and had served for a long time in the colonial army. In each case, the imperative of rapid Africanisation led to over-promotion at lightning speed. Amin was actually on the verge of being prosecuted for atrocities committed while serving in the King's African Rifles in the Northern Frontier District of Kenya, but was spared because he was one of only two Ugandans who could be promoted to head the army at independence.[75] Ironically, when Amin eventually decided on a pre-emptive strike against Obote, he was supported to the hilt by the intelligentsia and people of Buganda who hailed him as their liberator. Like Bokassa, Amin began by displaying an acute awareness of what was needed to consolidate popular support – and, although it now seems remarkable, he was highly successful. He firmed up his Buganda base by ensuring that the body of the deceased *Kabaka* was returned for a fitting burial in March 1971. Asian business leaders who had been alarmed by the 'Move to the Left' expressed their faith in the ability of Amin to restore a conducive commercial environment. Amin was also able to persuade some respected civilians to join the government, which signalled that this was not to be a mere military junta. Finally, the Western press played its part by giving a mostly favourable account of the new regime.

Such was the outpouring of praise that Amin began to believe that he genuinely was a man of destiny. This led him to take a more pro-active role in the decision-making process, presiding over issues which he did not understand in detail but to which he felt a gut reaction. His tendency to express himself in the most un-nuanced language endeared him to ordinary Ugandans who had not passed through secondary school, far less Makerere University, and who rather enjoyed his plain speaking. Intoxicated by the publicity, Amin decided to take on larger dragons, posing increasingly not merely as the saviour of Uganda but as the liberator of the entire African continent. The underside of the personalisation of Amin's rule was that he acted to physically eliminate anyone who was a potential threat to his position. Despite the bluster, he felt insecure from the start because he had come to power through his ethnic kinsmen, that is fellow Kakwa who numbered only some 60,000.[76] The Langi represented a large section of the army, as did the Acholi who Obote had been seeking to marginalise. Amin began by secretly murdering Langi officers and soldiers, and then extended the pogrom to include the Acholi as well. The full scale of these murders, conducted at a time when his political stock was high, did not come out until some time later. It eventually became clear that it was not merely soldiers who were the victims. Indeed, it is estimated that as many as 10,000 people had been liquidated by the end of 1971.[77] Moreover, this was just the beginning. An attempted invasion by Obote loyalists in September 1972 was followed by the elimination of many prominent civilians, including Chief Justice Benedicto Kiwanuka, alongside renewed pogroms within the army.

A crucial stage came around February 1972 when Amin jettisoned the Israelis, who had helped him to power, in favour of an alliance with the Arab world. In the context of the meteoric rise of the OPEC countries, this made a certain pragmatic sense because Uganda stood to benefit from the economic assistance which was being denied to him in the West. However, there was also a Muslim side to Amin's complex self-identification which began to have momentous internal consequences. Amin later claimed to be of Nubian origin, the latter consisting of the remnants of Sudanese troops from the nineteenth century who had come to be associated with Islam and petty trade.[78] In August, Amin dropped an even greater bombshell when he pronounced that the Asian community would have to leave the country within three months. Those Asians who were fellow Muslims were not spared, nor were those who possessed Ugandan citizenship. Much as Shagari bought popular support by expelling Ghanaian strangers from Nigeria in 1983, Amin was playing to the gallery. The difference was that whereas the Ghanaians were economic exiles from their stricken country, the Asian community controlled much of the business in Uganda, including both trade and manufacturing. By expelling the Asians, Amin was granted a windfall in the form of profitable businesses which could be handed out to loyal supporters. Unsurprisingly, the measure was economically disastrous as most of the enterprises collapsed, leading to consumer shortages of items like sugar and textiles which Asian entrepreneurs had previously supplied. The expulsions presented an embarrassing problem for the British government which was forced to absorb many of the Asian refugees. Not surprisingly, inter-governmental relations rapidly deteriorated, and reached a nadir when Amin proceeded to nationalise the assets of major British businesses, as part of his so-called Economic War to bring the economy under national control. Attacking British imperialism was always likely to be popular, although the enthusiasm began to wane as Ugandans felt the economic pinch.

By 1973, Amin was well on the way to turning the country into the worst-case scenario of personalised authoritarian rule. As in the case of the CAR, this was accompanied in the complete breakdown of state institutions. The armed forces was thoroughly disrupted by the shameless manner in which Amin used ethnicity as the principal criterion for promotion and secret executions as the means of getting rid of awkward leftovers. However, the problem was that the very boundaries of ethnic alignment were constantly mutating – providing a further example of why 'tribes' cannot be taken as a fixed quantity in Africa. Amin initially struck against so-called Nilotics in the army – Langi and Acholi – and advanced fellow West Nilers. However, this was swiftly followed by the emergence of another line of cleavage. As Amin began to play the Muslim card, he alienated groups from the West Nile who identified themselves as Christian. Purges against Alur, Lugbara and Madi soldiers and officers then followed, leading to a succession of counter-rebellions by the peoples affected. Amin's base was narrowed to that of the Kakwa, but even these were not to be trusted. In 1974, Brigadier-General Chalres Aruba, a Christian Kakwa, headed an attempted coup which Amin could only put down by calling on Nubian troops.

Increasingly, Amin's support base lay with the Nubians, but this was an extremely fluid category – Muslims from the West Nile tended to be assimilated to the Nubian label, but according to Amin himself people of different 'tribes' could become Nubian! Some of these Nubians were from Uganda, but many were actually Sudanese. To their ranks were added other southern Sudanese (non-Muslim) and Zaireans, veterans of other guerrilla wars with whom Amin had cultivated strong links. To all intents and purposes, therefore, Amin remained in power by relying on a mercenary force composed of non-Ugandans which made of three-quarters of the army. This amounted to the disappearance of a national army in the conventional sense of the term. While Amin surrounded himself with his elite Nubian units, 'the countryside [was] transformed into peripheral zones of operation for local military garrisons, under the command of functional warlords having power over life, death, and property in their territorial spheres'.[79] Not surprisingly, there was also a breakdown of the administrative infrastructure. Amin ceased to rely on his Cabinet or the structures of state administration which he found tiresome. Bureaucrats, who went unpaid, lived in constant fear and tended to lie low in Kampala. Decalo concludes that 'It is thus difficult to talk of Uganda having been "governed" by Amin, especially after 1975 because of his highly personalist style of rule, and as a consequence of the state of quasi-anarchy in the countryside.'[80]

Over 1975/76, there was a slight lull in the orchestrated violence – although killings continued at the local level – as Amin concentrated on his duties as OAU Chairman. Thereafter, Amin proclaimed himself 'Field-Marshal' and 'Life President' and resumed a reign of terror which was provoked by a series of plots. Amongst the casualties was Anglican Archbishop, Janani Luwum, who was killed for not having reported a Langi/Acholi conspiracy.[81] By 1978, the popular support for Amin had dwindled to practically nothing, even in Buganda and the West Nile, because most Ugandans had relatives or friends who had been murdered or who had been brutalised in some manner. However, ordinary Ugandans did not possess the means with which to remove the source of their oppression: after all many communities had been levelled for daring to stick their heads above the parapet. As in the CAR, there was therefore a withdrawal from the state. Communities reverted to subsistence, while those who lived close enough to the borders, especially that of Kenya, made a living out of the black market, or *magendo*.

The forces which finally overthrew Amin, like those which unseated Bokassa, came from outside the country. Amin had previously made border claims against both Kenya and Tanzania. When he decided to invade the Kagera salient in October 1978, Julius Nyerere (who had consistently supported Obote and refused to grant Amin any credence) was provided with the excuse he needed. Having recaptured the salient, the Tanzanian army marched on Kampala itself. The demoralised Ugandan forces melted away, while the Tanzanians were welcomed by the rural population as liberators. Following in the slipstream of the Tanzanian forces was a motley collection of fighters derived from the various opposition movements which had been given a home by Nyerere. While Amin retreated into a lengthy exile in Saudi Arabia, where he died in 2003, the United National Liberation Front (UNLF) was entrusted with forming a successor administration. This proved no simple task because the opposition groups were divided into so many factions, while their fighting forces were often out of control. Two Presidents, Yusufu Lule and Godfrey Binaisa were installed and then rapidly deposed when they proved incapable of straddling the various factions. Obote meanwhile was waiting for a convenient moment to retake the political stage, which he finally did in May 1980. In the December elections, Obote's UPC was triumphant, although victory was secured in an atmosphere of violence and intimidation.

Obote had not learned the lessons of his first stint as President any better than Dacko had. The difference was that whereas Dacko eventually went meekly, Obote launched a reign of terror of his own in an attempt to avoid history repeating itself. The West Nile was laid waste by the Obote forces in 1980 to punish this region for having given birth to Amin, although arguably it had suffered as much as the rest. The Uganda Patriotic Movement, which had been formed by Yoweri Museveni in time for the 1980 elections, rejected the results after having failed dismally even in the leader's home area of Ankole. Other members of the mainly Baganda Democratic Party (DP) were equally disinclined to accept an Obote Presidency. These opposition elements came together to form a movement committed to violent opposition, the National Resistance Movement (NRM) which set up an armed wing, the National Resistance Army (NRA). This meant that Buganda once more became the prime site of opposition to Obote. As the NRA embarked on a guerrilla insurgency, Obote's generals unleashed a pogrom in Buganda which matched the worst excesses of Amin. Obote was eventually deposed by his own generals before they were themselves pushed out by Museveni's army in 1986. It was only under Museveni that a modicum of stability emerged, as well see in Chapter 9.

The CAR and Ugandan cases demonstrate two general points. The first is that the depth of civilian political divisions may not merely have made military intervention possible, but also led exhausted populations to invest their trust in a single leader. Personal rule therefore began with a social contract of sorts, but one which by its very nature had no checks and balances. While personal rule could provide direction, the idiosyncrasies of the leader tended to be magnified the longer he was in office. Both Bokassa and Amin started with a popular mandate and ended up going off the rails completely. They turned violence and murder into something almost mundane and they impoverished their citizens. With the exception of some nationalist bombast, neither of them seriously addressed the affairs of state. Their education and abilities were hardly suitable to the task anyway. Amin was scarcely literate, while his Vice-President and Minister of Defence, General Mustafa Adrisi, later confessed that he was only able to read and write his name.[82] For the affairs of state, Bokassa and Amin substituted their own personal ambitions, fears and fixations. The second point is that if military rule tended to lead to greater internal fragmentation, a personal ruler often had a vested interest in destroying the very institution he had emerged from.

Our next pairing of examples, namely Zaire under Mobutu and Togo under Eyadéma, differs in the sense that there was a much more elaborate attempt to legitimise and institutionalise the usurpation of power by means of a combination of civilian co-optation and the installation of a hegemonic single party.

They may usefully be treated together because Eyadéma consciously modelled himself on his more charismatic Zairean mentor. In Zaire, or the Congo as it still was, Mobutu was presented with his opportunity as a result of renewed fratricidal struggles between civilian factions centered on Joseph Kasavubu and Moïse Tshombe respectively. Against the backdrop of another constitutional impasse, following Kasavubu's failed attempt to foist his own choice of premier on Parliament, Mobutu intervened for a second time on 25 November 1965 with the forewarning of the Americans. The new regime clothed itself in readily recognizable corrective colours, and promised to restore both political and economic stability. According to Mobutu, it would take five years to put the country back on track politically, at which point there would be a return to democracy. The takeover was even given the imprimatur of Parliament in return for the right to remain in existence. Although Mobutu assumed the formal position of head of state, his Cabinet was carefully selected to represent all regions of the country and to include elements of the main political factions. Furthermore, Mobutu assembled some of the best intellectual talent on offer as presidential staffers who briefed him on a daily basis.[83] On the economic front, the government began by introducing austerity measures and won much acclaim by managing to restore some order to public finances. In subsequent years, more ambitious plans for economic takeoff were drawn up, premised on an influx of foreign investment which would generate the resources to sustain three development poles at Kinshasa, Kisangani and southern Shaba (Katanga). Crawford Young and Thomas Turner contend that Mobutu's popularity was such that he would have won any freely contested election at the turn of the decade.[84]

Be that as it may, it did not take very long before the tell-tale signs of personalism began to manifest themselves. In October 1966, Mobutu dispensed with the post of premier, thereby concentrating full executive power on himself. From the start, Mobutu had also assumed a right to legislate by edict. When Parliament was dissolved in 1967, this meant that Mobutu was the sole law-giver for the next three years. Many of the most prominent politicians who had been brought into the ruling coalition, like Victor Nendaka and Justin Bomboko, had been sidelined by 1969. Equally, Mobutu began to rely less on his presidential staffers and to surround himself with 'yes-men' who were more inclined to pander to his whims. However, all of this was given the appearance of constitutional legitimacy when Mobutu founded a political party, the MPR (Mouvement Populaire de la Révolution) which was granted a monopoly under the 1967 constitution. The student movement was forced to dissolve and come under the youth wing of the party, the JMPR (Jeunesse de la MPR), while the labour movement was similarly annexed. In common with other one-party states, this was justified on the basis that the imperative of nation-building required the sublimation of sectional interests to the general will. After 1972, party cells were extended to the military, while hereditary chieftaincies lost much of their importance as the regime attempted to improve MPR penetration at the local level.

Formally speaking, the MPR was construed as 'the nation politically organised', while the Political Bureau became its supreme organ. In reality, both came to serve as the instruments of Mobutu. In the 1974 constitution, the primacy of the party was reiterated, but tellingly 'Mobutuism' was enshrined as the official ideology. Predictably, the structures of the MPR began to wither. In 1977, Mobutu seized on the legitimising potential of competitive elections held under one-party rule (as pioneered by TANU in Tanzania). That year, open contests were held for the legislature and for the Political Bureau itself. This exercise reinvigorated popular interest in politics, but it was not altogether consistent with the logic of personal rule. Parliamentarians began to display an unexpected independence, such as in 1979 when a group from Kasai Oriental ignored pressures from Mobutu and denounced army killings of diamond miners near Mbuji-Mayi.[85] In 1980, Mobutu decided to restrict the accountability of ministers to the legislature and terminated elections to the Political Bureau.

Compared to Bokassa and Amin, Mobutu was a sophisticated political operator. Although he resorted to naked violence when circumstances demanded it, he avoided the mistake of turning it into something routine. Those who displeased the President were generally demoted rather than liquidated. Many who were sent into the wilderness to contemplate the error of their ways were subsequently rehabilitated. A case in point is Nguza Karl-i-Bond who went from number two to being found guilty of treason (which meant a trip to the torture chambers) in 1977, only to be brought back as prime minister two years later. Over the next two decades, he repeated the cycle of disgrace and rehabilitation. Mobutu was the master of co-optation, and it is remarkable how many intellectuals and politicians passed through the revolving door at one point or the other. Mobutu also understood the importance of ideological legitimation for long-term survival. At first, he could remind his audience of the alternative of warring politicians, which threatened to unleash dangerous ethnic rivalries, but when this began to wear thin he had to find more positive reasons for accepting his rule. Interestingly, despite his role in the elimination of Lumumba, he began by presenting himself as the bearer of the radical nationalist mantle and elevated the murdered President to the position of a national martyr. In 1967, Mobutu also launched his N'Sele Manifesto which, with echoes of the Arusha Declaration, proclaimed a commitment to achieving economic independence from the stranglehold of foreign capital. Both of these measures were designed to appeal to that section of civilian opinion which lay outside the Kasavubu and Tshombe camps. The willingness to stand up to the Belgians over the inherited colonial debt and the divestiture of colonial state investments won much sympathy. The nationalisation of the giant UMHK corporation (Union Minière du Haut Katanga), and its replacement by a state corporation GECAMINES (Générale des Carrières et des Mines) in 1967 was regarded by many as a crowning victory, as was the nationalisation of land and mineral rights the previous year.

After the elimination of the last two giants, Tshombe and Kasavubu, from the political equation in 1969, Mobutu began to make himself become the focal point of a veritable personality cult.[86] As we have seen in an earlier chapter, African nationalists learned to play the ideological trick of the colonial masters back on themselves, asserting a common humanity at the same time as asserting an African essence which was somehow unique. The same formula was repeated by intellectuals within the *négritude* movement. Mobutu was intelligent enough to recognise that such a double positioning would serve his purposes equally well. The subtlety lay in representing different faces to different audiences, exploiting the lack of direct communication between them. Mobutu was acutely aware of the tremendous mineral wealth of the country and the importance of foreign mining capital in generating the resources which he needed for his political project. He had also risen to power with the patronage of the Americans, for whom he represented the surest bulwark against Soviet penetration. At the same time, Mobutu was aware of the risk of appearing to be a mere stooge of Western interests at a time when revolutionary ideas were gaining greater currency on the continent. Indeed, his own personal pride made him especially sensitive to the perceived arrogance of Westerners. Whereas some African leaders sought merely to strike a balance between accommodating foreign interests and nationalist sentiments (like Houphouët-Boigny) or were schizophrenic (like Hastings Banda in Malawi), Mobutu aspired towards a more holistic synthesis.

In 1971, Mobutu launched his 'authenticity' campaign. Significantly, he chose to do so not in Kinshasa, but in Dakar, the home of Senghorian *négritude*.[87] This programme was supposed to break the mental shackles of colonialism and allow Africans to take a pride in the indigenous cultures of Zaire– the newly chosen name for a country which had supposedly existed in embryo before the Belgians fixed its boundaries.[88] Whether they liked it or not, all Zaireans were required to renounce their Christian names and to adopt indigenous ones. Hence Joseph-Désiré Mobutu became Mobutu Sese Seko (for short), the 'all-conquering warrior who triumphs over all obstacles'.[89] Officials were required to replace their European suits with the *abacost*, a collarless affair akin to the Mao suit, with the mandatory Mobutu badge appended.[90] In addition to the *abacost*, Mobutu always appeared in public with a leopard-skin hat and a carved cane embodying symbols connoting power and courage. In drawing on 'tradition', Mobutu claimed to be acting as any chief would in relation to his subjects: showing firmness and benevolence as circumstances demanded. He was invariably accompanied by a vast troupe of performers who sang and danced in his honour, drawing on cultural traditions from different parts of the country. In 1974, authenticity mutated further into 'Mobutuism' and an MPR ideological institute was formed to disseminate this official ideology – no simple task, one imagines, given that Mobutu had failed to articulate a coherent body of ideas. However, Mobutuism was taken deadly seriously by agents of the regime who went to remarkable lengths to subordinate its principal rival in the form of the Christian churches. Mobutu, who had suffered personally at the hands of the missionaries, exacted his revenge on the churches who were castigated as instruments of European imperialism. In August 1971, the Catholic University of Louvanium was nationalised, followed by the schools three years later. In 1974, the regime ended the status of Christmas as a national holiday, replaced religious teaching in schools with that of 'Mobutuism' and restricted the exhibition of religious artifacts to the interior of churches while the images of Mobutu were everywhere.[91] In this most Christian of countries, the agents of Mobutu dared the churches to utter 'blasphemy' as they repeatedly likened Mobutu and the MPR to Jesus Christ and his Church.[92]

Although personalism did not lead to as rapid a collapse of state institutions as in the CAR, there was a creeping sclerosis which was starkly apparent by the mid-1970s. The cult of the leader reached a point where decision-making began to be seriously impaired. Government bureaucrats found it increasingly difficult to draw attention to policies which were not working, lest this be taken as a veiled criticism of *Le Guide*. Equally, it was in the interest of Ministers, who drew very substantial salaries and perks, to keep a low profile lest they fall victim to the next reshuffle. The armed forces also began to manifest signs of institutional decay, despite the fact that more than a tenth of the national budget was poured into expensive hardware and training programmes. Mobutu was pulled between conflicting impulses: creating an effective military would strengthen his hands against potential rebels, but it also heightened the chance of a successful coup. The result was that government policies tended to cancel themselves out. Although the army was repeatedly revamped, a succession of purges removed some of the best trained personnel. Moreover, Mobutu tended to duplicate structures in order to blunt potential threats to himself. Apart from the army itself, Mobutu created no fewer than seven other security agencies with overlapping functions.[93] Moreover, the military high command was promoted less on the basis of competence than perceived loyalty, with a marked preference for personnel drawn from Equateur province and from the President's own Ngbandi group.[94]

Then there was the phenomenon of corruption which consumed scarce resources and further eroded confidence in public institutions. When Mobutu seized power, he was a man of modest means, but within a few years he had begun to accumulate a spectacular fortune, much of which was stashed away in foreign bank accounts (so much for authenticity!). He freely raided the national bank, a practice which a parliamentary commission of 1979 had the courage to criticise in a single instance involving the siphoning off of $150 million. Within the country, his business empire (and that of his family) thrived, with his enormous agro-pastoral empire becoming the third-largest employer in the country by 1977. In addition, Mobutu was the largest shareholder in the Banque du Kinshasa, whilst holding stakes in many of the leading multinational companies.[95] Large sums of money was redistributed as patronage, as befitted the benevolent father of the nation. By contributing to this school or that clinic, Mobutu replaced impersonal state provision by a gift that was designed to create a moral debt to his person.[96] But the underlying reality was that Mobutu also became one of the richest men in the world (allegedly worth some $5 billion), at the same time as the road network fell apart, teachers went unpaid and health facilities all but collapsed. A large amount of graft by senior officials, including the organised smuggling of the country's minerals, was tolerated by Mobutu. These rewards were assumed to go with the job – which was prebendalism in its purest form – but peculation also gave Mobutu a hold over his officials who could be called to account if it was expedient to do so. Endemic corruption within the higher echelons of the military was one reason why the armed forces regularly found themselves without ammunition and fuel. Unpaid soldiers effectively preyed off the rural populations amongst whom they were garrisoned, which meant that they approximated much more to ruthless bandits than to members of a professional military.[97]

The honeymoon came to an end in 1974 as the country was plunged into economic turmoil. Some of the causes lay beyond the control of the regime: most notably, the collapse of the world copper price and the simultaneous hike in petroleum prices. But to a large extent, Mobutu was the architect of his own misfortune. Riding high on the initial economic achievements, Mobutu embarked on a massive public investment programme, which included dam construction on the lower Zaire River with a lengthy transmission line to Shaba and the creation of the Maluku steel plant whose feasibility was not properly assessed. The result was that the country was already over-committed when the external shocks hit. In November 1973, Mobutu also announced his intention to give substance to earlier proclamations of intent under what came to be known as 'Zairianisation'. The initial intention seems to have been one of taking over foreign-owned plantations, but against a backdrop of uncertainty Zairianisation was extended to commercial and industrial enterprises.[98] The mostly Greek, Portuguese and Pakistani owners were given three months to wind up their operations, following which the companies were handed over to Zaireans who had been screened by local officials. Little attempt was made to ensure that these enterprises went to people with business acumen, and in fact the principal beneficiaries were the politicians – most notably Mobutu himself. As in the case of Uganda, the immediate result of this sharing out of the booty was the collapse of the businesses in question, leading to acute consumer shortages and a public backlash. Mobutu attempted to salvage some credibility by joining in the attack on the freebooters and in December 1974, following a trip to China and North Korea, he announced a policy of 'radicalisation'. What began as a supposed war against the Zairean bourgeoisie ended up as an extension of Zairianisation to encompass the larger Belgian enterprises as well. In this case, parastatals were formed to take over the newly acquired enterprises. Because foreign personnel were kept on in a managerial capacity alongside the state employees, the running costs of these enterprises tended to escalate to the point where they became a drain on the exchequer. In 1975, Mobutu compounded his woes by embarking on a very expensive invasion of Angola in support of his FNLA allies, which ended in an embarrassing rout (see Chapter 7).

As the national economy contracted in real terms and the international debt piled up to around $3 billion, Mobutu came under pressure to change direction or risk being cut off. Beginning in 1976, Mobutu was forced to embrace stabilisation plans which reversed most of the initiatives of the past three years. Many enterprises were returned to their former owners and compensation terms were agreed for the rest, while many of the new state agencies were wound up. Two years later, the regime was forced to agree to an IMF appointee taking over the operations of the central bank, and to French and Belgian experts running the Ministry of Finance and the Customs department.[99] For a regime which had built much of its legitimacy on its nationalist posturing, these were bitter pills to swallow. Mobutu was even forced to make his peace with the Catholic church, which had previously been chastised for its critique of the leadership cult.[100] An even greater humiliation came in March 1977 when rebels of the FLNC (Front Pour la Liberation Nationale du Congo) drawn largely from

Tshombe's former Katangan gendarmerie, invaded Shaba. Because of the complete disarray of the Zairean army, Mobutu had to call on Moroccan troops flown in by France. In March 1978, when the rebels invaded for a second time (Shaba II), and seized the mining town of Kolwezi, Mobutu had to call on French and Belgian paratroopers to bail him out. These events demonstrated the extent to which Mobutu was dependent on his Western patrons.

'Authenticity' and Zairianisation were self-serving and ill-considered, but one of the spinoffs was unexpectedly fruitful. Amongst the beneficiaries of the nationalisation drive was Franco Luambo Makiadi, considered by most to be the king of Congolese music, who was rewarded with the only record production plant in Zaire. Under the cover of 'authenticity', Congolese music thrived as never before, with Franco literally and figuratively centre-stage. He was lionised by the regime and, as head of the musician's union, he was given the power to decide which musicians could travel abroad. Such was his mass appeal that he was inevitably called on to compose songs in praise of Mobutu, who he frequently escorted on his foreign travels. However, Franco also managed to produce enough songs on the eternal themes of love and hardship to retain his mass following. Moreover, some of the lyrics were susceptible to multiple interpretations, even if these were not necessarily intended. Fela and Franco represented radically different responses to the problems of dealing with the post-colonial power structure: whereas the one was abrasive and confrontational, the other was compromising and studiously ambiguous. What they shared was a cultural influence far beyond the boundaries of their respective countries.[101] As economic conditions deteriorated, many of the most talented musicians migrated to greener pastures to ply their trade in countries like Kenya and Togo where Congolese music reigned supreme.

Despite the retreat from Zairianisation, the regime was not able to recapture its winning ways. The economy actually contracted annually by several percentage points per annum, despite a steady increase in population. The erratic pattern of decision-making, and the highly venal nature of the regime, meant that there was a vast gulf between pronouncements and what actually transpired. Comparatively little of the revenues generated by the mining sector ended up in government coffers. Moreover, when the regime was short of resources to pay its workers, it resorted to printing money which meant that inflation soared to unprecedented levels.[102] Wage-earners could not survive on their formal incomes and therefore resorted to a range of stratagems to make ends meet. This was tacitly accepted by the regime, such that in popular discourse Article 15 of the constitution was held to read: 'débrouillez-vous' (fend for yourself').[103] As a consequence, the so-called 'informal economy' eclipsed the formal one, that is what was reflected in the official statistics. In the countryside, where communities could not acquire access to basic goods, there was a retreat from cash crop production into foodstuffs which could be consumed, sold covertly in local markets (avoiding official marketing mechanisms) or smuggled for hard currency.[104] Mobutu's power was increasingly confined to Kinshasa and the principal cities where the military was garrisoned, while much of the country was left to its own devices. The patrimonial system which Mobutu had created still hinged upon control of the mining enclaves. As long as the hens were continuing to lay the golden eggs, there was little need to engage with the rest of the country.

With the French, Belgians and Americans ever willing to act as the guarantors of the regime, Mobutu could afford to preside over a country where very little functioned. Despite the failure to comply with any of the economic targets, and the systematic evasion of the controls which were put in place, the Paris Club of creditor countries rescheduled Zairean debts no fewer than five times between 1976 and 1983. By this point, Zaire was in debt to the tune of $4 billion and $1 billion in arrears.[105] The reason for this boundless generosity clearly lay in geo-political considerations rather in than any realistic expectation that the government was likely to play by the rules. Meanwhile, the wealth disparities within the country became more pronounced than ever. In 1980, one commentator, who was in a position to know, summed up the Zairean condition under Mobutu when he declared that:

> After fifteen years of the power you have exercised alone, we find ourselves divided into two absolutely distinct camps. On the one side, a few scandalously rich persons. On the other, the mass of the people suffering the darkest misery.[106]

That person was none other than Field-Marshal Mobutu, whose personal fortune happened to be greater than the national debt!

The circumstances which underlay the usurpation of Lt.-Colonel (later General) Etienne Eyadéma in Togo were comparable to those in the Congo/Zaire. After his first intervention in 1963, Eyadéma had handed power back to the politicians as promised. A debilitating power struggle had ensued between President Grunitzky and his deputy, Antoine Meatchi. When the impasse threatened to spill on to the streets, Eyadéma was provided with the perfect excuse to step in – initially as a mediator in April 1967, and then as substantive ruler from 14 April. Like Mobutu, Eyadéma claimed that the selfishness of the politicians threatened to drive the country to destruction. And like Mobutu, he promised that his administration would be a provisional one, with power eventually being returned to the hands of properly elected politicians. A constitutional commission was even established to draw up the modalities. Eyadéma warned of a dangerous North–South divide in Togolese politics and in order to avoid the impression that his was merely a northern junta, he made a conscious effort to balance military with civilian representation (four as against eight) and to ensure that the composition of his Cabinet reflected the diversity of the country as a whole. However, the underlying reality was that, in the absence of a legislature, Eyadéma now commanded complete lawmaking and executive powers. At the start of 1969, Eyadéma carried out an elaborate theatrical ruse – which was so good that he repeated it in 1971 and 1976 – which consisted of pretending to return to the barracks, only to be 'dissuaded' by mass demonstrations pleading for him to stay on.[107] The leader, who only had the welfare of the nation at heart, not surprisingly bent to the 'popular will'. In January 1972, the usurpation was ratified in a referendum in which supposedly more than 99 per cent of the electorate voted in favour.

Eyadéma was acutely aware of where the challenges to his supremacy were likely to emanate from and he built his political defences accordingly. After the first three years of ruling with the assistance of a hand-picked Cabinet, he realised that there was a need to sink firmer roots in the South of the country, where there was still a tendency to regard him as an ignorant northerner who had personally murdered Olympio. His solution was to create a political party in November 1969, the RPT (Rassemblement du Peuple Togolais), to which all Togolese could belong. Edem Kodjo, a respected southern public servant, was brought in as secretary-general, although Eyadéma could ultimately not resist taking top slot for himself.[108] The first congress of the RPT was held in the important commercial town of Kpalimé in 1971, in an attempt to seduce this part of Eweland. Having blamed political parties for past excesses, it was necessary to market the RPT as a different kind of party, one which was dedicated to the goal of national unity. To complete the exercise, Eyadéma removed military personnel from Ministerial positions, filling them with civilians instead. On this basis, the regime could claim to have fully civilianised itself, which was important in terms of establishing the international credibility of the regime. Despite the claim to be democratising, the RPT actually set about strangling the associational life of the country. The party established a single women's movement, youth movement and trade union umbrella, rendering independent organisation virtually impossible.[109] Even the chiefs were brought into a party affiliate. As with most one-party states, this was justified on the basis that sectional interests – such as the wage demands of workers – should not be allowed to supersede the common interest. In January 1980, a constitution was finally promulgated, which provided for a legislature and elected party organs with clearly defined powers.

However, the underlying reality remained that this was a military regime to the core. Military officers filled many non-Ministerial slots, while the armed forces received a substantial chunk of the national budget. Fortunately for Eyadéma, there were relatively few soldiers or officers from the South to worry about, and these were eventually weeded out. Eyadéma made sure that future recruits would be drawn overwhelmingly from the North – in particular from his Kabré homeland and most particularly from his village of Pya. Each year, he used the annual wrestling competition to recruit young Kabrés into the army. Given the acute poverty of this part of the North, he could count on the unswerving loyalty of grateful recruits. The soldiers were carefully despatched to military camps dotted across the country where they could keep the citizens in thrall and where they would not pose a daily threat to the President.

Eyadéma also found additional means of consolidating his position. He was able to take advantage of a fortuitous boom in phosphate prices, which jumped by almost 5 times over 1973/74. He began by seeking a substantial state share in the mines, and after failing to secure their co-operation he embarked on outright nationalisation which generated a windfall. The revenues made it possible to embark on an ambitious range of infrastructural and directly productive projects which had a dual purpose. They were expected to generate further economic returns, but they were also intended to firm up support for the regime. A lot of money was pumped into the hitherto neglected north, with the Kabré town of Lama-Kara being the principal beneficiary. Northerners were also given privileged access to educational scholarships, thereby redressing the acute regional disparity in access to schooling and higher education. However, Eyadéma was astute enough to ensure that the South also benefited from road-building, other infrastructural work and improved social services. The capital of Lomé was itself the beneficiary of a building boom, in which plush international hotels, public buildings and markets were erected. Meanwhile, the paving of the main arterial route from the North to the South stood to benefit both parts of the country. Eyadéma was also singularly fortunate that Ghana began to sink deeper into economic crisis as the decade unfolded. By reducing import duties, he nourished the contraband trade into Ghana (where consumer goods were scarce) from which the market women of Lomé and other southern towns benefited greatly.

Finally, Eyadéma turned to Zaire, China and North Korea for some lessons in ideological legitimation. 'Authenticity' was borrowed *in toto*, as it was in Chad under François Tombalbaye before 1975. The orthography of place names was altered (very few towns had French or German names anyway) and citizens were invited to abandon Christian names for 'authentic' ones.[110] Eyadéma himself dropped Etienne in favour of Gnassingbé and required that public servants follow suit. Because it was impossible to acquire official documents while still bearing a European name, ordinary Togolese were forced to comply. At the same time, Eyadéma drew on traditional rulers as an additional source of legitimation. In the same way that he expected to be venerated as chief of the nation-writ-large, so the customary respect accorded to traditional rulers at the local level was to be upheld. Both based their authority on a combination of physical presence and their reputation for spiritual power. However, as Mobutu once pointed out, there could only be one chief in a given community. Practically, this meant that Eyadéma was prepared to depose traditional rulers who failed to perform as expected. The principle of heredity was not formally abandoned, but that still left a great deal of room for manipulation. The chiefs were expected to function as loyal instruments and most openly displayed the President's photograph in their palaces in order to avoid any ambiguity on this score. Those who had enough traditional weight behind them sought to use their strategic position to bargain on behalf of themselves and their communities, but the rest preferred to keep their heads down.[111]

Authenticity was closely associated with its ideological bed-fellow, the cult of the ruler. From Zaire, Eyadéma imported the whole panoply of praise singers and *animateurs* who materialised anywhere where *Le Guide* was in attendance.[112] Public speeches had to be laced with obsequious and repetitious references to the supreme foresight and benevolence of the great leader. In the style of Kim Il Sung of North Korea, imposing statues of Eyadéma were erected in Lomé and other urban centres. Moreover, the President's face was emblazoned on lapel-badges, which all officials were forced to wear, and even on wristwatches and drinks trays. When Eyadéma escaped a plane-crash at Sarakawa unscathed, this was worked up into an elaborate public myth in which fiendish imperialists had supposedly been thwarted.[113] A shrine was constructed at the crash site, visited by RPT pilgrims, which drew on elements of indigenous religion to promote the notion that Eyadéma possessed mystical – even divine – powers.[114] Apart from holding the mass of the population in awe, constant recitation of the Sarakawa 'miracle' was intended to serve as a deterrent to those who might want to make an attempt on the life of the President.[115]

How much of this was actually internalised by ordinary people is difficult to gauge because Togo provides a textbook example, à la James C. Scott, of the manner in which the perils of overt dissent necessitated the use of highly coded forms of expression.[116] In his excellent study, Comi Toulabor suggests that Eyadéma tapped into Togolese beliefs about the non-material world with a great deal of skill. However, he also reveals how resistance was expressed in so many subtle ways. In some cases, the adoption of 'authentic' names was provocative: choices such as 'Kesse Dufia' ('the monkey is ruler') and 'Dansomo' ('a snake is on the path') needed very little deconstruction. Toulabor also demonstrates that Ewe, being a tonal language, lends itself to subversive plays on words. Hence many of the crowds who ostensibly turned out to sing praises to Eyadéma were often mocking his pretensions – which included making allusions to his sexual preferences – all of which was achieved simply by varying the tones in the lyrics.[117] Although there was a great deal of complicity with the regime – born of fear and opportunism alike – the people of Togo also found ways of expressing their distance from the suffocating leadership cult.

As we have seen in the other case-studies, personal rule has a tendency to generate institutional breakdown. In the Togolese case, there certainly was a deterioration in the operation of state institutions. Eyadéma tended to promote members of his extended family, and beyond that trusted Kabrés, to the most strategic positions. This generated a considerable amount of resentment within the armed forces where more qualified officers were marginalised or (in extreme cases) liquidated. The resulting internal plots tended to draw Eyadéma into a even tighter circle of kinsmen. Although the Togolese armed forces never degenerated to the extent that the Ugandan army did, there were unmistakeable signs of internal malaise. Hence when the exiled opposition attempted an armed invasion in July 1986, Eyadéma found it wise to call on the assistance of French troops.[118] Equally, the quality of Ministerial appointees declined sharply after the first few years. Because these positions were not filled by soldiers, the Ugandan scenario of functionally illiterate Ministers did not transpire. However, the educated civilians who occupied these positions were increasingly sycophants who rose to the top by colluding in the great pretence. Like Mobutu, Eyadéma resorted to constant reshuffles in order to keep his appointees destabilised and thoroughly dependent upon him. Although corruption scarcely reached Zairean heights, those who held public office tended to accumulate as much as they could before they were removed. It was only after French threats to cut off aid that some attempt was made to address government corruption.[119] Finally, the insecurity of Ministers made it highly unlikely that anyone would oppose the inclination of the President to spend at will. When the short-lived phosphate boom came to an end, the government found itself unable to cover its expenses. The international debt mounted, reaching $1 billion by 1982. For a small country like Togo, the level of servicing was simply crippling. The inevitable result was that the IMF had to be called in and the proud economic nationalism of the 1970s was abruptly terminated. This, in turn, threatened to unravel the system of patronage upon which Eyadéma depended. Public employees and ordinary Togolese, who were forced to bear the brunt of austerity, began to find RPT rule less palatable, creating a mounting crisis of legitimacy for the regime to which we will return in Chapter 9.

6.2.4 Praetorian Marxism

In Chapter 5, we placed African socialism under the historical microscope. It will have been noticed that each of the governments concerned was civilian in character. By contrast, all of the regimes which embraced Marxism in some form of other (Marxism-Leninism or 'Maoism') were linked to the military. In the case of regimes which came to power through liberation war – such as FRELIMO in Mozambique – this is not too surprising because armed combat had a radicalising effect on the political movements, as we will see in Chapter 7. What is more intriguing is why regimes which came to power through coups d'état should have been drawn towards Marxism. On the face of things, the armed forces is the least likely candidate for a radical agenda, given its notion-ally apolitical and strictly hierarchical character. But in view of the permeability of the African military, and the frailty of its command structures, this cannot be taken for granted. Soldiers in Africa have been ideologically suggestible, and the rank-and-file especially so. However, this does not of itself resolve why Marxism proved seductive in Congo-Brazzaville, Benin, Ethiopia, Somalia and to a lesser extent Ghana and Burkina Faso. A superficially satisfactory answer is that military leaders had to try harder to justify their usurpations and were conse-quently driven further to the ideological extremes – hence African socialism was altogether too tepid to perform the task satisfactorily. On this view, Marxism represents a convenient ideological gloss – a form of 'signpost socialism' – which was reinforced by pragmatic Cold War alliances. An element of opportunism is certainly apparent in each of the cases we will consider. However, the adoption of Marxism was also born out of certain objective circumstances which radicalised the respective juntas, albeit without necessarily making social revo-lution a realistic possibility.

We begin with the case of Congo-Brazzaville which was the first to openly declare itself Marxist (1963) and a People's Republic (1969). The country shared certain legacies with the rest of former French Equatorial Africa (FEA), namely a highly exploitative experience of colonialism combined with pronounced levels of uneven development. However, it also embodied certain unique features. First of all, because Brazzaville had been the capital of FEA, it grew into a substantial urban centre which thoroughly dominated its rural hin-terland once the rest of the federation had been cut away. The combination of a self-confident urban elite and rapid rates of urbanisation during the war meant that Brazzaville was not only home to much of the national population, but also the cockpit of national politics.[120] Civil servants, students and unemployed city dwellers exercised a powerful influence upon Congolese politics which was true of very few other African countries. Significantly, it was amongst these urban constituencies that Marxism – closely associated with statist solutions to a myriad of social problems – established a popular constituency. The trade unions were heavily influenced by their French progenitors, that is the Communist, Socialist and Catholic federations, the first two of whom were decidedly to the left.[121] Equally, the Congo boasted the most educated population within Francophone Africa, one which was susceptible to international currents. The controversy surrounding events in neighbouring Congo-Kinshasa, and subsequently the Angolan liberation war, also had an impact upon political perceptions in Brazzaville. From urban society, leftwing ideas percolated into the armed forces which never had the time to properly insulate itself from urban society. The rural population for the most part lay outside the loop. At best, it was condescended to within political debate; otherwise, it was systematically neglected in the allocation of material resources.

What complicates any discussion of Congolese politics is the fact that ideological differences became thoroughly bound up with ethno-regional competition. The Bakongo sub-groups (the Lari and the Vili) had received a head-start in education and therefore tended to dominate the civil service and the professions. On the other hand, the relatively deprived northerners (Mbochi and Kouyous) were drawn disproportionately into the armed forces, initially at the base but increasingly also within the officer corps as well. Furthermore, the chronology of urbanisation engendered a pronounced divide within Brazzaville between the northern quarters like Poto Poto which were mostly populated by northerners (lumped together as 'Mbochi') and the southern quarters which were populated by the Bakongo. A series of ethnic clashes around the time of independence removed most of the grey areas in between. The permutations which emerged in the competition for power therefore turned on several axes at once: doctrinal (pro-Soviet, Maoist and so on), civilian-military and Mbochi-Bakongo (but often involving subsets of each).

The civilian government which brought the Congo to independence was led by Fulbert Youlou, a defrocked priest, whose political constituency lay with the Bakongo. French attempts to marginalise Youlou merely had the effect of raising his stock amongst the Lari, in particular, whose attachment to the quasi-religious cult of André Matsoua was rooted in the latter's perceived martyrdom at the hands of the colonial power in 1942.[122] Youlou succeeded in co-opting his main northern rivals and announced his intention to create a one-party state. His was the only Congolese regime which was decidedly conservative and pro-Western. For example, when it came to the crisis in the former Belgian Congo, Youlou came out against Lumumba and in support of Katangan secession. Not long after independence, many of the groups who had given Youlou their backing began to peel off. The Matsouanists, who rejected all governmental authority and refused to carry any identity cards or pay taxes, were the first to break ranks. Then the government, whose members were engaged in all manner of conspicuous consumption, made the mistake of taking on the trade unions. On 13–15 August 1963, strikes and street demonstrations swelled by unemployed youth paralysed Brazzaville, as the gendarmerie lost control of the situation. This urban insurrection, later dubbed 'Les Troises Glorieuses', brought the collapse of the administration when de Gaulle refused a plea for help. At this point, the tiny Congolese army – numbering only 1500 men and still largely under French officers – did not seize power for itself, but brokered the installation of a new government, headed by a former Youlou Minister, Alphone Massemba-Debat. However, some soldiers were included on the Conseil National de la Révolution (CNR), which also included leftwing trade unionists.

The founding myth of the new regime was that it had come to power through a popular revolution. Although Massemba-Debat was not particularly militant himself, the regime as a whole was dominated by self-professed Marxists of various descriptions. In July 1964, a new political party was founded, the MNR (Mouvement National de la Révolution), which spawned a series of integral wings for youth, workers and women and suppressed those which had previously existed. The army was itself converted into a People's Army, in which ideological commitment was demanded. And whereas officers had previously been sent to France for training, they were increasingly despatched to the Soviet Union instead. The government was not, however, a military regime in the true sense of the word. This did not come to pass until the removal of Massemba-Debat after he proved incapable of reconciling the various tendencies within the regime. The youth wing of the ruling party, the JMNR (Jeunesse de la MNR) quickly became a law unto itself, harassing all those suspected of harbouring 'bourgeois' tendencies. With financial aid from the Soviet and Chinese embassies, it began to train and equip its own militia which numbered 1100 by 1968. The JMNR usurped many of the functions of the gendarmerie and, when it threatened to eclipse the army as well, a backlash was always on the cards. A crucial moment came when the President attempted to arrest Captain Marien Ngouabi in July 1968. Massemba-Debat had once before tried to demote him and had been forced to backtrack by mutinous Kouyou soldiers. On this occasion, Ngouabi was freed by his men and Massemba-Debat was forced to accept his installation as chief of staff and head of the CNR. At the end of August, Ngouabi finally seized power after a bloody battle with the JMNR in which some 200 of the latter were killed.

Although the military had now taken over, the emphasis lay upon revolutionary continuity. Hence, far from trying to insulate the military, Ngouabi announced further steps to politicise the People's Army in 1969. A new political party, the PCT (Parti Congolais du Travail), was founded and in 1970 Ngouabi proclaimed the People's Republic of the Congo. The political structures of the PCT were closely modelled on the Communist parties of the Soviet bloc. In order to clear up any ambiguity as to the orientation of the regime, Ngouabi pointedly distanced himself from African socialism, declaring that 'there is only one socialism – scientific socialism, the foundations of which were laid by Marx and Engels'.[123] Although ideological rectitude was now the order of the day, the underlying reality was that this was a regime whose power base lay very much inside the military, which was in itself a northern preserve. The Ngouabi era was characterised by repeated purges, usually justified on ideological grounds, but which were rooted in his attempts to consolidate his political position. Amongst the casualties was Ange Diawara (reputedly of Maoist persuasions), who headed the People's Militia. He mounted an unsuccessful coup in 1972, allegedly with encouragement from members of the French Communist Party, and was eventually tracked down and killed. For the most part, however, political struggles were resolved without recourse to violence. Most members of the regime, civilian and military, were purged at some point, only to be rehabilitated at a later date. A case in point was Denis Sassou-Nguesso who was purged from the Politburo after the Diawara plot, but became a beneficiary of the 'systematic purge' of 1975–76. Radu and Somerville suggests that the reason why rehabilitation was so common was that the Congolese elite was so small that anything more far-reaching would have threatened the viability of the PCT itself.[124] The demise of Ngouabi in March 1977, assassinated by a suicide squad and members of his own guard under mysterious circumstances, did not lead to a change of direction.[125] He was succeeded by the next in the military chain of command, Yhombi-Opango (a Lari born in the North) with Sassou-Nguesso emerging as the strongman of the regime. When Yhombi-Opango forfeited the support of the party, he was forced to resign by the Central Committee and Sassou-Nguesso moved into the Presidency in September 1979. Whereas his predecessor had been less ideologically minded, Sassou-Nguesso was reputed to be a committed socialist. Certainly, the revolutionary rhetoric suggested that there was to be no change of direction. Some continuity also lay in the way in which Sassou-Nguesso embarked on a series of purges of his own, in response to real and imagined plots.

What, then, is one to make of Congolese Marxism? What has struck most outside observers is the vast gulf separating rhetoric from reality. Decalo, for example, refers to the disjuncture between the ubiquity of large posters of Ngouabi, demanding revolutionary discipline and asceticism, plastered 'to walls adjacent to supermarkets overflowing with luxury imports and lively cafes where the easy-going Brazzaville civil service meets to conduct lucrative "private affairs" during office hours'.[126] Moreover, despite the diatribes against Western imperialism, the links with France remained very close. It is tempting, therefore, to conclude that the Marxist rhetoric was just that: rhetoric. However, it would be a mistake to ignore the extent to which it also constrained the margin for manoeuvre for whoever happened to be in power. The fact of the matter is that urban pressure groups were both well-organised and willing to defend their interests by appealing to socialist principles. There was an overwhelming demand for free education which no government could resist. By 1979, the Congo could boast a 93 per cent school attendance rate, ranking it amongst the highest in the Third World. Students leaving secondary school expected to be able to attend University and there was a great deal of resistance when Ngouabi attempted to end automatic admission. The net result was that education became a major call on the national budget, with 7 per cent being consumed by grants alone in 1974.[127] Although there was a high dropout rate, there can be no doubting that in the case of education, a commitment to socialism meant something real. The problem was those who left University expected instant access to state employment, given the limited scale of the private sector. Public sector employment therefore swelled to accommodate the army of graduates without much reference to efficiency criteria. Urban workers came to expect job security and living wages, and to a large extent they were successful in prising concessions from the hands of governments who were well-aware that volatile urban youth could easily be drawn into any protests. In 1984, public sector salaries alone consumed 27 per cent of budgetary allocations. The manner in which the cake was cut tended had its consequences. The armed forces, not surprisingly took a hefty slice in the form of wages, leaving less for essential services. The budgetary allocations to health and infrastructure, for example, suffered. This was especially true of the countryside, thereby adding further impetus to the rural-urban drift.[128]

Ironically, the imperative of keeping highly politicised urban constituencies moderately content contributed to the widening gap between rhetoric and reality in other areas. Although the Congo was fortunate that petroleum exports came on stream when international prices were climbing, expenditures tended to accelerate even faster. When the oil price collapsed in the 1980s, the Sassou-Nguesso regime woke up to the reality that it could only cover part of its budgetary commitments. Despite fierce anti-imperialist diatribes, it was essential not to alienate the French who provided the bulk of the aid necessary to balance the books. Moreover, it was French oil companies which were generating the main source of state revenues. Despite Congolese appeals, the Soviet Union and China provided military aid, but furnished paltry sums in economic assistance. Because American interests in the Congo were fairly minimal, it was possible to maintain some ideological consistency by concentrating most of the anti-imperialist fire on that country. When Ngouabi and the Americans found themselves on opposite sides of the Angolan civil war in 1974, for example, the former seized the assets of Texaco and Mobil, although his successor later paid compensation. As economic conditions deteriorated in the 1980s, it became necessary to reach an accord, given the ability of Washington to block aid from the Bretton Woods institutions.[129] It was only at this point, when structural adjustment became unavoidable, that Sassou-Nguesso was finally forced to jettison the policies which had been pursued since the 1960s and to risk alienating urban interests. At this point, perhaps predictably, the politics of the Congo become an altogether more bruising affair.

The West African state of Benin bore certain similarities with Congo-Brazzaville. Both were characterised by high rates of education at independence, but with significant regional disparities favouring the southern regions. Indeed Dahomey, as it then was, had traditionally exported skilled manpower to other parts of French West Africa. In either case, French colonialism had done little to develop the economic resource base, which in the case of Dahomey was hardly abundant to start with. Finally, while Dahomey was much less highly urbanised than the Congo, Cotonou and Porto Novo were home to an assertive youth culture and well-organised trade unions which had demolished the fortunes of a string of politicians during the first years of independence. The cycle of crises leading up to the December 1972 coup have already been examined above. What remains is to consider why the junta led by Mathieu Kérékou adopted a leftwing agenda in the mid-1970s, and what consequences issued from that. None of this could have been predicted from the start. Although the coupmakers were junior officers who were dismayed by the conduct of the politicians and senior officers alike, none of them had previously shown any radical inclinations. In his first major speech, Kérékou articulated a nationalist position and explicitly eschewed all ideologies, stating categorically that '[y]ou see we do not want communism or capitalism or socialism. We have our own Dahomean social and cultural system, which is our own.'[130] However, this all changed in November 1974 when Kérékou defined Marxism-Leninism as the official ideology of the regime. Thereafter, the public discourse of the regime was broadly similar to that in Brazzaville.

This shimmy to the left has, because of its very suddenness, been viewed with a certain amount of scepticism. It has been seen as an attempt to win the sympathy of the civilian left and organised labour by borrowing some of their own language. It has also been interpreted as an attempt at wiping the political slate clean by, as it were, parachuting in a new social myth – a low-cost one at that, given that there was no bourgeoisie to actually do battle with.[131] Moreover, the language of socialism enabled the regime to deny the legitimacy of ethnic discourse which, given its northern hue, was potentially its Achilles heel. When the name of the country was changed to Benin, it was not for reasons of authenticity – because Dahomey would have served equally well – but in an effort to create a set of symbols with which northerners and southerners alike could identify. Chris Allen has also argued that Marxism-Leninism provided a template for the creation of new structures which would not be subject to the rules of clientelism which had previously turned civilian politics into such a free-for-all.[132] The grounds for scepticism are also strengthened by the manner in which the regime – which was still essentially military in character – subsequently turned on civilian groupings, most notably students, which attempted to outflank it on the left.[133] The periodic internal purges, which were dressed up in terms of right-wing deviationism or ultra-leftism, themselves smacked of more mundane struggles for power.

However, if the label of 'signpost socialism' seems to fit, one should not lose sight of the fact that certain practical consequences followed from the appropriation of Marxism. Words, after all, have a power of their own. The impact can be seen in relation to a number of policy initiatives. First of all, the Kérékou regime began by announcing its intention to free itself of the shackles of neo-colonialism. This led to a series of verbal tirades against France, and to the severing of relations for a time. This came at a cost because it meant forfeiting the budget subsidies which had hitherto balanced the books.[134] Even when relations with France were normalised, the country developed a much more diversified set of economic and political relations after 1974. The Soviet Union and North Korea mostly confined their assistance to military aid, but the Chinese became more economically involved in the country, as did other Western nations with the noteworthy exception of the United States. Secondly, the adoption of a socialist programme was quickly followed by the nationalisation of the assets of foreign companies, which were mostly French. Although compensation was paid, the Kérékou regime prided itself on having brought the economy under national control. No fewer than 125 new parastatals were set up and the government embarked on an attempt to promote industrial development (textiles, cement, sugar and agro-industries) which was hitherto virtually non-existent.[135]

Thirdly, the government dedicated itself to a more egalitarian allocation of state resources. After 1973, the educational system was revamped with a view both to extending access at all levels and (with echoes of Tanzania) providing something which was better suited to the requirements of the country.[136] In the area of public health, there was similarly a commitment to extending primary health care to the rural areas, through village health units, and bringing service provision under greater local control.[137] Fourthly, the regime expanded public employment threefold within the civil service and the parastatals, thereby partially mitigating some of the problems of urban (and educated) unemployment. At the same time, the private commercial sector was pretty much left to its own devices. Smuggling to and from Nigeria, especially at the height of the oil boom, provided an income for very many ordinary Beninois which it was wise not to tax or tamper with.[138] To a much greater extent than in the Congo, the issue of rural production was taken seriously and there were efforts to build upon the existing structure of co-operatives. At the village level, the Groupements Villageoises (village groups) provided inputs and marketing facilities (as well as playing a role in rural literacy campaigns), while above them GRVCs (Groupements Révolutionnaires à Vocation Coopérative) were set up in an effort to encourage peasants to work on collective farms.[139]

Finally, the regime created new political structures which were supposed to provide greater scope for popular participation.[140] On the face of things, the regime shed its military fatigues and became institutionalised through a vanguard party, the PRPB (Parti Révolutionnaire du Benin), which was founded in November 1975. Behind the scenes, however, the regime continued to be directed by military officers. The structures of the PRPB conformed to a familiar pattern, comprising a Political Bureau in effective control of policy; a much larger Central Committee; a Party Congress which was seldom convened; and an Assembly, which was elected from a single list of candidates designed to reflect different corporate groups, which met twice a year. The PRPB created separate integral wings for the trade unions, women and youth which enjoyed monopoly status and a guaranteed voice within the party. At the base, Committees for the Defence of the Revolution (CDRs) were established, with an equivalent set of committees at the workplace, to galvanise support for the policies of the regime. At the village level, revolutionary committees replaced the chiefs and were made up of a balanced ticket of elders, women and youth. This initiative, which was designed to undermine traditional power structures, mirrored those of the liberation movements in the former Portuguese territories (see Chapter 7). These village committees, in turn, elected commune councils. By contrast, the next two tiers, the district and provincial councils were chosen from above. Inevitably perhaps, democratic centralism meant that there was much greater popular input at the bottom than at the top, but this was nothing unique to Benin. Moreover, whereas national structures were dominated by a self-selecting leadership, there is some evidence to suggest that rural dwellers were able to take decisions which were not always to the liking of the authorities – most notably in resisting collectivisation.[141] The fact that this independence was tolerated was a sign that the regime accepted, or was resigned to, a broad measure of local autonomy.

The constraints facing Beninois socialism were not that different to those which pertained in the Congo. In each case, an expanded public sector, which was expected to provide the motor of development, turned into a vast drain on the government purse. Salaries alone were consuming as much as 70 per cent of the national budget by 1979, leaving precious little for infrastructural maintenance, not to mention material improvements. The parastatals were particularly inefficient, with most of the newly founded enterprises operating at far below capacity. Agriculture stagnated, partly because the budgetary allocation was comparatively small: for example, 11 per cent under the 1977–80 economic plan.[142] Moreover, the terms of trade provided a disincentive to cash crop farmers, while much of the food which was produced ended up in Nigeria. This forced Benin, like the Congo, to import greater quantities of foodstuffs to meet its urban requirements. The educational reforms were extremely costly, consuming about a third of the recurrent budget, and given the additional burden placed upon teachers, quality suffered. In fact, when a large part of the teaching profession fled the country in search of better conditions, much of the instruction had to be carried out by untrained teachers. Access was certainly expanded, with 64 per cent of primary-school age attending school and 19 per cent receiving a secondary education by 1984. However, any transformation was probably for the worse, given the deterioration of standards.[143] Again, while rural health care expanded on paper, its functionality at the village level was open to question because the budgetary allocation (7 per cent in 1983) was too small to enable the health centres to fulfil their remit.[144] Nevertheless, it was to the credit of the regime that life expectancy rose from around 37 to 49 years.

The mounting strain on public finances might have been eased by the discovery of offshore petroleum reserves, but by the time these came on stream in 1984 the price had plummeted and little benefit accrued. By the mid-1980s, the Kérékou regime was faced with increasingly intractable problems: the economy was shrinking in real terms, there was no money to pay public employees on a regular basis, and the country was so heavily indebted that it was unable to meet its service payments. The inevitable consequence was that the government had to approach the IMF for a bail-out package in 1984, and equally inevitably it was instructed to dismantle the entire edifice of state controls. The Kérékou regime was therefore placed in the peculiar position of attempting to proclaim its fidelity to socialism at the same time as it cut the number of parastatals in half, implemented a wage free and openly solicited foreign private investment. These measures were bound to alienate public sector employees, students and members of the armed forces, each of whom expressed its opposition in familiar ways: that is through strikes, demonstrations and plots. The political convulsions were as predictable as in the Congo, but as we shall see in Chapters 9 and 10 the outcomes were markedly different.

Whereas the Congo and Benin instances are broadly comparable, Ethiopia is in a category all of its own. The overthrow and murder of Emperor Haile Selassie; the seizure of the assets of the Crown and the ruling elite; the dismantling of the structures of imperial rule and the assault on the Orthodox Church were revolutionary by any yardstick. The social upheavals which accompanied this revolution, in the rural as well as the urban areas, were equally of a different order. In Chapter 4, we considered the factors underlying the overthrow of the monarchy. Here we will examine the subsequent passage of events in greater detail. There is a rich literature on this phase of Ethiopian history, in which there has also been some divergence of opinion as to what transpired after 1974. On the one hand, many leftwing activists and some academic commentators have seen the overthrow of the Emperor as a revolutionary act carried out through the agency, but not necessarily the complete foresight, of the urban population – that is, workers and students, but also teachers, taxi-drivers and the unemployed.[145] On this view, a gaping vacuum was created into which a section of the military inserted itself, mouthing Marxist slogans whilst converting a popular revolution into a military coup. On the other hand, there are those who have pointed out that the mutinies were the primary catalyst of the revolution, whereas the Confederation of Labour Unions (CELU) was confined to white-collar workers and conservative in orientation; the radical left was minuscule and mostly living outside the country; while the peasantry was ground down, not least by the grim realities of famine. Moreover, despite the violence which was subsequently unleashed upon the civilian radicals, it has been pointed out that the Derg implemented decisions which were revolutionary in character.[146] Whilst acknowledging the reality that the Derg was a military construct, I allow some latitude to the second interpretation, on the principle that once unleashed from the bottle, the genie of revolution could not always be contained.

In one respect, the Derg did appear similar to the Kérékou regime. That is, it did not have a clear sense of what it wanted to achieve when it proclaimed its existence in July 1974. At this point, the emerging inner council of junior officers and NCOs issued a policy statement, entitled *Ethiopia Tikdem* ('Ethiopia First') which was not exactly fire-breathing. Its list of short-term objectives anticipated the continuation of the monarchy and merely spoke of framing a new constitution, whilst its long-term plan advocated economic modernisation and equal treatment for the nationalities.[147] At best, therefore, it was nationalist in conception. Having abolished the monarchy and assumed full executive and legislative powers in September, the Derg went a step further and pronounced its commitment to something called 'Ethiopian Socialism'. This policy statement, which was supposed to clarify matters, enshrined economic nationalism as state policy. It was followed by the announcement of the nationalisation of private banks and insurance corporations, and the net was later widened to include commercial and industrial concerns. This was always likely to be popular because most of these enterprises were owned by expatriates. So far so statist, but the *Derg* was still struggling to define its objectives in the face of competing pressures. Remarkably, the first vice-chairman, Major Mengistu Haile-Mariam, and some of his colleagues began to take a crash-course from civilian radicals on the fundamental principles of Marxism and Leninism and the history of world revolution.[148] Mengistu, it seems, was a fast learner (despite his limited formal education) and in September 1975 the Derg swapped 'Ethiopian socialism' for the certainties of Marxism-Leninism.

The question arises as to why the Derg went down this particular pathway. For the sceptics, the language of Marxism merely provided a convenient cover for what was really a usurpation by the military – or rather a faction thereof. Although it is difficult to deny that the military discovered an appetite for power, it would be a mistake to assume that there was a preconceived plan that was being played out. In some respects, Mengistu and his colleagues found themselves adopting radical policies in order to placate highly assertive urban constituencies. In 1974, much of the exiled left returned to Ethiopia with a view to influencing the course of the revolution. Amongst the myriad of small splinter parties, two stood out as relatively coherent. The first was the Ethiopian People's Revolutionary Party (EPRP), which originally went under the name of the Ethiopian Communist Party. This party was founded by former University students from within Ethiopia who had gone into exile, where they did not always see eye to eye with those who had conducted their studies in Europe and North America. By 1973, the EPRP had already sent some of its militants for guerrilla training in Algeria, expecting that the campaign to overthrow 'feudalism' would be a protracted one. When the monarchy unexpectedly imploded in 1974, its Central Committee returned to Addis Ababa and through its paper, *Democracia*, attempted to add to the revolutionary momentum. Amongst the former students whose radicalism had been nurtured overseas, a rival organisation, the All-Ethiopian Socialist Movement (or Meison) had been founded in 1969. Although its own Central Committee members did not return until early 1975, the party was present on the ground and maintained a high profile through its own paper, *Voice of the Masses*. The EPRP and Meison were both explicitly Marxist, but they were also bitter rivals – the more so as they were competing for the same ideological space.[149] These organisations congratulated the Derg on its arrest of members of the *ancien régime* and the confiscation of their assets. They also shed no tears when 60 prisoners were executed in November, most of them political and military functionaries of Haile Selassie.[150] At the same time they were also fiercely critical of anything which deviated from their conception of revolution. The EPRP, in particular, insisted that the Derg should immediately transfer power to a 'Provisional People's Popular Government', comprising workers and peasants. When the Derg insisted that it had already constituted itself as the Provisional Military Administrative Council (PMAC), it was set on a collision course with the EPRP. In September 1975, when CELU attempted to mount a general strike in support of its own demand that the Derg resign, it was supported by the EPRP and the students.

While the regime came down hard on this emerging opposition, it also felt the need to respond to the charge that its socialist rhetoric was a figleaf designed to disguise the naked reality of military dictatorship. 'Ethiopian socialism' had been openly ridiculed in the leftwing press as essentially vacuous, and it was in an attempt to prove its critics wrong that the Derg embarked on a series of far more radical initiatives. The nationalisation measures only affected a small part of the national economy (some 71 firms), whereas the decision to embark on land reform had far-reaching implications. The slogan of 'Land to the Tiller' had been articulated by the student movement since the mid-1960s. In a country where much of the peasantry was landless and where tenants gave up much of their harvest to landlords, it was not difficult to attribute the rural crisis (including the famine) to entrenched class inequalities. Early in 1975, the Derg surprised many when it proclaimed the nationalisation of all rural land, the redistribution of use rights to those who worked it and a ban on the employment of labour. Only farmers who tilled the land were to be entitled to plots, and it was envisaged that a ceiling of 10 hectares would be placed on individual holdings. In order to reallocate the land, peasant associations were to be established with the helping hand of some 56,000 teachers and students who were despatched to the countryside under the *zemacha* (or 'campaign') – Mao's Red Book in hand.[151] At one fell swoop, this demolished the foundations upon which the *ancien régime* had rested, whilst weakening the Orthodox Church which had been a significant landholder in its own right. The civilian left was impressed, as were the students who immersed themselves in the realities of rural communities which they would never otherwise have thought to visit.[152] Even the EPRP conceded the historic significance of the land reform, while Meison activists cited it as a sound reason for dealing openly with the regime. The land reform had its analogue in the cities. In July, the government announced that all urban land would be nationalised along with property beyond the quota of one house per family. The stated intention here was to eradicate landlordism. As in the rural areas, popularly elected Urban Dwellers' Associations were created, known as *kebeles*, and to these fell the task of administering the rental of urban properties, providing local services and resolving disputes. The Minister of Urban Development and Housing, who was entrusted with overseeing the programme was, significantly enough, a member of Meison. This was a clear sign that the Derg had succeeded in convincing a section of the civilian left that it was serious about revolution. Although there were some unforeseen problems, most academic commentators agree that the reforms were more than cosmetic. In remote rural areas, the revolution may have been interpreted in the light of local history and social cleavages, but it was no less dramatic for that.[153]

The emerging relationship between Meison and the radical wing of the regime was consolidated by these events. When the Derg urged all revolutionary movements to enter into a common front, the EPRP entered negotiations but later drew back. On the other hand, Meison linked up with a number of other smaller leftwing groups and rallied behind Mengistu who seemed to represent the most radical force within the Derg. Members of the Joint Front were subsequently given leading roles in the Provisional Office for Mass Organisational Affairs (POMOA) which was set up to further the process of forging a single revolutionary party out of the member organisations in 1976. As Mengistu and Meison forged a closer bond, this widened the division with other members of the Derg who cautioned against cutting out the EPRP altogether. In the contest which ensued, Mengistu successfully eliminated his principal critics, only to be stripped of most of his formal powers by other members of the Derg in December 1976. In February 1977, a shootout at Derg headquarters ensued in which those who had previously disciplined Mengistu were physically eliminated. Mengistu quickly consolidated his position as Chairman of the Derg and concentrated all decision-making powers on himself, thereby ending the collegial system (however fictional in reality) which had hitherto prevailed.

Although Mengistu was a military strongman, it has to be remembered that Meison had conspired to bring about this very outcome. Its leaders calculated that by strengthening Mengistu's hand their own pet views on the revolution would triumph over those of the EPRP. At the end of the day, mutual loathing between factions of the civilian left created the very outcome which they had been seeking to avoid, namely a military usurpation. Whereas Meison was complicit with Mengistu, the EPRP did much to bring about the reign of terror which subsequently ensued. Having decided not to enter a leftwing front, the EPRP embarked on an ill-advised assassination campaign against supporters of the regime (including Meison) with effect from September 1976. This 'white terror' merely provided the regime with the excuse to embark on its own 'red terror' in which many supporters of the EPRP, but many others besides, were hunted down and physically liquidated. When Meison parted company with the regime in the latter part of 1977, it was included in the second round of the terror. According to one estimate, the final death toll on both sides may have been as high as 32,000, while another 30,000 had been arrested and subjected to torture.[154] In classic fashion, the revolution had begun eating its own children.

The results were devastating for the left. The EPRP was destroyed in Addis Ababa, and was reduced to a small guerrilla army in Tigray which later suffered in a turf war at the hands of the Tigrayan People's Liberation Front (TPLF). Meison was similarly decapitated. The remaining members of the Joint Front later suffered the same fate, starting with the Ethiopian Oppressed People's Revolutionary Struggle (June 1978), the Workers League (September 1978), the Ethiopian Marxist Revolutionary Organisation (June 1979) and finally the Revolutionary Flame. Ironically, the latter organisation had been founded by Mengistu himself, and consisted largely of members of the armed forces. However, when it was decided to dissolve all existing parties and create a new party from scratch, members of the Revolutionary Flame made the mistake of expressing their doubts about the wisdom of making one individual the focal point. The nay-sayers were purged for being 'anti-people elements', and in December 1979 a new Commission for the Organisation of the Ethiopian People's Workers Party (COPWE) was established, consisting of members handpicked for their loyalty to Mengistu.

By this point, a highly complex political topography – in which shifting factions within the Derg competed for influence and bartered with leftwing civilian organisations without – gave way to a flattened landscape which was thoroughly dominated by Mengistu who became the sole interpreter of revolutionary rectitude. In September 1984, a single party was finally established, which created the appearance of a constitutional regime which had shed its military robes. The Derg was formally wound up and a new set of institutions, including an elected legislature, a Central Committee and a Politburo took over. However, soldiers remained prominently placed within the upper echelons of government. In practice, Mengistu personally selected the most important officials of the regime who, in turn, chose others lower down the line. Although the peasant associations and urban associations persisted at the base, their formal powers were whittled down, while those of the party were augmented. Moreover, the regime depended heavily on its security agencies to secure compliance. Whereas the Congolese and Beninois regimes typically purged and quickly forgave, in the Ethiopian case falling foul of the leader was more likely to end in a painful death, even if the regime was 'not gratuitously brutal after the manner of an Amin or a Bokassa'.[155] The ability of the regime to demand compliance was enhanced by the fact that state institutions functioned in Ethiopia in a way that they did not in somewhere like the CAR. Despite a dramatic clearing out at the apex, the rest of the bureaucracy ticked over pretty much as before, the difference being that it was entrusted with the task of implementing 'scientific socialism'.

The siege mentality of the regime was greatly accentuated by its efforts to contain the guerrilla movements which were agitating for a change of government and/or secession. The national question had been the subject of heated debates in leftwing circles since long before the revolution. Some insisted that the central contradiction was one of class and that the oppression of the non-Amhara peoples was merely an epiphenomenal reflection of that reality. Once the national revolution was carried through, so the reasoning went, the sources of ethnic and regional antagonism would evaporate. Not surprisingly, Amhara radicals were attracted to this logic, in the same way that white Communists in South Africa were. Meison, which was largely made up of Oromos, who felt their second-class status all the more because of their numerical dominance, seems to have regarded the Ethiopian nation as salvageable. But for many others, the nationalities question had to be taken seriously alongside the question of class. The EPRP, which was composed largely of Eritreans and Tigrayans, actually emerged out of an earlier debate on this issue, in which its members had made precisely this point.[156]

Given that the Eritrean insurrection provided a catalyst for some of the original mutinies in 1974, there was inevitably a debate within the Derg about how best to resolve the national question. Whereas some members wished to open negotiations with the Eritrean liberation movements, others stood on the territorial integrity of Ethiopia. Although Mengistu was himself from a marginal 'nationality', he fell squarely into the second camp.[157] By contrast, the first Chairman of the Derg, Lt.-General Aman Andom, proposed negotiating with the Eritreans secessionists, for which he paid with his life.[158] Thereafter, the Derg attempted to strike a balance between acknowledging the existence of different nationalities – by for example appointing regional administrators from indigenous groups – whilst seeking to head off claims to secession. The defection of some dissident Derg members to the liberation movements, and the demise of Meison, had the consequence of making the regime much less accommodating. Increasingly, Mengistu made a convenient equation between counter-revolution and support for the various liberation movements. In the case of the Ethiopian Democratic Union (EDU), which sought a restoration of the old order and received the patronage of the Sudanese government, there was some plausibility to the argument. The same was true of the Eritrean Liberation Front (ELF) which was supported by the Arab states. However, the suggestion that the EPRP, the EPLF and the TPLF, all of which were Marxist in complexion, were really part of an elaborate imperialist conspiracy was evidently stretching a point. Nevertheless, the regime sought to acquire legitimacy by presenting itself as the defender of the historic Ethiopian nation against foreign intrigue.

The repulsion of the Somali invasion in 1977 was a crucial watershed. It came at the point when the United States had finally terminated its alliance with Addis Ababa and was seen to be backing the Somali cause. In order to quash this 'imperialist' invasion, Mengistu succeeded in winning the backing of the Soviet Union and Cuba. The weaponry which poured into Ethiopia, which was critical in the defeat of Somalia, was then turned on the liberation movements, whose own campaigns could be presented as extensions of a single grand conspiracy. By 1978, the circle was complete: any serious discussion of the national question was foreclosed as tantamount to flirting with counter-revolution. At the same time, a virulent Ethiopian nationalism was weaved into the fabric of a ready-made internationalist discourse of Marxism-Leninism. In the process, an overtly modernist regime began to appropriate and re-encode many of the symbols of the defunct Empire. The Orthodox Church came back into favour while evangelical Christianity, which had often provided the local support base for the revolution, was cast as 'foreign' and subjected to systematic harassment.[159] Most strikingly still, Mengistu began to adopt the trappings and mannerisms of the late Emperor, including sitting on something which looked suspiciously like a throne.[160]

Finally, let us conclude by considering the implications of Ethiopian Marxism for social equality and economic development. The land reform did remove one of the sources of the exploitation of the peasantry. The implications were more profound in the South, where northern settlers had battened onto the indigenous peoples and extracted part of their surplus. The land reform was quickly accompanied by the expulsion of these settlers, which is perhaps the best example of class- and nationality-based demands working in harmony. In the North, by contrast, the land reform had less dramatic consequences. In this land-short and barren part of the country, there were fewer substantial landlords to expropriate. When land was redistributed, the net effect was to subdivide it still further, without greatly easing the hardship of most peasant families.[161] The revolution also brought fresh demands upon the peasantry which have to be added into the equation. After 1978, the administration set quotas for grain which peasant associations were required to deliver at well below market prices, while coffee producers were squeezed more tightly.[162] Although still elected, the peasant associations increasingly functioned as instruments of intervention from above. One of their functions was to fulfil conscription quotas for the military; another was to implement the government's villagisation and resettlement plans.[163] Neither would have ranked very highly on a peasant list of priorities. Moreover, the pattern of spending which tended to concentrate social services – health, education and water supplies – on Addis Ababa was not greatly modified. At the same time, the Mengistu regime greatly expanded public sector employment within the parastatals and the civil service, whilst capping salary levels. In order to pay for the expanding state sector, the regime became more assiduous in taxing the private sector and urban dwellers once control of rentable property was brought fully under state control.[164] Indeed, the rigour with which the regime taxed its urban population makes Ethiopia rather unusual.

In economic terms, revolutionary socialism was less of a success. Given the acute poverty of the country, the regime was hardly playing with a full deck. However, the principal constraint was arguably of its own making. Having resolved to deal with the national question through force of arms, it was inevitable that defence allocations would consume a large part of the national budget. The extent to which the military, by far the largest in Africa, consumed national resources was unprecedented.[165] The returns on state investments in production were not particularly high. Although there were attempts to promote state farms and peasant co-operatives, with a view to eventually bringing about collectivisation, the former were very expensive and the latter were less productive than the individual farms which peasants doggedly defended. State intervention in the marketing of foodstuffs proved highly disruptive, not only because it lowered the returns to the producer, but also because internal controls prevented foodstuffs from being freely moved around the country. It is generally agreed that while the Ethiopian famine of 1984–85 was partly a consequence of adverse weather conditions, it was also a consequence of such injudicious state policies. For example, the ban on hired labour and the tying of peasants to particular associations condemned peasants in the poorest areas to remain shackled to their inadequate plots.[166] To this needs to be added the impact of perpetual warfare on the agricultural and pastoral economies of some of the most ecologically fragile regions. The famine was especially acute in the Tigrayan highlands where government forces were engaged in a ferocious war with the TPLF and the EPLF. Although the regime's management of the relief effort, and its attempt to resettle northern peasants in the lowlands, were sometimes unfairly criticised by a hysterical Western media circus, its efforts to stop relief reaching areas which were under rebel control undoubtedly added to the suffering.[167] Finally, the crisis of rural production was accompanied by a state industrial sector which did not perform as well as expected. The patchy overall performance, which belied the ambitious planning targets, is revealed in the statistics for growth in GDP: that is, somewhat over 5 per cent between 1978 and 1980, but −3.7 per cent for 1983–84 and −6.5 per cent for 1984–85 when the famine was at its zenith.[168] The Ethiopian experience of purposeful state intervention was not, therefore, markedly different to other parts of Africa where the shortcut to modernity was attempted.

Although the Mengistu regime was eventually held up as a grim instance of Afro-Stalinism, for a number of years the Ethiopian Revolution provided an inspiration for Africans seeking a radical alternative to the impasse in which their own countries found themselves. In Liberia, leftwing intellectuals and soldiers could perceive a certain similarity between the *ancien régime* in Ethiopia and the True Whig administration which had ruled for all but six years since 1870. The country was run by and in the interest of the Americo-Liberian elite, who benefited from American patronage, while 'indigenous' Liberians paid most of the taxes and were treated with the condescension characteristic of European colonial rulers elsewhere in Africa. Those upcountry Liberians who acquired an education were drawn towards revolutionary ideas which started to be espoused by MOJA (the Movement for Justice in Africa) and the Progressive People's

Party (PPP) during the 1970s. President William Tolbert, who succeeded William Tubman in 1971, lacked the latter's deft political touch and by the end of the decade, even the Americans accepted that the old order was unsustainable. The manner in which the regime collapsed bore more than a passing resemblance to the Ethiopian precedent. In April 1979, the government increased the price of rice which provoked widespread rioting and provided a cause which civilian radicals could exploit. Tolbert's concessions merely weakened the regime still further, and on 12 April 1980 soldiers mounted a coup in which he was killed. This was followed by the mass arrest of True Whig politicians and the execution of no fewer than 13 members of the government. The leaders of the coup had little sense of what they wanted to achieve and called on the expertise of civilian radicals from MOJA and the PPP who regarded the coup as a short-cut to power.[169] This was to prove as ill-judged as in Ethiopia, in that Samuel Doe, the co-chairman of the People's Redemption Council (PRC), began to dig in. Like Mengistu, he started by eliminating his rivals within the PRC, whilst surrounding himself with advisors who were dependent upon him. In the process, independently minded civilians were consigned to the sidelines. Doe followed up with a classic usurpation by putting himself forward for President in 1985 and rigging the election when it looked like he would be unable to win cleanly.

In Ghana, the lower ranks and junior officers within the army were similarly attracted to the clinical manner in which the Derg swept away the *ancien régime*. Again, many leftwing intellectuals believed that there was much to learn from the Ethiopian model, with the result that they too fell into very same trap as Meison and the EPRP. Hence, when Rawlings seized power again on 31 December 1981 and proclaimed a 'revolution', radicalised soldiers and civilians embraced a vision which owed much to Ethiopian precedents. And when Thomas Sankara came to power in Upper Volta in 1983, and changed the name of country to Burkina Faso ('Land of the Virtuous People') to signal a dramatic break with the past, he was not merely linking arms with Rawlings, but was also aligning himself with a radical military tradition which owed much to Ethiopian inspiration. In neither instance did the 'revolution' take root. Rawlings lost faith in the radical agenda and purged the leftwingers, while the immensely charismatic Sankara was physically eliminated in 1987. However, the revolutionary interlude in both countries represented a period of high idealism and mass political activism which has seldom been seen in Africa – and which has largely been airbrushed out of the official histories.

6.3   Conclusion

In this chapter, we have looked at why the African militaries left the barracks and, as it were, entered the Ministries. We have also sought to convey some sense of the considerable ideological and stylistic differences between military regimes. Whereas some were almost embarrassed to find themselves manning the controls and promised a timely exit, others stated their intention to remain as long as was necessary to clear up the mess left by the politicians. In many instances, this corrective agenda provided an excuse for the outright usurpation of power, as is so graphically illustrated in the instance of the CAR. In other cases, the usurpation was justified on the basis of a professed commitment to Marxism in which the vanguard party would transcend the civilian–military divide. Many countries experienced variants on all of these types, perhaps the best example being Benin. Finally, what we hope to have demonstrated is that there is little evidence to support the contention that military regimes have been more effective than their civilian counterparts. They have been just as prone to the personalisation of power and, at worst, they have been inordinately blood-thirsty. Their economic record has also been extremely poor, as Appendix 6.1 demonstrates.

Appendix 6.1 Economic performance of selected countries with a history of military governance, 1960–87

Country	1960–70	1970–79	1980–87
Ethiopia	4.4**	1.9	0.9
Somalia	1.0**	2.7	2.2
Ghana	2.1**	−0.1	1.4
Upper Volta/Burkina Faso	3.0**	−0.1	5.6
Benin	2.6	3.3	2.8
Zaire	3.6	−0.7	1.6
Central African Republic/Empire	1.9	3.3	2.0
Congo-Brazzaville*	2.7	2.9	5.5
Uganda	5.9**	−0.4	0.4
Togo	8.5	3.6	−0.5
Nigeria*	3.1**	7.5	−1.7

* includes oil ** civilian or mostly civilian

Source: Tables from World Bank, *World Development Report, 1981* (Washington, DC: World Bank, 1981), pp. 136–7; World Bank, *Sub-Saharan Africa: From Crisis to Sustainable Growth* (Washington: World Bank, 1989), pp. 222–3.

Second Liberation: Guerrilla Warfare, Township Revolt and the Search for a New Social Order

> Always remember that the people are not fighting for ideas, nor for what is in one man's mind. The people fight and accept the sacrifices demanded by the struggle in order to gain material advantages, to live better and in peace, to benefit from progress and for the better future of their children.
>
> Amílcar Cabral, leader of the PAIGC

> Parents, you should rejoice for having given birth to this type of a child. A child who prefers to fight it out with the oppressors rather than to be submerged in drunkenness, frustration and thuggery. A child who prefers to die from a bullet rather than to allow a poisonous education which relegates him and his parents to a position of perpetual subordination. Aren't you proud of the soldiers of liberation you have given birth to? If you are proud, support them! Do not go to work on Monday.
>
> Soweto Students' Representative Council call for stayaway, September 1976

Whereas the previous chapter dealt with the invasion of the political arena by the Armed Forces shortly after independence, here we are largely concerned with a different face of militarism: namely, the phenomenon of the liberation movement. In the Portuguese colonies, it required sustained guerrilla warfare before the last vestiges of European rule were removed from African soil in 1974/75. Apart from Djibouti, that only left white minority rule in Rhodesia (Zimbabwe) and South Africa, and the latter's dominion over South West Africa (Namibia). Here liberation wars were also fought, but with differential levels of success. In each of the cases under consideration, a retarded liberation also brought a significant reappraisal of basic objectives. Whereas the first generation of African leaders were only too happy to accept the reins of power from the departing colonial power, the initial optimism surrounding independence had dissipated by the end of the 1960s. The liberation movements therefore envisaged a different kind of freedom, which would not merely substitute black faces for white ones, but transform the very nature of power itself. In the

Portuguese territories, Rhodesia and (to a lesser extent) SWA, nationalists embarked on a 'people's war' – a term which signified that liberation would benefit the mass of the population, but equally that it would result from their active participation. As we will see below, this had important implications for the manner in which the fighting was conducted and for the engagement between the various liberation movements and their rural constituencies. In South Africa itself, the African National Congress (ANC) and the Pan-Africanist Congress (PAC) faced a much more formidable adversary. Here, the guerrilla option quickly appeared untenable, with the result that the liberation movements resorted to alternative strategies. This equally modified the very conception of what liberation meant in the South African context.

7.1 *Aluta continua*: wars of national liberation in the Portuguese colonies

As we have already seen in Chapter 1, the *Estado Novo* ruled out any possibility of a separate independence for Africans. The acceleration of decolonisation across the continent nevertheless forced the Portuguese to embrace limited reform in order to be able to hang on to their colonial possessions – closely mirroring French policy in the post-war period. In 1961, the formal distinction between *assimilados*, who enjoyed Portuguese citizenship, and the *indígenas* (or natives) was finally extinguished. This meant that, in theory at least, everyone became an equal citizen of overseas Portugal. At the same time, some of the worst abuses of compulsory cultivation and forced labour were eradicated.[1] Nevertheless, the underlying relationship between coloniser and colonised remained deeply ingrained in the mentalities and daily practices of Portuguese officials and settlers alike. The experience of racial prejudice was felt especially keenly by the *mestiços* (those of 'mixed race') and other *assimilados*, especially when urban jobs were snapped up by an influx of poorly educated (and often illiterate) Portuguese settlers.[2] There were substantial social barriers separating these indigenous elites from the rest of the population which for a long time inhibited their ability to establish any common cause.

Significantly, it was Africans who had been sent to study in Portugal who began to look upon colonial realities in a different way. Many of them were influenced by the Portuguese left which was active in spite of repression by the Salazar dictatorship. It was in Lisbon that Eduardo Mondlane and Marcelino Dos Santos from Mozambique first came into contact with Amílcar Cabral from the Cape Verde Islands and Agostinho Neto and Mario Pinto de Andrade from Angola.[3] These individuals were all to play a catalytic role in the anti-colonial struggles of their respective countries in the 1950s and 1960s – a struggle which was co-ordinated through the Conference of Nationalist Organisations of the Portuguese Colonies (CONCP) after 1961. The nationalists did not need to start from an entirely blank slate. The Portuguese Communist Party had established a branch in Angola as early as 1948, while in Guinea-Bissau the Front for the National Independence of Guinea (FLING) existed from 1953. There were also a number of regionally based organisations in each of the territories which were exploiting rural grievances. In Mozambique, there was a Mozambican-Makonde Union (MANU) which grew out of self-help and cultural associations catering to Makonde migrant workers in Kenya and Tanzania; a National Democratic Union of Mozambique (UDENAMO) which drew its membership from the South, which was the historic recruitment ground for the South African mines; and the National Union of Independent Mozambique (UNAMI) which was supported by indigenes of Tete Province working in Malawi.[4] In Angola the death of the Bakongo king in 1955 provoked a succession struggle, in which a Union of the Peoples of Northern Angola (UPNA) was formed to advance the claims of a Protestant successor in opposition to the candidate the Portuguese wanted to impose.[5] The challenge facing the new wave of nationalist leaders was to draw these various strands into a more coherent formation. The challenge was taken up in Mozambique and Guinea-Bissau, but proved too much for the nationalists in Angola.

In September 1956, Cabral and five of colleagues covertly launched what became known as the PAIGC (African Party for the Independence of Guinea and Cape Verde) in Bissau, the capital of Portuguese Guinea. In that same year, the Communist Party and other organisations in Angola merged to form the MPLA (Popular Movement for the Liberation of Angola), which Norrie MacQueen credits with being a 'genuine alliance between intelligentsia and proletariat'.[6] The MPLA established a following in Luanda and the surrounding Mbundu areas, but failed to make inroads into the North where the UPNA, under the leadership of Holden Roberto, attempted to widen its own appeal by renaming itself the Union of the Peoples of Angola (UPA) in 1958. Whereas the UPNA had initially championed the reunification of the Bakongo people divided by colonial borders (originally a pet project of Joseph Kasavubu as well), it was encouraged by the All-African People's Conference in Accra to embrace a more inclusive definition of its constituency.[7] In 1961, the UPA finally brought a number of non-Bakongo into leadership positions, including one Jonas Savimbi who was an Ovimbundu from the Huambo area. The UPA presented itself as the party of oppressed Africans, whilst casting the MPLA as a party led by relatively privileged *mestiços*. In Mozambique, the proliferation of regional movements and the scattering of their bases initially presented a formidable barrier to unity. But in June 1962 Julius Nyerere of Tanzania succeeded in persuading MANU, UDENAMO and UNAMI to merge as FRELIMO (Front for the Liberation of Mozambique). The first president of FRELIMO was Eduardo Mondlane, who enjoyed diplomatic protection from the Portuguese security service by virtue of being in the employ of the United Nations.

The leadership in each of the colonies was initially influenced by the strategies of nationalists elsewhere in Africa, and it would have been surprising if it had been otherwise. Hence the boycott, the strike and the demonstration were regarded as crucial weapons in the nationalist armoury. As it happened, they had underestimated the determination of the Portuguese to cling on. In Guinea-Bissau, the PAIGC initially placed its faith in the collective leverage of urban workers. After attempting to form a separate trade union which was all too easily penetrated by Portuguese intelligence, the PAIGC infiltrated the official union and then endeavoured to win the sympathy of dock workers, stevedores and sailors. In August 1959, the PAIGC was emboldened by the relative success of a strike by sailors to embark on a trial of strength at the Pidjiguiti docks. This resulted in a confrontation with the police which left 50 dockers dead. The following month, the PAIGC leadership admitted that it had miscalculated and decided to abandon its urban strategy in favour of mobilising the 'peasant masses'.[8] In Mozambique, the miscalculation did not lie in the choice of an urban focus, but rather in the form of protest. MANU enjoyed considerable success in infiltrating agricultural co-operatives in Makonde country, and in June 1960 it decided to stage a peaceful demonstration at the administrative headquarters at Mueda. In the violence which ensued, some 500–600 peasants were killed – which rather puts the Accra riots of 1948 into perspective.[9]

Given its urban origins, it is not surprising that the MPLA experience was closer to that of the PAIGC. In February 1961, there was an attempt by militants in Luanda, supported by local youth, to storm the prison and to release political detainees being held there.[10] In the midst of the ensuing white panic, the police gave settlers the licence to engage in a killing spree. Their choice of targets speaks volumes about their neuroses. In the words of David Birmingham:

> Violence was directed primarily against school-leavers, townsmen in Western dress, Portuguese speakers, and against the literate and the employed. Anyone who might remotely be thought of as a nationalist leader, or even supporter, was hauled out of bed and murdered in the street.[11]

Many of those who survived fled the city and took refuge in the hills, where they provided willing recruits for the MPLA. Like the PAIGC, the MPLA was forced to recognise that Portuguese control over Luanda was too entrenched to make urban resistance viable, and it therefore decided (in principle) to take to the bush. In the North, the UPA launched its own rural rebellion in the coffee-growing areas in March of that year, with even more disastrous consequences. The victimisation of Ovimbundu contract workers merely contributed to the ethnic fracturing of Angolan politics in the long run, although Savimbi remained loyal to the UPA. Roberto appears to have been trying to replicate the experience of the Belgian Congo, calculating that an outbreak of popular violence might force the Portuguese government to retreat and induce a flight of the settler population.[12] On this occasion, anywhere up to 50,000 people lost their lives in the Portuguese reprisals, while many more were forced to flee across the border to the Congo.[13] The refugee influx was a boon to the UPA which found itself in favour in Leopoldville after the installation of the Adoula government in July 1961.[14]

For good reasons, therefore, the various nationalist movements decided that their liberation would have to follow a different path to that of the French and British colonies. And because it would have to come through the barrel of a gun, they would have to be prepared to concede the loss of the cities in order to concentrate on the countryside. One advantage of embarking on the guerrilla option was that, as more African states achieved their independence, there was every chance of winning some material assistance as well as the offer of safe havens. All the liberation movements came to depend upon friendly countries through which they could communicate with the external world, channel funding and armaments, train cadres and plan their military operations. After the PAIGC decision to launch its guerrilla war, Cabral solicited the co-operation of the Sekou Touré regime in Guinea. There were already some small national-ist groupings operating in that country, and it therefore took some persistent lobbying within the corridors of power before the PAIGC eventually won offi-cial recognition. After a lukewarm initial response, Sekou Touré became a very committed supporter of the PAIGC. This enabled the latter to launch its first incursions into Guinea-Bissau in 1963. The PAIGC would sorely have liked to have opened a second front from Senegalese territory, but Senghor was intent on engaging in a dialogue with the Portuguese and denied it access.

In the case of Mozambique, FRELIMO could build upon the cross-border networks established by MANU and, having been formed through the good offices of Nyerere, it could also count on Tanzanian support. This enabled FRELIMO to launch attacks into Cabo Delgado and Niassa Provinces in the North of the colony in 1964. Later on, FRELIMO was able to open a second front in Tete Province, operating out of bases on Zambian soil. In Angola, the rival liberation movements competed for the recognition of neighbouring governments. The FNLA (the National Front for the Liberation of Angola), which arose out of a further relabelling of the UPA in 1962, enjoyed the back-ing of the Americans and the government in Leopoldville. The FNLA was nevertheless hostage to changing political fortunes within the Congo. Whereas Kasavubu was antagonistic to a rival Bakongo movement, the Adoula regime was supportive, while the Tshombe administration was openly pro-Portuguese. The Mobutu coup of 1965 was crucial, however, because it placed a pro-FNLA faction firmly in control in Leopoldville.[15] The MPLA was unceremoniously driven out of the capital in 1963, but this assured it of the sympathy of the government in Congo-Brazzaville. From here, the MPLA was able to launch an assault on the Cabinda enclave in 1964 where a highly fragmented Front for the Liberation of the Cabinda Enclave (FLEC) was already seeking to map out an autonomous future. That same year, Zambian independence afforded the MPLA an opportunity to open up a second front in the East of the country.[16] When Savimbi split from the FNLA in 1964 and formed UNITA (National Union for the Total Independence of Angola) two years later, he was equally denied access to Congo-Leopoldville. But for the first year UNITA was granted limited access through Zambia, which enabled its fighters to launch its first operations in east-ern Angola. However, its attacks on the Benguela railway directly clashed with Zambian interests and it was quickly expelled. UNITA lacked friendly neigh-bours and was therefore forced to scale down its operations. Indeed, the UNITA leadership even allegedly entered a secret truce with the Portuguese in 1972 which prioritised the struggle against the MPLA and the FNLA instead.

If neighbouring countries provided support which was crucial to sustaining a guerrilla war, there was also a need for an outer ring of alliances. The most important international patrons were the United States, the Soviet Union, China and various European countries. The liberation movements solicited material support, and to some extent tailored their messages in order to keep their patrons on side. The Kennedy administration decided to work towards Portuguese decolonisation and, surprisingly perhaps, began to channel covert assistance to the FNLA and FRELIMO in 1961.[17] At the end of the decade, however, American policy switched back to support for the Portuguese in line with Cold War calculations of the crudest kind. Most of the European members of NATO also backed Portugal, and sold her weapons, whereas the Nordic countries were generally more disposed towards the liberation movements. The Communist world was split as a result of the ongoing public rift between the Soviet Union and China. Hence whereas the MPLA was aided by the Soviet Union, the FNLA and UNITA looked to China in spite of their anti-Communist posturing. Again, the PAIGC was favoured by the Soviet Union, and given some support by Cuba and Vietnam. By contrast, FRELIMO received its weapons and military instruction from China, which is not unrelated to the fact that the latter was forging close links with Tanzania.[18] As Thomas Henriksen suggests, these various alliances did not require the liberation movements to toe any line particularly closely. On the contrary, the behaviour of the PAIGC and FRELIMO demonstrated that they had a capacity to be remarkably pragmatic in juggling with their more powerful patrons. The PAIGC, for example, abandoned terminology which was too redolent of the Soviet model because much of its funding was coming from the Nordic countries.

The Portuguese territories differed from the British and French colonies not only in that they had to fight for their liberation, but also because the very conception of liberation underwent a significant reformulation. The PAIGC, FRELIMO and the MPLA all subscribed to the principles of a 'people's war'. This was accompanied by serious power-struggles both within and between rival liberation organisations. In 1963, the MPLA lost its most prominent Marxist intellectual, Viriato da Cruz, as a result of distemper arising from the ascendancy of Agostinho Neto and concerns about the dangers of appearing too leftwing.[19] The split could not have come at a worse time because it coincided with an evaluation of the relative strengths of the liberation movements by an OAU mission. The result was that exclusive recognition, and so the all-important funding, was reserved for the FNLA. To make matters worse, the MPLA was expelled from Congo-Leopoldville. However, over 1963/64 the MPLA clawed its way back into contention on the basis of a more explicitly radical agenda. This change of orientation was related to the support it was now receiving from the avowedly Marxist regime in Brazzaville as well as from Cuba and the Soviet Union. Bolstered by the moral solidarity of FRELIMO and the PAIGC within CONCP, and with evidence of military operations in Cabinda to back up its claims, the MPLA was able to establish recognition by the OAU Liberation Committee towards the end of 1964. By contrast, the FNLA began to lose favour and forfeited OAU financial support in 1968. By this point, the FNLA was positioning itself as an orthodox nationalist movement which was opposed to the extension of Soviet influence, whereas the MPLA was openly talking the language of revolution.

In the PAIGC, there was an internal struggle over the direction of the war in 1964. Balanta fighters, who saw the struggle in purely military terms, resented interference by the radical wing of the movement which also happened to largely Cape Verdean in origin. At the Cassaca congress in February 1964, battle was joined and the Cabral faction came out on top. Amílcar Cabral swiftly consolidated his authority and emerged as by far the most sophisticated theoretician thrown up by the various liberation wars. The losers were ruthlessly purged and some lost their lives. As the PAIGC chalked up substantial military gains, it thoroughly eclipsed FLING and other smaller groupings. In Mozambique, FRELIMO underwent its own ideological disputes in the second half of the 1960s. As in the Balanta areas, a venerable tradition of popular resistance amongst the Makonde threw up local leaders who believed that they had the right to conduct their campaign as they saw fit, without the interference of a leadership which mostly came from the South of the country.[20] Matters came to a head at the second FRELIMO congress in 1968, where the left wing of the party again carried the day. Lázaro Kavandame, who headed the Makonde rebels, was expelled from the movement at start of 1969. A month later, Mondlane was assassinated in what appears to have been a fallout from the purge. However, this merely confirmed the move to the left. The leadership of FRELIMO was taken over by a triumvirate until 1970 when Samora Machel emerged as the undisputed president. Under Machel, FRELIMO did not mince its words as a movement of the left.

Underlying the concept of 'people's war' were a number of cardinal principles, which were derived from Marxism, but as filtered through Mao and the guerrilla movements of East and South-East Asia. The African organisations were only too willing to acknowledge their international debts, but insisted that they were not blindly following models derived from countries which embodied quite different experiences of colonialism. Considerable emphasis was therefore placed upon moulding Marxism to fit local circumstances. On this score, it is worth noting that these differed significantly as between the Portuguese territories as well.[21] The absence of settlers in Guinea-Bissau by contrast with their substantial – and indeed growing – presence in the other territories, was merely the most obvious difference. Again, the migrant labour system tied Mozambique into a wider regional complex in a way that was less true of Angola and not true at all of Guinea-Bissau and Cape Verde. Behind the idea of the 'people's war' lay, firstly, the principle that the rural masses were crucial to sustaining a successful guerrilla campaign, and secondly that they should be considered the ultimate beneficiaries of victory. The interpretation of flag decolonisation elsewhere was that many of the excesses of colonialism had simply been indigenised, whilst new vices had been added to the list. The narrow social base of the mainstream nationalist parties was seen as a contributing factor problem because it threw up politicians who were effectively unaccountable to the masses. By engaging the latter directly in the war effort, it was argued, they would become active participants in the political process.

The class composition of the nationalist leadership posed a trickier conundrum. Cabral accepted that the petite bourgeoisie had headed the nationalist parties in most African states and had profited most from the transfer of power. Why, then, should the outcome be any different in the Portuguese colonies? Cabral and his associates argued that fighting a prolonged war alongside the peasantry, and experiencing some of their suffering, would provide as much of a mind-altering experience for the petite bourgeoisie as for the peasantry. As a result, the latter might eventually be prevailed upon to commit 'class suicide'. The taking up of arms was not to be confused with mere militarism, with its preoccupation with success on the battlefield. Far more important was the political understanding which would emerge out of the struggle. Cabral once summed up the distinction by saying that 'we are armed militants and not militarists', a tag which had been pinned on the losers in the power-struggle.[22] Henriksen observes that whereas theoreticians of revolution in Asia often tended to regard military success as the key to garnering peasant support, the African liberation movements reversed the order of precedence. They were very careful to carry out extensive political education before they even started military operations in a given area. In the case of Mozambique, the military front was normally understood to lag 80 kilometres behind the line of prosyletisation, such was the concern for preparing the peasantry.[23]

The second related principle was that liberation was about the construction of a new kind of society which would be based on egalitarianism and mass participation. This not only meant sweeping away the last vestiges of colonialism, but also confronting tradition head-on. Class divisions could be partially attributed to the colonial impact, but the liberation movements did not shy away from tackling gender and generational inequalities which had indigenous roots. The liberation movements needed to persuade peasants of the superiority of their vision, which was a tall order when they merely passing through an area. The key was therefore held to lie in the carving out of 'liberated zones' where the restructuring of power relations could begin before the achievement of independence. The MPLA was the least successful on this score, although it did its best in the eastern sector. FRELIMO enjoyed considerable success in the Cabo Delgado and Niassa provinces, and by 1968 claimed to control up to 25 per cent of the total territory.[24] The Portuguese responded with Operation Gordian Knot in June 1970, which intended to push FRELIMO out of its northern strongholds and to create a defensive line by forcing the peasantry into protected villages or *aldeamentos*.[25] FRELIMO fighters melted across the Tanzanian border, but later re-entered the North and repeated the trick in the Tete province which they infiltrated through Zambia. Because Portugal needed to commit up to 20,000 troops to defence of the Cabora Bassa dam, this gave FRELIMO the run of much of the rest of Tete province.[26] Hence FRELIMO had some success in carving out liberated zones, although its more grandiose claims need to be taken with a pinch of salt. There were still large swathes of Mozambique where FRELIMO made little headway. In Nampula province, the Portuguese cleverly exploited Makua mistrust of the Makonde, and in Niassa they were able to appeal to Muslim sensibilities. The *aldeamentos* programme was most actively pursued in these areas, and with some success. FRELIMO made only partial inroads into the central belt, although it attacked the Beira railway, and it had scarcely infiltrated southern Mozambique prior to 1974.[27]

Where FRELIMO was able to establish liberated zones, steps were taken to create a parallel administration which would manage the sale of consumer goods, run schools and offer basic medical provision (mostly of the curative variety).

By 1970, for example, some 30,000 pupils were being taught within FRELIMO schools, and adult literacy programmes reached many more.[28] With Italian aid, FRELIMO also managed to set up a few hospitals and a much larger number of health posts. In return for bringing material benefits, FRELIMO attempted to secure peasant compliance with its vision of a modern, socialist society. As in Tanzania, the chiefs were considered tainted by their associations with the Portuguese (see Chapter 4). FRELIMO claimed that chiefs continued to command a disproportionate say within the liberated zones, and it took some time before their power was broken. In the place of 'autocratic' chiefs, weekly village meetings were institutionalised as a means of arriving at collective decisions and carrying out political education. At these meetings, the equal worth of youth and elders, and men and women, was emphasised. The Isaacmans observe that there was some male resistance to the involvement of women in combat roles, but FRELIMO endeavoured as best it could to integrate women at every level.[29] The leadership was also keen to persuade peasants of the benefits of collective farming, but outside of Cabo Delgado province the takeup was mostly tokenistic.[30] There was evidently a limit to how far the peasants, who had doggedly resisted Portuguese interference in their daily lives, were prepared to change their preferred ways of working the land and distributing the proceeds.

The most successful of the liberation movements was undoubtedly the PAIGC. Although Cabral was a Cape Verdean, there was no effort to take the war to the islands for logistical reasons.[31] The PAIGC also encountered problems in penetrating the Fula areas of the East, where the Portuguese once again rallied the forces of 'tradition'. But elsewhere the territorial gains of the PAIGC were impressive by any yardstick. The movement claimed to control around half of the territory of Guinea-Bissau by as early as 1965 and more than three-quarters by 1972.[32] The Portuguese were increasingly holed up in a string of fortified camps, which were linked by air transport. Within the liberated areas, the PAIGC established a basic social infrastructure which was designed to demonstrate the practical gains which it could confer on the peasantry. This was famously articulated in the Cabral quotation at the start of this chapter. The PAIGC was able to offer basic preventive health care, with a limited curative dimension. In 1964, the PAIGC had no doctors at its disposal, but with Nordic funding a number of hospitals were established and staffed by Cuban and Soviet doctors.[33] There was also a network of dispensaries which were designed to cater to soldiers, but which extended treatment to the local population.[34] In the educational sphere, the PAIGC aimed to provide four years of primary education, for girls as well as boys. There were also a number of better-resourced boarding schools, with a student body numbering in the hundreds, which perhaps underlies Mustafa Dhadha's description of the educational provision as 'in every sense elitist'.[35] Like FRELIMO, the PAIGC also set up 'people's stores' which sought to compete with the Portuguese in providing consumer goods at affordable prices.

On the other side of the equation, the PAIGC sought to exact compliance with its vision of a progressive society in which the peasant masses would be active and equal participants. The liberated zones were administered by means of village committees which consisted of five elected members, at least two of whom had to be women – once again, the exclusion of chiefs is noteworthy here.[36] Each committee member was given responsibility for a particular function: that is, local defence, agriculture, health, support services to the armed forces and record-keeping. This meant that many local services were placed under the everyday control of village officers who enjoyed the confidence of their constituents. The villages provided most of the foodstuffs with which to sustain the fighters, but Cabral's more ambitious plans for collective farming again remained a dead-letter. The villagers were organised into militias which were separate from the army but, in the face of Portuguese counter-insurgency operations, these were later upgraded and placed under the command of experienced military officers. The local defence forces were composed of both men and women, which once again reflected an abiding concern with gender equality. The judicial structures, which emerged through a process of trial and error, represented something of a half-way house. Elected tribunals at the village level were expected to be guided by customary law as long as this did not conflict with the priorities of the liberation movement. Cabral was, however, opposed to polygamy, and PAIGC officials were expected to comply faithfully with the prohibition on multiple marriages.[37]

Much of the literature on the PAIGC and FRELIMO which was written during the war presents a glowing account of people's power at work, which cannot be entirely trusted.[38] Because of a heavy reliance on party claims, with little attempt at critical verification, it is difficult to reconstruct a detailed picture of how peasants really perceived their encounter with FRELIMO. With the passage of time, something of a revisionist backlash has occurred. The later work uses many of the same sources, but passes them through a different set of intellectual filters. In some recent writing, the liberation movements are seen as having engaged with peasants in a more or less utilitarian fashion. Thus whereas Rudebeck emphasised the benefits which were conferred upon the inhabitants of liberated areas in Guinea-Bissau, Dhadha is more inclined to underline the manner in which the PAIGC used the peasants.[39] The truth of the matter is that the peasant–guerrilla relationship was bound to be a two-way negotiation in which both the 'liberators' and the 'liberated' hoped to gain something. Because it was a negotiated relationship, the liberation movements did not have things all their own way. Peasants were particularly adept at subverting pressures to give up the family farm in favour of collective labour on a community farm. Whereas Basil Davidson and an earlier generation of commentators wrote about peasant enthusiasm for revolutionary change, MacQueen has gone as far as to conclude that:

> ...with the possible exception of Guiné [Bissau], there can be no convincing evidence that the liberation movements carried a majority of their 'nations' behind them.[40]

The reason why the evidence is lacking is that African peasants had become past masters at the arts of dissimulation in the interests of survival.

The revisionist onslaught has also been directed at the military achievements of the liberation movements. Whereas sympathetic writers such as Patrick Chabal have emphasised the considerable skill with which the liberation movements modified their tactics over time, John Cann has presented the Portuguese military as the real innovators. In his view, the Portuguese had learned the lessons of counter-insurgencies in Asia and Africa and come up with a long-haul, low-cost formula which was viable for a relatively weak country like Portugal.[41] Whereas other writers have mentioned Portuguese strategies of winning hearts and minds only to dismiss them, Cann takes them seriously and argues that they were often quite successful. On the whole, he concludes, 'while it [Portugal] lost its colonies, it did not lose them because of military reasons'.[42] Once again there is a problem with this reading of the evidence. The impact of the *aldeamentos* policy in Mozambique was certainly profound (especially in the North), given that up to 1 million Mozambicans were corralled. Also, the use of black counter-insurgency units, in the shape of the elite forces and the mobile *flechas*, somewhat altered the complexion of the wars. But the fact of the matter is that the liberation movements were not banking on a final shootout like Diem Bien Phu which would force the Portuguese to capitulate. Cabral repeatedly stated that the PAIGC lacked the equipment to win a war, besides which it had no desire to risk the personnel in an all-out confrontation. Instead, the liberation movements aimed to grind the Portuguese down to the point when the financial and human costs became unbearable. As it turned out, this was a well-chosen strategy. Although perhaps half of the fighting force in Mozambique was African by the end, the costs to Portugal were nevertheless very great. Hence Cann is forced to concede that while overall Portuguese casualties were fairly low, at least by comparison with the Algerian and Vietnam wars, they were far higher than the French and the Americans incurred on a per capita basis.[43] Moreover, military expenditure was consuming over 17 per cent of the Portuguese budget by 1973, which was less than the French equivalent, but more than could be sustained by a relatively poor state.[44] The loss of a stomach for the fight within Portugal, as reflected in the non-appearance of conscripts, also proved crucial. This too had been anticipated by the liberation movements. In the final analysis, therefore, it does seem reasonable to conclude that the latter got their tactics right and effectively rendered the Portuguese position untenable. Whether the word 'victory' is used would seem to be a matter of semantics.

In the case of Guinea-Bissau, the PAIGC was in such a commanding position that it held elections within the country in 1972 and convinced much of the international community that it was the legitimate authority. The assassination of Cabral took some of the shine off the achievement, but the final outcome was not in doubt. In Mozambique, FRELIMO managed to hit the Beira railway and other communications routes, and its forces had come to within 400 kilometres of the capital by the end of 1973.[45] Only in Angola was the Portuguese military able to hold its own. The pressures which the Portuguese were under finally produced a startling turn of events in April 1974 when the regime in Lisbon was overthrown by many of the very same officers who had spent their careers fighting the colonial wars. Marcello Caetano, who had succeeded Salazar as Prime Minister in 1968, had gingerly embraced imperial reform, but had been reined in by his own right-wing. In 1970, he commissioned a paper from General António Spínola, the Governor-General of Guinea-Bissau, on the future of the African colonies. Spínola had written of the need to exchange the colonial relationship for a Lusophone community in which some powers would be devolved from Lisbon to the colonies. Spínola subsequently took up this theme in a book, entitled *Portugal and the Future*, which was published in 1974. The latter actually said little that could be considered new, but it was enough to scandalise the right because of its insistence (from one who knew) that the colonial wars were essentially unwinnable. Responding to the furore, Caetano sacked Spínola from his latest position as Deputy Chief of Staff, as well as Costa Gomes, his superior. By this point, rumblings of professional discontent were already emanating from the Armed Forces Movement (MFA), led by alienated junior and middle-ranking career officers who had corporate grievances of their own. On 24 April, these soldiers seized power and brought Spínola in as head of the Junta of National Salvation (JNS). Coups, it transpired, were not purely an African phenomenon.

Over the next few months, Spínola articulated his vision of a Lusophone community falling short of independence, whereas the MFA began to make the case for outright decolonisation. As it moved towards the left, the MFA came to have more in common with the liberation movements than with Spínola himself. In the colonies, the coup produced a collapse of army morale, while the PAIGC and FRELIMO stepped up their military campaigns. In consequence, the junta had very little margin for manoeuvre. In July, the MFA finally had its way when it succeeded in passing a law (Law 7/74) which accepted the right of self-determination up to and including independence. From this point onwards, Portuguese officials expended most of their energies on negotiating a peaceful withdrawal. Over September and October, the Portuguese finally recognised the independence which the PAIGC had proclaimed in 1973. This outcome was supported by the local branch of the MFA, and was actively endorsed by the Governor, Major Carlos Fabião, who had been initially been sent by Spínola to bring about the opposite result. Although the PAIGC also laid claim to being the popular party of Cape Verde as well, party negotiators agreed to a separate independence, without prejudice to eventual unification, which came about in November 1974. This was followed by the independence of Mozambique in June 1975 and of the small island group of São Tomé and Príncipe in July of that year. The independence of Angola in November 1975 was a far messier affair, as we will see below.

7.2 The second *chimurenga*: the liberation of Zimbabwe

The decision to embark on liberation warfare in Zimbabwe followed a very similar logic to that of the Portuguese territories, although its final trajectory was significantly different. The pioneer Zimbabwean nationalists, whose political base lay in the cities (especially Bulawayo), initially placed their faith in a pincer movement consisting of popular pressure from one flank and British pressure from the other. Because nationalist protest had yielded dividends in other British colonies, including Northern Rhodesia and Nyasaland, it was believed that the same tactics would work here as well. However, this underestimated the extent to which the settlers were prepared to disengage from the metropole

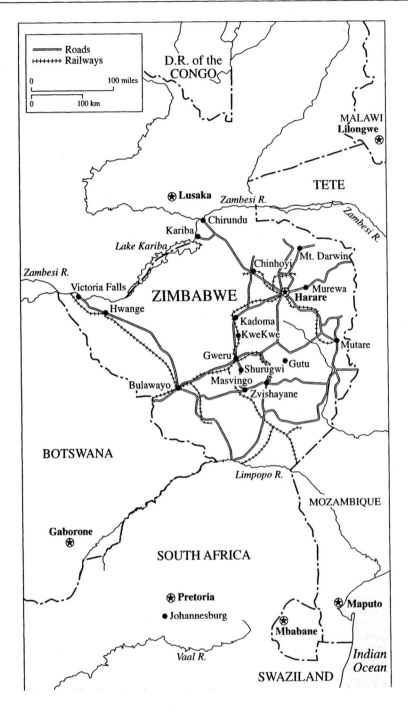

Map 5   Zimbabwe

in order to retain their minority privileges. Around half of the land (later reduced to a third) was reserved for the use of white farmers, who numbered 275,000 in the early 1970s, whereas 5 million Africans had to make do with rest.[46] And as in Kenya, the best land was reserved for settlers. Moreover, since 1923 the white community had enjoyed the privilege of internal self-government. As was noted in Chapter 1, the creation of the Central African Federation enabled the settlers to widen the field of their dominance to include Nyasaland and Northern Rhodesia as well. There was provision for some African representation in the Federal legislature, and in 1961 this was extended to the parliament of Rhodesia. However, because less than one per cent of Africans were eligible to vote, power was never likely to slip from white hands.[47]

The Southern Rhodesian African National Congress, which became the first truly national party in September 1957 was moderate in its demands and in tone, but was nevertheless proscribed two years later.[48] In 1960, the National Democratic Party (NDP) was formed, under the same leadership of Joshua Nkomo. The NDP was drawn into negotiations with the British and the Rhodesian government and, having apparently agreed to an unfavourable constitutional revision, turned around to reject it. This led to the banning of the NDP in December of the following year. Almost immediately, the Zimbabwe African People's Union (ZAPU) was formed to take its place. After some attempts at internal sabotage, the predictable banning order followed in September 1962. This pattern of events, in which conventional nationalist strategies seemed to make no headway, eventually led to a reappraisal of tactics. However, it also culminated in a lasting rupture within the nationalist movement. Militants, who perceived Nkomo as too vacillating and timorous, broke away to form the Zimbabwe African National Union (ZANU) in August 1963, under the leadership of Ndabaningi Sithole as President and Robert Mugabe as Secretary-General.[49] Both ZAPU and ZANU leaders came to the conclusion that armed struggle provided the only realistic route to liberation. The main leaders of both organisations were placed under detention, but the remainder were able to reach exile in Zambia. They began training military recruits for what was likely to be a protracted guerrilla war. In 1965, the year of Ian Smith's UDI, ZAPU infiltrated its first small units into the country where they carried out numerous acts of sabotage.[50] The following year, ZANU fighters engaged in their first fire-fight with the Rhodesian security force at Chinhoyi (or Sinoia), which later assumed iconic status in ZANU accounts of the liberation war.

Up until relatively recently, the literature on these rival movements has tended to draw sharp distinctions between ZANU and ZAPU to the detriment of the latter. One the one side, ZAPU is presented as a relatively conservative, Ndebele movement which pinned its hopes on winning a conventional war with the backing of the Soviet Union. Unkind critics have suggested that it sat tight in Lusaka, waiting for the tanks and aircraft to be handed over, rather than getting on with fighting with whatever resources it could muster. On the other side, ZANU is depicted as a movement of the Shona majority which, with Chinese backing, resorted to a classic 'people's war' strategy. ZANU is credited with being prepared to commit guerrillas to the field in the absence of sophisticated weaponry and, under the influence of FRELIMO, with making concerted effort to win the sympathy of the peasantry. The starkness of the contrast had been reinforced by the fact that journalistic and academic commentators have tended to gravitate to ZANU, whereas the activities of ZAPU have not received much in the way of detailed examination.[51] More than two decades after Zimbabwean independence, though, the distinctions have lost much of their sharpness as the historiographical imbalance has started to be redressed.[52]

In the early years, the armed wing of ZANU, the Zimbabwe African National Liberation Army (ZANLA), had only a handful of guerrillas to commit to the field. After the 1971 split within ZAPU, which we will come to presently, ZANLA gained a number of defectors, but even then it only had around 212 fighters as against the 600 which remained with the Zimbabwean People's Revolutionary Army (ZIPRA).[53] The transformation of ZANLA fortunes came with the opening up of liberated areas in the Tete Province by FRELIMO. The latter initially offered an alliance to ZAPU, but switched to working with ZANU because of the former's internal disarray. This meant that ZANLA fighters could profit from working alongside a seasoned guerrilla movement. Moreover, Tete offered the perfect base from which ZANLA could launch its own guerrilla operations across the north-eastern border from 1972. Over time, success brought fresh waves of recruits into ZANLA, enabling the latter to field a substantially larger force than ZIPRA by the end of the war.[54] The ideological position of ZANU mirrored that of FRELIMO, in the sense that both maintained that the pursuit of victory had to be accompanied by an effort to create an egalitarian, socialist society. Where ZANU differed was in the emphasis it placed on recapturing the land which had been lost to white settlement. Nevertheless, a number of commentators have remarked upon the fairly superficial commitment to Marxism on the part of the political leaders who remained steeped in a conventional discourse of nationalism.[55] It was within ZANLA that a more radical agenda gestated, but this remained a minority tendency and was eventually checked by purges against 'ultra-leftists'. The result was that while the guerrillas organised local support committees, there was minimal commitment to effecting a social revolution.

Immediately after the breakaway of ZANU, ZAPU distanced itself from the Marxist rhetoric of the 'splitters' and continued to insist on the priority of ending white minority rule. However, the resort to armed struggle had a similar effect on ZAPU thinking. Over 1967 and 1968, ZAPU and the South African ANC infiltrated units across the border to engage in joint military operations. However, these incurred heavy casualties and forced ZAPU to reconsider its whole approach to warfare. The operational collaboration with the ANC was terminated – in part because it provided an invitation to the South Africans to send in more of their own personnel – and ZAPU began to take seriously the need to cultivate the sympathy of the peasantry. The internal shift only took place after a bitter internal rift in 1971, which turned largely on the advisability of forming a united front with ZANU. The upshot was that one faction of the party, led by James Chikerema, broke away to form the Front for the Liberation of Zimbabwe (FROLIZI). The latter gained the support of some

ZANU elements who could also see the case for an alliance. The faction which remained in control of ZAPU embarked on a internal reorganisation of the party, the most important consequence of which was the creation of ZIPRA itself. From this point onwards, ZIPRA was committed to a strategy which sought to combine the purely military aspects of the war with a campaign to win over the peasantry. According to Jeremy Brickhill, ZIPRA was fortunate in being able to rely upon ZAPU party structures, which continued to exist clandestinely at the local level.[56] In the process, ZIPRA began to deploy a Maoist discourse of the 'people's war', whereas the political leadership continued to articulate a more conventional nationalism.

In the later stages, the organisational differences re-emerged, and this goes some way towards explaining why the two movements have been viewed in bi-polar terms. ZAPU tacticians began to insist upon the importance of building in some aspects of conventional warfare if they were to achieve outright victory. In this, they seem to have been guided less by Soviet advisors than the injunctions of Vietnamese strategists working within the paradigm of a 'people's war'. According to Dumiso Dabengwa, who occupied a leading position within ZIPRA, the Rhodesian security forces had been weakened to the point where it was considered that a change of tactics was in order. In particular, he maintains that liberated zones could best be defended by more conventional forces, while guerrilla fighters would open up new frontiers.[57] According to Brickhill, ZIPRA was planning a sustained military offensive when peace unexpectedly broke out in 1979. This analysis would tend to suggest that both ZANLA and ZIPRA aspired to the creation of liberated zones, but merely differed on the practicalities of creating and defending them.

For all their similarities, the two liberation movements did have a different recruitment profile. In the case of ZIPRA, the recruits were mostly male (only around 10 per cent were women) and lay between the ages of 18 and 25 years of age. The same was roughly true of ZANLA as well. However, Brickhill claims that ZIPRA recruits were unique in the extent to which they were drawn from an urban and proletarian milieu: he estimates that over 53 per cent of the intake had been in wage employment prior to enlistment, and many had previously been migrant labourers in South Africa.[58] By contrast, ZANLA recruited from amongst the ranks of the Shona peasantry, and increasingly so in the final stages of the war.[59] Even then, there was some similarity in the tensions which surfaced between different cohorts of recruits. Within ZANLA, the relationship between the 'veterans', derived from poor peasant backgrounds, and the more educated recruits who enlisted in large number later on, was often a fractious one. The same dynamic revealed itself within ZIPRA, especially when the latter created a formal distinction between the guerrilla wing and a better-equipped conventional army.[60]

The liberation movements in Zimbabwe shared with their Lusophone counterparts a dependence upon external patrons. The Zambians provided a home for ZAPU operations throughout the war, whereas ZANLA was forced to relocate itself to Mozambique after the controversial assassination of Herbert Chitepo in March 1975. In fact, this was not much of an imposition because (as we have seen) the independence of Mozambique provided ZANLA with easier access into Mashonaland. As I have already intimated, there was also a partition of international alliances. Whereas the Soviet Union favoured ZAPU, ZANU followed FRELIMO in allying itself with China. Where the Zimbabwean liberation movements were singular was in the extent to which they were subjected to political pressure from other African countries, including the newly liberated Portuguese territories. The OAU Liberation Committee and the so-called Frontline states bemoaned the failure of ZAPU and ZAPU to overcome their differences, and repeatedly insisted on the priority of forming a united front. This pressure elicited the outward appearance of compliance, but without any real commitment to unity, far less reunification. In 1967, for example, OAU intervention led the two movements to agree to the formation of a Joint Military Command. However, the ZAPU leadership reckoned that ZANU had nothing to bring to the table and conspired behind the scenes to ensure that it failed.[61] Following Zambian arm-twisting, the next effort came with the formation of FROLIZI by breakaway elements from the two existing movements in 1971. The prospect of OAU recognition for FROLIZI was sufficient to frighten the leadership of ZANU and ZAPU into the creation of a Joint Military Command in March 1972. However, on this occasion a buoyant ZANU felt that it had nothing to gain, and this initiative went the way of the first one. FROLIZI itself became more or less dormant when many of the ZANU defectors returned to the fold.

At the end of 1974, after the diplomatic intervention of the South African government and the Frontline states, the Smith regime released Sithole and Nkomo from detention in order to take part in a fresh round of negotiations. In December, the three liberation movements were bounced into signing a unity accord which brought them under the wing of the African National Council (ANC), which was to be temporarily headed by Bishop Abel Muzorewa.[62] This was a difficult pill to swallow because Muzorewa, who had initially enjoyed the confidence of many nationalists, had recently blotted his copybook by entering into secret negotiations with Smith. The brief interlude during which African political activity within Rhodesia was tolerated was characterised by fierce competition for ownership of the ANC between ZAPU and its rivals. However, after the failure of the Victoria Falls Bridge talks in August 1975, at which the ANC spoke for the liberation front as a whole, the likelihood of an internal settlement once again seemed very slim. Although Nkomo was still willing to give negotiations a chance, Mugabe, who had squeezed out Sithole as ZANU leader, was confirmed in his opinion that armed struggle was the only way forward.

The ANC itself concluded that liberation would only come through force of arms and set up the Zimbabwe Liberation Council (ZLC) with a view to creating a united military front. However, the latter was rapidly overtaken by yet another unification initiative. At the end of 1975, the Frontline states dropped Muzorewa and sponsored the formation of a joint Zimbabwean People's Army (ZIPA) which would combine members of ZANLA and ZIPRA units and operate out of Mozambique. When the war was restarted in 1976, after a two year intermission, it was ZIPA which stole the headlines.[63] The ZIPA initiative, which was born out of frustration with the bickering amongst the rival political leaderships, represented the high-point of radicalism within the liberation movement. Its leaders sought to break down ethnic particularism and exclusive loyalties to ZANU and ZAPU, and to combine an appreciation of the finer points of Marxism with military training at its Wampoa College. For a time, ZIPA threatened to become a third force, and at the 1976 Geneva Conference it was independently represented at the negotiations. However, tensions between ZANLA and ZIPRA elements soon resurfaced, and after the defection of the latter ZIPA itself imploded. In January 1977, Mozambique consented to the arrest of its leaders by the ZANU hierarchy who felt threatened by its radical posturing.

The Frontline States had not given up, however, and they subsequently forced ZANU and ZAPU into the formation of the Patriotic Front (PF). It was the PF which negotiated with the Smith regime at the Lancaster House talks of 1979 which brought the war to an end. However, as soon as national elections were scheduled for 1980 the two parties squared up to one another as rivals once more. In short, therefore, while the liberation movements were not in a position to reject the demands of the OAU Liberation Committee and the Frontline states, they came to believe in the efficacy of their own strategies for achieving liberation. The political leadership of ZAPU was more prepared to take negotiations seriously, whereas ZANU saw little point in talking after 1975.

Thus far, we have dealt at some length with the politics of the liberation movements. What remains is to consider how these movements engaged with their mass constituencies. By comparison with the Portuguese territories, a rich body of literature has emerged which enables one to draw more substantive conclusions about how guerrillas and peasants engaged with one another. A starting point is Terence Ranger's monograph which is very much concerned with how peasants viewed their world. Ranger contends that a revolutionary peasant consciousness was born out of a keen sense of dispossession as well as compulsion arising out of land 'betterment' schemes.[64] What the peasants of Makoni District wanted was to recover their land and their autonomy, and they were prepared to assist ZANLA guerrillas because the latter provided them with the means to this end. On the side of the guerrillas, Ranger shows how they were prepared to work through spirit mediums in order to win local legitimacy. The analysis is taken much further by David Lan in a fascinating study which delves into Shona belief. Like many African peoples, the Shona have imagined an unbroken link between the living and the dead.[65] The ancestors of deceased chiefs – the *mhondoro* – were thought to maintain an active presence in the living world and were closely associated with the fertility of the land through their power to deliver (or withhold) rain. The *mhondoro* expressed their wishes through mediums, who were (and are) ordinary men and women selected by the spirit in question, while in a state of possession. Like Ranger, Lan underlines a continuity of resistance from the first *chimurenga* of 1896, when certain spirit mediums co-ordinated the uprising, and the liberation war of the 1960/70s. Indeed, Lan observes that the Nehanda spirit, whose medium was executed in 1896, was sought out by ZANLA guerrillas in 1971. He also suggests that the mediums were vitally important in terms of legitimating the presence of guerrillas who did not normally hail from the area they were infiltrating.[66] Since both claimed to be working for the good of the land, Lan argues that the alliance was a natural one. By contrast, he claims, the chiefs were too implicated in the structures of state power to make attractive partners.

Interacting with spirit mediums was something of a learning experience for the guerrillas. In Tete Province, FRELIMO had taught the fighters to be sceptical about peasant beliefs which it dismissed as sheer superstition.[67] However, Lan maintains that because ZANLA was in a relatively vulnerable position – lacking any liberated zones of its own – it was forced to make greater compromises. According to Lan, the spirit mediums promised that if the fighters would observe particular prohibitions and taboos, the forces of nature would work for them. The notion that fighters could make themselves invisible, or would be alerted to the presence of the Rhodesian army by birds, soon became integrated into their approach to warfare (the similarity with the Mulelist rebels of the Congo is striking here).[68] By the end, guerrillas had been converted to the peasant world-view rather than the other way round.

Lan is not alone in subscribing to the crucial role played by spirit mediums in building local support for the liberation movements. Martinus Daneel has suggested that most guerrillas believed in the existence of a liberation council composed of spirit mediums who were directing the war effort.[69] Lan has been criticised, however, for representing a Shona belief system which is all too tidy, for underestimating the continuing legitimacy of many chiefs and for ignoring the doubts that some guerrillas entertained as to the reliability of mediums.[70] Most of this criticism qualifies Lan's model rather than overturning it. However, there are two more substantive objections. The first is that he exaggerates the extent to which Shona peasants continued to operate within a purely indigenous cosmological system. Lan dedicates a few pages to the churches in Dande, where he conducted his field-research, but mainly with a view to reiterating the survival of indigenous religion in the face of mission Christianity.[71] A more recent literature has, however, looked at Christian communities in greater detail and come to more ambiguous conclusions. The most finely textured account is offered by David Maxwell, who compares areas which came under Catholic and Protestant missionary influence.[72] At the Catholic Avila station, he observes that the missionaries left some space for local religion to breathe. Moreover, a folk Catholicism failed to develop here, whereas earlier Catholic missionaries had resacralised the landscape through pilgrimages and the recognition of holy places. This left the field open to the spirit mediums who could set themselves up as the guardians of the land.[73] At the Elim station, by contrast, indigenous belief systems had been attacked as diabolical by Protestant missionaries. The result was that the spirit mediums were rendered relatively impotent. When white missionaries withdrew to a safer location, the church was suddenly indigenised and the guerrillas began to look for allies within it. Here, the church–guerrilla relationship became an intimate one – much closer, Maxwell contends, than at Avila.[74] We can conclude that while Lan's Dande study is not necessarily typical, the spirit mediums did exercise an influence where the churches had not managed to establish a hegemonic position.

A second, and in many ways more damaging, criticism is that of Norma Kriger who points out that neither Lan nor Ranger actually listened very closely to their peasant informants. If they had, she contends, they would have noticed that the experience of dealing with guerrillas was more commonly one of coercion than of co-operation. Kriger's argument, which relates to ZANU operations in the North-east, rests on a couple of basic propositions. The first is that while ZANU made Maoist noises, it was actually more concerned with gaining peasant compliance than with transforming rural society.[75] This a point which we have touched on above, and it is worth merely reiterating the ideological direction of both ZANU and ZAPU (with the ZIPA exception) seems to have been considerably fuzzier than in the case of FRELIMO, the PAIGC or even the MPLA. A second point is that the Zimbabwean liberation movements failed to establish liberated zones inside the country because of the reach of the Rhodesian military machine. The net result, she argues, was that ZANU had limited utilitarian appeals with which to reach the peasantry. Even if there was talk of semi-liberated zones towards the end of the war, this seems uncontroversial.[76] On the other side, the guerrillas needed protection from possible informers, as well as foodstuffs and other provisions. Kriger describes the formation of village committees, consisting of married adults, and youth wings made up of unmarried adults over the age of fifteen. While the committees organised logistical support, the youth (or *mujibas*) were responsible for ferrying information between the 'comrades' and the villages.[77] Whereas sympathetic writers like Lan have emphasised the common purpose of guerrillas and peasants, Kriger maintains that the relationship was coercive. Poor villagers were forced to part with money, foodstuffs and livestock on pain of beatings or possible execution. Hence membership of the village committees was something which people avoided at all costs because of the personal risks associated with it.[78]

Kriger does not deny that the guerrillas garnered some peasant support, but she construes this as the playing out of tensions within communities.[79] Hence the youth used their relationship with the 'comrades' to reverse their traditionally subordination to parents and elders. She claims that many of the abuses were actually carried out by youth acting in the name of the guerrillas who had no particular interest in upsetting the generational hierarchy. Equally, she asserts that while ZANU was not especially concerned with promoting gender equality, aggrieved wives were able to use the guerrillas to get back at abusive husbands. And finally, the hierarchical relationships between chiefly and stranger clans could be reversed by taking control of the committees. As a result, Kriger sees the war as being fought less on the terrain of ZANLA than of intra-communal struggles. Moreover, she is at pains to point out that this all came at a tremendous cost in human lives: whereas the Rhodesian security forces were reported to have killed 3360 civilians (certainly an under-estimate), the guerrillas killed another 2751, many of whom were falsely accused of being sell-outs.[80] Kriger's revisionism is open to its own objections. Maxwell observes that the Mtoko District (where her research was conducted) was close enough to Harare to make a hearts-and-minds campaign uncommonly difficult. His contention is that in other theatres the guerrillas probably had less need to resort to compulsion.[81] Moreover, Kriger struggles to account for the massive vote in favour of ZANU in 1980.[82] But what she has done is to direct some of the focus away from the peculiarities of guerrilla warfare towards longstanding patters of social cleavage within rural communities. Moreover, subsequent research in Matabeleland has confirmed her picture of guerrilla violence.[83]

Returning to our story, the conclusion of the struggle for Zimbabwean liberation contained some unexpected twists. An 'internal settlement', which brought Muzorewa to power in 1979, was intended to resurrect the idea of racial partnership. Nevertheless, the war intensified on all fronts and for the first time guerrillas were able to operate over the greater part of the country. In fact, as many as 33 per cent of total deaths occurred during the final year.[84] The burden on the white population, in terms of military service, was becoming unsustainable despite the large-scale recruitment of Africans. Moreover, the share of total government expenditure consumed by the military had risen from 25 per cent in 1976 to as much as 47 per cent in 1979 – far exceeding the comparable burden on the Portuguese exchequer.[85] Towards the end of 1979, therefore, a fresh round of negotiations was held in London, which brought the PF to the negotiating table with Muzorewa and Smith. After a great deal of diplomatic brinkmanship, a constitutional agreement was hammered out. The Lancaster House deal conceded the principle of majority rule, but also wrote in certain guarantees for the white minority. A total of 20 parliamentary seats were reserved for whites, while limitations were placed on the ability of a new government to seize control of white lands. Moreover, the guerrillas were instructed to converge on designated assembly points in order to prevent possible interference with the projected elections.

The elections were held in February 1980, and resulted in ZANU-PF winning 63 per cent of the vote and 57 of the 80 common roll seats. PF-ZAPU, took 24 per cent of the vote and 20 of the seats, which were mostly located in Matabeleland. Muzorewa's United African National Council (UANC), which many had expected to perform well, took a little more than 8 per cent of the votes and a mere three seats. Sithole's version of ZANU came in a poor fourth with two per cent of the votes and no seats at all. As for the Rhodesian Front, it captured all 20 of the reserved seats. After a short period in which Zimbabwe became a British colony once more, formal independence followed in April. With echoes of Kenyatta's promises on the eve of Kenyan independence, incoming President Robert Mugabe, who whites had come to loathe as a Communist demagogue, assured them that 'we will ensure that there is a place for everyone in this country ... We want to ensure a sense of security for both the winners and the losers.'[86] What everyone knew at the time was that, unlike in Kenya, the land question had been swept under the plush red carpet.

7.3 The fruits of liberation: the limits to radical change

Although the various liberation movements professed a commitment to societal transformation, economic restructuring and popular empowerment, the environment in which they were forced to operate after independence could scarcely have been less favourable.

It is commonly thought that the PAIGC enjoyed the best prospects because it had succeeded in penetrating most of the countryside.[87] Moreover, because there was no settler population, Guinea-Bissau was spared the acute disruption that accompanied the Portuguese withdrawal elsewhere. Although Spínola, who was something of an expert on Guinea-Bissau, attempted to apply the brakes, Portuguese troops were in favour of negotiating a peaceful exit. Even the future of Cape Verde, which might have constituted a sticking point, ceased to pose a problem once PAIGC negotiators accepted that its future ought to be delinked from the independence of Guinea.[88] Despite a relatively trouble-free transition, Guinea-Bissau was nevertheless a very poor country – although positively affluent by comparison with the barren and drought-prone islands of Cape Verde. Much of the economic infrastructure which did exist had been destroyed in the course of the war. Chabal also argues that the assassination of Cabral in 1973 was a cruel blow because it eliminated the one person who had a clear vision of how the mistakes of other African countries could be averted and how development could be pursued in co-operation with the rural majority.[89] For Cabral, the future lay in the relocation of decision-making powers from Bissau to the provinces, and in the pursuit of 'agrarian socialism'. The obvious problem with this analysis is that it only confirms the impression of a party which was weakly institutionalised and dominated by a handful of leaders who were 'changeable only as a result of a death or a major party upheaval'.[90] Be that as it may, Chabal is correct to point out that under the Presidency of Amílcar's half-brother, Luís Cabral, the party quickly became detached from its rural moorings after independence in September 1974.

One reason is that the PAIGC was mesmerised by the challenge of winning over the population of the capital, Bissau, whose population had swelled to 90,000 (or one-seventh of the national total) as a result of the war. Although the PAIGC had begun as a party of the city, it had been cut off from the population of Bissau during the fighting. When PAIGC cadres moved into the capital, they found themselves in the midst of a population which was somewhat truculent. Perhaps because it needed to win the urbanites over, but also because it shared a misplaced vision of modernity, the PAIGC policies came to be skewed towards Bissau. It is remarkable, for example, that 66 per cent of the national budget in 1979 was expended on salaries, which were overwhelmingly urban, leaving precious little for social services such as health and education.[91] Moreover, the PAIGC departed significantly from its earlier insistence on the primacy of the countryside when it allocated 50 per cent of the national health budget to Bissau.[92] The government also invested much of its remaining resources in state enterprises, such as a Citroen car assembly plant, whose viability was questionable.[93] Most of the factories depended upon imported machinery and raw materials, which meant that they operated at a fraction of capacity when foreign exchange was in short supply (as it perennially was). The peasantry was also disadvantaged by a lack of investment in roads and river transport, low producer prices, and endemic shortages of consumer goods arising from the deficiencies of the People's Stores.[94] After some time, rural producers did what African peasants have often done in similar circumstances, that is they resorted to smuggling or stopped producing a marketable surplus. The performance of the agricultural sector was consequently weak, with a net decline of rice and groundnut production between the mid-1970s and the early 1980s, when a recurrence of drought further compounded the problem.[95]

The failings of government agricultural policy had knock-on effects elsewhere, not least on the urban cost of living – in that sense, subverting the political calculus which had driven government policy in the first place. A widespread sense of disillusionment with the Cabral regime set in, and in areas which had once actively supported the PAIGC the party died a death at the local level. At the same time, the leadership increasingly fell back upon more coercive expedients. The cracks in the edifice, which had been apparent for some time, finally opened up in November 1980 when João Vieira mounted a coup against Cabral. This ruptured the link with the Cape Verde wing of the PAIGC, whose historic dominance had long been a source of annoyance. The President of Cape Verde, Aristides Pereira, condemned the takeover in no uncertain terms and proceeded to launch a new party, the PAICV (Party for the Independence of Cape Verde) in 1981. This led to the expulsion of the Cape Verdeans from the PAIGC and to a final parting of the ways.

In Guinea-Bissau itself, the Vieira government reversed many of the policies which had been pursued since 1974. State investment in industry was radically pared back (the Citroen plant, for example, was put on ice); salaries were scaled back to a more manageable 59 per cent share of the total budget; and rural producer prices were raised. However, the administration was saddled with a crippling debt burden and was unlikely to be able to balance its budget for some time to come. The absolute dependence upon foreign aid donors meant that the regime had limited room to shape its own agenda. Despite an obvious desire to give credit to the PAIGC, Chabal observed in 1986 that 'The fate of Guinea-Bissau today is that of any other similar African country. The history of the armed struggle is less and less relevant.'[96] If Amílcar Cabral had lived to read these lines, he would have been more taken aback than anyone: for this was precisely the outcome which the PAIGC had tried to avoid.

In Mozambique, the portents were less favourable from the start. The Portuguese junta and FRELIMO were able to agree on a phased transition to independence which was intended to avoid the kind of chaos which had been witnessed in the Congo in 1960. However, this was jeopardised by the efforts of white hardliners to recruit non-FRELIMO elements in Beira and Maputo in support of an uprising designed at forestalling a handover to FRELIMO. The violence which erupted over September and October 1974, claimed many lives, led to a flight of the Portuguese population and brought about the collapse of many industrial and agricultural enterprises. When FRELIMO went on to nationalise rented property, there was a further Portuguese exodus, so that by the end of 1976 only around 10 per cent of their original number remained.[97] In view of the dislocation created by the war and the closing of Portuguese businesses – many of which were deliberately sabotaged by the departing owners – FRELIMO faced a formidable task in staving off economic collapse.

FRELIMO almost seemed to revel in having to fight a new phase of the liberation struggle. Many of the abandoned enterprises were brought under state ownership. Although this was a necessary expedient, the instincts of the government were already thoroughly statist. The party was beholden to a Marxist-Leninist tradition in which central planning and state control over productive activity had long been advocated as the best means to both optimise output and promote social equality. But as Margaret Hall and Tom Young suggest, the attraction of Marxism lay in its specific associations with modernity, whereas Portuguese rule was thought to have confined the African in the strait-jacket of tradition.[98] The platform of FRELIMO was therefore one which emphasised state control of industry and a commanding role for the state in agriculture. The first made some sense in view of the exodus of Portuguese entrepreneurs, but the second was distinctly unwise. Scarce government resources were ploughed into state farms, and to some extent into co-operatives, while peasants were effectively neglected. There was no land reform and indeed peasants were often forced to relinquish more of the most fertile lands. Moreover, when peasants did produce for market there was little in the way of consumer goods for them to purchase in return. From the peasant perspective, therefore, it was often the continuities rather than the changes which were most apparent.[99] The assumption was that state farms would necessarily prove their superiority over the peasant sector because of their application of scientific methods. This failed to take account of the extent to which peasants were agricultural innovators and it further ignored the record of failed state farms across Africa. In the final analysis, most state enterprises operated at far below capacity and tended to leak money. The advent of drought conditions in 1982/83 brought the agrarian crisis to a head when famine conditions emerged across the South.

In fairness, FRELIMO did succeed in clawing its way back from the economic turmoil surrounding the transition. Between 1975 and 1977, aggregate output is estimated to have risen by 5.5 per cent, and between 1977 and 1981 it rose by a further 11.6 per cent.[100] These were not spectacular rates of growth, but some of the indicators were at least pointing in the right direction. However, a sign of an underlying disequilibrium was that imports were outstripping exports, while the fiscal deficit was gathering pace. The proudest achievements of FRELIMO undoubtedly lay in the area of social services.[101] Despite the mass exodus of all but around 100 doctors after independence, the government was able to make primary and preventive health care much more widely available. In 1976, the World Health Organisation marvelled at the ability of the regime to reach 96 per cent of the population with a national vaccination campaign. Again, literacy rates increased from a national average of 10 per cent (whites included) to 25 per cent when the whites had mostly left.[102] These were unquestionable achievements, but in the absence of sustained economic growth, they were vulnerable in the long run.

The inability of FRELIMO to deliver the goods, literally as well as figuratively, played directly into the hands of its detractors. The tragic consequence was that Mozambique became embroiled in yet another war which exceeded that of the liberation struggle in its ferocity. After Mozambican independence, the Rhodesian Central Intelligence Organisation (CIO) co-opted former members of Portuguese military units, FRELIMO defectors and other dissident elements and trained them up as guerrilla fighters to be used against the Machel government.[103] This was the origins of RENAMO (the National Resistance of Mozambique) which commenced military operations within Mozambique in 1977. Following the death in action of André Matsangaíssa (a rusticated

FRELIMO member) in October 1979, Afonso Dhlakama emerged as its somewhat shadowy leader.[104] After Zimbabwean independence, RENAMO was taken over by the South Africans who provided a home and logistical support. From being a minor irritant, RENAMO rapidly evolved into a debilitating scourge in the early 1980s – beginning first in the central provinces of Manica and Sofala and then spreading to Inhambane, Gaza, Tete and eventually into Zambézia province.[105] RENAMO specifically targeted the infrastructural network of a country whose political geography was particularly difficult (See Chapter 2). It repeatedly hit the rail links from Nacala, Beira and Maputo, as well as the Maputo-Beira road. RENAMO also targeted the Umtali-Beira pipeline, the transmission lines from the Cabora Bassa dam and (worst of all) the hospitals and schools which FRELIMO had constructed as part of its social programme.[106] The underlying aim was to paralyse the administration, to further compound the economic crisis and thereby to undermine the credibility of the government.

Although South African support was crucial, RENAMO was also able to build upon the lessons of successful guerrilla insurgencies and to turn them back on FRELIMO. In particular, the rebels learned to exploit grievances arising directly out of government policy. At independence, there were large parts of the country where FRELIMO had scarcely made a dent. Although it tried to fill the gap by encouraging the formation of Dynamising Groups, many of these areas remained mistrustful of the government. Moreover, a compulsory villagisation programme which FRELIMO was determined to implement – another product of its misplaced concern with modernity – was unpopular in many parts of the country because it was so redolent of the *aldeamentos* policy of the Portuguese military. Again, FRELIMO had almost gone out of its way to antagonise the Christian churches, which it accused of complicity with the Portuguese, and had unnecessarily offended the Muslim minority. Given the longstanding hostility of FRELIMO to chiefs and spirit mediums – the one being regarded as 'feudal' and the other representing peasant 'superstition' – these were often natural allies for RENAMO as well. A study of Nampula province, carried out by Christian Geffray in the mid-1980s, confirmed the ability of RENAMO to exploit past mistakes, although the author also suggested that FRELIMO learned some lessons.[107] A good example was a reappraisal of official attitudes towards indigenous cultures. RENAMO appears to have copied from a ZANLA template in bringing spirit mediums on board.[108] Be that as it may, the devastation wrought by RENAMO raids eventually led to a fightback in some rural communities. In Zambézia, a peasant movement called Naparama emerged in the late 1980s which was led by one Manuel Antonio, a traditional healer.[109] Antonio launched a highly successful campaign against well-armed RENAMO units involving recruits armed only with spears and knives. His secret lay in fortifying his soldiers with 'traditional medicine' which was thought to render them impervious to bullets as long as they respected certain ritual taboos. Such ideas have long existed in the Zimbabwe–Mozambique borderlands, but the significant thing is that they had always been scoffed at by FRELIMO. However, after Naparama succeeded in capturing a number of RENAMO strongholds, government troops began to engage in joint operations and even to seek spiritual fortification themselves.

The resonances with the Kriger model are striking. Because RENAMO was not able to establish true liberated zones, it resorted to crudely coercive expedients. Minter's interviews suggest that the vast majority of fighters were forcibly recruited, and in the South this included child soldiers.[110] Those who signed up voluntarily tended to be the most marginalised sections of rural society. Moreover, RENAMO acquired a well-deserved reputation for being short on ideology and long on terror. The random violence unleashed against civilian populations – from killings to maimings and amputations – has been well-documented by many writers on the subject as well as by reputable human rights organisations. Hence Human Rights Watch Africa, reported that '[i]n the early 1980s, RENAMO acquired a reputation for savagery. It became particularly well-known for a policy of mutilating civilian victims, including children, by cutting off ears, noses, lips and sexual organs.'[111] While not disagreeing fundamentally, Nordstrom suggests that the list of perpetrators needs to be extended to include unpaid and underfed FRELIMO forces, renegade ex-government soldiers, private militias, armed bandits and protection-racketeers. Indeed, her list of war beneficiaries is remarkably similar to Ken Saro-Wiwa's fictionalised account of the Nigerian Civil War.[112] The big picture has also been somewhat refined on a regional basis. Robert Gersony, whilst working for the American State Department, distinguished between three RENAMO zones of operation: areas of destruction where the guerrillas killed anything that moved; areas of control, where peasants were systematically exploited; and areas of taxation where the overall burden was lighter.[113] Although there appear to have been striking differences within provinces, there were also significant differences between them. In those regions where FRELIMO was relatively well-entrenched, notably in Gaza province, RENAMO carried out countless atrocities which were designed to spread a climate of fear. But where the ruling party was historically weaker – such as in Manica and Sofala – RENAMO felt more secure, and consequently there was greater give-and-take between guerrillas and peasants.[114]

If the intention was to sow the utmost mayhem, RENAMO succeeded admirably. The destruction of infrastructure and the mining of the roads hit the economy hard. As a result, GDP fell at 8 per cent a year between 1980 and 1985. Moreover, RENAMO successfully widened its campaign to cover the greater part of the country. These stark realties forced the Machel government to jettison much of its radical programme in a fight for sheer survival. It began by seeking to build closer links with sympathetic Western countries like Italy and (bizarrely) Margaret Thatcher's Britain, in an attempt both to isolate RENAMO and attract vital economic aid.[115] The regime was forced to acknowledge that South African destabilisation had the potential to bring the country to its knees if it didn't come to a modus *vivendi*. In March 1984, Machel and P. W. Botha signed the Nkomati accord which committed the two governments to refrain from supporting armed dissidents against each other. In practical terms, this meant that the Mozambicans were forced to place restrictions on ANC activities. In return, the Botha regime was supposed to desist from supporting RENAMO, but the security agencies continued to provide a great deal of covert assistance. The result was that FRELIMO never gained the breathing-space it so desperately needed.

The change of direction in economic policy, which became somewhat easier to pursue after the untimely death of Machel in a plane crash in October 1986, was in many ways even more remarkable.[116] Under the leadership of Joaquim Chissano, the government adopted a Programme of Economic Rehabilitation (PRE) and signed an agreement with the IMF and the World Bank the following year. The PRE entailed the adoption of a series of market reforms corresponding to the standard Structural Adjustment package which most African countries were forced to embrace at about the same time. In subsequent years, the language of socialism was quietly dropped, as the regime embraced a new discourse of economic liberalism. In an obvious sense, the volte-face had been forced upon the FRELIMO regime. And yet Hall and Young may be correct to suggest that FRELIMO found the transition so effortless because they were swapping one vision of modernity for another which was no less coherent in its own terms.[117] During the 1990s, Mozambique became the extreme case of a country which was heavily indebted, dependent on foreign aid and over-run by Western Non-Governmental Organisations (NGOs).

On a more positive note, real progress was eventually made towards restoring the peace. The ending of South African rule in Namibia and the first stages in the dismantling of apartheid signalled to RENAMO that the external environment was likely to become less forgiving. Moreover, a severe drought in 1990 took its toll on populations in both the government and RENAMO areas. Given that FRELIMO had reconciled itself to multipartyism in 1989, RENAMO also had a weaker case for adhering to armed struggle. In October 1992, the two sides signed a peace agreement which provided for national elections and the formation a national army made up of elements from the two sides. Crucially, the UN decided to commit itself to making the agreement stick. The United Nations Organisation for Mozambique (ONUMOZ) despatched 7000 troops who had successfully completed a demobilisation by January 1994. Indeed, soldiers on both sides demanded that the process be accelerated in order to benefit from the compensation package.[118] The substantial presence of UN observers made it possible for the elections to proceed with remarkably little trouble. Chissano won the Presidency with 53.3 per cent of the vote to 33.7 per cent by Dhlakama, while FRELIMO won 129 seats to RENAMO's 112. FRELIMO had won in six of the eleven provinces, demonstrating that RENAMO was still a serious political force across much of the country, especially in the central belt. Proving the sceptics wrong, RENAMO made the transition to a mainstream political party, and in subsequent years expanded its support base. The successful transition did depend, however, on prodigious quantities of foreign aid, which came with conditions attached.

Looking back on the war itself, much of the misery had been inflicted on Mozambicans by FRELIMO, which had made some costly mistakes. But at least the government faced the public at the polls. The South African government, the American right (fronted by Jesse Helms) and RENAMO were arguably far more culpable, but the difference is that the first two did not have to pick up the tab in any sense. Those who did so in spades were the countless Mozambican victims: the five million displaced people; the orphans; those whose limbs had been blown or hacked off; and others who had lost close family members. It is difficult enough to quantify the mortality rates. Some sense of the enormity lies in a UNICEF estimate that as many as 494,000 children under the age of five died from war-related causes between 1980 and 1988.[119] If these figures are remotely accurate, then the global figure of 1 million dead is probably an undercount.[120] However, most of the suffering experienced by ordinary Mozambicans can never be reduced to such statistics. Although some anthropological research, such as that by Nordstrom, has tried to recapture the voice of ordinary Mozambicans, it remains sadly muffled.

The Mozambican experience of independence was grim enough. However, it was matched by the tortured history of post-colonial Angola. In this case, there was a seamless continuity from the colonial war to civil war. After the Portuguese coup, what transpired bore more than a passing resemblance to the débâcle in the Belgian Congo – which may be no accident, given that many of the same cast of characters took the stage. As in Mozambique, an immediate hitch was the unwillingness of the settler population to go along with the MFA agenda. A further outpouring of white vigilante violence in Luanda, and the black counter-response, helped to create a climate of insecurity which strengthened the resolve of the Portuguese military to secure a timely exit. Whereas the Portuguese authorities could hand over to FRELIMO and the PAIGC, there were three liberation movements in Angola which were furiously jockeying for position. Spínola and the conservative wing of the junta initially joined with Mobutu in an attempt to broker a broad coalition which would exclude the MPLA. On the other hand, the MFA and the leftist High Commissioner, Admiral Rosa Coutinho, were more favourably disposed to the MPLA.[121] In January 1975, the MPLA, the FNLA and UNITA finally signed the Alvor Agreement which was supposed to lead to the installation of a transitional government prior to the holding of national elections. Under this accord, the Portuguese would slowly withdraw, leading to the conferral of formal independence in November. However, the signing of the agreement was followed by an intensification of military clashes between the MPLA and FNLA in Luanda which the Portuguese were powerless to prevent. When the time came for their staged exit, they withdrew without seeking to transfer power to anyone in particular. By this point, the Alvor Agreement had already been torn up as a full-scale civil war erupted.

The rapid militarisation of Angolan politics in mid-1975 is inseparable from the politics of Cold War and South Africa's forward strategy – or what later came to be known as Botha's 'total strategy'. The implementation of any kind of political programme became a practical impossibility for the next three decades as rival movements and their international trainers slugged it out like out-of-shape heavyweight boxers. The first rounds of the contest over 1975/76 went to the MPLA. This could not have been foreseen at the start of 1974 when the movement was recovering from another round of splits and defections from within its military wing. At this point, the FNLA commanded many more fighters, and because it seemed to have a greater presence in the field, Daniel Chipenda led a defection. However, after the Portuguese coup, the Soviet Union followed the advice of the Portuguese Communist Party and began to channel substantial weaponry towards the MPLA, with the apparent complicity of the Countinho administration. Cuban military advisors, who arrived through Brazzaville, provided training in the use of this more sophisticated equipment. As yet another illustration of how the fates of Angola and Zaire were intertwined, up to 7000 Katangan secessionist exiles were recruited into the MPLA.[122] This provided an excuse for Mobutu to throw more than a thousand Zairian troops into the battle on the side of the FNLA. The United States had already decided to direct financial support to the latter in early 1975, and this was funnelled through Zaire. While the MPLA and the FNLA battled it out for control of Luanda, UNITA continued to formally abide by the Alvor Agreement. It lacked an external patron of its own, had relatively few fighters and was likely to prosper in any elections if it could harness the Ovimbundu vote.[123] However, as the military balance swung towards the MPLA, the United States decided to fund UNITA as well, which then joined forces with the FNLA and the Zaireans (who had their eyes on the oil-rich Cabinda enclave) in a big push designed to capture Luanda before the official date of independence.[124]

The stakes were further raised in August, when the South African Defence Force (SADF) advanced across the border from SWA in support of the anti-MPLA coalition. Pretoria claimed that it was acting with certain assurances from the United States, although this was later denied by the Secretary of State, Dr Henry Kissinger.[125] The South African push came close to dislodging the MPLA, but the commitment of Cuban forces proved crucial in holding the line. The pendulum then swung the other way when the FNLA gambled and was routed on the northern front. A further blow followed in December when the United States Congress came to know the extent of covert CIA funding for the war. Still haunted by nightmares of Vietnam, it passed the Tunney Amendment which blocked further transfers at a critical moment.[126] When the South Africans pulled back towards the border, clearly annoyed by American vacillation, the MPLA victory was guaranteed.

In February 1976, the MPLA seized the stronghold of Huambo, where UNITA and the FNLA had turned their guns on each other, forcing UNITA forces to scatter. The FNLA thereafter ceased to be a factor in the Angolan political equation, while UNITA retreated to the South-east to regroup. In February, the OAU officially recognised the People's Republic of Angola under MPLA control. Many member states, most notably Nigeria, had abandoned their objections to the MPLA as soon as the South Africans weighed in. The Kaunda regime in Zambia, which may have solicited this intervention in the first place, later made its own peace with the MPLA. Finally, sweet revenge followed in 1977 and 1978 when many of the same Katangan rebels who had fought for the MPLA took up arms against Mobutu in the Shaba province (see Chapter 6). Because his position no longer looked so secure, Mobutu was forced to come to his own modus *vivendi* with the Angolan government.

The MPLA which had never sunk deep roots outside Luanda and the Mbundu areas now faced a challenge in establishing its political legitimacy across the length and breadth of Angola. After its military victory in 1976, it attempted to repair much of the shattered economic and social infrastructure.

Unlike FRELIMO, it was fortunate in being able drawn on substantial oil revenues from the Cabinda enclave, as well as being able to call on the services of skilled Cuban personnel. The arrival of 400 Cuban doctors played an invaluable role in restoring basic health amenities, given that the country only had 100 doctors of its own.[127] Moreover, between 1973 and 1977 the number of children in primary schools doubled to one million, with a further 100,000 in secondary schools. As in Mozambique, national literacy campaigns also chalked up real successes. These material achievements also generated peace dividends as many former FNLA and UNITA supporters returned to their homes. However, the reality was that UNITA had not been eradicated. Indeed, it was primed to start fighting as soon as external funding was resumed. Savimbi withdrew to the remote south-eastern corner of the country and established a new military headquarters at Jamba in 1979. There UNITA could rely on South African air-cover, and because Jamba was close to the border it could be easily supplied.

However, the crucial factor in transforming the sagging fortunes of UNITA, and thus restarting the war, was the election of Ronald Reagan in the United States in 1980. Across the world, the Reagan regime decided that the cheapest and most effective way of fighting left-wing governments was by sponsoring insurgent movements of its own: backing the very activities it would prefer to call 'terrorism' elsewhere. Support for the Contras in Nicaragua had its parallel in backing for UNITA in Angola, which became overt after the repeal of the Clark Amendment, which had prevented further direct funding, in 1985.[128] Much like RENAMO, UNITA embarked on a war of attrition which exacted a heavy price from the civilian population, including its notional Ovimbundu constituency. Villages were routinely burned down and those inhabitants who were not killed on the spot were force-marched back to UNITA zones where they were either made to produce food or were dragooned into its army. The peasantry of the south-central provinces suffered most from these attacks and from the infestation of some 6 million landmines which earned Angola the dubious honour of having the highest per capita number of amputees in the world. By 1991, some 100,000 Angolans had perished on the battlefield, but this was dwarfed by the estimated 700,000 who had become the casualties of landmines, killings, famine and disease. Moreover, no fewer than 3 million out of a population of 10 million had been displaced.[129] Washington purported to believe that the perils of Communism were far greater.

The adoption of a new policy towards South Africa, which Assistant Secretary of State for African Affairs, Chester Crocker, euphemistically called 'constructive engagement', was also highly significant. On the face of things, this meant seeking to engage South Africa in a dialogue, but in practical terms it meant falling into line with Botha's own doctrine of 'total strategy'. When the South Africans intervened once more in Angola, they were therefore assured of the tacit support of the American government on the basis that their presence was essential to forestalling a Cuban-Soviet victory. From 1980, the SADF placed itself in effective occupation of much of Southern Angola: that is, large swathes of the Cunene and Cuando Cubango provinces. The Angolan government reported no fewer than 50 South African ground operations in 1981, the most extensive being Operation Protea which aimed at the creation of a buffer zone along the border.[130] In 1983, the SADF launched Operation Askari which was more ambitious in conception, but met with more effective MPLA resistance. In all of these operations, the SADF worked closely with UNITA, and indeed it executed many acts of sabotage in the latter's name.[131] Publicly, UNITA endeavoured to maintain a distance of sorts from the Botha regime. For example, Savimbi remarked rather memorably of the 1984 South African Constitution (see below) that 'Black men with flat noses can hardly agree with a constitution based on racial discrimination.'[132] However, all the evidence suggests that Savimbi leaned heavily on his South African patrons for routine assistance and backup when its positions were threatened. Hence when the MPLA launched an assault on Mavinga in 1987 with a view to forging a ring of air defences, the SADF weighed in on the side of UNITA.

This intervention proved to be a turning point. In 1988, the SADF despatched 6000 troops to assist UNITA in a joint assault on the MPLA stronghold of Cuito Cuanavale. The Cubans responded by sending in 50,000 troops of their own, with air support from Soviet pilots, which forced the South Africans to beat a hasty retreat, leaving UNITA forces to their own devices. For years, the Reagan government had insisted that the question of a South African withdrawal had to be linked to the removal of Cuban troops from Angolan soil. After the battle for Cuito Canavale, the external players began to assess the cost of perpetual warfare. To the consternation of Savimbi, the Americans, the MPLA, the South Africans and the Cubans signed a regional peace accord in 1988. This committed the Cubans to a phased withdrawal from Angola. At the same time, the SADF was to pull out of Namibia and allow elections in that country in 1989. On this occasion, the signatories actually carried out their commitments to the letter. But the small problem was that UNITA was not a signatory. Moreover, the American administration felt the need to sweeten the pill by offering UNITA greater aid, thereby ensuring that the Angolan war would continue. Indeed UNITA proceeded to intensify its military operations and spread its insurgency to the North of the country.

With the advent of Namibian independence in 1990, the United States and the Soviet Union began to press the two sides to come to a proper agreement. This culminated in the Bicesse accords of May 1991, under which it was agreed that demobilisation of the two armies would be supervised by the UN, while national elections were scheduled to take place within 18 months. However, the failure of the UN to commit enough resources to the exercise proved fatal because it enabled Savimbi to secretly maintain many of his forces under arms. When the September 1992 elections failed to go his way, contrary to his confident predictions, Savimbi was able to catch the MPLA off-guard and to seize control of 70 per cent of the country. On this occasion, he attempted to hold the cities and a number of provincial towns which had supported the MPLA in the elections. Although the Americans and the South Africans had ceased to arm UNITA, the latter managed to rearm itself by purchasing weapons which the Soviet successor states were only too happy to offload, using money derived from the sale of illicit diamonds.[133] By this point, the bad faith of the UNITA leadership had exhausted the patience of even the Americans, and the incoming Clinton administration decided to make a clean break with the *realpolitik* of the Reagan and Bush era. Clinton formally recognised the MPLA government, which had abandoned Marxism-Leninism in 1990, and began selling it weapons. This enabled the MPLA to roll back the UNITA offensive, albeit at great human cost (a further 100,000 dead). However, the Luanda government came under renewed pressure to find a negotiated settlement. This culminated in the Lusaka accords of 1994 which produced a power-sharing agreement, properly underwritten by the UN, in which UNITA would receive a number of Cabinet positions and provincial governorships. This was supposed to bring the 20-year war, which had by now claimed something close on 1 million lives, to a conclusion. As we shall see in a later chapter, though, even this was not the end of the Angolan tragedy.

The fortunes of Zimbabwe took a very different turn. By comparison with Angola and Mozambique, Zimbabwe was a haven of stability, but this came at the expense of the liberational aspirations to which ZANU had traditionally appealed. The first decade was marked by the entrenchment of social inequalities and of authoritarian tendencies within the regime. One explanation for why the revolution 'lost its way' is that the political leadership of ZANU-PF had always worn Marxism as a cloak of convenience which could be easily discarded when conditions so dictated.[134] But there were also more deep-seated reasons for the effective dilution of a commitment to socialism. The first is quite simply that the Lancaster House Agreement bound the hands of the Mugabe regime for the next ten years. The most important of the 'sunset clauses' were those which related to the critical question of land. Rural Africans were crammed into Tribal Trust Lands – or Communal Areas as they were renamed – where the population density stood at 28 people per square kilometre as against nine per square kilometre in white farming areas.[135] Moreover, while most of the Communal lands were located in the medium to poor lands of the centre and west – which had average or weak soils and were prone to drought – the 6000 white farms were (unsurprisingly) concentrated on the fertile and well-watered north-east. The legal deracialisation of land ownership in 1977 had done nothing to alter this highly unequal pattern of land distribution. But while peasant supporters of ZANU-PF looked to the government to allocate land, the 'Declaration of Rights' within the independence constitution stated that property could not be seized without good reason and adequate compensation. Furthermore, seizures required ratification by the courts.[136] The Mugabe regime was therefore bound by the 'willing seller–willing buyer' principle, which meant that it was reduced to buying up lands which whites wanted to sell, and at their full market value.

With British financial assistance underwriting half of the costs, the Mugabe government embarked on a limited process of land resettlement. This was supposed to move 18,000 families onto 1.1 million hectares within three years, but in 1982 the government revised its goals upwards with a view to resettling 162,000 families (or roughly one in five of the peasant population) on 5 million hectares.[137] The authorities were, however, unable to meet the ambitious targets they had set for themselves. They did acquire some 3.3 million hectares during the first decade, but no less than 44 per cent of this land was poor and much was not really suitable for agriculture.[138] Only 19 per cent of the acquired land fell within the fertile zone (what is called Natural Region 1). But even if more and better land had been available, the government would still have lacked the financial resources to render the more ambitious programme feasible. By the end of 1990, the number of resettled families stood at 52,000 which was far below the target figure, but it was an achievement of sorts. The small problem was, however, that the population of the Communal Areas was growing at such a pace that overall population pressure had not significantly abated by the end of the decade. As a result, peasants often occupied unused land rather than waiting for official approval. By the mid-1990s, there were some 500,000 squatters in effective occupation.[139]

Although land redistribution had failed to take place on the scale that peasants were clamouring for, the regime could point to substantial achievements in the agricultural sector. The white Commercial Farmers' Union argued against hasty land reform on the basis that the large-scale commercial farms were responsible for some 90 per cent of marketed output at independence. To reallocate land on a systematic basis, it was argued, would hit the principal export crops (tobacco, cotton, groundnuts, sugar and coffee) and endanger food security. As it happened, there was a substantial expansion in agricultural output in the years after independence which was almost wholly due to takeup within the peasant sector. The most spectacular increases were reflected in the increases in maize production: between 1979/80 and 1984/85, peasant communal farmers increased their marketed output from 18,260 tons (3.6 per cent of the total) to 341,673 tons (36.5 per cent), leading to conditions of national abundance. At the same time, the proportional contribution of the white commercial farmers to agricultural output fell significantly from 90 per cent to less than 80 per cent by the mid-1980s.These figures, which comprehensively demolished the assumption that peasants were inefficient farmers, nevertheless concealed some important variations. The bulk of the increase occurred in the fertile zones of Natural Regions 1 and 2, where some peasants were able to take advantage of equal access to inputs and markets. But in the poorer regions (Regions 3–5), there was little improvement. Participants in the settlement schemes often lost out doubly because they were allocated marginal lands and prohibited from engaging in wage employment which provided an important avenue through which peasant households could purchase agricultural inputs.[140] The agricultural revolution in Zimbabwe therefore concealed greater differentiation within the peasantry and the continuing hardship of many rural households.

A second consideration was that the bureaucratic structures of the Rhodesian state remained in place and were simply taken over by ZANU-PF. The element of continuity was obvious in relation to the functioning of Ministries, which ticked over as before, but it was even more starkly apparent in respect of agencies like the Police and the CIO. It would arguably have taken a greater measure of single-mindedness than the ZANU-PF possessed for the politicians to have reshaped the bureaucracy and the security apparatus. Although the government sought to bring local party supporters into elected District Councils, these were comparatively weak and were largely under the control of local civil servants. The result was that the rural administration functioned in a manner which rank-and-file supporters often found difficult to fathom. This was the case, for example, when peasants were turned off lands which they tried to occupy.

There was also a third legacy which had an important bearing on the outcome, and that was the history of rivalry between ZANU and ZAPU. Although ZAPU leaders such as Joshua Nkomo were given Ministerial positions, it did not take long before the relationship revealed signs of strain. The problems began within the Assembly Camps to which both sets of guerrilla fighters were supposed to report, as well as within the Zimbabwean National Army (ZNA) which was meant to absorb elements of each. In the early days of the transition, guerrilla fighters resented the powers which continued to be exercised by the white secu-rity forces whilst they were confined to camps. But increasingly, the problems turned on the animosity between ZANLA and ZIPRA fighters within the camps as they were being demobilised. After a number of clashes, in which ZIPRA tended to come off worst, many former guerrillas absconded. The perceived dis-crimination against ZIPRA fighters within the fledgling ZNA only added to a sense of a malaise which increasingly assumed ethnic overtones. Many former ZIPRA fighters crossed the borders into South Africa and Botswana in search of work. Predictably, the Botha regime recruited some of them into an insurgent army, dubbed Super ZAPU, which launched raids across the Botswana border. Others wanted nothing to do with the South Africans, but nevertheless attempted to fight a government which they regarded as bent on eliminating the Ndebele from the political equation. The Mugabe government interpreted the insurgency as evidence that the ZAPU leadership had not reconciled itself to electoral defeat. Although Nkomo protested his innocence and urged ZIPRA fighters to abide by the political accords, he was demoted within the Cabinet.

The government then proceeded to unleash a reign of terror within Matabeleland, in which the notorious Fifth Brigade was the principal culprit. This Brigade, which was trained by the North Koreans, physically eliminated ZAPU activists at the local level and anyone else who was perceived as being sympathetic to the 'dissidents'. At least 1500 people may have been killed in this manner. Through their own distorting lenses, the combatants of the Fifth Brigade, who were almost all ex-ZANLA fighters, interpreted themselves as the liberators of Zimbabwe and the 'dissidents' as merely the old enemy in another disguise. Apart from confirming gratuitous killing by the Fifth Brigade, Richard Werbner observes that peasants were brow-beaten into conforming with a vir-tual parody of the *pungwes* (or political gatherings) of the liberation war. Ndebele peasants found themselves forced to sing ZANLA war songs in Shona, as if speak-ing the Sindebele language itself was tantamount to dissidence. Famine relief was also deployed as a political weapon, and had to be consumed under military supervision. After having ruthlessly crushed the insurgency in Matabeleland, and come to terms with ZAPU in 1987, Mugabe declared an amnesty the following year and what remained of the rebels returned to civilian life.

The triple legacy of Zimbabwean independence was to have important consequences for the landscape of ideas which manifested itself over the first decade. First of all, the failure of ZANU-PF to follow through on promises of land reform contributed to a sense of disillusionment amongst party stalwarts.

Matters were not helped by revelations that senior politicians and civil servants were acquiring access to prime land, which had hitherto been farmed by whites under state leasehold, with loans from the Agricultural Finance Corporation.[141] Within a couple of years, the local structures of the party tended to ossify in a familiar manner. Secondly, whereas ZANU-PF had been hostile to the chiefs on the basis that they had collaborated with Rhodesian rule, traditional authority staged something of a comeback after 1980. The Mugabe government gave the chiefs ex officio representation on District Councils, and after the failure of community courts it formally restored the traditional courts in 1990.[142] But as important was the success with which the chiefs themselves exploited the weakness of the ruling party as a channel of popular communication. By posing as the spokesmen for peasants opposed to the reinvention of 'land betterment' in Communal Areas, and by taking an active part in campaigns to recapture lost lands, the chiefs were able to restore much of their local constituency.[143]

Finally, the first decade witnessed interesting mutations within the field of popular belief. Many families had lost loved ones during the liberation war, and in the Fifth Brigade's brutal invasion of Matabeleland. The spirits of those who had not received a proper burial were thought to roam free, inflicting further tribulations on the living. Within many communities, there was a perceived need to get the source of the affliction and, once the relevant spirit had been identified, to put it to rest. Whereas the *mhondoro* mediums communicated with the spirits of important ancestral spirits, the need to placate avenging spirits (or *ngozi*) led to the heightened importance of phenomena such as the *sangoma* cults in Matabeleland.[144] Moreover, many communities were polarised by the fact that members had participated in the maltreatment (or worse) of fellow villagers. The traditional churches had been forced to scale down many of their operations during the guerrilla warfare, which left a space into which new Pentecostal churches could assert themselves. After independence, there was an upsurge of witchcraft accusations, which is perhaps related to the greater inequalities that characterised many communities.[145] The Pentecostal churches regarded it as their mission to rehabilitate witches. Furthermore, Maxwell argues that the re-establishment of rural patriarchy, not least within the mainstream churches, made the Pentecostal churches more attractive to women and youth.[146] To the consternation of chiefs and spirit mediums, they openly attacked many practices which they regarded as un-Christian – underlining once again the importance of generational cleavages within Shona society. These various developments underscored the immense vitality of peasant culture in a part of Africa which had been more intensively colonised than most.

7.4 Amandla! The liberation struggle in South Africa

The challenge facing African nationalists in South Africa was even more daunting than in the other countries we have so far considered. In South West Africa, as will see, SWAPO faced the same enemy, but was assisted by the fact that South Africa's moral basis for being there was extremely weak. In the Portuguese territories, the liberation movements knew the colonial power was likely to withdraw once the costs of remaining became too great. In Rhodesia, the settlers posed a greater stumbling block because they fully intended to stay put, but because they were a small minority the liberation movements could escalate the war to the point when the latter would have to give in. In South Africa, the white population was much larger and every bit as obdurate. The election of the National Party (NP) in 1948 brought a regime to power which promised its supporters that it would make no concessions and ended up taking segregationism to its logical extreme in the shape of 'apartheid' (or separateness). Moreover, the South African state possessed powers of surveillance and control which were singular on the African continent, as well as the material resources to resist external pressures such as sanctions. The South African government was also fortunate in that it could use neighbouring states as a buffer against whatever guerrilla armies might be raised against it. Hence South African soldiers and police were sent to defend the Cabora Basa dam in Mozambique and to fight alongside the Rhodesian forces. After the fall of its northern allies, the South Africans clung on to SWA because this prevented it from being encircled by hostile states. Although the Frontline States gave the liberation movements their backing, the Pretoria regime had the means to make life extremely difficult for them if they harboured guerrillas. The states which were closest to South Africa, namely Botswana, Lesotho and Swaziland, were economically dependent upon it because they derived much of their revenue from membership of a common customs union.

For all of these reasons, the task facing nationalists was uniquely difficult. Nevertheless, the peculiarities of South Africa also presented a different set of possibilities for political organisation. The very substantial African population in the cities, which was continually augmented by 'illegal immigration' from the countryside, provided a focus for mass mobilisation which did not exist elsewhere in Africa. Moreover, there was a substantial African working class which had substantial weight of its own to throw behind the liberation cause. As we shall see, the main difference between the liberation struggle in South Africa was precisely that it was much less rural in character. After the early 1960s, the liberation movements paid relatively little attention to peasant struggles and concentrated on tapping into the energies of the urban masses. This, in turn, imparted a different shape to the ideologies and tactics of the South African liberation movements. None of this was pre-ordained, though, and it is part of the objective of this section to establish why opposition to apartheid eventually assumed the shape that it did.

But first of all, it is necessary to say something more about the specific manner in which racial domination and nationalism in South Africa influenced each other in the period before the 1950s. After its 1948 victory, the NP set about tightening up the loopholes which had emerged within segregationist practice, and then in the 1950s started constructing its grand project of apartheid at precisely the moment when colonial rule in the rest of Africa began to implode. The objectives of apartheid can most easily be gauged through the passage of interlocking pieces of government legislation.[147] The Population Registration Act of 1950 categorised all South Africans according to their supposed racial origins. The Group Areas Act of the same year insisted on the strict residential separation of each racial group, and in subsequent years many 'non-whites' were required to relocate to conform to the new geography of race. The destruction of District Six in the centre of Cape Town and the eviction of its Coloured population to the windswept Cape Flats, and the levelling of the African settlement of Sophiatown in Johannesburg, were merely the most famous instances. The Mixed Marriages Act and the Immorality Act were intended to police the boundaries of race by outlawing sex and marriage across the colour line.

Then there was the sharpening up legislation which was introduced to refine the existing structures of influx control. The law which required African men to carry a pass was extended to women and the Native Urban Areas Act (1923) was further amended in order to reduce the entitlement of Africans to reside in the cities. Only those who qualified under Section 10 of the Act were entitled to remain in the urban areas as of right. The rest were expected to return to their Bantustan (or homeland) if they remained out of work for longer than a period of 72 hours. Africans who fell foul of these regulations were liable to be 'endorsed out' (that is, evicted) to the homeland to which they notionally belonged. The Bantu Education Act (1953) separated educational provision on grounds of race, on the principle that Africans should only receive an education appropriate to the menial jobs which they would be expected to occupy. As Prime Minister Verwoerd bluntly put it: 'What is the use of teaching the Bantu child mathematics when it cannot use it in practice?'[148] At the level of higher education, a determined policy of 'retribalisation' meant not only that Coloured and Indians were expected to attend their own Universities – the University of the Western Cape and the University of Durban-Westville respectively – but also that Africans were sifted out according to their 'tribal' group. The University of Fort Hare was defined as Xhosa, while separate institutions were created for the Sotho, Pedi, Tswana and Venda at the University of the North (Turfloop) and for Zulus at the University College of Zululand at Ngoye. Finally, the Bantu Authorities Act attempted to introduce a system of indirect rule into the Bantustans, the implications of which have already been examined at some length in Chapter 4. The NP fully intended this battery of legislation to be implemented and a formidable maze of bureaucracy was created into carry it into effect. Although apartheid ideologues such as H. F. Verwoerd defended apartheid on the grounds that it embodied a realistic – even generous – policy of allowing each race and 'tribe' to develop along its own lines, all sides understood that it was really about maintaining white domination. In their unguarded moments, NP politicians defended apartheid on the basis that the accompanying hardships of forced removals and the like had to be accepted as part of the price for maintaining 'civilised society' in this corner of Africa.

Within this overall framework, there were some finer details which are often missed, but which are fundamental to an understanding of what underpinned apartheid. The NP was maintained in power after 1948 by a solid Afrikaner bloc vote. Although English-speaking whites initially remained loyal to the United Party (UP) and others later supported various manifestations of the Progressive Party (PP), most eventually switched to supporting the NP as well. In some respects, this was a bitter pill to swallow because English-speakers tended to look down upon Afrikaners – as reflected in the ubiquitous Van der Merwe joke, South Africa's variant on the Irish joke. In the final analysis, English-speakers were prepared to tolerate Afrikaner political hegemony in return for the protection of their own lifestyles and economic security. If the NP wanted to extend separate development to the creation of a separate educational system for Afrikaners, then this was acceptable to English-speakers as long as their schools were given equal resources. It was an unspoken assumption that jobs within the state sector would be reserved for Afrikaners, given the commitment of the NP to guaranteeing full employment for its core constituency. The greater part of the English-speaking white population was content in the knowledge that there were jobs a-plenty in the private sector. Over the course of the twentieth century, a racial pecking order also emerged in which Coloureds in the Cape and Indians in Natal both enjoyed a somewhat privileged position in relation to Africans, even as they were discriminated against by whites. For example, the NP government declared the Western Cape a 'Coloured labour preference area', which required employers to employ Coloureds in preference to Africans unless they could demonstrate special circumstances. The result was that the complexion of the working class of the Western Cape, especially within the textiles, food and canning industries, was Coloured rather than African. The protected status of Coloureds, which was reinforced by residential segregation, strengthened the objective underpinnings of Coloured identity even if the more politically aware sections of the population rejected the classificatory system imposed upon them.[149]

The 'non-white' section of the population had a long history of seeking to break down the structures of white domination. However, for the first part of the twentieth century its success was limited by two considerations. On the one hand, it proved difficult to dismantle the barriers between Africans, Coloureds and Indians which were in some respects a product of segregationist practices. On the other hand, the first political movements were led by small elites who purported to speak on behalf of the mass of the population but who were often socially separated from them. The Natal Indian Congress (NIC) tended to be led by urban professionals, like Mahatma Gandhi himself, but it sought to speak for Indian workers and petty traders as well. The leadership of the ANC (founded in 1912) was equally drawn from a narrow wedge of African society– that is doctors, lawyers, educationalists and the like – whose members had been nurtured by the mission school milieu. As a result, they subscribed to a rather Victorian view of social progress, which emphasised hard work and asceticism, and looked forward to a future society ordered according to merit. The mission schools were particularly influential in the Cape, and partly for this reason a belief in its version of liberal ideology ran deep. This was further reinforced by the emergence of a relatively prosperous peasantry in the Eastern Cape, at least until the 1913 Native Land Act began to bite.

Many educated Africans like Sol Plaatje, who was one of the founders of the ANC, had supported Britain in the South African War of 1899–1902 because they sincerely believed that this would lead to the extension of the colour-blind, but qualified, Cape franchise. They were bitterly disappointed when the African franchise remained confined to the Cape Province, and those who lived to see the complete revocation of African voting rights in 1936 were devastated. By this point, the assumption that Africans who could boast of the requisite education and a comfortable income would be permitted to join white society began to appear severely misplaced. But ANC leaders remained unsure of how to respond. The Communist Party of South Africa (CPSA) exerted some influence in the 1920s and 1930s, but this was not the liking of many more traditional ANC leaders. The emergence of factionalism within the party, along generational and ideological lines, further marginalised the ANC. According to Saul Dubow, the membership of the ANC may have fallen to as little as 1000 by the mid-1930s, at a critical historical moment, while the opposition mantle passed momentarily to an All-African Convention.[150]

The fortunes of the ANC were, however, transformed by two developments. The first was the enlistment of a new cohort at the end of the 1930s which could see the limitations of the ANC as presently constituted. The second was a new dynamism within the urban areas which was evident both in the cultural sphere and in a renewed spirit of popular resistance born of housing and social amenities which had failed to keep pace with the rural influx. Although the ANC was often observing from the sidelines, it was reinvigorated by urban campaigns, including a long-running bus boycott in Alexandra township, squatter protests on the Rand and strikes on the gold mines in 1946. The signal of a leadership shift came with the emergence of the ANC Youth League as a ginger group over 1943–44. The Youth League deplored the timidity of the ANC leadership which, they claimed, played into the hands of government. Under the intellectual leadership of Anton Lembede, the Youth League asserted a pride in being African and advocated that the party should embrace more direct forms of action. The ranks of the Youth League included many of the individuals who would come to dominate the movement for half a century: notably, Nelson Mandela, Walter Sisulu and Oliver Tambo, but alas not Lembede himself who died prematurely in 1947.[151] At the national conference of 1949, the year after the election of the NP government, the Youth League wrested control over the ANC leadership. Alfred Xuma was ousted as president by Dr James Moroka, while Sisulu assumed the position of secretary-general. The party also formally adopted the Youth League's *Programme of Action* which embraced the tactics of civil disobedience. Furthermore, the ANC resolved to boycott institutions like the Native Representative Council which had been established as a sop to compensate for the removal of the Cape African franchise.

Once in command of the ANC, the Youth Leaguers turned out to be more pragmatic than might have been expected. They had previously insisted on an exclusively African leadership, and for this reason had previously opposed Xuma's efforts to find common ground with the NIC. Many were also suspicious of any involvement with Communists partly on the grounds that these were largely white in complexion. But this ultramontane position was modified in the early 1950s in the face of a raft of apartheid legislation which had to be resisted in any way possible. In June 1950, the ANC organised a joint National Day of Protest and Mourning together with the NIC, the African People's Organisation (APO), the Communist Party and the Council of Non-European Trade Unions. The turnout was somewhat disappointing, but the initiative was nevertheless important in terms of forging a cross-racial alliance. Indeed it marked the beginning of the so-called 'Congress Alliance' which brought together a wide variety of political organisations which were opposed to apartheid. The high point was the launching of the Defiance Campaign in June 1952, which set out to challenge unjust laws by means of non-violent acts of civil disobedience, more or less along Gandhian lines. The principal target was the pass laws which were challenged by Africans destroying their passbooks and then presenting themselves for arrest with the intention of clogging up the system. In the Eastern Cape and Transvaal, the turnout was good, but in other parts of the country the response was more patchy. Nevertheless, the Defiance Campaign helped to re-establish the credentials of the ANC as the organisation which represented the interests of the African section of the population. It also cemented the cross-party alliance which reached its apotheosis at the Congress of the People in Kliptown in 1955. Here some 3000 delegates from a number of organisations – notably the ANC, the NIC, the Coloured People's Organisation and the white Congress of Democrats – adopted the Freedom Charter.

This seminal document provided the statement of principles on which the Congress Alliance was founded, and which the ANC continued to adhere until the end of the struggle against apartheid. The commitment to a multiracial future was apparent in the opening paragraph which proclaimed that South Africa belonged to all of its people regardless of race. It also insisted on equal access to educational provision and cultural expression. The Charter was most ambiguous in the paragraphs which touched on economic issues, reflecting the fact that its adherents ranged ideologically from Communists to orthodox liberals. The Charter spoke of state ownership of the commanding heights of the economy, and appeared to advocate the nationalisation of land, but other than that the terrain upon which the state and the private sector were expected to meet was left unclear. Since the Freedom Charter was never intended as a blueprint for a post-apartheid order, this is not too surprising. It was also good politics because a document which was more precise might have exposed ideological cleavages. As it happened, Marxists and liberals could both see their vision of a new South Africa reflected in the same document. In fact, the ANC came to internalise this ideological catholicism. Anticipating its proscription under the Suppression of Communism Act, the CPSA disbanded in 1950. It later re-established itself covertly as the South African Communist Party (SACP), which established an overlapping membership with the ANC. Whereas most ANC members remained nationalists first and foremost, a large proportion of senior executives were simultaneously SACP members. This arrangement ultimately became accepted as normal, assisted perhaps by the SACP's acceptance that since South Africa was afflicted by 'colonialism of a special type'. If the revolution had to wait its turn, then non-Communists felt more at ease than they might have done if the SACP had been more tinged with Trotskyism.

In the short run, however, the united front did produce its fallout. Within the ANC, there remained a certain body of opinion who worried that the leadership was abandoning its commitment to 'Africanist' principles in its enthusiasm to work with other parties. They were particularly suspicious of white activists. However, well-intentioned the latter might appear to be, it was argued, they would never be happy unless they were running the show. White Communists, who might have been expected to be more palatable to Africanists than their liberal counterparts, were actually regarded with greater suspicion because they seemed bent on detracting from what was a race issue by introducing questions of class. The Africanists were also critical of the fruits of the civil disobedience campaigns. In 1956, the government had responded with the arrest of the leaders on grounds of treason, thereby throwing the ANC into some disarray. Those who took over the running of the ANC lacked the political skills of those they were replacing, and stood accused of manipulating internal party elections. By the end of 1957, a dissident faction in the Transvaal, led by Potlake Leballo, was openly attacking way the ANC was run as well as the merits of the Congress Alliance. In November 1958, the split finally came into the open with the breakaway of the Africanists who had failed to take over the Transvaal provincial conference. The rebels issued a statement which stated that they stood by the 1949 Programme of Action and asserted fidelity to the original principles of the ANC Youth League. They also rejected the terms of the Freedom Charter. In April 1959, the Pan-Africanist Congress (PAC) was formally launched with Robert Sobukwe as president and Leballo as national secretary.

In her analysis of the formation of the PAC, Gail Gerhart points to a number of factors which influenced its orientation.[152] First of all, she observes that the secessionists were drawn from an age cohort below that of the ANC leadership, thus repeating a longstanding pattern of generational cleavages within the party. Secondly, the PAC was profoundly influenced by events unfolding elsewhere in Africa. It believed that its no-nonsense adherence to nationalism was in step with the dominant trends elsewhere and that it was the multi-racialism of the ANC which was outmoded. Africanists were inspired by the All-African People's Conference convened by Kwame Nkrumah in December 1958. The PAC's *Manifesto* pledged support for Nkrumah's dream of a United States of Africa, while its chosen flag consisted of a gold star against a black background, with Ghana at its epicentre. Whereas the ANC accepted that whites were in South Africa to stay, the PAC could claim that the size of the white population became quite insignificant when measured against that of a united Africa. As Sobukwe put it: 'We are not fourteen million. We are two hundred [and] thirty-two million.'[153] With some subtlety, Sobukwe rejected ANC charges that it was xenophobic by countering that it was meaningful to talk of non-racialism only once liberation had been achieved. Until that point, whites could not be trusted because their material interests lay in a perpetuation of the structures of racial domination, whatever their intellectual conversion. Although the PAC welcomed Coloureds into the fold, and Sobukwe believed that ordinary Indians should be accepted, the party remained suspicious of the Asian community.[154] Thirdly, an important strand in PAC thinking was drawn from the Africanism of Lembede and the Youth League of the 1940s. Sobukwe, in particular, insisted that liberation had to be as much psychological as physical in character. A pride in being African – and sharing in its historical and cultural achievements – was a necessary precondition for genuine liberation.

There is one final element which Gerhart regards as crucial in the makeup of the PAC, and which was in many respects its fatal flaw: this was its belief in the spontaneity of the masses. Whereas the ANC leadership tried to marshal popular protest from above, the PAC believed that it was in tune with the aspirations of ordinary Africans who experienced degrading treatment every day of their lives and were merely waiting for the opportunity to strike back. Comparing the membership of the two organisations, Gerhart concludes that the ANC and PAC profiles were broadly similar, except that the ANC was more popular amongst industrial workers, while the PAC had greater support amongst teachers and students. However, one other difference she notes is the attraction to the PAC of 'location boys', defined as 'a type of young, urbanised African who falls outside and somewhere in between the proletariat proper and the respectable middle class'.[155] These were young men who possessed some skills, but limited opportunities for advancement, and who therefore felt their exclusion all the more intensely. It was this 'volatile element' which found the PAC message of direct action most attractive. Although Sobukwe appreciated the coercive capacities of the state, Gerhart suggests that he became swept along with the enthusiasm for lighting the spark which would ignite the fires of popular anger.

Conscious of the fact that it was competing with the ANC for the loyalties of the people, the PAC decided to pre-empt the latter's anti-pass campaign, which was scheduled for 31 March 1960. The PAC planned an identical campaign of 'positive action' (again borrowing from a Ghanaian script) on 21 March, when PAC supporters would present themselves for arrest at police stations across the country. In some way that was never clearly thought through, it was believed that the campaign would provoke a mass uprising from below. However, the day of action had disastrous consequences when policemen at Sharpeville, outside Vereeniging, panicked and opened fire on the crowd which had gathered, killing 67 and wounding 168 others.[156] At Langa, near Cape Town, the killing of two other protestors was followed by further rioting. The result was without doubt a public relations disaster for the government which was haunted by Sharpeville for decades to come. But it also had devastating consequences for the PAC and the ANC alike. The government proceeded to crack down hard on the protests which erupted in the wake of the killings. Contradicting the faith which the PAC had placed in a mass uprising, the state was able to crush the resistance with comparative ease. It also rounded up most of the leaders who were thought to be behind the events, including Sobukwe and Leballo. As a result, the PAC was rendered virtually leaderless overnight. Indeed Gerhart observes that the police arrested officeholders down to the third and fourth levels, bringing about organisational collapse. Wasting little time, the government also pushed the Unlawful Organisations Bill through Parliament which enabled it to proclaim the ANC and the PAC banned organisations. This momentous act took the ANC by surprise as much as the PAC.

The first round had clearly gone to the government, and this demanded the kind of rethink which had occurred in different circumstances in Guinea-Bissau and Mozambique. The faith which the ANC and the PAC had placed in civil disobedience now seemed naively misplaced. In each case, therefore, a decision was taken to embark upon some form of armed struggle. In the case of the ANC, an armed wing was established in 1961 under the name of Umkhonto we Sizwe (meaning Spear of the Nation), or MK as it was more popularly known. The ANC began training guerrillas with a view to carrying out acts of sabotage within South Africa. As we have already seen, some of these later fought alongside ZANU inside Rhodesia. However, the MK suffered a terrible setback when its High Command was caught red-handed at Rivonia farm in 1963, following the earlier capture of Nelson Mandela. In the trial which ensued, the defence led by Bram Fischer managed to ward off the death sentence, but only at the cost of hefty prison sentences. Mandela himself was to spend the next 27 years in prison, 18 of them on Robben Island, along with Walter Sisulu, Govan Mbeki and others. Although Mandela became a powerful symbol for the ANC, thereby turning a disaster into something of a political resource, there is no escaping the fact that the ANC lost the services of its real leadership for close on three decades. MK continued to exist, but it had failed to fire a single shot within South Africa prior to 1976.[157] The reality was that the South African state was able to secure its borders relatively easily and succeeded in asserting a vice-like grip on the countryside. Thereafter, MK managed to carry out some bombings and high-profile acts of sabotage in the cities, but these hardly made more than a psychological ripple. Even once Zimbabwe and Mozambican independence had brought the frontline onto South Africa's own borders, there was never a realistic prospect of achieving liberation through guerrilla warfare. The ANC was therefore forced to look for ways of battening onto new forms of urban protest when these emerged in the 1970s and 1980s.

In the case of the PAC, the fallout from the events of 1960 were even more serious. Their talented leader, Sobukwe, was imprisoned for treason and then held under a special detention order until his premature death from lung cancer. What survived of the leadership retreated into exile where they aimed to commence guerrilla operations, but with even less success than the ANC. In later years, the PAC was riven by leadership struggles which rendered it ineffective. However, before the PAC vacated South African soil it engaged in one last attempt to engage the state head-on. With its national leadership in prison (like Sobukwe) or in exile, divisions emerged between the next tier and the lower echelons of the party. Eventually, it was decided to dissolve into smaller cells which would be less susceptible to police infiltration. Out of this new structure emerged a plan for a general insurrection which would be centered on the rural areas. As we saw in Chapter 4, there had already been widespread rural resistance to 'betterment schemes' and Bantu Authorities since the 1950s, but the main political organisations had not paid very much attention to them. The emergence of *Poqo* signalled the PAC's intention to switch its focus to rural insurrection.[158] Tom Lodge observes that *Poqo* had a limited following in the Transvaal and even less in the Orange Free State and Natal, but in the Cape Province and in the Transkei it enjoyed much greater success.[159] Lodge's assessment of its following in its Cape stronghold is was that it was very much a movement from below, being composed of 'the inmates of migrant workers' hostels, employer's compounds, as well as farm labourers'.[160] The migrant workers who formed the core constituency, spread the movement into the Transkei where there was already substantial opposition to collaborationist chiefs. *Poqo* bands had something in common with Mau Mau fighters, in terms of their youth, acute sense of deprivation and a willingness to resort to violence. And in each case, it was the decapitation of the political leadership which provided them with their chance to take control.

In November 1962, *Poqo* groups had already launched an attack on Paarl, in the Cape winelands, and others had been arrested en route to assassinate Chief Kaiser Matanzima. Responding to pressures from below, the exiled leadership eventually decided upon a co-ordinated general uprising which was scheduled to start in April 1963. Lodge describes the plan of action as follows:

> In each centre different groups would be assigned to attacks on police stations, post offices, power installations and other government buildings. Groups should then turn their attention to the white civilian population which they were to kill indiscriminately. The killings should go on for four hours and should then cease, when the insurgents should await further instructions.[161]

However, because the exiled leadership had chosen to use the official mail system, the police received detailed news of the plot and began arresting *Poqo* suspects en masse. The result was that the rebellion went off half-cock. By June 1964, no fewer than 1162 *Poqo* activists had been prosecuted. Lodge notes that *Poqo* activities continued spasmodically until 1968, but to all intents and purposes this sorry episode put paid to a strategy of liberation based on rural insurrection.[162]

In the wake of these trials of strength which had gone very badly for the liberation movements, the initiative very much lay with the government for the rest of the decade. Africans were forced to comply once again with the humiliating pass laws and other discriminatory legislation. The Vorster government had the principal ANC and PAC leaders safely tucked away behind bars, while the rest were languishing in an impotent exile. In fact, both organisations effectively ceased to operate within South Africa for the next decade. To cap it all, the defeat of internal opposition coincided with the start of a decade of economic boom – as South African growth rates hit 6 per cent per annum – which translated into rising living standards for whites.[163] This further strengthened white confidence in the direction which the NP had mapped out. The churches and the white University campuses continued to harbour opposition to apartheid, and Helen Suzman remained a highly effective critic within Parliament, but for the most part whites were comfortable with apartheid even if they were not always swayed by the grand statements. On the other side, the strictures associated with the tightening of influx controls, and the limits placed on African accumulation in the countryside and in the cities alike, assured that material prosperity was a racially exclusive experience.

In the early 1970s, just when the morale of the opposition had reached its lowest ebb, the tectonic plates of the South African polity began to shift – almost imperceptibly at first, but then with a compelling force which could not be ignored. After a series of political tremors on University campuses and at the workplace, resistance finally exploded in the townships of Soweto, which surround Johannesburg, in early 1976.[164] It is noteworthy that the banned political organisations were spectators in these events, as the way was led by groups which had not been part of the ANC and PAC campaigns of the 1950s. In what is still the most detailed examination of these events, Baruch Hirson identifies two developments which provided the dress-rehearsal for the main event. The first is the emergence of the Black Consciousness movement, which revived many of the Africanist themes which had been articulated by the ANC Youth League and subsequently by the PAC in the 1940s and 1950s. However, the bearers of the Black Consciousness banner were either University students, who were too young to have had direct experience of either organisation, or were people had long since parted company with their former colleagues who regarded them as sell-outs.[165] On the non-white University campuses, the South African Students Organisation (SASO) was formed in 1969 as a break-away from the National Union of African Students (NUSAS) which it claimed was too much under the control of white students. SASO aimed to represent Black students, defined so as to include not just African and Coloureds, but Indians as well. Having scored some success on the campuses, where SASO challenged the reality of inferior facilities and the authoritarian structures of University administration, it sought to spread its ideas to an urban constituency. In July 1972, SASO was one of the co-sponsors of the Black People's Convention (BPC) which sought to give greater organisational expression to Black Consciousness. Most of the other six co-sponsors came from Black theology organisations which were seeking to develop a form of religious expression which would break free of white structures and cultural aesthetics.

As an ideology, Black Consciousness was pretty amorphous, and its exponents did not necessarily agree of all the constituent ingredients. However, a number can be isolated. First of all, there was a concern with Black self-reliance, which was informed by a tradition of non-co-operation, but also drew on Tanzanian socialism and even on the Black Power strand within black American politics.[166] In practical terms, this translated into an unwillingness to work with whites, a policy of principled non-co-operation with apartheid structures, as well as an obsession with emancipating Blacks from their supposed psychological oppression.[167] The promotion of Black theology, which was written into the founding principles of the BPC fitted in here as well. The insistence on Black Consciousness being a 'state of mind' made it an easy target for left-wing critics who pointed out that it was an intellectual construct rather than a guide to action. At the same time, white liberals complained that much of its message amounted to the blackening of apartheid doctrine, with its insistence on distinct racial attributes.

Over time, Black Consciousness became less of an abstraction. Much as the PAC had previously drawn inspiration from the first wave of decolonisation, the Black Consciousness movement was invigorated by the sudden advent of independence in the Portuguese colonies. In September 1974, the BPC and SASO organised 'Viva Frelimo' rallies and further jubilation ensued when South Africa troops were forced to pull back from Angola at the start of 1976 (see above). Secondly, there was a concern with improving access to education, which often took a very practical form – such as SASO's promotion of literacy and other improvement projects. And thirdly, the Black Consciousness Movement advocated the promotion of Black business, and 'buying Black', as a means to liberation – echoing the agenda of Pan-Africanists in West Africa during the interwar period. There was some ambiguity on this score because the insistence on the virtues of African communalism, which was allegedly untainted by class divisions, did not sit easily with the advocacy of Black accumulation.[168] Steve Biko was damning about white liberals, but also impatient with those Marxists – especially white ones – who insisted that the South African struggle was really a matter of class. For Biko, it was all about racial domination which was why Coloured and Indians were to be counted in and whites were not to be trusted.

Hirson argues that there was nothing which SASO did on a day-to-day basis which was significantly different to the programmes of NUSAS. Moreover, he concludes that while banning and detentions had severely disrupted the movement by 1975, the marginality of SASO and the BPC in the events of 1976 was symptomatic of a failure to formulate a coherent political strategy and to speak in terms which were relevant to the masses.[169] Nevertheless, Gerhart makes the point that the Black Consciousness movement had shifted the political terrain to the extent that Gatsha Buthelezi, who had previously been taken seriously by opponents of the system, now seemed seriously out of step.[170] Moreover, the Black Consciousness movement helped to broker a closer association between Africans, Coloureds and Indians which was a substantial achievement in the light of previous divisions. Finally, Gerhart credits SASO leaders with injecting greater political consciousness into high school students which bore fruit in the Soweto rising.[171] The South African Students Movement (SASM), which was formed in Soweto in 1972, and the National Youth Organisation (NAYO) which followed in 1973, represented the first systematic attempts to organise school pupils. In each case, there were identifiable links to SASO and the Black Consciousness movement.

The second development, which was at least as important in setting the scene, was an upsurge in labour unrest during the early 1970s, after a decade of relative quiescence. One of the peculiarities of South African labour relations was that the apartheid regime and the employers had managed to ensure that most Africans remained non-unionised. Moreover, they were denied the right to strike. In the early 1970s, South Africa began to experience rapid inflation which arose partly out of wage increases paid to white workers in order to compensate for a shortage of skilled labour, and later out of global inflation following the OPEC oil embargo.[172] The steep price rises affected African workers most of all, because food and transportation costs rose fastest, and beginning in 1973 there was a veritable epidemic of strike activity.[173] The unrest began in the Durban docks and then spread to industrial establishments in Natal, before jumping to the textile industry nationwide, and the gold mines and the industrial enterprises of the Witwatersrand, before touching down in the car factories of East London in 1974. Hirson observes that these strikes were very difficult to resolve because there was often no union leadership to negotiate with. Indeed workers refused to appoint leaders for fear of victimisation. Apart from the wage increases, which were significant achievements in their own right, a lasting consequence was that the government was forced to design a system of industrial relations which included the right of Africans to strike. The strike wave had largely petered out by the outbreak of the Soweto rising, although some disputes continued simultaneously with it. The significance of the labour unrest lay above all in demonstrating the results which could flow from collective action after a decade of demoralisation.

The Soweto rising of 1976 was a far more substantial affair than the Sharpeville episode with which it has become mnemonically linked. It also embodied a very different cast of characters. The ANC and the PAC were scarcely involved until the later stages, and the leaders of the Black Consciousness movement were themselves fairly marginal to events, many having already been arrested by this point. Moreover, the trade unions had few points of contact with a phenomenon which was centered on the townships as a site of struggle. What is truly extraordinary about the 1976 rising was that it was led by school pupils, many of whom were in their early teens. Their targets were at first purely educational, but by the end of the year the focus of their attack had widened to include apartheid itself. Bantu Education had constituted one of the most hated aspects of the apartheid system because it blocked the remaining avenues for self-enhancement. By the end of the 1960s some of the contradictions inherent in the apartheid system began to surface. While it might make good Afrikaner politics to restrict African access to schooling, the reality was that the South African economy was becoming extremely short of skilled labour. The government therefore expanded educational provision for Africans, and most importantly widened secondary school access. In the ten year period after 1965, African secondary school enrolments jumped from 66,906 to 318,568, while total African enrolments leaped from 1.96 million to 3.68 million.[174] In Soweto itself, the number of secondary school enrolments rose from 12,656 in 1972 to 34,656 in 1976.[175] However, the Vorster regime remained extremely reluctant to finance adequate classroom accommodation, school books and other basic facilities. The inevitable outcome was that while many more Africans could gain access to a secondary education, what they received was of poor quality and manifestly inferior to what white children were receiving. The statistics speak for themselves: whereas the state spent 605 Rand annually on each white child, the equivalent was 125 Rand for Coloureds and 40 Rand for Africans.[176] In 1976, a crisis loomed in many schools when a reduction in the number of years Africans would spend in primary school produced a bottleneck in the first year of secondary school. Against this background, the spark which ignited open resistance was the announcement that Afrikaans would be introduced as the medium of instruction for half of the secondary school subjects, including maths. This sheer obtuseness of this official dictat, which scarcely made much sense in terms of apartheid ideology, evoked a storm of protest given that most Africans (unlike Coloureds) had no more than a smattering of Afrikaans.

On 16 June 1976, following a rash of boycotts in Soweto schools over the language issue, SASM organised a demonstration which was attended by some 15,000 pupils between the ages of ten and twenty.[177] After the police opened fire on the crowd, rioting broke out across Soweto which swept up workers returning home at the end of the day. The police resorted to the use of live ammunition and admitted to having killed 96 and wounding more than a thousand in only the first three days. As news of police violence spread, similar actions broke out elsewhere in the Transvaal and in the homelands, before eventually reaching the Western and Eastern Cape in August. According to Hirson, Natal remained relatively quiet and only the homelands of Transkei and Kwazulu were more or less immune from the upheaval.[178] Throughout South Africa, schools were closed down and a variety of student bodies, modelled on the Soweto Students Representative Council (SSRC), engaged in collective acts of resistance. Crowds of youths targeted government buildings and those of the Administration Boards, as well as beer halls, bottle stores (recognised liquor outlets) and shebeens (illegal outlets) for destruction. The choice of the first target needs little elaboration. The municipal beer halls and liquor outlets were attacked because they gathered the revenue on which much of the urban administration ran. However, the inclusion of shebeens also demonstrated a determination to confront the culture of hard drinking for which the youth blamed the enervation of the older generation.[179] Whereas in Zimbabwe, generational conflict was rooted in rural patriarchy, in the South African townships it was the emasculation of the Sharpeville generation which brought tensions to the fore.

The SSRC, which was made up of delegates from schools across Soweto, could only claim to represent the secondary school students. These were derived from a relatively privileged section of society, but the SSRC was surprisingly successful in winning wider support for many of its initiatives.[180] The mass of urban youths who had not had the opportunity to further their education often joined the protests even if they would not have been the beneficiaries of government concessions. Even the *tsotsis*, urban criminals who were widely feared, gave some backing to the protests. Looting could be seen as self-serving, and acts of violence conformed to a *tsotsi* mentality, but once the pupils had embarked on a head-on confrontation with the state, they were almost bound to attract the sympathy of *tsotsis* who were in constant conflict with the police themselves – a point which is brought out in 'Mapantsula', a film which traces the transformation of a *tsotsi* into a 'comrade' in the early 1980s.[181] It is therefore noteworthy that, according to Hirson, there was a decrease in urban crime at the time of the revolt.

Once the SSRC decided to widen its appeal, it also enjoyed some success in encouraging workers to comply with calls to stay at home. On three occasions over August and September, workers in Soweto brought the industrial heartlands of Johannesburg to a halt. Migrant workers living in the hostels were less easy to reach and the authorities eventually became alert to the divisive possibilities which lay in arming them against the students. However, other workers stayed away in sympathy, although as Hirson argues this was a tactic which needed to be used very sparingly. When the SSRC overplayed its hand, workers refused to comply, highlighting a lingering gap between young students and adult workers who were living close enough to the economic margins as it was. The small urban middle class was the most ambivalent of all. Many of its leading lights were members of the Urban Bantu Councils (UBCs) which acted in an advisory capacity to the Administration Boards. The SSRC scored a startling (if momentary) victory in forcing the Soweto UBC to resign in April 1977.[182]

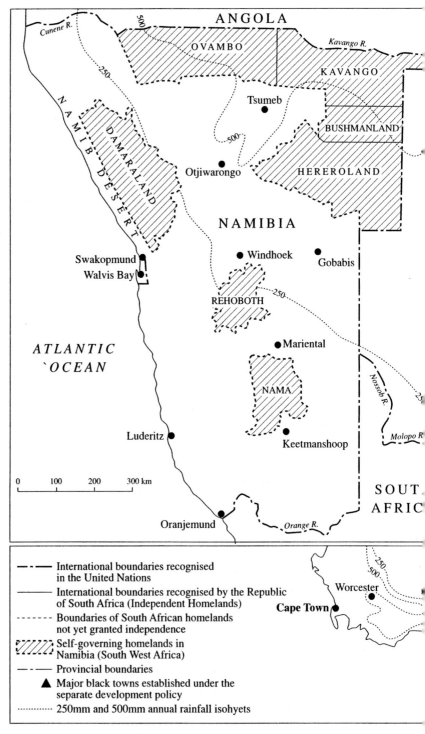

Map 6 African homelands in 1984
From Rodney Davenport and Christopher Saunders, *South Africa: A Modern History*, fifth edition
(Basingstoke: Macmillan (now Palgrave Macmillan), 2000), p. 433.

Reproduced with permission of Palgrave Macmillan.

In other parts of the country, student leaders also enjoyed some success in bringing Coloured students and urban residents out in sympathy, even if co-ordinating activities between physically segregated communities proved well-nigh impossible.

The SSRC campaign had started as a demand for the withdrawal of Afrikaans-medium education, and in this it was successful. The students also demanded an end to the Bantu Education system which the Vorster regime was obviously unwilling to countenance. When student activists attacked apartheid as an entire system they were focusing on a target which was far beyond their collective might. Hence members of the SSRC met with the ANC in exile, and the latter began to play more of a role behind the scenes. For its part, the NP imagined the playing out of a grand conspiracy and used every weapon in its armoury to crush the rebellion. Many hundreds of children and young people were killed – the official death toll was 195 killed and 410 injured, but a more realistic figure is 1000 killed and more than 5000 injured – while 21,435 were prosecuted for public order offences.[183] Eventually, the weight of government repression proved too great for the revolt to be sustained. The arrest of successive cohorts of student leaders, and the flight into exile of many others, brought about organisational fatigue. Moreover, urban workers were reluctant to be drawn into costly confrontation. In early 1977 the drift back to school began and the momentum dissipated.

The long-term consequences of the revolt were still profound. On the one side, the ANC gained many new members as up to five thousand student activists fled the country, as well as renewed 'street cred' within the country.[184] The Black Consciousness movement by contrast failed to consolidate its position in a way which might have been anticipated. Its principal organisations were banned in 1977 and many of its leaders were imprisoned, detained or, as in the case of Steve Biko, killed. When the Azanian People's Organisation (AZAPO) was formed the following year, it introduced a very different slant to Africanist politics. Finally, the PAC remained a moribund organisation given more to rhetorical flourishes, delivered from a safe distance, than action. On the other hand, the government recognised the need to engage in more serious effort to build structures of collaboration in the urban areas which could act as political shock-absorbers. This was to shape the next round of political struggles when the shortening cycle of resistance came around again in the mid-1980s.

With the resignation of John Vorster as Prime Minister in 1978, the NP embarked upon a change of direction which is sometimes as described as 'reform apartheid'. What this meant was that a new administration under P. W. Botha sought to dispense with those aspects of apartheid which were either considered unworkable or which attracted undue international opprobrium, whilst clinging on to what were considered to be the essentials. Even the latter were given a new verbal dusting to excise many of the words in the apartheid lexicon which were considered offensive: hence the language of separate development was replaced with the apparently more acceptable terminology of 'group rights' and consociationalism. Indeed, Botha proclaimed that apartheid itself was dead. However, not everyone in the NP could agree on what was expendable, and those who were inclined to look for the thin end of the wedge seceded to form the Conservative Party (CP) under the leadership of Andries Treurnicht in

1982. The latter had a serious point to make which was that if apartheid was an interlocking system – held in place by a closely knit web of laws and regulations– politicians tinkered with it at their peril. Even to tap into an international discourse of 'rights' was considered dangerous because it narrowed white South Africa's margins for manoeuvre. Botha was, however, able to persuade the majority of the party and the white electorate that they must, as he put it, 'adapt or die' As far as the 'non-white' majority was concerned, reform apartheid offered a combination of carrots and sticks.

As Robert Price maintains, reform and repression should not be considered as alternatives, but as opposite sides of the same coin: the one offering limited amelioration as the other lowered expectations about the feasibility of a more radical alternative.[185] On the repressive side of the equation, the government continued to ban and detain individuals who fraternised with proscribed organisations or who engaged in activities which were construed as threatening to the security of the state. On the reform side, the regime offered the possibility of co-optation to Coloureds, Indians and some Africans. The entire package, which included a mixture of inducements and threats against South Africa's neighbours, was dubbed 'total strategy'. The stated aim was to wage a multi-dimensional campaign against international and domestic threats to white rule in the 'ideological, military, economic, social, psychological, cultural, political and diplomatic fields'.[186] In order to mount this strategic response, the decision-making apparatus was itself restructured. The Prime Ministerial system was replaced with an executive Presidency, in which the incumbent would be advised by a State Security Council (which included the head of the Army, Police and intelligence services and some senior Cabinet Ministers) and a National Security Management System designed to improve implementation of government policy on the ground.

The government had been brought to this point by a combination of factors. Most obviously, there was the fallout from the Soweto uprising which had attracted unprecedented criticism from abroad and a UN arms embargo, but also a flight of the foreign capital. As result of political lobbying in Western countries, South Africa also found it difficult to raise loans from international banks. However, the even bleaker reality was that the South African economy had already begun to run into trouble before the events of 1976, pointing to deeper structural problems. The government was being told by private businessmen and its economic advisors alike that apartheid was itself to blame because Bantu Education policies had created a critical shortage of skilled labour; that influx control was both highly inefficient in allocating labour and was impeding the internal African market for manufactured goods; and that a poor international image was scaring investors away, whilst making it very difficult for South African industries to carve out other export niches. After 1976, when the growth rate fell back to 2.8 per annum, the boom years of the late 1960s seemed like a distant memory.

The Riekert Commission of Enquiry, which was set up to look into influx control, reported in 1978 and its recommendations played an important in reshaping apartheid doctrine. Riekert urged the government to abandon the fiction that all Africans were temporary sojourners in the cities and to render more meaningful the distinction between urban Africans (those who qualified under Section 10) and those who remained tied to their rural roots. It suggested that the former should be accorded complete mobility (to enable them to move in search of work), the right to bring their families with them, and the chance to buy their own houses. Out of this report emerged an about-turn in official policy – indeed a veritable heresy in Verwoerdian terms – which had as its centrepiece the nurturing of a stable African urban population, undergirded by a solid middle class which would have a stake in the maintenance of the system. These urban Africans would be encouraged to buy their own homes, they would be given greater freedom to establish their own businesses and money would be found to expand and improve their amenities. Moreover, whereas the urban areas had previously been run by white-run Administration Boards, real powers were to be devolved onto elected Community Councils. Following the advice of the Wiehahn Commission, which reported in 1979, fully urban Africans were to be permitted to join trade unions which would henceforth be formally registered. As in other parts of Africa in the 1940s and 1950s, these were considered preferable to a proliferation of unofficial unions which were not bound by any regulations and which could lend themselves to 'political agitation'. Under the right circumstances, it was reasoned, unions would concentrate on bread-and-butter issues. As for the majority of Africans, the government continued to insist that their homes were in the rural areas. Non-urbanised workers would preferably live in dormitory towns serving industry located on the edge of the homelands. But if they were needed in the 'white' cities they should be confined to hostels and other temporary accommodation. Hence the government remained as committed to the principle of influx control as before – as born out by the repeated destruction of squatter camps on the fringes of Cape Town – but hoped to shift some of the burden of implementation onto employers and landlords.

Much government thinking centered on recreating the preconditions for sustained economic growth. But there was evidently a political logic to the reform agenda as well. The underlying aim of these reforms was to divide the ranks of Africans and to render those who were given the inside track more amenable. Once they had a stake in the urban environment, it was thought, they too would have a vested interest in keeping their country cousins at bay. This would create some basis for a cross-racial alliance. However, the demographic realities of urban South Africa posed a perennial headache for the government. Even assuming that urbanisation could be checked, which was a tall order given the vast number of illegal arrivals who continued to flock to the cities, the whites would still be outnumbered. The Botha regime spoke of recognising the urban rights of 5 million urban Africans, but even these would have outnumbered the estimated 4.5 million whites. When 2.5 million Coloureds and 1 million Indians were added to the total, whites were destined to remain a clear minority and that was clearly disconcerting. For this reason, the Botha regime struggled to find a formula which would defeat the laws of simple arithmetic. In the interim, it introduced a new constitution in 1984 which brought Coloureds and Indians into the political process. A tricameral Parliament was set up in which each house would vote on 'own' issues while the three houses together would deliberate on areas of common concern. Conveniently, the white chamber was larger than the other two put together, which ensured that power would remain within white hands. Africans remained on the outside looking in, although the government spoke of creating African 'city-states' which might ultimately federate with the other three racial groups. No real progress had been made by the mid-1980s at which point a resurgence of internal opposition had overtaken the reform agenda.

For reform apartheid to bear the desired fruit, it was essential that enough 'non-whites' should accept the revised rules of the game. If it failed on this count, there was no realistic prospect that international pressure would subside and every chance that further outbreaks of resistance would send the South African economy into even deeper crisis. Reform was a calculated risk and one which ultimately proved unrewarding. One reason was that few people, either within South Africa or beyond its borders (with the exception of Reagan and Thatcher), was fooled by the talk of a new dispensation. For most critics, the reforms were clearly designed to reinvent white supremacy. Another reason was that the reforms took an excessive length of time to implement. Although a number of crucial policy changes had been announced before the close of the 1970s, it was only in 1986 that the Immorality Act, the Mixed Marriages Act and the 72-hour provisions of the Group Areas Act were actually repealed along with the pass laws.[187] By that point, it was too late for a political dividend to accrue because the townships were already in flames. Moreover, minimal progress was made in terms of infrastructural improvements within the townships, and pitifully few Africans managed to acquire their own homes.[188] At the same time, the authorities remained powerless to stem the tide of illegal urban migration which was an essential requirement for cultivating a category or 'urban insiders'.[189] Finally, the government expected many of the material improvements to follow indirectly from accelerated economic growth, rather than by means of increased public expenditure. However, this growth was itself contingent on the working through of many of the reforms. The vicious circle was one which the government could not escape, especially as the more auspicious economic omens of 1980, when the country registered a 5 per cent growth rate, turned out to be a temporary blip. Between the end of 1980 and the beginning of 1986, the economy had grown by a total of less than 4 per cent.[190] The rate of inflation had soared to 12 per cent by mid-1984 and an estimated 1.5 million Africans, or between 15 and 25 per cent of the black labour force, was unemployed.[191] Under these circumstances, 'urban insiders' were hardly likely to feel prosperous or thankful to the government. Indeed, attitude surveys conducted at the time pointed to a sense of alienation which was greater than ever before.

After the Soweto revolt died down, a period or relative tranquillity had ensued. But whereas the post-Sharpeville decade had been characterised by widespread demoralisation, this time it was as if opposition forces were merely catching their breath. At the turn of the 1980s, there was a remarkable efflorescence of associational life in the cities which eventually provided the political synthesis which had been lacking in 1960 and 1976. When Community Councils were forced to substantially increase rents, a myriad of local associations sprang up to mobilise non-payment campaigns on the basis that there were no decent amenities to point to. After some time, these associations banded together to form larger federations, spawning the new phenomenon of the 'civics' (or civic associations). The civics imposed a deep imprint on township politics because of the emphasis they placed on popular decision-making and public accountability. At the same time, workers who complained of steep rises in transport costs participated in a wave of bus boycotts, which again assumed a more organised character over time. There was also a revival of student activism within the secondary schools, led by the Congress of South African Students (COSAS) which was formed in 1979. From the early 1980s, there were a renewed outbreak of boycotts and school closures, as a new cohort of students complained about inferior facilities and consequently high failure rates.[192]

Finally, there was a resurgence of militancy within the labour movement as rising inflation ate into wage packets. Following government recognition of registered unions, workers resorted to repeated strike action over familiar grievances about pay and conditions – only now union recognition was added to the list. In 1982, a rash of wildcat strikes led to the highest number of workdays lost since 1973 and this was further exceeded in 1984. That year, the National Union of Mineworkers (NUM), which had won grudging recognition from the Chamber of Mines, engaged in a bitter strike which culminated in many deaths and injuries.[193] The labour movement, which was potentially a powerful player in South African politics, was however divided over the extent to which it was desirable to link up with wider struggles in the townships. Some independent general unions, like the South African Allied Workers Union (SAAWU) took the view that it was meaningless to distinguish between community and labour struggles and willingly pitched in. A number of these joined the United Democratic Front (UDF) in 1983. Other unions, especially those under the umbrella of the Federation of South African Trade Unions (FOSATU) were worried that they would compromise the interests of their members if they jumped aboard a bandwagon which was being driven by non-workers.[194] Nevertheless, once the township revolt began in earnest all trade unions inevitably became drawn into the politics of confrontation. In June 1985, the Confederation of African Trade Unions (COSATU) was formed by FOSATU, the NUM and a number of the independent unions. The new super-federation brought together 34 affiliated unions with a combined membership of more than 500,000 members, making it the largest in the country. Interestingly, despite the earlier caution of FOSATU affiliates, COSATU adopted an explicitly political orientation. Its first policy statement set the tone when it made a number of demands, including the removal of the SADF from the townships, the unbanning of proscribed organisations and the repeal of racist legislation.[195]

The actions of the civics, the student movement and the unions fed off each other and together generated a level of mass activism which was extraordinary by any standard – and certainly far in advance of what is encountered in most Western democracies. The countryside lagged behind, but by the mid-1980s the spirit of rebellion had spread to some rural areas with a tradition of resistance, like Sekhukhuneland. The various campaigns typically began by addressing single-issue grievances and bread-and-butter demands, but as they escalated and cross-fertilised each other they assumed the form of a frontal attack on the apartheid state. The formation of the National Forum and the UDF in 1983, both of which brought together a diverse range of civics, student associations, sporting bodies and trade unions, represented an important watershed in this respect.[196] These two broad fronts explicitly linked their campaigns to a longer tradition of opposition to the apartheid state. The UDF presented itself as a direct heir to the Congress Alliance of the early 1950s and openly subscribed to the inclusive principles of the Freedom Charter.[197] Although the UDF was never simply an ANC front, most of its members looked approvingly upon the grandfather of South African liberation movements. The National Forum, by contrast, represented a reworking of the Africanist tradition which had already mutated several times since the 1940s. The insistence on Black leadership was now married to Marxism (a significant step beyond Black Consciousness), leading to the insistence on the black working class as the only true agent of mass liberation. This position had been developed by AZAPO after 1978, but it also bore the accent of a distinctively Cape radical tradition dating back to the Non-European Unity Movement. It also enjoyed support within certain trade unions who established the Azanian Congress of Trade Unions (AZACTU) which remained outside COSATU. There was some overlap in membership between the UDF and the National Forum, but for the most part they differed openly in their approach to membership (the UDF allowed white affiliates whereas the NF did not), level of organisation (UDF structures were much more elaborate) and their very conception of liberation (a multi-racial democratic South Africa as opposed to a Black socialist state). Of the two, however, the UDF was the largest grouping by a significant margin.

Whereas the start of the Soweto revolt can be traced to one fateful day in June 1976, the revolt of the mid-1980s had been gathering a head steam since the start of the decade. If a moment needed to be isolated it would be the last week of August 1984 when a successful boycott of the Coloured and Indian elections to the tricameral Parliament was conducted.[198] A few days later, African protests broke out in townships to the northeast of Johannesburg and in the Vaal triangle to the south of the city. By the end of the first day, some fourteen people had been killed, the news of which brought more people onto the streets and into open conflict with the Police. From its epicentre in the Vaal triangle, the unrest spread to Soweto and the East Rand where township residents erected street barricades and engaged the police in pitched battles. In November, independent trade unions and civic groups joined forces to mount a two-day stayaway across the Transvaal which was the most successful action of this kind since the early 1950s.[199] Thereafter the contagion spread to the Eastern Cape, which became one of the fiercest battlegrounds over 1985. The townships of Port Elizabeth had a history of militancy which was reconfirmed in abundance, but what was more surprising was the intensity of the revolt in smaller towns across the region – such as one rural settlement where the Cradock Residents Association successfully mobilised an African population numbering 15,000 and turned the township into a virtual no-go area for the Police.[200] Finally, after some delay the uprising spread to the Durban area and the Western Cape in August 1985.

The pattern of the uprising was shaped by the dynamic interaction between the government and opposition forces. The latter resorted to a number of stratagems which were designed to break the structures of collaboration which the government was seeking to assemble. One objective was to cripple urban administration by forcing the membership of the Community Councils to resign en masse. Those who refused to comply were branded as traitors to the cause, their properties were destroyed and a good number were killed. In many areas, civics attempted to step in to the vacuum to operate an alternative administration. At the same time, youth endeavoured to turn the townships into 'liberated territory' by erecting street barricades, preventing the movement of traffic in and out, and engaging the Police in pitched battles. When riot Police failed to hold the line, the government sent in the SADF, thereby raising the stakes. As the revolt spread, troops freely resorted to the use of live ammunition and the virtually indiscriminate use of force. The declaration of a state of emergency in July 1985, initially covering 36 magisterial districts and eventually extended to the whole country in June 1986, granted immunity from prosecution to officials engaged in putting down the revolt. This effectively meant open season upon anyone found on the streets. The image which appeared on television screens across the world was one of well-armed soldiers, riding in armoured vehicles, firing at youths armed only with stones, bottles and petrol bombs. But when the uprising reached the Western Cape, the SADF began to come under small-arms fire, signalling a qualitative shift in the character of resistance.[201]

In 1986, the weight of government repression led to further modifications in opposition tactics. In the Eastern Cape, township residents engaged in a highly effective boycott of white businesses in order to persuade the latter to put pressure on the SADF to withdraw. The mass detention of community leaders also led to the emergence of street and area committees which would be less easy to break. These attempted to take over the affairs of the townships, dubbed 'liberated zones', and set up their own people's courts. The government's riposte was to fall back upon the tried-and-tested tactics of divide and rule. In some instances, Zulu policemen were used against rioters of other ethnic origins. In others, hostel workers were armed and unleashed against the 'comrades'. This became a particular feature of Kwazulu and Natal, where Inkatha joined forces with the government in seeking to drive UDF supporters out of townships like KwaMashu. The supreme irony of migrant workers being used to crush the supposed 'urban insiders' was scarcely noticed by a regime which was determined to crush the opposition. In many areas, ugly turf-wars ensued in which necklacing (involving the placing of a burning tyre over a victim) of people suspected of being either 'comrades' or 'collaborators' became a daily occurrence. For many urban residents, the stereotype of hostel dwellers was that of rural, innately conservative and politically ignorant barbarians. What tended to be forgotten was that it was migrant workers who had led the resistance to Bantu Authorities in the 1950s and who had been instrumental in the Western Cape *poqo* bands in the early 1960s.

The UDF recognised the dangers of hostel dwellers being turned against it and made some effort to regain the initiative by bringing them into the fold and then using them to spread insurrection to the countryside. In Sekhukhuneland, where migrant workers had established the highly successful Sebatakgomo association in the 1950s (see Chapter 4), this was a strategy which might have been expected to bear fruit. However, in an analysis which mirrors some of the Zimbabwean findings of Norma Kriger, Van Kessel observes that the resistance was already being led by youth (principally secondary school students) who were in open revolt against chiefs, parents and teachers. At a time of acute generational conflict, the youth tended to regard adult migrant workers as adversaries rather than allies.[202] Finally, government agents also posed as UDF or AZAPO supporters and carried out attacks on members of the other group, calculating (in many cases correctly) that this would precipitate tit-for-tat retaliation. By 1986 the government's riposte to opposition calls to render the townships ungovernable was to encourage a generalised state of violence which, it was calculated, would eventually intimidate and exhaust township dwellers. As a tactic for breaking the opposition, this worked passably well, but it came at an enormous social cost.

The cost for the victims who were caught in the crossfire between 'comrades' and vigilantes hardly needs stating. In the later stages of the revolt, the lines began to blur and many innocent people were the victims of one or other criminal outfit claiming to act in the name of the UDF or the forces of 'law and order'. But there was also a tremendous cost for the government in that it cemented the image of a country teetering on the brink of anarchy. Government restrictions on reporting came too late and were too leaky to prevent the images from getting out. One immediate result was a further flight of foreign capital – not for reasons of solidarity but simply because South Africa had become a high-risk proposition for investors. The currency plummeted, and the government was forced to introduce exchange controls and a moratorium on interest payment in order to steady the listing ship, but at some cost to business confidence. Because 'reform apartheid' was premised upon the recovery of economic buoyancy, the entire edifice which had been so carefully constructed by the new ideologues of the NP simply collapsed. There was no going back to classic apartheid for the NP, although the CP was arguing for doing so, but there was no obvious way forward either. In short, the Botha regime had reached a hegemonic crisis of epic proportions by 1986.

How much importance should be attached to the uprising of 1984–86? Sceptics point out that in the final event the opposition was ground down and that talk of a revolution was simply naive. But if the government seemed to emerge from the ruins more or less victorious, its reform package was in tatters which was precisely what the UDF and the National Forum had set out to achieve. As in the case of the Portuguese territories, victory did not have to come in a final conflagration: all that was required was to break down the other side's will to soldier on. The revolt of the mid-1980s was a critical turning point because white South Africans came to feel for the first time that the old order was no longer tenable or indeed in their self-interest. Intellectuals had been saying so for a long time, but now they were joined by businessmen (including Afrikaners who had once been loyal supporters) who openly criticised government policy and began meeting privately with the ANC. Ordinary whites were propelled in opposite directions – some to the right, others towards the centre – but a dramatic loss of confidence was manifested in so many telling ways, such as a growing refusal to respect orders for military conscription. This signalled the endgame of apartheid. As the 1980s drew to a close, the NP regime concentrated on trying to strengthen its hand sufficiently to be able to engage in negotiations with the very organisations which had been regarded as beyond the pale. We conclude this account in Chapter 9.

7.4   The end of South African rule in Namibia

Our final case is that of the struggle for the liberation of Namibia which could be seen as a hybrid of all the forms we have been considering. First of all, there were some echoes of the first wave of flag decolonisation during the 1950s and 1960s. SWA had been a League of Nations mandate on a par with the two Togolands, the two Cameroons, Tanganyika and Ruanda-Urundi. Prior to its dissolution in 1946, the League of Nations had invited the various mandatory powers to enter into trusteeship agreements with its successor, the United Nations. These various agreements presumed eventual 'self-government' or independence as the terminal point. Whereas the other territories duly received their independence in some shape or form, SWA missed out because of the intransigence of the administering power. South Africa refused to bring the territory under the trusteeship system, and in 1947 formally requested the UN to agree to its absorption on the grounds that it would never be capable of sustaining a separate independence.[203] If the UN had capitulated at this point, subsequent agitation for independence would probably have assumed a guise more like other anti-colonial movements. As it was, when the South Africans were rebuffed, they abandoned their plans for outright annexation, thereby confirming the status of SWA as something other than a colony. The result was that the hopes of the liberation movements came to be pinned on the intervention of the UN and the International Court of Justice (ICJ).

Under the NP regime, the South African position was that the UN possessed no legal standing with respect to the territory. However, when the UN requested the ICJ to deliver an advisory opinion, it ruled in 1950 that the mandate obligations remained intact even if the League of Nations had ceased to exist, and that future oversight should be exercised by the UN General Assembly. In other words, SWA remained an international responsibility. The only concession to the South Africans resided in the opinion that they were not obliged to enter into a formal trusteeship agreement. In subsequent years, the ICJ and the General Assembly played a crucial role in further weakening the foundations of South African rule. In 1966, the court ruled that Liberia and Ethiopia possessed no legal standing when they sought a definitive ruling that South African occupation was illegal. However, this decision was definitively reversed in 1971 when the court called on UN member states to recognise the illegality of South Africa's presence.[204] Two years later, the General Assembly declared that the South West African People's Organisation (SWAPO) was the 'authentic' voice of the Namibian people. This was further modified in 1976 so that SWAPO became both the 'sole and authentic' voice of Namibians. UN Resolutions 435 (1976) and 435 (1978) called on South Africa to withdraw its troops and demanded free elections to be held under UN supervision. For its part, SWAPO behaved as if it really were a government-in-waiting. It was granted membership or observer status within a number of UN agencies, was invited to join the Non-Aligned Movement and maintained diplomatic missions across the world.[205] Although the timing of independence remained an unknown, and eventually came much later than was expected, it was clear by the end of the 1970s that the days of South African rule were numbered. The latter sought to play for time, as they rifled through the shelves of recent African history to find a neo-colonial formula which would suffice.

Secondly, however, the very fact that South Africa was the administering power imparted a distinctively southern flavour to Namibian protest. One good reason was that apartheid legislation and practice was imported wholesale into SWA. This included colour bars, influx controls, residential segregation, differential educational provision and prohibitions on mixed marriages and sex across the colour line. Moreover, in 1964 the Odendaal Report recommended the division of the territory into Bantustans along South African lines. All of these measures were resisted in ways which mirrored reactions within South Africa itself. In December 1959, the residents of Windhoek's Old Location held out against being forcibly moved to the new Katatura township. This had tragic consequences when some 60 demonstrators were killed or wounded in a confrontation with the Police.[206] Meanwhile, in the rural areas migrant workers and the youth set themselves against 'traditional' authority in a manner which was equally redolent of South Africa in the 1950s.

In many cases, the links with South African movements were direct. The first significant nationalist organisation was the Ovambo People's Congress (OPC) which was established in 1957 by migrant workers and a smaller group of students in Cape Town, who found inspiration in the Freedom Charter.[207] The OPC transformed itself into the Ovambo People's Organisation (OPO) in 1959 and many of its leaders, including Sam Nujoma, were involved in the Katatura protests. In June 1960, the OPO finally repackaged itself as SWAPO in order to widen its nationalist appeal. Over subsequent years, South African influences became even more evident. Some Namibian students who attended University in South Africa were profoundly influenced by Black Consciousness ideas and brought them home. Moreover, the growing militancy of Namibian school students took some inspiration from south of the border. In 1971, Namibian students publicly demonstrated after the Bantu Commissioner, Jannie De Wet, made a statement rejecting the ruling of the ICJ. Many were arrested and subsequently excluded from school, in response to which their colleagues boycotted classes for many months. The SWAPO Youth League (SYL), which emerged out of these events, thereafter established itself one of the leading forces of internal opposition. Together with contract workers, many of these militant students returned to Ovamboland and engaged in open confrontation with the chiefly authority, which necessitated the deployment of the SADF. When the SYL and a contract workers' association co-ordinated a highly successful boycott of the elections for the Ovamboland legislature in August 1973, local activists were rounded up and handed over to the chiefs who proceeded to administer severe floggings. After Chief Elifas (Chief Minister of the

Ovambo homeland), who had administered some of the most brutal floggings, was assassinated in August 1975, a further crackdown ensued which forced many SYL activists fled into exile.[208] However, the vacuum was partially filled by the Namibian Black Students' Organisation (NABSO) which was constituted along Black Consciousness lines in 1975. Although NABSO was originally geared towards secondary school students, it later opened its doors to University students studying in South Africa.[209] Predictably, the outbreak of the Soweto uprising was followed by a parallel wave of boycotts aimed at the elimination of Bantu Education in Namibian schools.

It would, however, be a mistake to assume that Namibians were always following the lead of their South African counterparts. In December 1971, Namibian contract workers went on a two-month general strike when De Wet asserted that the contract system, which was operated by the South West African Native Labour Association (SWANLA), was based on the consent of the workers concerned. Apart from challenging this wilful misconception, the strikers made demands which included the right to move freely in search of jobs, to be paid at equal rates and to bring their families with them. Colin Leys and John Saul have concluded that '[b]etween a quarter and a half of the total contract workforce stopped work, making this action perhaps the single most important blow ever struck by Namibians for their own liberation'.[210] Importantly for our purposes, Hirson observes that news of the success of the Namibian strike emboldened workers in South Africa try similar action themselves, culminating in the surge of 1973.[211] Although SWA was never formally part of South Africa, therefore, it was so tightly enmeshed in its economic and political orbit that it was only natural that there should be a cross-fertilisation of resistance politics.

Finally, the Namibian opposition also came to embody some of the characteristics of liberation movements in the Portuguese territories and Zimbabwe. The OAU Liberation Committee channelled most of its resources to movements which seemed to be serious about mounting guerrilla warfare against the last bastions of white rule. SWAPO had already accepted the need for such a course of action in 1961 and its first combatants were sent abroad for military training the following year. By contrast, the South West African National Union (SWANU) had no structures in place and therefore found itself excluded from OAU patronage after 1965. Following a merger with the Caprivi African National Union (CANU) in 1964, SWAPO established itself as the pre-eminent national liberation movement, although its centre of gravity remained in the North. This was further cemented when, as we have seen, the UN endorsed SWAPO as the 'sole and authentic' voice of the Namibian people.

During the 1960s and 1970s, an undoubted cachet came to be attached to armed struggle, and it was not too surprising that SWAPO sought to join the illustrious company of Third World liberation movements. The official histories of SWAPO place the turning point at Omgulumbashe in August 1966 when the South African Police discovered its first military base and a shootout ensued. The fact that this was a military setback – not unlike ZANU's Chinhoyi – was conveniently glossed over within the heroic meta-narrative. Over the next two decades, SWAPO became fully committed to the pursuit of armed struggle through the instrument of the People's Liberation Army of Namibia (PLAN) and with the backing of the Soviet Union, Eastern Europe and China. The first military bases were provided by Tanzania and Zambia, but after the independence of Angola PLAN relocated to the adjoining border areas in 1976. Thereafter, the language of SWAPO came to closely mirror that of the liberation movements in the Portuguese colonies. In the words of Nujoma:

> The tactical principles followed by PLAN are based mainly on typical and scientific methods of guerrilla warfare. Ours is a people's war…The basic ideological principle of SWAPO is to build a classless non-exploitative society which allows no room, no loophole, for the exploitation of man by man.[212]

There also some similarities in the manner in which the Rhodesian and South African regimes sought to deal with the threat of guerrilla insurgency. With the South African Police already assisting the Rhodesians, the SADF was despatched to northern Namibia in the early 1970s with a mandate to curb guerrilla incursions and to punish local SWAPO sympathisers. The SADF did so with considerable brutality, but this paled into significance alongside what ensued after 1978 when the government created Koevoet ('crowbar' in Afrikaans) as a counter-insurgency unit. Koevoet is credited with responsibility for most of the killings which took place within Namibia.[213] Although the SADF had withdrawn from Angolan territory after its abortive intervention in 1975/76, it repeatedly struck at SWAPO bases well within the Angolan border. The most notorious occasion was in May 1978 when an air and paratroop assault on a SWAPO refugee camp at Cassinga left some 600 civilians dead. The government also recruited Angolans directly into 32 (Buffalo) Battalion in 1975 which was used against SWAPO as well as the MPLA government. In subsequent phases of the war, the government went further down the Portuguese route by attempting to recruit the bulk of its fighting force from within Namibia, thereby sparing white South African lives and giving the local population a stake in the war. The South West African Territorial Force, which was founded in 1980, comprised ethnic battalions and had up to 30,000 troops under arms by 1989.[214] The militarisation of Namibian society had profound consequences, not least for the Bushmen, a large proportion of whom exchanged their previous modes of existence as hunter-gatherers for military service as trackers and combatants. Finally, the South Africans also sought to win the war of hearts-and-minds by assuming direct responsibility for schools and hospitals and rewarding compliance.

At the same time as they were seeking to neutralise SWAPO as a fighting force, the South Africans were looking around for possible allies. The Bantustan initiative was evidently not winning international legitimacy, and so in September 1975 the Vorster government convened the Turnhalle Conference which brought white political representatives and the notional leaders of the different ethnic groups together. Significantly, this initiative occurred at precisely the moment when Ian Smith was being forced, under South African duress, to parlay with Zimbabwean nationalists. Whereas the Victoria Falls talks failed, the Turnhalle initiative culminated in the holding of elections in December 1978 which were won by the Democratic Turnhalle Alliance (DTA), a grand alliance of ethnic leaders. This attempt to undercut the leadership claims of SWAPO bore some fruit when CANU broke off and join the DTA. Although the South Africans were forced to restore direct rule in 1983 when the DTA Ministers resigned, a Transitional Government of National Unity was put in place two years later. This enabled the Botha regime to argue that significant powers were devolved upon elected leaders. As in the case of Zimbabwe-Rhodesia's 'internal settlement', the intention was to persuade many would-be nationalists that armed struggle was quite fruitless and that more would be gained from striking a bargain. At the same time, it was hoped to undercut SWAPO's claims to uphold democratic aspirations. Most of the international community agreed with SWAPO that the settlement was a cynical attempt to forestall genuine independence, but the Reagan administration was (as ever) more receptive. The doctrine of 'linkage' meant that no pressure would be brought to bear on South Africa in Namibia (and indeed Angola) until the Cubans withdrew from Angola. As we have already seen, this merely had the effect of escalating the regional conflict and delaying independence. At the end of the day, however, the South African 'internal settlement' proved as unworkable as in Rhodesia itself.

If the Namibian experience shared elements with the first wave of African decolonisation, the liberation wars and South African resistance politics, the balance between the three was uneven. The reality was that SWAPO, which came to dominate the opposition, was most at ease when pursuing its case within international fora. This meant that its leaders accorded secondary importance to the armed struggle, and looked with some suspicion upon popular movements which emerged within Namibia. On the first point, SWAPO found itself in an unenviable position because the SADF was mobile and commanded formidable firepower. This made it very difficult for PLAN – as for Umkhonto we Sizwe – to prosecute a successful guerrilla war within the borders of Namibia. Certainly, there was no realistic prospect of creating liberated zones. PLAN did launch many hit-and-run raids from Zambia into the Caprivi strip until it was forced to pack its bags in 1975. By then, it was already seeking to open a second front along the lengthy Angolan border when the victory of MPLA afforded it formal bases the following year. Between 1978 and 1980, PLAN managed to destabilise parts of Ovamboland, whilst launching guerrilla raids as far south as Windhoek.[215] However, these operations became unsustainable once the SADF began launching attacks deep inside Angola after 1980. After falling prey to South African attacks, PLAN was forced to relocate its bases hundreds of kilometres away from the Namibian border, with the result that its strikes became more episodic and less threatening. In the final stages of the war, it was the Cubans and the MPLA who were playing the major part in the fight against the South Africans, with SWAPO performing at best an auxiliary role. Finally, we have seen, the Namibian settlement came about because the Cubans and the South Africans had fought each other to a standstill and were keen to find an honourable exit in 1988.

But while SWAPO lacked the wherewithal to score the kind of military successes which other movements claimed, it was also predisposed to privilege the diplomatic route. As Lauren Dobell suggests, most of the SWAPO leaders were orthodox nationalists who did not wholeheartedly share the revolutionary agenda of the other movements. Significantly, SWAPO was closely associated with UNITA rather than the MPLA, and only switched sides in 1976 when it was expedient to do so. At about the same time, SWAPO began to swap its nationalist language for explicitly Marxist verbiage. Although this appeared to signal a move to the left, there is some reason for viewing this as a pragmatic response. Apart from a need to legitimise the MPLA alliance, SWAPO leaders felt they had to answer their critics within the party. By 1976, many PLAN fighters felt that the SWAPO leadership was not sufficiently committed to armed struggle and that it was neglecting its troops in the field. These dissident voices were joined by younger and more radical SYL members who had been part of the 1974/75 exodus. Having led the internal opposition, they expected to be taken seriously and sought to open up a debate within SWAPO. In particular, they demanded a party congress at which the future orientation of SWAPO might be thrashed out. Feeling threatened, the inner circle around Nujoma employed the Zambian army to arrest thousands of dissident troops, as well as SYM members and some members of the existing executive. Having ruthlessly purged the dissenters, the leadership nevertheless went on to borrow from their script. There was a repeat performance of this episode in the early 1980s when the war started to go badly for PLAN. SWAPO intelligence suspected the handiwork of South African spies and before long a full-scale witch-hunt was in progress. Thousands of ordinary PLAN fighters were detained, and it eventually transpired that many had been tortured.

The ambivalent attitude towards popular movements inside Namibia is more surprising, especially when South African parallels are borne in mind. As we have seen, the ANC was able to revitalise its flagging fortunes by tapping into labour, student and community struggles in the 1970s. All of these were present in Namibia as well, but SWAPO looked with some suspicion on political activity which it did not control. In other words, it took being the 'sole and authentic voice' of the Namibian people quite literally. This attitude was reflected, for example, in blunt criticism of labour leaders who sought to organise strikes without SWAPO authorisation.[216] According to Gretchen Bauer, the SWAPO leadership read the confrontation between the Polish government and Solidarity in the early 1980s as an illustration of the dangers of 'counter-revolutionary' tendencies infiltrating the labour movement.[217] As SWAPO turned in on itself, many of the unfortunate members who found themselves incarcerated (and worse) came from trade union backgrounds. Equally, voluntary associations which were committed to community development initiatives were often frowned upon, lest they ameliorate the conditions under which Namibians lived and thereby take the heat out of the struggle for national liberation. Even a promising grassroots women's organisation, the Namibia Women's Voice, was forced to close down because it was thought to compete with the SWAPO Women's Council.[218]

However, the most remarkable development was the subordination of church organisations to SWAPO. In Zimbabwe, many of the churches were sympathetic to the cause, but saw themselves as defending a higher truth as well. In 1978, the Council of Churches of Namibia (CCN), in this most Christian of countries, brought together all the main Protestant churches, with the Catholic Church maintaining an observer status. The CCN quickly established itself as an active supporter of SWAPO within the country. Indeed Philip Steenkamp goes as far as to describe the CCN as 'the internal religious wing of SWAPO'.[219] The role of the CCN in exposing government injustices was commonly agreed to be a very positive contribution. But the CNN also shied away from any actions or statements which could be construed as a criticism of SWAPO. According to Steenkamp, when the CCN gathered positive proof of torture against alleged spies in SWAPO prisons, it chose to sweep the embarrassment under the carpet. Any other course of action would, it was thought, present an all-too-easy easy target for the South African authorities. When the storm finally broke, the revelations did little for the credibility of the churches or the SWAPO leadership.

By stark contrast with the ongoing agonies in Angola, the denouement in Namibia was remarkably smooth. On the basis of the Cuban–South African agreements of 1988, the SADF withdrew from the territory whilst elections to a Constituent Assembly were scheduled to be held under UN auspices in line with Resolution 435. Although SWAPO was hoping for a comprehensive victory in the polls of November 1989, it received only 57.3 per cent of the vote.[220] The DTA came in second, albeit some way behind, with 28.6 per cent. The next largest party, the United Democratic Front (UDF), received only 5.6 per cent, while the rest of the vote was distributed amongst seven small parties. Under a system of proportional representation, this meant that while SWAPO commanded a majority of seats in the Constituent Assembly (41 out of 72), it lacked the two-thirds majority which would have enabled it to unilaterally determine the new constitution. The failure of SWAPO to live up to its proud claim to being the 'sole and authentic voice' of Namibians may have had something to do with the difficulty of making the transition from an exiled movement to a political party. However, what appears to have been more decisive was the revelations of the brutal treatment meted out in SWAPO camps. Many of those who were late recruits to SWAPO came from the South of the country, and it was these who were the most likely to be accused of being spies. In the South, the revelations produced a backlash against SWAPO, whereas it swept the board in Ovamboland. The DTA, on the other hand, performed best in the South whilst failing to make an impression in Ovamboland.

After the elections, the debate over the new constitution proceeded with a remarkable level of cross-party co-operation. Despite the rather dogmatic leanings of the SWAPO leadership, it eventually signed up to a constitution which contained a good many checks and guarantees of human rights. The incoming Nujoma government also committed itself to a programme of national reconciliation which spared Namibia the political chaos and white exodus which had marred Mozambican and Angolan independence. However, many on the left worried that SWAPO had conceded to much in its attempt to placate white commercial farmers and the mining companies. Given the pragmatism and ideological plasticity of SWAPO, the dropping of socialist rhetoric probably did not cause much of a *crise de conscience*.

On 21 March 1990, the South African flag was lowered and the new Namibian flag was hoisted in its place, signalling the final act of African decolonisation more than forty years after the process had begun in the Sudan. Amongst the seated dignitaries were Soviet Foreign Minister, Eduard Shevardnadze, and American Secretary of State, James Baker, who used the occasion to talk about ways of bringing the Angolan combatants to the negotiating table. The previous month, the South African government had initiated a radical rethink of its own when it released Mandela, unbanned the ANC and other proscribed organisations and signalled its willingness to negotiate an end to apartheid. In an important sense, therefore, Namibian independence signalled a watershed in the politics of the entire Southern African sub-region.

7.5 Conclusion

In this chapter, we have dealt with the second wave of African liberation. This differed from flag decolonisation of the 1950s and 1960s in that conventional nationalist strategies simply did not work where the colonial power was determined to stay put (as in the Portuguese territories and in SWA) or where white minorities were deeply entrenched (as in Rhodesia and South Africa). Each of the liberation movements learned the hard way that petitions and civil disobedience campaigns had their limitations outside of certain specific historical contexts. In the Portuguese territories and in Rhodesia, the liberation movements abandoned their urban bases, often after incurring heavy losses, and turned to guerrilla warfare with differing degrees of success. This meant establishing some sympathy amongst the peasant population, which was expected to provide material support and protection. By contrast, a 'people's war' was revealed to be a non-viable option in South Africa and even Namibia. Here the dominant pattern was urban-centered resistance in which workers and youth took the lead, often leaving the liberation movements trailing in their wake. Finally, the particular path to liberation had enduring consequences for politics in the post-liberation period in each of the cases we have examined.

8

Invasion of the Acronyms: SAPs, AIDS and the NGO Takeover

When did the IMF become an International Ministry of Finance? When did nations agree to surrender to it their power of decision-making?

President Julius Nyerere of Tanzania, 1980

When it comes to Africa, the outsiders have always behaved as if they know better than Africans what is good for Africa, and the result is that without the needed co-operation and support, Africa has particularly always been derailed from pursuing relentlessly and vigorously the agenda it has set for itself, whether it is the Monrovia Strategy, the Lagos Plan of Action or the Final Act of Lagos.

Adebayo Adedeji, Executive Secretary of United Nations Economic Commission for Africa

In the heat of decolonisation, the deceptively simple concept of 'development' was born. Whereas the interwar colonial regimes had been far more concerned with sound administration and with balancing their books, their post-war successors sought to morally rearm themselves by presenting the state as the harbinger of economic development and social improvement. At independence, African regimes commandeered the package, encouraged by newly established international organisations, like the World Bank and the tentacular agencies of the United Nations which proliferated after 1945. It became an unquestioned assumption that African countries would add annually to their GDP growth rates and their living standard indices as part of a global human progression. As we have seen, African rulers believed that they had to jet propel themselves if they were to catch up with the advance party.

During the 1960s and 1970s, it was possible to argue that Africans were making their own choices, even if these were informed by currents thinking within the burgeoning development industry. However, over the next two decades it often seemed as if the clock was being turned back. By the start of the 1980s, virtually every African country was manifesting signs of acute economic distress, reflected in a mounting and unsustainable debt burden, a permanent trade deficit and an acute fiscal crisis which meant that the state was unable to maintain basic infrastructure or fund essential social services. The signs were also visibly apparent on the ground, in the shape of an impoverished rural population and a swelling mass of urban dwellers struggling to make a living through petty trade and hustling. Whereas the rest of humanity still seemed to be on the virtuous path to progress, the African continent appeared to be marching in the opposite direction, led by false prophets and 'guides'.

Although most African leaders were reluctant to admit defeat, they were eventually forced to approach the International Monetary Fund (IMF) and the World Bank for relief. The IMF had a reputation of being less sympathetic, whereas the Bank had previously been involved in many of the development plans hatched by African regimes in the 1970s. But by the early 1980s, the mood within the Bank had become every bit as uncompromising as within the IMF. Together, the International Financial Institutions (IFIs) blamed the crisis squarely on inappropriate policies and poor implementation. In return for bailing out African states, therefore, they insisted upon the fulfilment of a long list of conditions, the net effect of which was to compel governments to cut back on public spending and to open their markets to foreign competition. Even the most principled socialist regimes, which had prided themselves on their achievements in raising living standards, were forced to comply. By the end of the 1980s, the freedom of action which seemed to come with independence had narrowed to the point of becoming a virtual fiction.

At the same time as Structural Adjustment Programmes (SAPs) were rolling back the frontiers of the state, Western Non-Governmental Organisations (NGOs) were moving into the vacuum. The NGOs, who saw themselves very much as the 'good guys' seeking to help ordinary Africans, became the moral and financial beneficiaries of a diagnosis which cast the state in the role of villain– or at best as a hopeless bundle of incompetence. As more external aid was channelled through the NGOs, the 'statishness' of African states was further eroded. Finally, the mid-1980s witnessed the outbreak of the global Acquired Immune Deficiency Syndrome (AIDS) pandemic which afflicted the African continent to a far greater extent than the rest of the world. The AIDS catastrophe, which could not have been predicted, wiped out many of the gains which had been made in the first decades of independence, whilst placing an intolerable burden on an already enfeebled state.

Many of the underlying processes were not confined to Africa, or even to the so-called Third World. Indeed the latest intellectual fashion pointed to the invisible hand of globalisation, in which it was argued there were both gains as well as losses. However, to many Africans – and especially intellectuals – they added up to a *de facto* recolonisation of the continent. The colonial metaphor was especially apt because Western assistance seemed to clothe itself in a dusted down version of the white man's burden. Whereas the European colonists had delivered Africans from pre-colonial despotism and 'inter-tribal warfare', their later twentieth-century counterparts saw themselves as delivering the benighted continent from autocratic and incompetent regimes who could not grasp elementary economics. Whereas the economists liked to suppose that they were the adepts of an objective science – embodied in statistics which were in turn assembled in elaborate models and matrices – the humanitarians purported to act in the name of a global humanity. Both were dealing in cultural universals, which distinguished them from the pronounced relativism which underwrote high colonialism. But the net effect was not dissimilar. That is, the abstract 'African' was construed as the victim of his/her rulers and in need of salvation – whether through the forces of the market or through charitable donation. The donor agencies and NGOs were, of course, sensitive to the accusation that they were over-reaching themselves and modified their language in the 1990s. The former began to insist on the importance of local 'ownership' of SAPs, whilst the NGOs attempted to express themselves through the voices of African partners. By stark contrast, Western media organisations – which were obsessed with famines, civil wars and emergencies – tended to state things as they saw them. The results sometimes made for uncomfortable viewing, listening and reading, but the media were characterised by much less verbal dissimulation.

It is more than usually difficult to write the history of the past twenty years because the events are too proximate: the sediment, as it were, has yet to settle. Moreover, while the sheer volume of information about Africa has grown exponentially, very little of it can be taken at face value. The statistics, which constitutes the basis on which structural adjustment is conventionally evaluated, are especially problematic. Aside from the larger question of the relationship between the numerals and reality, there is the simple fact that African governments have lacked the means to gather reliable statistics. On the other hand, the economists who fly in and out of capital cities usually have not the slightest knowledge of local languages or indigenous cultural constructions of the realities which they seek to change. Although NGOs have prided themselves on having an ear to the ground, their testimony is not necessarily plain, unvarnished truth either, given that they have developed their own blind spots and vested interests. With theses caveats in mind, this chapter will set out to assess the African experience of structural adjustment, the impact of AIDS and the contribution of NGOs.

8.1 Curse or cure? The structural adjustment regime

The sheer ubiquity of the crisis in the 1980s cut across ideological boundaries, taking in capitalist Côte d'Ivoire, socialist Tanzania and Marxist–Leninist Ethiopia. Even the oil-rich states, such as Nigeria and Congo-Brazzaville, found themselves deep in the mire, having been lured into a false sense of optimism by the oil boom. If so many states shared the same outward symptoms, one might reasonably have wondered whether they shared a common ailment. The so-called structuralists have argued that the common factor was a debilitating economic dependency, rooted in a subordinate position within the international division of labour. However, those who hovered at the bedside tended to see things rather differently. Those (mostly non-Africans) who shaped the reform agenda in the 1980s came to the opposite conclusion: namely that Africans states were sick because they had drunk from the same contaminated source. Even those who had apparently struck the right the balance in the 1960s, such as Kenya and Côte d'Ivoire, were seen as having lost their way over the next decade when they allowed state expenditure to run out of control. The key to restoring good economic health was therefore held to reside in getting back to the African capitalist policies of the 1960s: that is export-led development through open markets. The structuralist diagnosis was rejected as at variance with the evidence – namely a decade of genuine growth in some African states alongside the Asian miracle. Indeed, structuralism was seen as part and parcel of what had led African rulers astray in the first place. There is some truth to the charge. In the 1960s, Nkrumah and many other African leaders had followed the structuralist line in attempting to kick-start their economic takeoff. In retrospect, one might agree with their assessment of the dilemmas they faced, but fault them on the naiveté of their solutions. The very fact that a country like Ghana was so dependent on one commodity, cocoa, arguably should have dictated a greater measure of caution rather than precipitating a spending spree. Nevertheless, the vulnerability of African countries to commodity swings arguably *was* the common factor linking the experience of diverse African states.

In the 1980s, the structuralists were effectively run out of town. The initiative now lay with the advocates of neo-liberalism both in key Western capitals – as exemplified by Thatcherism in Britain and Reaganomics in the United States – and in the Bretton Woods institutions (the IMF and World Bank) themselves.[1] In the past, African governments had been able to shop around for aid, tapping foreign governments, international banks and the IFIs. But it was no longer a buyer's market. The banks and the bilateral donors were now refusing to come to terms on debt rescheduling or renewed lending until the IMF gave its seal of approval. Meanwhile, the IMF and the World Bank had begun to overlap in terms of their functions and to co-operate in formulating reforms which they considered necessary to resolve the crisis. This meant that any African government seeking a financial bail-out had to agree to a set of cross-conditionalities devised between them. Having done so, they might be eligible for an IMF basic credit facility, followed normally by a Structural Adjustment Facility (SAF) and possibly an Enhanced Structural Adjustment Facility (ESAF) which were specially designed for the poorest countries.[2] They might also be eligible for a Structural Adjustment Loan (SAL) and a Sectoral Adjustment Loan (SAL) from the World Bank. But failing to agree to the conditions, or cheating on the implementation, invited the ultimate sanction of being cut off from further assistance. In practical terms, that meant not being able to finance essential imports or to pay civil servant or army salaries, with all the political repercussions which might be expected to follow. Not surprisingly, most African regimes capitulated, however reluctantly. Between 1980 and 1989, some 36 countries had taken a total of 241 loans from the IFIs, and many more were to follow in the 1990s.[3]

On what assumptions, then, were SAPs devised and what precise differences were they supposed they make? In order to comprehend the underlying rationale, one need look no further than a landmark World Bank publication of 1981, entitled *Accelerated Development in Sub-Saharan Africa* – otherwise known as the Berg Report.[4] The latter began by recapitulating the generally poor economic performance of sub-Saharan Africa in the shape of '[s]low overall economic growth, sluggish agricultural performance coupled with rapid rates of population increase, and balance-of-payments and fiscal crises'.[5] It conceded that African countries had suffered external shocks – fallout from the economic downturn in the industrialised countries after 1974, rising energy prices and weak prices for the continent's primary products – but went on to place far greater blame on a string of ill-chosen policies. It singled out three in particular: namely a trade and exchange-rate regime which protected inefficient industries whilst penalising private agriculture; pricing and tax policies which similarly discriminated against agriculture; and insufficient attention paid to the manpower constraints which were bound to follow from the adoption of statist policies.[6] Whilst advocating an injection of real resources into stricken African economies, the Berg Report also urged far-reaching policy reforms, especially exchange-rate adjustments and price deregulation which would stimulate agricultural exports. In harmony with a growing tendency to blame the over-extension of the state, the report also took a stand on the controversial issue of service provision. It argued that while Africans tended to expect free health and education, the reality of the situation was that states simply did not have the means to pay for it. This meant that there was no realistic alternative to charging for these services.[7] Although the Berg Report was measured in its tone, what eventually blossomed as SAPs was rather less nuanced. The importance placed upon manpower development, for example, was mostly forgotten until the 1990s when 'capacity building' was rediscovered. Rolling back the state, which lurked behind most of the conditionalities, became an end in itself – as indeed it did in Thatcher's Britain.

Although the Berg Report identified what African countries had done wrong, it did not really provide a clear explanation for why so many had erred. Of course, many structuralists denied that they had, and instead blamed the two oil-shocks (1974 and 1979) and the global downturn which had thrown all reasonable calculations into disarray. Some resolutely maintain that the quest for accelerated development and the expansion of basic services were laudable in themselves, but that the chosen policies offered no solution to the vagaries of the international market.[8] This kind of answer was not, however, to the liking of the authors of the Berg Report who insisted that the reality was that African countries were producing fewer exports, even when the international prices should have been enticing. In truth, they could not have provided an answer to the conundrum without crossing on to the terrain of political analysis. One can, however, turn to another body of literature which is not reducible to the Bretton Woods agenda, but which drinks from a common pool of ideas. The classic statement is Robert Bates, *Markets and States in Tropical Africa*, which sought to explain the deeper political logic underlying dysfunctional economic policies.[9] Bates accepted the central premise that the African crisis was rooted in disincentives to agriculture, which he attributed to the influence exerted by urban interest groups demanding cheap raw materials, high wages and low-cost food. These could only be met by taxing export crops through marketing boards and imposing price control on foodstuffs and other rural produce. Whereas urban interest groups were easy to mobilise around their core interests, it was much more difficult to organise a disparate rural population – not least cash crop farmers who did not know how much their commodities were worth on the world market. However, Bates and others also observed that urban bias was ultimately self-defeating because once the price incentives were removed there was no reason for peasants to enter the market at all. The decline of marketed food and cash crops therefore tended to rebound upon urban constituencies in the long run. Within his model, Bates also sought to account for the differing preferences of African regimes, positing that those which were more favourably disposed to rural producers tended to derive from agrarian constituencies. Hence KANU in Kenya and the PDCI in Côte d'Ivoire were exceptional in being dominated by elites who kept one foot in the countryside and were therefore more supportive of pricing policies which tended to benefit peasants as well.

The IFIs eventually took up the idea of an 'urban coalition' dictating government policies and gave it their own gloss. In 1989, the World Bank published *Sub-Saharan Africa: From Crisis to Sustained Growth*, which simultaneously conceded a lack of sensitivity to the human dimensions of adjustment whilst incorporating urban bias and systemic corruption as factors accounting for economic failure.[10] This document also dropped a new ingredient into the discursive pot, which was the 'crisis of governance'. During the 1990s, Bank documents routinely appealed to lapses in governance to account for virtually every shortcoming within SAPs, thereby deflecting criticism away from the prescriptions and towards the implementation. Ironically, the very fact that these variables were not measurable, in the way that subsidies and price disincentives were, rendered them all the more attractive. Despite the intrusion of 'good governance' into Bank rhetoric, the implications were potentially anti-democratic: that is, if the peasantry was too weak to make its voice heard over the hubbub of urban interest groups, then SAPs might best be implemented by governments of honest men who were thoroughly insulated from popular demands. These implications became problematic after 1989, as 'pro-democracy' movements proliferated in Eastern Europe and Africa. The IFIs were therefore thrown back upon the nebulous concept of civil society. In a nutshell, the NGOs were expected to mobilise constituencies which were conducive to SAPs, whilst improving efficiency and exposing corruption and other lapses in governance. The shape-shifting character of the IFIs became apparent once again towards the end of the 1990s when lingering criticisms of the impact of adjustment on the poor, and renewed interest in Africa in Western capitals, led to the insistence on African governments drawing up Poverty Reduction Strategy Papers (PRSPs). These would ensure that aid was directed to the most needy sections of the population. The implication was that African governments had previously neglected the poor majority, which was a bit rich given that African foot-dragging hinged precisely on the argument that the poor would suffer from state withdrawal. In Kenya, for example, government opposition to liberalisation of the food trade rested on the argument that this would impair its ability to guard against a return of famine. However, this shift towards a 'poverty focus' perfectly illustrates the capacity of the Bretton Woods to endlessly reinvent structural adjustment, and to absorb external critiques without altering the fundamental premises.

The contents of the standard SAP package, which normally consisted of 'stabilisation', an 'adjustment' and a takeoff phase, can be summarised very briefly. Firstly, there was early pressure upon African governments to radically devalue their currencies. The Francophone states which used the CFA franc had no control over their own currencies, and when France devalued in 1994 this came as a genuine surprise – indeed a shock – to African leaders. In the Anglophone, Lusophone and Francophone countries which lay outside the franc zone (Zaire and Guinea), the real value of national currencies bore no relation to their official exchange rates. Indeed in Zaire, large parts of the country refused to accept the official currency. In much of Africa, systematic overvaluation could plausibly be linked to the penalisation of cash crop farmers whose remuneration was calculated at official currency rates. In a number of African countries, this provided one of the primary inducements to smuggling, which intensified the squeeze on official foreign exchange earnings. The ultimate aim of structural adjustment was to let the market decide exchange rates.

Secondly, African governments were encouraged to restore incentives to the farming population by raising producer prices in the short-term, but ultimately by implementing complete deregulation – a policy otherwise known as 'getting the prices right'. If world market prices were passed on to the farmers (less essential export duties), rather than mediated through inefficient marketing boards, then cocoa, coffee and groundnut farmers would have an incentive to raise their production. Equally, if the food prices were allowed to find their own level in urban markets, the farmers would be given an incentive to maximise their output. Thirdly, SAPs were supposed to involve a drastic scaling back of public sector employment, given that salaries typically consumed a large swathe of the overall budget. The supposedly bloated civil service was to be reduced by removing ghost workers from the payroll, retrenching surplus staff and capping new recruitment.[11] Equally, governments were expected to either close down or privatise parastatals.

Fourthly, the SAP package entailed a thorough liberalisation of the economy. The subsidies to local industry were to be ended, while an abolition of import licences would permit the easier importation of goods. Those industries which could not compete would be allowed to go under on the basis that they were probably not viable and that domestic consumers would benefit from being able to purchase goods more cheaply. On the other hand, the ending of protectionism and the return to a more stable economic climate was expected to lead to a resumption of foreign investment, after a decade of capital flight. Finally, the state was to abandon the welfarist pretensions which were associated above all with 'African socialism'. The users of medical and educational services were to pay part of the cost of provision in order to keep them ticking over. In sum, therefore, SAPs were expected to kill several birds with one stone: they were to lead to a reallocation of resources from consumption to production and, by stripping away the layers of regulation, they would narrow the opportunities for corruption and rent-seeking. Insofar as the ruling classes had grown fat on the latter pursuits, SAPs could also be sold as an instrument which would benefit the African peasantry while clipping the wings of corrupt bureaucrats.

There was undoubtedly a logical consistency to the SAP agenda, but what did it all add up to in practice? There is a remarkable level of disagreement about how much was accomplished and who actually benefited. There are three broad interpretations of what transpired in the 1980s and 1990s. First of all, the Bretton Woods institutions themselves maintained that SAPs had checked the rot and that those countries which stuck to the economic medicine performed far better than those which did not.[12] Elliot Berg also pointed out that the level of performance ought to be measured against the available alternatives rather than some ideal.[13] A World Bank report of 1994 ventured that faster growth was likely to have reduced poverty, notably in the rural areas, albeit without providing concrete supporting evidence.[14]

Secondly, critics (often of a structuralist persuasion) attacked SAPs across a broad front. The claim that the economies of countries which pursued SAPs experienced higher growth was contested on various grounds. It was pointed out that continental growth was less than spectacular and actually very disappointing by comparison with other regions of the world.[15] In 1989, the United Nations Economic Commission for Africa (UNECA) even found a negative correlation between GDP growth and the adoption of SALs.[16] Even World Bank statistics which pointed to sub-Saharan growth rates of 1.7 per cent in the 1980s and 2.0 per cent between 1990 and 1996 need to be set against a population growth rate of around 2.7 per cent. On these figures, the continent was actually becoming poorer in real terms. The critics also identified clear weaknesses in specific sectors. Whereas the World Bank was upbeat about agriculture, Mkandawire and Soludo have drawn attention to alternative statistics from the Food and Agriculture Organisation (FAO) and the African Development Bank (ADB) which convey a picture of stagnation.[17] In the case of food crops, what appears to have happened is that trade liberalisation eased the burden on urban consumers, while farmers bore the brunt of higher input prices and those in outlying areas encountered greater difficulties in selling their goods – an ironic reversal of what was supposed to have transpired. In the case of cash crops, for all the inefficiencies of state marketing, the controls on quality slipped and partially accounted for declining prices on the international market.[18]

In the case of industry, the World Bank contested popular wisdom that local industries had been driven to the wall and claimed a positive correlation between sticking to the programme and registering improvements in industrial performance. However, Mkandawire and Soludo make the valid point that there was almost bound to be some increase in output once scarce raw materials became available, but that the gains tended to evaporate in the face of competition from cheaper imports.[19] Another reality about adjustment, which is not disputed, is that African countries became vastly more indebted under the SAP regime. In 1980, African countries were in debt to the tune of $84 billion, but in 1992 this had risen to $150 billion, the servicing of which consumed around a fifth of annual export earnings. By 1996, the tally had risen further to $227 billion.[20] At the same time, critics linked the implementation of SAPs with increases in poverty. Retrenchment from the public sector and wage freezes were linked to the impoverishment of urban households wholly or partially dependent on wage-earnings. Equally, it was claimed that 'cost recovery' led to shrinking school enrolments and a narrowing of access to health facilities, not least in the rural areas. In 1990, UNICEF claimed that rising infant mortality rates could also be attributed to SAPs. By this point, even the World Bank was conceding that the burden was often falling on the least advantaged sections of society, with the result that some money was channelled into cushioning the blow. However, Mkandawire and Soludo are amongst those who maintain that these programmes were merely 'tacked onto the SAPs as an afterthought' without significantly altering the thrust of adjustment policies.[21]

Finally, whereas the critics maintained that adjustment medicine threatened to finish the patient off, a sceptical wing pointed to the gulf between theory and practice. Nicolas van de Walle, in particular, has argued that most SAPs were honoured in the breach, a point sometimes acknowledged in World Bank documents and also endorsed by Berg.[22] Van de Walle suggests that the measures which were implemented were those which enabled the authorities to shed uncomfortable burdens, or which enabled quick money to be made by the politicians (for example by cashing in on cut-price privatisations). On the other hand, the ruling elites dug their heels in when adjustment threatened their own core interests. Hence while governments faithfully cut back spending on social services, he asserts, most did not actually reduce the public sector payroll or deregulate the rural economy. Moreover, military expenditure continued to rise, even in countries not embroiled in conflict, while diplomatic expenses consumed swathes of national budgets. Going to the heart of the SAP agenda, Van de Walle also argues that, far from there having been a reduction of state spending, the injection of large sums of foreign aid had completely the opposite effect:

> Thanks in part to substantial donor support to state structures, twenty years of crisis have resulted in a bigger state that does less for its citizens, particularly its poor and rural ones.[23]

This interpretation meshes with the second one, in the sense that both see SAPs as promoting greater social inequality. The difference is that Van de Walle portrays African leaders not as helpless ciphers, but as sharp operators who learned to turn the reform process to their material advantage. This analysis dovetails with other works which have seen crisis and disorder as functional for African political elites.[24]

Assessing the veracity of these various claims is exceedingly difficult. Apart from the questionable nature of the statistics, different economic models tend to generate divergent results.[25] Moreover, if it is true that SAPs have not been fully implemented, then it is questionable whether one can judge their efficacy. Fortunately, as historians our concern resides less with the validity of particular economic models and rather more with what has happened in practice. On this basis, one can draw certain broad conclusions. The first is that the introduction of SAPs did not lead to spectacular rates of economic growth in Africa, and in real terms – that is, once population growth is factored in – the totality of African economies may well have contracted over the 1980s and 1990s. Nevertheless, the evidence would tend to support the contention that the fastest growing economies were those in adjusting countries like Ghana, Uganda and Tanzania (see Table 8.3). Kenya and Côte d'Ivoire, which had once been the darlings of the IFIs had been more resistant to adjustment and had performed rather worse overall – although political instability became a significant factor in the latter case. However, the variable performance of countries with significant mineral endowments owed more to world prices and the vagaries of production than SAPs. Hence whereas the Gabonese economy went into freefall as the oil began to dry up, Equatorial Guinea recorded a GDP growth rate of no less than 93.8 per cent in 1997 on the back of the latest African oil bonanza. However, experience would suggest that this absolute dependency on oil was likely to store up problems in the long run as Gabon discovered to its cost. The country which consistently turned up in World Bank documents as a stubborn non-reformer was the Democratic Republic of Congo (formerly Zaire). However, in this case the disastrous results are notional in the sense that a national economy had long since ceased to exist along with reliable statistics, which was merely confirmed by the *de facto* partition of the country in the late 1990s.

Secondly, the structuralist contention that there are inherent limitations to a strategy of maximising primary exports needs to be taken seriously. Although it may be true that there has not been a steady decline in the terms of trade for African countries, over the long run the trend has clearly been downwards – as even the IFIs were forced to admit. As Table 8.1 demonstrates, Africa's terms of trade continued to deteriorate through the adjustment period.[26] External indebtedness also grew (Table 8.2). Perversely, the designers of SAP programmes never seriously considered it a likely scenario that increased production of cocoa or coffee which negatively affect world prices. A third point is while African industry – born of import-substitution policies in the 1970s – was squeezed over the next two decades, the limited influx of foreign investment failed to compensate for the losses. The exception was in the mining sector, but the world prices for gold, diamonds and the like had a volatility of their own. The net result was the de-industrialisation of much of the African continent, with serious implications for urban employment and the balance of trade. Fourthly, far from increasing the viability of African states, the SAP years witnessed the escalation of foreign debts to the point when these threatened to become unsustainable. In that sense, African states were as economically vulnerable at the millennium as at the beginning of structural adjustment. Finally leaving aside the specific impact of the AIDS pandemic, most of the social indicators did not point to improving living standards for the mass of the population, and in many countries the poverty profile deteriorated in tandem with SAPs.[27] Moreover, the effective dismantling of state marketing boards for foodstuffs sometimes led not merely to lower producer prices, but also the running down of food reserves. For example, Zimbabwe only narrowly averted famine in 1991–92 when the Grain Marketing Board, in an attempt to minimise financial losses, failed to maintain an adequate food reserve as it had done in the past.[28] Although the poor were heavily concentrated in the rural areas, in many countries the figures for poverty and the physical manifestations of impoverishment suggested progressive deterioration in the cities during the 1990s.[29]

This broadly negative assessment covers the whole of sub-Saharan Africa, which is evidently not very helpful when one takes into account that some countries were embroiled in civil wars and stricken by drought in particular years. It may therefore be more instructive to consider the experience of particular African countries in more detail. We will choose two which were reasonably thorough in implementing SAPs, namely Ghana and Tanzania. Another obvious candidate would be Uganda, but we will reserve consideration of this country for our discussion of AIDS policy.

8.1.1 The Ghanaian experience of adjustment

Our first case-study is Ghana which was a most unlikely candidate for the paragon of adjustment virtue which it was later to be held up as. Although the economic downturn had begun in the 1960s, the next decade witnessed a catastrophic decline in the country's fortunes and in the living standards of its people. By 1981, industries were operating at around 25 per cent of capacity because of crippling shortages of raw materials and spare parts. Equally, the cocoa farmers had largely ceased to replant their lands and resorted to smuggling to Côte d'Ivoire and Togo, where at least they could purchase the consumer goods which had disappeared from Ghanaian markets. The attempt to enforce price controls in urban areas was a limited disincentive to food crop farmers, given the vitality of the black market. More crucial were the bottlenecks arising from the deterioration of the roads and an absence of serviceable vehicles, petroleum and spares. The travails of agricultural production and marketing were an important contributing factor to the inflation rate which hit 116 per cent in 1981. If ever there was a country in need of a change of direction, it was Ghana. However, the political environment was scarcely conducive to the Bretton Woods agenda. Flt.-Lt. Jerry Rawlings had returned to power through a military coup on 31 December 1981, promising 'nothing less than a revolution'. As in the case of Ethiopia in 1974 (see Chapter 6), the civilian left which had multiplied on the University campuses responded to the clarion call and provided active support for a regime whose legitimacy was initially tenuous.

As in Ethiopia, a rift quickly emerged between voluntarists, who insisted that the revolution had to spring from below, and pragmatists who were prepared to co-operate with the military once it had demonstrated its revolutionary intent.[30] Members of the June 4 Movement (JFM), who had initially been represented at the heart of the Provisional National Defence Council (PNDC), and within the co-ordinating structures of the People's Defence Committees (PDCs), were purged for 'ultra-leftism' at the end of 1982. That left the members of the New Democratic Movement (NDM) who accepted that an austerity package was necessary, but continued to oppose anything which smacked of a capitulation to the Bretton Woods institutions. However, some of the government's economic advisors, like Dr Joe Abbey, became convinced that there was no alternative to striking a deal. This position was supported by the incoming Secretary for Finance and Economic Planning, Dr Kwesi Botchway (allegedly an NDM member) towards the end of 1982. After a heated internal debate, Rawlings eventually came down on the side of the reformers. The fact that 1983

Table 8.1   Terms of trade for selected African countries (1987 = 100)

Country	1967	1980	1986	1991
Africa overall	124	142	127	84
Ghana	119	118	103	62
Côte d'Ivoire	107	114	120	67
Kenya	117	124	137	87
Nigeria	81	186	83	82
Tanzania	108	112	116	84

Source: Adapted from R. Lensink, *Structural Adjustment in Sub-Saharan Africa* (London and New York: Longman, 1996), Table 3.4, p. 48.

Table 8.2 African indebtedness under structural adjustment (billions US$)

Country	External debt 1980	Debt service ratio 1980*	External debt 1997	Debt service ratio 1997*
Africa overall	84.0	9.7	198.2	13.7
Ghana	1.4	13.2	6.0	29.5
Côte d'Ivoire	7.4	39.4	15.6	27.4
Kenya	3.4	21.6	6.5	21.5
Nigeria	8.9	4.1	28.5	7.8
Tanzania	2.6	21.5	7.2	12.9
Zambia	3.3	25.3	6.8	19.9

* As percentage of exports of good and services.

Source: Adapted from Nicolas Van de Walle, *African Economies and the Politics of Permanent Crisis*, Table 5.2, p. 221.

Table 8.3 Growth rates in GDP for selected countries, 1980–97

Country	1980–90	1990–97	1998–2000
Ghana	3.0	4.3	4.3
Uganda	3.1	7.2	5.6
Tanzania*	2.4	3.0	4.4
Côte d'Ivoire	0.9	3.0	1.7
Kenya	4.2	2.0	1.2
Zambia	0.8	−0.5	n/a
DR Congo	1.6	−6.6	n/a
Botswana	n/a	n/a	6.6
Gabon	0.6	2.6	−2.7
Equatorial Guinea	n/a	n/a	20.1
Nigeria	1.6	2.7	2.8

* For Tanzania, the lower estimates have been used for the early 1990s.

Sources: World Bank, *World Development Report: Knowledge for Development, 1998–99*, Table 11, pp. 210–11; OECD, *African Economic Outlook, 2001/2002*, Statistical annex, Table 2; Phil Raikes and Peter Gibbon, 'Tanzania', in Poul Engberg-Pedersen, Peter Gibbon, Phil Raikes and Lars Udsholt (eds), *Limits of Adjustment in Africa: The Effects of Economic Liberalisation*, p. 234.

was the worst year on record – in which the return of more than a million citizens (expelled from Nigeria) compounded the calamity of drought – no doubt helped to focus minds. The government signed up to its first three-year Economic Recovery Programme (ERP) in April. While leaders of the NDM were marginalised, or purged outright, policymaking was increasingly dominated by technocrats who lacked a political base of their own, but who were trusted by Rawlings to run the administration. Rawlings continued to represent the populist face of the regime, but left most of the day-to-day administration to trusted Ministers and civil servants.

The willingness of the PNDC to adhere to the rigours of the agreements won it a great deal of respect within the IMF and World Bank. Consequently, as the

SAP formula evolved, Ghana found itself in the vanguard of reform, whereas Côte d'Ivoire (with whom it was always compared) acquired the reputation of being a reluctant reformer.[31] In 1987, Ghana embarked on ERP II which began the adjustment phase proper, but at the same time the government pioneered a Programme of Action to Mitigate the Social Costs of Adjustment (PAMSCAD). In 1993, phase three followed, which was supposed to herald the transition from recovery to 'accelerated growth'. Over these two decades, the Ghanaian programmes followed a standard format. The regime progressively devalued the currency and eventually allowed the market to determine the exchange rate. It laid off thousands of public sector (and ghost) workers, especially in the Cocoa Marketing Board, where the payroll shrank from 101,000 in 1984 to 42,000 at the end of 1991.[32] The PNDC also dismantled price controls, abolished import licensing and endeavoured to raise cocoa producer prices to around half of the world price. It also pushed through controversial charges for health and education, (un)popularly known as 'cash and carry'. In the 1990s, the Rawlings regime embarked on the privatisation of state enterprises and a reform of the banking sector and set up a stock exchange (see Table 8.4).

In return, the IMF and World Bank injected large sums of money into the country. This initially went into rehabilitating the crumbling infrastructure and the importation of materials for the productive sectors of the economy. Although dramatic improvements in transportation and the ending of consumer shortages were welcomed, there remained considerable opposition to the programme as a whole. In the urban areas, inflation fell from a peak of 129 per cent in 1983 to 25 per cent by 1989. But the collapse of the cedi meant that for some years real wages continued to decline, while the thousands who were retrenched had to find alternative sources of income. Although PAMSCAD was supposed to ease the transition, the amount of money available was too limited to make a practical difference. Not surprisingly, the Trade Union Congress (TUC) opposed structural adjustment, although its leaders tried to avoid open confrontation with the government. While urban opinion was largely opposed, little support emanated from the rural areas. In effect, therefore, the SAP was pursued by a government which pointedly refused to listen to expressions of popular opinion. If there had been an open debate, there is little doubt that the SAP would never have got off the ground. Nevertheless, by the 1990s, when Rawlings finally gave way to demands for a return to electoral politics, none of the competing parties argued for a significant change of direction. Although structural adjustment still had the capacity to provoke protest – such as when the government sought to introduce Value-Added Tax (VAT) in 1995 – the opposition argued for better implementation rather than the outright abandonment of the SAP.

For many years, Ghana was touted as the 'star pupil' of the IMF and World Bank. This stellar quality lay not merely in the willingness of the government to embrace austerity, but also in the early record of adjustment. After 1983, food shortages disappeared, cocoa production rose substantially, there was a spectacular recovery of the gold mining sector and industries began to increase their capacity utilisation.[33] Moreover, the government was able to balance its foreign trade, while revenues and expenditures were brought into alignment. In short, the stabilisation plan appeared to have borne fruit. However, as Ghana moved into the 'accelerated growth' phase, the indicators began to paint a less favourable picture. The growth rate slowed to just over 4.6 per cent in 1998, and fell further to 3.7 per cent in 2000, which was only slightly above the estimated population increase of around 3.1 per cent.[34] Whereas agriculture was supposed to have been rejuvenated by price incentives, the results were disappointing. In the case of cocoa, the government unwisely put most of its eggs in the cocoa basket. Although planters did replant their old cocoa farms, rising production was accompanied by a decline in world prices. Indeed, the world price lost 68 per cent of its value between 1985 and 1992.[35] In the food sector, the rate of growth in the second half of the 1980s averaged a meagre 2.1 per cent. Although there was some improvement in the mid-1990s, growth had fallen back to the same level at the end of the decade. In forestry, the early years of the ERP witnessed a free-for-all in which much of the forest was destroyed – a classic instance of windfall gains which had serious environmental consequences and which could not be sustained in the long run.

After an early spurt, much manufacturing enterprise went out of business because of an inability to compete with cheaper imports. The producers of consumer goods like textiles were hardest hit, whereas the production of intermediate goods (cement, processed wood and iron and steel products) performed rather better.[36] However, after increasing by 14.5 per cent between 1984 and 1987, manufacturing growth as a whole slumped to 2.6 per cent between 1988 and 1995. In 2000, it grew by 3.8 per cent which was an improvement, but far beneath the government's optimistic projections of 8 per cent growth.[37] Liberalisation and a more attractive investment code was supposed to attract foreign investment into industry, but this never materialised. The exception was mining where substantial injections of fresh investment led to a considerable increase in gold output. Indeed gold had replaced cocoa as the main export earner by 1992. However, the gold boom itself gave way to a slump after 1994, with the result that even the mighty Ashanti Goldfields Corporation sank into debt.[38] To top it all, the fiscal deficit reappeared, the external debt soared to $6.93 billion in 2000 and the level of corruption increased noticeably.[39] In consequence, Ghana quietly dropped off the World Bank/IMF list of high performers, to be replaced by other countries like Uganda.[40]

Table 8.4 Ghanaian economic performance, 1972–2000 (percentage growth rates)

Sector	1972–75	1976–82	1983–86	1987–90	1991–95	1998–20
Agriculture	−2.3	1.4	1.5	1.3	2.7	3.7
Industry	1.9	−7.3	5.6	7.0	4.3	4.0
Services	0.2	1.2	5.7	7.9	6.1	5.2*

* Refers only to 1999 and 2000.

Sources: OECD, *African Economic Outlook, 2000–01*, pp. 156–8; Ernest Aryeetey and Jane Harrigan, 'Macroeconomic and sectoral developments since 1970', in Ernest Aryeetey, Jane Harrigan and Machiko Nissanke (eds), *Economic Reforms in Ghana: The Miracle and the Mirage* (Oxford, Accra and Trenton: James Currey, Woeli and Africa World Press, 2000), p. 24 (1998–20 column, added by author).

The central question is whether the Rawlings regime had deviated from the path of righteousness or the SAP formula was flawed to start with. Certainly, there is reason to believe that the need to solicit votes after 1992 led to a weakening of the government's resolve to keep public expenditure down.[41] However, it is difficult not to conclude that the ERP/SAP fell victim to its own internal contradictions. The initial rapid gains were of the one-off variety: manufacturing was bound to recover once inputs became available and control prices were removed, while the marketed output from agriculture was likely to increase once rural roads became motorable. However, there was a limit to the capacity of the market to resolve deeper structural constraints, which meant that production increases tended to level off quite quickly. Moreover, the pursuit of liberalisation at all costs was often counter-productive. For example, food crop farmers were faced with a substantially higher bill for fertiliser and other inputs once subsidies were removed, but found it almost impossible to access bank credit. The net result was that fertiliser and pesticide use declined from an already low base and yields remained unusually low.[42] The failure to offer any protection to the manufacturing sector, which was equally starved of credit, had adverse consequences of its own. The crucial point is that none of this was very surprising: indeed it had been widely predicted at the outset. However, the Rawlings regime had little joy in arguing the case for selective non-market intervention in the face of the rigid orthodoxy which prevailed within the Bretton Woods institutions. The latter continued to insist that free markets would necessarily stimulate agriculture and manufacturing, in the face of compelling evidence to the contrary.

If structural adjustment did not deliver rapid economic development, what of the social consequences? The underlying assumption was that as the economic cake expanded, all Ghanaians would ultimately benefit. However, by the turn of the millennium it was apparent that the cake was not expanding fast enough, while the share of the slices was becoming yet more unequal. For this reason, crude measures such as the rise in average per capita income should not be taken to mean that all Ghanaians necessarily became better off. In the rural areas, the financial constraints facing small farmers meant that most probably did not benefit from liberalisation to any great extent. In the urban areas, the informal sector sustained a majority of the urban population, but the competition was intense in the 1990s. Although in theory there was scope for the development of micro-enterprises, the reality is that aspiring entrepreneurs could not lay their hands on the start-up capital. On the whole, it is difficult to see where the increments in urban and rural incomes would come from except in regions which were favourably endowed – such as at the coast where niche tourism for African Americans was a novel departure.

A great deal of effort has gone into attempts to gather statistical evidence concerning the social impact of SAPs. However, there has been a lack of agreement as to what ought to be measured and by what instruments. Eboe Hutchful has rightly pointed out that the obsession with calibrating absolute poverty has tended to obscure the plight of Ghanaians hovering just above the notional poverty line.[43] Furthermore, there have been problems with reconciling the data sets. Be that as it may, it is worth highlighting some of the conclusions which have been reached. The figures released by the Ghana Living Standards Survey (GLSS) suggest that between 1987/88 and 1991/92 the incidence of poverty fell from 36.9 per cent to 31.5 per cent of the population after an initial increase, but that it continued to increase significantly in Accra.[44] The unprecedented phenomenon of street children in the capital bears out this finding impressionistically. In 1998, Ghanaian life expectancy stood at 59 years, which was above the African average and an improvement on the average of 45 years in 1960. Moreover, over the ten-year period from 1988 to 1998 infant mortality is estimated to have fallen from 77 to 60, while the percentage of immunised children is estimate to have risen from 31 to 55 per cent over the five years after 1988.[45]

Insofar as these figures can be trusted, they appear to disprove the assertion that structural adjustment led to mass impoverishment. However, it is worth underlining that the gains were fairly marginal as well as unevenly distributed. Although there was a real increase in spending on health, for example, the historic bias in favour of the cities was intensified.[46] Moreover, the share of health spending enjoyed by the poorest 20 per cent is thought to have fallen from 12 to 11 per cent between 1989 and 1992, at the same time as the richest 20 per cent increased their share from 31 to 34 per cent. Anyone who has lived in rural Ghana will be aware that people tend to avoid hospitals unless suffering from severe illness because of the burden of paying for treatment.[47] In the case of education, the story was a broadly similar one. The amount of money injected into education increased in line with its share of the national budget. Both primary and secondary school enrolments are thought to have increased between 1988 and 1993, from 79 to 88 per cent and from 37 to 39 per cent respectively.[48] However, the poorest 20 per cent of the population experienced a slight drop in their share of education expenditure. By the end of 1990s, when there was increasing concern at the effects of educational reform on teaching standards, those with money tended to send their children to private schools. Finally, while the proportion of women entering higher education rose, male and female enrolments from the North of the country were inordinately low[49] (see Table 8.5).

The picture is therefore a decidedly mixed one. Elliot Berg poses the legitimate question of whether the alternatives to adjustment would not have been worse. Certainly, there is reason to believe that if there had not been radical change of direction in 1983, most Ghanaians would probably have become progressively poorer over time. However, the Ghanaian experience also demonstrates the stubborn persistence of all the interlocking constraints identified by the structuralists. The deteriorating terms of trade, which wiped out the gains which should have followed from increased exports of cocoa and gold, is a salutary reminder of the 'Catch-22' which Nkrumah had warned of in the 1950s. Moreover, structuralists could have predicted that economic liberalisation would squeeze local industry while contributing to balance of payments problems. Matters were not helped by the conspicuous consumption of the Ghanaian *nouveaux riches* which did very little to stimulate local industry. Even the construction boom, which underpinned much of the vitality of the industrial sector, was based on rampant speculation. Finally, set against whatever social gains were recorded is the salutary fact that per capita income in Ghana in 1994 was significantly lower than it had been in 1980.[50] In short, this was no miracle.

Tanzania arrived at a similar destination, but through a rather different pathway. As we have seen in Chapter 5, the Arusha Declaration of 1967 was followed by the adoption of an avowedly socialist programme. The Nyerere vision was ambitious, and precisely for that reason it enjoyed the sympathy of the donor community – especially the Scandinavian countries, but also the World Bank which, under the presidency of Robert McNamara, was committed to the goal of achieving 'growth with equity'.[51] As a result, Tanzania became the largest recipient of foreign aid in sub-Saharan Africa during the 1970s. By the end of the decade, however, donor confidence in the Tanzanian experiment was beginning to wane as bureaucratic inefficiency and corruption became all too obvious and as substantial public investments seemed to yield almost no dividend. The crunch came in 1979 when the sudden end of the coffee boom was followed by a costly war against the Amin regime in Uganda and the second oil shock which doubled petroleum prices overnight.

At this point, an approach was made to the IMF and a standby credit was agreed, but this was terminated when the government was unable to respect the budget ceilings. In 1981, negotiations began with the World Bank which insisted on an agreement with the IMF. However, the latter insisted on tough conditions, such as a devaluation of at least 50 per cent and substantial budget cuts. Nyerere refused to give way over devaluation and instead the government launched its own National Economic Survival Programme in 1981/82. However, this attempt at home-grown austerity failed to arrest the slide. In an attempt to break the deadlock, the World Bank sponsored an international team of advisors to help design an adjustment programme which would be acceptable to all sides. The team was sympathetic to the Tanzanian position, but reasoned that without some devaluation any recovery effort was doomed to fail. The government cannibalised parts of the proposal and incorporated them into its own Structural Adjustment Programme (not to be confused with the real thing), but left out the proposed devaluation for the moment.[52] Meanwhile, within the regime, a vigorous internal debate was playing itself out between would-be reformers, like Finance Minister Cleopas Msuya, and committed socialists like Kigoma Malima (the Minister of Planning) and Nyerere himself.[53] Whereas the former accepted that the parallel economy was nurtured by state controls in the context of endemic scarcity, the latter argued that what was required was tougher action against smugglers and black marketeers. When attempts to enforce controls more rigorously led to goods simply disappearing from the market, the government was forced to reconsider its options. In 1984/85, the owners of foreign exchange were permitted to import goods without questions asked; the currency was devalued; and school fees were introduced.[54]

However, none of this tinkering failed to arrest a steadily deteriorating economic situation, and when even the Nordic countries began to scale back their own funding the message was clear. In 1985, the greatest obstacle was removed when Nyerere voluntarily retired and was succeeded by Ali Hassan Mwinyi. In 1986, President Mwinyi decided to cut a deal with the IMF and World Bank in the shape of a three-year ERP. In 1989, this was followed by a

Table 8.5 Ghanaian social indicators, 1988 and 1993

Indicator	1988	1993
Infant mortality (per 1000 births)	77	66
% children immunized	31	55
Gross primary enrolment rate	79	88
Gross secondary enrolment rate	37	39

Source: Adapted from Kweku Appiah, Lionel Demery and George Laryea-Adjei, 'Poverty in a changing environment', in Aryeetey et al. (eds), *Economic Reforms in Ghana*, Table 16.5, p. 317.

three-year Enhanced Structural Adjustment Programme (ESAP) or ERP II. These followed pretty much the same format as in Ghana. Under ERP I, the regime agreed to raise agricultural producer prices, devalue the currency, rein in public spending, maintain a tight monetary policy, improve revenue collection and free up the market for inputs and consumer goods. Under ESAP, these reforms were deepened, with the liberalisation of foreign investment, the financial sector and agricultural marketing. As in Ghana, foreign exchange bureaux were legalised, while the exchange rates was henceforth determined by a foreign exchange auction rather than by administrative fiat. In 1993, the third phase began with the replacement of three-year plans by a 'Rolling Plan and Forward Budget', in which the emphasis was on scaling down the civil service and privatising the parastatals.[55] There were some glitches, most notably over 1993–95 when the government was accused of corruptly granting tax exemptions and failing to do enough to raise revenues. The IMF responded by closing off the tap, while donors demanded the removal of Malima as Minister of Finance. Malima was duly sacrificed and Tanzania returned to the good books of the donor community. By the mid-1990s, the hardliners had been defeated, while rival political parties which were legalised from 1992 were themselves committed to the broad principle of structural adjustment.

Like the Ghanaians, the Tanzanians eventually complied with the most important conditionalities, whilst dragging their feet on some of the reforms which were the least acceptable. For some years, the decision to open up produce buying to private traders was stymied by local government authorities working in league with the co-operative unions. In the second half of the 1990s, as the donors began to attribute backsliding to a lack of perceived local 'ownership' of SAPs, some space was also created for the central government and interest groups to argue for, and occasionally win, modification of the terms.[56] On the whole, though, Tanzania was a country which dutifully took the economic medicine even when many considered it unpalatable – undoubtedly helped by the legislative majority wielded by the CCM. Hence, the public sector payroll was cut from 355,000 to 270,000 between 1993 and 1997, which was hardly likely to be a vote-winner. Again, despite moans of protest about the disposal of national assets to foreigners at knock-down prices, some 230 of the 383 parastatals which had been earmarked for privatisation or liquidation had been wound up by 1998.[57] Indeed, the assessment of the Bretton Woods institutions was that (the glitch apart) Tanzania had demonstrated a solid commitment to reform. The shortcomings were mostly attributed to a legacy of bureaucratic inertia rather than to a lack of political will. Indeed, in a striking reversal of the normal pattern, Tanzania began to contrasted favourably with Kenya.

In assessing the impact of structural adjustment, it is useful to distinguish once again between the economic results and the social consequences. As in Ghana, the devaluation of the currency and a shift towards market mechanisms did help to curb smuggling and shrink the black market – as did the greater availability of consumer goods. Again, the channelling of large sums of money into infrastructural improvement and into the regeneration of the industrial sector removed many of the production bottlenecks. This infusion of foreign aid also helped to soften opposition to structural adjustment within the CCM and within the wider society. As Raikes and Gibbon put it: 'Whatever the Tanzanian people want, it does not seem to be a return to the later Nyerere years: the shortages, the rationing, the waiting and the intrusion of officialdom into personal space and time.'[58] However, in the longer run the same mixed picture emerged as in Ghana. In terms of overall economic growth, the record was certainly more favourable than in the pre-adjustment period, but Tanzania never quite reached lift-off. In the early 1990s, the economy grew at less than 4 per cent, but in the latter part of the decade it topped 5 per cent.[59] This represented an improvement on the pre-adjustment years, but it was still disappointing in view of the fact that the much of the second economy – which may have previously accounted for as much as 30 per cent of economic activity – had been captured within official circuits.[60]

As in the case of Ghana, the weak link proved to be agriculture, which was supposed to be the linchpin of recovery. Between 1976–85 and 1986–95 official figures estimated an acceleration in agricultural growth from an average of 2.2 to 5.5 per cent annum. However, Ponte has revealed that the recurrent problem of inflated statistics worsened in the SAP years, with the result that these figures significantly exaggerate the divergence in performance.[61] Moreover, OECD statistics reveal that agricultural production grew slower than the rest of the economy, at 3 per cent, in 2000. Although there were years of comparative abundance, the production of foodstuffs never registered the increases which had been anticipated. As in Ghana, the removal of fertiliser subsidies and the liberalisation of supplies led to declining usage, with adverse consequences for crop yields. The story of cash crop production was equally mixed. Coffee exports rose from 13,600 tonnes in 1991 to 18,400 tonnes in 1998, but then began to decline again. The export of cashew nuts increased greatly; that of tea, tobacco and sisal grew more slowly; while tobacco exports were static.[62] Although the winding up of inefficient parastatals had its merits, the pressure on bank credit meant that peasant farmers were left out of the loop. In fact, the share of bank lending that went to agriculture as a whole fell from 8.3 per cent in 1990 to 4.6 in 1998.[63] In an instructive comparison of Morogoro and Songea Districts, Ponte found that peasants in the former were able to increase their farm incomes over the adjustment period by cultivating crops for the Dar es Salaam market, whereas the farmers in peripheral Songea became poorer as a result of the abolition of uniform national prices for food crops and the removal of the input subsidies.[64] The story of the industrial sector was also depressing. The contribution of mining and industry to GDP actually fell between 1980 and the period of ESAP. Although a gold mining boom did get underway, the manufacturing industry suffered. A mounting import bill for consumer goods supports the conclusion that 'some types of domestic production such as clothing and textiles, shoes, leather, sugar and oil were largely replaced by imports'.[65] Hence, the industrial infrastructure which was erected during the Nyerere years wilted under competition from cheaper imports.

Although structural adjustment was supposed to enable Tanzania to live within its means, the reality was that the country remained in the red throughout the 1990s. In years when the production of crops such as coffee expanded, the world market price simply declined, leaving the country no better off. One of the stock critiques of the Nyerere years was that 'self-reliant' Tanzania became more dependent on foreign aid and not less so. However, under structural adjustment the country became yet more dependent on the donors. While the latter were prepared to repeatedly reschedule the national debt, the size of the overall burden rose from $4.3 billion in 1986 to $7.97 billion at the end of 1999. At the same time, the large domestic debt increased as well, squeezing the amount of credit which was available for farmers and manufacturers.[66] By 1992/93, the greatest single item in the national budget – some 32 per cent – was set aside for debt repayment, compared to half that sum which was earmarked for health and education together.[67] In 1997, Christian Aid claimed that 'Tanzania now spends four times more on servicing external debt than it does on health'.[68] In a nutshell, more than a decade of structural adjustment had failed to really put Tanzania back on track. If the donors had chosen to pull the plug at any stage, Tanzania would have been plunged straight back into the crisis of the early 1980s.

Finally, if one turns to the social impact of SAPs, the picture is as confused as in Ghana. On government statistics, which were based on income and expenditure estimates, there was a reduction of poverty in the country as a whole, but this was partially offset by increases in urban poverty. However, the criteria and the figures themselves have been hotly contested, while opinion surveys which have sought to assess whether Tanzanians perceived themselves as better off after adjustment have yielded conflicting results.[69] What can be said is, firstly, that rural poverty almost certainly increased in areas which were disadvantaged by remoteness from the main lines of communication. Secondly, the retrenchment of urban labour and the over-crowded nature of the informal sector meant that life became appreciably harder for large sections of the urban population as well. Another way of measuring well-being is to focus on access to basic services. Whereas Nyerere's proudest achievement had been the progress towards universal primary education, enrolment is estimated to have fallen back from 93 per cent of the population in 1980 to 57 per cent in 2000.[70] However, as the budgetary allocation that went to education fell back to 2.5 per cent of the total in the mid-1990s, the greatest squeeze was placed on secondary and higher education. What that meant in real terms is very difficult to judge. Whereas only 6 per cent of Tanzanian children received a secondary education in government schools, the equivalent figure was 28 per cent for Kenya and 17 per cent for Uganda.[71] However, there was a proliferation of private secondary schools from the 1980s onwards, typically funded through community contributions, which accounted for more students than the formal system did. Hence, a study of nine districts in 1993 found that 60.9 per cent of secondary education was accounted for by religious organisations, District Development Trusts and the like. The deployment of statistics in relation to Tanzania, not least by the IFIs, has been so shoddy that they almost certainly undercount the secondary school population.[72]

In the case of health care, the state continued to play the dominant role overall, but government allocations were cut by about 15 per cent between 1990 and 1997 – in spite of the fact that the country was in the grips of the AIDS epidemic. The result was that the number of hospital beds shrank, while government hospitals regularly lacked basic equipment. However, the above study found that 43.5 per cent of hospitals were non-governmental, and these would have filled the gap to some extent.[73] When it comes to evaluating the health implications of structural adjustment, the figures are especially difficult to reconcile. Whereas access to health care supposedly expanded from 72 per cent of the population in 1980 to 93 per cent in 1995, figures released by the OECD give a much lower figures of 42 per cent in 2000, which would place Tanzania far below the continental norm.[74] On life expectancy, the figures for women in 1996 stood at exactly where they had been in 1980 (an average of 51.8 years), whereas there had been a modest improvement for men (49.2 as against 48.4 years). However, life expectancy apparently began to decline again at the end of the decade, as a consequence of the AIDS pandemic. In general, one can conclude that whereas SAPs arrested the spiral of economic decline, it did not issue in a new era of material improvement for most Tanzanians.

In both Ghana and Tanzania, the independence leaders had boasted that a generation was time enough for committed governments to forge modern economies and bring about significant improvements in living standards. At the start of the new millennium – after a decade-and-a-half of adjustment – the IFIs were talking down such rapid advances. Both countries were described as high achievers, but they experienced pretty modest growth over the 1980 and 1990s. Certainly, anything which might reasonably be described as 'development' was as far off at the start of the new millennium as ever. In the opinion of the IFIs, the ability to raise living standards in the face of rapidly rising populations depended on accelerated growth whose beneficial effects would trickle down. In the case of Ghana, where an estimated 30 per cent of the population lived below the poverty line, if per capita incomes were to grow at only 1 per cent per annum it would still take 34 years for that figure to be brought down to 10 per cent.[75] In the case of Tanzania, with an estimated 50 per cent living below the poverty line, the gradient was that much steeper.[76] When one takes account of the fact that per capita income in that country rose at an average of 0.6 per cent per year after 1986, the enormity of the task is apparent.[77] Moreover, the evidence of increasing inequality within these countries – both as between regions and as between households – would suggest that the trickle-down effect was likely to be much slower than the models would suggest.

In a nutshell, even the success stories were less than inspirational. On a continental scale, structural adjustment failed to unlock the development potential of the continent as much as the programmes which had been adopted after independence. At the start of the new millennium, the depressing reality was that Africa's position within the global economy seemed destined to condemn the majority of its people to perpetual impoverishment. In a neo-liberal reworking of Orwellian 'Newspeak', in which words mean their very opposite, Western countries continued to speak of eradicating poverty within a matter of decades whilst practicing blatant protectionism which ensured the opposite result.[78] For example, the hefty subsidies paid to a mere 25,000 American cotton producers were not merely greater than the entire GDP of Burkina Faso, but were also blamed for driving world prices downwards to the detriment of very large numbers of African farmers in countries like Burkina and Mali. Equally, European Union farm subsidies led to the production of non-economic crops like sugar beet at the expense of sugar producers in countries like Mozambique.[79] Free markets, it seems, were only for the poor.

8.2 False friends? The rise of Non-Governmental Organisations

In the 1980s and 1990s, a feature of the African landscape which was almost as striking as the ubiquity of SAPs was the proliferation of NGOs. These refer to associations, of a non-profit nature, which were formally distinct from the institutions of the state – both in Africa and in donor countries – as well as from the international agencies. It also makes sense to distinguish NGOs in the North (NNGOs) from NGOs grounded within Africa, and to distinguish the latter from other grassroots organisations (GROs). During the period in question, there was an expansion in the number, scope and public profile of NNGOs in the North. But at the same time, there was an exponential growth of NGOs on the African continent. These two phenomena were closely related, in that NNGOs sought out partners within Africa, while people on the continent were quick to spot the advantages of banding together and attaching themselves to NNGOs and donor agencies.

It is worth reminding ourselves that the rich associational life of contemporary Africa is not of recent provenance. In most African countries, there are long-established traditions of traders, women, youth and religious groups forming their own associations, often of considerable size and organisational complexity. In West Africa, the venerable market women of cities like Kumasi and Lomé have not merely dominated the trade in foodstuffs, textiles and other consumer items, but have been a political force to reckon with as well. Revolving credit association, or *tontines*, has similarly been a feature of many countries where access to bank credit has been hard to come by or where interest rates have been prohibitive. Again, male migrants to the cities and mining camps of Central and Southern Africa have historically paid their dues to burial associations to assure themselves of a fitting sendoff in their places of origin, should the worst come to pass. Finally, it is worth mentioning the vitality of hometown associations, which have been such a feature of southern Nigeria.[80] These have provided a mechanism for urban dwellers to contribute to the upliftment of their home areas in the shape of schools, clinics and the like. In some African countries, like Tanzania, this associational panorama was considerably narrowed after independence as the single-party endeavoured to eliminate possible sources of ethnic mobilisation and alternative foci of loyalty. In Kenya, by contrast, self-improvement, in the shape of *harambee*, became virtually a state ideology under Kenyatta. In fact, self-help was deeply inculcated in the fabric of most African countries. What was different about the 1980/90s was the emergence of NGOs floating above these primary associations and GROs. These spoke the language of the donors and tapped into their resource base.

The NGO explosion can itself be attributed to three developments which manifested themselves in the mid-1970s, but which came to full fruition over the next decade. The first is the flourishing of international humanitarian concern arising out of unprecedented material affluence in the West (despite the temporary setback of the oil crisis) and the growing sophistication of media technologies. The first substantive NGOs were formed in the post-war period and were primarily focused upon poverty alleviation in the West. The classic instance is Oxfam which was formed in 1942 to address famine conditions in Greece and which later became one of the largest international NNGOs, with an income of £91.8 million in 1997.[81] After African independence, Western audiences began to be bombarded with images of human suffering, to the extent that events on the continent were scarcely considered newsworthy unless they entailed pictures of abject misery. The first media famine arose out of the Biafran war, when the emotive images of starving children served as lethal ammunition in the propaganda war. The images of famine in the West African Sahel and in Ethiopia over 1972–74 were the next to be delivered to the doorsteps of Western audiences. However, nothing quite compared to the effects of the Ethiopian famine of 1983–85 when the most intimate pictures of human misery were relayed to Western television screens on a daily basis and for months on end. The Band-Aid initiative, in which popular entertainers performed to raise money for famine relief, set the tone for all subsequent emergencies. Although it was bad tactics to make potential givers feel responsible for African poverty, audiences were invited to reflect on how much difference even a small sum of money would make to families living on the margins of subsistence. Although relief agencies were only the tip of the NGO iceberg, their public campaigns did enable a host of other developmental NGOs to piggyback their own activities. In the OECD countries, the number of NGOs is estimated to have risen from 1600 in 1980 to 2970 in 1993, while their total spending is estimated to have risen from $2.8 billion to $5.7 billion over the same period– the equivalent to the national debt of many an African country.[82] Clearly not all of this activity was centered on Africa, but in the case of the European NGOs more than half (and rising) has gone to the poorest continent.[83] Developmental NNGOs have sought to persuade their constituents of the importance of acting pre-emptively in Africa to promote sustainable development, which would obviate the need for famine relief in the future. They have also lobbied their governments for an increase in the amount of development aid which is despatched to Africa, as well as for debt relief.

The second development is one we have already touched on, namely the tendency for the Bretton Woods institutions to blame African states for the crisis and to seek out other partners who were not tainted by association. As the state was rolled back, NNGOs were invited to play a more active part in the delivery of basic services like health and education, whilst they became the recipient of significant amounts of donor funding. The NGOs were seen as less bureaucratic and corrupt than state institutions and were therefore thought to provide better value for money. Within the OECD countries, the proportion of all aid which was channelled through NNGOs rose from 0.7 per cent in 1975 to around 5 per cent in 1993/94.[84] At the same time, the NNGOs came to account for as much as 14 per cent of total overseas aid.[85] When the World Bank began to admit that there might be social costs associated with adjustment, much of the money that went into mitigating the side-effects was channelled through these same bodies. Moreover, Western governments preferred to direct their own bilateral aid through favoured NNGOs, normally headquartered in their own capital city. By 1995/96, the British government was routing 9.3 per cent of its aid through agencies like Oxfam.[86] Many NNGOs became more reliant upon government sources than the voluntary contributions which kept them in the public eye. In the case of the Canadian and Swedish NGOs, as much as 70 and 85 per cent of their resources came through the Canadian International Development Agency (CIDA) and the Swedish International Development Authority (SIDA) respectively in the mid-1990s. The average for all NGOs is possibly in the region of 35 per cent.[87] In short, while African countries were becoming more dependent on NNGOs, the latter were leaning more heavily on Northern governments. This is significant in itself because it has meant that the aid being sent to Africa – partially offsetting the debt payments going in the opposite direction – actually emanated from governmental sources.

Finally, there was the tremendous demand for services in countries ravaged by economic crisis and the rigours of adjustment. In some instances, most famously in Tanzania, state failure led communities to embark on self-help initiatives to keep services running. However, it would be fallacious to suppose, as some political scientists has done, that when state money dried up communities could fill the gap themselves. More typically, service provision dried up. With the donors pushing the NNGOs, it made sense for African GROs to seek assistance from external sources. However, it did not take long before indigenous NGOs began to proliferate, seeking to insert themselves as intermediaries between external agencies and local communities. The rate of NGO expansion in most African countries is striking, although estimates vary wildly. In Ghana, where there had been ten registered NGOs in 1960, there were 350 of various descriptions in 1991.[88] In Kenya, the number of registered development-oriented NGOs is estimated to have increased sixfold between 1963 and 1988, reaching 291 – and if others are included the total was more like 400.[89] In the case of Uganda, Susan Dicklitch estimates that as many as between 700 and 1000 foreign and indigenous NGOs were registered by the mid-1990s.[90] In Tanzania, long established as a Mecca for donors, there were some 200 in 1993, but 813 two years later, although subsequent official estimates put the number at anywhere between 1800 and 8000.[91]

Aside from the numerical explosion, the range of NGOs operative in any one country was astonishing. There were the large international NGOs, with instantly recognisable names which sometimes worked through their own local chapters or through selected partners – examples would be Oxfam, World Vision, Christian Aid and Action-Aid. This bracket would also include the large Church-based NGOs such as the Catholic Relief Services and Lutheran World Relief. What is often forgotten in this is the similar contribution made by Islamic

NGOs, operating from other parts of the Muslim World like Saudi Arabia and the Gulf States, which sought to aid their co-religionists. There was also a myriad of smaller NNGOs which had specific remits, like Water Aid and the various AIDS charities. On the African side, there were NGOs which were committed to the empowerment of women, dealing with the impact of AIDS, assisting small farmers, delivering education, promoting environmental protection and mobilising support for marginalised groups like the handicapped, orphans, street children and minority peoples. The list was endless, while the scale ranged from organisations which turned over multi-million dollars budgets to those which were confined to a handful of part-time workers. In short, it would be mistaken to imagine that either NNGOs or African NGOs came in a single package.

For heuristic reasons it is helpful to maintain the distinction between NNGOs, international agencies, African NGOs and GROs. During the period in question, the first three represented the unequal sides of a triangle, in which there was close co-operation, but also a great deal of mutual ambivalence. The NNGOs were only too keen to be brought into development work at the bottom floor and for that reason they tended to identify with the rolling back of the state. Although they were construed by African governments as being potential fifth columnists, their relationship with the Bretton Woods institutions was seldom that simple – even if they enjoyed 'sweetheart relationships' with their own governments. The reality was that many of the NNGOs were critical of a dogmatic economism which they blamed for mass impoverishment and/or environmental degradation. For their part, the World Bank and IMF welcomed the willingness of NNGOs to take over many of the functions of the state and to run them more efficiently. From the late 1980s, Bank reports began to extol NNGOs as valued partners and a formal NGO–World Bank Committee, which was first established in 1984, was accorded much greater publicity.[92] Indeed some commentators began to question whether the NNGOs were not, in fact, losing their identity altogether on the basis that 'as NGOs get close to donors they become more like donors'.[93] On the other hand, there was an inherent incompatibility between their operating assumptions. Whereas the Bank was concerned with disbursing large sums of aid from above and was firmly wedded to its conventional performance criteria, many of the NNGOs were committed to the ideal of participatory development in which the views of the recipients were considered a crucial measure of success. When supposedly objective statistics was traded against subjective perception, there was no easy means of converting one currency into the other. The World Bank had little time for the NGO obsession with empowerment, especially when this threatened to complicate relations with the African governments concerned.

Not surprisingly, African NGOs welcomed the infusion of external resources whether these were channelled through the NNGOs or came directly through Northern governments and international agencies. However, there were tensions when the 'partners' insisted on strict monitoring of expenditure. Another source of resentment amongst the wider population was the amount of money which seemed to be spent on Pajeros and office equipment. In many African capitals, like Kampala, it was impossible not to be struck by the fleets of NNGO vehicles contributing to the interminable traffic jams. In many countries, the NNGO invasion also elicited unfavourable comment about the differential rates of remuneration which arose from their presence. NNGOs poached highly qualified personnel at higher rates of pay, leaving other public servants to bear the costs of civil service reform. On the other hand, NNGOs sometimes suspected their African partner NGOs of being more interested in accumulating perks at the endless round of workshops than the furtherance of a development agenda. These suspicions were not altogether unwarranted, given that the lure of money led many poorly paid public servants and academics to form NGOs as a means of improving their material conditions: in the trade these came to be known as 'briefcase NGOs'. Although Westerners treated NGO work as a career option, many certainly regarded it as a vocation. The relationship between many NGOs and the GROs lower down the food chain was often tenuous to say the least. Finally, given that so many NNGOs and NGOs were setting up shop, it was inevitable that there was fierce competition for the attention of the same limited set of donors. The result was that the rhetoric of pooling expertise often belied a reality of cut-throat competition, far removed from the supposedly humanitarian objectives which justified the existence of NGOs in the first place. One does not have to be entirely cynical to suppose that NGOs, like all human organisations, had an interest in perpetuating their existence. In a highly competitive environment, that meant doing down the opposition, whilst clinging doggedly to existing honeypots.

African governments also exhibited an ambivalent attitude towards the NGO community. Although they had to tolerate the periodic invasion of IMF and World Bank missions, they were under no such compulsion to defer to NNGOs. On the other hand, when NNGOs were providing significant material resources, they were relieving some of the burden from central government. In countries like Ghana, official enthusiasm for decentralisation was partly rooted in the expectation that District Assemblies would raise more of their own revenues through market tolls and local taxation. Later, these Assemblies were also encouraged to solicit additional support from NNGOs, rather than looking to central government. The shrewd calculation was that anything which led to the completion of local projects was likely to redound to the credit of the regime even when it had not actually stumped up the money. In fact, the Rawlings regime went a step further and converted the 31st December Women's Movement, which had been founded by Nana Konadu Rawlings (the President's wife), into an NGO in its own right. In this manner, the Rawlings government found ways on turning the NGO presence to its own advantage. In Tanzania, this process was taken even further. Not only were GROs sponsored and patronised by the ruling party, but it became common practice for District Councils to devolve some of their activities on to separate District Development Trusts – a process which Andrew Kiondo depicts as the 'privatisation' of local government.[94] These Trusts were empowered to raise revenues, through local taxes and crop cesses, in return for which they took over the construction and maintenance of local services such as roads, schools and health clinics. The NGOs and donor agencies, which assisted the District Councils, also provided much of the funding which made these initiatives viable. Whereas the councils themselves were statutory bodies, the Trusts were the creation of political and business elites, often resident in Dar es Salaam, who were not formally elected or accountable to the rest of the population. This arrangement was evidently to the liking of the Tanzanian government, many of whose members managed or sponsored their own funds, because it actually firmed up political links with the countryside.

Nevertheless, many African governments also regarded the NGOs as a potential threat. By usurping the functions of the state, they were infringing on national sovereignty. At the same time, the NGO rhetoric of empowerment often sounded like an invitation to citizens to stand up to authority. Although there was little reason to fear NGOs which organised women in the production of soap, there was good reason to be suspicious of human rights or environmental NGOs. The latter had the potential to bring the authorities into disrepute and to complicate relations with foreign donors. Governments therefore sought to deal with the NGOs through a combination of carrots and sticks. They could grant or withhold privileges, such as the right to import equipment duty-free, and they could choose to be co-operative or otherwise in relation to visa applications and residence permits. By insisting on formal registration, they could also force NGOs to agree to codes of conduct. While the NNGOs could call on the moral support of their embassies and donor agencies, local NGOs were typically placed in a more exposed position. They had to choose between steering clear of political controversy, in return for receiving favourable consideration from the authorities, and vocally presenting their case at the risk of arrest and physical intimidation. A good example of someone who learned to play the game was the director of the Ndugu Society in Kenya, Ezra Mbogori. When the Kenyan government introduced legislation to subject NGOs to tighter controls in 1991, the NNGOs and local NGOs joined forces to resist what they regarded as unwarranted interference. Mbogori was elected to a new lobby group, the NGO Standing Committee, which successfully challenged the government plan. However, the Ndugu Society itself stayed well clear of political controversy in its work with street children and slum dwellers, and was able to carry out resettlement schemes in Nairobi on the basis of its co-operative relationship with the local administration.[95]

How then should one evaluate the NGO balance-sheet? The claim that NGOs constituted a friend of democracy will be left over to the next chapter. Here we will confine our discussion to their socio-economic contribution. By the start of new millennium, after two decades of intense activity on the continent, the early flush of enthusiasm had mostly dissipated and the NGOs were widely indicted by their critics for making things worse. At the very least, one could argue that the NGOs found it extremely difficult to reconcile two of their principal aspirations, namely improving the lot of ordinary Africans and empowering the least advantaged groups in society. As the NGOs became the conduits for donor funding, they slipped into the habit of thinking that if yet more money could be raised, that would inevitably enable them to do even better work. The problem was that as NGOs began to function and sound more like businesses, they became bureaucratic, technocratic and top-heavy. Although they were accountable to the Western governments which were stumping up more of the cash, they were not actually accountable to anyone in Africa. Moreover, NGO fundraising in the West tended to project the most paternalistic images of the African continent which contributed to a misunderstanding of the causes of crises and thus to a repetition of many mistakes. Often, the voices of the recipients of relief were not listened to because they were assumed to be in need of salvation first.

One of the fiercest critics of the 'humanitarian international', Alex de Waal, has suggested that the activities of the worst kind of organisations have set the standard for all the rest:

> The agency most determined to get the highest media profile obtains the most funds from donors (both the public and donor governments). In doing so, it prioritises the requirements of fund-raising: it follows the TV camera, employs pretty young women to appear in front of the cameras, engages in picturesque and emotive programmes (food and medicine, best of all for children), it abandons scruples about when to go in and when to leave, and it forsakes co-operation with its peers for advertising its brand name. Agencies that are more thoughtful – a category that includes most non-operational agencies (mainly church-related agencies that work through local partners/clients), consortia, and a handful of the older secular agencies – fail to obtain the same level of public attention and suffer for it.[96]

In relation to the famine industry, which is the special focus of his study, the author presents NNGOs (and UN agencies) as contributors to starvation rather than as benign saviours. The basis for this accusation is partly that food aid has tended to be diverted to meet the needs of combatants in civil wars, thereby prolonging the agony. But the contention is also that famine has tended to be construed in highly technocratic terms, thereby skirting the political causes of such disasters. Hence, in the Ethiopian famine of the mid-1980s, De Waal maintains that the blame was wrongly placed on a devastating drought rather than the use of starvation as a weapon of war. The NGOs therefore despatched famine relief through Addis Ababa, very little of which reached the most distressed areas which were under rebel control, and much of which was appropriated by the Ethiopian army.[97] A few NGOs were prepared to quietly ship aid over the border through the Sudan into Tigray and Eritrea, but most were not prepared to break with the principle of respect for national sovereignty.[98]

The shortcomings of the relief NGOs are controversial because of the practical implications for millions of Africans. Although the developmental NGOs often failed in their allotted tasks, the consequences were usually less dramatic – although sometimes persistent. One tendency was for NNGOs to converge on a country, district or area of activity and to duplicate each other's activities. In Tanzania, for example, Kiondo found that NNGOs and donors were drawn to the same districts which had the longest tradition of voluntary activity, neglecting other parts of the country where the need was greater.[99] Another inevitable consequence of becoming beholden to donors was that larger NNGOs, managing substantial budgets, tended to become overly bureaucratic. The NGOs with the worst success rates tended to be those which attempted to leave all decision-making in the hands of expatriate personnel as they attempted to throw money at a problem. As time went on, and NGOs learned from some of the mistakes of top-down development, many agreed that Africans ought not be merely treated as helpless victims, but valued as people who could be helped to help themselves. Conversely, it was increasingly agreed that forging a dependent relationship was likely to lead to a point when the NGO and/or donor agency eventually withdrew and the scheme in question collapsed. The problem with many attempts at grassroots empowerment was that they over-estimated the resources which were at the disposal of the target-group – be it women, youth or the average rural household. Thus a scheme might function for as long as it was financially supported, only to implode when the target group was thrown back on its own resources – not because of a dependent mentality, but rather for simple for reasons of poverty.

After Zimbabwean independence in 1980, NNGOs poured into the country and many became engaged in income-generating projects. The underlying assumption was that there were market demands waiting to be satisfied, but that the poor lacked the starting capital and the expertise with which to be able to respond. NNGOs therefore stepped in with a view to providing training in skills like book-keeping, whilst providing the seed-money to get projects off the ground. According to one assessment of NGOs worldwide, the experience was salutary:

> For many people involved in rural development in Zimbabwe the term income-generation is now loaded with negative connotations, equated with income-loss and seen more as a means of avoiding rather than addressing the factors perpetuating rural poverty.[100]

If making money was more elusive than it initially seemed, a safer bet for NGOs appeared to lie in supporting peasant farmers. The same report examines the record of two longstanding schemes which were designed by local NGOs to assist farmer's groups in Zimbabwe. The first was started by Silveira House, which depended on foreign church funding, while the second was run by Christian Care which derived its resources from Christian Aid and other international donors.[101] Both initiatives dated from before independence and involved dispensing concessional credit to farmers. This automatically screened out the poorest households who were considered too much of a credit risk. Ultimately, the farmers' groups were successful, but only for as long as they were supported by the parent NGOs. When the latter removed the crutches, the groups collapsed. A crucial reason was that the commercial interest rates of the Agricultural Finance Corporation were prohibitive and repayment terms were inflexible, with the result that many farmers defaulted when the rains failed in the early 1980s. Whereas these farmers' groups significantly increased their yields during the 1970s, these could not be sustained over the following decade when the cost of fertiliser became prohibitive.[102] While such initiatives demonstrated the ability of NGOs to make a difference in the agricultural sector, the lesson is that even middling peasants farmers had difficulty in keeping their heads above water. In that sense, liberalisation was no more conducive to raising peasant production (or income) in Zimbabwe than it was in Ghana or Tanzania.

Another example of a scheme which was designed to empower and to provide money to Zimbabwean peasants was an innovative approach to nature conservation. Whereas in Kenya and Tanzania, the authorities went down the route of evicting people and fencing-off wildlife parks in which tourists could view game in its 'natural' habitat, the Zimbabwean and Namibian governments attempted to involve rural communities in the management of wildlife resources.[103] Despite the opposition of international animal rights lobbies and certain conservationist NNGOs, the Zimbabwean government position was that protecting species was compatible with hunting at sustainable levels – a realist stance which was endorsed by most local NGOs. The earlier wildlife parks, which constituted 12.7 per cent of the land area of the country, remained, but there were growing concerns about the viability of certain species. Hence NNGOs like the World Wildlife Fund (WWF) assisted white ranchers to set up their own wildlife conservancies, to which black rhino and other animals were transferred from the national parks.[104] The owners of these private conservancies attempted to win over neighbouring African communities, if only to minimise the risk of poaching. However, the latter remained on the outside looking in. Moreover, critics were not slow to observe that this was part of a wider game-plan by whites to cling to their ownership of the land.

A far bolder initiative was the creation of the Communal Areas Management Programme for Indigenous Resources (CAMPFIRE) which was designed to associate the population of the former reserves with the management of wildlife resources for the first time: rather than viewing people as a problem, the latter would become partners in harvesting a renewable resource. Wildlife would be reintroduced into these settled areas, to attract foreign hunters who would pay good money for the right to shoot the game. While the Parks Department would supervise the wildlife, local communities would be materially rewarded for tolerating the inconvenient presence of wild animals. The first CAMPFIRE schemes were established in areas of low population density in the Nyaminyami (north-west) and Guruve Districts (north) in 1989. These were such a success that 21 other districts joined the scheme over the next two years. In order to assist with the increasingly complex organisation and financing of CAMPFIRE, a Collaborative Group of NGOs was constituted, including the WWF and the Zimbabwe Trust.[105] These NGOs were, in turn, the recipient of funding from USAID and the British Overseas Development Administration. The local NGOs also lobbied against international animal rights initiatives, most notably the Convention on International Trade in Endangered Species of 1989 which purported to ban the ivory trade. The latter posed a direct threat to CAMPFIRE because if wealthy foreigners (especially Americans) could not return home with their trophies, they were unlikely to come to Zimbabwe to hunt in the first place.

The CAMPFIRE initiative began with great promise because local communities were directly involved in wildlife management through Ward Wildlife Committees and benefited materially from the money brought in by safari organisers. In 1989, it was reported that one ward in Dande (on the northern border) had received Z$47,000, and had divided the proceeds between a clinic, school furniture and individual payments of Z$200 to each of 102 ward households. The latter was estimated to represent 56 per cent of annual gross household income from the sale of cotton.[106] But despite some highly optimistic assessments, CAMPFIRE began to run into difficulties in the 1990s as questions of financial control acquired heightened salience. Predictably, the aid which was being channelled through the NGOs precipitated a scramble for resources which owed little to the founding objectives. Two commentators, with close first-hand experience, have concluded that 'in a few districts and wards it is probably true to say that CAMPFIRE is as much about leveraging foreign funds as it is about sustainable wildlife management and production'.[107] Another problem was that the revenues from safari operators were paid into the funds of the Rural District Councils (RDCs) before they were passed down to the ward level.[108] Under the pressure of structural adjustment (which began in 1990), the central government was forced to scale back what it sent to the RDCs. The latter, not surprisingly, began to divert the safari revenues for their own operating expenses or what local government bureaucrats considered was appropriate development expenditure. Although the RDCs were nominally vehicles of local democracy, they were at some physical and psychological remove from the base communities. Finally, when news spread about the rewards which were accruing to the pioneer CAMPFIRE communities, there was an influx of land-hungry settlers from further afield. As the population increased, the returns which made it profitable for individuals to support CAMPFIRE started to evaporate. Although this might be taken as an illustration of the free-rider principle, it appears that the host communities actively encouraged settlement in the belief that a higher population would attract basic amenities such as roads and schools.[109] This might be interpreted as a response to the usurpation of CAMPFIRE, but it is equally conceivable that family income was considered secondary to local services. In fact, it may well be that the long-term interest of indigenes and settlers alike lay in farming and cattle-keeping which was ultimately incompatible with wildlife conservation. This implication was not to the liking of conservationist NGOs who were more concerned with the preservation of endangered species than with peasant livelihoods, but in a land-short country like Zimbabwe hard choices are having to be made.

While the CAMPFIRE experience points to the complications which came with money, our final example is of an environmental NGO which achieved a measure of local empowerment on the back of minimal resources. The Green Belt Movement (GBM) was initiated by the National Council of Women of Kenya (NCWK) in 1977 in an effort to raise awareness of environmental issues. Under the leadership of Wangari Maathai, it blossomed into a highly successful grassroots NGO which aimed to reverse environmental degradation by promoting tree planting in rural communities. By the mid-1990s, it could boast 'over 50,000 members organised in over 2000 local community groups in 27 of the 42 administrative districts in Kenya'.[110] The simple operational principles were one key to success. Women who wished to participate were expected to form a group and then to apply to the GBM offices for affiliation. Once this was approved, the community would be subjected to a basic environmental awareness programme, in which the importance of tree-planting was outlined. Thereafter, the women's group set about establishing a nursery. When the seedlings were ready for transplantation, they would be entrusted to selected farmers and public institutions. After follow-up visits to ensure that the trees were progressing, the women's groups would be remunerated by the GBM for each one which survived. In planting an estimated ten million new trees, the programme made a significant contribution to arresting environmental degradation. The woodlands which were planted also provided a renewable resource which reduced the burden on women whose job it was to find firewood. Moreover, the programme enabled the participants to develop valuable skills.

Arguably, though, it was the limited scale of the GBM which preserved its strong participatory dimension. Despite the prolific growth of the GBM network, its annual budget in the early 1990s hovered somewhere between $30,000 and $70,000, based on initial support from the Royal Norwegian Embassy Development Corporation (NORAD) and later from the Netherlands Organisation for International Development Co-operation (NOVIB). The GBM did not even have a proper office, but operated out of the private Nairobi residence of Maathai herself. Moreover, there was no wholesale pumping of money into the communities in question. Ndegwa estimated, on the basis of his research in one district in 1992, that members were likely to earn an extra $12 a year. When set against an average annual household income of $400, this was significant, but hardly a windfall.[111] However, this did prevent the GBM from degenerating either into a scramble for resources or a bureaucratic exercise. Although Maathai herself assumed a prominent profile as an environmental campaigner, clashing openly with the Moi government, her more political activities were far removed from the women's groups at the village level.

The contribution of NGOs therefore varied significantly. Some single-issue NGOs, such as those dealing with landmine eradication, made an undeniably positive contribution. At the other extreme were De Waal's buccaneering NNGOs which sometimes made things worse. In between was a myriad of organisations which struggled to reconcile the ideals of social improvement and local empowerment. A number of AIDS-focused NGOs which we discuss more fully in the next section made sterling contributions, but they were also loosely accountable and inclined towards empire building.[112] In general, NGOs contributed to the weakening of the post-colonial state.

8.3 The curse of Ham? Africa and the AIDS pandemic

The final theme which we wish to consider in this chapter is the historical progression and societal impact of AIDS in Africa. This account is more than usually provisional, given that there is so much about the spread of the disease that is imperfectly understood and it is still too early to gauge the success of various efforts to arrest its advance.

The first indication that there was a new threat to humans came over 1979/80 when doctors in the United States began to encounter clusters of diseases which had hitherto been considered rare. Shortly thereafter, an increased incidence of Karposi's sarcoma (a form of cancer) was also being noticed in African hospitals in places like Lusaka. It was quickly established that there was a direct link between the proliferation of these illnesses and the breakdown in the immune system of the patients. By 1983, the Human Immunodeficiency Virus (HIV) which causes AIDS had been identified, at the point when the world was waking up to the implications of a truly global pandemic of epic proportions. The scale of the crisis which unfolded over the next two decades is unparalleled in the history of our species. It is estimated that by 2010, AIDS will have killed more people than all of the previous global pandemics – including the Black Death, smallpox in the sixteenth century and the devastating 1917/19 influenza outbreak – combined.[113]

In debates about HIV/AIDS, Africa quickly assumed a central importance. The emerging consensus was that the disease had its origins somewhere in Central Africa. There is broad agreement that HIV, which is closely related to viruses in monkeys, jumped to humans. This is nothing unusual in itself, as the periodic transmission of influenza between humans and pigs, often with fatal consequences, attests to.[114] It is most likely that the first carrier of the present virus came into contact with contaminated blood from a monkey, and then passed it on. Quite when the species jump took place has been the object of some speculation. It is conceivable that such an event had happened before, but that the virus had failed to take off because it was not transmitted to enough people. On this occasion, however, it spread along the main transport corridors across Africa and then to the world beyond.[115] As the global crisis unfolded, it was apparent that Africa was disproportionately affected – even if by the end of the 1990s regions of Asia, including China and India, appeared to be catching up fast. By mid-decade, Africa was still estimated to have 60 per cent of global infections, despite comprising only 10 per cent of the world's population.[116] The fact that Africa was apparently both the source and the epicentre of HIV/AIDS initially led to a great deal of uninformed speculation. Old colonial myths about the rampant promiscuity of Africans were dusted down and given a pseudo-scientific gloss. At the same time, many Africans were prepared to believe that HIV had been spread by the Americans or by colonial powers themselves, whether deliberately or by ill-advised experimentation.[117] Over time, many of the myths were exploded and something like a scientific consensus emerged, although a minority maintained that there was no proven link between HIV and AIDS. Controversially, this position was upheld by President Thabo Mbeki of South Africa.

Some African governments admitted the problem at a relatively early stage, whereas others sought to sweep it under the carpet. In Zambia, the Ministry of Health reported its first cases in 1984, but it was official policy to keep the scale of the crisis under wraps for fear of scaring off tourists who assumed a heightened importance as the mining economy continued its long decline. It was only after President Kaunda's son died of AIDS in 1987 that the attitude of his government changed.[118] The South African government response was the least responsible of all. Evidence given before the Truth and Reconciliation Commission (TRC) pointed to the deliberate spread of AIDS by agents of the apartheid state.[119] When the first deaths began to be reported in 1985, the regime allocated a tiny sum of money (some £200,000) to poorly formulated public education campaigns. Much of the dithering arose from a reluctance to promote the use of condoms for fear of offending Christian sensibilities. As late as 1991/92, when most African countries had an AIDS prevention plan in place, the South African response was still contradictory, underfunded and poorly executed. Despite the vastly greater wealth of that country, the government spent only one-third of what the Zambian, and possibly half of what the Mozambicans, allocated to AIDS control in 1991.[120] It was not until 1994 that a National AIDS Plan for South Africa was drawn up, seven years after Botswana had taken decisive action of its own.

Although HIV/AIDS was something altogether new, it actually tended to slide into some deeper historical grooves. Although some infection arose from contaminated blood supplies, HIV in Africa was spread overwhelmingly through heterosexual sexual activity. As a sexually-transmitted disease (STD), it has tended to replicate some of the transmission patterns of older scourges like syphilis.[121] Indeed, the two are directly related since medical research has demonstrated that people who have previously contracted STDs are more likely to acquire HIV by virtue of the resulting genital lesions. The comparison with the passage of STDs in colonial times has proved of some utility in modelling the spread of HIV/AIDS. Because the latter requires human carriers, it has pursued some very well-trodden routes of human migration. In Africa, there are established patterns of population movement, such as in Southern Africa where the migrant labour system has pumped people from distant rural areas towards the mines and cities, and back again. There are other patterns of population movement which became more of a feature after independence, as a consequence of rapid rates of urbanisation and the attraction of people towards centres of comparative economic prosperity. A good example of the latter would be the drift of people from Burkina Faso, and the Sahel countries in general, towards southern Côte d'Ivoire. Differential levels of economic success have also played a part in stimulating inter-regional trade. For example, endemic shortages in Uganda and Zaire gave rise to a lucrative smuggling trade from Kenya which had the capacity both to produce and to import consumer goods. Finally, successive liberation and civil wars in the three decades after 1970 led to the displacement of millions of Africans from their homes towards safer ground in neighbouring countries. Uganda and Tanzania were both recipients of large refugee flows from Rwanda. Each of these forms of migration have been linked to a greater or lesser extent with the spread of AIDS.

Cities have tended to exhibit much higher rates of infection than remote rural localities for some very simple reasons: they tend to attract people from a wide catchment areas, including those with a high incidence of previous infection, while the opportunities for sexual encounters tend to be greater. Prostitutes who are drawn to cities clearly represent the most important vectors, and the effect is compounded because they tend to work outside their home countries. The cities which have been growing fastest over the past 30 years, such as Abidjan and Kinshasa, have consequently tended to exhibit the most rapid rates of infection (see Table 8.6). In Southern Africa, the migrant labour system has played an important role in relaying AIDS back to the countryside. Males living in single-sex hostels in South Africa have commonly used prostitutes without recourse to condoms. On the other hand, the homosexual relationships forged between older mine workers and younger migrants is probably much less important, given an apparent preference for inter-crural over penetrative sex.[122] Rural localities which have consistently sent migrant workers to the mines have tended to manifest a higher prevalence of HIV/AIDS. In the South African context, this helps to explain the exceptionally high prevalence in Kwazulu-Natal. However, the Southern African migrant labour system is not the only example of urban–rural transmission. The Kilimanjaro region of Tanzania has also been acutely affected, given the propensity of Chaggas to travel far and wide in search of trading opportunities and employment.

Although Chagga perceptions of disease causality do not concur on every point with those of professional epidemiologists, Philip Setel has shown how migration away from Kilimanjaro is associated with a supposed weakening of Chagga cultural norms, thereby opening the way to unbridled sexual desire and ultimately HIV/AIDS.[123]

There is also good evidence to support the proposition that HIV/AIDS has followed trade routes. When infection rates are plotted on a map they often tend to cluster at particular points along main roads. Long-distance trade has the closest correlation with infection rates. Truckers plying these routes tend to rely on the services of prostitutes at their stopping-off points, thereby serving as sources of fresh infection. This is born out by the fact that the border towns which link Zimbabwe, Namibia and Botswana have manifested far higher rates of infection than the national averages.[124] In some cases, these match or even exceed the rates for the capital. In Botswana, for example, Francistown has recorded higher rates of infection (39.6 per cent) than Gaborone, and this reflects its strategic location on the route to Bulawayo in Zimbabwe. The story in East Africa is broadly similar. Southern Ugandan towns, notably Rakai and Masaka, have been the focal point of the AIDS outbreak in that country. Part of the reason is that this is an area along which traders have passed from Congo/Zaire and Rwanda to Kenya. During the Amin years, substantial fortunes stood to be made from the smuggling of goods (including everything from gold to coffee and consumer items) to and from Tanzania and Kenya. Border towns became a magnet for all kinds of people seeking to make a living from smuggling, prostitution and ancillary activities. At the start of the 1990s, southern Uganda still lay at the heart of a vibrant regional trade network. According to Bond and Vincent:

> Traders from Zambia purchase goods in Rwanda and refresh themselves at 'hotels' and bottle stores on the long journey home; Zairean prostitutes and Rwandan migrant labourers seek employment in the cities and on sugar and tea plantations in Uganda, desperately seeking a living wage that will permit them to make remittances to families at home; fishermen and traders ply the waters of Lake Victoria, crossing to and from the lakeshore villages in Kenya, Tanzania and southern Uganda. Pastoralists move freely across the northern part of Tanzania and southwestern Uganda.[125]

Just over the border in Tanzania, the story is very similar. The Bukoba district was a 'hot spot' right from the start of the pandemic, and HIV/AIDS seems to have spread from here to Dar es Salaam and then to have been fed back to other rural communities like those of Kilimanjaro. It would be a mistake, however, to regard all border towns as equally susceptible to the spread of HIV/AIDS. On Ghana's border with Togo, for example, the incidence of the disease has been amongst the lowest in the country despite a long history of profitable trade from Lomé and Kpalimé. The simple reason would appear to be that the trucking phenomenon is much less evident in this part of Africa. Much of the border trade is carried out by local people who buy and sell goods alongside their other activities without significantly altering other aspects of their daily lives.

Thirdly, as noted above, the incidence of HIV infection has been closely correlated with the displacement of populations through armed conflict of various kinds. In the midst of warfare, there is a much greater likelihood of forced sexual encounters. Moreover, the populations whose daily lives are rendered precarious are more likely to take chances, on the principle that STDs are the least of their worries. In southern Uganda, the turmoil of the Amin years, the Tanzanian invasion and Obote's reign of terror are popularly linked to the spread of HIV/AIDS. Across the continent, the military itself has been worst affected and has come to behave as what Robert Shell refers to as a 'Trojan horse' in relation to the rest of society. In Zimbabwe, possibly as many as 80 per cent of soldiers have been affected, while in Malawi 75 per cent of one sample of troops were estimated to be HIV positive.[126] In 1998, a South African insurance company came up with a prevalence rate of 40 per cent for its armed forces, which was far higher than officially admitted.[127] Soldiers are likely to have amongst the greatest range of sexual encounters, and the power that they wield over the lives of others gives them greater access. Hence garrison towns are typically a focal point for secondary outbreaks. The South African Defence Force (SADF) camps in northern Namibia attracted many sex-workers, and this is reflected in higher rates of infection in the surrounding areas today. Amongst the SADF soldiers based in Namibia, no fewer than 17.2 per cent were found to be HIV positive in 1994.[128] When they eventually returned to South Africa, they took AIDS back with them, as did the former fighters of Umkhonto we Sizwe who had been stationed in high-risk countries like Zambia and Tanzania. The African National Congress (ANC) refused to agree to a screening of its returnees, no doubt because that might have been interpreted as giving credence to the allegation of the white right that AIDS was a curse which was confined to homosexuals and blacks. In Namibia, the high incidence of AIDS in Ovamboland appears to be directly related to the return of former guerrillas and refugees to their homes from neighbouring countries.

Table 8.6 The fastest-growing African cities, 1950–2000 according to average annual growth rate

City	1950 population	2000 population	Annual average growth rate	World ranking
Abidjan	59,000	3,790,000	8.7	1st
Lusaka	26,000	1,653,000	8.7	2nd
Conakry	39,000	1,232,000	7.1	7th
Lagos	288,000	8,665,000	7.0	8th
Kinshasa	173,000	5,054,000	7.0	10th
Yaounde	50,000	1,420,000	6.9	12th
Dar es Salaam	78,000	2,115,000	6.8	13th
Nairobi	87,000	2,233,000	6.7	17th
Mogadisho	47,000	1,157,000	6.6	20th
Kampala	53,000	1,213,000	6.5	21st
Harare	84,000	1,791,000	6.3	24th
Luanda	138,000	2,697,000	6.1	28th

Source: United Nations Population Division, *World Urbanisation Prospects*.

It is also worth noting that there was a distinct regional pattern to the spread of the disease. Map 7 conveys some sense of the variations across African countries (but crucially not within them), on the basis of World Bank criteria: 'nascent' refers to countries with less than 5 per cent HIV prevalence in all sub-populations regarded as high risk; 'concentrated' refers to HIV prevalence of more than 5 per cent in one or more high-risk sub-population; and 'generalised' alludes to the spread of AIDS beyond the high-risk populations and where women attending urban ante-natal clinics have returned a higher than 5 per cent HIV prevalence rate.[129] As the map demonstrates, the countries worst hit were located in Central, Eastern and Southern Africa, where the HIV-I virus was prevalent. Whereas countries like Tanzania, Uganda and Zambia were amongst the worst affected in the first decade, the subsequent expansion into southern Africa was nothing short of catastrophic. Botswana recorded the highest rates of HIV infection (38.5 per cent of adults), while the figure for South Africa was around 19.94 per cent in 1999. By virtue of its much larger population, the takeoff in the latter country represented a far greater demographic onslaught. The first AIDS deaths were reported in South Africa in 1985. By 1999, the Department of Health was estimating that 3.6 million were already infected, with up to 150,000 people a year perishing from the disease. The forecasts were, however, even more alarming: by 2010, it was projected that around 6 million South Africans will have died from the disease, with the toll falling disproportionately on the black population.[130] In West Africa, a separate strain (HIV II) predominated, which was less virulent and had a longer life-cycle. Certain countries which have a recent history of warfare (Guinea-Bissau) or have been characterised by significant population flows (Côte d'Ivoire and Burkina Faso) were also registering high rates of infection by the end of the 1990s. The regional giant, Nigeria, seemed to have largely missed the first wave, but it may well be that ECOWAS troops returning from peacekeeping operations in Sierra Leone and Liberia will turn out to be the 'Trojan horse'. The estimated prevalence rate had risen to 5 per cent by 2000. Moreover, there were indications signs that HIV-I was making inroads into the sub-region.[131] Finally, it is worth mentioning that a third strain of the Virus (HIV III) has been reported from Cameroun, but did not have appear to have spread very far by the start of the new millennium.

The impact of the pandemic has been registered in a number of different forms. To start with, there is the demographic shock associated with the loss of an estimated 12 million people in sub-Saharan Africa over the 1990s.[132] This is equivalent to the obliteration of the entire population of a medium-sized African country. It also matches the number of Africans transported to the New World during the trans-Atlantic slave trade over three-and-a-half centuries.[133] The mortality rates have been higher amongst women, by a ratio of around 1.3 women (rising in some countries to 1.5) for every man lost.[134] This means that the long-term demographic impact is likely to be greater than if the gender balance was roughly equal. Secondly, the steady improvements in basic human indicators since independence have started to dip once more. Average life expectancy has fallen rapidly in many instances: in the South African case, from 63 years in 1990 to 56.5 years in 2000 and it is dropping fast.[135] By virtue of the proliferation of secondary illnesses associated with AIDS, the strain placed on public health facilities – already under pressure from the rigours of structural adjustment – has been considerable. Thirdly, the concentration of the disease upon the most sexually active section of the population, between 15 and 35 years, has had profound social consequences. The elderly have often being left to care for children orphaned by AIDS. In some countries, the female-headed household has itself been replaced by the child-headed household, as the adult population has been wiped out. The net effect has been the absolute impoverishment of whole communities in certain regions. Finally, the AIDS pandemic has had important economic consequences. In the countryside, the rising proportion of dependants to workers is likely to have had an impact on rural productivity in the most blighted communities. Moreover, in the cities and mining camps, productivity has been affected by recurrent illness and the death of skilled workers. Equally, the functioning of core state institutions has been impaired. The demise of much of the teaching profession, for example, has affected the quality of access to education in countries like Tanzania. The impact on education is a good example of the need to look at AIDS in a far more holistic fashion than has traditionally been done. The thinning out of the teaching ranks has serious implications for the improvement of the skills-base of African countries, whilst narrowing the perceived life-chances of youth. While African governments recognise the need to train more teachers to fill the gap, the net effect of SAPs is to pass the costs onto prospective trainees who have to balance the reality of low wages against the income-generating activities which can be married to teaching. Teachers are not the only group to have been affected. In Malawi and Zimbabwe, the illness and death of large numbers of civil servants, Members of Parliament and Cabinet Ministers has been officially acknowledged.[136] The fact that the most privileged sections of society have been felled is none too surprising because power and sexual access tend to go together. It does, however, challenge the generalisation that AIDS always feeds off poverty.

Finally, it would be worth saying something about the success associated with efforts to arrest the onward march of the epidemic. Although no cure has been found, there are drugs, such as AZT, which retard the onset of AIDS and minimise the likelihood of mothers infecting their children during birth or breast-feeding. The problem is that these drugs are very expensive and more than most countries can afford. In South Africa, 'the cost of treating a single terminal case of AIDS with an AZT cocktail per month is equivalent to placing 19 school children in primary school for a month'.[137] The crippling cost is one reason why President Mbeki held out against pressure to make AIDS drugs freely available to pregnant mothers, despite the counter-argument that the costs of caring for a larger infected population would work out greater in the long run. It was only after losing its case in court in March 2002, that the South African government capitulated the following year.[138] African governments have often had to slash their health budgets in order to conform to IFI conditionalities, which has made it very difficult for them to adequately finance the health care which is evidently needed. The World Bank insisted that the alternative, of bumping up subsidies to the health sector, would simply reintroduce distortions in the supply of public goods, by for example diminishing spending elsewhere.[139] The shortage of funds has led African government to embrace the NGOs as partners, and sometimes also to solicit the co-operation of 'traditional' healers who have often remained the first port of call for patients. However, their pooled resources have been manifestly inadequate, with the result that the amount of suffering has been far higher than it needed to be – especially when one recalls that debt repayment in a country like Tanzania is several times larger than the annual health budget.

Given that AIDS is transmitted through bodily fluids, condoms provide a relatively cheap and easy means of prevention. AIDS-prevention programmes have therefore focused on alerting youth to the importance of using condoms as well as to the causes of AIDS. Not all African leaders have felt very comfortable with championing the humble condom. In Kenya, for example, Daniel Arap Moi memorably confessed that 'I am shy that I am spending millions of shillings importing those things' and suggested that it would be better for Kenyans to abstain for sex for two years instead.[140] Religious leaders, whether Muslim or Christian, have often been opposed to the advocacy of condoms. The Catholic and Protestant churches have often been opposed on predictable grounds, but the new churches which have spread across Africa in the era of structural adjustment have themselves depicted AIDS as the 'wages of sin' and have preferred a message of sexual abstinence. Nevertheless, public awareness campaigns have been launched, using posters, advertisements as well as discussion and drama programmes on television and radio. Popular musicians and theatre companies have also played their part in disseminating the message. Zambia provides a good example of the range of stratagems which have been deployed. According to Bujra and Baylies:

> AIDS information was disseminated through the mass media, via messages on the front pages of national newspapers, a weekly newspaper column and a five minute slot in a religious radio broadcast. Posters were displayed in public places, AIDS song and drama contests were organised and street theatre performances given, announced by drums, introduced by humorous sketches and featuring plays about AIDS which encouraged discussion by the audience.[141]

A lot of effort has gone into disabusing people of popular myths about AIDS – such as that it can be cured through sexual intercourse with a virgin. They have also focused on modifying certain cultural practices which are seen as likely to contribute to infection – such as the ritual cleansing of a widow or widower by ensuring that he/she sleeps with a member of the deceased person's family.[142] The focus of much of the work has been the schools, given the risk posed to the youth. In Zambia, the formation of anti-AIDS clubs in the schools enjoyed some success, although these often withered after an initial burst of enthusiasm. In some noteworthy instances, the message seems to have got through, indicating a greater awareness of both cause and prevention. In many countries, the uptake in condom use has been noteworthy, although barriers have remained. Men the world over tend to associate condoms with diminished sexual pleasure, while women have often been reluctant to insist on their husbands using them because of the implication that they are not to be trusted. Apart from public education, a great deal of NGO energy has been directed towards mitigating the effects of AIDS. In Zambia, the Churches have played a leading role on the ground. One particularly successful initiative was launched by the Salvation Army's Chikankata Hospital in the South of the country. The hospital pioneered a home-care programme for AIDS-sufferers in 1987, which later provided a template for others to follow in Zambia and in Tanzania. Other NGOs dealt with the counselling of AIDS patients and the problems associated with caring for orphans. Be that as it may, the AIDS-centered NGOs were not immune to the shortcomings of NGOs in general. Bujra and Baylies, for example, observe that they have tended to cluster in the capital cities, while the size of their presence in the rural areas did not necessarily correlate with the scale of the outbreak.[143]

Two countries which are commonly cited as success stories are Senegal and Uganda. In the former case, the anticipated onset of an AIDS crisis failed to materialise, with only 0.95 per cent of the over-15 year population turning up HIV positive in 1994.[144] The Senegalese government was praised for responding relatively quickly to the threat. A National Committee for AIDS Prevention was established in 1988, which led to the accumulation of reliable data on the spread of the disease. However, the Senegalese authorities were actually rather reluctant to campaign too openly on sexual practices for fear of offending sensibilities in what is a staunchly Muslim country. At the same time, the religious authorities contributed comparatively little to the debate about AIDS, despite being by far the most influential societal group, until the mid-1990s. The remarkable success of checking the onset of the disease appears to derive from other factors. Although there was a low-intensity guerrilla insurgency in the Casamance region, Senegal has been a haven of political stability since independence. Moreover, the relatively strict moral code with respect to sexual practice, outside of Dakar and the tourist centres, is another factor in the equation. The point that trade is merely one variable amongst many is underscored by the low prevalence of AIDS in Kaolack, despite its centrality in the lucrative contraband trade with the Gambia. As the home of one branch of the Tijaniyya brotherhood, restraints on sexual activity are broadly respected. Finally, it may be significant that the Senegalese authorities have taken a pro-active line in regulating prostitution. Sex-workers have been required to register and to take regular AIDS tests, at the risk of penal sanctions. Precisely because the Senegalese state has functioned pretty effectively, these regulations have been more than a dead-letter.

Unlike Senegal, the history of Uganda has been one of recurrent crisis. The dislocation of populations and the growth of *magendo* (the black market) made Uganda an ideal site for the spread of HIV/AIDS. The outbreak started in Rakai, Kyotera and Masaka Districts and when it reached Kampala, it accelerated.[145] In the early years, Uganda came to symbolise the plight of the continent as a whole. In 1990, a team of American demographers impressed upon President Museveni that if the disease continued to spread at its present rate, the population would stand at 20 million in 2015 – that is 12 million fewer than what would otherwise have been the case. Museveni was duly impressed and threw his weight behind a massive public education campaign. A National AIDS Control Programme (NACP) had already been established to monitor the spread of the disease, but after 1990 the emphasis switched to an anti-AIDS campaign. The Uganda Aids Commission was established, drawing in the Churches and NGOs, and was charged with the task of co-ordinating an awareness programme. The object was to get Ugandans to talk openly about HIV/AIDS, to modify their sexual practices and to learn how to cope with the disease. NGOs were also active on the ground. Some set out to help AIDS victims. One woman, whose husband died from AIDS, set up The AIDS Support Organisation (TASO) which provided counselling and medical care in the Kampala area, employing people who were themselves HIV-positive. Another NGO, Action for Development toured schools with a view to educating girls about the dangers of unsafe sex.[146] Others became involved in theatre groups which (as in Zambia) toured the country, spreading the message through a participatory format.[147]

The evidence suggests that Ugandans did indeed take up the invitation to speak about sex. One study which compared Uganda with Zambia, Malawi and Kenya reported that 90 per cent of Ugandans engaged in open discussions about sex (far above the continental average), while there was a reduction of sexual activity amongst adolescents and a growing preference for delaying sex until after marriage.[148] In Uganda, the use of condoms also increased significantly. The result was that the rate of infection slowed quite significantly. The Ugandan seroprevalence rate fell from 18.5 per cent in 1995 to 9.5 per cent in 1998.[149] Although hotspots still remained, there is no doubt that this was a remarkable achievement, and one from which other countries had much to learn. However, in some countries AIDS campaigns do not seem have had the same effect. In South Africa, for example, rising mortality rates appear to have generated a certain fatalism which has militated against behavioural change. The lesson is that, unlike the condoms, one size does not fit all, and the success of national campaigns is likely to depend on the varied historical and cultural inheritances which prevail in different countries.

8.4 Conclusion

In this chapter, we have looked at the ways in which the relationship between African states and their peoples were radically altered over the last two decades of the twentieth century. The capitulation of African governments to the IFIs led to the acceptance of a diminished role for the state as an economic actor, as an employer and as provider of goods and services. This happened against the backdrop of the AIDS pandemic which placed a greater strain upon the whole range of institutions and public services. At the same time, NGOs which cut their teeth on disaster relief, began to muscle in on development activity and service provision. Aid money which had previously gone directly to governments was increasingly being channelled through the NGOs by the close of the 1990s. Although some governments resented the NGO intrusion, others welcomed the chance to shed themselves of some of the burden. The record of NGOs was an uneven one, with the worst ones acting as little more than business enterprises in their own right. However, some of the most fruitful contributions lay in the support they gave to AIDS-prevention campaigns in countries like Uganda. In October 2001, African leaders sought to recapture the initiative when they launched the New Partnership for Africa's Development (NEPAD). This was intended to signal an intention to assert African ownership over the development agenda, albeit in partnership with external donors. While accepting African responsibility for past failures, it also insists on the importance of its leaders embracing the realities of globalisation and fashioning realistic plans for economic development. The NEPAD approach is distinctive because it sees democracy, good governance, conflict resolution, poverty alleviation, the campaign against AIDS and African economic integration as a single integrated package. The donors have broadly welcomed this willingness to take responsibility, but at the time of writing there remain lingering doubts as to the coherence of the vision itself.

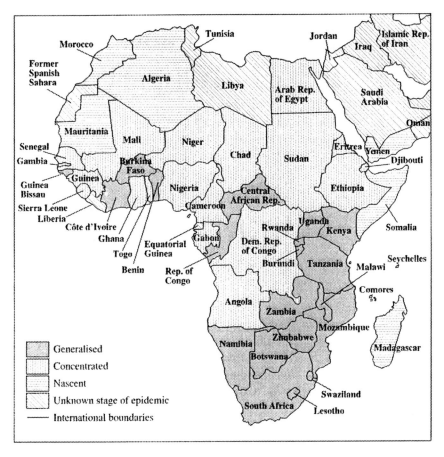

Map 7 HIV prevalence, 1997

From World Bank, *Confronting AIDS*, Statistical Appendix, Table 4. Every effort has been made to trace the copyright holder and the publisher will be pleased to make the necessary arrangement at the first opportunity.

9

Democracy Rediscovered: Popular Protest, Elite Mobilisation and the Return of Multipartyism

The winds from the East are shaking the coconut trees.
President Omar Bongo of Gabon on the knock-on effects of political events in
Eastern Europe

If the owners of socialism have withdrawn from the one-party system, who are the
Africans to continue with it?
Frederick Chiluba of Zambia

The last two decades of the twentieth century were not merely remarkable for the extent to which African states surrendered their autonomy in the face of aid conditionalities and the invasion of the NGOs. As striking was the rediscovery of competitive politics. Under one-party and military rule alike, the circles of decision-making had typically narrowed to nested cliques, even though the regimes in question often claimed to be looking out for the interests of the whole population and sometimes lured interest groups into quasi-corporatist structures. Large sections of African society which operated outside the charmed circle may have appeared to confer tacit consent on these arrangements by remaining overtly quiescent, but the silences often belied a more complex reality. Ordinary Africans concentrated their energies on getting by and, if they were lucky enough, exploiting the opportunities for rent-seeking which accompanied the African crisis. Many also found coded ways of deflating the pretensions of the powerful through carnivalesque humour. By the start of the 1980s, cynicism abounded, not least within the single parties and military coalitions themselves. In the 1980s and 1990s, however, the pendulum swung back again as significant sections of society weighed into politics with a gusto which had not been witnessed since the heydays of nationalism – and often exceeding it. The cities became the crucible of political opposition, whereas rural populations had learned not to reveal their hand prematurely. In some countries like

Congo-Brazzaville and Rwanda, there was a complete political breakdown, which we will address in the final chapter. However, across the greater part of the continent there was genuine movement in the direction of open debate and an attachment to constitutional order.

The dramatic events which unfolded from 1989 have been associated with the so-called 'third wave' of democratisation, as identified by Samuel Huntington.[1] However, even if one accepts the seminal importance of global transformations, such as the collapse of Communism in Eastern Europe, these only resonated across Africa because of the rot which had hollowed out incumbent regimes from within. Equally, when the tide finally receded, it did so more quickly in some countries than others and so left a different kind of residue on the political shoreline. In Benin and Zambia, incumbent regimes were voted out of office without further ado. As of 1990, no African government (outside of South Africa) had ever been removed through the ballot box, but within six years no fewer than 18 heads of state had been sent packing. However, the gains were both uneven and fragile. In some countries, such as Togo and Zaire, Machiavellian rulers found ways of fragmenting and frustrating the opposition forces, whilst resorting to naked violence when the tide went against them. The largest set of countries experienced something in between – that is, the opposition made significant inroads, and openings for political debate emerged, but the regime in office still held the decisive advantage. It is these different storylines which I will seek to follow in this chapter. In the first part, I will begin by setting out some of the factors which led to a re-enchantment with politics. In the second, I will trace some of the different trajectories through a series of case-studies.

9.1 The rediscovery of a popular voice

The story which I wish to tell has often been cast in terms of the resurgence of 'civil society', a term which now carries more than its fair share of baggage. Insofar as it refers to an associational life existing beyond the confines of the state, it is a useful shorthand. However, the concept of 'civil society' has been bandied about with such little analytical rigour that it has lost much of the precision which it once possessed. It should not be taken for granted that the associations in question have necessarily been opposed to the state, and nor should it blithely be assumed that they have always been gallantly fighting the cause of democratisation in Africa. The range of associations which have become more visible in Africa since the 1980s – NGOs, religious bodies, trade unions, women's groups and the media – have all played their part in shaping recent developments, but none have been unambiguous in their stance towards democracy. Here, I deploy 'civil society' sparingly and as a shorthand.

9.1.1   Of dinosaurs, crocodiles and father figures: crises of political legitimacy in the 1980s

Before looking more closely at the emergence of dissident voices, it makes sense to begin our account with the incumbent regimes themselves, for it was their legitimation crises which led to the realisation that many an emperor was sorely lacking in the clothes department.

I begin with those one-party regimes (*de facto* or *de jure*) which had been firmly ensconced since independence, and which were dominated by Presidential potentates like Kamuzu Banda in Malawi, Kenneth Kaunda in Zambia, Félix Houphouët-Boigny in Côte d'Ivoire, Omar Bongo in Gabon, Ahmadou Ahidjo in Cameroun and Julius Nyerere in Tanzania. These were leaders who had managed to hold sway for as many as three decades by virtue of their capacity to sniff out potential threats and to neutralise challengers using a mixture of carrots and sticks. These were also leaders who knew how to work their national and international audiences, sometimes directing different kinds of appeals to each in turn. As a medical doctor who had spent most of his life in Britain, Banda projected an image to the outside world of a sincerely conservative, pro-Western leader who was committed to the modernisation of his country. To his domestic audience, Banda projected a more traditionalist image.[2] As Michael Schatzberg suggests, African leaders tended to portray themselves as father figures in relation to their supposedly grateful wards.[3] The aim was to foreclose discussion and to instil awe by constantly rehearsing the pivotal role of the leader in nationalist history, that is once rival figures had been airbrushed out of the picture, as happened in Malawi. Some leaders appealed to their superior learning and erudition (notably Banda, Nyerere and Senghor) and to their intimate knowledge of the wider world. The grand ideological statements of these regimes, whether couched in the international vocabularies of socialism or capitalism, also constituted part of the tools of legitimation. To a greater or lesser extent, each of the leaders also insulated himself by nurturing relationships of personal loyalty and dependence.

The problem was that the spell only worked for as long as these leaders could be seen to pull the strings which made their underlings move. As they grew older and more out of touch, their ability to manage the show became as halting as their memories. This left some scope for trusted lieutenants to exercise power in their own right, and ultimately in their own self-interest. When Banda, who was already quite old when he became President, exhibited unmistakable signs of senility, effective power increasingly rested with his 'hostess', Madame Kadzamira, and her uncle John Tembo. The magic also began to wear off when it became abundantly clear that the leaders in question were not the colossuses bestriding the world stage that the state propaganda machinery made them out to be. Having to approach the IMF cap-in-hand, and then to sign up to conditions which negated everything which had been boasted of, visibly shrunk the 'father of the nation' before the country's eyes. Nyerere foresaw the problem and chose to resign his office when it became clear that there was no avoiding structural adjustment. Although the 'socialist' regimes ostensibly had the greatest ideological distance to travel, it was often the 'capitalist' ones (such as those of Kenya and Côte d'Ivoire) which felt the greatest sense of indignation because they refused to accept that they had ever deviated from the path of economic righteousness. The imposition of austerity measures, including retrenchment from the public sector and the introduction of user fees in schools and hospitals, naturally taxed the legitimacy of African governments. By the mid-1980s, many rulers were caught in a cleft stick because digging in was almost as unrewarding as embracing reform. In Zambia, where some 42 per cent of the population was urban, Kaunda was understandably wary of alienating city dwellers. In 1987, after pressure to reduce subsidies on maize-meal led to outbreaks of rioting on the Copperbelt, the government jettisoned the SAP and introduced its own New Economic Recovery Programme (NERP). However, it could not afford to go it alone for very long because the country was in such dire straits. When a reform package was finally relaunched in 1990, the economic situation had deteriorated to the point that UNIP had forfeited whatever popular support it had once enjoyed.

In the early 1980s, a number of Presidents chose retirement rather than preside over a steady decline. When Ahidjo stepped down in favour of Paul Biya in 1982, the oil revenues were starting to flow, but, the context was very different when Senghor made way for Abdou Diouf in Senegal in 1981, when Siaka Stevens handed over to General Joseph Momoh in Sierra Leone in 1985, and when Nyerere transferred power to Ali Hassan Mwinyi that same year. In all these countries, an acute economic crisis formed the all-important backdrop to the succession. Although the incoming President typically enjoyed a honeymoon period, he also faced problems of legitimacy. For a start, the nation could only have one founding father, and although some mileage could be made out of being the chosen son (or *dauphin*) this rather undercut his personal standing in the long-term. Although leaders sought ways of reinfantilising their citizens, the trope of the 'father figure' clearly had its limitations. Some found it preferable to project themselves as new brooms who would retain the basic format of the old regime, but sweep out the inner sanctums. Both Biya and Diouf were originally elevated for their reputed technocratic competence, and this gave them something to build upon. The successor also typically faced a Cabinet whose members did not necessarily owe any personal loyalty to himself. Having been passed over in the succession, they were not always entirely loyal. The new leader therefore needed to bide his time, slowly sidelining potential challengers, whilst cultivating grateful clients of his own. The economic backdrop was important here because a shrinking cake tended to place even greater limits on the ability to dispense patronage.

The first to negotiate the perils of succession was Daniel Arap Moi following the death of Kenyatta in 1978. As we saw in Chapter 5, Moi began by preaching continuity with the Kenyatta era, but once he was safely ensconced he proceeded to weed out those (mostly Kikuyu) politicians whose loyalty he doubted. Moi was fortunate in taking office against a backdrop of comparative prosperity. Unlike Moi, Biya had to come to deal with an ex-President who was very much alive and who refused to relinquish control over party structures. Biya also retained a large number of Ahidjo Ministers to start with, but this did not avert a falling out over who was ultimately in control. As early as June 1983, Ahidjo was plotting his return and when there was an abortive coup attempt in April 1984, his name was inevitably linked to the conspiracy. Having seen off the challenge, Biya was in a position to stamp his own authority on the government.[4]

The remaining transitions took place in the context of a dearth of material resources. In Senegal, the declining fortunes of the groundnut economy presented Diouf with enough headaches to tax his technocratic acumen, although he was fortunate in that Senghor chose voluntary retirement in France. Diouf played his hand more astutely than most, but his inability to resolve the structural weaknesses of the economy ultimately eroded his support base within the urban areas. In Senegal, opposition parties had been legal since the 1970s, but had failed to make significant inroads against the Parti Socialiste (PS). However, Abdoulaye Wade's Parti Démocratique Socialiste (PDS) began to gather momentum and in the 1988 elections commanded majority support in Dakar. In Tanzania, Mwinyi had to endure some carping from the sidelines by Nyerere, but his greatest priority lay in convincing Tanzanians that the austerity medicine was working. Mwinyi successfully served out his two terms and then transferred power to Benjamin Mkapa in 1995, thereby institutionalising the rotation of the highest office. This was progress of sorts, but the moral authority of Chama Cha Mapinduzi (CCM) was at its lowest ebb by the close of the decade.

Military governments faced difficulties of their own. The continent continued to be coup-prone during the 1980s. Hence, the death of Ahmed Sékou Touré in Guinea did not lead to an orderly succession within the single-party state – in part because that eventuality had always been considered a taboo subject – but rather to a military takeover by Colonel Lansana Conté in March 1984. In Nigeria the military regime of General Buhari was overthrown by a palace coup led by Ibrahim Babangida in 1985. The following year, Lt.-Colonel Justin Lekhanya toppled Leabua Jonathan in Lesotho. Finally, the overthrow of General Nimeiri led to a brief civilian inter-regnum in the Sudan before the re-establishment of military rule under General Omar Hassan Ahmad al-Bashir in 1989. Although military governance was evidently nothing out of the ordinary by the 1980s, these military regimes still needed to legitimise their seizures of power. As before, they variously passed themselves off as caretakers, reformers, or as the harbingers of a radically different social order. As always, the credibility of the caretakers hinged on their willingness to beat a reasonably rapid and orderly retreat to the barracks, while that of the reformers rested upon their ability to deal with the problems of national unity coupled with the economic crisis. Inevitably, because the perks of office were so juicy, there was a temptation for reformers to find reasons for staying on, thereby slipping into usurpatory mode.

Some of the military usurpers battened onto structural adjustment, insisting that a necessary period of austerity would best be managed by the men in khaki. They calculated (wisely) that there would be little pressure upon them to hand power back to the civilians if they could be seen to be implementing reform. In Ghana, Flt-Lt Jerry Rawlings clasped the structural adjustment agenda with both hands, insisting that there was nothing to be gained by rushing back towards multipartyism. Throughout the 1980s, the regime was praised by the international financial institutions (IFIs), and by Western governments, for its willingness to court unpopularity in the relentless pursuit of economic reform. In Nigeria, Babangida began by proclaiming a corrective agenda. He launched a national debate about structural adjustment and then proceeded to institute a 'home-grown' SAP which was supposed to restore economic equilibrium. At the same time, the junta promised to set in motion a staggered return to civilian rule, which would come to fruition in 1990. The ability of military regimes to appropriate the reform agenda had its down-side of course, namely that they were forced to impose policies which were deeply unpopular. Paring back expenditure on government salaries was contentious enough, but cutting back on military and police expenditure was potentially suicidal. Some military regimes failed to strike the right balance and succumbed to counter-coups, or were confronted with demands for a return to civilian rule.

The calculus was further complicated at the end of the 1980s when other certainties began to give way. The implosion of Communism in the Soviet Union and Eastern Europe had two important consequences. On the one hand, it gave heart to African 'movements for democracy', whilst rendering the legitimation of military regimes more difficult. On the other, it led to the abrupt termination of the Cold War which had kept certain military regimes in business. In Zaire, Mobutu had been cosseted because he was a useful pawn in American geo-politics. Despite stupendous levels of corruption, the Paris Club of donors had rescheduled debt repayments no fewer than seven times between 1976 and 1987.[5] After 1989, however, the United States and France felt able to adopt a tougher line, although this did not endure. At the same time, the demise of Communism also removed much of the ideological legitimation from avowedly Marxist regimes such as those in the Congo-Brazzaville and Benin. The financial patronage, which was never that great anyway, dried up as the Soviet Union sank into economic doldrums of its own.[6] At the same time, the cachet of belonging to a global Marxist fraternity turned into a liability. Significantly, the only military regime which spoke the language of revolution after 1989 was that of Sudan, and its version of revolution was an Islamic one.

At the end of the 1980s, the IFIs introduced the concept of 'good governance' into aid discourse which had implications for civilian and military regimes alike. It was open to a narrow technocratic interpretation, but in certain quarters it began to be equated with a respect for democracy. The donor community consequently added political conditionalities to an already lengthy list. In 1990, for example, the British government announced its intention to treat economic performance and political pluralism as part of a single package. In June of the same year, President François Mitterrand surprised his African colleagues at a summit in La Baule when he indicated that French aid would similarly be tied to political reform. In November 1991, the European Community (later renamed the European Union) laid down the principle that the future disbursements of aid would be tied to the furtherance of democracy and human rights. This was a highly significant development because the EC/EU and its members states accounted for roughly half of all aid to sub-Saharan Africa in the first part of the decade.[7] African governments which had hoped to insulate themselves from global winds of change were served notice that there was to be no business as usual. And because almost every African state was heavily aid-dependent, the leverage was potentially enormous.

Across the continent, African governments responded by bending with the winds from the East. While making concessions towards an incipient opposition, they conspired to render their position impregnable. The ideal scenario was to become formally elected – using as much chicanery as one could get away with. Although the presence of international election observers rendered blatant rigging more difficult, there was very little they could do about the enormous advantages of incumbency. Moreover, the fact that the Electoral Commission was often appointed by the President greatly facilitated gerrymandering in all its forms. In some cases, as will see, the flexible response worked a treat, whereas in others incumbent Presidents lost control of the reform agenda and ended up being voted out of office. However, those autocrats who weathered donor pressure in the early 1990s were often able to regain the initiative in subsequent years as Western governments lost interest in African democracy and began to place greater weight on stability. In France, *realpolitik* reasserted itself as early as November 1991. Mitterrand increasingly adopted the persona of a latter-day de Gaulle who, in the manner of an avuncular *paterfamilias*, was indulgent towards his African clients – provided they remained within the Francophone club and resisted the American sirens.[8] When Jacques Chirac assumed the Presidency in 1995, this tendency to place French national interest first was further consolidated. Within the EU, France saw to it that the lofty principles which had been laid down in the early 1990s were rendered a dead-letter.

9.1.2   *Rendering unto Caesar: religious bodies and discourses of democracy*

Potentially the greatest counterweight to one-party and military regimes was a vast panoply of religious associations – Christian, Muslim and to a lesser extent 'traditionalist' – to which most Africans had some level of attachment. If the Christians and/or Muslims spoke with one voice, depending on the religious makeup of each particular country, even the most intransigent government would have found the going tough. However, such unity of purpose was rarely achieved and governments learned to play Christian off against Muslim, as well as rival Muslim brotherhoods and Christian denominations off against each other. Where religious affiliation mirrored the ethno-regional division within a given country, the world of belief could never be entirely separated from the arena of partisan politics. Nevertheless, there was a qualitative shift in the relationship between religious bodies and the state in a number of African countries at the end of the 1980s.

To start with the Christian churches, most African countries hosted a number of competing denominations. In colonial times, there was often a fierce struggle for converts between the Catholics and the various Protestant denominations, of which the Anglicans, Lutherans, Methodists, Presbyterians and Baptists were the most important. The fairly close association between the Christian churches and the colonial power, as well as the strict racial hierarchy within the former, led to the breakaway of a number of African independent churches. Some of these, such as the Kimbanguists in the Belgian Congo and the Watchtower Society in Central Africa, rejected colonialism and all its works, whereas others were more tractable. After independence, the churches came to different levels of accommodation with the state. The Jehovah's Witnesses clashed with the political authorities in a number of countries because of their refusal to conform with the rituals of nationhood. As far as the others are concerned, there were instances where the mainstream churches were directly linked to the power structure – most notably in Liberia, where the politically dominant Americo-Liberians also happened to be the leading lights in the Protestant churches, and in Rwanda where the Catholic church co-operated with a succession of 'Hutu' regimes.[9] In many others, such as in Gabon and in Malawi, the mainstream churches adopted a theological position which avoided having to take a stand on social issues.[10] In Uganda, for example, the Catholic and Anglican churches were reluctant to criticise human rights abuses under Idi Amin, although the eventual murder of Archbishop Janani Luwum perhaps points to an obvious reason why.[11] In Kenya, the churches conspicuously failed to speak out against the detentions of government critics during the Kenyatta years. Gifford wryly observes that the Catholic Bishops so successfully resisted the introduction of sex education in schools that one is led to wonder what might have happened if they had decided to take up the issue of human rights.[12] Be that as it may, where churchmen were amongst the most vocal critics, these tended to be drawn from the mainstream churches rather than the independent ones. The mainline churches were in a potentially strong bargaining position, given the number of followers they commanded. However, it was almost as if the politicians and the churchmen recognised each other's strength and often steered clear of a take-on which could be damaging to both parties. While the independent churches often did represent the most marginalised sections of society, for precisely that reason they tended to be poorer and less well-organised. This made them more susceptible to offers of patronage by the political elite. Moreover, their own histories often chimed in with official nationalism, whereas the mainline churches were castigated as European fifth-columnists opposing 'African' ways of doing things.

During the 1980s, the picture became yet more complicated with the proliferation of Pentecostal churches, which took much of their inspiration and some of their resources from the United States. These churches came from nowhere to rival the mainstream churches in size. By the close of the 1990s, the Zimbabwe Assemblies of God Africa (ZAOGA) had almost as many members as the Catholic Church, despite the rather honourable role played by the latter in support of the liberation movements.[13] Given that Christian conversion (outside of Muslim areas) was virtually total by this point, the rise of the Pentecostals inevitably came at the expense of the churches which already existed. The mainline churches suffered from defections because their ingrained traditions often failed to deal with the everyday concerns of their congregations. As Birgit Meyer has brilliantly argued with respect to south-eastern Ghana, the reluctance of the Presbyterians to engage in too much discussion about the nature of the devil, for fear of detracting from the essential point about the greatness of God, left them vulnerable to new churches which attributed misfortune to malign forces such as witchcraft.[14] The Pentecostals won many converts because they were in the business of casting out the demons which many Christians blamed for their misfortune. However, the independent churches seem to have suffered much greater rates of defection than the mainline ones, and during the 1980s they themselves came under the spell of Pentecostalism.

It would be a mistake to assume that all Pentecostals sang from the same hymn-sheet, and in fact there were some significant differences between them. On the question of politics, they tended to adopt a rather ambiguous position. Many Pentecostals sought to keep their distance from the corruptions of politics and enjoined their flocks to concentrate on personal salvation – whereas the mainline churches at least professed to be interested in matters of social concern. Hence the Pentecostals, and other 'born agains', concentrated on building new moral communities in which adherents could immerse themselves totally. Some churches even colluded with the power structure on the principle that this would enable them to operate more freely in the far more important battle for human souls. There was also something of a fit between the behaviour of the political elite, which openly flaunted its wealth, and the message of certain Pentecostal churches that the accumulation of riches was in harmony with God's plan. The Faith Gospel movement, in particular, associated poverty with sinfulness and enjoined its members to aspire towards the accumulation of personal wealth. Whereas some of the older mainline churches had traditionally made a virtue of asceticism, these new churches were encouraging their members to enrich themselves in God's name and to exhibit their wealth at every opportunity – as well, of course, as donating generously to church coffers. In the words of Bishop Nicholas Duncan-Williams of the Christian Action Faith Ministries (CAFM), which made rapid strides in Ghana:

> God did not predetermine who would be rich and who would be poor. He sim-
> ply created His spiritual laws and freely gave them to everyone. Every person then
> has a choice – to implement the laws of poverty, or to implement God's spiritual
> laws of prosperity.[15]

The simple message that material reward would come naturally with acceptance of God's word went down well with many ordinary Africans who were struggling to make ends meet under the rigours of structural adjustment.

When noticeable cracks in the political monolith began to appear at the end of the 1980s, the mainline churches became much more assertive. In Malawi, the Presbyterians had put up with the authoritarianism of the Banda years with surprisingly little demur. But in the early 1990s, the churchmen found their voice as the regime started to wobble, and their contribution was an important catalyst in the eventual downfall of the regime. In Kenya, individual Bishops and ministers from within the Presbyterian and Anglican churches began to criticise the abuses associated with single-party rule and to lend their voices to demands for the holding of a national conference. When this provoked a furious response from the Moi regime, the Catholic church hierarchy rallied to the side of the Protestant churchmen. By contrast, the independent churches and the Pentecostalists were much less prepared to rock the boat. Indeed, some joined in the attack on the National Council of Churches of Kenya (NCCK) and openly backed the Moi Presidency.[16] In Ghana, it was the attempt to control the churches through the requirement of formal registration which united the Catholic and Protestant churches in opposition. A freeze on the activities of the Jehovah's Witnesses and the Mormons in 1989, and the banning of two local churches, was accompanied by the introduction of the Religious Bodies Registration Law which required all churches to register with the National Commission on Culture. In the face of a co-ordinated outcry, the Rawlings regime protested that the aim was merely to monitor suspect churches who fleeced and took sexual advantage of their members. However, the mainline churches detected an attempt to muzzle religious bodies as a whole and refused to comply. The government was eventually forced to beat a retreat and to withdraw the offending legislation, thereby signalling an important breach in the 'culture of silence'. The Christian Council subsequently followed up by demanding the release of political prisoners and the convention of a constituent assembly.[17] The Pentecostal church leaders, for their part, either lent their support to the regime or kept out of the political fray altogether. Duncan-Williams even conferred his blessing on Rawlings, although Mensa Otabil of the International Central Gospel Church (ICGC) was more overtly critical.[18]

If one is looking for a broad pattern, it is that the mainline churches only intervened once the power structure seemed vulnerable to attack, but when they did so their contribution was weightier than that of the independent and Pentecostal churches who were often apolitical or openly complicit. There are, however, some qualifications which still need to be made. In South Africa, the mainline churches played a consistently combative role, insisting that apartheid was a sin against God. The Kairos Document of 1985, which was South Africa's best approximation to liberation theology, laid primary emphasis upon uprooting apartheid as opposed to saving souls, although its militant tone worried many more orthodox clerics.[19] This set these churches in opposition to the Dutch Reformed churches, many of whose clerics had helped to influence apartheid doctrine. The pattern is, however, confirmed by the behaviour of the largest of the African independent churches, the Zion Christian Church, which gave President P. W. Botha a rapturous welcome in 1985, at a time of mounting turmoil in the townships. The other partial exception is Zambia, where the Catholic Church came to an accommodation with the Kaunda regime, and where the eventual religious backlash was led by those who tended to be associated with the 'born again' churches. Frederick Chiluba, who would go on to defeat Kaunda at the polls, was himself a 'born again' member of the United Church of Zambia (UCZ) who claimed to have received the gift of tongues.

Superficially, there is the world of difference between Christian and Muslim terms of engagement with the state. In principle, Muslims might be expected to favour the construction of a polity ordered according to the precepts of Shari'a law, whereas Christians have reconciled themselves to the secular state. Moreover, Muslims lacks a formal hierarchy like that of the Catholic Church through which they can formally negotiate with the power structure. One might therefore expect a relationship with the African state which is conflictual or at best evasive. In reality, there is not that much to differentiate Christian and Muslim interactions with the state. With the obvious exception of the Sudan and Northern Nigeria, African Muslims have reconciled themselves to the practical impossibility of forging an Islamic polity, even where they constitute the numerical majority. At the same time, the coherence and organisation of Muslim brotherhoods in many African countries means that something like a formal structure does in fact exist. The Sufi brotherhoods have their religious heads and a pecking order of holy men whose eminence is a function of birth and/or success in attracting disciples. In Northern Nigeria, the emirs were both traditional rulers and defenders of the faith. Although they lost much of their formal power after independence, as we have seen, the emirs remained extremely influential spokesmen for the Muslim cause.

In countries where Muslims were in the minority, they applied pressure upon the political authorities to respect their distinctive way of life, including rules concerning marriage, the family and inheritance. Muslims also sought recognition of the right to operate their own schools with adequate government support. Where brotherhoods were weak, Muslims tended to form Islamic associations in order to lobby for their preferred causes. In Kenya, where Muslims made up about a tenth of the total population, the National Union of Kenyan Muslims (NUKEM) campaigned on a range of issues, but most especially on recognition for Islamic schools.[20] Such bargaining necessarily meant an ongoing engagement with the power structure, normally behind the scenes and often on the latter's terms. Where Muslims constituted the majority, their spokesmen sometimes wielded considerable political influence. In Senegal, as we have already seen, the Socialists had to come to terms with the popular base of the Mourides and Tijanis. While the ruling party depended on the *marabouts* to bring out the voters and to secure compliance with official policy, the *marabouts* received money to build mosques and schools as well as displays of public deference. However, as Leonardo Villalón has demonstrated, this relationship was inevitably laced with a certain amount of tension because the state and the brotherhoods were also in competition with one another.[21] At the local level, *préfets* saw themselves as the bearers of modernity and resented having to approach the rural population through the marabouts. On the other hand, the marabouts were often critical of the corruption of the political elite. As in the cases where the Christian churches were well-organised, these two giants realised that they had to co-exist. When the state encroached too far, however, it could be openly rebuffed. For example, when the Senghor regime introduced a new family law in 1972, religious leaders lobbied against it on the grounds that it was incompatible with the Shari'a, and when that failed they threatened to thwart its implementation. In the end, they seem to have succeeded in rendering the offending legislation a dead-letter.[22]

In Nigeria, where Muslims and Christians stood at rough parity, the former lobbied government to put the brakes on campaigning by American evangelists. At the end of the 1990s, they also succeeded in persuading a number of northern state governments to declare the application of Shari'a law. The meting out of harsh punishments to women accused of engaging in extra-marital affairs provoked a furious debate over whether Nigeria truly was truly a secular state.[23] Whereas Muslims in Nigeria knew that they would never be able to win over the rest of the federation, radical Muslims in the Sudan succeeded in capturing power and declaring the existence of an Islamic state. The process began when General Nimeiri introduced Shari'a law in September 1983. Although it was suspended when he was overthrown two years later, it was reintroduced by the military government of Umar al-Bashir after 1989. The Muslim Brothers, led by Hassan al-Turabi, were able to ride to power on the back of this military junta, while the older brotherhoods were actually hostile to the National Islamic Front (NIF) regime. As we will see in the next chapter, Islamicisation was an important reason for the resumption of civil war in the South. These cases demonstrate that the relationship of Muslim leaders to the state was characterised by complicity as much as resistance. It was only when incumbent governments began to appear vulnerable that religious authorities began to assume a more critical position.

9.1.3 Voluntary associations: old, new and compromised

As we have noted at various points, the declaration of the one-party state was typically accompanied by the co-optation of trade unions and women's and youth groups. Their leaders sometimes received Ministerial positions and salaries, while in turn they were expected to discipline their members. Workers who could not depend on their unions to represent their demands often found other ways of redressing the balance – through absenteeism, moonlighting and helping themselves to public property. In the era of structural adjustment, official trade unions became more assertive while independent unions sprang up to oppose the reduction in salaries, layoffs and the removal of subsidies and allowances. In Zambia, the Zambian Congress of Trade Unions (ZCTU), led by Chiluba from 1974, had struggled to keep its distance from the Kaunda regime. In the context of adjustment, it sought to protect the material interests of its 400,000 members. However, in 1989, it finally broke cover by openly championing a return to multipartyism. Again, in Zimbabwe, where the labour movement had played almost no role in the Chimurenga, ZANU-PF brokered the formation of a single labour federation, Zimbabwe Congress of Trade Unions (ZCTU), in 1981. The government expected the ZCTU to moderate its demands, but as structural adjustment translated into falling real wages, organised labour displayed an unexpected independence. The decade of the 1990s was marked by an increasingly bitter rift between the ZCTU and ZANU-PF, culminating in a public sector strike in 1996 and a massive general strike in 1997.[24] In August 1999, the ZCTU crossed the Rubicon when it sponsored the creation of a political party, the Movement for Democratic Change (MDC) which was led by the ZCTU leader, Morgan Tsvangirai.

In Niger, the Union des Syndicats des Travailleurs du Niger (USTN) which had been completely docile similarly began by opposing a wage freeze and then jumped the political firebreak to campaign for a multiparty system. In November 1990 the union was able to bring as many as 100,000 people onto the streets of Niamey, thereby indicating that it was speaking for more than its official constituency.[25] In Benin, there was equally a progression from bread-and butter grievances, concerning the non-payment of salaries, to overtly political protest. In all of these instances, women's and youth associations played an active part alongside the unions. Market women often chafed against tax-gathering exercises, as well as the corruption and harassment of the police and municipal authorities. Students had a long history of cocking a snook at the authorities and had frequently put their lives on the line. In Zaire, after initially backing Mobutu, University students proved themselves to the bravest opponents of the regime, for which large numbers paid with their lives. For having dared to challenge Mobutu in 1969, they were forcibly recruited into the army in 1971, where they began to politicise ordinary soldiers before being disgorged from the belly of the beast once again.[26] It should come as no surprise, therefore, that students continued to lead the charge against the regime two decades later. As the momentum for an end to authoritarian rule gathered across Africa, even 'traditional rulers' jumped ship. Although they tended to be seen as creatures of the state, the reality was that they too had been forced to relinquish most of their capacity for autonomous action in the decades after independence.

The African business community, which was supposed to benefit from structural adjustment, was not always the most adept at making its own voice heard. Those business elites who had enjoyed 'sweetheart' deals with the regime in power stood to lose out from liberalisation. Others who were on the outside, however, had an interest in dismantling restrictive practices. Traders within the informal sector often felt threatened by economic reforms, such as efforts to improve revenue collection. In Ghana, the introduction of Value Added Tax (VAT) provided the occasion for violent protests in Accra, which were supported by traders and urban dwellers worried about the impact on consumer prices. In Senegal, traders formed an association, the Union Nationale des Commerçants et Industriels du Sénégal (UNACOIS) which used a combination of strikes (in tandem with the trade unions) and demonstrations to pressurise the government to dismantle monopolistic commercial practices and to exempt small traders from payment of VAT. The popular support which it commanded in Dakar forced the Diouf government to come to the negotiating table and to deregulate the marketing of rice in 1995.[27]

Most NGOs preferred to cast their work as 'non-political'. Nevertheless, there was a sub-class of NGOs which set out to perform an advocacy role. By taking up issues relating to government policy, and openly contradicting the authorities, these NGOs inevitably stepped into the political limelight. In the 1980s and 1990s, there was a proliferation of NGOs which campaigned on human rights (broadly defined) and did not shrink from exposing government shortcomings. Many were constituted by lawyers who had direct experience of the abuses of the justice system and spoke out more freely than before, in the knowledge that they enjoyed some backup from the donor community and from international watchdogs like Amnesty International and African Rights Watch. In Ghana, Kenya and Nigeria, lawyers had long been organised within Bar Associations which maintained a principled stance on human rights issues. The same was true of other professional associations, such as the Association of Recognised Professional Bodies (ARPB) in Ghana which had been the bane of successive regimes since the 1970s. The emerging advocacy NGOs tended to draw on the expertise and enthusiasm of the members of these professional associations, whilst providing a cutting edge of their own.

It would, however, be a mistake to concentrate purely on the proliferation of formal associations, which most Africans did not belong to. For some governments, the greatest headache was posed by urban youth who were not 'captured' in any formal organisation. The unemployed lived by their wits, and having been born long after independence, were not privy to the glory-days. Growing up at a time of endemic crisis, their alienation from the political system was a source of worry in many a Presidential palace. In many ways, the rest of the continent was following in the footsteps already trodden by South Africa in the 1970s. In a number of African capitals, nothing symbolised the erosion of government support more than the open contempt displayed by youth towards figures and symbols of authority. The urban crowd could take shape in a matter of minutes and was often highly volatile. In Senegal, for example, the youth of Dakar rioted after the 1998 elections which they believed had been rigged. It was partly in an attempt to domesticate unruly youth that the regime began channelling resources to reformist Muslim associations like Dahiratoul Moustarchidina wal Moustarchidaty ('those who seek the straight path'), which were thought to appeal to this popular constituency. The name of the game was to capture the youth in a religious vessel and thereby bring it into dialogue with government. Predictably, the association began to lose its popular following as soon as it became too close to government, with the result that its leader, Moustapha Sy, went into reverse gear. He regained his notoriety prior to the 1993 elections through a popular cassette recording in which he lambasted Diouf.[28]

9.1.4   *The media: fourth estate or servants of the state?*

Finally, it is worth drawing attention to the ambiguous role played by the visual, aural and print media. In the years immediately after independence, African governments, who were keen to impart their views to the wider public, invested in the kind of media infrastructure which was more elaborate than the colonial states had deemed necessary. Where they did not already exist, Information Ministries and/or Departments were established and given relatively generous budgetary allocations. Sometimes, as in Gabon, these were headed by the President himself. Their remit was to disseminate government information and sometimes to co-ordinate the activities of the various branches of the official media. An early innovation was the regular newsreel which would be shown in cinemas and would sometimes be taken round the rural areas by cinema vans specially purchased for that purpose. These eventually died out, to be replaced by television from the early 1960s. As with the earlier newsreels, television provided a powerful medium through which those in power could represent the world as they wanted it seen. In Zaire and Togo, television became a serviceable instrument in constructing the personality cult of the leader, with the former benefiting from French aid.[29] In Côte d'Ivoire, the regime was more subtle, but actively encouraged television because it recognised its political potential. As in much else, Nigerian television was in a league of its own. In 1983, the budget of the Nigerian Television Authority was about one-third that of the BBC, and this did not even include the multiplicity of affiliated stations in the individual states.[30] Interestingly, the South African government held out against television for a decade longer than the rest of the continent, for fear that it would be unable to control the medium effectively and that it might become dependent upon foreign programming whose images would be incompatible with apartheid doctrine. In Malawi, Banda never permitted television for the very same reasons, while the Gambia and Rwanda perhaps declined for simple cost reasons.

Television tended to be the most slavish of all the media and remained so even when governments lost their monopolies elsewhere. Although state channels increased their own reliance on foreign programming, this consisted mostly of long-dead 'soaps' and situation comedies which were dumped in Africa, rather along the lines of food aid.[31] The only real shift came with the availability of satellite television in the 1990s, which made it possible for audiences to tap into foreign news channels. However, the Africa content was normally very limited, the coverage of the largest networks like CNN was superficial and the audience in Africa was minuscule because it was usually only international hotels which could afford the subscriptions. The television revolution therefore had relatively few political spinoffs. Although opposition groups could produce their own videos cheaply enough, this format tended to be monopolised by the mass entertainment market. In Nigeria, the spectacular takeoff of the video industry was based on low-budget films dealing with love triangles and the occult, in which there was minimal political content. At best, these popular videos (and even some national television productions) made fun of Nigerian 'big men', but politics proper was a topic to be avoided. A far more important vehicle for dissidence was the clandestine audio cassette which could be played in city taxis and in vehicles plying the inter-city routes.[32]

Given that most rural households had limited access to television, radio was a sister medium which played a more significant role in reaching the national population.[33] There were only some 252 radio transmitters in sub-Saharan Africa in 1960, but in 1975 there were 458. More tellingly perhaps, whereas there were only 32 radios per 1000 people in 1965, this had risen to 164 by 1984.[34] In some cases, UNESCO sponsored efforts at bringing radio to the rural population and involving the latter in shaping the product – all as part of a broader development agenda. But normally, radio programming was centered on the capital city, while its reception was sometimes buttressed by relay stations in outlying urban centres. The news content tended to consist of a predictable round of official speeches and commentaries, with very little space for acknowledging the existence of dissident voices – far less reporting them. Because of the strategic importance of radio, most successful coup attempts involved the seizure of the state-owned radio station and were followed by a broadcast of the official rationale for the takeover.[35]

Although controlling national radio was a prerequisite of political domination, shortwave radio also enabled ordinary people to pick up broadcasts from neighbouring countries and even further afield. With French co-operation, the Gabonese government established a highly successful African service of its own in 1981, but 'Afrique No. 1' was geared towards popular music rather than current affairs. It also happened to be part-owned by President Bongo and members of his family. For many Africans, the British Broadcasting Corporation (BBC), the Voice of America (VOA) and Radio France Internationale (RFI) served as the most dependable source of information about everyday politics in their own countries. Often Ministers, who would not deign to be interviewed on their own radio stations, were to be heard on the BBC, seeking to rebut allegations which had been made in earlier news stories. Although governments sometimes attempted to ban foreign broadcasts, this was well-nigh impossible to enforce. In the 1990s, an important contribution to the opening up of political debate lay in the legalisation of private radio stations. In Mali, there were no fewer than 12 in operation by 1993.[36] In Accra, the most lively and informed debate took place on the discussion and call-in programmes on FM radio, and although the Regional stations were less daring they provided a forum for people in the rural areas which should not be under-estimated.

Finally, there were the print media, ranging from quality newspapers to simple broadsheets plastered to walls. After independence, governments were determined to control the print media, being fully cognizant of the role once played by the nationalist press. While state resources were pumped into building printing presses and training journalists, pressure was applied to private newspapers to refrain from overt criticism. In Senegal, after a state-of-the-art printing press was installed with French development aid, it was possible to exercise leverage by granting or withholding access to the machinery.[37] Where proprietors owned their own presses, pressure might take the form of restricting access to basic materials such as paper, and when all else failed it was always possible to find an excuse for closing newspapers down, invoking breaches of the libel laws. In Ghana, there were only two daily newspapers which continued to appear during the 1980s, the *People's Daily Graphic* and the *Ghanaian Times*, and both of these were state-owned. Their content was essentially a collage of government press releases and speeches by officials commissioning this or that development project. The independently minded newspapers, such as the *Catholic Standard*, had previously been forced to close down. In Zambia, the *National Mirror* survived as an interdenominational Christian newspaper, which maintained a critical distance from the government. However, the two main newspapers, the *Zambian Daily Mail* and the *Times of Zambia* were under state control.

Outside of South Africa, Nigeria was the one country which boasted a vigorously independent press after independence. The federal system lent itself to a more decentralised media structure, in which each state would typically own its own newspaper. There were also private newspapers which were the partisan instruments of political grandees, such as the *Tribune* which was in the pocket of Obafemi Awolowo. Because of the sheer size of the Nigerian reading public, there was real money to be made through the print media. Hence Nigeria threw up media tycoons like M. K. O. Abiola, whose publishing group published the *Concord* locally, but also the *African Concord* magazine from offices in London. The size and strength of the Nigerian press made it much less susceptible to manipulation by central government, although the down-side was that it tended to be highly partisan in tone. The Buhari regime was the first to attempt a crackdown on the press, by means of the notorious Decree No. 4 of 1984. This made it a crime to embarrass a public official, even if the printed allegations happened to be true. This piece of controversial legislation was repealed by Babangida, who promised a return to unfettered press freedom. However, an ominous sign that things might not be quite that simple came with the assassination on Dele Giwa, the editor-in-chief of the fiercely independent *Newswatch*, by means of a parcel bomb which many believed had been sent by government security agents.[38] As we will see below, the stalled transition in Nigeria led to an unprecedented attack on the print media in the 1990s. At the end of the 1980s, then, there was a veritable explosion of the print media in most African countries, as dozens of private papers suddenly hit the newsstands. Although many of these folded because of the stiff competition, large numbers survived by catering to the thirst of the urban reading public for news about politics. However, relatively few of these newspapers reached the rural areas, where the government press normally benefited from a better-funded distribution system.

Even during the most repressive years, urbanites had revelled in the trails of gossip and rumour known as *radio trottoir* (pavement radio), which had the capacity to propagate itself with remarkable speed. The private newspapers often collected this rumour and committed it to print, thereby lending it further credibility. But at the same time, the private papers initiated rumours of their own which then fed into the realm of the spoken word and underwent further mutations. The net result was that there was very little which government officials could say or do without fear of it appearing in print a few days later – often having become more grotesque as a result of successive retellings. For President and Ministers who were used to fawning journalists, it was profoundly unsettling to have their most intimate financial and sexual affairs dissected in public. It is surely no accident that many of the most successful newspapers also employed the most daring cartoonists, who mercilessly lampooned the highest officials in the land. In the case of Cameroun, where the private press had a field day after 1991, Achille Mbembe has highlighted the social significance of the cartoon. In *Le Messager*, Nyemb Popoli represented Paul Biya through the character 'Popaul' who combines all the pomposity of an African President with obsequiousness in relation to his Western masters. The President who is depicted in the most compromising positions, from the bedchamber to the toilet, was repeatedly set up as an object of public ridicule.[39] Although Mbembe is reluctant to read resistance into expressions of popular vulgarity, it is clear that getting away with printing these cartoons served as a standing invitation to other Camerounians to reject the pretensions of the ruling elite. Because the government was powerless to prevent the lowliest Camerounian from sharing in the laughter, its own hegemonic position was called into question. The Ghanaian cartoonist Jo Mini, who worked for the *Ghanaian Chronicle*, typically chose a different kind of target.[40] As Rawlings endeavoured to clothe himself in civilian respectability, Mini presented him as a boorish thug who winked at corruption at the highest levels of government. There was little subtlety in the humour, but the effect was very caustic. It worked so well because the cartoons reinforced the story lines in the pages of the *Chronicle*, which relayed a constant battery of rumours about abuse of office and waged a highly personalised attack on the Rawlings family. The Jo Mini and the Nyemb Popoli cartoons would have been simply unimaginable in the Ghana and the Cameroun of the 1980s.

9.2   Autumn of the patriarchs or a Prague Spring? Democratic openings and closures

It will be noticed that this broad sweep has made little mention of the peasantry. Yet in spite of the rapid pace of urbanisation, the bulk of the population in most countries was still rural. In most countries, however, the peasantry observed events from a remote distance. In fact, one reason why embattled regimes made the concessions they did was that they reckoned on the innate conservatism of the rural populace. They could be counted on to out-vote the noisy urbanites and put them squarely in their place. When this did not happen, as in Malawi, this was profoundly shocking. However, in many cases governments calculated the odds correctly. In what follows, we will plot the trajectories in greater detail.

9.2.1   The Lusophone states of West Africa: Cape Verde, São Tomé and Guinea-Bissau

Whenever the story about the return to multipartyism is recounted, the focus almost invariably falls on one Francophone and one Anglophone state, namely Benin and Zambia respectively. But the first breaches in the wall actually took place in two island statelets off the coast of West Africa, namely São Tomé and Príncipe and the Cape Verde islands. In both instances, the struggle for liberation from Portuguese rule had brought with it an ideological attachment to socialism, but nothing in the way of practical armed struggle. In both cases, the disappointments which followed independence led to a marked decline in support from the ruling party and ultimately to peaceful transitions which were scarcely noticed in the wider world.

In São Tomé, the reversal began with ideological divisions and purges within the ruling MLSTP (Movimento de Libertação de São Tomé e Príncipe) under Pinto da Costa. Although the latter shared a socialist platform, it had never exhibited the coherence of the parties in the other Lusophone states. In 1984, the failure of the MLSTP to make a go of statism led to a decision to abandon links with the Eastern Bloc and to embrace economic and political reforms. The MLSTP signalled this conversion by adding Partido Social Democrata (PSD) to its name. In December 1989, the Da Costa regime became the first in Africa to hold a national conference which endorsed multipartyism, and this was confirmed in a national referendum. This was followed by the creation of opposition parties and the breakaway of younger elements from the MLSTP/PSD to form the PCD-GR (Partido da Convergência Democrática – Grup de Reflexão). In January 1991, the PCD-GR won a majority of the seats in the legislative elections (33 to 50), which signalled that the political dominance of the MLSTP/PSD was over. Da Costa stood down as Presidential candidate and was not replaced. As a result, Miguel Trovoada, who had been purged from the regime in 1979, was elected unopposed, with the support of the PDC-GR and another opposition party. Trovoada was forced to govern through a legislature in which he could not count on a reliable body of support. After fresh legislative elections designed to resolve the impasse in 1994, the MLSTP/PSD emerged with virtual control of the legislature. Trovoada went on to defeat Da Costa in 1996, ensuring a prolongation of unstable government in which coalitions were made and unmade in quick succession.[41] However, the principle that the ballot box ought to be the sole determinant of the right to govern was firmly established.

In the Cape Verde islands, the rupture with Guinea-Bissau had led to the creation of a separate political party for the islands, the PAICV (Partido Africano da Independência de Cabo Verde). In 1988, the PAICV accepted the need for economic reform, but signalled its intention to cling to its political monopoly. However, two years later the law was changed to allow other parties to contest elections, an opening which was seized by the MPD (Movimento para a Democracia), which attracted some defectors from the ruling party. In January 1991, the MPD won a clear majority of the legislative seats, and in the Presidential elections which followed António Mascarenhas Monteiro won a landslide against Aristides Pereira with 73.4 per cent of the vote. In 1995, the MPD repeated its victory, and the following year Monteiro walked back into the Presidency as the only candidate. As in the case of São Tomé, democratic elections proved to be no panacea, or even a guarantor of 'good governance', but it did at least provide a mechanism for getting rid of politicians who had outstayed their welcome. By contrast with these Lusophone states, the democratisation of Equatorial Guinea was purely formal. Although opposition parties were permitted in theory, they faced so many practical obstacles that they opted to boycott the 1992 polls. In 1996, the opposition were persuaded to take part, but President Teodoro Obiang Nguema Mbasogo, who had been in office since 1979, manufactured a result which gave himself 97.8 per cent of the vote. Hence, Equatorial Guinea ranked amongst a handful of states where little meaningful political change occurred in the 1990s.

The course of democratisation also ran less smoothly in the state of Guinea-Bissau. Here the regime of Nino Vieira was carried on a tide of goodwill which followed the expulsion of the Cape Verdeans. However, the coup set a precedent and in subsequent years there was a succession of plots in which the perpetrators were shown no mercy (two mass graves were later found in 1999).[42] In 1991, the Vieira regime decided to embrace multipartyism, whilst seeking to ensure that power did not slip from its grasp. The transition period was marred by further coup plots and political brinkmanship which threatened to derail the entire process. Nevertheless, legislative and Presidential elections went ahead over July/August 1994, in which ethnicity became a significant line of division in a manner which it never had before. The ruling PAIGC succeeded in winning 62 out of 102 seats, but there were now three opposition parties in the legislature. More tellingly, Vieira was elected President with a narrow majority (52 per cent) over Kumba Yalla of the Social Renovation Party (PRS), and not everyone believed that this was an accurate tally. The fact that Yalla was himself an ex-PAIGC cadre underlined the extent to which the party of independence had fragmented. In the years which followed, a democratic veneer barely concealed an autocratic style of governance, conditioned by ad hoc responses to perceived opposition threats and internal party schisms. By the time Vieira was overthrown in 1998, the popularity he had once enjoyed had dissipated, while the PAIGC had gone the way of earlier nationalist parties.

9.2.2 Vive the National Conference: the Francophone states

In the Francophone states, 'pro-democracy' movements typically seized on the demand for a sovereign national conference, harking back to the Estates-General which launched the French Revolution.[43] The remarkable transformation which accompanied the national conference in Benin was widely reported by the media across Francophone Africa and led to copycat demands in the other countries. In a few cases, the results were replicated but in the majority of cases the opposition was less than successful in pulling off its own 'civilian coup d'état'.

9.2.2.1 The successful conferences: Benin, Congo, Niger and Mali

Although there is always a danger of writing with hindsight, the Kérékou regime was ripe for the taking. The regime was placed in an unusually precarious position by virtue of having very little in the manner of taxable resources to sustain the rapid expansion of the state apparatus in the 1970s. The fact that the country was only able to cover 15 per cent of its imports also meant that it was especially dependent on external aid. Although the government recognised that it could not continue as before, and embarked on its first economic restructuring in the early 1980s, it was reluctant to alienate urban interests which had shown their capacity to pull down governments in the past. Kérékou contrived to achieve the worst of all worlds. Although the government entered into negotiations with the IMF in 1984, it was unwilling to accept the conditions and proceeded to muddle through. The result was the regime ceased to be able to maintain social spending, especially in the area of education which many Beninois regarded as their best escape route. This provoked a series of violent confrontations with the students, who were also worried about their employment prospects. More seriously still, the government ceased to be able to pay its 50,000 workers on a reliable basis after the collapse of the banking system, whereas the well-connected were known to be salting away private fortunes. On repeated occasion over 1989, workers took to the streets alongside students and other urban dwellers, who began to demand a return to 'democracy'.

Realising that repression was not working, and that there was mounting restiveness in the army, Kérékou decided on a tactical retreat. He promised to legalise parties other than the PRPB (Parti Révolutionnaire du Peuple du Benin) and to convene a national conference, consisting of a wide range of social groups, to deliberate on changes to the constitution. Between 19 and 28 February 1990, the 500 conferees – consisting of a diverse band of government representatives, opposition politicians, trade unionists, women's leaders, churchmen and the like – set to work. One of their first acts was to declare the conference sovereign, thereby stripping the PRPB of its mandate to govern. Another was to elect the Archbishop of Cotonou, Isidore da Souza, chairman of the conference. The delegates then embarked on a searing attack on the Kérékou years, reducing the latter to tears at one point. Although Kérékou was allowed to remain the titular President, effective power was transferred to an interim government, with responsibility for organising fresh elections. The interim Prime Minister was Nicéphore Soglo, a former World Bank official.[44]

A new constitutional draft was approved by referendum at the end of 1990. This was followed by national elections over February and March 1991, in which Soglo roundly defeated Kérékou and his party.[45] While Kérékou slunk into retirement, Soglo assumed the Herculean task of seeking to implement structural adjustment, while hanging on to his popular base. Benin, a country which had once been a by-word for political instability, had become the model of a successful transition through the ballot box. In 1996, it repeated the trick when it became the first country to alternate its government. On this occasion, the beneficiary was none other than Kérékou himself, now professing to be a reformed character. Under the SAP, Soglo had chalked up some significant improvements, not least to the battered infrastructure of the country. Nevertheless, the economy of the country remained as fragile as ever. Moreover, core constituencies were alienated by the officious manner in which the technocrats went about administering the economic medicine. To make matters worse, Soglo was accused of spinning a new web of patronage in which many members of his immediate family were amongst the primary beneficiaries. The fact that Soglo did not attempt to prevent Kérékou from returning was in itself an encouraging sign. However, when Kérékou sought a renewal of his mandate in 2000, and won convincingly, the opposition cried foul, taking some of the shine off the earlier success.

The country which most resembled Benin was its ideological soul-mate, the People's Republic of Congo (formerly Congo-Brazzaville). Although the Congo had precious oil reserves, and thus profited from the second oil-hike of the late 1970s and early 1980s, the country continued to live well beyond its means. Faced with the threat of bankruptcy, the Sassou-Nguesso regime made its own approach to the IMF in 1986, but was unable to implement the reforms in full. With some 60 per cent of the Congolese population living in the urban areas, and with the state employing a quarter of the national workforce, it was very difficult for the government to comply and in 1990 the IMF and World Bank suspended their programmes due to perceived backsliding.[46] As in Benin, the regime found itself unable to pay its workers, leading the Congolese Federation of Labour to sever its links with the ruling party and to embark on strike action in the early months of 1990. The strikes quickly escalated into an organised campaign in support of the demand for the legalisation of opposition parties and for the holding of a national conference. In July, Sassou-Nguesso followed Kérékou in declaring the abandonment of Marxism–Leninism and an acceptance of multipartyism. He also gave way on the demands for a national conference. When the latter finally convened, between February and April, the similarity to the Benin pattern was uncanny. A wide array of social groups sent delegates; the proceedings were chaired by a bishop, Monsignor Ernest Kombo; the conference declared itself sovereign and Sassou-Nguesso was forced to live with an interim government headed by yet another former World Bank employee, André Milongo. Moreover, the delegates positively revelled in excoriating the leadership, including Sassou-Nguesso himself.

Finally, a new constitution was drafted and national elections were held between March and June 1992. Pascal Lissouba's UPADS (Union Panafricaine Pour la Démocratie Sociale) emerged with a plurality of seats in the legislative polls (albeit nothing like a majority) and a clear victory in the Presidential runoff. Bernard Kolélas and his MCDDI (Mouvement Congolais Pour le Développement et la Démocratie Intégrale) came in second. Sassou-Nguesso and the former ruling party, the PCT (Parti Congolais du Travail) followed in a rather forlorn third, while Milongo paid for his rather poor showing as interim Prime Minister by being confined to fourth place. As in Benin, therefore, a successful transfer of power had been executed through the ballot box. As we will see in greater detail in the next chapter, the hopes which accompanied these elections were not fulfilled in the longer term. Lissouba, who had entered a working alliance with Sassou-Nguesso of all people, fell out with the latter almost immediately. A process of musical chairs then ensued, as accords between the main parties were successively struck and broken. On each occasion when the music stopped, one party was left without a seat. In the latter part of the decade, large parts of Brazzaville were levelled as armed militias took to fighting the corner of their leaders. Although Sassou-Nguesso had the smallest electoral base, he proved the most adept at raising his own private army and ultimately succeeded in reclaiming power through the barrel of a gun in 1997. This outcome demonstrated that democratisation was no panacea, and was capable of heightening violent competition for power.

In Niger, which had been under military rule since 1974, there was a democratic opening at the start of the 1990s, but this did not endure either. After the death of General Seyni Kountché in November 1987, he was succeeded in office by General Ali Saïbou, who was ultimately chosen as a compromise candidate. Saïbou endeavoured to give the military regime a more acceptable face, but without necessarily intending to initiate a return to civilian rule. His problem was a familiar one, namely that the SAP which being operative since 1986 imposed hardships on urban workers and students who took to the streets of Niamey to voice their demands. In 1990, clashes between students and the army led to many deaths, which – coming at the time that they did – further politicised these constituencies. After a series of strikes, Saïbou endeavoured to regain the initiative by promising that there would be a return to multipartyism and that a national conference would be convened.

As in the other cases, a panoply of parties and associations sent delegates to the conference which was held between July and November 1991. However, the Armed Forces were merely accorded observer status. The conference followed that of Benin in requiring Saïbou to cohabit with an interim administration, but went further in preventing him from standing for the Presidency. Interestingly, the conference also came out against many of the SAP reforms, such as the reduction of expenditure on civil service salaries and a reallocation of educational expenditure towards the primary sector. This reflected the vocality of student and trade union representatives at the conference. In 1993, national elections were held. In the legislative poll, Saïbou's former party, the MNSD (Mouvement National Pour une Société de Développement) won the most seats overall, but fell a long way short of a majority. A coalition of the opposition parties commanded more seats and managed to capture the Presidency on the second round of voting. Mahamane Ousmane was duly installed and the military dutifully returned to the barracks. Although the people's voice had triumphed, Nigerian electoral democracy was always teetering on a knife's edge. When a vote of no confidence necessitated fresh legislative elections in 1995, the MNSD bounced back. Then, in January of the following year, Colonel Ibrahim Mainassara seized power in a military coup. He had himself elected in another set of elections, but then was promptly assassinated in April 1999. This prepared the way for yet another constitutional debate and fresh elections in which the MNSD won the Presidency once more, but commanded less than a majority of legislative seats.

The only other country where a national conference produced a change of government was in Mali, but here the circumstances were different to start with. The usurpatory military regime of Moussa Traoré, which had come to power as far back as 1968, was confronted by street protests in 1990, initiated in the first instance by women traders. Demonstrations in Bamako rapidly spread to a number of other urban centres. Traoré responded with ruthless repression, but failed to contain this popular insurrection. The crisis was resolved when a section of the army, led by Lt-Col. Amadou Toumani Touré, seized power and announced that there would be a return to civilian rule. The new government, which co-opted a number of civilians, yielded to demands for a national conference, which sat over July and August 1991. In this case, Toumani Touré chaired the conference, which refrained from declaring its sovereignty and from seeking to install an interim administration. The main job of the conference was to prepare the way for a return to constitutional rule, which all sides agreed was the desired end. The bitter denunciations which were a hallmark of the other conferences were directed at the ousted military rulers, whereas the good faith of Toumani Touré was mostly accepted. When national elections were held between February and April, he was not a candidate. Instead, the elections were won by a historian, Alpha Konaré, who went on to repeat the feat in 1997. Although the opposition parties complained about the lack of a level playing field, Mali could fairly be described as a functioning constitutional democracy. After serving two terms of office, as permitted under the constitution, Konaré stepped aside.

9.2.2.2 Abortive national conferences: Zaire, Togo, Gabon

In three other instances, those of Zaire and Togo and Gabon, the opposition forces were successful in calling for national conferences, but failed to unseat the great escapists who occupied the Presidencies. After repeated criticisms of the human rights record of his regime, Gnassingbé Eyadéma had established a National Human Rights Commission, headed by a party loyalist, Yao Agboyibor. Unexpectedly, the latter began to expose human rights violation in the public domain, which provided a space into which other human rights lobby groups could insert themselves. At the close of the decade, there was growing restiveness within the capital, especially as news about the collapse of other dictatorships began to filter through. The public humiliation of Kérékou – no friend of Eyadéma, but a President all the same – seems to been a particularly important catalyst. Moreover, Eyadéma came under pressure from the French to agree to the holding of a national conference. As Eyadéma made concessions to the opposition, such as permitting the first opposition newspapers to be published, strikes and youth demonstrations spread across the capital. Whilst purporting to be opening up, the regime resorted to cracking the whip. In the most notorious episode, a significant number of protestors were drowned in the Bé lagoon.

As the opposition demonstrated its capacity to paralyse Lomé – with the active participation of traders, dockers, taxi drivers and students – Eyadéma agreed to the holding of a national conference, but subject to certain conditions. The conference chose a religious leader to chair proceedings, namely Monsignor Kpodzro of Atakpamé. The conference also appointed Joseph Kokou Koffigoh, a human rights activist, as the head of an interim administration, while Eyadéma was confined to the Presidency. The delegates also gave vent to their feelings, exchanging a hitherto 'hidden transcript' for a very public denunciation of the dictatorship. Although most of the chiefs kept a low profile, the chief of Mission-Tové publicly stated what everyone knew but had not dared to say, namely that chiefs had been systematically bullied by the ruling party.[47] According to John Heilbrunn, the delegates became intoxicated with the thrill of vilifying Eyadéma, forgetting that he remained in effective control: 'it would not be until the "morning after" that local reformers would bitterly recall that Eyadéma held all the guns'.[48]

When the conference tried to declare its sovereignty, Eyadéma contended that this contravened the accord. He was able to counter-attack with the assistance of the army which he had packed with recruits from his home area. These had good cause to worry about what might happen if southern politicians, baying for revenge, should ever come to power. In December 1991, the army arrested Koffigoh, who was so chastened by the event that he effectively capitulated to Eyadéma. When Presidential elections were finally held in 1993, a number of opposition candidates were disqualified from standing, including Gilchrist Olympio – the son of the first President who Eyadéma once claimed to have shot – who stood much the best chance of victory. The other opposition candidates boycotted and Eyadéma was duly returned to office. Although the opposition parties won many legislative seats, Eyadéma had evidently weathered the storm. Only the French could have altered the result, but they were prepared to contract business as usual with the Togolese dictator. This pattern was repeated in 1998 when counting was stopped at the point when it seemed Olympio might actually win. A highly dubious result was subsequently announced. Finally, in 2003 Eyadéma changed the constitution and stole another election (Olympio was debarred) with even less criticism, at the very time when the United States was defending its policy of 'regime change' in Iraq on the basis of promoting democratic values abroad.

Given the close ties between Eyadéma and Mobutu Sese Seko, it is unsurprising that their political responses evolved along parallel lines. As we have already seen in Chapter 6, the Zairean legislature had displayed an unexpected independence after being elected on relatively more open terms in 1977. Thirteen parliamentarians came out openly to demand political reform in 1980, amongst them Etienne Tshisekedi. Despite systematic harassment and periods of detention, this small group broke away from the ruling party to form the UDPS (Union Pour la Démocratie et le Progrès Sociale) in 1982. The UDPS was illegal, but operated more or less above ground. As external and internal pressures accumulated, Mobutu announced the formation of a committee to engage in 'consultations' with the public over the political dispensation they preferred. Although Mobutu claimed that the overwhelming demand had been for limited reforms within the framework of the one-party state, he was apparently taken aback by the audacity with which ordinary citizens spoke truth to power: 'The problem, he was frequently told at public forums by people who no longer feared him, "is you Citizen President".'[49] In April 1990, Mobutu announced that he was over-riding the popular will and ending the monopoly of the Mouvement Populaire de la Révolution (MPR). This precipitated a scramble to form political parties. Sensing that the lion was losing his teeth, many of Mobutu's political associates decamped to join a motley array of splinter parties. However, as Nzongola-Ntalaja suggests, many were actually hedging their bets, intending to associate themselves with whoever eventually came out on top.

Although Mobutu hoped to resist demands for a sovereign national conference, this too was conceded as the clamour for change gathered momentum. The national conference opened in August 1991, but its business was immediately interrupted by rebellious soldiers and then closed down on the orders of Mobutu in January 1992. It was only reopened in April, but then sat until the end of the year, although the pro-Mobutu delegates had broken away by that point. In Zaire, no fewer than 2842 delegates attended the national conference. The patchwork of parties and associations which were represented coalesced into two larger blocs, the Sacred Union of the Radical Opposition (USOR) and the pro-Mobutu FPC (Forces Politiques du Conclave). The conference set itself an enormous task of poring over the entrails of Zairean history in order to discern what had gone wrong and then hammering out a constitutional framework which would, in turn, pave the way for fresh elections. The conference divided itself into 23 commissions, whose task was to report their findings back to the plenary sessions. An immediate concern was who would govern the country in the interim. Militants insisted that Mobutu was a criminal who ought to be stripped of all authority, while the President was equally intent on wrecking the conference. The chairman, Monsignor Monsengwo Pasinyi (the Archbishop of Kisangani), sought to resolve the standoff by brokering a compromise between Mobutu and the opposition forces. The deal which was struck behind closed doors, and which was to prove fateful in the long run, was then presented to the conference as a *fait accompli*. The conference was to appoint a provisional parliament or High Council of the Republic, while the national assembly would be suspended. It was also to appoint a provisional government which would be accountable to the High Council. Mobutu would remain the head of state, but would share power with the head of government. In August 1992, despite the furious machinations of Mobutu, Tshisekedi was duly elected as Prime Minister. Within the national conference itself, Mobutu was publicly vilified, the scenes of which provided riveting theatre for the masses on radio and television.

As Nzongola-Ntalaja (who was himself a delegate) has admitted, the opposition committed a number of fatal errors in their rush to squeeze through the narrow democratic aperture. The former constitution was never abrogated and the old legislature was simply 'suspended'. These oversights enabled Mobutu to close the national conference in December 1992, to resurrect the mothballed parliament and to appoint a Prime Minister of his own choosing.[50] Of course, he was only able to carry off this coup because he remained in effective control of the armed forces and because Western governments – notably the United States, France and Belgium – refused (as usual) to apply any countervailing pressure. Although the country now had two parallel administrations, the advantage clearly lay with Mobutu. Tshisekedi did enjoy one minor victory when the central bank issued a new 5 million Zaire banknote, which he declared was not legal tender. When traders in the capital refused to accept the notes, there were violent clashes with members of the armed forces at the end of January 1993.[51]

The deadlock was broken in September, but this enabled Mobutu to further consolidate his gains. It was agreed that the parallel administrations would merge once again: that is, a single legislature would be formed from the two parliaments, a new Prime Minister would be elected by it, and a constitution would be drafted prior to holding national elections. At this point, many of the waverers in the opposition jumped ship once more and voted for the Mobutu candidate, Léon Kengo wa Dongo, rather than Tshisekedi who was unacceptable to the President. In January 1994, the FPC was granted a majority of seats within a restructured legislature, thereby signalling the final closure of the democratic door.

Although an electoral commission was constituted, its independence was subverted by Mobutu, while the polls themselves were postponed from 1995 to 1997. By this point, the question of elections had become purely academic anyway. For one, Tshisekedi himself was preparing to boycott the process. More crucially, Laurent Kabila's army had begun its long march on the capital in October 1996 with a view to removing Mobutu through force of arms. The days of Mobutu Sese Seko were evidently numbered, as he was struck down with prostrate cancer in 1997 and had to leave the country for treatment. However, the opportunity which had been present for a return to constitutional rule was lost, with disastrous consequences. Much of the blame lies with the opposition politicians themselves, who took decisions and cut backroom deals without any reference to the rest of the population who became increasingly distant spectators. Time and again, Mobutu was able to buy off individuals who claimed to be on the side of change but caved in when Mobutu dangled the carrot of high office in front of them. Throughout his lengthy reign, Mobutu had cleverly played this game of co-optation, and the same card continued to come up trumps in the 1990s when the rules had supposedly changed. For example, Nguza Karl I Bond, who had been purged and then rehabilitated on successive occasions, was instrumental in the formation of the Sacred Union in July 1991. But in November, he was prepared to do the bidding of Mobutu by replacing Tshisikedi as Prime Minister and closing down the national conference. Nguza perhaps felt justified at leaving his colleagues in the lurch because in July Tshisekedi himself had come to a secret agreement with Mobutu, much to the surprise of his colleagues. If Mobutu had been faced with a purposeful opposition, united in its desire to dethrone him, it is doubtful whether he could have survived the early 1990s. As it was, he had studied and knew the personal weaknesses of his opponents, most of whom had been his clients at an earlier point. In many ways, it is not surprising that Mobutu held his challengers in such contempt, because he had repeatedly demonstrated that they were biddable.[52] Finally, the role of the West in bailing out Mobutu one more time cannot be ignored. If the United States and France had taken a principled stance in support of Tshisikedi, the subsequent history might have been different. But by this point, it had become a habit to play fast and loose in matters affecting Zaire, without very much concern for the interests of its hostage-citizens. The result was the country was eventually plunged into chaos, which we will consider in greater detail in the next chapter.

The questionable role of the French is also apparent in the case of Gabon, where the Elf oil corporation had long enjoyed a privileged position and Paris had underwritten the security of Omar Bongo. The French had intervened to restore Léon M'ba, when he was overthrown in February 1964, and had engineered the subsequent succession of Bongo. During the 1980s, the most significant challenge to the rule of the PDG (Parti Démocratique Gabonais) emanated from a movement within the Catholic church which began to insist on a more socially committed reading of the gospel. In 1981, Father Paul Mba-Abbesolé was instrumental in the formation of MORENA (Mouvement de Redressement Nationale), which demanded fundamental political reforms. That the church became the focus of an emergent critique of the regime is significant because Bongo had turned the manipulation of religion into a fine art. He had established a cosy relationship with the Catholic and Protestant hierarchies, even after his conversion to Islam in 1973. He had also positioned himself in important positions within the Bwiti and Ndjombe secret societies, thereby claiming protection from traditional spiritual forces. To cap it all, he had adopted a leading position within the two principal Masonic lodges.[53]

The roots of the malaise in Gabon were rooted in certain material facts of life. The country suffered greatly from the Dutch disease, in the sense that oil revenues had killed off other productive sectors of the economy, while there was a wholesale movement of population to the cities in search of public sector jobs. Whereas only 15 per cent of the population was urban in 1960, the figure was close to 75 per cent in 1990, with Libreville becoming the principal magnet. What this meant was that when oil revenues began to decline, there was less money to pay salaries and to fund the educational provision which Gabonese expected as of right. In 1990, students at the University clashed with the Police, while workers resorted to a series of debilitating strikes, which crossed the divide between the public and private sectors.[54] In order to recapture the initiative, Bongo indicated that he was prepared to contemplate an end to one-party rule and he agreed to the holding of a national conference in March 1990. However, this conference was very muted by comparison with Benin. Bongo was able to insist that he remain the substantive President and that the conference was merely advisory in character. Behind the scenes, he was engaged in secret negotiations with certain members of the opposition, which somewhat undercut the formal proceedings.

When Bongo formed a new government at the end of the conference, most of the posts went to members of the PDG, with a token inclusion of opposition politicians. All eyes were then turned on the legislative elections which were held in September and October 1993. These gave the PDG a slim majority, but mainly because the distribution of seats was weighted in favour of Bongo's home province of Haut-Ogooué. With Presidential elections scheduled for December, Bongo had every reason to be worried, especially as many of his long-term associates decided to stand against him. When the first results seemed to point towards a victory for Mba-Abbesolé, the Minister of the Interior simply declared Bongo the winner with a convenient 51 per cent of the vote. These results were later validated by the Constitutional Court, presided over by the alleged mistress of Bongo, and backed up by military force.[55] Once again, the external reaction was crucial to determining the viability of such outright manipulation. According to David Gardinier, the centre-right coalition in France, headed by Prime Minister Edouard Balladur, decided to back Bongo in return for his not making waves over the proposed devaluation of the CFA franc. He also makes a more serious allegation to the effect that the French assisted with vote-rigging in the two provinces where the PDG controlled the local administration.[56] The net result was that Bongo was able to literally steal a win. However, as in the case of Zaire, the opposition contributed to its own demise by succumbing to internal bickering and to the lure of petrol money. When Bongo convened a coalition government after the elections crisis, it was very much on his own terms.

9.2.2.3   The controlled release: Central African Republic, Guinea, Cameroun, Côte d'Ivoire, Burkina Faso and Chad

In the remaining cases we need to consider, the opposition failed to achieve the critical mass which was needed to bring about the holding of a national conference. In the Central African Republic (CAR), General André Kolingba had attempted to legitimise his usurpation of power in 1981 through the creation of a one-party state which was supposed to facilitate popular participation. In 1986, he had himself elected to the presidency under a new constitution and the following year legislative elections were held after a long period of abeyance. However, these limited reforms appeared to be little more than a subterfuge and at the turn of the decade students and intellectuals began to demand a return to multipartyism. In 1991, the CCCCN (Comité Coordonnateur pour la Convocation d'une Conférence Nationale) was established to campaign for a national conference. Kolingba attempted to get away with convening a 'national debate' instead, but this failed to persuade the most important opposition politicians who kept up the pressure and won some external backing.[57] Realising the dangers associated with holding a national conference, Kolingba agreed to hold Presidential and legislative elections instead, on the assumption that he would be able to manipulate the process to his advantage. When it became obvious in the polls of October 1992 that he was going to lose, he cancelled them, set up and interim administration and announced fresh elections for the following year. When he was heading for defeat once again, it appeared as if Kolingba intended to annul the elections for a second time. On this occasion, the French made a timely intervention by announcing a suspension of aid. This forced Kolingba to beat a retreat and ultimately to accept a humiliating exit in the first round – alongside David Dacko. The victor in the second round was Ange-Félix Patassé, a former Bokassa Prime Minister, who bested another veteran, Dr Abel Goumba. In the Parliamentary polls, Patassé's MPLC (Mouvement Pour la Libération Centrafricain) won 40 per cent of the seats and was therefore forced to construct a coalition government. On somewhat rickety foundations, a multiparty system was erected. Although the opposition had failed to push through a national conference, the demise of Kolingba arose from his clumsy political footwork and the eventual withdrawal of French support.

In Guinea, a culture of authoritarianism remained deeply ingrained. After five years at the helm of what was effectively a military regime, Lansana Conté announced the legalisation of political parties in 1989. However, it was not until December 1993 that the first multiparty elections were actually held. In the Presidential polls, Conté only managed 51.7 per cent of the vote, which was an indication that his popularity was far from assured. The crucial legislative elections were not held until as late 1995, when Conté's Parti de l'Unité et du Progrès (PUP) received 71 out of 114 seats. Although Guinea had gone through the democratic motions, the legitimacy of the regime remained weak at every level. Despite Conté's military background, mutineers actually came close to toppling him in 1996. Two years later, a second Presidential election was held and Conté claimed victory once again. On this occasion, international observers were critical of the harassment of opposition candidates and many other electoral irregularities, but concluded that the exercise had been an improvement on 1993.[58] This rather weak criticism probably owed something to the recognition that Guinea was one of the few countries in this part of West Africa which had avoided civil war (see Chapter 10). By such a pragmatic yardstick, Guinea seemed to be limping along tolerably well. Conté himself was quick to appreciate that conflicts within the sub-region could serve a useful political purpose at home. In September 2000, following incursions from the Liberian side of the border, Conté alleged that there was a great conspiracy to topple the government, involving Charles Taylor of Liberia, Blaise Compaoré of Burkina Faso and the opposition leader, Alpha Condé. Significantly, it was the latter who had presented him with the greatest challenge at the polls. By resurrecting a very old theme, in which fifth-columnists were supposedly everywhere, Conté tapped into a latent fear of foreigners which had been carefully instilled by Sekou Touré.[59] It is doubtful how many Guineans were persuaded that Condé was truly in league with foreign armies, but it reminded many that the authoritarianism of the present system was preferable to the devastation of Liberia ad Sierra Leone.

In Cameroun, Paul Biya was fond of pointing out that he had put the question of democracy on the agenda as far back as 1983, thereby precipitating his breach with Ahidjo. From that point, it was theoretically possible for more than one Presidential candidate to stand, while the principle of competition was later introduced into party structures and for the legislature itself. There was also a liberalisation of media restrictions. However, the catch was that Cameroun was to remain a one-party state, for the usual justification that this would sublimate latent ethnic divisions. While the limited reforms won Biya some initial support, these had ceased to satisfy many urban Camerounians by the end of the decade, when economic conditions had also taken a decisive turn for the worse. In 1990, a series of attempts to found opposition parties led to arrests and violence. As the pressure continued to mount, Biya conceded the legality of opposition parties at the end of that year. However, like Kolingba, Biya resolutely resisted demands for a national conference in the face of demonstrations, strikes and campaigns to bring the cities to a halt, billed as *opération villes mortes*. His resolve stiffened by the French, the most Biya was prepared to concede was a Tripartite Conference. The talks were held the following year, but opposition leaders refused to sign the final report on the basis that the exercise was a charade.

Biya endeavoured to maintain the initiative by bringing legislative elections forward to March 1992, which gave the opposition something to play for. With the question of a national conference off the agenda, Biya and his revamped Cameroun People's Democratic Movement (CPDM) set out to ensure that they triumphed at the polls. Although the CPDM managed less than an outright majority (88 out of 180 seats), it remained the largest party in the legislature and achieved a working majority by striking a deal with smaller parties. In the Presidential elections which followed in October, Biya achieved a slim majority of 39.9 per cent of the vote, as against 35.9 per cent won by John Fru Ndi of the Social Democratic Front (SDF) and 19.2 by Bouba Bello Maigari of the Union Nationale Pour la Démocratie et la Progrès (UNDP), to mention only the serious contenders. These elections were marred by widespread irregularities which were identified by credible external observers.[60] The protests which ensued, especially in the Anglophone west, were put down with some force.

The insouciance of France was a crucial factor in ensuring that Biya's gamble paid off. However, once again, it has to be recognised that the opposition proved to be its own worst enemy. The SDF boycotted the legislative polls and thereby gifted a number of crucial seats in the North-West Province to the CPDM. Moreover, the opposition parties failed to field a common Presidential candidate, thereby ensuring that Biya would retain his office. As in Gabon and Zaire, opposition politicians also proved extremely susceptible to bribery and co-optation. Even a fraction of the Union des Peuples du Cameroun (UPC), which had been the most consistent opponent of the ruling party, had been lured into collaborating with the CPDM in the legislature in return for scraps from the governing table. In subsequent years, personal and deep-seated ethnic rivalries prevented the opposition from rallying together to unseat Biya. The leadership of the UNDP, for example, was mistrustful of the pretensions of Fru Ndi and the SDF, and refused to participate in the Allied Front for Change which was established in 1994.[61] Instead, the party entered into an alliance with the CPDM which proved to be its undoing, as its support-base evaporated.[62] Equally, the growing expressions of alienation by Anglophone politicians helped to accentuate a latent line of cleavage within the body politic, which undercut the national appeal of Fru Ndi, who was himself an Anglophone from the North-West Province. This fracturing of the opposition, combined with a calculated policy of frustrating its attempts to organise and to gain equal access to the media, enabled the CPDM to repeat its electoral triumph in the legislative elections of 1997 – precipitating an opposition boycott of the Presidential elections which followed.[63] From this point, things went from bad to worse for the opposition. In 2002, the CPDM managed to increase its haul of legislative seats from 116 to 133 seats, while the SDF fell back from 43 to 21 seats, 19 of which were located in the North-West Province. When Fru Ndi decided that the SDF should take up its seats, rather than boycott the legislature and municipal councils, there was a spate of prominent defections from the party. By this point, the hopes of unseating the Biya regime had become but a distant prospect, as Cameroun returned to being dominated by one party.

In Côte d'Ivoire, as we have seen, Houphouët-Boigny had proved himself to be one of the shrewdest political operators in the political business. With a downturn in the economic fortunes of the country at the end of the 1970s, perhaps the most important instrument of personal rule, namely co-optation, had been rendered deeply problematic. Without the resources to buy off dissent, and with countervailing pressures from the IFIs to implement austerity measures, Houphouët was cornered. His initial response was to release some of the pressure through controlled political reform. From 1980, it became possible for more than one candidate to stand in legislative elections, and in the polls which followed there was a substantial turnover of personnel. However, Houphouët remained the sole Presidential candidate, while the principle of one-party rule remained inviolate. However, these reforms failed to satisfy students and teachers who bore much of the brunt of declining expenditure. Over 1982–83, the students', teachers' and lecturers' unions resorted to sustained strike action and forced the government on to the back foot. Although it subsequently recaptured some of the initiative, there was a renewed challenge at the end of the decade when Houphouët was forced to impose even more draconian austerity measures, including a halving of cocoa and coffee producer prices, salary cuts and substantial retrenchment from the public sector.[64] On this occasion when students and teachers demonstrated, they received support from the urban unemployed and even some social groups who had hitherto remained loyal: the list included 'bus drivers, dock workers, police, soldiers, and even doctors and dentists'.[65]

The bread-and-butter grievances fed into growing demands that the monopoly of the PDCI (Parti Démocratique de la Côte d'Ivoire) be brought to a timely end. In April 1990, Houphouët gave his response when he came out firmly against a national conference, but agreed to the holding of multiparty elections later in the year. This was vintage Houphouët in the sense that the he was well-aware that the opposition was ill-prepared to put up a credible challenge. Although Laurent Gbagbo succeeded in rallying other parties behind his candidacy, Houphouët beat him in less-than-fair elections by an order of 81.7 to 18.3 per cent. In the legislative poll, the PDCI also won 163 of the 175 seats. Although the opposition now had a toe-hold in parliament, where Gbagbo had himself secured a seat, its fundamental weakness had nevertheless been exposed. In the aftermath of these elections, the regime went out of its way to make it virtually impossible for opposition parties to mobilise their supporters, while Gbagbo himself received a two-year prison sentence for incitement in 1992.

So far so Biya. However, the unforeseen factor which threatened to upset everything was the confirmation that Houphouët was suffering from terminal prostate cancer in 1993. Such was the shadow cast by *Le Vieux* over the political life of the country that his sudden disappearance from the scene was bound to create a vacuum of enormous proportions. When he finally passed away in December, Henri Konan Bédié lost no time in claiming the presidency for himself as president of the legislature. Under the terms of the constitution, his tenure was supposed to last until the next set of elections. Bédié's game-plan was to milk his temporary advantage and thereby turn himself into the legitimate successor of *Le Vieux*. Finding himself out-manoeuvred, Alassane Ouattara resigned the post of Prime Minister, which he had held since 1990, and took up a senior position with the IMF in Washington. As the 1995 elections hove into view, the politicking came fast and furious. Bédié's supporters pushed through a new electoral code which stipulated that both parents of a prospective candidate had to be of Ivoirien nationality. The barely disguised intention was to disqualify Ouattara, on the basis that his father was a Burkinabé. Given that around a third of the population came from outside Côte d'Ivoire – and had made a seminal contribution to the expansion of cash crop production on which the entire 'miracle' had been based – this was as cynical as it was divisive. The net result was that the opposition parties resolved to boycott the elections, permitting Bédié to romp home on a much lower turnout. As we will see in the next chapter, this was a thoroughly Pyrrhic victory because the legitimacy of Bédié, which was shaky to start with, was further impaired. Moreover, the new President lacked the political savvy of his predecessor, and by unwisely choosing to stoke up ethnic divisions he unleashed forces which ended up devouring the PDCI and his own presidential pretensions.

Across the border in Burkina Faso – the new name for Upper Volta chosen by Thomas Sankara in 1984 – the final outcome bore some similarity, although the route taken was very different.[66] Sankara had articulated a radical populist position, in which the empowerment of women and the peasantry, had been placed at the top of the 'revolutionary' agenda, alongside some good old-fashioned nationalism. Sankara, who was rarely to be seen outside his military fatigues and who took pleasure in tweaking the nose of his French overlords, could not have cut a more different figure to the patrician Houphouët. In October 1987 – when the 'revolution' already in deep trouble because of its failure to carry critical constituencies like organised labour with it – Sankara was assassinated, quite possibly at the instigation of his friend, Blaise Compaoré.[67] Stepping into the limelight, Compaoré sought to reconcile many of the social groups which had been alienated by the revolution. Drawing an explicit parallel with *glasnost* in the Soviet Union, he also set in motion a process of reform in which independent political parties were made legal and press freedoms were reintroduced.[68] Compaoré tried to bind the parties which sprang up in 1989 into a Popular Front, but relatively quickly the latter found the embrace of the regime too suffocating and opted for an independent existence. To all intents and purposes, the Front consisted of Compaoré's own party, the ODP/MT (Organisation pour la Démocratie Populaire/Mouvement du Travail). The opening up of Burkinabé politics therefore preceded the political upsurge elsewhere on the continent.

Inevitably, however, these events had a direct impact on Burkina Faso where the opposition parties began to insist on the need for a national conference. As in Côte d'Ivoire and Cameroun, the government response was to call early elections at the end of 1991, after a referendum on the adoption of a new constitution. The opposition parties boycotted, thereby ensuring Compaoré of an easy victory in the presidential polls. When legislative elections were held in May 1992, the opposition parties took part, but the ODP/MT nevertheless emerged clutching 78 of 107 seats. In the years which followed, Burkina Faso exemplified the pattern of a qualified democracy. While the odds were stacked against the opposition parties, there was an independent and vocal press, while students and workers were permitted some freedom to strike and demonstrate against the effects of the SAP which came into effect in 1991 – although the former were on the receiving end of state violence in 1996. Unlike Côte d'Ivoire, Burkina Faso at least managed to avoid a fracturing of party politics along ethnic lines.

The story of democratisation in Chad was equally mixed. Ever since the mid-1960s, Chad had come to symbolise the abject failure of the post-colonial state. Between 1979 and 1982, when Goukhouni Weddeye was normally ruling the country – which effectively meant controlling N'Djamena – Chad had effectively ceased to function, although the international system kept up the pretence of statehood.[69] Hissein Habré enjoyed a greater measure of success in restoring central control after 1982, but with time he alienated many of his allies who complained of dictatorial tendencies. The dissidents included Idris Déby who crossed the border into Sudan in 1989, where he was permitted to mobilise his own rebel army in the Dafur region. When Habré allegedly entered into negotiations with American oil interests, he alienated his most powerful patron in the shape of France. Mitterrand who had come around to the merits of democracy in Africa now purported to find Habré unacceptable and offered covert support to Déby who invaded and seized the capital in December 1990 – rehearsing a very familiar script.

Déby was a most unlikely champion of democracy, having lived the life of a Chadian warlord, but shortly after coming to power he made encouraging noises. An independent press was permitted to operate and in January 1992 political parties were legalised. Between January and April of the following year, a national conference was convened, which asserted its sovereignty but without removing Déby from office. An interim prime minister was appointed and a new constitution was drafted. However, Déby fully intended to succeed himself and when (after some obvious stalling) Presidential elections were finally held in 1996, the opposition and international observers alike cried foul. Five years later, the story was repeated against a chorus of opposition protests. The Déby regime, which drew most of its support from the North, enjoyed little legitimacy in the South where rebels once more took up arms. But even in the North itself, one of Déby's associates, Youssouf Togoimi, rose up against the government and scored some military success. At the end of the 1990s, therefore, the survival of Chadian democracy was once more in question.

9.2.2.4   A special case: Senegal

The Senegalese trajectory differed in significant respects from that of the other Francophone states. As we have seen, Senghor had initiated a return to controlled multipartyism as far back as 1976, following which the opposition parties had endeavoured to convert popular dismay at the economic failings of the PS into votes. In 1983, Diouf had put the seal of legitimacy on the managed succession by winning 83.5 per cent of the Presidential vote. However, it did not take long before disillusionment set in. In the 1988 elections, Abdoulaye Wade, the leader of the PDS (Parti Démocratique Sénégalais), purported to believe that the party stood a genuine chance of winning, and when this failed to transpire there were violent demonstrations fomented by urban youth. These protests led to the declaration of a state of emergency and the conviction of Wade and others for incitement to commit violence. As events began to unfold elsewhere, the Diouf regime recognised the need to engage the opposition in a dialogue in order to keep the lid on things. The upshot was that Wade and other opposition leaders were granted an amnesty and brought into the government in 1991. Moreover, opposition demands that the electoral code be amended – by amongst things, granting equal access to the media and lowering the voting age from 21 to 18 years – were conceded by the PS. By making these concessions, the PS managed to avoid holding a national conference, although interestingly Wade distanced himself from this particular Francophone fashion.[70]

One consequence of the reforms was that the opposition convinced itself that victory was inevitable in the 1993 elections: any other result could be taken as proof of rigging.[71] Confirmation of the fact that PS dominance was crumbling came when the marabouts failed to issue their customary *ndigals*, or injunctions to their followers to vote for the governing party. However, disillusionment with the regime did not necessarily translate into opposition votes, especially as the newly enfranchised young voters generally opted to abstain. When the results of the Presidential polls were finally announced, and indicated a Diouf victory with 58.4 per cent of the vote, the opposition cried foul and the political system was rocked by a fresh bout of demonstrations and arrests. Moustapha Sy, who led the Moustarchadines into direct confrontation with the regime, was arrested along with opposition leaders and the movement was formally proscribed in February 1994.[72] By this point, the moral authority of the PS was at an all-time low, not helped by the devaluation of the CFA franc which took a further bite out of urban incomes. The latest round of brinkmanship ended when Wade re-entered negotiations with Diouf and joined the government in March 1995 as a Minister of State at the presidency. In return, Wade surprisingly dropped his demand for an independent electoral commission.

The reasons why Wade and the leaders of other parties like the Ligue Démocratique-Mouvement Pour le Parti du Travail (LD-MPT) agreed to enter a coalition are at first sight puzzling. Clearly, the PS was aiming to defuse potential sources of protest, whilst plotting its next triumph at the polls. For a leader like Wade, there was an obvious risk of ceasing to be seen as an alternative to the PS. However, as Beck points, participation also gave the opposition parties access to patronage which they could dispense to their followers lower down in order to keep them on the political hook.[73] This gamble eventually paid off when, having once more distanced himself from the administration, Wade finally succeeded in defeating Diouf in Presidential elections in 2000. Many observers feared the worst in the run-up to these polls, but when it became clear that Wade had won an overwhelming majority on the second round, Diouf accepted the verdict of the people with good grace.[74] The well-springs of PS supremacy, which were close on four decades old, had finally dried up. The final implosion of the PS, which was confirmed in the legislative elections of 2001, was arguably every bit as profound as the defeat of Kérékou a decade earlier. However, the historic victory also concealed the same underlying reality that the incoming regime faced an enormous task in seeking to satisfy raised expectations. Throughout the 2000 campaign, Wade was decidedly unclear about what he would do which was different. The campaign slogan of *Sopi!*, or change, was effective, but it scarcely amounted to a serious platform. Wade therefore faced the strong likelihood that voters would turn against him if he did not deliver the goods in short order.

9.2.3 The Anglophone states

Although there was inevitably some cross-fertilisation of ideas, it would be a mistake to underestimate the gulf separating the political cultures of the Francophone and the Anglophone countries. In each case, geographical proximity counted for less than established patterns of thinking about and practicing politics. Hence, the Benin model exerted less of an influence than one might expect upon the states of Anglophone West Africa. Because there were no Francophone states in Eastern or Southern Africa, there was even less chance of a crossover in these regions. The Anglophone states also diverged from each other to a far greater extent than their Francophone counterparts did, because they did not share such an intimate relationship with the former colonial power. Perhaps the most striking difference was that the opposition in the Anglophone states did not bother themselves unduly with demands for national conferences. In most cases, they proceeded directly to agitating for free elections, preceded if necessary by the holding of a referendum. Britain did not play a particularly pro-active role, although it became *de rigeur* for the Commonwealth to send election observers who either legitimated or attached health warnings to the final results. Finally, in those Anglophone countries which did undergo successful transitions, there was a strong sense of history repeating itself, as the liberators were seduced by the attractions of public office and had to be prised away from the levers of power.

9.2.3.1 Two qualified victories and a partial defeat: Zambia, Malawi and Zimbabwe

Amongst the Anglophone states, Zambia became as much of a beacon as Benin was for the Francophone ones. The overturning of the UNIP regime was, if anything, an even more remarkable feat because Kaunda was one of the founding generation of nationalist leaders with a better-than-average nose for politics. The problem facing UNIP was a simple one, namely that its practice of buying compliance from core urban constituencies became untenable as the mining economy descended into terminal decline. The living standards of most Zambians fell substantially over the course of the 1980s, due to a combination of rising unemployment (particularly in the mining areas), falling real wages and collapsing social services. Whereas UNIP had previously maintained subsidies on foodstuffs for urban dwellers, this became increasingly unsustainable and workers began to feel the pinch. In 1985, 1987, 1988 and 1989 there were illegal strikes across the public sector, as well as food riots in 1986 and 1990. In 1989, the ZCTU gave these protests a more explicitly political edge when it laid the blame for the suffering of Zambians squarely at the door of UNIP. In June of the following year, the doubling of maize meal prices led to further angry protests, which was accompanied by the torching of a national monument glorifying Kaunda's role in the freedom struggle.[75] Moreover, the mainstream churches became more overtly critical of the regime, particularly through the pages of the *National Mirror*, which was jointly owned by the Christian Council of Zambia (CCZ) and the Episcopal Conference of Zambia, and the Catholic Church's Bemba-language monthly *Icengelo*.[76]

Kaunda desperately sought to rekindle older loyalties to UNIP, whilst assiduously playing the Christian card to tap into revivalist currents sweeping the country. Hence in November 1990, he invited a number of African heads of state to join him in a prayer breakfast. Moreover, Kaunda sought to play for time. In July 1990, the National Interim Committee for Multiparty Democracy had been formed to campaign for immediate elections. Kaunda insisted on the importance of first holding a referendum, which he then sought to postpone for a year, supposedly to permit a proper voter registration exercise to be carried out. In this, as in much else, he was forced to give way after the opposition took to the streets to demand immediate multiparty elections. In January, the Committee transformed itself into a political party, the MMD (Movement for Multiparty Democracy) which proceeded to select Chiluba as its own Presidential candidate. The MMD flexed its muscles by holding a succession of mass rallies which demonstrated the depth of urban alienation from the regime.

However, Kaunda still held one trump-card. Although he had served the rural population poorly in the past, by forcing peasants to subsidise urban consumption, he gambled on the presumption that the MMD was a purely urban phenomenon. With the majority of the voters still residing in the countryside, the day might still be saved when the ballots were cast. The chiefs, in particular, were showered with patronage, including Toyota Land Cruisers, and some were even fielded as UNIP candidates.[77] Kaunda also made a special pitch for the women's vote. Unfortunately for him, UNIP structures had withered at the local level, whereas the MMD had managed to insinuate itself into even the more remote rural locations. When all else failed, UNIP resorted to blatant vote-buying and scare tactics, hinting at the possibility of a civil war if the opposition should ever come to power. As for the MMD, it did not promise a radically different set of policies, being firmly wedded to a neo-liberal agenda, so much as a cleaner leadership. The results of the October 1991 elections demonstrate the extent to which UNIP had forfeited its popular mandate. Only the Eastern Province remained loyal, whereas elsewhere the MMD swept the board in both the urban and the rural areas. In the legislative elections, the MMD won no fewer than 125 out of the 150 seats, while in the Presidential poll Kaunda was trounced by Chiluba who received close on 76 per cent of the votes case. Like Kérékou, Kaunda salvaged some residual respect by accepting defeat and bowing out gracefully.

Although Zambia had become the first Anglophone country to change its government through the ballot-box, it did not take very long before it was being held up as a model for a different reason. From an early point, it became evident that the MMD leadership was no less immune to the temptations of office than the UNIP grandees had previously been. Ministers revelled in the many perquisites of office, including sumptuous housing and chauffeured cars. This came with the territory, but it also contrasted with the plight of the average citizen. Moreover, MMD politicians went much further in their quest for accumulation. Some Ministers were forced to resign for alleged implication in drug-dealing in 1994, while many other allegations of corruption and abuse of privilege began to stick. Those who were sacked or resigned their offices split from the MMD and made some of the most damaging allegations, which the private press was only too happy to relay to a wider audience. Chiluba responded to the welter of allegations in a high-handed manner, as if corruption was logical impossibility in a country ruled by a devout born-again Christian such as himself. When Chiluba insisted on formally proclaiming Zambia a Christian country, against the inclinations of the mainline churches, the gap between the holier-than-thou rhetoric of the regime and the behaviour of its public representatives was too great for many to tolerate. In January 1995 the Catholic Commission on Justice and Peace (CCJP) linked the government to a culture of profiteering, in which it was supported by the Bishops.[78] The Christian Council was equally searing in its criticism. This brought the MMD into open confrontation with the churches as well as with the independent press, which was subjected to systematic harassment.

The Chiluba government responded with increasing paranoia to what it claimed was a grand conspiracy to return Kaunda to power. As early as 1993, the government claimed to have uncovered a UNIP plot to mount a coup, with foreign backing, and swiftly imposed a State of Emergency. This was the first of many alleged plots involving Kaunda, none of which stood up in court, and which were widely believed to have been fabrications. Chiluba, who had suffered at the hands of Kaunda, perhaps enjoyed exacting his revenge, and he was certainly determined to ensure that there would be no comeback. To the consternation of civil society groups, Chiluba was prepared to resort to questionable expedients to have things his own way. He first of all tried to have Kaunda deported on the basis that his parents were Malawians rather than Zambians, but after this provoked a storm of protest he fell back upon a 1996 amendment to the constitution which required a Presidential candidate to have both parents born in Zambia.[79] He refused to submit the new constitution to a referendum or even to enter into negotiations with civil society groups as had been advocated by the architect of the document.

These moves were seen as a transparent attempt to disqualify Kaunda who had come out of retirement in 1995. Further controversy surrounded the conduct of the urgently needed voter registration, subcontracted to an Israeli computer company, when it produced surprisingly low returns.[80] In June, following a series of bomb blasts, eight UNIP leaders were arrested and put on trial for treason. Against a backdrop of escalating violence, UNIP resolved to boycott the 1996 polls, alongside some other opposition parties. Given the resources which were at the disposal of the MMD, the result was a predictable landslide for the governing party against a number of smaller challengers, a number of whom had previously split from its ranks.[81] Although international monitoring groups signalled their lack of confidence in the exercise by refusing to send observers, three out of four internal monitoring bodies, issued detailed reports to back up their conclusion that the elections had not been free and fair.[82] The opposition parties, including those which had contested and those which had boycotted, cried foul and threatened to make the country ungovernable. Although Chiluba had won, the claim that Zambia was at the forefront of African democracies had worn rather thin by this point: 'At the end of 1996, democracy was barely surviving, and its future did not look promising.'[83]

After the polls, Chiluba continued to conjure up fresh conspiracies, supposedly involving hostile Western governments, and announced his intention to subject NGOs to closer monitoring. However, he had to respect some autonomy for opposition activity as the price for the resumption of foreign aid. However, following another attempted coup, a second State of Emergency was imposed in 1997 and Kaunda was imprisoned for some time. Two years later, against a backdrop of political machinations, the High Court finally ruled that Kaunda was not a citizen. This finally spiked Kaunda's hopes of 'doing a Kérékou'. The weakened opposition was reduced to playing a waiting game in the knowledge that the MMD had a history of internal divisions, which were likely to be exposed in the run-up to the third set of elections scheduled for 2001. For the reality was that Chiluba was only permitted two terms of office under the constitution. Any attempt to alter the constitution was likely to provoke an uproar, not least within the MMD where many budding successors were waiting in the wings. In the first half of 2001, the MMD leadership was openly divided over the issue. The Vice-President, Christon Tembo, and eight other Cabinet Ministers were expelled from the party for openly urging Chiluba to go quietly. They formed a breakaway party of their own, the Forum for Democracy and Development (FDD). As the churches, students and other associational bodies spearheaded a mass campaign against him, Chiluba was forced to accept the inevitable and to agree to go into retirement. For a second time, Zambians had succeeded in unseating an incumbent, if not the ruling party.

With his principal detractors now outside the party, Chiluba was free to handpick his successor at the head of the MMD. To universal surprise, he selected Levy Mwanawasa who had resigned as Vice-President in 1994 in protest against corruption. He was therefore regarded as a man of considerable integrity. The elections held at the end of 2001 were closely contested and might have been lost by the MMD if the opposition parties had presented a united front. However, due to the peculiarities of the electoral system, which made no provision for a second round of Presidential voting, Mwanawasa triumphed with a mere 29 per cent of the vote, to 27 per cent of Anderson Mazoka of the United Party for National Development (UPND) and 13 per cent for Tembo at the head of the FDD. The opposition complained of systematic irregularities and unsuccessfully contested the Presidential and Parliamentary results in the courts. In an attempt to be seen as his own man, Mwanawasa put together a government which was short on Chiluba loyalists. Moreover, he subsequently supported the removal of his predecessor's immunity from prosecution on charges of corruption. The turnover in the MMD leadership was a limited triumph of internal democracy over personalism, but whether the opposition would receive a fair crack of the whip in future remained to be seen.

The Malawian experience bore more than a passing similarity to that of its larger neighbour. Here, the political transformation of the early 1990s was bound to be still more profound given that Life-President Banda had treated Malawi as his personal estate after the purging his rivals in the Cabinet crisis of 1964.[84] Although the Malawi Congress Party (MCP) was supposedly supreme, the party was a creature of Banda. The regime enforced rigid censorship over the media and academic debate at the University, and policed the most intimate discussions of its citizens through a dense network of informers. Amongst the instruments of social control, the Malawi Young Pioneers (MYP) was a para-military organisation which was encouraged to regard itself as the equal of the police and the army. After a quarter of a decade of closure, the decompression which occurred once the first small puncture had been made, was spectacular.

The process began with a pastoral letter which was read from the pulpit of Catholic churches across the country in March 1992. This calculated attack on social inequality, injustice and mass impoverishment came like a bolt from the blue, given the relative quiescence of the churches in the past. Although the regime responded with threats and bluster, there was no disguising the fact that its presumed right to rule had been called into question. The University students immediately rallied to the side of the Bishops, inducing the government to close the campuses.[85] This turn of events provided the occasion for dissident politicians to gather in Zambia to co-ordinate demands for fundamental political reform. Chafukwa Chihana emerged from nowhere as the main leader of this group. When he returned to Malawi, he was promptly detained and became a symbol for the opposition. His supporters moved to establish the Alliance for Democracy (AFORD), while the United Democratic Front (UDF) was formed by ex-MCP politicians who had not attended the Lusaka meetings. As in Zambia, it was urban protesters who forced the pace through a series of rolling strikes and rioting in Lilongwe and Blantyre.

In the past, repression had worked because it had been targeted, but the mass movement which was beginning to take shape could not be dealt with in this way. Moreover, foreign donors indicated that they would respond to repression by shutting off the aid flow. Although the MCP initially refused to budge from its adherence to one-partyism, Banda eventually relented by agreeing to a referendum on the issue. This provided a focus for the opposition forces who knew that if they defeated Banda in June 1993, his moral authority was likely to evaporate. Banda used all the resources at his disposal in an attempt to snatch a victory, but the result was a decisive vote for multipartyism by a ratio of two to one. As the political game threatened to run away from him, Banda insisted that he was under no immediate obligation to organise elections. However, whatever room for manoeuvre the MCP still enjoyed rapidly dissipated. First of all, Banda himself had to be rushed to South Africa for medical treatment in October, arising from a brain tumour, leaving others in the MCP to manage the crisis.[86] Then in December, the Malawian army, which had been smarting at the favouritism displayed towards the MYP, turned on the latter in 'Operation Bwezani' and, having disarmed it, ran its members out of the country. The MCP now found itself forced to negotiate from a position of weakness when it came to shaping the constitutional revisions under which national elections would be held.

In the run-up to the elections, the opposition front cracked. As AFORD and the UDF came to see each others as rivals for a succession which was virtually in the bag, the former began to deflect its fire away from the MCP. Whereas AFORD held up Chihana as a man of bravery, it dredged up allegations that the UDF candidate, Bakili Mulizi, had once been convicted over the theft of six pounds as well as having served as Vice-President under Banda.[87] In the elections which followed on 17 May 1994, the MCP was roundly defeated, but not disastrously so. Banda, who had banked on women and rural voters, received 33 per cent of the vote, trailing behind Muluzi on 47 per cent, but ahead of Chihana on 19.5 per cent. One reason why the MCP did so well was that the political map had fragmented along ethno-regional lines, unlike in Zambia. The UDF triumphed on the basis of its support in the more populous south, the MCP clung on to the loyalties of the central belt and AFORD was confined to its northern stronghold. Banda gracefully accepted the verdict of the electorate, and withdrew from the fray with a surprising amount of goodwill on all sides. His death finally followed in 1997. Muluzi was duly installed as the new president and because the UDF did not command a parliamentary majority, a deal was struck with AFORD in which the latter was offered Ministerial appointments in return for support in the legislature.

As in Zambia, it did not take too long before some of the worst practices of the ousted regime began to repeat themselves. The fact that so many leading UDF figures were recycled MCP politicians suggests why this should not have been unexpected. Government Ministers were not slow in cashing in on the privileges of office and in cornering scarce resources for themselves.[88] Moreover, once UDF politicians had tasted the fruits of office, they were determined that power should not slip from their grasp. In the run-up to the second elections in 1999, AFORD cut its ties and joined forces with the MCP. The latter, proclaiming itself reformed, hoped to stage a comeback by fielding Gwanda Chakuamba, a former Banda prisoner of 25-years standing, as its Presidential candidate. Using all the resources which came with incumbency, including control of the country's new television network, Muluzi and the UDF were able to maintain their grip on power.[89] Although the opposition complained about the voters' register, AFORD agreed once more to re-enter an alliance with the UDF. During 1992, the issue of a third term soon became a key point of controversy, with the churches and many other associational bodies demanding that the terms of the constitution be respected. Although Muluzi attempted to find his way around the obstacles, he was eventually forced to capitulate along the lines of Chiluba.

In Zimbabwe, the Mugabe regime managed to parry the onslaught of domestic opposition, but only at the cost of aggravating social cleavages and precipitating an economic collapse. At the time of independence, the main challenger to the absolute dominance of ZANU-PF had been PF-ZAPU. However, the reign of terror which the Fifth Brigade conducted in Matabeleland in the mid-1980s led PF-ZAPU to throw in the towel. In 1987, the two parties signed a Unity Accord, which in reality meant that Joshua Nkomo's party was swallowed up. In the decade which followed, Zimbabwe formally operated a multiparty system, but ZANU-PF remained the only show in town. When Mugabe signalled his intention of formalising the one-party state in 1990, he faced spirited opposition from the ZCTU, but also from within the ranks of his own party. Edgar Tekere, who had a reputation of being a ZANU-PF firebrand, was amongst those who broke away to form ZUM (Zimbabwe Unity Movement) with a view to contesting the 1990 elections. Although ZUM fielded candidates in the majority of constituencies, it managed to win only two legislative seats, although it won a very respectable 23 per cent of the vote.[90] These figures demonstrated that there was some mileage in the electoral route and in subsequent years a number of other opposition parties were established. Most of these failed to make an impression, and in the 1995 elections it was rebel ZANU-PF candidates who gave the regime the greatest cause for concern.

Whereas the ZCTU had agreed to remain neutral during the polls of 1995/96, its decision to broker the formation of the MDC in September 1999 presented the government with a serious challenge. The MDC appealed to those interests which felt most alienated from the regime, especially urban workers, intellectuals, the youth, Ndebele peasants, white commercial farmers and their many farm labourers. ZANU-PF responded by raising the stakes. In 1997, the War Veterans Association had begun to place pressure upon the Mugabe regime to deliver compensation for sacrifices made during the second Chimurenga. The embattled government conceded a lump sum payment of Z$50,000 to each veteran plus a monthly pension, without giving much thought to where the money was going to come from. However, it was the veterans' demand for land which took the lid off a political brew which had been simmering since independence. Mugabe was quick to sense that taking up the land issue was likely to mollify the veterans and play well with the Shona peasant majority whose votes would be decisive in any future election. Hence 1471 white farms were earmarked for seizure in 1997, and two years later Mugabe indicated that no government compensation would be forthcoming. When the MDC attacked the government's approach, the ZANU-PF was able to claim that the MDC was in the pockets of white settlers.

The first real trial of strength came in February 2000, when a ZANU-PF constitutional amendment, which included the land seizure provisions, was put to a national referendum. On this occasion, the opposition forces scored a famous victory, although that did not prevent Mugabe from inserting the land provisions into the existing constitution. With legislative elections to follow in June, a vengeful government gave the green light for the War Veterans to invade the land. Moreover, the government deployed systematic violence against MDC supporters. Despite the intimidation, which rendered campaigning next to impossible across much of the country, the MDC performed extremely creditably, winning 57 seats to 62 by ZANU-PF. Significantly, all the Harare seats were won by the MDC. But while Tsvangirai had high hopes of defeating Mugabe in the March 2002 Presidential poll, the latter managed to claw his way back to victory, using every dirty trick in the political book. By no stretch of the imagination was this a fair election, although the South African Observer Mission did the ANC no favours by asserting that the people of Zimbabwe had made their considered verdict.[91]

The two sets of results did, however, underline the limitations of an urban-based opposition movement when much of the rural population was prepared to stick with ZANU-PF or (increasingly) preferred to abstain altogether. In 2003, Zimbabwe was locked in a downward spiral of epic proportions. The national economy was in tatters and possibly as many as a million peasants were teetering on the brink of famine. Moreover, insofar as the economic crisis was attributable to political causes, the situation looked set to deteriorate still further. Mugabe had cocooned himself in a circular logic which attributed all opposition to external conspiracies which justified the resort to extreme measures. If the military hierarchy had not been so preoccupied with profiteering from the war in the Congo (see Chapter 10), one might have said that Zimbabwe was ripe for a coup.

9.2.3.2 The great survivors: Multipartyism in Kenya and Tanzania

Our next pairing consists of two countries where well-established ruling parties managed to fend off an early challenge to their dominance, in large part due to the inability of the opposition politicians to submerge their differences. In Tanzania, the CCM managed to trounce the opposition in successive elections, whereas KANU eventually stumbled in the elections of December 2002. However, it was the bungled succession from the Moi Presidency, as much as the deft footwork of the opposition, which produced this outcome, as we shall see.

By the early 1990s, disillusionment with the Moi regime was deep-seated, due to falling living standards, rising urban unemployment, conflicts over land in which the government was seen to be partial and rampant corruption. To this has to be added a highly ruthless manner of dealing with awkward characters: the unexplained murder of Foreign Minister, Robert Ouko, in 1990 was a further illustration of the dangers of falling on the wrong side of the ruling clique.[92] Disillusionment was rife within KANU itself, where the existence of concentric circles of influence meant that entire factions and communities were cut out. The manner in which a Kalenjin bourgeoisie had been nurtured by Moi on state patronage, while Kikuyu businessmen were relegated to the sidelines, was a source of considerable resentment in Central Province which constituted the original heartlands of KANU.

At the start of the decade, a familiar coalition of churches, professional associations and civil society bodies found their voice and began to demand an to end to one-party rule. When Kenneth Matiba, Charles Rubia, Raila Odinga and others were detained in June 1990 for calling for reform, this prompted the donor community to adopt a much tougher line with the Moi regime, which in turn emboldened the incipient opposition. One product of the first cycle was the formation of the Forum for the Restoration of Democracy (FORD) which was conceived of as a broad anti-KANU front, encompassing radicals and moderates alike. Although Moi sought to hold the line, donors threatened to cut off aid unless he conceded the principle of multipartyism. The upshot was that he was forced to accept a change to the constitution. However, just as KANU appeared to be on the ropes, the opposition front began to fracture along lines which were partly ethnic, partly ideological and very largely personal.[93] To start with, not all opponents of the regime wanted to be associated with FORD, which they regarded as altogether too strident. Hence Mwai Kibaki, who had been a Finance Minister under Kenyatta and a Vice-President under Moi, led a secession of well-to-do Kikuyu politicians out of KANU and into the Democratic Party of Kenya (DP). More dramatically, FORD itself split into two separate political parties once multipartyism was conceded. On the one side, there was FORD-Kenya, which largely orbited around the person of Oginga Odinga, who still enjoyed the radical reputation which he had earned after his clash with Kenyatta. The 'Young Turks' who wanted to pursue a more progressive line remained loyal to Odinga, as did most Luo politicians who resented their perceived marginalisation at the hands of the Kikuyu and the Kalenjin elites. On the other side, there was FORD-Asili, which coalesced around Kenneth Matiba and which was regarded as more 'bourgeois' and Kikuyu in composition.[94]

Instead of presenting a single Presidential candidate at the 1992 elections, or reaching an agreement over the distribution of legislative seats, the opposition parties chose to fight each other. Needless to say, KANU already enjoyed enormous advantages of incumbency, including privileged access to the media and material resources, which the opposition could not hope to match.[95] Moi also stirred up ethnic violence against Kikuyu settlers in the Rift Valley in the hope of forging greater solidarity amongst non-Kikuyus. This was crucial to Moi's strategy of ruling Kenya through a coalition of ethnic minorities: the so-called KAMATUSA, which originally comprised the Kalenjin, Maasai, Turkana and Samburu, but was later broadened to include other minorities like the Luhya, the Somali and the Mijikenda.[96] By definition, this strategy left much of Kenya outside the fold and susceptible to opposition appeals. If the opposition parties had prioritised the defeat of KANU, the next decade might have looked very different. But while Moi only polled 36.4 per cent of the Presidential vote, this was enough because the rest of the votes were split between Matiba (26.2 per cent), Kibaki (19.1 per cent) and Oginga Odinga (17.6 per cent). Equally, KANU managed to capture 95 out of 188 seats, which provided a wafer-thin majority. But Moi was able to build on this majority by tempting opposition MPs to cross the carpet. Although KANU did not win all the by-elections which followed, it captured enough through promises of access to amenities, to reassert its national dominance.

The shortsightedness of opposition politicians, many of whom were former KANU loyalists, cost them dearly. Having failed to win public office, their local support began to melt away. Moreover, there was an eruption of disputes within each of the main parties as fresh contenders blamed the incumbent leadership for defeat. Moi gave a little nudge here and there to ensure that the opposition parties broke into warring factions. Kibaki survived a challenge from younger elements with the least damage done. FORD-Kenya was split by an inter-Luo power struggle after the death of Odinga in 1994, which was transformed into a bitter Luo-Luhya rift. The upshot was that the party segmented into two parties claiming to be the real FORD-Kenya – one led by Raila Odinga (the son of Oginga) and the other by Wamalwa Kijana. The party which suffered most of all was FORD-Asili which tore itself apart as Matiba refused to cede his dominance to a rival faction led by Martin Shikuku.[97] When Matiba lost control, he attempted to form another party, but this never got off the ground. Given the factional nature of KANU, it was to be expected that it suffered internal divisions of its own. The struggle between a so-called 'KANU A' and 'KANU B' was potentially damaging, but (as ever) Moi found ways of playing them off against each other.

Given the complete disarray in opposition ranks, it comes as no surprise that no broad front was forged in time for the elections in 1997, despite several attempts. The outcome was an even greater victory for the ruling party. Against a backdrop of ethnic violence, Moi increased his share of the vote to 40.4 per cent, while KANU secured a working majority with 108 out of a total of 210 seats. On this occasion, Kibaki came a close second with 30.9 per cent, while his DP won 39 seats. At the head of the National Development Party (NDP), Odinga came in third on 10.8 per cent, while the Wamalwa version of FORD-Kenya received 8.2 per cent. Next came Charity Ngilu of the SDP on 7.9 per cent, who had campaigned on an anti-poverty platform and was expected to do well, followed by a number of smaller parties.[98]

Ever since his succession, Moi had demonstrated his intimate knowledge of the fault-lines in Kenya politics and how to exploit them to optimal effect. However, there were signs that the KAMATUSA front was beginning to fragment, with KANU support being reduced to a pastoralist core. Moreover, the reality of the situation was that Moi was only permitted two terms under the constitution. This meant that his personal authority was always likely to dissipate as his tenure ran down. Be that as it may, Moi fully intended to preside over the choice of a successor to lead KANU and it became increasingly apparent that this was likely to be Uhuru Kenyatta, the son of the first President, who Moi brought into Parliament and then catapulted into a Ministerial position. Moi could claim to be broadening the appeal of KANU, given that Kenyatta was a Kikuyu and not another member of the KAMATUSA minorities. Equally, in March 2002, Moi pulled off a merger with Odinga's mostly Luo NDP, which had signalled its willingness to play ball soon after the elections – a further indication of the biddable nature of the opposition. The problem was that there were individuals within KANU who harboured their own designs on the Presidential nomination, including Odinga himself. When Moi began to campaign openly on behalf of Kenyatta, a number of Ministers chided the President and insisted that there should be an open contest. George Saitoti, the Vice-President, was sacked for daring to declare about his own intention to stand. Saitoti and Odinga then proceeded to form the 'Rainbow Alliance' within KANU to press for internal democracy. In the interim, the DP, Wamalwa's FORD-Kenya and Charity Ngilus's National Party of Kenya had united to form the National Alliance for Change which intended to present a unified challenge to KANU in 2002, with Kibaki as their common candidate. As the rift within KANU deepened, the Rainbow Alliance finally jumped ship, preparing the way for the creation of an expanded opposition front, the National Rainbow Coalition (NARC).

In the general elections of December 2002, the KANU bubble finally burst. Kibaki polled 62.2 per cent of the vote to 31.3 per cent by Kenyatta and 6 per cent by Simon Nyachae of FORD (a former 'KANU A' leader). In Parliament, NARC controlled 125 seats to 64 by KANU, 14 by FORD and seven by smaller parties. While Kenyatta and Moi accepted the verdict of the electorate, Kibaki proceeded to stitch together a government composed of leaders of all the parties which had participated in the alliance. Inevitably, these consisted of a large number of former KANU stalwarts of different generations – Kibaki was a first-generation politician, Saitoti was a product of Moi era (and a player in KANU B'), and Odinga was a recent convert. This profile somewhat qualifies the euphoric media depictions of a historic vote for the politics of change. In some respects, what had occurred was a shuffling of the KANU pack, with the Moi loyalists losing out to others who were steeped in older KANU traditions. Given that many Kikuyu politicians regarded KANU as their own creation, and never ceased to treat Moi as a KADU interloper, it almost seemed as if Kenyan politics had come full circle. The only anomaly was that the son of the first President found himself on the wrong side of the fence. Equally, the promise that NARC would tackle corruption and tidy up politics has to be regarded with some scepticism. Although the Kibaki regime was keen to reopen negotiations with the IMF, which had broken them off over corruption allegations in 2000, it was Saitoti (as Minister of Finance) who had played the pivotal role in the scam of 1992 which had thrown national finances into crisis and shattered the confidence of the IFIs.[99] Finally, given that NARC was a front rather than a party, it remained to be seem whether Kibaki could hold such a diverse team together.

In Tanzania, the CCM had long taken its monopoly of power for granted. Under Nyerere, the practice of allowing voters to choose between two candidates had enabled party bosses to maintain that it was possible to practice democracy within a one-party state, whilst avoiding the threats to national unity which multipartyism was likely to bring in its train. At the end of the 1980s, however, the moral authority of the CCM was at a low ebb. Tanzanians could not fail to be conscious of the deterioration of their material conditions. Moreover, when the government was finally forced to capitulate to the IFIs, it lost face. And even before the abrogation of the Leadership Code in 1991, a flurry of conspicuous consumption, just as ordinary Tanzanians were being advised to tighten their belts, rendered the rhetoric about a continuing commitment to probity and social equality particularly hollow. In the humour of the street, CCM was rendered as short for Chama Cha Majangili or 'Party of Crooks'.[100] Finally, in a country which was relatively open, Tanzanians would have been well-aware of developments unfolding elsewhere.

Curiously, however, there was no upsurge of popular protest in Tanzania, along the lines of Zambia, Malawi or indeed Kenya. Commentators who are broadly sympathetic to the CCM have been inclined to credit the regime with the lingering attachment of its citizens, while sceptics have suggested that Tanzanians had never known anything different.[101] The latter is scarcely convincing because neither had Malawians or Zambians. The learned behaviour of Tanzanians in finding ways of evading and beating the system, rather than challenging it head on, may account for some of the lack of activism. As far as the potential counter-elite is concerned, it may well be that the enthusiasm with which it members threw themselves into NGO activity detracted from political militancy. Be that as it may, it was ironically Nyerere himself who reopened the question of multipartyism in his ongoing capacity as CCM Chairman. Having consistently argued that a multiplicity of parties was potentially divisive as well as a luxury in a poor country, Nyerere publicly revised his opinion in February 1990. In his assessment, the party had atrophied because of the lack of an alternative and so would be toughened (and cleaned) up by having to defend its platform. Moreover, as he saw it, international pressures were only likely to intensify, and so it was better to jump rather than to be pushed – or, as he memorably put it, invoking a different metaphor: 'When you see your neighbour being shaved, wet your head to avoid a dry shave.'[102]

President Mwinyi, who finally took over the chairmanship of CCM from Nyerere shortly thereafter, was initially unconvinced by this revisionism. However, in February 1991 he set up a Presidential commission, headed by Chief Justice Francis Nyalali, to solicit popular opinion on the merits of multipartyism. With possible reform in the air, there was at last some stirring of activity outside of CCM circles. The National Committee for Constitutional Reform was established by professionals and intellectuals to lobby for a national conference. Another organisation which was founded with broadly similar objectives, but with a more radical edge, was the Civil and Human Rights Movement.[103] The Nyalali Commission eventually concluded that the majority of Tanzanians favoured the retention of the one-party state, but it nevertheless came out in favour of multipartyism on the basis that people wanted 'modifications' which were difficult to reconcile with the one-party system.[104] This recommendation was accepted by the Mwinyi government and, after the legalisation of opposition parties in December 1992, feverish attempts were made to establish political parties. As the country moved towards national elections in 1995, the opposition managed to mount several large rallies, especially in Dar es Salaam, which showed how a well-organised movement could give vent to popular alienation. Even so, the CCM regime was still operating within a wide margin for manoeuvre by comparison with President Moi. Interestingly, the fact that the tenure of Mwinyi was set to end, and could not be renewed under the constitution, did not greatly upset things. Such was the continuing respect attached to the opinion of Nyerere that his preferred choice of CCM candidate, Benjamin Mkapa, was selected ahead of Mwinyi's own client – a further illustration of the extent to which Tanzania was characterised by a rather unique political dynamic.[105]

Almost full three years after the acceptance of multipartyism, national elections were held and these were contested by thirteen political parties, of whom five could be considered national in coverage: the CCM, the National Convention for Construction and Reform (NCCR), the Civic United Front (CUF), Chadema and the United Democratic Party (UDP). Remembering that Zanzibar enjoyed a special status within the union, with its own President and legislature, the first round of elections was held there. Whereas the CCM stood by the advantages of the union between Zanzibar and the mainland, the CUF adopted a more autonomist position. Amidst some controversy over the fairness of the exercise, the CCM won by 26 to 24 seats and managed the most slender of victories in the Presidential poll, with the island of Pemba giving all its seats to the CUF.[106] In the national election which followed, however, the CCM won comfortably, although further questions were raised about the conduct of the poll – to the extent there needed to be a re-run in Dar es Salaam. Mkapa won 62 per cent of the vote, with Augustine Mrema of the NCCR managing a distant second on 28 per cent. The ruling party also captured as many as 219 out of 274 legislative seats. The only region where Mkapa was defeated was in Kilimanjaro, which was the home region of Mrema. The Chagga, who are famous in Tanzania for their business acumen, had never looked favourably on Tanzanian socialism and seized their opportunity to punish the CCM. But outside of Zanzibar, the CCM had proved itself to be by far the most coherent political force. Even in the capital city, which was safe opposition territory in most African countries, the CCM won with ease, with Mkapa capturing 72 per cent of the vote. In subsequent years, real politics was conducted inside the CCM, with MPs lobbying hard to attract NGOs and government spending for their home areas.

9.2.3.3 The populist response: the fate of democratic alternatives in Ghana and Uganda

In two Anglophone countries, Ghana and Uganda, the leaders set their faces against multipartyism, not on the basis that the one-party state was capable of doing a better job, but rather on the principle that political parties were themselves the enemies of democracy. For them, the pursuit of 'no-party democracy' was not a contradiction in terms, but an insight derived from bitter experience. In Ghana, which had tasted one-partyism under Nkrumah and multipartyism under Busia and Limann, Flt-Lt Jerry Rawlings maintained that parties tended to be the instruments of the wealthy, who alone could afford to have themselves elected and who then typically recouped their investments through graft. Rawlings could also point with some justification to the paralysis which had characterised the Third Republic, due to incessant infighting within the ruling party. In Uganda, Yoweri Museveni equated multipartyism with a history of ethnic chauvinism and violence which had made the lives of its people a misery. In both instances, the leaders in question spoke of forging a new kind of democracy, one in which power would rest with a conscientised populace rather than with professional politicians. However, in each case, the slow process of trial and error which was contemplated ran counter to the consensus that there was no realistic alternative to electoral pluralism. The response of Rawlings and Museveni was a significantly different one.

In Uganda, the National Resistance Movement (NRM) had been forged in the crucible of the war against Obote and the Okellos. After the seizure of Kampala in January 1986, the model of resistance councils was propagated across the country – much as FRELIMO had attempted to disseminate the 'dynamising groups'. The councils were directly elected at the primary level, and these proceeded to elect the membership of higher councils up to and (supposedly) including the National Resistance Council (NRC) which enacted the laws. However, the NRM at the summit left itself the freedom to co-opt individuals from all the political traditions and regions of Uganda. In February 1989, national elections were held for the village councils, followed by indirect elections to the higher tiers. The exercise was repeated in 1992, but the NRC remained unelected at this point.[107] Thereafter, the councils were converted into the building blocks of a decentralised system of local government, in which finances and responsibilities were devolved downwards.[108]

Political parties were not made illegal, and the Democratic Party (DP) and UPC (Uganda People's Congress) remained in business. Indeed, at various points they even joined the administration. However, they were not permitted to campaign or field candidates for election. Moreover, the primary elections were conducted by a queuing system rather than by secret ballot. Although the refusal to allow unfettered political competition was criticised inside the country and abroad, Museveni continued to insist that the system was thoroughly democratic in practice, and made for a more consensual system of decision-making. Like Rawlings, he insisted that formalistic definitions of democracy were misleading because they did not take account of the minimal conditions for the enjoyment of democratic rights. In his fifth anniversary speech in January 1991, Museveni stated the point thus:

> Whichever way democracy is defined, it must incorporate the rule of law, social justice, and the observance of basic human rights. You, no doubt, remember that during the second Obote regime, from 1980 to 1985, Uganda had a multi-party system complete with Parliament and Leader of the Opposition. That multi-party democracy did not embody the democratic elements I have referred to. The polarisation of society along ethnic and religious lines cannot form a basis of democracy and Uganda's recent history has proved this point again and again.[109]

This was an argument which possessed some force because, with the exception of parts of the North bordering on to Sudan, where the Lord's Resistance Army wreaked havoc, the country was enjoying stability and freedom from fear after two decades of extreme insecurity.[110] Moreover, while power had been won by the National Resistance Army, the regime bore the trappings of a civilian rather than a military regime.

Of course, Uganda was not immune to the pressures emanating from the external environment, including the donors. However, Museveni and his associates were not about to roll over and conform to the new political orthodoxies which, they argued, had proved unworkable in the past. The NRM won itself some breathing space with the donors by demonstrating its commitment to economic reform, whilst remaining largely free of complaints about human rights abuses. Nevertheless, Museveni appreciated the perils of standing still and therefore initiated a search for a new constitutional dispensation on the basis of popular consultation. In fact, an enabling law was passed as early as 1988, which provided for a Constitutional Commission to come up with concrete proposals. The Commission got off to the slowest start imaginable, in part because it was forced to operate with minimal resources.[111] However, the lack of headway also had a great deal to do with the remit of the Commission which was required to engage in a two-way discussion with the people (organised through their resistance councils) about what system of government they wanted. This was to be achieved through seminars and workshops held across the length and breadth of the country. The final product was a very detailed document – ten times longer than the American Constitution – which was accepted with minor changes by the Constituent Assembly which was elected to approve it in 1994.[112]

The 1995 constitution confirmed the principle that political offices should be filled by election, including that of the President, but left it to a referendum to decide whether political parties should be permitted to compete. The document also came down in favour of a unitary state, in which chiefs would exercise only 'cultural' rights. While the four monarchies of Buganda, Ankole, Bunyoro and Busoga were allowed to reconstitute themselves, they were to be on a par with other chieftaincies and no special privileges were reserved for them. Most Baganda, who had long been smarting at the abolition of their kingship by Obote, rejoiced when Mutebi II (who had been languishing in the Britain in the intervening years) was recognised as King of Buganda in 1993.[113] Despite the reservations of the government, the advocates of the monarchy set about restoring its former grandeur. Finally, the constitution was remarkable for the extent to which, as part of a concern for human rights, it enshrined gender equality as something to be actively pursued – going as far as to provide for 'affirmative action'. Amongst other things, a gender balance was to be maintained in all state bodies, including the legislature, placing Uganda far in advance of most countries in the world. This did not so much reflect the benevolence of the NRM as the relative success of the women's movement in Uganda in furthering its own agenda.[114]

Not everyone was impressed by the outcome. The two main parties, the DP and the UPC, interpreted the entire exercise as a cynical attempt on the part of Museveni to cling to power. Although the referendum of 2000 would decide their fate, they complained that it was impossible for them to campaign for their preferred option for as long as the restrictions on party activities remained in place. They eventually decided to mount a boycott, whereas some of the smaller parties sought to persuade the electorate to vote for the multiparty option. Needless to say, the NRM used the media and other state resources to make the case for retaining a no-party system. On a 52 per cent turnout, in which there was some voter abstention, this option won 91 per cent of the poll. Michael Bratton and Michael Lambright conclude that many Ugandans did not vote on the merits of the issue, but credited Museveni with heading an effective government and supported the government on that basis.[115] Insofar as the result was a vote of confidence in the NRM, this was no mean achievement, given that it had been in power since 1986. The authors also argue, on the basis of a pre-election survey, that many Ugandans were in favour of multipartyism in principle, but voted with the government because they had such a low opinion of the main parties. To that extent, Museveni had won Ugandans over to his view that the professional politicians were not to be trusted. The no-party elections which followed in 2001 led, not surprisingly, to victory for Museveni.

Whether Uganda had genuinely created an alternative model of democracy is open to question. Some have concluded that the NRM was a one-party state in all but name, albeit on the more benign end of the spectrum.[116] The revelations of high-level corruption surrounding privatisation, in which Museveni's own brother was complicit, are an illustration on the fact that important decisions continued to be made behind closed doors despite the best efforts of the legislature to monitor performance.[117] Nevertheless, it appears that the no-party system had won acceptance amongst war-weary Ugandans. It is no accident that the greatest levels of disaffection were apparent in the North, where the Museveni regime defeated Alice Lakwena's rebels in 1987, but was unable to crush the Lord's Resistance Army. The latter repeatedly crossed the Sudanese border to burn villages and seize the next cohort of child soldiers. Elsewhere, the social contract struck by the NRM rested upon its guarantee of peace and freedom from arbitrary violence, and some economic improvement.

Rawlings was as much of a dissenter on the question of democracy as Museveni was, but he struggled to shape a clear vision of what the alternative might look like. In the early days of the revolution, the People's and Workers' Defence Committees (P/WDCs) offered something akin to the Ugandan resistance councils. However, Rawlings did not appreciate what he regarded as efforts by the left to hijack them, and after a series of purges, the P/WDCs were replaced by Committees for the Defence of the Revolution (CDRs) at the end of 1984. Whereas the P/WDCs were supposed to be the building blocks of a new democratic order, the CDRs were relegated to a support role. The National Commission on Democracy (NCD) which was set up that same year under the chairmanship of D. F. Annan (a retired judge) was encouraged to look elsewhere for its inspiration. Annan, who also sat on the PNDC, was given the difficult task of hammering out proposals for a new dispensation which would not slavishly follow Western models. As Annan himself expressed his quest:

> We feel that a truly democratic system should take into consideration our tradition, history and culture. We must measure the performance of the modern political system since independence against our traditional system and see whether the modern period could not have been improved by an interrelationship with the traditional system ...[118]

In a strange way, the cultural relativism of the colonial period had come full circle. However, what sounded like a ringing endorsement of chieftaincy was actually nothing of the kind. To be sure, the PNDC abandoned its earlier anti-chiefly rhetoric, and made its separate peace with the Asantehene, but there was never any serious intention to build on 'traditional' institutions. What the regime appeared to envisage was working through new institutions which would incorporate some 'traditional' symbolism.

When the first fruits of these deliberations were revealed, there was nothing especially innovative about them. Picking up on an early promise, the regime announced that genuine grassroots democracy would arise out of a decentralisation of decision-making powers. Over 1988/89, the first elections were held to newly created District Assemblies (DAs) which were expected to assume enlarged responsibilities. Two-thirds of the membership was directly elected, but the remaining one-third was appointed by government. Wisely, the PNDC did not pack the DAs with its cadres, often selecting chiefs and other respected local figures instead. Nevertheless, a sound local government system did not a democratic dispensation make. In 1989, the Rawlings regime seemed to have the political situation well under control. It had managed to keep potential opposition under wraps through selective harassment rather than by outright repression. However, its sense of being on top of things led it to tread on toes which it would have been better advised to avoid. The Religious Bodies Registration Law of 1989 stung the churches into action and, once they found their voice, they proceeded to attack other aspects of PNDC rule. The PNDC also engaged in a vendetta against the acting head of the Trade Union Congress (TUC), L. G. K. Ocloo, and clashed with the Ghana Bar Association (GBA), which had long been a thorn in its side.[119] In August 1990, a broad coalition of anti-government intellectuals and politicians, from across the ideological divide, finally came together under the banner of the Movement for Freedom and Justice (MFJ). The objective was to target repressive laws and to campaign for a return to democracy. Although the MFJ campaign was less successful than in many other countries, in part because it pulled its punches, the mounting internal pressure fed off changes in the external environment.

Rather than be forced into a defensive position, the Rawlings regime decided to accelerate the momentum of reform from above. In 1990, the NCD was charged with organising seminars across the country to debate the contours of a new dispensation. When the NCD issued its report in the early part of 1991, opposition expectations of a rehash of PNDC principles were confounded. The NCD signalled that the overwhelming demand was for a return to multiparty-ism which it endorsed, subject to a caution about 'unacceptable features of party politics such as when parties become corporate vehicles of investment which must be recouped'.[120] In May, the PNDC accepted the NCD findings and set up a Committee of Experts to draft concrete constitutional proposals which would then be debated by a Consultative Assembly. The operative word here was 'consultative' because the PNDC was intent on reserving to itself the right to approve or amend the final document. It also wanted to avoid losing control of the agenda, as had happened in Benin. Although the opposition continued to cry foul, a number of its members participated in the proceedings, and most eventually expressed their satisfaction with the final document.

At this point, political parties were still proscribed, but as soon as it became clear that elections were on the way there was a feverish attempt to reconstitute old political networks under the cover of 'private clubs' and 'friendship societies'. The Nkrumahists, who had never ceased to regard themselves as Ghana's natural rulers, ended up forming a number of rival clubs, whereas most of the erstwhile supporters of the Progress Party (PP) rallied to the Danquah-Busia Memorial Club. While the intentions of Rawlings were still unclear, loy-alists established their own stalking-horse in the shape of the Eagle Club. In May 1992, the legal barriers came down and these clubs quickly converted themselves into fully fledged political parties. The Danquah-Busia Memorial Club reconstituted itself as the New Patriotic Party (NPP), and selected Professor Adu Boahen (a historian) as its Presidential candidate.[121] By contrast, the Nkrumahists remained split between the People's Heritage Party (PHP), the National Independence Party (NIP), the National Convention Party (NCP) and the People's National Convention (PNC) – the latter led by ex-President Limann who continued to insist that he was the legitimate leader of the Nkrumah family. On the government side, the National Democratic Congress (NDC) was inaugurated, pushing the Eagle Party into a support role alongside the NCP once the latter had been taken over. Why Rawlings had decided to set off down the somewhat risky electoral road is an interesting one. Throughout the transition period, he admitted to lingering reservations about multiparty-ism. However, he realised that he could not halt the momentum. He was also persuaded that he had nothing to fear from elections, the likelihood being that Ghanaians would vote for him in droves if given the chance.

In the national elections of November 1992, the polls were staggered. When the Presidential results revealed that Rawlings had won with 58.3 per cent of the vote, to 30.4 per cent by Boahen and 6.7 per cent by Limann, the opposi-tion cried foul and boycotted the Parliamentary election. The NPP later pub-lished a document entitled *The Stolen Verdict* which presented a less than convincing case for wholesale fraud. The Commonwealth Observer Group had, however, pronounced the elections 'free and fair, and free from fear', and the legitimacy of the results were mostly accepted outside of Ghana. The NPP had revealed itself to be a largely Ashanti phenomenon, while the rifts in the Nkrumahist ranks had proved to be as disastrous as predicted: the Limann chal-lenge had failed to materialise, while Kwabena Darko of the NIP and General Erskine of the PHP had managed a desultory 2.8 and 1.7 per cent respectively. The opposition decision to boycott the Parliamentary elections was a further blunder, as was subsequently admitted, because it conferred a monopoly of power on the NDC for the next four years. The only real voice which the opposition was left with was the private press which was unrelenting in its attacks on the government.

When the second set of elections came around in December 1996, the oppo-sition sought to avoid repeating the same mistakes. The NIP and the PHP merged to form the People's Convention Party (PCP), although the PNC con-tinued to stay outside the fold. The PCP and the NPP also reached an alliance over the Presidential polls, under which J. A. Kufuor (NPP) would be the joint candidate with K. N. Arkaah serving as his running-mate.[122] Unfortunately, the parties were unable to conclude a binding national agreement over the Parliamentary seats, which meant that they fought each other in many con-stituencies. As in 1992, the NDC enjoyed all the advantages of incumbency. It used state vehicles to move its supporters around and it enjoyed the lion's share of official media coverage. Moreover, the December 31st Women's Movement (DWM), which was headed by Mrs. Rawlings but posed as an NGO, provided a conduit for election funds, as well as a mechanism for harnessing female vot-ers. On this occasion, there would be no bandwagon effect as the Presidential and Parliamentary elections were held on the same day. Despite the optimism of the opposition, Rawlings took 57.4 per cent of the vote to 39.6 per cent by Kufuor and 3 per cent by Dr Edward Mahama who had been brought in to lead the PNC challenge. The NDC also emerged with a comfortable Parliamentary majority, having captured 133 out of 200 Parliamentary seats.

The NPP won 61 seats, which was far short of what it had been expecting. It remained a largely Ashanti phenomenon, but managed to make some inroads into the Eastern Region and performed well in Accra. The PNP took a mere five seats, while the PNC was confined to a single seat in the Northern Region.

The second term of Rawlings witnessed a progressive deterioration in the standards of governance. The President appeared to have become weary of politics, and distanced himself from much of the day-to-day administration. Meanwhile, a number of senior politicians within the NDC sought to cash in – ironically vindicating everything which Rawlings himself had said about the moral rot which would accompany electoral democracy. Moreover, the NDC itself became decidedly twitchy over the succession question, given that Rawlings was confined to two terms under the 1992 constitution. As in Kenya a couple of years later, the failure to address this issue to the satisfaction of party members proved the undoing of the NDC. Once Rawlings decided to advance the cause of his Vice-President, John Atta-Mills – who had been parachuted into the NDC in time for the 1996 race – those who felt cheated by the lack of a leadership election seceded. Goosie Tanoh, who at one point was being groomed for the succession, led the breakaway of the National Reform Party (NRP). Others who were less than enthusiastic about Mills, including Mrs. Rawlings, reduced their campaign funding. Moreover, the attempt by headquarters to impose candidates on the constituencies led to a grassroots revolt in which those who felt aggrieved stood against the official candidates – and in four cases actually won.

In the December 2000 polls, the NPP and the Convention People's Party (as the PCP had been renamed) were unable to reach an accord and fought the NDC separately. This was a high risk strategy, but on this occasion it paid off for the NPP.[123] The CPP performed dismally, ramming home the point that Nkrumahism meant very little to a young electorate which had no memory of the First Republic.[124] Kufuor, standing in his second election, scored 48.2 per cent on the first round, some way ahead of Mills on 44.5 per cent. None of the other candidates made a dent, and when the runoff was held Kufuor was the only likely winner. In the legislative elections, the NPP also won half of the seats and was soon assured of a governing majority. The defeat of the NDC owed a great deal to infighting within its ranks, and the public perception of corruption on a grand scale. Moreover, the NPP shed its rather stuffy image and appealed directly to the youth vote in a manner which paid dividends. The sluggish performance of the Ghanaian economy in the second half of the 1990s had exacerbated the problem of youth unemployment which the NPP promised to deal with. Nevertheless, despite gains across the board, the North and the Volta Region remained as detached from the Busia-Danquah tradition as they had always been.

The electorate had been enjoined to vote for 'Positive Change' which (as in Senegal) was a suitably vague slogan. What remained to be seen was whether the Kufuor regime would be able to retain the goodwill of the population, including the young majority, which it undoubtedly enjoyed in 2001 and 2002. It also remained to be seen whether the NDC would recover from the blow of electoral defeat. For most Ghanaians, though, these elections had demonstrated the beauty of the ballot box. Indeed the enthusiasm was so infectious that NDC politicians went out of their way to give the administration a chance, to the extent of praising Kufuor's first two years in office. Ghanaian politicians it seemed had fallen in love with one another.

9.2.3.4 The perpetual transition in Nigeria: 'Babangidocracy' and 'Abachange'

The African colossus, Nigeria, deserves special treatment in its own right, in that its staccato movement towards civilian rule bore many unique hallmarks. Nigerians had long taken a pride in their irrepressible private press and vibrant associational life, and often found the political timidity of other Africans incomprehensible. Nigerians, it used to be said, would simply not tolerate a Banda or a Mobutu. The obvious anomaly was, of course, that Nigeria had been ruled by the military for most of the period since independence. But even the soldiers appeared to accept their shaky legitimacy by claiming to be ushering in a return to civilian normality. It came as a great shock to many Nigerians, therefore, that at a time when other African countries were witnessing a democratic opening, their own country regressed. During the 1980s and 1990s, thousands of Nigerians lost their lives, not just in paroxysms of ethnic and religious rioting, but at the hands of the police and army. Moreover, journalists, human rights activists and aspirant politicians were repeatedly detained, harassed and (in some cases) subjected to judicial execution. Although the civil war years had been traumatic enough, the decade of the 1990s arguably represented the darkest hour of Nigerian independence because it seemed that things could only get worse.

In the mid-1980s, nobody would have predicted the painful journey which was about to follow. When General Ibrahim Babangida overthrew Muhammadu Buhari in August 1985, one of the reasons given was that the latter had failed to come up with detailed plans for a return to civilian rule. Whilst setting himself up as the first substantive military President, with complete personal control over appointments, Babangida promised that he would remain in office for only as long as was necessary to get the economy and democracy back on track.[125] Indeed, he was quick to set the date for the eventual handover at 1 October 1990. In January 1986, he appointed a Political Bureau which was expected to pore over the entrails of Nigerian history and to come up with 'blueprint' for a lasting democratic order. The Bureau received and collated no fewer than 27,324 submissions, which is an indication that Nigerians took the process very seriously.[126] It then came up with a voluminous set of recommendations, reflecting some of the pet schemes of its academic members. The government excised many of the proposals which appeared overly radical, but took on board some others, most notably the principle that the country should be run according to a two-party system. A Constitution Review Committee then drafted a new constitution, subject to certain 'no-go areas', which was then submitted to a Constituent Assembly for approval. Throughout this laborious exercise, the cream of the Nigerian intellectual establishment were involved in an ambitious – and arguably wrongheaded – attempt to fabricate the perfect constitutional document. Because the (supposedly) outgoing military government was expected to preside over the holding of a much-needed census, the formation of political parties, and the conduct of elections at the local, state and federal levels, the initial timetable soon became untenable. To the consternation of some watchdogs, the terminal date was pushed back to October 1992 and then to late August 1993. However, for as long as the transition was on course, most of the would-be politicians were prepared to tolerate some measure of delay.

However, the transition process quickly descended into something more approximating a farce. One underlying reason was the dubious assumption that it was possible to legislate for political stability by concocting the right constitutional formula. Within the Constituent Assembly, there was a predictable coming together of members who shared a common political outlook. On this basis, some 88 associations had been formed by July 1989, angling (as in Ghana) to seek formal registration as parties. However, under the new constitution only two nationally based parties would be allowed to stand, which was supposed to ensure competition whilst deterring organisation along ethnoregional lines. The National Electoral Commission (NEC) was not greatly impressed by the national spread of the parties which put themselves forward, with the result that the military dissolved all of them. In their place, it announced two parties of its own creation – one 'a little to the left' and the other 'a little to the right' – namely the Social Democratic Party (SDP) and the National Republican Convention (NRC). The exercise became almost surreal when the NEC drafted the manifestoes for the parties and the transition committee crafted their symbols.[127] More understandably, the government agreed to fund the creation of the two new parties in their infancy.

A reasonably well-executed census was held, and local government elections were successfully held in 1990.[128] Despite some disputes which reached the courts, and constant changes of mind over which old politicians were debarred from standing, the elections for state governors, the state legislatures and the federal legislature were also completed in 1992.[129] However, the process began to run into serious trouble when it came to the selection of the Presidential candidates within parties which were artificial constructs. In the first attempt at holding primaries, the losing candidates complained of vote-buying when ex-Major-General Shehu Yar'Adua and Adamu Ciroma looked set to take the SDP and NRC nominations respectively. In October 1992, the government took the drastic step of cancelling the primaries, disqualifying all of the candidates and dissolving the party executives. It then proceeded to organise fresh primaries, starting with nominations at the ward level and ending with national conventions. The net result was that the fabulously wealthy Yoruba, Moshood Abiola, captured the SDP nomination, while another businessman of Kanuri extraction, Alhaji Bashir Tofa, won the candidacy of the NRC. Both were Muslims. Up until this point, Osaghae maintains, it is probable that Babangida had intervened out of frustration at the behaviour of politicians which was at odds with the idealistic quest for a new breed of politician.[130] But beyond this point, all the indications were that Babangida was merely looking for an excuse to prolong his own stay in office. The spectacular levels of corruption which Babangida and his associate were engaged in provides one clear reason why this might have been so.[131]

In the run-up to the elections, shadowy pressure groups began to place newspaper advertisements and to issue statements calling for Babangida to remain in office. Amongst these was the Association for a Better Nigeria (ABN) which the junta claimed to disapprove of, but did not ban. On the eve of the Presidential election, the ABN secured a court injunction against the holding of the elections which nevertheless went ahead without any hitches on 12 June 1993. The unofficial results appeared to demonstrate that Abiola had won hands down. Significantly, he had polled well not just in the South, but in large parts of the North as well – indeed Abiola beat Tofa in his home state of Kano.[132] However, the ABN succeeded in securing a court order preventing the NEC from releasing the results. Then, on 23 June, the junta abruptly announced that the election had been terminated and that all legal proceedings were suspended. The military regime gave a number of reasons for the annulment, but the most revealing was that the top brass simply found Abiola unacceptable.[133] Given the limitations which had already been placed on who could compete, and the terms under which they could so, this was the final nail in the coffin of a smooth transition. The announcement was followed by widespread rioting, especially in Lagos and other parts of Yorubaland, and acts of civil disobedience designed to force Babangida to back down. However, this turn of events merely played into the hands of the junta. The more Abiola's supporters complained of a nefarious northern plot to prevent a Yoruba from assuming the presidency, the higher the ethnic stakes became. The northern support which Abiola had hitherto enjoyed fell away, even within the SDP, and politicians from the South-east proceeded to strike a deal with their northern counterparts who insisted that the annulment was not negotiable. Abiola did not help his cause by going into exile over August and September, just when his ingenuity in holding together a unstable front was most needed.

Meanwhile, Babangida endeavoured to fabricate support for a prolongation of his tenure by some biddable traditional rulers and other 'leaders of thought', whilst promising that another election would follow. Remarkably, Babangida had taken these momentous decisions without even consulting his colleagues, which evidently rankled. On 27 August the latter asked him to stand down. The junta now formally gave way to an Interim National Government (ING), headed by a civilian (and a Yoruba) by the name of Ernest Shonekan. However, General Sanni Abacha remained the Minister of Defence and was evidently the power behind the throne. Although Shonekan won some support abroad, where the pressure for sanctions was mounting, the ING enjoyed little real power. In November 1993, a court ruling that the ING was illegitimate because Babangida had signed the enabling decree after he ceased to be head of state, provided Abacha with the excuse he needed for an outright seizure of power. In a nutshell, a process which was supposed to have culminated in a resumption of civilian rule had ended in the installation of another military dictator – one who was known to have been biding his time for many years.

Abacha did the prudent thing and sought to distance himself from the Babangida legacy. A series of official probes were set up which (to no-one's surprise) revealed the spiriting away of millions of dollars of oil money, and some prominent individuals were placed on trial for corruption. This included even the Sultan of Sokoto, Ibrahim Dasuki, who had ridden to office on the coat-tails of Babangida and now became a casualty of the turnover.[134] The junta also offered prominent civilians some key Ministerial positions – including Abiola's erstwhile running-mate, Babagana Kingibe. Moreover, Abacha promised to address demands for a more equitable distribution of the oil money, and brought Buhari back to head a Petroleum Trust Fund. The leadership was quick to claim that it had been invited in by opposition groups to sort out the constitutional impasse. In fact, it would seem that Abiola entered into secret negotiations with Abacha, and agreed to suspend his agitation in the expectation that his victory would eventually be restored. However, Abacha proceeded to take Nigerians down a route which had become all-too-familiar by this point: namely yet another transition programme. All the elected bodies which had been so laboriously created under Babangida were summarily dissolved and the political parties were proscribed, casting the country – in snakes and ladders fashion – all the way back to 1996. Abacha promised another constitutional conference, which would come up with yet another constitutional document, on the basis of which the electoral process would resume from scratch.

It did not take long for the penny to drop that this was yet another attempt by a section of the military to keep its nose in the trough long enough to amass personal wealth. Abiola realised the mistake he had made in trusting Abacha and reverted to the demand that he be instated as President. In May 1994, a coalition of (mostly Yoruba) politicians came together under the wing of the National Democratic Coalition (NADECO) – which Toyin Falola has described as 'a strange gathering of political opportunists and committed democrats'.[135] On the first anniversary of the abortive election they issued an ultimatum to the government to resign and to recognise Abiola as the duly elected President. Abacha responded by banning NADECO, thereby precipitating a popular revolt in the South-west of the country, backed up by a series of crippling strikes. The most damaging of these was led by oil workers, organised within the National Union of Petroleum and Natural Gas Workers (NUPENG), which paralysed production and hence domestic supplies. This frontal challenge elicited an even more severe crackdown on the part of the junta. Large numbers of opposition figures were detained; Abiola himself was charged with treason; militant trade unions, including NUPENG, were dissolved; and three groups of newspapers were closed down. In March 1995, the government raised the stakes further by announcing the discovery of a coup plot, implicating Olusegun Obasanjo and Yar'Adua. The latter were sentenced to death by a special military tribunal, but the personal intervention of Nelson Mandela, through Desmond Tutu, led to a commutation of the sentences to life imprisonment. However, the death sentence passed on Ken Saro-Wiwa and eight other Ogoni activists in a separate case went ahead in November. The upshot was that Nigeria became a pariah state and was suspended from the Commonwealth, despite the solidarity extended some other African leaders like Jerry Rawlings.[136]

In fact, Abacha's ambitions went much further than even his civilian detrac-tors had imagined. As the transition process ground on, it became increasingly evident that he intended to stand for the presidency himself, borrowing a leaf from the Rawlings book. In September 1996, only five out of fifteen new political parties cleared the final hurdle for registration. Ominously, all of these were closely allied to elements within the junta. Over 1997 and 1998, these parties contested the local government elections, the legislative and gubernatorial elections across the 30 states (including six new ones), and the federal legislative elections. This left the choice of President. Against a backdrop of stage-managed rallies and the distribution of 'support Abacha' buttons, the five parties followed the script and plumped for Abacha as the single candidate.[137] However, the enthronement never took place because Abacha died suddenly on 8 June 1998, to widespread public rejoicing.

General Abdulsalami Abubakar stepped into the resulting vacuum, indicating his intention to perform no more than a traditional caretaking function. Abubakar did his best to distance himself from the Abacha legacy, dismissing most of the loyalists of the deceased general. However, before he could find a face-saving means to release Abiola, the latter also died under circumstances which many opponents of the military regarded as highly suspicious. The death of Abiola did spare Abubakar the embarrassment of having to deal with ongoing demands for restitution of the 1993 elections results. The recently elected bodies were once again dissolved, along with the five political parties, and the way was opened for freedom of political association. Eventually, the registration of nine political parties was approved, and these coalesced to form a final total of six. The Babangida project of cultivating a new class of politicians had evidently failed, as the leading lights were experienced politicians, often sporting a less than spotless record of public service.

The People's Democratic Party (PDP) managed to win the greatest number of state governorships, together with a majority in the House of Representatives and the Senate. When it came to the Presidential elections, Obasanjo of the PDP beat Olu Falae, a former Babangida associate standing on behalf of both the Alliance for Democracy (AD) and the All People's Party (APP). Although the culmination of the process was a return to civilian rule, the fact that Obasanjo was a retired General qualified the completeness of the transition. Moreover, he had won the presidency with the backing of much of the northern political and military establishment, while many Yoruba voters apparently regarded him as a stooge. The Obasanjo presidency was characterised by a state of almost perpetual crisis, as politicians at every level of the system pursued vendettas against each other, and as ethnic militias engaged in repeated bouts of fighting. Moreover, the religious divide became wider than ever when a number of northern states proclaimed the adoption of Shari'a law, despite the President's insistence that this was unconstitutional.

Towards the end of 2002, the course of Nigerian politics took a more peculiar turn when Obasanjo's main challenger for the next set of elections became none other than Muhammadu Buhari. The latter managed to secure the nomination of the All Nigeria People's Party in circumstances which were as controversial as the renomination of Obasanjo himself. Hence Nigerians were asked to choose between two retired Generals, which was a rather curious inversion of what is normally understood by democratisation. The willingness of civilians to tolerate the incursion of the Generals is, on the face of it, surprising. However, as more than one commentator has noted, it was politicians and intellectuals – particularly academics – who had repeatedly done the bidding of Babangida and Abacha, lending them the legitimacy which they craved.[138] In 2003, Obasanjo prevailed in an election vitiated by widespread fraud. To the relief of many, however, the predicted breakdown cataclysm was averted.

9.2.3.5 The old stagers: Botswana and the Gambia

As in the case of Senegal, there were two African countries which had enjoyed long periods of multipartyism prior to the continental movement of the early 1990s: namely Botswana and the Gambia. In the former case, the Botswana Democratic Party (BDP) had contested six elections between 1965 and 1989 and had won each them with ease against a fragmented opposition. Although the BDP exploited the advantages of incumbency to the full, the opposition was given a free hand to organise and to criticise the performance of the regime. The success of the BDP in holding on to its position rested on the conjuncture of a number of circumstances, largely of its own making. First of all, the regime had presided over extremely impressive rates of economic growth which brought substantial improvements in living standards to most of the population. Secondly, and somewhat ironically, President Seretse Khama and his successor, Ketumile Masire, had taken the politics out of development by investing the civil service with remarkable levels of operational autonomy. This minimised the kind of squabbling over the pork-barrel which tended to divide ruling parties in other African countries. Thirdly, the BDP and the civil service continued to work in alliance with the Tswana chiefs who remained the most influential players in the rural areas. Khama had carefully consolidated his position within the largest chiefdoms – those of his own group, the Bamangwato, and the Bakwena – which minimised the mathematical chances of defeat, and Masire endeavoured to keep the winning coalition together even though he himself belonged to a smaller Tswana group.[139]

However, by the early 1990s the ruling party began to encounter more serious challenges, which were equally of its making. External pressures were minimal, in that Botswana had dispensed with most forms of aid and was looked upon by Western governments as a model state. It was more a case of past success generating unforeseen problems. To start with, Botswana experienced possibly the fastest rate of urbanisation in Africa, estimated at 12.3 per cent between 1960 and 1994, which arose from the concentration of decision-making and much economic activity on the capital.[140] This swelling urban population began to encounter unemployment and housing shortages which had not initially been envisaged as a problem. Moreover, urban dwellers broke free of the pressures to support a rural bloc vote and embraced a more scurrilous form of political expression which was unimaginable in rural society. A related point is that the age profile of the population was very young, with as many as 44 per cent being beneath the age of 15 years. As in other countries, alienated youth ceased to be swayed by the arguments for a continuation of BDP rule, knowing (and caring) little of its past achievements. The fact the voting age was pegged at 21 years meant that there was little outlet for the frustration of urban youth who responded in more anomic ways.

Another development was assertiveness of interests which had previously been regarded as tame. The women's movement in Botswana became particularly bold in attacking forms of patriarchy, especially in the rural areas, which the BDP was accused of benefiting from. The San (or Bushmen) who had been treated as second-class citizens also began to assert their rights as 'first peoples'. The Botswana National Front (BNF) astutely brought the San into the party and fielded them as candidates in areas where they represented a significant minority or a numerical majority. One of the San complaints was about dispossession at the hands of ranchers who were closely allied to the ruling party. The participation of prominent BDP politicians in the land-grab, and the unwillingness of Masire to curb their excesses, became a source of considerable controversy in the early 1990s – as did revelations of blatant corruption in a regime which had always boasted of its high moral standards.

In the 1994 elections, the BDP was given a run for its money by the BNF. Three members of the Cabinet lost their seats. Although the BDP still won with 54.4 per cent of the vote and 27 of the 40 seats in parliament, this was its worst performance ever. Conversely, this was the best result achieved by the BNF which took all of the remaining 13 seats. Tellingly, the BDP was trounced in Gaborone, where the BNF won all four constituencies, and in other urban locations.[141] Whereas Botswana had always been a by-word for political stability, even this began to look fragile in the aftermath of the elections. In February 1995, demonstrations by University and school students in Gaborone led to clashes with police and an outbreak of youth unrest and student strikes across the country which were repressed with considerable brutality. The Botswana Federation of Trade Unions, the Women's NGO Coalition and the Catholic Church expressed solidarity with the students and accused the government of heavy-handedness. The BDP weathered this crisis and in 1998 it managed a successful leadership transmission from Masire, whose two terms under the constitution were up, to Festus Mogae. However, there was every sign that Botswana politics was likely to become more hotly contested than in the past when a broad social consensus had existed. Nevertheless, the future of multipartyism in Botswana still seemed much secure than in most African countries.

The same could not be said of the Gambia which followed a different path altogether. Like Botswana, the Gambia had managed a measure of political pluralism since independence, including regular elections. However, Dawda Jawara's People's Progressive Party (PPP) was very much in the driving seat. The regime was severely shaken in 1981 when it took Senegalese troops to reverse a coup. The price for this bail-out was a confederation which Jawara finally managed to extricate himself from in 1989. The subsequent public rift with Senegal meant that Jawara would no longer be able to rely on his more powerful neighbour to underwrite his security. This necessitated building up a loyal army and police force, which needed to be played off against each other. Although the PPP won the next set of elections in 1992, the popularity of the regime was lower than ever. Two years later, a section of the army seized power and, when the Senegalese sat on their hands, Captain Yahya Jammeh proceeded to set up an Armed Forces Provisional Ruling Council (AFPRC). When the junta signalled its intention of staying on until 1998 the donors suspended aid. Although Jammeh was forced to bow to external pressure, and to hold elections, there was nothing to stop him from trading in his fatigues for civilian clothes. In 1996, a new constitution was adopted and Jammeh retired from the army to form a political party, the Alliance for Patriotic Reorganisation and Construction (APRC). In the Presidential polls which followed, Jammeh won a clear majority. However, the old parties were banned from contesting while the new ones were spiked until a few weeks before the polls.[142] The prospects for democracy in the Gambia therefore looked rather poor at the start of the new millennium.

9.2.3.6 Kings and democrats: Lesotho and Swaziland

We turn now to the fate of democracy in two African countries where indigenous monarchies retained real power. Of the two, the Swazi monarchy was by far the most powerful. As we have already seen, Sobhuza II had resorted to the drastic step in 1973 of abrogating the constitution, declaring a state of emergency (which was never rescinded) and banning political parties. In 1978, Sobhuza introduced an Order-in-Council which created an alternative arrangement for choosing leaders, the so-called *tinkhundla* system. Swazis at the local level were permitted to elect representatives on an individual basis. These then constituted an electoral college which selected parliamentarians, to whom the king added ten appointees of his own. This indirectly elected assembly then chose ten members of the Senate, while the king added an equal number. The screening process ensured that it was only pliable politicians who reached the top. Moreover, the powers of the legislature were limited by virtue of the fact that the king continued to rule by decree. Underpinning this political structure was a willingness to use repression to deal with any dissent, on the basis that this was 'un-Swazi' and signalled a lack of respect for the king. Sobhuza, who had been king for some 61 years, finally died in 1982, unleashing a struggle for power within the court. This was finally resolved when his teenage son succeeded in 1986, as Mswati III. Those who hoped that the young king would break with the conventions of the Sobhuza years were soon to have their illusions shattered, as Mswati signalled his intention to continue ruling as the continent's last absolute monarch.

In 1983, in the midst of the crisis of the monarchy, the first attempt to mobilise support for radical change began with the formation of the People's United Democratic Movement (PUDEMO). The support for PUDEMO, which operated underground, came from students, workers and intellectuals who were disillusioned by the rampant corruption and abuse of power, including the seizure of valuable land by Ministers and royal favourites. Many of its sympathisers were active within the trade unions, including the Swaziland National Association of Teachers (SNAT), the Swaziland National Association of Civil Servants (SNACS) as well as the Swaziland Association of Students (SNAS). All of these drew inspiration from popular movements in South Africa. In 1990, the government arrested the leaders of PUDEMO and put them on trial for high treason, alleging that they had been plotting an insurrection.[143]

The collapse of the trial merely emboldened the incipient opposition, especially students at the national University.

Mswati attempted to recapture the initiative by setting up two enquiries to look into reform of the electoral system. However, hardliners within the regime insisted that any concessions represented the thin end of the wedge. In 1998, the Public Order Act was passed to enable the government to employ more drastic expedients, and Decree No. 2 of 2001 empowered the authorities to muzzle the press and to restrict the autonomy of the courts. Moreover, the President of PUDEMO, Mario Msuku, was once again placed on trial for treason. At the end of 2002, the regime found itself in open conflict with the judiciary, the labour movement, the churches and a resurgent PUDEMO over its refusal to rescind the 1973 legislation. The regime also incurred a great deal of negative publicity by announcing its intention to purchase a luxury jet at a time when many Swazis were facing the prospect of famine. Although the United States threatened to impose sanctions, external pressure failed to produce any movement in the direction of a constitutional monarchy.

In Lesotho, as we saw in Chapter 4, Leabua Jonathan had tamed the king, Moshoeshoe II. The Basotho National Party (BNP) operated a one-party state, not unlike that in many other African countries. The peculiarity of Lesotho was that it was surrounded by, and economically dependent upon South Africa and was therefore vulnerable to pressure from beyond its borders. From 1974, Jonathan offered his support to the ANC, which drew the ire of the South Africans. The latter retaliated by permitting Ntsu Mokhehle – hitherto a strident opponent of the apartheid regime – to set up the Lesotho Liberation Army (LLA) on their soil. The demise of Jonathan finally came in the context of a South African blockade in 1986. However, the coup which toppled the regime also had other causes. One was the feeling within the Lesotho Para-Military Force that Jonathan was practicing favouritism. Amongst the complainants was Major-General Justin Lekhanya, who did not mastermind the coup, but was its immediate beneficiary. Another reason was that Jonathan was believed to favour the ambitions of the Molapo royal house, from which he hailed, whilst undermining the dignity of Moshoeshoe II.[144] The king had his revenge by failing to come to the aid of Jonathan when the plot was revealed. Once the coup was complete, the king offered his seal of approval, commenting that under Jonathan 'human life was no more valuable than that of a house-fly'.[145] In the period of military rule which followed, Moshoeshoe II became in effect a co-ruler and an arbiter in the affairs of a factionalised junta. The perception that the king was siding against Lekhanya provoked another trial of strength in which Moshoeshoe came off second best. In March 1990 he was sent into exile in Britain to 'cool off', but after keeping up his invective he was stripped of his office in November – the first time that a Lesotho king had ever been dethroned. In his place, his son was installed as King Letsie III.

At this point, the military decided to initiate a return to civilian rule and convened a Constituent Assembly to that end. But before its work could be completed, a revolt by certain Captains forced the removal of Lekhanya in April 1991 and brought about the retirement of the upper echelons of the military. Major-General Ramaema, who was co-opted, made it clear that his task was to engineer a smooth exit, remarking that 'I am the driver of a lorry without a reverse gear. It will only shift forward.'[146] In March 1993, national elections were finally held in which the Basotho Congress Party (BCP), which had been robbed of victory in 1970, finally received its reward. The BNP, for which Lekhanya stood as a candidate, failed to win a single seat.[147] Under the terms of the transition arrangements, Moshoeshoe was brought back, but following his untimely death in a motor accident, Letsie III resumed the kingship for a second time in 1996. The king retained certain political prerogatives, notably the right to name one-third of the members of Senate, but in other respects Lesotho conformed to a conventional Westminster system.

The new democratic institutions could not have been more fragile. In 1997, the BCP split in two, in the wake of which Prime Minister Mokhehle founded a new political party, the Lesotho Congress for Democracy (LCD). In 1998, after Mokhehle had handed the baton to Pakalitha Mosisili, fresh elections were held. The LCD won a landslide in the face of opposition protests. The chaos which threatened when sections of the army began to take sides led SADC (the Southern African Development Conference), in the shape of South Africa and Botswana, to send in troops to restore 'order'. This became a highly messy operation, and an acute embarrassment to the South Africans. Nevertheless, it culminated in the installation of an interim administration, including the LCD and the opposition. In May 2002, fresh elections were held which were won by Mosisili and the LCD, against the backdrop of renewed opposition complaints. Whereas in Swaziland the pressing question was whether the monarchy would ever relinquish its grip on power, what was at issue in Lesotho was the ability of the politicians to sublimate their differences so that the army was not presented with a fresh excuse to intervene.

9.2.3.7 *Not so fast there: the making of a New South Africa*

Having indicated many of the pitfalls and reversals associated with democratisation across Africa, we conclude this survey with a comparative success story. At the start of the 1990s, there was every possibility that South Africa would slide deeper into chaos. Various branches of the security apparatus had established a measure of operational autonomy and were actively fomenting violence in an attempt to disable the opposition. Meanwhile, ANC supporters and Inkatha fought for control of Kwazulu/Natal.[148] That the apocalypse was averted owes everything to the willingness of the major protagonists to pull back from the brink. As early as 1989, President P. W. Botha had been engaged in exploratory talks with the country's most illustrious prisoner, Nelson Mandela. However, it fell to F. W. De Klerk, who ousted Botha in August of that year, to break with the National Party (NP) dogma that the ANC was nothing more than a terrorist organisation hell-bent on turning South Africa into a Communist satellite. The implosion of Communism in the Soviet Union and Eastern Europe came at a rather fortuitous moment. In February 1990, De Klerk surprised Parliament when he announced that he was unbanning the ANC, the South African Communist Party (SACP) and other proscribed organisations; repealing the state of emergency provisions; and releasing Mandela without conditions. Nine days later, Mandela walked free and a fresh chapter in South African history began.

South Africa became the only Anglophone country to go down the national conference route, although the participants were wrong in their belief that they were engaged in something altogether unique. The NP and the ANC set about negotiating the conditions under which political rights for all South Africans could be enjoyed whilst reassuring the minorities. De Klerk had cause to worry about being outflanked by the far-right, which was resolutely opposed to any negotiations. Equally, as the ANC began to operate above ground, it had to satisfy its own mass constituency by pushing for the rapid dismantling of apartheid. The instrument which was vested with responsibility for ushering in a negotiated settlement was the Convention for a Democratic South Africa (CODESA). This was a more exclusive club than that of other national conferences, in that only eight political organisations took their seats in 1991. The Pan-Africanist Congress (PAC) and Inkatha remained outside the negotiations, complaining about a secret compact between the ANC and the NP. Despite the conspiracy thesis, the relationship between the main parties was characterised by acute mistrust, and in 1992 the ANC withdrew from CODESA after the killing of its supporters at Boipatong by hostel dwellers, apparently aided by the police. However, in September of that year a further mass killing at Bisho (in the Ciskei) was followed by a resumption of the CODESA negotiations, lest the process break down completely. Crucially, the ANC conceded the formation of a Government of National Unity once national elections had been held. This reassured the NP that it would retain a measure of input into decision-making for the next five years. CODESA II culminated in agreement on a Interim Constitution, in which the NP support for federalism won out over the wishes of the ANC to concentrate power. However, it also led to the creation of an Independent Electoral Commission, which was placed beyond the control of De Klerk. In the run-up to the elections, a Transitional Executive Council was established to keep a check on the Cabinet. Finally, the design of the final constitution was to be delegated to the legislature which was elected in April 1994.[149]

The electoral stakes could not have been higher, but while there was many flaws in the execution, the polls passed off remarkably smoothly. For the vast majority of the population, this was the first time that they had ever voted, and the enthusiasm was palpable. Under the Interim Constitution, South Africa adopted a system of proportional representation, in which members were chosen from a party list rather than being elected from single-member constituencies. Simultaneous elections were held for the nine provincial legislatures and the National Assembly and Senate. As had been predicted, the ANC demonstrated its overwhelming popular appeal, winning 252 of the 400 seats in the National Assembly and control of seven provinces. By contrast, the PAC performed dismally, winning only five seats in the national legislature on the strength of 1.25 per cent of the vote. The NP emerged with 20.39 per cent of the national vote and control of the Western Cape, having successfully convinced Coloured voters that they would be the losers if a black government ran the province. Inkatha, which was only persuaded to participate at the last moment, won 10.54 per cent of the national vote, but control of

Kwazulu/Natal. The party of white liberals, the Democratic Party (DP) took only seven seats on the basis of 1.73 per cent of the vote, and was therefore excluded from the Government of National Unity. The right-wing Freedom Front managed a mere 2.17 per cent and was equally excluded. What was crucial was the margin of the ANC victory. Its 62.65 per cent share of the vote fell short of the two-thirds it would have needed to write the next constitution single-handedly. This meant that the ANC was forced to engage in dialogue with the other parties in drafting a document which did not eventually differ that much from the Interim Constitution.

On the back of the 1994 elections, Mandela was installed as President, while De Klerk became one of two Vice-Presidents. The Ministerial portfolios were distributed between the ANC, the NP and Inkatha as the only parties which had polled above 5 per cent. Although there were inevitable stresses, the Government of National Unity managed to transact its business in a consensual fashion. The political violence which had continued in the transition phase was brought under control and a new constitution was finalised at the end of 1996. This was a document with which all parties felt relatively happy, especially in its guarantees for individual rights and gender equality. The importance which was attached to judicial independence was underscored by the submission of the draft constitution to the Constitutional Court for approval. The latter in fact insisted on certain modifications, which had to be inserted.[150] After the adoption of the new constitution, the NP withdrew from the government, with a view to plotting its success at the next set of elections scheduled for 1999.

After 1994, the ANC appeared somewhat vulnerable for two main reasons. On the one hand, there were signs of division within the party at both the provincial and national levels. One ANC Minister, Bantu Holomisa, broke away after coming off second best in a private vendetta with Stella Sigacu, who he had once overthrown in a coup when she was Transkeian Prime Minister. Holomisa, who had a solid constituency within the party, joined Roelf Meyer (formerly of the NP) in creating the United Democratic Movement (UDM) which targeted corruption in government. Mandela's furtherance of the Presidential ambitions of Thabo Mbeki was also a source of internal discord. On the other hand, the ANC was unable to satisfy the aspirations of its popular constituency. In 1994, the government had launched the Reconstruction and Development Programme (RDP) which envisaged the injection of large sums of money into education, housing, land redistribution and other programmes designed to mitigate the legacy of apartheid. However, the leadership quickly realised that it lacked the resources to embark on such an ambitious programme. If it sought to make the business community pay for social improvement, there was every chance that capital would simply pull out. In 1996, the RDP was therefore subsumed by the Growth, Redeployment and Redistribution (GEAR) strategy. Whereas the RDP had been interventionist in tone, GEAR was premised on the attraction of foreign capital which would promote faster growth and thereby generate both jobs and the resources needed to pay for social amenities. The problem was that the trickle-down was painfully slow. One study estimated in 1998 that unemployment stood at around 24 per cent, and predicted that it would hit 40 per cent in ten years unless GEAR hit its target of 6 per cent growth per annum.[151] The problem was that GEAR consistently fell below those rates. Black South Africa continued, therefore, to be faced with massive unemployment, inadequate housing and a lack of basic amenities. To compound the malaise, a crime wave (born in part out of poverty) made the lives of urban dwellers a daily misery.

The adoption of neo-liberal policies placed the relationship between the ANC and its historic allies, the Congress of South African Trade Unions (COSATU) and the 'civics', under some strain.[152] However, an even greater worry was that voters would shop elsewhere or, more likely, not to turn out to vote at all. In fact, in 1999 the ANC increased its share of the national vote to 66.35 per cent, while the New National Party (NNP) slid back to 6.87 per cent, polling fewer votes than the DP on 9.56 per cent. However, the share of the population who voted was substantially smaller. It has been estimated that perhaps as many as 91 per cent of adults voted in 1994, but only 60 per cent did so five years later.[153] Admittedly, on this occasion voters had to make the effort to register, but still this lower turnout arguably reflected a growing sense of disenchantment with politics.

9.3 Conclusion

In a sense, South Africa was not so unlike the rest of Africa after all. In countries like Ghana and Senegal, where the opportunity to change governments by the ballot box had been seized with alacrity, the stark reality was that the victors were almost bound to disappoint their constituencies because they lacked the resources to deliver jobs and basic amenities. For that reason, the question of democracy became inseparable from the reality of Africa's marginalised position in the international division of labour. The New Partnership for Africa's Development (NEPAD), which was launched on the initiative of the new democrats – Thabo Mbeki, Olusegun Obasanjo and Abdoulaye Wade – was an attempt to link democracy to ambitious plans for continental economic renewal along broadly neo-liberal lines. In this, it enjoyed the support of the African Union, which replaced the OAU. Under NEPAD arrangements, African leaders were expected to police their own adherence to democratic norms through the African Peer Review Mechanism. Whether leaders would feel bound by the opinion of their colleagues, and whether moral pressure alone would suffice to significantly modify the behaviour of rogue Presidents and Generals, remained open questions at the end of 2003. As far as the West was concerned, there was no sign that the politics of self-interest was going to give way to something more altruistic. In 2003, the administration of George W. Bush courted a number of governments in Africa with extremely poor track records, such as Cameroun and Equatorial Guinea, with a view to protecting American oil interests. The imperative was to find an alternative to Middle Eastern oil which was potentially at risk from so-called Muslim fundamentalism. Across Africa, oil was negatively correlated with 'good governance' and there was nothing in the Bush overtures to suggest that the latest oil bonanza was going to lead to anything significantly better.

10

Millennial Africa: The National Question Revisited

I, Mohammed Siyad Barre, am singularly responsible for the transformation of Somalia and Mogadisho from a bush country and scruffy hamlet into a modern state and commodious city, respectfully. Consequently, I will not allow anyone to destroy me or run me out of here; and if they try, I will take the whole country with me.

President Barre of Somalia

He killed my Pa, he killed my Ma. I'll vote for him.

NPFL campaign song in Liberia, 1997

At the start of the new millennium, the configuration of Africa was more varied than at any point since the Scramble. In some countries, democratisation led to a reinvigoration of politics and an alleviation of political tensions. In others, the grim determination of incumbent regimes to cling to power at all costs, raised the real prospect of endemic civil unrest and renewed military intervention.[1] More seriously still, the viability of the state itself was thrown into question across much of the continent, as armed factions carved out their own territorial niches. In most cases, they aspired to ultimate control of the centre, but where no faction commanded a decisive advantage, there was often a de facto fragmentation into competing fiefdoms. Whereas the international community had once worked on the assumption that the globe was naturally composed of sovereign states, there was a greater willingness to live with the possibility that states might fall off the map altogether. In this chapter, we examine the playing out of the national question across the continent from the 1990s. We start by revisiting some of the political unions which had been forged around the time of independence (see Chapter 3). We then consider the experience of countries plagued by a long history of civil wars. After that, we turn to the contagion of warfare in Central and West Africa. Finally, the book concludes with some general observations about the pursuit of national reconciliation and the acceptance of diversity at the start of the new millennium.

10.1   Unhappy marriages: Cameroun, Zanzibar, Eritrea and Somalia

For the optimists, the success of territorial unions at independence provided living proof that there was life after colonial partition. In each case, however, disparate legacies remained a complicating factor, and the circumstances under which the unions were originally forged often provided scope for subsequent disagreement. When the marriages became seriously strained, the weaker partners spoke of regaining their freedom, while the dominant ones insisted on a binding contract.

In two of the four cases, that is Cameroun and Tanzania, marriages of convenience showed signs of real strain, but the threatened breakup up did not come to pass. The union between British Southern Cameroon and the Republic of Cameroun was always going to be difficult by virtue of the fact that the official languages, systems of education and administrative practices were quite different. Moreover, the fact that the Francophone east contained three-quarters of the population meant that this was not a marriage of equal partners. This was made abundantly clear in May 1972 when the Ahidjo regime brusquely abolished the federation, claiming it was divisive, and ushered in a unitary state in its place. In 1984, the country was renamed the Republic of Cameroun, dropping 'United' and thus reverting to what the Francophone part had been called prior to the union. Although English remained one of the official languages, the Anglophone segment simply became two provinces within a larger Francophone state. By the 1980s, the exploitation of oil reserves in the Anglophone South-West created an additional source of strain because of perceptions that the benefits were being monopolised by the Francophone majority.

The authoritarianism of the Ahidjo years was one reason why most Anglophones did not challenge these arrangements. But as some space for political expression opened up in the early 1990s, it became possible for Anglophone politicians to contest the terms under which they were governed. It is worth noting, however, that not all chose to do so as Anglophones. As we saw in the last chapter, the Social Democratic Front (SDF) was led by John Fru Ndi who was an Anglophone from the North-West Province. Although the SDF was the dominant force in the west, it was intent on projecting itself as a party of all Camerounians. In 1992, Fru Ndi ran Biya close, which demonstrated his appeal to a wider constituency. However, there was also a competing tendency which sought to mobilise the Anglophone population against the Francophones, demanding either the restoration of the federation or, failing that, outright secession. The militants managed to mobilise popular support through demonstrations and other forms of direct action.[2] In November 1991, when Biya convened his Tripartite Conference, some of the Anglophone delegates tabled a demand for a loose federation. They subsequently reconstituted themselves as the All Anglophone Conference (AAC) which went on to issue the Buea Declaration. The latter portrayed the Anglophones as an oppressed minority, and made detailed constitutional proposals of its own. At its second conference at Bamenda in 1994, the AAC moved towards a more explicitly secessionist position, despite the questionable advantages of belonging to a micro-state.[3] From this point onwards, the Southern Cameroons National Council (SCNC) became actively involved in campaigning for the breakup of Cameroun. The SCNC set 1 October 1996 as its date for independence, and although it came and went without much drama it laid down a marker.

The electoral failure of the SDF undermined the contention that Cameroun could be reformed from within, and lent greater weight to the SCNC position that there was no half-way house. However, Biya was astute in exploiting some longstanding rivalries between the two Anglophone provinces. Some politicians from the South-West, which had hitherto played second fiddle to the North-West, were promoted to senior positions in the government and the party, including that of Prime Minister. This probably had the effect of weakening the SDF rather than the SCNC which, if anything gained in strength at the close of the decade. In December 1999, Anglophone militants attempted to seize the radio station in Buea, and in subsequent years there were violent clashes on the anniversaries of 'independence day'. Although none of this seriously threatened the Camerounian state, there were signs that the 'Anglophone problem' was likely to become a serious headache.

The Tanzanian context was significantly different. Anglophone Camerounians resented the *de facto* marginalisation of English and fiercely resisted efforts at tampering with their separate educational system. By contrast, Nyerere had adopted Swahili, which belonged to the coast and the islands of Zanzibar and Pemba, as the national language of Tanzania. Moreover, Swahili cultural forms, including *taarab* music, enjoyed widespread acceptance on the mainland. Moreover, while there was little chance of an Anglophone becoming President of Cameroun, Ali Hassan Mwinyi succeeded Nyerere as President of Tanzania. Finally, whereas the Camerounians lost their separate political institutions when the federation was dissolved, Zanzibar retained its own legislature, President and administrative structures. In that sense, the reassertion of Zanzibari identity could not be attributed to the failure of the mainlanders to respect the terms of the union. The changing mood on the islands appears to be related to the conjuncture of two other factors. One was the impact of a globalised Islamic identity on Zanzibaris, especially amongst the Arabs and Shirazis on the island of Pemba. The latter had not forgotten the bloodshed surrounding the revolution of 1964. The second factor was mounting frustration with the politics of the CCM (Chama Cha Mapunduzi), after the fusion of the ruling parties on the mainland and Zanzibar in 1977. On the islands, opposition to the CCM assumed a distinctive character, in which aspects of history, religion, Arab culture and political dissidence formed a seamless whole.

The one similarity with Cameroun was that flawed elections added credibility to those who maintained that the ruling party was determined to cling to power at all costs. Despite an agreement between the CCM and Civic United Front (CUF), which was brokered by the Commonwealth Secretariat in June 1999, the former continued to act in a manner which made fair elections difficult on Zanzibar/Pemba. In the Zanzibari elections of 2000, the CCM claimed victory, but the Commonwealth Observer Group proclaimed that the process had been represented a 'colossal contempt for the Zanzibari people'.[4]

There was a marked increase in political tension on the islands, especially on Pemba where the CUF was the dominant force, enjoying the support of peasants who had long been on the receiving end of discriminatory pricing for cloves. The CUF announced it would boycott the Zanzibari legislature and staged mass demonstrations, demanding a re-run. In the confrontation which ensued, some 22 people were shot dead by the authorities and around 2000 refugees fled to Kenya. These events focused the attention of Amnesty International and Western governments upon events in Zanzibar and led the government to adopt a more conciliatory stance towards the CUF. In October 2001, the two sides signed an agreement accepting the need for a commission of enquiry to look into the violence. The parties also agreed to co-operate in ensuring fair elections in the future. What remained unclear was whether the CUF would be happy with winning control of political institutions on Zanzibar, or whether it would push for outright secession.

Whereas Anglophone Cameroun and Zanzibar remained consigned to their respective unions (however reluctantly), the Eritreans embarked on a successful war of liberation, achieving their complete independence from Ethiopia in May 1993. In Chapters 3 and 6, we looked at the origins of the federation and the first manifestations of resistance. Here we only need to recapitulate a couple of key points. One is that whatever support for union had originally existed – and there was some – dissipated rapidly once it became clear that Haile Selassie intended to treat Eritreans as his subjects. The compulsion to learn Amharic and to conform to Ethiopian ways of doing thing was a particular affront to educated Eritreans, especially teachers, students and civil servants. The dissolution of the federation in 1962 was the point of no return for nationalists who set out to win their independence through force of arms. It is also worth reiterating that cementing a sense of Eritrean nationhood was a tall order in view of the mutually reinforcing fault-lines which separated highlanders from lowlanders, agriculturalists from pastoralists and Christians from Muslims. There was nothing which made Eritrea in any sense 'natural', and as a political idea it arose out of Italian colonialism. Eritrean nationalists were acutely aware of this fact and sought to transcend its unwelcome implications in different ways. The first effective movement for independence, the Eritrean Liberation Movement (ELM) espoused a secular message, but was squeezed out by the Eritrean Liberation Front (ELF) which was a primarily Muslim in composition and made its affiliations with the Arab world. The ELF functioned as a loose federation of five separate armies which mobilised recruits along ethnic lines and fought almost exclusively in their own zones.[5]

By 1969, there was a growing sense of disillusionment with the leadership of the ELF, and a number of splinter groups emerged. The two most important were the Popular Liberation Front, made up of people from the east coast region, and the so-called Ala group which was composed of Tigrayans like Issayas Afeworki. In 1972, these two factions (and fragments of a third) came together, leading to the emergence of yet another movement, the Eritrean People's Liberation Front (EPLF). Like the ELM before it, the EPLF adopted a secular position and distanced itself from the Arabist orientation of the ELF. However, the EPLF faced its own internal crisis within a year when former

University students, who were steeped in Marxist conceptions of revolution, took the leadership to task, while others alleged ethnic particularism. The leadership came down hard on the dissidents, many of whom were later executed, to the embarrassment of many academic sympathisers to this day. The winning side – which enjoyed the luxury of writing the history – insisted that factionalism had been the downfall of Eritrean nationalism in the past and that the EPLF had to be founded on tight discipline and non-sectarianism. The EPLF stuck firmly to both of these principles over the years, and many commentators have attributed the remarkable success of the organisation to this fact.[6]

In other respects, though, the EPLF proved to be more chameleon-like. In its initial incarnation, the EPLF singled out American imperialism and Zionism as the mainstays of Ethiopian imperialism. The language of the movement became more overtly Marxist over the course of the 1970s, matching that of the Derg after the revolution. However, the EPLF toned down the rhetoric after 1978, once the Soviet Union began to actively arm the Derg. By 1987, the EPLF was sounding almost social democratic in its advocacy of a mixed economy, a multi-party political system and a referendum to determine the future of Eritrea.[7] Nor did the EPLF stand still when it came to formulating a military strategy. The early EPLF sought to prosecute a 'people's war', based on the active support of the peasantry. In areas which it liberated, it carried out land reform, promoted gender equality and sponsored Peoples' Assemblies which were vested with a wide range of responsibilities. Writing of an Assembly in liberated Keren in 1977, David Pool recalls that it 'introduced price controls, reduced the highest salaries and raised the lowest wages, and reduced rents for houses nationalised by the Ethiopian government'.[8] The EPLF suffered a setback in 1978, when the Ethiopians reached a peace agreement with the Somalis and then turned all their firepower on the rebels. The EPLF managed to survive this onslaught as well as the Red Star Campaign of 1982, and captured large numbers of Soviet tanks and other heavy equipment. In the latter part of the 1980s, the EPLF turned to prosecuting a conventional war, using the heavy weapons which it had captured. Whereas advocates of 'people's war' elsewhere in Africa warned of the political costs which would ensue from going down the conventional route, the EPLF claimed to be mindful of the need to build structures of popular power. Its semi-autonomous relief arm, the Eritrean Relief Association (ERA) also won considerable admiration amongst aid donors for the effectiveness with which it ferried food to the stricken areas.

The one respect in which the EPLF was ultra-sensitive was in respect of the national question. The EPLF insisted that the mass of Eritreans had never supported federation with Ethiopia, but had been sold down the river by their traditional rulers. According to this reading of history, the Eritreans were already a nation-in-waiting at the end of the Second World War, and their plight arose out of a combination of bad faith on the part of the British and the Americans, the irresponsibility of the United Nations, the duplicity of Haile Selassie and the genocidal inclinations of the Derg. In 1980, the EPLF finally eradicated the ELF and became the only serious contender for Eritrean support. An insistence on the singularity of the Eritrean predicament did, however, create multiple points of friction with other liberation movements which were also fighting the Derg. The EPLF expressed its willingness to co-operate militarily, but only on condition that these other organisations acknowledged the Eritrean right to independence. The EPLF was distinctly cool about anything which smacked of a secessionist agenda on the part of these other movements, lest this detract from the uniqueness of the Eritrean case. The fact that the EPRP saw their revolutionary objectives in pan-Ethiopian terms made them acceptable partners and rendered the Tigray People's Liberation Front (TPLF) suspect. Although the TPLF was an early beneficiary of EPLF training, relations soured when the former issued a manifesto which spoke of creating 'an independent democratic republic of Tigray'.[9] The fact that both the EPLF and the TPLF were seeking to mobilise Tigrinya-speakers might have been expected to divide them further. However, given that both movements broadly accepted the colonial line of partition, this proved to be much less controversial than the TPLF's insistence that all the 'nationalities' in Ethiopia and Eritrea should enjoy the right to self-determination up to and including secession. This was unacceptable to the EPLF which regarded such a position as a recipe for the very divisions which it had sought to transcend.[10]

There were also a number of other irritants in the relationship. The TPLF's attack on the Soviet Union as 'social imperialist' and its bizarre championing of the Albanian path to socialism, found little support with the EPLF. Secondly, the TPLF continued to champion the ideal of a 'people's war' and was overtly critical of the EPLF's adoption of conventional warfare. In a sympathetic analysis of the TPLF, John Young is at pains to demonstrate that the Kriger model of a guerrilla–peasant relationship underpinned by violence is wide of the mark, and that the organisation made conscious compromises with the peasantry – for example, in its attitude towards the Orthodox Church.[11] Certainly, the TPLF regarded itself as peasant-friendly and contrasted this with the *dirigisme* of the EPLF. Finally, the TPLF resented the manner in which the EPLF posed as the senior partner and treated its own guerrilla campaign with condescension. The nadir in their relationship came at the height of the famine in 1985 when the EPLF severed relations and prevented food aid from passing from Sudan through Eritrea, thus forcing the TPLF to construct its own road at short notice. This use of famine as a political weapon – something normally associated with the Derg – created an enmity between the leaderships of the two organisations which never really disappeared.[12]

Nevertheless, the EPLF and the TPLF recognised by 1988 that they would hasten the demise of the Derg if they pooled their resources. In 1988, the EPLF won their most decisive battle when they defeated the Ethiopians at the battle of Afabet – described rather extravagantly by Basil Davidson as 'the most significant victory in the history of liberation movements since Diem Bien Phu in 1954'.[13] In February 1989, the EPLF lent an armoured brigade which enabled the TPLF to take the town of Endaselasie and to capture thousands of Ethiopian troops. In 1990, the EPLF went on to seize Massawa and laid siege to large numbers of Ethiopian ground troops. Sensing that the end was in sight, the TPLF forged an alliance with the Ethiopian People's Democratic Movement (EPDM) and the Oromo People's Democratic Organisation (OPDO), giving birth to the EPRDF (Ethiopian People's Revolutionary Democratic Front). On 24 May 1991, the EPLF captured Asmara and four days later Addis Ababa itself fell. While Mengistu Haile-Mariam scurried into exile, the EPRDF and the EPLF co-operated within a Transitional Government of Ethiopia.

Rather than declaring a precipitous independence, the EPLF agreed to the holding of a referendum within two years to decide on the future of Eritrea. The EPLF naturally campaigned for independence, and while many EPRDF leaders apparently hoped that Eritreans would not sue for divorce, the result was overwhelming. When governments claim victory with 99.8 per cent of the vote, it is reasonable to suspect foul play. But in the Eritrean referendum, the result seems to have genuinely reflected the will of the people. This was a graphic demonstration of how the violence of the Derg had driven ordinary Eritreans into the arms of the nationalists. Some have seen Eritrean independence as a departure from the OAU principle that the colonially-derived boundaries should be considered sacrosanct. However, the EPLF denied that it *was* seceding on the basis that it had never really been part of Ethiopia. Moreover, Eritrea was actually reverting to an older set of colonial boundaries, namely those of Italian Eritrea.

Although the separation was a relatively amicable one, the relationship between Eritrea and Ethiopia deteriorated rapidly after 1993. On Eritrean independence, the two sides signed 25 protocols which were supposed to lead to a harmonisation of economic policies to the mutual benefit of both countries. However, within three years the agreements had broken down amidst mutual recriminations.[14] Whereas the Eritreans wanted complete freedom of trade and investment, which would benefit its nationals in Ethiopia, the EPRDF was inclined towards protectionism. In 1997, the Eritreans launched their own currency, the *nakfa*, and demanded that this be exchanged at parity with the Ethiopian *birr*. This the EPRDF would not accept and instead it insisted that trade between the countries be carried out in hard currency. For their part, the Eritreans stalled on the issue of allowing Ethiopia access to a port on the Red Sea. Finally, by seeking to promote industrial development in Tigray, the EPRDF seemed intent on undercutting Eritrean businesses. In May 1998, the war of words between the two governments escalated into a shooting war when the Eritreans moved into a disputed border zone at Badme. What followed was a conventional conflict in which heavy equipment and massed armies, made up of conscripts, engaged each other in pitched battles. By 2000, it is estimated that up to 70,000 troops had been killed in the fighting, while civilians caught on the wrong side of the border lost their property and were subjected to ill-treatment. The Eritreans had embarked on this risky course, believing that they were essentially invincible. However, the population of Eritrea was only 3.2 million, whereas the Ethiopians could call on a population of around 60 million. Having taken heavy losses, the Eritreans were eventually forced to sue for a humiliating peace. In December 2000, the Algiers Agreement was signed, which provided for arbitration over the disputed border zone. Whether this was just a border dispute is open to question.[15] Arguably, the war arose out of the clash of wills between two rival liberation movements who disagreed so fiercely because they had so much in common. The fact that the two Presidents, Issayas Afeworki and

Meles Zenawi, were both Tigrayans who allegedly originated from towns which were not that far apart, rather underscores the point.

The unravelling of the Somali Republic was, if anything, even more spectacular. As indicated in Chapter 3, the notion that the Somalis represented a nation by virtue of their shared language, cultural traditions and attachment to Islam has to be qualified by recognising that their society was arranged around powerful clan solidarities. Paradoxically again, it was the very fact of sharing a common cultural framework which made Somalis conscious of what made them distinct from other Somalis. If one conceives of Somali society in terms of a family tree, there were three overarching clan families, namely the Saar, Irir and Darod. Each of these segmented into clans which were a more important focus of identity. The Saar were comprised of settled agriculturalists located in the southern riverine areas: namely the Rahanwein and the Digil. The Irir sub-divided into the Dir, Isaaq and Hawiye. Finally, the Darod were made up of five clans: the Dolbahante, Mijerteen, Warsangali, Ogaden and Marehan.[16] These clans were, in turn, divided into a series of sub-clans, which did not necessarily see eye to eye. If one views Somalia spatially, these clan groupings were concentrated in particular regions of Somalia whose resource endowments also imparted deeper meaning to these divisions. The agriculturalists were, for example, looked down upon by the pastoralists, reflecting the importance attached to livestock as well as the slave origins of many farmers. The fact that certain clans spilled across the international borders was also a factor which helped to shape Somali identity politics. At independence, Somali nationalists tended to emphasise the points of convergence, and this became the basis for the pursuit of irredentist claims against Ethiopia, Kenya and Djibouti. However, it did not take long before northern Somalis began to complain about the nepotism of southerners from former Italian Somaliland, despite the fact that the Prime Minister, Ibrahim Egal, was from their part of the country.

The military coup of 1969 which brought General Siyad Barre to power, following the assassination of President Abdirashid Ali Shermaarke, led to a ratcheting up of state nationalism. Barre set out to promote mass literacy campaigns for the pastoral Somali using a Latinised script, whilst outlawing all overt references to clan affiliation. More fatally, at a time when the Derg was preoccupied with fighting the EPLF and the TPLF, Barre chose his moment in 1978 to invade the Ogaden with a view to bringing Ethiopian Somalis into the fold. The humiliating defeat which ensued killed off the likelihood of a 'Greater Somalia' ever being achieved, and unleashed latent tensions within the body politic. The honeymoon with Barre's increasingly personalist style of rule – in which the cult of the leader was accentuated – had long since dissipated. The rhetorical commitment to transcending clan loyalties, in particular, seemed like a thinly-veiled cover for Darod domination. Moreover, the modernist posturing of the regime meant that the lion's share of foreign aid and state resources were ploughed into Mogadisho, an urban enclave which had minimal connection with the pastoralist majority.[17] Indeed, the latter were squeezed by falling livestock prices as the hitherto safe Saudi market began to be opened up to international (especially Australian) competition.[18] Equally, as the capital grew by leaps and bounds – from 50,000 to more than a million inhabitants between

1960 and the mid-1980s – the profitability of food crop production led to a land grab which affected farming communities.[19] Finally, while the elite surrounding Barre made personal fortunes by squirreling away foreign aid and tapping the richest veins of accumulation, other regions of the country were effectively left to their own devices. Hence a mere 7 per cent of the foreign aid channelled to Somalia between 1985 and 1990 went to the North of the country where 35 per cent of the population lived.[20]

By the end of the 1970s, the Barre regime started to face overt challenges to its political monopoly, which tended to follow clan lines in the absence of other mechanisms for co-ordinating resistance. Expressions of dissent were quashed with considerable brutality, thereby widening the circle of malcontents to include much of the rural population. In 1978, on the back of military defeat in the Ogaden, colonels belonging to the Mijerteen sub-clan attempted to mount a coup, which misfired. Barre retaliated by launching indiscriminate reprisals against the entire Mijerteen population of the North-east. This guaranteed enduring Mijerteen enmity which the Somali Democratic Salvation Front (SSDF) attempted to tap into. Meanwhile, northern intellectuals, religious leaders and traders rallied to the banner of the Somaliland National Movement (SNM) in 1981. The SNM aimed to draw its support from Isaaq clansmen who were subjected to spoliation at the hands of large numbers of refugees from the Ogaden and ill-disciplined government troops. In 1988, Barre came to a deal with Mengistu whereby each would desist from aiding rebels from the other country. The net effect was to push SSDF and SNM rebels back into Somali territory where they began to engage the Barre regime directly. The SNM was able to fight its way into the main northern towns of Hargeisa, Burao and Berbera, to which Barre responded by arming non-Isaaq clans and bombing the former city to rubble. Between 1988 and 1990, the regime is estimated to have killed some 60,000 civilians in the northern towns and to have systematically persecuted Isaaq pastoralists.[21] In 1989, the rebellion spread across the South as the Somali Patriotic Movement (SPM) and the United Somali Congress (USC) mobilised Ogadeni and Hawiye supporters respectively, reducing the government army to a Marehan rump loyal to Barre. As the physical security of the regime crumbled, the population of Mogadisho itself took the streets. After Friday prayers on 14 July 1989, demonstrators clashed with the security forces, in which a significant number of protestors were killed. The extra-judicial execution of individuals of Isaaq affiliation precipitated the panicky withdrawal of Western agencies, removing any chance of external mediation.[22]

For the duration of the year, the capital became the site of intense fighting between the regime and its opponents. On 27 January 1991, Barre was finally forced to flee the city in a tank, from where he made his way to his native Gedo region. Barre was thereby reduced to the status of a regional warlord, but even this last stand was ill-fated and he was eventually forced into exile in Nigeria. This turn of events left the USC in effective control of the capital. However, when the civilian leadership of the USC announced the installation of Ali Mahdi Mohammed as interim president, the crisis took a new turn. The other movements concluded that there was no basis for forging a national consensus when the USC was intent on replacing Marehan with Hawiye domination. On the other hand, General Mohammed Aideed who belonged to the military wing of the USC, refused to recognise Ali Mahdi and proceeded to unleash his own forces in an attempt to seize the capital. The subsequent power struggle between sub-clan militias for control of Mogadisho led to carnage in the streets of the capital and to the dislocation of about one-third of its population.[23] These events provided the SNM with the excuse it needed to declare the secession of the North under the name of the Republic of Somaliland. The significant point to note is that the latter (like Eritrea) conformed to the boundaries of the former colony of British Somaliland, while the other movements were left to fight over the remains of former Italian Somaliland. Although the SNM was subsequently accused of practising Isaaq domination, and failed to win recognition from the international community (despite bringing Ibrahim Egal in as leader), it won favourable publicity by restoring peace in its area. By contrast, things went from bad to worse in Mogadisho and in the riverain zone where an acute famine ensued. It is estimated that some 350,000 people died over the course of the famine in 1992, while another million fled to refugee camps.[24]

Up until this point, the United Nations had done relatively little other than to broker a ceasefire in March 1992. In November, after considerable delay, 500 Pakistani peacekeepers were sent out under the remit of the United Nations Operations for Somalia (UNOSOM). Their restricted mandate meant that they were effectively paralysed, while much of the humanitarian food aid which reached Somalia went straight into the hands of the militias. In the closing stages of his presidency, George Bush finally offered to send in American troops, supposedly to create the conditions under which humanitarian operations could be carried out. Under the banner of 'Operation Restore Hope', American forces were given more robust rules of engagement. What followed was a public-relations disaster for the UN and a humiliation for the United States. After Aideed gratuitously killed a contingent of Pakistani troops, the Americans developed a fixation with the personality of this 'warlord' and forgot about the rest of Somalia. In a tit-for-tat vendetta with Aideed's forces, American troops ended up destroying property and killing yet more civilians, thereby uniting Somalis around hostility to the foreigner. The turning point was an incident in which a number of American soldiers were killed and their bodies dragged through the streets. The Clinton administration decided it was time to cut its losses. Although the UN remained, the idea that decisive foreign intervention could restore a governing authority to Somalia evaporated. In May 1995, the UN forces withdrew without having achieved their objective of putting Somalia back together again.

Subsequently, many commentators began to wonder whether Somalia might be better off without a central government if that meant revisiting the Barre years. The evidence of successful reconstruction in the absence of a state seemed to indicate that there were might be more workable alternatives. By 2003, Somalia had effectively been divided into three parts. In the North, the SNM stuck by its decision to secede on the basis that there were irreconcilable differences between the former British and Italian sections. In the North-east, the

SSDF created its own administration, and in 1998 the Puntland State of Somalia was proclaimed. This stopped short of secession and indeed the leadership argued for the recreation of Somalia on federal lines. In Somaliland and Puntland, the authorities faced many problems of governance, including in the latter case unruly militias made up of alienated youth. However, they both made significant strides in terms of restoring peace by bringing the traditional authorities into the process. Peace also brought economic recovery, while international NGOs provided much of the funding of basic social services.[25] There were some tensions over demarcation of the border between Somaliland and Puntland, but the two administrations went out of their way to resolve these without resorting to arms. The weak link remained the southern half of Somalia, including Mogadisho, which continued to be ravaged by warfare and banditry.

10.2   Running sores: civil wars in Sudan, Angola and Chad

We turn now to consider some of the most intractable conflicts in post-colonial Africa, where the national question seemed to lack a straightforward answer. In each case, longstanding ideological differences were reinforced by the discovery and exploitation of oil deposits which represented the price of victory as well as the means for incumbent regimes to finance their military operations.

In the aftermath of this historic Addis Ababa Agreement of 1972, Nimeiri enjoyed considerable support in the South of Sudan. The problem was that the main political organisations in the North were less than enthusiastic. The parties which had historically represented the two main Islamic communities – the Umma Party and what came to be known as the DUP (Democratic Unionist Party), drawing support from the Khatmiyya and the Ansar sect respectively – were lukewarm about an agreement which they thought would merely hasten the break-up of the Sudan. After the demolition on the Communist Party, its principal rival amongst educated Sudanese, the Muslim Brothers, acquired greater leverage in the politics of the North. They opposed the agreement, as well as the Constitution of 1973, on the basis that a secular state was incompatible with Islamic principles. Nimeiri faced serious challenges to his rule over 1975 and 1976, in which he was forced to rely upon the support of former southern rebels who had been integrated into the army. Although this should have made him grateful, Nimeiri was aware that it would be suicidal to remain on the wrong side of all the main northern political factions. As a result, he proclaimed a policy of National Reconciliation in 1977 in which Sadiq al-Mahdi, a former Umma Prime Minister, and Hassan al-Turabi of the Muslim Brothers were brought into the government. Although the former did not stay long, Turabi began to push from within for the adoption of overtly Islamist policies. This bore fruit in September 1983 when Nimeiri, desperately struggling to stay ahead of the game, introduced his September Laws which brought Shari'a law into force.[26] This set Nimeiri on a collision course with southern politicians who had many other additional reasons to feel aggrieved. In 1983, the carving up of the Southern Region into three separate units, which would be much weaker vis-à-vis the centre, was construed as a cynical attempt to weaken the South. Moreover, the central government redrew the internal borders in order to ensure that the emerging oilfields would fall within the northern domain. Finally, the government's pursuit of plans to channel the waters of the Nile southwards, through the Jonglei canal, was perceived as another instance of taking the South for granted.[27] The result was that while Nimeiri bought himself some breathing space in the North, he thoroughly alienated southern opinion.

Some guerrillas had remained under arms despite the Addis Ababa agreement and they were now joined by mass defections of southern soldiers in 1983. The new political organisation which emerged out of this process of realignment was the Sudan People's Liberation Movement (SPLM) and its armed wing, the Sudan People's Liberation Army (SPLA), both of which were led by Dr John Garang. Whereas the Anyanya had previously struggled for secession, the SPLM/SPLA claimed to be fighting on behalf of all the Sudanese for a country which would be liberated from religious sectarianism and regional inequalities.[28] The Nimeiri regime responded to the renewed insurgency by astutely exploiting American geo-political concerns. In its desire to isolate the Qaddafi regime in Libya, which sided with the rebels, the Reagan administration was only too happy to furnish Nimeiri with the weapons he needed to defeat the SPLA. The Nimeiri regime also armed Arab and southern minority militias against Dinka and the Nuer populations who were regarded as supporters of the SPLM, whilst simultaneously seeking to turn Nuer rebel units against Dinka ones. The net result was a considerable amount of low intensity violence over cattle, grazing and water, which was only loosely related to the larger political questions.

In April 1985, a series of street demonstrations in Khartoum led to the overthrow of Nimeiri and the installation of a Transitional Military Council which signalled its intention of returning the country to civilian rule. Although the new leadership was reluctant to repeal the September Laws, there were some indications that peace negotiations would resume. In March 1986, the SPLM entered talks with a delegation made up of representatives of northern parties, with the exception of the DUP and the National Islamic Front (as the Muslim Brothers were now calling themselves). The Koka Dam Declaration expressed support for the repeal of the September Laws and proposed a constitutional convention to resolve all the substantive points which divided Sudanese opinion. However, in the elections which ensued Sadiq al-Mahdi returned to power at the head of an Umma/DUP coalition, and pointedly distanced himself from the reforms. Indeed, he proceeded to resurrect an Islamist agenda, thereby making a continuation of the war a virtual certainty. At this point, even southern parliamentarians began to enter into secret negotiations with Garang. In the years which followed, the SPLA chalked up significant victories against government forces and to some extent succeeded in winning over and disabling the ethnic militias. Furthermore, 'non-Arab' minorities across the North began to join the banner of rebellion. For example, the Nuba, many of whom had been converted to Islam, started to join the SPLA around 1986, driven into its arms by government repression.[29]

The realisation that the war was not being won led to increasing dissension in Khartoum. In 1988, the DUP leadership reopened negotiations with Garang in which the Koka Dam proposals were reactivated alongside a proposal to suspend Shari'a law. When Sadiq al-Mahdi and the Umma party failed to play ball, the DUP withdrew from the coalition, to be replaced by the NIF. However, the army impressed upon Sadiq the need to find a negotiated settlement, and he was forced to restore his alliance with the DUP, while the NIF returned to opposition. Just as it seemed that a peace package might be in the offing, Sadiq was overthrown in another military coup on 1 July 1989. The incoming junta was headed by Colonel Umar al-Bashir and was made up of middle-ranking officers. Although Turabi was briefly detained, it quickly became apparent that the NIF was to be an active partner in the Revolutionary Council of National Salvation (RCC-NS). Indeed, many came to suspect that the coup had been a plot hatched by the NIF which had never managed to win enough votes to impose its own stamp on government.[30] Certainly, the new regime adopted a more virulently Islamist line as Turabi held sway, rendering an agreement with the SPLM highly unlikely.

This narrative of events hopefully demonstrates the futility of attempting to explain Sudanese politics purely in terms of a North–South/Christian–Muslim divide. In reality, there was constant jockeying for position between northern politicians, who were apt to reverse their stances on the national question if they thought they might gain some short-term political advantage. Equally, there was a long history of tensions within southern politics in which alleged Dinka domination (the latter making up a third of all southerners) became a recurrent theme. The almost unlimited scope for schism in both the North and the South made for a bewildering permutation of alliances, in which natural enemies occasionally joined forces. Because these alliances were inherently unstable, their potential for bringing about a permanent settlement was limited. Meanwhile, as the war trundled on and the military advantage passed back and forth, southern civilians found themselves on the receiving end of attacks from all sides. Government forces and its ethnic militias killed civilians, appropriated their cattle and drove them from the land. A number of human rights associations and observers of Sudanese affairs have also drawn attention to the manner in which displaced people were forced to labour on commercial farms. Indeed, many maintain that there has been a resurgence of slavery.[31] Although the SPLM/SPLA purported to represent the interests of the victims, it was also known to have attacked civilian populations. Importantly, the SPLA failed to establish the strong local structures of support which characterised many of the more successful guerrilla movements in Africa. In areas where its support-base was fragile, most notably in non-Dinka districts, the SPLA itself looked like an army of occupation – more or less as the Kriger model would predict. In the areas where it was politically well-established, it tended to work through chiefs rather than engaging in the social engineering attempted by other guerrilla movements. Moreover, the SPLA behaved like the northern government when it used refugees as bait with which to parlay for emergency food relief which a number of agencies shipped to the country under Operation Lifeline Sudan, in order to combat the perennial threat of famine.[32] Finally, the SPLA stood accused of recruiting child soldiers in the vast refugee camps which sprang up inside and outside the borders of the country.

These points are illustrated perfectly by the passage of events in the decade after 1990. By this point, the lack of internal democracy within the SPLM/SPLA led to growing dissatisfaction on the part of some commanders. Their decision to move against Garang in August 1991 was supported by the Sudanese government which had a vested interest in dividing southern ranks. The dissident faction failed to gain the support of the majority of SPLA units, leading to a permanent rift between what became known as SPLA-Mainstream and SPLA-United, the latter being led by Riek Machar. The breakaway faction began to receive direct assistance from the Khartoum government, despite insisting that it was still fighting for outright secession. It also threatened to turn the dispute into a Nuer-vs-Dinka issue. Meanwhile, the growing influence of Turabi in the Khartoum government led to the increasing alienation of the other civilian factions who rallied under the umbrella of the National Democratic Alliance (NDA). The Umma Party retreated from the position that Islamic law was non-negotiable and, with Eritrean mediation, negotiated directly with Garang, who had recovered from his initial setbacks, in 1994. The NDA even began to launch a guerrilla insurgency of its own.

The radical Islamic posturing of Turabi began to present problems for the Sudanese government as the United States found a new international enemy to replace the Soviet Union in the shape of 'Muslim fundamentalism'. The public defence of Iraq and the manner in which Osama bin Laden was permitted to set up commercial farms and military training camps in the Sudan began to attract critical attention, whereas the regime had previously benefited from decidedly uncritical American support. An ensuing power struggle at the centre was resolved when Bashir removed Turabi from the government in 2000 and brought Sadiq al-Mahdi back from exile (yet again) and into government. While the new ruling coalition remained committed to military solutions, Turabi bizarrely turned round to negotiate with Garang. By 2002, this unnatural alliance had collapsed, while breakaway factions of the SPLA had rejoined that organisation.

In the latter months of 2003, the chances of the war being brought to an end suddenly improved as Garang entered into negotiations with the Khartoum regime. Nevertheless, the fundamental problem remained that all the main northern parties continued to adhere to the position that Muslims were the majority and therefore should have the right to live in an Islamic state – despite their occasional willingness to dilute this stance in negotiations with the SPLM/SPLA. On the other side, the SPLA was prepared to accept the continuation of the Sudan, but wanted a loose federal arrangement in which southern rights would be guaranteed. The only realistic compromise would have been to allow the regions to decide whether or not they would accept Shari'a law. But apart from the fact that this was unacceptable to many Islamists, it created the same dilemma as in Nigeria over what would happen to non-Muslims living in the North. The alternative scenario in which the Southern Sudan was allowed to secede seemed less likely than ever at the start of the new millennium because of the growing importance of oil to the Sudanese economy. As in Nigeria, northern interests simply could not contemplate the loss of the revenue. While the Khartoum regime ethnically cleansed the indigenous peoples of the

oil-producing areas, by means of Arab militias, Canadian and Swedish companies dutifully paid substantial royalties into government coffers. Finally, it is
important to recognise the role of neighbouring states in either aiding or
narrowing the scope for guerrilla activity. The Derg gave the SPLA free rein to
operate inside Ethiopia in return for fighting against the Gambela People's
Liberation Front and the Oromo Liberation Front (OLF). Although the fall of
Mengistu presented the SPLA with some headaches to start with, the Islamist
agenda of the Bashir regime ensured that relations with both Ethiopia and
Eritrea would deteriorate. Equally, the Museveni regime sided with the SPLA,
in defence of the 'black Christian' minority, while the Sudanese offered support
to the Lord's Resistance Army. Because the Eritrean, Ethiopian and Ugandan
governments have all been active players in the larger game, any realistic peace
deal would need to embody a regional dimension.

The Angolan civil war was another one which trundled on despite several
mediation efforts and ceasefire agreements. Although the ending of the Cold
War and the demise of the apartheid regime removed the most important international parties to the conflict, Zaire continued to be a factor in the equation
because arms and fuel were routed through that country despite international
sanctions which aimed at bringing UNITA to the negotiating table. In Chapter 7,
we left Angola at the point in late 1994 when the Lusaka peace accord was
signed. Its prospects looked unpromising right from the start, given that Jonas
Savimbi refused to leave his rural base and deputed one of his subordinates to
attend the signing ceremony. Although UNITA was supposed to demobilise,
the next four years witnessed very little progress on that front. President José
Eduardo Dos Santos attempted to weaken Savimbi in 1997 by forming a government of national unity in which UNITA politicians were offered Ministerial
positions while their parliamentarians were persuaded to take their seats in
Luanda. These UNITA politicians, who came to enjoy the perks and privileges,
were understandably reluctant to restart the fighting and some broke away in
1998. As Savimbi himself prepared for a resumption of hostilities, the MPLA
government decided to strike first. The fighting which ensued was savage, even
by Angolan standards. UNITA blockaded a number of cities, and prevented
relief aid from getting through. But after an initial stutter, the military advantage swung decisively towards the government forces in 1999. Many UNITA
troops deserted or surrendered, while Savimbi was forced to fall back upon
hit-and-run tactics with which he began his chequered career. Within UNITA,
there were signs of war-weariness and when Savimbi was killed in an engagement in February 2002, the bulkiest obstacle to peace was suddenly removed.
By April, the UNITA leadership had signed a temporary ceasefire and in August
a peace was formally declared which was underwritten by the UN. As part of an
effort to make the agreement stick, some 5000 UNITA troops were integrated
into the Angolan armed forces, and another general amnesty was declared.
This concluded a war which had led to untold death and destruction, and
had displaced 1.4 millions (or just over 10 per cent of the population) from
their homes as of June 1999.[33] That left only the separatist insurgency
led by the Front for the Liberation of the Cabinda Enclave (FLEC) to be
resolved.

Commentators who have written about the later phases of the conflict have tended to confirm the observation that sustained warfare creates its own adepts and beneficiaries – the 'war-boys' – as well as its own internal dynamic. The Angolan war was originally underpinned by a mixture of ideological and ethnic differences, but over the decades the lines of division became progressively blurred. When the MPLA jettisoned Marxism-Leninism in 1990, and adopted economic liberalisation as state policy, it ceased to construe the world in a fundamentally different manner to UNITA. Indeed an ascetic strain gave way to what Hodges calls 'a rogue form of capitalism in which a handful of prominent families, linked politically to the regime … exploited opportunities for self-enrichment.'[34] Leading the way was Dos Santos who concentrated decision-making on the president's office and dispensed vast amounts of patronage.[35] As in other African countries, privatisation provided the perfect cover for MPLA politicians to enrich themselves. If Savimbi had ever come to power, it is doubtful that he would have behaved any differently, especially in view of his highly personalist style of leadership. Moreover, as the MPLA and UNITA used increasingly sophisticated weaponry to prosecute their feud, they ceased to view ordinary Angolans as anything other than cannon fodder and sources of food and manual labour – or, at worst, as enemies who needed to be eliminated. The international watchdog, Human Rights Watch, was almost equally damning of both sides, accusing them of engagement in forced movements, rapes, beatings and extra-judicial killings against civilian populations – crimes which are likely to remain unpunished because no provision was made in the final peace agreement for something like a Truth Commission.[36]

While protracted warfare tended to devalue human life, it also had to be funded. But what began as a means to an end tended to become an end in itself. The Angolan government was extremely fortunate in that it possessed vast oil resources, which were not easily targeted by UNITA because of their offshore location. As Angola became the continent's second largest oil-producer, a culture of corruption took hold at the highest levels. In many ways, continuation of the war served a convenient purpose because the diversion of oil revenues into special accounts could be justified as a necessary expedient for purchasing arms and the like. On the other side, the loss of external patrons in the early-1990s led UNITA to concentrate on control of the diamond fields, where civilians were often compelled to work. The diamonds were smuggled out via Kinshasa, Mbuji-Mayi, Brazzaville and Pointe Noire (Congo-Brazzaville), before ending up on the Antwerp market. The proceeds were then used to purchase weapons. After the UN had placed a ban on the sale of Angolan diamonds which did not have a government certificate of origin, many of the diamonds were sold to licensed buyers on the government side.[37] A further indication of the corrosive impact of the war economy is that government soldiers themselves trafficked in UNITA's diamonds in return for smuggling weapons to their supposed adversaries. The proceeds were used to build or purchase houses in Luanda which could be rented out to diplomats, oil workers and aid agencies at considerable profit.[38]

At the end of 2003, the future remained uncertain. It was by no means clear that the peace would hold or that Angola would make the transition away from a war economy. Moreover, the experience of Nigeria points to the ways in which the oil bonanza could heighten social inequalities and undermine the rural econ-omy. As a result of the war, agricultural production and marketing collapsed, while displaced populations congregated in the cities where half of the popula-tion now lives. Although some may return to the countryside, there is strong likelihood that urbanisation will turn out to be a permanent consequence of war. If the peace holds, thousands of demobilised soldiers are likely to join the ranks of the urban unemployed. On the other hand, it is questionable whether the MPLA, which never paid very much attention to the rural areas, will feel inclined to tilt the terms of trade in favour of rural producers. The social consequences are likely to be immiseration in the urban and rural areas alike. At the end of 1990s, the collapse of the health and educational systems co-existed with a boom in private facilities catering to those who had the means to pay. The elite sent their children overseas on state scholarships, which consumed as much as 18 per cent of educational expenditure in 1996, while 7 per cent of health expenditure was consumed by medical treatment abroad.[39] The prospects of a very wealthy urban elite, seeking to insulate itself from the grievances of a mass of urban poor and unmindful of poverty in the rural areas, were very real in 2003.

In the 1990s, Chad appeared to map out a different course. After almost con-stant warfare since 1965, the overthrow of Hissein Habré by Idris Déby in 1990 was followed by the transition to constitutional rule six year later. The slow process of democratisation was also accompanied by a resurgence of civil society along the lines identified in Chapter 9. The problem was that Déby's electoral vic-tory was not accepted as legitimate by all of his opponents or, for that matter, by most foreign observers. To complicate matters, southern feelings of domination and exclusion were accentuated as pastoralists from the drought-prone north were permitted to push southwards and as plans were set in motion to construct a pipeline to export oil from the Doba region via Cameroun.[40] Rebels began to operate across the South, and the banner of revolt soon began to be raised in parts of the North as well. Apart from movements which had a more or less political objective, much of the country was still subject to banditry and to warlordism for its own sake. In 2001, Déby was elected for a second term under circumstances which were no less controversial. The slide back towards chaos did, however, appear to have been arrested in 2002 when Déby signed a peace agreement with the northern-based Movement for Democracy and Justice in Chad (MDJT). This was followed up by a ceasefire agreement with the National Resistance Army in the East. Be that as it may, the highly factional and regionalised character of Chadian politics in this vast country means that the consensus is likely to be a highly fragile one. If fresh rebel movements spring up, and receive the support of the Libyan and Sudanese regimes (as in the past) there is every chance that war-fare will resume, given the endemic weakness of the central administration. As with the Great Lakes region, the outcomes in each country in this part of the Sahel are bound to have knock-on effect on the rest of the sub-region.

10.3 The contagion of violence: ethnicity and warlordism

Having considered the travails of the political unions, and some long-running civil wars, we turn now to consider a new manifestation of political disorder during the 1980s and 1990s. Many of the other conflicts had a regional dimension as guerrilla armies operated out of safe havens in neighbouring countries, and as refugees spilled in their tens of thousands across international borders. What was distinctive about the new conflicts was three things: first of all, they were characterised by a contagion effect as specific patterns of violence reproduced themselves beyond the original epicentres; secondly, these conflicts were often overtly genocidal, in which civilian populations became the explicit target as well as being active participants; and finally, many of these vicious wars (fought in a post-Cold War environment) did not turn on differences of ideology and religion, but on the struggle for material resources, especially mineral wealth. It is also worth adding that while foreign actors had taken an active interest in many of the older civil wars, the so-called 'international community' was forced to think long and hard about its level of commitment to certain of its universal values: most notably a common humanity which might over-ride traditional respect for state sovereignty. In the process, the cardinal OAU principle that African member states should not interfere in the internal affairs of fellow members went by the board, for better or worse. We begin this account with an analysis of the Great Lakes crisis, before shifting the focus to West Africa.

10.3.1 *From the Great Lakes to the Congo*

We begin with an account of the genocide in the small state of Rwanda, but tellingly our story unfolds in neighbouring Uganda. After the dramatic events of 1959, which came to glorified by the winning side as a 'revolution', much of the Tutsi population had fled to neighbouring countries, where they were joined by a fresh wave of refugees in 1972–73. The greatest number went to the twin-state of Burundi, where the Tutsi power structure (if not the monarchy) remained very much in place, but tens of thousands also sought refuge in Uganda, Tanzania and Zaire. By 1990, there were anywhere between 400,000 and 700,000 refugees, consisting of the original escapees and their children born in these countries.[41] These were not the first Rwandans to grow up elsewhere given that during colonial times Uganda became a magnet for people seeking work and farming land. The refugee communities tended to think of themselves as victims who had escaped death at the expense of their patrimony and many of them dreamed of eventually returning home – even if, in the case of second generation refugees they had never actually been to Rwanda. The refugees who believed that they had found safety in Uganda were inevitably caught up in the violence of the Amin years and the subsequent brutality associated with the second term of Milton Obote. When the latter targeted opponents of the UPC (Uganda People's Congress), he included the Rwandans whose Catholicism associated them with the Democratic Party (DP) tradition. Due to the persecution of the Rwandan exiles, many of them rallied to the rebellion launched by Yoweri Museveni in 1981. By the time the National Resistance Army (NRA) entered Kampala in 1986, around 3000 of the 14,000 fighters were actually of Rwandan origin.[42] Their profile was heightened by the fact that the commander-in-chief and Minister of Defence in the new administration,

Major-General Fred Rwigyema, was himself of Rwandan origin. The Rwandan presence in Museveni's army soon became a source of some controversy in Uganda, as critics began to insinuate that the President himself was a closet Rwandan who was turning the country over to foreigners.[43] Rwigyema became the most prominent casualty of a policy of nativism which Museveni had been forced to implement by 1989. As the refugees began to feel targeted once more, the idea of returning to Rwanda became ever more attractive.

Rwanda had been under military rule since July 1973 when Juvénal Habyarimana overthrew the presidency of Grégoire Kayibanda. In an even-handed account of his tenure, Gérard Prunier observes that while Habyarimana subscribed to the view that the 1959 revolution had been justified, and he continued to insist on ethnic quotas for higher education, he did not actively persecute Tutsis, a number of whom prospered in business. Mamdani goes further and credits Habyarimana with having shifted the emphasis from the colonially-derived discourse of racial difference – which cast the Tutsis as Hamitic aliens – to that of ethnicity in which they were construed as a minority, but Rwandan all the same.[44] In fact, Habyarimana spent more time worrying about intra-Hutu rivalries in a country where region and clan were important lines of cleavage.[45] The internal power struggles became increasingly bloody as competing cliques surrounding the ruler and his wife – one in a long line of fearsome African first ladies which included Maryam Abacha and Nana Konadu Rawlings – competed for diminishing spoils at the centre. In 1990, when François Mitterrand momentarily embraced the ideal of constitutional democracy for Africans, Habyarimana came under pressure to accept a greater measure of political pluralism. In 1974, Habyarimana had established the sole legal party, the National Revolutionary Movement for Development (MRND). The declaration of multipartyism therefore presented opponents of the regime with the opportunity to break cover. Parties were quickly formed and a series of demonstrations was organised to pressure the government to agree to the holding of a national conference and/or elections. The former PARMEHUTU party reconstituted itself as the Rwandan Democratic Movement (MDR), espousing a somewhat attenuated Hutu chauvinism. However, the latter was outdone by the overtly racist Coalition for the Defence of the Republic (CDR), while other parties such as the Social Democratic Party (PDS) articulated a more liberal vision. As in other African countries at the time, there was a proliferation of private newspapers which revelled in the exercise of their editorial independence. Even the Catholic Church, which had shied away from expressing criticism of government, became more assertive.[46]

The positions and popular standing of these various parties was profoundly affected by the actions of the Tutsi refugees. In 1987, the Rwandan Patriotic Front (RPF) had been formed in Uganda and began to plan an invasion of Rwanda, believing that the Habyarimana regime was in a greatly weakened position. Officers serving in the Ugandan army orchestrated a mass desertion of troops with as much equipment as they could carry with them, and while Museveni probably had some inkling that something was afoot, he was taken by surprise when 4000 soldiers crossed the Rwandan border at the end of September 1990. The launching of the war a couple of days later was anything but glorious. Rwigyema was killed, the RPF was soon routed and the remnants of the invasion force was forced to ask Museveni for safe passage back to Uganda. Major Paul Kagame then set about trying to rebuild the RPF in the Virunga mountains bordering Uganda. To make matters worse, Mitterrand forgot whatever doubts he might have entertained about the democratic credentials of Habyarimana by flying in troops. The latter played a crucial support role in subsequent fighting against the RPF, while the French shipped arms to the government side. The war had a catalytic effect on the unfolding political debate inside Rwanda, where the extremist tendency warned Hutus that the RPF wanted to deprive them of their birthright. The accusation that Habyarimana was too soft became easier to make once he decided that the revitalised RPF could not be defeated and entered into negotiations. Much that has been written about the subsequent genocide is somewhat teleological, in the sense that one is presented with an inexorable slide towards disaster. In reality, nothing made the genocide inevitable. The first planned massacres in the countryside and high-profile political assassinations in Kigali were warning signs, but there seemed to be every chance that 'democratisation' would take root as in some other Francophone countries.

In Kigali, Habyarimana did not yield to demands for a national conference or proceed with national elections. Instead, he brought opposition parties into a coalition government, thereby encouraging a jockeying for position at the centre. Quite possibly, he was modelling himself on the successful tactics of Mobutu next door. At precisely the same moment, the incoming government began negotiating a peace deal with the RPF at Arusha. The problem was that not all parties within the coalition wanted an agreement. The intransigent wing of the MRNDD (the party having added 'Democracy' to its title) and the CDR were determined that the negotiations should fail and began to ratchet up violence against Tutsis and moderate Hutus in an attempt to scupper them. The secret arming of party militias seems to have begun in the latter part of 1992, enjoying the support of sections of the army and the Presidential Guard. Indeed, Prunier suggests that the first vague plan for the carrying out of a genocide dates from this period.[47]

In January 1993, an agreement on the formation of a Broad-Based Transitional Government was nevertheless signed with the RPF. At once, militiamen went on a killing spree in the North-west, leading the RPF to resume the fighting. In February, the RPF pushed to within 30 kilometres at the capital, but stopped short for fear of drawing the French into open combat. This turn of events had dramatic consequences, and precisely those which the extremists had banked upon. On the one hand, it weakened the liberals who began to fret about what would happen to Hutus if the RPF should be victorious. On the other hand, the MRNDD and most of the opposition parties began to splinter, as so-called 'Hutu Power' factions came into the open, thereby creating a still more chaotic political situation. Habyarimana attempted to play all sides off against each other, in the hope of retaining his supremacy. Eventually, he decided to throw his lot in with the negotiators and on 4 August 1993 a fresh peace deal was signed with the RPF. This was more generous to the RPF than the first agreement had been. The establishment of a broad-based government was to follow, alongside the appointment of a transitional assembly and the integration of RPF fighters into the Rwandan army on the basis of a quota of 40 per cent of the troops and 50 per cent of the officer corps. Moreover, the Rwandan refugees were to be assisted to return to the country which they had been forced to leave decades before. To the 'Power' tendency, this amounted to a reversal of the 1959 Revolution.

Not surprisingly, there were many within the Rwandan army and the administration who looked with trepidation on the return of large numbers of Tutsis. Equally, peasants worried that returning refugees would demand the return of land and other properties. These genuine fears played into the hands of the extremists who hoped to drive the Hutu population into an ethnic laager. The gift which fell into their laps in September 1993 could not have been anticipated. In neighbouring Burundi, as we will shortly see in more detail, a separate democratisation exercise had led to free elections in June and the installation of the first Hutu President, Melchior Ndadaye. This seemed to present a model for Rwanda to emulate. However, on 21 October the President was kidnapped and executed by Tutsi soldiers, provoking wholesale bloodletting and a flight of some 200,000 Hutu refugees across the border into Rwanda. Even moderate Hutus in Rwanda began to worry about whether allowing the RPF back into the country would not be quite literally a fatal mistake. Predictably, the extremists put it about that the assassination demonstrated the sheer impossibility of reconciliation with murderous Tutsis. The result was that the implementation of the Arusha agreement stalled, the militias continued to arm themselves and the fragmentation of the political parties accelerated. Habyarimana also had a vested interest in stalling implementation of the Arusha agreement. In April 1994, he was invited to Dar es Salaam to meet with the Presidents of neighbouring states who chastised him for being an obstacle to the peace process. On the way home, the new President of Burundi, Cyprian Ntaryamira, hitched a ride on Habyarimana's plane. As it came in to land at Kigali on 6 April, the plane was hit by a missile, killing the Presidents of both countries.

While the assassination of the Burundian President could not have been foreseen, the elimination of Habyarimana was clearly calculated. Although the jury is still out on who might have carried out the assassination, the most likely suspects lay close to the dead President. The fact that well orchestrated killings began almost immediately within Kigali suggests that elements in the Presidential Guard and on the 'Power' end of the political spectrum found the assassination expedient: it removed someone whose commitment to the Hutu cause was vacillating and it could be used to justify a pogrom in his name. Significantly, the first victims of the killings in the capital included many who were regarded as being on the accommodationist wing of Rwandan politics – the *ibyitso* or 'accomplices'. This included the Prime Minister, Madame Agathe Uwilingiyimana, and most of the leadership of the PSD. With minimal delay, the killings spread to the countryside, and with a precision which suggested that the exercise had been carefully planned. Hit-lists had been rumoured to exist for some time and these were now used to track down perceived Hutu collaborators and anyone who happened to be Tutsi. The executions were typically carried out through the offices of the local administration and were physically carried out through the *Interahamwe* militias, but with the active participation of Hutu peasants who knew who the local Tutsis were. Throughout, the killers were egged on by the newspaper, *Kangura*, and the radio station, Radio Télévision Libre des Milles Collines (RTLMC) – confirmation that the liberalisation of the media could also be turned to less savoury ends.[48]

A recurring question in the vast literature on the Rwandan genocide was why so many ordinary peasants actively participated.[49] Many clearly did so for fear of being singled out as collaborators themselves, while many others willingly killed Tutsis, apparently believing that they were engaged in a zero-sum struggle for survival in which they had to kill or be killed. The argument that Rwandan peasants were used to obeying orders from above is rather less convincing. The active involvement of the Hutu peasantry does not mean, of course, that complicity was total. Many individuals actively helped their Tutsi neighbours by offering them hiding places and lending them their own identity documents at a time when such papers (which clearly stated whether the bearer was Hutu or Tutsi) literally became a death warrant. Although individual clergymen sought to protect Tutsis who sought refuge, the Catholic Church and the Protestant churches failed to speak out publicly, and the clergy were often counted amongst the killers – as indeed were doctors and teachers who liquidated their patients and pupils. Even human rights activists were implicated. Mamdani suggests that the Hutu middle class, which had emerged after the 1959 Revolution, actually had the most to lose from the Tutsi return, and therefore played a leading part in the genocide at every level.[50] This underlines the point that the killing was not the work of ignorant peasants who did not know better, but rather a calculated response on the part of highly educated individuals. As many commentators have observed, there were few international actors who emerged with clean hands either. The UNAMIR (United Nations Assistance Mission to Rwanda) soldiers were implicated in the sense that they literally watched people being killed because their rules of engagement did not entitle them to intervene. Moreover, as news of the killings spread, the UN dithered, to the evident exasperation of the Secretary-General, Boutros Boutros-Ghali.

On 8 April, the RPF restarted its war and advanced on the capital, from which the provisional government was forced to flee. As the government forces retreated in disarray, the militias endeavoured to kill as many Tutsis as they could before they were over-run. Given that the RPF was advancing from the North, the worst atrocities were carried out in the South and central regions which also happened to be those where there was the longest history of Hutsi-Tutu intermarriage.[51] The leaders who orchestrated the killings, including the prefects and burgomasters, then escaped across the borders as refugees, joining the flood of Hutu peasants fearing the anticipated RPF retribution. The RPF itself, whose numbers were swelled by many Tutsi recruits, sometimes carried out retributive killings of their own, but most commentators agree that the rebels avoided replicating government excesses and concentrated on sealing their military victory. The French deliberately muddied the waters by claiming that there was no state-sponsored genocide afoot, but merely a savage war in which both sides targeted civilians. The French attitude sprang in part from a perception that the RPF was the cat's paw of the Museveni regime in Uganda. Prunier lays particular emphasis upon a deep-seated paranoia about 'Anglo-Saxons' – for which read British and American – plotting against the French position in Africa, in which Museveni was viewed as a proxy.[52] When the French government launched Operation Turquoise in June, and carved out a so-called Safe Humanitarian Zone in the South, its avowed object was to protect innocent civilians. The RPF was understandably suspicious, as many of the perpetrators fled to the French zone, before making their way across the border to Zaire. This did not, however, prevent the RPF from taking Kigali and from installing a new government.

The RPF respected the Arusha accords to the extent of composing a legislature and a cabinet along the lines of the original agreement, with the exception that the MRNDD positions in the government went to the RPF, while Kagame was given the position of Vice-President. The President was Pasteur Bizimungu, one of the comparatively few Hutu members of the RPF, while other Hutu politicians like Faustin Twagiramungu of the moderate wing of the MDR became the Prime Minister. The withdrawal of the French after two months brought the entirety of the country under RPF control. The final victory precipitated further large-scale movements of population. While Hutus continued to pour over the border into Zaire, Tutsi exiles from an earlier era moved the other way from Burundi, Uganda and Zaire. Those who had left the country perhaps totalled some 2 million out of a total population of some 7 million, while perhaps some 400,000 travelled in the other direction. Meanwhile, those who had been eliminated in the genocide probably amounted to some 650,000 (Prunier and Chrétien favour a higher figure of 800,000), of whom the vast majority were Tutsis.[53] Although the *génocidaires* had not succeeded in wiping the Tutsis off the population map – given the number living in neighbouring countries – they had performed a pretty thorough job if it is true that Tutsis made up around ten per cent of the resident Rwandan population before the genocide. It is these proportions, as well as the single-mindedness of the perpetrators, which have tended to provoke comparisons with the Nazi holocaust against the Jews.

At this juncture, we pause to consider the passage of events in Burundi which had a dynamic of their own. The most obvious difference is that Burundian Hutus had failed to carry off a 'revolution' of their own. The armed forces and other state institutions remained highly Tutsi in composition which belied the official line that ethnicity was a form of false consciousness instilled by the colonial powers. As has already been seen in Chapter 4, there was a series of pogroms after independence as Hutus attempted to seize power in their own right. In 1972, one such unsuccessful attempt led to some 100,000 Hutus being exterminated in a foretaste of the Rwandan genocide, while many more fled across the borders.[54] After the overthrow of the Micombero regime in 1976, Colonel Jean-Baptiste Bagaza (a relative) mirrored the strategy of Habyarimana as he attempted to take the heat out of ethnicity and build a consensus on the back of sustained economic growth through foreign aid. Bagaza was himself overthrown by Major Pierre Buyoya in 1987, who was yet another

Hima Tutsi from the same *commune* in the South of the country.[55] By this point, militant Hutus had formed their own army, the Party for the Liberation of the Hutu People (PALIPEHUTU) which had (since 1980) been committed to the violent overthrow of the perceived Tutsi dictatorship. In August 1988, the movement launched an attack along the Rwanda border, provoking a vicious counter-response from the government forces which left thousands dead. Confronted by the prospect of a deteriorating security situation, Buyoya attempted to strike a lasting deal with moderate Hutus. In order to create the necessary goodwill, a Hutu Prime Minister was installed and half of the government portfolios were allocated to Hutus. Given that the latter probably made up around 85 per cent of the population, they were still under-represented. The educated elite was still overwhelmingly Tutsi in complexion, which reflected a longstanding policy of covertly screening access to educational institutions.[56] Responding to the nudge given by Mitterand at La Baule in 1990, Buyoya signalled his intention to embrace democracy. Indeed Burundi found itself at the forefront of the continental movement.

Naturally, it was difficult for Buyoya to publicly acknowledge that Hutus had been systematically discriminated against, and killed in their thousands after independence. The National Commission to Study the Question of National Unity fudged the contentious issues and contented itself with blaming the Belgians. To some extent, the Constitutional Commission on the Democratisation of Institutions and Political Life, which issued its report in August 1991, did the same. Nevertheless, it did explicitly raise the vexed question of what democracy might mean in the Burundian context. In February 1991, a Charter on National Unity was subjected to a referendum and was approved by 89 per cent of voters. This then prepared the way for the Constitutional Commission, which entrenched the principle of non-sectarianism and required political parties to subscribe to the Unity Charter. The constitution was then adopted by 97 per cent of voters in March 1992.[57] As in Rwanda, there was a proliferation of political parties seeking to inherit the political kingdom, the most important of which were FRODEBU (Front Pour la Démocratie au Burundi) and UPRONA (Union Pour le Progrès National). Buyoya, standing in the Presidential elections as the UPRONA candidate, evidently believed that his conciliatory stance would win enough Hutu support to grant him victory in the elections. Naturally, he also enjoyed the advantages of incumbency, including control of the patronage machine. His opponent was Melchior Ndadaye of FRODEBU which drew its support from the Hutu majority, but did include some Tutsis in its leadership. At the June 1993 polls, Buyoya came away with a third of the national vote, which suggests that many Hutu did indeed vote for him, but the clear winner on 65 per cent was Ndadaye who was duly installed as the first Hutu President of Burundi. In the legislative polls, FRODEBU similarly walked away with 65 of the 81 electoral seats. The peaceful conduct of these elections, together with Buyoya's acceptance of defeat, led to a sigh of relief within the country and a belief that democracy might just work in this most divided of societies.

However, as we have already seen, this was not to be the case. Tutsi supremacists within the army could not tolerate the presence of a Hutu President and promptly executed Ndadaye, as well as the President and Vice-President of the National Assembly in October 1993. This plunged Burundi into a maelstrom of violence in which Hutus massacred Tutsis in the countryside, while the army struck back against Hutus in general. Anywhere between 50,000 and 100,000 people may have been murdered at this time, around 60 per cent of them Tutsis, while Tanzania was the recipient of 500,000 new refugees.[58] From this point onwards, the central government was faced with a stubborn insurgency in the North, which tended to harden attitudes in the capital. The immediate power vacuum was filled by means of a legislative amendment to the Constitution which made it possible for the National Assembly to choose a successor rather than having to hold a fresh Presidential election. On 5 February, Cyprien Ntaryamira of FRODEBU was duly installed as President with Anetola Kanyenkiko of UPRONA as his Prime Minister. The government was a broad-based one, embracing Hutus and Tutsis of both parties. Unfortunately, everything was thrown into chaos once more when Ntaryamira was killed in the Rwandan plane crash in April 1994. By this point, the internal fragmentation of political parties in Rwanda was also replicating itself in Burundi. Militants within FRODEBU decided that the time for compromise was over and they variously joined Hutu militias or the CNDD (Conseil National Pour la Defense de la Démocratie) which resorted to arms, thereby adding to the PALIPEHUTU insurgency. The cross-fertilisation of Rwandan and Burundian politics is apparent in the influence of RTLMC broadcasts over the border, in which Hutu militiamen were exhorted to exterminate all Tutsis. The difference was that in Burundi, Tutsi militias were able to respond in kind.

In Bujumbura, the remainder of FRODEBU attempted to make a go of power-sharing. The various political parties struck a deal in which offices would be shared out between them. The net effect was in fact to significantly deflate the significance of FRODEBU, which had after all won the 1993 elections. FRODEBU and its allies were allocated 55 per cent of the Ministerial portfolios, while UPRONA and its allies received the rest.[59] By 1996, twenty FRODEBU parliamentarians had disappeared or were in exile, while its share of cabinet positions shrank still further.[60] On the other hand, UPRONA itself began to dissolve into moderate and extremist factions. As the political machinations unfolded at the centre, violence intensified both in the capital and in the countryside. By mid-1986, no fewer than eleven out of 15 provinces were caught up in what had escalated into a full-scale civil war.[61] The position of beleaguered Hutu President Ntibantuganya became untenable as well as unsafe, and in July he sought refuge at the American Embassy in Bujumbura. This provided the excuse for Buyoya to seize power for a second time, signalling the closure of democratic opening which had appeared at the start of the decade.

By this point, the Rwandan genocide was a matter of historical record and with Ntibantuganya warning that a repeat performance was imminent, the OAU felt impelled to act. The former President of Tanzania, Julius Nyerere, assumed personal responsibility for seeking to bring the warring sides to the negotiating table. This was evidently in the best interests of Tanzania because of the number of Burundians who had spilled over the border. The neighbouring states imposed economic sanctions on Burundi, which was economically paralysed by the political instability, demanding the legalisation of political parties, the restitution of the National Assembly and the commencement of negotiations without preconditions. Although Buyoya conceded the first two, bringing FRODEBU back into government, the third proved much more intractable. Indeed there was an intensification of fighting over the course of 1997, and in the midst of an escalating food crisis sanctions were lifted the following year. Nyerere nevertheless persisted with trying to bring about a negotiated settlement – his final contribution to the politics of this part of the continent – and after his death Nelson Mandela took up the baton. In 2000, the government signed a peace agreement with Tutsi militants, but the Hutu rebel movements merely intensified the fighting which directly impinged on the capital. The complicating factor was that Hutu rebels were operating out of the East of the former Zaire where another war had erupted. Eventually, an agreement was signed with the main Hutu rebel group in December 2002, but fighting nevertheless continued into 2003. As long as other rebels remained outside the negotiating process, there seemed little likelihood that the Burundian crisis would be resolved. Equally, the prospects for a solution depended upon events elsewhere in the Great Lakes region, given the extent to which the Hutu-Tutsi conflict had been regionalised. This brings us to a more detailed discussion of a fresh breakdown in Zaire which had experienced more than its fair share of civil war after independence.

In Chapter 9, we showed how Mobutu was thrown off balance at the start of the decade, but had recaptured much of the initiative by 1993. The Rwandan genocide presented the Zairean leader with the perfect opportunity to regain some of the attention which had once been heaped upon him in Western capitals, despite an atrocious record spanning three decades. As Hutu refugees poured across the border into eastern Zaire, the United Nations High Commission for Refugees (UNHCR) and other relief agencies needed the consent of Mobutu to deal with the humanitarian crisis. At the same time, the Americans and the French once more began to treat Mobutu as if he was an important player in the game. The stakes were, however, higher than they had ever been. The Hutu refugees arrived under the leaders who had masterminded the genocide and for whom the French had provided a safe exit. These political leaders established effective control over the refugee camps, which placed the relief agencies in the awkward position of having to work through people they knew were guilty of mass killings. Before leaving Kigali, they had emptied the banks of all their foreign exchange, which meant that they also commanded considerable economic resources. The *génocidaires* had no intention of sitting tight in Zaire and they were equally determined that the refugees should not return to Rwanda while the RPF was in power. What they attempted to do, therefore, was to carve out their own territory within Zaire, with the connivance of Mobutu who was not particularly sensitive to issues of sovereignty when so much of his country was only loosely administered. The Former Government of Rwanda (FGOR) therefore became a political reality within the borders of Zaire. The Mobutu regime sold the FGOR arms, some of which had previously seized by the French at the border and turned over to the Zairean authorities.

The new army which the FGOR recruited came to number some 50,000 troops.[62]

The FGOR took over where it had left off by mounting attacks within Rwanda and targeting Tutsi populations in Zaire. There was a substantial population of peoples of Rwandan and Burundian origin who were already living in North and South Kivu. Some had been there since the nineteenth century and had been divided from their kinsmen by the colonial borders. Others had been invited in by the Belgians as a captive source of labour in the interwar period, and had been allowed to form their own chieftaincies, while a third group consisted of refugees from Rwanda and Burundi. In 1972, the Mobutu regime had drawn a line by offering those refugees who had come between 1959 and 1963 full citizenship. This heightened the concerns of those communities which construed themselves as the indigenous peoples of the Kivus, such as the Nande and Hunde, who insisted that all the Banyarwanda and Barundi were aliens. In 1981, the government had rendered the position of the Banyarwanda highly insecure by insisting that only those who could demonstrate that their forebears had lived in Zaire prior to the colonial partition could claim citizenship. This placed Hutus and Tutsis in the same predicament because to be labelled a 'stranger' meant in effect the loss of inherent rights to land.[63] The manner in which the Hutus and Tutsis responded to their common plight, in opposition to the 'indigenes', offers a textbook example of the contextual nature of ethnicity. However, the alliance of Hutus and Tutsis came under stress whenever the political temperature rose in Rwanda and Burundi.

Moreover, the internal politics of Zaire also created after-shocks within the two Kivus. In 1992, the Sovereign National Conference upheld the 1981 Citizenship Law which placated the Nande and Hunde representatives, but condemned most Hutus and Tutsis to the status of foreigners. The Hutu response was to claim the mantle of indigeneity (disputed, of course, by the 'autochthons') whilst deflecting the charge of being alien on to the Tutsis.[64] The latter meanwhile attempted to downplay their Rwandan and Burundian origins by consciously identifying themselves as Banyamulenge. The latter was originally a more restricted term adopted by Burundian Tutsis in South Kivu who associated themselves with the land around the Mulenge hills rather than with their homelands. By 1993, the lines of cleavage were unstable, as vulnerable Tutsis variously sided with the 'autochthons' against the Hutus or with the Hutus against the 'autochthons'. When the FGOR arrived in Zaire, it began attacking Tutsis in the two Kivus as well as the Hunde. The net result was that the Tutsis were driven out of North Kivu where they had formed the numerical majority.[65] Tens of thousands of fled into Rwanda, where they were initially welcomed by the government, but were later classified as refugees and confined to refugee camps. In 1996, the FGOR and the Zairean army extended its 'ethnic cleansing' into South Kivu, but here the Tutsis found powerful patrons who helped them to fight back.

Laurent-Desiré Kabila had been involved in the Stanleyville regime's resistance to the Kinshasa regime in 1963–64 and had subsequently lived a shadowy existence in the Fizi enclave where he made money trading in gold. Despite setting himself up as the nemesis of Mobutu, he had also apparently had dealings with the Zairean leader, at one point liaising with the SPLA on his behalf.[66] As the FGOR allied itself with the Zairean army, Kabila's own rebel group began to establish links with the Banyamulenge and to receive material support from the RPF government in Rwanda. In October 1996, the RPF invaded Kivu and attacked the refugee camps which it accused of harbouring the perpetrators of genocide. Two months later, the Alliance of Democratic Forces for the Liberation of Congo/Zaire (AFDL) was formed out of four distinct rebel groups, including that of Kabila. The link between these developments is a source of some controversy. As far as Nzongola-Ntalaja is concerned, the Rwandan government had decided to take over eastern Zaire and sponsored the AFDL as a means of weakening its enemies.[67] On this view, Kabila was essentially the creature of the Rwandans. On the other hand, Reed regards the AFDL rebellion as having roots in southern and eastern Zaire, with the Rwandans merely providing 'critical, if not decisive, support to the AFDL'.[68] Nzongola-Ntalaja also asserts that the Rwandans deliberately targeted the ordinary Hutu population of eastern Zaire, in effect carrying out their own mini-genocide, whereas Mamdani blames the militias who had taken up arms against the Interahamwe and the Zairean government.[69] What is clear is that the AFDL made rapid strides, with both moral and material support from the Rwandan authorities. The AFDL quickly captured Bukavu and Uvira in South Kivu and Uvire and Goma in North Kivu, drawing on the support of militiamen from the 'autochthons' (the Mai-Mai), and the Banyamulenge. Interestingly, the AFDL was also bolstered by seasoned Angolan fighters whose origins lay within the old Katanga secessionist movement and who had subsequently gone over to the MPLA.[70] While most ordinary Hutu refugees made their way back to Rwanda, the FGOR retreated deeper into Zaire.

Kabila, who rapidly emerged as the dominating influence within the AFDL made it clear that he would stop at nothing short of the overthrow of Mobutu himself. As the Zairean government forces folded, the AFDL advance was faster than anyone could have imagined. By March, Kisangani had fallen, followed in quick succession by Mbuji-Mayi and then Lubumbashi. On 17 May 1997, a terminally-ill Mobutu fled the country, barely escaping being lynched by his own soldiers, and the AFDL marched into Kinshasa.[71] At this point, it appeared that two large birds had been killed with one stone: the *génocidaires* had been routed in the East and Mobutu had finally been consigned to history once and for all. The country was renamed the Democratic Republic of Congo (DRC), while the flag reverted to the one which had been run up the pole at independence.[72] Unfortunately, the euphoria which accompanied the AFDL victory proved all too temporary. Kabila, who ruthlessly eliminated his principal rivals within the AFDL, demonstrated a lack of sensitivity towards the political aspirations of his fellow citizens. He saw himself as the conqueror, to whom the spoils were (over)due. In Kinshasa, the population rejoiced at Mobutu's demise and hailed Kabila, but the opposition politicians were adamant that some upstart from the 'bush' should not steal a political victory which they had been working towards for years. They expected Kabila to form a broad-based government without delay. Instead, he suspended all political institutions, including the Sovereign

National Conference and conferred all legislative and executive power on himself. When it came to the distribution of Ministerial positions, the AFDL took nine out of thirteen for itself.[73] This put Kabila on a collision course with Etienne Tshisekedi, the leader of the Union for Democracy and Social Progress (UDPS), who aspired to Presidential office. While Kabila co-opted many discredited politicians, à la Mobutu, Tshisekedi was despatched to his home village.

One of the sticks which the opposition used to beat Kabila with was the prominence of Banyamulenge within the AFDL. As far as the Kinshasa politicians were concerned, the Banyamulenge were 'foreigners' who had no right dabbling in the politics of the country. This was precisely the criticism which had been levelled against Museveni after 1986, and Kabila responded in much the same manner. He began to sideline senior Tutsi officers and in July 1998 he dismissed all his Rwandan troops and ordered them out of the country. The demobbed Banyamulenge soldiers returned to the eastern DRC and raised the standard of rebellion against the leader they had helped to bring to power, under the name of the RCD (Rassemblement Congolais Pour la Démocratie). The Rwandan army was already operating inside the borders of the country, having won the right to fight Hutu rebels on Congolese soil. The Rwandans and the Ugandans now lent their support to the RCD, while Kabila turned to the Hutu militias for support. Like the EPLF, the RPF had emerged from the Rwandan civil war with an inflated sense of its own military prowess. This led it to engage in operations which were beyond its capacities as a small country. Once the Rwandan government had decided that Kabila had to go, they decided to launch an attack on Kinshasa to remove him from power in August 1998. Museveni would have preferred more subtle methods and failed to send many Ugandan troops at this critical moment. Kabila called on the assistance of the Angolans who successfully repulsed the attack. This forced the Rwandan and Ugandans back upon Plan B, which was to prosecute a war in the eastern Congo alongside local proxies, which would render Kabila's position untenable. Kabila responded by calling on the assistance of Angolan, Namibian, Zimbabwean and even (for a time) Chadian troops. The Congo crisis rapidly escalated into a full-blown regional war in the late 1990s.

It is worth pausing to consider why the Rwandan and Ugandan governments found it expedient to go down their chosen routes. John Clark rightly concludes that not too much should be read into their official claims that the Kabila regime was at best failing to deal with guerrilla attacks against their countries and at worst fomenting them with Sudanese support.[74] Given that no Congolese government had the means to secure the borders, it is possible that the Rwandans had decided that annexing the eastern Congo as a buffer zone was their best guarantee, as Nzongola-Ntalaja avers.[75] In October 1996, the Rwanda government spoke openly of 'Great Rwanda' which had supposedly been severed by colonial boundaries. Indeed the Rwandans advocated convening a 'Conference of Berlin II' to address the lingering anomalies.[76] The Ugandans were less explicit, but they were equally concerned with preventing future incursions by the Allied Democratic Forces (ADF). Insofar as the Rwandan intention went beyond merely removing Kabila, this ran counter to the OAU Charter on a second count. It was also bound to involve the

Rwandans in cleansing the Kivus of non-Tutsis. The chilling implications would not necessarily have deterred the RPF leadership which adopted the Israeli stance that, having survived a genocide once before, Tutsis had a moral right to stake whatever territorial claims were necessary to ensure their safety. If that meant displacing other peoples, that was a price which would have to be paid. Like Israel, the Rwandans were confident that the international community, and more particularly the United States, would do nothing to call them to order. After all, the Ugandans and the Rwandans were bulwarks against the Khartoum regime which was accused of sponsoring Islamic extremism. Although the Americans saw the Congo war as a dangerous adventure, they were hardly likely to use force to defend the integrity of the DRC. Putting it simply, the DRC was no Kuwait. On the other side, the Angolans had a vested interest in defending a friendly government in Kinshasa, which would prevent its own rebels from attacking the Cabinda enclave.[77] The Namibians and the Zimbabweans weighed in on the grounds that the DRC was a fellow member of the Southern African Development Community (SADC) which was under attack from hostile neighbours.

Whatever the reasons for initial involvement in the war, it did not take long before vested interests began to play a part in its prolongation. All of the armies became involved in pillaging the natural wealth of the DRC. Ugandan and Rwandan officers made themselves extremely wealthy trading goods into their respective zones and shipping valuable commodities out: especially gold, diamonds, timber and columbium tanatalite (coltan), an important component in the production of mobile telephones. The involvement of multinational companies at different stages of the chain demonstrates the extent to which the war was thoroughly global. Museveni's own half-brother, General Salim Saleh, was widely reputed to have made a fortune out of the war, while Rwandan generals profited in their own right. The Angolan and the Zimbabwean top brass also benefited, with much of the diamond production of Mbuji-Mayi being flown to Harare.[78] Finally, the Kabila regime was sustained by the deals which it struck with other mining companies. All of the wheeling and dealing helped to fuel a war economy in which private accumulation and the destruction of property went hand-in-hand.

The cut-throat nature of the competition also produced fallings-out amongst friends. In August 1999, the Rwandan and Ugandan armies began fighting each other, probably because of a clash of business interests between the commanders of the forces rather than differences over military strategy.[79] The rift between these allies reinforced divisions within the RCD. In May 1999, Ernest Wamba-dia-Wamba and 'progressives' within the RCD broke off after a successful leadership challenge and moved to Bunia, where they formed RCD-Mouvement de Libération (RCD-ML) under the patronage of the Ugandans. The rump, which was mostly composed of Congolese Tutsis, went under the name of RCD-Goma and fought with the support of the Rwandans.[80] The Ugandans also spawned a third rebel group, the Mouvement de Libération du Congo (MLC), which fought in the North-west of the country under the leadership of Jean-Pierre Bemba, which later merged with the RCD-ML group. To complete a confused picture, the Interahamwe continued to fight the Rwandan forces and their proxies, with Kabila's backing, and were joined by the 'autochthons'.

The latter were organised as Mai-Mai and Simba militias, having eventually decided that the Banyamulenge posed more of a threat than the Kabila regime itself did. By 1999, the Mai-Mai had begun to co-operate with the FDD (Forces de la Défense de la Démocratie) in its war against the Burundian government.[81] The net effect of all the fighting scarcely needs to be pointed out. Much of the DRC was turned into killing fields, and where civilians enjoyed some respite they were subjected to occupying armies who preyed off them in a thoroughly predatory manner.

In July 1999, the first faltering steps were made towards a peace agreement. The six African countries which had sent troops to the DRC signed the Lusaka Accords alongside the Kabila government, and were later joined by the MLC and the two RCD groups. This agreement provided for a ceasefire, the deployment of UN peacekeepers and the disarming of 'negative forces', including the FDD of Burundi. The second part of the agreement envisaged an 'inter-Congolese dialogue', leading to the creation of a national government. The commitment of the signatories to the agreement was, however, weak and very little progress was made. Nevertheless, the context was dramatically transformed in January 2001 when Kabila was murdered by one of his own child soldiers who had accompanied him from the East. One of his sons, Joseph Kabila, assumed the mantle of leadership despite his youth (he had just turned 30) and signalled his willingness to reach a political compromise. In April 2002, the government signed a deal with the MLC and three months later the Rwandans agreed to withdraw their forces in return for more rigorous efforts to disarm the Hutu militias. Finally, at the end of the year, all the main rebel groups signed an agreement with the Kabila regime which brought them into an interim government in July 2003. Unfortunately the deal, which was brought all the signatories to Kinshasa, did not include rival militias in Ituri district, north of Kivu. Despite the deployment of UN peacekeepers, there was an outbreak of hostilities between Hema and Lendu armies and their backers. As yet another example of the 'hutusification' of the Great Lakes region, the Hema-Lendu cleavage came to be construed as a timeless clash between pastoralists and agriculturalists and this was reinforced by the pattern of alliances. The genocidal impulse was also apparent in acts of ruthless extermination of civilians from the wrong 'tribe'. In September 2002, some 1200 Hema were murdered over a ten day period, while the Union des Patriots Congolais (UPC) retaliated against the Lendu and their supposed sympathisers in Bunia. The result was that the peace deal in Kinshasa failed to resolve the crisis in the eastern Congo. The human costs of this series of conflicts in the Congo are staggering. It is estimated that as many as three million people may have died up to mid-2003, including 50,000 in Ituri, making this the bloodiest conflict since the Second World War.

We conclude this account with a brief discussion of the civil wars which erupted in two other neighbouring countries in the 1990s, namely the Republic of Congo (as Congo-Brazzaville was renamed in 1997) and the Central African Republic (CAR). In each case, multipartyism had failed to provide a mechanism for peacefully resolving struggles over political power and the spoils which came with it. In the Congo, the spoils consisted of oil revenues. Between November 1993 and February 1994, there was fierce fighting in Brazzaville between militias belonging to President Lissouba and Bernard Kolélas, the 'Zulus' and the 'Ninjas' respectively.[82] After international mediation, peace was restored and in 1995 Lissouba brought some of the politicians from Kolélas' MCDDI (Mouvement Congolais Pour la Démocratie et le Développement Intégrale) into government. The next elections were scheduled for 1997, but Lissouba appeared to have his mind set on postponing them. After a violent incident involving rival supporters of Sassou-Nguesso and Jacques Yhombi-Opango in the northern town of Owando in May 1997, Lissouba unwisely sent troops to arrest the former leader. This provided the spark which ignited the second civil war between June and November, in which some 10,000 Congolese were killed.[83] The battle for Brazzaville pitted three militias against each other: that is, the 'Mambas' on the side of Lissouba, the Ninjas and Sassou-Nguesso's 'Cobras'. Each of these militias recruited from its chosen 'ethnic' constituency, but more specifically from amongst alienated urban youth which saw itself as throwing off the authority of elders. An indication of the widening of the conflict was the increased recruitment of fighters from smaller towns.[84] The French appear to have secretly despatched arms to Sassou-Nguesso, perhaps because Lissouba had dared to strike a deal with an American oil company in an area which Elf-Aquitaine regarded as its own patch. This forced Lissouba to look for other friends, and at this point Laurent Kabila sent some soldiers to help him out. Lissouba's fate was sealed, however, when the Angolan government, which had its own concerns about the activities of FLEC, sent in thousands of troops to fight on the side of Sassou-Nguesso.[85] The upshot was that the democratically elected President was chased into exile, with French collusion, while the leader who had fared worst at the polls in 1992 came back through force of arms. In 1999, a peace deal was signed and two years later a new constitution was adopted which put the country back on a conventional footing. However, Sasssou-Nguesso only succeeded in winning the elections of 2002 by ensuring that his principal rivals were debarred. The predictable result was a resumption of fighting in Brazzaville between the government forces and the Ninjas, until yet another peace deal was hammered out.

In the CAR, the elected government of Ange-Félix Patassé had to contend with a succession of army mutinies which came to a head in 1997 when the French ceased to billet their troops there. After two years of fighting, peace was restored and fresh elections were held in 1999. Patassé won again with considerable ease, as Kolingba once again failed to stage a successful comeback in civilian garb. In May 2001 there was a further coup attempt in which the army chief, François Bozise, was implicated. After his dismissal, troops loyal to him took up arms, and in October 2002 they began fighting for the removal of Patassé. Although they failed to unseat him, they did seize around 70 per cent of the territory. While the Libyans backed the President, the government of Chad was allegedly supporting the rebels, replicating an earlier line of cleavage. However, the forces which came to mean the most to the survival of Patassé were those of the MLC from the DRC. Bemba's troops were accused of acting as an ill-disciplined army of occupation, but Patassé depended on them to remain in power. This did the trick until March 2003 when Bozise finally succeeded in expelling the hapless Patassé and declaring himself President.

10.3.2 The path of rebellion in West Africa: Liberia, Sierra Leone, Guinea-Bissau and Côte d'Ivoire

Many of the same patterns unfolded in the West African sub-region as well: most notably, the linkage between civil war, the struggle for control over valuable resources traded on a global marketplace, and the habituation of youth (including children) to lives of violence. Moreover, the breakdown was typically preceded by a period in which the legitimacy of governments had reached a dangerously low ebb, often due to the narrowing of the circles of clientage as a result of the economic crisis of the 1980s and 1990s. In some countries, the threadbare fabric of administration also came apart, rendering it extremely difficult for the authorities to maintain control over their territory.

The crisis in West Africa had its epicentre in Liberia, which had always been the odd-one-out in a region where the division between Anglophone, Francophone and Lusophone states remained a real one. Although Liberia was Anglophone, it faced in the direction of the United States, to the extent that American dollars served as the national currency. The Americans had returned the compliment by headquartering the African division of the Central Intelligence Agency (CIA) on Liberian soil. The result was that even as the country headed towards the precipice, many Liberians mistakenly believed that the Americans would eventually intervene to restore order. The distancing of the Americans from the Liberian crisis brought a rude awakening. Finally, as the war spread beyond the borders of Liberia, the latter came to be seen as a threat to the stability of the entire sub-region. Although a full-blown regional war did not erupt in the manner of the Great Lakes, a number of countries backed different sides.

As with Rwanda, the story does not begin inside Liberia, but in the countries where refugees began congregating after Samuel Doe set about eliminating his principal challengers. In 1980, Doe had posed as the defender of the interests of the upcountry majority, although many Americo-Liberians were brought in as Ministers and as advisors. However, it did not take very long for divisions to emerge within the junta. The brains behind the coup was Thomas Quiwonkpa, a friend of Doe who had brought him in as co-chairman of the People's Redemption Council (PRC). While Quiwonkpa's power base lay within the army, which absorbed most of his attention, Doe started to tighten his grip over the PRC. With echoes of the rift between Sankara and Compaoré in Burkina Faso, these two close friends became progressively estranged. In 1983, Quiwonkpa realised that his life was in danger – Doe having executed other members of the junta in 1981 – and fled into exile. In November 1985, as Doe was engineering his election to the Presidency, Quiwonkpa infiltrated a group of rebels into the country and attempted to seize power in Monrovia. After jubilation in the capital at the apparent demise of Doe, the latter staged a fightback. Quiwonkpa was killed and his body paraded triumphantly around the city. This was followed by a government assault on Nimba County, where the civilian population was accused of harbouring sympathies for the rebels.

The pogroms carried out against the Gio as a group sowed the seeds of a feud with Doe's own Krahn people of Grand Gedeh County, despite the fact that many Krahns also felt that they had been marginalised. Although the language of tribalism became the stock-in-trade of Liberian politics, Stephen Ellis observes that some of the identities in question had very little historical depth to them.[86] The Krahn case, like that of the 'Niboleks' in the Congo, illustrates a more general point about ethnic identities in Africa, namely that these have often proven extremely mutable. By brutalising the population of Nimba County, and showing favour to Mandingos – renowned as traders and seen by many Liberians regarded as 'non-indigenous' – Doe forged the context in which competition for power could plausibly be read in ethnic terms.

The waves of political refugees who left Liberia for Côte d'Ivoire and other neighbouring countries wasted little time in plotting their revenge. What proved crucial was the support offered by an improbable alliance between Libya, Burkina Faso and Côte d'Ivoire. Félix Houphouët-Boigny had a personal score to settle. Doe had abducted and killed Adolphus Tolbert, the son of the late President, who was married to Houphouët's adopted daughter, despite a plea by the Ivoirien President to spare his life. The woman in question became a close associate of Compaoré, whose own wife happened to be a protégée of Houphouët.[87] Although the Compaoré-Houphouët axis was otherwise a rather unlikely one, it proved more enduring than the former's personal friendship with Thomas Sankara. To close the circle, the coup which killed Sankara and elevated Compaoré was carried out with the assistance of a group of dissident Liberian soldiers, including one Prince Johnson. Libya was a crucial factor in the equation because Qadaffi put his training camps at the disposal of a motley collection of would-be guerrillas, who assembled under the banner of the National Patriotic Front of Liberia (NPFL). Apart from the Liberian contingent, the NPFL trainees were made up of a good number of Burkinabé, Ghanaians, Nigerians and Gambians, including the soldiers who had failed to overthrow President Jawara of the Gambia in 1981.[88] Ellis suggests that Qadaffi's support for the overthrow of the Doe regime was motivated by the desire to get back at the Americans after having been bombed by them in 1986. An attack on Liberia amounted to revenge against the CIA which the Libyan President also blamed for his defeat in Chad.[89] Charles Taylor, who had worked for the Liberian junta before fleeing in 1983 (allegedly with $900,000 of state money), came to prominence as the go-between, liaising between the Libyans, other West African governments and scattered elements of the external opposition.[90] Taylor used this position to the elbow his way to leadership of the NPFL, despite his Americo-Liberian origins, eliminating many of those who had the misfortune to get in his way.[91]

The war for Liberia began on 24 December 1989, when some 150 NPFL rebels crossed the border from Côte d'Ivoire into Nimba County and attacked the government forces. The violence unleashed by the Armed Forces of Liberia (AFL) on civilians served to further alienate the Gio and Mano population. The NPFL did not have particularly clean hands either, and was blamed for the summary executions of large numbers of Mandingos and Krahns as it advanced. Within seven months, the guerrilla forces had closed in on Monrovia and it seemed merely a matter of time before the AFL was defeated, given the unwillingness of the Americans to intervene. By this point, the NPFL had split in two

Map 8 Liberia and Sierra Leone: principal ethnic groups

Adapted from Christopher Clapham, *Liberia and Sierra Leone: An Essay in Comparative Politics* (Cambridge: Cambridge University Press, 1976), p. 23.

and the most likely scenario was one in which the downfall of Doe would lead to a final showdown between the Independent National Patriotic Front of Liberia (INPFL), led by Prince Johnson, and Taylor's NPFL. However, an unexpected development was the decision by the Babangida regime in Nigeria to pursue a pro-active policy in Liberia, with the encouragement of the Americans. The formation of the Economic Community of West Africa States (ECOWAS) in the 1970s had been the initiative of the then Nigerian President, Yakubu Gowon. The Senegalese and Ivoirien leaders, in particular, had been wary of signing over too many powers to a body which might well be domi-nated by the largest Anglophone state, and they were encouraged to balance their membership with participation in the wider Francophone community. As a result, ECOWAS could point to relatively few achievements in the area of pro-moting closer regional integration. The Liberian crisis therefore provided the perfect opportunity for the Nigerians to reinvent ECOWAS. The other Anglophone West African leaders were worried that if the Liberian government was toppled, this would enable Libya to export its version of 'revolution' to other parts of the sub-region. They therefore supported the formation of an ECOWAS Monitoring Group (ECOMOG), which despatched troops to Monrovia in August 1990 with a view to enforcing a ceasefire. The first force commander was Lt.-General Arnold Quainoo, a member of the Rawlings regime who had been instrumental in reconstructing the Ghana armed forces. However, most of the soldiers were contributed by Nigeria. Not surprisingly, the leaders of Burkina Faso and Côte d'Ivoire opposed ECOWAS involvement, but Guinea was more enthusiastic because it hoped ECOMOG would defend the Mandingo population who lived on both sides of the border.

While Doe and his beleaguered officials were holed up in the Executive Mansion, ECOMOG forces secured the Monrovia Freeport. Whereas Prince Johnson welcomed the peacekeepers, Taylor was furious that the Nigerians had tried to rob him of his victory and he resolved to fight them at every turn. An unexpected development was the untimely death of Doe who was captured by Johnson's troops while making a call on Quainoo. He was tortured and finally finished off by Johnson's men, a gruesome episode which Johnson faithfully captured on a video tape which subsequently sold like hot-cakes. This was the high-water mark of Johnson's influence, and from this point onwards he became progressively less important to the power-play. The real protagonists were now the NPFL and ECOMOG who had come to regard each other as adversaries. After the replacement of Quainoo by a Nigerian General, Joshua Dogonyaro, the latter demonstrated his willingness to stand up to the NPFL. The ECOMOG forces might have rolled the NPFL all the way back. However, Babangida decided to refrain from a fight to the finish, thereby leaving Taylor's forces in de facto control of most of the country. This enabled Taylor to strengthen his position by systematically tapping the natural resources of the country, often in close association with French and American firms who provided the NPFL with logistical support and money in return for the right to remain in business. Hence large quantities of diamonds, gold, rubber and timber was exported through Ivoirien ports. As William Reno puts it:

> The breakdown of Doe's state and the rise of Taylor's warlord political authority was not strictly a consequence of Liberia's economic marginalisation; on the contrary, the organisation of Taylor's political authority moved it close to global economic networks and privatisation of markets.[92]

The number of links in the chain between the producer of alluvial diamonds in NPFL areas and the cutter in Antwerp was surprisingly few, confirming much conventional wisdom about the impact of globalisation processes on Africa. Whereas the administration which ECOMOG installed in Monrovia, under the name of the Interim Government of National Unity (IGNU), had almost no budget to work with and enormous debts to juggle, Taylor's revenues were estimated at upwards of $75 million per year.[93] Taylor used much of this money to purchase arms and communications equipment to remain in contact with the outside world, but at the same time many affiliated warlords and their commercial agents became fabulously wealthy. The quest for accumulation was not sullied by debates about the relative merits of capitalism or socialism. On the contrary, the NPFL exhibited an ideological agnosticism arising out of its attachment to a form of landborne piracy. As Reno also suggests, another characteristic of warlordism was that it was not inhibited by an obsession with territoriality. It thrived on the basis of trans-national commercial networks, in which the nodal points were capital cities separated by vast distances. However, the quest for new sources of accumulation led to the spilling of violence across borders. In March 1991, Taylor made a fateful decision when he despatched some of his best fighters to assist with an invasion of Sierra Leone, in which control of the diamond fields was an important objective.

In Sierra Leone itself, the government and its Nigerian allies decided that the most effective means of defeating the NPFL was to beat it at its own game. Mandingo and Krahn refugees were placed under arms and sent to exact their revenge on the NPFL. Hence the United Liberation Movement for Democracy in Liberia (ULIMO) came into being as a proxy guerrilla army. History repeated itself when ULIMO subsequently split along ethnic lines. Alhaji Kromah headed ULIMO-K which recruited Mandingos (or Mandinkas) in Sierra Leone, Guinea and as far afield as the Casamance region of Senegal. On the other hand, Roosevelt Johnson led the Krahn element in ULIMO-J, which went even further than the NPFL in combining business with fighting. Its soldiers were empowered to establish their own tolls and taxes, while the leadership exchanged guns in return for the diamonds they produced.[94] By 1992, the two ULIMO groups were making inroads within Liberia, with covert Nigerian support, thereby depriving the NPFL of some of its juiciest pickings along the border. There was a real possibility that the NPFL would unravel and so Taylor decided to gamble on a bid to seize Monrovia. He struck a secret deal with the INPFL which the latter failed to honour. In the battle which ensued, ECOMOG demonstrated its decisive military advantage over the NPFL. A somewhat chastened Taylor was therefore forced to come to the negotiating table, and in July 1993 a power-sharing agreement was signed between the AFL, ULIMO and the NPFL. However, none of the parties really trusted the other signatories, and behind the scenes everyone was preparing contingency plans for the next showdown. Meanwhile, the Nigerians covertly sponsored another proxy army outside the peace process, in the shape of the Liberian Peace Council (LPC). As Taylor sponsored a proxy of his own in Lofa County, fighting and self-enrichment continued across much of the country.

By 1995, it had become obvious to Taylor that he had no realistic chance of becoming President if he failed to make his peace with the Nigerians who alone had the capacity to thwart him. Although the ECOMOG operation was costing Nigeria dearly, many officers were engaged in highly profitable business deals of their own, selling arms and buying diamonds. However, the replacement of Babangida by Sanni Abacha removed the grudge factor from the contest. In August 1995, the Abacha regime convened a meeting at Abuja which brought together all the main protagonists once again. They hammered out a new peace deal which provided for a sharing of executive power between the parties within a Council of State. Taylor re-entered the capital in triumph, supposedly to play his part in the politics of compromise. In December 1995, however, fighting broke out once more when the NPFL leader took it upon himself to try to arrest Roosevelt Johnson with the support of ULIMO-K. A sign that times had changed was the support which ECOMOG now gave to the NPFL, although some Nigerian troops supplied ULIMO-K with arms as well. This rather farcical episode, which was something of an embarrassment to the Nigerians, led to ECOMOG forces taking the initiative once more. The latter established control over the entire country and promised to hold the ring in order that proper elections could be held.

Despite a challenge from Ellen Johnson-Sirleaf, who had remained outside the country during the war, Taylor won the Presidential elections in July 1997 with around three-quarters of the vote.[95] This result might appear somewhat bizarre, given the untold misery which Taylor had inflicted on the population. It is likely that many Liberians voted for Taylor in recognition of the likelihood that, like Savimbi, he would resume fighting if he was not victorious at the polls. The countries which had contributed most to ECOMOG, notably Nigeria and Ghana, were showing signs of fatigue and there was every chance that they would fail to intervene if the fighting did resume. As the duly-elected President, Taylor laid emphasis upon national reconstruction. For the first few years, he presided over a peaceful country, but there were renewed guerrilla incursions over the Guinea border in 1999. These were carried out by a group calling itself the Liberians United for Reconciliation and Democracy (LURD), which represented a fusion of ULIMO-K and ULIMO-J and fragments of other movements. The Liberian government claimed, with some reason, that LURD was being actively abetted by the regime of Lansana Conté in Guinea. Taylor now found himself in the reverse position of holding the capital, as rebels were given the run of the countryside. The Liberian regime was vulnerable after the UN Security Council imposed an arms embargo in 2001, following complaints that it was continuing to support the rebels in Sierra Leone. At the end of 2002, Taylor also stood accused of permitting al-Qaeda operatives to purchase diamonds on either side of the Sierra Leone border. By this point, even Taylor's historic alliances with Burkina Faso and Côte d'Ivoire were under strain. Early in 2003, LURD rebels demonstrated their improved fighting capacity when they occupied the towns of Tubmansburg and Bopolu, while a new Movement for Democracy in Liberia (MODEL) launched its own military campaign.[96] A bruising battle for Monrovia ensued which culminated in Taylor eventually being forced to accept a Nigerian offer of exile in August 2003. Liberian history had come full circle, but whether Taylor was actually a spent force, and whether he would be forced to stand trial for his part in the atrocities in Sierra Leone, was by no means certain.

In many respects, it is tempting to regard the Sierra Leonean conflict as merely a second front in Taylor's Liberian campaign. The NPFL leaders had encountered Sierra Leonean dissidents in exile across West Africa and while they were both undergoing training in Libya. When the Revolutionary United Front (RUF) started its war against the Freetown government in March 1991, its soldiers infiltrated across the border from Liberia, into Kailahun and Pujehun Districts, accompanied by some of the NPLF's own crack troops. Taylor had reasons for wanting to pull down the government of Joseph Momoh, who had failed to put his country at the disposal of the NPFL and had then swung behind the ECOMOG intervention in 1990.[97] Finally, while eastern Sierra Leone was rich in diamonds which could be used to finance the Liberian war, the NPFL could not be seen to simply invade a neighbouring state for fear of playing into the hands of ECOMOG. Taylor therefore had many reasons for arming a surrogate army next door. However, those who have studied the RUF insurgency have rejected the imputation that it was purely an extension of the NPFL. Instead, they have attributed the rise of the RUF to a mounting social crisis in Sierra Leone itself. The rule of the APC (All People's Congress) had followed the classic clientelist model, but as the economic crisis deepened in the 1980s, there was fewer resources to redistribute. Moreover, while politicians and merchants continued to amass fortunes in the illicit diamond trade, government revenues declined along with public services. Whether measured in terms of access to those services or real incomes, the lot of the average Sierra Leonean became noticeably poorer.[98] Disillusionment with the APC regime ran deep, even after Siaka Stevens made way for Joseph Momoh in 1985. This created an amalgam of forces which were hostile to the APC cabal, but had an inchoate vision of what might replace it.

The origins of the RUF has become a matter of some debate between scholars of Sierra Leone. Paul Richards lays the primary emphasis upon 'excluded intellectuals'. While it has been pointed out that there were precious few 'highly educated' individuals in the RUF leadership, the author seems to have had in mind the failures rather than the academic success stories.[99] The critics have preferred to see the RUF as a movement of 'lumpen' elements whose defining characteristic is the lack of a truly political consciousness. However, 'lumpen' is something of a dustbin category in itself and lacks precision. Indeed, the lexicon of African politics, which is mostly derived from other regions and periods, seems extremely ill-suited to describing social processes in countries like Sierra Leone at the close of the twentieth century. Moreover, some of Richards's critics have themselves gone on to examine the links between the 'lumpen' elements and other social categories. Ibrahim Abdullah and Patrick Muana, in particular, trace the emergence of a lumpen sub-culture in Freetown back to the 1940s, but observe a shift in its character during the late 1960s and 1970s.[100] We are told that in their own peri-urban spaces around Freetown, called *potes*, the youth consumed drugs, vented their frustrations and took solace in the anti-establishment messages of musicians like Bob Marley and Fela Kuti. The authors point out that students began to integrate into this milieux in the 1970s, borrowing much of its language and chic, whilst popularising pan-Africanist ideas and fragments of Third World Marxist thought in return.[101] By the mid-1980s, Sierra Leonean student politics was also borrowing ideas about revolution from North Korea and Libya. In 1985, the authorities purged militant students from the University (Fourah Bay College) as part of an attempt to curb Libyan influences, forcing many aspirant intellectuals to the margins of subsistence and inducing many to leave the country. Those who ended up in Ghana found Qadaffi's *Green Book* study clubs on the ground. Ghana certainly provided a staging post in the drift towards Burkina Faso and Libya.[102] Others continued their studies inside the country and were often consigned to remote rural localities as teachers where they were irregularly paid. As a result, the *pote* phenomenon reproduced itself in smaller towns in the interior, where a sense of exclusion also festered amongst the youth. Paul Richards insists that the political platform of the RUF, vague as it was, drew heavily on a historic sense of exploitation at the hands of outsiders, which the rebels intended to bring to world attention in a grand theatrical display.[103]

The enigmatic individual who emerged as the spokesmen of the RUF was Foday Sankoh, a corporal in the army who had been dismissed for his alleged involvement in a coup attempt in 1971, and had gone on to make a living as an itinerant photographer. Sankoh was habituated to plying the bush-paths in the East of the country, which later came in very useful. As has already been noted, some of the Sierra Leonean exiles were recruited for training in Benghazi (Libya) over 1987–88. The first group filtered back into Sierra Leone, but apparently disbanded without taking their revolutionary plans much further. However, Sankoh, Abu Kanu and Rashid Mansaray went on to enlist 'lumpen' elements as the first cohort of RUF fighters. Mansaray was closely connected with the NPFL and brought some of its fighters into the rebellion, while Sankoh established contacts with Taylor.[104] The third social group which was swept up by the RUF consisted of the diamond-winners located near to the Liberia border, who had long had a difficult relationship with the state. When the authorities placed the production and sale of diamonds in the hands of its favoured clients, often Lebanese businessmen, this threatened the small producers. This was the background to a revolt in the Pujehun District in 1982, which was put down with considerable force, thereby fostering a heightened sense of grievance.[105] It was no accident that when the RUF launched its first attacks across the border, Pujehun was one of the two Districts which was selected. In the surrounding communities which regarded themselves as the owners of the land, the RUF had more or a problem, not least because refugees from Liberia had got there first with stories of the extreme violence perpetrated by the rebels. The RUF did little to alter this opinion when it set about killing chiefs and elders in the villages, and abducting the youth. The latter were often forced to carry out murders themselves, so that they would be unable to return to their home communities. The abductees were also branded with the RUF logo, so that they would be unlikely to run away for fear of being killed by government troops, and were subjected to a socialisation process which encouraged them to think of the RUF as their substitute family. Within the RUF camps, the youth were provided with some very basic schooling and were relatively generously catered for with clothing and looted consumer goods. They were also offered a training in 'bushcraft' and a gradual apprenticeship into the rebel army. When these recruits went into battle, it was allegedly under the influence of crack cocaine and other drugs which were reputed to take away the fear. These child soldiers therefore became the fourth element in the RUF coalition, alongside the frustrated intellectuals, the 'lumpen' elements and the diamond-winners.

The war itself can be divided into four distinct phases, in which the balance of advantage shifted along with the strategies of the RUF.[106] The initial invasion caught the government by surprise and by June 1991 the RUF had over-run around a fifth of the country, although it failed to capture the important centre of Bo. But the violence inflicted by the rebels, especially those of non-Sierra Leonean origin, produced an inevitable backlash as villagers joined irregular forces mobilised by the army. Moreover, as we have seen, the Momoh government rallied Liberian exiles and these took to the field under the banner of ULIMO. By the early part of 1992, the RUF had been forced to retreat into a remote corner of Pujehun district and by the end of the year the war seemed almost over. But events had took an unexpected turn in March 1992 which enabled the RUF to stage a comeback. A mutiny by government troops on the front gave way to a fully-fledged coup which toppled Momoh and led to the creation of a military junta, the National Provisional Ruling Council (NPRC), made up of soldiers in their twenties and headed by a youthful Captain Valentine Strasser. The NPRC committed itself to the restoration of democracy and to a concerted military push if overtures towards peace yielded no returns. The populist coup-makers basked in the adulation which greeted them in Freetown, where the euphoria manifested itself in a veritable explosion of street art and civic activism.[107] Meanwhile, officers who had hitherto managed to avoid combat were despatched to the front. The loss of experienced officers, and the movement of ULIMO fighters into Liberia, enabled the RUF to drift back into the areas from which it had been cleared, although it continued to suffer fresh reverses in 1993.

By 1994, when the war entered its second phase, the picture had became confused. When the war started up, the army doubled in size to 6000 men, but Strasser increased it further to some 14,000 troops. Inevitably this meant that little attention was paid to the quality of intake or training.[108] Soon a new word was coined, that of 'sobel' – an amalgam of soldier and rebel – which pointed to the manner in which government troops by day resorted to banditry by night. The NPRC itself estimated that as many as a quarter of its soldiers were suspect. The RUF was able to exploit this situation by infiltrating its fighters behind government lines and then carrying out attacks in official army uniforms.[109] This undermined public confidence in the army and turned the RUF into an almost faceless enemy. Indeed, the RUF altered its tactics completely, eschewing set-piece battles in favour of fanning out across the country and engaging in hit-and-run raids which sapped public morale. This confirmed the lack of interest in actually creating 'liberated zones': the RUF was at war with the people as much as with the state, as was reflected in its trademark practice of burning villages and either killing or physically mutilating its occupants. The popular support which had been enjoyed by the NPRC evaporated, as the government seemed incapable of preventing the devastation. By the start of 1995, the RUF had demonstrated its capacity to strike in all parts of the country, and Freetown itself seemed the next likely target.

In 1995/96, the war entered its third phase as a new set of factors entered the political equation. On the one hand, the government recruited a South African company, Executive Outcomes, to assist with counter-insurgency operations, allegedly in return for a share of the diamond mining operations. This company, which was a hybrid between a commercial operation and a mercenary outfit, assisted with triangulating RUF radio communications, thereby making it easy to track the armed bands who typically set up their base camps in remote locations.[110] On the other hand, a new civil defence initiative was launched in the guise of the Kamajoi militias. As with the case of the Naparama movement which took on RENAMO in Mozambique (see Chapter 7), the Kamajoi was reworking of an older set of beliefs and institutional practices, in this case based on hunter's guilds amongst the Mende. These were thought to be the repository of spiritual powers, and the same belief in the ability to render oneself impervious to bullets was present. According to Muana, the Kamajoi initiates were not typically villagers, but peoples who had been drivers, craftsmen and labourers before the war started.[111] The Kamajoi were reputed to have an unequalled knowledge of the terrain and were trusted by the civilian population much more than the regular army. It is also noteworthy that the Kamajoi were deployed by the chiefs who, as in much of Africa, began recapturing some of their former societal significance. The Kamajoi–chiefly alliance began to chalk up some striking successes against the rebels in the South and east. By October 1996, the RUF headquarters had been captured with the loss of thousands of rebel lives, signalling that the pendulum had swung back once more.

This new context ultimately proved the undoing of Strasser when Brigadier Julius Maada Bio, who had begun to work with Executive Outcomes in retraining government troops, mounted a palace coup in January 1996.[112] The ostensible reason for the takeover was that the leadership was seeking excuses not to organise elections. Strasser was bundled into exile and the renovated NPRC arranged swift elections as promised. Ahmad Tejan Kabbah of the Sierra Leone People's Party (SLPP), which had brought the country to independence, was voted in as President, while the APC received a desultory 5.7 per cent share of the vote.[113] The campaigning was necessarily limited, given the determination of the RUF to disrupt the process, including amputating hands in order that people could not vote. The Kabbah regime was initially heavily dependent on Executive Outcomes for survival against the operations of the RUF and coup-plotters alike. However, the President decided to divest himself of his South African allies in February 1997, judging that the Kamajoi militias would be equal to the task of defeating the RUF. In May, the gamble went horribly wrong when 'sobel' elements in the army, led by Johnny Paul Koroma, seized power in Freetown, signalling the fourth phase in the conflict. Demonstrating that they had learned very little, many opposition politicians cynically backed the new administration.

Koroma was typical of the 'sobel' phenomenon, having only joined the army in the 1990s. The suspicion that sections of the army had long been playing a double-game were confirmed when Koroma proceeded to invite the RUF to join it. The army and the RUF, who were supposed to form a 'People's Army', then jointly set about pillaging Freetown and attacking the Kamajoi in the interior.[114] This redrawing of the battle lines signals more than anything the sheer unpredictably of the Sierra Leonean situation. Although the Nigerians became involved in fighting against the new coalition, with a view to restoring Kabbah, ECOWAS preferred to negotiate a solution with the Armed Forces Revolutionary Council (AFRC).[115] Eventually, after it became clear that the latter had no intention of coming to a peaceful settlement, ECOMOG forces were mandated to resort to more direct methods. This was backed up by the UN Security Council, which also approved an oil and arms embargo on the Freetown regime. Under sustained international pressure, the AFRC finally signed up to the Conakry Peace Plan which provided for the restoration of Kabbah, the release of Sankoh from detention in Nigeria and the granting of immunity to members of the AFRC. ECOWAS was vested with the difficult task of disarming the combatants, including what was by now a very notional Sierra Leonean army.[116] In February 1998, the ECOMOG forces took control of Freetown and placed Kabbah back in office. Although Koroma remained on board the peace train, the RUF reverted to type and in January 1999 came close to seizing control of the capital in a most vicious attack in which many civilians were maimed and executed by the rebels.

After the repulsion of the RUF, a fresh peace agreement was signed in Lomé in July 1999 which provided for the inclusion of the rebels in a national government. With echoes of Liberia, the deal quickly collapsed as the RUF preferred to push for a total victory. When the Nigerians withdrew their contingent in April 2000, the rebels proceeded to take a large number peacekeepers of the United Nations Mission in Sierra Leone (UNAMSIL) hostage, underlining their perception that the latter body would (unlike the Nigerians) be reluctant to fight. This was followed by a fresh assault on Freetown, drawing British forces into the fray against the RUF and the West Side Boys, another faction which had split off from the army. As the UN presence was augmented, and adopted more robust terms of engagement, the tide began to turn against the RUF. Meanwhile, the Guineans covertly mobilised another civilian militia, along the lines of the Kamajoi, which scored notable successes in the diamond-fields. Across the Liberian border, Charles Taylor came under sustained pressure to distance himself from the RUF, and the arms embargo which was imposed on Liberia began to be felt by the rebels in Sierra Leone. In the field, RUF fighters began to surrender their remaining weapons. Although the 2001 elections needed to be postponed, the return of some semblance of normality meant that elections could go ahead in May 2002, and these were won by Kabbah and the SLPP for a second time. The RUF was not a contestant and it seems unlikely that it will ever do a RENAMO and reinvent itself as a political party. The manner in which it had brutalised the civilian population was hardly likely to make it a vote-winner. Moreover, it had never attempted to build support along ethnic lines, and indeed it was in Mende country, where it was most firmly established, that the Kamajoi fightback occurred. The best hopes of the RUF lay in the resumption of hostilities at some point in the future. However, this would presumably require a different leadership. In January 2002, a UN Special Court was set up, on the request of the Sierra Leonean government, to try those accused of war crimes. The most prominent person to be placed before the court was Foday Sankoh himself, although his death in 2003 meant that he was never brought to book. The futures of Sierra Leone and Liberia remained as fused as ever, much like those of Rwanda and Burundi.

While these dramatic events were playing themselves out in Liberia and Sierra Leone, a different crisis was brewing in Guinea-Bissau. As we observed in Chapter 9, the movement towards a multiparty system had, if anything, heightened divisions within that country. These were in part ethnic, given that sections of the Balanta population felt excluded from the centres of power. Moreover, President Vieira was constantly looking over his shoulder at the military, from where innumerable plots continued to emanate. In early 1998, he decided to remove his military chief of staff, Ansumane Mané, who he probably suspected of plotting, despite the fact these were friends who had fought alongside each other in the liberation war. The excuse for removing Mané was that he was involved in running guns to Casamance separatists operating along the border with Senegal. At this point, a small digression is necessary. For the most part, the Senghor and Diouf regimes in Senegal had presided over an appreciable level of ethnic unity in that country. The spread of the Wolof language and the dissemination of the Muslim brotherhoods had played an important part in the integrative process, but they also produced a backlash in the southern reaches of Senegal. The Senegalese authorities perceived the geographical isolation of the Casamance as the crux of the problem and one reason for pushing for confederation with the Gambia was to resolve what was seen as a simple anomaly of colonial geography.[117] The trans-Gambian highway was supposed to bridge the divide between the two halves of Senegal, but it did not alter the perception that the Casamance was neglected. Militants, under the banner of the MFDC (Mouvement des Forces Démocratiques de Casamance), took up arms in support of their demand for independence in 1990, and staged incursions across the border. It seems that elements within the Guinea-Bissau army were indeed selling arms to the MFDC, either for profit or because they identified with the cause of peoples who straddled the border. Although Mané was quite possibly implicated, this was also a handy excuse to dispense with a potential threat. At the time, Vieria was seeking to enter the Francophone fold, having joined the West African Economic and Monetary Union (UEMOA) the previous year, and was susceptible to Senegalese pressure.

The dismissal was immediately followed by a mutiny in support of Mané, followed by pitched battles between rival factions of the army in June 1998. Unfortunately for Vieira, most of the army sided with the chief of staff, and despite raising his own militia, defeat was a virtual certainty. Hence Vieira called on the support of Senegal and Guinea, both of whom sent soldiers who engaged the rebels in battle. Vieira also appealed to ECOWAS, hoping that it would come to the defence of the elected government. In August, ECOWAS and the Community of Portuguese-Speaking Countries (CPLF) jointly brokered two successive ceasefires. Under the second of these, Senegalese and Guinean troops were to withdraw and be replaced with ECOMOG forces from neutral countries. The Nigerian leader, Abdulsalami Abubakar, was reluctant to commit his country to yet another peacekeeping exercise, with the result that the responsibility shifted to smaller states, notably Benin, Togo, the Gambia and Niger, none of whom possessed the logistical capacity to adequately perform the job.[118] In May 1999, Mané's forces simply ignored the ECOMOG contingent and proceeded to rout the forces loyal to Vieira, who was allowed to go into exile in Portugal. Presented with a fait accompli, the ECOMOG peacekeepers somewhat sheepishly packed their bags and went home. The war had led to some 3000 civilian mortalities, matched by the death of around 2000 soldiers on either side and of as many as 1000 Senegalese troops.[119]

In the aftermath, Mané declined to assume formal control, and an interim President and Prime Minister were installed, pending elections. These passed off peacefully between November 1999 and January 2000. On this occasion, Kumba Yalla was successful on the second round of balloting, while the PRS became the largest party in the legislature with 38 out of 102 seats. Yalla was forced to stitch together a coalition government which excluded the PAIGC, although the fractiousness of the system meant that he eventually became dependent on an alliance with the latter. Mané continued to regard the army as his fief, however, and following complaints of Balanta favouritism, embarked on a fresh revolt in November 2000. On this occasion, Mané was killed and order was restored. However, in September 2003 Yalla was finally deposed in a coup and a caretaker regime was installed. The Casamance remained a complicating factor. In Senegal, Abdoulaye Wade was elected on a platform of negotiating an end to the war in the South. In reality, despite the efforts of Yala to put pressure on the MFDC, the border zone remained as unstable as ever. In 2001, competing factions of the MFDC fought it out with each other, the Guinea-Bissau army and the Senegalese armed forces.[120] Although one faction of the MFDC declared an end to hostilities towards the end of 2003, the hardliners remained committed to secession.

Our final case is that of Côte d'Ivoire, long held up as a model of stability and sound administration. Houphouët-Boigny had, however, lumbered Ivoiriens with a political system which was highly personalised and in the succession problems which ensued the foundations of economic success were simultaneously destroyed. Henri Konan Bedié, who succeeded to the leadership of the PDCI (Parti Démocratique de la Côte d'Ivoire), lacked the same kind of authority and, in order to bolster his position he fatally chose to play the citizenship trump-card. Alassane Ouattara, who had been debarred from standing on the basis that his mother was a Burkinabé, absented himself from the country, but returned in 1999 with a view to standing in the 2000 polls. The debate as to whether Ouattara was really a foreigner stoked up ethnic and regional antagonisms in a country where about a third of the population originated from neighbouring states, most notably Burkina Faso. On 24 December 1999, Côte d'Ivoire experienced its first military coup, led by General Robert Gueï who promised to restore a sense of national unity and to preside over free and fair elections. The military genie had now been let out of the bottle, with disastrous consequences. Gueï set about creating a broad-based government, including representatives of Laurent Gbagbo's FPI (Front Patriotique Ivoirien) and Ouattara's RDR (Rassemblement des Républicains). However, the amity did not last for very long. Gueï, who had begun by attacking Bedié's exploitation of ethnic divisions, came down in favour of the view that Ouattara was indeed a foreigner, and as relations with the RDR deteriorated the party was excluded from the coalition. When the Constitutional Court confirmed that Ouattara was not eligible to stand for President, the RDR resolved to boycott the 2000 elections, along with the PDCI. Gbagbo, who clearly profited from this outcome, believed that the Presidency was his for the taking, but Gueï decided to stand for the highest office in his own right. When Gueï tried to manipulate the process and declare himself President, Ggagbo loyalists took the streets of the capital and managed to force Gueï, who failed to carry enough of the army with him, to capitulate. Gbagbo now claimed to be the duly elected President, but his legitimacy was in question, given that around 62 per cent of the population decided not to vote.[121] When the RDR insisted on there being a re-run of the polls, fighting broke out in Abidjan along ethno-regional lines.

The rest of the year marked a further poisoning of the political atmosphere. There was also a succession of coup attempts and clashes between supporters of the FPI and the RDR. The latter could point to its victory in local elections in March 2001, the first poll it did not boycott, as clinching evidence for its national support. On the other side, the FPI continued to stand by the election results of 2000. A Forum for National Reconciliation was convened in December 2001 – attended by Gueï, Gbagbo, Bedié and Ouattara – and some Ministerial positions were handed to the opposition, but there was little genuine reconciliation. In September 2002, a full-blown crisis erupted when some 750 demobilised troops attempted to seize power. At first, it seemed that this was a coup led by Gueï loyalists. However, the former military ruler was killed at an early point in the proceedings, possibly by the government side. Very quickly, the putsch assumed an ethnic and regional character when rebels, having failed to seize control of Abidjan, captured the towns of Bouaké and Korhogo and much of the North of the country, proclaiming the existence of a Mouvement Patriotique de Côte d'Ivoire (MPCI) and demanding the removal of Gbagbo. Meanwhile two smaller rebel movement took control of the west. The government and the Abidjan press now came to the conclusion that the conspiracy had been financed and aided by the Compaoré regime in Burkina Faso. The evidence for this thesis, apart from the fact that many northerners were of Burkinabé extraction, lay in the revelation that a number of the conspirators had fled there after the failure of earlier plots in 2001. Given Comaporé's history of fomenting rebellions in other parts of West Africa, there is some possibility that this was the case. If so, it would be a case of chickens coming to roost, in view of the PDCI regime's earlier support for the NPFL. Gueï himself had channelled arms sales to the Taylor regime, using dealers who were alleged to be linked the Taliban in Afghanistan.[122] However, this rebellion was evidently deeply rooted in the internal dynamics of Côte d'Ivoire. Northerners felt threatened by the discourse of *ivoirité* which threatened to strip them of their citizenship and so their rights to land. As in the eastern Congo, the stakes were higher than the question of who wielded power at the centre. The FPI pretended not to understand these concerns and posited a great Dioula/Muslim conspiracy to seize power. After the al-Qaeda attack on New York on 11 September 2001, it could conveniently link the rebellion to a global terrorist threat embodied by all Muslims. Although the RDR leaders distanced themselves from the rebellion, the regime believed that the hand of Ouattara lay behind it and many of its leading members were arrested and summarily executed.

After the initial military clashes, and acts of 'ethnic cleansing' on both sides – which produced a flood of refugees into neighbouring countries – the front lines sides stabilised. In effect, there was a stalemate: the rebels knew that

French forces would not allow them to move on Abidjan, while Gbagbo was aware that the French would not be drawn into a reconquest of Côte d'Ivoire. Short of partitioning the country, the only solution was to enter into negotiations. In January 2002, the Linas-Marcoussis accord was signed through the direct intercession of Jacques Chirac, Thabo Mbeki and the UN Secretary-General, Kofi Annan. It was agreed that a Government of National Reconstruction, representing all the parties, would be constituted and that some of the rebels would be taken back into the army. It was also agreed that the Constitution would be amended along with the naturalisation laws, thereby removing the barrier on the candidacy of Ouattara and meeting the concerns of many northerners. The interim government was also entrusted with taking action to prosecute the pushers of xenophobic reporting within the media – one of the least pleasant manifestations of the crisis which bore echoes of Rwanda.

The deal was widely interpreted as a humiliating defeat for Gbagbo, and there were demonstrations and riots in Abidjan against the peace deal. Most of the violence was directed against French persons and property. In the view of FPI supporters, the Chirac government had been less than impartial.[123] However, there was little that Gbagbo could do, but make the most out of the hand which he had been dealt. As he candidly put it: 'I did not win the war, and so there is therefore no option open to me but to talk peace.'[124] The prospects for actually reconciling the parties were actually rather slim, and towards the close of 2003 the accord had not been fully implemented. The rebel movements had withdrawn from the government and showed no signs of disarming. However, it was clearly understood that the outbreak of a full-scale civil war would be disastrous for everyone concerned, with knock-on effects on the entire sub-region. It would further complicate the search for peace in Liberia and Sierra Leone, and inundate Ghana, which had so far avoided the contagion effect, with refugees. At best, Burkina Faso would probably back one side and at worst become directly involved in the fighting. Because of the serious implications, other West African leaders, France and international agencies all had a vested interest in maintaining pressure on the various factions to keep their rivalries within bounds. For this to happen required a different kind of Ivoirien miracle.

10.4 The national question in focus

In this chapter, we have dwelt in some detail upon the political upheavals which afflicted all regions, if not all countries, from the 1980s onwards. This has not made for edifying reading, but it is important to relate because it marks the final demise of many of the confident assumptions which had been made about African states at independence. Voices of realism have begun suggesting that the nation-state project is dead and buried, and that the way ahead lies in thinking creatively about the alternatives. The case of the former Somalia, which has witnessed some genuine reconstruction in the absence of a functioning state, often serves as a point of reference. However, all too frequently there is an elision from what commentators believe is unsustainable about the post-colonial state to the assertion that alternative forms are already in the making. However, in southern Somalia, where there is the least approximation to a state, there has been the least post-war reconstruction. Across the greater part of the continent, the new millennium has witnessed attempts to reformulate the 'nation-state' model rather than to abandon it altogether, and there is reason to believe that there is greater mileage in this approach. We conclude, therefore, with a somewhat panoramic overview of attempts to revisit questions of identity and political authority in contemporary Africa.

A preliminary word of clarification is in order. In the vast outpouring of writings about Africa, most is cast in presentist mode and is normative in character. This has created a rather awkward fit between a discourse *about* Africa which is conducted in terms of the application of supposed cultural universals – like human rights and good governance – and a debate *within* Africa in which the emphasis tends to fall on alterity. If the one is unashamedly ahistorical, the other is heavily laced with claims about the past and their relevance for establishing present entitlements. Of course, the external discourse often intrudes into the internal debate – in part because the money for reconstruction, feeding refugees and the like is derived from beyond Africa, and in part because it can be deployed as ammunition by the protagonists. But when this language is borrowed, the terms are almost always re-encoded. With this caveat in mind, we turn to consider two issues which have featured prominently internal debate: namely, the path to post-conflict reconciliation and the interplay between conceptions of indigeneity and citizenship.

10.4.1 *Reconciliation and its malcontents*

One of the supposedly universal values which has been progressively refined over the second half of the twentieth century is that of the primacy of fundamental human rights. From the start, the UN enshrined human rights as a core concern of the international system. It is important to remind ourselves that the principle of equality was necessarily a construct of the post-war period, given that in a world of colonial overlords and colonised subjects there was an assumption of difference – 'trusteeship' was a feature of the post-1919 environment, to be sure, but equality certainly was not. The OAU was initially more concerned with guaranteeing the sovereign rights of its member states, but later adopted the language of international human rights discourse. The African Charter on Human and People's Rights, which was signed in 1981 and came into effect as late as 1986, finally brought that organisation into line with the UN.[125] Now, the corollary of a conception of fundamental human rights is the possibility of their infringement, and what steadily emerged in the latter part of the twentieth century was the principle that it was the responsibility of the international community to prevent serious violations, which (as in the case of the Iraqi Kurds) could over-ride respect for national sovereignty. In practice, though, intervention had much more to do with power politics than with a willingness to step in whenever and wherever human rights were being violated, as the Rwandan genocide of 1994 tragically demonstrated. However, the principle itself was established, and could be invoked as and when circumstances demanded. The next step was for the international community to establish mechanisms for trying those accused of gross violations of human rights. The trial of the Serb leader, Slobodan Milosevic, was intended to send out a clear signal that no head of state was immune to prosecution by an international court if he was in breach of the conventions. In the case of Africa, the Rwanda tribunal performed the same exercise, but without receiving quite the same measure of publicity.

There was inevitably a tension between the desire on the part of human rights lobbies to punish violations, and the political imperative of promoting reconciliation. The underlying problem was there was a growing gulf between the improved monitoring of agencies like Amnesty International and Human Rights Watch, and the instruments for enforcement. The UN, which had burnt its fingers on many occasions, was reluctant to be drawn into the role of continental policeman, while the capacities of regional organisations like ECOWAS and SADC was somewhat limited, even when the will was present. Moreover, while the ending of the Cold War wrought some important transformations in mentalities, the foreign powers which had the greatest interests in Africa – notably France, Britain and the United States – were often prepared to look the other way when the victims were in the enemy camp. As a consequence, the punishment of offenders was less about the application of high-minded principles than the winning side imposing its will. In Ethiopia, the EPRDF regime set up courts to try individuals who had perpetrated human rights abuses under the Derg. This was only possible because the Derg had been defeated on the battlefield. Ironically, however, the new regime was accused of violating the rights of many who were suspected of having supported the former regime. Rwanda and Sierra Leone sought to internationalise the process by involving the UN, but these trials only took place because the perpetrators had lost the war. The RPF regime failed to accept that murders carried out by its own forces should be covered by the trials, which only concerned the genocide. More tellingly, it continued to carry out human rights abuses of its own, in the knowledge that nobody was likely to take action. Indeed, Paul Kagame who was appointed to the Presidency in 2001 had himself been implicated (some three years earlier) by a UN investigation team in war crimes, possibly stretching to genocidal acts, within the DRC.[126] The popular saying that 'might is right' was vindicated year on year as perpetrators of mass killings often walked free provided they did not find themselves on the losing side.

Because it was the balance of political power which was the crucial determinant, combatants who were evenly matched tended to negotiate according to a political logic rather than a legalistic one. That is, they struck deals which were designed to further peace and hopefully reconciliation, and which were often rather silent when it came to considerations of justice and recompense. This was not a purely cynical calculation, given that a prolongation of open warfare could be expected to generate yet more deaths and human rights abuses. In the case of Mozambique, RENAMO had carried out many atrocities along the lines of the RUF in Sierra Leone. But because FRELIMO could not defeat RENAMO militarily, it had to settle for an agreement under which there would be a complete amnesty for the guerrilla movement. The alternative was a prolongation of the war, with all the consequences which ensue. The peace deal brought RENAMO fully into the political process and enabled Mozambicans to return to their everyday lives. In the 1999 elections, FRELIMO held onto the Presidency and a majority of the legislative seats, but RENAMO won a majority of votes in six of the eleven provinces of the country and demonstrated that it represented a credible alternative to the ruling party.

In the case of South Africa, where there were no outright victors, there was an attempt to address past violations through a Truth and Reconciliation Commission (TRC) which might be viewed as a halfway-house between the Rwandan and Mozambican models. The TRC had a broad mandate to investigate the planning or conduct of gross human rights violations, defined as 'killing, abduction, torture or severe ill-treatment of any person'. The TRC was not a court of law, and in fact the African National Congress (ANC) and the National Party (NP) had agreed on the principle of an amnesty for agents of the apartheid regime. The ANC accepted this deal because it recognised that prosecuting everyone who was guilty of human rights violations risked jeopardising the fragile consensus. When the Amnesty Committee was established, the applicants were required to make a full disclosure, but they were not forced to express any remorse for their crimes. Nor were they required to compensate their victims. A convenient myth was propagated by Desmond Tutu and the other architects of the TRC to the effect that a peculiarly African conception of justice was being applied, one which sought healing rather than retribution.[127] The tone of most of the literature on the TRC has been critical of a process which, it is argued, revealed limited truths and probably generated more bitterness than genuine reconciliation.[128] On this view, the halfway-house represented the worst of both worlds, in that the victims and their families were invited to dredge up bitter memories, only to be cheated of a genuine 'closure'. There is some merit in this complaint, but it is doubtful whether a more rigorous pursuit of the truth, let alone retribution, was politically feasible. The fudge served a useful purpose in facilitating a consolidation of South African democracy, warty myths and all.

By contrast, the Rwandan government was determined not to waver from bringing the perpetrators of the genocide to justice. It was in a much stronger position than the ANC, but it ran into constraints of a different kind. One practical difficulty was deciding where to draw the line. Although liquidation squads had operated in Kigali, most of the killing was carried out by ordinary Hutu peasants responding to exhortations by local officials and the incendiary propaganda of RTLMC. It was simply not possible to try everyone who had been complicit in the genocide, because that would have stigmatised the majority of the population and rendered reconciliation impossible. The circle was therefore narrowed to trap only those who had played a pro-active role. A division of labour was established between the International Criminal Tribunal which tried the principal architects of the genocide in Arusha (Tanzania), and the Rwandan courts which were expected to try the remaining perpetrators. However, conducting trials which conformed to 'international standards' required lengthy investigations which a war-ravaged Rwanda could scarcely afford. Both the Arusha tribunal and the Rwandan courts struggled to bring about as many successful convictions as they would have liked. As of March 2001, only 5301 people had been placed before the Rwandan courts, leaving some 110,000 still languishing in crowded and unsanitary detention centres. Remarkably, the Arusha tribunal had only managed to try eight people by the end of 2002. The irony of the situation was while the true architects of the genocide were treated relatively well, thousands of ordinary Hutus were subjected to life-threatening conditions within Rwanda, as they awaited trial.

As it eventually became apparent that the judicial system could not cope, the Rwandan authorities decided to make a bold departure from international legal norms. To the consternation of watchdogs like Amnesty International, they decided to place as many of the remaining cases before customary courts as possible. These *gacaca* courts were expected to try all but the most serious offenders, numbered at some 2900.[129] In effect, these were a hybrid between 'traditional' and formal courts, in that magistrates, who had been given a crash legal training, were to preside over them. It was inevitable that this innovation should involve a radical break with the internationally-sanctioned definitions of a fair trial – including the ability to mount a defence and uniform rules of evidence. However, localisation was the only realistic alternative to either letting the remaining detainees go free or keeping them permanently incarcerated and thereby falling foul of other human rights norms. More positively, the *gacaca* courts could also be presented as a means of not merely punishing offenders, but also healing local wounds. In that sense, there had been some movement from punishment towards the language of reconciliation.

In the case of Sierra Leone, the international tribunal was likely to concentrate on the leaders of the RUF, raising questions about what would happen to the large numbers of ordinary fighters who were also culpable. The reality of the situation was that rape, mutilation and summary executions had become a way of life for young men in the RUF, who had been mentally deadened by the repetition of acts of extreme violence and by the consumption of hard drugs. The simple mantra that criminals should be brought to justice begins to look rather facile when one takes account of the fact that these were very often victims themselves, having previously been abducted as children and forced to kill members of their own families. Here the reintegration of dysfunctional individuals back into society was arguably the greatest priority of all. In Somaliland and Puntland, where the emphasis lay on reconciliation rather than punishment, 'traditional leaders' played an important role in alleviating societal tensions – including the generational ones which were so starkly apparent in countries like Sierra Leone and the Congo (Brazzaville). They were certain lessons to be drawn from their experience, even if the processes were unlikely to be directly replicable. Although so-called 'traditional institutions' had themselves evolved greatly since independence, there was a much greater willingness to take them seriously at the start of the twenty-first century right across Africa.[130] On this point, Mamdani's rather jaundiced interpretation of chieftaincy seems inadequate.

10.4.2   Indigeneity, citizenship and pluralism

One of the apparent paradoxes of the 1990s was that, as state structures imploded and millions of Africans were uprooted from their homes – to be variously classified as displaced persons, refugees and economic migrants – discourses about citizenship and indigeneity took hold as never before. However, this was a thoroughly understandable development in that Africans became more concerned with drawing boundaries of inclusion and exclusion as control of resources assumed a heightened importance. Land, which had not been particularly scarce across most of the continent, was a key resource at the close of the twentieth century. There were also more symbolic resources, including linguistic and religious recognition, which were contested with just as much grim determination. The challenge for Africans at the start of the new millennium was to find viable mechanisms for reconciling these competing claims. Supposedly universal models have proven only of partial relevance. For example, the assumption that multipartyism would establish an arena in which conflicting demands could be reconciled failed to take account of the fact that in many countries pastoralists and hunter-gatherers were located at the margins of political life. The development of commercial ranching, settled agriculture and wildlife parks often infringed directly upon their livelihoods, but formal political institutions were of little use to them as instruments of redress. The NGOs sometimes helped to voice their concerns, but these had a tendency to arrogate the right to speak for the communities concerned.

The manner in which discourses of indigeneity played themselves out is revealing about the importance of power relations in cementing some claims and relegating others to the sidelines. In virtually every country, there are long-running disputes about who is truly autochthonous and who is not. Given that African oral traditions tend to consist of very complex stories of migration and settlement, there is no easy means of reconciling or deciding between such claims. However, particular groups had their versions validated by the colonial powers, typically through the recognition of chiefs. Those who did not receive their own chiefs, such as the Konkomba of northern Ghana, have since had much greater difficulty in asserting their claims to territory. Significantly, the discourse of indigeneity tended to leave out peoples who arguably had the greatest claims to being autochthonous, such as the San (or Bushmen) of Southern Africa and the Pygmies of Central Africa. In most countries, hunter-gatherers were treated as lesser peoples – at best quaint and at worst a nuisance – a perception which was rooted in their limited numbers and lack of organisation. The Twa of Rwanda are a case in point, being confined to a footnote in most accounts of political struggles in that country. The peoples who monopolised the claim to being the autochthons were Hutu nationalists, who had numbers on their side, rather than the Twa who did not.

Nevertheless, the basis for claiming entitlements underwent significant modifications at the end of the twentieth century. On the one hand, the mobilisation of so-called 'first peoples' across the globe enabled some marginalised minorities to organise themselves with the assistance of international lobby-groups. In Botswana, Namibia and South Africa, the cause of the San was taken up by organisations like Survival International, which placed pressure upon national governments to respect the rights of 'first peoples'. At the same time, the San slowly began to find a voice of their own. In South Africa, those who were removed from the Kalahari Gemsbok Park recruited lawyers to fight their corner. Their struggles, in turn, inspired the San of the Central-Kalahari Game Reserve in Botswana who the authorities wanted to resettle on the basis that their continued presence posed a threat to wildlife and hence to tourism. In 1994, they formed the 'First People of the Kalahari' which endeavoured to persuade the government to allow them to remain in the park. The campaign ultimately failed, and by the start of 2002 the entire community had been resettled elsewhere.[131] Nevertheless, the San could no longer be disregarded as before.[132] In South Africa, there was also a rediscovery of Khoi identity amongst peoples had been classified as Coloured during the apartheid era, thereby bringing an 'extinct people' back to life.

On the other hand, new citizenship claims were invoked to exclude groups of people who were defined as non-indigenous to a particular country. Hence many Banyamulenge, who regarded themselves as belonging in the eastern Congo, stood accused of being recent immigrants from Rwanda. Similarly, the Konkomba in northern Ghana were accused by the Dagomba and Nanumba of being recent arrivals from Togo, whereas there is evidence of their presence dating from the early colonial period. These claims were anachronistic in that they effectively read modern citizenship backwards into the pre-colonial period, but they were taken deadly seriously by all concerned. Whereas in much of the world, the assumption is that citizenship can be acquired, its grafting onto a reified conception of indigeneity has threatened to create a two-tier system: one in which 'honorary' citizens are tolerated as long as they do not over-reach themselves whereas the remainder are excluded. The Asians of Kenya and Tanzania have been unpopular, but escaped the fate of their Ugandan colleagues by ingratiating themselves with the power structure. In Côte d'Ivoire, by contrast, the political situation became so explosive because of southern perceptions that they were in danger of being outnumbered, and hence outvoted, by immigrants from the Sahel. Whereas the exclusion of Kenneth Kaunda from standing for the Presidency was a cynical attempt at playing the nationality card, the debarring of Ouattara was deeply rooted in real societal cleavages. In Zimbabwe, whites had failed to earn their national stripes by opposing black majority rule. Although the sun-set clauses which were inserted into the independence constitution tied the hands of the ZANU-PF government, the latter never regarded whites as genuinely Zimbabwean. In the views of Mugabe, the acute land shortage entitled the government to forcibly expropriate white farms and to redistribute the land to the real sons and daughters of the soil. Whereas this was widely interpreted as an illegal act, the Mugabe regime stood by the fact that the land had been forcibly seized from Africans in the first place. Ironically, by turning for support to the Blair government in Britain, the whites only seemed to confirm that that they were not really Zimbabwean.

At the same time as Africans were debating the boundaries of citizenship, they were also thinking in new ways about what it meant to share a common nationality. The instinct of African leaders immediately after independence was to regard lower order identities as a threat to the nation-building project. In some countries, like Ethiopia and Botswana, there was an attempt to promote one language and culture over the rest. In most other countries, the nation-building imperative was actively pursued through the educational system, but for the most part it was negatively construed: that is, suppressing the expression of ethnic solidarity. Indeed, one of the principal justifications for the one-party state was that it precluded mobilisation along ethnic lines. By the end of the twentieth century, there was a greater willingness to recognise that national identity could not be forged by suppressing ethnic identities, and indeed that they might have a positive side. In Botswana, there was a backlash against Tswana hegemony towards the end of the 1990s, as minority groups began to push for the recognition of their own paramount chiefs and equal statuses for their own languages. Jacqueline Solway plausibly argues that this was a consequence not of the failure of the state, but its very success.[133] Minorities had seized on educational opportunities and their representatives amongst the elite became increasingly confident of their own worth and that of their cultures. Whereas the identity of Botswana had once been bound up with Tswana culture, there was now a markedly greater level of polyphony.

In Ethiopia, the shift in public discourse has been even more striking. Having defeated the Derg, the EPRDF ushered in a new constitution in 1994 which built a recognition of 'nationality' differences into the fabric of the state, whereas the Eritreans were wedded to a more traditional conception of nation-building. Ethiopia was construed as an amalgam of diverse peoples, each of which was entitled to 'the unconditional right of self-determination, including the right of secession'. The map of federal Ethiopia was redrawn in such a way that each nationality was given its own region (nine in all), thereby creating problems of internal boundary definition.[134] The primacy of the Amharic language was downgraded, and the educational system was reconfigured to take account of the linguistic diversity of the country. Although Oromo nationalists thought they detected a sleight of hand, under which the TPLF in practice ran the show and made self-determination a practical impossibility, contemporary Ethiopia is very unlike the empire of old.[135]

The acceptance of difference was taken to the furthest extreme in South Africa. The liberation movements naturally rejected the apartheid classification system, and many accepted the term 'Black' as a catch-all category for peoples without political rights. However, since 1994, the Coloured category has regained currency, especially in the Western Cape. The system which has been put in place encourages South Africans to take a pride in their common nationality, but also gives them reasons for asserting their other group identities.[136] Provided the latter does not engender open conflict, the consensus is that this is a compromise which can be lived with. To external eyes, South Africa after the ending of apartheid was almost schizophrenic. This was most graphically reflected in the playing of the old national anthem and the ANC's 'Nkosi Sikelel 'iAfrika' (God Bless Africa) back-to-back at international rugby matches – one rehearsing a glorious Afrikaner history and the other embodying a Black Christian optic on African liberation. However, within the country there was an acceptance of the possible benefits of cultural bricolage and folly of trying to create a nationalist master-narrative. One might even say that South Africa has become the first truly post-modern nation.

We conclude by drawing attention to the betwixt-and-between position of the many Africans who were forced to take up residence abroad, whether as refugees or as so-called 'economic migrants'. An important dimension of what has transpired over the past half-century is the export of African population to the world beyond. Many cities in the United States, Canada and Europe had become home to large diaspora communities. In the case of Ghana, anywhere between 200,000 and 400,000 were resident in the United States in the mid-1990s.[137] Particular groups have tended to favour specific locales, often because of the strength of post-imperial ties – hence Mozambicans have gravitated to Lisbon and Camerounians to Paris. However, other communities have emerged out of the logic of chain-migration. A visitor to contemporary Florence, for example, is likely to be struck by the Senegalese presence. Similarly, Washington DC has became a favoured place of abode for Ethiopians and Eritreans, whereas many Ghanaians have headed for German cities. The latest recipient of immigrants have been post-apartheid South African cities, especially Johannesburg and Cape Town which have drawn peoples from across Central and West Africa.[138]

International migration has often been presented in negative terms. In Western Europe, governments complain of bogus refugees who are actually 'economic migrants' seeking a more prosperous life abroad. On the other hand, those who identify with Africa often bemoan the so-called 'brain drain' to the west. In fact, many of the stock arguments are wide of the mark. African immigrants have tended to fill the jobs that nationals won't perform, with a view to saving enough money to return home and start up in business. Often the West is seen not as a final resting place, but as a temporary exile. The identities of Africans have themselves been shaped by the experience of travel. Young men who journey to Paris to purchase natty clothing have generated an entire subculture, called the *Sape*.[139] The *sapeurs* are not mimicking Western styles, but tapping its material culture to make quite different statements about their identity. The same point could be made in relation to popular music. Whilst patronising their own nightclubs and musicians, Africans in the diaspora have also borrowed certain musical forms, reworked them and sent them home. Hence, *burgher* highlife in Ghana – so-called because it emerged in Hamburg – marries older musical forms and Western instrumentation to create a unique fusion. While it has dismayed the highlife purists, it has certainly been popular with Ghanaian youth. Equally, African American music has been domesticated in a number of African countries, where performers rap in Wolof or Twi, creating something quite distinctive.[140]

Even the diaspora communities which have become firmly rooted in Western soil have tended to retain close links with their countries of origin. Indeed, the sense of being exiled has tended to foster a heightened sense of identification with home. Hence Congolese might have been forced to leave a country in ruins, but abroad they have taken a tremendous pride in who they are. The music and the ever-changing dance styles, and the panache with which they are carried off, is something which has made the Congolese a focus of admiration across much of Eastern and Southern Africa. The contribution made by the diaspora also takes a more practical form. In Eritrea and the former Somalia, remittances from abroad have probably been a more important source of funding for reconstruction than external aid has been. Moreover, foreign investment has paled into insignificance by comparison.[141] Contrary to the 'brain drain' thesis, there has actually been a reskilling process which had been immensely beneficial to African countries where a modicum of stability has prevailed. Unfortunately, the diaspora has not always been given its fair due. Many African states still refuse to recognise dual nationality, with the result that citizens have been turned into 'foreigners' despite their self-identification and continuing support for kith and kin. However, countries such as Ghana and Eritrea are beginning to appreciate the tremendous resource which the diaspora community represents. If globalisation contains many pitfalls, there is also a sense in which it presents abundant opportunities.

Notes

Introduction: The Basis of Comparison

1. I focus on sub-Saharan Africa in a way which includes the Horn of Africa, but which excludes the Maghreb and Mauritania (for the most part). This is not to deny that there have historically been close links between parts of West Africa and Morocco and Algeria, or between the Sudan and Egypt. However, the dynamics of North Africa remain significantly different, and I am following fairly routine practice in making this selection. I have also left out the Indian Ocean islands (other than Zanzibar), whilst counting in the islands off the coast of West Africa, on the basis of the intimacy of their links with continental Africa.

2. Stephen Ellis, 'Writing histories of contemporary Africa', *Journal of African History* 43, 2002, pp. 1–2.

3. Jean-François Bayart, 'Africa in the world: a history of extraversion', *African Affairs* 99, 395, 2000.

4. Terence Ranger, 'The invention of tradition in colonial Africa', in E. Hobsbawm and T. Ranger (eds) *The Invention of Tradition* (Cambridge: Cambridge University Press, 1983) and 'The invention of tradition revisited: the case of colonial Africa', in Terence Ranger and Olufemi Vaughan (eds) *Legitimacy and the State in Twentieth-Century Africa* (London: Macmillan, 1993). See also the excellent collection, Leroy Vail (ed.), *The Creation of Tribalism in Southern Africa* (London: James Currey, 1989).

5. See the contributions to Carola Lentz and Paul Nugent (eds) *Ethnicity in Ghana: The Limits of Invention* (Basingstoke and New York: Macmillan and St Martin's Press, 2000).

6. James Fairhead and Melissa Leach, *Misreading the African Landscape: Society and Ecology in a Forest-Savanna Mosaic* (Cambridge: Cambridge University Press, 1996); Melissa Leach and Robin Mearns (eds) *The Lie of the Land: Challenging Received Wisdom on the African Environment* (London, Oxford and Portsmouth: IAI, James Currey and Heinemann, 1996); and M. Tiffen, M. Mortimore and F. Gichuki, *More People, Less Erosion: Environmental Recovery in Kenya* (Chichester: John Wiley, 1994).

7. For a good example of the first, see James C. McCann, *Green Land, Brown Land, Black Land: An Environmental History of Africa, 1800–1990* (Portsmouth and Oxford: Heinemann and James Currey, 1999). For a persuasive study of African peasants as relentless innovators, see Paul Richards, *Indigenous Agricultural Revolution: Ecology and Food Production in West Africa* (London: Hutchinson, 1985).

8. One noteworthy attempt to do so, with a strong ecological dimension, is Jean-Pierre Chrétien, *The Great Lakes of Africa: Two Thousand Years of History* (New York: Zone Books, 2003).
9. An example would be a website for the Mai-Mai, who are discussed in Chapter 10. Their website is www.congo-mai-mai.net

1 African Independence: Poisoned Chalice or Cup of Plenty?

1. The literature on each of these subjects is too exhaustive to even summarise here. However, some useful overviews are Crawford Young, *The African Colonial State in Comparative Perspective* (New Haven and London: Yale University Press, 1994); and John Hargreaves, *Decolonization in Africa* (London and New York: Longman, 1988).
2. Basil Davidson, *The Black Man's Burden: Africa and the Curse of the Nation-State* (London: James Currey, 1992).
3. Mahmood Mamdani, *Citizen and Subject: Contemporary Africa and the Legacy of Late Colonialism* (Kampala, Cape Town and London: Fountain, David Philip and James Currey, 1996).
4. Jean François Bayart, Stephen Ellis and Béatrice Hibou, *The Criminalisation of the State in Africa* (London, Bloomington, Indianapolis and Oxford: IAI, Indiana University Press and James Currey, 1999).
5. This was more convincingly argued in respect of Tanzania than for the continent as a whole. See Goran Hyden, *Beyond Ujamaa in Tanzania: Underdevelopment and an Uncaptured Peasantry* (London: Heinemann, 1980) and *No Shortcuts to Progress: African Development Management in Perspective* (London: Heinemann, 1983). An extreme case of state incapacity in colonial and post-colonial times alike is dealt with instructively in Joshua Forrest, *Lineages of State Fragility: Rural Civil Society in Guinea-Bissau* (Oxford and Athens: James Currey and Ohio University Press, 2003).
6. Patrick Chabal and Jean-Pascal Daloz, *Africa Works: Disorder as Political Instrument* (Oxford and Bloomington: James Currey and Indiana University Press, 1999), especially Chapter 1.
7. Chabal and Daloz, *Africa Works*, p. 16 do acknowledge a continuum, and accept that some former settler colonies may buck the trend, but they are otherwise reluctant to concede anything much to African states.
8. It did, however, lend a helping hand in contexts where the machinations of the Soviet Union were thought to lurk behind the forces of nationalism. See Wm Roger Louis and Ronald Robinson, 'The United States and the liquidation of the British Empire in Tropical Africa, 1941–1951', in Prosser Gifford and Wm Roger Louis (eds) *The Transfer of Power in Africa: Decolonisation 1940–1960* (New Haven and London: Yale University Press, 1982).
9. I am using Bhabha with a specificity here which is lacking in the actual text, which is often infuriatingly elusive and obtuse. Homi Bhabha, *The Location of Culture* (London and New York: Routledge, 1994).

10. Partha Chatterjee, *The Nation and its Fragments: Colonial and Postcolonial Histories* (Princeton: Princeton University Press, 1993), especially Chapter 2.

11. Michael D. Callahan, *Mandates and Empire: The League of Nations and Africa, 1914–1931* (Brighton and Portland: Sussex Academic Press, 1999).

12. Christopher Fyfe, 'Race, empire and the historians', *Race and Class* 33, 4, 1992.

13. Anne Phillips, *The Enigma of Colonialism: British Policy in West Africa* (London and Bloomington: James Currey and Indiana University Press, 1989).

14. Cary was not opposed to colonialism *per se*. He argued, however, that it could only be justified if it brought real benefits to Africans. See *The Case for Colonial Freedom and Other Writings* (Austin: University of Texas Press, 1962).

15. In the Northern Territories of the Gold Coast, for example, educational provision was restricted and its contents closely monitored in order to avoid a repetition of what were seen as the mistakes of Cape Coast and Accra. See R. Bagulo Bening, *A History of Education in Northern Ghana 1907–1976* (Accra: Ghana Universities Press, 1990), pp. 49–51.

16. On the ideology of French imperialism in this period, see Alice Conklin, *A Mission to Civilize: The Republican Idea of Empire in France and West Africa, 1895–1930* (Stanford: Stanford University Press, 1997).

17. Janet G. Vaillant, *Black, French and African: A Life of Léopold Sédar Senghor* (Cambridge, MA and London: Harvard University Press, 1990), pp. 49–56.

18. Vaillant, *Black, French, passim*. The very same contradictions were manifested by Barthélémy Boganda, the undisputed African leader of Oubangui-Chari until his untimely death. Boganda was a priest who was defrocked after taking a French wife. His demand was for equal treatment, which was considered radical by many Frenchmen in the colony, but he was also something of a Francophile.

19. Gerald J. Bender, *Angola Under the Portuguese: The Myth and the Reality* (London: Heinemann, 1978), pp. 3–9.

20. Quoted in Bender, *Angola*, p. 206.

21. Bender, *Angola*, p. 219.

22. In 1940, only 1012 Africans or less than 0.03 per cent of Africans in Angola could read and write. Bender, *Angola*, p. 220.

23. In 1950, there were only 30,000 black *assimilados* in Angola (a mere 0.7 per cent of the African population) and 5000 in Mozambique. Malyn Newitt, *Portugal in Africa: The Last Hundred Years* (London: C. Hurst, 1981), p. 138, Bender, *Angola*, p. 151.

24. For details, see Gervase Clarence-Smith, *The Third Portuguese Empire, 1825–1975: A Study in Economic Imperialism* (Manchester: Manchester University Press, 1985).

25. Allen Isaacman, *Cotton Is the Mother of Poverty: Peasants, Work and Rural Struggle in Colonial Mozambique, 1938–1961* (Portsmouth, London and Cape Town: Heinemann, James Currey and David Philip, 1996), also some of the contributions to Allen Isaacman and Richard Roberts (eds)

Cotton, Colonialism, and Social History in Sub-Saharan Africa (Portsmouth and London: Heinemann and James Currey, 1995).

26. Very little has been written on Spanish colonialism in the region, but see Max Liniger-Goumaz, *Small is Not Always Beautiful: The Story of Equatorial Guinea* (London: C. Hurst, 1986), Chapter 2.

27. Crawford Young, *Politics in the Congo: Decolonisation and Independence* (Princeton: Princeton University Press, 1965), p. 32.

28. Young, *Politics in the Congo*, p. 36.

29. Tekeste Negash, *Italian Colonialism in Eritrea,1882–1941: Policies, Praxis and Impact* (Uppsala: Acta Universitatis Upsaliensis, 1987), Chapter 2. This section summarises the thrust of this book.

30. Robert Hess, *Italian Colonialism in Somalia* (Chicago and London: University of Chicago Press, 1966).

31. Tekeste, *Italian Colonialism*, pp. 72–7.

32. Tekeste, *Italian Colonialism*, pp. 51–3.

33. On the impact of Italian rule on the agricultural economy, see Haile Larebo, *The Building of an Empire: Italian Land Policy and Practice in Ethiopia* (Oxford: Clarendon Press, 1994).

34. Alberto Sbacchi, *Ethiopia Under Mussolini: Fascism and the Colonial Experience* (London: Zed Press, 1985), p. 237. See also Alberto Sbacchi, *Legacy of Bitterness: Ethiopia and Fascist Italy, 1935–1941* (Lawrenceville and Asmara: Red Sea Press, 1997).

35. Tekeste Negash, *Eritrea and Ethiopia: The Federal Experience* (Uppsala and New Brunswick: Nordiska Afrikainstitutet, 1997), p. 55. These powers were looking to the possible return of Italy. Haile Selassie agreed to the Bevin-Sforza proposal of 1949 which would have partitioned Eritrea.

36. Ruth Iyob, *The Eritrean Struggle for Independence: Domination, Resistance, Nationalism, 1941–1993* (Cambridge: Cambridge University Press, 1995), p. 62.

37. Iyob, *Eritrean Struggle*, p. 77; Harold Marcus, *A History of Ethiopia* (Berkeley, Los Angeles and London: University of California Press, 1994), p. 158. There was also a small Pro-Italy Party.

38. Tekeste Negash, *Eritrea and Ethiopia*, pp. 54–61.

39. Iyob, *Eritrean Struggle*, p. 78.

40. I. M. Lewis, *A Modern History of Somalia: Nation and State in the Horn of Africa* (London and New York: Longman, 1980), p. 124.

41. Prior to the Italian invasion, the Ethiopians had exercised limited effective control over the Ogaden and held a dubious claim over the Haud. The Italians had placed all the Somali territories under a separate administration. These ambiguities were now resolved, although there was considerable Somali opposition to the imposition of Ethiopian rule. As for the Italians, they had hoped for a return of their former colony, but this has been successfully opposed by Somali nationalists. Lewis, *A Modern History*, pp. 125–31.

42. Lewis, *A Modern History*, pp. 148–55.

43. On Sudanese nationalism, see Mohamed Omer Beshir, *Revolution and Nationalism in the Sudan* (London: Rex Collings, 1974); and Peter

Woodward, *Condominium and Sudanese Nationalism* (London: Rex Collings, 1979). For a useful overview of British policy, see the introduction to Douglas H. Johnson, *British Documents on the End of Empire: Sudan, Part I, 1942–1950* (London: Her Majesty's Stationery Office, 1998).

44. Johnson, *British Documents*, p. xlvi.
45. Johnson, *British Documents*, p. xlviii. Elections to a new Legislative Assembly were held in 1948.
46. Johnson, *British Documents*, p. liii.
47. C. L. R. James, *Nkrumah and the Ghana Revolution* (London: Allison and Busby, 1977).
48. James, *Nkrumah*; Basil Davidson, *Black Star: A View of the Life and Times of Kwame Nkrumah* (London: Allen Lane, 1973); and David Birmingham, *Kwame Nkrumah: The Father of African Nationalism*, 2nd edition (Athens: Ohio University Press, 1998).
49. Kwame Nkrumah, *Ghana: The Autobiography of Kwame Nkrumah* (Edinburgh: Thomas Nelson, 1959).
50. An early critique from a more orthodox Marxist standpoint was, Bob Fitch and Mary Oppenheimer, *Ghana: End of an Illusion* (New York and London: Monthly Review Press, 1966); for a far more sophisticated version, see Colin Leys, *Underdevelopment in Kenya: The Political Economy of Neo-Colonialism* (London: Heinemann, 1975).
51. In a classic example of flawed methodology, John Flint proclaims that he has no apology to make for relying almost exclusively on Colonial Office files on the grounds that 'the dynamic for change ... lay there, and not in Africa'. Since the entire burden of the article is to prove this very point, the author effectively prejudges the issue. See his 'Planned decolonisation and its failure in British Africa', *African Affairs* 82, 328, 1983, p. 389.
52. Flint, 'Planned decolonisation', pp. 404–5; Robert Pearce, 'The Colonial Office and planned decolonisation in Africa', *African Affairs* 83, 330, 1984, p. 393.
53. Flint, 'Planned decolonisation', p. 411.
54. For more on this point, see Frederick Cooper, *Decolonisation and African Society: The Labor Question in French and British Africa* (Cambridge: Cambridge University Press, 1996), pp. 67–73.
55. Flint, 'Planned decolonisation', p. 407.
56. Flint, 'Planned decolonisation', pp. 398–9.
57. Pearce, 'Colonial Office', p. 80.
58. Quoted in Richard Rathbone (ed.) *British Documents on the End of Empire, Series B Volume 1: Ghana, Part I, 1941–1952* (London: Her Majesty's Stationery Office, 1992), p. 10.
59. For a detailed treatment of these memoranda, see R. D. Pearce, *The Turning Point in Africa: British Colonial Policy, 1938–48* (London: Frank Cass, 1982), pp. 147–76.
60. Pearce, 'Colonial Office', p. 86.
61. Quoted in Pearce, *Turning Point*, p. 167.
62. Hargreaves, *Decolonisation*, p. 101.

63. Yusuf Bangura, *Britain and Commonwealth Africa: The Politics of Economic Relations, 1951–75* (Manchester: Manchester University Press, 1983), p. 46.

64. Hargreaves, *Decolonisation*, p. 101.

65. Quoted in David Throup, *Economic and Social Origins of Mau Mau* (London, Nairobi and Athens: James Currey, Heinemann and Ohio University Press), p. 20.

66. Pearce, 'Colonial Office', p. 89.

67. Ibid., pp. 90–2.

68. Pearce himself suggests that there was less of a blueprint than a flexible plan which was expected to evolve with circumstances, including the rise of nationalism. Stated thus, the scale of the 1947 proposals would seem limited. *Turning Point*, p. 168.

69. The words are those of Ronald Robinson, quoted in Pearce, 'Colonial Office', p. 78.

70. The best account of this period remains the classic, Dennis Austin, *Politics in Ghana, 1946–1960* (London, Oxford and New York: Oxford University Press, 1964).

71. Colonial Office, *Report of the Commission on Enquiry into Disturbances in the Gold Coast, 1948*, p. 24.

72. Hargreaves, *Decolonisation*, p. 116.

73. For a history of the backlash in Ashanti, see Jean-Marie Allman, *The Quills of the Porcupine: Asante Nationalism in an Emergent Ghana* (Madison: University of Wisconsin Press, 1993).

74. As Crook indicates, the identification of the chiefs with the farmers' cause indicated that the British could no longer entirely rely on the traditional authorities. Richard Crook, 'Decolonisation, the colonial state and chieftaincy in the Gold Coast', *African Affairs* 85, 338, 1986.

75. Robert Tignor, *Capitalism and Nationalism at the End of Empire: State and Business in Decolonising Egypt, Nigeria and Kenya, 1945–1963* (Princeton: Princeton University Press, 1998), p. 235.

76. However, as the dominance of the Saros (of Sierra Leone extraction, albeit mostly of Yoruba ancestry) declined with the emergence of an indigenous educated elite, there was some relocation of the focus towards Nigeria in the 1930s. For a discussion, see Philip S. Zachernuk, *Colonial Subjects: An African Intelligentsia and Atlantic Ideas* (Charlottesville and London: University of Virginia Press, 2000), Chapter 4.

77. It granted an African unofficial majority in the Legislative Council, but only four of the 28 were directly elected. Regional councils were also set up.

78. On these events, see Richard Sklar, *Nigerian Political Parties: Power in an Emergent African Nation* (New York and Enugu: Nok, 1983 edition), pp. 72–83; and Carolyn A. Brown, *'We Were all Slaves': African Miners, Culture and Resistance at the Enugu Government Colliery* (Portsmouth, Oxford and Cape Town: Heinemann, James Currey and David Philip, 2002), Part II.

79. Harry Gailey, *A History of the Gambia* (London: Routledge and Kegan Paul, 1964), pp. 207–8.

80. See John Cartwright, *Politics in Sierra Leone, 1947–1967* (Toronto: University of Toronto Press, 1970) and his *Political Leadership in Sierra Leone* (London: Croom Helm, 1978), Chapters 2–3.

81. After the war, five out of eleven Executive Council members were settlers. Africans were not represented and only had one member of the Legislative Council. Throup, *Economic and Social Origins*, p. 45.

82. On the personality and influence of Mitchell, see Throup, *Economic and Social Origins*, especially Chapter 3.

83. Pearce, *Turning Point*, pp. 178–89.

84. In Kenya, Mitchell tried to garner white support for federation, but settler leaders were mistrustful of what they regarded as a plot to weaken their grip. Throup, *Economic and Social Origins*, pp. 48–52.

85. John Iliffe, *A Modern History of Tanganyika* (Cambridge: Cambridge University Press, 1979), p. 450.

86. Throup, *Economic and Social Origins*, p. 47.

87. The following sections on Tanganyika draw heavily on Iliffe, *Modern History*.

88. Jan Jelmert Jørgensen, *Uganda: A Modern History* (London: Croom Helm, 1981), pp. 142–5.

89. T. V. Sathyamurthy, *The Political Development of Uganda: 1900–1986* (Aldershot: Gower, 1986), p. 302.

90. Iliffe, *Modern History*, 499–503; Thomas Spear, *Mountain Farmers: Moral Economies of Land and Agricultural Development in Arusha and Meru* (Oxford, Nairobi and Berkeley: James Currey, Mkuki na Nyota and University of California Press, 1997), Chapter 11.

91. On the women's section, and the dynamic contribution of Bibi Titi Mohammed, see Susan Geiger, *TANU Women: Gender and Culture in the Making of Tanganyikan Nationalism, 1955–1965* (Portsmouth, Oxford, Nairobi and Dar es Salaam: Heinemann, James Currey, EAEP and Mkuki na Nyota, 1997). See also Cranford Pratt, *The Critical Phase in Tanzania, 1945–1968: Nyerere and the Emergence of a Socialist Strategy* (Cambridge: Cambridge University Press, 1976), Chapters 2–3.

92. Iliffe, *Modern History*, p. 567. As with all of the most successful nationalist organisations, there was a cross-fertilisation of local and national agendas.

93. Iliffe, *Modern History*, p. 510.

94. Ibid., pp. 517, 536.

95. Ibid., p. 536.

96. Sathyamurthy, *Political Development*, p. 325.

97. Ibid., p. 377.

98. Throup, *Economic and Social Origins*; Tabitha Kanogo, *Squatters and the Roots of Mau Mau* (London: James Currey, 1987); Frank Furedi, *The Mau Mau War in Perspective* (London: James Currey, 1989); Bruce Berman, *Control and Crisis in Colonial Kenya* (London: James Currey, 1990); Bruce Berman and John Lonsdale, *Unhappy Valley: Conflict in Kenya and Africa, Books One and Two* (London: James Currey, 1992); Wunyabari Maloba, *Mau Mau and Kenya: An Analysis of a Peasant Revolt* (Indiana

University Press, 1993); Greet Kershaw, *Mau Mau From Below* (James Currey, Ohio University Press, 1997); and E. S. Atieno Odhiambo and John Lonsdale (eds), *Mau Mau and Nationhood: Arms, Authority and Narration* (Oxford, Nairobi and Athens: James Currey, EAEP and Ohio University Press, 2003).

99.   Colony and Protectorate of Kenya, *The Origins and Growth of Mau Mau: An Historical Survey* [Corfield Report] (Sessional Paper No. 5 of 1959/60) (Nairobi, 1960).

100. On this period of Kenyan politics, see Keith Kyle, *The Politics of the Independence of Kenya* (Basingstoke and London: Macmillan (now Palgrave Macmillan), 1999) and the contributions to B. A. Ogot and W. R. Ochieng (eds) *Decolonisation and Independence in Kenya 1940–93* (London, Nairobi and Athens: James Currey, East African Educational Publishers and Ohio University Press, 1995).

101. In 1950, there were 129,000 whites and 1,960,000 Africans in Southern Rhodesia. The comparable figures for Northern Rhodesia were 36,000 and 1,849,000, while for Nyasaland they were 4000 as against 2,330,000. Hargreaves, *Decolonisation*, p. 78.

102. In Southern Rhodesia in 1951, the franchise requirement was an income of £240 per annum and occupation of property valued at not less than £500. Patrick O'Meara, 'Rhodesia/Zimbabwe: guerrilla warfare or political settlement', in Gwendolen M. Carter and Patrick O'Meara (eds), *Southern Africa: The Continuing Crisis* (London and Basingstoke: Macmillan (now Palgrave Macmillan), 1979), p. 23.

103. Pearce, 'Colonial Office', p. 88.

104. Prosser Gifford, 'Misconceived dominion: the creation and disintegration of federation in British Central Africa', in Gifford and Louis, *Transfer of Power*, p. 401.

105. 'Misconceived dominion', pp. 403–4.

106. In Nyasaland, for example, the Legislative Council was composed of 12 official members, five African non-officials and six non-African non-official members.

107. In Nyasaland, over 1300 Africans were detained and 51 were killed. Colin Baker, *State of Emergency: Crisis in Central Africa, Nyasaland, 1959–1960* (London and New York: Tauris, 1997), pp. viii–ix.

108. In the Gold Coast in 1957 and in Nigeria in 1958. On the Nigerian case, see Tignor *Capitalism and Nationalism*, p.280.

109. Bangura, *Britain*, pp. 48–53.

110. Tignor, *Capitalism and Nationalism*, Chapters 6–8.

111. Ibid., p. 275.

112. Bangura, *Britain*, p. 107.

113. Tignor, *Capitalism and Nationalism*, pp. 366–75.

114. Ibid., pp. 378, 385. In all, some 2.5 million acres reverted to Africans in the 1960s.

115. See Nicola Swainson, *The Development of Corporate Capitalism in Kenya, 1918–1977* (London: Heinemann, 1980).

116. Leys, *Underdevelopment*, Chapters 7–8.

117. Quoted in Bangura, *Britain*, p. 110.
118. Quoted in Vaillant, *Black, French and African*, p. 192.
119. Yves Person, 'French West Africa and decolonisation', in Gifford and Louis, *Transfer*, p. 144.
120. Quoted in Catherine Coquery-Vidrovitch, 'The transfer of economic power in French-speaking Africa', in Prosser Gifford and Wm. Roger Louis (eds), *Decolonisation and African Independence: The Transfer of Power, 1960–1980* (New Haven and London: Yale University Press, 1988), p. 107.
121. Cited in John Chipman, *French Power in Africa* (Oxford: Blackwell, 1989), p. 70.
122. According to Hargreaves, *Decolonisation*, p. 96, FIDES channelled 18 per cent of its finances into social expenditure, roughly the same into the productive sectors and 64 per cent into infrastructure between 1946 and 1956.
123. Ruth Schachter Morgenthau, *Political Parties in French-Speaking Africa* (Oxford: Clarendon Press, 1964), p. 40.
124. Henri Brunschwig, 'The decolonisation of French Black Africa', in Gifford and Louis, *Transfer*, p. 220.
125. Brunschwig, 'The decolonisation', p. 220. Tony Chafer, *The End of Empire in French West Africa: France's Successful Decolonisation?* (Oxford and New York: Berg, 2002), pp. 61–7.
126. On labour, see Fred Cooper, 'The Senegalese general strike of 1946 and the labor question in post-war French West Africa', *Canadian Journal of African Studies* 24, 1990 and ' "Our strike": anticolonial politics and the 1947–48 railway strike in French West Africa', *Journal of African History* 36, 1996.
127. For the English translation, see Sembène Ousmane, *God's Bits of Wood* (translated by F. Price) (London: Heinemann, 1970).
128. On the background to the UPC revolt in Cameroun, see Richard Joseph, *Radical Nationalism in Cameroun: Social Origins of the UPC Rebellion* (Oxford: Clarendon Press, 1977).
129. The ideas of Senghor are explored in Vaillant, *Black, French and African*.
130. Chipman, *French Power in Africa*, p. 80; Person, 'French West Africa', p. 148.
131. A thinly veiled depiction of Guèye's intervention on the side of the exploiters is to be found in *God's Bits of Wood*.
132. Hargreaves, *Decolonisation*, p. 141.
133. D. E. K. Amenumey, *The Ewe Unification Movement: A Political History* (Accra: Ghana Universities Press, 1989), pp. 70–2.
134. Chipman, *French Power in Africa*, p. 100.
135. Ibid., p. 106.
136. Ibid., p. 107.
137. On the Guinean rebuff to de Gaulle, see Lansiné Kaba, *Le 'Non' de la Guinée à de Gaulle* (Paris: Editions Chaka, undated).
138. Person, 'French West Africa', p. 169.

139. The majority party in Gabon, under Léon M'ba, initially declined the offer of independence, preferring to become an overseas department. Elikia M'Bokolo, 'Comparisons and contrasts in equatorial Africa: Gabon, Congo and the Central African Republic', in David Birmingham and Phyllis Martin (eds), *History of Central Africa: The Contemporary Years Since 1960* (Harlow: Addison Wesley Longman, 1998), p. 79.

140. Around a hundred people were killed on the streets of Brazzaville in February 1959. M'Bokolo, 'Comparisons and contrasts', p. 78. See also Rémy Bazenguissa-Ganga, *Les voies du politique au Congo: essai de sociologie historique* (Paris: Karthala, 1997), Chapters 1–4.

141. Crawford Young, *Politics in the Congo*, Chapter 3.

142. Jean Stengers, 'Precipitous decolonisation: the case of the Belgian Congo', p. 320. Only 1557 *cartes de mérite civique* and 217 *immatriculation* cards were issued. Crawford Young, 'Zaire, Rwanda and Burundi', *Cambridge History of Africa, Volume 8: From 1940 to 1975* (Cambridge: Cambridge University Press, 1984), pp. 705–6.

143. Young, *Politics in the Congo*, p. 28.

144. Young, 'Zaire, Rwanda and Burundi', p. 706.

145. After the 1994 genocide in Rwanda, the new government and many commentators in the West insisted that the distinction was merely that of cattle-keepers and farmers and that there had been free movement between the Hutu and Tutsi categories. This has been attacked as a convenient social myth. Johan Pottier insists, on the basis of an earlier body of scholarship, that the nineteenth-century king, Rwabugri, created a rigid Hutu–Tutsi division by introducing *uburetwa* (labour service) exclusively for Hutus. See *Re-Imagining Rwanda: Conflict, Survival and Disinformation in the Late Twentieth-Century* (Cambridge: Cambridge University Press, 2002), p. 117.

146. Young, 'Zaire, Rwanda and Burundi', p. 707.

147. Young, *Politics in the Congo*, pp. 61–5.

148. European Common Market Survey, cited in Young, *Politics in the Congo*, p. 62.

149. Young, 'Zaire, Rwanda and Burundi', pp. 749–50; Stengers, 'Precipitous decolonisation', p. 308.

150. Young, 'Zaire, Rwanda and Burundi', p. 750; Stengers, 'Precipitous decolonisation', p. 310.

151. Stengers, 'Precipitous decolonisation', p. 315.

152. Patrice Lumumba, *Le Congo, terre d'avenir: est-il menacé?*, quoted in Stengers, 'Precipitous decolonisation', p. 314.

153. Stengers, 'Precipitous decolonisation', pp. 324–35.

154. Quoted in Stengers, 'Precipitous decolonisation', p. 324.

154. Stengers, 'Precipitous decolonisation', p. 320.

156. For a table of the results, see Young, *Politics in the Congo*, p. 302.

157. Ibid., p. 305.

158. Young, 'Zaire, Rwanda and Burundi', p. 713.

159. Young, 'Zaire, Rwanda and Burundi', p. 716.

2 A Profile of Africa at Independence

1. For a useful collection dealing with the urban tradition, see David M. Anderson and Richard Rathbone (eds) *Africa's Urban Past* (Oxford and Portsmouth: James Currey and Heinemann, 2000).
2. Ieuan Ll. Griffiths, *The African Inheritance* (London and New York: Routledge, 1995), p. 99.
3. Figures are from Charles M. Becker and Andrew R. Morrison, 'The growth of African cities: theory and estimates', in Archie Mafeje and Samir Radwan (eds) *Economic and Demographic Change in Africa* (Oxford: Clarendon Press, 1995), pp. 112–15, and Anthony O'Connor, *The African City* (London: Hutchinson, 1983), p. 48.
4. On the evolution of highlife, see John Collins, *Highlife Time*, 2nd edition (Accra: Anansesem Publications, 1996). On the evolution of Congolese music, see Gary Stewart, *Rumba on the River: A History of the Popular Music of the Two Congos* (London and New York: Verso, 2000); and Bob W. White, 'Congolese rumba and other cosmopolitanisms', *Cahiers d'Etudes Africaines* XLII, 168, 2002.
5. Kenneth W. J. Post and George D. Jenkins, *The Price of Liberty: Personality and Politics in Colonial Nigeria* (Cambridge: Cambridge University Press, 1973).
6. For an extended treatment of this theme, see Frederick Cooper, *Decolonisation and African Society: The Labor Question in French and British Africa* (Cambridge: Cambridge University Press, 1996).
7. H. W. Singer, 'Demographic factors in Subsaharan African economic development', in Melville J. Herskovits and Mitchell Harwitz (eds) *Economic Transition in Africa* (London: Routledge and Kegan Paul), p. 258.
8. Griffiths, *Africa Inheritance*, p. 101; Anthony O'Connor, *African City* notes that Kigali had fewer than 10,000 inhabitants in 1962.
9. For a highly instructive account of the differential pace of educational advancement within the South, as well as between North and South, see Philip S. Zachernuk, *Colonial Subjects: An African Intelligentsia and Atlantic Ideas* (Charlottesville and London: University Press of Virginia, 2000), pp. 82–4, 92, 128.
10. Mahmood Mamdani, *When Victims Become Killers: Colonialism, Nativism, and the Genocide in Rwanda* (Kampala, Cape Town and Oxford: Fountain, David Philip and James Currey, 2001), pp. 111–12.
11. René Dumont, *False Start in Africa* (London: Andre Deutsch, first English edition 1966), p. 32.
12. Griffiths, *African Inheritance*, p. 75.
13. Griffiths, *African Inheritance*, pp. 75, 81; Jeffrey Herbst, *States and Power in Africa: Comparative Lessons in Authority and Control* (Princeton: Princeton University Press, 2000), p. 140. The membership of the European Union refers to the period prior to expansion.
14. Griffiths, *African Inheritance*, p. 76.
15. Herbst, *States and Power*, Chapter 5.
16. Griffiths, *African Inheritance*, p. 81.

17. Herbst, *States and Power*, p. 145.
18. Ibid. p. 154.
19. Griffiths, *African Inheritance*, p. 114.
20. Megan Vaughan, 'Exploitation and neglect: rural producers and the state in Malawi and Zambia', in David Birmingham and Phyllis M. Martin (eds) *History of Central Africa: The Contemporary Years Since 1960* (Harlow: Addison Wesley Longman, 1998), p. 179.

3 The Shape of Things to Come: Irredentism, Secessionism and the Pan-African Ideal

1. For a reproduction of this poster, see A. H. M. Kirk-Greene, *Crisis and Conflict in Nigeria: A Documentary Sourcebook, 1966–1970 – Volume 1, January 1966 – July 1967* (London: Oxford University Press, 1971), p. 99.
2. Ieuan Ll. Griffiths, *The African Inheritance* (London and New York: Routledge, 1995), p. 172.
3. Tekeste Negash, *Eritrea and Ethiopia: The Federal Experience* (Uppsala and New Brunswick: Nordiska Afrikainstitutet, 1997).
4. Ruth Iyob, *The Eritrean Struggle for Independence: Domination, Resistance, Nationalism, 1941–1993* (Cambridge: Cambridge University Press, 1995), pp. 89–90.
5. Tekeste, *Eritrea and Ethiopia*, p. 133.
6. In his view, it was the Eritrean police which unleashed a policy of systematic repression against the defenders of federation.
7. In October 1957, two pro-federalists, Mohamed Omar Kadi and Woldeab Wolde Mariam presented a petition to the UN. The former was given a prison sentence of ten years when he returned.
8. Iyob, *Eritrean Struggle*, p. 93.
9. Iyob, *Eritrean Struggle*, pp. 101–6.
10. John Markakis, *National and Class Conflict in the Horn of Africa* (London: Zed Press, 1990), p. 107.
11. Quoted in Alemseged Abbay, *Identity Jilted or Re-Imagining Identity?: The Divergent Paths of the Eritrean and Tigrayan Nationalist Struggles* (Lawrenceville and Asmara: Red Sea Press, 1998), p. 112.
12. Iyob, *Eritrean Struggle*, p. 104.
13. It should not be assumed that Ewes were necessarily opposed to integration with Ghana. Indeed it is doubtful whether Ewe identity was as deeply held as the leaders of the Ewe unification movement alleged. See Paul Nugent, *Smugglers, Secessionists and Loyal Citizens on the Ghana-Togo Frontier: The Lie of the Borderlands Since 1914* (Oxford, Athens and Accra: James Currey, Ohio University Press and Subsaharan Publishers, 2002), Chapters 4–5.
14. Victor Julius Ngoh, *Southern Cameroons, 1922–1961: A Constitutional History* (Aldershot: Ashgate, 2001), pp. 140–2.
15. Edwin Ardener, 'The nature of the reunification of Cameroon', in Arthur Hazlewood (ed.) *African Integration and Disintegration: Case Studies in*

Economic and Political Union (London, New York and Toronto: Oxford University Press, 1967), pp. 321–31.

16. The following section draws heavily on Michael F. Lofchie, 'The Zanzibari revolution: African protest in a racially plural society', in Robert I. Rotberg and Ali A. Mazrui, *Protest and Power in Black Africa* (New York: Oxford University Press, 1970).

17. Lofchie, 'Zanzibari revolution', p. 965.

18. Ibid., p. 967.

19. Cranford Pratt, *The Critical Phase in Tanzania, 1945–1968: Nyerere and the Emergence of a Socialist Strategy* (Nairobi, Oxford and New York: Oxford University Press, 1976), p. 180.

20. Janet G. Vaillant, *Black, French and African: A Life of Léopold Sédar Senghor* (Cambridge and London: Harvard University Press, 1990), p. 298.

21. Griffiths, *African Inheritance*, p. 166.

22. Mensah had become something like the official praise-singer of the Nkrumah government. This track is available on compact disc. E. T. Mensah, *Day By Day: Classic Highlife Recordings of the 1950s and 1960s* (London: RetroAfric, 1991).

23. Griffiths, *African Inheritance.*, p. 167.

24. A. I. Asiwaju, 'Partitioned culture areas: a checklist', in A. I. Asiwaju (ed.) *Partitioned Africans: Ethnic Relations Across Africa's International Boundaries 1884–1984* (London and Lagos: Christopher Hurst and University of Lagos Press, 1984), pp. 256–8.

25. Lesotho made a weak claim to the land in the Orange Free State. Griffiths, *African Inheritance*, p. 144. There were Swazis in Mozambique as well as South Africa.

26. See the revisionist contributions to Ali Jimale Ahmed (ed.) *The Invention of Somalia* (Lawrenceville: Red Sea Press, 1995). On the place of clan in Somali culture and political life, see the collection of essays by Ioan M. Lewis, *Blood and Bone: The Call of Kinship in Somali Society* (Trenton: Red Sea Press, 1994).

27. The Somali government went as far as cutting off diplomatic ties with Britain in spite of the loss of aid this entailed. Markakis, *National and Class*, pp. 186–7.

28. Markakis, *National and Class*, p. 175.

29. Markakis, *National and Class*, pp. 178, 189.

30. I. M. Lewis, *A Modern History of Somalia: Nation and State in the Horn of Africa* (Boulder and London: Westview Press, 1988), pp. 238–9.

31. Markakis, *National and Class*, p. 148.

32. Douglas Johnson, *The Root Causes of Sudan's Civil Wars* (Oxford, Bloomington, Indianapolis and Kampala: James Currey, IAI, Indiana University Press and Fountain Publishers, 2003), p. 30.

33. In July 1965, over a thousand citizens of Juba were massacred by government forces. Markakis, *National and Class*, p. 161.

34. Ibid., p. 164.

35. Simon Katzenellenbogen, *Railways and the Copper Mines of Katanga* (London: Oxford University Press, 1973).

36. Crawford Young, *Politics in the Congo: Decolonisation and Independence* (Princeton: Princeton University Press, 1965), p. 210.

37. Young, *Politics in the Congo*, p. 244.

38. The colonial conception of 'tribe' was one which regarded ethnicity as a given rather than as something which was constantly reworked and renegotiated. Although 'tribes' were not invented in any simple sense, nor could they be considered as timeless entities.

39. An excellent overview of these events is presented in Isodore Ndaywel è Nziem, *Histoire générale du Congo: de l'héritage ancien à la République Démocratique* (Paris and Brussels: De Boeck and Larcier, 1998), pp. 565–646.

40. Ndaywel, *Histoire générale*, pp. 577, 590.

41. Young, *Politics in the Congo*, p. 17.

42. Edgar O'Ballance, *The Congo–Zaire Experience, 1960–98* (Basingstoke and New York: Macmillan and St. Martin's Press, 2000), p. 25.

43. Young, *Politics in the Congo*, p. 336.

44. Crawford Young, 'Zaire: the anatomy of a failed state', in David Birmingham and Phyllis Martin (eds) *History of Central Africa: the Contemporary Years Since 1960* (Harlow: Addison Wesley Longman, 1998), p. 104.

45. Ludo De Witte, *The Assassination of Lumumba* (London and New York: Verso, 2001). American plans for the assassination of Lumumba had been in the air since August. The De Witte book, which went as far as to implicate the Belgian government and King Baudouin himself, produced a storm of controversy in Belgium. A Parliamentary commission was set up in 2000 to belatedly look into the accusations. The report, which was published the following year, was at pains to stress the context in which the events took place. Although it avoided identifying a smoking gun, its middle-of-the-road assessment was nevertheless a step beyond previous denials of Belgian involvement. The report states that: 'No single document, of which the commission is aware, indicates that the Belgian government or a member thereof gave the order to physically eliminate Lumumba; The investigation does not show that the Belgian authorities premeditated the murder of Lumumba when it attempted to transfer him to Katanga; It is very clear, though, that the physical safety of Lumumba was of no concern to the Belgian government. It deemed the safety of Lumumba less important than other interests.' Quoted in Edouard Bustin, 'Remembrance of sins past: unravelling the murder of Patrice Lumumba', *Review of African Political Economy* 93/94, 2002, p. 550.

46. Young, *Politics in the Congo*, p. 342.

47. At one point, Tshombe was even placed under arrest for two months after he walked out of talks in Leopoldville. Young, *Politics in the Congo*, p. 337.

48. Gisenga was amongst those who was opposed to the compromise and he endeavoured to mobilise resistance to it. However, most of the supporters of the Stanleyville administration rallied to the Adoula government and Gisenga himself was placed under arrest.

49. Ndaywel, *Histoire générale*, p. 602.

50. The underlying themes were self-reliance and the need to win peasants over to the side of the revolution. These were encapsulated in a code of conduct borrowed from a Vietnamese Communist Party manual attributed to Mao. Ndaywel, *Histoire générale*, p. 616; Benoît Verhaegen, 'Le rôle de l'ethnie et de l'individu dans la rébellion du Kwilu et son échec', in Catherine Coquery-Vidrovitch, Alain Forest and Herbert Weiss (eds) *Rébellions-révolution au Zaire 1963–1965, tome 1* (Paris: L'Harmattan, 1987), p. 162.

51. It was present in the Maji-Maji rebellion in German Tanganyika (1905–07), and recurred in the Mai-Mai movement in the eastern Congo at the end of the century.

52. Mulele himself was executed by the government in September 1968, having decided to return to Kinshasa in the knowledge that he was taking a large personal risk. Ndaywel, *Histoire générale*, p. 630.

53. For the second liberation, see the studies contained in Catherine Coquery-Vidrovitch, Alain Forest and Herbert Weiss (eds) *Rébellions-révolution au Zaire 1963–1965, 2 tomes* (Paris: L'Harmattan, 1987).

54. Ndaywel, *Histoire générale*, p. 620.

55. The head of the rebel state was Christophe Gbenye, while the position of Foreign Minister was bestowed on one Laurent Kabila, who was to loom large in the subsequent history of the Congo.

56. Wililunga B Cosma, *Fizi, 1967–1986: le maquis Kabila* (Brussels and Paris: Institut Africain and L'Harmattan, 1997).

57. Herbert Weiss, 'Collapsed society, surviving state, future polity', in William Zartman (ed.) *Collapsed States: The Disintegration and Restoration of Legitimate Authority* (Boulder: Lynne Rienner, 1995) pp. 166–7.

58. Young, 'Zaire: the anatomy', p. 730.

59. Obafemi Awolowo, *Path to Nigerian Freedom* (London: Faber and Faber reprint, 1947 edition), p. 47.

60. The best treatment remains Richard Sklar, *Nigerian Political Parties: Power in an Emergent Nation* (Princeton: Princeton University Press, 1963).

61. Colonial Office, *Report of the Commission Appointed to Enquire into the Fears of Minorities and the Means of Allaying Them* [Willinck Commission] (London: HMSO, 1958).

62. Whereas the AG supported the efforts of the UMBC, the NCNC allied itself to NEPU which appealed to the Hausa *talakawa* (or commoners) against the Fulani aristocracy.

63. Larry Diamond, *Class, Ethnicity and Democracy in Nigeria: The Failure of the First Republic* (Basingstoke: Macmillan, 1988). This section draws heavily on this monograph.

64. Diamond, *Class, Ethnicity and Democracy*, p. 106.

65. However, the NPC took most of the Ministerial slots and AG politicians were cut out entirely.

66. Diamond, *Class, Ethnicity and Democracy*, pp. 271–2.

67. Obasanjo had come to know Nzeogwu when then they were both serving with the Nigerian military contingent in the Congo. They apparently shared a dim view of the drinking excesses of their commanding officer,

then Lt.-Colonel Aguiyi Ironsi. Olusegun Obasanjo, *Nzeogwu* (Ibadan: Spectrum Books, 1987).

68. During the coup, Nzeogwu was quoted by a northern source as saying that those he wanted to eliminate were the likes of Azikiwe, Ahmadu Bello, Akintola, Okpara, Okotie-Eboe, and Orizu. This list contained the names of the most prominent Igbo politicians. Azikiwe was out of the country at the time. Sir Kashim Ibrahim quoted in D. J. M. Muffett, *Let Truth Be Told: The Coups d'Etat of 1966* (Zaria: Hudahuda Publishing, 1982), p. 35. Adewale Ademoyega, *Why We Struck: The Story of the First Nigerian Coup* (Ibadan: Evans Brothers, 1981), p. 60 presents a more benign version of the plot.

69. Ben Gbulie, *Nigeria's Five Majors: Coup d'Etat of 15th January 1966 First Inside Account* (Onitsha: Africana Educational Publishers, 1981), p. 58.

70. Muffett, *Let Truth Be Told*, p. 39–40.

71. The selective killing of officers does seem to have been envisaged. Obasanjo refers to a plan to eliminate Ojuwku. *Nzeogwu*, p. 94. Muffett, *Let Truth Be Told*, p. 58 quotes a newspaper interview given by Nzeogwu on 18 January in which he explicitly stated that Ironsi was supposed to have been killed. A highly jaundiced view of the coup plot is provided in A. M. Mainasara, *The Five Majors: Why They Struck* (Zaria: Hudahuda Publishing, 1982).

72. In reality, Ironsi was of an entirely different generation and mindset to that of the young Majors, who seem to have had a very low opinion of his abilities.

73. On a landmark study of the military before and after the coup, see Robin Luckham, *The Nigerian Military: A Sociological Analysis of Authority and Revolt 1960–67* (Cambridge: Cambridge University, 1971).

74. A. H. M. Kirk-Greene, *Crisis and Conflict – Volume 1, January 1966–July 1967* (London: Oxford University Press, 1971), p. 54.

75. Kirk-Greene, *Crisis and Conflict, Volume 1*, p. 54. One of his first acts was to release Awolowo and others who had been imprisoned under the civilian administration.

76. It is estimated that between May and September some 80,000–100,000 Easterners were killed. Eghosa Osaghae, *Crippled Giant: Nigeria Since Independence* (London: Christopher Hurst, 1998), p. 63.

77. On the Igbo presence in the North, see Douglas Anthony, *Poison and Medicine: Ethnicity, Power and Violence in a Nigerian City, 1966 to 1986* (Portsmouth, Oxford and Cape Town: Heinemann, James Currey and David Philip, 2002), Chapter 1.

78. Kirk-Greene, *Crisis and Conflict, Volume 1*, pp. 92–3.

79. Wayne Nafziger, *The Economics of Political Instability: The Nigerian-Biafran War* (Boulder: Westview Press, 1983), p. 105.

80. None of the tax on profits went directly to the East and only half of the rents and royalties did so. In 1967, if there had been no war, the East stood to receive £N9.4 million as opposed to the £N30 million which would have accrued if everything was paid over to the producing region. Nafziger, *Economics*, p. 106.

81. The companies in question were Shell-British Petroleum, Mobil and Gulf.

82. A compelling account of the secession from the minorities from point of view is offered in Ken Saro-Wiwa, *On a Darkling Plain: An Account of the Nigerian Civil War* (London, Lagos and Port Harcourt: Saros Publishers, 1989). This interpretation is confirmed by later research in the field. See Jones O. Ahuazem, 'Perceptions: Biafra, politics and the war', in Axel Harneit-Sievers, Jones Ahuazem and Sydney Emezue (eds) *A Social History of the Nigerian Civil War* (Enugu and Hamburg: Jemezie Associates and Lit Verlag, 1997), pp. 32–44.

83. The total number of deaths is estimated at anywhere between one and three million, with a further three million peoples becoming refugees and displaced persons. Osaghae, *Crippled Giant*, p. 69.

84. For a pro-Biafran account of the war, see Herbert Ekwe-Ekwe, *The Biafra War: Nigeria and the Aftermath* (Lewiston, Queenston and Lampeter, Edwin Mellen Press, 1990). For an insider view, see Alexander Madiebo, *The Nigerian Revolution and the Biafran War* (Enugu: Fourth Dimension Publishers, 1980).

85. John J. Stremlau, *The International Politics of the Nigerian Civil War, 1967–1970* (Princeton: Princeton University Press, 1977), p. 58.

86. Nafziger, *Economics*, pp. 105–6.

87. Frederick Forsyth wrote and spoke a great deal in support of the Biafrans. See, for example, *The Biafra Story* (London: Penguin, 1969).

88. The Biafrans had to make do with what they had, and this led to some small-scale inventions which was made much of. See Reuben N. Ogbudinkpa, *The Economics of the Nigerian Civil War and its Prospects for National Development* (Enugu: Fourth Dimension Publishers, 1985).

89. Wole Soyinka wrote a prison diary, published as *The Man Died: Prison Notes of Wole Soyinka* (London: Rex Collings: 1973). Fela's 'Viva Nigeria' has been re-released on CD as the *'69 Los Angeles Sessions* (London: Stern's, 1993).

90. Ekwe-Ekwe, *Biafra War*, p. 85. France sold arms to the Biafrans on the sly. Tekena Tamuno, 'Introduction: men and measures in the Nigerian crisis, 1960–70', in Tekena N. Tamuno and Samson C. Ukpabi (eds) *Nigeria Since Independence, the First 25 Years – Volume VI, The Civil War Years* (Ibadan: Heinemann Educational Books, 1989), p. 15. On the international dimension more generally, see Stremlau, *International Politics*.

91. This is brought out in an excellent BBC documentary, in the Timewatch series, entitled 'Biafra: Fighting a War Without Guns' (1995).

92. As early as September 1967, there were plans afoot to replace Ojukwu, which were dealt with mercilessly. From this point onwards, suspicions about the loyalties of senior officers became deeply embedded. See Bernard Odogwu, *No Place to Hide: Crisis and Conflict Inside Biafra* (Enugu: Fourth Dimension Publishers, 1985), Chapters 5–6; and Madiebo, *The Nigerian Revolution*, pp. 166–70, 379–81.

93. A. H. M. Kirk-Greene, *Crisis and Conflict in Nigeria: A Documentary Sourcebook, 1966–1970 – Volume 2, July 1967–January 1970* (London: Oxford University Press, 1971), pp. 143–4. Also Paul Obi-Ani, 'Post-civil war Nigeria: reconciliation or vendetta?' and Pat Uche Okpoko, 'Three

decades after Biafra: a critique of the reconciliation policy', both in Toyin Falola (eds) *Nigeria in the Twentieth Century* (Durham: Carolina Academic Press, 2002).

94. See Ahuazem and Emezue (eds) *A Social History of the Nigerian Civil War*, Axel Harneit-Seivers and Sydney Emezue, 'Towards a social history of warfare and reconstruction: the Biafran case', in Ifi Amadiume and Abdullah An-Na'im (eds) *The Politics of Memory: Truth, Healing and Social Justice* (London and New York: Zed, 2002) and other contributions to this volume; and Anthony, *Poison and Medicine*.

95. Lisette was of Caribbean origin. Sam C. Nolutshungu, *Limits of Anarchy: Intervention and State Formation in Chad* (Charlottesville and London: University Press of Virginia, 1996), p. 50.

96. Quoted in Nolutshungu, *Limits of Anarchy*, p. 61. For a comprehensive history of the movement, see Robert Buijtenhuijs, *Le Frolinat et les guerres civiles du Tchad (1977–1984): la révolution introuvable* (Paris and Leiden: Karthala and Afrika-Studiecentrum, 1987).

97. The emergence of a Mobutu axis was thought to signal a drift towards the United States, while warmer relations with Nigeria were also regarded with concern in Paris given previous French support for Biafran secession.

98. Nolutshungu, *Limits of Anarchy*, pp. 87–8.

99. Ibid., p. 130.

100. Because the relevant treaty had never been ratified, the legality of Libyan claims was dubious and in 1994 the International Court of Justice finally decided in favour of Chad.

101. On the first occasion, Nkrumah benefited from the fact that the only other head of state to attend was President Tubman of Liberia, although even then he did not have everything his own way. See W. Scott Thompson, *Ghana's Foreign Policy, 1957–1966; Diplomacy, Ideology, and the New State* (Princeton: Princeton University Press, 1969), pp. 31–9.

102. Klaas Van Walraven, *Dreams of Power: The Role of the Organisation of African Unity in the Politics of Africa, 1963–1993* (Aldershot: Ashgate, 1999), pp. 102–3.

103. Van Walraven, *Dreams of Power*, p. 106.

104. The Union Africaine et Malgache (UAM), the Organisation Africaine et Malgache de Co-opération Economique (OAMCE) and the Union Africaine et malgache de Défense (UAMD) were the most important. Van Walraven, *Dreams of Power*, p. 106.

105. Saadia Touval, *The Boundary Politics of Independent Africa* (Cambridge: Harvard University Press, 1972), p. 67.

106. The case for continental union was spelled out in Kwame Nkrumah, *Africa Must Unite* (London: Heinemann, 1963).

107. Van Walraven, *Dreams of Power*, p. 124.

108. For the text of the Charter, see Gino Naldi (ed.) *Documents of the Organisation of African Unity* (London and New York: Mansell, 1992), pp. 3–10.

109. Jon Woronoff, *Organising African Unity* (Metuchen: Scarecrow Press, 1970), p. 624. For an analysis of the Charter, see Gino Naldi, *The Organisation of African Unity: An Analysis of its Role* (London and New York: Mansell, 1989), pp. 4–14.

110. See the text in Naldi, *Documents*, p. 49.

111. Iyob, *Eritrean Struggle*, pp. 51–2.

112. Van Walraven, *Dreams of Power*, p. 312. A. G. G. Gingyera-Pincywa, 'The border implications of the Sudan civil war: possibilities for intervention', in Dunstan M. Wai (ed.) *The Southern Sudan: The Problem of National Integration* (London: Frank Cass, 1973), p. 134.

113. Van Walraven, *Dreams of Power*, p. 307.

114. Ibid., p. 24.

4 Modernity and Tradition, Power and Prestige: Monarchs, Chiefs and Politicians, 1956–74

1. Pierre Alexandre, 'The problems of chieftaincies in French-speaking Africa', in Michael Crowder and Obaro Ikime (eds) *West African Chiefs: Their Changing Status Under Colonial Rule and Independence* (Ile-Ife: University of Ife Press, 1970), p. 24.

2. For example, E. Adriaan, B. Van Rouveroy Van Nieuwaal and Werner Zips (eds) *Sovereignty, Legitimacy, and Power in West African Societies: Perspectives From Legal Anthropology* (Hamburg and New Brunswick: Lit Verlag and Transaction, 1998); E. Adriaan, B. Van Rouveroy Van Nieuwaal and Rijk Van Dijk (eds) *African Chieftaincy in a New Socio-Political Landscape* (Münster and London: Lit Verlag, 1999), and special issue of *Journal of Legal Pluralism*, 37–8, 1996.

3. Mahmood Mamdani, *Citizen and Subject: Contemporary Africa and the Legacy of Late Colonialism* (Kampala, Cape Town and London: Fountain, David Philip and James Currey, 1996).

4. Christopher Clapham, *Haile-Selassie's Government* (London: Longman, 1969), pp. 34–5.

5. Harold G. Marcus, *A History of Ethiopia* (Berkeley, Los Angeles and London: University of California Press, 1994), p. 161.

6. John Markakis, *Ethiopia: Anatomy of a Traditional Polity* (Oxford: Oxford University Press), Chapter 9.

7. There were no political parties and the turnout was typically very low, even in Addis Ababa. Markakis, *Ethiopia*, pp. 277–87.

8. Clapham, *Haile-Selassie's Government*, p. 39.

9. Markakis, *Ethiopia*, pp. 213–15.

10. Ibid., p. 215.

11. Ibid., pp. 223–7. The virtual absence of a national Budget contributed to the lack of financial discipline which had steered the country towards the financial rocks by 1968.

12. Edmond J. Keller, *Revolutionary Ethiopia: From Empire to People's Republic* (Bloomington and Indianapolis: Indiana University Press, 1988), p. 133.

13. Ibid., p. 166.
14. Ibid., pp. 171–2.
15. René Lefort, *Ethiopia: An Heretical Revolution?* (London: Zed Press, 1981), p. 55.
16. Andargachew Tiruneh, *The Ethiopian Revolution, 1974–1987: A Transformation From an Aristocratic to a Totalitarian Autocracy* (Cambridge: Cambridge University Press, 1993), p. 38.
17. Keller, *Revolutionary Ethiopia*, p. 184.
18. Ryszard Kapuscinski, *The Emperor: The Downfall of an Autocrat* (London: Picador, 1983).
19. Donald Donham, *Marxist Modern: An Ethnographic History of the Ethiopian Revolution* (Berkeley, Los Angeles and Oxford: University of California Press and James Currey, 1999), p. 25.
20. Andargachew, *Ethiopian Revolution*, p. 56.
21. In this case, it took the form of a debate about the basis of chieftaincy in Maale. Donham, *Marxist Modern*, pp. 38–45.
22. René Lemarchand, *Burundi: Ethnic Conflict and Genocide* (Cambridge: Cambridge University Press, 1994), pp. 37–9. This section draws extensively on Lemarchand.
23. Ibid., p. 53.
24. Ibid., pp. 92–3.
25. Richard Levin, *When the Sleeping Grass Awakens: Land and Power in Swaziland* (Johannesburg: Witwatersrand University Press, 1997), pp. 50–4.
26. After the buy-backs, half of the land remained alienated. Levin argues that the Swazi chiefs were able to extract labour and tribute through their control over this scarce factor of production. See *When the Sleeping Grass Awakens*.
27. Gabriele Winai Ström, *Development and Dependence in Lesotho, the Enclave of South Africa* (Uppsala: Scandinavian Institute of African Studies, 1978), p. 41.
28. Richard F. Weisfelder, *Political Contention in Lesotho, 1952–1965* (Maseru: Institute of Southern African Studies, 1999), pp. 15, 17. This section draws heavily on this source.
29. The election was indirect from the District Council level to the central legislature. Furthermore, women were disenfranchised by the requirement that voters had to be taxpayers. L. B. B. J. Machobane, *Government and Change in Lesotho, 1800–1966: A Study of Political Institutions* (Basingstoke: Macmillan, 1990), p. 296.
30. Weisfelder, *Political Contention*, pp. 35–6. This was despite the fact that Jonathan had been closely allied to the Regent and thus opposed to the Moshoeshoe faction.
31. The element which was loyal to the ANC seceded and – somewhat bizarrely – joined up with the MP to form the Marematlou Freedom Party (MFP).
32. Weisfelder, *Political Contention*, p. 48. *Report of the Basutoland Constitutional Commission, 1963* (Maseru: Basutoland Council, 1963).
33. From this point onwards, women could vote.

34. Chief Jonathan actually failed to win a seat until a BNP parliamentarian resigned his seat to make way for him. Machobane, *Government and Change*, p. 301. For a detailed analysis of these elections, see part II of Weisfelder, *Political Contention*.
35. Machobane, *Government and Change*, p. 304.
36. B. M. Khaketla, *Lesotho 1970: An African Coup Under the Microscope* (London: C. Hurst, 1971), p. 181.
37. Ström, *Development and Dependence*, p. 93. L. B. B. J. Machobane, *King's Knights: Military Governance in the Kingdom of Lesotho* (Roma: Institute of Southern African Studies, 2001), pp. 26–7.
38. The land committees contained four elected members, three government appointees and a chief. The chiefs retained control over cattle-post grazing grounds. James Ferguson, *The Anti-Politics Machine: 'Development', Depoliticisation and Bureaucratic Power in Lesotho* (Cambridge: Cambridge University Press, 1990), p. 131.
39. Ström, *Development and Dependence*, p. 96.
40. Writing in 1978, Ström asserted that 'Today a foreign aid expert or a state employee has a greater influence on how the land is used than a chief ever had', Ibid., p. 95.
41. Ferguson, *Anti-Politics Machine*.
42. This included some 8800 migrant workers in South Africa, 24,000 rural workers and 5400 urban workers. Levin, *When the Sleeping Grass Awakens*, p. 61. The section which follows draws heavily on Levin.
43. Levin, *When the Sleeping Grass Awakens*, pp. 65–70.
44. Each constituency contained three seats, all of which passed to the party which won a plurality of the votes.
45. Levin, *When the Sleeping Grass Awakens*, p. 78.
46. For an account which emphasises British interventionism, see P. K. Tibenderana, *Sokoto Province Under British Rule, 1903–1939* (Zaria: Ahmadu Bello University Press, 1988).
47. Richard L. Sklar, *Nigerian Political Parties: Power in an Emergent African Nation* (Princeton: Princeton University Press, 1963), p. 356.
48. Ibid., p. 362.
49. Ibid., pp. 335–8.
50. Jonathan T. Reynolds, *The Time of Politics (Zamanin Siyasa): Islam and the Politics of Legitimacy in Northern Nigeria 1950–1966* (San Francisco, London and Bethesda: International Scholars Publications, 1999), Chapter 1.
51. Insulting an Emir, or even referring to him in a campaign speech, was enough to attract a lengthy prison sentence from the Native Court. For examples, see Reynolds, *Time of Politics*, Chapter 1.
52. Usman dan Fodio was the founding leader of the Sokoto Caliphate. Bello was his great-great-grandson and hoped one day to succeed to position of Sultan. Reynolds, *Time of Politics*, p. 47.
53. Olufemi Vaughan, *Nigerian Chiefs: Traditional Power in Modern Politics 1890s–1990s* (Rochester and Woodbridge: University of Rochester Press, 2000), p. 71.

54. Alhaji Mahmood Yakubu, *An Aristocracy in Crisis: The End of Indirect Rule and the Emergence of Party Politics in the Emirates of Northern Nigeria* (Aldershot: Avebury, 1996), p. 189.

55. Indeed it was his apparent untouchability which led him to display open disrespect towards Regional ministers, and thus led to his spectacular downfall. Yakubu, *Aristocracy*, pp. 192–8.

56. Vaughan, *Nigerian Chiefs*, pp. 94–5.

57. Vaughan notes that a number of chiefs were appointed Ministers without portfolio over 1964/65. *Nigerian Chiefs*, p. 115.

58. Ibid., pp. 122–5. The Emirs were also permitted to replace nominated Native Authority councillors with their own appointees.

59. Ibid., p. 125.

60. Eghosa Osaghae, *Nigeria Since Independence: Crippled Giant* (London: C. Hurst, 1998), p. 91.

61. Vaughan, *Nigerian Chiefs*, p. 140.

62. Moreover, this was a government which began by courting traditional rulers. Osaghae, *Nigeria Since Independence*, p. 182.

63. For an overview of the trajectory of Ghanaian chieftaincy, see Donald I. Ray, 'Chief-state relations in Ghana – divided sovereignty and legitimacy', in Van Rouveroy and Zips, *Sovereignty*.

64. Richard Rathbone, *Nkrumah and the Chiefs: The Politics of Chieftaincy in Ghana, 1951–60* (Oxford, Accra and Athens: James Currey, F. Reimmer and Ohio University Press, 2000), pp. 52–5.

65. Ibid., p. 126.

66. Ibid., pp. 140–1. The regime also cunningly exploited the faultlines in Ashanti between the core and the Brong periphery when it carved out a separate Brong-Ahafo Region in 1958. See F. K. Drah, 'The Brong Political movement', in Kwame Arhin (ed.) *Brong Kyempim: Essays on the Society, History and Politics of the Brong People* (Legon: Institute of African Studies, 1979).

67. Equally, on the Ashanti queenmother's court, see Beverly J. Stoeltje, 'Narration and negotiation: a woman's case in the queenmother's court in Ghana', in Van Rouveroy and Zips, *Sovereignty*.

68. The chiefs were often able to profit personally from this control. See Sara S. Berry, *Chiefs Know Their Boundaries: Essays on Property, Power and the Past in Asante, 1896–1996* (Portsmouth, Oxford and Cape Town: Heinemann, James Currey and David Philip, 2001), p. 115.

69. Jan Jelmert Jørgensen, *Uganda: A Modern History* (London: Croom Helm, 1981), p. 149.

70. M. Crawford Young, 'The Obote revolution', *Africa Report*, June 1966, p. 10.

71. Phares Mutibwa, *Uganda Since Independence: A Story of Unfulfilled Hopes* (London: Hurst and Company, 1992), p. 19.

72. Young, 'Obote', p. 10.

73. Jørgensen, *Uganda*, p. 223.

74. Ibid., p. 224.

75. For a full analysis, see Young, 'Obote', p. 10.

76. Ibid., p. 8.

77. Joel Samoff, *Tanzania: Local Politics and the Structure of Power* (Madison: University of Wisconsin Press, 1974), p. 21.

78. In the case of Shambaai, for example, the rebels won control of the royal council, and forced the king into exile. Stephen Feierman, *Peasant Intellectuals: Anthropology and History in Tanzania* (Madison and London: University of Wisconsin Press, 1990), pp. 228–31.

79. In 1963, the African Chiefs Ordinance (Repeal) Act formally brought the end of chieftaincy. Some ex-chiefs were co-opted onto local councils as *ex officio* members, but they were there as individuals rather than as traditional authorities. William Tordoff, *Government and Politics of Tanzania: A Collection of Essays Covering the Period from September 1960 to July 1966* (Nairobi: East African Publishing House, 1967), p. 114.

80. Anthony Sillery, *Botswana: A Short Political History* (London: Methuen, 1974), pp. 183–4.

81. Anne M. O. Griffiths, *In the Shadow of Marriage: Gender and Justice in an African Community* (Chicago and London: University of Chicago Press, 1997), p. 35.

82. Ibid., p. 36.

83. For the Yoruba case, see A. I. Asiwaju, *Western Yorubaland Under European Rule, 1889–1945: A Comparative Analysis of French and British Colonialism* (London: Longman, 1976), p. 79. And for the Hausa instance, see William F. S. Miles, *Hausaland Divided: Colonialism and Independence in Nigeria and Niger* (Ithaca and London: Cornell University Press, 1994), Chapters 5–6. In another comparison between the Bakweri of British Cameroon and the Maka of French Cameroon, Peter Geschiere argues that it was actually the French who were more consistent in backing their created chiefs. However, the net result was the same, in that the Bakweri chieftaincy retained a good deal more vitality than its Maka counterpart. Peter Geschiere, 'Chiefs and indirect rule in Cameroon: inventing chieftaincy, French and British style', *Africa* 63, 2, 1993.

84. See extract in Pierre Alexandre, 'The problems', p. 65.

85. Ibid., p. 58.

86. The council member who acquired the most votes overall became the chief. See the decree of 26 December 1957, reproduced in Alexandre, 'The problems', pp. 62–3. On the events leading up to this episode, see Jean Suret-Canale, 'La fin de la chefferie en Guinée', *Journal of African History* 7, 3, 1966.

87. William Derman, *Serfs, Peasants and Socialists: A Former Serf Village in the Republic of Guinea* (Berkeley, Los Angeles and London: University of California Press, 1973), pp. 177–8.

88. Donal Cruise O'Brien, *The Mourides of Senegal: The Political and Economic Organisation of an Islamic Brotherhood* (Oxford: Clarendon Press, 1971), pp. 268–9.

89. Edward J. Schumacher, *Politics, Bureaucracy and Rural Development in Senegal* (Berkeley, Los Angeles and London: University of California Press, 1975), pp. 87–8.

90. Mamdani, *Citizen and Subject*.

91. For a useful overview of the literature on the relationship between segregationism and apartheid, see William Beinart and Saul Dubow, 'Introduction: the historiography of segregation and apartheid', in William Beinart and Saul Dubow (eds) *Segregation and Apartheid in Twentieth-Century South Africa* (London and New York: Routledge, 1995).

92. The term coined by the Stallard Commission, whose main ideas were enshrined in the Natives (Urban Areas) Act of 1923.

93. The classic statement of the position that apartheid was all about resolving the labour problem is Harold Wolpe, 'Capitalism and cheap lab our power in South Africa: from segregation to apartheid', *Economy and Society* 1, 1972, conveniently republished in Beinart and Dubow, *Segregation and Apartheid*.

94. Peter Delius, *A Lion Amongst the Cattle: Reconstruction and Resistance in the Northern Transvaal* (Portsmouth, Johannesburg and Oxford: Heinemann, Ravan Press and James Currey, 1996), p. 54.

95. For a discussion of resistance in Sekhukuneland, see Delius, *A Lion*, p. 59.

96. For a discussion of the farming lobby in the Eastern Cape, see Anne Kelk Mager, *Gender and the Making of a South African Bantustan: A Social History of the Ciskei, 1945–1959* (Portsmouth, Oxford and Cape Town: Heinemann, James Currey and David Philip, 1999).

97. Henry Kenney, *Architect of Apartheid: H. F. Verwoerd – An Appraisal* (Johannesburg: Jonathan Ball, 1980), p. 94.

98. For a fuller discussion, see ibid., pp. 93–6.

99. Verwoerd, quoted in ibid., p. 92.

100. Delius, *A Lion*, p. 141.

101. For details, see Tom Lodge, *Black Politics in South Africa Since 1945* (London and New York: Longman, 1983), pp. 273–9.

102. Ibid., pp. 279–83. For a detailed study of the Mpondo case, see Fred T. Hendricks, *The Pillars of Apartheid: Land Tenure, Rural Planning and the Chieftaincy* (Uppsala: Uppsala University, 1990).

103. An indication of how seriously the revolt was taken lies in the deployment of armoured vehicles and helicopters and the declaration of a state of emergency. William Beinart and Colin Bundy, 'State intervention and rural resistance: the Transkei, 1900–1965', in Martin Klein (ed.) *Peasants in Africa: Historical and Contemporary Perspectives* (Beverley Hills and London: Sage, 1980), p. 304.

104. Lodge, *Black Politics*, pp. 283–8.

105. On Matanzima, see Ivan Evans, *Bureaucracy and Race: Native Administration in South Africa* (Berkeley, Los Angeles and London: University of California Press, 1997), pp. 249–56.

106. Quoted in Robert M. Price, *The Apartheid State in Crisis: Political Transformation in South Africa 1975–1990* (New York and Oxford: Oxford University Press, 1991), p. 22.

107. Kenney, *Architect*, pp. 231–2.

108. Mzala, *Gatsha Buthelezi: Chief With a Double Agenda* (London: Zed Press, 1988), pp. 30–1. See also Gerhard Maré and Georgina Hamilton,

An Appetite For Power: Buthelezi's Inkatha and South Africa (Braam-fontein and Bloomington: Ravan Press and Indiana University Press, 1987).

109. Newell M. Stultz, *Transkei's Half Loaf: Race Separatism in South Africa* (Cape Town: David Philip, 1979), p. 82.

110. Mzala, *Gatsha Buthelezi*, p. 78.

111. Section 10 of the 1955 Natives (Urban Areas) Amendment Act stipulated that the only Africans with the right to remain in the urban areas were those who had been born there, had lived there continuously for 15 years or had worked for the same employer continuously for a minimum of 10 years.

112. Delius, *A Lion*, pp. 142, 151, 154.

113. Even Buthelezi accused chiefs of fleecing their people by 'charging for sites, arable land and services such as pensions' in 1978. Maré and Hamilton, *Appetite For Power*, p. 90.

114. Mzala, *Gatsha Buthelezi*, p. 85.

115. Ibid., pp. 112–13.

116. Maré and Hamilton, *Appetite for Power*, p. 89.

5 'Ism Schisms': African Socialism and Home-Grown Capitalism, 1960–85

1. Crawford Young, *Ideology and Development in Africa* (New Haven and London: Yale University Press, 1982), p. 183.

2. Partha Chatterjee, *The Nation and its Fragments: Colonial and Postcolonial Histories* (Princeton: Princeton University Press, 1993).

3. See, for example, Joel Barkan and John Okumu (eds) *Politics and Public Policy in Kenya and Tanzania* (New York: Praeger, 1979); Ahmed Mohiddin, *African Socialism in Two Countries* (London and Totowa: Croom Helm and Barnes and Noble, 1981); Joel D. Barkan (ed.) *Beyond Capitalism vs. Socialism in Kenya and Tanzania* (Boulder and London: Lynne Rienner, 1994).

4. 'Ujamaa – The Basis of African Socialism', reproduced in Julius K. Nyerere, *Ujamaa: Essays on Socialism* (Oxford and Dar es Salaam: Oxford University Press, 1968).

5. For an excellent discussion of Nyerere's ideas at this point, see Cranford Pratt, *The Critical Phase in Tanzania, 1945–1968: Nyerere and the Emergence of a Socialist Strategy* (Nairobi, Oxford and New York: Oxford University Press, 1978).

6. Ibid., pp. 131–2.

7. Ibid., p. 97.

8. By 1960, an estimated 2000 Tanzanians had been through secondary school, Tanzania did not have any University of its own, and by 1962 there were only 17 Tanzanians graduating from Makerere University in Tanzania and Royal College in Kenya. Pratt, *Critical Phase*, pp. 93–4. On colonial education policy, see Lene Buchert, *Education in the Development of Tanzania, 1919–1990* (London, Dar es Salaam and

Athens: James Currey, Mkuki na Nyota and Ohio University Press, 1994), Chapters 2, 4.

9. Pratt, *Critical Phase*, p. 174.

10. Ibid., pp. 134–66.

11. The most visible Chinese contribution was the construction of the Tanzania-Zambia railway.

12. Pratt, *Critical Phase*, p. 175.

13. Ibid., p. 238.

14. 'The Arusha Declaration', reproduced in Nyerere, *Ujamaa*, p. 25.

15. 'After the Arusha Declaration', a speech to TANU on 17 October 1967, reproduced in Nyerere, *Ujamaa*.

16. 'Arusha Declaration', p. 28.

17. Ibid., p. 29.

18. Ibid., p. 34.

19. Dean McHenry points out that local autonomy was somewhat in tension with the conception of the nation as the focus of self-reliance because the state would inevitably intrude into the affairs of village communities. Dean McHenry, *Limited Choices: The Political Struggle for Socialism in Tanzania* (Boulder and London: Lynne Rienner, 1994), pp. 161–3.

20. McHenry, *Limited Choices*, p. 30.

21. 'Education for Self-Reliance', in *Ujamaa*.

22. 'Socialism and Rural Development', September 1967, reproduced in *Ujamaa*, p. 131.

23. Pratt, *Critical Phase*, p. 79.

24. 'After the Arusha Declaration', pp. 163–70.

25. Issa G. Shivji, *Class Struggles in Tanzania* (London: Heinemann, 1976). However, not all those on the left were convinced by rather rigid Shivji's position. See, for example, the critique by John Saul, 'The state in post-colonial societies', reproduced in *The State and Revolution in Eastern Africa* (London: Heinemann, 1979), pp. 180–91.

26. Julius Nyerere, 'The Arusha Declaration ten year after', in Andrew Coulson (ed.) *African Socialism in Practice: The Tanzanian Experience* (Nottingham: Spokesman, 1979).

27. Nyerere, 'Arusha Declaration ten years after', p. 51.

28. Goran Hyden, *Beyond Ujamaa in Tanzania: Underdevelopment and an Uncaptured Peasantry* (London: Heinemann, 1980), p. 104.

29. Hyden, *Beyond Ujamaa*, pp. 132–3.

30. Nyerere, 'Arusha Declaration ten years after', p. 51.

31. David Leonard, cited in McHenry, *Limited Choices*, pp. 76–7.

32. The base year is not mentioned. McHenry, *Limited Choices*, p. 78.

33. Figures from McHenry, *Limited Choices*, p. 79.

34. Nyerere, 'Arusha Declaration ten years after', p. 50.

35. Rodger Yeager, *Tanzania: An African Experiment* (Boulder and Aldershot: Westview and Gower, 1982), p. 71.

36. Ibid., p. 28.

37. Buchert, *Education*, p. 112.

38. Only 2.4 per cent of fourteen to seventeen-year-olds were in government secondary schools in 1980. McHenry, *Limited Choices*, p. 84.

39. I am grateful to Steve Kerr, who has carried out doctoral research on Tanzanian teachers, for this point.

40. Ironically, the embattled Portuguese were forcing peasants on the other side of the border into fortified villages of their own. See Chapter 7.

41. Hyden, *Beyond Ujamaa*, pp. 101–2.

42. Yeager, *Tanzania*, p. 64.

43. On villagisation and Ujamaa villages, see Jannik Boesen, Birgit Storgård Madsen and Tony Moody, *Ujamaa – Socialism From Above* (Uppsala: Scandinavian Institute of African Studies, 1977); Michaela Von Freyhold, *Ujamaa Villages in Tanzania: Analysis of a Social Experiment* (London: Heinemann, 1979); Dean McHenry, *Tanzania's Ujamaa Villages: The Implementation of a Rural Development Strategy* (Berkeley: University of California, 1979); and Kjell J. Havnevik, *Tanzania: The Limits to Development From Above* (Uppsala and Dar es Salaam: Nordiska Afrikainstitutet and Mkuki na Nyota, 1993), Chapter 6.

44. Hyden, *Beyond Ujamaa*, Chapters 4–5.

45. The TAZARA railway also helped to open up these hitherto marginal areas. Stefano Ponte, *Farmers and Markets in Tanzania: How Policy Reforms Affect Rural Livelihoods in Africa* (Oxford, Dar es Salaam and Portsmouth: James Currey, Mkuki na Nyota and Heinemann, 2002), p. 49.

46. See the tables in Michael F. Lofchie, 'The politics of agricultural policy', in Barkan, *Beyond Capitalism*, pp. 142–3.

47. The Tanzanian maize producer received about $47.6 per metric ton in 1980 whereas a Kenyan farmer received $115. In the case of coffee, the differential was almost threefold, but it was twenty seven fold in the case of tea. Lofchie, 'Politics of agricultural policy', pp. 133–5. The importance of overvaluation of the Tanzanian shilling is underlined in Frank Ellis, 'Tanzania', in Charles Harvey (ed.) *Agricultural Pricing Policy in Africa: Four Country Case-Studies* (London and Basingstoke: Macmillan, 1988), p. 94.

48. McHenry, *Limited Choices*, p. 171.

49. For an insider account, see Ralph Ibbott, 'History of the Ruvuma Development Association', Tanzania, unpublished manuscript 1970.

50. Yeager, *Tanzania*, pp. 62–3.

51. In a study of the nationalised sisal industry, Dianne Bolton, *Nationalisation: A Road to Socialism? The Case of Tanzania* (London: Zed Press, 1985) argues that labour relations remained more or less the same as before.

52. Joel D. Barkan, 'legislators, elections, and political linkage', in Barkan and Okumu, *Politics*, p. 87.

53. Robert H. Bates, *Beyond the Miracle of the Market: The Political Economy of Agrarian Development in Kenya* (Cambridge: Cambridge University Press, 1989), p. 59.

54. Christopher Leo, *Land and Class in Kenya* (Toronto, Buffalo and London: Toronto University Press, 1984).

55. For a discussion of these companies, see Nicola Swainson, *The Development of Corporate Capitalism in Kenya, 1918–1977* (London: Heinemann, 1980), pp. 250–84.

56. In this novel, the protagonists are surprised to discover that the MP has bought the farm which belonged to the departing settler. Ngugi wa Thiong'o, *A Grain of Wheat* (London: Heinemann Educational Books, revised edition, 1988), p. 169. For a discussion of this and other writings on the land question, see David Maughan-Brown, *Land and Freedom: History and Ideology in Kenya* (London: Zed Press, 1985), Chapter 8.

57. Nicola Swainson, 'Indigenous capitalism in postcolonial Kenya', in Paul M. Lubeck (ed.) *The African Bourgeoisie: Capitalist Development in Nigeria, Kenya, and the Ivory Coast* (Boulder: Lynne Rienner, 1987), p. 142.

58. Ibid., p. 142.

59. Bates, *Beyond*, p. 58.

60. Ibid., pp. 59–63.

61. David Throup, 'The construction and destruction of the Kenyatta state', in Michael G. Schatzberg (ed.) *The Political Economy of Kenya* (New York, Westport and London: Praeger, 1987), p. 44.

62. Bates, *Beyond*, pp. 62–3.

63. Republic of Kenya, *African Socialism and its Application to Planning in Kenya* (Nairobi, 1965), p. 18.

64. Quoted in William Ochieng', 'Structural and political changes', in B. A. Ogot and W. R. Ochieng' (eds) *Decolonisation and Independence in Kenya 1940–93* (London, Nairobi and Athens: James Currey, EAEP and Ohio University Press, 1995), p. 100.

65. Ochieng', 'Structural and political changes', p. 86.

66. Kenya only became a *de jure* one-party state in 1982 when KANU needed to act to stop Odinga forming a Kenya Socialist Party.

67. The first victim, Pio Gama Pinto, was an advisor to Odinga prior to his death in 1965. E. S. Atieno-Odhiambo, 'Democracy and the ideology of order in Kenya', in Schatzberg, *Political Economy of Kenya*, p. 198.

68. On the significance of the *baraza* in Kenyan politics, see Angelique Haugerud, *The Culture of Politics in Modern Kenya* (Cambridge: Cambridge University Press, 1995).

69. Young, *Ideology and Development*, p. 216.

70. Benno J. Ndulu and Francis W. Mwega, 'Economic adjustment policies', in Barkan, *Beyond Capitalism*, p. 110.

71. World Bank figures, quoted by Lofchie, 'Politics of agricultural policy', p. 129.

72. Joel D. Barkan, 'Divergence and convergence in Kenya and Tanzania: pressures for reform', in Barkan, *Beyond Capitalism*, p. 22.

73. Michaela Von Freyhold, *Ujamaa Villages in Tanzania: Analysis of a Social Experiment* (London: Heinemann, 1979).

74. Swainson, 'Indigenous capitalism', pp. 150–2.

75. Ibid., p. 158.

76. R. Kaplinsky, quoted in Swainson, 'Indigenous capitalism', p. 152.

77. Colin Leys, *Underdevelopment in Kenya: The Political Economy of Neo-Colonialism, 1964–1971* (London: Heinemann, 1975); and 'Capital accumulation, class formation and dependency: the significance of the Kenya case', *Socialist Register* 1978.

78. Steven Langdon, 'Industry and capitalism in Kenya: contributions to a debate', in Lubeck, *African Bourgeoisie*.

79. Between 1978 and 1987, the national debt increased by 470 per cent. At this point, debt-servicing represented 37 per cent of exports. Robert Maxon and Peter Ndege, 'The economics of structural adjustment', in Ogot and Ochieng', *Decolonisation and Independence in Kenya*, p. 177.

80. Ndulu and Mwega, 'Economic adjustment policies', p. 101.

81. Colin Leys, *The Rise and Fall of Development Theory* (London and Bloomington: James Currey and Indiana University Press, 1996), p. 161.

82. Hence Leys notes that business forecasts for Kenya in the 1980s actually tended to be rather upbeat. Leys, *Rise and Fall*, p. 162.

83. Throup, 'Construction and destruction', p. 71. The most spectacular expansion took place in Meru, which grew from a mere 4,475 people in 1969 to 78,100 in 1989. Again, Machakos mushroomed from 6,312 to 116,000 over the same period. See the table in Richard Stren, Mohammed Halfani and Joyce Malombi, 'Coping with urbanisation and urban policy', in Barkan, *Beyond Capitalism*, p. 176.

84. Sharon Stichter, 'Women and the family: the impact of capitalist development in Kenya', in Schatzberg, *Political Economy of Kenya*, pp. 159–60.

85. Leo, *Land and Class*, pp. 172–7.

86. Michael Cowen, 'Commodity production in Kenya's Central Province', in Judith Heyer, Pepe Roberts and Gavin Williams (eds) *Rural Development in Tropical Africa* (New York: St Martin's Press, 1981).

87. Leo, *Land and Class*, p. 196.

88. Robert M. Maxon, 'Social and cultural changes', in Ogot and Ochieng', *Decolonisation*, pp. 127–8.

89. Maxon, 'Social and cultural', p. 130.

90. Ibid., pp. 134–5.

91. Ibid., p. 123.

92. Throup, 'Construction and destruction', pp. 34–5; Jennifer A. Widner, *The Rise of a Party-State in Kenya: From 'Harambee!' to 'Nyayo'* (Berkeley, Los Angeles and Oxford: University of California Press, 1992), pp. 51–66; also Peter Anyang' Nyong'o, 'State and society in Kenya: the disintegration of the nationalist coalitions and the rise of presidential authoritarianism 1963–1978', *African Affairs* 88, 1989, pp. 235–7.

93. Widner, *Rise of a Party-State*, p. 55.

94. Throup, 'Construction and destruction', p. 41.

95. According to Widner, patron–client ties also tended to cross cut ethnic divisions. *Rise of a Party-State*, p. 64.

96. Throup, 'Construction and destruction', pp. 50–2.

97. Widner, *Rise of a Party-State*, pp. 149–56.

98. B. A. Ogot, 'The construction of a national culture', in Ogot and Ochieng' *Decolonisation and Independence*, p. 220.

99. For a critical assessment of Tanzanian cultural policy, see Kelly M. Askew, *Performing the Nation: Swahili Music and Cultural Politics in Tanzania* (Chicago and London: Chicago University Press, 2002).

100. Quoted in Jon Woronoff, *West African Wager: Houphouët Versus Nkrumah* (Metuchen: Scarecrow Press, 1972), p. 13.

101. For example, Philip Foster and Aristide Zolberg (eds) *Ghana and the Ivory Coast: Perspectives on Modernisation* (Chicago and London: University of Chicago Press, 1971).

102. Quoted in Tony Killick, *Development Economics in Action: A Study of Economic Policies in Ghana* (London: Heinemann, 1978), p. 42.

103. Roger Genoud, *Nationalism and Economic Development in Ghana* (New York, Washington and London: Praeger, 1969).

104. Killick, *Development Economics*, p. 40.

105. Quoted by Dennis Austin, *Politics in Ghana, 1946–60* (Oxford: Oxford University Press, 1970), p. 40.

106. For a sustained Soviet comparison, see Robert E. Dowse, *Modernisation in Ghana and the USSR: A Comparative Study* (London: Routledge and Kegan Paul, 1969).

107. For example, Kwame Nkrumah, *Neo-Colonialism: The Last Stage of Imperialism* (Edinburgh: Thomas Nelson, 1965).

108. Douglas Rimmer, *Staying Poor: Ghana's Political Economy, 1950–1990* (Oxford: Pergamon Press, 1992), p. 62.

109. Ibid., p. 62.

110. Ibid., p. 86.

111. Jonathan Frimpong-Ansah, *The Vampire State in Africa: The Political Economy of Decline in Ghana* (London and Trenton: James Currey and Africa World Press, 1991), Table 5.9, p. 87.

112. Killick, *Development Economics*, p. 66.

113. Ibid., Chapters 2–3.

114. Richard D. Mahoney, *JFK: Ordeal in Africa* (New York and Oxford: Oxford University Press, 1983), pp. 164–70.

115. *Programme of the Convention People's Party For Work and Happiness* (Accra: Ministry of Information and Broadcasting, undated), p. 3.

116. *Ibid.*, pp. 9–10.

117. *Ibid.*, pp. 4, 31.

118. *Blueprint of our Goal: Osagyefo Launches Seven-Year Plan* (Accra: Ministry of Information and Broadcasting, 1964).

119. Rimmer notes that 63 per cent was still allocated to infrastructure and social services under the Plan. *Staying Poor*, p. 88.

120. *Seven-Year Plan for National Reconstruction and Development: Financial Years 1963/64 – 1969/70* (Accra: Planning Commission, 1964), p. 12.

121. According to Henry Bretton, *The Rise and Fall of Kwame Nkrumah: A Study of Personal Rule in Africa* (London: Pall Mall Press, 1967), p. 194, some 2000 people were detained between 1958 and 1966.

122. Hence Jeffries refers to the CPP as following a policy of state capitalism. Richard Jeffries, *Class, Power and Ideology in Ghana: The Railwaymen of Sekondi* (Cambridge: Cambridge University Press, 1978), p. 65.

123. Björn Beckman, *Organising the Farmers: Cocoa Politics and National Development in Ghana* (Uppsala: Scandinavian Institute of African Studies, 1976), p. 238.

124. Jeffries, *Class, Power and Ideology*, p. 68.

125. Elliot J. Berg, 'Structural transformation versus gradualism: recent economic development in Ghana', in Foster and Zolberg, *Ghana and the Ivory Coast*, p. 192; Rimmer, *Staying Poor*, p. 91; Killick, *Development Economics*, p. 83.

126. For a counterpoint to Berg, 'Structural transformation', see Reginald H. Green, 'Reflections on economic strategy, structure, implementation and necessity: Ghana and the Ivory Coast', in Foster and Zolberg, *Ghana and the Ivory Coast.*

127. Killick, *Development Economics*, Table 4.1, p. 68.

128. Ibid., p. 196.

129. For example, it is estimated that peasants were producing 0.490 tons per acre, while the SFC managed a mere 0.26 tons. Killick, *Development Economics*, Table 8.2, p. 193.

130. If the CPP had survived, it would have been faced with debt repayments equal to 19 per cent of export earnings by 1967. Killick, *Development Economics*, p. 110.

131. Rimmer, *Staying Poor*, p. 100.

132. Ibid., p. 103.

133. Killick, *Development Economics*, Table 4.5, p. 81. This reading of the evidence is shared by Jeffries, *Class, Power and Ideology*, Chapter 8.

134. This view is expressed in Beckman, *Organising*, pp. 236–7.

135. Karin Barber, John Collins and Alain Ricard, 'Three West African Popular Theatre Forms', in Karin Barber, John Collins and Alain Ricard (eds) *West African Popular Theatre* (Bloomington and Oxford: Indiana University Press and James Currey, 1997), p. 14; John Collins, *West African Pop Roots* (Philadelphia: Temple University Press, 1992), p. 41.

136. Barber, Johnson and Ricard, 'Three West African', pp. 19–20.

137. Catherine M. Cole, *Ghana's Concert Party Theatre* (Bloomington: Indiana University Press, 2001), pp. 155–6.

138. Jeffries, *Class, Power and Ideology*, p. 95.

139. Ibid., pp. 103–7.

140. On the theme of smuggling, see Paul Nugent, *Smugglers, Secessionists and Loyal Citizens on the Ghana-Togo Frontier: The Lie of the Borderlands From 1914* (Oxford, Athens and Accra: James Currey, Ohio University Press and Subsaharan Publishers, 2002), Chapter 7.

141. Jon Kraus, 'Political change, conflict, and development in Ghana', in Foster and Zolberg, *Ghana and the Ivory Coast*, p. 47.

142. Curiously, one of the earliest post-coup critiques of the experiment argued that not only had it been launched too late, but had not gone far enough. Bob Fitch and Mary Oppenheimer, *Ghana: End of an Illusion* (New York and London: Monthly Review Press, 1966), p. 84.

143. For these plots, see Aristide R. Zolberg, 'Political development in the Ivory Coast since independence' in Foster and Zolberg, *Ghana and*

the Ivory Coast, pp. 15–21; and Aristide R. Zolberg, *One-Party Government in the Ivory Coast* (Princeton: Princeton University Press, 1969).

144. An interim two-year plan was introduced for 1962/63, which prepared the ground for the main document, entitled 'Perspectives Décennales de Développement Economique 1960–69 et Projections 1970–75'. Woronoff, *West African Wager*, p. 209.

145. Ibid., p. 227.

146. Lynne Krieger Mytelka, 'Foreign business and economic development', in I. William Zartman and Christopher L. Delgado (eds) *The Political Economy of Ivory Coast* (New York: Praeger, 1984), p. 152.

147. I. William Zartman and Christopher L. Delgado, 'Introduction', in Zartman and Delgado, *Political Economy of Ivory Coast*, p. 13.

148. Quoted in Woronoff, *West African Wager*, p. 222.

149. Quoted in ibid., p. 221.

150. Woronoff, *West African Wager*, p. 221. There was also a substantial Lebanese community.

151. Gilles Michel and Michel Noel, 'The Ivorian economy and alternative trade regimes', in Zartman and Delgado, *Political Economy of Ivory Coast*, p. 83.

152. Berg, 'Structural transformation', p. 215.

153. Mytelka, 'Foreign business', p. 153.

154. Quoted in John Rapley, *Ivoirien Capitalism: African Entrepreneurs in Côte d'Ivoire* (Boulder and London: Lynne Rienner, 1993), p. 65.

155. Ibid., pp. 69–73.

156. Ibid., p. 56.

157. Richard E. Stryker, 'Political and administrative linkage in the Ivory Coast', in Foster and Zolberg, *Ghana and the Ivory Coast*, p. 91.

158. Ibid., p. 100.

159. Zolberg, 'Political development in the Ivory Coast', p. 25.

160. Tessilimi Bakary, 'Elite transformation and political succession', in Zartman and Delgado, *Political Economy of Ivory Coast*, p. 47.

161. Ibid., pp. 24, 46.

162. For a fascinating account, see Rapley, *Ivoirien Bourgeoisie*, Chapter 6.

163. Berg, 'Structural transformation', p. 215.

164. Young, *Ideology and Development*, p. 190.

164. Green, 'Reflections', p. 235.

166. Rapley, *Ivoirien Capitalism*, p. 79.

167. Ibid., pp. 82, 90.

168. Ibid., p. 97.

169. Ibid., p. 99.

170. Remi Clignet and Philip Foster, 'Convergence and divergence in educational development in Ghana and Ivory Coast', in Foster and Zolberg, *Ghana and the Ivory Coast*, pp. 273–5.

171. Quoted in Woronoff, *West African Wager*, p. 213.

172. Louise M. Bourgault, *Mass Media in Sub-Saharan Africa* (Bloomington and Indianapolis, 1995), pp. 116–17.

173. Bastiaan A. Den Tuinder, *Ivory Coast: The Challenge of Success* (Baltimore: John Hopkins University Press, 1978), p. 135.

174. L. Gbetibou and Christopher Delgado, 'Lessons and constraints on export crop-led growth: cocoa in Ivory Coast', in Zartman and Delgado, *Political Economy of Ivory Coast*, p. 139.

175. Michel and Noel, 'Ivorian economy', p. 86.

176. Michel and Noel, 'Ivorian economy', p. 88. For more on economic policy, see Bonnie Campbell, 'The Ivory Coast', in John Dunn (ed.) *West African States: Failure and Promise – A Study in Comparative Politics* (Cambridge: Cambridge University Press, 1978).

177. Mytelka, 'Foreign business', p. 158; Yves Fauré, 'Côte d'Ivoire: analysing the crisis', in Donal B. Cruise O'Brien, John Dunn and Richard Rathbone (eds) *Contemporary West African States* (Cambridge: Cambridge University Press, 1989), p. 62.

178. Young, *Ideology and Development*, p. 201.

179. Michael A. Cohen, 'Urban policy and development strategy', in Zartman and Delgado, *Political Economy of Ivory Coast*, p. 67.

180. Young, *Ideology and Development*, p. 202.

181. Bakary, 'Elite transformation', p. 47.

182. Fauré, 'Côte d'Ivoire', p. 71.

183. R. W. Johnson, 'Guinea', in John Dunn, *West African States: Failure and Promise – A Study in Comparative Politics* (Cambridge: Cambridge University Press, 1978), p. 40. Lansiné Kaba argues that Sekou Touré did not seek to apologise, but rather to sway part of French opinion towards Guinea. 'From colonialism to autocracy: Guinea under Sekou Touré, 1957–1984', in Prosser Gifford and Wm. Roger Louis (eds) *Decolonisation and African Independence: The Transfers of Power, 1960–1980* (New Haven and London: Yale University Press, 1988), p. 229.

184. Cited by Kaba, 'From colonialism to autocracy', p. 229.

185. Johnson, 'Guinea' p. 54. Lansiné Kaba, 'Cultural revolution and freedom of expression in Guinea', *Journal of Modern African Studies* 14, 2, 1976.

186. Claude Rivière, *Guinea: Mobilisation of a People* (Ithaca and London: Cornell University Press, 1970), p. 104.

187. Ibid., p. 105.

188. Ibid., p. 110.

189. Ibid., p. 111.

190. Ibid., pp. 185–6.

191. Ibid., p. 180.

192. Johnson, 'Guinea', p. 48.

193. Rivière, *Guinea*, p. 198.

194. Johnson, 'Guinea', p. 49.

195. Rivière, *Guinea*, p. 204.

196. Ibid., p. 119.

197. Ibid., Table 3, pp. 174–5.

198. Ibid., p. 229.

199. This came into the open in the alleged 'Foulah plot' of 1976. Thereafter the government became more obviously Malinké in complexion.

200. After the 1970 invasion, no fewer than 16 out of a total of 24 Ministers were arrested. Johnson, 'Guinea', p. 57. Perhaps the most famous casualty was the former OAU Secretary-General, Diallo Telli, who was found guilty of involvement in the 1976 plot and died in prison.
201. Under a decree of 1959, individuals were even prevented from owning radio sets. Rivière, *Guinea*, p. 126.
202. Johnson, 'Guinea', p. 50.
203. Ibid., p. 55.
204. Ibid., pp. 235–6.
205. Ibid., pp. 234–5.
206. Johnson, 'Guinea', p. 52.
207. Rivière, *Guinea*, pp. 127–8.
208. Ibid., p. 219.
209. These events are a classic illustration of James C. Scott's argument about the consequences which ensue when the powerless swap strategies of evasion for direct confrontation. See *Domination and the Arts of Resistance: Hidden Transcripts* (New Haven and London: Yale University Press, 1990). For a brief account of these events, see Young, *Ideology and Development*, pp. 172–3.
210. Kaba, 'From colonialism to autocracy', p. 240.
211. For that very reason, critics have argued that it actually validated a Eurocentric value system. Wole Soyinka once famously commented that 'a tiger does not speak of its "tigritude"': in others words, Africans who were not culturally alienated had no need to proclaim their *négritude*.
212. Young, *Ideology and Development*, p. 97. On the Senegalese model of 'socialism', see Irving Leonard Markovitz, *Léopold Sédar Senghor and the Politics of Negritude* (London: Heinemann, 1969). See also the collection of his writings, which are full of references to Marx and Engels. Mercer Cook (ed.) *Léopold Sédar Senghor on African Socialism* (New York and Praeger, 1964).
213. Catherine Boone, *Merchant Capital and the Roots of State Power in Senegal, 1930–1985* (Cambridge: Cambridge University Press, 1992), p. 115. Much of this section draws on Boone.
214. Ibid., p. 119.
215. Senghor was also worried about the extent to which Dia was attempting to centralise power.
216. Dia remained in prison until 1974. On the crisis, see Edward J. Schumaker, *Politics, Bureaucracy and Rural Development in Senegal* (Berkeley, Los Angeles and London: University of California Press, 1975), pp. 63–7.
217. Boone, *Merchant Capital*, p. 97.
218. Ibid., p. 108.
219. Ibid., p. 208.
220. Ibid., pp. 127–9.
221. For the book, see Sembène Ousmane, *Xala* (translated by Clive Wake) (London: Heinemann, 1976). The film was made in 1974.

222. Gerti Hesseling, *Histoire politique du Sénégal: institutions droit et société* (Paris and Leiden: Karthala and Afrika Studiecentrum, 1985), p. 62.

223. Schumacher, *Politics, Bureaucracy and Rural Development*, pp. 183–5.

224. John Waterbury, 'Dimensions of state intervention in the groundnut basin', in Mark Gersovitz and John Waterbury (eds) *The Political Economy of Risk and Choice in Senegal* (London and Totowa: Frank Cass, 1987), p. 189.

225. Sidi C. Jammeh, 'Politics of agricultural price decision-making in Senegal', in Gersovitz and Waterbury, *Political Economy of Risk*, p. 234.

226. Boubacar Barry, 'Neocolonialism and dependence in Senegal, 1960–1980', in Prosser Gifford and Wm. Roger Louis (eds) *Decolonisation and African Independence: The Transfers of Power, 1960–1980* (New Haven and London: Yale University Press, 1988), p. 290.

227. Boone, *Merchant Capital*, p. 179.

228. Ibid., pp. 124, 127.

229. Waterbury, 'Dimensions', p. 191.

230. Sheldon Gellar, *Senegal: An African Nation Between Islam and the West* (Boulder and Aldershot: Westview and Gower, 1982), p. 64.

231. Of course, the rampant smuggling of consumer items like sugar and textiles suggests that many Senegalese managed to avoid absorbing the costs. Boone cites an ex-official of the Ministry of Commerce as estimating in 1984 that 80 per cent of textiles were being smuggled. *Merchant Capital*, p. 243.

232. ONCAD took over the duties of the OCA in 1967.

233. Robert Fatton Jnr, *The Making of a Liberal Democracy: Senegal's Passive Revolution* (Boulder and London: Lynne Rienner, 1987), p. 80.

234. On his creative contribution, see David Murphy, *Sembene: Imagining Alternatives in Film and Fiction* (Oxford and Trenton: James Currey and Africa World Press, 2000).

6   Khaki Fatigue: Military Rule in Africa, 1960–85

1. David Goldsworthy, 'Armies and politics in civilian regimes', in Simon Baynham (ed.) *Military Power and Politics in Black Africa* (London and Sydney: Croom Helm, 1986), pp. 98–9, and in the same volume, Simon Baynham, 'Introduction: armed forces in Africa', p. 5. Lesotho had its first coup in 1986, the Gambia followed in 1994 and Côte d'Ivoire did so in 1999. At the time of writing, in 2003, that leaves only 13 countries which have not had a coup, although most have experienced plots. For a complete statistical analysis of coups and plots up to 2001, see Patrick J. McGowan, 'African military coups d'état, 1956–2001', *Journal of Modern African Studies* 41, 3, 2003.

2. For a leading example of a literature which is now rather dated, see Samuel Huntington, *Political Order in Changing Societies* (New Haven: Yale University Press, 1968).

3. Samuel Decalo, *Coups and Army Rule in Africa* (New Haven and London: Yale University Press, 2nd edition, 1990).

4. A point made some time ago by Samuel Finer, *The Man on Horseback: The Role of the Military in Politics* (London: Pall Mall, 1962).

5. Decalo, *Coups*, p. 214.

6. Timothy H. Parsons, *The 1964 Army Mutinies and the Making of Modern East Africa* (London and Westport: Greenwood, 2003); Nestor Luanda, 'The Tanganyika rifles and the mutiny of January 1964', in Eboe Hutchful and Abdoulaye Bathily (eds) *The Military and Militarism in Africa* (Dakar: CODESRIA, 1998).

7. Decalo, *Coups*, p. 159; Holger Bernt Hansen, *Ethnicity and Military Rule in Uganda* (Uppsala: Scandinavian Institute of African Studies, 1977), p. 81.

8. Eric A. Nordlinger, *Soldiers in Politics: Military Coups and Governments* (Englewood Cliffs: Prentice Hall, 1977), p. 39.

9. Decalo, *Coups*, p. 163.

10. Harlley and Deku had reason to fear they would be put on trial for their involvement in diamond smuggling, while Captain Akwasi Afrifa was due to face a court-martial. The creation of the POGR and a Special Intelligence Unit had alienated the leadership of the army and the police respectively. Finally, Nkrumah was suspected of favouring northerners and Nzemas (his own group) in an attempt to secure his position. The head of the POGR was Colonel Zanlerigu, a northerner.

11. Simon Baynham, *The Military and Politics in Nkrumah's Ghana* (Boulder and London: Westview Press, 1988), pp. 185–94.

12. At the very least, the CIA was being kept informed by the plotters. Paul Lee, 'The Western conspiracy that destroyed Nkrumah', *West Africa* 19–25 November 2001, pp. 11–17.

13. On the NLC, see Robert Dowse, 'Military and police rule' in Dennis Austin and Robin Luckham (eds) *Politicians and Soldiers in Ghana 1966–72* (London: Frank Cass, 1975).

14. Richard Rathbone, 'Ghana', in John Dunn (ed.) *West African States: Failure and Promise – A Study in Comparative Politics* (Cambridge: Cambridge University Press, 1978), p. 26.

15. On the shaping of the constitution, see Robin Luckham, 'The Constitutional Commission 1966–69', in Austin and Luckham, *Politicians and Soldiers.*

16. See Yaw Twumasi, 'The 1969 election', in Austin and Luckham, *Politicians and Soldiers.*

17. Naomi Chazan, *An Anatomy of Ghanaian Politics: Managing Political Recession, 1969–1982* (Boulder: Westview, 1983), p. 238.

18. These tensions were partly reflected in the unwillingness of these NRC members to defer to more senior officers, which is an example of the havoc which military rule has often played with military hierarchy.

19. For an insider account, see Kofi Awoonor, *The Ghana Revolution: Background Account From a Personal Perspective* (New York: Oases Publishers, 1984).

20. On cocoa smuggling, see Paul Nugent, *Smugglers, Secessionists and Loyal Citizens of the Ghana-Togo Frontier: The Lie of the Borderlands Since 1914* (London, Athens and Accra: James Currey, Ohio University Press and Subsaharan Publishers, 2002), Chapter 6. See also 'Educating Rawlings: the evolution of government strategy towards smuggling', in Donald Rothchild (ed.) *Ghana: The Political Economy of Recovery* (Boulder and London: Lynne Rienner, 1991).

21. Many of these abuses are identified in Mike Oquaye, *Politics in Ghana, 1972–1979* (Accra: Tornado Publications, 1980).

22. Chazan, *Anatomy*, p. 247.

23. Chazan, *Anatomy*, p. 250. See also Maxwell Owusu, 'Politics without parties: reflections on the Union Government debate', *African Studies Review* 22, 2, 1979.

24. Chazan, *Anatomy*, p. 264.

25. This argument is well-put in Eboe Hutchful, 'Institutional decomposition and junior ranks' political action in Ghana' in Hutchful and Bathily, *The Military*.

26. On this aspect of the AFRC, see Barbara Okeke, *4 June: A Revolution Betrayed* (Enugu and Oxford: Ikenga, 1982).

27. Whereas the First and Second Republics had followed the Westminster model, the Third was based on a mixture of the Westminster and the Presidential systems.

28. Very few former Biafran officers were integrated back into the Nigerian army.

29. Gavin Williams and Terisa Turner, 'Nigeria', in Dunn, *West African States*, p. 153.

30. Eghosa Osaghae, *Crippled Giant: Nigeria Since Independence* (London: C. Hurst, 1998), p. 70.

31. Williams and Turner, 'Nigeria', p. 159.

32. The one lasting achievement for which Gowon is recognised was his instrumental role in the formation of the Economic Community of West African States (ECOWAS).

33. Williams and Turner, 'Nigeria', p. 160.

34. The description of Osaghae, *Crippled Giant*, p. 78.

35. Shehu Othman, 'Nigeria: power for profit – class, corporatism, and factionalism in the military', in Donal Cruise O'Brien, John Dunn and Richard Rathbone (eds) *Contemporary West African States* (Cambridge: Cambridge University Press, 1989), p. 121.

36. On the Kaduna Mafia, see Othman, 'Nigeria', pp. 122–4.

37. Osagahe, *Crippled Giant*, pp. 97–8.

38. Othman, 'Nigeria', p. 121.

39. Osagahe, *Crippled Giant*, p. 85.

40. Gunilla Andrae and Bjorn Beckman, *The Wheat Trap: Bread and Underdevelopment in Nigeria* (London: Zed Press, 1986).

41. Interestingly, Fela's record 'Zombie' (1976) which ridiculed the unthinking mentality of soldiers was a great hit in Acheampong's Ghana at the time. Fela was initially invited to join the planning committee for FESTAC, but fell out with the other members and went on to organise his own

'counter-FESTAC'. The eventual cost of the jamboree was 140 million Naira, which was roughly the same amount in dollars. Michael Veal, *Fela: The Life and Times of an African Musical Icon* (Philadelphia: Temple University Press, 2000), pp. 151–4.

42. Bissalla apparently resented the promotion of Mohammed, Obasanjo and Danjuma into positions over his head. There was also an element of Middle Belt solidarity. If the coup had succeeded, it would allegedly have led to mass executions of the top brass. Osaghae, *Crippled Giant*, pp. 88–90.

43. Osaghae, *Crippled Giant*, p. 127.

44. Ibid., pp. 128–9.

45. Ibid., pp. 155–6.

46. For an analysis, see Richard Joseph, *Democracy and Prebendal Politics in Nigeria: The Rise and Fall of the Second Republic* (Cambridge: Cambridge University Press, 1987).

47. For some very good analyses of the Maitatsine revolts, see Paul Lubeck, 'Islamic protest under semi-industrial capitalism: "Yan Tatsine explained"', *Africa* 5, 4, 1985; Niels Kastfelt, 'Rumours of Maitatsine: a note on political culture in Northern Nigeria', *African Affairs* 88, 1989; and Mervyn Hiskett, 'The Maitatsine riots in Kano, 1980: an assessment', *Journal of Religion in Africa* 17, 3, 1983.

48. Kastfelt, 'Rumours', p. 84.

49. The core of the movement consisted of young men who had traditionally migrated to the cities where they attended Koranic schools and begged for alms. These *gardawa* were increasingly perceived as a social nuisance by the elite, while many of the means of earning money were closed to them.

50. Kastfelt, 'Rumours', p. 83.

51. Otwin Marenin, 'The Anini saga: armed robbery and the reproduction of ideology in Nigeria', *Journal of Modern African Studies* 25, 2, 1987.

52. The subsequent Babalakin Commission into the elections confirmed wholesale rigging on all sides. Osaghae, *Crippled Giant*, p. 150. On these elections, see also Joseph, *Democracy*, Part III.

53. Quoted, Osaghae, *Crippled Giant*, p. 169.

54. Ibid., p. 172.

55. The fact that Buhari had royal connections in Daura helped.

56. Osaghae, *Crippled Giant*, p. 180.

57. On the reasons for their falling out, see Othman, 'Nigeria', pp. 138–9.

58. The third member of the trio, who I do not have the space to cover here is Macias Nguema of Equatorial Guinea whose excesses were legendary. For details, see Samuel Decalo, *Psychoses of Power: African Personal Dictatorships* (Boulder and London: Westview Press, 1989), who compares the three in detail.

59. Thomas O'Toole, *The Central African Republic: The Continent's Hidden Heart* (Boulder and London: Westview Press and Gower, 1986), pp. 41–2.

60. Didier Bigo, *Pouvoir et obéissance en Centrafrique* (Paris: Karthala, 1988), pp. 96–7.

61. O'Toole, *Central African Republic*, p. 50.

62. Bigo, *Pouvoir*, p. 108.
63. O'Toole, *Central African Republic*, p. 52.
64. Bigo, *Pouvoir*, pp. 118, 121.
65. Ibid., p. 108. The French footed much of the bill for the coronation.
66. Bigo cites the example of a sub-lieutenant who was elevated to général d'aviation for having slapped a Frenchman who showed a lack of respect. Bigo, *Pouvoir*, pp. 83, 110–11.
67. Ibid., p. 136.
68. Decalo, *Psychoses*, p. 164.
69. Bigo, *Pouvoir*, p. 98.
70. Decalo, *Psychoses*, p. 164.
71. Bigo, *Pouvoir*, p. 120. On the Libyan connection, see Brian Titley, *Dark Age: The Political Odyssey of Emperor Bokassa* (Liverpool: Liverpool University Press, 1997), pp. 79–80.
72. O'Toole, *Central African Republic*, p. 53.
73. O'Toole, *Central African Republic*, pp. 54–5. Emmanuel Germain, *La Centrafrique et Bokassa, 1965–1979: force et déclin d'un pouvoir personnel* (Paris: L'Harmattan, 2000), pp. 243–52. Brian Titley suggests that the fall of the Shah of Iran, alongside a number of other dictatorships in 1979, was a precipitating factor in the challenge to Bokassa. *Dark Age*, p. 105.
74. Although there were up to 1,500 French troops in the country, they failed to prop up Dacko.
75. Phares Mutibwa, *Uganda Since Independence: A Story of Unfulfilled Hopes* (London: C. Hurst, 1992), p. 80. This section draws substantially on this source.
76. Mutibwa, *Uganda Since Independence*, p. 79.
77. Decalo, *Coups*, p. 165.
78. This identity had tended to absorb many peoples who were not actually the descendants of the original Nubians. Hansen, *Ethnicity*, pp. 79–80.
79. Decalo, *Coups*, p. 169.
80. Ibid., p. 177. By contrast, Mutibwa suggests that many members of the civilian elite were actually complicit in the nightmare which the country endured. *Uganda Since Independence*, p. 121.
81. Mutibwa, *Uganda Since Independence*, p. 112.
82. Ibid., p. 123. Likewise Master-Sergeant Samuel Doe, who came to power in Liberia in 1980 was virtually illiterate.
83. Crawford Young and Thomas Turner, *The Rise and Decline of the Zairean State* (Madison and London: University of Wisconsin Press, 1985), p. 61. In this section, I draw extensively on this study.
84. Young and Turner, *Rise and Decline*, p. 63.
85. Ibid., p. 207.
86. Tshombe was abducted from his European exile and died under dubious circumstances in an Algerian prison in June. Kasavubu also allegedly died of natural causes, but many believe he was poisoned by agents of the regime. Young and Turner, *Rise and Decline*, p. 58 and footnote 31, p. 420.

87. Young and Turner, *Rise and Decline*, p. 210.

88. Ironically, 'Zaire' was itself a Portuguese corruption of a local term. The work of two Belgian historians, Placide Tempels from the colonial period and Jan Vansina from the present were mined for evidence to support the claim that the Congo had, in a sense, always existed. Young and Turner, *Rise and Decline*, pp. 213–14.

89. Or in the long-version, Sese Seko Kuku Ngbendu wa za Banga. However, his wife apparently neglected to change her French name of Marie-Antoinette.

90. Short for 'à bas le costume occidental' (down with Western dress). Young and Turner, *Rise and Decline*, p. 117.

91. The schools were later returned because of the chaos which ensued. Thomas M. Callaghy, *The State-Society Struggle: Zaire in Comparative Perspective* (New York and Guildford: Columbia University Press, 1984), p. 305.

92. As Mobutu himself put it, 'I am power with a capital P. Power is myself, not the church'. Callaghy, *State-Society Struggle*, p. 304.

93. Georges Nzongola-Ntalaja, *The Congo From Leopold to Kabila: A People's History* (London and New York: Zed Books, 2002), pp. 154–6.

94. Young and Turner, *Rise and Decline*, pp. 266–7. By contrast, Katangans came to be seen as a threat to the regime, having been at the centre of a series of mutinies.

95. Ibid., pp. 179–81.

96. For a discussion of the ideological underpinnings, see Michael Schatzberg, *The Dialectics of Oppression in Zaire* (Bloomington and Indianapolis: Indiana University Press, 1988), Chapter 5.

97. On the military as bandits, see Schatzberg, *Dialectics*, Chapter 4.

98. Young and Turner, *Rise and Decline*, p. 330.

99. Nzongola-Ntalaja, *Congo*, p. 151.

100. Schatzberg, *Dialectics*, p. 118.

101. In Nigeria, most politicians tended to steer clear of politics. Ebenezer Obey did so, but he did produce one album which consisted of two sides in praise of Obafemi Awolowo. When Franco died, he was given a lavish state funeral by Mobutu. I am grateful to Tom Salter for insights on this point. For a study of Franco, see Graeme Ewens, *Congo Colossus: The Life and Legacy of Franco and OK Jazz* (North Walsham: Buku Books, 1994).

102. Whereas two Zaires traded for one United States dollar in 1974, the latter was equivalent to seven million Zaires by 1993.

103. This is sent up in a classic comedy, 'La Vie Est Belle' (Director: Mweze Nwangura, 1987). This Belgian co-production stars the musician, Papa Wemba, in the lead role.

104. Catherine Newbury, 'Survival strategies in rural Zaire: realities of coping with the crisis', in Nzongola-Ntalaja (ed.) *The Crisis in Zaire: Myths and Realities* (Trenton: Africa World Press, 1986), p. 103; Janet MacGaffey, *Entrepreneurs and Parasites: The Struggle for Indigenous Capitalism in Zaire* (Cambridge: Cambridge University Press, 1987); and Janet MacGaffey *The Real Economy of Zaire: The Contribution of Smuggling*

and Other Unofficial Activities to National Wealth (London and Philadelphia: James Currey and Pennsylvania University Press, 1991).

105. Callaghy, *State-Society Struggle*, pp. 198–201.
106. Crawford Young, 'Zaire: the anatomy of a failed state', in David Birmingham and Phyllis M. Martin (eds) *History of Central Africa: The Contemporary Years Since 1960* (London and New York: Longman, 1998), p. 123.
107. Comi Toulabor, *Le Togo sous Eyadéma* (Paris: Karthala, 1986), p. 93. The same ruse was performed as late as July 2002 and repeated *ad nauseam* on Togolese television.
108. Kodjo went on to become OAU secretary-general in 1978.
109. Toulabor, *Le Togo*, pp. 91–2.
110. Tombalbaye similarly changed the name of Fort-Lamy to the more 'authentic' N'Djamena.
111. For a detailed analysis, see E. Adriaan B. Van Rouveroy Van Nieuwaal, *L'Etat en Afrique face à la chefferie: le cas du Togo* (Paris and Leiden: Karthala and Afrika-Studiecentrum, 2000).
112. The cultural dominance of Congolese music, and the spell cast by Mobutu, meant that the Togolese initially imported directly from Zaire. Franco even performed a praise song to Eyadéma when he accompanied Mobutu to Togo in 1972. Toulabor, *Le Togo*, p. 201.
113. This was supposed to have been hatched by the company which wished to retain control of the phosphate industry.
114. For an analysis of the religious symbolism, see Toulabor, *Le Togo*, Chapter 4.
115. Of the new hotels constructed in Lomé, one was called 'Sarakawa' and the other (a vast white elephant) 'Hotel 2 février' to commemorate the date of his triumphal return to the capital.
116. Scott, *Domination and the Arts of Resistance*.
117. Comi Toulabor, 'Political satire past and present in Togo' *Critique of Anthropology* 14, 1, 1994.
118. Decalo, *Coups*, p. 236.
119. Ibid., p. 230.
120. More than half of the population lived in the capital and the three other main towns. Decalo, *Coups*, p. 43, which was remarkable by African standards.
121. Michael S. Radu and Keith Somerville, 'The Congo' in Chris Allen, Michael S. Radu, Keith Somerville and Joan Baxter, *Benin, The Congo, Burkina Faso: Politics, Economy and Society* (London: Pinter Publishers, 1988), p. 163.
122. Remarkably, Matsoua was elected deputy to Paris in 1945 and again in 1951. Death, it seems, was no impediment. Decalo, *Coups*, p. 52.
123. Radu and Somerville, 'The Congo', pp. 172–3.
124. Radu and Somerville, 'The Congo', p. 194. At one point in 1972, PCT membership had fallen to 160, while only three of the nine member Politburo remained. Decalo, *Coups*, p. 71.
125. It was later claimed that Sassou-Nguesso was behind the assassination.
126. Decalo, *Coups*, pp. 41–2.

127. Radu and Somerville, 'The Congo', pp. 211–12.

128. By the 1980s, over 65 per cent of the population was urbanised. The 1983 census revealed that Brazzaville itself contained 521,000 people out of a national total of 1.62 million. Radu and Somerville, 'The Congo', pp. 156, 206–7.

129. Ibid., 'The Congo', p. 227.

130. Quoted in Chris Allen, 'Benin', in Allen et al., *Benin, the Congo, Burkina Faso*, p. 63.

131. Decalo, *Coups*, p. 117.

132. Allen, 'Benin', pp. 117–30.

133. In June 1975, there were demonstrations against Kérékou after the killing of Captain Michel Aikpé, a member of the regime who was regarded as a friend of the left. These were harshly repressed. There was also a series of clashes with the students over the years, as the regime attempted to impose austerity measures. Allen, 'Benin', pp. 36, 71–2.

134. The budget was permanently in deficit to the tune of around 20 per cent at this point. Allen, 'Benin', p. 75.

135. Allen, 'Benin', p. 79.

136. Teaching was to be in local languages and to involve practical subjects, most notably agriculture, alongside book learning. Political education was also inserted into the curriculum. Allen, 'Benin', p. 105.

137. Ibid., pp. 109–12.

138. Ibid., p. 100.

139. Ibid., p. 81.

140. A full discussion is to be found in ibid., Chapter 3.

141. Ibid., p. 73.

142. Ibid., p. 84.

143. Ibid., p. 108.

144. Interestingly, traditional healers, who it was hoped might be brought on board, kept their distance as a result of the public campaign against traditional religion (including *vodun*) as tantamount to witchcraft.

144. For example, John Markakis and Nega Ayele, *Class and Revolution in Ethiopia* (Nottingham: Spokesman, 1978), Chapter 4.

146. Fred Halliday and Maxine Molyneux, *The Ethiopian Revolution* (London: Verso, 1981), pp. 90–1, 96–7.

147. Andargachew, *The Ethiopian Revolution,1974–1987* (Cambridge: Cambridge University Press, 1993), p. 66.

148. Ibid., p. 133.

149. For a revealing account of these groupings, see ibid., pp. 134–43.

150. However, a sign of things to come was the execution of some military personnel, including members of the *Derg* itself, who were the casualties of internal power struggles.

151. For a more detailed account, see René Lefort, *Ethiopia: An Heretical Revolution?* (London: Zed Press, 1981), Chapter 3.

152. However, many of these students were later arrested for being over-zealous. Many who returned to Addis Ababa enlisted in the leftwing organisations.

153. Clapham argues that the land reform is what made it a genuine revolution. Christopher Clapham, *Transformation and Continuity in Revolutionary Ethiopia* (Cambridge: Cambridge University Press, 1988), p. 50. For a fascinating study of what the revolution meant at the rural periphery, see Donald L. Donham, *Marxist Modern: An Ethnographic History of the Ethiopian Revolution* (Berkeley, Los Angeles and Oxford: University of California Press and James Currey, 1999).

154. Halliday and Molyneux, *Ethiopian Revolution*, pp. 123, 223.

155. Clapham, *Transformation*, p. 128.

156. Andargachew, *Ethiopian Revolution*, p. 137; Halliday and Molyneux, *Ethiopian Revolution*, pp. 126–7.

157. There is some dispute as to his origins. While some have described him as Oromo, it is also claimed that he was half Amhara and half from one of the despised 'black' *shankala* groups. Halliday and Molyneux, *Ethiopian Revolution*, p. 116.

158. Crucially, he was of Eritrean extraction.

159. This is brought out in the Maale case-study. Donham, *Marxist Modern*, Chapter 7.

160. The fact that Mengistu was reputedly of slave origins, however, seemed to underline the democratisation of monarchy. Donham, *Marxist Modern*, p. 146.

161. For an analysis, which also highlights significant local variations, see Dessalegn Rahmato, *Agrarian Reform in Ethiopia* (Trenton: Red Sea Press, 1985), especially pp. 52–6.

162. Clapham, *Transformation*, pp. 126, 168–71.

163. In 1985, the government embarked on a campaign to force peasants to give up their scattered settlement patterns in favour of living in villages where it would be easier to provide them with services. Although there seems to have been less coercion deployed than in Tanzania, many of the same problems recurred. The advantages for peasants were limited.

164. Clapham, *Transformation*, pp. 124–5.

165. By the mid-1980s, the armed forces numbered some 300,000 people and boasted a thousand tanks and four airborne brigades. Much of the personnel consisted of conscripts. Ibid., p. 109.

166. Ibid., p. 165.

167. The fact that the regime was celebrating the tenth anniversary of the revolution when the famine broke out was a stroke of bad timing or bad luck, depending on one's view. For a measured assessment of the regime's response to the famine, see ibid., pp. 189–94.

168. Ibid., p. 118.

169. J. Gus Liebenow, *Liberia: The Quest for Democracy* (Bloomington and Indianapolis: Indiana University Press, 1987), pp. 214–17.

7 Second Liberation: Guerrilla Warfare, Township Revolt and the Search for a New Social Order

1. In May 1961, the compulsory cultivation of cotton in Mozambique, which had been perhaps the most hated aspect of Portuguese rule, was ended. However, the promotion of the settler option meant that Africans were still needed as farm labour. Allen Isaacman, *Cotton is the Mother of Poverty: Peasants, Work and Rural Struggle in Colonial Mozambique, 1938–1961* (Portsmouth, London and Cape Town: Heinemann, James Currey and David Philip, 1996), p. 242.

2. In Angola, the Portuguese population rose from 44,083 in 1940 to 78,826 in 1950 and 172,529 in 1960. Malyn Newitt, *Portugal in Africa: The Last Hundred Years* (London: C. Hurst, 1981), p. 164.

3. Mondlane had studied at Witwatersrand University in South Africa, but was deported in 1949. The Portuguese sent him to study in the metropole the following year, apparently to get him out of the way. He subsequently left to the United States, where he became the first Mozambican to complete a Ph.D. Allen Isaacman and Barbara Isaacman, *Mozambique: From Colonialism to Revolution, 1900–1982* (Boulder and Aldershot: Westview Press and Gower, 1983), p. 81.

4. Isaacman and Isaacman, *Mozambique*, p. 80.

5. Norrie MacQueen, *The Decolonisation of Portuguese Africa: Metropolitan Revolution and the Dissolution of Empire* (Harlow: Addison Wesley Longman, 1997), p. 19.

6. MacQueen, *Decolonisation*, p. 19.

7. Fernando Andresen Guimarães, *The Origins of the Angolan Civil War: Foreign Intervention and Domestic Political Conflict* (Basingstoke and New York: Macmillan and St Martin's Press, 1998), p. 49. The most complete study of the various liberation movements remains John Marcum, *The Angolan Revolution: Exile Politics and Guerrilla Warfare (1962–1976)* (Cambridge, Mass. and London: MIT Press, 1978).

8. Mustafah Dhada, *Warriors at Work: How Guinea Was Really Set Free* (Niwot: University Press of Colorado, 1993), pp. 4–5.

9. The Mueda episode was not unprecedented. In 1953, some 1,000 Africans were killed in the course of a week on the plantation islands of São Tomé and Principe. MacQueen, *Decolonisation*, p. 17.

10. The MPLA claimed the credit, but it has been suggested that the activists concerned were more inclined towards the UPA, which was making the running at this time. Guimarães, *Origins*, p. 45.

11. David Birmingham, *Frontline Nationalism in Angola and Mozambique* (London and Trenton: James Currey and Africa World Press, 1992), p. 36.

12. Guimarães, *Origins*, p. 53.

13. MacQueen, *Decolonisation*, p. 24. There were something in the region of 300,000 refugees in the Congo by the end of 1963.

14. Apparently, Roberto (who had grown up in Leopoldville) used to play football together with him.

15. Like Mobutu, Holden Roberto, was apparently on the CIA payroll from 1961. Roberto was a close friend and was married to the sister-in-law of Mobutu.

16. MacQueen, *Decolonisation*, p. 32.

17. Ibid., pp. 54–5.

18. Thomas H. Henriksen, 'People's war in Angola, Mozambique, and Guinea-Bissau', *Journal of Modern African Studies* 14, 3, 1976, p. 392.

19. On the early travails of the MPLA, see Guimarães, *Origins*, pp. 65–75. Mario de Andrade left as well, but rejoined the fold in 1964.

20. There is a suggestion that the Makonde rebels tended to be dominated by the richer and middle peasants. Mondlane, Machel and Joaquim Chissano were all southerners, despite the fact that FRELIMO had limited success there. Merle L. Bowen, *The State and the Peasantry: Rural Struggles in Colonial and Postcolonial Mozambique* (Charlottesville and London: University Press of Virginia, 2000). On the tradition of resistance in Guinea-Bissau, see Joshua Forrest, *Lineages of State Fragility: Rural Civil Society in Guinea-Bissau* (Oxford and Athens: James Currey and Ohio University Press, 2003).

21. For example, Guinea-Bissau differed from Angola and Mozambique in having no settler population to speak of.

22. Patrick Chabal, *Amilcar Cabral: Revolutionary Leadership and People's War* (Cambridge: Cambridge University Press, 1983), p. 106.

23. Henriksen, 'People's war', p. 382.

24. Isaacman and Isaacman, *Mozambique*, p. 86.

25. According to Isaacman and Isaacman, roughly half of the population of these provinces was pushed into villages. *Ibid.*, p. 101.

26. Margaret Hall and Tom Young, *Confronting Leviathan: Mozambique Since Independence* (London: C. Hurst, 1997), p. 22.

27. Bowen, *State and Peasantry*, p. 50.

28. Isaacman and Isaacman, *Mozambique*, p. 94.

29. Ibid., pp. 91–2.

30. Bowen, *State and Peasantry*, p. 53.

31. On this point, see Chabal, *Amilcar Cabral*, p. 104.

32. Ibid., p. 124.

33. Dhada, *Warriors at Work*, p. 135.

34. Chabal, *Amilcar Cabral*, p. 119. This is given a more cynical gloss by Dhada, *Warriors at Work*, p. 135.

35. Dhada, *Warriors at Work*, p. 136.

36. For a more detailed discussion, see Chabal, *Amilcar Cabral*, pp. 107–10.

37. Dhada, *Warriors at Work*, pp. 118–19.

38. The writings of Basil Davidson stand out. See, for example, his revision of a 1969 text, *No Fist is Big Enough to Hide the Sky: The Liberation of Guinea-Bissau and Cape Verde* (London: Zed Press, 1981).

39. Lars Rudebeck, *Guinea-Bissau: A Study of Political Mobilisation* (Uppsala: Scandinavian Institute of African Studies, 1974); Dhada, *Warriors at Work*.

40. MacQueen, *Decolonisation*, p. 58.

41. John Cann, *Counterinsurgency in Africa: The Portuguese Way of War* (Westport: Greenwood Press, 1997), p. 187.

42. Ibid., p. 187.

43. Cann estimates that there were 8,90 Portuguese deaths. Ibid., pp. 191–2.

44. Ibid., p. 191.

45. Isaacman and Isaacman, *Mozambique*, p. 105.

46. Norma J. Kriger, *Zimbabwe's Guerrilla War: Peasant Voices* (Cambridge and Harare: Cambridge University Press and Baobab Books, 1992), p. 1.

47. Kriger, *Zimbabwe's Guerrilla War*, p. 59.

48. The SRANC arose from a merger of the City Youth League, centered on Salisbury (Harare) and the African National Congress of Southern Rhodesia which was Bulawayo-based. The SRANC was not pressing for early independence, but wanted an extension of the franchise and the ending of discriminatory legislation.

49. For a summary of the case against Nkomo as stated by Ndabaningi Sithole, see Masipula Sithole, *Zimbabwe: Struggles Within the Struggle (1957–1980)* (Harare: Rujeko, 1999), pp. 39–43.

50. Dumiso Dabengwa, 'ZIPRA in the Zimbabwe war of national liberation' in Ngwabi Bhebe and Terence Ranger (eds), *Soldiers in Zimbabwe's Liberation Wars* (London, Portsmouth and Harare: James Currey, Heinemann and University of Zimbabwe Publications, 1995), p. 27.

51. A standard pro-ZANU work is David Martin and Phyllis Johnson, *The Struggle for Zimbabwe: The Chimurenga War* (London: Faber, 1981).

52. Further elaboration of this point may be found in Ngwabi Bhebe and Terence Ranger, 'Volume introduction: soldiers in Zimbabwe's liberation war', in Bhebe and Ranger, *Soldiers*. For an excellent account of the war in Matabeleland, see Jocelyn Alexander, JoAnn McGregor and Terence Ranger, *Violence and Memory: One Hundred Years in the 'Dark Forests' of Matabeleland* (Oxford, Portsmouth, Cape Town and Harare: James Currey, Heinemann, David Philip and Weaver Press, 2000).

53. Fay Chung, quoted in Bhebe and Ranger, 'Introduction' in Bhebe and Ranger, *Soldiers*.

54. By the ceasefire in December 1979, ZANLA had 20,000 fighters to the 8,000 of ZIPRA. Kriger, *Zimbabwe's Guerrilla War*, p. 92. Brickhill concedes that ZIPRA had about half the fighting force of ZANLA, but claims that it operated over as wide an area by the conclusion of hostilities. Brickhill, 'Daring', p. 70.

55. For example, Lionel Cliffe and Colin Stoneman, *Zimbabwe: Politics, Economics and Society* (New York: Frances Pinter, 1989), pp. 38–9; and Ibbo Mandaza, 'The state and politics in the post-white settler colonial situation', in Ibbo Mandaza (ed.) *Zimbabwe: The Political Economy of Transition* (Dakar: CODESRIA, 1986), p. 29.

56. Jeremy Brickhill, 'Daring to storm the heavens: the military strategy of ZAPU 1976 to 1979', in Bhebe and Ranger, *Soldiers*, pp. 68–9. This interpretation is supported by Alexander, McGregor and Ranger, *Violence and Memory*, Chapters 6 and 7.

57. Dabengwa, 'ZIPRA', p. 35. Dabengwa was head of the National Security Organisation and Secretary of the War Council, the body which was the most influential on a day-to-day basis.

58. Brickhill, 'Daring', p. 66. Urban workers also provided important logistical support for ZIPRA fighters. Alexander, McGregor and Ranger, *Violence and Memory*, p. 162.
59. Bhebe and Ranger, 'Volume introduction', in Bhebe and Ranger, *Soldiers*, pp. 8–11.
60. Brickhill, 'Daring', p. 55.
61. Dabengwa, 'ZIPRA', pp. 29–30.
62. An ANC had been founded within Rhodesia in 1971 when the British negotiated the release of ZANU and ZAPU leaders as part of a package which would have involved a vote on the independence issue. Muzorewa was chosen by the two sides to head the new ANC because of his lack of partisan affiliations.
63. For a positive reappraisal of ZIPA, see David Moore, 'The Zimbabwe People's Army' strategic innovation or more of the same?', in Bhebe and Ranger, *Soldiers*.
64. Terence Ranger, *Peasant Consciousness and Guerrilla War in Zimbabwe* (London: James Currey, 1985).
65. David Lan, *Guns and Rain: Guerrillas and Spirit Mediums in Zimbabwe* (London, Berkeley and Los Angeles: James Currey and University of California Press, 1985).
66. This was deliberate ZANLA policy. Lan, *Guns and Rain*, p. 164.
67. Lan, *Guns and Rain*, p. 208.
68. Lan, *Guns and Rain*, p. 158.
69. Quoted in Ngwabi Bhebe and Terence Ranger, 'Volume introduction: society in Zimbabwe's liberation war', in Ngwabi Bhebe and Terence Ranger, *Society in Zimbabwe's Liberation War* (Oxford, Portsmouth and Harare: James Currey, Heinemann and University of Zimbabwe, 1996), p. 11.
70. M. F. C. Bourdillon, 'Guns and rain: taking structural analysis too far?', *Africa* 57, 2, 1987; Janice McLaughlin, 'Avila mission: a turning point in church relations with the state and with the liberation forces', in Bhebe and Ranger, *Society*; Jocelyn Alexander, 'Things fall apart, the centre can hold: processes of post-war political change in Zimbabwe's rural areas', in Bhebe and Ranger, *Society*.
71. Lan, *Guns and Rain*, pp. 39–42.
72. David Maxwell, *Christians and Chiefs in Zimbabwe: A Social History of the Hwesa People c.1870s–1990s* (Edinburgh and London: Edinburgh University Press, International Africa Institute, 1999). Also 'Christianity and the war in eastern Zimbabwe: the case of the Elim mission', in Bhebe and Ranger, *Society*.
73. Maxwell, *Christians*, p. 130.
74. By contrast, McLaughlin, 'Avila mission', presents a rather more positive picture of the role of the Avila mission in supporting the liberation movement. In Matabeleland, the relationship between the churches and ZIPRA was never a comfortable one. Presumably, this points to a failure of the churches to establish their supremacy over indigenous religion. Hence in Matabeleland, the Mwali shrines were visited by guerrillas. Terence

Ranger and Mark Ncube, 'Religion in the guerrilla war: the case of southern Matabeleland', in Bhebe and Ranger, *Society*.

75. Kriger, *Zimbabwe's Guerrilla War*, p. 100.
76. It is also worth noting that even in the refugee camps of Zambia and Mozambique, the liberation movements did not provide access to education until as late as 1977 because they simply lacked the personnel to maintain them. Once founded, the camp schools received favourable reports. Bhebe and Ranger, 'Volume introduction', in Bhebe and Ranger, *Society*, pp. 19–20. On ZANU's educational policies, see Fay Chung, 'Education and the liberation struggle', in Bhebe and Eranger, *Society*.
77. Kriger, *Zimbabwe's Guerrilla War*, pp. 116–21.
78. Rural elites, including master farmers in the Tribal Trust Lands (or reserves) and independent farmers in the Purchase Areas were particularly prone to accusations of disloyalty because they were more closely associated with the structures of the Rhodesian state. Whereas Africans were only supposed to farm in the reserves within South Africa, in Rhodesia a separate category of land was set aside for 'native purchase'. This provided some opportunities for sections of the African community.
79. On this theme, see Kriger, *Zimbabwe's Guerrilla War*, Chapter 5.
80. Kriger, *Zimbabwe's Guerrilla War*, p. 157.
81. Maxwell, *Christians and Chiefs*, pp. 145–6
82. Kriger, *Zimbabwe's Guerrilla War*, p. 165.
83. Richard Werbner, 'In memory: a heritage of war in south-Western Zimbabwe', in Bhebe and Ranger, *Society*, p. 195.
84. Kriger, *Zimbabwe's Guerrilla War*, p. 92.
85. Ibid., p. 112.
86. Ibid., p. 217.
87. Patrick Chabal, 'Revolutionary democracy in Africa: the case of Guinea-Bissau', in Patrick Chabal (ed.) *Political Domination in Africa: Reflections on the Limits of Power* (Cambridge: Cambridge University Press, 1986), p. 84.
88. MacQueen, *Decolonisation*, pp. 110–15.
89. Chabal, 'Revolutionary democracy', pp. 86–7.
90. Rosemary E. Galli and Jocelyn Jones, *Guinea-Bissau: Politics, Economics and Society* (London and Boulder: Frances Pinter and Lynne Rienner, 1987), p. 71.
91. Ibid., *Guinea-Bissau*, p. 91.
92. Ibid., p. 186.
93. Ibid., pp. 119–20.
94. The country had only 400 kilometres of tarred roads at the time of independence, and this had only marginally risen to 550 kilometres by 1983. Ibid., p. 112.
95. Rice production stood at around 93,000 tonnes in 1976, but had fallen 80,000 by 1981, while groundnut production fell from around 41,000 to 30,000 tonnes. Galli and Jones, *Guinea-Bissau*, p. 110.
96. Chabal, 'Revolutionary democracy', pp. 101–2.

97. Hall and Young, *Confronting Leviathan*, pp. 49–50.

98. Ibid., p. 64.

99. The case for continuity, based on local-level research, is made in Bowen, *State Against the Peasantry*.

100. William Minter, *Apartheid's Contras: An Inquiry into the Roots of War in Angola and Mozambique* (London: Zed Press, 1994), p. 25.

101. For a positive assessment, which also recognised some of the underlying problems, see Joseph Hanlon, *Mozambique: The Revolution Under Fire* (London: Zed Press, 1984), Chapter 8.

102. Minter, *Apartheid's Contras*, p. 22.

103. The re-education camps had been set up to deal with enemies of the revolution. Amongst them was Kavandame who was imprisoned and later executed when it seemed possible that he might be sprung from jail.

104. Matsangaíssa had been found guilty of theft of a car and sent to a re-education camp from which he escaped in 1976.

105. Hall and Young, *Confronting Leviathan*, p. 128.

106. Ibid., pp. 128–9.

107. Christian Geffray, *La cause des armes au Mozambique: anthropologie d'une guerre civile* (Paris: Karthala, 1990).

108. In this connection, it may be significant that RENAMO roots went deepest in the Shona-speaking areas of Manica province bordering on to Zimbabwe. The Ndau dialect of Shona even became something approximating to the RENAMO *lingua franca* despite the fact that it was spoken by only around 7 per cent of Mozambicans.

109. On this phenomenon, see Carolyn Nordstrom, *A Different Kind of War Story* (Philadelphia: University of Pennsylvania Press, 1997).

110. Minter, *Apartheid's Contras*, pp. 174–6.

111. Quoted in James Ciment, *Angola and Mozambique: Postcolonial Wars in Southern Africa* (New York: Facts on File, 1997), p. 194.

112. Carolyn Nordstrom, *A Different Kind of War Story*.

113. A discussion of the Gersony model may be found in Alex Vines, *RENAMO: From Terrorism to Democracy in Mozambique?* (London: James Currey, 1991), pp. 91–7.

114. This regional pattern is apparent from a map of atrocities produced by Vines, *RENAMO*, p. 98.

114. Britain provided some military training for the government forces.

116. The South Africans were accused of complicity in the crash. The truth has yet to emerge.

117. Hall and Young, *Confronting Leviathan*, Chapter 9.

118. Malyn Newitt, 'Mozambique', in Patrick Chabal, David Birmingham, Joshua Forrest, Malyn Newitt, Gerhard Seibert and Elisa Silva Andrade, *A History of Postcolonial Lusophone Africa* (London: C. Hurst, 2002), p. 224.

119. Quoted in Minter, *Apartheid's Contras*, p. 3.

120. This figure is cited in Vines, *RENAMO*, p. 1.

121. In October 1974, the MFA and the MPLA launched joint military operations in Cabinda in order to drive out FLEC separatists. MacQueen, *Decolonisation*, p. 173.

122. Guimarães, *Origins*, p. 103. The rest of this section draws substantially on this book.
123. The Ovimbundu constituted around 36 per cent of the population.
124. The Americans funded the FNLA and UNITA to the tune of $64 million. Guimarães, *Origins*, p. 107.
125. Marcum, *Angolan Revolution*, p. 271.
126. George Wright, *The Destruction of a Nation: United States' Policy Toward Angola Since 1945* (London and Chicago: Pluto Press, 1997), pp. 669–70.
127. Minter, *Apartheid's Contras*, p. 23. For a eulogy to the Cubans, see Victoria Brittain, *Death of Dignity: Angola's Civil War* (London and Chicago: Pluto Press, 1998), pp. 7–8.
128. On the campaign trail, Reagan clearly expressed his intention to provide Savimbi with weapons and he was true to his word. Savimbi himself rejoiced in the outcome.
129. These figures are drawn from Ciment, *Angola and Mozambique*, p. 87.
130. Ciment, *Angola and Mozambique*, p. 71.
131. This was confirmed, for example, when a South African commando was intercepted in Cabinda in 1985 and spilled the beans.
132. Quoted in Ciment, *Angola and Mozambique*, p. 71.
133. Ciment, *Angola and Mozambique*, p. 211. Tony Hodges, *Angola: From Afro-Stalinism to Petro-Diamond Capitalism* (London, Lysaker, Oxford, Bloomington and Indianapolis: IAI, Fridjtof Nansen Institute, James Currey and Indiana University Press, 2001), p. 15.
134. The term is that of André Astrow, *Zimbabwe: A Revolution That Lost its Way?* (London: Zed, 1983).
135. Jeffrey Herbst, 'The dilemmas of land policy in Zimbabwe', in Simon Baynham (ed.) *Zimbabwe in Transition* (Stockholm: Almqvist and Wiksell, International, 1992), pp. 130–1. The Riddell Commission Report of 1981 estimated that there were 2 million more people in these areas than the land could sustain.
136. Sam Moyo, *The Land Question in Zimbabwe* (Harare: SAPES Trust, 1995), p. 107.
137. Herbst, 'Dilemmas', pp. 132–3.
138. Sam Moyo, 'The land question', in Ibbo Mandaza (ed.) *Zimbabwe: The Political Economy of Transition, 1980–1986* (Dakar: CODESRIA, 1986), p. 121.
139. Ibid., p. 119.
140. Daniel Weiner, 'Land and agricultural development', in Colin Stoneman (ed.) *Zimbabwe's Prospects: Issues of Race, Class, State, and Capital in Southern Africa* (London and Basingstoke: Macmillan, 1988), p. 73.
141. Moyo, *Land Question*, pp. 113–14.
142. Alexander, 'Things fall apart', p. 187.
143. Ibid., p. 188.
144. This is examined in Richard Werbner, 'In memory'. See also his more detailed study, *Tears of the Dead: The Social Biography of an African Family* (London and Edinburgh: Edinburgh University Press and International Africa Institute, 1991).

145. There is a vast literature on witchcraft in post-colonial Africa which has pointed to the ways in which material success are often attributed to the sacrifice of an individual's kin. For a study which takes Cameroun as its focus, see Peter Geschiere, *The Modernity of Witchcraft: Politics and the Occult in Postcolonial Africa* (Charlottesville: University of Virginia Press, 1997).

146. Maxwell, *Christians and Chiefs*, pp. 196–200.

147. An excellent discussion along these lines can also be found in Robin Cohen, *Endgame in South Africa? The Changing Structures and Ideology of Apartheid* (London and Paris: James Currey and UNESCO Press, 1986).

148. Quoted in Baruch Hirson, *Year of Fire, Fire of Ash – The Soweto Revolt: Roots of a Revolution?* (London; Zed Press, 1979), p. 45.

149. To non-South Africans, the term 'Coloured' is often a highly confusing one. It refers to a community which has emerged out of fragments of the indigenous Khoi peoples of the Cape intermixed with the descendants of slaves, some of whom came from other parts of Africa, but the majority of whom actually originated from the Dutch East Indies. The Cape Malays, who constitute a sub-set of the Coloured communities are distinctive in the South African context by being Muslims, Islam having been brought from South-East Asia. Most of the Coloureds speak Afrikaans, albeit with significant differences of accent and vocabulary from the Afrikaners themselves.

150. Saul Dubow, *The African National Congress* (Johannesburg: Jonathan Ball, 2000), p. 18.

151. For an appraisal of his thought and influence, see Gail M. Gerhart, *Black Power in South Africa: The Evolution of an Ideology* (Berkeley and London: University of California Press, 1979), Chapter 3.

152. Ibid., Chapter 6.

153. Quoted in ibid., p. 208.

154. Ibid., pp. 280.

154. Ibid., pp. 223–4.

156. On the Sharpeville episode, see Philip Frankel, *An Ordinary Atrocity: Sharpeville and its Massacre* (New Haven and London: Yale University Press, 2001).

157. Dubow, *African National Congress*, p. 75.

158. *Poqo* means something like 'pure', repeating the self-reliance theme of the PAC.

159. Tom Lodge, 'The Poqo insurrection', in Tom Lodge (ed.) *Resistance and Ideology in Settler Societies – Southern African Studies Volume 4* (Johannesburg: Ravan Press, 1986) p. 188.

160. Ibid., p. 189.

161. Ibid., p. 192.

162. Ibid., p. 195.

163. These growth rates, compared with an average of 4.8 per cent in the 1950s, were matched only by Japan amongst the industrialised countries. Robert M. Price, *The Apartheid State in Crisis: Political Transformation in South Africa 1975–1990* (New York and Oxford: Oxford University

Press, 1991), p. 34. But when measured against other newly industrial-ising countries the growth was perhaps not as spectacular as it initially sounds. Terence Moll, 'Did the South African economy "fail"?' *Journal of Southern African Studies* 17, 2, 1991.

164. Soweto is itself an acronym for South-Western Townships, which signals that it is not a place in itself.

165. A case in point was the Association for the Educational and Cultural Advancement of the African People of South Africa (ASSECA) which was led by two former ANC members. Hirson, *Year of Fire*, pp. 77–8.

166. Frantz Fanon was another obvious influence. For a discussion, see Gerhart, *Black Power*, pp. 274–7.

167. As the SASO Policy Manifesto of July 1971, put it: 'The Blackman must build up his own value systems, see himself as self-defined and not defined by others.' The document is reproduced in Thomas G. Karis and Gail Gerhart (eds) *From Protest to Challenge: A Documentary History of African Politics in South Africa, 1882–1990: Nadir and Resurgence, 1964–1979* (Bloomington, Indianapolis and Pretoria: Indiana University Press and UNISA Press, 1997), pp. 481–2.

168. The ambiguities are apparent in the Mafeking Manifesto, the BPC's statement on economic policy, dated 31 May 1986. Karis and Gerhart, *From Protest to Challenge*, pp. 548–50. The similarities with African Socialism are also striking.

169. Hirson, *Year of Fire*, p. 119.

170. Gerhart, *Black Power*, pp. 295–6.

171. Ibid., p. 297.

172. The inflation rate reached 12 per cent in 1973 and 14 per cent in 1974.

173. Whereas in 1972 there had only been six strikes affecting 5,000 workers this rose to 161 strikes involving 60,000 workers between January and April 1973. Price, *Apartheid State*, pp. 46, 53.

174. Hirson, *Year of Fire*, p. 98.

175. Price, *Apartheid State*, p. 51.

176. Hirson, *Year of Fire*, p. 220.

177. For details of the first stages, see Hirson, *Year of Fire*, Chapter 20.

178. Ibid., p. 239.

179. Hjalte Tin, 'Children in violent spaces: a reinterpretation of the 1976 Soweto uprising', in Abebe Zegeye (ed.) *Social Identities in the New South Africa: After Apartheid - Volume One* (Cape Town and Maroelana: Kwela Books and SA History Online, 2001), p. 141.

180. These were children who enjoyed Section 10 rights.

181. See Clive Glaser, *Bo-Tsotsi: The Youth Gangs of Soweto, 1935–1976* (Portsmouth, Oxford and Cape Town: Heinemann, James Currey and David Philip, 2000), Chapter 7. 'Mapantsula' (Director: Oliver Schmitz, 1988) was shot underground.

182. Hirson, *Year of Fire*, pp. 272–3.

183. For the death statistics, see Hirson, *Year of Fire*, p. 185 and Price, *Apartheid State*, p. 48.

184. Dubow, *African National Congress*, p. 82.

185. Price, *Apartheid State*, p. 91.

186. As defined by Botha when he was Defence Minister in 1977. Defence White Paper, quoted in ibid., p. 87.

187. Ibid., p. 128.

188. In 1987, some 86 per cent of houses in the townships remained without electricity. And by 1986, only 19 per cent of the housing stock had been sold off. Ibid., pp. 111–14.

189. This was not for want of trying. In the early 1980s, there was a marked increase in arrests under the pass laws, numbering 206,022 in 1982. Ibid., p. 126.

190. Ibid., p. 158.

191. Martin Murray, *South Africa: Time of Agony, Time of Destiny* (London: Verso, 1987), p. 252.

192. By May 1984, perhaps as many as 220,00 students were boycotting classes. Ibid., p. 246.

193. Ibid., pp. 252–3.

194. This is discussed more fully in ibid., Chapter 3.

195. Ibid., p. 193.

196. For histories of the UDF, see Jeremy Seekings, *The UDF: A History of the United Democratic Front in South Africa, 1983–1991* (Cape Town, Oxford and Athens: David Philip, James Currey and Ohio University Press, 2000); and Ineke Van Kessel, *'Beyond Our Wildest Dreams': The United Democratic Front and the Transformation of South Africa* (Charlottesville and London: University Press of Virginia, 2000).

197. Some of the patrons of the UDF were familiar faces from the 1950s, like Albertina Sisulu and Archie Gumede. Murray, *South Africa*, p. 216.

198. Only 18 per cent of Coloureds and 13 per cent of Indians voted. Murray, *South Africa*, pp. 244–5.

199. Murray, *South Africa*, p. 260.

200. For the Cradock story, see ibid., pp. 273–4.

201. Ibid., p. 347.

202. Van Kessel, *Beyond*, pp. 112–13.

203. Laurent C. Kaela, *The Question of Namibia* (Basingstoke, London and New York: Macmillan and St Martin's Press, 1996), p. 14.

204. Lauren Dobell, *SWAPO's Struggle for Namibia, 1960–1991: War By Other Means* (Basel: Schlettwein Publishing, 1998), p. 40.

205. Ibid., p. 66.

206. Ibid., p. 31.

207. Ibid., p. 29.

208. Colin Leys and John S. Saul, 'SWAPO inside Namibia', in Colin Leys and John S. Saul (eds) *Namibia's Liberation Struggle: The Two-Edged Sword* (London and Athens; James Currey and Ohio University Press, 1995), pp. 72–3.

209. Sipho S. Maseko, 'The Namibian student movement: its role and effects', in Leys and Saul, *Namibia's Liberation Struggle*, p. 117.

210. As a result of the strike, SWANLA was abolished. Leys and Saul, 'SWAPO inside Namibia', p. 72. A useful analysis of the contract labour system is

Rauha Voipio, 'Contract work through Ovambo eyes', in Reginald Green, Marja-Lissa Kiljunen and Kimmo Kiljunnen (eds) *Namibia: The Last Colony* (Harlow: Longman, 1981).

211. Hirson, *Year of Fire*, pp. 130–3.

212. Anon., 'The state of the liberation struggle: an interview with SWAPO President Sam Nujoma', in Green et al., *Namibia*, p. 175.

213. Lionel Cliffe, *The Transition to Independence in Namibia* (Boulder and London: Lynne Rienner, 1994), p. 24.

214. Ibid., p. 34.

215. Susan Brown, 'Diplomacy by other means: SWAPO's liberation war', in Leys and Saul, *Namibia's Liberation Struggle*, p. 29; John S. Saul and Colin Leys, 'SWAPO: the politics of exile', in Leys and Saul, *Namibia's Liberation Struggle*, p. 54.

216. Leys and Saul, 'SWAPO inside Namibia', p. 84 cite an occasion in 1988 when Nujoma allegedly told the head of the Mineworkers' Union of Namibia, which was engaged in a strike at the Rossing mine, that it was not up to the union to decide when to strike.

217. Gretchen Bauer, *Labor and Democracy in Namibia, 1971–1996* (Athens and Oxford: Ohio University Press and James Currey, 1998), pp. 59–60.

218. Leys and Saul, 'SWAPO inside Namibia', pp. 81–3.

219. Philip Steenkamp, 'The churches', in Leys and Saul, *Namibia's Liberation Struggle*, p. 99.

220. For an analysis of the results, see Cliffe, *Transition*, Chapter 8.

8 Invasion of the Acronyms: SAPs, AIDS and the NGO Takeover

1. In the past, the World Bank had participated actively in large-scale development projects in Africa. Without acknowledging its complicity in the crisis, it turned round to blame African governments for poor policy choices.

2. For a clear account of the differences between these various loan packages, see Robert Lensink, *Structural Adjustment in Sub-Saharan Africa* (London and New York: Longman, 1996), Chapters 4–5.

3. Nicolas Van de Walle, *African Economies and the Politics of Permanent Crisis, 1979–99* (Cambridge: Cambridge University Press, 2001), p. 7.

4. World Bank, *Accelerated Development in Sub-Saharan Africa: An Agenda for Action* (Washington: World Bank, 1981). The principal author, Elliot Berg, had contributed to the debate comparing the Ivoirien and Ghanaian economic models in the 1960s. He had lauded the success of Ivorian capitalism. See Chapter 5.

5. Ibid., p. 4.

6. Ibid., p. 4.

7. Ibid., p. 43.

8. Thandika Mkandawire and Charles C. Soludo, *Our Continent, Our Future: African Perspectives on Structural Adjustment* (Dakar, Ottawa, Trenton: CODESRIA, IDRC and Africa World Press, 1999), pp. 28–30.

9. Robert H. Bates, *Markets and States in Tropical Africa: The Political Basis of Agricultural Policies* (Berkeley, Los Angeles and London: University of California Press, 1981).

10. Eboe Hutchful, *Ghana's Adjustment Experience: The Paradox of Reform* (Geneva and Oxford: UNRISD and James Currey, 2002), p. 55 astutely observes that the Bank was giving way to its critics on the lack of a social angle at the same time as it shifted the blame back onto African governments.

11. In fact, most African bureaucracies were not excessively large by international standards. Van de Walle, *African Economies*, pp. 91–2.

12. This is baldly stated at the opening to World Bank, *Adjustment in Africa: Reforms, Results, and the Road Ahead* (Washington: World Bank, 1994) p. 1.

13. Elliot Berg, 'African adjustment programs: false attacks and true dilemmas', in Daniel M. Schydlowsky (ed.) *Structural Adjustment: Retrospect and Prospect* (Westport and London: Praeger, 1995), p. 92.

14. *Adjustment in Africa*, pp. 163–7.

15. Mkandawire and Soludo, *Our Continent*, p. 52.

16. Michael Barratt Brown, *Africa's Choices After Thirty Years of the World Bank* (London: Penguin, 1985), p. 81. UNECA was one of the fiercest critic of SAPs.

17. Mkandawire and Soludo, *Our Continent*, pp. 51–2.

18. For an overview of the impact of structural adjustment on African agriculture, see Stefano Ponte, *Farmers and Markets in Tanzania: How Policy Reforms Affect Rural Livelihoods in Africa* (Oxford, Dar es Salaam and Portsmouth: James Currey, Mkuki na Nyota and Heinemann, 2002), Chapter 2.

19. Mkandawire and Soludo, *Our Continent*, pp. 56–9.

20. Barratt Brown, *Africa's Choices*, p. 84, Van de Walle, *African Economies*, p. 6. However, the debt burden was expected to decline towards the end of the century when more countries joined the HIPIC (Highly Indebted Poor Countries) initiative.

21. Mkandawire and Soludo, *Our Continent*, pp. 74–5. Interestingly, Berg himself adopts the same view, arguing that the effect has been to 'weaken the intellectual foundations of the program.' 'African adjustment', p. 7.

22. Van de Walle, *African Economies*, Chapter 2; A World Bank report of 1990 observed that 45 per cent of conditions were not fully met. Berg, 'African adjustment', p. 101.

23. Ibid.

24. For example, see Patrick Chabal and Jean-Pascal Daloz, *Africa Works: Disorder as Political Instrument* (London, Oxford and Bloomington: IAI, James Currey and Indiana University Press, 1999).

25. Alongside the national archives, the statistical service is normally one of the most benighted branches of the African state.

26. Lensink, *Structural Adjustment*, p. 48. Putting it very simply, if Ghana, Côte d'Ivoire and Cameroun opted to maximise their output of cocoa

(alongside Brazil and Malaysia), the net effect is likely to be a glut on the cocoa market and a substantial decline in the world price – although droughts and frosts might produce temporary upswings.

27. David E. Sahn, Paul A. Dorosh and Stephen D. Younger, *Structural Adjustment Reconsidered: Economic Policy and Poverty in Africa* (Cambridge: Cambridge University Press, 1997) have conducted a sober analysis of the impact of economic policies on the poor and conclude that the latter were 'small net gainers' under SAPs. This is a more positive assessment than my own, but it is hardly a ringing endorsement of SAPs.

28. Alex de Waal, *Famine Crimes: Politics and the Disaster Relief Industry in Africa* (London, Oxford and Bloomington: African Rights, IAI, James Currey and Indiana University Press, 1997), pp. 60–4.

29. The percentage of the 'extremely poor' in Zambia rose from 27 per cent to 36 per cent between 1996 and 1998. Lusaka and the Copperbelt both experienced this phenomenon. Oliver Saasa, *Aid and Poverty Reduction in Zambia: Mission Unaccomplished* (Uppsala: Nordiska Afrikainstitutet, 2002), pp. 29–30.

30. For the energies released by the revolution, see Paul Nugent, *Big Men, Small Boys and Politics in Ghana: Power, Ideology and the Burden of History, 1982–1994* (London: Frances Pinter, 1996), Chapter 2.

31. Elliot Berg, Patrick Guillaumont, Jacky Amprou and Jacques Pegatienan, 'Côte d'Ivoire', in Shantayanan Devarajan, David R. Dollar and Torgny Holmgren (eds) *Aid and Reform in Africa: Lessons From Ten Case-Studies* (Washington: World Bank, 2001).

32. Hutchful, *Ghana's Adjustment*, p. 68.

33. Gold production increased fivefold in the decade after 1984, which meant that mining superseded cocoa as the leading export. Hutchful, *Ghana's Adjustment*, p. 84.

34. *African Economic Outlook, 2001/2002* (Paris: OECD and African Development Bank, 2002), p. 155; Ernest Aryeetey, 'Macroeconomic and sectoral developments since 1970', in Ernest Aryeetey, Jane Harrigan and Machiko Nissanke (eds) *Economic Reforms in Ghana: The Miracle and the Mirage* (Oxford, Accra and Trenton: James Currey, Woeli and Africa World Press, 2000), p. 17; also Tony Killick, 'Fragile still: the structure of Ghana's economy, 1960–94', Table 3.1, p. 55.

35. Hutchful, *Ghana's Adjustment*, p. 69.

36. Yaw Asante, Frederick Nixson and G. Kwaku Tsikata, 'The industrial sector and economic development', in Aryeetey et al., *Economic Reforms*, pp. 248–9. In the 1990s, Accra and Kumasi underwent a construction boom of extraordinary proportions. Much of the building was carried out on behalf of returnees from North America and Europe. The building boom largely accounts for the vitality of the intermediate goods sector of industry.

37. This was the projection in the government's '2020 Vision' document. *African Economic Outlook*, p. 156.

38. Hutchful, *Ghana's Adjustment*, pp. 85–6.

39. *African Economic Outlook*, p. 162.

40. However, in a World Bank document of 2001 Ghana is still ranked along-side Uganda as one of the 'successful reformers'. Devarajan et al., *Aid and Reform in Africa.*

41. The resignation of Botchway may also have removed one of the individuals who had endeavoured to keep the SAP on track.

42. Hutchful, *Ghana's Adjustment*, p. 73.

43. This is the critique offered by Hutchful, *Ghana's Adjustment*, p. 121.

44. Kweku Appiah, Lionel Demery and George Laryea-Adjei, 'Poverty in a changing environment', in Aryeetey et al., *Economic Reforms*, pp. 314–15. Poverty was defined as an income of less than 32,981 cedis in 1987/88 prices. Hutchful, *Ghana's Adjustment*, pp. 120, 124.

45. Hutchful, *Ghana's Adjustment*, p. 139. Appiah, Demery and Laryea-Adjei, 'Poverty', p. 317.

46. The urban areas received 48.7 of health spending in 1992. Hutchful, *Ghana's Adjustment*, p. 130.

47. Although the fees do not sound like much, they have represented significant outlays for ordinary Ghanaians. For confirmation on this point, see Lynne Brydon and Karen Legge, *Adjusting Society: The World Bank, the IMF and Ghana* (London and New York: Tauris, 1996), p. 150.

48. Appiah, Demery and Laryea-Adjei, 'Poverty', p. 317. However, the primary school enrolment rate for 1999 is cited as being 82.8 per cent, which suggests that the gains were not maintained. *African Economic Outlook*, p. 165. It is not clear whether private schools are included.

49. Gender and regional inequality had a reinforcing effect. In 1998/9, only 27 of the 1033 women admitted to the University of Ghana came from the three northern regions. Hutchful, *Ghana's Adjustment*, p. 137.

50. With 1960 as the base year, the index of per capita income stood at 89 in 1980 and 83 in 1994. Tony Killick, 'Fragile still? the structure of Ghana's economy 1960–94', p. 57.

51. Arne Bigsten, Deogratias Mutalemwa, Yvonne Tsikata and Samuel Wangwe, 'Tanzania', in Devarajan et al., *Aid and Reform*, p. 295. McNamara became a close friend of Nyerere.

52. John Loxley, 'The devaluation debate in Tanzania', in Bonnie K. Campbell and John Loxley (eds) *Structural Adjustment in Africa* (Basingstoke: Macmillan, 1989), pp. 23–5. By the mid-1980s, the official rate of exchange for the cedi (pegged to the dollar) was seven times its parallel rate. Bigsten and Danielson, 'Tanzania', p. 47.

53. Bigsten et al., 'Tanzania', pp. 318–19.

54. Phil Raikes and Peter Gibbon, 'Tanzania', in Poul Engberg-Pedersen, Peter Gibbon, Phil Raikes and Lars Udsholt (eds) *Limits of Adjustment in Africa: The Effects of Economic Liberalisation* (Copenhagen, Oxford and Portsmouth: Centre for Development Research, James Currey and Heinemann, 1996), pp. 220–2.

55. Peter Gibbon, 'Merchantisation of production and privatisation of development in post-*Ujamaa* Tanzania', in Peter Gibbon (ed.) *Liberalised Development in Tanzania* (Uppsala: Nordiska Afrikainstitutet, 1995), p. 14.

56. For example, concerned citizens managed to alter the terms under which the National Bank of Commerce was split up. Bigsten et al., 'Tanzania', p. 326.

57. Ibid., pp. 333–4. The total number of parastatals numbered 450 in 1985. The fact that the buyers were often Asians heightened popular sensitivity.

58. Raikes and Gibbon, 'Tanzania', p. 217.

59. *African Economic Outlook*, p. 281.

60. Gibbon, 'Merchantisation', p. 15. This estimate is derived from T. L. Maliyamkono and M. S. D. Bagachwa, *The Second Economy in Tanzania* (London, Nairobi, Athens and Dar es Salaam: James Currey, Ohio University Press, Heinemann Kenya and ESAURP, 1990).

61. Ponte, *Farmers and Markets*, pp. 68–71.

62. Bigsten and Danielson, *Tanzania*, p. 59.

63. Bigsten and Danielson, *Tanzania*, p. 73. On the other hand, more loans went in the direction of trading.

64. Ponte, *Farmers and Markets*, Chapter 6.

65. Bigsten and Danielson, *Tanzania*, p. 63.

66. Ibid., *Tanzania*, p. 52.

67. Raikes and Gibbon, 'Tanzania', p. 249.

68. Quoted in Janet Bujra and Carolyn Baylies, 'Responses to the AIDS epidemic in Tanzania and Zambia', in Carolyn Baylies and Janet Bujra (eds) *AIDS, Sexuality and Gender in Africa: Collective Strategies and Struggles in Tanzania and Zambia* (London and New York: Routledge, 2002).

69. Ponte, *Farmers and Markets*, p. 142.

70. *Africa Economic Outlook*, p. 289.

71. Bigsten and Danielson, *Tanzania*, p. 84. Tanzania supposedly had the lowest government secondary school enrolment in Africa in 2000. *Africa Economic Outlook*, p. 289.

72. I am grateful to Steve Kerr for assistance in trying to untangle this knot.

73. Andrew S. Z. Kiondo, 'When the state withdraws: local development, politics and liberalisation in Tanzania', in Gibbon, *Liberalised Development*, pp. 160–1.

74. Bigsten and Danielson, *Tanzania*, p. 85; *Africa Economic Outlook*, p. 289.

75. If per capita incomes grew at 3 per cent, it would take 12 years. Appiah, Demery and Laryea-Adjei, 'Poverty', p. 318.

76. A different definition of poverty is used in Tanzania, namely the ability to consume 2100 calories per day. Bigsten and Danielson, *Tanzania*, p. 22.

77. Ibid., p. 22.

78. The British government's poverty reduction strategy, as promoted by the Department for International Development (DfID), is particularly sold on this idea. However, the underlying philosophy is a rather tired liberal orthodoxy which makes enormous assumptions.

79. Gumisai Mutume, 'Mounting opposition to Northern farm subsidies: African cotton farmers battling to survive', *Africa Recovery* 17, 1, May 2003.

80. Much of the literature deals with the Igbo, but for a Yoruba study see Lillian Trager, *Yoruba Hometowns: Community, Identity and Development in Nigeria* (Boulder and London: Lynne Rienner, 2001).

81. Michael Jennings, ' "Development is a very political thing in Tanzania": Oxfam and the Chunya Integrated Development Programme, 1972–76', in Ondine Barrow and Michael Jennings (eds) *The Charitable Impulse: NGOs and Development in East and North-East Africa* (Oxford and Bloomfield: James Currey and Kumarian Press, 2001), p. 111.

82. Ondine Barrow and Michael Jennings, 'Introduction: the charitable impulse', in Barrow and Jennings, *Charitable Impulse*, p. 4.

83. Research cited in Alan Fowler, 'NGOs and the globalisation of social welfare: perspectives from East Africa', in Joseph Semboja and Ole Therkildsen (eds) *Service Provision Under Stress in East Africa* (Copenhagen, Nairobi, Dar es Salaam, Kampala, Portsmouth and London: Centre for Development Research, EAEP, Mkuki na Nyota, Fountain Publishers, Heinemann and James Currey, 1995), p. 57.

84. Barrow and Jennings, 'Introduction', p. 4.

85. Fowler, 'NGOs', p. 57.

86. Barrow and Jennings, 'Introduction', p. 5.

87. David Hulme and Michael Edwards, 'NGOs, states and donors: an overview', in David Hulme and Michael Edwards (eds) *NGOs, States and Donors: Too Close for Comfort?* (London and New York: Macmillan, St. Martin's Press and Save the Children Fund, 1997), p. 7. Fowler, 'NGOs', p. 57.

88. Kojo Amanor, Aloysius Denkabe and Kate Wellard, 'Ghana: country overview', in Kate Wellard and James G. Copestake (eds) *Non-Governmental Organisations and the State in Africa* (London and New York: Routledge, 1993), p. 187.

89. The lower figure comes from James C. Copestake, 'Kenya: country overview', in Wellard and Copestake, *Non-Governmental Organisations*, p. 92. The higher estimate is from Fowler, 'NGOs', p. 60.

90. Susan Dicklitch, *The Elusive Promise of NGOs in Africa: Lessons From Uganda* (Basingstoke and New York: Palgrave, 1998), pp. 125–6.

91. Tim Kelsall, 'Donors, NGOs and the state: governance and "civil society" in Tanzania', in Barrow and Jennings, *Charitable Impulse*, p. 135.

92. Paul J. Nelson, *The World Bank and Non-Governmental Organisations: The Limits of Apolitical Development* (London and New York: Macmillan and St. Martin' s Press, 1995), pp. 56–9.

93. Hulme and Edwards, 'NGOs, states and donors', p. 8.

94. Andrew S. Z. Kiondo, 'When the state withdraws', p. 163.

95. See Stephen N. Ndegwa, *The Two Faces of Civil Society: NGOs and Politics in Africa* (West Hartford: Kumarian Press, 1996), Chapters 3–4.

96. De Waal, *Famine Crimes*, pp. 138–9.

97. On the famine, see ibid., Chapter 6.

98. For an account of the NGOs which were prepared to break with the consensus, see Ondine Barrow, 'International responses to famine in Ethiopia,

1983–85: Christian Aid and political economy framework for action', in Barrow and Jennings, *The Charitable Impulse*.

99. Kiondo, 'When the state withdraws', p. 162. The lack of co-ordination is also identified in the Ugandan case. Dicklitch, *Elusive Promise*, pp. 167–8.
100. Roger C. Riddell and Marc Robinson with John de Coninck, Ann Muir and Sarah White, *Non-Governmental Organisations and Rural Poverty Alleviation* (Oxford: Clarendon Press, 1995), p. 243.
101. Riddell and Robinson, *Non-Governmental Organisations*, Chapter 10.
102. The impact of structural adjustment on the price of agricultural inputs would only have made matters worse in the 1990s.
103. For the Tanzanian case, see Don Brockington, *Fortress Conservation: The Preservation of the Mkomazi Game Reserve, Tanzania* (London, Oxford, Dar es Salaam, Bloomington: IAI, James Currey, Mkuki na Nyota and Indiana University Press, 2002).
104. Rosaleen Duffy, *Killing for Conservation: Wildlife Policy in Zimbabwe* (London, Oxford, Bloomington and Harare: IAI, James Currey, Indiana University Press and Weaver, 2002), p. 82.
105. Ibid., p. 106.
106. Riddell and Robinson, *Non-Governmental Organisations*, p. 272.
107. Brian Jones and Marshall Murphree, 'The evolution of policy on community conservation in Namibia and Zimbabwe', in David Hulme and Marshall Murphree, *African Wildlife and Livelihoods: The Promise and Performance of Community Conservation* (Oxford and Portsmouth: James Currey and Heinemann, 2001), p. 48.
108. Ivan Bond, 'Campfire and the incentives for institutional change', in Hulme and Murphree, *African Wildlife*, pp. 229–30.
109. James Murombedzi, 'Committees, rights, costs and benefits: natural resource stewardship, and community benefits in Zimbabwe's CAMP-FIRE Programme', in Hulme and Murphree, *African Wildlife*, p. 251. Even the more favourable assessment observed that people intended to invest the money in cattle.
110. Ndegwa, *Two Faces*, p. 81. This section draws heavily on this account.
111. Ibid., pp. 90–1.
112. Bujra and Baylies, 'Responses to the AIDS epidemic', pp. 43–5.
113. Robert Shell, 'Halfway to the holocaust: the economic, demographic and social implications of the AIDS pandemic to the year 2010 in the Southern African region', in Robert Shell, Kristina Quattek, Martin Schönteich and Greg Mills, *HIV/AIDS: A Threat to the African Renaissance* (Johannesburg: Konrad Adenauer Stiftung, 2000), p. 10.
114. 'The Hong Kong Flu, for example, held seven genes from a human virus, and one gene from a duck virus, that met inside a pig to produce an entirely new hybrid.' Alan Whiteside and Clem Sunter, *AIDS: The Challenge for South Africa* (Cape Town: Human and Rousseau and Tafelberg, 2000), p. 5.
115. The earliest tissue sample bearing AIDS dates from 1956 in Kinshasa.
116. Douglas Webb, *HIV and AIDS in Africa* (London, Cape Town and Pietermaritzburg: Pluto Press, David Philip and University of Natal Press, 1997), p. 2.

117. One view is that HIV might have been spread in the course of polio vaccination campaigns in Central Africa in the 1950s, in which the vaccine was cultivated on the kidneys of monkeys. Ed Hooper cited in Whiteside and Sunter, *AIDS*, p. 6.

118. Webb, *HIV and AIDS in Africa*, p. 85.

119. Tony Barnett and Alan Whiteside, *AIDS in the Twenty-First Century: Disease and Globalisation* (Basingstoke and New York: Palgrave, 2002), p. 154.

120. Webb, *HIV and AIDS in Africa*, p. 76.

121. For a series of comparisons, see Philip W. Setel, Milton Lewis and Maryinez Lyons (eds) *Histories of Sexually Transmitted Diseases and HIV/AIDS in Sub-Saharan Africa* (Westport and London: Greenwood, 1999).

122. Webb, *HIV and AIDS in Africa*, p. 91.

123. Philip W. Setel, *A Plague of Paradoxes: AIDS, Culture and Demography in Northern Tanzania* (Chicago and London: University of Chicago Press, 1999), p. 58.

124. Webb, *HIV and AIDS in Africa*, pp. 12–19.

125. George C. Bond and Joan Vincent, 'Living on the edge: changing social structures in the context of AIDS', In Holger Bernt Hansen and Michael Twaddle (eds) *Changing Uganda; The Dilemmas of Structural Adjustment and Revolutionary Change* (London, Kampala, Athens and Nairobi: James Currey, Fountain Press, Ohio University Press and Heinemann, 1991), p. 121.

126. Webb, *HIV and AIDS in Africa*, p. 106.

127. Greg Mills, 'AIDS and the South African military: timeworn cliché or timebomb', in Shell et al., *HIV/AIDS*, pp. 69–70.

128. Shell, 'Halfway to the holocaust', p. 12.

129. Whiteside and Sunter, *AIDS*, p. 46.

130. Shell, 'Halfway to the holocaust', p. 11.

131. Barnett and Whiteside, *AIDS in the Twenty-First Century*, p. 125.

132. Whiteside and Sunter, *AIDS*, p. 44.

133. The demographic loss associated with the slave trade is a matter of some debate. One problem lies in estimating how many Africans died during the course of enslavement and transportation to the coast.

134. Whiteside and Sunter, *AIDS*, p. 45; Webb, *HIV and AIDS in Africa*, p. 9. Many of the mortalities have been a consequence of pregnant mothers passing the disease to their babies.

135. Shell, 'Halfway to the holocaust', p. 11.

136. Barnett and Whiteside, *AIDS in the Twenty-First Century*, p. 297.

137. Shell, 'Halfway to the holocaust', p. 17.

138. In 2003, the World Trade Organisation (WTO) also finally dropped its objection to countries importing cheaper generic drugs.

139. World Bank, *Confronting AIDS: Public Priorities in a Global Epidemic* (New York: Oxford University Press, 1997), pp. 196–206.

140. Barnett and Whiteside, *AIDS in the Twenty-First Century*, p. 318. Even Museveni declared himself not to be an admirer of the condom.

141. Bujra and Baylies, 'Responses to the AIDS epidemic', pp. 36–7.

142. This was a cultural practice in parts of Uganda and Zambia. Tony Barnett and Piers Blaikie, *AIDS in Africa: Its Present and Future Impact* (London: Belhaven Press, 1992), p. 156.

143. Bujra and Baylies, 'Responses to the AIDS epidemic', p. 45.

144. Charles Becker and René Collignon, 'A history of Sexually Transmitted Diseases and AIDS in Senegal: difficulties in accounting for social logics in health policy', in Setel, Lewis and Lyons, *Histories*, pp. 78–84.

145. Bond and Vincent, 'Living on the edge', p. 118. For a detailed account of the susceptibility of Uganda, see Tony Barnett and Piers Blaikie, *AIDS in Africa*, Chapter 5.

146. Barnett and Blaikie, *AIDS in Africa*, pp. 157–8.

147. Marion Frank, *AIDS-Education Through Theatre: Case Studies From Uganda* (Bayreuth: Bayreuth African Studies, 1995).

148. Barnett and Whiteside, *AIDS in the Twenty-First Century*, pp. 319–20.

149. Ibid., p. 115.

9 Democracy Rediscovered: Popular Protest, Elite Mobilisation and the Return of Multipartyism

1. Samuel Huntington, *The Third Wave: Democratisation in the Late Twentieth Century* (Norman: Oklahoma University Press, 1991). He dates the first wave to 1828–1926 and the second to 1943–62.

2. While traditional healers were frowned upon, the President appropriated their symbols and powers for his own repertoire of power. I am grateful to John Lwanda for sharing his insights into the mind of Banda.

3. Michael Schatzberg, *Political Legitimacy in Middle Africa: Father, Family, Food* (Bloomington and Indianapolis: Indiana University Press, 2001).

4. On the Biya succession, see Victor Le Vine, 'Leadership and regime change in perspective', in Michael G. Schatzberg and I. William Zartman (eds) *The Political Economy of Cameroon* (New York: Praeger, 1986), pp. 35–49.

5. Thomas Turner, 'Zaire: flying high above the toads: Mobutu and stalemated democracy', in John F. Clark and David E. Gardinier (eds) *Political Reform in Francophone Africa* (Boulder and Oxford: Westview Press, 1997), p. 253.

6. Margot Light, 'Moscow's retreat from Africa', in Arnold Hughes (ed.) *Marxism's Retreat in Africa* (London: Frank Cass, 1992).

7. Gorm Rye Olsen, 'Europe and the promotion of democracy in post Cold war Africa: how serious is Europe and for what reason?', *African Affairs* 97, 1998, pp. 344–5.

8. It is surely no accident that the 'father figure' role adopted by de Gaulle and Mitterrand was mirrored by African Presidents in relation to their own populations.

9. President Tolbert was Chairman of the Baptist Convention. Paul Gifford, *African Christianity: Its Public Role* (London: C. Hurst, 1998), p. 48.

10. François Ngolet, 'Ideological manipulations and political longevity: the power of Omar Bongo in Gabon since 1967', *African Studies Review* 43, 2, 2000, pp. 60–1.

11. Under Milton Obote's second Presidency, which was every bit as violent as the Amin years, the Catholic and Anglican church hierarchies found it difficult to stand shoulder-to-shoulder as religion and partisan politics became intertwined. The Anglican church became heavily compromised in its relations with the Obote regime once it had chosen a pro-UPC Archbishop. M. Louise Pirouet, 'The churches and human rights in Kenya and Uganda since independence', in Holger Bernt Hansen and Michael Twaddle (eds) *Religion and Politics in East Africa: The Period Since Independence* (London, Nairobi, Kampala and Athens: James Currey, EAEP, Fountain Publishers, Ohio University Press, 1995), p. 254.

12. Paul Gifford, 'Some recent developments in African Christianity', *African Affairs* 93, 373, 1994, p. 523.

13. On ZAOGA, see David Maxwell, 'Christianity without frontiers: Shona missionaries and transnational Pentecostalism in Africa', in David Maxwell and Ingrid Lawrie (eds) *Christianity and the African Imagination: Essays in Honour of Adrian Hastings* (Leiden, Boston and Cologne: Brill, 2002).

14. Birgit Meyer, *Translating the Devil: Religion and Modernity Among the Ewe in Ghana* (Edinburgh and London: Edinburgh University Press/ International Africa Institute, 1999).

15. Quoted in Gifford, *African Christianity*, p. 79.

16. For more detail, see David Throup, ''Render unto Caesar the things that are Caesar's: the politics of church-state conflict in Kenya, 1978–1990', in Hansen and Twaddle, *Religion and Politics*.

17. Paul Nugent, *Big Men, Small Boys and Politics in Ghana: Power, Ideology and the Burden of History, 1982–1994* (London and New York: Frances Pinter, 1995), pp. 188–9. However, church leaders subsequently played a less prominent political role than in other countries.

18. Rijk Van Dijk, 'Contesting silence: the ban on drumming and the musical politics of Pentecostalism in Ghana', *Ghana Studies* 4, 2002, p. 49. See also Akosua K. Darkwah, 'Aid or hindrance? Faith Gospel theology and Ghana's incorporation into the global economy', in the same issue.

19. The document was produced by the Institute for Contextual Theology. John W. de Gruchy, 'Grappling with the colonial heritage: the English-speaking churches under imperialism and apartheid', in Richard Elphick and Rodney Davenport (eds) *Christianity in South Africa: A Political, Social and Cultural History* (Berkeley: University of California Press, 1997), pp. 168–9.

20. Donal Cruise O'Brien, 'Coping with the Christians: the Muslim predicament in Kenya', in Hansen and Twaddle, *Religion and Politics*, p. 206.

21. Leonardo Villalón, *Islamic Society and State Power in Senegal: Disciples and Citizens in Fatick* (Cambridge: Cambridge University Press, 1995), pp. 219–22.

22. Villalón, *Islamic Society*, pp. 228–9. In Kenya, Muslims equally refused to be bound by the Law of Succession Act of 1992. A. B. K. Kasozi,

'Christian-Muslim inputs into public policy formation in Kenya, Uganda and Tanzania', in Hansen and Twaddle, *Religion and Politics*, p. 233.

23. In 2002, the unwise decision to hold the Miss World contest in Nigeria led to widespread violence and rioting, which underlined the lack of a consensus over religion.

24. Brian Raftopoulos, 'The labour movement and the emergence of opposition politics in Zimbabwe', in Brian Raftopoulos and Lloyd Sachinkoye, *Striking Back: The Labour Movement and the Post-Colonial State in Zimbabwe 1980–2000* (Harare: Weaver Press, 2001), pp. 10–12.

25. John Wiseman, *The New Struggle For Democracy in Africa* (Aldershot: Ashgate, 1996), p. 46.

26. Georges Nzongola-Ntalaja, *The Congo From Leopold to Kabila: A People's History* (London and New York: Zed Books, 2002), pp. 178–9.

27. Ibrahima Thioub, Momar Coumba-Diop and Catherine Boone, 'Economic liberalisation in Senegal: shifting politics of indigenous business interests', *African Studies Review* 41, 2, 1998, pp. 75–81.

28. Villalón, *Islamic Society*, pp. 239–42.

29. Thomas Turner, 'Zaire', p. 251. On Zairean television, the image of Mobutu floated through the ether, signifying his almost God-like properties.

30. However, salaries and running expenses consumed 98 per cent of the budget. Louise M. Bourgault, *Mass Media in Sub-Saharan Africa* (Bloomington and Indianapolis, 1995), p. 136.

31. Bourgault, *Mass Media*, pp. 106–7. However, it is likely that even the most unchallenging American comedies did have some impact on perceptions in Africa.

32. Musical cassettes often carried a political message. For a Ghanaian example, examining the use of allegory, see Kwesi Yankah, 'Nana Ampadu, the sung tale metaphor and protest discourse in contemporary Ghana', in Luise White, Stephan Miescher and David William Cohen (eds) *African Words, African Voices: Critical Perspectives in Oral History* (Bloomington and Indianapolis: Indiana University Press, 2001).

33. Even in Côte d'Ivoire, which could boast the highest proportion of television ownership, some 82 per cent of people in Abidjan enjoyed access in 1987, as against 22 per cent of rural dwellers. Bourgault, *Mass Media*, pp. 119–20. The lack of electricity was not necessarily a problem because people in rural Senegal have run television off a car battery in order to be able to watch their favourite soap operas, especially Brazilian ones.

34. Bourgault, *Mass Media*, p. 75. See also the contributions to Richard Fardon and Graham Furniss (eds) *African Broadcast Cultures: African Radio in Transition* (Oxford, Harare, Cape Town and Westport: James Currey, Baobab, David Philip and Praeger, 2000).

35. The struggle between Senghor and Mamadou Dia was played out over the airwaves. Moussa Paye, 'The regime and the press', in Momar Coumba Diop, *Senegal: Essays in Statecraft* (Dakar: CODESRIA, 1993), pp. 326–7.

36. Bourgault, *Mass Media*, p. 100.

37. Paye, 'The regime and the press', p. 342.

38. Tunji Dare, 'The press', in Larry Diamond, Anthony Kirk-Greene and Oyeleye Oyediran (eds) *Transition Without End: Nigerian Politics and Civil Society Under Babangida* (Boulder and London: Lynne Rienner, 1997), pp. 453–4.

39. Achille Mbembe, *On the Postcolony* (Berkeley and London: University of California Press, 2001), Chapter 4.

40. For a sample of his cartoons, see Alex Akurgo (ed.) *Jo Mini and the Rawlings Story: The Remarkable Odyssey of a Humble Man who Drew the Battle Lines Against Indiscipline in an African State* (Accra: Blue Volta, 2002).

41. For details on these elections, see Helga Fleischhacker, 'São Tomé and Príncipe', in Dieter Nohlen, Michael Krennerich and Bernhard Thibaut (eds) *Elections in Africa: A Data Handbook* (Oxford: Oxford University Press, 1999), p. 412. Between 1991 and 1999, no fewer than eight governments were formed. Gerhard Seibert, 'São Tomé e Príncipe', in Patrick Chabal, David Birmingham, Joshua Forrest, Malyn Newitt, Gerhard Seibert and Elisa Silva Andrade, *A History of Postcolonial Lusophone Africa* (London: C. Hurst, 2002), p. 307.

42. Joshua Forrest, 'Guinea-Bissau', in Chabal et al., *History of Postcolonial Lusophone Africa*, p. 252.

43. For an early account, focused on Benin, see F. Eboussi Boulaga, *Les conférences nationales: une affaire à suivre en Afrique noire* (Paris: Karthala, 1993). See also Samuel Decalo, 'Benin: the first of the new democracies', in Clark and Gardinier, *Political Reform*.

44. Given that the adoption of a SAP accompanied the political transition, this was a significant consideration.

45. Soglo took 67.73 per cent of the Presidential vote.

46. John F. Clark, 'Congo and the struggle to consolidate', in Clark and Gardinier, *Political Reform*, pp. 66, 76.

47. E. Adriaan B. Van Rouveroy Van Nieuwaal, *L'état en Afrique face à la chefferie: le cas du Togo* (Paris and Leiden: Karthala and Afrika-Studiecentrum, 2000), p. 49.

48. John R. Heilbrunn, 'Togo: the national conference and stalled reform', in Clark and Gardinier, *Political Reform*, p. 237.

49. Nzongola-Ntalaja, *Congo*, p. 186.

50. Nzongola-Ntalaja, *Congo*, pp. 201–2. See also Gauthier de Villers, Jean Omasambo Tshonda, *Zaïre: la transition manquée (1990–1997)* (Tervuren and Paris: Institut Africain-CEDAF and L'Harmattan, 1997).

51. Turner, 'Zaïre', in Clark and Gardinier, *Political Reform*, p. 258.

52. Mobutu apparently knew Machiavelli's *The Prince* inside out. Certainly, his behaviour suggested that he had taken its advice to heart.

53. For a discussion, see Ngolet, 'Ideological manipulations', pp. 58–63.

54. David Gardinier, 'Gabon: Limited reform and regime survival', in Clark and Gardinier, *Political Reform*, pp. 151–2.

55. Nelson N. Messone and Jean-Germain Gros, 'The irony of wealth: democratisation in Gabon', in Jean-Germain Gros (ed.) *Democratisation*

in Late Twentieth-Century Africa: Coping With Uncertainty (Westport and London: Greenwood Press, 1998), p. 139.

56. Gardinier, 'Gabon', p. 156. If true, it would not have been the first time. The French had previously rigged elections in Côte d'Ivoire and Togo in the 1950s.

57. Thomas O'Toole, 'The Central African Republic: political reform and social malaise', in Clark and Gardinier, *Political Reform*, pp. 116–17.

58. Mike McGovern, 'Conflit régional et rhétorique de la contre-insurrection', *Politique Africaine* 88, 2002, p. 87.

59. Ibid., pp. 94–8.

60. Joseph Takougang, 'Cameroon: Biya and incremental reform' in Clark and Gardinier, *Political Reform*, p. 172.

61. Takougang, 'Cameroon', p. 176. The CPDM won 109 out of 180 seats.

62. UNDP representation in the legislature dropped from 68 in 1992 (when it was the largest opposition party because of the SDF boycott) to 13 in 1997 and a single seat in 2002.

63. Tatah Mentan, 'Cameroon: a flawed transition to democracy', in Gros, *Democratisation*, pp. 50–3.

64. For an enlightening discussion, see Dwayne Woods, 'Côte d'Ivoire: the crisis of distributive politics' in Leonardo A. Villalón and Phillip A. Huxtable (eds) *The African State at a Critical Juncture: Between Disintegration and Reconfiguration* (Boulder and London: Lynne Rienner, 1998), p. 227.

65. Robert J. Mundt, 'Côte d'Ivoire: continuity and change in a semi-democracy', in Clark and Gardinier, *Political Reform*, p. 190.

66. 'Burkina Faso' was an amalgam of Moré and Peul words, translating roughly as 'Land of the Virtuous People'.

67. Conveniently perhaps, the individuals who might have been able to reveal the truth of what happened were killed after an alleged coup attempt in 1996. Christopher Wise, 'Chronicle of a student strike in Africa: the case of Burkina Faso, 1996–1997', *African Studies Review* 41, 2, 1998, p. 22.

68. Laura E. Boudon, 'Burkina Faso: the "rectification of the revolution"' in Clark and Gardinier, *Political Reform*, p. 132.

69. Robert Buijtenhuijs, 'Chad in the age of warlords', in David Birmingham and Phyllis M. Martin (eds) *History of Central Africa: The Contemporary Years Since 1960* (London and New York: Longman, 1998), p. 28.

70. Linda J. Beck, 'Senegal's Enlarged Presidential Majority: deepening democracy or detour?', in Richard Joseph (ed.) *State, Conflict and Democracy in Africa* (Boulder and London: Lynne Rienner, 1999), p. 199.

71. Leonardo Villalón and Ousmane Kane, 'Senegal: the crisis of democracy and the emergence of an Islamic opposition' in Villalón and Huxtable, *The African State*, p. 149.

72. Ibid., p. 144.

73. Beck, 'Senegal's Enlarged Presidential Majority', pp. 203–13.

74. In the run-off, Wade won 58.7 per cent of the vote to 41.3 per cent by Diouf, with the votes of the other opposition candidates passing as a block

to the former. See Richard Vengroff and Michael Magala, 'Democratic reform, transition and consolidation: evidence from Senegal's 2000 presidential election', *Journal of Modern African Studies* 39, 1, 2001.

75. Michael Bratton, 'Economic crisis and political realignment in Zambia', in Jennifer Widner (ed.) *Economic Change and Political Liberalisation in Sub-Saharan Africa* (Baltimore and London: John Hopkins University Press, 1994), p. 117.

76. Gifford, *African Christianity*, p. 192.

77. Bratton, 'Economic crisis', p. 119.

78. Gifford, *African Christianity*, p. 211.

79. Ibid., p. 209. He was descended from missionary parents from the then Nyasaland. Ironically, doubts were raised about Chiluba's own credentials, amidst persistent rumours that he had actually been born in the Belgian Congo.

80. Jeremy Gould, 'Contesting democracy: the 1996 elections in Zambia', in Michael Cowen and Liisa Laakso (eds) *Multiparty Elections in Africa* (Oxford: James Currey, 2002), p. 303.

81. Chiluba took 73 per cent of the vote, while the MMD won 61 per cent and 131 of the 150 seats, which reflected voting for 'rebel' candidates. However, only 33 per cent of eligible voters turned out (or 59 per cent registered voters).

82. Gould, 'Contesting democracy', p. 304.

83. Michael Bratton and Daniel N. Posner, 'A first look at second elections in Africa with illustrations from Zambia', in Joseph, *State, Conflict and Democracy*, p. 403.

84. Colin Baker, *Revolt of the Ministers: The Malawi Cabinet Crisis, 1964–1965* (London and New York: I. B. Tauris, 2001).

85. Jan Kees Van Donge, 'Kamuzu's legacy: the democratisation of Malawi', *African Affairs* 94, 375, 1995, p. 230.

86. Sam Mchombo, 'Democratisation in Malawi: its roots and prospects', in Gros, *Democratisation*, p. 34.

87. Van Donge, 'Kamuzu's legacy', p. 251.

88. Hence, the reputed founder of the UDF, Brown Mpinganjira, was catapulted from a position of relative penury to a Ministerial position, ownership of a fleet of vehicles and propriety over a 350-acre farm which had formerly belonged to the MYP. Harri Englund, 'Winning elections, losing legitimacy: multi-partyism and the neopatrimonial state in Malawi', in Cowen and Laakso, *Multi-Party Elections*, pp. 176, 185.

89. Banda had refused to agree to the creation of a television station for fear that Malawians would succumb to foreign influences.

90. Equally, it won 22 per cent in the Presidential polls. Tandika C. Nkiwane, 'Opposition politics in Zimbabwe: the struggle within the struggle', in Adebayo Olukoshi (ed.) *The Politics of Opposition in Contemporary Africa* (Uppsala: Nordiska Afrikainstitutet, 1998), p. 98.

91. Tandeka C. Nkiwane, 'Observing the observers', in Henning Melber (eds) *Zimbabwe's Presidential Elections 2002: Evidence, Lessons and Implications* (Uppsala: Nordiska Afrikainstitutet, 2002), p. 57.

92. An enquiry was set up, but was dissolved when it began to implicate senior officials.

93. For a detailed analysis, see David Throup and Charles Hornsby, *Multi-Party Politics in Kenya: The Kenyatta and Moi States and the Triumph of the System in the 1992 Election* (Oxford, Nairobi and Athens: James Currey, EAEP and Ohio University Press, 1998).

94. Karuti Kanyinga, 'Contestation over political space: the state and the demobilisation of opposition politics in Kenya', in Olukoshi, *Politics of Opposition*, p. 60.

95. After the polls, it transpired that the party had financed its campaign through corrupt deals with foreign businessmen and by raiding the National Social Security Funds.

96. Michael Cowen and Karuti Kanyinga, 'The 1997 elections in Kenya: the politics of communality and locality', in Cowen and Laakso, *Multi-Party Elections*, p. 132. On these elections, see Throup and Hornsby, *Multi-Party Politics*, Chapters 9–11.

97. On these various splits, see Kanyinga, 'Contestation', pp. 67–79.

98. No fewer than 26 parties contested these elections, although most did not field Presidential candidates.

99. Cowen and Kanyinga, 'The 1997 elections', p. 153. Throup and Hornsby, *Multi-Party Politics in Kenya*, p. 563.

100. Mwesiga Baregu, 'The rise and fall of the one-party state in Tanzania', in Widner, *Economic Change*, p. 169.

101. Two rather different impressions are created by Jean-Germain Gros, 'Leadership and democratisation: the case of Tanzania', in Gros, *Democratisation*, which emphasises the positive legacy and influence of Nyerere; and Baregu, 'Rise and fall', p. 70 in which the emphasis is on the lack of a known alternative and coercion.

102. Quoted Baregu, 'Rise and fall', p. 169. In fact, the Norwegians made further aid conditional upon multipartyism in 1991.

103. Ibid., pp. 171–2.

104. Tuulikki Pietilä, Saanna Ojalammwi-Wamai and Liisa Laakso, 'Elections at the borderland: voter opinion in Arusha and Kilimanjaro, Tanzania', in Cowen and Laakso, *Multi-Party Elections*, p. 280.

105. Gros, 'Leadership and democratisation', p. 105.

106. The Arab population on Pemba was substantially greater and the lingering African-African divide partly explains the split. A. N. Kweka, 'The Pemba factor in the 1995 general elections', in C. K. Omari (ed.) *The Right to Choose a Leader: Reflections on the 1995 Tanzanian General Elections* (Dar es Salaam: DUP, 1996).

107. Holger Bernt Hansen and Michael Twaddle 'Uganda: the advent of no-party democracy', in John Wiseman (ed.) *Democracy and Political Change in Sub-Saharan Africa* (London: Routledge, 1995), pp. 140–1.

108. Aili Mari Tripp, *Women and Politics in Uganda* (Oxford, Kampala and Madison: James Currey, Fountain Publishers and University of Wisconsin Press, 2000), p. 66.

109. Speech reproduced in Yoweri Museveni, *What is Africa's Problem? Speeches and Writings on Africa by Yoweri Kaguta Museveni* (Kampala: NRM Publications, 1992), p. 99.

110. For the forerunner to the Lord's Resistance Army, see Heike Behrend, *Alice Lakwena and the Holy Spirits: War in Northern Uganda, 1896–97* (Oxford, Kampala, Nairobi and Athens: James Currey, Fountain Publishers, EAEP and Ohio University Press, 1999). Lakwena was Joseph Kony's cousin.

111. Oliver Furley and James Katalikawe, 'Constitutional reform in Uganda: the new approach', *African Affairs* 96, 383, 1997, p. 247.

112. Ibid., p. 257.

113. On the restoration, see Pierre Englebert, 'Born-again Buganda or the limits of traditional resurgence in Africa', *Journal of Modern African Studies* 40, 3, 2002.

114. For an elaboration of this argument, see Tripp, *Women and Politics.*

115. Michael Bratton and Gina Lambright, 'Uganda's 2000 referendum: the silent boycott', *African Affairs* 100, 400, 2001, p. 443.

116. Tripp, *Women and Politics*, p. 67. However, this author also identifies some of the limitations placed on the media and the NGOs.

117. Roger Tangri and Andrew Mwenda, 'Corruption and cronyism in Uganda's privatisation in the 1990s', *African Affairs* 100, 398, 2001.

118. Quoted in Nugent, *Big Men*, pp. 140–1.

119. Ibid., pp. 180–6.

120. Quoted in ibid., p. 199.

121. This was a reward for the courage which he had displayed in a series of sell-out public lectures in 1988, in which he had taken the regime to task.

122. Arkaah had been Rawlings's running-mate in 1992, but had fallen out with Rawlings who had allegedly assaulted him in a Ministerial meeting.

123. For an analysis of these elections, see Paul Nugent, 'Winners, losers and also-rans: money, moral authority and voting patterns in the Ghana 2000 elections', *African Affairs* 100, 400, 2001.

124. George Hagan took a mere 1.8 per cent of the vote, while the party was reduced to a single Parliamentary seat.

125. Two useful collections dealing with the Babangida years are Paul A. Beckett and Crawford Young (eds) *Dilemmas of Democracy in Nigeria* (Rochester and Woodbridge: University of Rochester Press, 1997); and Larry Diamond, Anthony Kirk-Greene and Oyeleye Oyediran (eds) *Transition Without End: Nigerian Politics and Civil Society Under Babangida* (Boulder and London: Lynne Rienner, 1997).

126. Oyeleye Oyediran, 'The Political Bureau', in Diamond, Kirk-Greene and Oyediran, *Transition Without End*, p. 88.

127. Eghosa Osaghae, *Crippled Giant: Nigeria Since Independence* (London: C. Hurst, 1998), p. 221.

128. The census produced a lower-than-expected tally of 88.5 million. The number of local government areas was increased from 301 to 589, while

the number of states was increased by two. In 1991, another nine were created, bringing the total to 30.

129. In July 1992, SDP beat the NDP by 52 to 39 Senate seats and by 314 to 275 House of Representatives seats. However, the NDP won 16 of the 30 governorships.

130. Osaghae, *Crippled Giant*, p. 237.

131. The unexpected windfall which arose from the hike in oil prices, resulting from the Gulf War, was paid into special 'off-shore accounts' which were drained in unexplained ways.

132. These results are reproduced in Bola A. Akinterinwa, 'The 1993 Presidential election imbroglio' in Diamond, Kirk-Greene and Oyediran, *Transition Without End*, p. 267.

133. It also cited a conflict of interest, in that the federal government happened to be indebted to Abiola's company, ITT, to the tune of $200 million. He had been a major supplies of signals equipment to the Nigerian Armed Forces. Curiously, Abiola had formerly been a close associate of Babangida.

134. Dasuki was removed and replaced with the candidate he had defeated, namely Alhaji Maccido.

135. Toyin Falola, *The History of Nigeria* (Westport and London: Greenwood, 1999), p. 203.

136. The extent to which Rawlings had 'gone soft' was revealed by his fraternisation with Abacha, whose venality and brutality far exceeded that of Acheampong.

137. Falola, *History of Nigeria*, p. 202.

138. Paul Beckett, 'Legitimising democracy: the role of the highly educated elite', in Beckett and Young, *Dilemmas of Democracy*, Osaghae, *Crippled Giant*, pp. 257–8.

139. John D. Holm and Steffan Darnolf, 'Democratising the administrative state in Botswana', in York Bradshaw and Stephen N. Ndegwa (eds) *The Uncertain Promise of Southern Africa* (Bloomington and Indianapolis: Indiana University Press, 2000), p. 126.

140. Holm and Darnolf, 'Democratising', p. 148, footnote 8.

141. Kenneth Good, 'Towards popular participation in Botswana', *Journal of Modern African Studies* 34, 1, 1996, p. 62.

142. The APRC equally claimed victory in the legislative elections the following year. Petra Bendel, 'Gambia', in Nohlen, Krennerich and Thibaut (eds) *Elections in Africa*, p. 412.

143. Richard Levin, *When the Sleeping Grass Awakens: Land and Power in Swaziland* (Johannesburg: Witwatersrand University Press, 1997), pp. 205–12.

144. L. B. B. J. Machobane, *King's Knights: Military Governance in the Kingdom of Lesotho, 1986–1993* (Roma: Institute of Southern African Studies, 2001), p. 65.

145. Ibid., p. 66.

146. Quoted in ibid., p. 126.

147. Ulf Engel, 'Lesotho', in Nohlen, Krennerich and Thibaut (eds) *Elections in Africa*, p. 496.

148. For a good account of the terminal period, see Martin J. Murray, *The Revolution Deferred: The Painful Birth of Post-Apartheid South Africa* (London: Verso, 1994).

149. On the transitional arrangements, see T. R. H. Davenport, *The Transfer of Power in South Africa* (Cape Town: David Philip, 1998), Chapter 1.

150. The only real difference between the interim and final constitution was that the Senate was replaced by a National Council of Provinces and the provision for power-sharing was removed. Adrian Guelke, *South Africa in Transition: The Misunderstood Miracle* (London and New York: I. B. Tauris, 1999), p. 169.

151. Lawrence Schlemmer and Charisse Levitz, *Unemployment in South Africa: The Facts, the Prospects and the Exploration of Solutions* (Johannesburg: South African Institute of Race Relations, 1998). On the route taken, see Patrick Bond, *Elite Transition: From Apartheid to Neoliberalism in South Africa* (London, Sterling and Pietermaritzburg: Pluto Press and University of Natal Press, 2000).

152. On the 'civics', see Glenn Adler and Joy Steinberg (eds) *From Comrades to Citizens: The South African Civics Movement and the Transition to Democracy* (Basingstoke and New York: Macmillan and St. Martin's Press, 2000).

153. Stephen Rule, 'Outcome of the election', in Yvonne Muthien (ed.) *Democracy South Africa: Evaluating the 1999 Election* (Pretoria: HSRC, 1999), pp. 107–8.

10 Millennial Africa: The National Question Revisited

1. Military coups remained a recurrent feature of the post-1990 period. Between 1991 and 2001 there were 47 coup attempts, of which 13 were successful. Patrick J. McGowan, 'African military coups d'état, 1956–2001', *Journal of Modern African Studies* 41, 3, 2003, p. 352.

2. Piet Konings and Francis B. Nyamnjoh, 'The Anglophone problem', *Journal of Modern African Studies* 35, 2, 1997, pp. 216–17.

3. Konings and Nyamnjoh, 'The Anglophone problem', pp. 218–20.

4. Greg Cameron, 'Zanzibar's turbulent transition', *Review of African Political Economy* 92, 2002, p. 324. On the relationship between Tanzania and the Zanzibar, see T. L. Maliyamkono (ed.) *The Political Plight of Zanzibar* (Dar es Salaam: Tema Publishers, 2000).

5. Ruth Iyob, *The Eritrean Struggle for Independence: Domination, Resistance, Nationalism, 1941–1993* (Cambridge: Cambridge University Press, 1995), p. 111.

6. For example, Iyob, *Eritrean Struggle*, p. 119; David Pool, 'The Eritrean People's Liberation Front', in Christopher Clapham (ed.) *African Guerrillas* (Oxford, Kampala, Bloomington and Indianapolis: James Currey, Fountain Publishers and Indiana University Press, 1998), p. 34.

7. Iyob, *Eritrean Struggle*, p. 132.

8. Pool, 'Eritrean People's Liberation Front', p. 31. On land reform, and other efforts to win peasant support, see David Pool, *From Guerrillas to*

Government: The Eritrean People's Liberation Front (Oxford and Athens: James Currey and Ohio University Press, 2001), Chapter 4.

9. John Young, 'The Tigray People's Liberation Front', in Clapham, *African Guerrillas*, p. 38.

10. John Young, *Peasant Revolution in Ethiopia: The Tigray People's Liberation Front, 1975–1991* (Cambridge: Cambridge University Press, 1997), p. 153.

11. Ibid., pp. 141–2.

12. Like the EPLF, the TPLF set up its own relief agency which acquired a favourable reputation.

13. Davidson in a BBC radio interview, as quoted by Alemseged, *Identity Jilted*, p. 123.

14. For an analysis of the disputes, see Tekeste Negash and Kjetil Tronvoll, *Brothers At War: Making Sense of the Eritrean-Ethiopian War* (Oxford and Athens: James Currey and Ohio University Press, 2000), Chapter 5.

15. The border issue is discussed in contributions to a special issue of the *Eritrean Studies Review* 3, 2, 1999, and in Tekeste and Tronvoll, *Brothers at War*, Chapter 4.

16. This information is drawn from Terence Lyons and Ahmed I. Samatar, *State Collapse, Multilateral Intervention, and Strategies for Political Reconstruction* (Washington: Brookings Institution, 1995), p. 9. Confusingly, not all academic commentators follow the same usage. Anna Simons, for example, refers to six clan-families: Rahanwein, Darod, Hawiye, Isaaq, Digil and Dir. Anna Simons, 'Somalia: the structure of dissolution', in Leonardo A. Villalón and Phillip A. Huxtable (eds) *The African State at a Critical Juncture: Between Disintegration and Reconfiguration* (Boulder and London: Lynne Rienner, 1998), p. 57.

17. Somalia had the highest proportion of pastoralists in the world.

18. Lyons and Samatar, *State Collapse*, p. 15.

19. Lee V. Cassanelli, 'Explaining the Somali crisis', in Catherine Besteman and Lee V. Cassanelli (eds) *The Struggle for Land in Southern Somalia: The War Behind the War* (Boulder and London: Westview and Haan, 1996), p. 22. Mogadisho was the twentieth fastest-growing city in the world. See Table 8.6.

20. Charles Geshekter, 'The death of Somalia in historical perspective', in Hussein M. Adam and Richard Ford (eds) *Mending Rips in the Sky: Options for Somali Communities in the 21st Century* (Lawrenceville and Asmara: Red Sea Press, 1997), p. 79.

21. Geshekter, 'death of Somalia', p. 79.

22. Simons, 'Somalia', p. 67.

23. Ahmed I. Samatar, 'The curse of Allah: civic disembowelment and the collapse of the state in Somalia', in Ahmed I. Samatar (ed.) *The Somali Challenge: From Catastrophe to Renewal?* (Boulder and London: Lynne Rienner, 1994), p. 126.

24. Lyons and Samatar, *State Collapse*, p. 33.

25. In the case of Puntland, see WSP Somali Programme, *Rebuilding Somalia: Issues and Possibilities for Puntland* (London: Haan, 2001).

26. Douglas Johnson, *The Root Causes of Sudan's Civil Wars* (Oxford, Bloomington, Indianapolis and Kampala: James Currey, IAI, Indiana University Press and Fountain Publishers, 2003), p. 56. This section draws heavily on this work.

27. Ibid., pp. 47–9.

28. The fact that Ethiopia was its major patron was probably a factor in the equation, in that the Derg was fighting for the territorial integrity of its own country and could not be seen to be sponsoring secessionism elsewhere. Johnson, *Root Causes*, pp. 62–5.

29. On the Nuba dimension, see Leif Manger, 'The Nuba mountains: battleground of identities, cultural traditions and territories', in Maj-Britt Johannsen and Niels Kastfelt (eds) *Sudanese Society in the Context of Civil War* (Copenhagen: University of Copenhagen, 2001).

30. Francis Mading Deng, 'War of visions for the nation', in John Voll (ed.) *Sudan: State and Society in Crisis* (Bloomington, Indianapolis and Washington: Indiana University Press and The Middle East Institute, 1991), pp. 32–3.

31. Jok Madut Jok, *War and Slavery in Sudan* (Philadelphia: University of Pennsylvania Press, 2001); Johnson, *Root Causes*, pp. 157–9. As in Mauritania, Western perceptions of the rise of Islamic fundamentalism and the incidence of slavery fed off each other and generated a great deal of negative publicity in the west.

32. The manner in which food aid fed the combatants, and thus sustained the war, is a telling criticism of the aid industry. Alex de Waal, *Famine Crimes: Politics and the Disaster Relief Industry in Africa* (London, Oxford and Bloomington: African Rights, IAI, James Currey and Indiana University Press, 1997), pp. 148–50.

33. Tony Hodges, *Angola: From Afro-Stalinism to Petro-Diamond Capitalism* (London, Norway, Oxford, Bloomington and Indianapolis: IAI, Fridjt of Nansen Institute, James Currey and Indiana University Press, 2001), p. 22.

34. Ibid., p. 13.

35. David Birmingham, 'Angola', in Patrick Chabal, David Birmingham, Joshua Forrest, Malyn Newitt, Gerhard Seibert and Elisa Silva Andrade, *A History of Postcolonial Lusophone Africa* (London: Christopher Hurst, 2002), pp. 178–9.

36. 'Human Rights Watch World Report, 2003: Angola', http:www.hrw.org/w2k3/africa1.html

37. Human Rights Watch, *Angola Unravels: The Rise and Fall of the Lusaka Peace Process* (New York, Washington, London and Brussels: Human Rights Watch, 1999), pp. 135–6.

38. Birmingham, 'Angola', p. 184.

39. Hodges, *Angola*, p. 41.

40. Robert Buijtenhuijs, 'Chad in the age of warlords', in David Birmingham and Phyllis M. Martin (eds) *History of Central Africa: The Contemporary Years Since 1960* (London and New York: Longman, 1998), p. 39.

41. The estimates vary wildly. Mahmood Mamdani, *When Victims Become Killers: Colonialism, Nativism, and the Genocide in Rwanda* (Kampala,

Cape Town and Oxford: Fountain Publishers, David Philip and James Currey, 2001), p. 161.

42. Gérard Prunier, *The Rwanda Crisis: History of a Genocide* (London: C. Hurst, 1995), p. 70.

43. Museveni had a Rwandan grandmother.

44. Prunier, *Rwanda Crisis*, p. 76; Mamdani, *When Victims Become Killers*, p. 190.

45. Ibid., pp. 85–7.

46. On the churches, see Saskia Van Hoyweghen, 'The disintegration of the Catholic Church of Rwanda: a study of the fragmentation of political and religious authority', *African Affairs* 95, 380, July 1996. On the political parties, see Jordane Bertrand, *Rwanda, le piège de l'histoire: l'opposition démocratique avant le génocide (1990–1994)* (Paris: Karthala, 2000).

47. Prunier, *Rwanda Crisis*, pp. 168–9.

48. The same could be said of their use of imagery and songs derived from popular culture. For a dossier on their contribution, with examples of incendiary cartoons, see Jean-Pierre Chrétien (ed.) *Rwanda: les médias du génocide* (Paris: Karthala, 1995).

49. For detailed evidence on the killings, see Africa Rights, *Rwanda: Death, Despair and Defiance* (London: African Rights, 1995).

50. Mamdani, *When Victims Become Killers*, p. 231.

51. Ibid., p. 219.

52. Prunier, *Rwanda Crisis*, pp. 277–80.

53. The estimates have varied between half a million and a million. The demographer, William Seltzer suggests a figure of 657,000, extrapolating from the 1991 census data. Chrétien estimates that three-quarters of the Tutsi resident in Rwanda were killed. Anywhere between 10,000 and 50,000 Hutus may also have been killed. Mamdani, *When Victims Become Killers*, pp. 5, 283, footnote 1; Prunier, *Rwanda Crisis*, pp. 312, 325; Jean-Pierre Chrétien, *The Great Lakes of Africa: Two Thousand Years of History* (New York: Zone Books, 2003), p. 332.

54. For a much-praised study of the Burundian exiles in Tanzania, see Liisa H. Malkki, *Purity and Exile: Violence, Memory and National Cosmology Among Hutu Refugees in Tanzania* (Chicago and London: University of Chicago Press, 1995).

55. Christian P. Scherrer, *Genocide and Crisis in Central Africa: Conflict Roots, Mass Violence and Regional War* (Westport and London: Praeger, 2002), p. 222.

56. Léonce Ndikumana, 'Institutional failure and ethnic conflicts in Burundi', *African Studies Review* 41, 1, 1998, pp. 38–9.

57. Pascal Rutake and Joseph Gahama, 'Ethnic conflict in Burundi', in Okwudiba Nnoli (ed.) *Ethnic Conflicts in Africa* (Dakar: CODESRIA, 1998), p. 98.

58. Prunier, *Rwanda Crisis*, p. 199. Malkki, *Purity and Exile*, p. 285.

59. Barnabé Ndarishikanye, 'The question of the protection of minorities in Burundi', *Issue* 26, 1, 1998, p. 8.

60. Filip Reyntjens, *La guerre des Grands Lacs: alliances mouvantes et conflits extraterritoriaux en Afrique centrale* (Paris and Montreal: L'Harmattan: 1999), p. 43.

61. Ibid., p. 46.

62. Wm Cyrus Reed, 'Guerrillas in the midst: the Former Government of Rwanda (FGOR) and the Alliance of Democratic Forces for the Liberation of Congo-Zaire (AFDL) in eastern Zaire', in Clapham, *African Guerrillas*, p. 140.

63. Koen Vlassenroot, 'Identity and insecurity: the building of ethnic agendas in South Kivu', in Ruddy Doom and Jan Gorus (eds) *Politics of Identity and Economics of Conflict in the Great Lakes Region* (Brussels: VUB University Press, 2000), pp. 265–6.

64. Mamdani, *When Victims Become Killers*, p. 247.

65. Reed, 'Guerrillas in the midst', pp. 143–4.

66. Nzongola-Ntalaja, *The Congo*, p. 225. On the Kabila phenomenon, see Jean-Claude Willame, *L'Odysée Kabila: trajectoire pour un Congo nouveau?* (Paris: Karthala, 1999).

67. Ibid., p. 226.

68. Reed, 'Guerrillas in the midst', p. 147.

69. Nzongola-Ntalaja, *The Congo*, p. 226.

70. Ibid., p. 226.

71. The troops even fired on Mobutu's plane as it took off. The tense closing moments of his reign are alluded to in ibid., p. 214.

72. For the changing symbols of nationhood, including flags, postage stamps and banknotes, see the colour reproductions in Isodore Ndaywel è Nziem, *Histoire générale du Congo: de l'héritage ancien à la République Démocratique* (Paris and Brussels: De Boeck and Larcier, 1998).

73. Martin Kalulambi Pongo, 'Dreams, battles and the rout of the elite in Congo-Kinshasa: the mourning of an imagined democracy', *Issue* 26, 1, 1998, p. 22.

74. John F. Clark, 'Explaining Ugandan intervention in Congo: evidence and interpretations', *Journal of Modern African Studies* 39, 2, 2001, p. 272.

75. Nzongola-Ntalaja, *The Congo*, p. 227.

76. Filip Reyntjens, 'The new geostrategic situation on Central Africa', *Issue* 26, 1, 1998, p. 12.

77. The other side was also alleged to be in league with UNITA. Nzongola-Ntalaja, *The Congo*, p. 238.

78. Members of Mugabe's own family allegedly profited from the war, much like those of Museveni. Nzongola-Ntalaja, *The Congo*, pp. 239–40.

79. Clark, 'Explaining Ugandan intervention', p. 282. Some 200 civilians were killed in the fighting.

80. However, many Banyamulenge began to wonder about the wisdom of being tied to the Rwandan cause and there were clashes with Rwandan troops in January 1999. Vlassenroot, 'Identity and insecurity', p. 279.

81. Vlassenroot, 'Identity and insecurity', p. 277.

82. The term 'Nibolek' does not represent an ethnic label per se, since it is an amalgam of the first two syllables of the districts of Niaria, Bouenza and

Lekoumou. Identification with the south segmented into 'Nibolek' and 'Tchek' with the latter tending to support Kolélas' MCDDI and the former Lissouba's UPADS.

83. John F. Clark, 'Foreign intervention in the Civil War of the Congo Republic', *Issue* 26, 1, 1998, p. 31.

84. Rémy Bazenguissa-Ganga, 'The political militia in Brazzaville', *Issue* 26, 1, 1998, p. 39.

85. The opposed positions of Dos Santos and Kabila provide just about the only example of where regional alliances did not translate from one context to another.

86. The 'Krahn' speak very different dialects, and merge into other peoples who might or might not be considered Krahn depending on the criteria employed. Moreover, those living on the Ivoirien side of the border have adopted a different ethnonym altogether. Stephen Ellis, *The Mask of Anarchy: The Destruction of Liberia and the Religious Dimension of an African Civil War* (London: C. Hurst, 1999), pp. 31–6.

87. Ellis, *Mask of Anarchy*, p. 66.

88. Ibid., p. 71.

89. Ibid., pp. 69–70.

90. Doe had requested the extradition of Taylor and he was imprisoned by the American authorities in 1984, pending extradition. In circumstances which remain unclear, he managed to break out, making him a wanted man in the United States.

91. Jackson Doe, who was reputed to have won the 1985 election was one of the people allegedly killed by Taylor's own hand. Ellis, *Mask of Anarchy*, p. 85.

92. William Reno, *Warlord Politics and African States* (Boulder and London: Lynne Rienner, 1998), p. 94.

93. Ellis, *Mask of Anarchy*, p. 90; Reno, *Warlord Politics*, pp. 98–9.

94. Reno, *Warlord Politics*, p. 105.

95. Around 80 per cent of eligible voters turned out to vote. Ellis, *Mask of Anarchy*, p. 109.

96. It has been pointed out that LURD had little in the way of a programme and was not very effective militarily. William Reno, 'La "sale petite guerre"du Liberia', *Politique Africaine* 88, December 2002. This proved not to be the case. While LURD enjoyed mostly Mandingo support, MODEL was apparently supported by Krahns, replicating something of the earlier ULIMO-K/ULIMO-J divide.

97. Momoh's attempts to extract his pound of flesh from the NPFL is referred to in Ellis, *Mask of Anarchy*, p. 71.

98. On the political economy of corruption in Sierra Leone at this time, see William Reno, *Corruption and State Politics in Sierra Leone* (Cambridge: Cambridge University Press, 1995).

99. Yusuf Bangura, 'Understanding the political and cultural dynamics of the Sierra Leone war: a critique of Paul Richards's *Fighting for the Rain Forest*', *Africa Development* 22, 3/4, 1997, pp. 126–7. A more telling criticism of Richards is that in his attempt to demonstrate that the RUF

violence was not irrational, he underplayed the element of sheer ruth-
lessness and capriciousness of the rebels. Richards was seeking to refute
Robert Kaplan's apocalyptic vision of an anarchic post-Cold War world,
in which he drew on Sierra Leone as an example.

100. Paul Richards, *Fighting for the Rain Forest: War, Youth and Resources in
Sierra Leone* (London, Oxford and Portsmouth: International Africa
Institute, James Currey and Heinemann, 1996), pp. 25–8; Ibrahim
Abdullah and Patrick Muana, 'The Revolutionary United Front of Sierra
Leone: a revolt of the lumpenproletariat', in Clapham, *African
Guerrillas*, pp. 173–6.

101. Abdullah and Muana, 'The Revolutionary United Front', pp. 173–5.

102. The importance of Gaddafi's *Green Book* has, however, been disputed on
the basis that none of the students who were influenced by it actually
joined the RUF. Ibrahim Abdullah, 'Bush path to destruction: the origin and character of the Revolutionary United Front (RUF/SL)', *Africa
Development* 22, 3/4, 1997, p. 71.

103. Richards, *Fighting*, p. 32.

104. Both Kanu and Mansaray were eventually executed by Sankoh over
1991/92 for supposed disloyalty.

105. Much of the money which the Lebanese diamond dealers made was actu-
ally channelled into the competing factions in the civil war in Lebanon.
It was this which, in turn, led the Israelis to become interested in Sierra
Leone. Richards, *Fighting*, pp. 20–2.

106. A concise overview of the war is John L. Hirsch, *Sierra Leone: Diamonds
and the Struggle for Democracy* (Boulder and London: Lynne Rienner,
2001).

107. Joseph A. Opala, ' "Ecstatic revolution": street art celebrating Sierra
Leone's 1992 revolution', *African Affairs* 93, 371, 1994.

108. Lansana Gberie, 'The May 25 coup d'état in Sierra Leone: a militariat
revolt?', *Africa Development* 22, 3/4, 1997, p. 155.

109. Abdullah and Muana, 'The Revolutionary United Front', p. 183.

110. Ibid., p. 185.

111. Patrick K. Muana, 'The Kamajoi militia: civil war, internal displacement
and the politics of counter-insurgency', *Africa Development* 22, 3/4,
1997, p. 88.

112. Reno, *Warlord Politics*, pp. 130–1.

113. Jimmy D. Kandeh, 'Transition without rupture: Sierra Leone's transfer
election of 1996', *African Studies Review* 41, 2, 1998, p. 101.

114. Gberie, 'May 25 coup', p. 152.

115. Few commentators failed to spot the irony of a military regime in Nigeria
fighting to restore civilian rule in Sierra Leone.

116. Members of the AFRC had ceased to even wear military uniforms.
Gberie, 'May 25 coup', pp. 155–6.

117. The nightmare scenario for the Senegalese authorities would have been
the formation of an 'axis of the 3 Bs', that is Banjul (Gambia) Bignona
(Casamance) and Bissau. The confederation was an attempt at gaining
the initiative. Ousseynou Faye, 'La crise casamançaise et les relations du

Sénégal avec la Gambie et la Guinée-Bissau (1980–1992)', in Momar-Coumba Diop (ed.) *Le Sénégal et ses voisins* (Dakar: Sociétés-Espaces-Temps, 1994), p. 199.

118. Adekeye Adebajo, *Building Peace in West Africa: Liberia, Sierra Leone and Guinea-Bissau* (Boulder and London: Lynne Rienner, 2002), pp. 120–4.

119. Joshua Forrest, 'Guinea-Bissau', in Chabal et al., *History of Postcolonial Lusophone Africa*, p. 258.

120. Adebajo, *Building Peace*, p. 130. In January 2003, there was renewed fighting well inside Senegal. Chris Simpson, 'Blood and confusion in Casamance', *West Africa* 10–16 February 2003.

121. Richard Banégas and Bruno Losch, 'La Côte d'Ivoire au bord de l'implosion', *Politique Africaine* 87, 2002, p. 150.

122. Reno, 'La "sale petite guerre"', p. 70.

123. Gbagbo was alleged to have offended the French by becoming too close to American business interests.

124. Quoted in Ibrahim Seaga Shaw, 'Peace deal in Côte d'Ivoire', *West Africa* 3–9 February 2003, p. 11. This article also includes details of the agreement.

125. On the Charter, see Malcolm Evans and Rachel Murray (eds) *The African Charter on Human and People's Rights: The System in Practice, 1986–2000* (Cambridge: Cambridge University Press, 2002).

126. Filip Reyntjens, 'Briefing: the Democratic Republic of Congo, from Kabila to Kabila', *African Affairs* 100, 2001, p. 317.

127. Richard A. Wilson, *The Politics of Truth and Reconciliation in South Africa: Legitimising the Post-Apartheid State* (Cambridge: Cambridge University Press, 2001); and Lyn S. Graybill, *Truth and Reconciliation in South Africa: Miracle or Model?* (Boulder and London: Lynne Rienner, 2002).

128. For example, Mamdani comments that 'The unintended consequence has been to drive a wedge between the beneficiaries and the victims of apartheid. In doing so, the TRC has failed to open a social debate on possible futures for a post-apartheid South Africa', in 'The truth according to the TRC', in Ifi Amadiume and Abdullahi An-Na'im (eds) *The Politics of Memory: Truth, Healing and Social Justice* (London and New York: Zed, 2000), p. 183.

129. Human Rights Watch, *World Report 2002*, at http:www.hrw.org.wr2k2/africa9.html

130. In Rwanda, there were calls for the restoration of the monarchy. The RPF regime was very worried about this development and was reported to have taken repressive measures against would-be monarchists, many of whom were former supporters of the movement. On the role of traditional institutions in peacemaking, see I. William Zartman (ed.) *Traditional Cures for Modern Conflicts: African Conflict 'Medicine'* (Boulder and London: Lynne Rienner, 2000). On the Somali case, see the chapter by Ken Menhaus, 'Traditional conflict management in contemporary Somalia'.

131. Robert K. Hitchcock, ' "We are the first people": land, natural resources and identity in the Central Kalahari, Botswana', *Journal of Southern African Studies* 28, 4, 2002, p. 820.

132. Some even became candidates for the opposition BNF in District-level elections, although the day when a San legislator was elected still seemed a long way off.

133. Jacqueline Solway, 'Navigating the "neutral" state: "minority" rights in Botswana', *Journal of Southern African Studies* 28, 4, 2002.

134. Christopher Clapham, 'Controlling space in Ethiopia', in Wendy James, Donald L. Donham, Eisei Kurimoto and Alessandro Triulzi (eds) *Remapping Ethiopia: Socialism and After* (Oxford, Athens and Addis Ababa: James Currey, Ohio University Press and Addis Ababa University Press, 2002), p. 29.

135. The negative assessment of democracy under the EPRDF enjoys some academic support. Hence it was not until 2000 that federal elections were held, and these seem to have been less than fair, having also been boycotted by groups like the OLF. For a generally negative assessment, see the contributions to Siegfried Pausewang, Kjetil Tronvoll and Lovise Aalen (eds) *Ethiopia Since the Derg: A Decade of Democratic Pretension and Performance* (London and New York: Zed, 2002).

136. There is a rapidly growing literature to match the rapid identity shifts in South Africa. A useful collection is Abebe Zegeye (eds) *Social Identities and the New South Africa: After Apartheid, Volume One* (Cape Town: Kwela Books and South African History Online, 2001).

137. Emmanuel Akyeampong, 'Africans in the diaspora: the diaspora and Africa', *African Affairs* 99, 2000, p. 211.

138. On immigration to South Africa, and the experience of the immigrants themselves, see Alan Morris and Antoine Bouillon (eds) *African Immigration to South Africa: Francophone Migration of the 1990s* (Pretoria: Protea and IFAS, 2001); and Jonathan Crush and David A. McDonald (eds) *Transnationalism and New African Immigration to South Africa* (Cape Town: Southern African Migration Project, 2002).

139. On the *Sape* phenomenon, see Justin-Daniel Gandalou, *Au coeur de la sape: moeurs et aventures des Congolais à Paris* (Paris: L'Harmattan, 1989). On the Congolese diaspora in Paris, see Janet MacGaffey and Rémy Bazenguissa-Ganga, *Congo-Paris: Transnational Traders on the Margins of the Law* (London, Oxford, Bloomington and Indianapolis: IAI, James Currey and Indiana University Press, 2000).

140. Reggae was also indigenised at an earlier point. For some articles on this theme, see Mai Palmberg and Annemette Kirkegaard (eds) *Playing with Identities in Contemporary Music in West Africa* (Uppsala: Nordiska Afrikainstitutet, 2002).

141. According to Emmanuel Akyeampong, private remittance outstripped foreign direct investment in every year between 1983 and 1990. In the latter year, it amounted to as much as $201.9 million as against $14.8 million. 'Africans in the diaspora', p. 211.

Bibliography

1 Documentary and statistical sources

Basutoland, *Report of the Basutoland Constitutional Commission, 1963* (Maseru: Basutoland Council, 1963).

Belgium, *Parliamentary Committee of Enquiry in Charge of Determining the Exact Circumstances of the Assassination of Patrice Lumumba and the Possible Involvement of Belgian Politicians: Summary of the Activities, Expert's Report and Full Conclusions* (2001) www.dekamer.be/commissions/LMB/indexF.html

Colony and Protectorate of Kenya, *The Origins and Growth of Mau Mau: An Historical Survey* [Corfield Report] (Sessional Paper No. 5 of 1959/60) (Nairobi, 1960).

Ghana, *Programme of the Convention People's Party for Work and Happiness* (Accra: Ministry of Information and Broadcasting, undated).

——, *Blueprint of our Goal: Osagyefo Launches Seven-Year Plan* (Accra: Ministry of Information and Broadcasting, 1964).

——, *Seven-Year Plan for National Reconstruction and Development: Financial Years 1963/64–1969/70* (Accra: Planning Commission, 1964).

Great Britain, Colonial Office, *Report of the Commission on Enquiry into Disturbances in the Gold Coast, 1948.*

——, *Report of the Commission Appointed to Enquire into the Fears of Minorities and the Means of Allaying Them* [Willinck Commission] (London: HMSO, 1958).

Johnson, Douglas H., *British Documents on the End of Empire: Sudan, Part I, 1942–1950* (London: Her Majesty's Stationary Office, 1998).

Karis, Thomas G. and Gerhart, Gail (eds), *From Protest to Challenge: A Documentary History of African Politics in South Africa, 1882–1990: Nadir and Resurgence, 1964–1979* (Bloomington, Indianapolis and Pretoria: Indiana University Press and UNISA Press, 1997).

Kirk-Greene, A. H. M., *Crisis and Conflict in Nigeria: A Documentary Sourcebook, 1966–1970, Volume 1, January 1966–July 1967* (London: Oxford University Press, 1971).

——, *Crisis and Conflict in Nigeria: A Documentary Sourcebook, 1966–1970, Volume 2, July 1967–January 1970* (London: Oxford University Press, 1971).

OECD, *African Economic Outlook, 2001/2002* (Paris: OECD and African Development Bank, 2002).

Rathbone, Richard (ed.), *British Documents on the End of Empire, Series B Volume 1: Ghana, Part I, 1941–1952* (London: HMSO, 1992).

Republic of Kenya, *African Socialism and Its Application to Planning in Kenya* (Nairobi, 1965).

United Nations Population Division, *World Urbanization Prospects,* various years.

World Bank, *Accelerated Development in Sub-Saharan Africa: An Agenda for Action* [Berg Report] (Washington, DC: World Bank, 1981).

——, *Adjustment in Africa: Reforms, Results, and the Road Ahead* (Washington, DC: World Bank, 1994).

——, *Confronting AIDS: Public Priorities in a Global Epidemic* (New York: Oxford University Press, 1997).

——, *World Development Report: Knowledge for Development, 1998–99* (New York and Oxford: Oxford University Press, 1999).

2 Books

Abebe Zegeye (ed.), *Social Identities and the New South Africa: After Apartheid, Volume 1* (Cape Town: Kwela Books and South African History Online, 2001).

Adebajo, Adekeye, *Building Peace in West Africa: Liberia, Sierra Leone and Guinea-Bissau* (Boulder and London: Lynne Rienner, 2002).

Ademoyega, Adewale, *Why We Struck: The Story of the First Nigerian Coup* (Ibadan: Evans Brothers, 1981).

Adler, Glenn and Steinberg, Joy (eds), *From Comrades to Citizens: The South African Civics Movement and the Transition to Democracy* (Basingstoke and New York: Macmillan (now Palgrave Macmillan) and St Martin's Press, 2000).

African Rights, *Rwanda: Death, Despair and Defiance* (London: African Rights, 1995).

Ahmed, Ali Jimale (ed.), *The Invention of Somalia* (Lawrenceville: Red Sea Press, 1995).

Akurgo, Alex (ed.), *Jo Mini and the Rawlings Story: The Remarkable Odyssey of a Humble Man Who Drew the Battle Lines Against Indiscipline in an African State* (Accra: Blue Volta, 2002).

Alemseged Abbay, *Identity Jilted or Re-Imagining Identity? The Divergent Paths of the Eritrean and Tigrayan Nationalist Struggles* (Lawrenceville and Asmara: Red Sea Press, 1998).

Alexander, Jocelyn, McGregor, JoAnn and Ranger, Terence, *Violence and Memory: One Hundred Years in the 'Dark Forests' of Matabeleland* (Oxford, Portsmouth, Cape Town and Harare: James Currey, Heinemann, David Philip and Weaver Press, 2000).

Allman, Jean-Marie, *The Quills of the Porcupine: Asante Nationalism in an Emergent Ghana* (Madison: University of Wisconsin Press, 1993).

Amenumey, D. E. K., *The Ewe Unification Movement: A Political History* (Accra: Ghana Universities Press, 1989).

Andargachew Tiruneh, *The Ethiopian Revolution, 1974–1987: A Transformation From an Aristocratic to a Totalitarian Autocracy* (Cambridge: Cambridge University Press, 1993).

Anderson, David M. and Rathbone, Richard (eds), *Africa's Urban Past* (Oxford and Portsmouth: James Currey and Heinemann, 2000).

Andrae, Gunilla and Beckman, Bjorn, *The Wheat Trap: Bread and Underdevelopment in Nigeria* (London: Zed, 1986).

Anthony, Douglas, *Poison and Medicine: Ethnicity, Power and Violence in a Nigerian City, 1966 to 1986* (Portsmouth, Oxford and Cape Town: Heinemann, James Currey and David Philip, 2002).

Asiwaju, A. I., *Western Yorubaland Under European Rule, 1889–1945: A Comparative Analysis of French and British Colonialism* (London: Longman, 1976).

Askew, Kelly M., *Performing the Nation: Swahili Music and Cultural Politics in Tanzania* (Chicago and London: Chicago University Press, 2002).

Astrow, André, *Zimbabwe: A Revolution That Lost Its Way?* (London: Zed, 1983).

Atieno Odhiambo, E. S. and Lonsdale, John (eds), *Mau Mau and Nationhood: Arms, Authority and Narration* (Oxford, Nairobi and Athens: James Currey, EAEP and Ohio University Press, 2003).

Austin, Dennis, *Politics in Ghana, 1946–1960* (London, Oxford and New York: Oxford University Press, 1964, reprinted 1970).

Awolowo, Obafemi, *Path to Nigerian Freedom* (London: Faber and Faber, reprint of 1947 edition).

Awoonor, Kofi, *The Ghana Revolution: Background Account From a Personal Perspective* (New York: Oases Publishers, 1984).

Baker, Colin, *State of Emergency: Crisis in Central Africa, Nyasaland, 1959–1960* (London and New York: I. B. Tauris, 1997).

——, *Revolt of the Ministers: The Malawi Cabinet Crisis, 1964–1965* (London and New York: I. B. Tauris, 2001).

Bangura, Yusuf, *Britain and Commonwealth Africa: The Politics of Economic Relations, 1951–75* (Manchester: Manchester University Press, 1983).

Barkan, Joel D. (ed.), *Beyond Capitalism vs. Socialism in Kenya and Tanzania* (Boulder and London: Lynne Rienner, 1994).

—— and Okumu, John (eds), *Politics and Public Policy in Kenya and Tanzania* (New York: Praeger, 1979).

Barnett, Tony and Blaikie, Piers, *AIDS in Africa: Its Present and Future Impact* (London: Belhaven Press, 1992).

—— and Whiteside, Alan, *AIDS in the Twenty-First Century: Disease and Globalization* (Basingstoke and New York: Palgrave (now Palgrave Macmillan), 2002).

Barratt Brown, Michael, *Africa's Choices After Thirty Years of the World Bank* (London: Penguin, 1985).

Bates, Robert H., *Markets and States in Tropical Africa: The Political Basis of Agricultural Policies* (Berkeley, Los Angeles and London: University of California Press, 1981).

——, *Beyond the Miracle of the Market: The Political Economy of Agrarian Development in Kenya* (Cambridge: Cambridge University Press, 1989).

Bauer, Gretchen, *Labor and Democracy in Namibia, 1971–1996* (Athens and Oxford: Ohio University Press and James Currey, 1998).

Bayart, Jean François, Ellis, Stephen and Hibou, Béatrice, *The Criminalization of the State in Africa* (London, Bloomington, Indianapolis and Oxford: IAI, Indiana University Press and James Currey, 1999).

Baynham, Simon, *The Military and Politics in Nkrumah's Ghana* (Boulder and London: Westview Press, 1988).

Bazenguissa-Ganga, Rémy, *Les voies du politique au Congo: essai de sociologie historique* (Paris: Karthala, 1997).

Beckett, Paul A. and Young, Crawford (eds), *Dilemmas of Democracy in Nigeria* (Rochester and Woodbridge: University of Rochester Press, 1997).

Beckman, Björn, *Organising the Farmers: Cocoa Politics and National Development in Ghana* (Uppsala: Scandinavian Institute of African Studies, 1976).

Behrend, Heike, *Alice Lakwena and the Holy Spirits: War in Northern Uganda, 1896–97* (Oxford, Kampala, Nairobi and Athens: James Currey, Fountain Publishers, EAEP and Ohio University Press, 1999).

Bender, Gerald J., *Angola Under the Portuguese: The Myth and the Reality* (London: Heinemann, 1978).

Bening, R. Bagulo, *A History of Education in Northern Ghana 1907–1976* (Accra: Ghana Universities Press, 1990).

Berman, Bruce, *Control and Crisis in Colonial Kenya* (London: James Currey, 1990).

—— and Lonsdale, John, *Unhappy Valley: Conflict in Kenya and Africa, Books One and Two* (London: James Currey, 1992).

Berry, Sara S., *Chiefs Know Their Boundaries: Essays on Property, Power and the Past in Asante, 1896–1996* (Portsmouth, Oxford and Cape Town: Heinemann, James Currey and David Philip, 2001).

Bertrand, Jordane, *Rwanda, le piège de l'histoire: l'opposition démocratique avant le génocide (1990–1994)* (Paris: Karthala, 2000).

Beshir, Mohamed Omer, *Revolution and Nationalism in the Sudan* (London: Rex Collings, 1974).

Bhabha, Homi, *The Location of Culture* (London and New York: Routledge, 1994).

Bigo, Didier, *Pouvoir et obéissance en Centrafrique* (Paris: Karthala, 1988).

Birmingham, David, *Kwame Nkrumah: The Father of African Nationalism* (Athens: Ohio University Press, 2nd edition, 1998).

——, *Frontline Nationalism in Angola and Mozambique* (London and Trenton: James Currey and Africa World Press, 1992).

Boesen, Jannik, Madsen, Birgit Storgård and Moody, Tony, *Ujamaa – Socialism From Above* (Uppsala: Scandinavian Institute of African Studies, 1977).

Bolton, Dianne, *Nationalization: A Road to Socialism? The Case of Tanzania* (London: Zed, 1985).

Bond, Patrick, *Elite Transition: From Apartheid to Neoliberalism in South Africa* (London, Sterling and Pietrmaritzburg: Pluto Press and University of Natal Press, 2000).

Boone, Catherine, *Merchant Capital and the Roots of State Power in Senegal, 1930–1985* (Cambridge: Cambridge University Press, 1992).

Boulaga, Eboussi F., *Les conférences nationales: une affaire à suivre en Afrique noire* (Paris: Karthala, 1993).

Bourgault, Louise M., *Mass Media in Sub-Saharan Africa* (Bloomington and Indianapolis: Indiana University Press, 1995).

Bowen, Merle L., *The State and the Peasantry: Rural Struggles in Colonial and Postcolonial Mozambique* (Charlottesville and London: University Press of Virginia, 2000).

Bretton, Henry, *The Rise and Fall of Kwame Nkrumah: A Study of Personal Rule in Africa* (London: Pall Mall Press, 1967).

Brittain, Victoria, *Death of Dignity: Angola's Civil War* (London and Chicago: Pluto Press, 1998).

Brockington, Don, *Fortress Conservation: The Preservation of the Mkomazi Game Reserve, Tanzania* (London, Oxford, Dar es Salaam, Bloomington: IAI, James Currey, Mkuki na Nyota and Indiana University Press, 2002).

Brown, Carolyn A., *'We Were all Slaves': African Miners, Culture and Resistance at the Enugu Government Colliery* (Portsmouth, Oxford and Cape Town: Heinemann, James Currey and David Philip, 2002).

Brydon, Lynne and Legge, Karen, *Adjusting Society: The World Bank, the IMF and Ghana* (London and New York: Tauris, 1996).

Buchert, Lene, *Education in the Development of Tanzania, 1919–1990* (London, Dar es Salaam and Athens: James Currey, Mkuki na Nyota and Ohio University Press, 1994).

Buijtenhuijs, Robert, *Le Frolinat et les guerres civiles du Tchad (1977–1984): la révolution introuvable* (Paris and Leiden: Karthala and Afrika-Studiecentrum, 1987).

Callaghy, Thomas M., *The State–Society Struggle: Zaire in Comparative Perspective* (New York and Guildford: Columbia University Press, 1984).

Callahan, Michael D., *Mandates and Empire: The League of Nations and Africa, 1914–1931* (Brighton and Portland: Sussex Academic Press, 1999).

Cann, John, *Counterinsurgency in Africa: The Portuguese Way of War* (Westport: Greenwood Press, 1997).

Cartwright, John, *Politics in Sierra Leone, 1947–1967* (Toronto: University of Toronto Press, 1970).

——, *Political Leadership in Sierra Leone* (London: Croom Helm, 1978).

Cary, Joyce, *The Case for Colonial Freedom and Other Writings* (Austin: University of Texas Press, 1962).

Chabal, Patrick, *Amilcar Cabral: Revolutionary Leadership and People's War* (Cambridge: Cambridge University Press, 1983).

—— and Daloz, Jean-Pascal, *Africa Works: Disorder as Political Instrument* (Oxford and Bloomington: James Currey and Indiana University Press, 1999).

Chafer, Tony, *The End of Empire in French West Africa: France's Successful Decolonization?* (Oxford and New York: Berg, 2002).

Chatterjee, Partha, *The Nation and Its Fragments: Colonial and Postcolonial Histories* (Princeton: Princeton University Press, 1993).

Chazan, Naomi, *An Anatomy of Ghanaian Politics: Managing Political Recession, 1969–1982* (Boulder: Westview, 1983).

Chipman, John, *French Power in Africa* (Oxford: Blackwell, 1989).

Chrétien, Jean-Pierre (ed.), *Rwanda: les médias du génocide* (Paris: Karthala, 1995).

——, *The Great Lakes of Africa: Two Thousand Years of History* (New York: Zone Books, 2003).

Ciment, James, *Angola and Mozambique: Postcolonial Wars in Southern Africa* (New York: Facts on File, 1997).

Clapham, Christopher, *Haile-Selassie's Government* (London: Longman, 1969).
——, *Transformation and Continuity in Revolutionary Ethiopia* (Cambridge: Cambridge University Press, 1988).
Clarence-Smith, Gervase, *The Third Portuguese Empire, 1825–1975: A Study in Economic Imperialism* (Manchester: Manchester University Press, 1985).
Cliffe, Lionel, *The Transition to Independence in Namibia* (Boulder and London: Lynne Rienner, 1994).
——, and Stoneman, Colin, *Zimbabwe: Politics, Economics and Society* (New York: Frances Pinter, 1989).
Cohen, Robin, *Endgame in South Africa? The Changing Structures and Ideology of Apartheid* (London and Paris: James Currey and UNESCO Press, 1986).
Cole, Catherine M., *Ghana's Concert Party Theatre* (Bloomington: Indiana University Press, 2001).
Collins, John, *West African Pop Roots* (Philadelphia: Temple University Press, 1992).
——, *Highlife Time* (Accra: Anansesem Publications, 2nd edition, 1996).
Conklin, Alice, *A Mission to Civilize: The Republican Idea of Empire in France and West Africa, 1895–1930* (Stanford: Stanford University Press, 1997).
Cook, Mercer (ed.), *Léopold Sédar Senghor on African Socialism* (New York and Praeger, 1964).
Cooper, Frederick, *Decolonization and African Society: The Labor Question in French and British Africa* (Cambridge: Cambridge University Press, 1996).
Coquery-Vidrovitch, Catherine, Forest, Alain and Weiss, Herbert (eds), *Rébellions-révolution au Zaire 1963–1965, 2 tomes* (Paris: L'Harmattan, 1987).
Cosma, Wililunga B., *Fizi, 1967–1986: le maquis Kabila* (Brussels and Paris: Institut Africain and L'Harmattan, 1997).
Coulson, Andrew (ed.), *African Socialism in Practice: The Tanzanian Experience* (Nottingham: Spokesman, 1979).
Crush, Jonathan and McDonald, David A. (eds), *Transnationalism and New African Immigration to South Africa* (Cape Town: Southern African Migration Project, 2002).
Cruise O'Brien, Donal, *The Mourides of Senegal: The Political and Economic Organization of an Islamic Brotherhood* (Oxford: Clarendon Press, 1971).
Cruise O'Brien, Rita (ed.), *The Political Economy of Underdevelopment: Dependence in Senegal* (Beverly Hills and London: Sage, 1979).
Davenport, T. R. H., *The Transfer of Power in South Africa* (Cape Town: David Philip, 1998).
Davidson, Basil, *Black Star: A View of the Life and Times of Kwame Nkrumah* (London: Allen Lane, 1973 edition).
——, *No Fist Is Big Enough to Hide the Sky: The Liberation of Guinea-Bissau and Cape Verde* (London: Zed, 1981).
——, *The Black Man's Burden: Africa and the Curse of the Nation-State* (London: James Currey, 1992).
De Waal, Alex, *Famine Crimes: Politics and the Disaster Relief Industry in Africa* (London, Oxford and Bloomington: African Rights, IAI, James Currey and Indiana University Press, 1997).

De Villers, Gauthier and Omasambo Tshonda, Jean, *Zaire: la transition manquée (1990–1997)* (Tervuren and Paris: Institut Africain-CEDAF and L'Harmattan, 1997).

De Witte, Ludo, *The Assassination of Lumumba* (London and New York: Verso, 2001).

Decalo, Samuel, *Psychoses of Power: African Personal Dictatorships* (Boulder and London: Westview Press, 1989).

——, *Coups and Army Rule in Africa* (New Haven and London: Yale University Press, 2nd edition, 1990).

Delius, Peter, *A Lion Amongst the Cattle: Reconstruction and Resistance in the Northern Transvaal* (Portsmouth, Johannesburg and Oxford: Heinemann, Ravan Press and James Currey, 1996).

Den Tuinder, Bastiaan A., *Ivory Coast: The Challenge of Success* (Baltimore: John Hopkins University Press, 1978).

Derman, William, *Serfs, Peasants and Socialists: A Former Serf Village in the Republic of Guinea* (Berkeley, Los Angeles and London: University of California Press, 1973).

Dessalegn Rahmato, *Agrarian Reform in Ethiopia* (Trenton: Red Sea Press, 1985).

Dhada, Mustafah, *Warriors at Work: How Guinea Was Really Set Free* (Niwot: University Press of Colorado, 1993).

Diamond, Larry, *Class, Ethnicity and Democracy in Nigeria: The Failure of the First Republic* (Basingstoke: Macmillan (now Palgrave Macmillan), 1988).

——, Kirk-Greene, Anthony and Oyediran, Oyeleye (eds), *Transition Without End: Nigerian Politics and Civil Society Under Babangida* (Boulder and London: Lynne Rienner, 1997).

Dicklitch, Susan, *The Elusive Promise of NGOs in Africa: Lessons From Uganda* (Basingstoke and New York: Palgrave (now Palgrave Macmillan), 1998).

Dobell, Lauren, *SWAPO's Struggle for Namibia, 1960–1991: War By Other Means* (Basel: Schlettwein Publishing, 1998).

Donham, Donald, *Marxist Modern: An Ethnographic History of the Ethiopian Revolution* (Berkeley, Los Angeles and Oxford: University of California Press and James Currey, 1999).

Dowse, Robert E., *Modernization in Ghana and the USSR: A Comparative Study* (London: Routledge and Kegan Paul, 1969).

Dubow, Saul, *The African National Congress* (Johannesburg: Jonathan Ball, 2000).

Duffy, Rosaleen, *Killing for Conservation: Wildlife Policy in Zimbabwe* (London, Oxford, Bloomington and Harare: IAI, James Currey, Indiana University Press and Weaver, 2002).

Dumont, René, *False Start in Africa* (London: Andre Deutsch, 1st English edition, 1966).

Ekwe-Ekwe, Herbert, *The Biafra War: Nigeria and the Aftermath* (Lewiston, Queenston and Lampeter: Edwin Mellen Press, 1990).

Ellis, Stephen, *The Mask of Anarchy: The Destruction of Liberia and the Religious Dimension of an African Civil War* (London: C. Hurst, 1999).

Evans, Ivan, *Bureaucracy and Race: Native Administration in South Africa* (Berkeley, Los Angeles and London: University of California Press, 1997).

Evans, Malcolm and Murray, Rachel (eds), *The African Charter on Human and People's Rights: The System in Practice, 1986–2000* (Cambridge: Cambridge University Press, 2002).

Ewens, Graeme, *Congo Colossus: The Life and Legacy of Franco and OK Jazz* (North Walsham: Buku Books, 1994).

Ezenwa-Ohaeto, *Chinua Achebe: A Biography* (Oxford, Bloomington and Indianapolis: James Currey and Indiana University Press, 1997).

Fairhead, James and Leach, Melissa, *Misreading the African Landscape: Society and Ecology in a Forest-Savanna Mosaic* (Cambridge: Cambridge University Press, 1996).

Falola, Toyin, *The History of Nigeria* (Westport and London: Greenwood, 1999).

Fardon, Richard and Furniss, Graham (eds), *African Broadcast Cultures: African Radio in Transition* (Oxford, Harare, Cape Town and Westport: James Currey, Baobab, David Philip and Praeger, 2000).

Fatton Jnr, Robert, *The Making of a Liberal Democracy: Senegal's Passive Revolution* (Boulder and London: Lynne Rienner, 1987).

Feierman, Stephen, *Peasant Intellectuals: Anthropology and History in Tanzania* (Madison and London: University of Wisconsin Press, 1990).

Ferguson, James, *The Anti-Politics Machine: 'Development', Depoliticization and Bureaucratic Power in Lesotho* (Cambridge: Cambridge University Press, 1990).

Finer, Samuel, *The Man on Horseback: The Role of the Military in Politics* (London: Pall Mall, 1962).

Fitch, Bob and Oppenheimer, Mary, *Ghana: End of an Illusion* (New York and London: Monthly Review Press, 1966).

Forrest, Joshua, *Lineages of State Fragility: Rural Civil Society in Guinea-Bissau* (Oxford and Athens: James Currey and Ohio University Press, 2003).

Forsyth, Frederick, *The Biafra Story* (London: Penguin, 1969).

Foster, Philip and Zolberg, Aristide (eds), *Ghana and the Ivory Coast: Perspectives on Modernization* (Chicago and London: University of Chicago Press, 1971).

Frank, Marion, *AIDS-Education Through Theatre: Case Studies From Uganda* (Bayreuth: Bayreuth African Studies, 1995).

Frankel, Philip, *An Ordinary Atrocity: Sharpeville and its Massacre* (New Haven and London: Yale University Press, 2001).

Frimpong-Ansah, Jonathan, *The Vampire State in Africa: The Political Economy of Decline in Ghana* (London and Trenton: James Currey and Africa World Press, 1991).

Furedi, Frank, *The Mau Mau War in Perspective* (London: James Currey, 1989).

Gailey, Harry, *A History of the Gambia* (London: Routledge and Kegan Paul, 1964).

Gandalou, Justin-Daniel, *Au coeur de la sape: moeurs et aventures des Congolais à Paris* (Paris: L'Harmattan, 1989).

Galli, Rosemary E. and Jones, Jocelyn, *Guinea-Bissau: Politics, Economics and Society* (London and Boulder: Frances Pinter and Lynne Rienner, 1987).

Gbulie, Ben, *The Fall of Biafra* (Enugu: Benlie Publishers, 1989).

——, *Nigeria's Five Majors: Coup d'Etat of 15th January 1966, First Inside Account* (Onitsha: Africana Educational Publishers, 1981).

Geffray, Christian, *La cause des armes au Mozambique: anthropologie d'une guerre civile* (Paris: Karthala, 1990).

Geiger, Susan, *TANU Women: Gender and Culture in the Making of Tanganyikan Nationalism, 1955–1965* (Portsmouth, Oxford, Nairobi and Dar es Salaam: Heinemann, James Currey, EAEP and Mkuki na Nyota, 1997).

Gellar, Sheldon, *Senegal: An African Nation Between Islam and the West* (Boulder and Aldershot: Westview and Gower, 1982).

Genoud, Roger, *Nationalism and Economic Development in Ghana* (New York, Washington and London: Praeger, 1969).

Gerhart, Gail M., *Black Power in South Africa: The Evolution of an Ideology* (Berkeley and London: University of California Press, 1979).

Germain, Emmanuel, *La Centrafrique et Bokassa, 1965–1979: force et déclin d'un pouvoir personnel* (Paris: L'Harmattan, 2000).

Geschiere, Peter, *The Modernity of Witchcraft: Politics and the Occult in Postcolonial Africa* (Charlottesville: University of Virginia Press, 1997).

Gifford, Paul, *African Christianity: Its Public Role* (London: C. Hurst, 1998).

Glaser, Clive, *Bo-Tsotsi: The Youth Gangs of Soweto, 1935–1976* (Portsmouth, Oxford and Cape Town: Heinemann, James Currey and David Philip, 2000).

Graybill, Lyn S., *Truth and Reconciliation in South Africa: Miracle or Model?* (Boulder and London: Lynne Rienner, 2002).

Griffiths, Anne M. O., *In the Shadow of Marriage: Gender and Justice in an African Community* (Chicago and London: University of Chicago Press, 1997).

Griffiths, Ieuan Ll., *The African Inheritance* (London and New York: Routledge, 1995).

Guelke, Adrian, *South Africa in Transition: The Misunderstood Miracle* (London and New York: I. B. Tauris, 1999).

Guimarães, Fernando Andresen, *The Origins of the Angolan Civil War: Foreign Intervention and Domestic Political Conflict* (Basingstoke and New York: Macmillan (now Palgrave Macmillan) and St Martin's Press, 1998).

Hall, Margaret and Young, Tom, *Confronting Leviathan: Mozambique Since Independence* (London: C. Hurst, 1997).

Halliday, Fred and Molyneux, Maxine, *The Ethiopian Revolution* (London: Verso, 1981).

Hanlon, Joseph, *Mozambique: The Revolution Under Fire* (London: Zed, 1984).

Hansen, Holger Bernt, *Ethnicity and Military Rule in Uganda* (Uppsala: Scandinavian Institute of African Studies, 1977).

Hargreaves, John, *Decolonization in Africa* (London and New York: Longman, 1988).

Haugerud, Angelique, *The Culture of Politics in Modern Kenya* (Cambridge: Cambridge University Press, 1995).

Havnevik, Kjell J., *Tanzania: The Limits to Development From Above* (Uppsala and Dar es Salaam: Nordiska Afrikainstitutet and Mkuki na Nyota, 1993).

Hendricks, Fred T., *The Pillars of Apartheid: Land Tenure, Rural Planning and the Chieftaincy* (Uppsala: Uppsala University, 1990).

Herbst, Jeffrey, *States and Power in Africa: Comparative Lessons in Authority and Control* (Princeton: Princeton University Press, 2000).

Hesseling, Gerti, *Histoire politique du Sénégal: institutions, droit et société* (Paris and Leiden: Karthala and Afrika Studiecentrum, 1985).

Hess, Robert, *Italian Colonialism in Somalia* (Chicago and London: University of Chicago Press, 1966).

Hirsch, John L., *Sierra Leone: Diamonds and the Struggle for Democracy* (Boulder and London: Lynne Rienner, 2001).

Hirson, Baruch, *Year of Fire, Fire of Ash – The Soweto Revolt: Roots of a Revolution?* (London: Zed, 1979).

Hodges, Tony, *Angola: From Afro-Stalinism to Petro-Diamond Capitalism* (London, Lysaker, Oxford, Bloomington and Indianapolis: IAI, Fridjtof Nansen Institute, James Currey and Indiana University Press, 2001).

Human Rights Watch, *Angola Unravels: The Rise and Fall of the Lusaka Peace Process* (New York, Washington, London and Brussels: Human Rights Watch, 1999).

Huntington, Samuel, *Political Order in Changing Societies* (New Haven: Yale University Press, 1968).

——, *The Third Wave: Democratisation in the Late Twentieth Century* (Norman: Oklahoma University Press, 1991).

Hutchful, Eboe, *Ghana's Adjustment Experience: The Paradox of Reform* (Geneva and Oxford; UNRISD and James Currey, 2002).

Hyden, Goran, *Beyond Ujamaa in Tanzania: Underdevelopment and an Uncaptured Peasantry* (London: Heinemann, 1980).

——, *No Shortcuts to Progess: African Development Management in Perspective* (London: Heinemann, 1983).

Ibbott, Ralph, *History of the Ruvuma Development Association*, Tanzania: unpublished manuscript, 1970.

Iliffe, John, *A Modern History of Tanganyika* (Cambridge: Cambridge University Press, 1979).

Isaacman, Allen, *Cotton is the Mother of Poverty: Peasants, Work and Rural Struggle in Colonial Mozambique, 1938–1961* (Portsmouth, London and Cape Town: Heinemann, James Currey and David Philip, 1996).

—— and Isaacman, Barbara, *Mozambique: From Colonialism to Revolution, 1900–1982* (Boulder and Aldershot: Westview and Gower, 1983).

—— and Roberts, Richard (eds), *Cotton, Colonialism, and Social History in Sub-Saharan Africa* (Portsmouth and London: Heinemann and James Currey, 1995).

Iyob, Ruth, *The Eritrean Struggle for Independence: Domination, Resistance, Nationalism, 1941–1993* (Cambridge: Cambridge University Press, 1995).

James, C. L. R., *Nkrumah and the Ghana Revolution* (London: Allison and Busby, 1977).

Jeffries, Richard, *Class, Power and Ideology in Ghana: The Railwaymen of Sekondi* (Cambridge: Cambridge University Press, 1978).

Johnson, Douglas, *The Root Causes of Sudan's Civil Wars* (Oxford, Bloomington, Indianapolis and Kampala: James Currey, IAI, Indiana University Press and Fountain Publishers, 2003).

Jok, Jok Madut, *War and Slavery in Sudan* (Philadelphia: University of Pennsylvania Press, 2001).

Jørgensen, Jan Jelmert, *Uganda: A Modern History* (London: Croom Helm, 1981).

Joseph, Richard, *Radical Nationalism in Cameroun: Social Origins of the UPC Rebellion* (Oxford: Clarendon Press, 1977).

——, *Democracy and Prebendal Politics in Nigeria: The Rise and Fall of the Second Republic* (Cambridge: Cambridge University Press, 1987).

Kaba, Lansiné, *Le 'Non' de la Guinée à de Gaulle* (Paris: Editions Chaka, undated).

Kaela, Laurent C., *The Question of Namibia* (Basingstoke, London and New York: Macmillan (now Palgrave Macmillan) and St Martin's Press, 1996).

Kanogo, Tabitha, *Squatters and the Roots of Mau Mau* (London: James Currey, 1987).

Kapuscinski, Ryszard, *The Emperor: The Downfall of an Autocrat* (London: Picador, 1983).

Katzenellenbogen, Simon, *Railways and the Copper Mines of Katanga* (London: Oxford University Press, 1973).

Keller, Edmond J., *Revolutionary Ethiopia: From Empire to People's Republic* (Bloomington and Indianapolis: Indiana University Press, 1988).

Kenney, Henry, *Architect of Apartheid: H. F. Verwoerd – An Appraisal* (Johannesburg: Jonathan Ball, 1980).

Kershaw, Greet, *Mau Mau From Below* (London: James Currey and Ohio University Press, 1997).

Khaketla, B. M., *Lesotho 1970: An African Coup Under the Microscope* (London: C. Hurst, 1971).

Killick, Tony, *Development Economics in Action: A Study of Economic Policies in Ghana* (London: Heinemann, 1978).

Kriger, Norma J., *Zimbabwe's Guerrilla War: Peasant Voices* (Cambridge and Harare: Cambridge University Press and Baobab Books, 1992).

Kyle, Keith, *The Politics of the Independence of Kenya* (Basingstoke and London: Macmillan (now Palgrave Macmillan), 1999).

Lan, David, *Guns and Rain: Guerrillas and Spirit Mediums in Zimbabwe* (London, Berkeley and Los Angeles: James Currey and University of California Press, 1985).

Larebo, Haile, *The Building of an Empire: Italian Land Policy and Practice in Ethiopia* (Oxford: Clarendon Press, 1994).

Leach, Melissa and Mearns, Robin (eds), *The Lie of the Land: Challenging Received Wisdom on the African Environment* (London, Oxford and Portsmouth: IAI, James Currey and Heinemann, 1996).

Lefort, René, *Ethiopia: An Heretical Revolution?* (London: Zed, 1981).

Lemarchand, René, *Burundi: Ethnic Conflict and Genocide* (Cambridge: Cambridge University Press, 1994).

Lensink, Robert, *Structural Adjustment in Sub-Saharan Africa* (London and New York: Longman, 1996).

Lentz, Carola and Nugent, Paul (eds), *Ethnicity in Ghana: The Limits of Invention* (Basingstoke and New York: Macmillan (now Palgrave Macmillan) and St Martin's Press, 2000).

Leo, Christopher, *Land and Class in Kenya* (Toronto, Buffalo and London: Toronto University Press, 1984).

Levin, Richard, *When the Sleeping Grass Awakens: Land and Power in Swaziland* (Johannesburg: Witwatersrand University Press, 1997).

Lewis, I. M., *A Modern History of Somalia: Nation and State in the Horn of Africa* (London and New York: Longman, 1980; Boulder and London: Westview Press, 2nd edition, 1988).

——, *Blood and Bone: The Call of Kinship in Somali Society* (Trenton: Red Sea Press, 1994).

Leys, Colin, *Underdevelopment in Kenya: The Political Economy of Neo-Colonialism* (London: Heinemann, 1975).

——, *The Rise and Fall of Development Theory* (London and Bloomington: James Currey and Indiana University Press, 1996).

Liebenow, J. Gus, *Liberia: The Quest for Democracy* (Bloomington and Indianapolis: Indiana University Press, 1987).

Liniger-Goumaz, Max, *Small is Not Always Beautiful: The Story of Equatorial Guinea* (London: C. Hurst, 1986).

Lodge, Tom, *Black Politics in South Africa Since 1945* (London and New York: Longman, 1983).

Luckham, Robin, *The Nigerian Military: A Sociological Analysis of Authority and Revolt 1960–67* (Cambridge: Cambridge University Press, 1971).

Lyons, Terence and Samatar, Ahmed I., *State Collapse, Multilateral Intervention, and Strategies for Political Reconstruction* (Washington, DC: Brookings Institution, 1995).

MacGaffey, Janet, *Entrepreneurs and Parasites: The Struggle for Indigenous Capitalism in Zaire* (Cambridge: Cambridge University Press, 1987).

——, *The Real Economy of Zaire: The Contribution of Smuggling and Other Unofficial Activities to National Wealth* (London and Philadelphia: James Currey and Pennsylvania University Press, 1991).

—— and Bazenguissa-Ganga, Rémy, *Congo-Paris: Transnational Traders on the Margins of the Law* (London, Oxford, Bloomington and Indianapolis: IAI, James Currey and Indiana University Press, 2000).

MacQueen, Norrie, *The Decolonization of Portuguese Africa: Metropolitan Revolution and the Dissolution of Empire* (Harlow: Addison Wesley Longman, 1997).

Machobane, L. B. B. J., *Government and Change in Lesotho, 1800–1966: A Study of Political Institutions* (Basingstoke: Macmillan (now Palgrave Macmillan), 1990).

——, *King's Knights: Military Governance in the Kingdom of Lesotho* (Roma: Institute of Southern African Studies, 2001).

Madiebo, Alexander, *The Nigerian Revolution and the Biafran War* (Enugu: Fourth Dimension Publishers, 1980).

Mager, Anne Kelk, *Gender and the Making of a South African Bantustan: A Social History of the Ciskei, 1945–1959* (Portsmouth, Oxford and Cape Town: Heinemann, James Currey and David Philip, 1999).

Mahoney, Richard D., *JFK: Ordeal in Africa* (New York and Oxford: Oxford University Press, 1983).

Mainasara, A. M., *The Five Majors: Why They Struck* (Zaria: Hudahuda Publishing, 1982).

Maliyamkono, T. L. (ed.), *The Political Plight of Zanzibar* (Dar es Salaam: Tema Publishers, 2000).

Maliyamkono, T. M. and Bagachwa, M. S. D., *The Second Economy in Tanzania* (London, Nairobi, Athens and Dar es Salaam: James Currey, Ohio University Press, Heinemann Kenya and ESAURP, 1990).

Malkki, Liisa H., *Purity and Exile: Violence, Memory and National Cosmology Among Hutu Refugees in Tanzania* (Chicago and London: University of Chicago Press, 1995).

Maloba, Wunyabari, *Mau Mau and Kenya: An Analysis of a Peasant Revolt* (Indiana University Press, 1993).

Mamdani, Mahmood, *Citizen and Subject: Contemporary Africa and the Legacy of Late Colonialism* (Kampala, Cape Town and London: Fountain, David Philip and James Currey, 1996).

——, *When Victims Become Killers: Colonialism, Nativism, and the Genocide in Rwanda* (Kampala, Cape Town and Oxford: Fountain, David Philip and James Currey, 2001).

Marcum, John, *The Angolan Revolution: Exile Politics and Guerrilla Warfare (1962–1976)* (Cambridge, MA and London: MIT Press, 1978).

Marcus, Harold, *A History of Ethiopia* (Berkeley, Los Angeles and London: University of California Press, 1994).

Maré, Gerhard and Hamilton, Georgina, *An Appetite For Power: Buthelezi's Inkatha and South Africa* (Braamfontein and Bloomington: Ravan Press and Indiana University Press, 1987).

Markakis, John, *Ethiopia: Anatomy of a Traditional Polity* (Oxford: Oxford University Press, 1974).

——, *National and Class Conflict in the Horn of Africa* (London: Zed, 1990).

—— and Ayele, Nega, *Class and Revolution in Ethiopia* (Nottingham: Spokesman, 1978).

Markovitz, Irving Leonard, *Léopold Sédar Senghor and the Politics of Negritude* (London: Heinemann, 1969).

Martin, David, and Johnson, Phyllis, *The Struggle for Zimbabwe: The Chimurenga War* (London: Faber, 1981).

Maughan-Brown, David, *Land and Freedom: History and Ideology in Kenya* (London: Zed, 1985).

Maxwell, David, *Christians and Chiefs in Zimbabwe: A Social History of the Hwesa People c.1870s–1990s* (Edinburgh and London: Edinburgh University Press, International Africa Institute, 1999).

Mbembe, Achille, *On the Postcolony* (Berkeley and London: University of California Press, 2001).

McCann, James C., *Green Land, Brown Land, Black Land: An Environmental History of Africa, 1800–1990* (Portsmouth and Oxford: Heinemann and James Currey, 1999).

McHenry, Dean, *Tanzania's Ujamaa Villages: The Implementation of a Rural Development Strategy* (Berkeley: University of California, 1979).

McHenry, Dean, *Limited Choices: The Political Struggle for Socialism in Tanzania* (Boulder and London: Lynne Rienner, 1994).

McLuckie, Craig W., *Nigerian Civil War Literature: Seeking an 'Imagined Community'* (Lewiston, Queenston and Lampeter: Edwin Mellen, 1990).

Meyer, Birgit, *Translating the Devil: Religion and Modernity Among the Ewe in Ghana* (Edinburgh and London: Edinburgh University Press/International Africa Institute, 1999).

Miles, William F. S., *Hausaland Divided: Colonialism and Independence in Nigeria and Niger* (Ithaca and London: Cornell University Press, 1994).

Minter, William, *Apartheid's Contras: An Inquiry into the Roots of War in Angola and Mozambique* (London: Zed, 1994).

Mkandawire, Thandika and Soludo, Charles C., *Our Continent, Our Future: African Perspectives on Structural Adjustment* (Dakar, Ottawa, Trenton: CODESRIA, IDRC and Africa World Press, 1999).

Mohiddin, Ahmed, *African Socialism in Two Countries* (London and Totowa: Croom Helm and Barnes and Noble, 1981).

Morgenthau, Ruth Schachter, *Political Parties in French-Speaking Africa* (Oxford: Clarendon Press, 1964).

Morris, Alan and Bouillon, Antoine (eds), *African Immigration to South Africa: Francophone Migration of the 1990s* (Pretoria: Protea and IFAS, 2001).

Moyo, Sam, *The Land Question in Zimbabwe* (Harare: SAPES Trust, 1995).

Muffett, D. J. M., *Let Truth Be Told: The Coups d'Etat of 1966* (Zaria: Hudahuda Publishing, 1982).

Murphy, David, *Sembene: Imagining Alternatives in Film and Fiction* (Oxford and Trenton: James Currey and Africa World Press, 2000).

Murray, Martin, *South Africa: Time of Agony, Time of Destiny* (London: Verso, 1987).

——, *The Revolution Deferred: The Painful Birth of Post-Apartheid South Africa* (London: Verso, 1994).

Museveni, Yoweri, Mutibwa, Phares, *Uganda Since Independence: A Story of Unfulfilled Hopes* (London: C. Hurst, 1992). *What is Africa's Problem? Speeches and Writings on Africa by Yoweri Kaguta Museveni* (Kampala: NRM Publications, 1992).

Mzala, *Gatsha Buthelezi: Chief with a Double Agenda* (London: Zed, 1988).

Nafziger, Wayne, *The Economics of Political Instability: The Nigerian–Biafran War* (Boulder: Westview Press, 1983).

Naldi, Gino, *The Organization of African Unity: An Analysis of its Role* (London and New York: Mansell, 1989).

—— (ed.), *Documents of the Organization of African Unity* (London and New York: Mansell, 1992).

Ndaywel è Nziem, Isodore, *Histoire générale du Congo: de l'héritage ancien à la République Démocratique* (Paris and Brussels: De Boeck and Larcier, 1998).

Ndegwa, Stephen N., *The Two Faces of Civil Society: NGOs and Politics in Africa* (West Hartford: Kumarian Press, 1996).

Nelson, Paul J., *The World Bank and Non-Governmental Organizations: The Limits of Apolitical Development* (London and New York: Macmillan (now Palgrave Macmillan) and St Martin's Press, 1995).

Newitt, Malyn, *Portugal in Africa: The Last Hundred Years* (London: C. Hurst, 1981).

Ngoh, Victor Julius, *Southern Cameroons, 1922–1961: A Constitutional History* (Aldershot: Ashgate, 2001).

Nkrumah, Kwame, *Ghana: The Autobiography of Kwame Nkrumah* (Edinburgh: Thomas Nelson, 1959).

——, *Africa Must Unite* (London: Heinemann, 1963).

——, *Neo-Colonialism: The Last Stage of Imperialism* (Edinburgh: Thomas Nelson, 1965).

Nolutshungu, Sam C., *Limits of Anarchy: Intervention and State Formation in Chad* (Charlottesville and London: University Press of Virginia, 1996).

Nordlinger, Eric A., *Soldiers in Politics: Military Coups and Governments* (Englewood Cliffs: Prentice-Hall, 1977).

Nordstrom, Carolyn, *A Different Kind of War Story* (Philadelphia: University of Pennsylvania Press, 1997).

Nugent, Paul, *Big Men, Small Boys and Politics in Ghana: Power, Ideology and the Burden of History, 1982–1994* (London: Frances Pinter, 1996).

——, *Smugglers, Secessionists and Loyal Citizens on the Ghana–Togo Frontier: The Lie of the Borderlands Since 1914* (Oxford, Athens and Accra: James Currey, Ohio University Press and Subsaharan Publishers, 2002).

Nyerere, Julius, *Ujamaa: Essays on Socialism* (Oxford and Dar es Salaam: Oxford University Press, 1968).

Nzongola-Ntalaja, Georges, *The Congo From Leopold to Kabila: A People's History* (London and New York: Zed, 2002).

O'Ballance, Edgar, *The Congo–Zaire Experience, 1960–98* (Basingstoke and New York: Macmillan (now Palgrave Macmillan) and St Martin's Press, 2000).

Obasanjo, Olusegun, *Nzeogwu* (Ibadan: Spectrum Books, 1987).

O'Connor, Anthony, *The African City* (London: Hutchinson, 1983).

Odogwu, Bernard, *No Place to Hide: Crisis and Conflict Inside Biafra* (Enugu: Fourth Dimension Publishers, 1985).

Ogbudinkpa, Reuben N., *The Economics of the Nigerian Civil War and its Prospects for National Development* (Enugu: Fourth Dimension Publishers, 1985).

Ogot, B. A. and Ochieng', W. R. (eds), *Decolonization and Independence in Kenya 1940–93* (London, Nairobi and Athens: James Currey, East African Educational Publishers and Ohio University Press, 1995).

Okeke, Barbara, *4 June: A Revolution Betrayed* (Enugu and Oxford: Ikenga, 1982).

Omotoso, Kole, *Achebe or Soyinka: A Study in Contrasts* (London: Hans Zell, 1996).

Oquaye, Mike, *Politics in Ghana, 1972–1979* (Accra: Tornado Publications, 1980).

Osaghae, Eghosa, *Crippled Giant: Nigeria Since Independence* (London: C. Hurst, 1998).

O'Toole, Thomas, *The Central African Republic: The Continent's Hidden Heart* (Boulder and London: Westview and Gower, 1986).

Palmberg, Mai and Kirkegaard, Annemette (eds), *Playing With Identities in Contemporary Music in West Africa* (Uppsala: Nordiksa Afrikainstitutet, 2002).

Parsons, Timothy H., *The 1964 Army Mutinies and the Making of Modern East Africa* (London and Westport: Greenwood, 2003).

Pausewang, Siegfried, Tronvoll, Kjetil and Aalen, Lovise (eds), *Ethiopia Since the Derg: A Decade of Democratic Pretension and Performance* (London and New York: Zed, 2002).

Pearce, R. D., *The Turning Point in Africa: British Colonial Policy, 1938–48* (London: Frank Cass, 1982).

Phillips, Anne, *The Enigma of Colonialism: British Policy in West Africa* (London and Bloomington: James Currey and Indiana University Press, 1989).

Ponte, Stefano, *Farmers and Markets in Tanzania: How Policy Reforms Affect Rural Livelihoods in Africa* (Oxford, Dar es Salaam and Portsmouth: James Currey, Mkuki na Nyota and Heinemann, 2002).

Pool, David, *From Guerrillas to Government: The Eritrean People's Liberation Front* (Oxford and Athens: James Currey and Ohio University Press, 2001).

Post, Kenneth W. J. and Jenkins, George D., *The Price of Liberty: Personality and Politics in Colonial Nigeria* (Cambridge: Cambridge University Press, 1973).

Pottier, Johan, *Re-Imagining Rwanda: Conflict, Survival and Disinformation in the Late Twentieth Century* (Cambridge: Cambridge University Press, 2002).

Pratt, Cranford, *The Critical Phase in Tanzania, 1945–1968: Nyeyere and the Emergence of a Socialist Strategy* (Cambridge: Cambridge University Press, 1976).

Price, Robert M., *The Apartheid State in Crisis: Political Transformation in South Africa 1975–1990* (New York and Oxford: Oxford University Press, 1991).

Prunier, Gérard, *The Rwanda Crisis: History of a Genocide* (London: C. Hurst, 1995).

Ranger, Terence, *Peasant Consciousness and Guerrilla War in Zimbabwe* (London: James Currey, 1985).

Rapley, John, *Ivoirien Capitalism: African Entrepreneurs in Côte d'Ivoire* (Boulder and London: Lynne Rienner, 1993).

Rathbone, Richard, *Nkrumah and the Chiefs: The Politics of Chieftaincy in Ghana, 1951–60* (Oxford, Accra and Athens: James Currey, F. Reimmer and Ohio University Press, 2000).

Reno, William, *Corruption and State Politics in Sierra Leone* (Cambridge: Cambridge University Press, 1995).

——, *Warlord Politics and African States* (Boulder and London: Lynne Rienner, 1998).

Reynolds, Jonathan T., *The Time of Politics (Zamanin Siyasa): Islam and the Politics of Legitimacy in Northern Nigeria 1950–1966* (San Francisco, London and Bethesda: International Scholars Publications, 1999).

Reyntjens, Filip, *La guerre des Grands Lacs: alliances mouvantes et conflits extraterritoriaux en Afrique centrale* (Paris and Montreal: L'Harmattan: 1999).

Richards, Paul, *Indigenous Agricultural Revolution: Ecology and Food Production in West Africa* (London: Hutchison, 1985).

——, *Fighting for the Rain Forest: War, Youth and Resources in Sierra Leone* (London, Oxford and Portsmouth: IAI, James Currey and Heinemann, 1996).

Riddell, Roger C. and Robinson, Marc with John de Coninck, Ann Muir and Sarah White, *Non-Governmental Organizations and Rural Poverty Alleviation* (Oxford: Clarendon Press, 1995).

Rimmer, Douglas, *Staying Poor: Ghana's Political Economy, 1950–1990* (Oxford: Pergamon Press, 1992).

Rivière, Claude, *Guinea: Mobilization of a People* (Ithaca and London: Cornell University Press, 1970).

Rudebeck, Lars, *Guinea-Bissau: A Study of Political Mobilization* (Uppsala: Scandinavian Insitute of African Studies, 1974).

Saasa, Oliver, *Aid and Poverty Reduction in Zambia: Mission Unaccomplished* (Uppsala: Nordiska Afrikainstitutet, 2002).

Sahn, David E., Dorosh, Paul A. and Younger, Stephen D., *Structural Adjustment Reconsidered: Economic Policy and Poverty in Africa* (Cambridge: Cambridge University Press, 1997).

Samoff, Joel, *Tanzania: Local Politics and the Structure of Power* (Madison: University of Wisconsin Press, 1974).

Saro-Wiwa, Ken, *On a Darkling Plain: An Account of the Nigerian Civil War* (London, Lagos and Port Harcourt: Saros Publishers, 1989).

Sathyamurthy, T. V., *The Political Development of Uganda: 1900–1986* (Aldershot: Gower, 1986).

Sbacchi, Alberto, *Ethiopia Under Mussolini: Fascism and the Colonial Experience* (London: Zed, 1985).

——, *Legacy of Bitterness: Ethiopia and Fascist Italy, 1935–1941* (Lawrenceville and Asmara: Red Sea Press, 1997).

Schatzberg, Michael, *The Dialectics of Oppression in Zaire* (Bloomington and Indianapolis: Indiana University Press, 1988).

——, *Political Legitimacy in Middle Africa: Father, Family, Food* (Bloomington and Indianapolis: Indiana University Press, 2001).

Scherrer, Christian P., *Genocide and Crisis in Central Africa: Conflict Roots, Mass Violence and Regional War* (Westport and London: Praeger, 2002).

Schlemmer, Lawrence and Levitz, Charisse, *Unemployment in South Africa: The Facts, the Prospects and the Exploration of Solutions* (Johannesburg: South African Institute of Race Relations, 1998).

Schumacher, Edward J., *Politics, Bureaucracy and Rural Development in Senegal* (Berkeley, Los Angeles and London: University of California Press, 1975).

Scott, James C., *Domination and the Arts of Resistance: Hidden Transcripts* (New Haven and London: Yale University Press, 1990).

Seekings, Jeremy, *The UDF: A History of the United Democratic Front in South Africa, 1983–1991* (Cape Town, Oxford and Athens: David Philip, James Currey and Ohio University Press, 2000).

Setel, Philip W., *A Plague of Paradoxes: AIDS, Culture and Demography in Northern Tanzania* (Chicago and London: University of Chicago Press, 1999).

——, Lewis, Milton and Lyons, Maryinez (eds), *Histories of Sexually Transmitted Diseases and HIV/AIDS in Sub-Saharan Africa* (Westport and London: Greenwood, 1999).

Shivji, Issa G., *Class Struggles in Tanzania* (London: Heinemann, 1976).

Sillery, Anthony, *Botswana: A Short Political History* (London: Methuen, 1974).

Sithole, Masipula, *Zimbabwe: Struggles Within the Struggle (1957–1980)* (Harare: Rujeko, 1999).

Sklar, Richard, *Nigerian Political Parties: Power in an Emergent African Nation* (New York and Enugu: Nok, 1983 edition; first published Princeton: Princeton University Press, 1963).

Spear, Thomas, *Mountain Farmers: Moral Economies of Land and Agricultural Development in Arusha and Meru* (Oxford, Nairobi and Berkeley: James Currey, Mkuki na Nyota and University of California Press, 1997).

Stewart, Gary, *Rumba on the River: A History of the Popular Music of the Two Congos* (London and New York: Verso, 2000).

Stremlau, John J., *The International Politics of the Nigerian Civil War, 1967–1970* (Princeton: Princeton University Press, 1977).

Ström, Gabriele Winai, *Development and Dependence in Lesotho, the Enclave of South Africa* (Uppsala: Scandinavian Institute of African Studies, 1978).

Stultz, Newell M., *Transkei's Half Loaf: Race Separatism in South Africa* (Cape Town: David Philip, 1979).

Swainson, Nicola, *The Development of Corporate Capitalism in Kenya, 1918–1977* (London: Heinemann, 1980).

Tekeste Negash, *Italian Colonialism in Eritrea, 1882–1941: Policies, Praxis and Impact* (Uppsala: Acta Universitatis Upsaliensis, 1987).

——, *Eritrea and Ethiopia: The Federal Experience* (Uppsala and New Brunswick: Nordiska Afrikainstitutet, 1997).

—— and Tronvoll, Kjetil, *Brothers At War: Making Sense of the Eritrean–Ethiopian War* (Oxford and Athens: James Currey and Ohio University Press, 2000).

Thompson, W. Scott, *Ghana's Foreign Policy, 1957–1966: Diplomacy, Ideology, and the New State* (Princeton: Princeton University Press, 1969).

Throup, David, *Economic and Social Origins of Mau Mau* (London, Nairobi and Athens: James Currey, Heinemann and Ohio University Press).

—— and Hornsby, Charles, *Multi-Party Politics in Kenya: The Kenyatta and Moi States and the Triumph of the System in the 1992 Election* (Oxford, Nairobi and Athens: James Currey, EAEP and Ohio University Press, 1998).

Tibenderana, P. K., *Sokoto Province Under British Rule, 1903–1939* (Zaria: Ahmadu Bello University Press, 1988).

Tiffen, M., Mortimore, M. and Gichuki, F., *More People, Less Erosion: Environmental Recovery in Kenya* (Chichester: John Wiley, 1994).

Tignor, Robert, *Capitalism and Nationalism at the End of Empire: State and Business in Decolonizing Egypt, Nigeria and Kenya, 1945–1963* (Princeton: Princeton University Press, 1998).

Titley, Brian, *Dark Age: The Political Odyssey of Emperor Bokassa* (Liverpool: Liverpool University Press, 1997).

Tordoff, William, *Government and Politics of Tanzania: A Collection of Essays Covering the Period from September 1960 to July 1966* (Nairobi: East African Publishing House, 1967).

Toulabor, Comi, *Le Togo sous Eyadéma* (Paris: Karthala, 1986).

Touval, Saadia, *The Boundary Politics of Independent Africa* (Cambridge: Harvard University Press, 1972).

Trager, Lillian, *Yoruba Hometowns: Community, Identity and Development in Nigeria* (Boulder and London: Lynne Rienner, 2001).

Tripp, Aili Mari, *Women and Politics in Uganda* (Oxford, Kampala and Madison: James Currey, Fountain Publishers and University of Wisconsin Press, 2000).

Vail, Leroy (ed.), *The Creation of Tribalism in Southern Africa* (London: James Currey, 1989).

Vaillant, Janet G, *Black, French and African: A Life of Léopold Sédar Senghor* (Cambridge and London: Harvard University Press, 1990).

Veal, Michael, *Fela: The Life and Times of an African Musical Icon* (Philadelphia: Temple University Press, 2000).

Van de Walle, Nicolas, *African Economies and the Politics of Permanent Crisis, 1979–1999* (Cambridge: Cambridge University Press, 2001).

Van Kessel, Ineke, *'Beyond Our Wildest Dreams': The United Democratic Front and the Transformation of South Africa* (Charlottesville and London: University Press of Virginia, 2000).

Van Rouveroy Van Nieuwaal, E. Adriaan B., *L'état en Afrique face à la chefferie: le cas du Togo* (Paris and Leiden: Karthala and Afrika-Studiecentrum, 2000).

—— and Van Dijk, Rijk (eds), *African Chieftaincy in a New Socio-Political Landscape* (Münster and London: Lit Verlag, 1999).

—— and Zips, Werner (eds), *Sovereignty, Legitimacy, and Power in West African Societies: Perspectives From Legal Anthropology* (Hamburg and New Brunswick: Lit Verlag and Transaction, 1998).

Van Walraven, Klaas, *Dreams of Power: The Role of the Organization of African Unity in the Politics of Africa, 1963–1993* (Aldershot: Ashgate, 1999).

Vaughan, Olufemi, *Nigerian Chiefs: Traditional Power in Modern Politics 1890s–1990s* (Rochester and Woodbridge: University of Rochester Press, 2000).

Villalón, Leonardo, *Islamic Society and State Power in Senegal: Disciples and Citizens in Fatick* (Cambridge: Cambridge University Press, 1995).

Vines, Alex, *RENAMO: From Terrorism to Democracy in Mozambique?* (London: James Currey, 1991).

Von Freyhold, Michaela, *Ujamaa Villages in Tanzania: Analysis of a Social Experiment* (London: Heinemann, 1979).

Webb, Douglas, *HIV and AIDS in Africa* (London, Cape Town and Pietermaritzburg: Pluto Press, David Philip and University of Natal Press, 1997).

Weisfelder, Richard F., *Political Contention in Lesotho, 1952–1965* (Maseru: Institute of Southern African Studies, 1999).

Werbner, Richard, *Tears of the Dead: The Social Biography of an African Family* (London and Edinburgh: Edinburgh University Press and International Africa Institute, 1991).

Whiteside, Alan and Sunter, Clem, *AIDS: The Challenge for South Africa* (Cape Town: Human and Rousseau and Tafelberg, 2000).

Widner, Jennifer A., *The Rise of a Party-State in Kenya: From 'Harambee!' to 'Nyayo'* (Berkeley, Los Angeles and Oxford: University of California Press, 1992).

Willame, Jean-Claude, *L'Odysée Kabila: trajectoire pour un Congo nouveau?* (Paris: Karthala, 1999).

Wilson, Richard A., *The Politics of Truth and Reconciliation in South Africa: Legitimizing the Post-Apartheid State* (Cambridge: Cambridge University Press, 2001).

Wiseman, John, *The New Struggle For Democracy in Africa* (Aldershot: Ashgate, 1996).

Woodward, Peter, *Condominium and Sudanese Nationalism* (London: Rex Collings, 1979).

Woronoff, Jon, *Organizing African Unity* (Metuchen: Scarecrow Press, 1970).

——, *West African Wager: Houphouët Versus Nkrumah* (Metuchen: Scarecrow Press, 1972).

Wright, George, *The Destruction of a Nation: United States Policy Toward Angola Since 1945* (London and Chicago: Pluto Press, 1997).

Yakubu, Alhaji Mahmood, *An Aristocracy in Crisis: The End of Indirect Rule and the Emergence of Party Politics in the Emirates of Northern Nigeria* (Aldershot: Avebury, 1996).

Yeager, Rodger, *Tanzania: An African Experiment* (Boulder and Aldershot: Westview and Gower, 1982).

Young, Crawford, *Politics in the Congo: Decolonization and Independence* (Princeton: Princeton University Press, 1965).

——, *Ideology and Development in Africa* (New Haven and London: Yale University Press, 1982).

——, *The African Colonial State in Comparative Perspective* (New Haven and London: Yale University Press, 1994).

—— and Turner, Thomas, *The Rise and Decline of the Zairean State* (Madison and London: University of Wisconsin Press, 1985).

Young, John, *Peasant Revolution in Ethiopia: The Tigray People's Liberation Front, 1975–1991* (Cambridge: Cambridge University Press, 1997).

Zachernuk, Philip S., *Colonial Subjects: An African Intelligentsia and Atlantic Ideas* (Charlottesville and London: University of Virginia Press, 2000).

Zolberg, Aristide R., *One-Party Government in the Ivory Coast* (Princeton: Princeton University Press, 1969).

3 Book and journal articles

Abdullah, Ibrahim, 'Bush path to destruction: the origin and character of the Revolutionary United Front (RUF/SL)', *Africa Development* 22, 3/4, 1997.

—— and Muana, Patrick, 'The Revolutionary United Front of Sierra Leone: a revolt of the lumpenproletariat', in Christopher Clapham (ed.), *African Guerrillas* (Oxford, Kampala, Bloomington and Indianapolis: James Currey, Fountain Publishers and Indiana University Press, 1998).

Ahuazem, Jones O., 'Perceptions: Biafra, politics and the war', in Axel Harneit-Sievers, Jones Ahuazem and Sydney Emezue (eds), *A Social History of the Nigerian Civil War* (Enugu and Hamburg: Jemezie Associates and Lit Verlag, 1997).

Akinterinwa, Bola A., 'The 1993 Presidential election imbroglio' in Larry Diamond, Anthony Kirk-Greene and Oyeleye Oyediran (eds), *Transition Without End: Nigerian Politics and Civil Society Under Babangida* (Boulder and London: Lynne Rienner, 1997).

Akyeampong, Emmanuel, 'Africans in the diaspora: the diaspora and Africa', *African Affairs* 99, 2000.

Alexander, Jocelyn, 'Things fall apart, the centre can hold: processes of post-war political change in Zimbabwe's rural areas', in Ngwabi Bhebe and Terence Ranger (eds), *Society in Zimbabwe's Liberation War* (Oxford, Portsmouth and Harare: James Currey, Heinemann and University of Zimbabwe, 1996).

Alexandre, Pierre, 'The problems of chieftaincies in French-speaking Africa', in Michael Crowder and Obaro Ikime (eds), *West African Chiefs: Their Changing Status Under Colonial Rule and Independence* (Ile-Ife: University of Ife Press, 1970).

Allen, Chris, 'Benin', in Chris Allen, Michael S. Radu, Keith Somerville and Joan Baxter (eds), *Benin, The Congo, Burkina Faso: Politics, Economy and Society* (London: Pinter Publishers, 1988).

Amanor, Kojo, Denkabe, Aloysius and Wellard, Kate, 'Ghana: country overview', in Kate Wellard and James G. Copestake (eds), *Non-Governmental Organizations and the State in Africa* (London and New York: Routledge, 1993).

Anon., 'The state of the liberation struggle: An interview with SWAPO President Sam Nujoma', in Reginald Green, Marja-Lissa Kiljunen and Kimmo Kiljunnen (eds), *Namibia: The Last Colony* (Harlow: Longman, 1981).

Anyang' Nyong'o, Peter, 'State and society in Kenya: the disintegration of the nationalist coalitions and the rise of presidential authoritarianism 1963–1978', *African Affairs* 88, 1989.

Appiah, Kweku, Demery, Lionel and Laryea-Adjei, George, 'Poverty in a changing environment', in Ernest Aryeetey, Jane Harrigan and Machiko Nissanke (eds), *Economic Reforms in Ghana: The Miracle and the Mirage* (Oxford, Accra and Trenton: James Currey, Woeli and Africa World Press, 2000).

Ardener, Edwin, 'The nature of the reunification of Cameroon', in Arthur Hazlewood (ed.), *African Integration and Disintegration: Case Studies in Economic and Political Union* (London, New York and Toronto: Oxford University Press, 1967).

Aryeetey, Ernest, 'Macroeconomic and sectoral developments since 1970', in Ernest Aryeetey, Jane Harrigan and Machiko Nissanke (eds), *Economic Reforms in Ghana: The Miracle and the Mirage* (Oxford, Accra and Trenton: James Currey, Woeli and Africa World Press, 2000).

Asante, Yaw, Nixson, Frederick and Tsikata, G. Kwaku, 'The industrial sector and economic development', in Ernest Aryeetey, Jane Harrigan and Machiko Nissanke (eds), *Economic Reforms in Ghana: The Miracle and the Mirage*

(Oxford, Accra and Trenton: James Currey, Woeli and Africa World Press, 2000).

Asiwaju, A. I., 'Partitioned culture areas: a checklist', in A. I. Asiwaju (ed.), *Partitioned Africans: Ethnic Relations Across Africa's International Boundaries 1884–1984* (London and Lagos: C. Hurst and University of Lagos Press, 1984).

Atieno-Odhiambo, E. S., 'Democracy and the ideology of order in Kenya', in Michael G. Schatzberg (ed.), *The Political Economy of Kenya* (New York, Westport and London: Praeger, 1987).

Bakary, Tessilimi, 'Elite transformation and political succession', in I. William Zartman and Christopher L. Delgado (eds), *The Political Economy of Ivory Coast* (New York: Praeger, 1984).

Banégas, Richard and Losch, Bruno, 'La Côte d'Ivoire au bord de l'implosion', *Politique Africaine* 87, 2002.

Bangura, Yusuf, 'Understanding the political and cultural dynamics of the Sierra Leone war: a critique of Paul Richards's *Fighting for the Rain Forest*', *Africa Development* 22, 3/4, 1997.

Barber, Karin, Collins, John and Ricard, Alain, 'Three West African popular theatre forms', in Karin Barber, John Collins and Alain Ricard (eds), *West African Popular Theatre* (Bloomington and Oxford: Indiana University Press and James Currey, 1997).

Baregu, Mwesiga, 'The rise and fall of the one-party state in Tanzania', in Jennifer Widner (ed.), *Economic Change and Political Liberalization in Sub-Saharan Africa* (Baltimore and London: John Hopkins University Press, 1994).

Barkan, Joel D., 'Legislators, elections, and political linkage', in Joel D. Barkan and John Okumu (eds), *Politics and Public Policy in Kenya and Tanzania* (New York: Praeger, 1979).

——, 'Divergence and convergence in Kenya and Tanzania: pressures for reform', in Joel D. Barkan (ed.), *Beyond Capitalism vs. Socialism in Kenya and Tanzania* (Boulder and London: Lynne Rienner, 1994).

Barrow, Ondine, 'International responses to famine in Ethiopia, 1983–85: Christian Aid and political economy framework for action', in Ondine Barrow and Michael Jennings (eds), *The Charitable Impulse: NGOs and Development in East and North-East Africa* (Oxford and Bloomfield: James Currey and Kumarian Press, 2001).

—— and Jennings, Michael, 'Introduction: the charitable impulse', in Ondine Barrow and Michael Jennings (eds), *The Charitable Impulse: NGOs and Development in East and North-East Africa* (Oxford and Bloomfield: James Currey and Kumarian Press, 2001).

Barry, Boubacar, 'Neocolonialism and dependence in Senegal, 1960–1980', in Prosser Gifford and Wm Roger Louis (eds), *Decolonization and African Independence: The Transfers of Power, 1960–1980* (New Haven and London: Yale University Press, 1988).

Bayart, Jean-François, 'Africa in the world: a history of extraversion', *African Affairs* 99, 395, 2000.

Baynham, Simon, 'Introduction: armed forces in Africa', in Simon Baynham (ed.), *Military Power and Politics in Black Africa* (London and Sydney: Croom Helm, 1986).

Bazenguissa-Ganga, Rémy, 'The political militia in Brazzaville', *Issue* 26, 1, 1998.

Beck, Linda J., 'Senegal's enlarged presidential majority: deepening democracy or detour?', in Richard Joseph (ed.), *State, Conflict and Democracy in Africa* (Boulder and London: Lynne Rienner, 1999).

Becker, Charles and Collignon, René, 'A history of Sexually Transmitted Diseases and AIDS in Senegal: difficulties in accounting for social logics in health policy', in Philip W. Setel, Milton Lewis, and Maryinez Lyons (eds), *Histories of Sexually Transmitted Diseases and HIV/AIDS in Sub-Saharan Africa* (Westport and London: Greenwood, 1999).

—— and Morrison, Andrew R., 'The growth of African cities: theory and estimates', in Archie Mafeje and Samir Radwan (eds), *Economic and Demographic Change in Africa* (Oxford: Clarendon Press, 1995).

Beckett, Paul, 'Legitimizing democracy: the role of the highly educated elite', in Paul Beckett and Crawford Young (eds), *Dilemmas of Democracy in Nigeria* (Rochester and Woodbridge: University of Rochester Press, 1997).

Beinart, William and Bundy, Colin, 'State intervention and rural resistance: the Transkei, 1900–1965', in Martin Klein (ed.), *Peasants in Africa: Historical and Contemporary Perspectives* (Beverly Hills and London: Sage, 1980).

—— and Dubow, Saul, 'Introduction: The historiography of segregation and apartheid', in William Beinart and Saul Dubow (eds), *Segregation and Apartheid in Twentieth-Century South Africa* (London and New York: Routledge, 1995).

Bendel, Petra, 'Gambia', in Dieter Nohlen, Michael Krennerich and Bernhard Thibaut (eds), *Elections in Africa: A Data Handbook* (Oxford: Oxford University Press, 1999).

Berg, Elliot J., 'Structural transformation versus gradualism: recent economic development in Ghana', in Philip Foster and Aristide Zolberg (eds), *Ghana and the Ivory Coast: Perspectives on Modernization* (Chicago and London: University of Chicago Press, 1971).

——, 'African adjustment programs: false attacks and true dilemmas', in Daniel M. Schydlowsky (ed.), *Structural Adjustment: Retrospect and Prospect* (Westport and London: Praeger, 1995).

——, Guillaumont, Parick, Amprou, Jacky, and Pegatienan, Jacques, 'Côte d'Ivoire', in Shantayanan Devarajan, David R. Dollar and Torgny Holmgren (eds), *Aid and Reform in Africa: Lessons From Ten Case-Studies* (Washington, DC: World Bank, 2001).

Bhebe, Ngwabi and Ranger, Terence, 'Volume introduction: Soldiers in Zimbabwe's liberation war', in Ngwabi Bhebe and Terence Ranger (eds), *Soldiers in Zimbabwe's Liberation Wars* (London, Portsmouth and Harare: James Currey, Heinemann and University of Zimbabwe Publications, 1995).

—— and Ranger, Terence, 'Volume introduction: Society in Zimbabwe's liberation war', in Ngwabi Bhebe and Terence Ranger, *Society in Zimbabwe's Liberation War* (Oxford, Portsmouth and Harare: James Currey, Heinemann and University of Zimbabwe, 1996).

Bigsten, Arne, Mutalemwa, Deogratias, Tsikata, Yvonne and Wangwe, Samuel, 'Tanzania', in Shantayanan Devarajan, David R. Dollar and Torgny Holmgren (eds), *Aid and Reform in Africa: Lessons From Ten Case-Studies* (Washington, DC: World Bank, 2001).

Birmingham, David, 'Angola', in Patrick Chabal, David Birmingham, Joshua Forrest, Malyn Newitt, Gerhard Seibert and Elisa Silva Andrade (eds), *A History of Postcolonial Lusophone Africa* (London: C. Hurst, 2002).

Bond, George C. and Vincent, Joan, 'Living on the edge: changing social structures in the context of AIDS', in Holger Bernt Hansen and Michael Twaddle (eds), *Changing Uganda: The Dilemmas of Structural Adjustment and Revolutionary Change* (London, Kampala, Athens and Nairobi: James Currey, Fountain Press, Ohio University Press and Heinemann, 1991).

Bond, Ivan, 'Campfire and the incentives for institutional change', in David Hulme and Marshall Murphree (eds), *African Wildlife and Livelihoods: The Promise and Performance of Community Conservation* (Oxford and Portsmouth: James Currey and Heinemann, 2001).

Boudon, Laura E., 'Burkina Faso: the "rectification of the revolution"' in John F. Clark and David E. Gardinier (eds), *Political Reform in Francophone Africa* (Boulder and Oxford: Westview Press, 1997).

Bourdillon, M. F. C., 'Guns and rain: taking structural analysis too far?', *Africa* 57, 2, 1987.

Bratton, Michael, 'Economic crisis and political realignment in Zambia', in Jennifer Widner (ed.), *Economic Change and Political Liberalization in Sub-Saharan Africa* (Baltimore and London: John Hopkins University Press, 1994).

—— and Lambright, Gina, 'Uganda's 2000 referendum: the silent boycott', *African Affairs* 100, 400, 2001.

—— and Posner, Daniel N., 'A first look at second elections in Africa with illustrations from Zambia', in Richard Joseph (ed.), *State, Conflict and Democracy in Africa* (Boulder and London: Lynne Rienner, 1999).

Brickhill, Jeremy, 'Daring to storm the heavens: the military strategy of ZAPU 1976 to 1979', in Ngwabi Bhebe and Terence Ranger (eds), *Soldiers in Zimbabwe's Liberation Wars* (London, Portsmouth and Harare: James Currey, Heinemann and University of Zimbabwe Publications, 1995).

Brown, Susan, 'Diplomacy by other means: SWAPO's liberation war', in Colin Leys and John S. Saul (eds), *Namibia's Liberation Struggle: The Two-Edged Sword* (London and Athens: James Currey and Ohio University Press, 1995).

Brunschwig, Henri, 'The decolonization of French Black Africa', in Prosser Gifford and Wm Roger Louis (eds), *The Transfer of Power in Africa: Decolonization 1940–1960* (New Haven and London: Yale University Press, 1982).

Buijtenhuijs, Robert, 'Chad in the age of warlords', in David Birmingham and Phyllis M. Martin (eds), *History of Central Africa: The Contemporary Years Since 1960* (London and New York: Longman, 1998).

Bujra, Janet and Baylies, Carolyn, 'Responses to the AIDS epidemic in Tanzania and Zambia', in Carolyn Baylies and Janet Bujra (eds), *AIDS, Sexuality and Gender in Africa: Collective Strategies and Struggles in Tanzania and Zambia* (London and New York: Routledge, 2002).

Bustin, Edouard, 'Remembrance of sins past: unravelling the murder of Patrice Lumumba', *Review of African Political Economy* 93/94, 2002.

Cameron, Greg, 'Zanzibar's turbulent transition', *Review of African Political Economy* 92, 2002.

Campbell, Bonnie, 'The Ivory Coast', in John Dunn (ed.), *West African States: Failure and Promise – A Study in Comparative Politics* (Cambridge: Cambridge University Press, 1978).

Cassanelli, Lee V., 'Explaining the Somali crisis', in Catherine Besteman and Lee V. Cassanelli (eds), *The Struggle for Land in Southern Somalia: The War Behind the War* (Boulder and London: Westview and Haan, 1996).

Chabal, Patrick, 'Revolutionary democracy in Africa: the case of Guinea-Bissau', in Patrick Chabal (ed.), *Political Domination in Africa: Reflections on the Limits of Power* (Cambridge: Cambridge University Press, 1986).

Chung, Fay, 'Education and the liberation struggle', in Ngwabi Bhebe and Terence Ranger (eds), *Society in Zimbabwe's Liberation War* (Oxford, Portsmouth and Harare: James Currey, Heinemann and University of Zimbabwe, 1996).

Clapham, Christopher, 'Controlling space in Ethiopia', in Wendy James, Donald L. Donham, Eisei Kurimoto and Alessandro Triulzi (eds), *Remapping Ethiopia: Socialism and After* (Oxford, Athens and Addis Ababa: James Currey, Ohio University Press and Addis Ababa University Press, 2002).

Clark, John F., 'Congo and the struggle to consolidate', in John F. Clark and David E. Gardinier (eds), *Political Reform in Francophone Africa* (Boulder and Oxford: Westview Press, 1997).

——, 'Foreign intervention in the Civil War of the Congo Republic', *Issue 26*, 1, 1998.

——, 'Explaining Ugandan intervention in Congo: evidence and interpretations', *Journal of Modern African Studies* 39, 2, 2001.

Clignet, Remi and Foster, Philip, 'Convergence and divergence in educational development in Ghana and Ivory Coast', in Philip Foster and Aristide Zolberg (eds), *Ghana and the Ivory Coast: Perspectives on Modernization* (Chicago and London: University of Chicago Press, 1971).

Cohen, Michael A., 'Urban policy and development strategy', in I. William Zartman and Christopher L. Delgado (eds), *The Political Economy of Ivory Coast* (New York: Praeger, 1984).

Cooksey, Brian, Court, David and Makau, Ben, 'Education for self-reliance and harambee', in Barkan, Joel D. (ed.), *Beyond Capitalism vs. Socialism in Kenya and Tanzania* (Boulder and London: Lynne Rienner, 1994).

Cooper, Fred, 'The Senegalese general strike of 1946 and the labor question in post-war French West Africa', *Canadian Journal of African Studies* 24, 1990.

——, ' "Our strike": anticolonial politics and the 1947–48 railway strike in French West Africa', *Journal of African History* 36, 1996.

Copestake, James C., 'Kenya: country overview', in Kate Wellard and James G. Copestake (eds), *Non-Governmental Organizations and the State In Africa* (London and New York: Routledge, 1993).

Coquery-Vidrovitch, Catherine, 'The transfer of economic power in French-speaking Africa', in Prosser Gifford and Wm Roger Louis (eds), *Decolonization and African Independence: The Transfer of Power, 1960–1980* (New Haven and London: Yale University Press, 1988).

Cowen, Michael, 'Commodity production in Kenya's Central Province', in Judith Heyer, Pepe Roberts and Gavin Williams (eds), *Rural Development in Tropical Africa* (New York: St Martin's Press, 1981).

—— and Kanyinga, Karuti, 'The 1997 elections in Kenya: the politics of communality and locality', in Adebayo Olukoshi (ed.), *The Politics of Opposition in Contemporary Africa* (Uppsala: Nordiska Afrikainstitutet, 1998).

Crook, Richard, 'Decolonization, the colonial state and chieftaincy in the Gold Coast', *African Affairs* 85, 338, 1986.

Cruise O'Brien, Donal, 'Coping with the Christians: the Muslim predicament in Kenya', in Holger Bernt Hansen and Michael Twaddle (eds), *Religion and Politics in East Africa: The Period Since Independence* (London, Nairobi, Kampala and Athens: James Currey, EAEP, Fountain Publishers and Ohio University Press, 1995).

Dabengwa, Dumiso, 'ZIPRA in the Zimbabwe war of national liberation' in Ngwabi Bhebe and Terence Ranger (eds), *Soldiers in Zimbabwe's Liberation Wars* (London, Portsmouth and Harare: James Currey, Heinemann and University of Zimbabwe Publications, 1995).

Dare, Tunji, 'The press', in Larry Diamond, Anthony Kirk-Greene and Oyeleye Oyediran (eds), *Transition Without End: Nigerian Politics and Civil Society Under Babangida* (Boulder and London: Lynne Rienner, 1997).

Darkwah, Akosua K., 'Aid or hindrance? Faith Gospel theology and Ghana's incorporation into the global economy', *Ghana Studies* 4, 2002.

Decalo, Samuel, 'Benin: the first of the new democracies', in John F. Clark and David Gardinier (eds), *Political Reform in Francophone Africa* (Boulder and Oxford: Westview Press, 1997).

De Gruchy, John W., 'Grappling with the colonial heritage: the English-speaking churches under imperialism and apartheid', in Richard Elphick and Rodney Davenport (eds), *Christianity in South Africa: A Political, Social and Cultural History* (Berkeley: University of California Press, 1997).

Deng, Francis Mading, 'War of visions for the nation', in John Voll (ed.), *Sudan: State and Society in Crisis* (Bloomington, Indianapolis and Washington: Indiana University Press and The Middle East Institute, 1991).

Dowse, Robert, 'Military and police rule', in Dennis Austin and Robin Luckham (eds), *Politicians and Soldiers in Ghana 1966–72* (London: Frank Cass, 1975).

Drah, F. K., 'The Brong political movement', in Kwame Arhin (ed.), *Brong Kyempim: Essays on the Society, History and Politics of the Brong People* (Legon: Institute of African Studies, 1979).

Ellis, Frank, 'Tanzania', in Charles Harvey (ed.), *Agricultural Pricing Policy in Africa: Four Country Case-Studies* (London and Basingstoke: Macmillan (now Palgrave Macmillan), 1988).

Ellis, Stephen, Writing histories of contemporary Africa', *Journal of African History* 43, 2002.

Engel, Ulf, 'Lesotho', in Dieter Nohlen, Michael Krennerich and Bernhard Thibaut (eds), *Elections in Africa: A Data Handbook* (Oxford: Oxford University Press, 1999).

Englebert, Pierre, 'Born-again Buganda or the limits of traditional resurgence in Africa', *Journal of Modern African Studies* 40, 3, 2002.

Englund, Harri, 'Winning elections, losing legitimacy: multi-partyism and the neopatrimonial state in Malawi', in Michael Cowen and Liisa Laakso (eds), *Multiparty Elections in Africa* (Oxford: James Currey, 2002).

Fauré, Yves, 'Côte d'Ivoire: analysing the crisis', in Donal B. Cruise O'Brien, John Dunn and Richard Rathbone (eds), *Contemporary West African States* (Cambridge: Cambridge University Press, 1989).

Faye, Ousseynou, 'La crise casamançaise et les relations du Sénégal avec la Gambie et la Guinée-Bissau (1980–1992)' in Momar-Coumba Diop (ed.), *Le Sénégal et ses voisins* (Dakar: Sociétés-Espaces-Temps, 1994).

Fleischhacker, Helga, 'São Tomé and Príncipe', in Dieter Nohlen, Michael Krennerich and Bernhard Thibaut (eds), *Elections in Africa: A Data Handbook* (Oxford: Oxford University Press, 1999).

Flint, John, 'Planned decolonization and its failure in British Africa', *African Affairs* 82, 328, 1983.

Forrest, Joshua, 'Guinea-Bissau', in Patrick Chabal, David Birmingham, Joshua Forrest, Malyn Newitt, Gerhard Seibert and Elisa Silva Andrade (eds), *A History of Postcolonial Lusophone Africa* (London: C. Hurst, 2002).

Fowler, Alan, 'NGOs and the globalization of social welfare: perspectives from East Africa', in Joseph Semboja and Ole Therkildsen (eds), *Service Provision Under Stress in East Africa* (Copenhagen, Nairobi, Dar es Salaam, Kampala, Portsmouth and London: Centre for Development Research, EAEP, Mkuki na Nyota Fountain Publishers, Heinemann and James Currey, 1995).

Furley, Oliver and Katalikawe, James, 'Constitutional reform in Uganda: the new approach', *African Affairs* 96, 383, 1997.

Fyfe, Christopher, 'Race, empire and the historians', *Race and Class* 33, 4, 1992.

Gardinier, David, 'Gabon: limited reform and regime survival', in John F. Clark and David E. Gardinier (eds), *Political Reform in Francophone Africa* (Boulder and Oxford: Westview Press, 1997).

Gberie, Lansana, 'The May 25 coup d'état in Sierra Leone: a militariat revolt?', *Africa Development* 22, 3/4, 1997.

Gbetibou, L. and Delgado, Christopher, 'Lessons and constraints on export crop-led growth: cocoa in Ivory Coast', in I. William Zartman and Christopher L. Delgado (eds), *The Political Economy of Ivory Coast* (New York: Praeger, 1984).

Geschiere, Peter, 'Chiefs and indirect rule in Cameroon: inventing chieftaincy, French and British style', *Africa* 63, 2, 1993.

Geshekter, Charles, 'The death of Somalia in historical perspective', in Hussein M. Adam and Richard Ford (eds), *Mending Rips in the Sky: Options for Somali Communities in the 21st Century* (Lawrenceville and Asmara: Red Sea Press, 1997).

Gibbon, Peter, 'Merchantisation of production and privatisation of development in post-*Ujamaa* Tanzania', in Peter Gibbon (ed.), *Liberalised Development in Tanzania* (Uppsala: Nordiska Afrikainstitutet, 1995).

Gifford, Paul, 'Some recent developments in African Christianity', *African Affairs* 93, 373, 1994.

Gifford, Prosser, 'Misconceived dominion: the creation and disintegration of federation in British Central Africa', in Prosser Gifford and Wm Roger Louis (eds), *The Transfer of Power in Africa: Decolonization 1940–1960* (New Haven and London: Yale University Press, 1982).

Gingyera-Pincywa, A. G. G., 'The border implications of the Sudan civil war: possibilities for intervention', in Dunstan M. Wai (ed.), *The Southern Sudan: The Problem of National Integration* (London: Frank Cass, 1973).

Goldsworthy, David, 'Armies and politics in civilian regimes', in Simon Baynham (ed.), *Military Power and Politics in Black Africa* (London and Sydney: Croom Helm, 1986).

Good, Kenneth, 'Towards popular participation in Botswana', *Journal of Modern African Studies* 34, 1, 1996.

Gould, Jeremy, 'Contesting democracy: the 1996 elections in Zambia', in Michael Cowen and Liisa Laakso (eds), *Multiparty Elections in Africa* (Oxford: James Currey, 2002).

Green, Reginald H., 'Reflections on economic strategy, structure, implementation and necessity: Ghana and the Ivory Coast', in Philip Foster and Aristide Zolberg (eds), *Ghana and the Ivory Coast: Perspectives on Modernization* (Chicago and London: University of Chicago Press, 1971).

Gros, Jean-Germain, 'Leadership and democratization: the case of Tanzania', in Jean-Germain Gros (ed.), *Democratization in Late Twentieth-Century Africa: Coping With Uncertainty* (Westport and London: Greenwood Press, 1998).

Hansen, Holger Bernt and Twaddle, Michael, 'Uganda: the advent of no-party democracy', in John Wiseman (ed.), *Democracy and Political Change in Sub-Saharan Africa* (London: Routledge, 1995).

Harneit-Seivers, Axel and Emezue, Sydney, 'Towards a social history of warfare and reconstruction: the Biafran case', in Ifi Amadiume and Abdullah An-Na'im (eds), *The Politics of Memory: Truth, Healing and Social Justice* (London and New York: Zed, 2002).

Heilbrunn, John R., 'Togo: the national conference and stalled reform', in John F. Clark and David E. Gardinier (eds), *Political Reform in Francophone Africa* (Boulder and Oxford: Westview Press, 1997).

Henriksen, Thomas H., 'People's war in Angola, Mozambique, and Guinea-Bissau', *Journal of Modern African Studies* 14, 3, 1976.

Herbst, Jeffrey, 'The dilemmas of land policy in Zimbabwe', in Simon Baynham (ed.), *Zimbabwe in Transition* (Stockholm: Almqvist and Wiksell, International, 1992).

Hiskett, Mervyn, 'The Maitatsine riots in Kano, 1980: an assessment', *Journal of Religion in Africa*, 17,3, 1983.

Hitchcock, Robert K., ' "We are the first people": land, natural resources and identity in the Central Kalahari, Botswana', *Journal of Southern African Studies* 28, 4, 2002.

Holm, John D. and Darnolf, Steffan, 'Democratizing the administrative state in Botswana', in York Bradshaw and Stephen N. Ndegwa (eds), *The Uncertain Promise of Southern Africa* (Bloomington and Indianapolis: Indiana University Press, 2000).

Hulme, David and Edwards, Michael, 'NGOs, states and donors: an overview', in David Hulme and Michael Edwards (eds), *NGOs, States and Donors: Too*

Close for Comfort? (London and New York: Macmillan (now Palgrave Macmillan), St Martin's Press and Save the Children Fund, 1997).

Hutchful, Eboe, 'Institutional decomposition and junior ranks' political action in Ghana', in Eboe Hutchful and Abdoulaye Bathily (eds), *The Military and Militarism in Africa* (Dakar: CODESRIA, 1998).

Jammeh, Sidi C., 'Politics of agricultural price decision-making in Senegal', in Mark Gersovitz and John Waterbury (eds), *The Political Economy of Risk and Choice in Senegal* (London and Totowa: Frank Cass, 1987).

Jennings, Michael, ' "Development is a very political thing in Tanzania": Oxfam and the Chunya Integrated Development Programme, 1972–76', in Ondine Barrow and Michael Jennings (eds), *The Charitable Impulse: NGOs and Development in East and North-East Africa* (Oxford and Bloomfield: James Currey and Kumarian Press, 2001).

Johnson, R. W., 'Guinea', in John Dunn (ed.), *West African States: Failure and Promise – A Study in Comparative Politics* (Cambridge: Cambridge University Press, 1978).

Jones, Brian and Murphree, Marshall, 'The evolution of policy on community conservation in Namibia and Zimbabwe', in David Hulme and Marshall Murphree (eds), *African Wildlife and Livelihoods: The Promise and Performance of Community Conservation* (Oxford and Portsmouth: James Currey and Heinemann, 2001).

Kaba, Lansiné, 'Cultural revolution and freedom of expression in Guinea', *Journal of Modern African Studies* 14, 2, 1976.

——,'From colonialism to autocracy: Guinea under Sekou Touré, 1957–1984', in Prosser Gifford and Wm Roger Louis (eds), *Decolonization and African Independence: The Transfers of Power, 1960–1980* (New Haven and London: Yale University Press, 1988).

Kandeh, Jimmy D., 'Transition without rupture: Sierra Leone's transfer election of 1996', *African Studies Review* 41, 2, 1998.

Kanyinga, Karuti, 'Contestation over political space: the state and the demobilisation of opposition politics in Kenya', in Adebayo Olukoshi (ed.), *The Politics of Opposition in Contemporary Africa* (Uppsala: Nordiska Afrikainstitutet, 1998).

Kasozi, A. B. K., 'Christian–Muslim inputs into public policy formation in Kenya, Uganda and Tanzania', in Holger Bernt Hansen and Michael Twaddle (eds), *Religion and Politics in East Africa: The Period Since Independence* (London, Nairobi, Kampala and Athens: James Currey, EAEP, Fountain Publishers, Ohio University Press, 1995).

Kastfelt, Niels, 'Rumours of Maitatsine: a note on political culture in Northern Nigeria', *African Affairs*, 88, 1989.

Kelsall, Tim, 'Donors, NGOs and the state: governance and "civil society" in Tanzania', in Ondine Barrow and Michael Jennings (eds), *The Charitable Impulse: NGOs and Development in East and North-East Africa* (Oxford and Bloomfield: James Currey and Kumarian Press, 2001).

Killick, Tony, 'Fragile still: the structure of Ghana's economy, 1960–94', in Ernest Aryeetey, Jane Harrigan and Machiko Nissanke (eds), *Economic Reforms in Ghana: The Miracle and the Mirage* (Oxford, Accra and Trenton: James Currey, Woeli and Africa World Press, 2000).

Kiondo, Andrew S. Z., 'When the state withdraws: local development, politics and liberalisation in Tanzania', in Peter Gibbon (ed.), *Liberalised Development in Tanzania* (Uppsala: Nordiska Afrikainstitutet, 1995).

Konings, Piet and Nyamnjoh, Francis B., 'The Anglophone problem', *Journal of Modern African Studies* 35, 2, 1997.

Kraus, Jon, 'Political change, conflict, and development in Ghana', in Philip Foster and Aristide Zolberg (eds), *Ghana and the Ivory Coast: Perspectives on Modernization* (Chicago and London: University of Chicago Press, 1971).

Kweka, A. N., 'The Pemba factor in the 1995 general elections', in C. K. Omari (ed.), *The Right to Choose a Leader: Reflections on the 1995 Tanzanian General Elections* (Dar es Salaam: DUP, 1996).

Langdon, Steven, 'Industry and capitalism in Kenya: contributions to a debate', in Paul M. Lubeck (ed.), *The African Bourgeoisie: Capitalist Development in Nigeria, Kenya, and the Ivory Coast* (Boulder: Lynne Rienner, 1987).

Lee, Paul, 'The Western conspiracy that destroyed Nkrumah', *West Africa* 19–25 November 2001.

Le Vine, Victor, 'Leadership and regime change in perspective', in Michael G. Schatzberg and I. William Zartman (eds), *The Political Economy of Cameroon* (New York: Praeger, 1986).

Leys, Colin, 'Capital accumulation, class formation and dependency: the significance of the Kenya case', *Socialist Register* 1978.

—— and Saul, John S., 'SWAPO inside Namibia', in Colin Leys and John S. Saul (eds), *Namibia's Liberation Struggle: The Two-Edged Sword* (London and Athens: James Currey and Ohio University Press, 1995).

Light, Margot, 'Moscow's retreat from Africa', in Arnold Hughes (ed.), *Marxism's Retreat in Africa* (London: Frank Cass, 1992).

Lodge, Tom, 'The Poqo insurrection', in Tom Lodge (ed.), *Resistance and Ideology in Settler Societies – Southern African Studies Volume 4* (Johannesburg: Ravan Press, 1986).

Lofchie, Michael F., 'The Zanzibari revolution: African protest in a racially plural society', in Robert I. Rotberg and Ali A. Mazrui (eds), *Protest and Power in Black Africa* (New York: Oxford University Press, 1970).

——, 'The politics of agricultural policy', in Joel D. Barkan (ed.), *Beyond Capitalism vs. Socialism in Kenya and Tanzania* (Boulder and London: Lynne Rienner, 1994).

Louis, Wm Roger and Robinson, Ronald, 'The United States and the liquidation of the British Empire in Tropical Africa, 1941–1951', in Prosser Gifford and Wm Roger Louis (eds), *The Transfer of Power in Africa: Decolonization 1940–1960* (New Haven and London: Yale University Press, 1982).

Loxley, John, 'The devaluation debate in Tanzania', in Bonnie K. Campbell and John Loxley (eds), *Structural Adjustment in Africa* (Basingstoke: Macmillan (now Palgrave Macmillan), 1989).

Luanda, Nestor, 'The Tanganyika rifles and the mutiny of January 1964', in Eboe Hutchful and Abdoulaye Bathily (eds), *The Military and Militarism in Africa* (Dakar: CODESRIA, 1998).

Lubeck, Paul, 'Islamic protest under semi-industrial capitalism: Yan Tatsine explained', *Africa* 5, 4, 1985.

Luckham, Robin, 'The Constitutional Commission 1966–69', in Dennis Austin and Robin Luckham (eds), *Politicians and Soldiers in Ghana 1966–72* (London: Frank Cass, 1975).

Mamdani, Mahmood, 'The truth according to the TRC', in Ifi Amadiume and Abdullahi An-Na'im (eds), *The Politics of Memory: Truth, Healing and Social Justice* (London and New York: Zed, 2000).

Mandaza, Ibbo, 'The state and politics in the post-white settler colonial situation', in Ibbo Mandaza (ed.), *Zimbabwe: The Political Economy of Transition* (Dakar: CODESRIA, 1986).

Manger, Leif, 'The Nuba mountains: battleground of identities, cultural traditions and territories', in Maj-Britt Johannsen and Niels Kastfelt (eds), *Sudanese Society in the Context of Civil War* (Copenhagen: University of Copenhagen, 2001).

Marenin, Otwin, 'The Anini saga: armed robbery and the reproduction of ideology in Nigeria', *Journal of Modern African Studies* 25, 2, 1987.

Maseko, Sipho S., 'The Namibian student movement: its role and effects', in Colin Leys and John S. Saul (eds), *Namibia's Liberation Struggle: The Two-Edged Sword* (London and Athens: James Currey and Ohio University Press, 1995).

Maxon, Robert M., 'Social and cultural changes', in B. A. Ogot and W. R. Ochieng' (eds), *Decolonization and Independence in Kenya 1940–93* (London, Nairobi and Athens: James Currey, EAEP and Ohio University Press, 1995).

—— and Ndege, Peter, 'The economics of structural adjustment', in B. A. Ogot and W. R. Ochieng' (eds), *Decolonization and Independence in Kenya 1940–93* (London, Nairobi and Athens: James Currey, EAEP and Ohio University Press, 1995).

Maxwell, David, 'Christiantity and the war in eastern Zimbabwe: the case of the Elim mission', in Ngwabi Bhebe and Terence Ranger (eds), *Society in Zimbabwe's Liberation War* (Oxford, Portsmouth and Harare: James Currey, Heinemann and University of Zimbabwe, 1996).

——, 'Christianity without frontiers: Shona missionaries and transnational Pentecostalism in Africa', in David Maxwell and Ingrid Lawrie (eds), *Christianity and the African Imagination: Essays in Honour of Adrian Hastings* (Leiden, Boston and Cologne: Brill, 2002).

M'Bokolo, Elikia, 'Comparisons and contrasts in equatorial Africa: Gabon, Congo and the Central African Republic', in David Birmingham and Phyllis Martin (eds), *History of Central Africa: the Contemporary Years Since 1960* (Harlow: Addison-Wesley Longman, 1998).

McGovern, Mike, 'Conflit régional et rhétorique de la contre-insurrection', *Politique Africaine* 88, 2002.

McGowan, Patrick J., 'African military coups d'état, 1956–2001', *Journal of Modern African Studies* 41, 3, 2003.

Mchombo, Sam, 'Democratization in Malawi: its roots and prospects', in Jean-Germain Gros (ed.), *Democratization in Late Twentieth-Century Africa: Coping With Uncertainty* (Westport and London: Greenwood Press, 1998).

McLaughlin, Janice, 'Avila mission: a turning point in church relations with the state and with the liberation forces', in Ngwabi Bhebe and Terence Ranger (eds), *Society in Zimbabwe's Liberation War* (Oxford, Portsmouth and Harare: James Currey, Heinemann and University of Zimbabwe, 1996).

Menhaus, Ken, 'Traditional conflict management in contemporary Somalia', in I. William Zartman (ed.), *Traditional Cures for Modern Conflicts: African Conflict 'Medicine'* (Boulder and London: Lynne Rienner, 2000).

Mentan, Tatah, 'Cameroon: a flawed transition to democracy', in Jean-Germain Gros (ed.), *Democratization in Late Twentieth-Century Africa: Coping With Uncertainty* (Westport and London: Greenwood Press, 1998).

Messone, Nelson N. and Gros, Jean-Germain, 'The irony of wealth: democratization in Gabon', in Jean-Germain Gros (ed.), *Democratization in Late Twentieth-Century Africa: Coping With Uncertainty* (Westport and London: Greenwood Press, 1998).

Michel, Gilles and Noel, Michel, 'The Ivorian economy and alternative trade regimes', in I. William Zartman and Christopher L. Delgado (eds), *The Political Economy of Ivory Coast* (New York: Praeger, 1984).

Mills, Greg, 'AIDS and the South African military: timeworn cliché or time-bomb', in Robert Shell, Kristina Quattek, Martin Schönteich and Greg Mills (eds), *HIV/AIDS: A Threat to the African Renaissance* (Johannesburg: Konrad Adenauer Stiftung, 2000).

Moll, Terence, 'Did the South African economy "fail"?', *Journal of Southern African Studies* 17, 2, 1991.

Moore, David, 'The Zimbabwe People's Army: strategic innovation or more of the same?', in Ngwabi Bhebe and Terence Ranger (eds), *Soldiers in Zimbabwe's Liberation Wars* (London, Portsmouth and Harare: James Currey, Heinemann and University of Zimbabwe Publications, 1995).

Moyo, Sam, 'The land question', in Ibbo Mandaza (ed.), *Zimbabwe: The Political Economy of Transition, 1980–1986* (Dakar: CODESRIA, 1986).

Muana, Patrick K., 'The Kamajoi militia: civil war, internal displacement and the politics of counter-insurgency', *Africa Development* 22, 3/4, 1997.

Mundt, Robert J., 'Côte d'Ivoire: continuity and change in a semi-democracy', in John F. Clark and David E. Gardinier (eds), *Political Reform in Francophone Africa* (Boulder and Oxford: Westview Press, 1997).

Murombedzi, James, 'Committees, rights, costs and benefits: natural resource stewardship and community benefits in Zimbabwe's CAMPFIRE Programme', in David Hulme and Marshall Murphree (eds), *African Wildlife and Livelihoods: The Promise and Performance of Community Conservation* (Oxford and Portsmouth: James Currey and Heinemann, 2001).

Mutume, Gumisai, 'Mounting opposition to Northern farm subsidies: African cotton farmers battling to survive', *Africa Recovery* 17, 1, May 2003.

Mytelka, Lynne Krieger, 'Foreign business and economic development', in I. William Zartman and Christopher L. Delgado (eds), *The Political Economy of Ivory Coast* (New York: Praeger, 1984).

Ndarishikanye, Barnabé, 'The question of the protection of minorities in Burundi', *Issue* 26, 1, 1998.

Ndikumana, Léonce, 'Institutional failure and ethnic conflicts in Burundi', *African Studies Review* 41, 1, 1998.

Ndulu, Benno J. and Mwega, Francis W., 'Economic adjustment policies', in Joel D. Barkan (ed.), *Beyond Capitalism vs. Socialism in Kenya and Tanzania* (Boulder and London: Lynne Rienner, 1994).

Newbury, Catherine, 'Survival strategies in rural Zaire: realities of coping with the crisis', in Nzongola-Ntalaja (ed.), *The Crisis in Zaire: Myths and Realities* (Trenton: Africa World Press, 1986).

Newitt, Malyn, 'Mozambique', in Patrick Chabal, David Birmingham, Joshua Forrest, Malyn Newitt, Gerhard Seibert and Elisa Silva Andrade (eds), *A History of Postcolonial Lusophone Africa* (London: C. Hurst, 2002).

Ngolet, François, 'Ideological manipulations and political longevity: the power of Omar Bongo in Gabon since 1967', *African Studies Review* 43, 2, 2000.

Nkiwane, Tandika C., 'Opposition politics in Zimbabwe: the struggle within the struggle', in Adebayo Olukoshi (ed.), *The Politics of Opposition in Contemporary Africa* (Uppsala: Nordiska Afrikainstitutet, 1998).

——, 'Observing the observers', in Henning Melber (ed.), *Zimbabwe's Presidential Elections 2002: Evidence, Lessons and Implications* (Uppsala: Nordiska Afrikainstitutet, 2002).

Nugent, Paul, 'Educating Rawlings: the evolution of government strategy towards smuggling', in Donald Rothchild (ed.), *Ghana: The Political Economy of Recovery* (Boulder and London: Lynne Rienner, 1991).

——, 'Winners, losers and also-rans: money, moral authority and voting patterns in the Ghana 2000 elections', *African Affairs* 100, 400, 2001.

Obi-Ani, Paul 'Post-civil war Nigeria: reconciliation or vendetta?', in Toyin Falola (ed.), *Nigeria in the Twentieth Century* (Durham: Carolina Academic Press, 2002).

Ochieng', William, 'Structural and political changes', in B. A. Ogot and W. R. Ochieng' (eds), *Decolonization and Independence in Kenya 1940–93* (London, Nairobi and Athens: James Currey, EAEP and Ohio University Press, 1995).

Ogot, B. A., 'The construction of a national culture', in B. A. Ogot and W. R. Ochieng' (eds), *Decolonization and Independence in Kenya 1940–93* (London, Nairobi and Athens: James Currey, EAEP and Ohio University Press, 1995).

Olsen, Gorm Rye, 'Europe and the promotion of democracy in post Cold War Africa: how serious is Europe and for what reason?', *African Affairs* 97, 1998.

Okpoko, Pat Uche, 'Three decades after Biafra: a critique of the reconciliation policy', in Toyin Falola (ed.), *Nigeria in the Twentieth Century* (Durham: Carolina Academic Press, 2002).

O'Meara, Patrick, 'Rhodesia/Zimbabwe: guerrilla warfare or political settlement?', in Gwendolen M. Carter and Patrick O'Meara (eds), *Southern Africa: The Continuing Crisis* (London and Basingstoke: Macmillan (now Palgrave Macmillan), 1979).

Opala, Joseph A., ' "Ecstatic revolution": street art celebrating Sierra Leone's 1992 revolution', *African Affairs* 93, 371, 1994.

Osuntokun, Akinjide, 'Review of literature on the Nigerian civil war', in Tekena N. Tamuno and Samson C. Ukpabi (eds), *Nigeria Since Independence, the First 25 Years, Volume VI, The Civil War Years* (Ibadan: Heinemann Educational Books, 1989).

Othman, Shehu, 'Nigeria: power for profit – class, corporatism, and factionalism in the military', in Donal Cruise O'Brien, John Dunn and Richard Rathbone (eds), *Contemporary West African States* (Cambridge: Cambridge University Press, 1989).

O'Toole, Thomas, 'The Central African Republic: political reform and social malaise', in John F. Clark and David E. Gardinier (eds), *Political Reform in Francophone Africa* (Boulder and Oxford: Westview Press, 1997).

Owusu, Maxwell, 'Politics without parties: reflections on the Union Government debate', *African Studies Review* 22, 2, 1979.

Oyediran, Oyeleye, 'The Political Bureau', in Larry Diamond, Anthony Kirk-Greene and Oyeleye Oyediran (eds), *Transition Without End: Nigerian Politics and Civil Society Under Babangida* (Boulder and London: Lynne Rienner, 1997).

Paye, Moussa, 'The regime and the press', in Momar Coumba Diop (ed.), *Senegal: Essays in Statecraft* (Dakar: CODESRIA, 1993).

Pearce, Robert, 'The Colonial Office and planned decolonization in Africa', *African Affairs* 83, 330, 1984.

Pietilä, Tuulikki, Ojalammwi-Wamai, Saanna and Laakso, Liisa, 'Elections at the borderland: voter opinion in Arusha and Kilimanjaro, Tanzania', in Michael Cowen and Liisa Laakso (eds), *Multiparty Elections in Africa* (Oxford: James Currey, 2002).

Pirouet, M. Louise, 'The churches and human rights in Kenya and Uganda since independence', in Holger Bernt Hansen and Michael Twaddle (eds), *Religion and Politics in East Africa: The Period Since Independence* (London, Nairobi, Kampala and Athens: James Currey, EAEP, Fountain Publishers and Ohio University Press, 1995).

Pongo, Martin Kalulambi, 'Dreams, battles and the rout of the elite in Congo-Kinshasa: the mourning of an imagined democracy', *Issue*, 26, 1, 1998.

Pool, David, 'The Eritrean People's Liberation Front', in Christopher Clapham (ed.), *African Guerrillas* (Oxford, Kampala, Bloomington and Indianapolis: James Currey, Fountain Publishers and Indiana University Press, 1998).

Radu, Michael S. and Somerville, Keith, 'The Congo', in Chris Allen, Michael S. Radu, Keith Somerville and Joan Baxter (eds), *Benin, The Congo, Burkina Faso: Politics, Economy and Society* (London: Pinter Publishers, 1988).

Raftopoulos, Brian, 'The labour movement and the emergence of opposition politics in Zimbabwe', in Brian Raftopoulos and Lloyd Sachinkoye (eds), *Striking Back: The Labour Movement and the Post-Colonial State in Zimbabwe 1980–2000* (Harare: Weaver Press, 2001).

Raikes, Phil and Gibbon, Peter, 'Tanzania', in Poul Engberg-Pedersen, Peter Gibbon, Phil Raikes and Lars Udsholt (eds), *Limits of Adjustment in Africa: The Effects of Economic Liberalization* (Copenhagen, Oxford and Portsmouth: Centre for Development Research, James Currey and Heinemann, 1996).

Ranger, Terence, 'The invention of tradition in colonial Africa', in E. Hobsbawm and T. Ranger (eds), *The Invention of Tradition* (Cambridge: Cambridge University Press, 1983).

——, 'The invention of tradition revisited: the case of colonial Africa', in Terence Ranger and Olufemi Vaughan (eds), *Legitimacy and the State in Twentieth-Century Africa* (London: Macmillan (now Palgrave Macmillan), 1993).

—— and Ncube, Mark, 'Religion in the guerrilla war: the case of southern Matabeleland', in Ngwabi Bhebe and Terence Ranger (eds), *Society in Zimbabwe's Liberation War* (Oxford, Portsmouth and Harare: James Currey, Heinemann and University of Zimbabwe, 1996).

Rathbone, Richard, 'Ghana', in John Dunn (ed.), *West African States: Failure and Promise – A Study in Comparative Politics* (Cambridge: Cambridge University Press, 1978).

Ray, Donald I., 'Chief–state relations in Ghana – divided sovereignty and legitimacy', in E. A. B. Van Rouveroy Van Nieuwal and Werner Zips (eds), *Sovereignty, Legitimacy, and Power in West African Societies: Perspectives From Legal Anthropology* (Hamburg and New Brunswick: Lit Verlag and Transaction, 1998).

Reed, Wm Cyrus, 'Guerrillas in the midst: the Former Government of Rwanda (FGOR) and the Alliance of Democratic Forces for the Liberation of Congo-Zaire (AFDL) in eastern Zaire', in Christopher Clapham (ed.), *African Guerrillas* (Oxford, Kampala, Bloomington and Indianapolis: James Currey, Fountain Publishers and Indiana University Press, 1998).

Reno, William, 'La "sale petite guerre" du Libéria', *Politique Africaine* 88, December 2002.

Reyntjens, Filip, 'The new geostrategic situation in Central Africa', *Issue*, 26, 1, 1998.

——, 'Briefing: the Democratic Republic of Congo, from Kabila to Kabila', *African Affairs* 100, 2001.

Rule, Stephen, 'Outcome of the election', in Yvonne Muthien (ed.), *Democracy South Africa: Evaluating the 1999 Election* (Pretoria: HSRC, 1999).

Rutake, Pascal and Gahama, Joseph, 'Ethnic conflict in Burundi', in Okwudiba Nnoli (ed.), *Ethnic Conflicts in Africa* (Dakar: CODESRIA, 1998).

Samatar, Ahmed I., 'The curse of Allah: civic disembowelment and the collapse of the state in Somalia', in Ahmed I. Samatar (ed.), *The Somali Challenge: From Catastrophe to Renewal?* (Boulder and London: Lynne Rienner, 1994).

Saul, John, 'The state in post-colonial societies', in John Saul, *The State and Revolution in Eastern Africa* (London: Heinemann, 1979).

—— and Leys, Colin, 'SWAPO: the politics of exile', in Colin Leys and John S. Saul (eds), *Namibia's Liberation Struggle: The Two-Edged Sword* (London and Athens: James Currey and Ohio University Press, 1995).

Seibert, Gerhard, 'São Tomé e Príncipe', in Patrick Chabal, David Birmingham, Joshua Forrest, Malyn Newitt, Gerhard Seibert and Elisa Silva Andrade (eds), *A History of Postcolonial Lusophone Africa* (London: C. Hurst, 2002).

Shaw, Ibrahim Seaga, 'Peace deal in Côte d'Ivoire', *West Africa* 3–9 February 2003.

Shell, Robert, 'Halfway to the holocaust: the economic, demographic and social implications of the AIDS pandemic to the year 2010 in the Southern African region', in Robert Shell, Kristina Quattek, Martin Schönteich and Greg Mills (eds), *HIV/AIDS: A Threat to the African Renaissance* (Johannesburg: Konrad Adenauer Stiftung, 2000).

Simons, Anna, 'Somalia: the structure of dissolution', in Leonardo A. Villalón and Phillip A. Huxtable (eds), *The African State at a Critical Juncture: Between Disintegration and Reconfiguration* (Boulder and London: Lynne Rienner, 1998).

Simpson, Chris, 'Blood and confusion in Casamance', *West Africa* 10–16 February 2003.

Singer, H. W., 'Demographic factors in Subsaharan African economic development', in Melville J. Herskovits and Mitchell Harwitz (eds), *Economic Transition in Africa* (London: Routledge and Kegan Paul, 1964).

Solway, Jacqueline, 'Navigating the "neutral" state: "minority" rights in Botswana', *Journal of Southern African Studies* 28, 4, 2002.

Steenkamp, Philip, 'The churches', in Colin Leys and John S. Saul (eds), *Namibia's Liberation Struggle: The Two-Edged Sword* (London and Athens: James Currey and Ohio University Press, 1995).

Stengers, Jean, 'Precipitous decolonization: the case of the Belgian Congo', in Prosser Gifford and Wm Roger Louis (eds), *The Transfer of Power in Africa: Decolonization 1940–1960* (New Haven and London: Yale University Press, 1982).

Stichter, Sharon, 'Women and the family: the impact of capitalist development in Kenya', in Michael G. Schatzberg (ed.), *The Political Economy of Kenya* (New York, Westport and London: Praeger, 1987).

Stoeltje, Beverly J., 'Narration and negotiation: a woman's case in the queen-mother's court in Ghana', in E. A. B. Van Rouveroy Van Nieuwal and Werner Zips (eds), *Sovereignty, Legitimacy, and Power in West African Societies: Perspectives From Legal Anthropology* (Hamburg and New Brunswick: Lit Verlag and Transaction, 1998).

Stren, Richard, Halfani, Mohammed and Malombi, Joyce, 'Coping with urbanization and urban policy', in Joel D. Barkan (ed.), *Beyond Capitalism vs. Socialism in Kenya and Tanzania* (Boulder and London: Lynne Rienner, 1994).

Stryker, Richard E., 'Political and administrative linkage in the Ivory Coast', in Philip Foster and Aristide Zolberg (eds), *Ghana and the Ivory Coast: Perspectives on Modernization* (Chicago and London: University of Chicago Press, 1971).

Suret-Canale, Jean, 'La fin de la chefferie en Guinée', *Journal of African History* 7, 3, 1966.

——, 'The Fouta-Djalon chieftaincy' in Michael Crowder and Obaro Ikime (eds), *West African Chiefs: Their Changing Status Under Colonial Rule and Independence* (Ile-Ife: University of Ife Press, 1970).

Swainson, Nicola, 'Indigenous capitalism in postcolonial Kenya', in Paul M. Lubeck (ed.), *The African Bourgeoisie: Capitalist Development in Nigeria, Kenya, and the Ivory Coast* (Boulder: Lynne Rienner, 1987).

Takougang, Joseph, 'Cameroon: Biya and incremental reform' in John F. Clark and David E. Gardinier (eds), *Political Reform in Francophone Africa* (Boulder and Oxford: Westview Press, 1997).

Tamuno, Tekena, 'Introduction: men and measures in the Nigerian crisis, 1960–70', in Tekena N. Tamuno and Samson C. Ukpabi (eds), *Nigeria Since Independence, the First 25 Years, Volume VI, The Civil War Years* (Ibadan: Heinemann Educational Books, 1989).

Tangri, Roger and Andrew Mwenda, Andrew, 'Corruption and cronyism in Uganda's privatization in the 1990s', *African Affairs* 100, 398, 2001.

Thioub, Ibrahima, Coumba-Diop, Momar and Boone, Catherine, 'Economic liberalization in Senegal: shifting politics of indigenous business interests', *African Studies Review* 41, 2, 1998.

Throup, David, 'The construction and destruction of the Kenyatta state', in Michael G. Schatzberg (ed.), *The Political Economy of Kenya* (New York, Westport and London: Praeger, 1987).

——, ' "Render unto Caesar the things that are Caesar's": the politics of church–state conflict in Kenya, 1978–1990', in Holger Bernt Hansen and Michael Twaddle (eds), *Religion and Politics in East Africa: The Period Since Independence* (London, Nairobi, Kampala and Athens: James Currey, EAEP, Fountain Publishers, Ohio University Press, 1995).

Tin, Hjalte, 'Children in violent spaces: a reinterpretation of the 1976 Soweto uprising', in Abebe Zegeye (ed.), *Social Identities in the New South Africa: After Apartheid, Volume 1* (Cape Town and Maroelana: Kwela Books and SA History Online, 2001).

Toulabor, Comi, 'Political satire past and present in Togo', *Critique of Anthropology* 14, 1, 1994.

Turner, Thomas, 'Zaire: flying high above the toads: Mobutu and stalemated democracy', in John F. Clark and David E. Gardinier (eds), *Political Reform in Francophone Africa* (Boulder and Oxford: Westview Press, 1997).

Twumasi, Yaw, 'The 1969 election', in Dennis Austin and Robin Luckham (eds), *Politicians and Soldiers in Ghana 1966–72* (London: Frank Cass, 1975).

Van Dijk, Rijk, 'Contesting silence: the ban on drumming and the musical politics of Pentecostalism in Ghana', *Ghana Studies* 4, 2002.

Van Donge, Jan Kees, 'Kamuzu's legacy: the democratization of Malawi', *African Affairs* 94, 375, 1995.

Van Hoyweghen, Saskia, 'The disintegration of the Catholic Church of Rwanda: a study of the fragmentation of political and religious authority', *African Affairs* 95, 380, July 1996.

Vaughan, Megan, 'Exploitation and neglect: rural producers and the state in Malawi and Zambia', in David Birmingham and Phyliis M. Martin (eds), *History of Central Africa: The Contemporary Years Since 1960* (Harlow: Addison Wesley Longman, 1998).

Vengroff, Richard and Magala, Michael, 'Democratic reform, transition and consolidation: evidence from Senegal's 2000 presidential election', *Journal of Modern African Studies* 39, 1, 2001.

Verhaegen, Benoît, 'Le rôle de l'ethnie et de l'individu dans la rébellion du Kwilu et son échec', in Catherine Coquery-Vidrovitch, Alain Forest and

Herbert Weiss (eds), *Rébellions-révolution au Zaire 1963–1965, tome 1* (Paris: L'Harmattan, 1987).

Villalón, Leonardo and Kane, Ousmane, 'Senegal: the crisis of democracy and the emergence of an Islamic opposition' in Leonardo A. Villalón and Phillip A. Huxtable (eds), *The African State at a Critical Juncture: Between Disintegration and Reconfiguration* (Boulder and London: Lynne Rienner, 1998).

Vlassenroot, Koen, 'Identity and insecurity: the building of ethnic agendas in South Kivu', in Ruddy Doom and Jan Gorus (eds), *Politics of Identity and Economics of Conflict in the Great Lakes Region* (Brussels: VUB University Press, 2000).

Voipio, Rauha, 'Contract work through Ovambo eyes', in Reginald Green, Marja-Lissa Kiljunen and Kimmo Kiljunnen (eds), *Namibia: The Last Colony* (Harlow: Longman, 1981).

Waterbury, John, 'Dimensions of state intervention in the groundnut basin', in Mark Gersovitz and John Waterbury (eds), *The Political Economy of Risk and Choice in Senegal* (London and Totowa: Frank Cass, 1987).

Weiner, Daniel, 'Land and agricultural development', in Colin Stoneman (ed.), *Zimbabwe's Prospects: Issues of Race, Class, State, and Capital in Southern Africa* (London and Basingstoke: Macmillan (now Palgrave Macmillan), 1988).

Weiss, Herbert, 'Collapsed society, surviving state, future polity', in William Zartman (ed.), *Collapsed States: The Disintegration and Restoration of Legitimate Authority* (Boulder: Lynne Rienner, 1995).

Werbner, Richard, 'In memory: a heritage of war in south-western Zimbabwe', in Ngwabi Bhebe and Terence Ranger (eds), *Society in Zimbabwe's Liberation War* (Oxford, Portsmouth and Harare: James Currey, Heinemann and University of Zimbabwe, 1996).

White, Bob W., 'Congolese rumba and other cosmopolitans', *Cahiers d'Etudes Africaines*, XLII, 168, 2002.

Williams, Gavin and Turner, Terisa, 'Nigeria', in John Dunn (ed.), *West African States: Failure and Promise – A Study in Comparative Politics* (Cambridge: Cambridge University Press, 1978).

Wise, Christopher, 'Chronicle of a student strike in Africa: the case of Burkina Faso, 1996–1997', *African Studies Review* 41, 2, 1998.

Woods, Dwayne, 'Côte d'Ivoire: the crisis of distributive politics', in Leonardo A. Villalón and Phillip A. Huxtable (eds), *The African State at a Critical Juncture: Between Disintegration and Reconfiguration* (Boulder and London: Lynne Rienner, 1998).

Wolpe, Harold, 'Capitalism and cheap labour power in South Africa: from segregation to apartheid', *Economy and Society*, 1, 1972.

WSP Somali Programme, *Rebuilding Somalia: Issues and Possibilities for Puntland* (London: Haan, 2001).

Yankah, Kwesi, 'Nana Ampadu, the sung tale metaphor and protest discourse in contemporary Ghana', in Luise White, Stephan Miescher and David William Cohen (eds), *African Words, African Voices: Critical Perspectives in Oral History* (Bloomington and Indianapolis: Indiana University Press, 2001).

Young, Crawford, 'The Obote revolution', *Africa Report*, June 1966.

——, 'Zaire, Rwanda and Burundi', *Cambridge History of Africa, Volume 8: From 1940 to 1975* (Cambridge: Cambridge University Press, 1984).

——, 'Zaire: the anatomy of a failed state', in David Birmingham and Phyllis Martin (eds), *History of Central Africa: the Contemporary Years Since 1960* (Harlow: Addison-Wesley Longman, 1998).

Young, John, 'The Tigray People's Liberation Front', in Christopher Clapham (ed.), *African Guerrillas* (Oxford, Kampala, Bloomington and Indianapolis: James Currey, Fountain Publishers and Indiana University Press, 1998).

Zartman, I. William and Delgado, Christopher L., 'Introduction', in I. William Zartman and Christopher L. Delgado (eds), *The Political Economy of Ivory Coast* (New York: Praeger, 1984).

Zolberg, Aristide R., 'Political development in the Ivory Coast since independence', in Philip Foster and Aristide Zolberg (eds), *Ghana and the Ivory Coast: Perspectives on Modernization* (Chicago and London: University of Chicago Press, 1971).

4   Literature

Achebe, Chinua, *Girls at War and Other Stories* (London: Heinemann, 1972).

Emecheta, Buchi, *Destination Biafra* (Oxford: Heinemann, 1982).

Ike, Chukwuemeka, *Sunset at Dawn: A Novel About Biafra* (London: Harvill, 1976).

Ngugi wa Thiong'o, *A Grain of Wheat* (London: Heinemann Educational, revised edition, 1988).

Okpewho, Isidore, *The Last Duty* (Harlow: Longman, 1976).

Ousmane, Sembène, *God's Bits of Wood* (translated by F. Price) (London: Heinemann, 1970).

——, *Xala* (translated by Clive Wake) (London: Heinemann, 1976).

Saro-Wiwa, Ken, *Sozaboy: A Novel in Rotten English* (Harlow: Longman, 1994).

Soyinka, Wole, *The Man Died: Prison Notes of Wole Soyinka* (London: Rex Collings, 1973).

5   Internet sites

Human Rights Watch, *World Report 2002*, www.hrw.org.wr2k2/africa9.html

Human Rights Watch, *World Report 2003*, www.hrw.org/w2k3/africa1.html

Mai-Mai, www.congo-mai-mai.net

6   Discography

Fela Anikulapo Kuti, *'69 Los Angeles Sessions* (London: Stern's, 1993).

——, *Zombie* (Wrasse Records edition, 2001).

E. T. Mensah, *Day By Day: Classic Highlife Recordings of the 1950s and 1960s* (London: RetroAfric, 1991).

7   Documentaries and film

BBC, 'Biafra: Fighting a War Without Guns' (*Timewatch*, 1995).

Xala (Director: Sembène Ousmane, 1974).

La Vie Est Belle (Director: Mweze Nwangura, 1987).

Mapantsula (Director: Oliver Schmitz, 1988).

Index

Printed in the United States
41951LVS00001B/43-141

9 780333 682739